DICTIONARY
OF
AMERICAN HISTORY

DICTIONARY
OF
AMERICAN
HISTORY

REVISED EDITION

VOLUME IV

Jockey Hollow–National Union for Social Justice

Charles Scribner's Sons · New York

Printed in the United States of America
Library of Congress Catalog Card Number 76-6735
ISBN 0-684-13856-5 (set)

ISBN 0-684-15071-9 (vol. 1)   ISBN 0-684-15075-1 (vol. 5)
ISBN 0-684-15072-7 (vol. 2)   ISBN 0-684-15076-X (vol. 6)
ISBN 0-684-15073-5 (vol. 3)   ISBN 0-684-15077-8 (vol. 7)
ISBN 0-684-15074-3 (vol. 4)   ISBN 0-684-15078-6 (Index)

EDITORIAL STAFF

LOUISE BILEBOF KETZ, *Managing Editor*

JOSEPH G. E. HOPKINS, *Editorial Adviser*

COPY EDITORS

PATRICIA R. BOYD

NORMA FRANKEL

ROBERT HAYCRAFT

LELAND S. LOWTHER

PROOFREADERS

MARGARET DONOVAN

ROGER GREENE

PAULINE PIEKARZ

ANDREW J. SMITH

DORIS A. SULLIVAN

MARSHALL DE BRUHL, *Director, Reference Editorial*

DICTIONARY OF AMERICAN HISTORY

Jockey Hollow–National Union for Social Justice

JOCKEY HOLLOW, an area used by horse traders for herding their animals, was the site of the encampment of the Continental army under Gen. George Washington during the winter of 1779–80. Located about four miles southwest of the general's headquarters at Morristown, N.J., ten brigades of some 12,000 men were hutted there. Shortage of food and clothing, and cold, caused acute suffering. There, early in 1781, occurred the mutiny of the Pennsylvania troops, which threatened for a time the independence movement.

C. A. TITUS

"JOE BOWERS," a song about the folk hero of the forty-niners. Dated around 1850, the song is a document straight from American soil.

> My name it is Joe Bowers,
>   And I've got a brother Ike;
> I come from old Missouri—
>   Yes, all the way from Pike.

To the words and haunting tune of this homely ballad oxen pulled a nation westward. Nobody knows absolutely who Joe Bowers was or who immortalized him. Specifically he was a "Piker" who had left home and "Sally" to make a stake in "Califony"; in a larger way he embodied the feelings and dreams of every emigrant to the West.

[W. E. Connelley, *Doniphan's Expedition.*]

J. FRANK DOBIE

JOHN, FORT, the name given to Fort Laramie when it was bought by the American Fur Company, after John B. Sarpy, a partner in the company. Built on the Laramie River in Wyoming Territory in 1834, it was described later in the decade by Frederick Wislizenus as a rectangle, 80 by 100 feet, protected by cottonwood pickets 15 feet high, having towers on three sides. The name "Fort John" never became popular, and the fort was still referred to as Laramie. Business transactions conducted by the American Fur Company were recorded as having taken place at Fort John.

[H. M. Chittenden, *History of American Fur Trade of the Far West.*]

CARL L. CANNON

JOHN BIRCH SOCIETY, an ultraconservative organization, founded in 1958 by Robert H. W. Welch, Jr., a retired Massachusetts businessman. It was named after John Birch, a Fundamentalist Baptist missionary from Georgia. Welch never knew Birch, who, while serving as a U.S. intelligence officer, was killed by Chinese Communists ten days after V-J Day, 1945, thereby making him the first hero of the cold war, according to the society. The declared aim of the society is to fight communism on a so-called intellectual basis apparently by adopting some of communism's own most vicious and ruthless tactics. Among other ancillary elements of its program are its advocacy of a return to minimum federal government

1

JOHNS HOPKINS UNIVERSITY

and the abandonment of the Federal Reserve System, the Commodity Credit Corporation, and the veterans' hospitals. Violence is not advocated, but a number of public men and others have been charged by the society with being "dedicated agents" of "the Communist conspiracy." The organization is composed of a semisecret network of cells of "Americanists" throughout the country. The society publishes a journal, *American Opinion,* eleven times a year. Its main headquarters are in Belmont, Mass.

THOMAS ROBSON HAY

JOHNS HOPKINS UNIVERSITY, a private, non-sectarian institution of higher learning, was established in 1876 in Baltimore, Md., as a unique experiment that combined the European, especially German, approach to higher education with its emphasis on advanced study and serious research, and the traditional American approach with its emphasis on the liberal arts and the classics. It also included the first graduate school in the United States. The university was founded by the Quaker merchant Johns Hopkins, who requested that his bequest of $7 million be divided equally for the creation of a university and a hospital in his native city. At the time that he drafted his will in 1867, Hopkins appointed a board of twelve trustees and secured the incorporation of the university, but the trustees' duties did not really begin until after his death in 1873.

The trustees installed Daniel Coit Gilman as the first president of the university on May 1, 1875. Gilman had studied in Berlin, where he had become enthusiastic about the new German university system. In the year before Johns Hopkins opened Gilman traveled on the Continent and in England to recruit a research faculty. In England he enlisted the mathematician J. J. Sylvester and the biologist Henry Newell Martin, who was then T. H. Huxley's assistant. In the United States, Gilman secured the appointment of Henry A. Rowland, a young American who, after his appointment, worked in Berlin briefly with Hermann von Helmholtz and who later revolutionized the science of spectroscopy. Gilman offered the professorship of chemistry to Ira Remsen, who had studied medicine in the United States and then had studied at Munich under Justus von Liebig and had taken a Ph.D. at Göttingen. For the humanities Gilman turned to a southern scholar, Basil L. Gildersleeve, as professor of Greek. Gilman's last senior appointment was that of the Oxford-trained classicist Charles D. Morris.

In October 1876 Johns Hopkins University opened

for classes in a modest collection of buildings located in downtown Baltimore. Among Gilman's educational innovations from Europe was an emphasis on teaching laboratories, student research, and the seminar. The original faculty was soon augmented by some newcomers who were to leave their impress on the development of the university: the philosophers George S. Morris and Charles Sanders Peirce; the mathematician-astronomer Simon Newcomb; the Leipzig Semitic scholar Paul Haupt; the economist Richard T. Ely; and the psychologist G. Stanley Hall. The southern poet and musician Sidney Lanier, who joined the faculty in 1879 to lecture on William Shakespeare, the English novel, and prosody, may have been one of the first "writers in residence" in an American university.

While students and masters gathered in such groups as the philological, historical, scientific, and archaeological associations, the Mathematical Society, or Peirce's Metaphysical Club, the young university also quickly became a center for new journals, usually the first in their fields in the United States. In 1879 Remsen founded the *American Chemical Journal.* Sylvester followed in 1878 with the *American Journal of Mathematics.* Gildersleeve in 1880 inaugurated the *American Journal of Philology.* H. C. Adams, who was rapidly establishing a new school of historical studies, initiated a monographic series, *JHU Studies in Historical and Political Science,* two years later. A. L. Frothingham, Jr., a fellow at the university, began the *American Journal of Archaeology* in 1885. A. Marshall Elliott, who had founded the Modern Language Association of America in December 1883 and had become its first secretary, launched another pioneer philological journal in 1886, *Modern Language Notes.* Finally, Hall began the *American Journal of Psychology* in 1887.

The need for a central publication agency was early recognized by Gilman. The result was the founding of the Johns Hopkins University Press in 1878, the oldest of the North American university presses in continuous operation.

Although the establishment of a medical school and hospital was integral to Johns Hopkins' testamentary bequest, their creation occupied a period of many years and the energies of Gilman and two pioneers of American medicine, John Shaw Billings and William H. Welch. In 1883 Billings accepted a Hopkins appointment to lecture on public health, medical education, history, and jurisprudence. Together with Remsen in chemistry and Martin in physiology, Billings and Welch constituted the first medical faculty almost

2

a decade before the opening of the medical school itself. As a blueprint for the overdue reform of U.S. medical training, they conceived the first premedical program, projected a rigorous four-year medical course, drew upon British and German innovations in the design of the hospital buildings and laboratory facilities, and developed a coherent relationship between the preclinical and clinical sciences as well as between patient care, teaching, and research.

The progress of the hospital's construction was slowed by the growing financial difficulties of the Baltimore and Ohio Railroad, which suspended dividends on common stock, on which Hopkins depended for its endowment income. The hospital finally opened its doors in May 1889. Welch was joined at this time on the staff by his three colleagues: William Osler, as physician in chief; William S. Halsted, as surgeon in chief; and Howard A. Kelly, as gynecologist and obstetrician. Henry Mills Hurd, a psychiatrist and medical reformer, was appointed the first superintendent. The first medical residency system in the United States was established on Osler's initiative. The School of Nursing was established under Isabelle Hampton later that year. In 1893 the medical school with Welch as its dean admitted its first students; this was made possible by an emergency fund raised by Mary E. Garrett and her associates with the provision that women be admitted on equal terms with men. This shrewd philanthropy brought to the medical school such students as Florence R. Sabin and Gertrude Stein.

As at the graduate school, new journals appeared at the medical school, among them the *Bulletin of the Johns Hopkins Hospital* (1889), Welch's *Journal of Experimental Medicine* (1896), and J. J. Abel's *Journal of Pharmacology and Experimental Therapeutics* (1909). The first in a long series of adaptations in the medical curriculum was made in 1898 when the elective system was instituted for the first time.

Although Osler left Hopkins for the Regius professorship at Oxford in 1905, the impulse of the four doctors—Welch, Osler, Halsted, and Kelly—had already been effectively communicated to the next generation. Thus, the tradition of Halsted was continued by a brilliant succession of surgeons, including John M. T. Finney and Harvey Cushing. The pathologists George H. Whipple and Joseph Erlanger (both Nobel laureates) extended the work of Welch and others in the laboratory, while Welch's early students Jesse W. Lazear and Walter Reed achieved notable results in the new fields of public health and epidemiology. New services and departments were established, such

as the Henry Phipps Psychiatric Clinic under Adolf Meyer in 1910. In 1922 Elmer V. McCollum, who had earlier identified vitamin A, discovered vitamin D in the medical school's laboratories; and pioneer work in biomedical statistics, preventive medicine, public health administration, and epidemiology was initiated throughout the 1920's. In 1926 Welch transferred his energies to yet another field, the establishment of the Institute of the History of Medicine and a central medical library, which were dedicated in October 1929. The medical institutions later were supplemented by yet another division with the creation in 1971 of the School of Health Services; the first students in the program to train for new kinds of health care were admitted in 1973.

While the Johns Hopkins University began as a frankly experimental venture, by the time Gilman retired in 1901 most of his priorities and goals of twenty-five years earlier had been realized. Gilman was succeeded as president by Ira Remsen, during whose administration (1901–13) plans were made to move the undergraduate, graduate, and extension school from downtown Baltimore to the present Homewood campus in the northern part of the city, a move that was finally made in 1916. Remsen's successor, Frank J. Goodnow, headed the university from 1913 to 1929. The fourth president, Joseph Ames, directed the university during the difficult depression years 1929–35. He was succeeded by Isaiah Bowman, who served as president from 1935 to December 1948; during his administration the university assumed responsibility for the Applied Physics Laboratory in Silver Spring, Md., which developed the proximity fuze and made important contributions in space and biomedical engineering. Detlev W. Bronk served as the sixth president (1949–53). During his first year he was instrumental in the founding of a department of biophysics, and the following year the university assumed responsibility for a new division, the School of Advanced International Studies (SAIS) in Washington, D.C. During the administration of Bronk's successor, Lowell Reed (1953–56), SAIS activities were extended to a center in Bologna, Italy, the first American graduate school in Europe.

Milton S. Eisenhower became president of Johns Hopkins in 1956. During his first administration (1956–67) new departments were established in social relations, statistics, and the history of science; the faculties of engineering and philosophy were combined into the division of arts and sciences; the evening college sponsored an influential graduate pro-

gram in the history of ideas; the medical school instituted a new accelerated curriculum; and the finances of the university were put on a solid basis, while a major program of building and renovation—including a new central library and extensive medical facilities—almost doubled the space available for teaching and research. During the administration of Lincoln Gordon (1967–71), the university began the Center for Metropolitan Planning and the Greater Homewood Corporation and admitted women to the undergraduate school. In 1971–72 Eisenhower returned from an active retirement to see the university successfully through a period of academic and financial transition. He was succeeded in February 1972 by Hopkins' tenth president, the German-born scholar Steven Muller. For the first time since a brief tenure by Gilman, this office was combined with that of the presidency of the hospital.

Celebrating its centennial in 1976, Johns Hopkins remained by tradition and design one of the smallest of the major American universities. The total enrollment of all divisions was just under 10,000. Approximately 3,000 of these were resident students in the Faculty of Arts and Sciences, of whom roughly two-thirds were undergraduates and one-third were graduate students. There were also some 5,000 students enrolled in the evening college, slightly more than half of whom were pursuing graduate degrees. Another 1,200 students were in the medical divisions.

[Alan M. Chesney, *The Johns Hopkins Hospital and the Johns Hopkins School of Medicine;* John C. French, *A History of the University Founded by Johns Hopkins;* Hugh Hawkins, *Pioneer: A History of the Johns Hopkins University, 1874–1889;* Robert P. Sharkey, *Johns Hopkins: A Centennial Portrait of a University.*]

RICHARD MACKSEY

JOHNSON AND GRAHAM'S LESSEE V. McINTOSH, 8 Wheaton 544 (1823), established the constitutional principle that grants of land made to private individuals by Indian tribes are invalid. The issue arose when successors to the grantees of a large tract of land in Illinois and Indiana, made by certain chiefs of the Illinois and Piankashaw in 1773 and 1775, challenged the ownership of a portion of the tract by William McIntosh, whose title derived from the U.S. government in 1818. The opinion of the Supreme Court presents an exhaustive survey of the attitudes of governments respecting the Indian tribal ownership and disposition of the soil.

M. M. QUAIFE

JOHNSON-CLARENDON CONVENTION (Jan. 14, 1869) covered American claims against the British from 1853 onward, without precise allusion to damages done to northern shipping during the Civil War by the *Alabama* and other Confederate raiders built or armed by the British. British concessions were so slight that the convention was rejected in the Senate, Apr. 13, 1869, by a vote of fifty-four to one. Settlement of Civil War claims was thereby postponed until the Treaty of Washington, 1871, and the subsequent, arbitrated Geneva award (1872).

[Louis Martin Sears, *A History of American Foreign Relations.*]

LOUIS MARTIN SEARS

JOHNSON COUNTY WAR. *See* **Rustler War.**

JOHNSON DOCTRINE, an expansion of the Roosevelt Corollary to the Monroe Doctrine enunciated on May 2, 1965, by President Lyndon B. Johnson in justification of his dispatch of U.S. Marines in April of that year to quell civil disorders in the Dominican Republic. It stated that "the American nations . . . will not permit the establishment of another Communist government in the Western Hemisphere." The doctrine was amplified by a resolution of the House of Representatives on Sept. 20, 1965.

JACOB E. COOKE

JOHNSON HALL, built in 1761–62, the last home of Sir William Johnson, colonial superintendent of northern Indian affairs, was a magnificent building for its day, 60 feet wide, 40 feet deep, and two stories high; it had wide clapboards cut to resemble blocks of stone. Situated half a mile from Johnstown, N.Y., and flanked on both sides by stone blockhouses, the hall was the scene of many important conferences between the British and Indians and the mecca for all travelers of note in the Mohawk Valley. Restored almost to its original appearance by the State of New York, it is the museum of the Johnstown Historical Society.

[Arthur Pound, *Johnson of the Mohawks.*]

EDWARD P. ALEXANDER

JOHNSON'S ISLAND, in Sandusky Bay, Lake Erie, was used as a prison for captured Confederate officers from 1862 to the end of the Civil War. The numbers of prisoners confined there fluctuated greatly in 1862 and 1863 because of exchanges but increased in the closing months of the war until more than 3,000 were on the island. The proximity of Johnson's Island to Canada, where Confederate agents were stationed, invited plots and attempts to escape, in which members of northern antiwar secret societies (*see* Canada, Confederate Activities in) were also involved. The most amazing rescue attempt came in September 1864, when Confederate agents planned to seize the lake gunboat *Michigan,* release 2,600 prisoners on the island, capture Sandusky, go by train to Columbus, Ohio, and release the prisoners at Camp Chase. This plot was foiled by the arrest of Capt. Charles H. Cole as he was about to seize the gunboat. An accomplice, John Yates Beall, seized a passenger steamer but had to flee with it to Canada.

[Whitelaw Reid, *Ohio in the War,* vol. II.]
EUGENE H. ROSEBOOM

JOHNSTOWN FLOOD occurred simultaneously with lesser floods in twenty Pennsylvania counties in the spring of 1889, and resulted from the collapse of the Conemaugh Reservoir during a period of exceptionally heavy rainfall. The dam, constructed in 1852 as part of the Pennsylvania canal system and immediately abandoned, had been rebuilt during 1879–81 to a height of 80 feet by Pittsburgh sportsmen to quadruple the size of the reservoir, situated 275 feet above the Johnstown low flats; but they skimped the work and omitted the original discharge pipes and spillway.

On Friday morning, May 31, 1889, after a night of heavy rain, engineers feared the dam would collapse, but their emphatic warnings were disregarded by many inhabitants of Conemaugh Valley as exaggerated. At 3:30 P.M. the earthen walls of the dam yielded, quickly inundating the entire valley in a powerful downward thrust. Halted by the Pennsylvania railway viaduct, just above Johnstown proper, the flood receded, causing destructive vortices, inducing a huge conflagration in the Cambria Iron Works, and annihilating most of Johnstown and its suburbs. Over 2,500 persons perished. Property losses totaled over $10 million. Generous assistance came immediately from almost every civilized country, furnishing $3,742,818.

Recriminations were severe. The *London Chronicle* declared that the disaster revealed the shoddiness of American engineering. In New York City a newspaper controversy raged over the construction of the Quaker Bridge dam. To these attacks American engineers replied that the Conemaugh Reservoir did not even represent the best professional practices of an earlier generation, being the only dam in the United States over 50 feet in height without a central wall of masonry or puddle. Despite popular demands for an official investigation, none was held. The Pennsylvania legislature permitted the legal consolidation of the Johnstown area for more effective civic cooperation.

[David G. McCullough, *The Johnstown Flood.*]
HARVEY WISH

JOINT COMMISSIONS. The arbitration of international disputes by joint commissions is usually distinguished from the negotiation of formal treaties by more than one diplomatic agent—such as the Definitive Treaty of Peace of 1783; the termination of Franco-American hostilities by the Convention of 1800; the Louisiana Purchase of 1803; the Treaty of Ghent of 1814; the Webster-Ashburton Treaty of 1842; and the Peace of Paris of 1898. Most arbitrations are the work of joint commissions, as indicated in the monumental six-volume work on international arbitration by John Bassett Moore. Since its publication in 1898, further cases have arisen for settlement, notably the Alaskan boundary dispute of 1903.

Of the numerous arbitrations to which the United States has been a party, some of the more important ones were conducted for the following purposes: for settling pre-Revolution American debts to the British, British spoliation claims, and the Maine-Canada boundary, under the Jay Treaty of 1794; for settling French spoliation claims in 1803, 1831, and 1880; for determining various articles under the Treaty of Ghent; for claims of American citizens against Mexico, in 1839, 1849, and 1868; for U.S. claims against Colombia in 1861 and against Peru in 1863; and for Spanish claims in 1871. Most significant of all was the Alabama Claims dispute, leading to the Geneva award of 1872. To these may be added fact-finding commissions as an indispensable adjunct of modern diplomacy.

Since the mid-20th century there have been increasing reservations toward the use of joint commissions to settle international disputes. In 1946 the United States accepted the compulsory jurisdiction of the International Court (except in domestic matters), but it continued its reluctance to accept any other binding arbitration.

[John Bassett Moore, *History and Digest of the International Arbitrations to Which the United States Has Been a Party.*]
LOUIS MARTIN SEARS

JOINT COMMITTEE ON RECONSTRUCTION. On Dec. 4, 1865, in the Thirty-ninth Congress, Thaddeus Stevens, representative from Pennsylvania, moved the appointment of a joint committee from House and Senate to report conditions on which the late "so-called Confederate states" might be received back into the Union. Stevens and the Radical Republicans, displeased with President Andrew Johnson's plan of reconstruction, expected to take the matter from his hands and to formulate a plan of their own.

The committee was appointed Dec. 13, 1865, with the following membership: from the Senate, William P. Fessenden (chairman), James W. Grimes, Ira Harris, Jacob M. Howard, Reverdy Johnson, and George H. Williams; from the House, John A. Bingham, Henry T. Blow, George S. Boutwell, Roscoe Conkling, Henry Grider, Lot M. Morrill, Andrew J. Rogers, Thaddeus Stevens, and Elihu B. Washburne. The chief work of the committee was the formulation of the Fourteenth Amendment and of the Reconstruction Act of Mar. 2, 1867. In modified form the Congress adopted these measures as reported, and they became the basis of southern reconstruction. The committee expired with the end of the Thirty-ninth Congress, Mar. 2, 1867.

[Benjamin B. Kendrick, *The Journal of the Joint Committee of Fifteen on Reconstruction.*]

HAYWOOD J. PEARCE, JR.

JOINT OCCUPATION, a term used to designate the agreement reached by the United States and Great Britain with regard to Oregon Country under the Convention of 1818. Having mutually determined the northern boundary of the Louisiana Purchase as far west as the Rocky Mountains the parties were unable to determine the boundary west of the mountains because of rival claims to the Oregon Country. It was agreed that the nationals of either nation could trade and settle in the region for a period of ten years. On Aug. 6, 1827, the agreement was renewed, to continue until one party gave a year's notice of termination. Following the popular excitement characterized by the "fifty-four forty or fight" campaign in 1846, Congress instructed President James K. Polk to serve notice upon Great Britain that the agreement was to end. The settlement of the boundary question by treaty, June 15, 1846, ended the joint occupation of Oregon (*see* Oregon Treaty of 1846).

[Charles H. Carey, *A General History of Oregon, Prior to 1861.*]

ROBERT MOULTON GATKE

JOINT RESOLUTIONS. *See* **Resolutions, Legislative.**

JOINT-STOCK LAND BANKS were chartered under the authority of the Federal Farm Loan Act, approved July 17, 1916. These banks were financed with private capital and were permitted to make loans in the states in which they were chartered and one contiguous state. About eighty-seven charters were granted, but not all of the banks opened for business. The joint-stock banks had their largest growth both in number and volume of business in the better agricultural areas—Iowa, Illinois, Minnesota, Missouri, Texas, and California. At first the law did not limit the size of loans, but the act was amended in 1923 limiting the size of loans to one borrower to $50,000. All loans were required to be made for agricultural purposes. Land was appraised by federal government appraisers, and the amount of a loan was limited to a percentage of the value of the appraised land and buildings. They were permitted to issue tax-exempt bonds up to twenty times their capital. These banks did a thriving business during the World War I land booms but declined rapidly with the less profitable conditions of agriculture in the late 1920's. Many of the banks failed. Accusations of mismanagement sprang up, and many of the banks reorganized or liquidated. The Emergency Farm Mortgage Act of 1933 ordered the joint-stock land banks liquidated. To aid in carrying out the liquidation of these banks the Farm Credit Act of 1933 provided the Land Bank Commission with $100 million for two years, and renewed the provision for two more years in 1935.

[Farm Credit Administration, *Annual Reports* (since 1933); Federal Farm Loan Board, *Annual Reports* (1916–1933); Ivan Wright, *Farm Mortgage Financing.*]

IVAN WRIGHT

JOLLIET AND MARQUETTE DISCOVERY. Louis Jolliet was a native of New France who, after being educated at the Jesuit schools of Quebec, embarked on a career of exploration in the far western country of the 17th century. On one of his voyages to Lake Superior in 1669 he met the Jesuit missionary Jacques Marquette, then at the mission of Sault Sainte Marie. Three years later the authorities of New France commissioned Jolliet to undertake the discovery of the great central river of the continent, which the Indians had described and spoken of as the Mississippi. Jolliet requested that Marquette be appointed chaplain of the expedition, and late in the autumn of 1672 set out for the Northwest to prepare for the voyage. Jolliet found Marquette at the mission of Saint Ignace on the north shore of Mackinac Strait. Together they prepared maps and planned for the discovery during the ensuing winter; the map Marquette then drew still exists, showing the route of his discovery that he traced on it.

On May 17, 1673, the two explorers left Saint Ignace in two canoes with five voyageurs, "fully resolved to do and to suffer everything for so glorious an undertaking." They went by way of Lake Michigan, Green Bay, and the Fox River (see Fox-Wisconsin Waterway), a route that was well known as far as the upper villages on the Fox. At the Mascouten, village guides were obtained to lead them to the portage. Friendly Indians tried to dissuade the explorers, enlarging on the difficulties of the voyage; but the travelers pressed on, and a month from the time of departure their canoes shot out from the Wisconsin into a great river, which they instantly recognized as the one they sought. Marquette wished to name the river the Conception for the Immaculate Conception of the Virgin Mary; Jolliet called it first the Buade, after Louis de Buade, Comte de Frontenac, governor of New France. Ultimately he christened it the Colbert, for the prime minister of France; but the Indian name persisted.

The two explorers in their canoes drifted down the river as far as the Arkansas; they met few Indians, and these for the most part friendly. They saw no monsters except painted ones on the cliffs high above the stream (see Alton Petroglyphs). They encountered no falls or whirlpools, and the voyage, while memorable, was not dangerous. From the Arkansas they turned back upstream, fearing to encounter Spaniards on the lower river. Acting on Indian advice, they did not return to the Fox-Wisconsin waterway, but ascended the Illinois and the Des Plaines, portaging at Chicago to Lake Michigan (see Chicago Portage). They were thus the first white men to stand on the site of that city.

Returning by Lake Michigan and Green Bay to the mission at De Pere, Marquette remained there to regain his health. Jolliet, after a winter of exploring around the lake, went in 1674 to Canada to report his discovery. Just before he reached Montreal, his canoe overturned in the rapids, and he lost all his journals, notes, and maps and saved his life only with difficulty. Thus Marquette's journal has become the offi-

cial account of the voyage, and Jolliet's share has been somewhat minimized. Jolliet was an expert mapmaker, later the official hydrographer of New France; his maps of the expedition, however, were drawn from memory, and the Jesuit maps superseded his. The discovery was widely heralded in France and formed the basis for the exploration and exploitation of the Mississippi Valley by Robert Cavelier, Sieur de La Salle, and other French voyagers in the late 17th century.

[Louise Phelps Kellogg, *French Régime in Wisconsin and the Northwest.*]

LOUISE PHELPS KELLOGG

JONATHAN, or Brother Jonathan, nicknames for a typical American. The story, unknown until 1846, attributing them to George Washington's affection for Jonathan Trumbull, the prominent Connecticut politician who was once secretary on his staff, is without foundation. In 1643 an English satirist, alluding to the monuments to Queen Elizabeth then common in London churches, declared that "her *Epitaph* was one of my Brother *Jonathan's* best *Poems,* before he abjured the *University,* or had a thought of *New-England.*" In a London satirical print entitled "The Yankie Doodles Intrenchments Near Boston 1776," a besieger says, "I Swear its plaguy Cold Jonathan." On vacating Bunker Hill, Mass., during the Revolution the British left images of hay labeled, "Welcome, Brother Jonathan." Throughout the Revolution the terms were employed by Loyalists and British soldiers in mild derision of patriots, but were avoided by the patriots themselves. After 1783 the terms were often applied by New Englanders to country bumpkins, and by 1812 they had become established as national sobriquets.

ALBERT MATTHEWS

JONES ACT, or Organic Act of the Philippine Islands, passed by Congress on Aug. 29, 1916, provided for the government of the Philippines and committed the United States to the future independence of the archipelago. All inhabitants who were Spanish subjects on Apr. 11, 1899, and their descendants were designated as citizens. The right to vote was given to all male citizens over twenty-one years of age who could read and write. The two houses of the Philippine congress were made wholly elective; the president of the United States was to appoint, subject to confirmation by the Senate, justices of the Philippine supreme court and a governor-general. (*See also* Philippine Islands.)

[W. Cameron Forbes, *The Philippine Islands;* Dean C. Worcester, *The Philippines, Past and Present.*]

JOHN COLBERT COCHRANE

JONES COUNTY, SECESSION OF, from the state of Mississippi during the Civil War, was first related by G. N. Galloway, historian of the Sixth Army Corps, in the *Magazine of American History* (1886), and it assumed importance when accepted by Albert Bushnell Hart (*New England Magazine,* December 1891). No evidence in documents or the memory of inhabitants supports the story. It apparently derives from the known antisecession sentiment of the county, a piney-woods area where there were no plantations, few blacks, and a small population and from the formation there in 1862 of a company of 125 raiders who cooperated with the Union army.

[Alexander L. Bondurant, "Did Jones County Secede?," *Publications of the Mississippi Historical Society,* vol. 1; Goode Montgomery, "Alleged Secession of Jones County," *Publications of the Mississippi Historical Society,* vol. 8.]

MACK SWEARINGEN

JONES V. VAN ZANDT, 5 Howard 215 (1846), followed *Prigg* v. *Pennsylvania* in sustaining the federal Fugitive Slave Law of 1793, despite arguments of prominent antislavery advocates Salmon P. Chase and William H. Seward, based on the Ordinance of 1787 and the "inexpedience and invalidity of all laws recognizing slavery." The Court unanimously declared that the Constitution in one of its "sacred compromises" not only made slavery a political question to be settled by each state for itself but also required each to allow the restoration of the slave property of others.

[J. W. Schuckers, *Life and Public Services of Salmon Portland Chase;* Charles Warren, *Supreme Court in United States History.*]

LAWRENCE A. HARPER

JORNADA DEL MUERTO, in English "journey of death," was a ninety-mile strip of desert extending from Valverde, Texas , to El Paso del Norte, later shortened to El Paso (Texas). The road follows a dry plain where soapweed grows high and the grass is dry from lack of moisture. Many tragedies occurred on the *jornada* during the Spanish era because of the absence of water.

CARL L. CANNON

JOUETT'S RIDE. Capt. John Jouett, Jr., was spending the night of June 3, 1781, at Cuckoo Tavern, Louisa, Va., when he saw Col. Banastre Tarleton with a detachment of British troops go by in the direction of Charlottesville, where the Virginia legislature was in session after having fled from Richmond on the approach of Gen. Charles Cornwallis. Jouett, who knew the countryside, rode by hidden paths the forty-five miles to Charlottesville before dawn, to warn the legislature, thus saving four signers of the Declaration of Independence—Thomas Jefferson, Thomas Nelson, Jr., Richard Henry Lee, and Benjamin Harrison—in addition to Patrick Henry and Edmund Randolph.

[Mary Mallet Elliott, *Colonial Days in Virginia.*]

JAMES ELLIOTT WALMSLEY

JOURNALISM. *See* **Newspapers.**

JOURNAL OF CONGRESS, the official record of the proceedings of the legislative branch of the U.S. government. The Continental Congress in 1774 appointed Charles Thomson as secretary; he kept a manuscript journal recording its resolves and other decisions and also the attendance of the members. This journal was published contemporaneously in thirteen volumes. Thomson also kept a secret journal that was not published until 1821. These journals, together with information from auxiliary records and papers, were used in the thirty-four-volume Library of Congress edition of the *Journals of the Continental Congress,* published 1904–37, to reconstruct the fuller story of the activities of the Congress from 1774 to 1789. The Constitution provides that "each House shall keep a Journal of its Proceedings." In the earliest congresses the journals were printed in parts and distributed during the session. At the end of each session since 1789 verbatim reports have been published with indexes, one or more volumes for each house. After the burning of the Capitol in 1814, when all printed copies belonging to both houses were destroyed, the journals of the first thirteen congresses were reprinted (1820–26). Until 1861 the journals were printed by contract and thereafter by the Government Printing Office under the authority of each house. They are also substantially incorporated in the *Annals of Congress* (covering 1789–1824), in the *Register of Debates* (1824–37), in the *Congressional Globe* (1833–73), and in the *Congressional Record* since 1873. The Senate also keeps an executive journal, which has been published from time to time.

[L. F. Schmeckebier, *Government Publications and Their Use*.]
ROSCOE R. HILL

JUCHEREAU'S TANNERY was established by Louis Juchereau de St. Denys on or near the site of the present city of Cairo, Ill., in 1702. At its height the establishment included a missionary priest, more than a hundred tradesmen, and many Mascouten hunters. Decline commenced in the summer and fall of 1703, when an epidemic caused the death of St. Denys and many of his men. Lambert Mandeville, second in command, attempted to carry on the enterprise, but in 1704 it was abandoned.

[C. W. Alvord, *The Illinois Country, 1673–1818*.]
PAUL M. ANGLE

JUDAISM, AMERICAN. The completion of the Christian reconquest of Iberia signaled the expulsion of over 150,000 Jews from Spain in 1492 and Portugal in 1497. Some of these Spanish and Portuguese Jews, known as Sephardim, settled as crypto-Jews in the Iberian colonies in the Western Hemisphere. A flourishing settlement developed in Brazil after the Dutch captured the area in 1630. When the Portuguese returned in 1654, Jews were obliged to migrate. Twenty-three of them landed in Dutch New Amsterdam (New York), establishing the first Jewish community in North America.

Other Jews came to North America, mostly from northern Europe, for economic advancement and greater freedom. Although they frequently had to struggle to obtain political and religious liberties, by the mid-1700's they enjoyed greater freedom in the English colonies than anywhere else in the world. With the outbreak of the American Revolution in 1775, remaining civic disabilities were gradually overcome. New York was the first state to enfranchise Jews completely, in 1777; New Hampshire, in 1877, was the last.

Although Jews of Germanic descent, known as Ashkenazim, constituted the majority of American Jews by the 1720's, the Sephardim dominated the spiritual tone of Jewish life. All six congregations founded in the United States before 1800 followed the Sephardic ritual. The synagogue, center of all forms of Jewish community life, was characterized by a dignified orthodoxy. As there were no rabbis in the United States before 1840, services were led by a *hazzan* (cantor), whose status became equated with that of a Protestant minister.

By the end of the 18th century the 2,000–3,000 Jews in America had for the most part prospered. Many were involved in mercantile activities, and several had amassed considerable wealth. The French Revolution and Napoleonic Wars brought a halt in immigration, and by 1815 a rather homogeneous American Jewish community had taken shape.

Immigration from Germany after Napoleon's defeat achieved mass proportions by the 1840's and changed the entire nature of American Jewry. In 1850 there were about 50,000 Jews in the United States; in 1880, over 250,000. By then the community was overwhelmingly Germanic in origin, Americanized by choice, Reform in belief, solidly middle class in stature, and rather evenly settled throughout the United States.

Most immigrants had settled initially on the East Coast and become peddlers, clerks, and artisans. Soon moving inland, they followed expanding trade routes into the Middle and Far West, establishing Jewish communities along the way. Gradually many of them became shopkeepers, merchants, wholesalers, and bankers, as well as professional men. Rising status was facilitated by broad social acceptance of Jews before the Civil War and by the tremendous industrial and financial expansion of the postwar period.

The Ashkenazic migration brought not only its poor but also increasingly its educated middle-class laymen and scholarly rabbis, whose penchant for religious reform challenged the intellectual and religious fabric of post-colonial Judaism. Classical Reform, particularly as it developed in the free American environment from the 1840's to 1890, emphasized the progressive nature of Jewish law and interpreted prophetic Judaism as a faith rather than a national identity. Extensive changes were made in the tone and content of services, prayers, and traditional rituals.

Of the influential rabbis who gave the Reform movement substance and institutional form, Isaac Mayer Wise was the most important. Having come to the United States in 1846, Wise established himself in Cincinnati in 1854; he issued a modern Hebrew prayer book in 1857 and played the major role in organizing the liberal Union of American Hebrew Congregations in 1873, the Hebrew Union College in 1875, and the Central Conference of American Rabbis in 1889.

Attempts by traditionalists—most notably Isaac Leeser, *hazzan* of the Sephardic congregation of Philadelphia—to stem the tide and organize parallel institutions met with scant success. By 1881 only 12 of the 200 major congregations were of the Orthodox or proto-Conservative variety. As a result of the proliferation of congregations and secular Jewish social, charitable, and mutual aid societies—particularly the powerful B'nai B'rith organization, founded in 1843—the synagogue was no longer the center of Jewish life. The theological and practical reforms occasioned by growing American secularization diluted the intensity of American Judaism.

Once again, however, the existing paradigm of Jewish life was transformed. Although Jews from Eastern Europe had lived in the United States for a long time, the mass migration set in motion by serious pogroms in the Russian empire in 1881 and debilitating anti-Jewish legislation in 1882 caught the American Jewish community unprepared. Between 1881 and 1924, when severely restrictive immigration quotas were established in the United States, nearly 2.4 million Jews arrived. By 1925 the American Jewish community of over 4 million had become the most powerful Jewish community in the world.

The new arrivals were characterized by religious orthodoxy, political radicalism, and Zionist leanings. At a time in which upper-class social and economic anti-Semitism was making its first noticeable appearance in the United States, the prospect of a massive migration of the "unwashed" at first frightened many American Jews, apprehensive about their status. Nonetheless, a number of relief organizations, immigration aid societies, and school programs were established by American Jews at the turn of the century to aid the newcomers and facilitate their acculturation, indicating that American Jews had maintained their ethnic identity.

The great majority of newcomers settled in the congested slums of New York City, Chicago, Philadelphia, Baltimore, Rochester, Boston, and Cleveland. In New York—where 46 percent of American Jews still lived in 1939—the largest urban community of Jews in history was consolidated. In these slums Jews formed a proletariat, particularly in the garment industry. Such Jews—notably Samuel Gompers, David Dubinsky, and Sidney Hillman—took the lead in establishing powerful trade unions to ameliorate sweatshop conditions. After bitter struggles that brought impressive gains from employers, most of whom were also Jewish, these unions increasingly worked in cooperation with management after World War I to bring about mutually beneficial improvements.

Although many Eastern European Jews came from communities that were isolated from modernity, they had an intense respect for learning. They worked diligently to improve their status and sacrificed much to obtain excellent secular educations for their children. A fusion of the Germanic and Eastern European Jewish community began and was accelerated by the need to combat increasing anti-Semitism in the United States, the growing proclivity of American Jews toward Zionism following the Balfour Declaration in 1917, the rise of Adolf Hitler in the 1930's, and the necessity of working together for relief of oppressed Jewish communities in Central and Eastern Europe. Increasingly, established Jews and newcomers worked together in such organizations as B'nai B'rith, the American Jewish Committee, the American Jewish Congress, the United Jewish Appeal, and the Zionist Organization of America. By the outbreak of World War II the acculturation of the newcomers was far advanced. Many had obtained middle-class status and most had moved from the slums, although the Great Depression and intensified discrimination had slowed this process.

Despite rising anti-Semitism Jews began to play a much greater role in American politics, serving on the local and national level. Louis D. Brandeis, Felix Frankfurter, and Benjamin Cardozo earned great distinction as Supreme Court justices, and several Jews became governors of major states. As the Democrats became the party of urban-oriented reform, Jews flocked to its support. President Franklin D. Roosevelt attracted widespread loyalty among Jews, and they played a prominent role during his administration. On the eve of the destruction of European Jewry, a relatively well-organized, secure, and yet highly self-conscious American Jewish community of about 5 million had developed.

The newcomers expanded the cultural and religious horizons of American Jewry and American culture. In New York and other major cities a vital, secularist Yiddish literature, press, and theater flourished from the 1910's into the 1930's. Together with such organizations as the Arbeter Ring (Workmen's Circle), the Yiddish cultural movement gave a sense of identity to Jews and provided an effective means of hastening acculturation. During the 1920's and 1930's Jews also began to play an important role in the mainstream of American culture, particularly in the area of motion picture entertainment, in which Jewish producers and entrepreneurs took a leading role.

Although the confrontation of traditional Orthodoxy and modern, secular American culture most frequently led to rapid secularization, numerous small

Orthodox synagogues sprang up. Between 1880 and 1916 the number of synagogues nearly quadrupled; almost all of the new ones were Orthodox. Parallel institutions developed quickly. In 1887 the Orthodox established a talmudical academy in New York, which merged with a *yeshiva* ("high school") in 1915 and became Yeshiva College in 1928. They quickly took over the moderate Union of Orthodox Jewish Congregations, founded in 1898, and established the Union of Orthodox Rabbis in 1902 and the Rabbinical Council of America in 1935.

The newcomers also gave vitality to the previously ineffective middle ground, Conservative Judaism, which permitted change within traditional continuity. The Jewish Theological Seminary Association, founded in 1887, was revitalized by the great scholar Solomon Schechter, who was persuaded to come to the United States from England in 1902. In 1913 Schechter founded the Conservative United Synagogue of America. The central organization for Conservative rabbis, the Rabbinical Assembly of America, was established in 1919.

Under the impact of the growth of Jewish life in Palestine, Hitler's impact in Europe, and the influence of Eastern European Jews in the United States, Reform Judaism took a conservative turn. The Central Conference of American Rabbis adopted a more traditional statement of principles in 1937 and published a somewhat more traditional prayer book in 1940.

At the same time Jewish education, especially in the form of afternoon schools, began to reflect a new synthesis of religion, modern Hebrew culture, and Zionism. The Reconstructionist movement—founded in 1935 by Mordecai Kaplan, a professor at the Jewish Theological Seminary—stressed the role of Judaism as a "religious civilization" and advocated the centralization of Jewish community life to include all varieties of Jewishness. Although it never attracted a large number of formal adherents, Reconstructionism exercised a deep impact on American Jewry. Jewish community centers—such as the Young Men's Hebrew Association—also expanded rapidly in the 1920's and thereafter, and centralized Jewish community councils were established in many cities.

The decimation of European Jewry during World War II stimulated an increasing Zionism among American Jews, and they played a crucial role in obtaining support for the establishment of the state of Israel in 1948 and in its preservation and growth. In the approach and aftermath of World War II the community was augmented by over 200,000 highly educated German Jews and intensely religious Eastern European Jews, including many Hasidim.

Postwar prosperity brought the acceleration of earlier developments: the fusion of the Germanic and Eastern communities was nearly completed, as was the acculturation of American Jewry. Except for many of the aged and certain pockets of poorer Orthodox Jews, the great majority of American Jews achieved middle- and upper-middle-class status.

This process was facilitated by the decline in anti-Semitism, which, being associated with nazism, came to be considered un-American. During the 1950's American Jews succeeded in breaking down the quota system in most colleges and universities, and by the 1960's 80 percent of Jews of college age attended college and 13 percent attended graduate school. Jews flocked into the professions, most noticeably law, medicine, accounting, and teaching; although 6 million Jews constituted only 3 percent of the population of the United States in 1970, about 10 percent of American college professors were Jews. As a result Jews played a role in American cultural life far more significant than their numbers would imply, and topics of Jewish interest became prominent in all areas of culture and communications.

The postwar years also saw a tremendous expansion in synagogue construction, particularly as substantial numbers of Jews moved into newer urban or suburban areas. Although the Conservative movement made the greatest gains, all three major branches of American Judaism, of comparable size and strength, benefited. Jewish education became more professional, and about 80 percent of Jewish children received some form of religious education. The day-school movement, mainly under the aegis of the Orthodox, experienced great growth, although it still reached only 80,000 children in 1970. In an era of growing Jewish-Christian dialogue, Judaism became accepted as one of the "three American religions."

By the end of the 1960's the longstanding Afro-American–Jewish alliance in the fight for civil rights was severely undermined as militant blacks frequently singled out Jews as their oppressors. Many Jews came to fear they might have to pay a disproportionate price for Afro-American progress in professional jobs and in colleges and universities, as a result of affirmative action programs. The Israeli military victory in June 1967, which saw an outpouring of support and financial aid from American Jews, as well as the immigration of 17,000 Jews to Israel from July 1967 to the end of 1970, did not elicit the hoped-for response from American churches and the American public. The New Left, in particular, attacked Israel and Zionism in terms that aroused fears of rising left-wing anti-Semitism. Moreover, young Jews as well as many Jewish leaders criticized the American Jewish community for its growing conservatism and materialism. There were, at the same time, signs that the Jewish community was on the threshold of a cultural, and perhaps spiritual, renaissance. There was a significant growth in Judaic studies in major colleges and universities and a considerable increase in the quality and quantity in all forms of Jewish scholarship and cultural activity. Newer and older forms of worship and social organization were being experimented with. The Israeli experience, moreover, exercised a highly beneficial impact on the Jews' self-image, and there was strong support for aiding the beleaguered Soviet Jews. In a mixed state of anxiety and optimism, American Jewry entered, during the 1970's, an intense process of reevaluation and transition.

[Nathan Glazer, *American Judaism;* Jacob Neusner, *American Judaism;* Howard M. Sachar, *The Course of Modern Jewish History;* C. Bezalel Sherman, *The Jew Within American Society;* Judd L. Teller, *Strangers and Natives: The Evolution of the American Jew From 1921 to the Present.*]

ROBERT I. WEINER

JUDICIAL REVIEW is the power of courts to hold that legislative enactments or executive decisions violate a written constitution. The world's oldest and leading practitioners of judicial review are the courts of the United States, all of whom have the power to refuse to enforce statutes or executive orders that they find to be contrary to the Constitution. Although the U.S. Constitution makes no direct statement on the subject, it has always been assumed that American courts, when confronted with conflicting rules of law, must prefer the law of superior obligation to a rule of inferior standing. For the Supreme Court this thesis was first spelled out by Chief Justice John Marshall, in 1803, in the celebrated case of *Marbury* v. *Madison* (1 Cranch 137). In holding a portion of an act of Congress unconstitutional, he reasoned that either the Constitution is the "superior paramount law, unchangeable by ordinary means, or it is on a level with ordinary legislative acts" and that there is no middle ground between these alternatives. If the Constitution is the superior paramount law, then a statute contrary to it cannot be law. If, however, the Constitution is alterable at the will of the legislature, then it

must be regarded as an absurd attempt to limit power that is by its nature illimitable. "It is emphatically the province and duty of the judicial department," Marshall reasoned, "to say what the law is." If the Constitution is superior to legislation, then the Constitution, and not an ordinary statute, must supply the rule of decision when the Constitution and a statute conflict with each other. He added that since judges must take an oath to support the Constitution, they are obliged to invalidate any statute that conflicts with it.

Since most countries that have written constitutions do not practice judicial review, the proposition that a written constitution necessitates judicial review is clearly the embodiment of certain political theories not universally accepted. While it is agreed that a written constitution takes precedence over a conflicting statute, it does not follow necessarily that judges must have the power so to declare. Furthermore, members of Congress and the chief executive also take oaths to support the Constitution, and since constitutional interpretation is neither a mechanical nor an automatic process, there is no a priori reason that legislators and executive officials cannot make their own readings of the fundamental law. But historically the seeds of judicial review are deeply implanted in American experience. As Justice Oliver Wendell Holmes observed in 1927, "Research has shown and practice has established the futility of the charge that it was a usurpation when this court undertook to declare an act of Congress unconstitutional" (*Blodgett* v. *Holden,* 275 U.S. 142, 147). In fact, the American doctrine of judicial review was the natural result of practices and ideas that were well known when the Constitution was written: during the colonial period many colonial statutes were disallowed by the Board of Trade in the name of the crown, and the Privy Council had the authority to annul colonial statutes in the course of ordinary litigation, often doing so when sitting as an appellate court. Above all, during the revolutionary period the American colonies appealed to doctrines of natural rights inherent in a body of natural law that was regarded as superior in obligation to acts of Parliament. Furthermore, at the time the government was being formed, there was widespread distrust of legislative power and a deep conviction that security from the abuse of such power would be found in such contrivances as written constitutions, the separation of powers, and checks and balances. Most of the leading members of the Constitutional Convention of 1787 and many members of the early congresses indicated in one way or another that they accepted the propriety of judicial review. In addition, many state appellate courts rendered decisions prior to 1803 holding state statutes invalid on constitutional grounds.

Judicial review has often been criticized as being undemocratic because it gives appointed, life-tenure judges the power to frustrate the popular will. It has been characterized as dangerous because it tends to minimize the responsibility of legislative bodies and to discourage popular interest in public affairs. It has also been described as ineffective, since many judicial decisions can be ignored, evaded, or circumvented by new legislative formulas. Many jurists in other countries take the view that judicial review violates the theory of the separation of powers; that it unwisely establishes the supremacy, not of the Constitution, but of the judiciary; and that it has the unfortunate consequence of involving the courts in politics. They question the wisdom of permitting judges to exercise so much power over the elected legislature through the manipulation of phraseology that is general and open to a variety of interpretations. Even so, while the exercise of judicial review in particular cases is often the subject of lively and even bitter controversy, the institution itself is accepted as a normal part of the governmental scene in the United States. This acceptance is based in substantial measure on the requirements of the U.S. government as a federal system, for there are bound to be conflicts of jurisdiction between central and local governments and it has been found desirable to authorize the highest court of the land to serve as an umpire to settle these disputes in a rational and peaceful manner.

That the U.S. Supreme Court has recognized the extraordinary character of judicial review is reflected in the fact that in its entire history it has invalidated only about 100 acts or parts of acts of Congress. It has also ruled unconstitutional about 750 state statutes and state constitutional provisions, and this is but a tiny fraction of the enormous body of constitutional and statute law in the fifty states. Clearly—and this is equally true for the state supreme courts and the lower federal courts—the power of judicial review has been exercised sparingly, in accordance with a well-developed philosophy of judicial self-restraint through which the judges have imposed limitations upon their own powers.

The Court has frequently called attention to the "great gravity and delicacy" of its function in ruling on the validity of acts of Congress. Thus, since the jurisdiction of the Court is limited to actual cases involving real controversies between adversary parties, it declines to give advisory opinions. Nor will the Court anticipate a question of constitutional law before it is essential to do so, and it will not formulate a rule of constitutional law broader than is required by the precise requirements of the case. In addition, the Court will not rule on a constitutional issue, even though properly presented in the record, if the case may be disposed of on some other ground, since it prefers statutory construction to constitutional interpretation. Nor will the Court rule on the validity of a statute on the complaint of one who fails to show that he is injured by its operation or who has taken benefits under it, such as sums of money from the public purse.

The Court insists that the constitutional issue raised must be specific and live; it will not entertain an abstract general issue, such as an invocation of the Constitution as a whole. The issue must be substantial, and not trivial, and must be of central significance in the case. If the constitutional question is political in character—for example, whether a state government is "republican" in form—the Court defers to the judgment of the legislative and executive branches of the government and thus considers the issue nonjusticiable. In addition, the Court will not usually inquire into—much less evaluate—the motives of the legislators who voted for a challenged statute. Nor will the Court rule a statute invalid on vague grounds—as being, for example, unwise, unfair, undemocratic, contrary to the spirit of the Constitution, or in violation of principles of natural law. Finally, there is a presumption in favor of the validity of challenged legislation: since it is assumed that the legislative body did not intend to violate the Constitution, the burden of proof rests upon those who challenge the constitutionality of statutes.

The history of judicial review of the U.S. Supreme Court indicates that this power has been exercised unevenly. The Marshall Court considered the validity of many federal statutes, but the net effect of its decisions was to uphold a broad exercise of powers by the national government; Marshall and his colleagues were Federalists in politics and nationalists in spirit, and through a vigorous assertion of the doctrine of implied powers, they created the juristic foundations of a governmental system that endured. It was not until more than fifty years after the *Marbury* decision that the Court held an act of Congress invalid, in the controversial *Dred Scott* case (1857), in a vain effort to dampen the fierce quarrels that soon led to the Civil War.

During Reconstruction the Supreme Court used its judicial powers frequently and vigorously to reduce the possible bite of the Civil War amendments to the Constitution—the Thirteenth, Fourteenth, and Fifteenth—in order to preserve the traditional federal system. The Court insisted that those amendments were not intended to enlarge the powers of the national government to the point at which the states would be "fettered and degraded." Accordingly, the Court invalidated a large body of federal legislation through highly technical and rather literal interpretation of relevant constitutional provisions.

A handful of state statutes were held unconstitutional during the pre–Civil War years, but most such decisions came later. Of the roughly 750 state laws and constitutional provisions held unconstitutional by the Supreme Court, about 650 involved cases decided after 1870.

The second great period of the Court's activism was during the years that Chief Justice Melville W. Fuller presided over the deliberations, 1888–1910, when its principal constituency was the conservative business community. The Court read laissez-faire economics into the Constitution as a limitation upon both federal and state legislative power. The high-water mark of conservative activism was reached in the years 1934–36, when the Court held thirteen New Deal statutes—most of them of major significance—to be unconstitutional. The Court's determined frustration of the will of the president and Congress led to a tremendous public controversy and to an attempt to pack the Court by increasing its membership. Although the attempt failed, the Court changed course abruptly in the spring of 1937 and relieved the pressure that had been generated, by sustaining the constitutionality of various state and federal laws dealing with such subjects as the relief of farm debtors, minimum wages, the right of labor to collective bargaining, and a national social security system. The important decisions of 1937 launched what has often been described as a judicial revolution, for since then the invalidation of federal statutes of a reform character relating to the economy has practically come to a halt. Only a few acts of Congress have been ruled invalid since 1937.

Under the leadership of Chief Justice Harlan F. Stone (1941–46), the Court began, albeit hesitantly, to be particularly concerned with the protection of basic civil liberties. Owing to the pressure of the cold war the Court, under Chief Justice Fred M. Vinson (1946–53), yielded to the government in respect to issues involving loyalty. Under Chief Justice Earl Warren (1953–69) the Court committed itself whole-heartedly to a strong civil liberties position. The

meaning of the due process clause of the Fourteenth Amendment as a limitation upon the states was expanded, especially in the area of the rights of the accused in criminal cases: for example, the right to counsel, freedom from compulsory self-incrimination and unreasonable searches and seizures, and trial by jury—which the federal Bill of Rights had secured against the national government since its adoption in 1791—were absorbed into the due process clause as limitations upon the states. In addition, notable decisions were rendered in the field of free speech, freedom of the press, the right of association, and freedom of religion. The Court also gave new life to the equal protection clause of the Fourteenth Amendment by striking out against racial segregation, malrepresentation in legislative bodies, and the denial of rights to indigent defendants because of their poverty, such as the right to take an appeal from a conviction. With the appointment by President Richard M. Nixon, during his first three years in office, of a new chief justice, Warren E. Burger, and three new associate justices, the Court began gradually to shift ground, and it was noticeable by the end of the 1971–72 term that the civil-libertarian ardor of the Warren Court had begun to cool.

Clearly the power of judicial review is exercised within the context of society's political, social, and cultural setting. The principle of *stare decisis,* the following of precedents in the interest of legal stability, sets limits to discretion. Similarly judges are inclined to show considerable deference to legislative bodies and are by no means indifferent to the prevailing facts of political life. In considerable measure they are confined by the demands of well-articulated legal procedures and by the techniques and thought patterns of their calling. They are subject to a continuous stream of informed criticism from the learned profession to which they belong. Judges are also under pressure to treat problems and persons in a uniform way, so that the demands of equality guide the processes of judicial decisionmaking in significant measure. Furthermore, each judge is influenced by his own sense of judicial integrity—that is to say, by the image he has concerning his expected role in society.

Court decisions are often set aside by later statutes or constitutional amendments, and even overturned by the Court itself. And judges realize that compliance with their decisions is neither automatic nor always substantial. Lower courts have a way of modifying decisions of higher appellate courts through the construction of ambiguous language, and many decisions, such as those of the Supreme Court relating to prayer and Bible-reading in the public schools, are simply ignored in many places. Certainly implementation of the 1954 decision against racial segregation in the public schools has been slow and spotty and has encountered great resistance all the way from the White House and Congress to the lowliest of local school boards. There are, accordingly, many good reasons why judges should heed Justice Felix Frankfurter's admonition in a 1958 decision that the Court "must observe a fastidious regard for limitations on its own power, and this precludes the Court's giving effect to its own notions of what is wise or politic" (*Trop v. Dulles,* 356 U.S. 86, 120). But there have always been judges who actively promote those objectives they regard as necessary and desirable. The tension between those who take an activist position and those who practice judicial self-restraint is at the very core of the exercise by courts of the power of judicial review.

[Charles L. Black, *The People and the Court: Judicial Review in a Democracy;* Leonard W. Levy, ed., *Judicial Review and the Supreme Court.*]

DAVID FELLMAN

JUDICIARY of the United States has its historical background in the legal and political institutions of England. The tribunals set up in the colonies were similar to those of the mother country, and acts of Parliament and the principles of the common law and equity were enforced in the new country as in the old, with the added responsibility on colonial courts of enforcing the enactments of colonial assemblies. The judiciary in the colonies was inadequate in significant respects.

For the large part, these inadequacies did not result from the inherent characteristics of the judiciary as an institution, but rather because of the subjection of judicial institutions, procedures, and rulings to the will and purposes of England. Several of these inadequacies are outlined in the Declaration of Independence as complaints against the king.

Colonial and Constitutional Origins. At the base of the colonial judiciary was the office of justice of the peace, for dealing with minor civil and criminal matters. Above that office was the court usually known as the county court, having original jurisdiction in more important matters. A right of appeal to the colonial assembly existed in some colonies, analogous to appeal to the House of Lords in England. There was in some cases a right of appeal from colonial courts to the judicial committee of the Privy Council in England.

After the colonies became independent states, their court systems remained fundamentally the same, except for the development of courts of appeals with full-time professional judges.

Whereas no provision for an adequate federal judiciary had been included in the Articles of Confederation, all the proposed plans of government submitted to the Constitutional Convention of 1787 provided for a national judiciary distinct from the judicial systems of the states. The adoption of the federal Constitution introduced two major breaks with the past: state judiciaries were subordinated to the federal judiciary in that the Constitution and federal laws and treaties were made the supreme law of the land, and an independent judiciary was explicitly created under the doctrine of the separation of powers. The early establishment of the principle of judicial review in 1803 emphasized the prestige and authority of the judiciary as an independent branch of government.

The first three articles of the Constitution, which were drafted to provide for a high degree of separation of powers, provided respectively for the establishment of the legislative, executive, and judicial branches of the government. Section 1 of Article III provided that the judicial power of the United States should be vested in a Supreme Court and such inferior courts as Congress might establish. It provided also that all federal judges were to hold office during good behavior and that their salaries were not to be diminished during their service in office. By Article II, dealing with the executive, the president was authorized to nominate, and, by and with the advice and consent of the Senate, to appoint Supreme Court judges. Section 2 of Article III prescribed the content of federal judicial power. Within the limits of that power the original jurisdiction of the Supreme Court was defined, while the jurisdiction of particular federal courts was left to congressional determination. Six articles in *The Federalist,* all written by Alexander Hamilton, analyzed and defended the judiciary provisions, and the proposed Constitution was adopted. The first ten amendments (Bill of Rights), added in 1791 to meet criticisms voiced in the ratifying conventions, included additional prescriptions with respect to the courts and the protection of individual rights.

The judiciary provisions of the Constitution were given effect in the Judiciary Act of 1789, enacted after eleven states had ratified the Constitution. The judicial system was headed by a Supreme Court consisting of a chief justice and five associate justices. Below the Supreme Court were three circuit courts, which had no judges of their own but were conducted by two Supreme Court judges and a district judge. Below the circuit courts were thirteen district courts, for each of which a district judge was to be appointed by the president in the same manner in which the Supreme Court judges were appointed. The districts established were coterminous with state lines except that two states were each divided into two districts.

The Supreme Court was given the jurisdiction allotted to it by the Constitution and appellate jurisdiction in certain cases from decisions of the circuit courts and the highest state courts. The circuit courts had original jurisdiction in cases involving large sums of money and serious offenses and in some instances appellate jurisdiction over cases originating in the district courts. In the early years the major portion of the work of the circuit courts was with cases involving state laws, in which federal jurisdiction depended on the fact that the parties were citizens of different states. The district courts were given original jurisdiction in minor offenses against federal laws and in a wide range of admiralty cases, the latter making up the burden of their work in early years.

The Federal Judiciary. The federal judiciary has seen a steady expansion of business—stemming from increases in territory, population, and legislation; the development of an increasingly complex society; and a growing inclination toward litigation. The district courts have undergone drastic jurisdictional changes, assuming in 1891 all the trial court responsibility originally allocated to both them and the circuit courts. Such change naturally resulted in their proliferation, and by 1973 the district courts in the United States numbered ninety-four as compared with thirteen in 1789; thirty-five times as many district judges (both active and retired but active) were required to conduct them. The circuit court system was modified repeatedly from 1801 until the early part of the 20th century, particularly as the jurisdiction of the district courts expanded. With the abolishment of circuit trial court jurisdiction in 1891, the circuit courts assumed increased appellate jurisdiction, and permanent judges were provided for the new circuit courts of appeals. In the interim the membership of the Supreme Court was altered several times, being increased to an all-time high of ten in 1863 and established at nine in 1869. It was not until 1891, however, that Supreme Court justices were relieved of obligations to ride circuit and much of their appellate jurisdiction.

To enable the Supreme Court to keep up with the growing stream of important cases, it was necessary to make further jurisdictional reductions from time to time, particularly by limiting the classes of cases that might be taken to the Supreme Court as a matter of right, in contrast with those that might be accepted or rejected by the Court after a preliminary scrutiny to determine their public importance. Provisions with respect to appellate jurisdiction are exceedingly complex. For example, some cases are taken directly from the district courts to the Supreme Court. Some go from the district courts to the circuit courts of appeals and then to the Supreme Court. Some cannot go beyond the circuit courts of appeals. Some go directly to the Supreme Court from special courts of three district judges made up for the trial of particular cases. Some cases from territorial courts go to circuit courts of appeals. With the exception of a few agencies that have special procedures, orders of independent regulatory commissions, such as the Civil Service Commission, the Atomic Energy Commission, the Federal Trade Commission, and the National Labor Relations Board, are reviewable by circuit courts of appeals. Cases involving federal questions go to the Supreme Court from the highest state courts having jurisdiction over them. The purpose of Congress in prescribing the appellate jurisdiction of the several courts is to provide for the expeditious appeal to the highest court of cases of greatest public importance, while moving those of less importance at a slower pace and limiting the right of appeal with respect to them or cutting it off altogether. In the mid-20th century concern emerged that judicial decisions have maximum finality at early stages, that appellate workloads be reduced, and that the process of bringing appeals be less complex; there was substantial pressure for reform.

Although the federal judiciary, in a narrow sense, consists only of the several courts created pursuant to the provisions of Article III of the Constitution, the exercise of certain powers requires Congress to create other tribunals to exercise judicial functions—for example, the powers to govern territories, to grant patents, and to appropriate money to pay claims against the United States. These tribunals are known as legislative courts, in contrast with the so-called constitutional courts organized under Article III. These courts include those established in the territories of the United States, the Court of Claims, the Court of Customs and Patent Appeals, and the Tax Court of the United States. (The courts of the District of Columbia were once regarded as legislative, but are now considered constitutional courts.) Bearing some resemblance to legislative courts are numerous independent agencies, such as the Interstate Commerce Commission, the Federal Trade Commission, and the National Labor Relations Board, which exercise functions seemingly judicial in character (commonly called quasi-judicial) although they are usually not classified as judicial tribunals.

The appointment of federal judges by the president with the consent of the Senate has been criticized from time to time, but there has been no serious movement for popular elections, such as the movement that took place in connection with state judges. The provision for lifelong tenure during good behavior has been regarded by many as a serious defect in the judicial system. Many judges have proved unwilling to resign from the bench even after reaching the stage of senility. In 1869 and 1919 Congress authorized various procedures for federal judges, other than members of the Supreme Court, to continue to receive full pay if they resigned after reaching seventy years of age with ten years on the bench—but this promise of continued compensation did not bring about resignations. The second of these acts authorized the president to appoint an additional judge for each judge eligible for retirement who did not resign or retire, if he had suffered permanent mental or physical disability for the performance of his duties. A proposal to make such appointments automatic rather than dependent on findings of disability, and to include the Supreme Court along with other federal courts, was much debated in connection with a bill submitted to Congress by President Franklin D. Roosevelt in 1937. The bill proposed that for each Supreme Court justice who failed to retire at age seventy, the president could appoint an additional justice until the total membership of the Court reached fifteen. The proposal failed, but during the period of debate a measure was enacted providing for the retirement of Supreme Court judges according to the procedure already prescribed for the judges of the lower courts. A constitutional amendment authorizing compulsory retirement of judges at a fixed age has been much discussed and has attracted widespread support but has never been implemented in regard to federal judges, except that chief judges of circuit and district courts are required to step down from their administrative duties at the age of seventy.

A barrier to efficiency in the federal courts has been the technicality and diversity in rules of practice. In 1792 Congress empowered the Supreme Court to adopt uniform rules of practice for the federal courts in equity and admiralty cases, and in 1898 the same power was given with respect to bankruptcy cases. Concerning actions at law, however, it was provided in the Conformity Act of 1872 that the federal courts should conform "as near as may be" to the practice currently in effect in the state courts. State practice varied widely. Federal practice, therefore, varied from state to state and was often archaic and cumbersome. After many years of agitation Congress in 1934 authorized the Supreme Court to adopt and promulgate uniform rules of civil procedure for the federal courts—which rules became effective in 1938, marking an outstanding achievement in judicial reform. These rules have undergone revision and similar rules of criminal and appellate procedure have been adopted. In 1973 new federal rules pertaining to evidence were adopted.

The expansion of the work of the federal courts and the increase in the number of courts and judges created a need for central coordination of the judiciary. An act of Congress in 1922 provided for a Judicial Conference of the senior circuit judges, to be presided over by the chief justice of the United States. Later representative district and special judges were added to the council's membership. Pursuant to the act, the conference met annually, and it was charged with making policy related to all aspects of the administration of the federal courts.

The Administrative Office Act of 1939 fundamentally changed the federal judicial system. The Judicial Conference was given a central administrative arm, the Administrative Office of the United States Courts. (Formerly the Justice Department had served in the housekeeping role for the U.S. judiciary.) Circuit councils were also created as regional administrative structures. Although manned by all the U.S. circuit appellate judges, the circuit councils never assumed the vast administrative power conferred on them. In 1971 Congress allocated each circuit a circuit court executive as staff. Previously (1967) Congress had also established the Federal Judicial Center as a research and development center for the U.S. courts.

State, County, and Municipal Courts. The state judicial systems differ greatly among themselves and from the federal system in matters of appointment, tenure, jurisdiction, organization, and procedure. Until the Jacksonian era the selection of state judges was made almost entirely by state legislatures or by some system in which they had indirect control; as late as 1974, in a little over half of the states, including a number of the original thirteen and other older states, judges of appellate courts and courts of general jurisdiction were selected by legislatures or governors or by cooperation between governors and legislatures or senates. The Jacksonian movement toward popular election of judges had prevailed in other states. Both methods are generally regarded as defective in that they involve the judiciary in politics in some measure and often fail in selecting the best personnel; a nonpartisan appointive-elective method (Missouri or Kales plan) was thus evolved and found favor in many states in the last half of this century. Tenure of judicial service varies greatly from state to state and from court to court; some states provide for lifetime appointment, as is true of the federal system, but some have provided means for removing judges before the expiration of their terms. In slightly over half of the states judicial qualification commissions were operative in the 1970's. The machinery of impeachment, although increasingly available in those states, remained cumbersome to use. In other jurisdictions removal was even more difficult. Thirty-three states provided maximum age limits (generally seventy, but up to seventy-five, depending on the state and the level of the court) for mandatory retirement of judges. In all but eleven states provisions existed for calling judges for service after retirement.

The highest state appellate courts rarely have original jurisdiction. Moreover, in order to relieve the highest courts of excessive burdens, almost half of the states have added intermediate appellate courts between them and the courts of original and general jurisdiction.

The expansion of court work and the increase in the number of tribunals created a need for centralized control of the judiciaries of the states. In the 1920's and 1930's a number of states, some in advance of the federal government and some later, organized judicial councils to aid in bringing order from the confusion. The judicial councils, although a great improvement, have generally proven to be a weak administrative model hindered by infrequent meetings, a lack of staff, and an inability to act authoritatively. The replacement of justice-of-peace courts with municipal courts within cities, beginning in the 1920's, was, however, a step toward increased efficiency and consistency. In the 1960's and 1970's court structure was being modified by the establishment of unified state court systems, with central administrative responsibility vested in the state's chief justice and supreme court—including the provision of centralized administrative staffs to assist the supreme courts in exercising their responsibilities. Efforts were being made to eliminate overlapping jurisdictions and the need for trial *de novo* and to simplify and solidify the administrative structure. Although state constitutional amendments have usually been required, over half of the states had adopted the unified state court model by

1973, and it was expected that the remainder would follow.

The geographical jurisdiction of general trial courts over criminal cases and civil disputes is usually organized on a county or multicounty basis, while municipal courts are organized on the basis of the city or borough. General trial courts have subject matter jurisdiction over felony criminal cases, all juvenile, domestic relations, and probate cases, and civil actions involving claims in excess of $5,000. Municipal courts generally have jurisdiction over the remainder of state cases, including criminal misdemeanors, local ordinances, and minor civil cases. The municipal court jurisdiction is similar to that originally assigned to the lay justice of the peace, who still survives with minor dissatisfaction in rural areas and in a few urban centers. One increasingly popular way of simplifying this complex web of geographical and subject matter jurisdictional responsibility is the consolidation of all state trial courts into a single-level trial court to be organized in a county or multicounty area with separate internal divisions to deal with specialized subject matter areas. In the 1960's and 1970's this approach to unifying state court systems was increasingly adopted. In addition, professional managers are increasingly employed by courts, and only six did not have professional state court administrative staff by 1973. Almost every trial court of ten or more judges employed a professional manager.

Complexities of procedure have embarrassed the states as well as the federal government. In the middle of the 19th century a movement was started for the codification of procedure with some elimination of unnecessary technicalities. An attempt at broad simplification was made in the 1920's and 1930's, led by the American Law Institute. After World War II significant progress occurred in the form of model codes promulgated by the American Bar Association and with groups of lawyers. In 1973 all but three states operated under Modern Rules of Criminal and/or Civil Procedure; some states lacked either civil or criminal improvement but had reformed the practice in the remaining area. The problem was more apparent with respect to modern rules of criminal procedure: thirteen states lacked modern criminal rules.

The Status Quo and Reform. Although there is no complete separation of powers in any state or in the federal government, the several judiciaries have maintained their strength against legislative and executive departments. There have been popular outbursts against particular courts at particular times but rarely against the courts as institutions. Nevertheless, there is great concern about the courts' ability to keep pace with the acute increase in litigation.

Increasingly efforts at reform are directed toward diverting case flow away from the courts: examples include no-fault insurance to cut down on the numerous tort cases that result from automobile accidents, efforts to deal with so-called victimless criminal cases with nonadjudicatory procedures, and efforts to simplify the issues of proof and liability in domestic relations litigation. Courts are attempting to increase their administrative and management capacities through the employment of skilled managers, improved judicial structure, and the application of modern management technology and procedures. Although the prestige and power of the courts are often strained because of both the volume of work and the explosiveness of the issues that must be resolved (particularly at the U.S. Supreme Court and other appellate courts), their pivotal position within government seems assured. In general courts have continued to maintain their integrity, ensure the protection of fundamental individual rights against the excesses of the executive and legislature, and preserve the tradition of government by law rather than men.

[American Law Institute, *A Study of the Business of the Federal Courts;* Peter Graham Fish, "The Circuit Councils; Rusty Hinges of Federal Judicial Administration," *The University of Chicago Law Review,* vol. 37 (1968); E. Friesen, E. Gallas, and N. Gallas, *Managing the Courts;* S. Goldman and T. Jahnige, *The Federal Courts as a Political System;* National Conference on the Judiciary, *Justice in the States;* Roscoe Pound, "Principles and Outline of a Modern Unified Court Organization," *Judicature,* vol. 23 (1940).]

GEOFFREY S. GALLAS

JUDICIARY ACT OF 1789, implementing the judiciary clause of the Constitution, first organized the federal judiciary. It provided for a Supreme Court of six members, three intermediate circuit courts comprising two Supreme Court justices and a district judge, and thirteen district courts, corresponding roughly to state boundaries, with a judge for each.

Probably most important was Section 25 granting the Court, through writs of error, the right to hear and decide appeals from state courts in three categories of cases: (1) Where the validity of a federal law, treaty, or authority, under the federal Constitution, was questioned and the state court decided against its validity; (2) where the validity of a state law or authority was similarly questioned and the state court upheld state against federal authority; (3) where a litigant set

up rights, privileges, or exemptions under the federal Constitution, treaty, or statute and had such contention denied by the state courts.

In the act is established the doctrine of judicial review of state legislation, first exercised in the case of *Fletcher* v. *Peck* (1810). The section, through its assignment of jurisdiction to the Supreme Court on writs of error in cases of conflict between state and federal authority, also became one of the strongest bulwarks of federal power against the attacks of the states' rights school. Asserted by the Court in the cases of *Martin* v. *Hunter's Lessee* (1816) and *Cohens* v. *Virginia* (1821), the right to hear appeals under the section was firmly established, to the chagrin of immediate advocates of states' rights and to the permanent enhancement of the Court's prestige and of federal authority. Later decisions reviewing state legislation—notably the Dartmouth College case (1819), *McCulloch* v. *Maryland* (1819), and *Gibbons* v. *Ogden* (1824)—exerted powerful influence on American social and economic development.

[Charles Warren, *The Supreme Court in United States History.*]

L. ETHAN ELLIS

JUDICIARY ACT OF 1801 has been erroneously viewed principally in the light of the election of 1800, leading to the frequent assertion that the outgoing Federalists erected new posts to provide offices for Federalists and perpetuate nationalism through the judiciary. Judicial reform was needed, had for some time been considered, was recommended by John Adams in 1799, and had been carefully prepared. The act (1) reduced the membership of the Supreme Court to five and relieved its justices of circuit court duty; (2) set up six circuits, five presided over by three circuit judges each and the sixth by a circuit and a district judge; and (3) established five new judicial districts. Incoming Democratic-Republicans derided the incumbents as "midnight judges," asserted that the judiciary had become a hospital for decayed politicians, and repealed the act in 1802. This action, at least as partisan as that of 1801, restored the Judiciary Act of 1789 to full force. The repeal debate thoroughly canvassed the issue of judicial review, set forth the Jeffersonian theory of legislative supremacy, and furnished the political setting for the Supreme Court's decision in *Marbury* v. *Madison* in 1803.

[Max Farrand, "The Judiciary Act of 1801," *American Historical Review,* vol. 5.]

L. ETHAN ELLIS

JUILLIARD V. GREENMAN, 110 U.S. 421 (1884), a case in which the Supreme Court upheld the implied power of Congress to make U.S. government notes legal tender (and therefore money) in peacetime as well as in wartime. In the case of *Hepburn* v. *Griswold* (1870) the Court had held the legal-tender acts of 1862 and 1863 unconstitutional, but in 1871, after two new justices had been appointed by President Ulysses S. Grant, the Court reversed this decision and upheld the legal-tender acts as a war measure—giving rise to the charge that Grant had packed the Court. *Juilliard* v. *Greenman* upheld the acts without reference to the war power, and in this decision all the members concurred except Justice Stephen J. Field. In this case the Court inferred the power from the express power to borrow money and the implied power to issue bills of credit.

[H. E. Willis, *Constitutional Law.*]
HUGH E. WILLIS

"JUKES" FAMILY. In 1874 Richard L. Dugdale, who was investigating county jails for the Prison Association of New York, found in a jail in a certain hilly county six persons, blood relations, who were guilty of theft, burglary, rape, and murderous assault. He further learned that of twenty-nine males, immediate kin of these six, seventeen were criminals and fifteen had been convicted of some sort of offense and had received a total of seventy-one years of sentences. Of the women, 52 percent were harlots in some measure. This led him to a remarkable study in heredity, a two-century record of a degenerate family, which he called the Jukes to protect its more worthy members. He traced it back to a man who settled in that area between 1720 and 1740. Intermarriage or cohabitation among themselves and with immediate neighbors with similar backgrounds had brought about an appalling record of crime, licentiousness, imbecility, and public dependency. Dugdale's report was published in 1875. In 1915 a continuation of it to that date by Arthur H. Eastabrook was published by the Carnegie Institution. Eastabrook studied 2,820 persons, including about 1,200 considered by Dugdale, and, despite an improvement in conditions, found 366 paupers, 171 criminals, 282 intemperates, and 277 harlots. The total expense to the state in prison, institutional, and relief costs for the Jukes was estimated at $2,093,685.

[Richard L. Dugdale, *The Jukes;* Arthur H. Eastabrook, *The Jukes in 1915.*]

ALVIN F. HARLOW

JUMPING-OFF PLACES, a term used to describe the towns along the border of American frontier settlement where emigrants completed their outfitting for the journey across the Plains during the 1840's and 1850's. Independence, Mo., was the best known of these places. Among the others were Council Bluffs, Iowa; Saint Joseph, Mo.; and Fort Smith, Ark.

DAN E. CLARK

JUNIOR COLLEGES. *See* **Education.**

JUNIUS, LETTERS OF, were published in the *London Public Advertiser* from Jan. 21, 1769, to Jan. 21, 1772. The unidentified writer who signed himself "Junius" was possibly Sir Philip Francis, a prominent disaffected British government official. A well-informed Whig, Junius poured brilliantly slanderous invective upon Tory-minded English ministers, especially Augustus Henry Fitzroy, Duke of Grafton, for a "series of inconsistent measures" that allegedly ruined England and drove the colonies "into excesses little short of rebellion." Vehement, lucid, frequently reprinted in colonial and other English newspapers, the letters were polemic masterpieces with such extraordinary knowledge and appreciation of contemporary colonial opinion that they lent moral support to the early revolutionary cause. Junius opposed the tea duty, but upheld the legality of the Stamp Act, and prophesied (Dec. 19, 1769) that the colonies aimed at independence.

[*Cambridge History of English Literature,* vol. X.]
RAYMOND P. STEARNS

JÜRGEN LORENTZEN **PRIZE CASE.** In 1861 the U.S. warship *Morning Light,* commanded by Capt. H. T. Moore, captured the Danish bark *Jürgen Lorentzen* sailing from Rio de Janeiro to Havana, Cuba, in the course of the blockade of the Confederacy. The papers of the bark stated that further orders might be received at Havana. Moore, suspecting the bark was bound for a Confederate port, took it to New York City. The Danes complained of ill treatment. An investigation turned out favorably for the *Jürgen Lorentzen.* A joint Danish-American commission was established to ascertain the damages and Congress made provision for the settlement.

[S. P. Fogdall, *Danish-American Diplomacy.*]
S. P. FOGDALL

JURY TRIAL is the characteristic mode of determining issues of fact at common law. It developed by a process of evolution that dates far back into the Middle Ages. It came to be so highly regarded as a procedure devised for the protection of the rights and liberties of the people that the eminent English legal historian Sir William Blackstone characterized it as "the glory of the English law." It was transplanted from England to the American colonies and became an integral part of their legal system in both civil and criminal common law cases, with the exception that a more summary procedure was allowed in petty cases. The Constitution of the United States as proposed in 1787 contained, in Article III, Section 2, the provision that "The Trial of all Crimes, except in cases of Impeachment, shall be by Jury." No mention was made of jury trial in civil cases. The omission was much criticized, and it was argued by some that the failure to include the requirement of jury trial in civil cases was in effect to abolish it. In No. 83 of *The Federalist* Alexander Hamilton refuted this argument and attempted to show that the subject was one much better left to legislation than to constitutional statement. The Constitution was adopted without any provision for jury trial in civil cases, but in the articles of amendment adopted soon afterward to quell the fears of those concerned about the omission of a bill of rights a provision was included to the effect that in common law suits involving more than twenty dollars the right of trial by jury should be preserved. The Sixth Amendment elaborated on the subject of jury trial in criminal cases by providing that "the accused shall enjoy the right to a speedy and public trial, by an impartial jury of the State and district wherein the crime shall have been committed. . . ."

In the several states the procedure of jury trial has continued to evolve since the date of the establishment of the federal government. Some states, for instance, have not adhered rigidly to the old common law requirement that the jury be composed of not more or less than twelve persons and the requirement that the verdict be unanimous. For the federal government, on the other hand, these changes are held to be forbidden by the Constitution. The courts have held that the constitutional phrases mean now what they meant when they were adopted, to the extent that juries must be of twelve persons and verdicts must be unanimous.

Jury trial has not been required in cases involving petty offenses, and in all cases, including cases involving serious crimes, the right of trial by jury may be waived by the parties. The constitutional requirement does not extend to equity cases or to civil cases arising out of statutes. The jury system has undergone serious criticism in the 20th century, partly because of the clogging of court calendars and the inadequacy of juries in dealing with complex questions beyond the limits of their experience. There has therefore been some tendency to avoid jury procedure wherever possible.

[William Anderson, *American Government;* John M. Mathews, *The American Constitutional System.*]

CARL BRENT SWISHER

JUSTICE, DEPARTMENT OF, was established June 22, 1870, by act of Congress. However, the office of attorney general had been created by Congress at the birth of the Republic in the Judiciary Act of 1789. It reached cabinet rank when the first attorney general, Edmund Randolph, attended his initial cabinet meeting on Mar. 31, 1792.

For many years the attorney general served almost solely as the legal counsel to the president and had no department as such. The other cabinet departments had their own solicitors who handled their legal affairs and argued their cases. In the country's various district courts, the U.S. district attorneys who tried federal cases were completely independent of the attorney general. His staff was so small that special counsel had to be retained in trying important cases. He had no official established office of his own; he was permitted to continue his outside law practice; and he was often absent from Washington in pursuit of that practice for long periods of time. Such a situation worked against the development of a unified legal policy for the United States and against any effort to evoke from the courts the consistent body of interpretive law needed by the young nation.

The proliferation of federal offenses proscribed by statute and the growth of civil litigation between private parties and the government transformed the office of attorney general. By the Civil War he was conducting most federal cases, both civil and criminal. He had an office and a growing staff and was devoting all his time to the task. Direction of U.S. attorneys and U.S. marshals had been transferred from the courts to his office. This trend was formalized by the act of Congress of June 22, 1870, that created the Department of Justice under the attorney general; put him in charge of substantially all federal prosecution and litigation; and established a solicitor general to argue government cases, especially before the Supreme Court.

Thus the president was given a legal arm responsible for enforcing federal laws and protecting federal legal interests and at the same time capable of seeking consistent lines of interpretation from the courts. Thus also an organization came into being that could be charged with additional legal duties as they might arise from future legislation—and as early as 1871 the federal prison system was placed under the department's jurisdiction. The growth of laws specifying federal criminal offenses necessitated a Criminal Division, established in 1909. Increased federal interest in developing the public lands brought creation of the Lands Division (later the Land and Natural Resources Division) in 1910. Other legislation, such as the antitrust laws of the late 19th and early 20th centuries, created the need for special offices. In the extensive departmental reorganization of 1933, several of these offices were made into divisions, including the Antitrust Division, the Tax Division, and the Claims Division (later the Civil Division). The process of elevating working groups to formal status continued; the Internal Security Division was created in 1954 and the Civil Rights Division in 1957. As legislation for the protection of the public continued to increase, further special offices were created—the Pollution Control Section in the Land and Natural Resources Division (1970), the Consumer Affairs Section in the Antitrust Division (1971), and the Economic Stabilization Section in the Civil Division (1971).

Meanwhile, enforcement duties were added to the department's litigative work. An investigative arm, the Bureau of Investigation (later the Federal Bureau of Investigation) was created in 1908. The Immigration and Naturalization Service was transferred from the Department of Labor to the Department of Justice in 1940. Antinarcotics enforcement was concentrated in the Department of Justice with the creation of the Bureau of Narcotics and Dangerous Drugs in 1968. In 1972 the president stepped up the federal effort against illegal drugs by creating within the Department of Justice the Office for Drug Abuse Law Enforcement, to coordinate all such federal and state efforts, and the Office of National Narcotics Intelligence, to be a clearinghouse for information on the drug traffic.

In the 1960's the department was assigned service functions beyond its traditional litigative and enforcement duties. The Office of Criminal Justice, charged with examining and proposing improvements in the entire criminal justice process, was created in 1964. Providing federal financial aid to help states and lo-calities upgrade their criminal justice systems was the task given in 1965 to the Office of Law Enforcement Assistance (a program greatly enlarged under the Law Enforcement Assistance Administration in 1968). The Community Relations Service, created by the Civil Rights Act of 1964 and charged with assisting minority groups in a variety of community problems, was transferred from the Department of Commerce to the Department of Justice in 1966.

Thus the expansion of the Department of Justice flowed directly from the American public's continually expanding use of federal legislation to solve economic and social problems. By the mid-1970's the Department of Justice had become by far the largest law office in the world, with a staff of more than 30,000 persons in the United States and its territories.

[Homer Stille Cummings and Carl McFarland, *Federal Justice;* Luther A. Huston, *The Department of Justice;* Albert George Langeluttig, *The Department of Justice of the United States;* U.S. Department of Justice, *Annual Report of the Attorney General* (1970).]

RICHARD KLEINDIENST

JUSTICE OF THE PEACE, originally a medieval English official authorized to keep the peace and try felonies and trespasses at the king's suit and in more recent times to deal with numerous other affairs of local government. The office flourished in the colonies from the beginning. The justice exercised both a criminal and a civil jurisdiction, the former through the courts of Quarter or General Sessions, the latter by statutory authority, such as acts of South Carolina and Massachusetts of 1683 and 1692, respectively, that authorized the justices to try all manner of debts, trespasses, and other matters involving not more than forty shillings, or, in Virginia, "one hogshead of tobacco not exceeding 350 pounds." In Maryland the justices of the peace of a county made up the county court, and later some of their number, known as "justices of the quorum," were designated for court service by the governor. In New York the justices gradually supplanted the old Dutch commissaries. In North Carolina they were given exclusive jurisdiction over the crimes of slaves.

In most of the colonies the justices in court sessions exercised sweeping local executive and administrative powers, drew up the levy, collected the tax, appointed road commissioners and supervised highways, made disbursements, granted licenses to keep taverns and retail liquors, and appointed and controlled administrators, executors, and guardians.

They generally took acknowledgments of deeds and depositions and performed marriage ceremonies, but they seldom exercised the sweeping authority of the English justices of levying wage assessments of laborers.

While the institution still exists in some states, the justice's criminal jurisdiction has been curtailed, and he is in the main a committing magistrate. An appointive officer in colonial times, he is now generally elected, with compensation from fees paid by parties losing in litigation. As in colonial days he is usually a layman. By World War I justices of the peace no longer existed in most urban areas.

[H. L. Osgood, *American Colonies in the 17th Century,* vol. II; C. H. Smith, "The Justice of the Peace System in the U.S.," *California Law Review,* vol. 15.]

RICHARD B. MORRIS

JUVENILE COURTS. The formal inception of a specialized juvenile court in the United States occurred on July 1, 1899, with the implementation of an Illinois legislative act establishing the juvenile court division of the circuit court for Cook County. The civic leaders who propelled this reform sought to separate children and youth from the ugly conditions in prisons and to improve their opportunities for constructive citizenship. Conceptual forerunners of the juvenile court were the equity jurisdiction of the English Court of Chancery, common-law traditions limiting or prohibiting the criminal liability of juveniles below certain ages, and the doctrine of the inherent power of a state to protect the welfare of children. Influenced by these precedents, various American institutions developed in the 19th century: privately operated houses of refuge, where juveniles toiled long hours in manufacturing tasks within an overall repressive environment, first in New York and then in other eastern cities in the 1820's and 1830's; probation, first in Massachusetts in 1868; and separate hearings for juveniles accused of criminal violations, first in Massachusetts in 1879.

The Illinois legislation not only established separate courts for juveniles but also incorporated other 19th-century reforms in juvenile justice. Since the intent was to help rather than to hurt, legal proceedings were kept simple and summary and lawyers were eschewed as unnecessary. Social workers and behavioral scientists were invited into the court to assist the judge in making and carrying out the most appropriate disposition of the cases. Court wards who were to be confined were to be segregated from adult offenders and placed in training and industrial schools—and some were placed in private foster homes and institutions. Probation officers were employed to facilitate a child's adjustment in his own home.

Colorado passed a similar statute in 1903, formalizing and extending a Denver juvenile court that, under Judge Ben Lindsey, had been hearing juvenile cases separately prior to 1899, under a preexisting juvenile disorderly persons act. Specialized juvenile courts were quickly created in the larger cities of the East and Midwest, and by 1925, a juvenile court in some form existed in every state except two.

Constitutional challenges to juvenile court practice and procedure were consistently overruled until the 1960's. Concerns that children were denied a right to bail, to counsel, public trials, jury trials, immunity against self-incrimination, and could be convicted on hearsay testimony or by only a preponderance of the evidence, were swept aside by state appellate court rulings that juvenile proceedings were civil in nature, and that their purpose was to obtain rehabilitation rather than to order punishment. Legislative reform in California and New York in 1961 and 1962, respectively, began to place a more regularized procedure on the historically informal juvenile court practices. Research studies into the juvenile justice system had shown that juvenile court judges not infrequently lacked legal training; that probation officers were undertrained and that their heavy caseloads often prohibited meaningful social intervention; that children were still regularly housed in jails; that juvenile correctional institutions were often, in reality, little more than breeding grounds for further criminal activity; and that juvenile recidivist rates were high.

In 1967 the U.S. Supreme Court ruled (*In re Gault*) that constitutional due process protected the juvenile whose liberty was threatened by juvenile court action and mandated formal rather than informal fact-finding hearings, together with the juvenile's right to be represented by an attorney and to avoid self-incrimination. The Court ruled in 1970 that the criminal system's principle of proof beyond a reasonable doubt must be utilized in juvenile court trials, but also in 1971 that juveniles were not entitled to a jury trial under the Constitution.

These Supreme Court rulings stimulated an ongoing legal challenge of juvenile court practice and procedure and the beginning of a conspicuous role for lawyers in juvenile courts. The lawyer began to replace the judge and probation officer as the advocate for the child. Benevolent intentions and broad juvenile court jurisdiction still apply, however. Juvenile noncriminal offenses—running away, habitual truancy, and incorrigibility—remain subject to sanction in all the states.

Although the customary maximum age limit for juvenile court jurisdiction is the eighteenth birthday, public concerns regarding the extent and seriousness of juvenile violations of the law stimulated efforts in the 1970's to lower the age, to make more serious offenses subject exclusively to criminal rather than juvenile court sanction, and to encourage the application of the juvenile code provision of many states for the discretionary transfer of juveniles from juvenile to criminal court jurisdiction. An oppositional movement sought to narrow juvenile court jurisdiction by transferring primary responsibility for minor offenses to social service agencies and by extending the array of available community service alternatives for juvenile rehabilitation to avoid the necessity for state institutional commitment.

In the 1970's juvenile courts in all the states had jurisdiction over dependent and neglected children as well as juvenile law violators (delinquents) and youths who commit noncriminal offenses (status offenders). Nearly a fourth of those courts also had jurisdiction over the voluntary relinquishment of children and their adoption and over the determination of paternity and support proceedings.

For all juvenile matters there appeared to be a conceptual trend away from an independent juvenile court toward a specialized juvenile or family court division of the court of general trial jurisdiction.

[O. Ketcham and M. Paulsen, *Cases and Materials on Juvenile Courts;* H. H. Lou, *Juvenile Courts in the United States;* A. M. Platt, *The Child Savers: The Invention of Delinquency;* T. Rubin, *Three Juvenile Courts: A Comparative Study.*]

TED RUBIN

KADIAK ISLAND. *See* **Kodiak Island.**

KAKIATE PATENT, located in what is now Rockland County, N.Y., was purchased from the Indians on June 25, 1696, by Daniel Honan and Michael Hawdon. Known as the Hackyackawck or Kakiate patent, it was confirmed by Gov. Benjamin Fletcher. Quarrels over the northern boundary with the owners of the Chesecocks patent delayed partition and settlement.

[David Cole, *History of Rockland County.*]

A. C. FLICK

KALAMAZOO CASE (*Charles E. Stuart et al.* v. *School District No. 1 of the Village of Kalamazoo,* 30 Michigan 69) was decided by the Michigan Supreme Court in 1874. Charles E. Stuart and other citizens of the village of Kalamazoo sought to restrain the school authorities from collecting taxes for the support of a public high school and a nonteaching superintendent. The opinion of the court, written by Chief Justice Thomas M. Cooley, held that the levying of taxes for these purposes was consistent with the educational policy of Michigan since 1817 and was legal under the provisions of the constitution of 1850. Education beyond the rudiments, it was affirmed, had never been regarded by the state as having a merely cultural value, but rather as being "an important practical advantage" to be supplied to rich and poor alike at the option of the school district. The decision confirmed the right of the state to establish, at public expense, a complete system of education from the elementary school through the university, and, as such, constituted an important precedent in many other states.

WILLIS DUNBAR

"KALLIKAK" FAMILY, the fictitious surname of two New Jersey kinship groups investigated and described by the American psychologist Henry Herbert Goddard (1866–1957). The study originated in the detailed genealogical history of an inmate at the training school for retarded children founded and directed by Goddard. The "bad blood" branch of the family, resulting from the illegitimate union during the Revolution of a soldier and a feebleminded girl, yielded 480 known descendants, 143 of whom were retarded. This group comprised criminal, alcoholic, illegitimate, epileptic, blind, deaf, and insane offspring as well; only 46 members were normal. The "good blood" branch, derived from a subsequent marriage to a normal woman, consisted almost entirely of normal individuals, many of whom were superior or prominent. On the basis of Mendelian laws of heredity, Goddard concluded that feeblemindedness is inherited as a recessive unit character. Considered an important contribution to the literature of genetics, the study later came to be regarded as having underplayed the influence of societally conditioned and environmentally determined factors in mental ability.

[H. H. Goddard, *The Kallikak Family.*]

JOEL HONIG

KANAWHA, BATTLE OF THE. *See* **Point Pleasant, Battle of.**

KANAWHA SALT WORKS. Although known to the native Indians, colonists did not learn of the presence of salt along the Kanawha River, near the present city of Charleston, W. Va., until 1755. The land on which the salt springs were located was bought by Joseph Ruffner in 1794, and leased by him to Elisha Brooks, who built a furnace there in 1797, beginning the first salt industry west of the Allegheny Mountains. Later the Ruffner brothers took over the saltmaking, improving the methods and drilling the first deep well in 1808. By 1817 there were twenty brine wells and thirty furnaces producing 600,000 to 700,000 bushels of salt per year. Bitter competition caused the organization of a ''Salt Trust'' in 1817 in an attempt to control production and to regulate prices. Impetus was given the business by the use of coal under the furnaces (1817) and the introduction of a patent steam furnace (1835). Saltmaking was the dominant industry in the Kanawha area for more than fifty years. Its decline is attributed to the discovery of stronger brine more accessible to western markets and the attraction of capitalists to more lucrative industries.

[Ruth W. Dayton, *Pioneers and Their Homes in the Upper Kanawha.*]

INNIS C. DAVIS

KANSAS, popularly known as the ''Sunflower State,'' was admitted to the Union on Jan. 29, 1861. It is located in the geographic center of the United States, and it is the site of the geodetic datum of North America from which all the United States, Canadian, and Mexican maps are made. Rectangular in shape (207 miles from north to south and 403 miles from east to west), Kansas has a total area of 82,264 square miles. There are rich deposits of oil, gas, coal, lead, zinc, and salt. The northern part of the state lies in the Smoky Hill–Kansas rivers watershed; the southwestern part lies in the Arkansas River basin; and the southeastern part is drained by the large tributaries of the Missouri and Arkansas rivers.

When the first white men arrived in Kansas, the resident Indian tribes were the Kansa, Osage, Wichita, Pawnee, and Pueblo. Hunter tribes of Kiowa, Comanche, Arapaho, Cheyenne, and Apache roamed over western Kansas. Archaeologists have uncovered many relics of the early Indian cultures. The Pawnee Indian Village Museum in Republic County is one of the best-preserved sites.

The recorded history of Kansas began when Francisco Vásquez de Coronado's expedition from Mexico reached the highlands of central Kansas in 1541.

The sword of a member of the expedition, found in Kansas, is now in the museum of the Kansas State Historical Society in Topeka. From 1682 to 1739 several French explorers crossed the area as they sought to reach Spanish settlements in the Santa Fe area. England, France, and Spain claimed the area at various times, but real interest in exploration did not come until the purchase of the Louisiana Territory from France by the United States in 1803. The area was well explored in the decades to follow. Meriwether Lewis and William Clark touched the northeastern border on their way to the Pacific. Zebulon M. Pike traversed the breadth of Kansas on his journey to the Southwest in 1806. Stephen H. Long led an expedition into the region in 1819, and reported it a sandy wasteland. Fur trappers Jacob Fowler, Sylvester Pattie, and Jedediah Strong Smith contributed to the geographic knowledge of the area, and John C. Frémont explored the region ahead of several official expeditions.

Preterritorial Kansas was on the way to the West. The Santa Fe Trail was used regularly after 1821. Pioneers on their way to Oregon and California opened new overland routes. The need for frontier defense led to the establishment of Fort Leavenworth (1827), Fort Scott (1842), and Fort Riley (1853); contingents from these forts opened new roads and trails to western and southwestern forts. Fort Larned and Fort Hays are good examples of modern restoration.

Since Kansas was regarded as an arid land, nearly one-fourth of the state's present area was set aside by the federal government as a permanent home for the Indians. Some twenty tribes were sent to this reserved area by the Indian removal acts of 1830 and 1850.

When Kansas was organized as a territory in 1854 under the Kansas-Nebraska Act, the primary incentive was not settlement and development for its own sake; it was rivalry between the North and the South, partly over a railroad to the Pacific and partly over the issue of the extension of slavery. The creation of this new territory was a signal for proslavery forces to make a bid for it to become a new slave state. Thus began the six-year period when the area was referred to as ''Bleeding Kansas.'' This brief period was marked by the work of the New England Emigrant Aid Company, which brought over 2,000 settlers to Kansas to help make it a free state; James H. Lane's militia, which raided the proslavery districts of the state; and civil war in Kansas, as members of the Free-State party received ''Beecher's Bibles'' (rifles) from the East and proslavery men, together with ''border ruffians,'' sacked Lawrence, in retaliation for which John Brown and six others carried out the Pottawatomie massacre, killing five proslavery Kansans at Pottawatomie Creek. The Indian's land vanished rapidly as federal legislation and Indian treaties opened the territory of eastern and southern Kansas to white settlement. During the territorial period four constitutions were drafted. The first three failed, largely because of the fight over slavery. The fourth, adopted in 1859 and usually referred to as the Wyandotte Constitution, made Kansas a free-soil state in 1861. This constitution remains the foundation of government in Kansas.

Kansas faced severe drought and famine in 1860, and the strain of the Civil War shortly after admission to statehood. With fewer than 30,000 men between the ages of eighteen and forty-five, the state furnished over 20,000 men for the Union army, supplying eighteen regiments and three batteries in addition to two black infantry regiments and a black battery. The raid by William C. Quantrill, a Confederate commander, was the most destructive episode of the war. After sacking several border towns, Quantrill's forces invaded Lawrence. Approximately 200 buildings were burned and 150 citizens killed. The biggest engagement was the Battle of Mine Creek in 1864, in which Confederate Maj. Gen. Sterling Price was badly defeated; this defeat crushed the South's bid for the control of the West. After the war Indian tribes were removed to Indian Territory, but Kansans were harassed by Indian raids until the late 1870's.

On July 10, 1860, the first "iron horse" on Kansas soil carried passengers from Elwood to Wathena. Liberal state and federal aid between 1864 and 1890 led to the creation of more than 200 railroad companies and the building of more than 8,700 miles of track. The Union Pacific in 1869 and the Santa Fe in 1872 reached the western border of Kansas. The railway towns of Baxter Springs, Abilene, Wichita, Ellis, Newton, and Dodge City became the western terminals for the "long drive" of Texas cattle. During the same period hard winter wheat was introduced into the agricultural economy, and abundant mineral resources were exploited. Kansas' industries—wheat, railroads, cattle, gas, oil, lead, zinc, and coal—became prime essentials in the nation's economy. Kansas greatly increased its industrialization during World War I and continued to expand afterward. By the mid-1970's Kansas produced about one-fifth of the nation's wheat. Livestock production was of even greater value. Airplanes, farm machinery, and numerous industrial goods were among the state's major manufactures. Its industrial income is derived mainly from oil, natural gas, coal, salt, clay products, and stone.

Politically, the history of Kansas has been basically Republican at both the state and the national level. But the economic problems that arose in adjusting to a new environment frequently led the voters to join political movements outside the mainstream. Kansas furnished leadership and supported issues in the Granger movement (1870's), the Farmer's Alliance (1880's), the Populist revolt (1890's), and the Progressive movement (1901–17). Kansas was indeed a heartland for populism and progressivism. Legislative pioneering in the state is found in the granting of equal property rights and local voting rights to women, a long experiment with prohibition, an early antitrust act (1889), a blue-sky law to protect investors in securities (1913), the direct primary, and the system of referendum and recall. Later leadership was shown in the merit system for state employees (1941), city manager plans, a legislative council, the appointment of supreme court justices, and the private and public support of mental health programs. Kansas has given the nation a president (Dwight D. Eisenhower, 1953–60), a vice-president (Charles Curtis, 1929–32), and an unsuccessful presidential nominee (Alfred M. Landon, 1936). Leaders with roots in Kansas who have made national cultural contributions include the journalist William Allen White; the artists John Steuart Curry, Henry Varnum Poor III, and Sven Berger Sandzen; and the authors Dorothy Canfield Fisher, Damon Runyon, and Edgar Lee Masters.

In 1970 Kansas had a population of 2,249,071, some 4,000 manufacturing firms, 38,000 miles of pipelines, 8,000 miles of railroads, 820 miles of interstate highways, 1,000 state and local parks, and nearly 400 square miles of surface water. Irrigation from deep wells and from impounded water sources was greatly increased in the 1960's.

[Louise Barry, *The Beginning of the West: Annals of the Kansas Gateway to the American West, 1549–1854;* John D. Bright, ed., *Kansas: The First Century;* Paul W. Gates, *Fifty Million Acres: Conflicts Over Kansas Land Policy, 1854–1890;* Homer E. Socolofsky and Huber Self, *Historical Atlas of Kansas;* William F. Zornow, *Kansas: A History of the Jayhawk State.*]

A. BOWER SAGESER

KANSAS, PROHIBITION IN. Kansas was opened for settlement just eight years after the enactment in 1846 of the first Maine Prohibitory Law, prohibiting the manufacture and sale of alcoholic beverages, and the prohibition idea was brought to Kansas by New

Englanders. As early as 1856 Rep. John Brown, Jr., son of the antislavery crusader, presented to the free-state legislature a memorial from a group of Topeka women petitioning for passage of a ''Maine law.'' While no action was taken, sentiment grew until 1880, when the people adopted a prohibition amendment to the state constitution by a vote of 92,302 to 84,304.

For twenty-six years enforcement was resisted in certain localities where saloons were operated under a system of city fines, collected in lieu of licenses. Carry A. Nation advertised this flagrant violation by leading a band of women zealots in saloon-smashing raids, commencing at Kiowa in south-central Kansas, in 1899 (see Hatchet, Carry Nation's). Enforcement became more effective in 1906 when Gov. Edward W. Hoch and Fred S. Jackson, state attorney general, hit on the plan of ousting local authorities who failed to keep their oath to support the state constitution. They replaced such officers with vigilant officials, who invoked the padlock law of 1901. This provided for the closing of buildings used for liquor sales and threw the burden of enforcement on property owners, who had to keep liquor from their premises or face loss of rent.

Success of enforcement stimulated neighboring states to adopt the Kansas plan. But when the federal government enacted Prohibition, a reaction set in. Resentment in large eastern population centers against the Eighteenth Amendment spread to Kansas. Following the repeal of national Prohibition in December 1933, Kansas juries, in many instances, failed to convict liquor dealers. The prohibition situation gained new strength in 1934 when a state repeal amendment was defeated by 436,678 votes to 347,644. Beer was legalized in 1937 when the legislature declared by statute that any beverage containing not more than 3.2 percent alcohol is nonintoxicating. In 1948 the state prohibition amendment was finally repealed.

[T. E. Stephens, *Prohibition in Kansas.*]

BLISS ISELY

KANSAS BORDER WAR. *See* **Border War.**

KANSAS CITY, a city in western Missouri at the confluence of the Missouri and Kansas rivers. The city is an outgrowth of two frontier settlements, Westport and the Town of Kansas.

About 1800 Louis Bartholet (or Bertholett) established a trading camp there, but the first permanent settlement was a trading post at Randolph Bluffs, built by François Chouteau in 1821. Floods submerged this post in 1826, causing it to be moved two miles upstream to a point near the mouth of the Kansas. The place became important because, at the apex of the big bend of the Missouri, it was the nearest water approach to the Santa Fe and California trails.

On the Santa Fe Trail, a few miles west of Independence, its terminus, John McCoy laid out Westport in 1833. It was four miles south of the mouth of the Kansas River. A company headed by William Sublette, noted fur trader, platted the Town of Kansas on the river above Chouteau's warehouse in 1838, but a clouded title prevented its development until 1846, and it was called derisively Westport Landing. Charles and William Bent and Ceran St. Vrain, fur traders, hauled merchandise directly from the Town of Kansas to Fort Bent in Colorado in 1845 and by the next year the settlement was competing for its share of the Santa Fe trade with Independence, Westport, and Leavenworth, its strategic location being a deciding factor.

In 1853 the name was changed to the City of Kansas and in 1889 to Kansas City. During the border difficulties preceding the admission of Kansas to statehood, it was a focus of proslavery activity, and near Westport the Civil War battle of that name was fought on Oct. 23, 1864. Kansas City became a railroad and packing center after the Civil War and absorbed Westport. Kansas City, Kans., a separate municipality, is separated from Kansas City, Mo., only by the Kansas-Missouri state line.

Since the beginning of the 20th century, Kansas City has developed into an important manufacturing city. It is a major railway terminus, shipping livestock, chemicals, and grain to all parts of the United States. Kansas City is the second largest city in Missouri and in 1970 had a population of 507,330.

[A. Theodore Brown, *Frontier Community: Kansas City to 1870;* C. W. Whitney, *Kansas City, Missouri: Its History and Its People, 1808–1908.*]

PAUL I. WELLMAN

KANSAS-COLORADO WATER RIGHTS. In the decade 1875–85 Kansas and Colorado developed irrigation systems by appropriation and diversion of water from the Arkansas River and by pumping water from the underground water supply in the river valley. Kansas claimed that the excessive use of water in Colorado endangered Kansas crops in midsummer and lessened the supply of groundwater. In 1901

Kansas filed suit against Colorado contending on the principle of riparian ownership that the state and its citizens suffered material damage from such illegal diversion. The Supreme Court in *Colorado* v. *Kansas,* 320 U.S. 383 (1907), recognized that each state had rights to the water—but the Court could not force a settlement. Litigation continued until 1943, when the Court recommended settlement of the dispute through the compact clause of the Constitution (Article I, Section 10). The dispute was resolved in 1949 with the federal approval of the Arkansas River Compact. The building of the John Martin reservoir, near Lamar, Colo., was the key to this compact. Under the compact Colorado uses 60 percent of the normal flow of the river and Kansas 40 percent. The compact is administered by a commission of seven members, three from each state and one from the federal government. This approach was so effective that Kansas later entered river compacts with Nebraska, Oklahoma, and Missouri.

A. BOWER SAGESER

KANSAS COMMITTEE, NATIONAL. After the sack of Lawrence on May 21, 1856, during civil war in Kansas Territory over the slavery issue, emigrant aid societies and Kansas relief committees sprang up throughout the free states. On July 9, 1856, representatives of these groups and of older organizations like the New England Emigrant Aid Company and the New York State Kansas Committee met at Buffalo, N.Y., and formed a National Kansas Committee with headquarters in Chicago. It raised and spent some $200,000, sending arms, supplies, and recruits to the Free-State (antislavery) party in Kansas.

[W. E. Connelley, *A Standard History of Kansas and Kansans.*]

SAMUEL A. JOHNSON

KANSAS FREE-STATE PARTY originated at the Big Springs Convention, Sept. 5, 1855. Opponents of slavery in the territory, defeated in previous elections, saw the necessity of consolidating all shades of antislavery opinion. A platform, largely the work of James H. Lane, ridiculed the charge of abolitionism and urged Whigs and Democrats to unite in a party devoted to the exclusion of slavery and of free blacks. Other resolutions, prepared by former Gov. Andrew Reeder, repudiated the "spurious" proslavery legislature. A subsequent convention, meeting at Topeka on Sept. 19, called an election of delegates to a constitutional convention and provided for the appoint-

ment of an executive committee which, with Lane as chairman, exercised the power of a provisional government and directed the party's quest for statehood. Factionalism appeared at Big Springs and became even more pronounced in the convention that framed the constitution. In the formative period of the party, Lane headed the conservative group and strongly hinted that his course was approved by the administration of President Franklin Pierce. Charles Robinson, Kansas agent of the New England Emigrant Aid Company, led the radical wing. The chief tests of strength came over the endorsement of popular sovereignty, which was defeated; and over the exclusion of free blacks, which was referred to the voters and approved along with the Topeka Constitution. The Wakarusa War in December hastened Lane's transition to radicalism and gave him undisputed leadership of the western element in the territory. The Free-State party failed in its major purpose of obtaining immediate statehood. Ignoring the Lecompton movement, begun by the legislature in Lecompton, it captured control of the territorial legislature in 1857. Although the party endorsed Republican doctrine in 1856, it was not supplanted by a Republican organization until Horace Greeley, one of the founders of the Republican party, visited the territory in 1859.

[W. H. Stephenson, *The Political Career of General James H. Lane.*]

WENDELL H. STEPHENSON

KANSAS-NEBRASKA ACT. Three important areas of concern are reflected in the enactment of the Kansas-Nebraska bill in 1854 and the repeal of the Missouri Compromise of 1820: (1) the basis of the struggle surrounding the bill, that is, why it was being proposed; (2) the political complexities involved in its enactment; and (3) the ensuing ramifications.

The historical context of the bill is complex, but frontier expansion was a major factor. With the Compromise of 1850 settling the slavery issue in New Mexico and Utah, it had been hoped that further controversy over slavery would be avoided. But it soon arose again, largely because of schemes for building a transcontinental railroad to the Pacific coast.

Four cities vied to become the terminus of the railroad: Chicago, Saint Louis, Memphis, and New Orleans. The argument in favor of the latter two cities was that lines extending from either of them would go through already settled territory, Texas and the Southwest. To justify building the railroad from a northern city, the "Great American Desert" would have to be settled.

Northern, antislave forces were traditionally more favorable to such programs as homesteading and internal improvements than were southerners. Moreover, expanding in the area west of Missouri and Iowa would benefit the northern economy, particularly because the Great Plains territory was suitable for farming. Further, the building of a northern transcontinental railroad through the Kansas-Nebraska region would present a tempting prospect for lucrative investment of capital, more abundant in the North than in the South.

The actual enactment of a Kansas-Nebraska bill illustrates the fact that the issue of frontier expansion permeated many issues of the day, dictating political alignments and policies on many questions. The bill was introduced by Sen. Stephen A. Douglas of Illinois, a Chicago resident who wanted his region to be the eastern terminus of the proposed railroad to the Pacific. (There is no clear evidence that Douglas had any personal interests in a Chicago-based line.) Although Douglas is usually regarded as the bill's author, there is significant evidence that the political reason for the bill's introduction lay more in the infighting taking place in the Democratic party in Missouri in 1853–54 than in Douglas' interests, which happened to coincide with territorial expansion into Kansas and Nebraska.

Missouri's influential Sen. David R. Atchison was seeking reelection in 1854, and his chief opponent was former Sen. Thomas Hart Benton, currently a member of the House of Representatives. Benton was a leader of slavery restrictionists, with support mostly in the eastern part of Missouri. Atchison, from the western area, had a much stronger proslavery constituency. Both men supported territorial expansion into Kansas and Nebraska, and both favored building a railroad to the Pacific through the region. Atchison also wanted to repeal the Missouri Compromise, which prohibited slavery north of 36°30' north latitude, for repeal would allow his slaveholding constituents to move into the new Kansas and Nebraska territories with their human property.

For repeal of the Missouri Compromise, the support of President Franklin Pierce was essential—and with Pierce's support enactment of the Kansas-Nebraska bill was likely. The president was in a difficult political situation: the Senate support that he needed for the confirmation of his appointments and ratification of his treaties was in jeopardy because some of his political appointments had angered southern partisans, and many of them felt the president had free-soil leanings—a notion far from the facts. Pierce

could ill afford defections in the Senate in this tenuous situation, and Atchison, as president pro tempore of the Senate, was in a position of power and not unwilling to take advantage of the president's predicament. Unlucky Pierce decided he had little choice but to support the Kansas-Nebraska bill—and once he gave his support, he worked hard for its approval, for he did not want to risk the loss of prestige that would accompany the defeat of his first administration measure.

Here Douglas, chairman of the Senate Committee on Territories, entered the picture directly and importantly. He reported the bill for territorial organization of Kansas and Nebraska out of his committee in January 1854, including a provision that, by indirection, repealed the Missouri Compromise. The bill asserted that the Compromise of 1850 had superseded the 1820 principle that 36°30' north latitude was the northern demarcation line for slave states; the bill also stated that the question of slavery in the territories should be settled by the people living in them.

This language conveniently favored Atchison in his senatorial campaign and faced Benton with a difficult dilemma. If Benton voted for the bill, he would betray his antislavery sympathies; but if he voted against it, he would be defaulting on his promise to work for expansion into Kansas and Nebraska. He voted against the bill and suffered defeat in the race with Atchison. The final bill explicitly repealed the Missouri Compromise, and the possibility of slavery in the new territories was made real.

The political ramifications of the enactment of the Kansas-Nebraska bill reached deeply into the general political climate in which it was passed. Support for it from southern members of Congress was nearly unanimous. Northern Democrats were seriously split, half of their votes in the House going for the measure and half against it. Nearly all northern Whigs opposed the bill.

This severe political division fractured the structure of the political party system. The Whig party was essentially destroyed in the South. The Democrats were so seriously divided that their tenuous congressional majority became highly vulnerable. A coalition of anti-Nebraska Democrats, northern Whigs, Know-Nothings, and nativist groups joined the newly organized Republican party, making it a viable political force. By 1856 the Whigs had all but disappeared, and the Republican party was able to confront the weakened Democrats with strong opposition.

In addition to these basic political changes, the Kansas-Nebraska Act had direct ramifications.

Kansas and Nebraska were promptly opened for settlement in 1854. Although Nebraska remained relatively quiet, Kansas, the destination of most of the new settlers, became a political hotbed. Settlers came to Kansas not only to develop the frontier but also—and perhaps more importantly—to lend their weight in the determination of whether Kansas would be free or slave.

The administration of the new territory further complicated Pierce's political difficulties. Immediately, the first governor he appointed for Kansas, Andrew H. Reeder, a Pennsylvania Democrat with southern sympathies, was the source of an endless series of problems for Pierce. Reeder became deeply involved in speculation in Kansas lands. His personal interests led to charges that he cheated Indians, and, worse still, he was unable to satisfy either proslavery or antislavery groups because both suspected his motives.

Thus, from the outset, political stability was lacking in Kansas. The absence of effective, overall, political control of the territory spawned bitter conflict. From the South, proslavery Missourians traveled into Kansas to vote in favor of slavery—and they sometimes came in armed bands. Groups in the North and East, such as the Emigrant Aid Company, helped so large a number of antislavery settlers into the territory that it was generally thought that an honest referendum of actual settlers would not permit slavery in Kansas. But Missouri raiders entering the territory in great numbers made an honest count impossible. In these circumstances a proslavery legislature was elected in 1855, and slavery was legalized. The weight of influence of the roving Missourians on the final tally is uncertain, but the antislavery forces repudiated the vote, wrote their own constitution banning slavery, and then chose a governor and legislature, centered in the town of Lawrence. The stage was thus set for violent confrontation. Proslavery posses, consisting mostly of Missourians, were formed and arrested the free-state leaders. The town of Lawrence was sacked, and some lives were lost. Revenge was taken, and the conflict escalated until some 200 people were killed.

The situation was a difficult one for Pierce to handle. He found he could only give his lawful support to the duly elected proslavery legislature, not to the free-state insurgents. At the same time he wanted to avoid direct intervention because he felt that the people of Kansas themselves should be responsible for maintaining order. Accordingly, he condemned the free-state faction, but also attacked the Missouri invaders. He ordered a halt to civil disorders and urged Kansans to bring peace to the territory through their own efforts. His attempt to end the crisis without intervention failed, and federal troops were brought in to restore order. Not until September 1856, near the end of Pierce's term, did the Kansas situation begin to stabilize.

In every respect the Kansas-Nebraska Act, incorporating the repeal of the Missouri Compromise, stands as a far-reaching piece of legislation. The basis of its proposal exemplifies the serious problems posed by frontier expansion. The complexities of its enactment illustrate the depth of political division in the country at the time and show, through Pierce's predicament, the difficulties of leading the nation and avoiding civil conflict during that period. Finally, the ramifications of the act not only drew the battle lines in the settlement of Kansas but also had an immeasurable effect on American party structure.

[James C. Malin, *The Nebraska Question, 1852–1854;* R. F. Nichols, *Disruption of the Democracy;* Robert R. Russel, "Kansas-Nebraska Bill, 1854," *Journal of Southern History,* vol. 29.]

JEANNETTE P. NICHOLS

KANSAS PACIFIC RAILROAD, a railroad system extending from Kansas City to Cheyenne, Wyo. Originally chartered by the Kansas territorial legislature in 1855 under the name of the Leavenworth, Pawnee and Western Railroad, it was included in the Pacific Railway Act of 1862 and given the right to connect with the Union Pacific at the 100th meridian. The route was changed in 1864. In 1863 Gen. John C. Frémont and Samuel Hallett secured control of the road and changed its name to Union Pacific Railway Company, Eastern Division. After many factional difficulties the road passed into the control of a group of men headed by John D. Perry, who built to Denver and connected it with the Union Pacific at Cheyenne by the use of a subsidiary road, the Denver Pacific. Although operated under financial difficulties throughout the period of its history as an independent system, it served as an outlet for the Texas cattle trade and brought many immigrants to Kansas, thus aiding greatly in the rapid settlement of that state. In 1880, largely through the efforts of Jay Gould, it was consolidated with the Union Pacific to form the Union Pacific Railway Company.

[Nelson Trottman, *History of the Union Pacific;* Henry K. White, *History of the Union Pacific Railway.*]

WALDO CRIPPEN

KANSAS STRUGGLE began in May 1854 with the passage of the Kansas-Nebraska bill, which repealed the slavery-extension restriction of the Missouri Compromise (1820) and applied the doctrine of popular sovereignty to the two territories. Competition for the rich lands of Kansas began immediately. Emigrant aid societies were formed in the East to promote settlement, but the lure of opportunity, a more potent factor than promotion, brought settlers from every section, especially from Missouri and the Old Northwest. Important proslavery settlements were made along the Missouri River; free-state migrants sought homes in the Kansas Valley. In elections for a delegate to Congress in November 1854 and for a territorial legislature in March 1855, there was illegal voting on both sides, but the proximity of Missouri gave the proslavery party an advantage and it won both contests. A slave code was enacted, friction developed between the legislature and Gov. Andrew Reeder, and he was replaced by Wilson Shannon.

Antislavery men, now a majority of the population, assembled at Big Springs in September to form the Free-State party, and a few weeks later inaugurated the Topeka movement for statehood, with James H. Lane as chairman of an executive committee. A *de facto* government, set up early in 1856 with Charles Robinson as "governor," unsuccessfully sought recognition from Congress. At Washington, D.C., acrimonious debates over Stephen A. Douglas' proposal to authorize a constitutional convention culminated in Charles Sumner's "Crime against Kansas" speech, May 19–20, and in Preston S. Brooks's assault on the Massachusetts senator. Open warfare in the territory had been narrowly averted the previous December by Shannon's intervention to prevent "border ruffians" from attacking Lawrence, Kans. As Sumner was making his speech, proslavery men again appeared at Lawrence and destroyed considerable property. This act was avenged by John Brown, who, with sons and neighbors, murdered five proslavery advocates. Such proceedings greatly aroused public sentiment in both North and South and led to renewed activity of aid companies and committees. Sporadic outbreaks continued and "Bleeding Kansas" caused Shannon's removal in favor of John W. Geary, who established peace, and thereby contributed to James Buchanan's election to the presidency.

Robert J. Walker, appointed governor in March 1857, realized that slavery was doomed and labored to save Kansas for the Democratic party. Free-State men declined to participate in the framing and ratification of the Lecompton Constitution, which guaranteed protection of slave property already in Kansas regardless of the decision on the slavery clause. Walker's rejection of fraudulent votes in the October election gave the Free-State party control of the legislature but cost the governor his position. A special session early in 1858 provided a referendum on the whole Lecompton Constitution. As proslavery men declined to vote, it was rejected almost unanimously. Despite the hostility of the great majority of actual settlers, Buchanan recommended that Kansas be admitted under this constitution. The Senate approved, notwithstanding Douglas' opposition; but his following in the House helped to defeat the admittance of Kansas there. Congress then passed the compromise English bill, offering Kansas a gift of land upon becoming a state, but the bribe was rejected. The state was finally admitted in March 1861.

[Alice Nichols, *Bleeding Kansas;* L. W. Spring, *Kansas, The Prelude to the War for the Union;* W. H. Stephenson, *The Political Career of General James H. Lane.*]

WENDELL H. STEPHENSON

KAPOSIA, BATTLE OF, also known as the **Battle of Pine Coulie.** Late in June 1842, about a hundred Chippewa of various bands, coming overland from Lake Saint Croix, established an ambush on the east bank of the Mississippi opposite Little Crow's Sioux village of Kaposia on the site of South Saint Paul, Minn. Premature firing killed two Sioux women, giving the alarm. In a running fight lasting several hours the Chippewa were repulsed after heavy cost in casualties to the Sioux.

[W. W. Folwell, *A History of Minnesota.*]

WILLOUGHBY M. BABCOCK

KASKASKIA, metropolis of the Illinois Country in the 18th century, was founded in April 1703 when the Jesuit Gabriel Marest moved the Mission of the Immaculate Conception from the site of the present city of Saint Louis to the right bank of the Kaskaskia River seven miles above its then junction with the Mississippi. With him went the Kaskaskia tribe of the Illinois Indians, former inhabitants of the Great Village of the Illinois.

For fifteen years Kaskaskia was primarily an Indian village in which a few French lived permanently, while more drifted in and out. Growth commenced in 1717, when it became a part of the district of Louisiana. In 1723 its white inhabitants numbered 196; in 1752, 350 whites and 246 blacks were enumerated. By 1770, after the high point of its 18th-century growth had been passed, it was said to contain 500 whites and nearly that many blacks.

Meanwhile the French and Indian villages had been separated by Pierre Duque Boisbriant in 1719. The population of the latter fluctuated greatly, but the trend was steadily downward. By the end of the century only a handful of Indians remained.

Under Boisbriant, commandant from 1718 to 1724, the characteristic land system of the French village was established—large commons, and common fields in narrow strips. Throughout the French period agriculture flourished, and grain was shipped as far as Detroit and New Orleans. Especially notable was the plantation of the Jesuits, which had become an "extensive estate" by 1763, when the order was dissolved.

During the last third of the 18th century many changes took place in Kaskaskia. In 1765, after the cession of the Illinois Country to Great Britain, a British garrison was established there, and traders and their employees replaced in part the former inhabitants, who moved across the Mississippi. On July 4, 1778, British rule ended with George Rogers Clark's capture of the town. For a decade after the Revolution, American rule was ineffective, and Kaskaskia was sunk in anarchy. During these years its population declined to such an extent that only 349 white inhabitants were counted in a census taken in 1787.

By 1800 Kaskaskia had recovered somewhat, and had become perhaps half American. The creation of Illinois Territory in 1809, and its designation as the territorial capital, resulted in further revival. In the following decade growth continued, and by 1818, when it became the first state capital, Kaskaskia had regained its former position as the metropolis of Illinois. But its primacy was short-lived. When the state offices were removed to Vandalia in 1820 rapid decline set in, and the town soon sank into somnolence. A disastrous flood in 1844 almost destroyed it and led to the removal of the county seat three years later. In 1881 the Mississippi broke through the tongue of land on which Kaskaskia stood and began to flow through the channel of the Kaskaskia River. Gradually it encroached upon the town site. By 1910 it had obliterated the ancient settlement.

[C. W. Alvord, *The Illinois Country, 1763–1818;* S. J. Buck, *Illinois in 1818;* J. H. Burnham, "Destruction of Kaskaskia by the Mississippi River," *Transactions of the Illinois State Historical Society* (1914).]

PAUL M. ANGLE

KASSERINE PASS, BATTLE OF. In a series of engagements in Tunisia during World War II that reached a climax near the Algerian border at the Kasserine Pass, combined Italian and German forces in February 1943 drove American and French troops back about fifty miles from the mountains called the Eastern Dorsale to the Western Dorsale. The events grew out of two actions: the British victory at El Alamein on Oct. 23, 1942, which precipitated the retreat of German Gen. Erwin Rommel's army across Libya and into southern Tunisia; and the Anglo-American invasion of French North Africa on Nov. 8, 1942, which prompted the Axis nations to dispatch troops from Italy to northern Tunisia. By January 1943 Rommel's troops, pursued by Lt. Gen. Bernard L. Montgomery's Eighth Army, were settling into the Mareth positions, and Gen. D. Juergen von Arnim held Bizerte and Tunis against Lt. Gen. Kenneth Anderson's First Army, composed of British, French, and American units.

The Americans were inexperienced and overconfident, and the French lacked modern and mechanized weapons and equipment. There were too few men for the large area they defended, and the forces were thinly dispersed. Yet the roads and railways from Algeria made support for larger forces impossible.

The battle opened Jan. 30, 1943, when Arnim overwhelmed the French at Faïd Pass, and the Americans failed to restore the situation. Arnim attacked again on Feb. 14 and marooned American forces on Lessouda and Ksaira hills. At Sidi bou Zid he soundly defeated the U.S. First Armored Division, which lost ninety-eight tanks and about half its combat effectiveness in two days. Allied troops abandoned Gafsa, Fériana, and Thélepte after destroying equipment and supplies, including facilities at two airfields, and the Americans were forced out of Sbeïtla.

Hoping to gain a great strategic victory by a wide envelopment through Tebéssa to Annaba (Bone), which would compel the Allies to withdraw from Tunisia, Rommel continued the offensive on Feb. 19. He thrust north from Sbeïtla toward Sbiba and sent two columns through the Kasserine Pass, one probing toward Tebéssa, the main effort toward Thala. After fierce fighting, all were stopped by heroic and determined defensive work.

On Feb. 22 a disappointed Rommel sent his units back to the Mareth positions to prepare for Montgomery's inevitable attack. Unaware of Rommel's withdrawal, the Allies moved cautiously forward, retook the Kasserine Pass on Feb. 25, and found the Italians and Germans gone.

The Americans learned their lessons and restructured their training programs. Maj. Gen. George S. Patton, Jr., replaced Maj. Gen. Lloyd R. Fredendall at the head of the II Corps and restored the fighting spirit of the troops. Gen. Harold Alexander instituted a better command system for the ground forces, and the French were rearmed and reequipped. Less than three months later the Allies defeated the Italians and Germans and won control over all of North Africa.

[Martin Blumenson, *Kasserine Pass.*]
MARTIN BLUMENSON

KASSON TREATIES, named after John Adams Kasson, charged with their negotiation, were treaties of reciprocity authorized under the Dingley Act of 1897. They provided for reciprocal tariff concessions with other nations. Treaties were negotiated with Denmark, the Dominican Republic, Nicaragua, Ecuador, Argentina, France, and Great Britain for certain of its smaller colonies on this side of the Atlantic. None of the treaties was ratified by the Senate of the United States.

[U.S. Tariff Commission, *Summary of the Report on Reciprocity and Commercial Treaties.*]
DEXTER PERKINS

KAYODEROSSERAS PATENT. Through sixty years colonial New York's relations with the Mohawk were affected adversely by the Kayoderosseras, or Queensborough, patent. This huge tract of about 300,000 acres formed a rough parallelogram stretching twenty-five miles along the north shore of the lower Mohawk River, with a width northward of twenty-two miles and touching the Hudson River at the Third Falls. The patent was applied for in 1703, and granted later to thirteen persons. Ownership became highly involved and title was disputed by tribal leaders alleging fraud. In 1768 joint efforts by Gov. Sir Henry Moore and Indian Superintendent Sir William Johnson effected a settlement under which the patentees released part of the land and the Mohawk received $5,000 in compensation for the balance.

ARTHUR POUND

KEARNEYITES, followers of Denis Kearney, a California labor agitator, who, in 1877, organized the Workingmen's party of California as a protest against widespread unemployment, dishonest banking, inequitable taxation, land monopoly, railroad domination, Chinese coolie labor competition, and other economic and political evils of the day. Fifty-one Kearneyites were elected delegates to the California constitutional convention of 1879, but they appear to have had little direct influence in the convention. The new constitu-

tion seemed to meet, at least partially, the demands of the Kearneyites; and Kearney himself advocated its ratification. By the presidential campaign of 1880 Kearney's party had practically disappeared.

P. ORMAN RAY

KEARNY, FORT. With a view to protecting the frontier Congress passed a law on July 2, 1836, providing for the opening of a military road from some point on the Mississippi near its junction with the Des Moines River, to the Red River. In accordance with this act, in the spring of 1838 Col. Stephen W. Kearny and Nathan Boone selected a site (present Nebraska City) for a fort on the Missouri River. A military post named Fort Kearny was established there in the spring of 1846, but was abandoned two years later in favor of a new Fort Kearny on the Platte. Lt. W. P. Woodbury was the founder of Fort Kearny on the Platte. This location on the Oregon Trail, near Grand Island, was selected to furnish protection for emigrants who might be en route and to keep the Indians at peace. In 1851 the War Department, because of lack of appropriations, seriously considered abandoning this post. However, the Indian troubles that followed made the idea impracticable, and the fort remained in use until 1871, by which time travel on the Oregon Trail had ceased and the Indian fighting frontier had been pushed farther west. For several years the Fort Kearny reservation remained under the control of the U.S. government. By act of Congress on July 21, 1876, the land was surveyed and offered for sale to "actual settlers at a minimum price in accordance with the provisions of the homestead laws."

[Lillian M. Willman, "The History of Fort Kearny," *Publications, Nebraska State Historical Society,* vol. 21.]
LILLIAN M. WILLMAN

KEARNY, FORT PHIL, principal military post on the Bozeman Trail, was built by Col. H. B. Carrington in the Bighorn foothills on Piney Fork, in northern Wyoming. Construction, starting in July 1866, was opposed by the Sioux, whose warriors harassed it constantly. In the first six months of its existence, Indians made fifty-one hostile demonstrations before the fort, killed 154 persons, and drove off 700 head of stock.

The Fetterman disaster of Dec. 21 reduced the garrison to perilous weakness, but Portugee Phillips, a frontiersman, rode 236 miles to Fort Laramie and secured help. The Wagon Box Fight, Aug. 2, 1867, ended in sharp defeat for the Sioux, but at no time were there enough troops at Fort Phil Kearny for anything but defense. The fort was burned by Indians after its abandonment under the terms of the Treaty of Fort Laramie in 1868.

[Frances Courtney Carrington, *My Army Life;* J. P. Dunn, *Massacres of the Mountains.*]

PAUL I. WELLMAN

KEARNY-FRÉMONT QUARREL. The quarrel between Gen. Stephen Watts Kearny and Col. John C. Frémont in 1847 had its inception in January in the appointment of Frémont as governor of California and the removal of Kearny from the command of all forces in California except a small force of dragoons by Commodore Robert F. Stockton, who was following Navy Department orders. Kearny protested the appointment of Frémont and warned him that he was disobeying the orders of a superior officer. New instructions arrived in March, ordering Kearny to set up a government, but Frémont continued to act as governor in Los Angeles. Frémont's actions led to his arrest and trial by court-martial. The charges brought against him by Kearny were mutiny from Jan. 17 to May 9, 1847; disobedience to orders; and conduct prejudicing good order and military discipline. The trial began in Washington, D.C., on Nov. 2, 1847, and continued until Jan. 31, 1848. The verdict was guilty with a recommendation for clemency. President James K. Polk pardoned Frémont and restored him to his position in the army, but he refused to accept either the verdict or the restoration of rank and resigned from the army.

[Cardinal Goodwin, *John Charles Frémont, An Explanation of His Career;* Allan Nevins, *Frémont, Pathmaker of West.*]

CARDINAL GOODWIN

KEARNY'S MARCH TO CALIFORNIA. Gen. Stephen Watts Kearny left Santa Fe on Sept. 25, 1846, and marched to conquer and possess California. He took with him 300 dragoons, baggage, wagons, and provisions enough for sixty-five days, but left all the horses, which he substituted with mules. The column marched down the valley of the Rio del Norte, and coming near Socorro, N.Mex., on Oct. 6, met the famous scout Kit Carson on the way to Washington, D.C., with dispatches. These messages, from Commodore Robert F. Stockton and John C. Frémont, announced the conquest of California, and Kearny decided to reduce his force, depending on the additional

troops routed by sea for future campaigns. He sent 200 of his force back, ordered Carson to accompany him as a guide, and sent the dispatches forward by Thomas Fitzpatrick. The party soon found itself beset with hardships unexpected and almost beyond endurance. It was faced with the lack of provisions and water, and had to abandon the wagons. Near the Gila River it found evidence of many horses and the remains of a large camp. Reconnaissance revealed only a small party of Mexicans traveling to Sonora, but from them they learned that the Mexicans in California had succeeded in expelling the Americans from Santa Barbara, Los Angeles, and other places. On Dec. 6 Kearny attacked a large force of the enemy at San Pasqual. Kearny and his staff, plus about forty dragoons, led the pursuit and became separated from the others, who were mounted on broken-down mules. Discovering their dilemma, more than 150 Mexicans turned on them and did much damage with their lances. In fifteen minutes of hand-to-hand fighting, the Americans drove them off. With 100 dragoons Kearny, twice wounded, fought his way through some 900 miles of grueling campaign, to reach San Diego, Calif., on Dec. 12, 1846, with a loss of thirty-three men killed and wounded.

STELLA M. DRUMM

KEARNY'S MISSION TO CHINA. Dispatched to the Far East in 1842 to protect American trading interests in China, Commodore Lawrence Kearny arrived in Canton at the close of the Anglo-Chinese War, generally known as the Opium War. After issuing a statement through the American consul that the United States would not under any circumstances sanction trade in opium, Kearny sent a note to the Chinese high commissioner on Oct. 8, 1842, expressing the hope that in any new arrangements governing foreign trade that might be made as a result of the war, the trade and citizens of the United States would be "placed upon the same footing as the merchants of the nation most favored." The reply of the Chinese high commissioner gave assurances that this would be done. By establishing the most-favored-nation doctrine as the standard for American trade relations with China, subsequently incorporated in Cushing's Treaty, the first U.S. treaty with China, this exchange of notes constituted the genesis of the open door doctrine proclaimed by Secretary of State John Hay some fifty-seven years later.

[Tyler Dennett, *Americans in Eastern Asia.*]

FOSTER RHEA DULLES

0

KEARSARGE AND *ALABAMA* ENCOUNTER

(June 19, 1864). The Confederate ship *Alabama,* 1,050 tons, 8 guns, 149 men, and commanded by Capt. Raphael Semmes, arrived at Cherbourg, France, on June 11, 1864, for repairs and to land prisoners of war. Three days later, while the Confederates were awaiting Napoleon III's permission to use the imperial dry dock, the U.S.S. *Kearsarge,* 1,031 tons, 8 guns, 162 men, and commanded by Capt. John A. Winslow, entered port for the purpose of securing the released captives. Winslow's intention was denied by the French authorities, and he withdrew beyond the neutrality limits. Meanwhile, Semmes sent him word that he intended to come out and offer combat as soon as he could take on coal.

The engagement, fought five days later, on Sunday morning, within sight of crowds gathered on the Norman cliffs, was one of the most deliberately staged naval conflicts in world history. The *Alabama,* choosing to circle, fired the opening gun at 10:57 A.M. The battle was decided by superior speed and ammunition. The *Kearsarge,* fresh from overhauling in a Dutch dockyard, enjoyed every advantage of condition over the *Alabama,* whose bottom was foul and powder dull after twenty-two months spent continuously at sea. The *Alabama* was badly hit on its seventh rotation and turned toward Cherbourg, thereby presenting its port broadside. Winslow ordered a raking fire, and the sinking *Alabama* surrendered at 12:24 P.M.

The *Kearsarge*'s loss was one killed and two wounded; the *Alabama*'s, nine killed, twenty-one wounded, and ten drowned. Little effort was made by Winslow to rescue the Confederates, most of whom were taken from the water by the boats of French and British spectators.

[W. M. Robinson, Jr., *The Alabama-Kearsarge Battle.*]
WILLIAM M. ROBINSON, JR.

KEELBOAT,

a type of craft that was used on American rivers, chiefly in the West. The earliest keelboat seems to have been a skiff with a plank nailed the length of the bottom to make the boat easier to steer, but by about 1790 the keelboat had become a long narrow craft built on a keel and ribs, with a long cargo box amidships. It was steered by a special oar and propelled by oars or poles, pulled by a cordelle, or occasionally fitted with sails. Keelboats were 40 to 80 feet long, 7 to 10 feet in beam, 2 feet or more in draft, with sharp ends. A cleated footway on each side was used by the pole men. The success of Henry

M. Shreve's shallow draft steamboats drove the keelboats from the main rivers by about 1820, except in low water, but they were used quite generally on the tributaries until after the Civil War. The chief utility of the keelboat was for upstream transportation and for swift downstream travel. It was used extensively for passenger travel.

[L. D. Baldwin, *Keelboat Age on Western Waters.*]
LELAND D. BALDWIN

KEGS, BATTLE OF THE,

the derisive name given to indiscriminate British firing, at Philadelphia, Pa., on Jan. 7, 1778, on David Bushnell's crudely built mines. These mines were designed to float down the Delaware River to explode upon contact with the British warships. No ships were harmed, but one gunpowder-filled keg exploded, killing four British sailors. The alarmed British garrison fired furiously on every floating object. The panic did not subside until nightfall. Francis Hopkinson, one of the signers of the Declaration of Independence, wrote a poem commemorating the battle ("The Battle of the Kegs") shortly after the event.

[John F. Watson, *Annals of Philadelphia,* vol. II.]
HARRY EMERSON WILDES

KEITH CONTROVERSY,

religious in origin, had political repercussions that added to contemporary unrest in Pennsylvania. The quarrel began in 1691 when George Keith, a Quaker leader formerly prominent in England, violently criticized the Pennsylvania Friends' Meetings on doctrinal grounds and on the basis of their failure to strictly observe the established discipline. Thomas Lloyd, a Quaker minister and William Penn's deputy governor, led the opposition to Keith. In 1692 Keith and his followers formed a separatist meeting, calling themselves "Christian Quakers." Keith was forbidden to preach by the regular meeting and also ran afoul of civil authority because of a seditious pamphlet he wrote attacking a Quaker magistrate. Keith went to England in 1693 to plead the orthodoxy of his group. The London Yearly Meeting, however, disowned him in 1695. As separatists, the Keithians in Pennsylvania formed a faction antagonistic to the proprietary government, but their influence faded out as the century closed.

[Rufus M. Jones, *The Quakers in the American Colonies.*]
RUTH E. STILSON

KELLOGG-BRIAND PACT,

also known as the **Pact of Paris,** an agreement signed in Paris by fifteen nations on Aug. 27, 1928. Eventually nearly all other governments adhered to the treaty. It grew out of negotiations that were begun between the United States, represented by Secretary of State Frank B. Kellogg, and France, represented by the foreign minister Aristide Briand. Article I provides that the parties renounce war as an instrument of national policy in their relations with one another. Article II provides that the settlement of disputes between the parties shall never be sought except by pacific means. Connected with the text of the pact are certain interpretations by Kellogg which were included as a part of the negotiations and which made clear that the treaty did not prevent wars of self-defense, that it was not inconsistent with the Covenant of the League of Nations, and that it did not interfere with the rendering of aid under the Locarno treaties and the so-called treaties of neutrality.

[D. H. Miller, *The Peace Pact of Paris: A Study of the Briand-Kellogg Treaty;* J. T. Shotwell, *War as an Instrument of National Policy and Its Renunciation in the Pact of Paris.*]

BENJAMIN H. WILLIAMS

KELLY'S FORD. On Nov. 7, 1863, the Union army under Gen. George G. Meade, moving forward in the early stage of the Mine Run Campaign, attacked the Confederate works on the Rappahannock River at Kelly's Ford, Va., and at the crossing of the Orange and Alexandria Railroad, a short distance above the ford. Both actions were successful, and the Army of the Potomac crossed the Rappahannock the next day.

[R. U. Johnson and C. C. Buel, eds., *Battles and Leaders of the Civil War,* vol. IV.]

ALVIN F. HARLOW

KELLY'S INDUSTRIAL ARMY was one of a number of "industrial armies" born of the panic of 1893. It was organized during the depression of the 1890's in California by Charles T. Kelly. Consisting of an army of 1,500 men, most of them unemployed, it left California aboard railroad boxcars in the spring of 1894 to join with Jacob S. Coxey's "army," in Washington, D.C. Coxey's army of 500 men had marched from Ohio to bring attention to the plight of the unemployed and to press for relief legislation.

At Council Bluffs, Iowa, the railroad ejected "General" Kelly's army, and after camping in the mud for a week and being fed by sympathizers, the army started on foot for Washington. The remnant of

the army that reached the capital joined the ranks of Coxey's army.

[I. M. Tarbell, *Nationalizing of Business.*]

CARL L. CANNON

KEMPER RAID. Many Americans in West Florida, led by the Kemper brothers—Reuben, Nathan, and Samuel—expected the United States to take possession of that region under the Louisiana Purchase treaty of 1803. Goaded by their disappointment when this did not happen and smarting under private grievances against certain Spanish officials, the Kempers headed a raiding party of about 100 in an abortive attempt to seize control of the region for the United States in 1804. Although this scheme failed, their intrigues produced an almost constant state of alarm in West Florida until it became independent and was annexed to the United States in 1810.

[Stanley C. Arthur, *Story of the Kemper Brothers.*]

WALTER PRICHARD

KENDALL V. UNITED STATES, 12 Peters 534 (1838), held that administrative officers must conform to the law when entrusted by Congress with purely ministerial duties having no executive or discretionary character. Postmaster General Amos Kendall had maintained that he was responsible only to the president in performing such duties with respect to certain postal claims, but the Court unanimously overruled his argument because its acceptance would clothe the president with dispensing powers not contemplated by the Constitution. There was a difference of opinion as to whether the circuit court of the District of Columbia could command Kendall's obedience by a writ of mandamus, the majority holding that it could by virtue of its general common-law powers. President Andrew Jackson's opponents made political capital of the decision, and President Martin Van Buren criticized it in his annual message to Congress, but the law remained unchanged.

[C. Warren, *Supreme Court in United States History;* W. W. Willoughby, *Constitutional Law.*]

LAWRENCE A. HARPER

KENESAW MOUNTAIN, BATTLE OF (June 27, 1864). As Union Gen. William Tecumseh Sherman advanced southward from Chattanooga, Tenn., in his campaign to Atlanta, he usually was able by flanking movements to force Gen. J. E. Johnston, his opponent, to retire without serious fighting. As he neared

Atlanta, Sherman came upon the Confederate army, drawn up with its center occupying the crest of Kenesaw Mountain. He decided on a frontal attack. After a furious cannonade, the Union troops moved forward, but were everywhere repulsed with heavy losses. Several days later Sherman resumed his flanking movements, forcing Johnston southward to the line of the Chattahoochee River. The unnecessary assault on Kenesaw Mountain was one of Sherman's few serious errors in the campaign.

[R. U. Johnson and C. C. Buel, eds., *Battles and Leaders of the Civil War*, vol. IV.]

THOMAS ROBSON HAY

KENNEBEC RIVER SETTLEMENTS. The English idea of colonizing what was later called the Province of Maine dates from the return of David Ingram, survivor of a crew marooned on the Gulf of Mexico in 1558, who started homeward on foot, walked the length of the Atlantic seaboard, and was picked up at Norumbega on the Penobscot. His tales of jewels and furs fired English imaginations. Queen Elizabeth sent her great captains Sir Walter Raleigh, John Davys, and Adrian Gilbert westward. The Virginia Company was formed. Bartholomew Gosnold (1602), Martin Pring (1603), and George Weymouth (1605) visited the Maine coast and reported rich resources there.

In 1607 the Popham plantation was established at the mouth of the Kennebec. But in 1608, because of the severity of the winter, the death of its leader, George Popham, and idleness and factionalism on the part of the colonists, it was abandoned.

The next settlements are shadowy. The settlers were unchurchly men, without patents, and no records were kept. Since the 16th century English fishermen had been busy along the coast; by 1615 they were using Monhegan Island and Pemaquid Point as bases for curing fish. A mutinous crew built a village on Monhegan. The Pilgrims of Plymouth got supplies from English fishermen there in the lean year of 1622. Fishermen were undoubtedly the first permanent settlers on the Kennebec. In 1625 the first deed drawn up in Maine was given to John Brown of New Harbor by Abnaki sagamores. Brown had probably been there for some time. Abraham Shurt settled on Monhegan in 1626. By this time, there were some families on the Kennebec. Before 1630 Thomas Purchase had selected Pejepscot Falls (Brunswick) for a settlement. The Pilgrims established a trading post at Cushenoc, far up the Kennebec, and encountered bitter competition with nearby settlers. According to an early Maine historian, there were eighty-four families near the Kennebec's mouth in 1630. There was a stout fort at Pemaquid. The Lygonia and Plough patents to Kennebec lands are dated 1630 and 1631. A settlement sprang up on Sheepscot Bay. John Parker acquired the lower west bank of the Kennebec in 1648; he bought Georgetown Island from Robinhood, a Kennebec chief. Robert Gutch bought, and settled in 1661 on, the site of what is now Bath. These settlements on or near the Kennebec flourished until the Indian wars, when, at one time or another, most of them except Monhegan were destroyed and had to be rebuilt by former inhabitants or newcomers.

[Henry S. Burrage, *The Beginnings of Colonial Maine;* R. P. T. Coffin, *Kennebec, Cradle of Americans;* Wilbur D. Spencer, *Pioneers on Maine Rivers.*]

ROBERT P. TRISTRAM COFFIN

KENNEBEC TRADING POST. Trading was the first link that bound Maine to the Massachusetts Bay Colony. From 1622 on, the Pilgrims of Plymouth traded in the Kennebec River region. William Bradford obtained an exclusive patent to river land at Cushenoc, now Augusta, head of tide, and built a palisaded station that became known as the Kennebec Trading Post. A brisk trade went on, particularly bartering for Indian furs. By 1633 the Pilgrims had sent enough beaver fur overseas to be made into hats for European gentlemen to pay all their debts. The Pilgrim control of the river lasted until 1661.

[R. P. T. Coffin, *Kennebec, Cradle of Americans.*]

ROBERT P. TRISTRAM COFFIN

KENNEDY, JOHN F., ASSASSINATION. On Nov. 22, 1963, at 12:30 P.M. (central standard time), President John F. Kennedy was assassinated while riding in a motorcade in Dallas, Tex. Also in the motorcade were Texas Gov. John B. Connally, Vice-President Lyndon B. Johnson, and Mrs. Kennedy. Kennedy's car was approaching a triple underpass beneath three streets—Elm, Commerce, and Main—and heading for the Stemmons Freeway when three shots rang out from the sixth floor of the Texas Public School Book Depository on Elm Street. The president was shot twice, in the lower neck and, fatally, in the head. Gov. Connally, in the same car, was also hit and seriously, though not fatally, wounded. Kennedy was killed instantly, though he was rushed to Parkland Hospital where extraordinary efforts were made to revive him; he was pronounced dead at 1 P.M. Within an hour Lee Harvey Oswald, a twenty-four-year-old

KENNEDY, ROBERT F., ASSASSINATION

Dallas resident, was arrested as a suspect in the murder of a Dallas policeman; before midnight Oswald was charged with Kennedy's murder. Oswald worked at the depository building and was located at the scene of the crime; he was also the purchaser and owner of the murder weapon. The assassin was never brought to trial; within forty-eight hours of his capture he was fatally shot by Jack Ruby of Dallas. A presidential commission under Chief Justice Earl Warren concluded that Oswald was the assassin and that he had acted alone.

[*Report of the President's Commission on the Assassination of President Kennedy;* William Manchester, *Death of a President.*]

AIDA DIPACE DONALD

KENNEDY, ROBERT F., ASSASSINATION. At exactly 12:16 A.M. (Pacific standard time) on June 5, 1968, in the Ambassador Hotel in Los Angeles, Sen. Robert F. Kennedy was shot three times. He was fatally wounded by one bullet, which tore into the right side of his head and severely damaged his brain. Kennedy quickly lapsed into a coma, and he was officially pronounced dead at 1:44 A.M., June 6, after brain surgery. The senator's assailant was a twenty-four-year-old emigrant from Jerusalem and an Arab nationalist, Sirhan B. Sirhan. He was caught with the murder weapon in his hand and was convicted and sentenced to death for his crime. The sentence was commuted to life imprisonment in 1972, and he remained in prison in California.

AIDA DIPACE DONALD

KENSINGTON STONE was brought to light by a Swedish immigrant, Olof Ohman, on his farm in Kensington, Minn., in 1898. The stone bears a long inscription in runic characters telling of the difficulties of a party of eight Goths and twenty-two Norwegians on a journey of exploration "from Vinland to the west" and reporting that they had just found ten of their party dead and bloodstained. The survivors recorded that they had another party of ten "by the sea to look after our ships" fourteen days' travel away. These events supposedly took place in the year 1362, but 19th-century scholarly opinion dated the inscription to the 19th century.

The subject of the stone's authenticity was reopened in 1907 by H. R. Holand and argued by him for the rest of his life, but his elaborate historical conjectures foundered on a lack of evidence. He could not shake the conviction of philologists and runol-

ogists that the character of the runic letters and the mode of their cutting proved them to be of modern origin. In books and articles since 1967 O. G. Landsverk and A. Mongé have sought to prove the inscription's authenticity by a demonstration of its cryptographic nature. It is said to be a runic puzzle concealing information about who carved the runes and when. The claim has found little favor with orthodox expert opinion. The Kensington Stone is now the central feature of the Rune Stone Museum in Alexandria, Minn.

[H. R. Holand, *A Pre-Columbian Crusade to America;* O. G. Landsverk, *Ancient Norse Messages on American Stones;* T. J. Oleson, *Early Voyages and Northern Approaches.*]

GWYN JONES

KENT ISLAND COLONY. *See* **Claiborne Settlement.**

KENT STATE PROTEST. In April 1970 Kent State University (21,000 students) in Kent, Ohio (28,000 population), was markedly less radical than comparable institutions across the United States. In 1968 it had experienced some disturbances under pressure from Students for a Democratic Society, and in 1969 there had been some mass disturbances resulting in arrests. But by 1970 the campus was quiet and even lethargic.

Opinions differ sharply about what triggered trouble on the night of Friday, May 1, 1970. Activists insist that students were outraged by President Richard M. Nixon's invasion of Cambodia. The average student argues that it was a case of traditional spring fever. That night students and many casual hangers-on gathered at a string of bars on North Water Street, far from the campus, and proceeded to create a minor disturbance. City police responded late and inexpertly. A real riot developed, in which damage estimated at either $10,000 or $100,000 was done. A curfew was imposed.

On Saturday night students convened in mass on the campus and burned down the Reserve Officers' Training Corps (ROTC) building, an outdated, frame relic of World War II, whose value was stated by authorities to be $100,000; by real estate men, less than $5,000. Students refused to allow city firemen to fight the blaze. During the fire a detachment of more than 400 Ohio National Guardsmen rode into town to restore order.

On Sunday a picnic atmosphere prevailed, and most observers judged the crisis to be over. That night

38

some students broke curfew to create a minor disturbance at the main gate to the campus. In general, however, both students and Guardsmen conducted themselves well and tensions relaxed.

On Monday, May 4, the legal position governing the campus was confused. No one knew precisely who was in charge, how far the authority of the National Guard ran, or what edicts were in effect. About 2,000 students gathered casually, but Gen. Robert Canterbury, commanding the Guardsmen, believed that an order of his had outlawed such assembly. The riot act was read, repeatedly and in all areas, but the students ignored it. Canterbury thereupon gave the order for his troops to clear the campus.

At 11:59 A.M. 113 Guardsmen wearing gas masks, carrying M-79 tear-gas launchers, and armed with M-1 high-powered rifles (deadly at two miles) set forth. With bad luck they marched into a cul-de-sac at the football field. Hemmed in by a high wire fence, they fell into confusion while students threw rocks at them, lobbed back their own gas cannisters, and subjected them to strident and obscene verbal abuse. Distances were so great that no Guardsmen were hurt.

The Guardsmen had no option but to retreat. Students interpreted the retreat as victory, and some pursued the soldiers. Canterbury claimed that rampaging students "threatened the lives of my men," but numerous photographs taken at the time by journalism students fail to confirm his statement. At 12:24, with an escape route open before them, the Guardsmen suddenly wheeled, turned back to the area where they had been humiliated, and fired for thirteen seconds, discharging fifty-five M-1 bullets, five pistol shots, and one blast from a shotgun. At this moment the student nearest the Guardsmen was twenty yards distant.

Thirteen students were struck by bullets, eleven men and two women. Four were killed—Allison Krause, Sandra Scheuer, William Schroeder, and Jeff Miller. The closest was 265 feet away, the farthest, 390 feet. Of the thirteen students hit, the majority had had no possible connection with the disturbances; they had been passing to their next class.

A state grand jury was convoked. It quickly exonerated the Guardsmen, then brought in thirty-one indictments covering forty-three different offenses allegedly committed by twenty-five young people. The jury then added a long, intemperate obiter dictum, castigating the university and its professors. A federal court of review ordered the obiter dictum to be deleted but allowed the indictments to stand. Belatedly, the trials started, but after one young man was found guilty of obstructing firemen, public opinion found the judicial process so offensive that the state wisely decided to drop all charges. In 1974 a federal judge in Cleveland dismissed a criminal trial of seven selected Guardsmen accused of firing on the students.

A major consequence of the Kent State tragedy was the closing down, in sympathy, of some 700 colleges and universities. Many did not reopen during the spring term. This was probably the largest nationwide protest in American history.

[James A. Michener, *Kent State.*]

JAMES A. MICHENER

KENTUCKY, the fifteenth state of the Union, was formed from the trans-Appalachian territory of Virginia. Geographically the state encompasses three distinct topographical areas that have distinct bearings on its history. The eastern-northeastern third of the state lies within the isolative folds of the Cumberland-Appalachian plateau. This mountainous region, which was originally heavily forested, is veined with innumerable streams. The inner dome, or Bluegrass plateau, lies near the center of the state, comprising approximately a fourth of its area. To the southwest lies the largest of the three sections, which includes the southwestern Mississippian embayment and the Jackson Purchase area. The two latter sections have made major social and economic contributions to the state in the field of agriculture; the mountainous plateau has contributed timber and minerals.

Kentucky is truly a border state in all the broad implications of the term. It was the first state organized on the Ohio River frontier and forms a political and economic link between the North and the South, having some of the characteristics of both regions. The discovery and earliest exploration of the territory are shrouded in obscurity. No doubt the region was crossed by ancient trails used by animals, Indians, and later white explorers and settlers. On record is the land-hunting expedition of Thomas Walker of Albemarle County, Va., who led his party through Cumberland Gap in April 1750. He and his party explored the upper Cumberland Valley and traveled out of the state eastward across the Big Sandy country. A year later Christopher Gist of Maryland, an agent of the Ohio Land Company, crossed the Muskingum-Miami areas of the Ohio and turned southward by way of the Big Bone Lick below the Ohio River and crossed out of Kentucky by way of the upper Kentucky Valley.

Between 1750 and 1768, traders from the upper

Ohio and from the Carolinas were in the Kentucky country. There were also some white captives of the Indians who were unwilling visitors to the region. Most dramatic of the earliest explorations were those of the various parties of long hunters who came out from the Carolinas to wander up and down the stream valleys in search of skins and furs. These have left at least a documentary trace of their presence.

The actual dawning of Kentucky history followed the French and Indian War, especially after 1768. In the period of serious exploration (1768–74), the names of such woodsmen as John Finley, Daniel Boone, Simon Kenton, James Harrod, and the Mc-Afee brothers became indelibly associated with the western country. Boone became a human symbol of pioneering and settlement. The settlement of Kentucky also involved scores of other prominent pioneers and leaders.

In 1774 Harrod led a party of Pennsylvania traders up the Kentucky River and overland to establish the first settlement in Kentucky. Called Harrodsburg, the settlement was at the head of the Salt River in present-day Mercer County. The following spring, after Lord Dunmore's War, Boone and Richard Henderson of the Transylvania Company established Boonesborough south of the Kentucky River in present-day Madison County. For the next three decades pioneer settlements appeared in rapid succession all over Kentucky.

Kentucky's pioneer beginnings coincided with the outbreak of the American Revolution. As a result the area was caught in constant Indian raiding from both above and below the Ohio, much of this stimulated by the British in the Great Lakes and Upper Ohio posts. Thus, the opening chapters of the state's history bore a heavy stamp of war and violence. George Rogers Clark organized his Northwest campaign at Harrodsburg and the Falls of the Ohio. Boone, Benjamin Logan, John Bowman, and others defended the home front against ever-threatening raids. The history of these years set the pattern for the future of the state.

The western country was a landed frontier, and the availability of abundant virgin land attracted more than 70,000 settlers overland by 1790. The story of conflict and confusion over land claims is almost as dramatic as that of Indian fighting. Kentucky was to become a rural state primarily dependent on agriculture and livestock production. The decade 1782–92 saw the Kentucky pioneers engaged in a fairly complex political struggle to establish local county governments, to separate the region west of the mountains from the political control of Virginia, and to establish an independent commonwealth. Throughout ten conventions (1784–92), Kentuckians debated a multiplicity of issues and were motivated by an equal number of political impulses. Kentucky entered the Union on June 1, 1792, under a constitution that reflected little if any of the substance of nearly a decade of debate and dispute—nor did it contain much that could be labeled original or innovative.

From the time Kentucky became a state, its citizens were actively concerned with such national issues as the Genêt mission, the negotiation of trade and reciprocity agreements with Britain and Spain, and the growing national partisan struggles. The westerners were predominantly Jeffersonian in outlook; they clearly demonstrated this in the adoption of the Kentucky Resolution in 1798 and later in almost militant support of the Louisiana Purchase. From the outset, politics in Kentucky has had a strong personal flavor and been a popular preoccupation, and the state has produced such major figures as Isaac Shelby, John C. Breckinridge, Humphrey Marshall, George Nicholas, John Adair, Henry Clay, and Richard M. Johnson.

The western phases of the War of 1812 were heavily supported by the Kentucky political contingent in both the statehouse and Congress and by the volunteer militia in the field. The names of Clay and Johnson were of importance among the ''war hawks'' and of Shelby, William Whitley, Joseph Hamilton Daviess, Adair, and Green Clay in military affairs. Kentucky troops fought on a broad front, most successfully in Michigan and New Orleans. The war produced a generous new crop of military-hero politicians who played active roles in the next quarter of a century. Beyond this it had an enormous bearing on the social and economic development of Kentucky. The runaway inflation after 1815 saw the state banking system overexpanded and then bankrupted in the biting depression of 1819. Also, many people migrated westward from the state in these years, giving Kentucky the title of ''mother of the greater westward movement.''

Between 1820 and 1860, Kentucky generally prospered. Its agriculture reached a high degree of development, and farmers became affluent, especially in the Bluegrass. Such institutions as the churches, the press, the schools, the legal profession, and the medical profession grew and matured. Two doctors, Ephraim McDowell and Benjamin Dudley, made medical history in pioneering surgical procedures, and the Transylvania Medical School had its brief moment of brilliance. Yet these were decades of frustration and failure for universities and colleges. Slavery with all its attendant social and economic problems created a considerable amount of social and political friction and division. Never did Kentucky reflect its border location more markedly than in the troubled history of slavery.

The Civil War placed a severe strain on Kentucky; technically the state was neutral, but actually it was sharply divided internally in sentiment and in support of the war. Approximately 35,000 volunteers fought with the Confederacy, and more than twice that number with the Union. An appreciable number of officers of general rank fought on both sides, and both Abraham Lincoln and Jefferson Davis were born in Kentucky. Socially, economically, and politically Kentucky's interests were divided between the sections. State boundaries were violated by both armies, and Kentucky was subject to almost constant skirmishing and guerrilla raiding. The most important battle fought on state soil was at Perryville on Oct. 8, 1862.

In the post–Civil War era Kentucky made sectional political adjustments, exploited its rich timber and mineral resources, and reestablished trade and industry. The most serious challenges were those of building railroads through all parts of the state, opening highways, organizing a public school system, and maintaining law and order. Also, establishing a state university, developing towns and cities, and developing acceptable markets for farm products were major priorities.

This period of Kentucky history was marred by constant political infighting in which both major parties, including two factions of the Democratic party, sought to grasp political control. Bloody violence, especially among the isolated coves of the Appalachian highlands, marred state history. This was especially true where the great family and community blood feuds were fought over a period of years, to the eternal embarrassment and disgrace of the state.

In more positive and civilized veins, Kentucky in the postwar era produced many such top-quality newspaper men as Henry Watterson, W. C. P. Breckinridge, Samuel Roberts, Irvin S. Cobb, Arthur Krock, and Tom Wallace. A fairly long list of distinguished authors, among them James Lane Allen; John Fox, Jr.; Anna Fellows Johnston; Robert Penn Warren; Eleanor Mercein Kelly; Jesse Stuart; Elizabeth Madox Roberts; and Harry Caudill, has offset the stigma of the state's reputation for feudists and self-seeking politicians.

Kentucky entered the 20th century on a note of tragedy. In 1900 governor-elect William Goebel was murdered. This incident almost led to civil war in Kentucky and cast a shadow across both state politics and social relations for two decades. There followed the so-called Black Patch War (1906–08), in which tobacco farmers in the western part of the state revolted against the discriminatory practices of the purchasing companies. These marketing conditions also effected the burley farmers of central Kentucky, who by 1920 organized a cooperative marketing system in which tobacco was sold on an open auction floor, a practice still in use.

From 1908 on Kentucky was to be engaged in a major crusade to improve its educational system. It resulted in the organization of a system of universal education, the passage of compulsory attendance laws, the consolidation of school districts, and the accreditation of teachers. All of this was accompanied by increases in public financial support of schools. Hand-in-glove with the educational reforms was the drive after 1918 to organize a modern highway authority and to build roads. By 1975, Kentucky had an extensive system of intrastate roads and perhaps the most extensive system of toll roads in the nation. Every section of the state is now served by a modern four-lane road, a fact that has wrought a revolution in internal communications in Kentucky.

Since 1920 Kentucky has shifted from its old agrarian economic base to a more highly industrialized one. World War I gave great impetus to the development of coal mining, especially in the eastern field. Both the western and eastern coalfields have been highly productive since the 1920's. Since 1940 an active issue in the state has been the controversy over strip mining, a practice that has great potential for destroying land, streams, homes, and the future of already poverty-stricken areas. Nevertheless, coal is one of Kentucky's most important resources, and during the energy crisis of the 1970's it assumed a much more important economic position.

Out on the Ohio River frontier, or "crescent," Kentucky has become highly industrialized. Among the significant industries are nuclear-produced electricity, hydroelectricity, whiskey, tobacco, textiles, small tools, electric typewriters, glass, electronics, automobiles and trucks, paper, packing, and chemicals. The thermonuclear power plant on the Ohio River south of Paducah was one of the first such plants put in operation in the nation. A major chemical industry has grown up about Calvert City, just below the great Kentucky Dam on the Tennessee River. Lexington, Louisville, Ashland, Paducah, Owensboro, and Bowling Green have become industrial centers. Small fabricating and manufacturing plants have been located in the county seats. Although agriculture is still of major importance in the state's economy, 20th-century Kentucky has become both urban and industrialized.

Two world wars and the Korean War, the automobile and motor truck, mechanized agriculture, modern industry, and hard-surfaced modern roads have intensified the Ohio River frontier spread of urban communities. The balance has tipped in favor of urban and rural nonfarm dwellers. Appalachian Kentucky has lost many of its pioneer-rural characteristics and is socially and economically more dependent on outside resources. Kentucky, along with the rest of Appalachia, has been an area of local and national concern in drives against poverty, lack of economic opportunity, and deprived social betterment. This condition has provoked almost endless debate in Congress, in the state legislature, and among the public in general. Major efforts have been made by various public agencies to bring about a reversal of the traditional way of life in this mountainous area.

The state's population in 1970 was 3,219,311.

[Thomas D. Clark, *A History of Kentucky,* and *Kentucky, Land of Contrast.*]

THOMAS D. CLARK

KENTUCKY, INVASION OF. In July 1862, following the lull after the Battle of Shiloh, Confederate Gen. Braxton Bragg moved his army from northern Mississippi to the vicinity of Chattanooga, Tenn., preparatory to beginning a movement through middle Tennessee into Kentucky. Much of both states was strongly prosouthern. A successful movement to the Ohio River, it was hoped, would bring many recruits into the Confederate ranks, open rich resources to the southern cause, and relieve the pressure on Gen. Robert E. Lee in Virginia. Interior lines would give a controlled, well-led army an opportunity to reach the Ohio in advance of any large Union force.

Bragg's army left Chattanooga late in August and marched rapidly northward, arriving at Bowling Green, Ky., in mid-September. Gen. Don Carlos Buell, commanding the Union defense, hastily gathered troops to oppose Bragg. On Sept. 14 the Confederate leader unnecessarily digressed to attack Munfordville. He wasted five valuable days, and Buell made good use of this time.

When Bragg finally resumed his march, instead of hurrying to Louisville, his proper objective, which was only weakly garrisoned, he went to Bardstown.

Buell rapidly concentrated his forces at Louisville. The first phase of the campaign was over. Up to this point the advantage had been with Bragg. While Buell prepared to march southward, Bragg waited for an army under Edmund Kirby-Smith coming from eastern Kentucky. While he was waiting, Bragg went to Frankfort to help inaugurate a secession governor of Kentucky. The ceremony completed, he returned to his army.

Confused by Buell's energy, Bragg was uncertain. He decided to move eastward toward Kirby-Smith. Buell had gained the initiative. On Oct. 8, 1862, Bragg, gathering his now scattered troops, unexpectedly encountered Buell's army near Perryville. A bloody battle followed, considering the numbers involved. Only portions of the two armies were engaged. Bragg achieved a tactical success, but after dark withdrew to join Kirby-Smith. Two days later it was decided to leave Kentucky rather than chance defeat in enemy territory.

Divided command, unnecessary diversions, and Buell's aggressive leadership all contributed to failure. Nothing of importance had been accomplished. Buell's army had not been defeated nor had the Kentuckians been persuaded to rise in revolt.

[R. U. Johnson and C. C. Buel, eds., *Battles and Leaders of the Civil War,* vol. III.]

THOMAS ROBSON HAY

KENTUCKY AND VIRGINIA RESOLUTIONS. *See* **Virginia and Kentucky Resolutions.**

KENTUCKY CONVENTIONS. In 1784 the Kentucky frontier, then part of Virginia, was subject to frequent Indian attacks. In that year a convention of representative delegates was called to meet in Danville to petition Virginia for assistance. Between 1784 and 1790 nine conventions were held. A tenth convention met in April 1792 to frame the constitution.

The first nine conventions were not held in vain. Specific gains were made in broadening Virginia's laws for frontier defense and in passing four enabling acts. These latter acts gave the Kentuckians three privileges: first, they provided specific rules for registry of land; second, they established definite terms of separation; and, third, they secured Kentucky representation in the Congress of the Confederation. In the numerous debates, pioneer statesmen were able to clarify many issues that faced the western people. Navigation and trade rights down the Mississippi River were partially guaranteed, the Spanish conspiracy was defeated, and a fairly democratic constitution was drafted. Perhaps the most important accomplishment of all was the excellent political training early Kentucky leaders secured as delegates to the conventions.

[W. E. Connelley and E. M. Coulter, *History of Kentucky*.]

T. D. CLARK

KENTUCKY COUNTY, created by the Virginia assembly on Dec. 31, 1776, on petition of the Harrodsburg settlers, presented by George Rogers Clark and John Gabriel Jones. The new county included all of Fincastle County south of the Ohio River and west of the Big Sandy River and Cumberland Mountains. It was divided into three counties in 1780.

[Temple Bodley, *History of Kentucky*.]

W. C. MALLALIEU

KENTUCKY'S NEUTRALITY DOCTRINE. When the secession of the southern states began in 1860, neutrality was considered by Kentucky, Tennessee, and Maryland; but Kentucky was the only state to attempt to apply the doctrine. On May 16, 1861, the Kentucky house of representatives resolved that the state would "take no part in the civil war now being waged, except as mediators and friends to the belligerent parties; and that Kentucky should, during the contest, occupy the position of strict neutrality." Four days later Gov. Beriah Magoffin issued a strict neutrality proclamation, warning all armed forces against entering Kentucky. The pronouncement was made complete on May 20, when the Kentucky senate ratified neutrality.

Kentucky based its position on a long period of training and experience. Occupying a frontier between North and South, it had never been completely a part of either. Largely southern in tradition, kindred, and sentiment, it was bound to the North by economic ties and national aspirations. For years it had been fed on Henry Clay's doctrine of compromises, to be followed by the similar teachings of John J. Crittenden. In 1861, feeling that the cotton South had precipitated the crisis without consulting the border states, and believing that by remaining neutral it could stay the forces of war, Kentucky attempted to apply its system of neutrality until early September, when warring forces swamped it from all sides.

[E. M. Coulter, *The Civil War and Readjustment in Kentucky*; E. C. Smith, *The Borderland in the Civil War*.]

E. MERTON COULTER

KENTUCKY V. DENNISON, 24 Howard 66 (1861). The state of Kentucky petitioned for mandamus in the U.S. Supreme Court to compel the governor of Ohio to "honor a requisition of the Governor of Kentucky for the surrender of a violator of a state law relative to slaves." The Court, in early 1861, held the duty of the Ohio governor mandatory but also denied the federal government power to coerce him to perform the act. Otherwise, the Court asserted, the federal government could destroy the states.

[Carl B. Swisher, *Roger B. Taney*; Charles Warren, *The Supreme Court in United States History*.]

PHILIP G. AUCHAMPAUGH

KERMIS, or kermess, was an annual fair brought by the Dutch settlers to New Netherland in the 17th century. The first regular kermis in New Amsterdam began in October 1659 and lasted six weeks. As in the Low Countries, stalls were built for the exchange of goods, and dancing, processions, lovemaking, and drinking made it a time of hilarious merrymaking that sometimes offended the more puritanical and led to restrictive legislation.

[M. W. Goodwin, *Dutch and English on the Hudson*; G. A. Wumkes, *Kermissen*.]

HAROLD E. DAVIS

KERNSTOWN, BATTLE AT (Mar. 23, 1862). Obeying instructions to detain Union forces in the Shenandoah Valley to prevent their moving to reinforce Gen. George B. McClellan, Gen. Thomas J. ("Stonewall") Jackson engaged Gen. James Shields's division at Kernstown, Va., four miles south of Winchester. Union Gen. Nathan Kimball, commanding on the field after Shields was wounded, repulsed Jackson, who retreated up the valley toward Swift Run Gap.

[R. U. Johnson and C. C. Buel, eds., *Battles and Leaders of the Civil War*, vol. II.]

ROBERT S. THOMAS

KEROSINE OIL. Americans knew something of petroleum deposits as early as 1700, when Richard Coote, Earl of Bellomont, governor of New York, ordered samples brought from an oil spring "eight miles beyond the Senek's furthest castle." Sir William Johnson in 1767 saw the "curious oyl" from Cuba, N.Y., and Pennsylvania settlers knew that Indians sank pits along branches of the Allegheny to procure petroleum for medicine. Soon after the Revolution men digging salt wells along the Allegheny, Kanawha, and other streams found oil, then regarded as a nuisance. But in 1833 Benjamin Silliman, Sr., describing the oil springs near Cuba, N.Y., stated that the product was useful as a liniment for bruises, rheumatism, and sores, and that much larger quantities of medicinal "Seneca Oil" were being distributed from Venango County, Pa. In 1849 Samuel M. Kier of Pittsburgh opened an establishment at 363 Liberty Street, Pittsburgh, and began selling "Kier's Petroleum or Rock Oil, Celebrated for its Wonderful Curative Powers" in bottles on a large scale. Meanwhile other men were taking steps destined to reveal the true value of the oil. James Young of Glasgow, Scotland, in 1847 learned of a petroleum spring in Derbyshire, England, and distilled from it both lubricating and illuminating oils. When it gave out he turned to the distillation of oil from coal. In Prince Edward Island, Canada, as early as August 1846, Abram Gessner distilled kerosine (which he so named from the Greek *keros,* wax, and *elaion,* oil) from local coal. He shortly brought his process to the United States and took out patents that he sold to the North American Kerosene Gas Light Company of New York, which began commercial manufacture in March 1854. Joshua Merrill began manufacturing kerosine from coal in Boston in 1852, and in 1856 was employed by Samuel Downer as chemist for the Downer Works in South Boston, where he experimented with bitumens and Cuban *chapapote,* or asphalt. Kerosine works were erected that same year at Cloverport, Ky., using cannel coal from the vicinity, while another establishment was opened in Perry County, Ohio. By 1859 the country had between fifty and sixty companies making kerosine from coal, shale, and other carbons. The business was growing rapidly and was crowding such older illuminants as whale oil and camphine, a rectified oil of turpentine, out of the markets. It was a short step to turn from coal to petroleum.

Although Kier had begun distilling kerosine or "carbon oil" from petroleum in 1850, he had made little headway, and the effective pioneer was Col. A. C. Ferris of New York. Ferris in Pittsburgh during 1857 saw a tin lamp burning kerosine and realized its possibilities. Obtaining most of the output of the Tarentum, Pa., wells, he began shipping it in quantity to New York, where various manufacturers distilled it. In 1858 the crude-petroleum business of the United States amounted to 1,183 barrels; Ferris handled most of it. Then in 1859 E. L. Drake made his momentous oil strike in western Pennsylvania, and the supply of crude oil rapidly grew enormous. Works for making kerosine from coal died or were converted into oil refineries. By 1860 more than 200 patents had been granted on kerosine lamps. Within a few years kerosine became the world's principal illuminant, penetrating even China. About 1880 a safe kerosine stove was perfected by the Standard Oil Company and furnished an important new use for the product. Meanwhile by-products of kerosine manufacture, such as paraffin, vaseline, and lubricating oils, had taken an important place in American life.

During the 20th century, additional uses were found for kerosine—as an ingredient in jet engine fuel, for domestic heating, as a cleaning solvent and insecticide, and, still, for illumination. In 1972 approximately 2.3 billion barrels (42 gallons each) of kerosine were produced in the United States.

[B. R. F. Bacon and W. A. Hamor, *The American Petroleum Industry;* M. L. Eakin, *Technology in the Early Development of the Petroleum Industry in Western Pennsylvania;* James D. Henry, *History and Romance of the Petroleum Industry;* Sir Boverton Redwood, *Petroleum.*]

ALLAN NEVINS

KETCH, a small yawllike vessel with two masts—main and mizzen—used originally as a yacht but later used in navies as a bomb vessel because of the clear space forward of the mainmast. The *Intrepid,* a Tripolitan ketch captured and used by Stephen Decatur in 1804, exploded in Tripoli harbor later that year. It is the most famous ketch in American naval annals.

[G. W. Allen, *Our War With the Barbary Corsairs.*]

WALTER B. NORRIS

KETTLE CREEK, BATTLE OF (Feb. 14, 1779). After Savannah had fallen to the British at the close of 1778, British troops quickly overran Georgia until they were rebuffed on Kettle Creek in upcountry Wilkes County. Patriots under John Twiggs, John Dooly, Elijah Clarke, and Andrew Pickens surprised and scattered about 700 Loyalists. Nine Americans and seventy British were killed. The British retired from Augusta, and loyalism in Georgia and South Carolina was severely checked.

[C. C. Jones, Jr., *The History of Georgia.*]

H. B. FANT

KEY WEST, in Florida, is the southernmost city of the continental United States. It is said to be named from a corruption of the Spanish Cayo Hueso ("bone key") because of heaps of human bones found there by 18th-century visitors. Grant of the island was made to Juan Pablo Salas on Aug. 26, 1815, by Don Juan de Estrada, Spanish governor of Florida. Salas sold his grant to John W. Simonton of Mobile, Ala., on Jan. 19, 1822, and the latter soon disposed of three-fourths of his rights to four other persons. The first settlers, who were chiefly from South Carolina and Saint Augustine, Fla., came in 1822. In that year the city became a major ship salvaging center. Key West has always been a key military point for the United States and a navy station and Coast Guard base are maintained there. The city has also developed into a popular fishing resort. The 1970 population was 27,563.

[Jefferson B. Browne, *Key West, The Old and the New.*]
W. T. CASH

KIDDER MASSACRE. On June 29, 1867, Lt. L. S. Kidder, Second Cavalry, with eleven men, left Fort Sedgwick, Colo., with dispatches for Gen. George A. Custer, supposedly camped at the forks of the Republican River. Custer had moved, and in following his trail Kidder, in July, encountered 500 Cheyenne under Roman Nose. Surrounded in a gully on Beaver Creek, Kidder and all his men were killed.

[E. B. Custer, *Boots and Saddles.*]
JOSEPH MILLS HANSON

KIDNAPPING OF FREE BLACKS. The kidnapping of northern free blacks to be sold into slavery in the South was a common and, in some instances, organized business notwithstanding laws to the contrary in southern states. Kidnappers were not easily punished because blacks were disqualified as witnesses. Whole families were often kidnapped, but children most frequently. One enterprising Philadelphian gained a livelihood courting and marrying mulatto women and then selling them as slaves.

In 1793 and 1850 Congress passed fugitive slave laws that empowered federal officers to seize runaway slaves in free-soil states and return them to their masters. The summary character of these laws, and the lust of federal magistrates for fees, made it easy for unscrupulous persons to seize free blacks and hasten them into slavery under pretext of law. Free-soil states passed statutes that afforded some protection to free blacks. These laws usually went so far as to nullify the Constitution.

[W. H. Collins, *The Domestic Slave Trade of the Southern States.*]
LLOYD C. M. HARE

KILBOURN V. THOMPSON, 103 U.S. 168 (1880), a Supreme Court case in which it was declared that Congress had no "general power of making inquiry into the private affairs of the citizens," and that since the inquiry being conducted was judicial rather than legislative, the House could not hold Hallett Kilbourn in contempt for refusing to answer questions. Kilbourn could sue the House's sergeant at arms, John G. Thompson, who arrested him, but not representatives advocating his arrest. Subsequent cases have held that in legislative matters Congress has "the power of inquiry—with the power to enforce it."

[W. W. Willoughby, *Constitutional Law.*]
LAWRENCE A. HARPER

KILLDEER MOUNTAIN, BATTLE OF (July 28, 1864). On July 23, 1864, information reached Gen. Alfred Sully's northwestern Indian expedition on the upper Heart River (N.Dak.) of a heavy concentration of Indians on Knife River. Coraling his heavy wagons and accompanying emigrant train, with 2,200 mounted men and light wagons carrying provisions and supplies, Sully marched northward, and on July 28 found the united Sioux forces, estimated at some 5,000, strongly posted on Killdeer Mountain (N.Dak.), in rugged, timbered country.

With dismounted men as skirmishers, supported by light artillery, flanking cavalry, and reserves, Sully pushed forward, while the rear guard protected the wagons. Through skillful use of cavalry charges, while artillery shelled the ravines, the mountain was reached and fully occupied by dark, together with the abandoned Indian camp. Vast quantities of Indian provisions and equipment were destroyed. Sully's casualties were fifteen killed and wounded; the Indian losses were estimated at upward of 100.

WILLOUGHBY M. BABCOCK

KING, MARTIN LUTHER, ASSASSINATION. On Apr. 4, 1968, in Memphis, Tenn., the Rev. Dr. Martin Luther King, Jr., a clergyman and an outstanding leader of the nonviolent movement for civil rights in the United States, was assassinated. He had gone to Memphis on Apr. 3 to prepare the community for a march on Apr. 8 in support of the striking Sanitation Worker's Union. An earlier march on Feb. 28 had been broken up by police, and another, led by King on Mar. 28, had ended in violence. Preparing to leave the Lorraine Motel on the evening of Apr. 4, King went out on the second-floor balcony and was hit by a bullet fired from a rooming house across from the motel. He died one hour later (7:05 P.M.) at Saint Joseph's Hospital.

President Lyndon B. Johnson, addressing the nation over television, proclaimed Apr. 7 a national day of mourning. The U.S. flag was ordered to be flown at half-staff at all federal facilities until King's interment. Many public schools, libraries, and businesses were closed as memorial services and marches were held throughout the nation.

King's body was flown to Atlanta, Ga., where he was born, and there lay in state at Sister's Chapel of Spelman College and later at Ebenezer Baptist Church, of which he was minister. On Apr. 9, after funeral services at the church, the casket was placed on a crude flatbed faded green farm wagon and pulled three and a half miles through the streets of Atlanta by two mules. The funeral cortege consisted of between 50,000 and 150,000 persons, including national leaders. It ended at Morehouse College, from which King had received his bachelor's degree, and there a final eulogy was given prior to temporary interment at Southview Cemetery.

The assassination, the second but not the last for the violence-filled 1960's, was followed by an outbreak of rioting, looting, and arson in black districts of more than a hundred cities across the nation. Thousands were injured and forty-six people were killed in the wave of violence that followed the King assassination. In the nation's capital the outbreak of racial violence, one of the worst in the city's history, devastated several blocks and brought about the death of ten people and the injury of more than a thousand others.

The search for the alleged assassin, one of the most extensive in police history, ended on June 8 when James Earl Ray was arrested at Heathrow Airport, London. After extradition to the United States, Ray pleaded guilty on Mar. 10, 1969, to the charge of murder and was sentenced to ninety-nine years in prison. Several appeals by Ray for a new trial were refused, but on Oct. 21, 1974, he was granted a review based on his claim that his lawyers coerced him to plead guilty.

[Gerold Frank, *An American Death;* Coretta Scott King, *My Life With Martin Luther King Jr.;* William Miller, *Martin Luther King, Jr.*]

JOYCE A. SWEEN

"KING COTTON" was an expression much used by southern authors and orators before the Civil War. The idea appeared first as the title of a book, *Cotton Is King,* by David Christy in 1855. In a speech in the U.S. Senate, Mar. 4, 1858, James H. Hammond declared, "You dare not make war upon cotton! No power on earth dares make war upon it. Cotton is king." The phrase expressed the southern belief that cotton was so essential that those who controlled it might dictate the economic and political policies of the United States and of the world.

[F. L. Owsley, *King Cotton Diplomacy;* J. A. B. Scherer, *Cotton as a World Power.*]

HALLIE FARMER

KING GEORGE, FORT, a cypress plank blockhouse built on the lower Altamaha River in Georgia in 1721, by Col. John Barnwell of South Carolina. The fort initiated a system of American defenses endorsed by the English Board of Trade to offset French expansion. Until it was burned in 1725, it challenged Spanish claims to a region that James E. Oglethorpe later dominated from Frederica, Ga.

[J. T. Lanning, *The Diplomatic History of Georgia.*]

H. B. FANT

KING GEORGE'S WAR (1744–48). Nominally at peace from 1713 to 1744, France and England developed irreconcilable colonial conflicts over boundaries of Acadia in Canada and northern New England and possession of the Ohio Valley. When England's commercial war with Spain (1739) merged into the continental War of Austrian Succession (1740–48), England and France, first fighting as "auxiliaries" on opposite sides, threw off the mask and declared war (Mar. 15, 1744). The French at Louisburg (Cape Breton Island) first learned of the war on May 5, 1744, surprised and captured Canso on May 13 but failed to take Annapolis (Port Royal). In retaliation New Englanders captured Louisburg (June 15, 1745), in the most daring and decisive victory in the colonial war, and planned, with English aid, to attack Quebec and Montreal simultaneously. Seven colonies cooperated to raise forces, ready in 1746, but promised English help did not arrive and the colonials finally disbanded the next year. Meanwhile, France had sent a great fleet in June 1746 to recapture Louisburg and devastate English colonial seaports, but storms, disease, and the death of the fleet's commander frustrated the attempt. A second fleet, sent May 1747, was defeated on the open sea by combined British squadrons. Gruesome raids along the New England–New York borders by both conflicting parties and their Indian allies characterized the remainder of the war, with no result except a temporary check on frontier settlement. Weary of futile, costly conflict, the warring parties signed the Peace of Aix-la-Chapelle in October 1748, granting mutual restoration of conquests (Louisburg for Madras, India), but leaving colonial questions unsolved.

[H. L. Osgood, *The American Colonies in the Eighteenth Century;* Francis Parkman, *A Half-Century of Conflict.*]
RAYMOND P. STEARNS

KING PHILIP'S WAR (1675–76). No longer of value to New Englanders, who, by 1660, produced their own food and valued fishing and commerce above fur trade, Indians played little part in New England economy. Their lands were coveted and their presence denounced, as New Englanders pushed the frontier forward. Conversely, Indians suspected English motives, chafed under English laws, and resented missionary efforts. When Massasoit died (1662), new Indian leaders rejected friendship with the English, ignored the fate of the Pequot, and were suspected of conspiring against New Englanders.

Chief conspirator was Massasoit's second son, Metacom, or Philip, sachem of the Wampanoag after his elder brother Alexander died (1662). Philip renewed the peace covenant with Plymouth Colony, but repeated reports of plots with the Narragansett, the French, and others led Plymouth (1671) to demand an account. Philip haughtily protested peaceful intentions, and agreed to surrender firearms. Sullen peace followed, but the Wampanoag surrendered suspiciously few arms. When three Wampanoag were executed for the murder of John Sassamon, a Christian Indian informer, the warriors attacked and plundered nearby farms. Philip's alliances were not concluded, but the English were unprepared and widely scattered. On June 18, 1675, Wampanoag marauders provoked Swansea settlers to begin hostilities. Swift, devastating raids on Swansea and neighboring towns threw the colonists into panic, intensified when the militia found no Indians to fight—for the Indians never made a stand. The war was a series of Indian raids with retaliatory expeditions by the English.

The English counterattack was ill planned and indecisive and antagonized other tribes. Jealous colonial commanders and troops cooperated badly, the soldiers were poorly equipped and ignorant of Indian warfare, and the troops lacked scouts to track the enemy and refused at first to employ friendly Indians. When combined Plymouth and Massachusetts forces drove Philip from Mount Hope into Pocasset swamps

(June 30), he easily slipped into central Massachusetts. Then, suspicious of the Narragansett, colonial forces raided their country and compelled a few lingerers to sign a treaty of neutrality on July 15, but the warriors, led by Canonchet, had joined in Philip's War. The English sale of captives into West Indian slavery and the slaughter of innocent Christian Indians drove Nipmuck, Abnaki, and even some converted Indians into opposition—though they never united under one leader.

Before the end of 1675, disaster overtook New England on all sides. Mendon, Brookfield, Deerfield, Northfield, and other towns were devastated, abandoned, or both; two colonial forces were ambushed and destroyed (Sawmill Brook, Sept. 3; Muddy Brook, Sept. 18). Similar raids devastated New Hampshire and Maine settlements. The English in turn destroyed the Narragansett in the Great Swamp Fight. As winter came on, the Indians encamped at Quabaug and Wachusett. Philip and a small band wintered at Scaticook, near Albany, in hopes of gaining aid from the Mohawk and the French.

In 1676 the war turned temporarily against the English. Planning to attack the eastern settlements in order to concentrate English forces there while they planted crops in the Connecticut Valley, the Indians (Feb. 9) fell on Lancaster—where Mary Rowlandson was captured—and threatened Plymouth, Providence, and towns near Boston. Meanwhile, the colonies reorganized their forces, destroyed Narragansett food supplies (December–January, 1675–76), and, though they temporarily fell into the Indian strategic trap, captured and executed Canonchet on Apr. 3. The Mohawk threatened to attack the valley Indians from the west, thereby helping the English; and (May 18–19) Capt. William Turner with 180 men surprised and massacred the Indians at Deerfield and broke their resistance in the valley. By the end of May the tide had turned in the west. Capt. Benjamin Church, assisted by able scouts, harried Philip and his followers in swamps near Taunton and Bridgewater. They captured his wife and son on Aug. 1, surrounded his camp, and shot and killed Philip as he tried to escape on Aug. 12.

Philip's death marked the end of the war, though hostilities continued in New Hampshire and Maine, where the Abnaki and others, supplied with French arms and encouragement, wreaked havoc on settlement after settlement. On Apr. 12, 1678, articles of peace were signed at Casco, Maine, with mutual restoration of captives and property. Since June 1675, sixteen towns in Massachusetts and four in Rhode

Island had been destroyed, no English colonist was left in Kennebec County (Maine), and all along New England frontiers, expansion had been retarded. But the Indians no longer posed a threat to the colonists in southern New England. Thereafter their struggle was confined to the northeast and northwest, where it merged with the struggle between the colonists and France for control of the continent.

[James Truslow Adams, *The Founding of New England;* George W. Ellis and John E. Morris, *King Philip's War.*]
RAYMOND P. STEARNS

KING'S COLLEGE. *See* **Columbia University.**

KING'S FERRY, an old ferryboat service crossing the Hudson River from the southwest side of Verplanck's Point in Westchester County to Stony Point in Rockland County, both in New York. During the revolutionary war this territory was much disputed on both sides of the river. On Sept. 22, 1780, Maj. John André, attempting to regain the British lines after his conference with Benedict Arnold, crossed from Stony Point to Verplanck's Point on the King's Ferry.

[Robert Bolton, Jr., *History of Westchester County.*]
A. C. FLICK

KING'S MESSENGER was a royal official during colonial times for the arresting of prisoners of state. When the Regicides—Edward Whalley, William Goffe, and John Dixwell—fled to New England on the accession of Charles II, two king's messengers were sent to arrest them.

[Thomas Hutchinson, *History of Massachusetts.*]
R. W. G. VAIL

KING'S MOUNTAIN, BATTLE OF (Oct. 7, 1780). In the autumn of 1780 Maj. Patrick Ferguson, in command of a detachment of about 1,000 soldiers from the British army of Gen. Charles Cornwallis, made a foray into the western part of North Carolina. The "mountain men," as the dwellers in the backcountry were called, had been stirred up by the ill conduct of the British troops in the South; and from the western Carolinas and Virginia, as well as from the present states of Kentucky and Tennessee, about 2,000 American frontiersmen gathered under the leadership of Col. Isaac Shelby, Col. William Campbell, Col. John Sevier, Maj. Joseph MacDowell, and Maj. Joseph Winston. Hearing of this possible resistance,

Ferguson beat a hasty retreat, but the American forces caught up to him at an eminence called King's Mountain, which is in what is now York County, S.C., about a mile and a half south of the North Carolina boundary. Here Ferguson took his position atop the mountain on Oct. 6. The next day he was entirely surrounded by the Americans. On the afternoon of Oct. 7 the Americans attacked up the mountain from all sides. The part of the ridge occupied by the British was extremely narrow. The Americans, equipped with long rifles, but without bayonets, assaulted the hill, and the British tactics consisted of charging down the side of the hill with bayonets. The cover of trees and shrubs was such that the Americans were able to retreat only a little way and conceal themselves while the British had to retreat to the summit and charge down the other side of the mountain. As Henry ("Light Horse Harry") Lee pointed out, the hill was "more assailable by the rifle than defensible by the bayonet," and the British lost heavily from rifle fire as they tried successively to regain the height. After about an hour's fighting, Ferguson was struck by several bullets, one of which killed him. Capt. Abraham De Peyster succeeded to the command, and observing that he was being overwhelmed, raised the white flag. The British force was composed principally, not of regulars, but of Loyalists, and the bitterness felt by the mountain men against their erstwhile Tory neighbors was exceedingly deep. There were charges of atrocities on both sides, possibly with some justification. Practically all the British were either killed, wounded, or captured, and they lost over 1,000 stand of arms to the Americans. The significance of the battle was best pointed out by Sir Henry Clinton, the British commander in chief, who wrote that this battle "proved the first Link of a Chain of Evils that followed each other in regular Succession until they at last ended in the total Loss of America."

[L. C. Draper, *King's Mountain and Its Heroes.*]
RANDOLPH G. ADAMS

KING'S PROVINCE was that portion of the mainland of Rhode Island between the Pawcatuck River and Narragansett Bay, known as the Narragansett Country and claimed by Rhode Island, Connecticut, and Massachusetts. In an attempt to settle the controversy, a royal commission, in 1665, named this territory the King's Province and placed it under the jurisdiction of Rhode Island. Connecticut still claimed authority over it, but the matter was settled when Sir Edmund Andros took possession of both colonies. In 1729 this territory became Kings County, Rhode Island; the name was changed in 1781 to Washington County.

[S. G. Arnold, *History of Rhode Island;* C. W. Bowen, *Boundary Disputes of Connecticut.*]

R. W. G. VAIL

KINGSTON, formerly known as Esopus, is a city in southeast New York, on the Hudson River. It was settled in 1652 by Thomas Chambers, who was followed by Dutch settlers. Soon afterward it became the scene of the Esopus War, and was later a center for trade and the third largest town in the colony. During the Revolution, when the British took New York City, the Provincial convention moved to Kingston in February 1777 and adopted and proclaimed the first New York constitution in April 1777. Gov. George Clinton took office in July, the legislature met in August, and the courts opened in September. After the British approached in October and burned the town, the government left and never returned. The senate house (built 1676) still stands. An active industrial city in the 20th century, the 1970 population of Kingston was 25,544.

[M. Schoonmaker, *The History of Kingston.*]

AUGUSTUS H. SHEARER

KING'S WOODS. In parts of colonial New England surveyors of the king's woods marked with a broad arrow all pine trees two feet or more in diameter suitable for use as masts in the Royal Navy. Even after the land had passed into private hands, trees previously so marked were reserved to the crown, thus taking from the colonists much of their best timber. Tactless enforcement of the law by the surveyors, especially in Maine and New Hampshire, where pines were more plentiful, caused friction that contributed to the growth of sentiment for independence. Various specific stands of timber were set aside for this purpose, including the township of Kingswood, N.H., chartered by the royal governor in 1737 for the "Encouragement of Setling a new Plantation for the Encrease of Naval Stores," including the production of hemp, pitch, tar, and turpentine, the crown reserving "all Mast Trees growing on said Tract of land."

[Joseph J. Malone, *Pine Trees and Politics;* Robert E. Pike, *Tall Trees, Tough Men.*]

R. W. G. VAIL

KING WILLIAM'S WAR (1689–97). This first of the French and Indian wars was already smoldering

on the New England frontier when England declared war with France in May 1689. Angry at the plundering of Saint Castin's Trading House, the French had incited the Abnaki tribes of Maine to destroy the rival English post of Pemaquid and to attack the frontier settlements. The revolution in England, which forced James II from his throne, was followed by revolt against his representatives in the northern English colonies. The Dominion of New England split into ten or twelve independent parts, each jealous of its own frontiers. In New York, the civil and military officers of Albany, the key point for Indian relations, were at odds with Jacob Leisler, who had usurped control of the southern part of the province.

In Canada conditions were little better. When Louis de Buade, Comte de Frontenac, arrived in 1689 to begin his second term as governor, he found the colony terror-stricken by Iroquoian raids. To revive the courage of the French and to regain the allegiance of his Indian allies, he sent out during the winter of 1690 three war parties: the first destroyed Schenectady, the second attacked and burned the little settlement of Salmon Falls on the New Hampshire border, and the third forced the surrender of Fort Loyal, an outpost at the site of the present city of Portland, Maine.

Terror spread throughout the English colonies, and Massachusetts raised a fleet of seven ships, under the command of Sir William Phips, who captured and plundered Port Royal, Nova Scotia. In May 1690, at the invitation of Leisler, representatives of Massachusetts, Plymouth, Connecticut, and New York met in New York City. A united attack by land on Montreal was planned with the promised cooperation of the Iroquois; Massachusetts and the other New England colonies undertook to attack Quebec at the same time by sea. Both expeditions were failures. Although a small number of New York and Connecticut troops under the command of Fitz-John Winthrop set out from Albany, they were unable to advance farther than the foot of Lake Champlain. Phips, who commanded the New England fleet, fared no better. Realizing that neither their financial resources nor their military organization was equal to the task, the leaders of the northern English colonies made repeated appeals to the English government for help. In response, in 1693, a fleet was dispatched under the command of Sir Francis Wheeler. This fleet, after operating in the West Indies, reached Boston with fever-stricken crews, and as no preparations had been made to cooperate with it, nothing was accomplished. Frontenac, also, made urgent appeals for help, with no better luck. The French squadron sent to capture Boston was delayed by head winds, ran short of provisions, and could do nothing.

With both the French and English colonies thus thrown back on their own resources, the results were altogether favorable to the French. Their numerous Indian allies were always available for raids on the English frontier. Pemaquid, which had been rebuilt, was again captured by the French, and the New England frontier suffered cruelly. New York suffered less, but the Iroquois, frightened by French attacks, were with difficulty held to their alliance. The Treaty of Ryswick (1697) ended the fighting, but did little to settle the questions under dispute.

[Herbert L. Osgood, *American Colonies in the 18th Century*.]

A. C. FLICK

KINKAIDERS. Before 1904 homesteaders generally avoided the western third of Nebraska because of its aridity and poor soil. Some Nebraskans thought that if the homestead unit were enlarged settlers might be attracted to that part of their state. In 1904 they persuaded Congress to adopt the Kinkaid Act, which increased the size of the homestead unit in the western part of Nebraska to 640 acres. A great rush of settlers, called Kinkaiders, went into the region, but they met disappointment from the outset. Unproductive soil, drought, dust storms, warfare with cattlemen and sheepmen, and insufficient capital defeated the settlers. Within a few years there was an exodus of small farmers from the section.

[Marie Sandoz, *Old Jules*.]

PAUL W. GATES

KINSEY REPORT. In 1948 Alfred C. Kinsey, professor of zoology at Indiana University, and his associates published the results of their interviews with more than 5,000 American males concerning sexual behavior (*Sexual Behavior in the Human Male*). In 1953 a comparable book on almost 6,000 females (*Sexual Behavior in the Human Female*) was published. Both books, constituting what was popularly known as the Kinsey Report, created a sensation. Many hundreds of articles and books discussed the research and the findings. Because Kinsey's in-depth interviews were so numerous, his statements carried far more weight than earlier and similar studies based on small samples. The lesson the public learned was that in the 1940's astonishingly high numbers of de-

viations from conventional norms of sexual conduct occurred in the United States. If the Kinsey sample was at all representative (which some doubted), premarital, extramarital, animal, homosexual, oral-genital, and other types of sex "outlets" (Kinsey's term) had been practiced by large segments of the population. Dramatic class differences in behavior patterns also appeared. The reports engendered much opposition from critics who said that reporting a high incidence of deviation from monogamous-marriage missionary-position intercourse would encourage more deviation. Those commentators who claimed that great changes in sexual standards occurred after the appearance of the books looked back to them as both cause and symptom. Others felt the reports simply led to more openness about common, but formerly hidden, sexual practices.

[Wardell B. Pomeroy, *Dr. Kinsey and the Institute for Sex Research*.]

JOHN C. BURNHAM

KIOWA, American Indians of the Plains, provide a classic example of the culture of that area. Dependence on the bison, aggressive raids for horses, war patterns, the vision quest, and Plains technology, including the use of buckskin and the tipi, were all characteristic of the Kiowa as well as their Plains neighbors. Despite small numbers, an estimated 2,000 in 1780, the Kiowa, always fiercely resistant to the inroads of settlers, moved slowly through the Plains in their search for hunting territory and horses. Tradition has it that they originated at the headwaters of the Missouri, or at least, like their neighbors, the Comanche, in the northern Basin. On a gradual movement southward through the 18th century, ostensibly in quest of horses and guns, the Kiowa moved from the Black Hills to the Arkansas River. Conflicting at first with the Arapaho and Comanche, they formed an alliance with the Comanche. With them, they raided far into Mexico and terrorized sections of present Oklahoma and Texas during the 1860's and 1870's.

The Kiowa differ from the Comanche in several respects. Their culture tended to place somewhat more emphasis on wealth, especially in terms of rank associated with possession of horses and Spanish goods. Although both the Kiowa and the Comanche spoke Uto-Aztecan languages, they were far from mutually intelligible, the Comanche speaking Shoshonean, while the Kiowa spoke a form of Uto-Aztecan allied to Tanoan. The Kiowa are not to be confused with the Kiowa-Apache, a tribe in western Texas that sometimes interacted with both the Kiowa and the Comanche but that had Apache origins and spoke an Athapascan language.

[Elden Johnson, "The Kiowa," in R. F. Spencer, J. D. Jennings, and others, eds., *The Native Americans;* B. Mishkin, *Rank and Warfare Among the Plains Indians.*]

ROBERT F. SPENCER

KIOWA, FORT, was built on orders of the American Fur Company about 1822. It was near Fort Lookout, on the right bank of the Missouri River about ten miles above the present site of Chamberlain, S.Dak. It consisted of a range of log buildings of four rooms, storehouse, blockhouse, and wooden tower. It was abandoned after the decline of the fur trade.

[H. M. Chittenden, *History of American Fur Trade of the Far West.*]

CARL L. CANNON

KITCHEN CABINET, a title derisively applied by President Andrew Jackson's political enemies to an informal group of advisers who were credited with exercising more influence on the president than his regular cabinet. From 1829 until 1831, when the cabinet was reorganized, the Kitchen Cabinet, or "lower cabinet," as it was often called, was especially influential. Thereafter, Jackson relied less on his informal advisers and more on regular members of the cabinet. The most important members of the Kitchen Cabinet were Amos Kendall, Francis Preston Blair, Sr., William B. Lewis, A. J. Donelson, Martin Van Buren, and John H. Eaton.

[John Spencer Bassett, *The Life of Andrew Jackson.*]

ERIK MCKINLEY ERIKSSON

KITTANNING CAMPAIGN (August and September 1756). During the French and Indian War the Delaware village of Kittanning, on the Allegheny River, was a base for Indian raids on the Pennsylvania frontier. In retaliation, Col. John Armstrong led some 300 men from Fort Shirley at Aughwick, Pa., against the Delaware. In a surprise attack, the militia and volunteers burned the thirty log houses of the town, destroyed ammunition and supplies, released eleven white prisoners, and killed thirty or forty Indians. Although Armstrong's losses almost equaled those of the enemy, the victory heartened the settlers and prevented further raids from Kittanning.

[C. H. Sipe, *Indian Wars of Pennsylvania.*]

SOLON J. BUCK

KLAMATH-MODOC. The Klamath and Modoc spoke dialects of the same language and preserved a tradition of relationship, but they differed somewhat from each other in habitat and ecological adaptation. Both spoke the Klamath-Modoc, or Lutuamian languages, a branch of the Penutian phylum, which relates northward from California into the Plateau, as well as southward. The Klamath lived in the lakes and marshes of south-central Oregon, and the Modoc at the edges of the Basin in northeastern California. In 1780 there were about 1,200 Klamath and 4,500 Modoc.

Although wild-seed gathering and hunting characterized both tribes, the Klamath exploited the marshlands in which they lived, depending on seeds and roots of lake plants, whereas the Modoc, in a much less well-watered area, gathered a variety of dry seeds, following generally the patterns of the Great Basin. Otherwise, the life patterns were similar. Each tribe lacked any sense of extended political organization. Following the Californian configuration, small hamlets, isolated small communities with a few communally inhabited semisubterranean winter earth lodges, were the rule among them. Family life was centered in the hamlet. Petty and community chiefs were present, but their functions were largely those of speaker and moral leader. In neither tribe were religious ceremonials, art—except perhaps basketry—and social organizations elaborated. Although both tribes shared elements of the cultures of the three seed-gathering areas—California, the Basin, and the Plateau—at whose boundaries they stood, their position was marginal to each and marked by simplicity of institutions.

Contact with the United States came after 1830. The tribes were relegated to the Klamath Reservation in Oregon in 1864. When some of the group resisted, leaving the reservation under the leadership of Kintpuash (Captain Jack), attempts were made to subdue them. The Modoc War of 1872–73, following a series of atrocities on both sides, involved the military operation of evicting the tribesmen from the northern California lava beds. The contemporary Klamath-Modoc have been closely involved in the litigation surrounding the termination of reservation status.

[Verne F. Ray, *Primitive Pragmatists: The Modoc Indians of Northern California;* Theodore Stern, *The Klamath Tribe: A People and Their Reservation.*]

ROBERT F. SPENCER

KLONDIKE RUSH. On Aug. 16, 1896, gold was discovered on Bonanza Creek of the Klondike (Ton-Dac) River, a tributary of the Yukon River in Canada's Yukon Territory, by George Carmack and his two Indian brothers-in-law, allegedly on a tip from Robert Henderson. Carmack made his discovery known at the town of Forty Mile, and the miners from there and other settlements came up and staked claims. At the confluence of the two streams, which was fifty miles east of the Alaskan border, Joseph Ladue laid out Dawson City.

News of the discovery reached the United States in January 1897, and in the spring of that year a number of persons made preparations to depart by boat by way of Saint Michael up the Yukon or up the Inside Passage to Lynn Canal and over the Chilcoot and White passes and from there down the upper tributaries of the Yukon. On July 14, 1897, the steamer *Excelsior* arrived at San Francisco with $750,000 in gold; on July 17, the *Portland* arrived at Seattle with $800,000. No other compelling news event was before the country when the ships arrived, and the press played up the gold strike. Thousands of inquiries were received by chambers of commerce, railroads, steamship lines, and outfitting houses, and these agencies, seeing the commercial possibilities, began a well-financed propaganda campaign that precipitated the rush.

The peak of the rush occurred during 1897–99, when some 100,000 persons left for Alaska. The passage to the Klondike was facilitated by the progressive construction of the White Pass and Yukon Railroad from Skagway to White Horse. The miners worked their claims for the coarse gold and then sold them—principally to the Guggenheim Exploration Company, which sent up dredges and introduced scientific methods of gold recovery. By 1900, $27 million in gold per year was being taken from the region, but it declined thereafter as the richer deposits were exhausted.

The Klondike Rush had far-reaching economic results, particularly for Alaska. Those who were unable to secure claims on the Klondike spread over Alaska, finding gold at Nome, Fairbanks, and at numerous lesser places. Many turned to other pursuits. Taken together, the participants in the rush were the principal factor in the diffuse settlement of Alaska and the economic development of the territory.

[Tappan Adney, *Klondike Stampede;* Jeannette P. Nichols, "Advertising the Klondike," *Washington Historical Quarterly* (1922); Clarence L. Andrews, *The Story of Alaska*.]
                                                    V. J. FARRAR

KNIGHTS OF LABOR,

KNIGHTS OF LABOR, a secret league founded by Uriah Stevens and other garment workers in Philadel-

phia in December 1869. For a time the order grew slowly, but during the early 1880's it became an open organization and its membership increased in spectacular fashion. In 1886 it included between 600,000 and 700,000 persons. Organized into mixed local and district assemblies, its aim was to weld the whole labor movement into a single disciplined army. All gainfully employed persons except lawyers, bankers, professional gamblers or stockbrokers, saloon keepers, and (prior to 1881) physicians were eligible.

The natural consequence of this all-inclusive membership and of the structural arrangements of the order was a bent in the direction of political action and broad social reform. The underlying premise was that of an abundance of opportunity to be shared among all workers of hand and brain, and the mission of the producing classes was conceived to be to regain for themselves and to protect this opportunity.

Several factors contributed to the rapid decline of the Knights of Labor after 1886. Of immediate and circumstantial character were the unsuccessful outcome of the strike policy, the internal friction, and the depletion of union finances resulting from the failure of the producers' cooperatives supported by the Knights. Of more basic importance were the structural characteristics of the order and the fallacies in assumption. The centralized control and the mixed character of local and district assemblies inevitably invited difficulties with the job-conscious trade unions affiliated in the Federation of Organized Trades and Labor Unions (called American Federation of Labor after 1886). These unions had evolved a program of worker control of jobs that attracted and held the mass of skilled craftsmen, and by 1890 their federated organization overshadowed the Knights of Labor.

[Gerard N. Grob, *Workers and Utopia: A Study of Ideological Conflict in the American Labor Movement, 1865–1900;* Terence Powderly, *The Path I Trod*.]
                                            ROYAL E. MONTGOMERY

KNIGHTS OF THE GOLDEN CIRCLE, a secret order first recruited in the South, was formed about 1855 by George Bickley, a Cincinnati physician, to support proslavery policies and promote conquest of Mexico. During the Civil War the organization was introduced into Indiana as an order of Peace Democrats, or Copperheads, to oppose President Abraham Lincoln's war policy. Although connected with many acts of minor violence, the order did not promote any serious plots against the federal government. It was reorganized in 1863 as the Order of American

Knights and in 1864 as the Sons of Liberty. The Sons of Liberty were involved in the Northwest conspiracy in 1864. Soon thereafter the organization declined in importance and eventually ceased to exist.

[Mayo Fesler, "Secret Political Societies in the North During the Civil War," *Indiana Magazine of History,* vol. 14.]

CHARLES H. COLEMAN

KNIGHTS OF THE GOLDEN HORSESHOE.

Gov. Alexander Spotswood of Virginia undertook a western journey in the summer of 1716 that is considered one of the romantic episodes connected with the exploration of the western wilderness. On Aug. 20 he left Williamsburg on his adventurous journey. Leisurely the governor and his associates wended their way in a westerly direction up the valley of the Rappahannock River. It was a picturesque cavalcade made up of gentlemen, rangers, pioneers, and Indians, followed by the packhorses and servants. At night they bivouacked "under the canopy." The forests provided an abundance of fresh meat, and a marvelous assortment of liquors had been brought along. At the end of some two weeks the party gained the summit of the Blue Ridge Mountains. Here they gazed on the beauty of the panorama that spread itself before their eyes, and offered one toast after another. Two peaks were named—Mount George and Mount Alexander. The Indian name of the Shenandoah River was changed to the Euphrates. A bottle was buried on its banks containing a document to the effect that the region was taken in the name of the king. When he returned to Virginia Spotswood had some miniature gold horseshoes made; one of these was presented to each of the gentlemen who accompanied him. Hence the participants in the enterprise were designated Knights of the Golden Horseshoe.

[Philip A. Bruce, *The Virginia Plutarch,* vol. I.]

JAMES E. WINSTON

KNIGHTS OF THE WHITE CAMELIA,

an organization that arose in New Orleans in 1867 and spread rapidly over the South with the aim of maintaining the supremacy of the white race, which was threatened by Radical Reconstruction. A secret organization, it was much like the Ku Klux Klan in its aims and in having councils along state, county, and community lines.

[Walter Lynwood Fleming, *The Sequel of Appomattox.*]

HAYWOOD J. PEARCE, JR.

KNOW-NOTHING PARTY. *See* **American Party.**

"KNOW YE" PARTY.

Because of revolutionary war debts and a depreciated paper currency worth only sixteen cents on the dollar (1785–86), Rhode Island passed a forcing act in May 1786 compelling creditors to accept payment in paper money at face value. If they refused payment, the money could be deposited with the court, which then issued a certificate discharging the debt. These certificates were published in the newspapers and began with the words "Know Ye." The party advocating paper money became known as the Paper Money, or "Know Ye," party. The forcing act made business conditions so bad that the state was sometimes referred to as Rogue's Island but the act was declared unconstitutional in September 1786 in the case of *Trevett* v. *Weeden.*

[John Fiske, *Critical Period of American History.*]

R. W. G. VAIL

KNOX, FORT (Indiana). From 1763 to 1777, Vincennes, in present-day Indiana, though under British sovereignty, had no civil government. In May 1777, the town was officially occupied and the small stockaded Fort Sackville was built, but not permanently garrisoned. It was occupied for George Rogers Clark in 1778, but abandoned in December on the approach of a British force. Captured by Clark on Feb. 23, 1779, it was renamed Fort Patrick Henry. A small garrison remained for a few years. In 1788, when the Northwest Territory was organized, Maj. J. F. Hamtramck built a new fort and changed the name to Fort Knox, after Secretary of War Henry Knox. The post was again abandoned after Gen. Anthony Wayne's victory in 1794 at Fallen Timbers in northwest Ohio.

[L. P. Powell, *Historic Towns of the Western States.*]

THOMAS ROBSON HAY

KNOX, FORT (Kentucky). In 1918 an army camp called Camp Knox was established in Kentucky, thirty-one miles southwest of Louisville. Made permanent in 1932 as Fort Knox, the post became the main repository of U.S. gold in 1937. Billions of dollars worth of gold are kept in the two-story granite, steel, and concrete vault by the Treasury Department; the door of the vault weighs more than 20 tons. The fort is also known for its training of armored divisions and for Godman Army Air Field, which is part of the military reservation.

KNOX V. LEE

KNOX V. LEE. See **Legal Tender Cases.**

KNOXVILLE, SIEGE OF (November–December 1863). After the Battle of Chickamauga Confederate Gen. Braxton Bragg's Army of Tennessee laid siege to the defeated Army of the Cumberland in Chattanooga. Early in November Confederate Gen. James Longstreet's command was detached toward Knoxville to capture Gen. Ambrose E. Burnside and occupy Knoxville. Longstreet was delayed and Burnside retired into Knoxville without mishap. Longstreet arrived on Nov. 17 and laid siege to the town. On Nov. 29 he unsuccessfully assaulted Fort Sanders. Hearing of Bragg's defeat at Chattanooga, Longstreet withdrew on Dec. 3 into winter quarters in southwest Virginia. In the spring he rejoined Gen. Robert E. Lee's army (*see* Wilderness, Battles of the). Longstreet's detachment was unnecessary. Nothing had been accomplished beyond depriving Bragg, at a critical period, of needed men and a skillful leader.

[R. U. Johnson and C. C. Buel, eds., *Battles and Leaders of the Civil War,* vol. III.]

THOMAS ROBSON HAY

KODIAK ISLAND, also known as Kadiak Island, is located in the Gulf of Alaska east of Alaska Peninsula. Here, in 1784, fifteen years before the founding of Sitka on the mainland, Grigori Shelikof established the first Russian settlement in North America. The island is the habitat of the Kodiak bear and the king crab. It is also the site of a U.S. naval base.

[Hector Chevigny, *Lost Empire.*]

OSGOOD HARDY

KOMANDORSKIYE ISLANDS, BATTLE OF THE (Mar. 26, 1943). During World War II, while bringing reinforcements to the Japanese-occupied island of Attu in the western Aleutians, Vice Adm. Moshiro Hosogaya's task force of four cruisers and four destroyers ran into an American force barely half as strong under Rear Adm. Charles H. McMorris. For more than three hours on the morning of Mar. 26, 1943, the two groups fought a long-range gun and torpedo duel in the seas south of the Komandorskiye Islands near Kamchatka peninsula. Although badly outgunned, McMorris tried to get through to the transports Hosogaya was escorting. Unable to do so, he exchanged fire at ranges of eight to twelve miles with his foe, inflicting as much damage as he re-

ceived, and finally broke off the action when his sole heavy cruiser was crippled. A bold torpedo attack by American destroyers saved the cruiser from complete destruction and helped persuade Hosogaya, already worried about possible American bombing attacks, to retire to the west. Damage on both sides was fairly even, but the failure of the Japanese reinforcements to get through made the battle an American victory.

[Samuel Eliot Morison, *History of United States Naval Operations in World War II,* vol. VII.]

STANLEY L. FALK

KOREA, WAR WITH (1871). Undeclared hostilities in Korea in 1871 resulted from the murder of Americans who had illegally entered closed ports, and from the subsequent refusal of the Koreans to open their kingdom to foreign trade.

By ancient custom, violation of Korean seclusion was a capital offense. In August 1866, W. B. Preston, an American merchant of Chefoo, China, dispatched the armed schooner *General Sherman* to Ping-yang (now Heijo) in the extreme northwest of Korea to open trade. The schooner grounded on a sandbar in the Ping-yang River. The Koreans, acting by royal command, burned the ship and murdered the entire crew.

The U.S.S. *Shenandoah,* sent from Chefoo to investigate, was denied all communication with the capital on the ground that it had not come "in obedience to direct instructions from the sovereign of the United States." On the advice of George F. Seward, consul general at Shanghai, a punitive expedition was authorized. Rear Adm. John Rodgers was instructed to take Frederick F. Low, American minister to China, to the Korean capital to demand an audience with the king and to secure satisfaction for the *General Sherman* affair. The *Monocacy,* the *Palos,* and four steam launches arrived at the mouth of the Han River (then called Salée, or Seoul, River) on May 26, 1871. Local officials were advised that the squadron was friendly and sought merely to survey the coast and to confer with the king. When no favorable reply was received, the ships started upriver. On June 1, masked batteries situated on either side of the stream suddenly opened fire. Two Americans were wounded. The Americans returned the fire, silenced the batteries, and shelled the ravines in which the Koreans sought cover. The Korean loss is unknown. The *Monocacy* then struck a rock and was compelled to withdraw.

The guardian-general of Fu-ping prefecture formally complained of the American penetration of

Korean waters, but declared himself too humble a person to dare communicate the American message to his king. The Americans answered by sending a second expedition on June 10 to reduce the Korean forts. Five batteries were taken and burned. In the battles, which occurred on June 11, 250 enemy dead were left on the field. The American loss was three killed and nine wounded. But no satisfactory reply was given the American requests for an audience, and on July 2 Edward B. Drew, acting secretary of legation at Peking, announced that the squadron would withdraw to consult with Washington concerning further steps. No treaty was secured until 1882.

[Homer B. Hulbert, *The Passing of Korea.*]
HARRY EMERSON WILDES

KOREAN WAR (1950–53). The Soviet land grab of Japanese Manchuria during the last week of World War II was halted in Korea by the American occupation northward to the thirty-eighth parallel of the Korean peninsula. The parallel became the divider between zones of trusteeship scheduled to end within five years by the establishment of an independent, united Korea. By late 1947, because of the cold war that had begun, the United States despaired of forming a provisional government and invoked the jurisdiction of the United Nations, which in November sought to arrange Korea-wide free elections. The North Koreans, refusing to participate, established in February 1948 a Soviet-satellite form of government called the Democratic People's Republic (DPR) of Korea. The following July UN-sponsored measures resulted in the creation of the Republic of Korea (ROK), with Syngman Rhee as president.

Shortly afterward U.S. military government formally ended, but left forces at Rhee's UN-endorsed request to maintain order pending the development of a ROK army. To the majority of the UN General Assembly, Rhee's government had the legal status for ruling all Korea; the Soviet bloc claimed the same for the DPR. The views were irreconcilable. Through revolts, sabotage, and the inexperience of his administration Rhee found his political power waning in the May 1950 elections. The North Koreans, ostensibly seizing an opportunity to win by legitimate methods, in early June masked plans for military action by asking the UN to supervise elections for an all-Korea government. Then, on June 25, 1950, the North Korean army, trained and armed by the Russians, suddenly attacked across the parallel with 100,000 troops plentifully supplied with tanks, artillery, and modern equipment.

By then U.S. military commitments had been reduced to 500 advisers training the 95,000 recruits of the new ROK army, which was neither fully trained nor well equipped. The North Koreans advanced irresistibly, ignoring a UN cease-fire order. President Harry S. Truman accepted a mandate to intervene and authorized Gen. Douglas MacArthur to commit U.S. occupation forces in Japan. Other disputes had caused the Soviet delegate to boycott the UN Security Council, which on June 27 appealed for military units from the fifty-three member nations who had condemned the North Koreans as aggressors. The ROK and U.S. forces were joined by substantial or token contingents from Australia, Belgium, Canada, Colombia, Ethiopia, France, Great Britain, Greece, Luxembourg, the Netherlands, New Zealand, the Philippines, South Africa, Thailand, and Turkey.

At the outset, except for U.S. Air Force sorties from Japan and U.S. Navy carrier strikes, the ROK army fought desperately alone. Seoul, the capital, fell on June 28. On July 7, 700 men, constituting the first UN aid in ground action, spearheaded the understrength U.S. Twenty-fourth Infantry Division being airlifted from Japan to Pusan. The U.S. First Cavalry Division landed on July 18, a U.S. Marine brigade on Aug. 2, and the U.S. Second Infantry Division and Fifth Regimental Combat Team on Aug. 3. These sufficed to stiffen the battered ROK formations and to check North Korean momentum. A perimeter was established enclosing a meager 500 square miles hinged on Pusan.

MacArthur, commanding the UN forces as of July 8, exploited UN sea and air supremacy to plan a bold "end run" around the victorious North Koreans, which would cut their communications by striking amphibiously at Inchon, the port of Seoul, and the invaders' logistic base. On Sept. 15, 1950, U.S. Marines took Inchon and established a firm beachhead. On Sept. 17 American forces captured Seoul. Almost simultaneously the UN forces at Pusan commanded by U.S. Gen. W. H. Walker broke out of the perimeter and advanced northward toward Seoul, meeting a southward drive of the marines on Sept. 26. The North Koreans, fatally overextended and hit in rear and front, became disorganized and fragmented. As they retreated, MacArthur was authorized by a large majority of the UN membership to pursue across the thirty-eighth parallel into North Korea and to demilitarize the aggressors. Pyongyang, the DPR capital, fell on Oct. 19. Terrain features and overconfidence began to divide the advancing, road-bound UN troops into eastern and western segments. Between these, a gap of 80 miles opened as they neared the Yalu River, which formed the border with Red China.

Since the Korean War was dominated by the possibility of a third world war, Red China observed the letter of neutrality but freed large numbers of "volunteers" in organic formations that suddenly and skillfully struck between the UN columns. In turn caught overextended, the UN forces were compelled to retreat. Pyongyang was given up on Dec. 5 and Seoul on Jan. 4, 1951, before the Red Chinese attack was checked. The retreat was brightened by the famous march-to-sea evacuation at Hungnam by the U.S. Marines: against great odds, the marines brought out their casualties and equipment and remained battle-ready.

MacArthur was forbidden to strike across the Yalu, and nuclear armament, still a U.S. monopoly, was withheld. Under these conditions, the war could not be concluded on satisfactory military terms, especially after increasing numbers of Soviet-built jet fighters based on trans-Yalu fields began to contest command of the air. MacArthur's objective became the destruction of Communist forces actually in Korea. This was to be achieved by Operation Killer, wherein control of territory was subordinated to the purpose of creating tactical situations in which maximum losses could be inflicted. In two months Operation Killer restored a defensible battle line slightly north of the parallel. But the trans-Yalu area remained a secure staging and regroupment area for the Communists. MacArthur's publicized conviction that the war could not be won without decisive measures against Red China itself led President Truman to replace him with Gen. M. B. Ridgway on Apr. 11, 1951.

A few trials of strength failed to restore decisive movement to the war of attrition. Peace negotiations commenced at Kaesong in July 1951, were resumed at Panmunjom in October 1951, and dragged out to an armistice signed on July 27, 1953.

In general, except for a slightly rectified frontier, the *status quo ante bellum* was restored and the basic problem of Korean unity left unsolved. Both sides claimed victory. On balance, if strategic and tactical victory remained out of the grasp of the military on either side, the war was a political success for the UN, which had undeniably (1) fielded an international fighting force to oppose aggression, (2) held the aggressors back from their objective, and (3) confined the conflict to limited and nonnuclear bounds. Some students of the Soviet scene contend that there was an even greater long-range victory, insofar as the soli-

darity of the Communist bloc might be undermined by Communist yielding on the fundamental issue of prisoner-of-war exchange, which was the main cause for delay in reaching an armistice. In the course of World War II, Western powers had conceded the Soviet demand of forced repatriation of Soviet nationals wherever and however found. At Panmunjom UN representatives established the principle of voluntary repatriation of prisoners of war. It was underscored by the decision of 114,500 Chinese and 34,000 North Korean prisoners not to return to their homelands, while only 22 Americans elected to stay with their captors.

The United States put 1.6 million servicemen into the war zones. Losses were 54,246 killed, 4,675 captured, and 103,284 wounded. The war cost the United States about $20 billion. After the first few months the American public became almost apathetic toward the war, in strong contrast to the national patriotism that burned through World War II. President Truman set the tone with his description of it as a "police action."

[R. E. Appleman, W. G. Hermes, and J. F. Schnabel, *The United States Army in the Korean War;* Carl Berger, *The Korea Knot;* M. W. Cagle and M. E. Wolfe, *The Sea War in Korea;* Mark W. Clark, *From the Danube to the Yalu;* R. F. Futrell, *United States Air Force in Korea, 1950–53;* L. M. Goodrich, *Korea;* S. L. A. Marshall, *Porkchop Hill;* John Miller and others, *Korea, 1951–1953;* Lynn Montross and N. A. Canzona, *U.S. Marine Operations in Korea;* J. W. Spanier, *The Truman-MacArthur Controversy and the Korean War.*]

R. W. DALY

KOREAN WAR, AIR COMBAT IN (June 25, 1950–July 27, 1953). When the Democratic People's Republic of Korea (North Korea) invaded the Republic of Korea (South Korea) on June 25, 1950, the North Korean army was supported by a small but effective force of Russian-built aircraft. In the emergency, President Harry S. Truman directed the U.S. Far East Command to act as the United Nations Command and assist in repelling the Communist aggression. The U.S. Air Force's Far East Air Forces and the U.S. Navy's Seventh Fleet and First Marine Air Wing were the major elements of UN air power, which also included Royal Australian and South African air force fighter squadrons, Royal Thai and Royal Hellenic air force troop carrier detachments, and a growing Republic of Korea air force.

The Korean conflict has been called the first jet air war, and in the initial weeks American jet pilots quickly destroyed the North Korean air force, so establishing an air superiority that was critical during the summer months of 1950 as UN ground forces were driven into a perimeter around Pusan in southeastern Korea. By Sept. 15, 1950, the combination of UN ground defenses, strategic air attacks against North Korea, air interdiction operations against extended enemy supply lines, and very strong close air support decimated the initially victorious North Korean army. This permitted a UN amphibious invasion of the Inchon-Seoul area and a march into North Korea, which turned into retreat in November 1950 when Chinese Communist MIG-15 jet fighters appeared at the Yalu River and overwhelming Chinese armies poured into Korea.

After November 1950 the Communist MIG-15's sought to establish air superiority, but their efforts were thwarted by U.S. Air Force F-86 Sabre fighter screens, which destroyed 792 MIG's in air-to-air combat at a cost of 78 F-86's shot down. UN air power also provided extensive close air support to outnumbered ground forces and, equally important, proved effective in interdicting the movement of Communist troops and supplies to the battle area. By June 1951 the Communist ground offensives were defeated and the following month truce talks began. After the talks stalemated in mid-1952, UN air forces were authorized to wage air pressure attacks inside North Korea, culminating in the destruction of several irrigation dams and resultant flooding. Early in 1953 President Dwight D. Eisenhower indicated that the United States might act even more forcefully; this warning may have led the Communists to accept the military armistice agreement ending hostilities on July 27, 1953.

During the three-year Korean War, UN air forces flew a total of some 1,040,708 air sorties of all kinds and expended approximately 698,000 tons of ordnance in combat. The effect of air power was indicated by the senior North Korean truce negotiator, Lt. Gen. Nam Il, who stated in August 1951, "Without the support . . . by your air and naval forces, your ground forces would long ago have been driven out of the Korean peninsula by our powerful and battle-skilled ground forces."

[James A. Field, Jr., *History of U.S. Naval Operations: Korea*; Robert F. Futrell, *The United States Air Force in Korea, 1950–1953*.]

ROBERT FRANK FUTRELL

KOSSUTH'S VISIT. Lajos Kossuth, Hungarian revolutionary leader, landed in New York City in December 1851. His visit to the United States was in response to an invitation extended by a joint congressional resolution, signed by President Millard Fillmore. Everywhere he went, from New York and Washington, D.C., to Saint Louis and New Orleans, he received great ovations, reminiscent of the visit of the Marquis de Lafayette a quarter of a century earlier. Although the American government did not render official aid, Kossuth aroused nationwide support for the revolutionary causes for which he was fighting.

JOHN W. OLIVER

KOSZTA CASE. Martin Koszta, following the Hungarian Revolution of 1848, fled first to Turkey, and then to the United States (*see* New Buda). After taking out first citizenship papers, he returned to Smyrna in Asiatic Turkey, where he was kidnapped by the Austrians. On July 2, 1853, an American warship intervened, but his captors surrendered him to the French consul general. Upon strong representations by Secretary of State William L. Marcy, Koszta was released.

[Andor Klay, *Daring Diplomacy: The Case of the First American Ultimatum*.]

LOUIS MARTIN SEARS

KU KLUX ACT, one of the Force Acts, was passed Apr. 20, 1871, as the result of Republican efforts to give the president extraordinary powers to maintain the Republican governments in southern states. The president, Ulysses S. Grant, used his power to suspend the writ of habeas corpus only once, on Oct. 17, 1871, in nine South Carolina counties. Federal troops were to be used in destroying the Ku Klux Klan and other "conspiracies" aimed against enforcement of the Fourteenth Amendment, and cases were to be tried in federal courts. The act was declared unconstitutional in *United States* v. *Harris* (1882).

[Walter Lynwood Fleming, *Documentary History of Reconstruction*, vol. II.]

HAYWOOD J. PEARCE, JR.

KU KLUX KLAN. 19th Century. As a movement, the Ku Klux Klan was relied upon by southern whites to recoup their prestige, destroyed by the Civil War and Radical Reconstruction. Spontaneously organized in May 1866 in Pulaski, Tenn., by a group of young veterans, it had a potential for intimidating freedmen that was soon discovered. Its quick flowering over the

South was encouraged by unprecedented economic, political, and social conditions.

At least one design of Radical Reconstruction was to abolish the once dominant political power of the agrarian South by attaching the recently enfranchised freedmen to the Republican party. With leading southern whites disfranchised and with elections conducted by federal troops, state and local governments were soon in the inexperienced and unscrupulous hands of ex-slaves, carpetbaggers, and scalawags. As a group, the blacks had new powers they did not always use wisely, and they often fell into wanton indiscretions. Long used to sharp social distinctions and to a semblance of honest government, southern whites turned to secret means to rectify the new order of things, which was protected by federal bayonets.

At Nashville, in 1867, the Ku Klux Klan was organized into the "Invisible Empire of the South" ruled by a Grand Wizard; the Realms (states) were ruled by Grand Dragons; the Provinces (counties) were headed by Grand Titans; the individual Dens were under the authority of a Grand Cyclops. The Dens had couriers known as Night Hawks. Secret, the organization wanted to protect the white people from what they felt was humiliation by freedmen and to open the way for the reassertion of the supremacy of the whites politically and socially.

Most of the Klan's work was directed against blacks who, according to the Klan, were behaving obstreperously. To intimidate the superstitious and to escape being identified by federal troops, the Klansmen covered their bodies in white robes, masked their faces, wore high, cardboard hats, and rode robed horses with muffled feet. One of their favorite practices was to ride out of woods, surprising blacks walking home in the darkness from meetings of the Union League, an organization that sought to direct their votes into the proper Republican channels. The Klan invariably rode at night.

The Klan also intimidated carpetbaggers and scalawags and played unseen influential roles in many trials in the South. It was responsible for floggings, lynchings, and other acts of violence and lawlessness. It was formally disbanded in the spring of 1869, but it did not die.

In April 1871, a joint select committee of seven senators and fourteen representatives was selected "to inquire into the Conditions of Affairs in the late Insurrectionary States. . . ." In 1871 the Ku Klux Act was passed, empowering the president to use federal troops and to suspend the writ of habeas corpus in an effort to abolish the "conspiracy" against the federal government in the South. The gradual resumption of political power by whites saw the activities of the Klan decline.

HAYWOOD J. PEARCE, JR.

20th Century. As was its predecessor, the reborn Klan has been a secret, fraternal, and vigilante organization for native-born, white, Protestant Americans. In 1915, prompted by southern negrophobia and D. W. Griffith's epic movie version ("The Birth of a Nation") of Thomas Dixon's *The Clansman* (1905), an Alabama fraternalist, "Col." William J. Simmons, recreated the Klan at a Stone Mountain, Ga., ceremony.

After World War I, two supersalesmen, Edward Y. Clarke and Elizabeth Tyler, began hard-sell merchandising. To everyone's amazement, the Klan spread nationwide. At its mid-1920's peak, it had perhaps 3 million members. It marched, elected, and sometimes terrorized from Maine to California. It helped choose at least sixteen U.S. senators and eleven governors, although few high officeholders were actual members. It was strongest in Georgia, Alabama, Louisiana, Texas, Indiana, Ohio, Pennsylvania, and New York.

The Klan was the great fraternal lodge for the old-stock Americans of the 1920's, sworn to protect small-town values from foreigners, immorality, and change. The enemy was the outsider-alien, symbolized by Roman Catholicism. Although the Klan did well in inland and western cities, its violence was primarily restricted to the South and Southwest and mainly directed against fellow white, natural-born, Protestants in the name of threatened morality. The Klan was a major issue and force at the Democratic Convention and in the election of 1924. Nevertheless, poor leadership and internal conflict, combined with violence, community disruptiveness, corruption, and immorality, soon destroyed its power.

The depression-era Klan discovered communism, the Jews, and the Congress of Industrial Organizations, but its ranks were thin, and its influence outside of the Southeast was gone. The Dallas dentist Hiram W. Evans, who wrested the Klan away from Simmons in 1922, sold it to a Terre Haute, Ind., veterinarian, James A. Colescott, in 1939. Back taxes, bad publicity over German-American Bund connections, and World War II temporarily retired the Klan.

When its postwar resuscitator, Atlanta obstetrician Samuel Green, died in 1949, the Klan fragmented chaotically until a Tuscaloosa rubber worker, Robert M. Shelton, Jr., brought some order and unity in the

1960's and 1970's. Despite occasional violence and friends in office in Alabama and Georgia, the Klan offered little resistance to integration. Violence, particularly the murders of three civil rights workers (1964) and Viola Liuzzo (1965), helped bring civil rights laws, surveillance by the Federal Bureau of Investigation, some convictions, thinned ranks, and community rejection.

DAVID M. CHALMERS

[David M. Chalmers, *Hooded Americanism, The History of the Ku Klux Klan.*]

KWAKIUTL. Resident on the northern coasts of Vancouver Island and sections of the adjacent mainland of western Canada, the Kwakiutl are the best known of the native tribes of the Northwest Coast culture area. Their fame arises not so much from any historical role they may have played as from the detailed ethnographic studies of them by the distinguished anthropologist Franz Boas and his students. Kwakiutl culture was one of the most vivid and dramatic in aboriginal native America.

The Kwakiutl speak a language usually classified as Wakashan, related to those of the Nootka at the south and to the Bella Bella on the mainland. (The broader relationships of Wakashan are still being analyzed.) Although the Kwakiutl lacked political solidarity, they were bound together not only by language but also by socioeconomic networks based principally on the potlatch, a system of exchanges of property that enhanced social status and rank. The twenty-five villages of the Kwakiutl—with a population of perhaps 4,500 on Vancouver Island prior to contact with Europeans about 1775—interacted with each other by passing property, food, manufactured objects, and surplus materials of all kinds from hand to hand within a defined system of social rank, and concepts of property and status became somewhat more elaborate among them than among the more northern peoples of the area, such as the Haida, Tlingit, and Tsimshian. Local ''chiefs,'' men able to validate social position by feasting others of like status and by presenting goods collected by family and household effort, created cooperative activities within communities but strong competition between communities. The wealth complex reached an extreme among the Kwakiutl, whose system of credit, borrowing, and interest suggests an incipient capitalism.

Like others on the Northwest Coast, the Kwakiutl, dependent on the salmon and maritime village organization, stressed spirit visions and experiences. As with wealth, the Kwakiutl appear to have systematized their religious institutions more than did other tribes; they emphasized secret religious societies whose winter activities and initiations stood side by side with the potlatches in importance. The giving away of wealth and the dances of the secret clubs have led some to stress the competitive or individualistic elements in the culture, while others have stressed the cooperative, or ''amiable,'' side, the fact that related people cooperated to amass wealth.

[Franz Boas, *Ethnology of the Kwakiutl*, Bureau of American Ethnology Annual Report (1921), and *The Social Organization and the Secret Societies of the Kwakiutl Indians*, U.S. National Museum Reports (1895); Helen Codere, *Fighting With Property*, American Ethnological Society, memoir 18.]

ROBERT F. SPENCER

LABADISTS, followers of the French religious reformer Jean de Labadie, belonged theologically to the Calvinist school. A colony settled in Bohemia Manor, Md., in 1683 under the leadership of Augustine Herrmann and another was established shortly thereafter in New York.

[Bartlett B. James, *The Labadist Colony in Maryland.*]

JULIAN P. BOYD

LA BALME'S EXPEDITION. French Col. Augustin Mottin de La Balme appeared in the West in the summer of 1780. What credentials he carried is not known. He proposed a raid against the British at Detroit, and, enrolling in Illinois a body of the French inhabitants, crossed the Wabash, where he was joined by a party from Vincennes, captured by George Rogers Clark the previous year. They advanced in October to the Miami village where Fort Wayne, Ind., now stands. This village and the traders' stores were pillaged; then, not feeling strong enough to attack Detroit, La Balme began a hasty retreat. The Miami under Little Turtle pursued and gave battle. La Balme was killed and his men dispersed. This defeat long rankled in the breasts of the French and aided in destroying French prestige in the western country.

[C. W. Alvord, ed., *Kaskaskia Records*, Illinois Historical Collections, vol. V; L. P. Kellogg, *British Régime in Wisconsin and the Northwest.*]

LOUISE PHELPS KELLOGG

LA BAYE. *See* **Green Bay.**

LA BELLE FAMILLE, BATTLE OF (July 24, 1759). In response to the massive British campaign to end the French and Indian War in 1759, 1,200 French soldiers and a large force of Indians marched down the portage road to relieve Fort Niagara, N.Y. They were intercepted at La Belle Famille (Youngstown, N.Y.) by the British and Indians and utterly routed; only 200 of the French escaped capture or death.

[Frank H. Severance, *An Old Frontier of France.*]
Robert W. Bingham

LABOR. Unsuccessful in attempts to utilize native American Indians as a labor force, the sponsors of the American colonies in the 17th century looked to western Europe for their source of supply. Impoverished or propertyless laborers were induced to migrate to the far from utopian Middle Atlantic and southern colonies through the promise of a better life. The laborers of the New World were recruited as workers for chartered companies (in Virginia until 1624), as indentured servants, as redemptioners in the 18th century, or as apprentices. An agreement stipulating that after the period of servitude the laborer would receive his freedom, and possibly land besides, proved attractive to the unemployed and hopeless in western Europe, who came from England; from northern Ireland, where many Scots had settled; and from the western states of Germany.

Convicts, debtors, stranded seamen, and African slaves, as well as many who were kidnapped, were also brought to the colonies as involuntary laborers to meet the insatiable demand for hands. At first almost all the work was performed on the soil; but with growing population and consequent specialization of function, demand arose in urban centers, such as Boston, Philadelphia, New York, Baltimore, and Charleston, for mechanics, artisans, apprentices, and wage laborers.

Throughout the colonial period, and in fact throughout the history of the United States until 1920, labor was in short supply. During the 17th and 18th centuries, impressment and cooperation were often resorted to in order to meet labor needs. Roof raising and barn building were usually cooperative community activities, and crops were saved from ruin in some of the New England colonies by authorizing constables to impress mechanics and artisans to harvest the neighborhood fields.

Labor shortages required in some instances colonial controls over wages. John Winthrop, governor of Massachusetts, remarks in his *Journals* that the cu-

pidity of the artisans in the colony knew no bounds. In 1633, as a consequence of high wage demands, the Massachusetts General Court set a maximum wage for most skilled mechanics. Employers and employees violating this law were to be penalized, as were workers who refused to toil. Three years later, after the general penalties were removed and the law proved inoperative, the towns were given jurisdiction over wage determinations. Hours of toil were the traditional agricultural norm, sunup to sundown.

Common interests of artisans resulted in some degree of organization in the 17th century, but it was not until the end of the 18th century that labor unionism, as now understood, came into being. During the agitation regarding taxation and home rule that rocked the colonies after the French and Indian War, urban laborers were to be found in the forefront of the anti-Parliament cause. The Sons of Liberty in New York recruited many of its members from among workers, and the Boston Massacre was in large part the outgrowth of a labor conflict.

The appearance of merchant-capitalists, organized into associations of master employers seeking to reduce costs and increase profits by undercutting wages and extending hours of labor, caused laborers, most often skilled workmen, to turn to organization for protection. As early as the 1780's, short-lived local craft groups were founded, but not until the 1790's did more permanent unions appear. In 1792 the Philadelphia shoemakers formed a protective organization, and in 1794 the Typographical Society of New York was founded. In addition to the usual union aims found in later organizations, such as higher wages, shorter hours, and better working conditions, these bodies of workmen also sponsored fraternal benefits for sickness and burials.

These early unions, concentrated in the few large urban centers, invented some of the techniques later used extensively by labor organizations. Strikes, boycotts, business agents, collective bargaining, and the closed shop appeared early in the history of trade unionism. More usual, however, were attempts, such as that made by the New York typographers, to control the number and duration of apprenticeships in order to protect wage standards and work quality.

Employers' associations, organized both to protect the interests of employers and to combat the unionized artisans, early questioned the legal right of workers to combine into labor organizations. They argued that the English common law on this point was applicable in the United States in the absence of any statute law: it held that any combination of workers whose aim was to improve their financial lot constituted a conspiracy against the public weal. From the turn of the 19th century until 1815 in almost all of a number of separate conspiracy trials the contention was upheld. As a result of these decisions the embryonic labor unions formed at the end of the 18th century soon foundered and disappeared.

The force of these conspiracy decisions, particularly those in the Philadelphia cordwainers' (1806) and New York cordwainers' (1809–10) cases, was not overcome until a new political climate prevailed. Although democracy under President Andrew Jackson did not completely free unions from legal disabilities, it gave an impetus to more liberal interpretations of labor's rights. The decision written by Massachusetts' chief justice Lemuel Shaw in the 1842 case of *Commonwealth* v. *Hunt,* recognizing the legality of unions and their right to strike for a closed shop, was the most important case in eliminating the effects of the earlier conspiracy decisions upon trade unions.

During the first half of the 19th century wage scales in the United States for both skilled and unskilled labor were generally from one-third to one-half higher than those for similar workers in western Europe. The unskilled factory worker received from 90 cents to $1.00 a day, which was approximately half the amount received by a skilled worker. Farm workers received up to $15.00 a month with board and from 50 cents to $1.50 a day without board. Even though these wages were often inadequate to support a family unless more than one member of the family was working, most of the evils associated with the introduction of the factory system in England were avoided. Hours of labor continued to be extremely long during this period, generally varying between twelve and fifteen actual work hours a day; and the early factory mills were frequently unhealthy and unsanitary work places.

Initially the newly formed textile factories recruited their labor force from among single women, daughters of New England farmers, who worked for marriage dues or for a trousseau. Led by Francis Cabot Lowell, who set up his factory in Waltham, Mass., in 1813, factory owners attempted to introduce sorority-like living in the factory dormitories, and many foreign visitors commented favorably on such arrangements. Overlooked by these visitors was the excessive paternalism—the minute supervision of the workers' lives by the employer, including the requirement that they purchase goods in the company stores and worship in the company churches.

Increased immigration from western Europe during the 1840's and renewed agreements among employers about wages, hours, conditions, and blacklists ended the Waltham system. The growing competition for jobs and the extended use of child labor in the factories, coupled with the depressing effects of the panic of 1837, resulted in wage reductions for factory workers and increased paternalistic supervision over their lives by the employers.

The extension of democratic ideals in the 1820's created a more favorable climate for trade union organizational success. Renewed trade union activity found expression in the first recorded strike of women workers, when in 1824 the Pawtucket, R.I., women weavers left work for higher wages. In Philadelphia, Boston, New York, New Orleans, and Paterson, N.J., carpenters, weavers, tailors, cordwainers, cabinetmakers, masons, stevedores, hatters, and riggers formed fairly stable trade unions. The recognition by many of the workmen that, regardless of craft, they had many problems in common, prompted fifteen Philadelphia unions in 1827 to form the first city central trade council, the Mechanics Union of Trade Associations. By 1836 thirteen other cities had followed the Philadelphia mechanics' lead.

Under the leadership of Thomas Skidmore and William Leggett in New York and John Ferral and William English in Philadelphia, labor sought to achieve certain of its objectives through political action. In 1828, first in Philadelphia and then in New York and Boston, workingmen's parties were formed. Among their goals were the reduction of the workday to ten hours, abolition of imprisonment for debt, abolition of prison contract labor, enactment of mechanics' lien laws, curbs on banks and other monopolies, universal education, and free public land to settlers. In a few years these parties disappeared, either having been absorbed by the Jacksonian Democrats or the Whigs or forming radical factions (Locofocos) of the New York and Pennsylvania Democratic party.

Despite organized labor's support of Andrew Jackson, the first use of federal troops in a labor dispute was ordered under his administration, in January 1834. When Irish workers on the Chesapeake and Ohio Canal in Maryland struck for a closed shop and violence ensued, Jackson directed the War Department to halt the "riotous assembly" and restore peaceful conditions at the canal works. In that same year the New York General Trades Union, a city central, called a convention of delegates from other city centrals to discuss nonpolitical trade union objectives.

From this meeting emerged the first national federation of labor organizations, the National Trades Union, under the leadership of Ely Moore, a New York printer and union leader who was elected to Congress from New York and served as labor's first congressman from 1834 to 1839. The depression that followed the panic of 1837 saw the disappearance not only of the National Trades Union but also of the various city centrals and almost all of the local trade unions.

Social panaceas, utopianism, and the ten-hour-day movement dominated the thinking of labor during the next decade and a half. Associationism of either the Fourierist or the Owenite variety captured the imagination of the leaders of labor, and cooperation of the Rochdale variety was attempted unsuccessfully in both production and consumption by elements of organized labor. Labor was also attracted to the agrarian reform movement espoused by George Henry Evans, editor of the *New York Working Man's Advocate*. Evans called for free homesteads, and many workers believed his plan to be the answer to their propertyless state. Lack of success of these reform attempts slowly alienated the workers, and they turned increasingly to the more immediate economic gains that they hoped to achieve through trade unionism.

The ten-hour-day movement was, on paper, more successful. In 1836, as a result of the initiative of Moore and the National Trades Union, Jackson's secretary of the navy ordered a ten-hour day in the Philadelphia Navy Yard. President Martin Van Buren in 1840 extended the ten-hour day to laborers working on federal public works. Ten-hour legislation was passed in seven states during the 1840's and 1850's, but in all cases loopholes in the laws allowed workers to toil longer if they contracted a longer workday. By 1860, although the ten-hour day was widely accepted for skilled craftsmen, it was still not the norm for unskilled workers.

The improved economic conditions spurred on by increased industrialization and fortuitous gold finds in California caused a resurgence of labor union activities. Many locals were formed, and some ten national unions were organized in the 1850's. In 1852 the National Typographical Union was founded—and still prospered in the late 20th century; the iron molders formed a national union under the leadership of William Sylvis in 1859. The hat finishers (1854), journeymen stonecutters (1855), cigarmakers (1856), and machinists and blacksmiths (1859) were organized. Rejecting utopias and stressing immediate eco-

nomic gains, these unions were so solidly formed that even the panic of 1857 did not destroy all of them.

The outbreak of the Civil War occasioned a severe labor shortage, since industrial expansion was needed in the midst of large-scale military recruitment from among labor's ranks. Congress, in 1864, authorized the importation of contract labor to fill this need. Inflation, a usual partner of war, caused real wages to decline by one-third from 1860 levels by 1865. Although few strikes were called by unions during the war, labor considered the Conscription Act of 1863 to be unfair and consequently displayed some sympathy for the Irish laborers who rioted against the draft in New York.

Favorable wartime conditions acted as a further spur to trade union organization. National organizations and city centrals expanded their hold; an attempt was even made in Louisville, Ky., in 1865 by delegates from eight city centrals to form a national federation of unions, but the International Industrial Assembly of North America that they envisioned never came into being. During and immediately after the war the railway brotherhoods were founded—by the locomotive engineers in 1863, the railway conductors in 1868, and the firemen in 1873. The shoemakers' organization, the Order of the Knights of St. Crispin, started in 1867, had attained a membership of over 50,000 by 1870. The introduction of machinery into the shoe trade transformed the industry by allowing unskilled hands to replace skilled shoemakers, and the Crispins sought to overcome this eventuality by creating producers' cooperatives. Failure of these ventures to succeed spelled the doom of the Knights of St. Crispin early in the 1870's.

The iron molders under Sylvis and the anthracite coal miners, organized into a Workingmen's Benevolent Association by John Siney in 1868, were the two most powerful unions during the period immediately after the Civil War. Both organizations were weakened in the early 1870's, however—the molders by concerted employer opposition and the miners by increasing competition from immigrant labor. At their height, both unions could claim a membership of over 300,000 each.

Encouraged by the national unions and by local associations of workers and reformers seeking to establish the eight-hour day—a movement pioneered by Ira Steward of Boston—a national organization of labor, the National Labor Union, was established in Baltimore in 1866. Under the leadership of Sylvis of the Molders and Richard F. Trevellick of the Ship Carpenters and Caulkers International, the National

Labor Union concentrated upon producers' cooperatives and national political action to achieve its aims. The failure of the cooperatives and the minimizing of trade union methods and objectives caused many of the national unions to withdraw from the federation after Sylvis' death in 1869. In 1872 the organization converted itself into the National Labor Reform party, which nominated David Davis of Illinois for president. Davis' withdrawal, after failing to capture the nomination of the Democratic party, resulted in the collapse of both the party and the National Labor Union. This short-lived federation was not a complete failure, for through its efforts Congress passed a law in 1868 limiting the hours of federal employees (laborers and mechanics) to eight a day. Furthermore, the National Labor Union was the first body of organized American workers to make contact with its European counterparts, when it sent a delegate to the First International in Basel, Switzerland, in 1869 to discuss means of limiting migration of European workmen to the United States.

During the depression following the panic of 1873 the trade unions lost a substantial number of members, with the result that of the thirty national unions in existence in 1873, fewer than ten were able to survive. More significantly, the growth of the corporate form of industrial organization forced a wider separation of workers from employers. Consequently impersonal corporations did not consider the human price of layoffs, wage cuts, and other means of extracting more labor from workmen at lower costs. Defensive actions by workers, organized or unorganized, often resulted in violence and other manifestations of labor turbulence. Before the depression had run its course, armed clashes between workers, private police, and federal and state militia had become commonplace.

One casualty of the depression was the miners' union. In its absence anarchy ruled the anthracite fields. In eastern Pennsylvania a secret organization of Irish miners, called by the newspapers of the time Molly Maguires but actually an outgrowth of a fraternal order, the Ancient Order of Hibernians, was accused of spreading violence. Certain members of the group were charged with murdering opponents, not only miners competing for the jobs of their members but also foremen and mine bosses carrying out the policies of the Philadelphia and Reading Railroad, the operators of the local mine fields. As a result of the testimony of a Pinkerton detective, James McParlan, twenty-four Molly Maguires were convicted of murder in 1875 and ten were hanged in 1876, even though the evidence still seems spurious.

A series of wage reductions sparked a militant labor demonstration in 1877, when a general strike tied up the railroads of the country. Strikes and spontaneous work stoppages began on July 17 on the Baltimore and Ohio Railroad system, and before the month was over, it had spread to the Pennsylvania, the New York Central, and many western lines. At Martinsburg, W. Va., the strikers clashed with the state militia, and after nine persons were killed, President Rutherford B. Hayes dispatched federal troops to restore order. General rioting followed at Baltimore, Pittsburgh, Chicago, and Saint Louis. The violent climax of the strike was reached in Pittsburgh, where on July 21 the strikers, joined by sympathetic bystanders, fought a pitched battle with a company of Philadelphia militiamen, which had been called in because the Pittsburgh militia was considered sympathetic to the strikers and thus unreliable. After surrounding the defeated state troops in a railroad roundhouse, the enraged mob burned down machine shops, destroyed the Union depot, and damaged property valued at $5 million. Twenty-six people were killed in Pittsburgh before the federal troops put down the disturbances and broke the strike. Many state legislatures reacted to the violence of the great strikes of 1877 by reenacting conspiracy laws; labor reacted by turning to politics and, temporarily at least, to radical movements.

The Greenback party was the immediate recipient of labor's support as locally organized workingmen's parties combined with the Greenbackers to form the National Greenback Labor party at Toledo, Ohio, in 1878. Although this party elected fifteen members to Congress and gained over a million votes in 1878, its success was short-lived. The resumption of specie payment on Jan. 1, 1879, and the cleavage between the aims of the currency reformers and the labor people in the party caused its rapid decline.

Marxian and Lassallean socialism had some influence on the labor movement after 1876, and the headquarters of the First International was moved to New York City. The Marxists organized a workingmen's party in 1876, and a year later its name was changed to Socialist Labor party. This party attempted to work within the trade union movement but succeeded only among unions that had a high proportion of German immigrants among their members, as did the cigarmakers' and furniture workers' unions. In 1878–79 the Marxists, through their short-lived International Labor Union, attempted unsuccessfully to organize unskilled textile workers in Fall River, Mass., and Paterson, N.J. In Chicago the Socialists had some success in the city trades council, but it was dissipated in 1880 as a result of the friction between the Marxists and the newly formed anarchist faction within the labor movement.

In San Francisco the Workingmen's Party of California, under the domination of Denis Kearney, gained some political success with its program to restrict Chinese immigration. Anti-Chinese riots in 1877 were stimulated by this party and it elected a mayor of San Francisco in 1879. Although the party had disintegrated by 1881, its anti-Chinese agitation bore fruit in the passage of the Chinese Exclusion Act of 1882.

Antagonism to labor organizations that dominated the public mind throughout the depression years led to the prevalence of secret societies and orders among workers. The one labor group that had a rapid rise in membership and influence and equally rapid decline in the 1880's, the Noble Order of the Knights of Labor, began as a secret society. Founded in 1869 by a group of Philadelphia garment cutters led by Uriah S. Stephens, it did not gain strength until after the violence of 1876–77. By 1881 the Knights of Labor had a membership of 19,000, which increased to 111,000 in 1885 and to some 700,000 a year later.

In form the Knights resembled a national union of all workers. Organized into local and district assemblies, some of which were limited to a single craft but most of which were not, the Knights of Labor was a highly centralized group; the assemblies were directly responsible to the general executive board and the grand master workman. All gainfully employed persons except lawyers, bankers, gamblers, stockbrokers, saloon keepers, and physicians were eligible for membership.

Under the leadership of Terence V. Powderly, grand master workman from 1879 to 1893, the secret nature of the order was abolished in 1881; and for a short time it was the most powerful single labor organization in the United States. It favored the eight-hour day, advocated such reforms as the graduated income tax and prohibition of imported contract labor, sponsored consumers' and producers' cooperatives, and condemned the growing monopolistic power of banks and railroads. Despite Powderly's emphasis on the boycott and arbitration as the means for achieving labor's economic advances, a spontaneous strike movement among the Knights' railroad members in the system controlled by Jay Gould resulted in large additions to the order's ranks.

After a number of successful strikes conducted by the Knights against western railroads in 1884 and 1885, Gould agreed to discontinue discriminatory practices against members of the order. A year later, when the Texas and Pacific Railroad did not live up to the agreement, the district assembly immediately involved, led by Martin Irons, called another strike against the Gould system over the objections of Powderly. Marked by violence, arrests, and pitched battles, the strike was doomed to failure by Gould's adamant refusal to arbitrate the dispute as requested by Powderly. The failure of the Knights in this strike and in other actions in 1886, coupled with the growing antilabor sentiment that stemmed from the public reaction to the Haymarket riot of May 4, 1886, resulted in the serious decline of the order as a labor organization.

Even before the demise of the Knights the craft unions, favoring a less centralized and more job-oriented form of organization, had deserted the order. The growing dominance of the agrarian western members of the Knights culminated in the replacement of Powderly by James R. Sovereign of Iowa in 1893, and the order virtually ceased to exist as a labor organization.

The brief but spectacular career of the Knights of Labor was not devoid of results. Many weak unions were strengthened, and some new unions were established through affiliation with the Order. Its lobbying activities were instrumental in the passage of the Foran Act in 1885, which aimed at cutting off the migration to the United States of contract labor. The House of Representatives established a standing Committee on Labor in 1883, and in 1884 the federal Bureau of Labor was created to gather data. The railway strikes conducted by the Knights prompted Congress to pass a law in 1888 calling for the settlement of railway labor disputes by arbitration if both parties agreed. Most important, the Knights emphasized once again that only through organization could labor achieve even minimum economic benefits.

The eight-hour movement, strongly endorsed by all segments of organized labor, reached its climax in May 1886. The national unions set the first of that month as the deadline for achieving an eight-hour day. Labor demonstrations were called for as the day approached, and clashes with the police were commonplace. Aroused by the shooting of several workmen in Chicago, the anarchist newspaper *Die Arbeiter Zeitung* called for a mass meeting of protest at the Haymarket. Although the circulars issued were inflammatory, the speeches were innocuous. Despite the mayor's advice, a city police captain, leading 180 policemen, advanced on the meeting and ordered the crowd to disperse. A bomb was thrown and caused the death of seven policemen and the injury of many. Fears of an anarchist plot made impartial investigation impossible. Eight anarchists were convicted on a conspiracy charge. After four had been hanged and one had committed suicide, Gov. John Peter Altgeld in 1893 pardoned the three surviving prisoners on the ground that they had not received a fair trial. Branded as radical in consequence of the Haymarket incident, the eight-hour movement suffered a serious setback.

In the wake of the disastrous effects that the depression years of 1873–79 had upon the national trade unions, many leaders of labor began considering means to make their organizations more effective. Realizing that lack of central control, absence of strike funds, striving after monetary reforms, and advocating social panaceas had not achieved results, Samuel Gompers and Adolph Strasser of the New York Cigarmakers Union in particular began looking to the British trade unions and their Trades Union Congress as models. After a catastrophic strike of long duration had virtually destroyed the Cigarmakers Union in 1877, Gompers and Strasser reorganized it along British lines. Centralized control of the locals, effective collection of strike funds, and concern only for the immediate economic objectives of the cigar-workers were the principal guides of this "new unionism."

To the promoters of the new unionism, the reorganization of the Cigarmakers Union was only a first step. In emulating the British Trades Union Congress, they felt that a national federation of trade unions embodying the principles of business unionism was essential in order to mold labor unity for defensive action against aggressive employer groups on a national scale, to lobby for favorable legislation, and to prevent the dissipation of the energies of organized labor in political and utopian schemes. Consequently Gompers and Strasser seized upon a call for a national convention of laboring groups issued by two secret societies in 1881 to accomplish this aim. On Nov. 15, 1881, the Federation of Organized Trades and Labor Unions was formed in Pittsburgh. For a short time this federation and the Knights of Labor tried to cooperate, but when the essentially anti-trade-union approach of the Knights was reflected in its sanctioning of trade assemblies or dual unions competing with federation affiliates, the trade unions called another convention, at Columbus, Ohio. There on Dec. 8, 1886, the American Federation of Labor (AFL) was organized, and the Federation of Organized Trades and Labor Unions was disbanded.

From the beginning of the AFL until 1924, with the exception of one year, Gompers served as its president. Organized on the principle that each constituent national union was autonomous, the federation had only those powers that were delegated to it by the constitution or by the convention. City central unions and state federations coordinated economic and political actions of the AFL affiliates on the local or state level and also joined with the executive council in helping to organize new craft unions. Coordinating councils or departments within a single industry, such as the building trades department, consisted of delegates from the various unions in that industry. They sought to promote their common interests and to settle any jurisdictional disputes between member unions. The executive council, consisting of a president, several vice-presidents, a treasurer, and a secretary, administered the affairs of the federation between annual conventions. A per capita tax on all members provided funds for the work of the federation.

Through collective bargaining and through the use of such weapons as the strike, boycott, and picketing, the AFL sought to improve the economic status of the members of its affiliates. It sought public support through a campaign to popularize the union label among consumers. Being an organization of craft unions whose members were mainly skilled workers, the AFL stressed job security, favored the curbing of immigration, espoused the enactment of national and state laws favorable to labor, demanded relief from technological unemployment, and endeavored to achieve these objectives through collaboration with employer and consumer groups. It rejected independent political action, seeking only to lobby on behalf of its members. Only rarely did the federation deviate from its political principle of rewarding its friends and punishing its enemies.

The AFL made slow progress in its attempted organization of workmen in the beginning. The membership of its affiliated unions rose from somewhat less than 200,000 in 1886 to slightly more than 1,750,000 in 1904. Gompers, as president, vigorously acted as organizer, conciliator, and peacemaker within labor's ranks. Jurisdictional conflicts between member unions were resolved, and in the 1890's the electrical workers, teamsters, musicians, and building laborers were formed into national unions. Despite this activity the proportion of workers organized in unions lagged behind the growth of the labor force. With rapid industrialization utilizing unskilled immigrant labor, the AFL persisted in concentrating its attention on the skilled crafts. Only the United Mine Workers (UMW), founded in 1890 as a result of an amalgamation of the AFL miners with those affiliated with the Knights, was initially organized along industrial lines, and it succeeded in winning over Slavic and Italian miners in the bituminous fields after a successful strike in 1897.

More typical was the experience of the Amalgamated Association of Iron, Steel, and Tin Workers. In 1890 this union, which restricted its membership to skilled workers, claimed a total of 24,000 members in the steel industry. In 1892 the union had a contract with the Carnegie Company at Homestead, Pa., which was to be renegotiated. Henry Clay Frick, manager of the steel works, realizing that the union did not represent the majority of the Homestead workers, who were mainly Slavic unskilled laborers, refused to accord recognition to the union and ordered a reduction in wages. The strike that followed had the support of the entire labor force of the steel works, but Frick hired some 300 Pinkerton guards to keep the mills open for strikebreakers. On the night of July 6, as the strikebreakers were being brought to Homestead on river barges, the strikers prevented the guards from landing, and a battle broke out in which a number of deaths occurred. Although the Pinkertons surrendered, the state militia was summoned, and under its protection the strike was broken even though it dragged on for four more months. Thus, organized labor's first struggle with large-scale capital ended in failure; the Amalgamated Association of Iron, Steel, and Tin Workers lost support in other steel mills and the steel industry was destined to be free of union controls for many more years.

The Coeur d'Alene district of northern Idaho was rocked by violence at the same time as was Homestead. A strike of lead and silver miners who became part of the Western Federation of Miners, a sometime AFL affiliate, was marked by pitched battles, the dynamiting of a mill, and the proclamation of martial law when the owners sought to run their mines with strikebreakers and sweeping injunctions. Federal and state troops restored order, and the strike was broken, but in 1894 and again in 1899 the events of 1892 were repeated.

Concern over the failure of the AFL unions and the railroad brotherhoods to attempt to recruit large numbers of unskilled workers into their ranks caused some to question the basic premises of craft union philosophy. The Socialists in particular were critical of the job-conscious approach to unionism of the AFL under Gompers and its focus on skilled labor. Largely as a result of their efforts, Gompers was defeated for the presidency of the federation in the election of

1894, but when his successor proved unequal to the task of supervising the loose federation during his one-year term in 1895, Gompers was returned to office. Failing in their attempt to capture the AFL, the Socialists, led by Daniel De Leon, sought to win control of the almost defunct Knights of Labor. In 1895, when this effort failed, the Socialist Labor party established an independent federation, the Socialist Trade and Labor Alliance. This deliberate creation of a "dual federation" alienated many Socialists who believed it to be a cardinal sin in the labor movement. Many defected from the Socialist Labor party and in 1897 formed a rival organization, the Social Democracy. In 1900 this organization united with another moderate faction of the Socialist Labor party to create a new group, the Socialist Party of America, which became the largest Socialist group in the United States and continued to challenge Gompers' policies, but from within the ranks of the constituent unions of the AFL.

The failure of the railroad brotherhoods to create a federation of railroad unions after the unsuccessful strike on the Burlington Railroad in 1888 caused Eugene Victor Debs, a former secretary of the Brotherhood of Locomotive Firemen, to attempt a new type of organization. In 1893 the American Railway Union was founded as an industrial union open to all railroad workers, including the unskilled switchmen and maintenance workers who had been ignored by the brotherhoods. Despite the depression that followed the panic of 1893 and resulted in widespread unemployment, the new American Railway Union was able to attract a membership of 150,000 after it had conducted a successful strike against the Great Northern Railroad in April 1894. Before it had time to consolidate its gains, the union was forced almost immediately into a strike by members working for the Pullman Company, and the strike quickly assumed nationwide proportions.

Wage reductions averaging 25 percent ordered by the Pullman Company to offset the heavy losses caused by the depression were not matched by any reductions of rents or fees charged the workers living in the town run by the company, Pullman, Ill. Disgruntled, about 4,000 employees joined the American Railway Union, and on May 11, 1894, they quit work. The Pullman Company, receiving revenues from the rental of its equipment to the railroads, was not willing to arbitrate or negotiate a settlement with the union. The union, therefore, called upon its members on the railroads not to handle Pullman cars. As a result of this boycott call, twenty-four railroads centering in Chicago were tied up, and by June 28 the whole West was affected. By June 30 the railroads of the entire country were affected.

The strike seriously curtailed the movement of mail; consequently, at the request of the railroads' association of general managers, Richard Olney, President Grover Cleveland's attorney general, secured injunctions against the union's interference with interstate commerce. Defiance of the injunction of July 2 led to the arrest of Debs and the ordering of federal troops into Chicago by Cleveland. Gov. Altgeld protested against this violation of states' rights, and the presence of the federal troops triggered mob violence and destruction of railroad property. Riots were reported as far west as Oakland, Calif., and federal troops were ordered to strike duty there. By July 13 some trains were running under military guard, and a week later the strike was broken. Thus, the first and only attempt to create a single railroad union ended in failure. More significant was the dramatic and successful use of an injunction to curb the strike. The U.S. Supreme Court upheld the right of federal judges to issue such injunctions in the case *In re Debs,* 158 U.S. 564 (1895), and for many years organized labor campaigned to abolish the use of injunctions by federal and state courts in labor disputes.

Labor leaders, disappointed by the results of the Pullman strike and by the march on Washington of a jobless army led by Jacob S. Coxey for unemployment relief and federal work projects in 1894, turned once more to political action. Debs, who spent six months in prison, read Marxist literature and became a Socialist. Other labor leaders attempted a coalition with the Populists. The AFL remained true to its nonpolitical position, and when the depression subsided after 1897 and the Populist party virtually disappeared after the election of 1896, it was prepared to take advantage of better times to continue its organization of skilled workmen into labor unions.

From 1898 to 1904, a time called the honeymoon period of capital and labor, the AFL unions received wide recognition from employers and were able to increase membership substantially—with the assistance of such middle-class organizations as the National Consumers' League, National Civic Federation, National Child Labor Committee, and American Association for Labor Legislation. The organizational success of AFL unions, as well as the new progressive mood of the nation, were reflected in the action of President Theodore Roosevelt when John Mitchell, the president of the UMW, in attempting to organize the anthracite miners, called a strike in 1902: Roose-

velt compelled the mine owners to accept arbitration by a commission appointed by the president, and the commission's award of a 10 percent wage increase for the anthracite miners was the first known example of the federal government's intervention in a labor dispute on the workers' behalf. A number of new national unions chartered by the AFL were founded during this period; notable among them was the International Ladies' Garment Workers' Union (ILGWU), organized in 1900.

Trade union success caused a noticeable stiffening of attitudes among some employers. The National Association of Manufacturers (NAM), organized in 1895, spearheaded a campaign against trade unionism by sponsoring an open-shop drive that appreciably slowed down union organizational achievements after 1904. The unions were dealt a heavy blow by the courts during this open-shop campaign, when boycotts were ruled to be violations of the Sherman Antitrust Act. The D. E. Loewe Company of Danbury, Conn., was awarded triple damages under the Sherman Act when the Supreme Court in 1908 upheld its contention that the 1902 boycott of its wares initiated by the hatters' union was illegal (*see* Danbury Hatters' Case). Gompers was cited for contempt of court in 1909 in another boycott case, that against the Buck Stove and Range Company, decided in 1911.

At the same time, the AFL trade union concepts of craft exclusiveness and autonomy were challenged from the left. In Chicago, in June 1905, delegates from the Western Federation of Miners and from Daniel De Leon's Socialist Trade and Labor Alliance and some individual Socialists, notably Debs, joined to found the Industrial Workers of the World (IWW), with the objective of uniting all workers, regardless of skill, race, or ethnic origin, into one centralized industrial organization. Emphasizing the class struggle, the IWW called for the abolition of the wage system and stressed direct action, the general strike, boycott, and sabotage as the means of accomplishing this end. Factionalism and defections weakened the organization from the beginning, but after the elimination of the De Leon faction in 1908, William D. Haywood and Vincent St. John were able to achieve a certain measure of success for the industrial union. In the West the unskilled metal miners and migratory lumber, shipping, and farm laborers were organized. In the East the "Wobblies" provided English-speaking leadership for immigrant workers, especially those in textile factories. Under Haywood's leadership these textile workers won wage increases after strikes at Lawrence, Mass., in 1912 and Paterson, N.J., in

1913. The IWW's syndicalist philosophy, its rejection of collective bargaining, and its extreme tactics prevented any but the most desperate workers from joining, so that at its height in 1913 the organization did not have more than 70,000 members. Federal prosecutions of its leaders during World War I, coupled with effective vigilante action, notably at Centralia, Wash., eliminated the IWW as an effective labor federation, but not before it had called attention to the need for organizing the millions of unskilled workers who were flocking to the labor force to man new mass industries. Furthermore, the attention it paid to the migratory farm and lumber workers in the West underscored the problems of this underprivileged group.

Meeting the challenge of both the open-shop, antiunion employer groups and the militant advocates of industrial unions, Gompers sought to emulate the British Labor Representation Committee by appealing to Congress and to the two major parties for a redress of labor's grievances. Rebuffed by Congress and the Republican party, the AFL unofficially supported the Democratic party in the presidential campaigns of 1908 and 1912. That not all the workers followed Gompers' lead can be seen in the large vote polled for Debs, the Socialist candidate for president, who received nearly 900,000 votes in 1912. Nevertheless, Woodrow Wilson's election as president in 1912 and his subsequent use of Gompers as his unofficial and official labor adviser meant that organized labor for the first time had access to an administration that paid serious attention to its needs.

Class-conscious appeals to create a classless society by appropriating the means of production through revolutionary action, which was the main appeal of the IWW, the various Marxist-based Socialist movements, and independent radicals, failed to attract large numbers of American workers. The myth of social mobility and the reality of geographical mobility, as seen in the large turnover rates of workers in major industries and in the movement of large numbers of workers into and out of industrial centers, prevented class-conscious appeals from being heeded by the American working class. Massive immigration from eastern and southern Europe, the major source for new recruits to the industrial labor force at the beginning of the 20th century, created ethnic cleavages within the working class, further diluting the class appeals of the radicals. The willingness of the major political parties to absorb and legitimize the more attractive features of the radical programs of the Socialists also reduced the effectiveness of the class-oriented messages to the workers.

The early years of the 20th century saw a marked change in the public attitude toward the problems of the worker, and during this era protective legislation for labor's benefit was enacted in most states as well as at the national level. State laws were passed limiting child labor, setting standards for hours and wages for women workers, providing controls over sanitary and safety conditions in factories, and attempting to establish systems of accident insurance. Uncertain about the reception these laws would receive from a usually hostile Supreme Court, many states postponed such legislation until their constitutionality was determined. On the basis of the argument that the state's police powers gave it jurisdiction to protect its children, the state child labor laws were invariably upheld. A New York law limiting the labor of bakers to ten hours a day was declared unconstitutional on the ground that it restricted the worker's freedom of contract (*Lochner* v. *New York,* 1905). When an Oregon statute limiting the maximum working hours for women was challenged, the Supreme Court, following the sociological arguments submitted in favor of the law by Louis D. Brandeis, upheld it (*Muller* v. *Oregon,* 1908). By 1917 thirty-nine states had such laws on their statute books. In 1911 Wisconsin set up an industrial commission to establish safety and health standards in the factories. New York revamped its factory laws after the tragic Triangle fire in March 1911 killed more than 140 women shirtwaist workers. In 1912, Massachusetts established a minimum-wage board with authority to establish minimum wages for women and minors. Although the first workmen's compensation laws of Maryland (1902), Montana (1909), and New York (1910) were upset by the courts, those framed after 1910 met the tests of constitutionality, not only accomplishing their explicit purpose but also providing an economic incentive for employers to improve industrial safety in their factories.

Under friendly pressure from the Wilson administration, Congress passed several laws favorable to labor. In 1913 the Newlands Act created a four-member Board of Mediation and Conciliation for the settlement of railroad labor disputes. In 1915 the La Follette Seamen's Act regulated conditions for maritime workers. A year later the Adamson Act established an eight-hour day and time-and-a-half pay for overtime for workers on interstate railroads. During the same year the Keating-Owen Act sought to bar the products of child labor from interstate commerce, but the Supreme Court in 1918 ruled against this law. A subsequent act passed in 1919 sought to tax the products of child labor out of existence, but this too was declared unconstitutional in 1922. During the period 1913–21 labor's cause found particular support in the fact that the Department of Labor, created in 1913, was headed by a labor leader, William B. Wilson, a former official of the UMW.

Of greatest concern to organized labor was the use by the courts of the Sherman Antitrust Act to frustrate its organizational drives; injunctions and prohibitions against secondary boycotts were often justified through the use of the law. Consequently, when the Wilson administration in 1914 sponsored a revision of the antitrust laws, the resulting Clayton Antitrust Act contained provisions that prompted Gompers to call it "the Magna Carta of labor." Under the act's provisions, labor was not to be considered a commodity; labor organizations were not to be held illegal combinations in restraint of trade; and the injunction was not to be used in labor disputes except when necessary to prevent irreparable property damage. Strikes, boycotts, and peaceful picketing were recognized as legal rights of labor under federal jurisdiction, and jury trials were mandated in contempt cases except where the offense was committed in the court's presence. Judicial interpretation soon substantially weakened most of the labor provisions of the Clayton Act (*Duplex Printing Press Company* v. *Deering,* 1921), making possible a renewal of the campaign against trade unions after the end of World War I.

During World War I the number of organized workers increased from 2.75 million in 1916 to 4.25 million in 1919. This gain resulted partially from favorable action of government agencies responsible for maintaining war production and partially from the workers' better bargaining position as labor scarcity grew during the war. To offset this shortage of available workmen, approximately a million women were recruited into the labor force; countless thousands of blacks migrated North from the rural South, and the U.S. Department of Labor expanded the activities of its employment service. Since the AFL enthusiastically supported the war effort, officers of the federation were appointed to most of the war boards organized by the government. Gompers was appointed to the Council of National Defense and the Advisory Committee on National Defense. The Mediation Commission and the War Labor Board were created in 1917 and 1918, respectively, to settle disputes and maintain continuous production. The Railroad Wage Commission and adjustment boards were established to ensure unhampered movement of the railroads even after the federal government took over their operation. Through these means strikes were kept to a minimum and the trade unions grew in importance and size. In recognition of labor's role in winning the war, an international conference was sponsored by the victorious powers in Washington in 1919, out of which came the recommendation that an organization to promote the international improvement of labor conditions be created under the auspices of the League of Nations. Thus was established the International Labor Organization.

Although the standard workday, in the main, declined to the desired eight-hour norm during the war and money wages rose appreciably, real wages had declined from 1913 levels by 1919. By 1920, however, real wages had risen some 12 percent above the 1913 levels. The failure of wages to keep significantly ahead of rising prices, coupled with the public's growing hostility to organized labor because of the opposition of labor's left wing to the war, meant a resurgence of labor unrest after the armistice.

In 1919 over 4 million wage earners were involved in strikes, as compared to 1.25 million the year before. The bituminous coal strike called by John L. Lewis, who became president of the United Mine Workers the following year, was broken by an injunction secured by Attorney General A. M. Palmer under a wartime measure. A railroad shopmen's strike collapsed under government opposition. A general strike tying up Seattle and a policemen's strike in Boston spread a fear of radicalism. The most significant strike, in 1919, was one called under AFL auspices against the U.S. Steel Corporation. The strikers sought to end the notorious twelve-hour day in the steel industry and to gain union recognition, collective bargaining rights, and wage increases. The adamant refusal to bargain by Judge Elbert H. Gary, chairman of the board of U.S. Steel; the successful use of black strikebreakers; and the division of the strike committee into twenty-four craft committees spelled the doom of the walkout. The steel corporation effectively called the public's attention to the alleged radicalism of the leader of the strike, William Z. Foster.

The 1920's, a decade of massive economic growth resulting from the expansion of new industries and the increase of productivity, was also a decade of rapid decline of organized labor. Paradoxically, the decade of prosperity that saw real wages and per capita income rise, except for the textile workers and the coal miners, saw the membership of labor unions decline from 5 million in 1921 to 3.4 million in 1929. Unions lost another 500,000 members during the depression years from 1929 to 1933. This decline can be attributed to the failure of defensive strikes during the sharp recession of 1921; to the resurgence of strong, organized opposition to unions by employer associations; and to the unfavorable decisions rendered by the federal courts. Furthermore, the continued failure of the craft-oriented leadership of the AFL to organize the growing army of unskilled labor allowed this task to be taken over by a new militant revolutionary movement working within the ranks of labor, the Communists.

Manufacturers' associations and chambers of commerce conducted a successful open-shop drive. Company unions, organizations founded and controlled by management, grew in number and influence; by 1926 some 400 such unions had a membership of 1.4 million, and by 1935, 2.5 million. Labor spies and agents provocateurs were used in increasing number to destroy legitimate unions. Expansion of freely given fringe benefits, such as medical services, vacations with pay, profit-sharing devices, insurance and pension schemes, and promotion of stock ownership by employers, helped to discourage workers from remaining in unions. Finally, effective publicity campaigns blamed organized labor for the high cost of living and for increased radical and Communist activities.

The actions of the Supreme Court in rejecting labor's contention that the Clayton Act protected it from injunction proceedings (*Duplex Printing Press Company* v. *Deering,* 1921) and the overturning of a Washington, D.C., minimum-wage law for women (*Adkins* v. *Children's Hospital,* 1923) convinced the AFL leadership that it must reverse its traditional attitude to political action. Consequently, the AFL joined with the railroad brotherhoods, disgruntled liberals, reformers, farm groups, and Socialists in endorsing the candidacy of Sen. Robert M. La Follette of Wisconsin for president of the United States on the Progressive party ticket in the 1924 election. La Follette polled 4.8 million votes, more votes than any previous or subsequent third-party presidential candidate except George Wallace in the 1968 election. The unwillingness of La Follette's supporters to create a permanent third party—an unwillingness reinforced by the hostility of the AFL leadership to independent political action—ended this hopeful effort, even though Farmer-Labor parties in some states, notably Minnesota, were able to challenge the two major parties successfully and in some cases even to displace one of the major parties.

William Green of the UMW succeeded Gompers as president of the AFL after the latter's death in 1924, but the policies of the federation remained unchanged. Jurisdictional claims among rival affiliates of the federation frustrated Green's hope to organize the automobile industry, and the hoped-for extension of unionism into the newly born southern industries was thwarted in part by the failure of the AFL unions to contribute funds for this purpose.

Agitation for industrial unionism and for militancy came from the Communists who, under William Z. Foster, set up a Trade Union Education League. Seeking to take over existing unions, the Communists succeeded with the furriers and came close to success in the needle-trades unions. Failing to control these unions, they sought to create dual unions but then reverted to their "boring from within" tactics. Under Communist leadership, several violent strikes were conducted in the textile mills in Gastonia and Marion, N.C., in 1929, but they were just as unsuccessful as the strikes conducted at the same time by the AFL United Textile Workers Union.

Civil war in the West Virginia coalfields early in the decade; the Herrin massacre, in which strikebreakers were killed in retaliation for the murder of two strikers by mine guards in Williamson County, Ill., in 1922; and the internal conflict between the Communists and John L. Lewis decimated the ranks of the UMW. The membership in that union dwindled from 500,000 in 1921 to not quite 150,000 in 1933.

The economic collapse of the nation that began in 1929 found the labor movement completely unprepared to cope with the disastrous consequences. Unemployment surpassed 13 million by 1933, and countless millions of workers were employed only part-time. Although employment had declined 35.4 percent from 1926 levels by 1933, the total national payroll had declined 56 percent. Local relief organizations and private charitable institutions sought to ameliorate some of the more extreme effects of the depression, but soon their funds were exhausted. Families doubled up in apartments, and some were forced to improvise dwellings by using packing cases and boxes. The Communist party organized hunger marches, but the largest demonstration, by veterans in Washington in 1932 demanding the payment of bonuses, was not run by Communists. Until 1932 President Herbert Hoover sought to extend aid indirectly by assisting needy businesses and expecting that this maneuver would affect workers. When the extent of the need became clear, the president authorized direct federal assistance by means of loans to the states for emergency relief.

Union membership declined during the early years of the depression—AFL membership by nearly 1 million from 1929 to 1933. In the face of the depression, Green had the federation reconsider its opposition to legislation establishing compulsory welfare schemes. In 1932 the AFL began advocating a compulsory system of unemployment insurance as well as large-scale public works projects, while attempting to hold the line on wages. In that same year, Wisconsin enacted the first unemployment insurance law in the United States. A Congress more friendly to organized labor than previous postwar Congresses passed the Norris–La Guardia Act in 1932, which curtailed the federal courts' power to issue injunctions against unions conducting peaceful strikes and made antiunion ("yellow-dog") employment contracts unenforceable in the courts.

In the depths of the depression the New Deal of President Franklin D. Roosevelt came into being, with the announced objectives of "relief, recovery, and reform." Seeking to minimize the effects of unemployment, Congress authorized, and the new administration set up, the Federal Emergency Relief Administration under Harry L. Hopkins, with an initial appropriation of $500 million for direct grants to the states. The Civilian Conservation Corps was authorized by Congress for the purpose of providing work for jobless young people. Under the National Industrial Recovery Act (NIRA) the Public Works Administration headed by Secretary of the Interior Harold L. Ickes was established with an authorized fund of $3.3 billion. The cautious approach of the administrator prevented the rapid expansion of public works, and the Civil Works Administration was created to employ 4 million jobless on public works in order to cushion the economic distress of the winter of 1933–34. With the passage of the National Employment Service Act the U.S. Employment Service was expanded and the state bodies were coordinated with the federal agency. These measures sought to minimize the effects on the worker of joblessness while at the same time they sought to expand employment, even if it was under public auspices. In 1935 the federal government withdrew from the area of direct relief when Congress created the Works Progress Administration (WPA)—after 1939 the Works Projects Administration—with Hopkins as administrator, for the purpose of establishing a massive national public works program for the jobless. During its lifetime until 1943 the WPA spent $11 billion and employed 8.5 million different people on some 1.4 million projects. These measures of relief were necessary, for

despite efforts at recovery it was not until the defense and war production demands of the 1940's caused industry to boom that the rolls of the unemployed declined appreciably.

To improve the security of the American worker, the New Deal enacted a series of measures that resulted in the establishment of a system of social reforms closely paralleling the systems in operation in western Europe for a number of decades. The codes of industrial self-regulation drawn up under the National Recovery Administration, established under the NIRA, prescribed minimum wages and maximum hours and eliminated child labor. The Walsh-Healey Government Contracts Act of 1936 sought to establish fair labor standards among contractors accepting government work. In 1938 the Fair Labor Standards Act established minimum wages, maximum hours, and abolition of child labor for all businesses engaged in interstate commerce. To provide for the further security of the wage earner, a joint federal-state system of unemployment insurance financed by a tax on employers' payrolls, coupled with a system of old-age and survivors' insurance financed by a payroll tax on both employers and employees, was adopted as the Social Security Act of 1935.

Strengthening the power of organized labor was a further objective of the New Deal. Section 7(a) of the NIRA proclaimed the workers' "right to organize and bargain collectively through representatives of their own choosing" and prohibited the employers from any "interference, restraint, or coercion" on this process. The National Labor Board, chaired by Sen. Robert F. Wagner of New York, was created to settle differences arising from this act, and in 1934 this board was authorized to hold elections of employees to determine their bargaining representatives. Section 7(a) raised expectations among workers and unionists. Although some organizing successes were made among garment workers and coal miners, the NIRA stimulated the successful expansion of company unions and gave inordinate power to large corporate employers through the codemaking provisions of the act. When the automobile labor codes were interpreted in favor of the Big Three auto makers, labor's disillusionment with the NIRA was complete. Frustrated high expectations triggered massive strikes in Toledo, San Francisco, and Minneapolis during the spring and summer of 1934 that tied up those cities and almost resembled class-war. Federal and state governmental intervention resolved these strikes, and beginnings were made in collective bargaining in these heretofore open-shop cities.

Although the NIRA was invalidated by the Supreme Court in 1935 (*Schechter* v. *United States*), Congress reenacted the labor provisions of Section 7(a) in the same year by passing the Wagner-Connery National Labor Relations Act. A new three-man National Labor Relations Board (NLRB) was created by this act with the function of supervising elections of workers, designating the appropriate bargaining agents, and holding hearings to determine unfair employer practices. The board was authorized to issue cease-and-desist orders, which were made enforceable through the federal circuit courts of appeals.

Reacting to the stimulus of New Deal legislation and favorable governmental actions, the labor movement reawakened from its decade-long lethargy to begin a massive organizational drive. Supported by a shift of public opinion, noncompany union membership increased from 3 million in 1933 to 4.7 million in 1936; to 8.2 million in 1939; to 15.4 million in 1947; to 17 million in 1953; and to 21 million in 1972.

The almost defunct national unions affiliated with the AFL made rapid organizational progress on the heels of the passage of the NIRA. The three industrial unions within the AFL—the UMW, the ILGWU, and the Amalgamated Clothing Workers of America—reestablished themselves as effective bodies of organized workers through the membership drives they conducted as early as 1933. The executive council of the AFL and its national convention authorized an organizing campaign in the mass production industries, but when it became clear that the newly recruited members were to be distributed among existing craft unions, no appreciable headway was made. At the 1935 AFL convention the delegates split on the question of craft versus industrial unions for the mass production industries; and after the traditional craft-oriented position of the federation won out, the minority leaders established the Committee for Industrial Organization (CIO)—after 1938 the Congress of Industrial Organizations—with John L. Lewis of the UMW as chairman. Although the AFL, after warning the dissidents, first suspended and then expelled the unions that went along with the minority, the existence of a militant rival federation in the CIO caused the leaders of the older federation to intensify and make more forceful their own organizing drives. Consequently, as the CIO successfully carried out its efforts in the mass production industries, the AFL unions also continued to expand. The Teamsters Union, for example, grew from 95,000 to 350,000 in the 1930's and became the largest union in the AFL.

Financed from the coffers of the UMW, the CIO set up organizing committees to establish unions for rubber, automobile, steel, electrical, and texile workers. Using a dramatic technique, the sit-down strike—a device whereby the workers remained in the plants rather than vacating them and giving the companies an opportunity to utilize strike-breakers—the CIO United Automobile Workers Union (UAW) was able to receive recognition from the General Motors Corporation and the Chrysler Corporation early in 1937. By September the automobile union had bargaining agreements with every automobile producer except the Ford Motor Company and boasted of a membership of over 300,000. Even Ford finally capitulated and recognized the union in 1941. Earlier sit-down strikes were successful in establishing union control in the rubber industry, and the CIO organizers had some measure of success in establishing unions and attaining bargaining agreements in the electrical industry, among the West Coast longshoremen, and in the maritime trades.

After careful spadework the Steel Workers' Organizing Committee, led by Philip Murray, then vice-president of the UMW, was ready to tackle U.S. Steel in 1937. The time was right, for the government had become friendly to labor, and public opinion had been aroused against management by the disclosures resulting from the inquiry into industrial espionage and violence by a Senate committee chaired by Robert M. La Follette, Jr. Rather than risk a strike, U.S. Steel capitulated to the union, and in March 1937 its subsidiaries signed agreements granting union recognition, wage increases, and the forty-hour week. It was expected that the rest of the steel companies, known collectively as Little Steel, would follow the lead of U.S. Steel, but except for Inland Steel, which agreed to recognize the union in July 1937, the others offered stiff resistance. The strike that followed was marked by violence; special deputies of Republic Steel killed two strikers in Massillon, Ohio, and the South Chicago police killed ten strikers and wounded many at the Republic Steel plant on Memorial Day 1937. The investigation by La Follette's committee into the strike revealed that the companies had violated the Wagner-Connery Act, maintained an army of spies, and collected weapons for use against the strikers; and the NLRB demanded that the companies bargain in good faith with the union. In 1941 Little Steel capitulated. Thus, when the United States entered World War II, the entire steel industry was organized, and the steel workers' union reported over 600,000 members.

Not so successful was the attempt to penetrate the southern cotton mills by the Textile Workers Organizing Committee, headed by Sidney Hillman and financed by his Amalgamated Clothing Workers of America. Local opposition, which often resulted in violent attacks against the union organizers and which was reinforced by vigilante groups, frustrated this first all-out attempt to bring the benefits of unionism to the South.

Organized labor recognized its debt to the Roosevelt administration. In 1936 John L. Lewis contributed heavily to Roosevelt's reelection campaign; the New York labor leaders organized the American Labor party as a vehicle for garnering votes for the president; and the AFL cautiously and quietly worked for the president's reelection through labor's Nonpartisan League. The situation was quite different in 1940 when Roosevelt ran for a third term. Lewis, piqued that he did not become the president's labor adviser and critical of Roosevelt's international policies, backed Republican Wendell L. Willkie for the presidency. Although Lewis was supported within the CIO by the Communists, who, in obedience to the party line, also opposed Roosevelt's policy of aiding the Allies, the majority of the members, led by Hillman, supported the president. When Roosevelt won, Lewis, as he had threatened, resigned as president of the CIO and was replaced by Philip Murray, a former colleague in the UMW whom he had chosen to head the steel workers' union.

Production and employment boomed with the increase of U.S. defense spending and shipments of war materials to the Allies in 1940. The necessity for continuous production at the same time that the labor unions were militantly expanding their influence dictated vigorous executive actions. Hillman was made codirector of the Office of Production Management in 1941, and in the same year, the National Defense Mediation Board was established. With no effective powers to enforce decisions and with labor split on foreign policy questions, this body soon proved ineffective. Strikes of coal miners in April and September 1941 raised Roosevelt's ire and caused public opinion to turn against the unions for subordinating the nation's interests to their own.

When the United States entered the war, a no-strike pledge was given at a conference of labor leaders called by Roosevelt. The National War Labor Board (NWLB), with powers to enforce decisions, was created in January 1942. To the demand of the unions for the spread of the closed shop in war industries, the NWLB devised a compromise of "maintenance of membership" by which unionized workers were obliged to remain in their unions in order to continue employment. By the war's end some 4 million workers were employed under such conditions.

The necessity of holding the wage and price levels stable caused further difficulty for the NWLB, and in July 1942 the board devised the Little Steel formula, by which it tied wage increases to rises in the cost of living after January 1941. Roosevelt ordered the freezing of wages and prices in April 1943, causing discontent within the ranks of labor. Lewis dramatized this discontent by refusing to appear before the NWLB and calling a strike of soft-coal and anthracite miners in May 1943. The seizure of the mines by the federal government under the president's war powers quickly halted the strike but not before Congress acted in haste in passing the Smith-Connally War Labor Disputes Act over the president's veto. In December 1943, the railroads were temporarily taken over by the army in the face of a strike threat.

Despite strikes and seizures the time lost in wartime walkouts was exceptionally small. The dramatic challenge of government authority by Lewis, however, caused some public revulsion; many southern and western states outlawed the closed shop during the war period, and the way was opened for more restrictive legislation after the war.

The need to expand the labor force during wartime was met by the increased utilization of women workers and the opening of opportunities for black workers. To curb discriminatory employment, the Fair Employment Practice Committee (FEPC) was established by executive order in June 1941, and in May 1943 the government required nondiscrimination clauses in all war contracts. Attempts to make the national FEPC permanent failed to pass the Senate after the war, but by 1946 five states had created such commissions.

The CIO's political activities during the war were more vigorous than those attempted by the AFL. Avoiding the prohibition against the use of union funds for political purposes, which was part of the Smith-Connally Act, the CIO organized the Political Action Committee to work for Roosevelt's reelection in 1944 and to support congressional candidates favorable to labor's cause, and Hillman was asked to give labor's approval before Harry S. Truman was nominated for the vice-presidency by the Democratic party in 1944. The AFL, although supporting Roosevelt in 1944, continued to refuse to give him its open endorsement.

The end of the war saw the beginning of a cyclic

increase in wages and prices that frightened the public into an antiunion attitude, even though the responsibility of labor for this inflationary spiral was not exclusive. Strikes to keep up with the rising cost of living were widespread in 1945 and 1946, the most dramatic being the two strikes of the miners in 1946. The second resulted in the union's being held in contempt of court and fined $3.5 million (sustained by the Supreme Court in 1947, but the fine reduced to $700,000). When the railroads under government control were struck by the brotherhoods in 1946, President Truman threatened to draft the strikers. Walter Reuther, president of the UAW, demanded the right to inspect the company's books during the 1945–46 strike against General Motors, to determine whether the firm could raise wages without raising prices. In all cases the wage demands of the workers were met when government boards, intervening in the strikes, recommended both wage raises and price increases. A new means of increasing compensation, which had its origin during the war, was expanded in the postwar period when fringe benefits in the form of pension plans, insurance, and vacation grants became part of the collective bargaining agreement.

The inflationary spiral, the feeling that unions had grown too powerful with the help of favorable legislation, the existence of a few corrupt labor officials, and the control of some unions by Communists resulted in public hostility to unions that was translated into congressional action. In June 1947 the Taft-Hartley Act was passed over Truman's veto. Designed as a measure to redress the balance between union and management rights, the act modified the Wagner-Connery Act by changing the structure of the NLRB, by limiting some of the unions' freedoms, and by spelling out the rights of employers in industrial disputes. The act prohibited the closed shop, forced the unions to wait sixty days before striking, ended the system whereby employers collected union dues (checkoff), made the unions liable for broken contracts and damages during strikes, and required union leaders to take an oath that they were not members of the Communist party. The U.S. Conciliation Service was removed from the Department of Labor and made an independent body, the Federal Mediation and Conciliation Service.

Organized labor called the new law a "slave labor act" and campaigned for its repeal. Although the need for amending the act was proclaimed by one of its sponsors, Sen. Robert A. Taft of Ohio, before his death in 1953 and by Republican President Dwight D. Eisenhower repeatedly during both of his administra-

tions, 1953–61, only minor changes were made in its provisions. In response to the antiunion climate, many states adopted right-to-work laws, which outlawed union shops as well as closed shops. Effective political activity of labor, however, limited these laws almost exclusively to nonindustrial states.

Several factors paved the way for the long-desired merger of the AFL and CIO: the purge of the Communists from the CIO in 1949 and 1950; the appearance of new presidents of the rival federations when George Meany and Walter Reuther succeeded Green and Murray; and the beginning of vigorous anticorruption activity by the AFL, as reflected in the expulsion of the International Longshoremen's Association in 1953. During the Korean War the two federations formed the United Labor Policy Committee, and in 1953 they approved a "no-raiding" agreement. Negotiations removed jurisdictional obstacles, sought to remove the racially discriminatory policies of some AFL unions, and guaranteed the principle of industrial organization. The merger occurred in 1955, and the new federation, calling itself the AFL-CIO, elected Meany president and Reuther head of the industrial union department. Autonomy of affiliates was recognized, with equality of status between industrial and craft unions specifically stated in the constitution. The executive council was given authority to investigate and suspend affiliates accused of corruption or control by totalitarian groups. At the time of the merger the AFL-CIO consisted of 6 trade and industrial departments, 139 national unions, 50 state or territorial federations, 60,000 local unions, 1,000 city central bodies, and approximately 16 million members.

The most urgent task facing the merged federation was the elimination of corrupt elements from the labor movement. An effort was made in the creation of an ethical practices committee, which investigated and recommended the expulsion of a number of national unions—notably the Teamsters Union in 1957. Even so, evidences of sharp practices uncovered in the labor and management field in 1957 by a Senate committee headed by John L. McClellan resulted in legislation that further restricted the freedom of action of organized labor. The Landrum-Griffin Labor Management Reporting and Disclosure Act of 1959 restricted secondary boycotts, called for precise controls over union elections, demanded strict reporting of a union's financial transactions, outlawed extortion picketing, authorized state jurisdiction over labor disputes not handled by the NLRB, and modified union security provisions for the construction and garment industries. Labor reluctantly accepted this law, pledging to continue its efforts to clean its own house.

From 1960 to 1975 American labor faced many challenges resulting from social, economic, and political changes. Automation seemed to threaten the job security of production-line workers and the stability of industrial unions in coal mining, meat-packing, transportation, and steel and auto production, where new technologies threatened to displace skilled and semiskilled workers. The competition of new entrants into the industrial labor force, principally women and racial minorities, constituted a major challenge to the labor movement. The shift of workers from blue-collar to white-collar and service occupations seemed to some to suggest that the labor movement had reached the limits of its possibilities for growth. The growth of multinational corporations and the consequent removal of jobs to foreign countries with prevailingly low wages threatened the traditional free-trade stance of the labor movement. The rise of a middle-class, student-based counterculture protest movement, primarily aimed at halting the U.S. involvement in wars in Southeast Asia, threatened to isolate the labor movement from its traditional liberal political support base. Protest militancy among young workers constituted a major challenge to collective-bargaining concerns of both labor and management. The elusiveness of full employment and especially the growth of unemployment, exceeding the 9 percent level during the 1974–75 recession, further challenged the economic and political creativity of organized labor. These challenges were posed at a time when a new leadership was increasingly emerging within labor's ranks and the principles of collective bargaining and labor's political response were being questioned by its rank-and-file members and by the society at large.

Although union membership grew from over 18 million in 1956 to close to 21 million in 1972, it did not keep up with the growth in the nonagricultural labor force; it constituted some 34 percent in 1956 and only 26.7 percent in 1972. Numerical membership growth took place during those years in manufacturing, nonmanufacturing, and governmental unions; but the most spectacular growth was to be seen in the last category. In 1956 unions of public employees had 915,000 members, which was 5.1 percent of total union membership. By 1972, organized public employees numbered 2.46 million, constituting 11.8 percent of total union membership. Manufacturing unions suffered a 6 percent proportionate decline, from 48.8 percent in 1956 to 42.8 per-

cent in 1972, whereas nonmanufacturing unions declined less than 1 percent in their proportionate share of union members, from 46.1 percent in 1956 to 45.4 percent in 1972.

Public-sector employment grew spectacularly during the 1960's as a consequence of new federal, state, and municipal programs, and the labor movement's continuing success in organizing public employees shows that union organizing techniques can be effectively applied outside private-sector, profit-oriented enterprises. It should be emphasized that the public-sector work force encompasses not only relatively secure civil servants, such as teachers and clerical workers, but also a numerically larger number of unskilled and semiskilled service workers, such as street cleaners, postal workers, garbage collectors, prison guards, hospital workers, and janitors, many of whom are black and underpaid in comparison with their private-sector counterparts.

President John F. Kennedy's Executive Order No. 10988, issued Jan. 17, 1962, gave federal employees the right to organize and bargain collectively. This established the legal foundation for labor organization among federal governmental employees and stimulated the rapid growth of public-sector bargaining. State and municipal employees were granted similar rights when state legislatures passed public employee labor relations acts, as did Wisconsin in 1959, Michigan in 1965, New York in 1967, and Minnesota in 1971; more than half the states had passed such laws by 1975. Although most of the laws provide for peaceful, orderly resolution of conflicts through agencies modeled after the NLRB, many states allow for a limited right to strike if the public employer refuses to abide by an arbitration award (Minnesota, 1973). Despite restriction of their right to strike, public employees have used the strike weapon widely, and sometimes illegally, as did the Memphis garbage men in 1968; the postal workers in 1970; and the Minneapolis schoolteachers in 1971. So successfully have public-sector unions responded to their members' felt needs that the American Federation of State, County, and Municipal Employees (AFSCME), founded in 1936 but greatly expanded under the leadership of Jerry Wurf after 1964, had become the eleventh largest national union by 1971, with some 550,000 members; the American Federation of Government Employees (federal government jurisdiction) ranked as the seventeenth largest union, with some 300,000 members.

Also in the public sector, the unionization of teachers grew significantly in the 1960's and early

1970's, under the aegis of the American Federation of Teachers (AFT). After the militancy of the AFT affiliate in New York City succeeded in winning a collective bargaining agreement there in 1961, union organization spread into almost every major school system in the country. The AFT grew in membership from 50,000 in 1960 to 250,000 in 1973; the AFL-CIO, recognizing this growth, elected Albert Shanker, AFT president since 1947, to its executive council in 1973. Teacher militancy and strikes became an annual event wherever recalcitrant school boards sought to economize on school budgets. Labor militancy even affected the National Educational Association (NEA), and this venerable professional association increasingly took on trade union characteristics; although efforts to create a merger between the AFT and the NEA had not come to fruition by 1975, they had been effected at the state level in New York and Florida. Even college and university faculties began to move toward unionization: only five colleges had collective bargaining agreements in 1966, whereas 288 colleges were organized in 1973. In 1972 the American Association of University Professors (AAUP) joined the organizational scramble for college and university bargaining rights for faculty with the AFT and the NEA.

Convinced of the necessity for political action, three organizations of public employees—the AFSCME, the NEA, and the International Association of Fire Fighters—formed the Coalition of American Public Employees (CAPE) in 1973. In addition, since the AFT sought full participation of the labor movement in any political coordination of unions of public employees, it prevailed upon the AFL-CIO to create a public employee department within the federation and urged AFSCME to leave CAPE as a means of stimulating AFT-NEA merger.

During the 1960's increasing militancy among the rank-and-file membership led to leadership upheavals within many unions. James Carey, longtime leader of the electrical workers (IUE), was replaced by Paul Jennings in 1964; David McDonald was replaced by I. W. Abel as president of the steelworkers (USWA) in 1965; and Arnold R. Miller replaced W. A. "Tony" Boyle as president of the UMW in 1972, after the murder of Joseph A. Yablonski and his family during a bitter rank-and-file contest within that union in 1969. (In April 1974 Boyle was found guilty of murder and sentenced to life imprisonment.) A number of prominent leaders retired, such as David Dubinsky of the ILGWU and Jacob Potofsky of the Amalgamated Clothing Workers of America. These

leadership changes did not stop the criticism of the AFL-CIO for alleged inaction in organizing the unorganized low-income, unskilled workers; and this, together with the criticism of the "hawkish" stance of the federation on cold war foreign policy, led the UAW to discontinue its affiliation with the AFL-CIO in 1968. Reuther then joined with Frank E. Fitzsimmons, acting president of the Teamsters—whose president, James R. Hoffa, had been sent to jail in 1967 for jury tampering—to form the Alliance for Labor Action (ALA). The purpose of the alliance was to stimulate social action and promote organization, but not to form a rival federation to the AFL-CIO. With Reuther's death in 1970, the ALA lost its spark and disappeared.

Despite these criticisms, successful efforts to organize unskilled workers were attempted. Although most elements of the Great Society program inaugurated by President Lyndon B. Johnson were directed toward fighting poverty and ameliorating conditions for the nonworking poor, the Equal Opportunity Act of 1964 and the Civil Rights Act of 1964 were fully supported by the labor movement. Even when these acts compelled unions to open apprenticeship training programs to nonwhites and led to breaking down racial employment bars, the labor movement sought to educate its membership to compliance. As a consequence, the decade saw a large influx of black members into the labor movement. From 1954 to 1969 the number of black craftsmen more than doubled, increasing from 300,000 to 750,000, and operatives increased from 1.3 to 2.1 million. By 1970 more than 3 million black workers belonged to trade unions. It is noteworthy that the civil rights leader Rev. Martin Luther King, Jr., was killed while assisting black sanitation workers to organize in Memphis in 1968. The 1974 amendment to the National Labor Relations Act extending NLRB jurisdiction to health-care institutions laid the basis for the recruitment of larger numbers of low-paid, unskilled, nonwhite service workers into drug and hospital workers unions.

A particularly significant effort was made to organize agricultural field hands in California by the United Farm Workers (UFW), under the leadership of César Chávez and with the assistance of the AFL-CIO. After much organizing effort and through the use of the boycott, the UFW succeeded in winning some collective bargaining contracts with leading grape and lettuce growers in California in 1968. By 1972 the Teamsters succeeded in displacing the UFW as the bargaining agent for many California harvest hands, and the boycott was reestablished. The struggle took on some of the characteristics of a Mexican-American (Chicano) civil rights action. Despite support from religious, student, and civil rights groups, Chávez' efforts were not successful. The passage by the California legislature in 1975 of a collective bargaining act granting agricultural workers the right to choose their own bargaining agent through a secret ballot promised to help resolve this jurisdictional dispute and lead to full organization of farm workers. The victory of the Amalgamated Clothing Workers in its dispute with the Farah firm of El Paso, Tex., in 1974, after a long nationwide boycott, further increased the number of low-paid semiskilled Chicano garment workers among the ranks of the organized workers.

Throughout the 1960's and 1970's the political activities of the labor movement, primarily through the AFL-CIO Committee on Political Education (COPE), directed its efforts toward electing federal and state public officials who would further their favored progressive social programs, aimed at achieving full employment, tax reform, low-income housing, low-cost public transit, national health insurance, consumer protection, and aid to education. Modestly successful in congressional elections and able to divert their members' defection to the George C. Wallace presidential candidacy in 1968, the labor movement was not able to translate its successes into significant legislative enactments. The alliance forged by the New Deal, whereby the labor movement became an integral part of the Democratic party coalition, was splintered during George McGovern's presidential candidacy of 1972, but it emerged intact. The support by labor movement leadership of the Vietnam policies of President Johnson and President Richard M. Nixon lost it the support of the left-liberal critics within and outside the Democratic party. When antiwar demonstrators were attacked by New York City construction workers in 1970, the cord tying the labor movement to the left-liberal political coalition was symbolically rent; and Nixon's appointment of Peter J. Brennan, president of the New York City and New York State Building and Construction Trades Councils, to be secretary of labor in 1973 suggested that the labor-liberal coalition was at an end. But those who accepted this suggestion were premature, for a rift developed between the Nixon administration and the labor movement over the administration's economic antiinflation program; Meany reiterated labor's progressive domestic reform programs and read Brennan out of the labor movement.

The popular image of the American worker that emerged in the late 1960's and early 1970's persisted into the mid-1970's, when he was still seen by many as a racist and reactionary. Attitudinal survey research, voting records, and the legislative program of the labor movement were helping to destroy this misconception, however, even as it was being dispelled by the young worker, increasingly critical of his work environment and seeking to make his work more meaningful.

A strike by automobile workers in the Chevrolet automobile manufacturing plant at Lordstown, Ohio, in 1971 awakened interest in questions of work satisfaction. The plant was the most highly automated in the industry, and its workers were among the youngest. Their militancy and willingness to use sabotage as a weapon in their industrial dispute underscored the fact that wildcat (unauthorized) strikes were increasingly favored among younger workers, because of their feelings of helplessness in the face of increasing mechanization, bureaucratization, and centralization of management and union authority. In response to the Lordstown phenomenon labor and management, with the assistance of government agencies, investigated "worker alienation," "blue-collar blues," and "white-collar woes." To help resolve problems that were identified, efforts were sought to increase work satisfaction and to decrease the depersonalization of the worker by decentralizing the assembly line; some suggested increased worker participation in corporate or job decisionmaking. These efforts ended when the economy took a tailspin in 1973 and unemployment became the problem of the mid-1970's.

The environmental movement of the late 1960's and early 1970's gave rise to a major debate over environmental protection vis-à-vis jobs. The economic impact of an environmental protection program was often ignored or the burden of sacrifice fell on the workers. Even so, the labor movement generally supported public programs to prevent ecological damage and to insure a healthy environment. It insisted that environmental blackmail not be used as a weapon and reminded the environmental activists that occupational health and safety for workers was itself an environmental concern. Through these efforts the Occupational Safety and Health Act of 1970 was passed, which authorized the establishment of safety and health standards for the workshop, to be enforced through an agency of the Department of Labor. The labor movement also insisted that the debate over jobs vis-à-vis environment could only be resolved through a strategy of full employment.

Even though the Full Employment Act of 1946 established full employment as a national goal, it was an increasingly elusive objective in the mid-1970's. With unemployment rising above 9 percent in 1975 and economists modifying their definitions of "acceptable" unemployment levels upward, achieving full employment was the major challenge for American labor and for American society at large.

[Irving Bernstein, *The Lean Years*, and *The Turbulent Years*; David Brody, *The Steelworkers: Non-Union Era*; John R. Commons and associates, *History of Labor in the United States*; Theodore Draper, *The Roots of American Communism*; Sidney Fine, *Sit-Down*; Philip Foner, *History of Labor*, vol. IV; Eli Ginzberg and Hyman Berman, *The American Worker in the Twentieth Century*; Gerald Grob, *Workers and Utopia*; Andrew Levison, *The Working Class Majority*; Richard B. Morris, *Government and Labor in Early America*; Joseph G. Rayback, *History of American Labor*; David Shannon, *The Socialist Party: A History*; Lloyd Ulman, *Rise of the National Trade Union*; Norman Ware, *The Industrial Worker, 1840–1860*.]

HYMAN BERMAN

LABOR, DEPARTMENT OF, established as the tenth executive department by departing President William Howard Taft on Mar. 4, 1913. Demands for a department of labor had originated with a conference of labor representatives held in Louisville, Ky., in 1865 to deal with post–Civil War labor problems, and the National Labor Union took up the demands. Following the example of Massachusetts in 1869, thirteen other states established bureaus of labor by 1883. In 1884, the Bureau of Labor was established by statute in the Department of the Interior "to collect information upon the subject of labor." The Knights of Labor and the American Federation of Labor continued the pressure for a department. In partial response, the Bureau of Labor was elevated to an independent, but noncabinet, status as the Department of Labor in 1888. Legislation in 1903 established the Department of Commerce and Labor with cabinet status, with the Bureau of Labor continuing to study labor conditions. Renamed the Bureau of Labor Statistics, the bureau was installed in the new Department of Labor in 1913.

The mission of the new department was to "foster, promote and develop the welfare of wage-earners, to improve their working conditions, and to advance their opportunities for profitable employment." Besides the Bureau of Labor Statistics, the department included the Children's Bureau and the Bureau of Immigration and Naturalization, with the addition of the Conciliation Service in 1918 and the Women's

Bureau by statute in 1920. With labor legislation directed at the problems of economic depression in the 1930's the department acquired significant administrative responsibilities for the first time. The Wagner-Peyser Act established the U.S. Employment Service in the department in 1933. Administration of working conditions for construction workers was assigned under the Davis-Bacon Act of 1931 and for other workers under the Public Contracts Act of 1936. Administration of national minimum-wage levels was assigned under the Fair Labor Standards Act of 1938.

Proposals to enhance the department at the end of World War II were realized in the period from 1958 to 1970 with legislation for newly emerging problems. The Welfare and Pension Plans Disclosure Act and the Labor-Management Reporting and Disclosure Act were passed in 1958–59. The impact of technology on the growing labor force resulted in the department's development of national manpower policies under the Manpower Development and Training Act of 1962. And the development of national standards of work-place safety and health was added under the Occupational Safety and Health Act of 1970.

The Department of Labor remains the smallest of the executive departments, with a staff that increased from about 5,000 in 1930 to 7,100 in 1960 and to 12,700 in 1972. Growth in the responsibilities of the department is reflected in a budget of $4.5 billion in 1972, as against $11 million in 1930 and $1.2 billion in 1961. This growth has been accompanied by functional organization, with assistant secretaries bearing line responsibility for such individual organizations as the Manpower Administration, the Labor-Management Services Administration, the Employment Standards Administration, and the Occupational and Safety Administration. The Bureau of Labor Statistics remains a separate administrative entity.

The role of the Department of Labor as the representative of a specific interest—namely, workers—has been a matter for periodic discussion. Although the first three secretaries of labor, from 1913 to 1933, had been officials of labor unions, since 1933 the backgrounds of the secretaries have been more diverse, including social work; government administration; and legal, academic, and management specialization in labor-management relations. The department has continued to figure in reorganization proposals. In 1967 President Lyndon B. Johnson proposed the merger of the departments of Labor and Commerce. In 1970 President Richard M. Nixon proposed a comprehensive reorganization of the executive branch, with new, functionally oriented cabinet departments superseding several existing departments, including the Department of Labor.

[U.S. Department of Labor, *Annual Reports,* and *Twenty-Five Years of Service, 1913–1938.*]

JOSEPH P. GOLDBERG

LABOR CONTRACTS, FOREIGN. *See* **Contract Labor, Foreign.**

LABOR DAY. On May 8, 1882, Peter J. McGuire, carpenters' union founder, proposed to the New York City Central Labor Union the designation of an annual "labor day." He recommended the first Monday in September, midway between the Fourth of July and Thanksgiving Day. A parade and a festival were sponsored by the New York group the following Sept. 5. Oregon was the first state officially to designate a labor day holiday (1887), and thirty-one states had followed this example when President Grover Cleveland signed the bill passed by Congress, June 28, 1894, designating the first Monday in September as Labor Day and a federal legal holiday. As organized labor became accepted, the holiday changed to a summer holiday. There were fewer great parades, demonstrations, and workers' convocations, which labor leaders used as public forums.

[P. J. McGuire, "Labor Day—Its Origin and Significance," *American Federationist* (1897).]

IRVING DILLIARD

LABOR IN THE COLONIES. Slave labor, introduced in Virginia in 1619, in time became popular in the tobacco and rice colonies, and, as did indentured servitude and apprenticeship, existed to some extent in all the colonies. Some of the involuntary servants, such as convicts, declared William Eddis, "groaned beneath a worse than Egyptian bondage" (*Letters From America*). Other servants, particularly those in the voluntary group, were well treated. "There is no master almost," said English historian John Hammond, "but will allow his servant a parcel of clear ground to plant some Tobacco in for himself." The French writer M. G. J. de Crèvecœur (*Letters From an American Farmer,* 1782) believed that American mechanics served an apprenticeship even when there were no guilds, but Benjamin Franklin thought that apprenticeship was designed to secure a constant supply of labor.

The scarcity of labor is evident from the use of labor impressment and labor cooperation. In New En-

gland, legislation occasionally gave constables power to compel artificers and mechanics to work in the harvest fields of their neighbors to save crops. Under labor cooperation, the men of the neighborhood, well fed by the women, usually cooperated in the construction of a house, the erection of a barn, or the accomplishment of some other big task.

Hours of work were usually from daylight until dark. Remuneration was fair, partly because of the abundance of free or cheap land, but legislation at times interfered with wages. In Massachusetts a law in 1633 set a maximum wage of two shillings a day for most skilled mechanics when they boarded themselves and fourteen pence when their employers supplied board. Constables with two associates each were allowed to set wages for inferior workers in the same trades. Employers who paid more than the maximum wage, laborers who received more, and workers who remained idle were subject to penalties. The penalty against the employers was soon dropped because of the scarcity of laborers, but when the penalty against the employees was removed, another law, in 1636, gave the towns jurisdiction in the determination of wages. When prices declined sharply in 1640, the legislators ordered laborers, under penalty of fine, to accept wages corresponding with reduced prices.

During most of the colonial period wages varied from twenty-five cents a day to four times that amount, the lowest wages usually including board. Writing of his experience in the colonies in 1748, the Swedish botanist Peter Kalm reported that a manservant of ability in Pennsylvania received from sixteen to twenty pounds a year in currency and a maidservant received half as much. Both received their food, but neither received clothing. Andrew Burnaby, about a decade later, likewise commented favorably on the prosperity of workers and the dearth of beggars. Crèvecœur, citing the best board at seven shillings a week, or "less than four shillings sterling," complained of the high wages demanded by laborers: "You must give them what they ask" and "Many times have I given from five to eight shillings per day to a cradler."

[J. R. Commons, *Documentary History of American Industrial Society;* James Oneal, *The Workers in American History;* U. B. Phillips, *Life and Labor in the Old South;* U. B. Phillips, *Plantation and Frontier Documents, 1649–1863.*]

WALTER W. JENNINGS

LABOR LEGISLATION AND ADMINISTRATION. For a century, from the beginnings of industrialization to the depression of the 1930's, the legal protection of labor was considered the exclusive responsibility of the states. The federal government confined its protective efforts to its own employees, to persons working for government contractors, and to those engaged in interstate transportation. This was because congressional authority in the private sector is limited to commerce, and the Supreme Court until 1937 interpreted commerce as excluding all manufacturing and most distributive industries.

Even state protections were slow in coming, because of the popular faith in individual competitiveness. The first reforms obtained by the early "working men's parties" extended the elective franchise to nearly all male citizens, provided free universal education, abolished imprisonment for debt, and gave employees assurance of prompt payment of wages due. The objective was clearly "equal opportunity."

With the development of technology, an increase in occupational injuries led the industrial states gradually to adopt safety laws enforced by factory inspections (Massachusetts was first in 1877). But these laws usually applied only to extrahazardous occupations and were difficult to enforce. Hence, the toll from accidents continued, leaving survivors and the maimed generally without adequate compensation until the adoption of compulsory "no-fault" workmen's compensation insurance (first in Wisconsin, 1911; in virtually all the states by 1920).

In addition to safety legislation, there were early attempts to protect the health of industrial workers by state laws reducing excessive hours of work. At first, such laws were applied only to women but later also to men. The Supreme Court ruled uncertainly as to the constitutionality of these statutes—deciding by close votes and then reversing itself—until 1917 when, in *Bunting* v. *Oregon,* the Court clearly affirmed the propriety of such laws for both men and women in manufacturing generally.

The most strongly resisted reforms were those intended to assist the disadvantaged—those whose bargaining power in the unregulated labor market was weakest (that is, children and women). Although Pennsylvania established a minimum age (twelve) for child labor as early as 1848, many states by 1900 still had no such statutes; and in 1923 only a handful of states had protective legislation for women workers. In that year, the Supreme Court curbed even the power of the states to adopt minimum wage legislation for women and children. It held in *Adkins* v. *Children's Hospital* that such laws abridged freedom of contract in violation of the due process clauses of the Constitution.

This appears to have been the high-water mark of juridical individualism, for everything was changed by the collapse of the public faith in an unregulated market system during the Great Depression. Reflecting this change in public opinion, the Supreme Court reversed itself as to the powers both of the states and of the federal government. In *West Coast Hotel* v. *Parrish* (1937), the Court overruled the *Adkins* decision and upheld the state of Washington's minimum-wage statute. At the same time, Congress, under the leadership of President Franklin D. Roosevelt, was writing into federal law most of the reforms that had been creeping through the legislatures of the progressive states; and the Supreme Court, in a series of dramatic reversals, upheld the constitutionality of these new measures.

A system of compulsory public insurance for the unemployed and for retired workers was provided in the Social Security Act (1935) and was upheld in *Carmichael* v. *Southern Coal and Coke Company* and other cases in 1937. A schedule of minimum wages and compulsory overtime rules was made applicable to both men and women in the Fair Labor Standards Act (1938); extensive rules limiting the employment of children were also included. This statute was found constitutional in *United States* v. *Darby Lumber Company* (1941), in which the commerce power of Congress was applied to the regulation of working conditions in manufacturing whenever the operation "affects" interstate or foreign commerce. From this time, the way was open for almost unlimited development of a dual federal and state system of regulating working conditions.

The outcome of this significant change, although delayed by a sluggish recovery from the depression and by the need for direct government controls during World War II, was the adoption in the 1950's and 1960's of an elaborate system of labor laws having two new objectives: (1) to extend basic protections, such as occupational safety, minimum wages, and social security, to virtually every category of labor; and (2) to introduce new programs to strengthen the positions of groups of disadvantaged workers—the technologically displaced, women, and ethnic minorities. The latter may be illustrated by the Manpower Development and Training Act (1962), the Equal Pay Act (1963), and the "equal employment opportunity" sections of the Civil Rights Act (1964).

The new statutes immediately proved cumbersome in administration—first, because of their extensive coverage and, second, because of the lack of a comprehensive manpower policy. The goals of equal opportunity, special protections, and compensatory aid were contradictory. Many of the older protections for women workers had to be repealed or nullified in order to ensure equality of treatment; while "equal opportunities" for the ethnic minorities had to be supplemented by unequal compensatory services known as "affirmative action" programs. Thus, labor legislation, although freed from constitutional barriers in the first half of the 20th century, was beset in the second half by problems of scale and of unbalanced objectives.

[Sar A. Levitan et al., *Human Resources and Labor Markets;* John G. Turnbull et al., *Economic and Social Security;* Clair Wilcox, *Toward Social Welfare;* U.S. Department of Labor, *Growth of Labor Law in the United States.*]

JOHN L. BLACKMAN, JR.

LABOR PARTIES. The policy of support for independent parties representing specifically working-class interests, pursued by organized labor in most industrialized nations, has been eschewed by the national spokesmen of American labor during the 20th century. Nevertheless, on several occasions since the early 19th century, city and state labor organizations have initiated and supported labor parties, and even at a national level the "labor party question" has been a live issue from time to time.

The world's first labor parties appeared in a number of American cities after 1828, usually on the initiative of newly founded city labor organizations. They supported a variety of causes important to working men but failed to develop into a national force and did not survive the depression that began in 1837. Since then the city labor party has been a recurring phenomenon. The movement in New York between 1886 and 1888, for instance, attracted national interest by supporting the candidacy of Henry George for mayor. Similar labor parties appeared at the same time in Chicago and other cities and occasionally grew to state level organizations. In 1900 organized labor in San Francisco promoted a Union Labor party.

The first labor organization of national scope, the National Labor Union, formed a short-lived political party between 1870 and 1872. As well as supporting demands of labor such as the eight-hour day, its platform reflected the then-current greenback agitation, demonstrating the connection with farmers' movements that characterized most labor politics in the late 19th century. Thus, the Greenback Labor party, founded nationally in 1878, received the support of

the Knights of Labor, whose division into district and local assemblies was admirably suited to political activity. T. V. Powderly, the best-known leader of the Knights, was elected mayor of Scranton, Pa., on a Greenback Labor ticket in 1878 and was later active in the founding of the Populist party in 1889. By then, the American Federation of Labor (AFL) was replacing the Knights as the chief national labor organization. Although an important minority of the members of the new organization advocated support of the labor populists, the AFL convention of 1894 rejected this policy, partly owing to the parliamentary tactics of its president, Samuel Gompers.

Meanwhile, some Socialist trade unionists, chiefly of German origin, had founded the Socialist Labor party in 1877. Their party sometimes participated in the various movements already discussed, but Socialist doctrines often caused dissension, which contributed to the demise of "united labor" parties. After the foundation of the more moderate Socialist Party of America in 1901, its members within the AFL constantly argued for endorsement of the Socialist party, but they never succeeded. Had the AFL followed the example of the British Trade Union Council in forming a labor party in 1906, as seemed a possibility after several adverse court decisions, many Socialists would probably have supported it.

After World War I a labor party finally did emerge. Initiated by several state federations of labor and city centrals, the National Labor party was formed in 1919, and it renewed the earlier policy of alliance with farmers' groups by organizing the Farmer-Labor party the following year. The AFL remained aloof. Only in 1924 did it join a coalition of farmers, labor groups, and Socialists in support of Robert M. La Follette's presidential candidacy under the banner of the Conference for Progressive Political Action (CPPA). Disappointing hopes for a new national party, the CPPA disintegrated after the election. The Farmer-Labor party survived in Minnesota, and small minorities of trade unionists continued to support the Socialist Party of America, the Socialist Labor party, and the Communist party (under different names). The American Labor party (now the Liberal party) was a means by which mainly old-guard Socialists of the garment trades could support Franklin D. Roosevelt and still retain a separate identity from the Democratic party. In general, the state of the American Left since 1924 has made the traditional "nonpartisan" policy of the AFL seem all the sounder. Adopted in 1906, this policy has aimed at "rewarding friends and punishing enemies" irrespective of party. In practice it has usually involved close alliance with the Democratic party.

Explanations usually offered for the failure of labor parties stress American sociocultural patterns inimical to class-based parties and a political system that is flexible enough to absorb all third-party movements. Less optimistic explanations might include the ethnic and racial divisions within the working class and the minority status of labor within American society. The role played by leaders of the AFL during its formative period should not be overlooked in explaining American developments.

[C. M. Destler, *American Radicalism, 1865–1901;* W. M. Dick, *Labor and Socialism in America;* Nathan Fine, *Labor and Farmer Parties in the United States, 1828–1928.*]

W. M. DICK

LABOR UNIONS. *See* **Labor.**

LABRADOR FISHERIES, off the coast of Labrador, Canada, first attracted the cod and whale fishermen of New England during the colonial period. The Definitive Treaty of Peace, 1783, granted to American fishermen liberal privileges along the Labrador coast. Soon many codfishing vessels sailed each year from New England to Labrador. Restrictions placed later on American use of English colonial fisheries little affected those of Labrador, but as the economy of New England changed, fewer and fewer American fishermen found it worthwhile to make the voyage to Labrador for cod. Fishing on the Labrador coast is now limited to the months from June to October and is conducted by the people of the east coast of Newfoundland.

[Harold A. Innis, *The Cod Fisheries: The History of an International Economy.*]

F. HARDEE ALLEN

LACOLLE MILL, BATTLE OF (Mar. 30, 1814). Defending their position in Canada during the War of 1812, the British had stationed 200 troops at a stone mill on the Lacolle River, five miles north of the international boundary. Taking a force of 4,000 from Plattsburgh, N.Y., Gen. James Wilkinson marched against this outpost. The defenders stoutly resisted. With slight losses they repulsed his ill-directed attack. Threatening weather and 200 casualties caused Wilkinson to retreat.

[J. R. Jacobs, *Tarnished Warrior.*]

JAMES RIPLEY JACOBS

LACONIA GRANT. As John Mason and Sir Ferdinando Gorges were dividing their Province of Maine, Samuel de Champlain, governor of New France, was brought to London a prisoner. They saw a chance to secure part of the rich fur trade formerly held by France and obtained a new grant of land from the Council for New England on Nov. 17, 1629. The area, believed to contain many lakes, was named the Province of Laconia. Its indefinite limits ran from Lake Champlain westward halfway to Lake Ontario and north to the Saint Lawrence, embracing the land west and northwest of Maine. The proprietors were authorized to cross other lands and to take as a coastal station as many as 1,000 acres of ungranted land. Mason, Gorges, and six others formed the Laconia Company to develop the grant and sent settlers to the Piscataqua. Despite their proximity to the fine harbor at Portsmouth, N.H., and several attempts to find a trade route to Laconia, none was successful, and the grant was never located. A second patent of Nov. 13, 1631, included land on both banks of the Piscataqua and the Isles of Shoals. The company failed to pay, and in 1634 it was dissolved and its assets divided among the partners.

[W. H. Fry, *New Hampshire as a Royal Province;* C. W. Tuttle, *Captain John Mason.*]

HERBERT W. HILL

LADD'S PEACE PLAN. In his *Essay on a Congress of Nations,* published in Boston in 1840, William Ladd, a New England philanthropist and reformer, proposed a periodic congress of nations for formulating international law and for promoting the general welfare of nations and a related but independent court for settling disputes by judicial decision or by arbitration. The plan proposed a league of nations, not a mere league of sovereigns; and it was designed to promote peace, not merely to preserve the *status quo.* Its essential features were in part realized in the Hague conferences of 1899 and 1907 and the establishment of the League of Nations and Permanent Court of International Justice after World War I.

[Merle Curti, *The American Peace Crusade, 1815–1860;* Georg Schwarzenberger, *William Ladd.*]

MERLE CURTI

LADIES' REPOSITORY, a monthly periodical devoted to "literature and religion," was published by the Methodist Book Concern from 1841 through 1876 (thirty-six volumes) and continued for four more years as the *National Repository*. Started at Cincinnati under the editorship of Leonidas L. Hamline, a Methodist clergyman, it speedily became prosperous, at one time boasting 30,000 subscribers.

[W. H. Venable, *Beginnings of Literary Culture in the Ohio Valley.*]

EUGENE H. ROSEBOOM

LAE AND SALAMAUA. On Mar. 8, 1942, a few months after the United States entered World War II, the Japanese seized the ports of Lae and Salamaua, on the northeast coast of New Guinea. From there they dominated eastern New Guinea, threatened Allied shipping in the Coral Sea, and secured their flank for further advances. Unable to exploit this position to the fullest, the Japanese nevertheless possessed in Lae and Salamaua important bases that would have to be eliminated if any Allied counteroffensive were to succeed.

Gen. Douglas MacArthur's forces began an attack on Salamaua at the beginning of July 1943, hoping to divert Japanese strength from the defense of Lae, the more important of the two ports. Two months of fierce combat ensued, before a combined American-Australian attack resulted in the seizure of the Salamaua airstrip, still five miles from the town. Overcoming a Japanese counterattack, the Allied force finally captured Salamaua on Sept. 12. Although the cost in casualties was high, the drive on Salamaua succeeded in forcing a significant diversion of enemy troops from the Lae area.

On Sept. 4, after a heavy naval and air bombardment, Australian troops stormed ashore east of Lae. A day later, American paratroops dropped and seized Nadzab, northeast of Lae, where they were joined by other Australian forces. Although Japanese survivors of the Salamaua garrison retreated to Lae after the fall of Salamaua, the Lae defenders found themselves in an ever-tightening vise. Faced with the prospect of being crushed between two forces, the Japanese decided to withdraw inland. Allied troops converging on Lae met only delaying forces and seized the town on Sept. 16.

The fall of Lae and Salamaua, coupled with other Allied victories, forced the Japanese to withdraw their strategic defensive perimeter further westward on the coast. The advancing Allies, on the other hand, were able to accelerate the timetable for their offensive.

[John Miller, Jr., *Cartwheel: The Reduction of Rabaul,* United States Army in World War II.]

STANLEY L. FALK

LA FAMINE, TREATY OF (Sept. 5, 1684). Gov. Le Febvre de La Barre of New France, in charge of an expedition against the Seneca, was met at La Famine, at the confluence of the Salmon and Connecticut rivers, by the Onondaga orator Otreouati (also known as Grangula or Haaskouan) and fourteen deputies from the Onondaga, Oneida, and Cayuga nations. Otreouati countered all of La Barre's accusations, demanded the withdrawal of the army, and reserved the right to make war upon the Illinois. Although enraged by this defiance, La Barre was forced by sickness throughout the army to make peace and withdraw his army to Montreal.

[E. B. O'Callaghan, *The Documentary History of the State of New York.*]

ROBERT W. BINGHAM

LAFAYETTE, FORT, was situated on a shoal at the Narrows entrance to New York harbor. Construction began in 1812, and the fort was adapted only for guns of small caliber. During the Civil War it was used as a prison for political offenders, several thousand of whom were confined there at one period. Impaired by fire in 1868, it was replaced by fortifications mounting considerably larger armament.

[W. B. Hesseltine, *Civil War Prisons.*]

W. B. HESSELTINE

LAFAYETTE ESCADRILLE, a squadron of volunteer American aviators who fought for France before U.S. entry into World War I. Formed on Apr. 17, 1916, with 7 pilots, it was first known as the Escadrille Américaine, but the name was changed after German protest to Washington. A total of 267 men enlisted, of which 224 qualified and 180 saw combat. Since only 12–15 pilots made up a squadron, many flew with French units; but all were deemed members of the Lafayette Flying Corps. They wore French uniforms and most had noncommissioned officer rank. On Feb. 18, 1918, the squadron was incorporated into the U.S. Air Service as the 103rd Pursuit Squadron. The volunteers were credited with downing 199 German planes. Nineteen men were wounded, 15 were captured, 11 died of illness or accident, and 51 were killed in action.

[Arch Whitehouse, *Legion of the Lafayette.*]

CHARLES B. MacDONALD

LAFAYETTE'S VISIT TO AMERICA. In February 1824, President James Monroe invited the Marquis de

Lafayette—Marie Joseph du Motier—to visit the United States. Lafayette accepted, but would not permit a government vessel to be sent for him, as Congress wished. He sailed, however, in an American ship and reached New York on Aug. 16, 1824. He was so reduced in fortune that he feared he could not meet the expense of a long stay, but to his surprise he was not permitted to pay for anything during his visit. After a tumultuous reception in New York and a four-day stay he toured New England, visited Albany, N.Y., and returned to New York City twice. Then he traveled slowly southward through Philadelphia and Baltimore, making leisurely stays everywhere. After a long stop at Washington, D.C., where all government officials joined in doing him honor, he visited Thomas Jefferson at Monticello and went southward through the coastal states and then westward to New Orleans. Coming northward into the Middle West, he suffered shipwreck when a steamboat sank with him on the Ohio below Louisville, Ky., but despite his age (sixty-seven) he came through the disaster without severe shock. His progress everywhere was met by ovation; bands and military escorts went miles along the roads to meet him; and banquets and fetes greeted him at every stop. He visited Braddock's Field, Lake Erie, Niagara, and other American war scenes, after which he returned to Boston for the celebration of the fiftieth anniversary of the Battle of Bunker Hill. He visited New York City for the fourth time, and finally returned to Washington, from which he sailed for home on Dec. 7, 1825, having spent nearly sixteen months in the United States. A steamboat carried him from Washington to the frigate *Brandywine*, which awaited him at the mouth of the Potomac, and on that vessel he returned to France. Congress made him a gift of $200,000 in cash and a township of land.

[John Foster, *Sketch of General Lafayette on His Late Visit to the United States.*]

ALVIN F. HARLOW

"LAFAYETTE, WE ARE HERE." Following U.S. entry into World War I, the American Expeditionary Forces, commanded by Gen. John J. Pershing, landed in France on June 28, 1917—and on July 4, 1917, Paris enthusiastically celebrated American Independence Day. A battalion of the U.S. Sixteenth Infantry was reviewed by President Raymond Poincaré and then marched to the Picpus Cemetery, where several speeches were made at the tomb of the Marquis de Lafayette, honoring his heroic service in the cause of the American Revolution. Pershing was present but spoke very briefly, having designated Col. Charles E. Stanton of his staff to speak for him. The historic words uttered on that occasion, "Lafayette, nous voilà" ("Lafayette, we are here"), have been popularly, but erroneously, attributed to Pershing. He himself stated that they "were spoken by Col. Stanton, and to him must go the credit for coining so happy and felicitous a phrase."

[John J. Pershing, *My Experiences in the World War.*]

JOSEPH MILLS HANSON

LA FOLLETTE PROGRESSIVE PARTY. As a part of the Progressive movement that had begun in the United States about 1908, Sen. Robert M. La Follette of Wisconsin took the lead in forming in 1922 the Conference for Progressive Political Action. It was a loose federation of various Progressive groups in the country, such as the farmers' Nonpartisan League, the Farmer-Labor party, the Single Tax League, and several labor organizations, including the sixteen railroad brotherhoods. The purpose at first was not to organize another political party, but to secure the election of Progressives to Congress, regardless of party, and to promote the enactment of liberal legislation.

A national convention was held in Cleveland, Ohio, July 4–6, 1924, at which, in view of the dissatisfaction with the presidential nominations made by both major parties, La Follette was nominated for president and Sen. Burton K. Wheeler of Montana, a Democrat, for vice-president. The new party, officially named the Progressive party, although generally known as the La Follette party, was also endorsed by the Socialist party and by the American Federation of Labor. The platform was largely a reproduction of La Follette's personal views on public questions, with particular emphasis on the needs of agriculture and labor. The party polled nearly 5 million votes—about 17 percent of all votes cast—chiefly in the Middle and Far West; it displaced the Democratic party as the second party in eleven states and carried Wisconsin. The results were disappointing to La Follette and the other leaders of the movement, and plans for a permanent party organization were abandoned. La Follette died the following year.

[Fred E. Haynes, "The Significance of the Latest Third Party Movement," *Mississippi Valley Historical Review*, vol. 12; Harold L. Varney, "An American Labor Party in the Making," *Current History*, vol. 20.]

CLARENCE A. BERDAHL

LA FOLLETTE'S SEAMEN'S ACT. *See* **Seamen's Act of 1915.**

LA GALETTE, FORT. Shortly after the foundation of the mission of La Présentation, at the mouth of the Oswegatchie, near the modern city of Ogdensburg, N.Y., in 1749, the French missionary François Picquet, founder of the mission, persuaded the governor of Canada to build a substantial fort. It was intended as a protection for Montreal against invasion from the Oswegatchie. One of the last French strongholds in New York, it was captured by British Gen. Jeffrey Amherst in 1760.

[Francis Parkman, *Montcalm and Wolfe.*]

A. C. FLICK

LAIRD RAMS, two double-turreted, ironclad steamers, one equipped with a ram and each armed with four 9-inch rifled guns, ordered in 1862 by James D. Bulloch, Confederate naval agent, from John Laird and Sons, shipbuilders, of Birkenhead, England. They were designed for use in breaking the Union blockade during the Civil War. The North, which then had no ships able to cope with them, feared that the British government would allow them to put to sea. John Slidell, a Confederate agent, fearing their seizure by the British, transferred them to Messrs. Bravay and Company, a French firm, but arranged for their resale to the Confederacy after they were beyond British jurisdiction. They were both launched in the summer of 1863.

On Sept. 1, 1863, Lord John Russell, British foreign secretary, wrote Charles Francis Adams, American minister to Great Britain, that his government could not interfere with the vessels but would watch them carefully. Adams replied on Sept. 5 in a letter: "It would be superfluous in me to point out to your lordship that this is war." Meanwhile, on Sept. 3, Russell, suspecting that the ironclads were destined for the Confederacy, and influenced by the Union victories of Gettysburg and Vicksburg, ordered the ships detained. In October 1863 they were formally seized by the British government, which, in May 1864, purchased them for the royal navy. (*See also* Alabama Claims.)

[C. F. Adams, *Charles Francis Adams;* Montague Bernard, *A Historical Account of the Neutrality of Great Britain During the American Civil War.*]

LOUIS H. BOLANDER

LAISSEZ-FAIRE, a term originated by the disciples of the 18th-century school of economists in France known as the Physiocrats and given added meaning and widespread influence in the last quarter of the century by the Scottish economist Adam Smith.

Translated literally as "let (people) do (as they choose)," and freely as "let things alone," the term designates a doctrine that was a reaction against restrictions imposed on trade by the medieval guilds and the mercantilism of the 16th and 17th centuries. The theory rests upon the assumption that the economic well-being and progress of society are assured when individuals are free to apply their capital and their labor without hindrance by the state. In obedience to his own self-interest the individual, it is believed, will always do what conduces to his own best advantage and the general well-being of the community. State intervention through such agencies as protective social legislation and restrictions on freedom of trade is condemned as socially injurious. The doctrine of laissez-faire involves not only a negative social policy of nonintervention but also a positive philosophy that recognizes a natural order in which harmony of individual and social interests is the rule.

In the United States there has never been an undivided allegiance to this doctrine, either theoretically or practically. The tariff, which has been an established policy almost from the foundation of American sovereignty, is a contravention of the principle of individualism expressed in the doctrine of laissez-faire. The same can be said concerning the antitrust legislation represented in the Sherman Antitrust Act (1890) and the Clayton Act (1914). Numerous examples of protective labor legislation, such as minimum-wage laws, workmen's compensation statutes, hours legislation, and social security laws, belied professed allegiance to the principle of laissez-faire during the first half of the 20th century, and after World War II it was espoused by only a small minority of Americans.

[Henry C. Adams, *Relation of the State to Industrial Action;* O. F. Boucke, *Laissez-Faire and After;* John Dewey, *Individualism Old and New.*]

GORDON S. WATKINS

LAKE CHAMPLAIN, strategically located on the New York–Vermont border and extending six miles into Canada, was discovered in 1609 by Samuel de Champlain. The lake quickly became the gateway between French Canada and the English colonies. Lake George drains into Lake Champlain by cascades and a 30-foot falls at Ticonderoga. Lake Champlain is now a link in the Hudson–Saint Lawrence waterway, and the surrounding region is a noted resort area.

Early Clashes. Both English and French colonial forces, augmented by their Indian allies, found Lake Champlain a convenient route for expeditions into enemy territory. As early as the 1640's the French were fortifying the Richelieu River at the northern end of the lake. French expeditions swung down the lake to the west against Schenectady, N.Y., and to the east again against Deerfield, Mass., and other New England outposts. The English retaliated. As time went on, the rival expeditions became larger and more organized. England launched three successive but ineffectual campaigns northward in 1690, 1709, and 1711, in which land forces under governors John Winthrop and Sir Francis Nicholson were to cooperate by way of Lake Champlain with sea forces sent into the Saint Lawrence region. The establishment of Fort Carillon at the southern end of the lake in 1756 gave the French control of the pathway until the French and Indian War.

French and Indian War. Fort Saint Frédéric, built by the French on the western shore of Lake Champlain in 1731, was the base for French and Indian raids against New England and New York during the mid-18th century. With the outbreak of hostilities between France and England in 1754, it became one of the prime military objectives of the British. Sir William Johnson, major general of the New York militia, was sent against the fort. At the southern end of Lake George, on Sept. 8, 1755, he repulsed an attack by the French under Gen. Ludwig August Dieskau, but failed to follow up his advantage by moving against Fort Saint Frédéric. The expedition has been described as ''a failure disguised under an incidental success.''

In the fall of 1755 a fort was laid out at Ticonderoga as an outpost for the defense of Fort Saint Frédéric, but the British campaign of 1756 under Gen. John Campbell, Earl of Loudon, and Col. John Winslow did not get beyond the British Fort William Henry, situated at the southern end of Lake George. Meanwhile, partisan warfare was at its height: not a week passed without a raid against the New England frontier, and Maj. Robert Rogers and his rangers were harassing the French posts. On Mar. 19, 1757, the French under the governor of Canada, Pierre François de Rigaud, Marquis de Vaudreuil, failed to take Fort William Henry, but on Aug. 9, after a week's siege, the fort was surrendered to French field marshal Louis Joseph de Montcalm. The Indian allies of the French massacred a part of the garrison.

An expedition led by British Gen. James Abercromby against Ticonderoga met disastrous defeat on July 8, 1758, but in the next year Gen. Jeffrey Amherst compelled the French to blow up Fort Carillon at Ticonderoga and Fort Saint Frédéric and to retreat to Isle aux Noix at the northern end of Lake Champlain. After a long delay Amherst moved against Isle aux Noix, but operations had to be suspended late in October because of inclement weather. In 1759 Rogers and his rangers conducted a daring raid on the village of the Saint Francis Indians, and in the following year there were attacks and reprisals about the French forts at Isle aux Noix and at Saint Johns and Chambly, north of Lake Champlain on the Richelieu River. In August 1760 Gen. William Haviland drove Montcalm's aide-de-camp, Louis Antoine de Bougainville, and the French from Lake Champlain, and the fall of Montreal on Sept. 8 brought the fighting to an end.

The Revolution. At the beginning of the American Revolution both Americans and British were determined to control Lake Champlain. Commanded by Col. Ethan Allen, the American Green Mountain Boys seized Ticonderoga and Crown Point (formerly Fort Saint Frédéric) on the lake in May 1775 but were unable to hold Saint Johns. During the summer the expedition against Canada under Gen. Richard Montgomery, using Crown Point as a base, moved on to capture Saint Johns and Montreal but was repulsed at Quebec on Dec. 21. In the spring of 1776 Benjamin Franklin, Samuel Chase, Charles Carroll of Carrollton, and Father John Carroll passed through the Champlain Valley on their way to Montreal to seek without success to win Canada to the American cause. The commander of the British forces in Canada, Sir Guy Carleton, Baron Dorchester, in the following autumn moved down Lake Champlain with a strong flotilla but was delayed off Valcour Island by the determined stand of Gen. Benedict Arnold and his seagoing farmer boys; cold weather set in before the British could take the forts.

In 1777 British Gen. John Burgoyne's well-equipped army appeared on the lake (*see* Burgoyne's Invasion), compelled Gen. Arthur Saint Clair to evacuate Ticonderoga, beat the retreating Americans at Hubbardton, and captured Skenesboro, N.Y. As Burgoyne marched on to eventual defeat at Saratoga, N.Y., Col. John Brown of Pittsfield, Mass., unsuccessfully attempted to seize Ticonderoga and to capture the supplies on Diamond Island in Lake George. After Burgoyne's defeat at Saratoga in October 1777, the British continued to control the Champlain Valley, though they did not usually garrison the forts. In 1780 Gen. Frederick Haldimand was seeking to induce Vermont to join the British. In the same year Sir John Johnson passed up the lake on his way to raid the Mohawk Valley, and during 1781 a British fleet cruised about. In 1783, while awaiting the signing of the peace treaty, George Washington visited Ticonderoga and Crown Point.

War of 1812. As in previous wars, Lake Champlain was teeming with martial activity during the War of 1812. England was threatening the United States from the north by both land and water, and considerable bodies of U.S. regulars and militia, supported by a naval force, were stationed at Burlington, Vt., and Plattsburgh, N.Y., and other spots along the lake.

In command of the American fleet was Lt. Thomas Macdonough. On June 3, 1813, the Americans lost two vessels to the English. The next month, British Col. John Murray, with over 1,400 troops and marines, destroyed several military buildings near Plattsburgh. A few days later, Aug. 2, three British ships appeared off Burlington, but were driven off by Macdonough's ships and the shore battery. At about the same time the English burned the abandoned barracks and other government property at Swanton, Vt. Macdonough sought out the English fleet, but it declined battle. Gen. Wade Hampton, with several thousand men, crossed the border and was defeated by a smaller body of English. On the morning of Mar. 30, 1814, the American army, 4,000 strong, advanced for an unsuccessful attack upon Lacolle Mill, just north of the international boundary.

Meanwhile Macdonough, elevated in rank to commodore, had gone into winter quarters at Vergennes, at Otter Creek, Vt., and was strengthening his fleet. On Apr. 14 the British fleet attacked the battery at the mouth of the creek and was repulsed. Land skirmishes during the summer were frequent. In the fall came the general advance of the English, the decisive engagement taking place on Sept. 11, 1814, when the governor-general of British North America, Sir George Prevost, led more than 14,000 troops against an American force of some 4,700 regulars and militia under Gen. Alexander Macomb, who had taken up their position on the south bank of the Saranac River near Plattsburgh. At the same time the British fleet attacked Macdonough off nearby Cumberland Head. The American land force and naval force were both victorious, and the outcome had an important bearing on the peace signed at Ghent in December of the same year.

[W. H. Crockett, *A History of Lake Champlain;* Edward P. Hamilton, *Fort Ticonderoga: Key to a Continent,* and *The French and Indian Wars;* Charles A. Jellison, *Ethan Allen, Frontier Rebel;* P. S. Palmer, *History of Lake Champlain.*]

LEON W. DEAN
EDWARD P. ALEXANDER

LAKE GEORGE, BATTLE OF (Sept. 8, 1755). William Johnson, major general of the New York militia, moved north against the French Fort Saint Frédéric in midsummer 1755, the second year of the French and Indian War. At the southern end of Lake George his encamped force was threatened by Gen. Ludwig August Dieskau commanding 1,700 French and Indians. On Sept. 8 Johnson sent 1,200 men south to locate the French. Division proved costly; the French drove the surprised Americans back with severe losses, killing Col. Ephraim Williams and Hendrik, a Mohawk chieftain.

At the camp barricades the reunited provincials beat off repeated charges; the day ended with the French retreating. Both commanders were wounded; Dieskau was captured. Provincial forces lost 260 killed, 91 wounded; the French, about as many, including most of the regulars. The battle is regarded as a draw. Johnson could not proceed, and capture of their commander stopped the French offensive.

[Edward P. Hamilton, *The French and Indian Wars.*]
ARTHUR POUND

LAKE OF THE WOODS BOUNDARY PROBLEM was projected by the Definitive Treaty of Peace of 1783, which provided that the northern boundary should extend westward from the "most northwestern point" of the Lake of the Woods, in northern Minnesota, to the Mississippi. Since such a line was geographically impossible, it was agreed in 1818 that the boundary should be drawn south from the northwest point of the lake to forty-nine degrees north latitude—an arrangement that resulted in the creation of the Northwest Angle.

T. C. BLEGEN

LAKES, GREAT. *See* **Erie, Lake; Great Lakes; Huron, Lake; Michigan, Lake; Ontario, Lake; Superior, Lake.**

LAKES-TO-GULF DEEP WATERWAY. In 1673 Louis Jolliet noted the favorable possibilities for a canal to connect the Great Lakes with the Des Plaines, Illinois, and Mississippi rivers. The actual construction of a canal was urged by Albert Gallatin in 1808 and Peter B. Porter in 1810. Aided by a right-of-way and a land grant provided by Congress, the state of Illinois in 1848 completed the Illinois and Michigan Canal. The cost was about $6.6 million.

The first 30-mile section of this waterway, to a point below Lockport, was rendered obsolete by the completion in 1900 and the extension, finished in 1910, of the Chicago Sanitary and Ship Canal. Sponsored by the Chicago Sanitary District and representing an investment of $36,820,878, this new canal had a width of over 160 feet and a depth of 24 feet. Its construction gave additional impetus to the long-standing movement to develop a Lakes-to-Gulf deep waterway. In 1889 the legislature of Illinois had suggested a channel depth of 14 feet. A depth of 24 feet was demanded by some groups active during the transportation crisis of 1906–07 and the conservation movement of 1908. Congress could not be persuaded to provide federal support for these proposals. Consequently, in 1921, the state of Illinois started construction, made possible by a $20 million bond issue authorized in 1908, of five locks and four dams between Lockport and Utica. Taken over in 1930 by the federal government, which spent $7,407,707 finishing the structures, the project was completed in 1933 with a channel depth of 9 feet.

A similar minimum depth was achieved in the Illinois Waterway below Utica and in the Mississippi River to Cairo, Ill., by dredging and construction. Locks and dams at Peoria, La Grange, and Alton, Ill., were completed during 1938–39. Near Saint Louis, Mo., a lateral canal with locks was opened in 1953, and a dam was finished in 1964. Improvement of the Calumet-Sag route from the sanitary canal to Lake Calumet, begun in 1955, was scheduled for completion in 1977. This segment was slated to be the primary connection of the Illinois Waterway to Lake Michigan. Total federal investment in these projects was $203,604,094 for the Illinois Waterway (through the fiscal year 1974) and $230,641,000 for the Mississippi River from the Missouri River to Cairo, Ill. (as of June 30, 1975).

Six additional large locks and other improvements are planned for the section of the waterway between Lockport to La Grange. Estimated cost at 1974 prices is $626,894,000. Building a new dam and large twin locks at Alton has been proposed. The 1974 cost estimate is $424 million. The Army Corps of Engineers in 1973 estimated that the cost of increasing the channel depth to 12 feet between Chicago and Cairo would be about $514,190,000. These new authorizations, proposals, and studies are in part related to the great achieved and expected increases in barge traffic. Factors contributing to this growth include the economic expansion of the areas adjacent to the waterway and the substantial improvement during the 1960's and 1970's in the efficiency of barges, towboats, and related equipment.

[G. F. Barrett, *The Waterways From the Great Lakes to the Gulf of New Mexico;* U.S. Army Engineer Division, North Central, *Water Resource Development in Illinois.*]

MARCUS WHITMAN

LAME-DUCK AMENDMENT, the name applied to the Twentieth Amendment (1933) to the Constitution of the United States, which abolished so-called lame-duck sessions of Congress, from December of even-numbered years until the following Mar. 4. These sessions acquired their nickname because they included numerous members who had failed of reelection (the lame ducks) a month before the session opened. Yet the law permitted them to sit and function until their terms ended, while a newly elected Congress, with a fresh popular mandate, stood by inactive and unorganized, usually for thirteen months. In the last lame-duck session, opening in December 1932, there were 158 defeated members sitting in the Senate and House. The amendment, sponsored by Sen. George W. Norris of Nebraska, did away with the lame-duck session by moving back the day on which terms of senators and representatives begin from Mar. 4 to Jan. 3, and by requiring Congress to convene each year on Jan. 3—about two months after election. The amendment also set back the date of the president's inauguration to Jan. 20. Other provisions related to the choice of president under certain contingencies.

P. ORMAN RAY

L'AMISTAD SLAVE CASE. *See Amistad* Case.

LAMP, INCANDESCENT. As early as 1820 scientists all over the world had begun to work on the development of an incandescent lamp, but it remained for Thomas A. Edison at Menlo Park, N.J., on Oct. 21, 1879, to make the first successful high resistance carbon lamp, which embodied almost all the basic features of lamps commonly in use today.

The first carbon lamp was inefficient in comparison with present-day lamps, giving only 1.7 lumens (light units) per watt (unit of energy). The carbon lamp was gradually improved through minor changes in construction, many of which were introduced by American inventors, so that by 1906 it produced 3.4 lumens per watt. In 1905 Willis R. Whitney, head of the Research Laboratory of the General Electric Company at Schenectady, N.Y., succeeded in changing the character of the carbon filament to give it metallic characteristics, and for a few years the Gem lamp, which produced 4.25 lumens per watt, was on the market. In 1904 two Austrian chemists, Alexander Just and Franz Hanaman, patented a tungsten filament lamp that was remarkable from the standpoint of efficiency, giving 7.75 lumens per watt, but was extremely fragile and could be used only under special conditions. At that time it was believed impossible to draw tungsten wire, but in 1910 William D. Coolidge of the General Electric Research Laboratory succeeded in making ductile tungsten. This was at once used in lamps and the drawn wire tungsten filament lamp shortly superseded all other forms, being both efficient and strong.

All lamps up to this time operated filaments in a vacuum. In 1913, after much experimentation and fundamental research, Irving Langmuir, one of Whitney's assistants, discovered that with the largest sizes of lamps, if the filaments were coiled and the bulbs filled with inert gases, such as nitrogen or argon, the efficiency could be increased, to as high as 20 lumens per watt. As was the case with the carbon lamp, gradual, constant improvement has taken place with tungsten lamps, many American scientists contributing their bit. Gas filling and double coiling of filament have since been introduced into smaller sizes.

The cost of the incandescent lamp has constantly been reduced and efficiency increased. In 1907 the 60-watt lamp gave 8 lumens per watt and lost 25 percent of this light before burning out. Thirty years later the 60-watt lamp produced 13.9 lumens per watt and emitted 90 percent of its original light at the end of its life. By 1970 developments had brought the number of lumens produced in a tungsten-filament lamp to 40, the maximum obtainable before the filament melts. Although fluorescent lamps provide more light with greater efficiency, incandescent lamps continue to be used because of their simplicity and low cost.

[Illuminating Engineering Society, *Handbook;* William Thomas O'Dea, *Social History of Lighting.*]
A. L. POWELL

LANCASTER, FORT, a trading post on the South Platte River, Colo., in use during the early 19th century. It was noted by John Charles Frémont during his exploration of the region in 1843 as a trading post of a Mr. Lupton, with plenty of livestock, and was in fact more nearly a ranch. It was apparently synonymous with Fort Lupton, and was of adobe construction. By 1857 it was abandoned.

[F. S. Dellenbaugh, *Frémont and '49.*]
CARL L. CANNON

LANCASTER, TREATY OF (June 22–July 4, 1744), negotiated in Pennsylvania, settled disputes between the Six Nations and Maryland and Virginia over land claims. Commissioners from Maryland and Virginia and representatives of the Six Nations, except the Mohawk, were present. Conrad Weiser acted as interpreter. For considerations of goods and money, the Six Nations surrendered claims to a large region in the western parts of Maryland and Virginia. Even more important, the Six Nations were won to the support of England in the ensuing struggle of that nation with France (*see* King George's War).

J. PAUL SELSAM

LANCASTER PIKE, the first turnpike built in the United States, was begun in 1791, completed in 1794, and freed from tolls, by state purchase, in 1917. Need for a public highway to connect Philadelphia with Lancaster, Pa., had been felt since the founding of the latter town by Scotch-Irish and German immigrants in 1730. In 1770 commissioners were appointed to lay out a 60-foot road, but the plan failed, probably because of war conditions. William Bingham then secured a charter for the Philadelphia and Lancaster Turnpike Company, offering for public sale 1,000 shares of stock, $300 par, to be one-tenth paid up at once. The offering was heavily oversubscribed, and the surplus was reduced by a lottery. In 1807 the charter was made perpetual.

The Lancaster Pike opened the interior of the continent to settlement. Conestoga wagons rumbled over it westward in great numbers. A twelve-hour night stage service connected Philadelphia with Lancaster beginning with the spring of 1798. The Pike, however, lost heavily when the main line of the Pennsylvania Railroad, begun in 1846, paralleled its course. Free roads built by the state close by the Lancaster Pike also cut away its trade. The perpetual charter was, accordingly, surrendered.

[Charles I. Landis, "History of the Philadelphia and Lancaster Turnpike," *Pennsylvania Magazine of History and Biography,* vol. 42; Thomas B. Searight, *The Old Pike.*]
HARRY EMERSON WILDES

LAND. *See* **Soil.**

LAND, INDIAN CONCEPT OF OWNERSHIP OF.
To the Indian encountered by European settlers in the New World, land was not susceptible of individualistic sale and transfer. Tecumseh, chief of the Shawnee, said, "Sell a country! Why not sell the air, the clouds, the great sea as well as the land?" Land was an integral, inseparable part of nature, which sustained the beings that lived upon it. These beings lived by hunting and fishing in the unity of nature. An Ohio Valley Indian told the missionary David McClure, in 1772, "When you white men buy a farm, you buy only the land. You don't buy the horses and cows, and sheep. The elks are our horses, the buffaloes are our cows, the deer are our sheep."

The only Indian concept that corresponded at all to the European concept of land ownership was that geographic sections of that unity of nature were capable of being used particularly by different tribes. Friction and warfare could thus come about between groups. But as for individuals, Indians believed, according to the 18th-century missionary John Heckewelder, that the "Great Spirit made the earth and all that it contains for the common good of mankind. . . . Everything was given in common to the sons of men. Whatever liveth on the land, whatsoever groweth out of the earth, and all that is in the rivers and waters . . . was given jointly to all, and every one is entitled to his share."

Under such conditions it is easy to understand the reluctance with which Indians consented to the cession of their land at treaties (*see* Indian Land Cessions).

[F. W. Hodge, *Handbook of American Indians*.]
RANDOLPH C. DOWNES

LAND, LEASING OF AMERICAN INDIAN. Although Indian reservation land cannot be sold without an explicit act of Congress, it became possible for tribes or individual Indian owners of land allotments to lease land to outsiders, under the Trade and Intercourse Act of 1834. Tribal councils may also lease tracts of land as well as mineral rights. For example, the Laguna of New Mexico have leased uranium rights on their reservation to the Anaconda Copper and Mining Company. Many Indians have chosen to lease their farmlands to non-Indians rather than to cultivate them themselves. On the Fort Apache Reservation in Arizona at Hawley Lake, non-Indians have been granted ninety-nine-year leases for lots on which to erect vacation cabins. Structures built on Indian land revert to the tribes when the lease expires.

[William A. Brophy and Sophie D. Aberle, *The Indian: America's Unfinished Business*.]
KENNETH M. STEWART

LAND ACT OF 1796, the first great land act adopted by the U.S. government. It established the office of surveyor general and reenacted the rectangular system of survey with townships of six miles square and sections of 640 acres that the Confederation had embodied in the Land Ordinance of 1785. Half of the townships were to be offered in 5,120-acre blocks, and the smallest unit that could be bought was 640 acres. The lands were to be sold at public auction to the highest bidder at or above the minimum price of $2 per acre. Full payment was required within a year after purchase, and a 10 percent reduction was offered for advance payment. Although it was the basic law of the American land system, the act of 1796 was a failure from the start because the high minimum price and the large unit of entry deterred purchasing.

[B. H. Hibbard, *History of the Public Land Policies*; P. J. Treat, *The National Land System*.]
PAUL W. GATES

LAND ACT OF 1800. *See* **Harrison Land Act.**

LAND ACT OF 1820. The credit system in the disposition of the public lands inaugurated by the Land Act of 1796 and extended by the Harrison Land Act of 1800 had become an evident failure by 1820. Large numbers of settlers found it impossible to make the deferred payments on their lands. Other hard-working farmers, seeing that nothing happened to those who failed to meet their obligations, decided to let their own installments lapse. Arrearages piled up rapidly, and Congress was forced to pass law after law for the relief of the settlers. After considerable agitation Congress enacted the law of Apr. 24, 1820, abolishing the credit system. The minimum price at the public auctions and at private sale thereafter was reduced from $2 to $1.25 per acre, the entire amount to be paid at the time of purchase. The smallest purchasable unit of land was fixed at 80 acres.

[B. H. Hibbard, *History of the Public Land Policies*.]
DAN E. CLARK

LAND BANKS. *See* **Agriculture.**

LAND BOUNTIES. Lacking well-filled treasuries but possessing abundant supplies of land, the American colonies and, after the Revolution, the states and the national government all granted land bounties instead of cash subsidies to reward military service in past wars, to encourage enlistment in pending wars, and to aid various special groups. Virginia gave more generous bounties than any other colony or state, and a special Virginia military district was reserved north of the Ohio to fulfill these grants. During the Revolution Congress promised land bounties to British deserters and to enlisted officers and men. Again, during the War of 1812 and the Mexican War land bounties were offered as inducements to enlist and as rewards for service (*see* Bounties, Military). Land bounties were also granted to Canadian refugees in the Revolution, to earthquake victims, to Polish exiles, and to a number of other groups and individuals whose appeals to Congress received strong political support. The warrants for the many millions of acres of land thus granted were generally sold for small sums to speculators who used them to accumulate great tracts. The military tracts of Illinois, Arkansas, and Missouri, in which land bounties of the War of 1812 were located, were frequently called speculators' deserts. (*See also* Land Scrip.)

[Thomas Donaldson, *The Public Domain.*]
PAUL W. GATES

LAND DISTRIBUTION BILL, CLAY'S. Land policies, tariff rates, and public revenue questions were inseparable in the United States during the years 1834 to 1842. The old policy of using the public lands as a major source of income for the government remained in effect, and throughout the boom years 1834 to 1837 federal revenues were enormously swollen by receipts from land sales. Faced with a surplus, the politicians sought means to rid the treasury of its unwanted millions. The West wished the federal government to dispose of its public domain by ceding it to the states, by granting free homesteads, or by selling the land at low rates; the Old South opposed liberalization of the land policy and favored a lower tariff as a means of reducing the federal revenue; the Northeast opposed tariff reduction and a liberal land policy, and favored the proposal made by Sen. Henry Clay of Kentucky for the distribution of the net proceeds from the public land sales among the states. Clay's distribution bill, first introduced in 1832, provided that 10 percent of the net proceeds of the land sales be distributed to the states in which they were located and that the remaining 90 percent be distributed among all the states and territories in proportion to their population. To gain support for this measure the advocates of distribution made a concession to the West by adding to Clay's bill a provision for preemption. Before the bill was adopted in 1841, it was further provided that if tariff rates were raised above the 20 percent level they reached in that year, distribution would automatically be suspended. In 1842 the tariff was raised, and Clay's great political measure was suspended. (*See also* Surplus Revenue, Distribution of.)

[B. H. Hibbard, *History of the Public Land Policies.*]
PAUL W. GATES

LAND GRANT ACT. *See* **Morrill Act.**

LAND GRANTS, COLONIAL. Claims to land as between European governments rested upon discovery, exploration, and occupation, which, when completed, vested the title in the sovereign of a particular nation. According to this European concept it was the prerogative of the sovereign who had taken title— and of him alone—to terminate the claims of native Americans; the title to all English America was in the king, and from him all later titles stemmed. Royal land grants took the form of charters, and the whole Atlantic seaboard, except Florida, was, between 1606 and 1732, parceled out to the London and Plymouth companies; the Council for New England; James, Duke of York; William Penn and associates; George Calvert, Lord Baltimore; Edward Hyde, Earl of Clarendon, and associates; and James Oglethorpe and associates. From some of these in turn came grants to individuals and groups, which were gradually incorporated into regular colonial governments with boundaries based upon the earlier charters. Many of the original grants ran westward to the sea and became the foundation for the western claims of the original states, which were finally surrendered to the national government between 1778 and 1781 (*see* Western Lands).

Local land titles came from the colonial government or the proprietor, depending on who held the direct title from the king. The practice of New England was for the general court in each colony to grant a considerable tract, called a township, to a body of settlers, who in turn issued deeds to individual settlers. This practice tended to prevent speculation in vacant lands and engrossment.

In Maryland there were some manorial grants of

1,000 acres or more, although most of the grants were small and made to actual settlers. The practice in Pennsylvania was to grant land to actual settlers in small parcels but to retain title to vast acreage in the settled areas. Thus the proprietor not only held title to the ungranted regions but was also the largest land-owner in the developed eastern counties and collected rents as from any other private estate.

In Virginia there was at first a system of grants based on headrights—fifty acres for each person arriving in Virginia—and belonging to the individual who paid the transportation. This led to abuses and gradually degenerated into a simple fee system at the land office. Anyone who could pay the fees could acquire original title to as many acres as he could pay for. Under this system large plantations grew up that were far too big to be fully cultivated, such as those of the Byrds, Fairfaxes, Randolphs, and Spotswoods.

Grants were not infrequently used to promote settlements in the backcountry. These were usually conditioned upon the transportation and settlement of a minimum number of families within a limited time. The best known is the Ohio Company grant of 500,000 acres near the Forks of the Ohio in 1749. The practice was common on a smaller scale in all of the colonies south of Maryland.

In New York and South Carolina there were vast individual grants and extensive engrossment. In New York the practice had begun under the Dutch by the creation of the patroon estates, which were recognized as valid by the English. Henry Hyde, Viscount Cornbury, and other royal governors issued enormous grants to their favorites. In this way the Van Rensselaer, Philipse, Van Cortlandt, and Livingston estates were built up and perpetuated, paving the way for the serious antirent difficulties in New York, 1839–46.

To be valid, a grant had to come from the colonial government in which the land was situated. Undefined boundaries led to conflicts over titles, such as the troubles in Vermont where settlers claimed land under grants from both New York and New Hampshire and such as the bitter dispute in the Wyoming Valley where settlers from Connecticut were expelled as trespassers by those with titles from Pennsylvania (see Yankee-Pennamite Wars).

Land grants as bounties for military service became especially important after 1750. The Virginia grants were made in what is now West Virginia. Individual soldiers or officers could either use their warrants or sell them; the purchaser in turn could use them singly or in groups. Thus George Washington came into possession of his vast western properties by purchasing Virginia military warrants (see Washington's Western Lands). The British government made extensive military grants in the Floridas after their acquisition from Spain.

Indian titles were presumed to be extinguished by the local colonial government as the representative of the king before land was granted to individual settlers. This was not always the case, and after 1750 there was a growing custom of frontiersmen purchasing lands directly from the Indians and securing confirmation later. In other instances settlers secured grants before Indian titles were extinguished—this being one of the causes of Pontiac's War. The Proclamation of 1763 was issued to stop encroachments of this kind. On the other hand, the expansion into Kentucky and Tennessee in the late 1760's and in the 1770's was based upon the assumption that Indian titles alone were valid—particularly as manifested in the undertakings of Daniel Boone, Richard Henderson, and James Robertson.

The vast interior of the continent tempted Americans and Englishmen to seek grants to the rich lands west of the mountains. On the eve of the Revolution patents were pending in England for proprietary grants to form four new colonies in the region west of the Alleghenies and south and east of the Ohio and Mississippi rivers. These were called Vandalia, Transylvania, Georgiana, and Mississippi. Large additional purchases from the Indians north of the Ohio River also awaited confirmation.

Colonial land grants were not limited to the eastern part of the United States. Spain and France made grants similar to those made by England. When new areas came under the control of England, or later of the United States, the earlier foreign colonial land grants were accepted as valid. As many of these had very obscure descriptions, the boundaries became elastic and were used as the foundation for claims to large tracts of government lands. One of the most famous of these is the Maxwell land grant in Colorado and New Mexico, which involved litigation as late as 1887. Many of the large landed estates of the southwestern part of the United States go back to old Spanish colonial land grants confirmed after annexation to the United States (see Land Grants, Spanish and Mexican).

[C. W. Alvord, *Mississippi Valley in British Politics*; Evarts B. Greene, *The Foundations of American Nationality*.]

O. M. DICKERSON

LAND GRANTS, SPANISH AND MEXICAN, more commonly called private land claims, were grants made by predecessor governments in areas later acquired by the United States. They ranged all the way from small town-plots in present-day Detroit, Natchez, and Los Angeles to great colonization grants containing hundreds of thousands of acres. Included were choice spots for urban growth and some of the richest and most productive cotton and sugar-cane land of the South and the best of the valley land in California.

The title records of these early grants before American control were in poor shape, some of them being entirely lost. Most grants had been made on conditions, and in many instances these had not been fulfilled. When these areas came under American jurisdiction, there was a scramble for the most promising locations, which had been going begging just a few years before. All the grants had to be tested in the courts by American judges attempting to apply Spanish and Mexican law and American equity. Unfortunately, the swift rise in land values encouraged the fabrication of grants through forged documents and professional witnesses who, for a fee, would swear to anything the lawyers asked of them. Harried by the load of claims to be investigated, inadequate staff, and low pay, the government attorneys and judges were often overwhelmed by the highly skilled and extraordinarily able lawyers employed at high fees by the claimants, and some questionable claims were thus confirmed. Although it took a generation before the cost of the claims was patented, it is doubtful that any number of them with an equitable or other legal basis was rejected. Altogether 20,059 claims were confirmed for a total of 30,519,605 acres. The largest numbers of claims were in Louisiana, Missouri, and Mississippi, and the largest acreages, in New Mexico, California, and Louisiana. The larger claims in Florida, Louisiana, and California contributed to a concentrated pattern of land ownership that survived into the last third of the 20th century.

[Paul W. Gates, *History of Public Land Law Development.*]

PAUL W. GATES

LAND GRANTS FOR EDUCATION. The practice of making land grants to aid in supporting public schools was generally followed by the American colonies. The Confederation, borrowing from the New England land system, provided in the Land Ordinance of 1785 that the sixteenth section (640 acres) of each township, or one thirty-sixth of the acreage of the public land states, should be granted to the states for public schools. New states after 1848 were given two sections, or 1,280 acres, in each township, and Utah, Arizona, New Mexico, and Oklahoma were given four sections in each township when they entered the Union. At the same time, they were also given a minimum of two townships, or 46,080 acres, to aid in founding "seminaries of learning," or state universities. Such great institutions as the universities of Michigan, Wisconsin, and Indiana benefited from these grants.

The next important step in federal aid to education came in 1862 as the result of an energetic campaign undertaken by Jonathan Baldwin Turner of Illinois, the farm and labor journals, and Horace Greeley through the *New York Tribune*. The Land Grant College Act, generally called the Morrill Act, was fathered in the House of Representatives by Justin Smith Morrill of Vermont. This measure gave each state 30,000 acres of public land for each representative and senator it had in Congress, to aid in establishing colleges of agriculture and mechanical arts. States that had no public lands received scrip that could be exchanged for public lands open to entry elsewhere. As a result of this act agricultural colleges were established in every state, with two each in southern states because of their insistence on segregation. Special land grants have also been made to endow normal schools, schools of mining, reform schools, and a women's college.

Congress was unusually generous in sharing its public lands with Alaska for education and other purposes upon the state's admission to the Union in 1959. In place of numerous grants for education, internal improvements, and public buildings, Congress granted a total of 103,350,000 acres to be allocated as the new state wished. It also promised 5 percent of its net return from all land sales in the state for schools.

This liberal distribution of the public lands reflects the ever-growing interest of the American people in free public education. It encouraged the states early to create schools and aided in financing them when local resources were unequal to the task. It also eased the path of those of a later generation who favored direct money grants for education, for it was difficult for conservative opponents to hold—although some did—that the practice of granting land for schools for more than a century was not sufficient constitutional precedent for money grants. Altogether, an area much larger than that of California was given the states for public education. The first public land states recklessly mismanaged their bounty, while others, such as Minnesota, so managed theirs as to build up a large endowment for education.

[Paul W. Gates, *History of Public Land Law Development.*]

PAUL W. GATES

LAND GRANTS FOR RAILWAYS. The liberality with which Congress subsidized canal construction by land grants suggested to early railroad promoters that they might also obtain land donations to aid their enterprises. Most persistent were the advocates of a central railroad for Illinois to connect the extreme northwestern and southern parts of the state. When, in 1850, the proposed railroad scheme was made intersectional by a plan to extend it to the Gulf of Mexico, Congress adopted a measure that gave Illinois, Mississippi, and Alabama a broad right-of-way through the public lands for a railroad and alternate sections for a distance of six miles on both sides of the road, amounting to 3,840 acres for each mile of railroad. The government-reserved sections within the twelve-mile area were to be priced at double the ordinary minimum of $1.25 an acre, which enabled strict constructionists to maintain that building the road would assure the government as much return from half the land as it might receive for the whole without the line. Furthermore, the government was promised free transportation for troops and supplies and rate concessions for transporting mails.

Swift completion of the Illinois Central Railroad's portion of the intersectional line, which was made possible by the early sale of part of the lands, aided in opening to settlement areas hitherto inaccessible and gave a great impetus to immigration (promoted by extensive advertising), to farm and urban development, and to rising real estate values in Illinois. This spectacular success produced a scramble for railroad land grants in all existing public land states. Numerous land grants were made between 1850 and 1871, totaling, with state land grants, 176 million acres, or more than the area of Texas.

Most important and grandest in their conception were the transcontinental railways, which were to connect the Mississippi Valley with the new communities on the Pacific coast. First of the transcontinentals to be chartered and given a land grant, plus loans (in 1862), were the Union Pacific, to build west

from Omaha, and the Central Pacific, to build east from Sacramento. They met at Ogden, Utah, in 1869. In 1864 the Southern Pacific, the Atlantic and Pacific (a portion of which later became part of the Atchison, Topeka and Santa Fe), and the Northern Pacific were generously endowed with land, the latter receiving 39 million acres.

All land grant railroads undertook extensive advertising campaigns at home and abroad to attract immigrants to their lands, which were sold on easy credit at prevailing prices. When settlers found it difficult to meet their payments, especially in the poor years after 1873 and in the late 1880's, complaints against the policies of the land grant railroads began to be made. Forfeiture of their undeveloped and unsold land was demanded. Reformers condemned the land grants as inconsistent with the free homestead policy, and in 1871 they succeeded in halting further grants. Continued agitation over the large amount of land claimed by railroads that was not in the hands of developers led to the General Forfeiture Act of 1890, which required the return to the government of land along projected lines that had not been built. But this measure had no effect on the earned grants by construction of the lines. When the railroads succeeded in 1940 in inducing Congress to surrender the government's right to reduced rates for government traffic, it was proposed that the railroads be required to return the unsold portion of their grants to the public domain, but Congress did not so provide. Retention of these unsold lands by the railroads has been a sore point with many westerners, and agitation for compelling the forfeiture of these lands continued in the mid-1970's.

Land grants had encouraged capitalists to invest in railroads and enabled the lines so benefited to advance far beyond the zone of settlement. More than anything except the free land given to homesteaders by the government, they contributed to the rapid settlement of the West.

[Federal Coordinator of Transportation, *Public Aids to Transportation;* Paul W. Gates, *History of Public Land Law Development;* Robert E. Riegel, *The Story of the Western Railroads.*]

PAUL W. GATES

LANDGRAVE, a German title proposed for the second order of provincial nobility provided for in the Fundamental Constitutions of Carolina by the lords proprietors. Their inability to enforce the Constitutions made the title of little meaning save as an occasion for gifts of land to favorites, and as a title for the governors.

[E. McCrady, *South Carolina Under the Proprietary Government.*]

R. L. MERIWETHER

LAND OFFICE, U.S. GENERAL, was organized in 1812 as a bureau in the Treasury Department, to manage the public lands of the United States. The increasing burdens of the secretary of the treasury—who had to provide for surveying western lands, adjudicating the conflicting private land claims arising from the policies of previous foreign governments, and settling conflicting land claims arising from poorly drafted legislation—brought about the creation of the office of commissioner of the General Land Office. The commissioner's responsibility for more than a billion acres of land and for the patenting of tracts to hundreds of thousands of buyers made him a powerful political figure and made the Land Office one of the largest and most important of federal bureaus. The issuing of patents, the settling of contested claims, and the drafting of instructions amplifying upon, and clarifying, the public acts were delayed, causing confusion and controversy. Able and honest administrators, including John and Joseph Wilson and William A. J. Sparks, made notable records, but weaker men tolerated inefficiency and corruption. Despite complaints from the West and from Congress, the office received little attention. As revenue from the public land became diminishingly important, the office seemed less related to the Treasury Department. In 1849 it was transferred to the newly created Department of the Interior, where it was associated with the Office of Indian Affairs, the Bureau of Patents, the Bureau of Pensions, and the Office of Agricultural Statistics. Under the Department of Interior, it made detailed reports on minerals, agricultural possibilities, and forests of the West, which constitute a major source for historians of that section.

Consonant with a change in the attitude of Congress, the General Land Office became increasingly settler-minded until free lands were provided by the Homestead Act of 1862. No bureaucrat likes to have his responsibilities and staff reduced. Consequently, when large timbered areas of the public lands were being withdrawn from entry under the Forest Reserve Act of 1891 for conservation and public management, which they had never had, the commissioner of the General Land Office was not happy. Yet these reser-

vations remained under his control until 1905, when they were transferred to the National Forest Service under Gifford Pinchot in the Department of Agriculture.

By the forfeiture of the land grant of the Oregon and California Railroad in 1916 for failure to conform to the provisions of the granting act, 2,891,000 acres of richly endowed Douglas fir land in Oregon were returned to the Department of the Interior, enabling it to begin its own forestry development policies. After Harold Ickes became secretary of the interior in 1933, the department became ardently conservationist in administering the grazing districts created under the Taylor Grazing Act of 1934, and the Oregon and California Railroad lands. By 1947 the land disposal responsibilities of the General Land Office, which had been chiefly concerned with transferring public lands into private ownership rather than with conserving them in public ownership, were largely over. Its activities were transferred to the new Bureau of Land Management. Thereafter, the bureau administered the remaining public lands, the 140 million acres in grazing districts, the Oregon and California Railroad forest lands, and the leasing and sale of mineral rights. The bureau's aims are to protect the public lands from thoughtless exploiters and to develop and preserve the lands for economic use, recreation, wildlife, and scenic beauty.

[Paul W. Gates, *History of Public Land Law Development;* Malcolm J. Rohrbaugh, *The Land Office Business: The Settlement and Administration of American Public Lands, 1789–1837.*]

PAUL W. GATES

LAND ORDINANCES. *See* **Ordinances of 1784, 1785, and 1787.**

LAND POLICY. Because the new government of the United States needed revenue, the Land Ordinance of 1785 was passed, decreeing that the public lands should be sold for what was then a high price, $1.00 an acre—raised to $2.00 an acre in 1796 and lowered to $1.25 after 1820. Not until 1811 did the revenue from land sales amount to as much as $1 million, but thereafter it increased, until in 1836 the public lands produced 48 percent of the revenue of the federal government. As late as 1855 the income from this source was 17 percent of the total federal income. Western settlers insisted it was unfair to require them to pay

$1.25 an acre for raw land, a price that added heavily to the capital cost of making a farm. Supported by Horace Greeley and his powerful *New York Tribune* and by eastern workingmen, the demand for free land gradually won converts. In 1862 they won their objective with the adoption of the Homestead Act. This act was just one of the many steps Congress had taken, and was to take, to make pioneering on the public lands of the West attractive.

Congress, responsive to western interests, had previously aided the building of canals, roads, and railroads in the public land states by generous grants of land. It had also made grants of land for public schools and for the construction of public buildings, state universities, agricultural colleges, and other public institutions, on the assumption that such grants enhanced the value of the remaining lands and encouraged their sale and settlement. All such institutions were expected to sell their lands to produce the greatest possible revenue at the same time that the United States was giving land to settlers. Through these lavish donations, free grants to settlers, and huge purchases by speculators, the public lands were rapidly alienated. Although much land was still publicly owned in 1890, it was a poor remnant of a once-proud heritage, and the superintendent of the census could say, "The Frontier is gone."

Little thought was given to the consequences of this speedy transfer of lands to private ownership until the threatened exhaustion of the forest resources of the Great Lakes states and the rising price of timber raised fundamental questions about the wisdom of past disposal policies. By the turn of the century, conservation of the remaining resources under federal ownership was being vigorously advocated by John Muir, Gifford Pinchot, and Theodore Roosevelt. National forests were set aside as permanent reservations under controlled management. Places of special scenic beauty were created national parks; Yellowstone was the first, in 1872. In 1934 the remaining rangelands in public ownership were organized into management districts under the Taylor Grazing Act, thereby virtually ending the era of free land. The United States thus entered a new era, in which it cherished, and indeed largely added to, national parks and monuments, recreational areas, forests, and wilderness areas by purchasing lands that had previously passed into private ownership.

[Paul W. Gates, *History of Public Land Law Development*.]

PAUL W. GATES

LANDS, PUBLIC. *See* **Public Domain; Public Land Commissions; Public Land Sales; Public Land States.**

LANDSCAPE ARCHITECTURE, the shaping and planting of a garden or tract of land. American landscape architecture has been dominated by two styles: the classical, or formal; and the picturesque, or informal. The classical sprang from the Renaissance and is distinguished by straight paths, straight rows of trees, clipped shrubbery, flower bedding, fountains, formal bodies of water, and the use of architecture and sculpture. The picturesque, originating in 18th-century England, is characterized by winding paths, irregular planting, spreading lawns, and irregular bodies of water, and little, if any, architecture and sculpture.

The first American gardens, mostly for vegetables, had plain geometric designs. In the 18th century, gardens became elaborate, especially in the South. The best surviving examples are at Middleton Place outside Charleston, S.C.; at Hampton near Towson, Md.; and George Washington's garden at Mount Vernon near Washington, D.C.

The classical style bowed out as the picturesque caught on in the 1840's. Andrew Jackson Downing, who favored the picturesque, laid out private estates along the Hudson River and promoted the style in several popular books. His successors Frederick Law Olmsted and Calvert Vaux adopted the picturesque style in 1858 for Central Park in New York City, and from that time on, the style has been the dominant one for urban parks. In the 1960's and 1970's it was also found along parkways and in suburban developments.

Although the picturesque style has prevailed since the 1840's, it was swept aside by the classical—at least in the private section—during the American Renaissance (1880–1930). The World's Columbian Exposition of 1893 proved to be the most important single factor in making it popular. The best examples of the classical style are the gardens of Villa Viscaya in Miami, Fla., by Diego Suarez; the gardens of Dumbarton Oaks in Washington, D.C., by Beatrix Farrand; the grounds of San Simeon, Calif., by Julia Morgan; and Grant Park in Chicago, Ill., by Edward Herbert Bennett. The same exposition promoted flower bedding and show conservatories in urban parks; both survive in midwestern cities. Olmsted Brothers (the son and stepson of Frederick Law Olmsted), the nation's most successful landscape firm from 1900 to 1940, designed in both styles, their best-known work being Fort Tryon Park in New York City.

Since 1930 there have been very few new classical gardens. Many variations on the picturesque and what might be termed modernistic landscapes have been designed. This last is recognized by its irregular levels, eccentric architectural shapes, and the use of horizontal evergreens.

[Winifred Starr Dobyns, *California Gardens;* Louis H. Frohman and Jean Elliot, *A Pictorial Guide to American Gardens;* Alice G. B. Lockwood, ed., *Gardens of Colony and State;* Norman T. Newton, *Design on the Land;* Laura Wood Roper, *FLO: A Biography of Frederick Law Olmsted.*]

HENRY HOPE REED

LAND SCRIP and land warrants came to constitute a kind of land-office money acceptable for entry of public lands. Congress never drew any clear distinction between the two in the forty-nine statutes (mostly between 1820 and 1880) that authorized issues of scrip, some directly, others only after trial of claims before special commissions or the courts. Congress placed restrictions on the use of certain kinds of scrip, making them less valuable than scrip that had no such limitations. Scrip was used primarily to reward veterans, to give allotments to half-breed Indians, to make possible exchanges of private land for public land, to indemnify people who had lost valid claims through errors of the General Land Office, and to subsidize agricultural colleges.

The greatest volume of scrip or warrants was given to soldiers of the American Revolution, the War of 1812, the Mexican War, and finally, in 1855, to veterans of all wars who had not previously received a land bounty or who had received less than 160 acres. Warrants of the first two wars were to be located in military tracts set aside for that purpose; those of the Mexican War could be entered anywhere on surveyed public land open to purchase at $1.25 an acre. A total of 68,300,652 acres were thus conveyed to 426,879 veterans, their heirs, or their assignees.

In treaties with the Choctaw (1830) and Chickasaw (1832) of Mississippi and Alabama these Indians were given several million acres in individual allotments and land scrip, all of which became the object of speculation by whites, including a number of prominent political leaders. It was evident that the allotments and scrip were included to gain approval for land cessions from powerful white traders into whose hands the allotments and scrip promptly fell.

For the next thirty years treaties with Indian tribes were almost impossible to negotiate without the inclusion of similar provisions for allotments and scrip, so powerful were the traders in the negotiations.

Three issues of scrip to two bands of Chippewa and Sioux half-breeds in the 1850's and 1860's similarly fell into the hands of speculators, who used them to acquire valuable timberland in Minnesota and California that they would otherwise have been unable to acquire legally. The amount issued—for 395,000 acres—was small compared with issues of other forms of scrip, but this issue had few limitations on its use and thus became one of the most highly valued forms of scrip.

In the Morrill Act of 1862, Congress granted each state 30,000 acres for each member it had in the House and Senate, to aid in the establishment of colleges of agricultural and mechanical arts. Land was given to states containing public domain; other states were given scrip that they had to sell to third parties to enter land in public domain states. As had military warrants, the scrip—for 7,700,000 acres—fell well below the basic price of public lands when the states unloaded their allotments, thereby reducing the cost of public land to settlers and speculators and minimizing the endowment of the colleges.

The next major scrip measure was the Soldiers' and Sailors' Additional Homestead Act of 1872, which allowed veterans of the Civil War to count their military service toward the five years required to gain title to a free homestead and authorized those who had homesteaded on less than 160 acres to make an additional entry to bring their total acreage to 160 acres. Assignable scrip was issued for the additional acreage allowed. It was greatly in demand because it could be used to enter the $2.50-an-acre reserved land within the railroad land grant areas and to acquire much-sought-after timberland that was not otherwise open to purchase. In 1877 the scrip was being used to enter recently ceded Mille Lac Indian lands in Minnesota, worth from $10 to $30 an acre.

Other measures were enacted to indemnify holders of public-land claims that were confirmed long after the land had been taken up and patented to settlers; the claimants were provided with scrip equivalent to the loss they had sustained. Indemnity scrip for some 1,265,000 acres was issued, most of which was subject to entry only on surveyed land open to purchase at $1.25 an acre. The chief exceptions were the famous Valentine scrip for 13,316 acres and the Porterfield scrip for 6,133 acres, which could be entered on unoccupied, unappropriated, nonmineral land, whether surveyed or not. These rare forms of scrip could be used to acquire town and bridge sites, islands, tracts adjacent to such booming cities as Las Vegas, or water holes controlling the use of large acreages of rangelands, and they came into great demand. Their value reached $75 to $100 an acre in 1888.

Least defensible of all the scrip measures were the carelessly drawn Forest Management Act of 1897 and the Mount Rainier Act of 1899, which allowed owners within the national forests and Mount Rainier National Park to exchange their lands for public lands outside the forests and park. Under these provisions it was possible for the railroads and other owners to cut the timber on their inside lands and then surrender the cutover lands for the "lieu scrip" that could be entered on the best of the forest lands still in the public domain. It was charged that some national forests, and possibly Mount Rainier National Park, were created to enable inside owners to rid themselves of their less desirable lands for high stumpage areas outside. The Weyerhaeuser Company acquired some of its richest stands of timber with Mount Rainier scrip. After much criticism the exchange feature was ended in 1905.

As the public lands rapidly diminished and the demand for land to own intensified, values of scattered undeveloped land increased, and so did the value of the various forms of scrip, without which it was impossible to acquire these tracts, as public land sales had been halted in 1889. The peak prices of the 19th century seemed small in the 20th century, when speculators bid up quotations to $500, $1,000, and even $4,000 an acre. By 1966, administrative relaxation had wiped out some of the distinctions between types of scrip; Valentine, Porterfield, and Sioux Half-Breed were all accepted for land having an appraised value of $1,386 an acre, and Soldiers' and Sailors' Additional Homestead and Forest Management lieu scrip could be exchanged for land having a value from $275 to $385 an acre. At that time 3,655 acres of the most valuable scrip and 7,259 acres of that with more limitations on use were outstanding.

[House Committee on Public Lands, *Satisfaction of Scrip Rights,* Hearing of the Subcommittee on Public Lands . . . on the Satisfaction of Scrip and Similar Rights (89th Congress, 1966); Paul W. Gates, *History of Public Land Law Development.*]

PAUL W. GATES

LAND SPECULATION. The favorite object of speculation in America before the era of big business was the public lands. They could be bought cheaply in large quantities and withheld from market—if one had sufficient capital to carry them—until rising prices brought profits to the investors. Memories of high land values in the Old World and of the social prestige enjoyed by the possessor of broad acres, combined with the natural land hunger of all races, produced in the American people an insatiable lust for land.

Land speculation began with the first settlements in America. The proprietors of Virginia, disappointed at the meager returns from their investment, granted themselves great tracts of land from which they hoped to draw substantial incomes. Similarly, the Penns and Calverts in Pennsylvania and Maryland and the early proprietors of New York, New Jersey, and the Carolinas speculated in lands in an imperial way. Later in the colonial period a new crop of land companies composed of English and colonial speculators sought both title to and political control over great tracts in the Mississippi Valley. The Mississippi, the Georgiana, the Wabash, the Indiana, the Loyal, and the Ohio land companies attracted some of the ablest colonial leaders into their ranks, among them George Washington, Richard Henry Lee, Benjamin Franklin, the Whartons, and George Croghan. The struggles of these rival companies for charters and grants played an important role in British colonial policy during the years before the Revolution. Company rivalries were matched by the rival land claims of the colonies. One of the most notable was the conflict between Connecticut and Pennsylvania for the Wyoming Valley, which Connecticut granted to the Susquehanna Land Company. In western Virginia, Richard Henderson and his Transylvania Company, which claimed title to a great tract received from the Indians, came into conflict with Virginia and were successful in having only a small part of the area confirmed to them.

Most influential colonials tried their luck at speculating, either through the land companies or on their own account. George Washington was a large landowner in Virginia, Pennsylvania, and the Ohio country; Robert and Gouverneur Morris, William Duer, Oliver Phelps, Nathaniel Gorham, and William Johnson acquired princely domains in Pennsylvania, New York, and Maine. The Morrises negotiated a number of large purchases and resold tracts to others; perhaps the largest of them went to the Holland Land Company. This company was composed of Dutch capitalists who bought the Holland Reserve in western New York and were busily engaged in settling it during the first third of the 19th century. In the meantime, most of upstate New York was parceled out among speculators. Among the most prominent of the speculators were the Wadsworths of the Genesee country, John Jacob Astor, and Peter Smith, father of Gerrit Smith. These men, unlike Robert Morris, were able to retain their lands long enough either to resell at high prices or settle tenants on them.

The largest purchase and the most stupendous fraud was the sale in 1795 of 21.5 million acres of western lands in Yazoo River country by the legislature of Georgia to four companies for one and a half cents an acre. The next legislature canceled the sale, but the purchasers, frequently innocent third parties, waged a long fight to secure justice, claiming that the obligation of the contract clause in the federal Constitution prevented the Georgia legislature from reversing the original sale. The Supreme Court, in *Fletcher* v. *Peck* (1810), agreed with this interpretation. The Yazoo frauds became a *cause célèbre* in which John Randolph, Thomas Jefferson, John Marshall, and other notables took prominent parts.

Undeveloped Lands. When the public domain of the United States was created by the donations of the states with western land claims, speculative interests converged upon Congress with requests to purchase tracts of land north of the Ohio. In fact, the craze for land speculation was partly responsible for the adoption of the Northwest Ordinance of 1787, which set up a government for the ceded territory north of the Ohio. A group of New England capitalists known as the Ohio Company of Associates wished to buy a tract of land in southeastern Ohio for a New England settlement. To get the measure through Congress, it seemed necessary to enlarge the original project and to create a second organization, the Scioto Company, which was composed of members of Congress and other influential people who planned to buy some 5 million acres of land. The formation of the Scioto Company enlarged support for the enactment of the Northwest Ordinance, but the company itself was a failure because it could not fulfill its contract with the government. The Ohio Company of Associates did, however, succeed in planting a little New England outpost at Marietta on the Ohio River. In 1788 John Cleves Symmes of New Jersey also bought a large tract from Congress. These purchases virtually defeated the purpose of the Land Ordinance of 1785, which authorized the sale of land at $1.00 an acre, or a third more than the Scioto Company paid, and the Land Act of 1796, which raised the price to $2.00 an acre, because the speculators whom Congress had allowed to acquire large tracts of land at lower prices than were offered to individual settlers were able to undersell the government.

There were three great periods of land speculation after the creation of the public domain: 1817–19, 1834–37, and 1853–57. Outstanding easterners such as Daniel Webster, Caleb Cushing, Edward Everett, Amos Lawrence, Moses and John Carter Brown, and James S. Wadsworth and southerners such as John C. Breckinridge, John Slidell, Eli Shorter, and William Grayson bought western lands in large quantities. Land companies again were organized, and they entered great tracts embracing entire townships. The New York and Boston Illinois Land Company acquired 900,000 acres in the Military Tract of Illinois; the American Land Company had great estates in Indiana, Illinois, Michigan, Wisconsin, Mississippi, and Arkansas; and the Boston and Western Land Company owned 60,000 acres in Illinois and Wisconsin.

The Homestead Act of 1862 did not end land speculation; some of the largest purchases were made after it was passed. William S. Chapman alone bought over 1 million acres of land in California and Nevada; Henry W. Sage, John McGraw, and Jeremiah Dwight, benefactors of Cornell University, entered 352,000 acres of timberland in the Northwest and the South; and Francis Palms and Frederick E. Driggs bought 486,000 acres of timberland in Wisconsin and Michigan. Not until 1889 were effective steps taken to end large speculative purchases, and by that date the government had parted with its best lands. At the same time, the canal and railroad land grants and the lands given to the states for drainage and educational purposes were also attracting a great deal of speculative purchasing.

The accumulation of vast quantities of land in advance of settlement created many problems for the West, some of which have never been satisfactorily settled. The Indians were pushed back more rapidly than the actual needs of the population dictated and the frequent clashes between settlers and Indians might have been avoided had there been more social control of westward expansion and land purchases. In some places "speculators' deserts" were created where large amounts of land were owned by absentee proprietors who withheld them from development while waiting for higher prices. Settlers were widely dispersed because they could not find land at reasonable prices close to existing settlements. The problem of providing transportation facilities was consequently aggravated, and as a result of the importunities of settlers, thousands of miles of railroads were built through sparsely settled country, which could provide but little traffic for the roads.

Nevertheless, the speculators and land companies were an important factor in the development of the West. Their efforts to attract settlers to their lands through the distribution of pamphlets and other advertising literature describing the western country lured thousands from their homes in the eastern states and the countries of northern Europe to the newly developing sections of the West. They also aided in building improvements, such as roads, canals, and railroads, to make the life of the immigrant easier.

Land speculators were often unpopular and regarded unfavorably in newly opened areas because they often left their holdings undeveloped. But local people, actively selling and improving their holdings and thus contributing to the growth of the town and country, were shown every favor, were popular, and were frequently elected to public office.

The land reform movement with its corollary limitation of land sales had as its objective the retention of the public lands for free homesteads for settlers. Beginning in 1841, sales were restricted to 160 or 320 acres by new land acts—such as the Pre-emption Act (1841), the Graduation Act (1854), the Homestead Act (1862), the Timber Culture Act (1873), and the Timber and Stone Act (1878). But the cash sale system was retained, although after 1862 very little new land was opened to unrestricted entry and large purchases could be made only in areas previously opened to sale. Although reformers had tolerated the granting of land to railroads in the 1850's and 1860's, they later turned against this practice and began a move to have forfeited the grants unearned by failure to build railroads. In the midst of a strong revulsion against what were called "monopolistic" landholdings by railroads, cattle kings, and lumber companies in 1888–91, Congress adopted the Land Forfeiture Act of 1890, which required return of unearned grants to the public domain, and enacted other measures to end the cash sale system, to limit the amount of land that an individual could acquire from the government to 320 acres, and to make it more difficult to abuse the settlement laws. However, through the use of dummy entrymen and the connivance of local land officers, land accumulation continued.

Urban Property. Speculation in urban property was not so well structured as was speculation in rural lands, but it was widely indulged in and subject to the same excesses in periods of active industrial growth and to a similar drastic deflation in values following the economic crises of 1837, 1857, 1873, and 1930–33. During the boom years, prices for choice real estate in New York and other rapidly growing cities skyrocketed, only to decline when depression brought economic activity to a grinding halt. Fortunes were made in New York, Philadelphia, and Chicago from swiftly rising real estate values by old-line families. Among the parvenus, the best known is John Jacob Astor; the great wealth he accumulated enabled his family to rise to the top of the social ladder. With remarkable prescience, between 1800 and 1840 Astor invested $2 million, made from his trade with China and from returns in his land business, in land in Greenwich Village and elsewhere in Manhattan, but outside New York City limits. He acquired the fee simple to the land bought from Aaron Burr and George Clinton and took long-term leases on land from Trinity Church. After dividing the acreage bought from Clinton into blocks and lots, he waited until the demand rose and then began selling. His profit from these sales was substantial, but in later years he concentrated on granting long leases on his property. By his death his rent roll alone was bringing in $200,000 annually. His estate, valued at from $18 million to $20 million, mostly invested in real estate that was rapidly appreciating, had made him the richest man in the country. In two successive generations the family fortune, still concentrated in Manhattan real estate, increased to $50 million and $100 million. Other New York families were enjoying like successes in the burgeoning real estate market. The purchase in 1929 by John D. Rockefeller, Jr., of a long-term lease from Columbia University for the 11-acre tract on which he built Rockefeller Center was the most spectacular real estate transaction up to that point. He was able to get an eighty-seven-year lease for a ground rent of $3.3 million a year. With other city property this acquisition placed the Rockefeller family among the largest owners of New York property.

In every dynamically growing city, similar increases in land values have occurred, to the profit of those whose families by wisdom or good luck acquired land early. In Chicago, for example, lots on State Street between Monroe and Adams climbed from $25 per front foot in 1836 to $27,500 in 1931, a depression year. The families of Potter Palmer, Walter L. Newberry, and George M. Pullman were representative of the new rich in the Windy City.

Each generation produced its new millionaires—those who had the foresight to buy land in promising urban centers when prices were low. The spendthrift life style of the new millionaires and of their children aroused resentment, especially among the followers of Henry George. To tax the unearned increment in rising land values for the social good, George proposed a single tax on land so that the enhanced value of land that stemmed from society's growth would benefit the government directly. He also criticized the concentration of rural land ownership in a few hands, which was most marked in California in his day. Appropriately, George had his largest following in New York, where economic pressures had pushed land values to high figures. To further his reforms George offered himself as an independent candidate for mayor in New York in 1886. Without any party machine to fight for him and protect his interests at the polls, he still won 30 percent of the vote, against 41 percent for Tammany's candidate and 23 percent for Theodore Roosevelt, the Republican candidate. By that time George was the best-known economist in the country. Few people in America or Great Britain were unaware of his single-tax proposal and his strictures on the unearned increment that was making so many millionaires.

For everyone who turned to land and tax reform there were several who tried to emulate—on a smaller scale—the achievements of the Astors, the Schermerhorns, and the Hetty Greens by getting in on the ground floor of promising municipalities. In some states—particularly Illinois, eastern Iowa, and Kansas—town-site promoters took up hundreds of quarter sections of public land; laid out their blocks and lots; prepared alluring lithographed maps showing imagined buildings, factories, and homes; and peddled their towns, blocks, and lots in older communities that had long since given up the prospect of becoming miracle cities. Most of these dream cities never flourished; but a few, with aggressive leadership, managed to become the county seat, the territorial or state capital, or a railroad center or to acquire the U.S. land office, a religious college, or a state university or other public institution, and they grew moderately.

Among the major promoters of towns and cities were the land-grant railroads, which created station sites every 10 or 15 miles along their routes and offered numerous advantages to persons and institutions for locating in the vicinity. The officers of the Illinois Central alone laid out thirty-seven towns in Illinois, and the transcontinental railroads created far more communities around their stations. In fact, the struggle of town promoters to bring railroads and state and federal institutions to their communities constitutes one of the central themes of western American history. Some of these once-flourishing cities or towns have become ghost towns; few have gone on to flourish and grow.

The United States did not accept Henry George's view that profits from rising land values should be used for the public good, but it has increasingly sought to restrict property owners' rights by zoning regulations in both rural and urban areas. The outstanding illustration of such action is New York State's Adirondack Park Agency Act of 1971, intended to protect the wild character of the Adirondacks. The law curbs the creation of subdivisions with numerous small sites for second homes.

[Thomas P. Abernethy, *Western Lands and the American Revolution;* Everett Dick, *The Lure of the Land;* Paul W. Gates, *History of Public Land Law Development;* Homer Hoyt, *One Hundred Years of Land Values in Chicago;* Shaw Livermore, *Early American Land Companies: Their Influence Upon Corporate Development;* Gustavus Myers, *History of the Great American Fortunes;* Kenneth Wiggins Porter, *John Jacob Astor, Business Man;* Sidney Ratner, ed., *New Light on the History of Great American Fortunes: American Millionaires of 1892 and 1902.*]

PAUL W. GATES

LAND SURVEYING. *See* **Public Lands, Surveying of.**

LAND SYSTEM, NATIONAL. The American land system was established, almost as a matter of course, as an adaptation of European land systems brought over by the colonists or, in some instances, imposed by England or Holland on their respective colonies. The land in the English colonies, according to English law, in the first instance, belonged strictly to the crown.

Land was granted liberally to single individuals, groups of individuals, or joint-stock companies, proprietors who undertook settlements. These proprietors in turn granted land to settlers, generally freely, but often under the stipulation that rents should be paid. Down through these patentees, sometimes three or four in succession, title to the land passed into the hands of occupier and tiller. The latter usually paid little if anything for it, in the way of a purchase price, and was in many colonies granted a fee simple title. Such was the case in the New England colonies. In most of the others there was an attempt to collect quitrents in the form of very small payments, such as a halfpenny per acre or a shilling per hundred acres. Money being scarce, provision was made for payment in kind, usually in wheat or tobacco.

LAND TENURE

There was much difficulty attendant upon the collection of the rental payments, and gradually efforts to make collections were discontinued, although by then title to much land had been lost. This was no great calamity, since land was so plentiful, and the colonies so anxious to have it settled that almost anyone who wanted land could get it. Land, thus, came to be widely distributed in ownership, and held in fee simple, and most such land served at once as homestead and farm.

Two general land systems prevailed, so far as the character of the holding was concerned. In New England the holding was patterned after the farms of England and consisted of several separate pieces of land, altogether making a small unit. There was the home lot, usually in a village; a modest-size tract of arable land; a smaller piece of meadow, in typical localities where such were available; a wood lot; and a share in a common, generally used for pasturage and available for feeding all kinds of farm animals, but sometimes also including woodland, in which case the ownership of individual wood lots was obviated. The surveying was done in advance of distribution of the parcels, and the distribution carried out by lot. Thus the whole procedure was democratic in the extreme.

In the South the farm was different in character. To begin with, it was large. The grants of land were generally, to a family, a few hundred acres, and not infrequently, to the influential, a few thousand acres, some reaching the equivalent of a modern township. These tracts were surveyed privately, and the sites chosen by the grantee virtually at will. Through these liberal grants, coupled with the adaptation of the country to large-field undertakings in the growing of staple products, the foundation was laid for the plantation system, which long characterized the South.

The basic system of the North was found suitable for settlers as they moved westward, but the complications characterizing the New England holding were done away with, even before the Green Mountains were reached. Farms came to be of one piece, and the village idea was abandoned as fear of the Indians disappeared. For a long time the farms of the North were small because each family did most of its own work and, until about the middle of the 19th century, with comparatively little machinery.

The land system in the United States is adapted to a regime of extreme, individualistic, private ownership (see Land Titles), modified originally by the power of taxation and subsequently by zoning ordinances. Zoning implies, and embodies, the right of the public to decide, in general terms, the use to which land shall be put: whether or not, for example, a given tract, large or small, shall be provided with schools or roads, or shall be designated as forest, or recreational land.

Through the first quarter of the 20th century the general policy respecting land was to put the public domain into the hands of the user as fast as possible, but since that time the trend has been in a contrary direction.

[B. H. Hibbard, *A History of the Public Land Policies;* Payson J. Treat, *The National Land System, 1785–1820.*]
BENJAMIN HORACE HIBBARD

LAND TENURE, as here considered, applies to both farm and urban property and the status of the occupant or farmer who holds it either temporarily or permanently. The two classes of people from the tenure standpoint are the owner, or landlord, and the tenant, or lessee. British, French, Spanish, and Dutch efforts to establish colonies in North America produced a hodgepodge of land grants that included great manorial estates operated by tenants, large plantations operated by slaves, and small family farms operated by their owners. Outside New England, tenures were patterned most closely on models from the Old World, with some modernization of the manorial system as the objective. Lands were held in entail and passed by primogeniture, and they were subject to payment of quitrents. But even in those colonies in which large estates flourished, particularly in Virginia and South Carolina, the abundance of land available for settlement and the increasing liberality in granting land to small owners weakened the old system. Individual or family settlement replaced group or promoted and directed settlement. Many large estates, with their custom of primogeniture and entail and the obligation of quitrents, disappeared in the American Revolution. But in the Hudson River valley the only surviving Dutch manor—Rensselaerwyck—and a number of large English grants, operated by tenants, continued until the mid-19th century. In the antebellum South, tenancy existed to some extent, but it was not common. The better land tended to pass into the hands of planters who farmed them with their indentured servants or slaves. In the upland and hilly tracts and the piney woods areas of the South, yeoman farmers owned their small tracts.

In New England self-government, the nature of the land, and the nature of the inhabitants led to the establishment of small family farms and little tenancy, despite the tendency of the legislatures to grant numerous townships to speculators. Only on a few estates, such as that of John Winthrop the younger in Connecticut, did tenancy gain a foothold.

After 1865 the freedmen, lacking the means to begin farming on their own and eventually abandoned by northern Reconstructionists, had no alternative but to accept small (40-acre) allotments of land with a mule, plow, and means of subsistence from a landlord, not uncommonly their former owner, with whom they agreed to share the crop. Since the landlord provided everything, he resorted to crop liens to protect his equity; state laws helped further to tie the sharecropper to the land in virtual peonage. The number of sharecroppers increased, until by 1930 they constituted 43 percent of the farmers of Mississippi, 38 percent of those of Georgia, and 31 percent of those of Arkansas. The proportion of all tenant-operated farms for those states was 72, 68, and 63 percent, respectively, the highest in the country. In the sixteen states of the South sharecroppers and cash tenants constituted 55 percent of the farm families, but in the principal cotton counties the number of tenant-operated farms ranged up to 94 percent. Although cotton prices had been unfavorable during the 1920's, economic conditions had forced croppers to concentrate on planting cotton, using the same primitive methods of plantation farming in use a century earlier. The boll weevil and other parasites multiplied, soils became exhausted, yields declined, and the croppers became the most poverty stricken of all elements in the population. Cotton growing was a sick industry. With depression prevailing throughout the cotton belt in the post–World War I years, leaders of the cotton industry sought government aid to reduce soil losses, eliminate the boll weevil, and raise the price of cotton by subsidizing its sale abroad, but there were few to speak for the croppers, white or black.

In the newer states of the upper Mississippi Valley, especially on the better prairie soils, tenancy began to appear during the first generation of development. Contributing to the emergence of tenancy was the public land policy of permitting, and indeed encouraging, large speculative purchases, which had the effect of making land more expensive to those who used it. Pioneer settlers had to begin their farm operations heavily in debt for the land itself just when they needed all their capital to erect their cabins, fence their cultivated land, purchase livestock and farm machinery, and carry themselves for a year or more until their farming began to pay.

Tenancy data, first collected in 1880, startled many Americans, who had assumed that the public land

system with its free homesteads was making come true Thomas Jefferson's dream of a nation of farm owners. Instead, it appeared that in the richest of the prairie counties of Indiana and Illinois, from one-third to one-half of all the farms were operated by tenants. Furthermore, the statistics revealed that most blacks had lost the gains of emancipation. As sharecroppers they were tied to their allotments, with little hope of improving their condition. Shocked by the publication of the data on farm tenancy, a group of land reformers succeeded in inducing Congress to ban alien ownership of land, to enforce the forfeiture of unearned railroad land grants, to limit individual acquisition of public lands to 320 acres, and to repeal or correct laws that were so misused as to permit capitalists to enter land through the use of dummy entrymen.

Land economists in the agricultural colleges and the U.S. Department of Agriculture continued to look on tenancy as an unavoidable—and, in fact, benevolent—development, since it made for easy transfer of ownership of farms within families from father to son. The Bureau of the Census was persuaded in 1930 to collect data showing family relationship between tenants and owners. The results showed that for the entire country 20 percent of the tenants were related to the landlords, but that in the upper Mississippi Valley the range was between 28 and 37 percent. In counties where permanent landlordism was firmly entrenched, the figure was as low as 19 percent. From these data it was deduced that over the years many tenant sons of owners would climb the ladder to ownership. Furthermore, it was argued that interest on the capital invested in the land and property taxes were such heavy burdens that tenants were actually "glad to have a landlord to furnish a farm, keep buildings in repair, [and] assume responsibility for a considerable part of current cash expenses." None of these arguments explains away the obvious existence of permanent tenancy or the fact that tenants on the whole do not make as responsible farmers as owner-operators and that tenants strive to become ·owners. The Great Depression, following a decade of nearly disastrous farm prices, revealed that the agricultural ladder to farm ownership was working in reverse, that owners were slipping down into the ranks of tenants and even to farm laborers. Concern was expressed for the preservation of single-family farm ownership, as conducive to the preservation and improvement of the fertility of land and the maintenance of improvements.

Congress aggravated the condition of the tenants by the crop-reduction program of the Agricultural Adjustment Act of 1933, for although this program arranged for benefit payments to be made to landlords, it did not require the landlords to share these benefits with their tenants. Thousands of sharecroppers were dismissed by their landlords, who not only refused to divide the payments with them but also decided that on the reduced acreage they were no longer needed. The plight of the croppers led to the creation of the Southern Tenant Farmers Union and a demand for government assistance to aid tenants to buy small tracts. This in turn led to the adoption of the Bankhead-Jones Farm Tenant Act of 1937, which provided moderate funds for low-cost government loans to help tenants in purchasing land and getting started as independent proprietors; but southern opposition to a program that offered help to blacks dried up the funds.

With technological changes in agriculture, including the perfection of the cotton picker, the sharecropper was no longer essential and level land became a major advantage. Cotton growing began to be centered increasingly in Texas, Mississippi, Arkansas, and California, where cotton was produced on large farms. Since the crop control program of the original Agricultural Adjustment Administration and later measures for controlling the production of basic agricultural commodities had made many allotments too small to warrant the use of modern machinery, well-capitalized farmers and corporation farms bought adjoining farms to increase the acreage of their crops. Technology and the crop control program combined with other government boons, particularly irrigation projects, to bring about a rapid increase in the average size of farms and to eliminate thousands of farm families from rural life. Many farmers elected to go to the cities, where during the labor shortage of 1942–57, high wages were available in industrial jobs. The number of farms fell from 6,288,646 in 1930 to 2,730,000 in 1970, and the average size of farms expanded from 156.9 acres in 1930 to 351.6 acres in 1964. Tenancy declined from 42.4 percent in 1930 to 17.1 percent in 1964. However, 11 percent of the farmers who owned land in 1930 and 24.8 percent of those who owned land in 1964 were also renting additional tracts of land. The small-scale, part-time, or diversified farmer was being eliminated. Corporation farming was moving into the rural scene in what some feared was an alarming way, although some of the newer corporate farm experiments proved unprofitable and were quickly abandoned.

In the dryer regions of the West, water rights—whether they depended on adjacent streams, distant mountain reservoirs, or underground sources—were essential for successful farming. Land in the San Joaquin and Imperial valleys of California, which has water rights, is highly productive and valuable, whereas land in the Owens Valley, which is equally susceptible to irrigation, is mostly desert because the available water has been appropriated by Los Angeles. It is the ownership of water rights that most affects land values in the Far West.

State policies have dominated the water question, but the federal government has dealt with mineral rights. The United States has experimented with reserving the mineral rights from lands it was alienating. In 1862 and 1864 it retained ownership of all minerals other than coal and iron from lands thereafter granted to railroads. In Theodore Roosevelt's administration many millions of acres of public lands were withdrawn from all forms of entry, because they were suspected of containing valuable minerals. In 1910 and 1914 homesteading was allowed on these withdrawn lands, but subsurface rights were retained by the government. Thus, in rural areas a complex of tenures was being created that boded ill for the future, when coal or other minerals would begin to be extracted from farmland on which a lifetime of human labor had already been expended to make it productive. There then arises the question of who is responsible for the damage done to operating farms by strip mining.

Urban tenures did not escape this complexity, as witness the drilling for oil and gas in Oklahoma City and in Long Beach, Calif. Also, in larger cities owners of desirable business locations may lease the bare site at a "ground rent" for long periods, ranging from twenty to ninety-nine years. At the end of the leasing period, ground and buildings revert to the owner of the fee unless some provision is included in the contract for compensation for the improvements. An analysis of 313 long-term leases in Detroit showed that 307 gave the buildings and improvements free to the lessor when the lease expired, while six called for some payment by the lessor. Three parties are involved in ownership and use: the fee owner of the ground; the lessee of the ground, who might or might not own the buildings on it; and the tenants renting space therein. A fourth type came into existence with the sale of the air rights over railroads, which may have great value in high-rental areas. One of the biggest examples of a ground-rent lease was that of John D. Rockefeller, Jr. He leased the ground on which he built Rockefeller Center from Columbia University for an annual payment of $3.3 million.

[Murray R. Benedict, *Farm Policies of the United States, 1790–1950;* Marshall Harris, *Origins of Land Tenure System in the United States;* Land Planning Committee to the National Resources Board, "Farm Tenancy in the United States," *Certain Aspects of Land Problems and Government Land Policies*.]

PAUL W. GATES

LAND TITLES. In the United States land titles are called, in the terminology of English law, "allodial" or "fee simple," which terms have come to be used synonymously in the United States. "Allodial" means free of rent or services demanded by some lord or other claimant, leaving the exclusive right to land, or real estate, in the hands of an owner, subject only to the demands of the state or to the demands of some third party to which the right of eminent domain has been granted. "Fee simple," used in contrast to "fee tail," means free of any condition or limitation imposed respecting the exclusive right to real property, exclusive ownership limited only as noted in the definition of "allodial."

Titles as recognized in the English-speaking world are required to go back to grants made by the state, and, to be perfect, must show that at no time, no matter how remote, has any claim been left unsatisfied or unacknowledged. Names must be meticulously correct and all formally attested by notaries.

The title must start with a grant, or, in case of direct conveyance of title to an individual, with a patent. A patent is in every respect a deed, giving the recipient full fee-simple ownership. Where a grant, usually of a larger tract, is made to a company, such as a colonizing company or a railroad, the company comes into possession of the land in fee simple and can therefore sell, passing all rights possessed on to the buyer.

This type of title is found in all parts of the country that at any time belonged to the federal government as a part of the public domain, about half the whole area of the country. In the thirteen original states the land systems varied. In many colonies the old English tradition prevailed under which it was assumed that all land titles were vested in the crown. Thus the rulers of the 17th century granted land to colonies, to colonizing companies, and to individuals. In general the colonial authorities were given the right to grant land to individuals. Thus the title came from the king to the colony, and from the colony to a town, or land company, and from the town or company to the individual. In several colonies the right of primogeniture prevailed, but it had disappeared almost entirely before 1800.

In the case of settlement on land before it became U.S. territory, as with the Florida and Louisiana purchases and the Mexican cession, an agreement was made to the effect that bona fide settlers should be respected in their titles. In the Spanish territory of the Southwest the Spanish grants were lavish and vague, and although the titles to these lands are now on a par with other titles of the country, they became such through court action, involving, in many cases, much litigation, some of which was not settled until the 20th century (*see* Land Grants, Spanish and Mexican).

The most unfortunate feature of U.S. land titles is the insistence, supported by the legal profession and court decisions, of the requirement of a complete schedule of all transfers, called an abstract of title, showing all transfers from the beginning to date. The result has been in numerous cases that certain small tracts of land, usually pieces split off from larger tracts, are not worth the cost of the abstracts. A way out of this difficulty is provided in the Torrens system, involving the registration of titles and a state guarantee of their validity. It is used in several states on a voluntary basis but has not made great progress. It has come into use to a considerable extent in England and other parts of Europe. In the United States the federal government grants the title in the first place, county governments keep records of transfers, but it is left to the individuals to keep such titles valid and correct.

[Jacques Dumas, *Registering Titles to Land;* L. C. Gray, *History of Agriculture in Southern United States to 1860;* Edward L. McKenna, *State Insurance of Land Titles in the United States*.]

BENJAMIN HORACE HIBBARD

LANE V. OREGON, 4 Wallace 71 (1869), a case in which the U.S. Supreme Court ruled that the Legal Tender Act of 1862 could not interfere with state taxation. Under the Constitution the state has its own government and controls the problems pertaining to taxation. It was a victory for states' rights and strict construction.

[J. W. Ellison, "The Currency Question on the Pacific Coast During the Civil War," *Mississippi Valley Historical Review* (June 1929).]

J. W. ELLISON

LANGLEY AERONAUTICAL LABORATORY. Although the United States is credited with the invention of the world's first airplane in 1903, at the opening of World War I in 1914 very little fundamental aerodynamic research was being conducted in the United States. In 1915, primarily through the efforts of Charles D. Walcott, secretary of the Smithsonian Institution, Congress established the National Advisory Committee for Aeronautics (NACA). This committee, containing unpaid members from various governmental and nongovernmental areas interested in aviation, was made responsible for overcoming the deficiency. Within two years, construction began on the Langley Memorial Aeronautical Laboratory (renamed Langley Aeronautical Laboratory in 1948 and Langley Research Center in 1958) near Hampton, Va. The laboratory officially opened on June 11, 1920.

Laboratory personnel, led by Director Henry J. E. Reid for thirty-four years, centered most of their efforts on fundamental aspects of aeronautical research. With a staff numbering less than 300 professionals until World War II, the Langley researchers investigated airfoil shapes, propulsion systems and placement, materials for use in airplane construction, landing gears, structures, and aircraft instrumentation. The parent organization, NACA, published the results of this research in the form of technical reports, available to both military aviation branches and civilian aircraft companies.

Also, laboratory personnel over the years designed and constructed many innovative research tools, the most important of which was a series of wind tunnels, including a wind tunnel unaffected by the scaled-down size of an airplane model, a tunnel for the investigation of spinning problems, and a tunnel large enough to allow testing of a full-size airplane. These innovations significantly increased the safety of testing; radical design changes could be investigated without endangering the life of a test pilot.

During World War II, fundamental research at Langley was reduced while laboratory engineers carried out a series of "clean-up" tests on military aircraft. Slight design changes increased the maximum velocity and overall efficiency of the airplanes employed by the armed services. Near the end of the war, laboratory engineers began a joint venture with the Army Air Service and the navy that resulted in the development of a research airplane known as the X-1, which, on Oct. 14, 1947, became the first aircraft to achieve level flight faster than the speed of sound.

After World War II, Langley engineers, while maintaining their traditional interest in fundamental research in aerodynamics, played a major role in the U.S. space program and eventually became one of the many installations of the National Aeronautics and Space Administration.

Langley engineers have won many awards over the years. The Collier Trophy, emblematic of superior achievement in aviation development, was first awarded to Langley in 1930 for research headed by Fred E. Weick resulting in the development of a cowling for an air-cooled airplane engine. In addition to winning the Collier Trophy four more times, Langley researchers won most other major scientific awards at one time or another. Virtually every airplane flown in America is in part based on research originally conducted at the Langley Laboratory.

[G. F. Gray, *Frontiers of Flight: The Story of NACA Research.*]

MICHAEL D. KELLER

LANSING-ISHII AGREEMENT was concluded by an exchange of notes between Robert Lansing, U.S. secretary of state, and Viscount Kikujiro Ishii, head of a Japanese special mission to the United States, on Nov. 2, 1917. Its ostensible purpose was to reconcile conflicting points in American and Japanese policy in the Far East as a measure of cooperation in World War I, but Japan also undertook to win from the United States what Ishii termed Japan's "paramount interest" in China. Lansing opposed this move, and on Oct. 31 he and Ishii put Lansing's interpretation of Japan's "special interests" in a secret protocol, which stated that "The Governments of Japan and the United States will not take advantage of the present conditions [World War I] to seek special rights or privileges in China which would abridge the rights of the subjects or citizens of other friendly states." The secret protocol was not made public until 1935. Two days later, on Nov. 2, in their exchange of notes the men publicly expressed the two governments' reaffirmation of the Open Door policy and of the territorial integrity of China. Ambiguously, the notes also included a statement of U.S. recognition that Japan had "special interests in China, particularly in the part to which her possessions are contiguous." Acting as if the secret protocol did not exist, Ishii subsequently insisted that the "special interests" clause in the agreement implied definite acknowledgment of Japan's special position in Manchuria. Ishii's interpretation was generally accepted in the Far East, and the agreement was widely condemned in China as a betrayal of the principles of the Open Door. Without the secret protocol the Lansing-Ishii agreement seemed to nullify the Open Door and China's independence, but the agreement served as a temporary public concession to

Japan. Its ambiguity was recognized at the time of the Washington Conference of 1921–22, and on Mar. 30, 1923, a further exchange of notes between the American and Japanese governments declared that ''in the light of the understanding arrived at by the Washington Conference,'' the correspondence between Lansing and Ishii would be considered cancelled and ''of no further force or effect.''

[K. Ishii, *Diplomatic Commentaries;* Robert Lansing, *War Memoirs.*]

FOSTER RHEA DOUGLAS

LAOS, INTERVENTION IN (1954–74). In 1954, at an international conference at Geneva under UN auspices, the former French colony of Indochina was partitioned, and a unified, independent Laos was established. The government of Laos was to encompass all political factions, including the Communist Pathet Lao. By August 1956 the government of Laotian Prime Minister Souvanna Phouma had reached agreement with the Pathet Lao for a coalition government and a neutralist foreign policy. American policymakers, however, opposed a coalition government and a neutralist policy. In an effort to change the direction of Laotian policy, the United States periodically suspended aid to the government but, as this seemed counterproductive, increasingly turned to covert intervention in Laotian political affairs. U.S. action was motivated by a commitment to the containment of communism and a belief that if one country fell to the Communists, another and then another would also fall, the so-called domino theory.

Following Communist successes in the May 1958 elections, the United States began to aid various anti-Communist political groups, and thus fractured the non-Communist elements into right and neutralist factions, provoking more political instability. After 1958, however, the United States began to direct its support to right-wing elements within the Laotian army. Army support was necessary for the survival of the Laotian government, and since the army was dependent on U.S. aid, it increasingly reflected American opposition to neutralism and communism, making continued coalition government impossible.

When civil war began in September 1960, the United States channeled its aid to right-wing army leaders rather than to Souvanna Phouma. As a consequence he opened diplomatic relations with the Soviet Union and moved to bring the Pathet Lao into the government. American activity seemed to be undermining its policy goals, but the administration of President John F. Kennedy looked with some favor

on the neutralization of Laos and relaxed pressure on Souvanna Phouma. In July 1962 the Pathet Lao, the rightists, and the neutralists agreed to a government of national union and a neutralist foreign policy. Unable to agree on military matters, however, the coalition broke up in April 1963. Souvanna then asked for, and received, U.S. help against the military operations of the Pathet Lao.

Beginning in 1964, American policy in Laos was linked with, but subordinated to, events in Vietnam. U.S. intervention increased in degree and in kind through the training of Meo tribesmen for guerrilla activity (40,000 by 1970) and the introduction of Thai mercenaries (21,400 in Laos by 1972) and through the development of a clandestine army independent of the regular Laotian army, to fight the Communist forces in Laos without the commitment of American ground combat troops. No U.S. ground combat troops were used in Laos, although American military personnel received hazardous-duty pay, but for the next seven years the United States fought a secret war in Laos, supporting ground troops and bombing the Ho Chi Minh Trail and Communist positions in northern Laos.

The secret war diminished with the one in Vietnam (except that the early bombing pauses in Vietnam were marked by increases in the air war over Laos). In February 1974 a new Laotian coalition government was formed. All foreign troops were ordered from Laos; as had been the case in 1956, the coalition included the Communists and favored a neutralist foreign policy. Following the final Communist victory in South Vietnam, the influence of Laotian neutralists and Communists increased. In the spring of 1975 they forced the withdrawal of the administrators of the American aid program and a further reduction in American influence in Laos.

[Charles A. Stevenson, *The End of Nowhere: American Policy Toward Laos Since 1954,* and *United States–Vietnam Relations, 1945–67.*]

PHILIP W. WARKEN

LA POINTE, TREATY OF (Oct. 5, 1842), provided for the cession by the Chippewa to the United States of the western half of the upper peninsula of Michigan and a large tract in northern Wisconsin, extending westward to Minnesota. The cession opened the rich mineral deposits of the Lake Superior region to white exploitation, and the settlement and development of the copper country was at once begun.

M. M. QUAIFE

LAPWAI INDIAN COUNCIL. *See* **Nez Perce War.**

LAPWAI MISSION was established in November 1836, by the Rev. and Mrs. Henry Harmon Spalding, co-workers of the physician-missionary Marcus Whitman, at a site eleven miles above Lewiston, Idaho, where the Lapwai Creek empties into the Clearwater River. There Spalding had the first white home, church, school, flour mill, sawmill, blacksmith shop, and loom in what is now Idaho. In 1839 the mission secured a printing press from Hawaii and sent it to Lapwai, the first press in the Pacific Northwest. The mission was closed after the murder of Whitman and twelve of his companions by Indians in 1847. In 1871 the Presbyterian Church resumed the work.

[Nard Jones, *The Great Command: The Story of Marcus and Narcissa Whitman and the Oregon Country Pioneers.*]
CORNELIUS JAMES BROSNAN

LARAMIE, FORT, was established in June 1834, by William Sublette and Robert Campbell, fur traders who had come to Wyoming from St. Louis, Mo. The first structure, built of logs, was named Fort William for the senior founder. Located near the junction of the Laramie and North Platte rivers, in the land of the Sioux and Cheyenne, it became the trade center for a large area, serving white trappers and Indians alike. The American Fur Company purchased the fort in 1836. They replaced the log stockade with adobe walls in 1841 and christened the structure Fort John, but the name did not take; ''Fort Laramie'' supplanted it.

First missionaries to Oregon and earliest overland emigrants used this fort, on the Oregon Trail, as a supply and refitting depot. The growing emigrant tide, greatly augmented by the goldseekers of 1849, demanded protection from Indians. The government purchased the post from the trading company on June 26, 1849, for $4,000 and converted it into a military fort. New wooden and adobe buildings were erected. It became the great way station on the principal road to the Far West. The Grattan and the Harney incidents near the fort in 1854 and 1856 foreshadowed the general Indian war that followed, and Fort Laramie became headquarters for the military campaigns. When the Indians were subdued and placed on reservations, need for the fort ended. It was abandoned Apr. 20, 1890. The site of the post and the few surviving buildings were proclaimed a national monument on July 16, 1938. In April 1960 it became a national historic site.

[L. R. Hafen and F. M. Young, *Fort Laramie and the Pageant of the West, 1834–1890.*]
LeRoy R. HAFEN

LARAMIE, FORT, TREATY OF (1851). In 1849 Thomas Fitzpatrick, first Indian agent to the tribes of the upper Platte and Arkansas, requested authorization and funds for a general treaty with his wards. In February 1851, Congress responded with a $100,000 appropriation. Couriers were sent to the Indians appointing a council for Sept. 1 at Fort Laramie in Wyoming. Sioux, Cheyenne, Arapaho, and Shoshone were the principal tribes that gathered, forming perhaps the largest Indian council ever assembled in the West. For twenty days negotiations continued, being prolonged to await arrival of the wagon train of presents. Indian feasts and demonstrations occurred daily. Companies of soldiers placed between tribes hereditarily hostile to one another averted conflict. The treaty as signed provided for peace, for territorial boundaries for individual tribes, for a $50,000 annuity to the Indians, and permitted establishment of forts and roads in the Indian country. The treaty was amended and approved by the U.S. Senate but never ratified by the Indians.

[L. R. Hafen and W. J. Ghent, *Broken Hand, The Life of Thomas Fitzpatrick.*]
LeRoy R. HAFEN

LARAMIE, FORT, TREATY OF (1868). In 1866 the Sioux had agreed to permit the opening of the Bozeman Trail to Montana. Before negotiations were completed, Col. Henry B. Carrington arrived with troops and began erection of forts on the new road. The Indians objected, attacks began, and war ensued (*see* Red Cloud's War). Peace advocates in the East now won ascendancy with the slogan ''cheaper to feed than to fight the Indians.'' The government changed policy and in 1867 sent peace commissioners, but the hostile Indians refused to negotiate while the new forts remained. The commissioners came again in April 1868, acceded to Indian demands, and drafted a treaty. They agreed to withdraw the Bozeman Trail forts and to recognize the country north of the North Platte and east of the Big Horn Mountains in northern Wyoming as unceded Indian territory in which no whites might settle. All that part of present South Dakota west of the Missouri River was formed into a Sioux reservation. To induce Indians to settle upon it, the government agreed to construct an agency building, a schoolhouse, a sawmill, a gristmill, and other facilities on the Missouri River and to furnish food supplies for four years and clothing for thirty years. The Indians promised to refrain from capturing and killing whites and attacking coaches and wagon trains and to withdraw all opposition to the construction of railroads being built across the Plains. Some of the Indians signed the treaty in April, but Red Cloud and the distrusting bands refused to sign until November, after the hated forts in the Powder River country had been abandoned. With these concessions made and with annuities provided, generally peaceful relations prevailed until gold discoveries in the Black Hills brought a new white tide into Dakota and precipitated the wars of the mid-1870's.

[L. R. Hafen and F. M. Young, *Fort Laramie and the Pageant of the West, 1834–1890;* George E. Hyde, *Red Cloud's Folks.*]

LeRoy R. Hafen

LARNED, FORT, was established on the Pawnee fork of the Arkansas River, in Kansas, Oct. 22, 1859. It was named for Col. B. F. Larned, then paymaster-general of the U.S. Army. Built first of adobe, it was later reconstructed of stone. Gen. Winfield Scott Hancock used it as a base for his expedition against the Cheyenne in 1867, and troops operated from it in the Dull Knife campaign of 1878. The post was abandoned in the latter year.

Paul I. Wellman

LA SALLE, EXPLORATIONS OF. Until New France became a royal colony in 1663, its development was slow. Following this change, a period of marked progress set in. The Iroquois were subdued, industry and commerce were fostered, and geographical expansion was vigorously prosecuted.

Foremost in promoting this renaissance of New France were Intendant Jean Talon and Gov. Louis de Buade, Comte de Frontenac. Among the great explorers of the period, the most notable was Robert Cavelier, Sieur de La Salle, who came to Canada in 1666 and began near Montreal the development of a seigniory. Soon, however, his active mind became absorbed in the possibilities inherent in the Indian trade, and the coming of Frontenac as governor in 1672 offered him an opportunity to exploit them.

Frontenac was an imperialist, and the fur trade offered the prospect of recouping his ruined fortune. In 1673 he founded Fort Frontenac on the site of present-day Kingston, Ontario, in the Iroquois country, and the next year sent La Salle to France to enlighten Louis XIV concerning his expansionist designs. The king approved his plans, and La Salle returned with a patent of nobility for himself and the grant of Fort Frontenac as a seigniory.

In 1677 La Salle again went to France to seek royal approval of a far greater design: he desired to establish a colony in the country south of the Great Lakes and to this end desired a trade monopoly of the region to be developed and authority to build forts and govern it. The king was willing to approve all but the idea of colonizing, and in 1678 La Salle was back in New France making preparations for the actual invasion of the West, to be launched the following season. A small vessel, the *Griffon,* was built above Niagara, and in August 1679, La Salle set sail for Green Bay. From there the *Griffon* was sent back to Niagara, laden with furs, while La Salle himself journeyed southward by canoe around Lake Michigan to the mouth of the Saint Joseph River.

There he tarried until December, building Fort Miami and awaiting the return of the *Griffon,* which had vanished. At length he ascended the Saint Joseph to South Bend, Ind., where he crossed to the Kankakee and descended that stream and the Illinois to Lake Peoria, where he built Fort Crèvecoeur and a vessel in which to descend the Mississippi. He also dispatched Franciscan missionary Louis Hennepin and two companions to explore the upper Mississippi, while he himself set out in midwinter for distant Fort Frontenac to procure badly needed supplies.

Iroquois raids and other obstacles were encountered, but La Salle doggedly fought on, and the close of 1681 found him again at Fort Miami ready to renew his push for the sea. Descending the Illinois, he reached the Mississippi on Feb. 2, 1682, and on Apr. 9 was at the Gulf of Mexico, where with fitting ceremony he formally claimed the entire Mississippi Valley for his king and named it Louisiana.

The way to Mexico was open, and the realization of his plans seemed assured, when Frontenac was replaced by a new governor who proved a bitter enemy of La Salle. Facing utter ruin, he again went to France to appeal to his monarch in person. His requests were approved, and in 1684 he sailed for the Gulf of Mexico, equipped with men and means to establish a post on the lower Mississippi to serve as the southern outlet of his colony. He was unable to find the river's mouth, however, and the colonists were landed on the coast of Texas, where most of them eventually perished (see Saint Louis of Texas; La Salle, Spanish Searches for). La Salle himself was murdered by mutineers in 1687 while still trying to find the Mississippi and establish contact with his post in Illinois. Although his life closed in seeming failure, his dream survived, and in the following century Louisiana became the fairest portion of New France.

[Pierre Margry, Découvertes et Établissements des Français dans l'ouest et dans le sud de l'Amérique Septentrionale; Francis Parkman, The Discovery of the Great West.]

M. M. QUAIFE

LA SALLE, SPANISH SEARCHES FOR. The alarm felt by the Spaniards over La Salle's intrusion in the Gulf of Mexico was revealed by the intensity of their search for his colony. Between 1685 and 1688 five maritime expeditions combed the Gulf coast, but failed to find the French settlement in Texas. By land, one expedition searched westward from Florida; four expeditions, led by Alonso De Leon, went northeastward from Mexico; and a number of minor searches were instituted by provincial officials. On his fourth expedition De Leon, in 1689, found the remains of La Salle's colony, three months after it had been destroyed by Indians.

[Carlos E. Castañeda, The Finding of Texas.]

C. T. NEU

LAS ANIMAS LAND GRANT. On Dec. 9, 1843, the Mexican government granted to Cornelio Vigil and Ceran Saint Vrain a tract of 4 million acres lying southwesterly from the Arkansas River to the Sangre de Cristo Mountains with the valleys of the Huerfano and the Purgatoire (Animas) rivers as side lines. It was one of the many large grants made by Mexico to settle and protect the border. On June 21, 1860, Congress confirmed only 97,651 acres of this grant on the ground that a grant of more than eleven square leagues to one individual was illegal under Mexican law. Dissatisfied claimants appealed unsuccessfully to a special court of private land claims from 1891 until 1904 and finally to the U.S. Supreme Court.

[L. R. Hafen, "Mexican Land Grants in Colorado," Colorado Magazine (May 1927).]

PERCY S. FRITZ

LASSEN'S TRADING POST AND RANCH, near the mouth of Deer Creek in northeastern California,

stood at the head of Sacramento Valley and was an important center both in early exploration and in the gold rush. It was named after Peter Lassen, an early pioneer. John Charles Frémont was using the ranch as headquarters for exploring the region when war was declared against Mexico in May 1846.

[F. S. Dellenbaugh, Frémont and '49.]

CARL L. CANNON

LAST ISLAND CATASTROPHE. Last Island, in the Gulf of Mexico opposite the mouth of Bayou Lafourche, which had become a favorite summer resort for Louisiana families who wished to escape the intense heat of the interior, was devastated by a tropical hurricane on Sunday, Aug. 10, 1856. More than 100 persons perished.

[Walter Prichard, ed., "The Last Island Disaster of August 10, 1856," Louisiana Historical Quarterly, vol. 20.]

WALTER PRICHARD

LATIN AMERICA, U.S. RELATIONS WITH. With the beginning of the Latin-American wars for independence in 1810, leaders of the newly formed governments sought U.S. recognition and support. President James Madison issued a neutrality proclamation on Sept. 1, 1815, that had the effect of conceding belligerency rights to the rebellious colonies, with whom many in the United States strongly sympathized; but the American government withheld diplomatic recognition from any of the new countries until after a treaty with Spain for U.S. annexation of Florida had been ratified and the trend of military events in South America pointed clearly to victory for the independence forces. The first new nation accorded diplomatic recognition by the United States was Colombia in June 1822, and similar action was soon taken with respect to Mexico, the Federation of Central America, Brazil, Chile, the United Provinces of La Plata, and Peru. United States opposition to any effort on the part of European powers to reestablish colonial rule was articulated in the Monroe Doctrine in 1823, and the concept was gradually extended to signify that the American government viewed the entire Western Hemisphere as an area of special concern in its foreign policy.

Early efforts to initiate general discourse between the American republics in the interest of mutual assistance and support came to naught. Simón Bolívar convened a conference at Panama in 1826, but U.S. delegates did not arrive and resolutions adopted by delegates of the four participating states were never ratified. With final defeat of the Spanish army in Upper Peru (now Bolivia), threat of further European impositions subsided. Soon U.S. relationships with Latin America focused on issues deriving from national expansion across the North American continent and establishment of American economic and military hegemony in the Caribbean region. War with Mexico in 1846–48 ended with that country ceding its extensive northern territories to the United States, and various gestures were made toward the possible annexation of Cuba and the Dominican Republic. A diplomatic conflict with Great Britain over control of a canal route across the Central American isthmus resulted in eventual British withdrawal from a dominant role in the Caribbean and cleared the way for the United States to construct a canal at Panama after efforts by a French company to do so under a concession from the Colombian government failed. The preeminence of the United States in the Caribbean area was firmly established by the Spanish-American War in 1898–99, which concluded with the annexation of Puerto Rico and the creation of a protectorate status over a nominally independent Cuba.

North American investments and trade became important in Mexico and Cuba in the latter part of the 19th century, but commercial relationships with the rest of Latin America remained of minor importance. European capital and trade were predominant in South America, and commercial and intellectual leaders of the southern continent continued to look to Europe and to travel there for business and study.

The first important step toward closer relations with the Latin-American republics as a group was initiated by Secretary of State James G. Blaine. In 1889, at the beginning of Benjamin Harrison's administration, Blaine presided over the First International Conference of American States convened in Washington, D.C., by invitation of the United States. Blaine's chief purpose in calling the conference was to promote trade, but the Latin-American delegates came with political objectives in mind, such as the mutual guarantee of the sovereignty of small and weak states. An adopted resolution supporting compulsory arbitration of pecuniary claims was never ratified, and about the only lasting result of the conference was the creation in Washington of a Commercial Bureau of American Republics, which later became the Pan American Union.

Subsequent inter-American conferences at Mexico City in 1901–02, Rio de Janeiro in 1906, and Buenos Aires in 1910 accomplished little apart from the adop-

tion of resolutions of commercial significance, many of which were never ratified by the signatory governments. A growing hostility toward the American government was manifest as early as the second conference, reflecting in part a strong resentment of its increasingly interventionist role in the affairs of neighboring republics in the Caribbean area. Argentine statesmen were the most articulate spokesmen for Latin-American opposition to U.S. policies and actions. Although the Pan American Union was created by resolution of the Buenos Aires meeting in 1910, the location of its headquarters in Washington and the chairing of its governing board by the U.S. secretary of state suggested all too obviously that Pan-Americanism was largely an invention of the United States designed to further American commercial and political interests.

The United States began to show an increased interest in the internal affairs of the Caribbean and Central American republics soon after the Spanish-American War. Once the American government decided to build the Panama Canal, security of the waterway and its approaches made it imperative that states in the vicinity not be permitted to fall under the domination of a potentially hostile power. In accordance with Theodore Roosevelt's corollary to the Monroe Doctrine, the United States undertook to eliminate political disorder and financial mismanagement in several states whose internal difficulties exposed them repeatedly to European intervention. To restore order and assure that governments met their international obligations, the American government sent military forces into Cuba frequently, into Haiti in 1915, into the Dominican Republic in 1916, and into Nicaragua in 1912 and repeatedly in 1926–27. In 1914 and in 1916, during Mexico's turbulent revolution, the United States intervened militarily in that country. These actions, coming on the heels of Roosevelt's forceful separation of Panama and its canal route from Colombia, created fear and distrust of American intentions.

World War I for a time distracted attention from Latin-American differences with the United States and brought about improved political relationships as well as a marked increase in commercial activity. North American capital discovered new opportunities in Central and South American mines, railroads, and public utilities, and the pace of investment quickened during the 1920's. A number of governments borrowed heavily from American banks to undertake public improvements. Opposition to the interventionist policy of the United States continued to be expressed at the fifth and sixth inter-American conferences, however. The sixth meeting, held at Havana in 1928, unleashed a wave of acrimonious attack on American policies, particularly its intervention in Nicaragua. American quarantine of Argentine beef because of hoof-and-mouth disease caused further complaint.

U.S. policy began to change during the administration of President Herbert Hoover, and he withdrew the remaining marines from Nicaragua just before the end of his term in 1933. He also took steps to end the American military presence in Haiti, which had continued since the 1915 intervention. President Franklin D. Roosevelt specifically repudiated intervention, announcing instead the Good Neighbor policy in his inaugural address. Secretary of State Cordell Hull, at the seventh inter-American conference in Montevideo in 1933, signed a convention that specifically forbade intervention by any state in the external or internal affairs of another. Subsequently, the United States terminated its military protectorates over Cuba and Panama.

Latin-American relations with the United States rapidly improved, and at a special conference at Buenos Aires in 1936 and the eighth inter-American conference at Lima in 1938 a far more cordial atmosphere prevailed. Both conferences, the first of which was attended by Roosevelt, were used to strengthen peacekeeping machinery in the hemisphere. Steps to lower trade barriers through reciprocal agreements were proposed by the United States and welcomed by the other countries, but implementation proved a slow process.

When World War II broke out in Europe, the foreign ministers of the American republics held meetings to formulate hemispheric defense policy and forestall the spread of Axis influence in the Americas. After Japan's attack on Pearl Harbor, a meeting at Rio de Janeiro in January 1942 recommended that the American governments break off diplomatic relations with the Axis powers. All did so promptly except Chile and Argentina. Eventually, both countries took the recommended step, but Argentina was ruled by a pro-Axis government until the end of the war and the rupture of relations constituted a meaningless gesture that only masked continued Argentine sympathy for the German Nazi regime. In contrast, Brazil sent an expeditionary force to join in the Italian campaign, where it saw active combat, and Mexico sent an air squadron to the Pacific theater.

Plans for strengthening the inter-American system were formulated at a conference held at Mexico City in 1945. These resulted in the Inter-American Treaty of Reciprocal Assistance signed at a conference at Rio de Janeiro in 1947 and in the creation of the Organization of American States (OAS) at the ninth inter-American conference at Bogotá in 1948. The 1947 treaty pledged the signatory countries to aid any American state that became the victim of attack in the Western Hemisphere, and the charter of the OAS created a regional organization within the framework of the newly created United Nations system to promote political, economic, and cultural cooperation among the member states. The "supreme organ" of the OAS was to be the inter-American conference, to meet every five years. Between conferences, major problems were to be dealt with by meetings of the ministers of foreign affairs or by the council of the organization, sitting in Washington with a representative from each state. A number of technical organizations and specialized agencies were to function under the supervision of the OAS, and the Pan American Union became its secretariat. After 1948, the peacekeeping machinery of both the Rio treaty and the council was called upon repeatedly to settle disputes that threatened or had caused armed strife between member states, principally in the Caribbean area.

At the Bogotá conference in 1948, U.S. alarm over the threat of Communist subversion was already manifest. With a left-leaning government in power in Guatemala, the tenth inter-American conference at Caracas in 1954 devoted much of its attention to the efforts of the American government to secure approval of a resolution supporting collective action against any Communist threat. Secretary of State John Foster Dulles was successful, but only after bitter exchanges with the Guatemalan representative, with whom many sympathized, and the conference adjourned under a cloud of renewed resentment against the United States. No subsequent inter-American conference was held. One scheduled for Quito in 1960 was postponed indefinitely. In 1967 an extraordinary conference of the OAS in Buenos Aires approved a reform protocol, which, among other innovations, modified the charter to substitute an annual general assembly for the inter-American conference. The assembly's membership is composed of representatives of the member states.

The leftist Guatemalan government was shortly overthrown by revolution, but with the emergence of a Communist regime in Cuba after Fidel Castro's overthrow of Fulgencio Batista in 1959 and the Soviet Union's subsequent support of the Castro government, the Communist threat became a reality few could question. The United States sought to mobilize support against Castro in meetings of the foreign ministers but encountered widespread opposition. Having broken diplomatic and commercial relations with Cuba, the American government supported an abortive invasion by counterrevolutionary forces in April 1961, but both the effort and its failure further undercut Latin-American sympathy for the U.S. position. Secretary of State Dean Rusk obtained a vote to exclude the Cuban government from participation in the inter-American system in January 1962, but only during and after the Soviet effort to install long-range nuclear missiles in Cuba in October of that year was anything approaching a united front achieved. Before ordering the successful interdiction of weapons delivery on Oct. 23, President John F. Kennedy obtained from the OAS council a resolution demanding Soviet withdrawal from Cuba of all weapons with offensive capability. Subsequently, all Latin-American countries with the exception of Mexico broke diplomatic and commercial relations with the Castro regime.

The United States intervened militarily in the Dominican Republic in April 1965 to prevent what it feared would be a Communist takeover, and OAS support for the action was sought and obtained only after initiation of the invasion. Adverse reaction throughout Latin America was eased by the subsequent arrival of Brazilian military forces, as well as token troops from Costa Rica, Nicaragua, and Honduras, and the placing of a Brazilian general in charge of the "peacekeeping" force. Withdrawal took place after a new election in 1966.

In 1970 a Socialist-Communist government of Marxist ideology was elected in Chile, and it moved rapidly to expropriate the properties of American mining companies and other enterprises. A new Cuba-type crisis was avoided by the Chilean government's continued adherence to constitutional form and by moderation on the part of the United States. The almost complete solidarity in the isolation of Cuba was soon broken by Chile's reestablishment of full diplomatic and commercial relations with Castro's government, and in mid-1972 Peru followed Chile's example. By early 1973 even the American position appeared to be softening when, after President Richard M. Nixon embarked on a policy of détente with the People's Republic of China and the Soviet Union, an agreement between Cuba and the United States to curtail aircraft hijacking was arranged through intermediaries. By early 1975 the effort to maintain Cuba's isolation was virtually dead as

country after country reopened embassies in Havana.

In September 1973 the Chilean armed forces overthrew the Marxist government of President Salvador Allende, who committed suicide rather than surrender. Congressional inquiries in the United States subsequently brought to light U.S. Central Intelligence Agency involvement in financing anti-Communist groups in Chile both prior to and during Allende's rule. Although few Latin-American governments had openly sympathized with the Chilean Marxist regime, this revelation did little to improve the U.S. image in the region.

Both the Nixon administration and that of President Gerald Ford, who succeeded Nixon in the summer of 1974, were criticized by many Latin-American leaders as neglectful of their countries' interests, particularly their economic and development needs. A new American trade law became a lightning rod for attacks upon U.S. policy, and in spite of Secretary of State Henry A. Kissinger's talk of "opening a new dialog" little progress had been made by mid-1975. Furthermore, a seeming impasse in negotiations with Panama over a new canal treaty posed the possibility of new difficulties over that explosive issue.

The American government's program to extend technical aid and economic assistance to the less-developed countries of the world after World War II aroused hopes in Latin America of rapid economic and social progress. Technical and military assistance was provided, but the administration of Dwight D. Eisenhower made clear to Latin-American governments that they would have to look to private American capital to finance their industrialization programs. Loans from the World Bank or the Export-Import Bank might be obtained for suitable projects. This policy proved highly unpopular because Latin-American leaders saw government grants and loans flow from the United States to Asian and Middle Eastern countries more immediately threatened by Communist blandishments and subversion. Even the relatively modest aid program the United States did offer to Latin America seemed to favor pro-American dictatorships rather than countries seeking to couple economic and social development with structural reforms and popular democracy.

In the face of mounting unpopularity throughout Latin America, the American government accepted a proposal from President Juscelino Kubitschek of Brazil for a new effort at closer cooperation, and following a meeting of the foreign ministers of the American republics in Washington in 1958, the Inter-American Development Bank was launched in 1959, with the

United States contributing a significant part of the capital. This move was followed in March 1961 by President Kennedy's proposal for the Alliance for Progress, the charter of which was approved at Punta del Este, Uruguay, in August of the same year. The alliance involved a massive effort to combine national development planning with basic social, educational, land-tenure, and taxation reforms, all of which were to be financed by a strong infusion of public and private capital from abroad and a major effort to stimulate domestic investment in development programs. A special committee of nine was set up under OAS auspices to approve development programs and set loan and other assistance priorities.

In spite of an auspicious beginning and some significant successes, the goals of the alliance proved far more difficult to achieve than its creators had anticipated. Government instability, resistance to social and economic reforms, financing below promised levels by the United States, and vacillation in American aid policy all served to impede progress and to create gradual disillusionment in both the United States and Latin America. A meeting of presidents of the participating countries at Punta del Este in 1967 sought to revive waning enthusiasm; but President Lyndon B. Johnson spoke without the support of Congress, and his colleagues knew it. American attention was focused on other parts of the world. The incoming Nixon administration in 1969 showed no inclination to revive the moribund Alliance for Progress.

The Good Neighbor policy, the emergence of the United States as a world power second to none after World War II, and the Alliance for Progress each contributed to a gradual, but increasingly significant, political, economic, and cultural orientation of Latin America toward the United States. Thousands of Latin-American students choose to pursue their education in the United States rather than Europe, and business and commercial ties have grown steadily closer. On the other hand, opposition to the American government's policies has also increased, stemming in part from a fear of American economic power and military interventionism and, rather paradoxically, from a sense of neglect and the relatively low priority accorded Latin America in American international concerns. A growing sense of national power and cultural autonomy has come to infuse the outlook of such countries as Brazil, Mexico, and Argentina. The sudden and dramatic increase in the price of oil dictated by the Organization of Petroleum Exporting Countries after the Arab-Israeli War of 1973 poured unexpected riches into the coffers of both Venezuela and Ecuador. New discoveries in Mexico gave promise of sharp income increases for that country also, while exploration for new petroleum resources was intensified throughout the hemisphere. By mid-1975 it seemed clear that new centers of power were emerging that could not fail to alter old relationships permanently and affect the American role in the region. The form that the new relationships might take, however, remained obscure.

[Norman A. Bailey, *Latin America in World Politics;* Howard F. Cline, *The United States and Mexico;* John C. Dreier, *The Organization of American States;* Yale H. Ferguson, ed., *Contemporary Inter-American Relations;* Federico G. Gil, *Latin American–United States Relations;* Lincoln A. Gordon, *A New Deal for Latin America: The Alliance for Progress;* Simon G. Hanson, *Dollar Diplomacy Modern Style;* George C. Lodge, *Engines of Change: United States Interests and Revolution in Latin America;* William Manger, ed., *The Alliance for Progress—A Critical Appraisal;* J. Lloyd Mechan, *A Survey of United States–Latin American Relations,* and *The United States and Inter-American Security, 1889–1960;* James Petras et al., "The United States and Latin America," in James Petras, ed., *Latin America: From Dependence to Revolution;* Robert F. Smith, *The United States and Cuba: Business and Diplomacy, 1917–1960;* Víctor L. Urquidi, *The Challenge of Development in Latin America;* U.S. Department of State, *The Story of Inter-American Cooperation: Our Southern Partners.*]

WENDELL G. SCHAEFFER

LATIN-AMERICAN REPUBLICS, RECOGNITION OF. Both the government of the United States and public opinion were openly sympathetic to the cause of Latin-American independence from the beginning of the revolution against Spain in the early years of the 19th century. In 1810, during President James Madison's administration, Joel Poinsett was sent to Buenos Aires and Chile to promote commercial relations with the colonies and to express the friendly feeling of the United States. Other agents and consuls were sent in the following years. Officially the United States was neutral in the war, but private citizens engaged in filibustering and many Latin-American privateers were fitted out in American ports despite official opposition.

The uncertain character of the struggle postponed for some years any serious consideration of diplomatic recognition. In 1817, however, three commissioners were sent to Buenos Aires to investigate the propriety of entering into relations with the government there. They returned with conflicting reports and no action was taken. Later in the same year Rep.

Henry Clay began ardently to advocate recognition in a series of speeches in Congress, chiefly perhaps with the idea of causing embarrassment to the Monroe administration. In 1821 he procured the passage of a resolution in the House of Representatives expressing sympathy with Latin America and a readiness to support the president when he felt that the time for recognition had come.

Meanwhile Monroe and John Quincy Adams, his secretary of state, had proceeded cautiously in the matter, though the president had spoken sympathetically of the Latin-American cause in his message to Congress in 1819. The treaty with Spain for the purchase of Florida, signed Feb. 22, 1819 (*see* Adams-Onís Treaty), was still pending, and the administration did not wish to offend Spain until this matter was finally disposed of by the exchange of ratifications on Feb. 22, 1821. By that time the patriots in South America had won a series of important victories, and later in the same year Mexico proclaimed its independence. Strong Spanish forces still held the greater part of Peru, but the revolution in Spain had made their situation difficult.

On Mar. 8, 1822, Monroe recommended in a message to Congress that the Latin-American republics be recognized. A bill authorizing diplomatic missions to them was signed by the president on May 4, and on June 19 Manuel Torres was formally received by the president as chargé d'affaires from Colombia. In the following months the United States also entered into diplomatic relations with Argentina, Chile, Mexico, Brazil, and Central America.

[W. R. Manning, *Diplomatic Correspondence of the United States Concerning the Independence of the Latin-American Nations;* F. L. Paxson, *The Independence of the South American Republics.*]

DANA G. MUNRO

LATIN-AMERICAN WARS OF INDEPENDENCE
(1808–25). From the beginning of the Latin-American independence movement the government and people of the United States took a keen interest in it. Their interest was centered more on Spanish America than on Brazil, where the movement began late, was of short duration, and ended in the establishment of a monarchy, and where British influence was at all times paramount. Though their interest in the wars of independence rose and fell with developments in Latin America, Europe, and the United States itself, from 1815 to 1825 no other problem in U.S. foreign relations received more sustained attention than this one did. Practically everyone was theoretically in

favor of Latin-American independence; but there was a great divergence of opinion as to whether the United States should do anything to promote it. As early as 1808 President Thomas Jefferson's cabinet asserted that the United States had a common interest with the revolutionists in excluding European influence, commercial as well as political, from the Western Hemisphere. European complications and the War of 1812 prevented the development of the larger policy implicit in this view; but after 1815 Henry Clay made himself its champion in Congress and urged the United States to give open encouragement to the revolutionists.

The supporting arguments were both political and economic: sympathy (on the analogy of the American Revolution) for peoples struggling to be free; interest in spreading the "American system" of liberty and republican government, and the American doctrine of neutral rights over the whole Western Hemisphere to counterbalance the Holy Alliance and England; and interest in destroying the commercial monopoly of the European colonial systems. Important economic benefits were promised the United States: markets for its agricultural produce and manufactures; cargoes for its ships; a larger supply of specie; and facilities for its China trade. Less was said about the considerable profit derived during the war from the munitions trade with the revolutionists and from privateering under their flags. Many Americans (notably John Quincy Adams, secretary of state from 1817 to 1825) were skeptical about most of these political and economic benefits; gave less weight to them than to the danger of European retaliation against any unilateral action by the United States in favor of the revolutionists; and were opposed on principle to the United States engaging in a crusade for democracy in any foreign country whatever. Other obstacles were the territorial interests of the United States in Florida, Texas, and Cuba, and the antislavery measures of some of the new states.

The divergence of views in the United States often cut across party, sectional, and occupational lines, though generally speaking Clay's views seem to have found most support among agrarians of the interior and Adams's among southern planters and eastern merchants engaged in trade with England and the Continent. Monroe and probably most other Americans took a position somewhere between those of Adams and Clay. After 1825 the end of the wars of independence, the lessening of the military threat from Europe, widespread disillusionment about Latin America (sharpened by the successes of the British), and absorption in domestic affairs brought about a long-continued decline of interest on the part of the United States in the southern republics.

[C. C. Griffin, *The United States and the Disruption of the Spanish Empire*; J. F. Rippy, *Rivalry of the United States and Great Britain Over Latin America*; A. P. Whitaker, *The Interest of the United States in Latin America*.]

A. P. WHITAKER

LATIN SCHOOLS, the earliest type of educational institutions set up in the American colonies, grew out of the influence of the Renaissance and were patterned on the Latin schools of England. These schools appeared in all the colonies except Georgia, but reached their greatest growth in New England. An attempt to establish a Latin school in Virginia was made as early as 1621, but the Great Massacre of the following year and the failure of the Virginia Company ended the project. The first successful attempt to establish a Latin school was made in Boston in 1635; it was the principal school in that city for nearly a half century. The purpose of these schools was to prepare boys for college. The Massachusetts law of 1647 requiring a grammar school in every town of fifty families stimulated these schools, which quickly appeared also in neighboring colonies. Latin schools were planned, supported, and managed by the well-to-do. Tuition fees were generally charged, and the curriculum, confined almost entirely to a study of Latin and Greek but which included the study of religion and mathematics, was intended to teach boys to read and write Latin and possibly to speak it. Some of these schools had distinguished teachers. The Latin schools had begun to decline in importance by the middle of the 18th century, when they began to give way to the academies.

[E. P. Cubberley, *Public Education in the United States*; Edgar W. Knight, *Education in the United States*.]

EDGAR W. KNIGHT

LATITUDINARIANS is the name applied to a school of thought in the Church of England in the 18th century that emphasized the fundamental principles of the Christian religion rather than any specific doctrinal position. In America the name has been given to such religious leaders as have not been primarily concerned about the interpretation of a creed and have been liberal in their judgments of those who hold other than standard views.

WILLIAM W. SWEET

LATROBE'S FOLLY, the name given by engineers and the general public to the Thomas Viaduct, the

Baltimore and Ohio Railroad's stone arch bridge over the Patapsco River, near Relay, Md., designed by and constructed under the direction of Benjamin H. Latrobe, Jr., in 1832. His engineering contemporaries insisted that the bridge could not be built, that it would not stand up under its own weight, let alone the weight of the 6-ton locomotives then in service, with their trains. But the viaduct was a complete success, to the extent that a century after its construction 300-ton engines were passing over it in safety.

[Edward Hungerford, *The Story of the Baltimore and Ohio Railroad, 1827–1927*.]

JULIUS H. PARMELEE

LATTER-DAY SAINTS, CHURCH OF JESUS CHRIST OF, more commonly known as **Mormons.** The Mormons are members of an American religious movement that originated in the "burned-over" district of western New York during the Second Great Awakening. The church was founded in 1830 by Joseph Smith, who claimed to have discovered and translated the Book of Mormon on the basis of visions from heaven. After his work was finished, Smith maintained that the golden plates on which the message had been written were taken away into heaven. The Book of Mormon purports to be the history of certain of the lost tribes of Israel that fled to America after the conquest of their homeland. After Christ's Resurrection, these tribes were visited by Him and lived as Christians until, after a series of disasters and wars, they either lost the faith or were destroyed. Within the framework of the history, many of the burning questions of 19th-century evangelicalism, such as the nature of holiness, were raised and settled. The early success of the movement is partially attributable to its ability to provide authoritative solutions to the issues of the day.

After the publication of Smith's initial revelation, the Mormons moved in 1831 to Kirtland, Ohio, where Smith hoped to found an ideal community. Unfortunately, the movement rested its fortunes on a shaky, and possibly illegal, bank that collapsed during the panic of 1837. Some Mormons fled to Missouri, where they quickly became unpopular with the "gentile" (non-Mormon) population. In part, this antagonism was deserved, as the Mormons had boasted that they would soon be in complete political control of the state.

The Mormons next attempted to establish their ideal community in the town of Nauvoo, Ill., a new city said to have been planned by Smith. By 1843, it was the largest town in the state. The Nauvoo period was crucial in the development of Mormon doctrine.

It was during this time that Smith received the revelations that separated Mormonism from other frontier evangelical movements. The most important of these modifications was Smith's vision of the Temple and his elaboration of its sacerdotal system, which bears some relationship to Masonic rites. Smith also came to teach that there was more than one God, that Christ was a separate deity, that the goods and relationships of this life would continue in the next, and that polygamy conformed to the will of God. The rumor that the community was ready to begin to implement this latter revelation, plus gentile resentment of the community's political power, provoked the attack that carried Smith prisoner to Carthage, Ill. He was murdered there by a band of masked gunmen on June 27, 1844.

The death of the community's prophet caused a crisis within the movement, but Brigham Young (1801–77), who had been Smith's second in command and *de facto* leader of the group, was able to reorganize those who remained. He led the survivors on a march across the Great Plains to form the state of Deseret in the valley of the Great Salt Lake. Here, isolated from outside influences, the Mormons were able to build their Zion. Tightly organized by Young, they built an island of prosperity that virtually became an independent nation. After the Mexican War, the Mormons were forced to abjure the practice of polygamy and admit non-Mormons to the territory.

In the 1970's the Mormons were one of the fastest-growing religious groups in the United States, with every Mormon male being obligated to spend at least two years as a missionary. Their influence remains worldwide, and they have churches throughout Europe. Although the Temple at Salt Lake City is still the center of the faith, several new temples are being planned. There were four Mormon denominations in the mid-1970's: Church of Jesus Christ of Latter-Day Saints, the main body, with a membership of approximately 3.3 million; Reorganized Church of Jesus Christ of Latter-Day Saints, 179,763 members; Church of Latter-Day Saints (Bickertonites), 2,439 members; and Church of Christ, 2,000 members.

[Nels Anderson, *Desert Saints: The Mormon Frontier in Utah;* Leonard J. Arrington, *Great Basin Kingdom: An Economic History of the Latter-Day Saints;* William Muelder, *The Mormons in American History;* Brigham Roberts, *A Comprehensive History of the Church of Jesus Christ of Latter-Day Saints;* Richard Vetterli, *Mormonism, Americanism and Politics.*]

GLENN T. MILLER

LAURENS, FORT, on the Tuscarawas River, in northeastern Ohio, was erected in 1778 by Gen. Lachlan McIntosh, to serve as an advance base for an expedition against Detroit. Hostile Indians harassed it in the fall of 1778, and its garrison would have starved but for the friendly Delaware. The next spring a seige by Indians under a British officer was raised only by a relief expedition. Soon thereafter, when Col. Daniel Brodhead succeeded McIntosh in the West, Fort Laurens was abandoned.

[S. J. and E. H. Buck, *The Planting of Civilization in Western Pennsylvania.*]

SOLON J. BUCK

LAUSANNE AGREEMENT. At a conference of the European allies of World War I at Lausanne, Switzerland, in 1932, the creditors of Germany for reparations under the Treaty of Versailles effected the last write-off of the staggering total originally imposed on the defeated enemy. They conditionally canceled nine-tenths of the obligations still surviving under the Young Plan and lumped the total due into one easily supportable bonded indebtedness of $750 million bearing 5 percent interest, to be redeemed at the rate of 1 percent per annum, plus service on the international loans to Germany previously made under the Dawes Plan and Young Plan. The signatories signed among themselves a "gentleman's agreement" that they, on their part, would not ratify the treaty until a "satisfactory settlement is obtained between them and their own creditors." That is, they made the Lausanne Agreement dependent on cancellation of their debts to the United States. The U.S. government never accepted the arrangement; but at President Herbert Hoover's suggestion in 1931 an all-round moratorium for one year on international debts, including those to the United States, was agreed to, for the purpose of easing a desperate economy. At the expiration of the year all debtor nations defaulted, except Finland. Germany later resumed service to certain creditors of its obligations on the Dawes Plan and Young Plan loans, but only on exchange conditions favorable to itself.

[Samuel Flagg Bemis, *Diplomatic History of the United States;* Harold G. Moulton and Leo Pasvolsky, *War Debts and Reparations.*]

SAMUEL FLAGG BEMIS

LA VÉRENDRYE EXPLORATIONS. In 1728 Pierre Gaultier de Varennes, Sieur de La Vérendrye, was stationed by the French government of Canada at a small outpost on Lake Nipigon, thirty-five miles north of Lake Superior. There he heard from the Indians of a river flowing west into a salt sea. He knew nothing of the Rocky Mountains and he conceived the idea of an overland commerce between Lake Superior and the Pacific Ocean to bring the goods of the Far East to France by way of Montreal. The cost of this route could, he was sure, be defrayed from the profits of his fur trade.

Obtaining from the governor-general of Canada a trade monopoly in this vast territory, he established a line of posts westward from Lake Superior to Lake-of-the-Woods and Lake Winnipeg, and up the Red and Assiniboine rivers. On the latter stream he built Fort La Reine, now Portage la Prairie, at the point where the old Indian trail from the Great Plains led across the river northward to York Factory on Hudson's Bay. In 1738, in search of the westward-flowing river, he led a party south from this point to Star Mound in Canada. This was the First Mountain mentioned in his journal and was the site of an abandoned Hidatsa village on the old trail. He next recorded passing Turtle Mountain on the north side and from this point his guides led him far out of his course to an ancient Hidatsa site on Antler Creek. From this point he went directly south to a fortified Hidatsa village he called Fort La Butte, recently identified as near Minot, N.Dak. While there he sent his son to a second Hidatsa village, a day's journey distant, located on the Missouri at Old Crossing.

In 1742 La Vérendrye sent his two sons from Fort La Reine across the Missouri River at Old Crossing. From the account in their journal, the party traveled west and southwest until they came within sight of the Big Horn Mountains, west of the Black Hills. Here, on the banks of the North Platte River (erroneously called by their guides the Missouri), they buried a lead plate inscribed with the date and the names of three of the party (*see* La Vérendrye Plate). From their own account the party returned by the same route over which they had already traveled. It is worthy of note that after crossing the Missouri again they spoke of Fort La Butte as being a day's journey from Old Crossing.

[O. G. Libby, "Vérendrye's Visit to the Mandans in 1738–39," *Collections* of the State Historical Society of North Dakota (1908); Francis Parkman, *A Half Century of Conflict*.]

O. G. LIBBY

LA VÉRENDRYE PLATE. A sheet of lead, 7 inches by 8 inches in size, buried upon the hill at the junction of the Bad and Missouri rivers in Fort Pierre, S.Dak., Mar. 30, 1743, by the sons of Pierre Gaultier de Varennes, Sieur de La Vérendrye, to certify the French claim to the upper Missouri Valley. It was recovered by a party of schoolchildren on Feb. 17, 1913. Incised on the obverse is an inscription relating to the then existing French and Canadian governments. On the reverse are scratched the names of those present when the plate was deposited. It is now in possession of the South Dakota Historical Society, Pierre.

[L. J. Burpee, *Journals and Letters of La Vérendrye*; P. Margry, *Découvertes et Établissements des Français*, vol. VI.]

DOANE ROBINSON

LAWRENCE, a twenty-gun brig built by Capt. Oliver Hazard Perry at Erie, N.Y., in 1813, and his flagship at the Battle of Lake Erie. In July 1815 it was sunk as useless, but it was raised in 1875 and exhibited at the Centennial Exhibition until accidentally destroyed by fire.

[W. W. Dobbins, *History of the Battle of Lake Erie*.]

WALTER B. NORRIS

LAWRENCE, SACK OF (May 21, 1856), was the beginning of actual civil war in the Kansas conflict (*see* Border War). A proslavery grand jury had indicted several of the free-state leaders for treason and had started legal action against the New England Emigrant Aid Company's Free-State Hotel, believed to have been built as a fort, and the newspapers *Herald of Freedom* and *Free State* as nuisances. A U.S. marshal appeared before the village with a posse of 700–800 men to serve the warrants. Having made his arrests unopposed, he relinquished his posse to the proslavery sheriff, S. J. Jones, who, since the Wakarusa War, had sought the destruction of this "hotbed of abolitionism." Led by Jones and former Sen. David R. Atchison of Missouri, the mob entered the town and, making a pretext of the grand jury presentment, burned the hotel and wrecked the newspaper offices. Accounts disagree about how much more property was destroyed or stolen. A few days later abolitionist John Brown retaliated in the Potawatomie massacre, while, at the request of Gov. Wilson Shannon, troops were sent to Topeka to effect the dispersal of a free-state legislature. News of the sack aroused the entire North, led to the formation of the National Kansas Committee, and provided the Republican party with the issue of "Bleeding Kansas."

[Richard Cordley, *A History of Lawrence, Kansas*; L. W. Spring, *Kansas, The Prelude to the War for the Union*.]

SAMUEL A. JOHNSON

LAWRENCE RADIATION LABORATORY, on the Berkeley campus of the University of California, was named in honor of its first director, Ernest O. Lawrence. In the early 1930's several nuclear particle accelerators were devised, none more successful than Lawrence's cyclotron. His first few machines were small, just a few inches in diameter; the largest component was the electromagnet needed to turn the particles in their circular paths. Even before one machine was completed, Lawrence seemed always to be thinking of the next to be built, each larger than the last so that the particles could be accelerated to higher energies. When toward the end of 1931 he retrieved from an unused radio transmitter a 75-ton magnet whose 27-inch-diameter pole faces determined the size of the next cyclotron, he installed it in an old frame warehouse near the Berkeley physics building. This structure he christened the Radiation Laboratory, a name made official in 1936, when the university's regents designated it a separate administrative unit of the physics department. Upon Lawrence's death in 1958, the name was changed to the Lawrence Radiation Laboratory and later to the Lawrence Berkeley Laboratory, to distinguish it from the Lawrence Livermore Laboratory, created in 1952, where classified military research is performed.

During the 1930's the laboratory's primary activity was the study of nuclear reactions. Protons, deuterons, and other particles were accelerated to energies—a few hundred thousand electron volts at first but later several million electron volts—sufficient to disrupt target nuclei and produce neutrons, new artificially radioactive isotopes of stable elements, and the first artificial element, technetium. Lawrence's brother, John, initiated biological investigations in 1935; and other important work in nuclear chemistry, engineering, detection and recording, linear acceleration, and other scientific fields was performed. This wide-ranging experimental activity, coupled with theoretical work done by a group under J. Robert Oppenheimer, made the Radiation Laboratory probably the most exciting place in the United States for the study of nuclear physics. Certainly it was a major factor in raising the level of American science to a position of world eminence.

Work on a 184-inch cyclotron was interrupted by World War II, during which the large magnet and much of the laboratory's efforts were devoted to problems involving construction of the first atomic bombs. The first two elements heavier than uranium, neptunium and plutonium, were produced there in the early 1940's. By the end of 1946, the 184-inch ma-

chine, called a synchrocyclotron, was completed, incorporating a new principle conceived by Edwin M. McMillan (and independently by V. I. Veksler in the Soviet Union), who succeeded Lawrence as laboratory director. This principle permitted acceleration of particles to relativistic velocities, and hence greater energy, with the resulting ability to produce mesons in the nuclear collisions. In the next generation of much larger particle accelerators was the proton synchrotron, completed in 1954, with which energies of billions of electron volts were exceeded and antiparticles, such as the antiproton, were discovered.

Prior to World War II, funding for such research came from university and private foundation sources. Since 1942, support has come from the federal government, mostly via the Atomic Energy Commission. As part of the University of California, faculty and graduate students conduct research in the laboratory. Nobel Prizes have been awarded to Lawrence, McMillan, Glenn T. Seaborg, Owen Chamberlain, Emilio Segrè, Donald A. Glaser, Melvin Calvin, and Luis W. Alvarez for their work at the laboratory.

LAWRENCE BADASH

LAWRENCE RAID. *See* **Quantrill's Raid.**

LAWRENCE SCIENTIFIC SCHOOL, established at Harvard University in 1847 by a gift of $50,000 from industrialist Abbott Lawrence, who wished to support applied science in eastern Massachusetts. The school existed until 1906 but enjoyed only mixed success, since Harvard presidents Edward Everett and Charles W. Eliot did not favor applied subjects in their liberal arts university. Everett thought the school would be a means for bringing a German university to Cambridge and from the start tried to direct the school into advanced studies of pure science. His first move was to bring Eben N. Horsford, one of Justus von Liebig's best American students, to the school to teach pure and applied chemistry in Lawrence Hall, the school's new laboratory. His second move was to appoint Louis Agassiz, the eminent Swiss naturalist, to teach zoology and geology rather than the mining engineering Lawrence would have preferred. It is generally thought that Agassiz dominated the school, but his position was insecure and very few of the students worked with him, although several of those who did later became eminent: Joseph LeConte, Alexander Agassiz, Frederick W. Putnam, Alpheus Hyatt, Edward S. Morse, and A. E. Verrill. The school was most popular as an engineering school under Henry L. Eustis. Many of his students went on to have important careers in railroading and mining around the world, most notably James D. Hague, James P. Kimball, Sidney Fuller, and John D. Van Buren. Other scientists, such as Simon Newcomb, Harvey W. Wiley, Charles F. Chandler, John D. Runkle, and Thomas M. Drown, also attended the school.

The school had an uneven history. Starting off with high hopes, it had only modest enrollments in the 1850's and went into a decline in the 1860's from which it did not recover until the late 1880's. Since it was unable to compete with the Sheffield Scientific School at Yale and the Massachusetts Institute of Technology (MIT), then in Boston, Eliot tried repeatedly to transfer its programs to MIT. After several such attempts failed, Nathaniel S. Shaler, a Lawrence alumnus and Agassiz's successor on the faculty, became dean in 1891 and devoted himself to building up the school. Despite his success (the enrollment reached 584 in 1902, an all-time high) and a 1903 bequest of approximately $30 million from shoe manufacturer Gordon McKay, Eliot tried another merger with MIT in 1904. To protect the new endowment and to preserve a place for applied science at Harvard, Shaler agreed in 1906 to dissolve the Lawrence Scientific School and send its remaining undergraduate programs to Harvard College in return for a new Graduate School of Applied Science, which survives.

[Hugh Hawkins, *Between Harvard and America, The Educational Leadership of Charles W. Eliot;* James Lee Love, *The Lawrence Scientific School in Harvard University, 1847–1906.*]

M. W. ROSSITER

LAWRENCE STRIKE of textile workers in Lawrence, Mass., against a wage cut that employers alleged was necessitated by legislation curtailing working hours, lasted from Jan. 11 to Mar. 14, 1912. Perhaps its most sensational feature was the success of the Industrial Workers of the World (IWW) in organizing the polyglot mass of low-paid mill workers into a militant cooperative body. The IWW had until then been a minor factor in eastern labor disputes, and its appearance in New England created widespread perturbation. The strike involved most of the lawless practices common in American industrial warfare but resulted in important successes for the strikers. Increased wage scales were granted, result-

ing in improved standards in other New England textile centers.

[P. F. Brissenden, *The I. W. W., A Study of American Syndicalism.*]

W. A. ROBINSON

LAW SCHOOLS. From the colonial period until well beyond the end of the Civil War, lawyers were trained by apprenticeship. Some Americans went to London to study at the Inns of Court, but their training, too, was chiefly by apprenticeship. After the United States won independence, some law schools developed. The best known of them was the Litchfield School in Connecticut (1784–1833). By the beginning of the 19th century, there were a dozen schools, in all of which study was heavily based on Sir William Blackstone's *Commentaries on the Laws of England.* Established colleges showed some interest in law study; the first law professor was George Wythe, Thomas Jefferson's teacher, appointed at William and Mary in 1779. For prestige and the power to grant degrees, some law schools attached themselves loosely to colleges, as was the case at Harvard in 1817 and at Yale in 1824; by 1840, there were nine university-affiliated law schools, with a total enrollment of 345, about half of them at Harvard. Study at these law schools was far from rigorous, even at Harvard after the appointment of Joseph Story, associate justice of the Supreme Court, as law professor in 1829.

By 1860 there were twenty-one law schools. Although Columbia had great influence after Theodore W. Dwight came there in 1858, it was overshadowed by Harvard, especially after Christopher Columbus Langdell became dean in 1870. Langdell introduced the case and the Socratic methods of study, which became the pattern for many schools. In 1896, Harvard Law School introduced electives. It was not until 1899 that Harvard made law a three-year course of study, and it took ten more years before law became a graduate course of study at Harvard, which also pioneered with strict entrance requirements and rigorous annual examinations. These reforms greatly influenced law schools generally.

But criticism was widespread, too: the case method was repetitive; while the case book was useful to teach the common law, it was not as useful for teaching statutory law; only the exceptional student participated in the Socratic debate; the case method encouraged a large ratio of students per professor and, so, fed the profit motive; the schools neglected legal history, clinical experience, systematic study, and scholarship; there was more to the law than could be learned from a study of appellate court opinions.

Columbia in the 1920's introduced functionally organized courses in legal economics and trade regulation, which attempted to deal with law as a social science, but the experiment failed, in part because law teachers and the legal profession generally believed that law schools should be devoted to teaching for the profession rather than to research. In the 1930's there was experimentation at Yale, which even before then tried to depart from the Langdell pattern by introducing into its curriculum nontechnical—that is, nonprofessional—subjects. In the 1930's, Yale was dominated by a spirit of legal skepticism and by the idea that law should be used for social engineering. In 1937, Chicago offered the option of a four-year curriculum, with courses in economics, accounting, ethics, psychology, English constitutional history, and political theory, but this course of study was dropped in 1949; Minnesota had a similar option, which it discontinued in 1958. Yale in 1933 offered a program combined with the Harvard School of Business Administration, but this was dropped in 1938 because of lack of enrollment.

At most law schools, teaching proceeded untouched by any drive for reform; professors kept their eyes on bar examinations and used case books, although the teaching approach was modified by the use of some textbooks and lectures. A tendency developed to replace the pure case books with books called "Cases and Other Materials"; and electives were added to allow seminars, without, however, displacing the large lecture courses. In the 1960's and 1970's more teaching was offered in the public-law area—administrative law, labor law, tax law, poverty law, law and medicine, law and science and technology, civil rights, civil liberties, law and society, housing and planning law, consumer rights, and social legislation. Courses oriented toward problems rather than cases were introduced. Clinical legal education was started in the 1940's, and interest in such work was intensified in the 1960's and 1970's. But on the whole, law schools saw themselves as being essentially professional schools rather than research institutions and, so, remained teaching institutions with, naturally, a strong interest in preparing their students for the bar examinations.

The American Bar Association (ABA), founded in 1878, almost from its beginning showed an interest in legal education. In 1900 the Association of American Law Schools (AALS) was established for the purpose of setting standards for its institutional members.

These organizations represented only the elite of the law profession or of the law schools; real power rested in the state legislatures and courts. Accordingly, many night, part-time, and even proprietary schools were allowed to develop; their clientele were the disadvantaged groups, including the recent immigrants and their children. The ABA and the AALS were generally hostile to these schools—a hostility that was sometimes openly ethnic or racist. The legislatures were not eager to destroy these schools; but what the ABA and the AALS could not accomplish was accomplished by the Great Depression and the World War II selective-service draft. In 1935 there were 127 unapproved schools, but by 1947 there were only 47. In 1972 there were 28 unapproved law schools, 18 of them in California.

In the 1960's law school enrollment went up sharply; by 1973 it reached 106,000 at the 151 approved schools, and 82,000 college graduates applied for 37,000 first-year places. Further, new law schools were being established. The increase in interest in law school education was ascribed to many things: the legal profession appeared to be a lucrative one; with decreased interest in graduate study in the humanities and the social sciences, young people tended to look to the professional schools; many young people looked with favor upon a legal career devoted to consumer protection, the rights of disadvantaged persons, and government or public service; and women and blacks were being admitted to law schools in unprecedentedly large numbers—the number of women enrolled in 1973 was nine times that in 1963, and the total minority group enrollment in 1973 was almost three times that of 1969 (when comprehensive national figures were first collected). The fall of 1973 was the first time that there was not a single unfilled seat in the entering class of an approved law school. Law schools have almost completely pushed out study by apprenticeship. In 1951 thirty-five states still permitted qualification by apprenticeship study; but by 1974 the number was reduced to ten, and of the latter, four required at least one year of law school study.

While the law schools appeared to be secure and prosperous, critical appraisal of legal education continued unabated, especially in the face of jurimetrics (electronic, computer retrieval), games theory, symbolic logic, and the involvement of the law with moral and political questions, such as abortion, civil disobedience, school busing, and reapportionment.

[Association of American Law Schools, "Training for the Public Profession of the Law: 1971," *Proceedings,* part

1; A. Chroust, *Rise of the Legal Profession in America*; A. J. Harno, *Legal Education in the United States*; H. L. Packer and T. Ehrlich, *New Directions in Legal Education*; A. Z. Reed, *Training for the Public Profession of Law*, and *Present-Day Law Schools in the United States*; R. B. Stevens, "Two Cheers for 1870: The American Law School," in B. Bailyn and D. Fleming, eds., *Law in American History*.]

MILTON R. KONVITZ

LAWS, CONCESSIONS AND AGREEMENTS. *See* **West Jersey Concessions.**

LEAD INDUSTRY first became commercially important to the United States in 1750, when sustained lead mining and smelting began in Dutchess County, N.Y., and at what later became known as the Austinville mine in Virginia. The demand for lead bullets and shot in the revolutionary war prompted the working of several small deposits in Massachusetts, Connecticut, Maryland, Pennsylvania, and North Carolina. The domestic availability and relative ease of smelting of lead ores contributed a great deal to early frontier development and to sustaining the revolt against the English crown.

Some petty lead production in connection with a 1621 iron furnace project in Virginia has been reported, but later investigators were never able to find any evidence of lead occurrences in the vicinity. French trappers discovered lead in the upper Mississippi Valley about 1690, and by 1763 the district near Galena, Ill., had become a regular producer of lead. The French-Canadian Julien Dubuque arrived in 1774, made peace with the local Indians, and operated lead mines and furnaces in Iowa, Wisconsin, and Illinois until his death in 1810. The Fox and Sauk Indian tribes continued to mine and smelt the ore until the 1820's, when they were largely dispossessed by white venturers using black slaves and under strong military protection. This situation was, in part, the cause of the Black Hawk War.

In 1797 Moses Austin migrated from the Virginia district bearing his name (Austinville) to southeast Missouri, where lead had been mined sporadically at Mine La Motte and other mines by early French explorers since about 1724. Austin set up a large furnace and shot tower on the banks of the Mississippi River in 1798 and by 1819 was producing 3 million pounds of lead per year. With the Louisiana Purchase in 1803, these areas came under the control of the United States.

The simple log furnace—consisting of a crib of logs in which was piled the lead ore, topped by more logs to be burned—was of poor smelting efficiency. Thus, when Peter Lorimier built a Scotch hearth in 1834 near Dubuque, Iowa, this new technology greatly lowered production costs in the lead industry through improved productivity. Development of the frontier lead region from Galena into southern Wisconsin and Dubuque proceeded rapidly, so that by 1845 the district had a population of nearly 10,000 and reportedly produced 54,495,000 pounds of lead, which was taken by boat to New Orleans or by prairie schooner to the Erie Canal and thence by boat to eastern markets. Perhaps more than any other factor, early mining and commerce in lead accounted for opening the upper Midwest to settlement and civilization.

From 1845 until the 1860's, domestic lead production continued to be primarily from shallow galena (lead sulfide) workings in three districts: Austinville, Wisconsin-Illinois-Iowa, and southeast Missouri. Deeper mining had to await renewed exploration during the war periods of the 20th century. Throughout the Civil War all these areas were largely controlled by the Confederacy, so that the Union had to rely on the melting of lead gutters, pewter housewares, and lead pipe and on purchase from foreign sources.

In the 1860's and early 1870's, new developments rapidly shifted the locus of the lead industry. With the westward surge of miners and prospectors to the Rocky Mountains following the gold rush of the 1850's came discoveries of lead as a host mineral for some of the silver and gold values. In 1863 lead associated with silver was discovered in Little Cottonwood Canyon in Utah. Completion of the transcontinental railroad in 1869 gave the needed impetus to the growth of the intermountain lead-silver industry, including several smelters in Montana, Idaho, Utah, Nevada, California, and Colorado. Rich silver-lead ore was discovered at Leadville, Col., in 1876, and for a time this was the world's largest lead-producing area. The large high-grade ore body found at Bunker Hill, Idaho, in 1885 was the basis for the development of the Coeur d'Alene as an important lead-silver-zinc producing area.

Mining these western lead carbonate ores proved to be much more hazardous to health than mining the lead sulfide ores of the central and eastern states. The carbonate dust was more easily assimilated into the human body, causing "lead colic," which was most debilitating. In response to the problem, the lead industry initiated the practice of industrial hygiene, using dust respirators and providing a free ration of milk daily to the mine and smelter workers.

At the same time that many new discoveries of lead ore were being made in the West, the shallow occurrences in the southeast Missouri district were being exhausted. In 1869 the first diamond drill to be used in the United States was brought into the district from France and deeper, horizontally bedded deposits of lead ore were located at depths of 120 feet and more, with thicknesses of up to 500 feet. This area of nearly pure lead ore was destined to become one of the largest in the world and a source of great strength to the United States through the wars of the 20th century. Since 1904, southeast Missouri has been the leading lead-producing area in the United States.

In 1872 the railway from Saint Louis to Joplin, Mo., in the vicinity of which new ore bodies had been discovered, was completed, and the zinc-lead mining activity began to accelerate. About 1895 natural gas discoveries were made in the Kansas and Oklahoma part of the Joplin, or tristate, district, providing cheap fuel for zinc smelting and further stimulating mining activities. Since lead was a coproduct of zinc in the ore, lead production was also augmented and several smelters were constructed in the area and in the vicinity of Saint Louis.

The lead blast furnace first came into use in the United States in the late 1860's in areas of Nevada, Utah, and Montana, as lower-grade and more-complex lead ores required new technology. Gradually, in the older mining regions the old furnace, reverberatory, and hearth methods of smelting became outdated. With new concentrating methods of tabling, jigging, and doing selective flotation, the fine grinding of the ore required to permit upgrading produced unsuitable feed material for the smelters. Adoption of a new technique—sintering (desulfurizing and agglomerating) the fine ore concentrate, then reducing it to lead bullion in a blast furnace—again gave the lead industry an economic boost. Requiring greater amounts of capital, the new technologies were catalysts for a period of consolidation into a few large companies within the lead mining and smelting industry around the turn of the century.

Having provided the lead needs of the nation during the first half of the 20th century, the older mining districts (Illinois-Wisconsin, Joplin, southeast Missouri "old lead belt," Austinville) gradually became depleted, so that a new find was most welcome. Such was the case with the discovery of a "New Lead Belt" (some 50 miles from the Old Lead Belt) called the Viburnum Trend in southeast Missouri during the late 1950's. As the mines were developed and came into full production, between 1966 and 1974, Missouri lead output more than tripled, approaching a

half million tons, or 80 percent of the total U.S. lead production. Indicative of this major shift in mine production is the fact that two new lead smelters were built and the capacity of a third was doubled in Missouri, while two historic western smelters were being abandoned.

Once made into a metal, lead is almost indestructible. Water pipes, cisterns, and baths of the pre-Christian era in Rome and artifacts of the earlier Egyptian and Phoenician civilizations have been found almost completely intact. Large-scale peacetime reuse of lead became significant in the United States about 1907. Secondary recovery now accounts for half the domestic lead supply. In 1974 the United States used 1.5 million short tons of lead, which was supplied by 510,000 tons recycled from scrap and 670,000 tons from domestic mines, the remainder coming from imports (31 percent from Peru, 26 percent from Canada, 18 percent from Mexico, 11 percent from Australia, and 14 percent from other countries).

The importance of lead and its compounds to the average American may be illustrated by the strong reliance of the automobile on lead-acid storage batteries and organic lead antiknock compounds in gasoline. Lead-tin alloys are used for soldering radiators, electrical connections, and tin cans. Sheet lead is used increasingly in shielding from nuclear and X-ray radiation and from noise. The corrosion resistance of lead to acids, moisture, and atmosphere accounts for its use in chemical process equipment, electrical cable sheathing, plumbing, and architectural units. Lead compounds are used as paint pigments, metal primers, ceramic glazes, and insecticides. Use of the metal because of its density varies from ballast in the keel of a sailboat to shot and bullets for military and sporting ammunition. Lead and lead compounds can constitute a biological hazard if not properly handled. Excessive ingestion and inhalation of lead compounds can result in illness or death in humans. As a result, regulations have been established for permissible levels of lead in paints and emissions into the atmosphere.

[Carl H. Cotterill and J. M. Cigan, eds., "Extractive Metallurgy of Lead and Zinc," *Proceedings of AIME World Symposium on Mining and Metallurgy of Lead and Zinc,* vol. 2 (1970); Wilhelm Hofmann, *Lead and Lead Alloys;* D. O. Rausch and B. C. Mariacher, eds., "Mining and Concentrating of Lead and Zinc," *Proceedings of AIME World Symposium on Mining and Metallurgy of Lead and Zinc,* vol. 1 (1970).]

CARL H. COTTERILL

LEADVILLE MINING DISTRICT of Colorado, named for a lead carbonate ore that abounded in the region and contained large amounts of silver, is located near the headwaters of the Arkansas River. The first settlement resulted from the discovery in 1860 of rich placer deposits in California Gulch, which yielded over $3 million in gold before they were exhausted in 1867. For nearly ten years sporadic prospecting was carried on, which finally culminated, in 1875, in the discovery of the true nature of the carbonate ore by W. H. Stevens and A. B. Wood. Then occurred a mining rush on a grand scale. The Little Pittsburg, Matchless, Robert E. Lee, and other famous mines were developed. On Jan. 26, 1878, the city of Leadville was organized with H. A. W. Tabor, who was to become the district's best-known bonanza king, as the first mayor. During the period 1858–1925 the district produced nearly $200 million in silver and over $50 million in gold. Molybdenum was also discovered in the district, and by 1960, 90 percent of the world's supply was being produced at Climax, twelve miles north of the present city of Leadville.

[Don L. Griswold and Jean H. Griswold, *The Carbonate Camp Called Leadville;* G. F. Willison, *Here They Dug Gold.*]

GEORGE L. ANDERSON

LEAGUE OF ARMED NEUTRALITY. *See* **Armed Neutrality of 1780.**

LEAGUE OF NATIONS, formed on the basis of the first twenty-six articles of the Treaty of Versailles, which ended World War I. The idea of a world government or association of nations was not new—ancient Greece had its Amphictyonic League, and in modern times numerous proposals for a parliament of man had been advanced—but the idea remained inchoate until the ravages of a world war persuaded the nations to take formal steps to create such an organization.

In the United States the most active wartime proponents of the league idea belonged to a group known as the League to Enforce Peace. Numbering among its members such prominent figures as former President William Howard Taft, the League to Enforce Peace favored a postwar association of nations that would guarantee peace through economic and military sanctions. In 1916, President Woodrow Wilson spoke before this group and set forth his own developing ideas on the subject. The president included self-determination and freedom from wars of aggression as fundamental prerequisites of a stable peace. Most im-

portant, he wanted to see the United States take the lead in a "universal association of the nations to maintain the inviolate security of the highway of the seas for the common and unhindered use of all the nations of the world, and to prevent any war begun either contrary to treaty covenants or without warning and full submission of the causes to the opinion of the world—a virtual guarantee of territorial integrity and political independence." In subsequent speeches both before and after the United States entered the war in April 1917, Wilson elaborated on these themes. He called for "a peace without victory," a peace based on open diplomacy, arms reduction, removal of economic barriers between nations, and impartial settlement of colonial claims. Such a peace, he said, must be maintained not by entangling alliances or a balance-of-power system but by a concert of power in which the Monroe Doctrine would become "the doctrine of the world."

Not all Americans shared the vision of Wilson or the League to Enforce Peace. Some people believed in the general concept of a league but opposed giving a league any physical power over its members. Others rejected outright any league that would transform the Monroe Doctrine from its original character or violate the nation's tradition of isolationism except when directly threatened. Questions of physical force versus the power of public opinion, national sovereignty versus possible world government, and moral versus legal obligations to other nations underlay the great debate.

By autumn of 1918, as the war drew to an end, debate over a peace settlement intensified. The off-year congressional elections assumed added importance because of the Senate's constitutional power to approve or reject treaties. Fearful that the Democrats would lose their slim majorities in both houses of Congress, Wilson appealed to the voters to elect Democrats to office. Republicans called the appeal gross partisanship and cited Wilson's earlier pledge to adjourn politics until the war was over. When the votes were counted, Republicans had won both the Senate and the House. Significantly, the new majority leader in the Senate and chairman of the Foreign Relations Committee was Henry Cabot Lodge, a man whose ideology and personality clashed with the president's.

Relations between Wilson and his critics, both within Congress and outside, deteriorated further when the president announced that he would attend the peace conference and would not take either a senator or a prominent Republican to serve with him on the American commission. Such actions, following closely upon the election results, were regarded as unwise and partisan even by some of Wilson's closest advisers.

At the peace conference, Wilson revealed skills as a courageous negotiator in the face of Old World opposition to his ideas. Battling those who wanted to postpone discussion of a league until the spoils of war had been divided, Wilson succeeded in getting the League of Nations tentatively adopted. The heart of the League of Nations Covenant was Article X, which stated that the signatory nations agreed ''to respect and preserve as against external aggression the territorial integrity and existing political independence'' of all members. Other key articles were Article VIII, calling for the reduction of national armaments; Article XI, making ''any war or threat of war . . . a matter of concern'' to the league; Article XII, proposing arbitration or submission to the executive council of disputes between members; Article XVI, providing for economic and, if necessary, military sanctions against members violating Article XI; Article XVIII, entrusting the league with supervision of the arms trade when necessary for the common good; and Article XXII, establishing a mandate system over formerly German colonies.

The league structure consisted of a nine-member executive council, an assembly of all the members, the Permanent Court of International Justice, and a secretariat. In addition, various commissions were established to oversee particular areas of concern. When the final Treaty of Versailles was signed with Germany in June 1919, the Covenant of the League of Nations made up the first section of the treaty. By thus integrating the league with the general peace settlement, Wilson believed that any mistakes could be rectified later through the league.

Wilson's attempt to persuade the Senate to approve the treaty and thereby bring the United States into the league became one of the classic executive-legislative struggles in American history. Lodge united the Republican senators and a few Democrats behind a series of reservations to the treaty, the most important of which disavowed U.S. obligations to uphold the peacekeeping articles of the league unless Congress should so provide. Wilson rejected these reservations, contending that they were unnecessary and contrary to the spirit of the league and that because they made substantive changes in the treaty, they would necessitate reopening the peace conference. He agreed to accept a few ''interpretations'' to the treaty that would not change its substance. This impasse over reserva-

tions reflected real or perceived ideological differences over the future direction of American foreign policy as well as senatorial jealousy of its prerogatives and the partisanship of Republicans and Democrats.

Had Wilson been willing to accept the Lodge-backed reservations, the Senate would have approved the treaty, the reservations probably would have been accepted by the other powers, and the United States would have joined the League of Nations. Wilson, however, believed that to enter the league under such circumstances would be both dishonorable and possibly fatal to the league's success, depending as it would on an attitude of trust and cooperation. In March 1920, the Senate failed to give the Treaty of Versailles the necessary two-thirds approval.

The United States maintained informal relations with the league in the 1920's and 1930's and, at times, acted jointly with the world body. Whether its membership in the organization, either as Wilson wished or with reservations, would have strengthened the league sufficiently to allow it to cope with the problems that led to World War II is an unanswerable question. Most historians have been dubious, given the enormity of the problems and the lack of commitment to universal collective security. Nevertheless, the league served as an example—both negatively and positively—for those who founded the United Nations after World War II. The league had ceased to function politically early in 1940, and its physical assets were turned over to the United Nations in April 1946.

[Thomas A. Bailey, *Woodrow Wilson and the Great Betrayal;* D. F. Fleming, *The United States and the League of Nations;* Warren F. Kuehl, *Seeking World Order;* N. Gordon Levin, *Woodrow Wilson and World Politics;* Arthur Link, *Wilson the Diplomatist;* Ralph Stone, *The Irreconcilables and the Fight Against the League of Nations;* J. Chalmers Vinson, *Referendum for Isolation.*]
RALPH A. STONE

LEAGUE OF UNITED SOUTHERNERS, an organization of southern leaders created in 1858 by Edmund Ruffin, a Virginia planter, and William L. Yancey, an Alabama politician, to promote southern political unity and to spread propaganda for secession. It met with such indifference that the founders, in 1859, abandoned it. Some of the local clubs remained to campaign effectively for secession in 1860–61.

[Avery Craven, *Edmund Ruffin, Southerner.*]
HENRY T. SHANKS

LEAGUE OF WOMEN VOTERS OF THE UNITED STATES, founded in 1920 to help the newly enfranchised women make intelligent use of voting privileges, has become an outstanding agency for nonpartisan political education and a sponsor for legislation and policies judged by the league to be desirable for public welfare. The league strongly supported the Equal Rights Amendment, presented to the states for ratification in 1972.

LOUISE B. DUNBAR

LEARNED SOCIETIES are organizations with members whose primary interest is the study and advancement of knowledge, including particularly the exchange of information, in various areas of intellectual interest and endeavor. Although bodies comparable to learned societies had been established far back in history—for example, Plato's Academy, Aristotle's Lyceum, and the Alexandrine Library and Museum (300 B.C.–A.D. 600)—modern learned societies originated in western Europe in the 16th and 17th centuries. These societies grew out of, and were committed to, a way of thought that is called empirical or experimental. They played a large part in the scientific revolution that ushered in the modern world. The best known and most influential of this group have been the Royal Society of London, founded in 1660, and the French Académie des Sciences, founded in Paris in 1666. The members of these societies were, theoretically, catholic in their interests but actually concentrated on contemporary practical and scientific questions.

The first learned society founded in the United States was the American Philosophical Society (1743), whose origins have been traced to a club set up by Benjamin Franklin in Philadelphia in 1727. It was followed by the establishment of the American Academy of Arts and Sciences in Boston in 1780, John Adams being its prime mover. Both of these societies were patterned after their European counterparts. Membership has always been relatively small and honorific, including persons of distinction in all fields of intellectual endeavor, and concomitantly, societal interests have embraced all areas of knowledge.

A few national societies were founded prior to the Civil War by those who were interested in a particular branch of knowledge represented by the society. They include the American Antiquarian Society, founded in Worcester, Mass. (1812), and the American Statistical Association, in Boston (1839). A larger number of local and regional societies of this type were also created during this period. For example, the oldest historical society in America, the Massachusetts Historical Society, was founded in Boston in 1791, and the Chemical Society of Philadelphia, in 1792. Still, no more than about 100 societies of national or regional significance were organized before 1860, and their membership tended to be restricted to men of affairs and interested professionals.

The sweeping changes ushered in by the Civil War—political, economic, and social—saw increasing specialization in American life, which in turn was reflected in the character and number of American learned societies. American universities, strongly influenced in this period by the structure and development of German universities, created many new departments devoted to particular disciplines. Faculty members began to form societies for the exchange of information and other activities regarding these disciplines. Increasing urbanization facilitated the ease with which these academicians could organize and meet and also fostered the need for the training of personnel in their disciplines to solve burgeoning urban problems. Consequently, a flood of specialized societies organized after the Civil War. While such local and regional societies, numbering in the thousands, played significant roles at their respective levels, much greater importance was assumed by the approximately fifty national specialized learned societies spanning all of the disciplines in the natural sciences, social sciences, and humanities. Included are such societies as the American Chemical Society (1876), the American Historical Association (1884), the American Economic Association (1885), the American Psychological Association (1892), the American Anthropological Association (1902), and the American Society of Parasitologists (1924). A major difference between these specialized societies and earlier ones is that they have been open to all interested persons and some now have memberships in the thousands. An exception to these trends was the founding in 1898 of the National Institute of Arts and Letters and in 1904 of its affiliate, the American Academy of Arts and Letters. Membership is honorific and limited to 250 and 50 citizens, respectively, with notable achievements in arts, literature, and music.

With the increase in number of specialized societies, an awareness gradually developed of the need to span gaps between disciplines and to coordinate knowledge and societal efforts at the national level. The Medieval Academy of America (1925) and the Renaissance Society of America (1954) were set up to cut across different disciplines in their respective periods of study. Founded in 1848, the American Association for the Advancement of Science had developed into a coordinating entity by the 1870's. Other societies in various areas of the natural sciences include the Federation of American Societies for Experimental Biology (1912), the American Institute of Physics (1931), the American Institute of Biological Sciences (1948), and the American Geological Institute (1948). In the period during and shortly after World War I three overall coordinating councils were formed: the National Research Council (1916), natural sciences; the American Council of Learned Societies (1919), humanities and social sciences; and the Social Science Research Council (1923), social sciences. Each of these coordinating organizations includes learned societies as members, and the individual societies play a considerable role in the administration, activities, and operations of the larger bodies.

Before World War I the relationship of American learned societies to their counterparts abroad was informal and spasmodic. In the post–World War I and post–World War II periods three international councils were formed to coordinate the activities of learned societies from various countries. They are the International Research Council (1919), after 1931 known as the International Council of Scientific Unions; the International Academic Union (1919), which in 1954 became a subsidiary of the International Council for Philosophy and Humanistic Studies; and the International Social Science Council (1952). These three councils, although they have marked differences in their relationship to member societies of various countries, play analogous roles in the international field—in the natural sciences, humanities, and social sciences—to those played by the various national councils in the domestic.

American learned societies have been financed in various ways. Most of the local and regional societies rely primarily on membership dues or contributions. National learned societies also rely on members for a basic percentage of their expenses, but they look, too, to universities, government, industry, and philanthropic foundations for support. Since World War II, governmental and industrial support of learned societies has increased to millions of dollars annually. Initially, most of this aid was directed toward the natural science societies. Beginning in the 1960's, sums made available to societies active in the humanities and social sciences have increased noticeably. A few of the older societies have endowments from which they draw considerable income for their operating ex-

penses. The American Philosophical Society, for example, in 1974 had assets in excess of $15 million.

[Joseph C. Kiger, *American Learned Societies.*]
JOSEPH C. KIGER

LEASEHOLD, a system of land tenure characteristic of the southeastern portion of the colony and state of New York during the late 18th century and the first half of the 19th century. The tenant was bound to a perpetual payment of rent in money, produce, or labor, or all three. In the central part of the state and on the land included in the Holland Purchase in the six western counties, the system of long-term sales, whereby the title of the land did not pass until the final payment, was also upon occasion spoken of as leasehold. This leasehold system was abolished by the middle of the 19th century by the constitution of 1846 and the decisions of the courts (*see* Antirent War).

[A. C. Flick, ed., *History of the State of New York,* vol. VI.]
A. C. FLICK

LEATHER INDUSTRY. The tanner's art evolved from antiquity. Leather production had been reduced to well-established techniques by the 11th century A.D., but the chemical principles involved were not defined until the 19th century. Primitive societies preserved hides and skins with grease and smoke. The American Indians processed their raw hides by means of the chamois method, which utilized animal fats, livers, and brains; the white buckskin that resulted was much admired by the colonists as well as the Indians.

Massachusetts had tanneries before 1650. Later, townsfolk in Connecticut complained bitterly of the unpleasant piling of foul-smelling animal remains in "tann-hills." In the Middle Colonies the presence of the leather crafts was coincidental with settlement. The governors of New Sweden stressed the need for more tanners and curriers. An abundance of hides, plus quantities of bark for tanning, made the Middle Atlantic region the leading leather-producing area. In the South, the tannery was a common feature of all well-managed plantations.

By 1840, the census of manufacturers reported 8,229 tanneries in the United States. They were widely scattered small operations taking place in small towns and employing local labor. Regional characteristics that affected other industries had little effect on the appearance of tan vats, beaming sheds,

LEATHER INDUSTRY

or bark mills. The tanning agent—hemlock bark in the north and oak bark in the middle and southern regions—and the availability of skilled craftsmen varied from place to place.

Change occurred slowly in the American tanning industry. Steam came late to the leather factory, and when it did, steam power was unspectacularly harnessed to old techniques. It was used routinely for grinding bark, for softening foreign hides, and for giving motion to many machines that washed, glazed, and finished leather. Chemically and mechanically, some Americans sought to speed and ease the manufacture of leather, but generally the immigrant tanner with a knowledge of Europe's methods contributed most to this quest.

Rudimentary tanning facilities for washing, fleshing, liming, beaming, tanning, and drying had been the same everywhere. The craft persisted as a manual operation and the basic tools—the beam, the fleshing knife, and the tanner's hook—remained unchanged. The horse-powered bark mill retained its simple form. Tanning began with a prolonged washing of the hides in water to remove dirt, blood, and flesh. The hides were then placed in vats containing a lime-and-water solution, which loosened the hair on the hides. The hides were then placed on a sloping beam or bench and scraped by a downward motion with a beaming knife. After these preliminaries, hides were put into the tan vats. Tannin was obtained from the bark of sumac, oak, or hemlock trees. Bark and hides were placed in alternate layers in vats or pits and then covered with water. The conversion of raw hides to sole leather often required two years.

David Macbride, a Dublin physician; Armand Sequin of France; and Sir Humphry Davy of England were among the earliest men to improve the tanning process significantly. By 1840 their methods were employed by American tanners. Until the 1850's improvements in American tanning processes were mechanical rather than chemical. The leather industry changed after the Civil War. Many procedures were mechanized, interest in the chemical aspects of tanning increased, and steam power turned most of the machinery. Also, large tanneries profited from the division and specialization of labor and the timesaving aspects of machines.

The demand for shoes, harnesses for animals, belts for machines, and upholstery for carriages and automobiles created an immense market. Midwestern meatpackers, who entered the leather business in the 1890's, contracted tanners to process hides at fixed prices and hold the leather until market prices were

suitably high. The consolidation of big business did not bypass the leather industry. In 1917, the meatpackers, shoe manufacturers, and two large corporations tanned approximately 40 percent of the cattlehide leather made in America. The most important contributions to the technology of tanning after 1850 were the chrome processes of Jackson Schultz, Robert Foerderer, and Martin Dennis. The chrome process was an inorganic method using chromate salts instead of bark extract as the tanning agent. This process reduced tanning time and established the usefulness of chemical research in the leather industry.

The leather industry boomed during World War I, but thereafter, the demand for leather dropped drastically. An industrywide recession lasted until 1933, but full prosperity did not return until production was stimulated by World War II. The prosperity was short-lived: excess capacity, competition from substitute materials, and a lack of reliable foreign sources for hides curtailed production.

The Eagle Ottawa Leather Company of Grand Haven, Mich., developed solvent tanning in the late 1950's. The result was a uniformly soft piece of leather, but the costs of the process to date have proved too high for its universal use. Synthetic leather was developed in the 1960's. A product called Corfam was developed by E. I. du Pont de Nemours and Company. Initially a failure in the United States, by the 1970's it had become a marketing success in Europe, notably in Poland. The polyvinyls have been more successful in production and in the marketplace.

The leather industry has changed slowly since the 17th century from a time-consuming, backbreaking, and odious handicraft to a process speeded by advances in machinery and chemistry.

In the United States, by the mid-1960's, there were 3,695 establishments engaged in leather tanning and finishing and the production of industrial leather belting, footware, gloves, luggage, handbags, and other personal leather items. Collectively, the industry employed over 300,000 persons and produced over $5 billion worth of leather goods annually. Imports of leather in these years totaled $123 million, compared to an export of hides valued at $62 million.

[Lucius F. Ellsworth, *The American Leather Industry;* Edgar M. Hoover, Jr., *Location Theory and the Shoe and Leather Industries;* David Macbride, "An Improved Method of Tanning Leather," *Philosophical Transactions of the Royal Society of London,* vol. 68 (1778); Charles H. McDermott, ed., *A History of the Shoe and Leather Industries of the United States;* Peter C. Welsh, *Tanning in the United States to 1850.*]

PETER C. WELSH

LEATHERWOOD GOD. Leatherwood Valley in Guernsey County, Ohio, was the scene of a camp meeting in 1828. During the meeting a mysterious stranger appeared, who later gave his name as Joseph C. Dylks. With a tremendous voice he would shout ''Salvation!'' and then make a strange sound like the snort of a frightened horse. He claimed to be a celestial being. Men and women began to believe him, and he made bolder claims—that he could perform miracles and that he was the true Messiah. He disappeared from the community as mysteriously as he had appeared.

[R. H. Tanneyhill, *The Leatherwood God.*]
HARLOW LINDLEY

LEAVENWORTH, a city in northeast Kansas, on the Missouri River. In 1827 Col. Henry Leavenworth built Fort Leavenworth, three miles from the present site of the city, to protect settlers traveling along the Santa Fe Trail. Squatters from across the river at Weston, Mo., moved into the area in June 1854, and soon formed a town association. Leavenworth was incorporated in 1855 and received title to its site in November 1856. Accessible by the Missouri River and overland trails, it became the headquarters of the freighting firm of Russell, Majors and Waddell and the terminus of a number of overland mails. The Kansas border troubles brought a reign of terror to the town. Siding with the Union during the Civil War, the town prospered. With the advent of the railroads during the 1860's, Leavenworth became an important commercial center. The 1970 population was 25,147. (*See also* Leavenworth, Fort.)

[H. M. Moore, *Early History of Leavenworth.*]
RALPH P. BIEBER

LEAVENWORTH, FORT. In 1824 some citizens of Missouri, at the suggestion of Sen. Thomas Hart Benton, petitioned Congress for a military post at the Arkansas River crossing of the Santa Fe Trail to protect traders journeying to New Mexico. Although no action was then taken, Secretary of War James Barbout in 1827 decided to erect a fort near the western boundary of Missouri, which would, at least in part, meet the wishes of the petitioners. On Mar. 7 the adjutant-general ordered Col. Henry Leavenworth to select a site for the cantonment, an assignment he completed on May 8. It was named Cantonment Leavenworth. Because of an epidemic of malaria between 1827 and 1829, it was almost evacuated in May

1829; but late in that summer it was reoccupied. During 1832 it was renamed Fort Leavenworth.

The post became important as a starting point for a number of military expeditions to the Far West, as a meeting place for Indian councils, and as a supply depot for forts and camps on the frontier. Before 1846 its garrison usually included portions of the Sixth Infantry or First Dragoons. It rose to national prominence during the Mexican War, when the Army of the West was organized there and began a long march to occupy the Far Southwest (*see* Kearny's March to California). Throughout the 1850's it continued to be a point of departure for many military expeditions. Occupying a strategic position in the West during the Civil War, it was at various times headquarters of the Department of the West, the Department of Kansas, and the Department of Missouri. The Fort Leavenworth military reservation was the seat of an arsenal between 1859 and 1874, and it was the U.S. Disciplinary Barracks between 1874 and 1895 and 1906 and 1929. To the military post were added the U.S. Army Command and General Staff School in 1881 and a federal penitentiary in 1895.

[E. Bandel, *Frontier Life in the Army, 1854–1861;* E. Hunt and W. E. Lorence, *History of Fort Leavenworth, 1827–1937.*]
RALPH P. BIEBER

LEAVENWORTH AND PIKES PEAK EXPRESS was launched by W. H. Russell and J. S. Jones to serve the Pikes Peak region of Colorado after the discovery of gold near Cherry Creek in 1858 (*see* Pikes Peak Gold Rush). The meager first discoveries hardly warranted establishment of an expensive express, but the first coach reaching Denver, May 7, 1859, received news of important finds that saved the stageline venture. The first route, a new one along the Republican River, was changed to the Platte River Trail in June 1859. The express ran weekly. Fare to Denver was $100, board included; letters twenty-five cents, newspapers ten cents. The Central Overland California and Pikes Peak Express absorbed the Leavenworth and Pikes Peak Express in 1860.

[L. R. Hafen, *The Overland Mail, 1849–1869.*]
LEROY R. HAFEN

LEAVENWORTH EXPEDITION. At the Arikara villages on the upper Missouri a party of the Rocky Mountain Fur Company under Gen. William Henry Ashley, en route to the Yellowstone, was attacked on June 2, 1823, and thirteen men were killed. Informed of this outrage, Col. Henry Leavenworth promptly started up the Missouri from Fort Atkinson, at Council Bluffs, Nebr., with six companies of the Sixth Infantry and some artillery. Joined on the way by Joshua Pilcher's party of the Missouri Fur Company, by Ashley's survivors, and 750 Sioux, Leavenworth reached Grand River, Aug. 9. The next day he attacked the Arikara fortified villages, forcing their submission.

[Doane Robinson, *Encyclopedia of South Dakota.*]
JOSEPH MILLS HANSON

LEBANON, U.S. LANDING IN. Under the threat of civil war in May 1958 from dissidents encouraged by the United Arab Republic and reinforced by guerrillas from neighboring Syria, President Camille Chamoun of Lebanon in early July appealed to the United States for military forces to maintain order. By directive of President Dwight D. Eisenhower, approximately 5,600 U.S. Marines landed on Lebanese beaches on July 15 and 16 and secured port facilities and the international airport at Beirut. U.S. Army troops from stations in Germany began landing by air on July 19, with the last of a force totaling 8,500 arriving by sea on Aug. 5. The overall commander was Maj. Gen. Paul D. Adams. Although the populace cheered the troops, Lebanese army officers were bitter at first, the landings apparently having forestalled a coup d'etat aimed at replacing Chamoun with the army commander, Gen. Fuad Shehab. Only an occasional minor encounter between dissidents and American troops occurred. On July 31 the Lebanese Chamber of Deputies elected Shehab president, but Chamoun refused for several weeks to resign, so that Shehab was not inaugurated until Sept. 23. At that point the Lebanese army acted firmly to restore and maintain order, and the last U.S. forces departed on Oct. 25.

[Jack Shulimson, *Marines in Lebanon—1958.*]
CHARLES B. MACDONALD

LEBOEUF, FORT, WASHINGTON'S MISSION TO. In 1753 the French erected forts Presque Isle and LeBoeuf in northwest Pennsylvania and, seizing an English trader's house at Venango, converted it into a fort. Gov. Robert Dinwiddie of Virginia selected the youthful George Washington to deliver a letter to the French demanding their withdrawal. With frontiersman Christopher Gist and five others, Washington traveled from Wills Creek over the trail later known as Braddock's Road to the forks of the Ohio and

thence to Logstown. Guided by friendly Indians, the party then proceeded to Venango and LeBoeuf. The commandant at LeBoeuf received Dinwiddie's letter and answered that he would forward it to Duquesne. Washington and his companions noted the strength of fort and garrison and the large number of canoes there, indicating a contemplated expedition down the Ohio.

After two narrow escapes from death on the return journey, Washington arrived at Williamsburg Jan. 16, 1754, and delivered to Dinwiddie his journal and the French reply to Dinwiddie's demand. The journal, published and widely reprinted in the colonies and in England, not only helped arouse the English against the French advance but also brought Washington for the first time to the attention of the world.

[C. H. Ambler, *Washington and the West;* Francis Parkman, *Montcalm and Wolfe.*]
SOLON J. BUCK

LECOMPTON CONSTITUTION. From Sept. 7 to Nov. 8, 1857, during the dispute over the admission of Kansas to the Union as a free or slave state, a convention of proslavery Kansans met at Lecompton and framed a state constitution. Antislavery men had abstained from voting at an election of delegates on the preceding June 15. The constitution that was framed provided for the usual forms and functions of a state government, but an article covering slavery declared slave property inviolable, denied the power of the legislature to prohibit immigrants from bringing in slaves or to emancipate them without compensation and the owner's consent, and empowered the legislature to protect slaves against inhuman treatment. The schedule provided for a vote on the alternatives, a "constitution with slavery" or a "constitution with no slavery," the latter actually meaning no interference with slavery. Other provisions prevented amendment before 1865 and placed responsibility for canvassing returns upon the presiding officer.

On Dec. 21 the slavery clause was approved, 6,226 to 569 (although it was later learned that 2,720 of the votes were fraudulent), antislavery men declining to vote. The antislavery legislature (there being two legislatures—one proslavery and one antislavery—operating in Kansas at the time) called an election for Jan. 4, 1858, at which time the Lecompton Constitution was rejected, 10,226 to 162.

Against the advice of some of his friends, President James Buchanan recommended on Feb. 2 that Kansas be admitted to the Union under the Lecompton Constitution. The constitution was approved by the U.S. Senate, but Republicans, Democratic allies of Sen. Stephen A. Douglas, and others united to defeat it in the House. A compromise bill was suggested by Rep. William H. English of Indiana. It provided for a referendum in which Kansans would vote on the acceptance of a government land grant to Kansas, rather than on the constitution. If the Kansans accepted the land grant (5 million acres of land), Kansas would become a state under the proslavery Lecompton Constitution. If rejected, statehood would be postponed until the territory had a larger population. On Aug. 2 the Kansans rejected the land grant, 11,300 to 1,788, thereby expressing their opposition to the Lecompton Constitution.

[W. E. Connelley, *A Standard History of Kansas and Kansans;* D. W. Wilder, *Annals of Kansas.*]

WENDELL H. STEPHENSON

LECTURE DAYS were midweek gatherings in the colonial New England churches for sermons on doctrinal points. In 1633 the general court ordered the lectures confined to afternoons so that the people would not lose a full working day, and in 1639 it attempted to reduce their number. When the clergy protested, it rescinded the order, but shortly thereafter lectures were generally abandoned. The Boston lecture continued to be given at the First Church by ministers of the city in rotation until 1845, when the church resumed control in order to exclude the controversial Unitarian Theodore Parker, whereupon the institution died of inanition.

PERRY MILLER

LEDERER'S EXPLORING EXPEDITIONS. John Lederer, a German traveler, made tours of western exploration in 1669 and 1670 for Sir William Berkeley, governor of Virginia and one of the proprietors of Carolina. Lederer, starting from the site of Richmond, claimed to have reached the summit of the Appalachian Mountains, but in fact he reached only the eastern foothills of the Blue Ridge. In a town of the Occaneechi he met "stranger Indians" who said they lived two months' distance to the west and who described their country as marked by waves (mountain ranges). Lederer conjectured that "the Indian Ocean does stretch an arm or bay from California into the continent as far as the Apalataean Mountains." The explorer reached as far south as upper South Carolina, visiting a number of Indian tribes, some of

whose customs he recorded in a book published in London in 1672.

[John Lederer, *The Discoveries of John Lederer, in Three Several Marches From Virginia, to the West of Carolina, and Other Parts of the Continent;* James Mooney, *The Siouan Tribes of the East.*]

SAMUEL C. WILLIAMS

LEDO ROAD. *See* **Burma Road and Ledo Road.**

LEE, FORT, originally called Fort Constitution, was built on Gen. George Washington's orders on the summit of the palisades of New Jersey opposite Fort Washington, on Manhattan Island, during the summer of 1776. The two forts, with obstructions placed between them in the Hudson River, were intended to prevent the passage of enemy vessels, but they failed in this purpose. After the fall of Fort Washington (1776) Fort Lee, with large stores, was abandoned when Gen. Charles Cornwallis crossed the Hudson.

The present borough of Fort Lee (Bergen County) was incorporated in 1904. During the years 1907–19 it was known as the motion-picture capital of the world. No motion pictures have been made there since 1923, but Fort Lee is now one of the world's largest film-processing centers. The population in 1970 was 30,631.

[George Bancroft, *History of the United States of America,* vol. V.]

C. A. TITUS

LEECH LAKE, INDIAN COUNCIL AT. On Feb. 16, 1806, Maj. Zebulon M. Pike, who had been sent by Gen. James Wilkinson to reconnoiter to the source of the Mississippi, held a council with local Chippewa bands at the North West Company's trading post on Leech Lake in north central Minnesota. The Indians agreed to make peace with the Sioux, to yield up their British flags and medals, and to send two warriors to Saint Louis with Pike.

[Elliott Coues, ed., *The Expeditions of Zebulon Montgomery Pike.*]

GRACE LEE NUTE

LEECH LAKE UPRISING (1898). The previously friendly Pillager band of Chippewa in northern Minnesota had, by 1898, been irritated beyond patience. Being haled long distances to court as liquor witnesses and then abandoned caused the Pillagers to resist apprehension as material witnesses. U.S. sheriffs called in troops to help make arrests. Regular soldiers from Fort Snelling crossed Leech Lake to corral the fugitives. A gun accidentally discharged by a raw recruit upset a tense situation. General shooting followed. Soldiers, pinned to the ground in a clearing, and under hostile fire from noon to dark on Oct. 5, suffered several casualties before being rescued two days later. Reinforcements rushed up; and the Pillagers withdrew. Troops were withdrawn, and agents induced many Indians to surrender; executive clemency reduced the prison sentences.

[E. Colby, "Our Last Indian War," *Infantry Journal* (1936).]

ELBRIDGE COLBY

LEGAL TENDER is anything that, by law, a debtor may require his creditor to receive in payment of a debt, in the absence of the appearance in the contract itself of an agreement for payment in some other manner. The tender is an admission of the debt and in some jurisdictions, if refused, discharges the debt.

There were two periods of American history when the question of legal tender was an important political issue. The first was in the period between 1776 and 1789; the second was in the years just after the Civil War. In the first period the question was whether the states should be permitted to print currency and require its acceptance by creditors regardless of its severe depreciation in value. In the second period the question was whether Congress had power, under the Constitution, to cause the issuance of paper money (greenbacks) that would be legal tender in payment of private debts.

The amount of circulating medium in the newborn states was insufficient to finance a costly war. Nearly every state early had recourse to the printing presses in order to meet its own expenses and the quota levies made by the Continental Congress. At first these issues were small and notes passed at their face value. Soon, however, they began to depreciate, and the state legislatures resorted to laws requiring the acceptance of state bank notes at par. In Connecticut, for example, in 1776, the legislature made both Continental and state notes legal tender and ordered that anyone who tried to depreciate them should forfeit not only the full value of the money he received but also the property he offered for sale. Attempts were also made at price regulation. The South particularly went to excess in the abuse of public credit. Virginia, for example, practically repudiated its paper issues at the close of the Revolution.

The leaders in business and finance in the states were not slow to see the undesirability of a repetition of this financial orgy. Therefore when the Constitutional Convention met in 1787 there was general agreement upon the desirability of providing for a single national system of currency and of prohibiting note issues by the states. Accordingly Article I, Section 10, of the Constitution contains the following prohibitions upon the states, "No state shall . . . coin Money; emit Bills of Credit; make any Thing but gold and silver Coin a Tender in Payment of Debts; pass any . . . ex post facto Law or Law impairing the obligation of Contracts."

The question raised after the Civil War related to the constitutionality of the Legal Tender Act passed by Congress in 1862. It was alleged that Congress, in requiring the acceptance of greenbacks at face value was violating the Fifth Amendment, which forbade the deprivation of property without due process of law (*see* Legal Tender Cases). But the Supreme Court had the power to make paper money legal tender, since the Constitution itself clearly denies such powers to the states.

[Allan Nevins, *The American States During and After the Revolution;* Charles Warren, *The Supreme Court in United States History.*]

HARVEY WALKER

LEGAL TENDER ACT (1862). To provide funds to carry on the Civil War, Congress issued fiat money. By the act of Feb. 25, 1862, and by successive acts, the government put into circulation about $450 million of paper money dubbed "greenbacks." No specific gold reserve was set aside, nor was any date announced for their redemption. To insure their negotiability, Congress declared these notes legal tender in "payment of all taxes, internal duties, excises, debts, and demands of every kind due to the United States, except duties on imports, and of all claims and demands against the United States . . . and shall also be lawful money and legal tender in payment of all debts, public and private, within the United States." Wall Street and the metropolitan press opposed this measure. On the Pacific coast the law was frequently evaded through the passage of acts allowing exceptions on the basis of specific contracts. In 1870 the Supreme Court declared the Legal Tender Act unconstitutional and void in respect to debts contracted prior to its passage, but after two vacancies were filled the Court reversed its decision (*see* Legal Tender Cases).

[Joseph Ellison, "The Currency Question on the Pacific Coast During the Civil War," *Mississippi Valley Historical Review* (June 1929); W. C. Mitchell, *A History of the Greenbacks With Special Reference to the Consequences of Their Issue, 1862–1865.*]

J. W. ELLISON

LEGAL TENDER CASES involved the question of the constitutionality of the measures enacted by the U.S. Congress during the Civil War for the issue of treasury notes to circulate as money without provision for redemption. The constitutional question hinged not on the power of the government to issue the notes but on its power to make them legal tender for the payment of debts, particularly those contracted before the legislation was enacted. The Supreme Court ruled on the question first on Feb. 7, 1870, in the case of *Hepburn* v. *Griswold* (8 Wallace 603). The majority of the Court held that Congress had no power to enact the legal-tender provisions. The vote of the Court members, when taken in conference, had been five to three, with the obvious senility of Justice Robert C. Grier, one of the majority, casting doubt on the weight of his opinion. He retired before the decision was announced, leaving the alignment at that time four to three. The opinion against the constitutionality of the legislation was written by Chief Justice Salmon P. Chase, who as the secretary of the treasury had shared responsiblity for the original enactments.

Nominations of two new members of the Supreme Court were sent to the Senate on the day on which the decision was announced. At the ensuing term, over the protest of the four members who had previously constituted the majority, the Court heard the reargument of the constitutional question in another case. On May 1, 1871, the Court reversed the *Hepburn* decision in *Knox* v. *Lee* and *Parker* v. *Davis* (12 Wallace 457), which are listed in the U.S. Reports under the title of Legal Tender Cases. The question whether President Ulysses S. Grant deliberately packed the Court to bring about a reversal of the original decision is still a matter of debate.

Some of the notes issued were withdrawn by the Treasury, but some were reissued under a later statute enacted without reference to wartime conditions. This statute was upheld on Mar. 3, 1884, in *Juilliard* v. *Greenman.*

[Carl B. Swisher, *Stephen J. Field: Craftsman of the Law;* Charles Warren, *The Supreme Court in United States History.*]

CARL BRENT SWISHER

LEGION OF MERIT. *See* **Decorations, Military.**

LEGISLATURE. Central to democracy, the legislature serves as a link between the desires and needs of the people and the performance of their government. This very centrality frequently makes it the most criticized government organ. Legislative bodies on the national, state, and local levels have shown infinite variety in detail, but great similarity in broad outline. The U.S. Congress has provided the norm. It operates under a constitutional system of separation of powers in which the chief executive is popularly elected, rather than being chosen by and from the legislature. As a result, the president and others of the administration are excluded from direct participation in Congress. The legislature is bicameral, with a Senate that gives equal representation to each state and a House of Representatives that has members apportioned on the basis of each state's population. The two major policial parties, Democratic and Republican, elect the overwhelming majority of the members of both houses. Their parliamentary members choose their own leaders, and the party with a majority organizes each house. More than in most systems, in which the executive is part of the legislature, the party leaders have to share their power with the leaders of the standing committees of the two houses.

All state constitutions provide for separation of powers. Nearly all have bicameral legislatures. Georgia, Pennsylvania, and Vermont experimented with unicameralism in their early history. Nebraska has been operating with a single chamber since 1934. Various bases of representation have been used, with population and units of local government the most common. The U.S. Supreme Court, in *Baker* v. *Carr* (1962) and *Reynolds* v. *Simms* (1964), insisted on a population base for state representation and acted to ensure that legislative districts are frequently redrawn to comply with the principle of one man, one vote. Some have party organizations that are more powerful than those of Congress; others, especially where the two national parties do not approach equality, are less party oriented. Minnesota and Nebraska have abandoned partisan legislative elections.

Local governments have departed furthest from the traditional pattern. In the 20th century a number of local governments, especially those of middle-sized cities, have experimented with unification of powers. The manager form of government provides for a chief executive chosen by, but not from, the legislature, much as superintendents are chosen by school boards. The great majority of local governments have abandoned bicameralism. They have also frequently departed from the pattern of electing legislators from single-member districts, in many cases choosing them citywide. Less likely to have two-party competition, many local governments have organized their elections on a nonpartisan basis.

[William J. Keefe and Morris S. Ogul, *The American Legislative Process: Congress and the States.*]

GEORGE GOODWIN, JR.

LEHIGH VALLEY RAILROAD. *See* **Railroads, Sketches.**

LEISLER REBELLION (1689). The revolution in England that forced James II to abdicate was followed by uprisings in America. On May 31, 1689, Fort James on Manhattan Island was seized, and shortly afterward Capt. Jacob Leisler usurped complete control of southern New York. The following spring, at his suggestion, representatives from Massachusetts, Connecticut, and New York met in New York City to concert measures for a united offensive against Canada. Leisler assumed energetic charge of operations, but lack of cooperation from the other colonies and his own tactlessness spoiled his efforts. In March 1691 Col. Henry Sloughter was commissioned governor of New York by William and Mary. Leisler was tried for treason and executed. Agitation caused a further examination of the case in England, resulting in a reversal of the attainder and restoration of his estates.

[A. C. Flick, ed., *History of the State of New York*, vol. II.]

A. C. FLICK

LEISY V. *HARDIN*. *See* **Original Package Doctrine.**

LEND-LEASE. Put in its simplest terms, lend-lease was a subsidy for America's allies that provided the economic and military aid they needed in order to fight effectively during World War II. Its primary purpose was to provide the sinews of war for Great Britain, the Soviet Union, China, and various members of the British Commonwealth of Nations, although many smaller participants also received lend-lease goods. By the close of the war a total of $47.9 billion of lend-lease aid had been extended by the United States to thirty-eight different countries—most of it in the form of military supplies, although a substantial amount of agricultural goods, raw materials, and manufactured goods also was distributed. Even exchanges of certain scientific information, par-

ticularly between Britain and the United States, fell under the provisions of the Lend-Lease Act of 1941.

Domestic politics and the reluctance of the administration of President Franklin D. Roosevelt to force the aid issue with the so-called isolationists made the subterfuge of lend-lease necessary. After the fall of France in June 1940, the new British prime minister, Winston S. Churchill, warned the American government that Britain could not pay cash for war materials much longer. Unfortunately for England, American law (the Johnson Debt-Default Act of 1934) required any nation at war to pay cash for goods purchased in the United States. This law, a reaction to American intervention in World War I as well as a slap at those nations who had refused to pay their debts from that war, had widespread support in the Congress, and the Roosevelt administration chose not to attempt a repeal. Suspicion that Great Britain and its empire possessed vast amounts of hidden wealth, plus the upcoming presidential election of November 1940, combined to delay any action designed to relieve Britain's financial crisis. Not until after the election, when the British made both public and private pleas for aid, did Roosevelt instruct the Treasury Department and Secretary Henry Morgenthau, Jr., to draw up legislation that would provide Britain and any other nation fighting Germany with the goods to do the job. Knowing that Germany planned to attack the Soviet Union, Roosevelt asked for a bill to provide a broad grant of power that would permit the president to designate the recipients of aid. The highly successful campaign for public support began with Roosevelt's famous analogy of lending one's garden hose to a neighbor to enable him to put out a fire in his house—told at his press conference of Dec. 17, 1940.

Roosevelt's full motives are difficult to determine. He and his advisers were fully convinced that Britain's survival was essential to American national security and that that alone justified their action. In addition, it is clear that he saw the Lend-Lease Act as a key extension of presidential powers—a grant he needed in order to carry out his policies without constant congressional interference. There is also some evidence that Roosevelt hoped that lend-lease would make full military intervention by the United States unnecessary, although few of his cabinet and military advisers believed that. If he did see lend-lease as a sly means of involving America in the European war, as the isolationists claimed, he never said so either publicly or privately.

Roosevelt's sense of timing was perfect. After full

and heated debate in Congress, the bill received overwhelming support, with most of the opposition coming from Republicans who voted against anything Roosevelt proposed. The legislation gave the president the authority to "lease, lend, or otherwise dispose of" anything to any country he specifically designated as assisting in the war effort. Repayment terms were left up to the president, and although the inference was that goods were being lent or leased, the reality was that the bulk of the debts was written off with nominal repayment, since Roosevelt and his successor, Harry S. Truman, considered the military efforts of recipients as a fair exchange.

In essence the lend-lease program was the precursor of America's postwar foreign aid. The United States frequently used it to prop up unstable governments against internal subversion or to bribe smaller nations into joining the alliance against the Axis countries. The long-term effect of lend-lease was extensive. Not only did it constitute a declaration of economic warfare against Germany and lead inevitably to convoying and a naval confrontation with Germany, but it also eliminated the nasty problem of war debts that had clouded the international scene in the interwar years. Logistically it proved to be essential to the development of effective aid programs to America's allies, since it brought virtually all military and economic assistance during the war into a single organization. It was also a major step in the growth of presidential war powers, for Congress retained only a financial veto and a requirement for regular reports. All attempts to limit the scope of the act were labeled as isolationist during the congressional debates and were easily defeated or emasculated. The only loose end left by lend-lease was the failure to negotiate a settlement with the Soviet Union. That settlement was a casualty of the cold war and was not resolved until 1972, as part of an overall Soviet-American trade package.

[George Herring, *Aid to Russia, 1941–1946;* Warren F. Kimball, *The Most Unsordid Act: Lend-Lease, 1939–1941;* Edward Stettinius, *Lend-Lease: Weapon for Victory.*]

WARREN F. KIMBALL

LETTERS FROM A PENNSYLVANIA FARMER. *See* **Farmer's Letters, Dickinson's.**

"LET US HAVE PEACE." In his letter of May 29, 1868, accepting the Republican nomination for the presidency, Gen. Ulysses S. Grant endeavored to speak a word to calm feelings excited by civil war,

reconstruction, and impeachment. His phrase "Let us have peace" became the keynote of his successful campaign.

[J. F. Rhodes, *History of the United States Since the Compromise of 1850.*]

THEODORE M. WHITFIELD

LEVER ACT (Aug. 10, 1917), sponsored by Rep. A. F. Lever of South Carolina to mobilize food and fuel resources for World War I, authorized price fixing of commodities and licensing of producers and distributors and prohibited "unfair" trade practices. Subsequently the Price-Fixing Committee, the Food and Fuel Administrations, and the Grain Corporation were created by executive orders to administer the law.

[F. M. Surface, *The Grain Trade During the World War.*]

MARTIN P. CLAUSSEN

LEVY, an English project in the early years of the 19th century to recruit recent British arrivals in the United States and Canada for an enterprise against Napoleon's French possessions in the West Indies. Charles Williamson, a British officer captured during the Revolution and former agent of the Pulteney Associates, was delegated to organize the Levy in 1803. He proposed to cooperate with Francisco de Miranda in an attack against Spanish possessions in Florida, Mexico, and South America. The Levy may have been offered to Aaron Burr but no organization was ever effected. Miranda and Burr both failed; Williamson returned to England.

[T. R. Hay, "Charles Williamson and the Burr Conspiracy," *Journal of Southern History* (1936).]

THOMAS ROBSON HAY

LEWES, BOMBARDMENT OF, a British attempt to stop shipping in the Delaware River and on Delaware Bay during the War of 1812. On Mar. 14, 1813, a squadron of ten British vessels anchored off Lewes, on Delaware Bay, ravaged shipping, demanded provisions, and threatened to destroy the town if the provisions were not received. By delaying their reply, the Americans gained time to march militia to complete the construction of batteries. On Apr. 6 the British squadron began firing at the town and continued until ten o'clock at night. Firing began again at daybreak and continued until five or six o'clock in the afternoon. The British shots passed high over the town,

LEWIS AND CLARK CENTENNIAL EXPOSITION

with the result that after twenty-two hours of bombardment, during which nearly 900 shots and bombs were fired, no one at Lewes was killed or wounded and only a few houses were damaged. Shortly afterward the British vessels withdrew.

[J. Thomas Scharf, *History of Delaware.*]
LEON DEVALINGER, JR.

LEWIS AND CLARK CENTENNIAL EXPOSITION, held at Portland, Oreg., from June 1 to Oct. 15, 1905, commemorated the historic expedition of Meriwether Lewis and William Clark in opening up the Oregon country to settlement. It occupied 402 acres on the site of Willamette Heights. The federal government and nineteen states participated. Statuary and exhibits were sent from the Louisiana Purchase Exposition of the previous year. Twice the anticipated number of visitors attended and made it a conspicuous financial success.

FRANK MONAGHAN

LEWIS AND CLARK EXPEDITION (1804–06). The problem that Meriwether Lewis and William Clark undertook to solve in 1804 had originated with the dawn of American history. Christopher Columbus had been intent on finding a new way to the Orient, and the accidental discovery of America had been for him a great tragedy. As soon as contemporaries perceived that America barred the way to the Indies, they took up the task of finding a way around or through the troublesome continent, and for centuries this goal afforded one of the chief incitements to further American exploration. President Thomas Jefferson was deeply interested in scientific discoveries, and the Louisiana Purchase in 1803 afforded him a pretext for sending an expedition to explore the western country.

Lewis, Jefferson's private secretary, was appointed to command the expedition, and he associated his friend, William Clark, younger brother of Gen. George Rogers Clark, in the leadership. The party was assembled near Saint Louis late in 1803 in readiness to start up the Missouri River the following spring. In the spring of 1804 it ascended the river by flatboat and keelboat to the group of Mandan and Arikara towns in west central North Dakota.

There the winter was passed, and on Apr. 7, 1805, while the flatboat returned to Saint Louis, the explorers, in six canoes and two keelboats, set their faces toward the unknown West. Besides the two leaders, the party included twenty-six soldiers; George Drouillard and Toussaint Charbonneau, in-

terpreters; Clark's servant, York; and Charbonneau's Indian slave companion, Sacajawea, and her infant son.

On Nov. 7, 1805, the explorers gazed upon the Pacific Ocean. They had ascended the Missouri and its Jefferson fork to the mountains, which, by a rare combination of skill, perseverance, and luck they had crossed to the Snake; thence down the Snake and the Columbia to the sea. The winter was passed in a shelter (named Fort Clatsop) near present-day Astoria, Oreg., and in March 1806 the return journey was begun. After crossing the Rockies the explorers separated into three groups to make a more extensive examination of the country than a single party could accomplish. Thus both the Missouri and the Yellowstone rivers were descended, near whose junction the groups reunited. From here the party passed rapidly downriver to Saint Louis, on Sept. 23, 1806, where the expedition ended.

A great epic in human achievement had been written. Thousands of miles of wilderness had been traversed; an important impulse to the further extension of American trade and settlement had been supplied; and important additions to the existing body of geographical and scientific knowledge had been made.

[Bernard DeVoto, *The Course of Empire;* Donald Jackson, ed., *Letters of the Lewis and Clark Expedition With Related Documents, 1783–1854;* Ernest S. Osgood, *The Field Notes of Captain William Clark.*]
M. M. QUAIFE

LEXINGTON, a name given to four American ships: (1) A Continental brig that, under Capt. John Barry, captured the British sloop *Edward* in April 1776, off Chesapeake Bay. In 1777 it cruised about Ireland under Henry Johnson, but was captured in September of that year. (2) A store ship that, under Lt. Theodorus Bailey, captured San Blas, Mexico, in 1848, in the final naval operation of the Mexican War. (3) A Union sidewheeler, later armored, that fought at Belmont, Miss., Fort Henry, Tenn., and on the Red River, 1861–63. At Shiloh it saved Gen. Ulysses S. Grant's army from being driven back in utter defeat the first day of the battle. (4) A World War II aircraft carrier that participated in the Battle of the Coral Sea, May 7–8, 1942, the first major check to Japan's advance in the Pacific. The *Lexington* was so badly damaged that it had to be sunk by an American destroyer.

[G. W. Allen, *The Naval History of the American Revolution;* R. U. Johnson and C. C. Buel, eds., *Battles and Leaders of the Civil War,* vol. I.]
WALTER B. NORRIS

LEXINGTON, SIEGE OF (Sept. 12–20, 1861). After the Battle of Wilson's Creek, Confederate Gen. Sterling Price of the Missouri State Guard moved his army of 1,500 men northward toward Lexington, Mo., the most important town on the Missouri River between Saint Louis and Saint Joseph and located in the midst of counties that had large slave populations. Lexington was defended by 2,640 men under Union Col. J. A. Mulligan, who entrenched on a hill around the Masonic College. Price surrounded him and, cutting him off from the town, the river, and his water supply, constructed a breastwork of hemp bales that enabled him to move within close range of the defenders in comparative safety. On Sept. 20 Mulligan surrendered, after hopes of reinforcement were gone and his men were suffering from thirst. Price captured commissary stores valued at $100,000 and considerable war materials, but he abandoned Lexington in the face of superior Union forces. Losses on each side were comparatively light.

[R. U. Johnson and C. C. Buel, eds., *Battles and Leaders of the Civil War*, vol. I.]

W. FRANCIS ENGLISH

LEXINGTON AND CONCORD. On the evening of Apr. 18, 1775, the British military governor of Massachusetts sent out from Boston a detachment of about 700 regular troops to destroy military stores collected by the colonists at Concord. Detecting the plan, the Whigs in Boston sent out Paul Revere and William Dawes with warnings. The detachment consequently found at Lexington, at sunrise on Apr. 19, a part of the minuteman company already assembled on the green. At the command of British Maj. John Pitcairn, the regulars fired and cleared the ground. Eight of the Americans were killed and ten were wounded. The regulars marched for Concord after but a short delay.

At Concord the Americans, outnumbered, retired over the North Bridge and waited for reinforcements. The British occupied the town, held the North Bridge with about a hundred regulars, and searched for stores. Of these they found few; but the smoke of those they burned in the town alarmed the watching Americans, and, reinforced to the number of about 450, they marched down to the bridge, led by Maj. John Buttrick. The regulars, seeing them, hastily formed on the farther side to receive them and began to take up the planks of the bridge. Buttrick shouted to them to desist. The front ranks of the regulars fired, killing two Americans and wounding more. Buttrick gave the famous order, "Fire, fellow soldiers, for

God's sake, fire!" The response of his men and their continued advance were too much for the British, who (with two killed and several wounded) broke and fled. The Americans did not follow up their success, and after a dangerous delay the British marched for Boston about noon.

At Meriam's Corner their rear guard was fired upon by the men of Reading, and from there to Lexington a skirmish fire was poured upon the British from all available cover. By the time they reached that town the regulars were almost out of ammunition and completely demoralized. They were saved from slaughter or surrender only by the arrival of a column from Boston, under Sir Hugh Percy, with two fieldpieces that overawed the militia and gave the regulars time to rest. When they marched on again, the militia closed in once more and dogged them all the way to Charlestown, where before sundown the regulars reached safety under the guns of the fleet.

The casualties of the day bear no relation to its importance. Forty-nine Americans and seventy-three British were killed; the total of those killed and wounded of both sides was 366. But the fighting proved to the Americans that by their own method they could defeat the British. In that belief they stopped the land approaches to Boston before night, thus beginning the siege of Boston.

[Major John R. Galvin, *The Minute Men: A Compact History of the Defenders of the American Colonies, 1645–1775*; John Shy, *Toward Lexington: The Role of the British Army in the Coming of the American Revolution*.]

ALLEN FRENCH

LEXINGTON AND OHIO RAILROAD, chartered Jan. 27, 1830, to be built from Lexington, Ky., to some point on the Ohio River. Louisville was selected as the western terminus, and in 1831 the first rail was laid. In 1835 the road was completed to Frankfort. In 1842 the company failed financially. The state of Kentucky leased the line and equipment to a private company, and in 1852 the road was completed between Lexington and Louisville.

[T. D. Clark, "The Lexington and Ohio Railroad—A Pioneer Venture," *Kentucky State Historical Register* (1933).]

T. D. CLARK

LEXOW COMMITTEE, appointed by the New York State Senate on Jan. 30, 1894, to investigate the New York City Police Department, revealed widespread organized graft, called the "system." The system had been evolving for half a century, and, although it was not politically organized, it found special protection under the Tammany Hall leadership of Richard Croker, beginning about 1886. Opponents of the system "were abused, clubbed and imprisoned, and even convicted of crime on false testimony by policemen and their accomplices." Legitimate businesses, from pushcart peddlers to steamship companies, were forced to pay graft. But the underworld was the chief source of revenue, estimated at $7 million annually. Monthly levies were collected—from saloons ($2 to $20), poolrooms ($200), policy shops ($20), bawdy houses ($5 per inmate)—and each new brothel paid, on the average, $500 to open. The graft was divided: 20 percent to the patrolman-collector; from 35 to 50 percent to the precinct commander; the rest to the inspector. It was also testified that it cost $300 to become a patrolman; $300 to be promoted to roundsman; $1,600 to be made a sergeant; and as much as $15,000 for a captaincy. The comparative success of the committee, of which Clarence Lexow, a Republican, was chairman, was brought about chiefly by its fearless counsel, John W. Goff, a Democrat. In the ninth month of the committee's labors, the Republicans, after being out of office for several years, swept the city and state in the elections. One of the new police commissioners was Theodore Roosevelt.

DENIS TILDEN LYNCH

LEYTE GULF, BATTLE OF (Oct. 23–25, 1944). As the first step in recapturing the Philippines from the Japanese, a huge American armada descended on Leyte Island in mid-October 1944. The invasion force, Vice Adm. Thomas C. Kinkaid's Seventh Fleet, included some 700 combat, support, and transport vessels and 500 aircraft. Supporting it was the Third Fleet, under Adm. William F. Halsey, a powerful force of nearly 100 modern warships and more than 1,000 planes. Japanese naval units, sixty-four warships operating in accordance with a defensive plan called *Sho* ("Victory"), immediately moved to oppose the invasion. From the north, a decoy group of aircraft carriers under Vice Adm. Jisaburo Ozawa sought to lure Halsey away so that a powerful battleship force under Vice Adm. Takeo Kurita and a smaller cruiser force under Vice Adm. Kiyohide Shima could move through the central Philippines and fall upon the exposed American amphibious assault units in Leyte Gulf. The Japanese effort was weakened, however, by the fact that they had lost most of their supporting aircraft in the preceding week.

Kurita's force left Borneo on Oct. 22 in two groups. The larger group, thirty-two ships under Kurita himself, would pass through the Sibuyan Sea and San Bernardino Strait in order to enter Leyte Gulf from the north. A much smaller force under Vice Adm. Shoji Nishimura moved through the Sulu Sea toward Surigao Strait, the southern entrance to Leyte Gulf, which he planned to enter simultaneously with Kurita. To back up Nishimura's attack, Shima left Formosan waters at the same time.

Early on Oct. 23, two American submarines attacked Kurita, sinking two heavy cruisers and badly damaging a third. Alerted by this contact, planes from Halsey's carriers began hitting Kurita the next day. In five separate strikes, they sank the 64,000-ton superbattleship *Musashi,* crippled a heavy cruiser, and damaged many of their other targets. At the same time, land-based Japanese aircraft managed to sink one of Halsey's carriers and damage a cruiser. But Kurita, badly shaken by Halsey's attacks and fearing more blows, turned back just as he was approaching San Bernardino Strait. Late in the day, he reversed course again and headed once more for Leyte Gulf, too late for his planned rendezvous with Nishimura and Shima.

To the south, Kinkaid was ready to intercept Nishimura in Surigao Strait. The American battleships and cruisers formed a line across the northern end of the strait—thus capping the "T" of Nishimura's advance—while destroyers and motor torpedo boats were stationed ahead to attack the Japanese flanks. First contact came about midnight of Oct. 24–25, and within a few hours Nishimura was destroyed. Of two Japanese battleships, a heavy cruiser, and four destroyers that entered Surigao Strait, only a badly damaged cruiser and destroyer managed to escape. Only a single U.S. destroyer was damaged, mistakenly struck by American fire. Shima's small force, which arrived shortly thereafter, was also warmly greeted, but escaped with only small damage. Pursuing American ships and planes sank another cruiser and destroyer before what was left of the two Japanese forces could get completely away.

Meanwhile, before dawn on Oct. 25, Kurita's force debouched from San Bernardino Strait and headed for Leyte Gulf. Halsey, who should have intercepted him, had rushed north to attack Ozawa, in the mistaken belief that Kurita had been crippled and that Ozawa's carriers now constituted the main threat. He was unaware that Japanese aircraft losses had left Ozawa with barely 100 planes. Shortly after sunrise, Kurita struck Kinkaid's northernmost unit, a small force of escort carriers and destroyers. For more than two hours, in a confused, running fight, the tiny American force fought off the powerful Japanese fleet. American destroyers made repeated attacks to cover the fleeing escort carriers, whose planes constantly harassed Kurita. Suddenly, Kurita broke off his attack. Although he had sunk one escort carrier and three destroyers, he had suffered considerable damage himself. Convinced that he was being attacked by heavy units of the American fleet, aware of the destruction of Nishimura and Shima, and believing that he could no longer reach Leyte Gulf in time to do significant damage, the Japanese commander concluded that he should save what was left of his fleet for another day. He turned north and made good his escape. The Americans were harassed by a few land-based suicide planes, which sank another escort carrier, but otherwise Kinkaid was out of danger. Far to the north, Halsey struck Ozawa's decoy force. By afternoon on Oct. 25, in the final action of the far-flung battle, he had sunk four Japanese carriers, a cruiser, and two destroyers.

The great one-sided American victory destroyed the Japanese fleet as an effective fighting force. It also ensured the conquest of Leyte and cleared the way for the invasion and ultimate recapture of all the Philippine Islands.

[Stanley L. Falk, *Decision at Leyte;* Samuel Eliot Morison, *History of United States Naval Operations in World War II,* vol. XII.]

STANLEY L. FALK

LIBBY PRISON was, after the prison at Andersonville, Ga., the most notorious of Confederate prisons. When the captives from the first Battle of Bull Run arrived in Richmond in the summer of 1861, Gen. John H. Winder, provost marshal of the city, commandeered a number of vacant tobacco warehouses, among them one belonging to the firm of Libby and Son. Commissioned officers were confined there until after the fall of Richmond in 1865. The prison contained eight rooms, 103 by 42 feet, each equipped with a stove upon which the prisoners cooked their rations. After the failure of the cartel for the exchange of prisoners, Libby became crowded, and a shortage of food supplies during December 1863 and January 1864 caused extensive suffering among the inmates. In February 109 officers escaped through a tunnel, and 61 made their way to the Union lines. On Feb. 28 and Mar. 4, 1864, two cavalry raids were made on Richmond for the purpose of releasing the prisoners (*see* Dahlgren's Raid). As a result of these events the Confederates established a new prison for officers at

Macon, Ga., in May 1864. Thereafter Libby Prison was used only as a temporary station for captives en route to Macon.

[William B. Hesseltine, *Civil War Prisons: A Study in War Psychology.*]

W. B. HESSELTINE

LIBEL in Anglo-American law includes defamatory matter in some such permanent form as writing, printing, or painting, the less permanent or oral form being designated as slander. In Tudor and Stuart England published libels attacking public officers were rigorously dealt with, and as a result a distinction developed between civil suits for libel and criminal prosecutions. In the latter, truth did not constitute a defense. In some measure English political libel suits were paralleled in colonial America. The most celebrated prosecution was that of John Peter Zenger, New York printer, in 1735. In this case the prosecution contended that only the fact of publication could be determined by the jury, while the court was to determine whether the publication was libelous. Andrew Hamilton, counsel for the prisoner, persuaded the jury to judge both law and fact and secured Zenger's acquittal. This trial has generally been regarded as the first great victory for the freedom of the press in America. Reports of the trial were widely circulated in Great Britain and its colonies, but in neither English nor colonial law was the Zenger case considered a precedent.

The Sedition Act of 1798 allowed the defense to give evidence of the truth of the matter contained in the publication charged as a libel, the jury having the right to determine the law and the fact. Although the law expired in 1801, the whole question was brought to a head by the famous trial in New York of Harry Croswell, publisher of the *Hudson* (N.Y.) *Wasp,* for a libel on President Thomas Jefferson. As a result of Alexander Hamilton's arguments, the same ruling as in the Zenger case prevailed, and a precedent was set for the American common law. In 1805 a statute was enacted by New York State embodying the result of this decision, permitting the defendant to give truth in justification, provided it was published "with good motives and for justifiable ends."

While technically at common law oral defamation was a tort rather than a crime, in the colonial courts a flood of criminal prosecutions, as well as civil suits, for defamatory utterance gave unusual color and vitality to the court minutes of that period. In modern times criminal slander is not recognized in law, and civil suits for oral defamation have greatly declined in number and frequency. There is still judicial disagreement concerning whether oral defamation through the means of radio and television is libel or slander.

[J. C. Gatley, *Libel and Slander in a Civil Action;* W. S. Holdsworth, *History of English Law,* vols. III, V, VII.]
RICHARD B. MORRIS

LIBERALISM. The specific objectives of liberals vary from one generation to the next and are sometimes subject to vigorous debate even within a generation, but their basic philosophy has been constant throughout American history. Believing in the rationality of man and the dignity of the individual, committed to freedom, equal justice, and equal opportunity, liberals have always been reformers with little reverence for tradition and great faith in the power of human intelligence to establish a more just society. They have distrusted power and privilege, felt sympathy for the exploited and deprived, and relied upon rational and enlightened social and economic policies to rehabilitate even the lowest elements of society.

The Anglo-American liberalism of the 18th and 19th centuries, traceable to John Locke and Adam Smith, was a reaction against powerful monarchies that oppressed the masses and dispensed special privileges to a favored few. It espoused a strictly limited, decentralized government. The natural rights of the individual—most frequently identified as rights to life, liberty, property, and the pursuit of happiness—had to be protected from the state. This supposition underlay the American Revolution, the Bill of Rights, Jeffersonian Democracy, Jacksonian Democracy, and the antislavery movement. The liberal conviction that all men have basic rights and are entitled to basic opportunities led liberal reform to be identified with popular, democratic movements; on the other side of the coin was the necessity to protect natural rights even against the will of the majority. Overall, the liberalism of the antebellum American republic was a persuasion well suited to an individualistic agrarian society hardly touched by the forces of industrial capitalism.

In the late 19th century liberalism began to find new definitions in response to the rapid growth of monopolistic corporate power. As private power structures appeared to be the greatest threats to the natural rights of the individual, the state emerged as a protector. Laissez-faire no longer seemed a viable formula for a newly complex society with increasingly visible injustices. Workers, farmers, and intellectuals all

began to develop the ideal of a strong activist government affirmatively promoting the welfare of its citizens.

The Populist movement, primarily the vehicle of depressed southern and midwestern farmers, advocated a wide range of reforms. The multifaceted Progressive movement of the early 20th century, more urban and middle class in its constituency, indicated the maturation of the new liberalism. The Progressives struggled for a variety of measures designed to bring government closer to the people. They sought to curb corporate power through either trust-busting (the New Freedom) or trust regulation (the New Nationalism). They formulated the beginnings of a social welfare state that would work for the goals of human dignity and equal opportunity through active government programs in behalf of the underprivileged.

The New Deal was based squarely upon the intellectual heritage of progressivism. Its most important achievements were the adoption of a vast body of reform legislation and the building of a durable liberal political coalition. Its failures involved problems the Progressives had been unable to solve—most notably corporate concentration—or had not faced—for example, mass unemployment. The New Deal erected a rudimentary social welfare state, recognized struggling minorities, and established a rough system of countervailing power that strengthened agriculture and labor in what had been a corporate-dominated society. Perhaps most important, it brought forth a political coalition, based on labor and the urban lower classes, that would provide the sustenance for successor liberal movements—the Fair Deal, the New Frontier, and the Great Society.

In its approach to diplomacy American liberalism has faced the dilemma inherent in the use of liberal idealism as the guideline for dealing with an illiberal world. Not prone to think in terms of national self-interest or power politics, most liberals have been able to accept war only if it could be justified as essential to a quest for the near-total fulfillment of an international liberal vision. Those who supported the two great world wars of the 20th century, for example, did so in the belief that the outcome of each would be a planet safe for democracy and free from oppression. In both cases the imperfect results disillusioned many. After World War I most liberals turned to isolationism, but after World War II, impressed by the horrors of Stalinist communism and by the surface idealism of U.S. foreign policy, they reluctantly supported the cold war.

By the last third of the 20th century liberalism was in some measure in disrepute. Large, expensive neo–New Deal social welfare programs appeared to have achieved scant success in resolving the discontent of the underprivileged. The unhappy American venture in Vietnam, brought to its peak by a liberal president, had divided the liberal movement and left it without a solid foreign policy orientation. Liberal reformers faced the task of redefining their objectives at home and abroad.

[E. F. Goldman, *Rendezvous With Destiny;* L. Hartz, *The Liberal Tradition in America;* R. Hofstadter, *The Age of Reform.*]

ALONZO L. HAMBY

LIBERAL REPUBLICAN PARTY was the result of revolt of the reform element in the Republican party during President Ulysses S. Grant's first administration (1869–73). It advocated a conciliatory policy toward the South (*see* Reconstruction) and civil service reform and condemned political corruption. Some members of the party favored tariff revision. The movement was led by B. Gratz Brown, Carl Schurz, Charles Sumner, Charles Francis Adams, and Horace Greeley. Greeley was named for president and Brown for vice-president in 1872, and both candidates were later endorsed by the Democrats. In the ensuing campaign Greeley was overwhelmingly defeated by Grant.

[Edward Stanwood, *A History of the Presidency From 1788 to 1897.*]

GLENN H. BENTON

LIBERATOR, a weekly antislavery newspaper edited by William Lloyd Garrison and published in Boston, Jan. 1, 1831, to Dec. 29, 1865. Its circulation never exceeded 3,000. The annual subscription price was $2. Although never a success financially, this paper was largely influential in turning the antislavery movement from the advocacy of gradual emancipation to a demand for immediate, uncompensated emancipation. It greatly aided Garrison's work in organizing the New England Anti-Slavery Society in 1832 and the American Anti-Slavery Society in 1833. In its first issue he sounded its keynote in these words: "I am in earnest—I will not equivocate—I will not excuse—I will not retreat a single inch; and I will be heard!"

[Edward Channing, *A History of the United States.*]

ASA E. MARTIN

LIBERIA lies on the western coast of Africa and is the continent's oldest republic. The area is approximately 43,000 square miles, mostly dense tropical rain forest. The estimated population in 1973 was 1,650,000. Nearly the entire population is indigenous, comprising about twenty ethnic groups, of which the interior Kpelle and coastal Bassa and Kru peoples account for over half the total. Two percent belong to the Americo-Liberian elite, descended from liberated slaves and black American freedmen repatriated to Africa in the 19th century through the efforts of the American Colonization Society.

Since the founding of Liberia in 1822, the United States has maintained a policy of relative detachment. The colony declared itself independent in 1847, but the United States, embroiled in controversy over slavery, withheld recognition until 1862. American naval vessels occasionally assisted Liberian colonists in police actions against recalcitrant indigenes. In 1909 and 1915 the U.S.S. *Chester* was sent to rescue American missionaries and Liberian officials during Kru rebellions.

Relatively prosperous during the mid-19th century, Liberia became territorially overextended and declined disastrously when faced with European commercial and colonial competition. British and French traders and diplomats reduced Liberian territory by one-third before the United States quietly applied pressure around 1900 to preserve Liberian independence. Germany and even Poland cast covetous eyes on the struggling republic. By 1912 Liberia was badly in default to European creditors, and in return for a loan from the United States agreed to accept American customs officers and a military mission. Heavy investment by the Firestone Tire and Rubber Company in Liberian rubber plantations after 1926 partially alleviated financial strains. The United States suspended diplomatic relations from 1930 to 1935 over alleged forced labor abuses and cooperated with Liberian and League of Nations authorities in investigating the charges. United States influence peaked during World War II when the Liberian capital, Monrovia, became a major supply depot. Exports of high-grade iron ore began to revolutionize the country in the 1960's. European and Asian influence and capital now compete heavily with American.

The Liberian constitution replicates the U.S. form: a bicameral legislature with the lower house apportioned somewhat according to the population in nine counties and four territories. The True Whig party has ruled continuously since 1877, perpetuating Americo-Liberian oligarchy. Legislative and judicial branches have atrophied and power has been concentrated in the executive, especially under President William V. S. Tubman (1944–71). Tubman's National Unification Plan, supposed to close the gap between the oligarchy and indigenous peoples, was only a marginal success.

[R. L. Buell, *The Native Problem in Africa,* vol. II; Sir Harry Johnston, *Liberia,* vol. I; J. G. Liebenow, *Liberia: The Evolution of Privilege.*]

RONALD W. DAVIS

LIBERTY, CONCEPT OF. Liberty may be understood as a relationship between men living in society under government. Aristotle maintained that liberty is not desirable for its own sake, but always for the sake of something else. Otherwise it would be a formal and empty category. Every liberty that is liberty for something necessarily limits liberty and therefore establishes a distinction between liberty and license. It makes liberty dependent on the end for which it is intended. Whatever virtue can be ascribed to liberty, Aristotle would say, derives from its ability to contribute to moral and intellectual excellence. Therefore moral and intellectual excellence must be regarded as liberty's end, not merely its instrument. The tendency of Thomas Hobbes, John Locke, and Charles de Secondat, Baron de Montesquieu, was to give liberty a more central place than Aristotle did in their construction of ideal regimes.

The concept of liberty, as it is presently understood, has its roots in modern natural-right teaching. According to that teaching, developed primarily by Hobbes and Locke, the right to liberty is a necessary inference from the right of self-preservation, or is conceived as implicit in the exercise of that primary or natural right. From this point of view, the activities of the state should be directed toward providing security for life and for liberty, with the people as a whole judging the legitimacy of the exercise of that authority.

According to Locke, the best safeguards for the liberties of individuals are provided by a well-constructed constitution that, in almost all domestic concerns, subordinates the executive power to law and ultimately to a legislative assembly limited to the making of laws, with its representatives elected by the people for short periods of tenure. His great theme was liberty, and his great argument was that there is no liberty where there is no law. In a system such as Locke constructed, in which the decisive political power is in the hands of the majority, the political conflict between the majority-rule aspect of the regime and liberty is always a danger, for majorities do not always respect the liberties of minorities.

Montesquieu accordingly argued that liberty's crucial requirement is the separation of the powers of government—into legislative, executive, and judicial powers—so that they rest in different hands. If any two or all are combined in the same hands, power is too concentrated and insufficiently checked. Montesquieu's idea was that the wrong that a man or a body of men can do is lessened if one or two of the other bodies is in a position not necessarily dominated by the same intention and can use its power and pressure to slow down and act as a check on the other body.

The Locke-Montesquieu view of liberty became a part of the fundamental law inscribed in the American Constitution. On the basis of the Constitution, the American regime places central emphasis on individual liberty enforced through law and the delicate processes of government, which include separation of powers and a system of checks and balances.

MORTON J. FRISCH

"LIBERTY, SONG OF," was written in 1768 by John Dickinson, the Pennsylvania statesman often called the penman of the Revolution, to unite Americans against British oppression by expressing in popular verse his convictions of the necessity of colonial union. The song enjoyed immense popularity among the Sons of Liberty and played an important part in creating that unanimity of thought and action that Dickinson believed essential to the preservation of American liberty.

[M. C. Tyler, *The Literary History of the American Revolution.*]

JOHN C. MILLER

LIBERTY BELL. Ordered at a cost of £60 by the Philadelphia provincial council in 1751 for the golden jubilee of William Penn's Charter of Privileges, the bell now known as the Liberty Bell was cracked in testing upon arrival and recast by John Pass and Charles Stow of Philadelphia. It was installed in the Philadelphia state house and proclaimed American independence following the reading there on July 8, 1776, of the Declaration of Independence. During the years 1777–78, it was hidden from the British in Allentown, Pa. Rung frequently for celebrations, the bell was first strained tolling the obsequies of Chief Justice John Marshall in 1835 and was fatally cracked and silenced during the celebration of George Washington's birthday in 1846. It was first called the Liberty Bell by members of the antislavery movement in 1839. The Liberty Bell weighs over 2,080 pounds, and is inscribed "Proclaim Liberty throughout all the land unto all the inhabitants thereof." It is now housed in Independence National Historical Park.

[J. B. Stoudt, *The Liberty Bells of Pennsylvania.*]
JULIAN P. BOYD

LIBERTY BOYS. *See* **Sons of Liberty, (American Revolution)**

LIBERTY CAP, with a sharp-pointed apex tilted forward, was much used in the late 18th century. Probably Phrygian in origin, and apparently used in Rome as a token of manumission, a cap of this form was used by revolutionists in France after 1789. The red cap, or *bonnet rouge,* of the extremists became notorious (*see* Jacobin Clubs). With the extension of French revolutionary sentiment in America in the next decade, radical Jeffersonian Republicans sometimes donned liberty caps.

ALFRED P. JAMES

LIBERTY-CAP CENT, a U.S. coin, about an inch in diameter, struck by the U.S. mint at Philadelphia, 1793–96. On the obverse is a bust of Liberty with a pole over the left shoulder surmounted by a liberty cap.

THOMAS L. HARRIS

LIBERTY LOANS. Upon the entry of the United States into World War I in April 1917, it at once became apparent that large sums in excess of tax receipts would be needed both to provide funds for European allies and to conduct the war activities of the nation. To obtain the necessary funds, the Treasury resorted to borrowing through a series of bond issues. The first four issues were known as liberty loans; the fifth and last was called the victory loan.

The issues were brought out between May 14, 1917, and Apr. 21, 1919, in the total amount of $21,478,356,250. The separate issues were as follows: first liberty loan, $2 billion; second liberty loan, $3,808,766,150; third liberty loan, $4,176,516,850; fourth liberty loan, $6,993,073,250; and victory loan, $4.5 billion. The liberty loans were long-term bonds bearing from 3.5 to 4.25 percent interest, and the vic-

tory loan consisted of two series of three- and four-year notes bearing interest at 3.75 and 4.75 percent. The issues were all oversubscribed.

The disposal of this vast amount of obligations was accomplished by direct sales to the people on an unprecedented scale. Liberty loan committees were organized in all sections of the country, and almost the entire population was canvassed. Four-minute speakers gave high-powered sales talks in theaters, motion picture houses, hotels, and restaurants. The clergymen of the country made pleas for the purchase of bonds from their pulpits. Mass meetings were held upon occasion, and the banks assisted by lending money, at a rate no higher than the interest on the bonds, to those who could not afford to purchase the bonds outright. In this way it was possible to secure the funds wanted and to obtain oversubscriptions on each issue.

[D. R. Dewey, *Financial History of the United States;* A. D. Noyes, *The War Period of American Finance.*]
FREDERICK A. BRADFORD

LIBERTY PARTY, the first antislavery political party, was formed by opponents of William Lloyd Garrison's abolitionists in 1839. James G. Birney, the party's candidate for president in 1840, won about 7,000 votes in the election. In 1844 he won more than 62,000, drawing enough votes from Henry Clay to give New York and the election to James K. Polk. In 1848 the party nominated John P. Hale, but he withdrew and the party merged with the Free Soil organization. The leaders of the Liberty party included Salmon P. Chase, Gerrit Smith, Myron Holley, and Charles Torrey.

[T. C. Smith, *History of the Liberty and Free Soil Parties in the Northwest.*]
THEODORE W. COUSENS

LIBERTY POLES, or liberty trees, were symbols before which Sons of Liberty assembled and "pledged their fortunes and their sacred honors in the cause of liberty" during the period just before the American Revolution. Numerology played a part in the erection of liberty poles, particularly the numbers ninety-two and forty-five. The former symbolized the issue of John Wilkes's newspaper that had criticized the king, and the latter symbolized the votes in the Massachusetts legislature in 1768 against rescission of the circular letter to the other twelve colonies calling for united action against British abuses of power. Ninety-two Sons of Liberty raised a liberty pole forty-five feet high or dedicated a tree with ninety-two branches after seventeen had been lopped off in detestation of the seventeen Tories who had voted to rescind the circular letter.

The best-known liberty pole was erected in New York City in 1766, with approval of the royal governor, in celebration of repeal of the Stamp Act. Raised in harmony, it soon became the focus of brawls between British soldiers and Liberty Boys, attended by street fights and bloodshed.

The original liberty tree was an elm at the intersection of Washington and Essex streets, Boston; it was a rallying place for Sons of Liberty who met under its boughs, denounced British oppression, drank toasts, sang songs, and hanged unpopular officials in effigy. It was cut down by British soldiers in 1775 and converted into fourteen cords of firewood.

[W. C. Abbott, *New York in the American Revolution;* Justin Winsor, *Memorial History of Boston.*]

LLOYD C. M. HARE

LIBERTY SHIP. *See* **Merchant Marine; Shipbuilding.**

LIBRARIES. From their beginnings libraries in the United States have been characterized by diversity of size, type, and resources. Although sharing the basic functions of acquiring, organizing, preserving, and disseminating recorded knowledge, they have served a variety of clienteles and thus have had different focuses.

After the founding of the Harvard College Library in 1638 libraries developed sporadically until well into the 18th century. Capt. Robert Keayne willed a sum to the city of Boston in 1655 for various public purposes, including a town library, and the city met the conditions of his bequest by erecting a public building in which a room was set aside for a library. This library was destroyed by fire in 1747. Some years later a number of church-related libraries were established along the Atlantic seaboard by Thomas Bray, a clergyman who spent a few months in the colonies under the sponsorship of the Anglican church in 1689; the largest of these libraries was in Annapolis, Md. At the turn of the century libraries were established with the founding of William and Mary College and Yale College in 1693 and 1701, respectively. A few New England towns inherited small collections, as had Boston from Keayne, but no provision was made for their expansion or upkeep and they passed out of existence.

Not until 1731 did the next significant library development occur, with the founding of the first subscription library by Benjamin Franklin. Having organized the Junto, a social club for intellectual discussion and debate, he soon realized that a library was necessary to support the club's activities and astutely arranged for the members to pool their personal book collections to form the Library Company of Philadelphia. Other social libraries were soon founded in Durham and Lebanon, Conn., and in 1750 the Redwood Library, which is the oldest library in the United States, was erected in Newport, R.I.

As the country turned increasingly from agriculture to manufacturing and mercantile pursuits the need for greater access to educational materials in population centers found expression in social libraries. The social library was the basis for the first library movement in the United States and was to dominate the library scene for well over a hundred years. It was of two basic types: proprietary and subscription. The proprietary library was, in effect, a joint-stock company, whereas the subscription library was a corporation to which a member paid an annual fee for service. Proprietary libraries levied assessments on shareholders and in some cases permitted others to use the library for an annual fee. Between 1733 and 1850 more than 1,000 social libraries were established, mostly in New England, but also in Ohio, Kentucky, and Indiana as the population moved westward. Although these collections were small and members few, the fees were low enough to make the organizations attractive to many classes of society. There were, for example, social libraries for mechanics, clerks, juveniles, and factory workers. The major weaknesses, lack of continuity beyond the founding group and uncertain financial support—common to all voluntary associations—contributed to the decline of the social library and its replacement by the free, public, tax-supported library in the mid-19th century.

Free public libraries for juveniles had been founded in Salisbury, Conn., in 1803 and in Lexington, Mass., in 1827. But it was Peterborough, N.H., that first took advantage of state education funds to found a free public town library, opened in 1833 and supported by annual appropriations; as of the mid-1970's it was still in operation. The primacy of Peterborough in introducing a new library organization concept was overshadowed in 1852 when the Boston Public Library came into being. The report of its trustees issued in July of that year is still recognized as the most comprehensive statement of purpose, functions, and objectives for the modern American public library. It was nearly half a century later before the endowment trusts of John Jacob Astor, James Lenox, and Samuel J. Tilden were combined in 1895 to make possible the New York Public Library.

Encouraged by a commitment to free, popular education and permissive state legislation, public libraries quickly began to spread out, absorbing or supplanting social libraries. Several of the states followed the pattern set by New York in permitting school districts to levy a tax to establish and support public libraries. As the Civil War approached, the concept of the public library had just been established, and although the nation boasted more than 500 libraries only those at Harvard and Yale could count as many as 50,000 volumes. Literary societies were still important in campus life, providing for the library needs of their members with collections often rivaling those of the college libraries.

Several developments significant in modern library history occurred in the pivotal year 1876. At a meeting held during the Centennial Exposition in Philadelphia, Oct. 4–6, a group of librarians voted on the third day of the conference to form the American Library Association. Among them was Melvil Dewey, then not yet twenty-five years of age and only recently graduated from Amherst College, who was to be a dominant force in the library world for the next thirty years. In the same year the U.S. Office of Education issued its first report on libraries, *Public Libraries in the United States of America: Their History, Condition and Management,* in two parts. The first part contained the results of a survey of over 3,800 public libraries. The second part comprised Rules for a Printed Dictionary Catalogue by Charles Ammi Cutter, librarian of the Boston Athenaeum. These rules were quickly adopted by libraries for both printed and card catalogs. The first library periodical, *Library Journal,* was founded in 1876 and Dewey's famous decimal classification scheme, the most widely used library classification system in the world, first appeared in the same year.

In 1900 the library school at Columbia College had produced its first graduates, and Herbert Putnam had moved from the Boston Public Library to begin his impressive forty-year career as Librarian of Congress. Within a few years every major type of library was represented in the United States and most were well established, headed by the Library of Congress. Under Putnam it assumed a dual role, serving the U.S. Congress and functioning as a national library. From 1850 to 1876 the Library of Congress collection grew from 50,000 volumes to about 300,000 volumes; by 1974 its collections held nearly 74 million items, including books and pamphlets, as well as slides, films, prints, sheet music, manuscripts, and art reproductions. The Library of Congress defines its scope as universal, but the growth of other major federal libraries, including the National Library of Medicine and the National Agricultural Library, has tended to diminish the significance of that claim.

Closely related to the Library of Congress by their support for research, but separate in development, are the many research libraries in the United States. University libraries dominate this category, although a few research libraries—such as the Newberry Library in Chicago, the Henry E. Huntington Library in San Marino, Cal., and the Library Company of Philadelphia—remain private and independent. Still others, although independently controlled, have become associated with universities, for example, the John Carter Brown Library at Brown University and the William L. Clements Library at the University of Michigan. The university research library developed in response to an increased emphasis on research and graduate work, as exemplified by Johns Hopkins University under Daniel Coit Gilman. The growing demands of scholarly research are reflected in the fact that in 1876 only two libraries—Harvard and Yale—held more than 100,000 volumes, whereas by 1891 the number had grown from two to five; by the early 1970's more than fifty university libraries contained over 1 million volumes.

From their beginnings in the late 19th century through the first half of the 20th century, school libraries had minimal educational influence, primarily because elementary and secondary education remained textbook oriented until the 1940's. With the passage of the National Defense Education Act in 1958 massive financial assistance became available to school libraries, and in 1965 the Elementary and Secondary Education Act augmented that assistance. With those new sources of funds—and guided by standards and the concept of the school media center—such libraries soon came to constitute the largest category of libraries and continue a growing, vital force in American education.

More than 10,000 U.S. libraries are devoted to special subject matter or a specialized clientele. Among these are libraries of private companies—banking, insurance, research, manufacturing—and those associated with public institutions, including government agencies.

The urban public library is the prototype library in the United States. It serves, or has served, all the clientele served by other libraries. It has pioneered in the development of most of the significant concepts of American librarianship, for example, the open shelf, by the Cleveland Public Library, and subject divisional organization, by the Providence Public Library. In the latter part of the 20th century, however, costs and diminishing income, combined with ambiguity of purpose, reduced the capability of public libraries to respond quickly to changing public needs.

After 1956 the federal government began to play an increasingly influential role in library development. Federal funds supported extended service to rural areas, construction of new facilities, training of new librarians, and extensive research into library problems. By the mid-1970's the sharing of responsibility for library service by federal, state, and local government brought U.S. libraries of all types to the verge of launching a national library system capable of equalizing library resources and services to all Americans.

[Jean Key Gates, *Introduction to Librarianship;* Douglas M. Knight and Nourse Shepley, eds., *Libraries at Large;* Jesse H. Shera, *Foundations of the Public Library: The Origins of the Public Library Movement in New England, 1629–1855.*]

ROBERT WEDGEWORTH

LIBRARY OF CONGRESS, established by the same act of Congress, approved Apr. 24, 1800, that made provision for the removal of the government of the United States to the new federal city, Washington, D.C. It provided for ''the purchase of such books as may be necessary for the use of Congress'' and for ''fitting up a suitable apartment'' in the Capitol to house them. The original collections of the library, obtained from London, consisted of 152 works in 740 volumes and a few maps. To administer them, Congress, in an act of Jan. 26, 1802, provided that a librarian be appointed, and three days later President Thomas Jefferson named John James Beckley, clerk of the House of Representatives, who held both posts until his death.

When British troops burned the Capitol in 1814, the library of some 3,000 volumes was lost. To replace it, Congress purchased Jefferson's personal library, consisting of an estimated 6,487 books, for $23,950. This fine collection, far-ranging in subject matter, was ''admirably calculated for the substratum of a great national library,'' proponents of its purchase contended. In 1851 a Christmas Eve fire destroyed some 35,000 volumes, including two-thirds of the Jefferson library. By the end of 1864, the

collections had grown to some 82,000 volumes, but they were far from distinguished, and national only in the sense that the government owned them. Then Congress, in less than three years, passed four laws that cast the library in the mold of greatness: an act of Mar. 3, 1865, requiring the deposit in the library of a copy of all books and other materials on which copyright was claimed, with loss of copyright for failure to deposit; an act of Apr. 5, 1866, transferring to the Library of Congress the Smithsonian Institution's unique collection (40,000 volumes plus future increments) of scientific materials and transactions of learned societies, gathered from all over the world; an act of Mar. 2, 1867, strengthening international exchange of official publications and making the library the beneficiary; and an appropriations act of Mar. 2, 1867, providing $100,000 for the purchase of the Peter Force collection of Americana—the first major purchase since the Jefferson library and the library's first distinguished research collection. The 19th century also saw the creation (1832) of the Law Library in the Library of Congress, the assignment (1870) to the library of responsibility for the administration of the copyright law, and the first substantial gift to the library by a private citizen—Dr. Joseph Meredith Toner's collection of medical literature and of materials for the study of American history and biography, which was accepted by Congress in 1882.

In 1897 the library, which had grown to nearly a million volumes, moved from the Capitol to its own building. In preparation, Congress, in an appropriations act of Feb. 19, 1897—the nearest to an organic act the library has—provided for the appointment of the librarian by the president, by and with the advice and consent of the Senate, and vested in the librarian the authority to make regulations for the government of the library and to appoint members of the staff ''solely with reference to their fitness for their particular duties.''

The collections are housed in the ''old'' or main building; in the annex, which was occupied in 1939; and in rental space. Some are scheduled to be moved late in 1978 to the Library of Congress James Madison Memorial Building, authorized by Congress in 1965 for construction on a Capitol Hill site adjacent to the main building and to the Cannon House Office Building.

The functions of the library were extended by Congress until it became, in effect, the national library, serving the Congress, federal agencies, other libraries, and the public. It provides research and reference services to the Congress; for example, 210,893 requests were directed in 1974 to the Congressional Research Service, one of the six departments of the library, by members and committees of Congress. The library's comprehensive collections are open to adults for reference use, and some reference service is provided by mail. The use of the book collections is extended through interlibrary loan for persons unable to locate the research materials they need in libraries in their own regions, and is further extended through the Photoduplication Service, from which various types of photocopies of unrestricted materials can be purchased.

The library contains the national Copyright Office for the registration of claims to copyright, and its collections are enriched from the copyright deposits. It is the United States partner in the official, intergovernmental exchange of publications and has thousands of exchange agreements with private research institutions throughout the world. It also purchases materials, obtains them through official transfer, and receives gifts to the nation in the form of personal papers, rare books, and other valuable materials.

During the 20th century, the Library of Congress emerged as a library "universal in scope, national in service," as Librarian Herbert Putnam termed it. By June 30, 1974, the collections totaled almost 74 million items and constituted unparalleled resources for research. They included more than 16 million books and pamphlets on every subject and in a multitude of languages. Among them are the most comprehensive collections of Chinese, Japanese, and Russian materials outside the Orient and the Soviet Union; over 2 million volumes relating to science and technology and nearly as many legal materials, outstanding for foreign as well as American law; the world's largest collection of aeronautical literature; and the most extensive collection of incunabula in the Western Hemisphere, including a perfect copy of the Gutenberg Bible printed on vellum. The manuscript collections totaled more than 31 million items relating to American history and civilization and included the personal papers of twenty-three presidents. The music collections, from classical to modern, contained more than 3.4 million volumes and pieces, in manuscript form and published. Other materials included more than 3 million maps and views; 8.4 million photographic items, from the Civil War photographs of Mathew B. Brady to date; 428,000 recordings, including folksongs and other music, speeches, and poetry read-

ings; 174,000 fine prints and reproductions; newspapers and periodicals from all over the world; and motion pictures, microfilms, and many other kinds of materials.

The library plays a central role in a national program for the preservation of library materials, working with other libraries, library associations, and technical agencies and associations. It is also taking the lead in the automation of library processes.

Thousands of libraries throughout the world use the subject-classification system and cataloging codes developed by the library. Since 1901 the library has made its printed cards available to other libraries, and more recently it has offered bibliographic information in book form as well, including by 1975, 350 volumes of *National Union Catalog, Pre-1956 Imprints*. Since 1966 cataloging data in machine-readable form also have been distributed to libraries and library networks through the MARC (MAchine-Readable Cataloging) Distribution Service; and the MARC format has been accepted as a national and international standard. A program started in 1971, Cataloging in Publication, is providing publishers with cataloging data that can be printed in the published book; in 1975 such information was available in most of the trade books issued by American publishers.

Both acquisitions and cataloging for the Library of Congress and other U.S. libraries have benefited from two special programs authorized by Congress. In the 1960's, under Public Law 480, as amended, the Library of Congress acquired for itself and some 350 other U.S. libraries, through the use of surplus U.S.-owned foreign currencies, over 16 million books and serial pieces published abroad. Through the National Program for Acquisitions and Cataloging, begun under the Higher Education Act of 1965, the library promptly acquires other foreign materials and speeds up its cataloging service by utilizing the cataloging done in the countries of origin for their own national bibliographies.

The Pratt-Smoot Act in 1931 authorized the library to establish a free, nationwide library service for adult blind readers; in 1952 the act was amended to permit service to blind children as well; and in 1966 the service was extended to all persons unable to read conventional printed materials because of physical or visual limitations. The library in the mid-1970's served over 300,000 readers through fifty-three cooperating regional libraries.

The Library of Congress Trust Fund Board, created by an act of Congress on Mar. 3, 1925, accepts—

with the approval of the Joint Committee on the Library—and administers gifts and bequests that enable the library to develop tools for research, to enrich its collections, to issue special publications, and to present cultural programs in the fields of music and literature. Concerts and literary programs presented in the library's Coolidge Auditorium are made available to a national radio audience through such gifts, and exhibits of items from the collections, shown first in the library's own exhibit halls, are circulated to libraries and museums throughout the country with the help of a fund established by a gift.

There had been eleven librarians of Congress by the mid-1970's: John J. Beckley, 1802–07, and Patrick Magruder, 1807–15, both of whom served as clerk of the House of Representatives; George Watterston, 1815–29, the first to hold the separate post of librarian; John Sylva Meehan, 1829–61; John G. Stephenson, 1861–64; Ainsworth Rand Spofford, 1864–97; John Russell Young, 1897–99; Herbert Putnam, 1899–1939; Archibald MacLeish, 1939–44; Luther Harris Evans, 1945–53; and L. Quincy Mumford, 1954–74.

ELIZABETH HAMER KEGAN

LICENSE CASES, 5 Howard 504 (1847), involved laws of three states fixing conditions of, and requiring licenses for, the sale of certain goods imported from other states. In upholding the laws the U.S. Supreme Court weakened the doctrine of exclusive federal control of interstate commerce as laid down in *Gibbons* v. *Ogden* in 1824. That earlier doctrine was reasserted, however, with modifications, when, in *Cooley* v. *Port Wardens* (1851), the Court held that with reference to subjects not demanding uniformity, states might impose regulations on interstate commerce until Congress exercised its right to establish uniform regulations.

[W. W. Willoughby, *The Constitutional Law of the United States.*]

J. HARLEY NICHOLS

LICENSES TO TRADE. In colonial times licenses to trade granted in various colonies reflected the English common law, which recognized the power of the sovereign to regulate the "common callings," such as innkeeping, carrying goods and persons, or operating a bridge. By the 19th century the scope of licenses to trade, now granted by states and municipalities, extended to a much wider variety of occupations and began to include professions such as medicine and ar-

chitecture. The growing concern of the states in the regulation of business after the Civil War led to reliance on licenses to trade for the control of such diverse industries as ice manufacture and the operation of grain elevators. As late as the early 1930's, the U.S. Supreme Court effectively limited control of business by holding the due process clause of the Constitution to be a bar to much of such state action, including the issuance of restrictive licenses to trade. As the New Deal progressed in the 1930's, the Supreme Court retreated, so that by the 1970's wide areas of the economy were affected by state licensing without serious constitutional doubts.

The growth of huge, national corporations, however, began to weaken the effectiveness of state licensing of trade as a means to control business, so that it is now federal licensing of trade that has become effective in banking, electric power, gas distribution, telecommunications, and interstate transport in the air and on highways, for example.

At the municipal level licenses to trade continue much more as a reflection of local concerns with sanitation and orderly trade. While licenses to trade, and concomitant inspection of products in some cases, have usually been justified on the basis of guaranteeing quality and service, they have been perceived by many as primarily efforts to protect local tradespeople from outside competition. Revenue produced by the customary fees is not a substantial portion of local revenues. Some critics note the representation of local business on city licensing agencies, such as a plumbing board to regulate plumbing installations, and see the threat of a return to the medieval guild system, in which the public interest might not be represented. In many states local licensing of trade is frequently subject to state laws and increasing state supervision.

WILLIAM TUCKER DEAN

LIFE EXPECTANCY. The life span is the greatest number of years that a human being can live. Although the life span has remained unchanged, the average length of life, or the expectation of life at birth, has increased greatly in the United States since the colonial period. Life expectancy is the result of mortality at successive ages. It expresses the trend in the expectation of survival or, conversely, the trend in the rates at which individuals fail to survive. A life table (also called a mortality table) shows the probability of surviving from any age to any subsequent age in terms of the age-specific death rates prevailing at a particular time and place. Assuming that a group of some stated age will experience the mortality rates of a given life table, the expectation of life shows the average remaining years per person if the mortality rates of the life table remain constant.

Unfortunately, until the 1930's reasonably complete records of death had not been kept for the entire United States. As a result, only fragmentary data are available for the historical analysis of death rates in the United States throughout a long period of its history. During the colonial period the recording of vital statistics was not a government function. Records of births and deaths were kept by families and churches. Except for the limited evidence provided by family Bibles, diaries, gravestones, and similar sources, there are practically no vital statistics for the 17th century, nor is the situation much better for the 18th century. National vital statistics before 1860 must be accepted with caution.

Although primary responsibility for registration of births and deaths has rested with the states, most of them neglected this matter before 1910. Mortality statistics for the years up to 1900 are fragmentary and exist for only a few states and cities. Accurate death records began to be kept in New York in 1804. Mortality statistics were published by Boston in 1813, Philadelphia in 1825, and Baltimore in 1836. For about thirty years around 1900, complete records of deaths are available for what is known as the "original" death registration area, comprising ten states (Connecticut, Indiana, Maine, Massachusetts, New Hampshire, New Jersey, New York, Michigan, Rhode Island, Vermont). During this period these states included about 40 percent of the people in the United States. After 1910, the number of states requiring registration of births and deaths increased rapidly up to 1929, when it included all but South Dakota and Texas. In 1933 the birth and death registration areas included all the states for the first time. Since then, accurate and reasonably complete recording of births and deaths has been secured for the whole United States.

The earliest American life table, for Massachusetts and New Hampshire, was prepared by Edward Wigglesworth, a clergyman, in 1789 and was published in 1793. It was based on information from sixty-two communities and dealt with 4,983 deaths, of which 1,942 (39.2 percent) occurred during the first five years. This table was used for many years in Massachusetts for legal and actuarial purposes. In 1857, E. B. Elliots, an actuary, published in the *Proceedings* of the American Association for the Advancement of Science the first "Massachusetts Life, Population and Annuity Table," which he had constructed for the New England Life Insurance Company in Boston. Further advances were made by John Shaw Billings, a physician, who founded the surgeon general's library and who had charge of vital statistics in the censuses of 1880 and 1890. Through his efforts mortality schedules of probability were first used by the census office as a supplement to mortality enumeration. In connection with the census of 1880, Billings also constructed a number of local life tables. About the same time, in 1881, Levi W. Meech, an actuary, developed the American Experience Table from the records and experience of thirty insurance companies. A revised edition was issued in 1886. The value of this table was limited, because life insurance experience cannot fully substitute for general population data. Moreover, the large population changes of this period caused by immigration made all mortality tables less than satisfactory. For these reasons, Samuel W. Abbott, a physician and for many years secretary of the Massachusetts Board of Health, arranged for the publication in 1898 of the Second Massachusetts Life Table, based upon the experience of the period 1893–97. Abbott used the table as an index of the health status of the people of the state. A comprehensive and trustworthy national life table was first prepared in 1910 by Samuel Lyle Rogers, director of the census from 1915 to 1921, and James W. Glover, of the University of Michigan. The table was based on the estimated population as of July 1, 1910, and on the reported deaths during 1909–11 from the original death-registration states and certain selected states.

Although mortality data for the nation as a whole are limited and fragmentary before the early 20th century, it is clear from a review of the available information that a huge reduction in death rates and a corresponding increase in life expectancy at birth have been achieved since the colonial period. In the 17th century, life expectancy at birth is believed to have been between 25 and 30 years. Numerous dangers surrounded infancy and childhood. Infections were most fatal among infants and young children. Inadequate hygiene, inappropriate infant feeding, and incompetent medical assistance caused a high death rate. It has been estimated that during the colonial period half of all children died before the age of 10. Harvard graduates from 1658 to 1690 had a total of 808 children, of whom 162 died before maturity, a mortality rate of 20 percent for this group. The genealogical records of Hingham, Mass., indicate that of 827 persons whose ages were known, 276 died before the age of 21, a mortality rate of 33.3 percent. Infant mortality accounted for the major portion of these deaths.

During the early period of settlement, deaths were caused chiefly by respiratory conditions and malnutrition (scurvy) in winter and gastrointestinal disorders and malaria in summer. Later in the 17th century and during the 18th century these conditions remained endemic. Tuberculosis was probably also present but to what extent is not clear. Epidemics of smallpox, "throat distemper" (diphtheria and streptococcal infection), and yellow fever devastated communities and caused numerous deaths, but on the whole the endemic diseases were the more important killers.

The Hingham records indicate that life expectancy was relatively good for those who reached the age of 21. It seems to have been 41.3 years for males and 39.7 years for females. Indeed, a number of Hingham inhabitants attained a ripe old age. Of 827 persons listed for the 17th century whose length of life is recorded, 105 lived to 80 or over, 19 reached 90 or over, and 3 became centenarians.

The high death rate among infants and children was more than balanced by a maximum birthrate, and large families were common. Although the evidence concerning the expectation of life for women who bore many children is not conclusive, it is likely that there was a high maternal mortality. As an instance, Cotton Mather married his first wife when she was 16; she bore him ten children and died at the age of 32. There were women who had large families and attained old age, but their proportion in the population is unknown.

The average length of life around the time of the Revolution was probably about 35 years. A summary of Wigglesworth's life table (1789) shows the following life expectancies:

At birth	28.15 years
5 years old	40.87 years
20 years old	34.21 years
50 years old	21.16 years
65 years old	12.43 years

If the parish bills from Philadelphia for the 1780's are at all representative, the general mortality pattern remained unchanged throughout the 18th century. Almost half of all deaths occurred in the first decade of life, with the following two decades the next most fatal.

At the beginning of the 19th century, some observers felt that health conditions were improving, but the evidence on declining mortality is sketchy and uncertain. Between 1820 and 1850, rising death rates were reported from large cities, a consequence largely of immigration, poverty, and rapid urban growth. Nevertheless, estimates based on data for several states place the expectation of life around 1850 at about 40 years. Figures for Massachusetts are illustrative of a slight rise.

Expectation of life (*years*) in Massachusetts

	1789	1855
Males	34.5	38.7
Females	36.5	40.9

The gross mortality in American cities of the mid-19th century was kept high by certain infectious diseases—typhoid and typhus fevers, diarrhea and dysentery, smallpox, tuberculosis, diphtheria, scarlet fever, measles, and whooping cough. Malaria was largely eliminated from New England and the Middle Atlantic area, but remained a major plague in the Middle West and the South. Pneumonia was a significant cause of death in winter, and nutritional conditions persisted among the poorer classes, including slaves and, later, freedmen in the South.

A gradual improvement in health conditions began after the Civil War and accelerated after 1900 as a result of improved living conditions and, more specifically, of sanitary reform and the application of microbiological discoveries. Beginning about 1870, a continuing downward trend in mortality ensued because of a decline in the frequency of such communicable diseases as smallpox, diphtheria, typhoid and typhus fevers, tuberculosis, and malaria. As an example, the death rate for diphtheria among children up to 10 years of age in New York City was 785 per 100,000 in 1894, declining to less than 300 in 1900, and in 1920, when active immunization of schoolchildren began, it fell below 100. By 1940 the disease had been virtually eliminated, with the mortality rate at 1.1 per 100,000. The experience of Providence, R.I., with scarlet fever from 1865 to 1924 shows that the death rate of children aged 2 to 4 years decreased from 691 to 28.3 per 100,000 during this period. Typhoid mortality in New York City fell from 40 per 100,000 in 1870 to about 2 per 100,000 in 1920. Similarly, in three large cities the death rate from tuberculosis was almost 400 per 100,000 in 1880, but by 1920 it had dropped to 100.

Initially, the saving of lives was limited chiefly to children over 5. The mortality of infants and children under 5 years of age did not decrease materially until about 1900. At the turn of the century, largely because of improper feeding, poor sanitation, overcrowding, and poverty, the common killers among infants were diarrhea and pneumonia. As infant feeding improved, clean milk and water became available, and social conditions were ameliorated, infant mortality declined. In New York City the infant death rate in 1885 was 273 per 1,000 live births; by 1915 it had dropped sharply to 94 per 1,000. Similarly, in New Haven, Conn., the death rate from infant diarrhea dropped from 205 per 200,000 in 1881 to 19 in 1926.

The increase in life expectancy since 1900 has been striking, as can be seen in the table below. Women gained more than men during this period. In 1900, women lived an average of two years longer than men; by the mid-1960's they lived, on the average, seven years longer.

Not all Americans have experienced the same improvement in life expectancy. In 1900, expectation of life at birth for nonwhites was 33 years, 14.6 years less than that of whites. By 1965, the life expectancy for nonwhites had risen to 64 years, but was still 6.9 years below that of whites. This difference resulted from a higher infant and maternal mortality among blacks, as well as higher death rates from certain infectious diseases. During the period 1933–65 the infant mortality rate for both whites and nonwhites declined at a rapid rate. Nonetheless, black infant mortality still remained greater than that for whites. In 1966 infant mortality for whites was 20.6 per 1,000 live births; for nonwhites it was 38.7 per 1,000. A larger gap existed for maternal mortality. In 1965, the white maternal mortality rate was 22.4 per 100,000 live births; the black rate was 90.2 per 100,000.

As infectious diseases declined and life expectancy at birth increased, the number of people living on into middle and old age began to mount. In 1900, only 13 million people, or 18 percent of the population, were over 45 years old. Fifty years later this group comprised 43 million people, or 30 percent of the population. In consequence, the rate at which persons in the upper adult group have died has risen. This rise was caused by a major realignment of the principal causes of death, in which the chronic, noncommunicable diseases (cardiovascular and renal conditions, malignant neoplasms, diabetes mellitus, and bronchopulmonary disorders) became most significant. An analogous shift has occurred in infancy and childhood, where congenital malformations as well as accidents and other violence have tended to replace infectious diseases as causes of death.

The combined effect of these changes has been to slow down the rate of decline of the overall death rate. Reduction in the role of cardiovascular disease as a cause of death would no doubt yield a considerable increment in the average life expectancy. For the future, significant increases in longevity will result from a lowering of the mortality rates for the chronic, noncommunicable diseases.

[Louis I. Dublin and Alfred J. Lotka, "Trends in Longevity," *Annals of the American Academy of Political and Social Science,* vol. 237 (1945); E. B. Greene and Virginia D. Harrington, *American Population Before the Federal Census of 1790;* P. H. Jacobson, "An Estimate of the Expectation of Life in the United States in 1850," *Milbank Memorial Fund Quarterly,* vol. 35 (1957); Edgar Sydenstricker, "The Vitality of the American People," in *Recent Social Trends: Report of the President's Research Committee on Social Trends;* Conrad Taeuber and Irene Taeuber, *The Changing Population of the United States;* Edward Wigglesworth, "Observations on the Longevity of the Inhabitants of Ipswich and Hingham," *American Academy of Arts and Sciences Memoirs,* vol. I (1785).]

GEORGE ROSEN

Average Number of Years of Life Remaining at Specified Ages: United States, 1900–02 and 1966

Age at beginning of year	Average number of years of life remaining		Increase in average remaining lifetime (in years)
	1900–02	1966	
Birth	49.2	70.1	20.9
1	55.2	70.8	15.6
5	55.0	67.1	12.1
25	39.1	48.0	8.9
65	11.9	14.6	2.7

LIFEGUARD, WASHINGTON'S, a corps of infantry and cavalry attached to the person of Gen. George Washington and responsible also for the safety of baggage and papers. Organized in 1776, it was augmented at Valley Forge by the addition of 120 picked men as a model corps to be trained by Baron Friedrich von Steuben. The membership was selected of men ''with uniforms and arms,'' of soldierly bearing, ''neat and spruce.'' Its official title was the Commander in Chief's Guard.

[G. W. P. Custis, *Recollections of Washington.*]
LLOYD C. M. HARE

LIFE INSURANCE. *See* **Insurance.**

LIFESAVING SERVICE. In 1789 the Massachusetts Humane Society began erecting huts on dangerous and lonely portions of that state's coast for the shelter of persons escaped from shipwrecks. In 1807 the society established at Cohasset the first lifesaving station in America and soon afterward another at Lovell's Island, both in the area of Boston Bay. It continued to be the only organized agency in the nation for saving life and property from the sea until 1837, when Congress authorized the president to employ ships to cruise along the shores and render aid to distressed navigators. Rep. William A. Newell of New Jersey, after having seen many bodies wash ashore from a wreck off Barnegat in his home state, introduced a bill in 1848 for aiding shipwrecked persons. An appropriation of $10,000 was made, and eight lifesaving stations were set up between Sandy Hook and Little Egg Harbor, N.J. The crews were all volunteers from the vicinity, but they were under the direction of officers appointed by the Revenue Marine Service and the Life Saving Benevolent Society of New York, organized in 1849. This society awarded medals for bravery and otherwise aided the work. Another appropriation in 1849 financed the establishment of four more stations on the New Jersey and Long Island coasts, all with volunteer crews. Sumner I. Kimball, chief of the Revenue Cutter Service, induced Congress in 1870–71 to appropriate $200,000 and to authorize the organization of a government lifesaving service, under control of the Treasury Department. On Jan. 28, 1915, this service lost its identity, being merged with the Revenue Cutter Service to form the U.S. Coast Guard. It then had 203 stations on the coasts of the Atlantic and Gulf of Mexico, 62

on the Great Lakes, 19 on the Pacific coast, and one at the falls of the Ohio River at Louisville, Ky.

[T. B. M. Mason, ''The Preservation of Life at Sea,'' *Journal of the American Geographical Society* (1879).]
ALVIN F. HARLOW

LIGHTHOUSE BOARD. Although the federal government took control of navigational aids in 1789, they were not made the responsibility of a special administrative entity. Before 1820 the commissioner of revenue supervised them; from then until the creation of the Lighthouse Board, they were under the wing of the fifth auditor of the treasury, Stephen Pleasanton. Dissatisfaction with his regime resulted in the formation in 1851 of a board that recommended the creation of the Lighthouse Board to govern federal aids to navigation. Two naval officers, two army engineers, and two civilians made up the board; except for the years 1871–78, when Joseph Henry was chairman, the board was headed by commissioned officers. Technical officers on detail supervised construction and routine operations in the field. The board itself operated through committees supervising particular aspects of the work. Under Henry's leadership, for example, an Experiments Committee conducted research on the production, propagation, and reception of light and sound to improve existing navigation aids. With the decline of the American merchant marine after the Civil War, the board's relative importance declined, as did its innovating role. In 1910 the board was supplanted by the Bureau of Lighthouses. The board was an early example of civil-military cooperation in scientific and technical areas that was all but forgotten when similar bodies became important in the next century.

[George Weiss, *The Lighthouse Service, Its History, Activities and Organization.*]
NATHAN REINGOLD

LIGHTING. Domestic lighting in America prior to about 1815 was provided by a variety of devices, including lamps fueled by oil derived from animal or vegetable sources, tallow or bayberry candles, and pinewood torches. The late 18th-century chemical revolution associated with Antoine Lavoisier included a theory of oxidation that soon stimulated dramatic improvements in both lamp design and candle composition. These included a lamp with a tubular wick and shaped glass chimney invented in the early 1780's by Aimé Argand, a student of Lavoisier, and introduced into the United States during the administration of George Washington. The Argand lamp was approximately ten times as efficient as previous oil lamps and was widely used in lighthouses, in public buildings, and in the homes of the more affluent citizens. European chemists also isolated stearine, which was used in "snuffless candles," so called because they had self-consuming wicks. The candles became available during the 1820's and were produced on a mass scale in candle factories.

After an efficient means of producing inflammable gas from coal was discovered by European scientists, a new era of lighting began during the first decade of the 19th century. The first large-scale use of illuminating gas was both for street lighting and in textile factories in England. Baltimore became the first American city to employ gas streetlights in 1816, but the gaslight industry did not enter its rapid-growth phase until after 1850. Capital investment increased from less than $7 million in 1850 to approximately $150 million in 1880. The central generating station and distribution system that became standard in the gaslight industry served as a model for the electric light industry, which emerged during the last two decades of the century. Improvements such as the Welsbach mantle kept gas lighting competitive until World War I. Rural residents continued to rely on candles or oil lamps throughout most of the 19th century because coal gas could not be economically distributed in areas of low population density. The discovery of petroleum in Pennsylvania in 1859 soon led to the development of the simple and comparatively safe kerosine lamp, which continued to be used in isolated areas in the United States until the mid-20th century.

Certain deficiencies of the gaslight, such as imperfect combustion and the danger of fire or explosion, made it seem vulnerable to such late 19th-century electric inventors as Thomas A. Edison. Two competing systems of electric lighting developed rapidly after the invention of large self-excited electric generators capable of producing great quantities of inexpensive electrical energy. The American engineer-entrepreneur Charles F. Brush developed an effective street-lighting system using arc lamps beginning in 1876. One of Brush's most important inventions was a device that prevented an entire series circuit of arc lamps from being disabled by the failure of a single lamp. Brush's first commercial central arc-light stations were installed in 1879. Because of its high intensity, the early arc light was primarily useful in street lighting or in large enclosures such as train stations.

Edison became the pioneer innovator of the incan-

descent-lighting industry. Beginning in 1878 Edison made an intensive study of the gaslight industry and determined that he could develop an electric system that would provide equivalent illumination without some of the defects and at a competitive cost. His reputation already was such as to enable him to obtain adequate financial backing to support the necessary research and development. Crucial to his success was the development of an efficient and long-lived high-resistance lamp, a lamp that would allow for the same necessary subdivision of light that had been achieved in gas lighting but not in arc lighting. Edison and his assistants at his Menlo Park, N.J., laboratory solved this problem by means of a carbon filament lamp in 1879. The successful introduction of the incandescent lamp on a commercial scale at the Pearl Street (New York City) generating station in 1882 was a tribute to Edison's use of organized systems research. All the components—not only the lamp but also the generator, distribution system, fuses, and meters—were regarded as elements of a carefully engineered light-and-power system.

The thirty-year period after 1880 was a time of intense market competition between the gaslight, arc light, and incandescent light industries and between the direct-current distribution system of Edison and the alternating-current system introduced by George Westinghouse. Significant improvements were made in each of the competing lighting systems during this period, but incandescent lighting with alternating-current distribution ultimately emerged as the leader. The General Electric Company, which was organized in 1892 by a consolidation of the Edison Company and the Thomson-Houston Company, became the dominant lamp manufacturer, followed by Westinghouse.

An important event in the history of electric lighting was the formation of the General Electric Research Laboratory under Willis R. Whitney in 1900. A dramatic improvement in the incandescent lamp was achieved by William D. Coolidge of this laboratory in 1910 with the discovery of a process for making ductile tungsten wire. The more durable and efficient tungsten lamps quickly supplanted the carbon filament lamp. Irving Langmuir, also a General Electric scientist, completed development of a gas-filled tungsten lamp in 1912. This lamp, which was less susceptible to blackening of the bulb than the older high-vacuum lamp, was introduced commercially in 1913 and was the last major improvement in the design of incandescent lamps.

Development of a new type of electric light began

at General Electric in 1935. This was the low-voltage fluorescent lamp, which came on the market in 1938. The fluorescent lamp had several advantages over the incandescent lamp, including higher efficiency and a larger surface area, which provided a more uniform source of illumination with less glare. It also required special fixtures and auxiliary elements. This lamp has come into wide usage, especially in office buildings and schools and as a desk lamp. High intensity mercury-vapor lamps came into general use for street lighting after World War II.

[Arthur A. Bright, Jr., *The Electric-Lamp Industry: Technological Change and Economic Development From 1800 to 1947;* William T. O'Dea, *The Social History of Lighting.*]

JAMES E. BRITTAIN

LIGONIER, FORT, at the site of the Pennsylvania town so named, was built by Col. Henry Bouquet in 1758, as Gen. John Forbes's expedition made its way slowly westward toward Fort Duquesne. After the Battle of Grant's Hill, French and Indians attacked Bouquet at Ligonier but were repulsed (*see* Loyalhanna, Battle of the). Thereafter the fort was an important link in the chain of communications between eastern Pennsylvania and Fort Pitt. During Pontiac's War (1763–64) Ligonier was the only small fort west of the mountains in Pennsylvania that did not fall in the early attacks; its retention made possible the relief of Fort Pitt by Bouquet's forced march in 1763.

[S. J. and E. H. Buck, *The Planting of Civilization in Western Pennsylvania;* C. H. Sipe, *Fort Ligonier and Its Times.*]

SOLON J. BUCK

LIMA CONFERENCE. *See* **Latin America, U.S. Relations With.**

LIMITATIONS, STATUTES OF. *See* **Statutes of Limitations.**

LIMPING STANDARD, a term formerly used to describe the monetary standard of the United States in the latter part of the 19th and early 20th centuries. The standard was no longer bimetallic because the general revision of the Coinage Laws Act of 1873 (later called the Crime of '73) had eliminated free coinage of the silver dollar. Yet it was more than a gold standard, because the Bland-Allison Act of 1878

and later the Sherman Silver Purchase Act of 1890, laws passed in an unsuccessful effort to restore bimetallism, gave the silver dollars authorized by Congress status as "standard" money. These coins were full legal tender. This status became particularly significant in 1893 at the time of the "endless chain" of redemption of currency in gold coin. The treasury was legally entitled to redeem currency in either gold or silver dollars, instead of just in gold as it was doing. But exercising this right, as the pro-silver people, such as William Jennings Bryan and Sen. Henry M. Teller, desired, would have indicated to the world that the United States was abandoning the gold standard. A precipitous drop in the foreign exchange value of the dollar would have followed, since at that time the gold value of silver in a silver dollar was only about 52 cents.

[P. Studenski and H. Krooss, *Financial History of the United States.*]

DONALD L. KEMMERER

LINCOLN, ASSASSINATION OF. On Apr. 14, 1865, at 10:15 P.M., while attending a performance of "Our American Cousin" at Ford's Theatre in Washington, D.C., President Abraham Lincoln was shot in the back of the head by John Wilkes Booth. As soon as the fatal nature of the wound was apparent, Lincoln was carried to a lodging house opposite the theater. There, without regaining consciousness, he died at 7:22 on the following morning.

Despite the fact that Booth broke his leg in jumping from the presidential box to the stage, he made his way from the theater, and, with David E. Herold, escaped from Washington in the direction of Virginia before midnight. They first went to the house of Dr. Samuel A. Mudd, who set Booth's leg, and then to the Potomac River, where they hid in a pine thicket waiting their chance to cross to Virginia. During their wait, a farmer, Thomas A. Jones, brought them food. All the forces of the government were directed toward his capture, but hysteria, greed for the reward, and incompetence hindered the pursuit to such an extent that it was not until Apr. 26 that Booth and Herold were surrounded in a tobacco shed on the farm belonging to Richard H. Garrett, near Port Royal, Va. There Herold surrendered, but Booth defied his captors and was shot—possibly by Boston Corbett, possibly by his own hand.

Before the death of Booth the government had implicated nine persons in the assassination—George A. Atzerodt, Lewis Payne, Herold, Mary E. Surratt and her son John H. Surratt, Edward Spangler, Samuel Arnold Mudd, Michael O'Laughlin, and Booth. All except John H. Surratt were tried before a military commission, May 9–June 30, 1865. All were found guilty, although the verdict in the case of Mary Surratt was certainly a miscarriage of justice. Atzerodt, Payne, Herold, and Mary Surratt were hanged on July 7. Arnold, Mudd, and O'Laughlin were sentenced to life imprisonment while Spangler was given six years; the four were imprisoned in Fort Jefferson, Dry Tortugas, in the Florida Keys. Jones and Garrett were not indicted. John H. Surratt was brought to trial in 1867, but the jury failed to agree, and his case was later dismissed. By Mar. 4, 1869, President Andrew Johnson had pardoned all the imprisoned men, except for O'Laughlin, who had died in 1867.

The assassination of Lincoln was a national tragedy in the broadest sense. It removed a president who was averse to vindictive measures, and by transforming widespread northern inclination to leniency into a passion for retribution, it gave Reconstruction its popular sanction.

[D. M. DeWitt, *The Assassination of Abraham Lincoln and Its Expiation;* Otto Eisenschiml, *Why Was Lincoln Murdered;* Lloyd Lewis, *Myths After Lincoln.*]

PAUL M. ANGLE

LINCOLN COUNTY WAR, a struggle that began in 1876 between two rival groups of ranchers and businessmen in southeastern New Mexico. One faction was headed by Maj. L. G. Murphy and the other by John Chisum and Alexander A. McSween. A series of murders and depredations culminated in July 1878 in a three-day battle at the town of Lincoln, in which McSween and several others were killed. William H. Bonney, better known as Billy the Kid, was a prominent figure in this struggle.

[Walter Noble Burns, *Saga of Billy the Kid.*]

EDWARD EVERETT DALE

LINCOLN-DOUGLAS DEBATES took place between Republican Abraham Lincoln and the Democratic incumbent, Stephen A. Douglas, during the senatorial campaign in Illinois in 1858. Douglas' opening speeches in his reelection drive, with their effective frontal attack on Lincoln's "house divided" doctrine, alarmed Lincoln's managers and led him to issue a formal challenge to Douglas: "Will it be agreeable to you to make an arrangement for you and myself to divide time, and address the same audiences during the present canvass?" Douglas' speaking dates

were already set through October, but he agreed to one debate in each of seven congressional districts.

About 12,000 gathered at Ottawa, Aug. 21, for the first debate, which was preceded and followed by parades and punctuated by shouts and cheers. Douglas was well dressed, with a ruffled shirt, a dark blue coat with shiny buttons, and a wide-brimmed soft hat. Lincoln wore a rusty, high-topped hat, an ill-fitting coat, and baggy trousers so short as to show his rusty boots. Their speaking manners likewise contrasted. Douglas talked fast and steadily, in a heavy voice. He would shake his long, black hair and walk back and forth across the platform with great effectiveness. Lincoln's voice was light, almost nasal, and at the start had an unpleasant timbre, but carried well. Both gave a sense of profound earnestness.

Douglas' theme at Ottawa was the sectional bias, the strife-fomenting nature, of Republican doctrine. He read a series of resolutions he mistakenly believed had been adopted when the party was formed in Illinois in 1854 and pressed Lincoln to deny his endorsement of them. Douglas likewise assailed Lincoln's own position on the slavery issue, and Lincoln seemed troubled by his questions.

Lincoln went to Freeport for the second debate on Aug. 27 determined to impale Douglas on the horns of a dilemma. There he asked the famous Freeport questions, related to the Supreme Court's ruling in the Dred Scott case. Either Douglas must accept the Supreme Court's decision, which would mean that slavery could go anywhere, or he must cease urging the sanctity of Supreme Court decisions. It was not a new issue for Douglas, who was more realist than dialectician. "Slavery cannot exist a day," he answered, "or an hour, anywhere, unless it is supported by local police regulations." This was an effective counter in the debate.

The other debates were hard fought and colorful, but Ottawa and Freeport had set the tone for the rest of them. The third took place on Sept. 15 at Jonesboro, a little town deep in "Egypt," the southernmost region of the state, where neither antagonist had many partisans. At Charleston, three days later, the crowd was fairly evenly divided. Lincoln, smarting under Douglas' charges that he favored equality for blacks, toned down his earlier statements. Thereupon Douglas said his opponent's views were "jet black" in the North, "a decent mulatto" in the center, and "almost white" in Egypt.

On Oct. 7 the fifth debate took place at Galesburg, an abolitionist stronghold. On Oct. 13 the two men grappled at Quincy, and the last debate was two days

155

later at Alton. There Lincoln and Douglas epitomized again their points of view. Lincoln repeated the charge that Douglas looked to "no end of the institution of slavery." But Douglas said: "I care more for the great principle of self-government, the right of the people to rule, than I do for all the Negroes in Christendom. I would not endanger the perpetuity of this Union."

Lincoln lost the election, but the debates brought his name to the attention of people outside Illinois. His defeat cannot necessarily be attributed to the debates, since at that time congressional senators were not elected by popular vote, but by a joint ballot of the state legislatures. Lincoln and Douglas were, therefore, actually campaigning for the election of state legislators from their own parties. There were some Republican victories in the 1858 election, but one-half of the state legislature had been elected in 1856, a year when the Democrats were strongly in power.

[Paul Angle, ed., *Created Equal—The Complete Lincoln-Douglas Debates of 1858;* Robert W. Johannsen, *Stephen A. Douglas;* Allan Nevins, *The Emergence of Lincoln.*]

GEORGE FORT MILTON

LINCOLN HIGHWAY. The idea of a coast-to-coast highway originated with Carl G. Fisher of Indianapolis in 1912, when the automobile was in comparative infancy and when there was no system of good roads covering even one state. In September 1912 Fisher laid the proposition before the leaders of the automobile industry, and, giving $1,000 himself, obtained pledges of more than $4 million for construction. To add a patriotic touch, he gave the name "Lincoln" to the proposed road in 1913, and the Lincoln Highway Association was formed to further the project. States and individuals the country over made contributions and cement manufacturers donated material for "demonstration miles." By an act of 1921 the federal government increased its aid to states in road building, which greatly helped this project. From Jersey City the route chosen passed through Philadelphia, Gettysburg, and Pittsburgh, Pa., and Fort Wayne, Ind.; near Chicago; through Omaha, Nebr., Cheyenne, Wyo., Salt Lake City, Utah, and Sacramento, Calif. It ended in San Francisco. The original course was 3,389 miles, later cut by more than 50 miles. Work began in October 1914 but proceeded slowly. When the association closed its offices on Dec. 31, 1927, and $90 million had been spent, the road was usable throughout its length, although there

were still sections of gravel and some even of dirt, which were slowly improved thereafter. In 1925 the road became U.S. Highway 30.

[Lincoln Highway Association, *The Lincoln Highway.*]

ALVIN F. HARLOW

LINDBERGH KIDNAPPING CASE. On the night of Mar. 1, 1932, the eighteen-month-old son of Col. Charles A. Lindbergh was abducted from his parents' country home near Hopewell, N.J. The kidnapper climbed to the window of the second-story nursery by a ladder brought with him. He left a note demanding $50,000 ransom. After some futile attempts at closer contact with him, John F. Condon, a retired New York teacher, acting as intermediary, succeeded in having two night interviews with the man in a cemetery. On the second occasion, Apr. 8, the money was paid the kidnapper upon his promise to deliver the child—a false promise, as the child had been slain immediately after the abduction. Its body was found on May 12 near the Lindbergh home. The serial number of every note of the ransom money was made public. On Sept. 15, 1934, a carpenter named Bruno Hauptmann passed one of the bills at a New York filling station and was arrested. More than $14,000 of the ransom money was found concealed about his house. At his trial at Flemington, N.J., in January-February 1935 the ladder was identified as having been made with plank taken from his attic. He was convicted, and executed on Apr. 3, 1936.

[Anne Morrow Lindbergh, *Hour of Gold, Hour of Lead;* Sidney B. Whipple, *The Lindbergh Crime.*]

ALVIN F. HARLOW

LINDBERGH'S ATLANTIC FLIGHT. The first nonstop flight between New York and Paris, and the first one-man crossing of the Atlantic by air, was made by Charles A. Lindbergh, May 20–21, 1927. Previously, several attempts had been made to win the prize of $25,000 offered by Raymond Orteig in 1919 for the first continuous flight between New York and Paris over the Atlantic. In 1926 René Fonck had crashed when taking off from Roosevelt Field, Long Island, N.Y.; two American naval officers had been killed on a trial flight; and two French aviators had been lost over the Atlantic while attempting the difficult east-to-west crossing.

Backed by a group of Saint Louis businessmen, Lindbergh supervised the construction of a Ryan monoplane, christened the *Spirit of St. Louis.* It had a wing spread of 46 feet and a chord of 7 feet, weighed

5,135 pounds, and was propelled by a 225-horsepower Wright Whirlwind motor. On the morning of May 20, 1927, taking advantage of an area of high pressure reported over the Atlantic, Lindbergh took off from Roosevelt Field with a load of 425 gallons of gasoline. Encountering fog and sleet, the aviator was compelled to fly blind part of the way at an altitude of 1,500 feet. Later he dropped closer to the water, flying at times ten feet above the waves. Sighting the coast of Ireland, he turned his course toward France. After flying over England, he crossed the English Channel and at ten o'clock in the evening saw the lights of Paris. After circling the Eiffel Tower, he made for the Le Bourget airfield, where he landed, after having flown 3,605 miles in thirty-three hours and thirty minutes.

The reception of the young aviator in the capital of France was enthusiastic and demonstrative. Under the guidance of Myron T. Herrick, the American ambassador at Paris, Lindbergh made a favorable impression on the French public. A round of fetes in his honor failed to mar his attractive modesty, and he became a symbol of daring, courage, and international fraternity. In Brussels, Berlin, and London he was received with equal enthusiasm. He returned to the United States from Cherbourg on the U.S.S. *Memphis,* sent by command of President Calvin Coolidge.

[Charles E. Lindbergh, *The Spirit of St. Louis.*]
KENNETH COLEGROVE

LIND'S AMERICAN TOUR. After opening at Castle Garden in New York City, Sept. 11, 1850, Jenny Lind, the Swedish nightingale, toured the eastern United States. Under the astute management of P. T. Barnum, she gave ninety-five concerts, the last one on June 9, 1851. Tickets were auctioned before the concerts and often sold at fantastic prices, one at $650. Miss Lind received $176,675 for her services, and Barnum cleared over $500,000. Thereafter the singer gave a number of concerts under her own management before returning to Europe in 1852.

[P. T. Barnum, *Struggles and Triumphs.*]
ALVIN F. HARLOW

LIND'S MISSION TO MEXICO. After the overthrow of President Francisco Madero of Mexico in February 1913, the government of the United States refused to recognize the government set up by Victoriano Huerta. In August 1913 John Lind of Minnesota was commissioned by President Woodrow Wilson as his personal representative in Mexico City, to use his influence to set up a constitutional government worthy of recognition. Lind's efforts failed despite months of ''watchful waiting'' at Veracruz, and he returned to the United States in April 1914.

[G. M. Stephenson, *John Lind of Minnesota.*]
G. M. STEPHENSON

LINEN INDUSTRY. Flax was the principal textile fabric in colonial America, where it was raised and made into linen on the farm. Some colonies subsidized its manufacture into sailcloth. For two centuries dressed flax and yarn were common articles of barter; homespun was familiar merchandise in country trade; and linsey-woolsey, made of flax and wool, was a common clothing fabric.

With the coming of the cotton gin and of Arkwright machinery, cotton displaced flax. Small linen mills were established subsequently, but few were permanent, and none grew into sizable enterprises. The most successful manufactured thread and canvas. The Civil War cotton shortage stimulated efforts to revive the industry, but the high cost of dressing domestic flax and duties on imported fiber prevented its extension. Some linen goods, mostly thread and towels, are still manufactured in America, but the industry is a minor one, and most of the linen products now used in the United States are imported from Northern Ireland, the remainder from such countries as Belgium and Japan.

[Victor S. Clark, *History of Manufactures in the United States.*]
VICTOR S. CLARK

LINGAYEN GULF. Situated on the northwest coast of Luzon Island in the Philippines, Lingayen Gulf is a natural landing area for any invader. Its excellent wide beaches give easy access to a broad central plain leading south to Manila and the great natural harbor of Manila Bay. In World War II, the gulf suffered two invasions: the first, in 1941, by the Japanese; the second, three years later, by the returning Americans.

In December 1941, the shores of Lingayen Gulf were defended by Filipino and American troops commanded by Gen. Douglas MacArthur. The Filipinos, who constituted the bulk of these forces, were poorly trained and equipped. Moreover, Japanese victories in the initial weeks of the war had denied the defenders the air and naval support so vital for their defense. In contrast, the invasion force of Lt. Gen. Masaharu Homma was well trained, adequately supplied, and supported by strong naval and air units. Homma's troops began landing before dawn on Dec. 22 along the eastern shore of Lingayen Gulf, site of the best beaches. The convoy had overshot its planned anchorage, and high winds and rough waves made for difficulties. Yet the absence of significant opposition more than balanced these problems. A few artillery rounds and ineffective attacks by a handful of American submarines and bombers were all the defenders could muster. Homma quickly secured his initial objectives and began to drive inland. A day later, MacArthur issued the order to withdraw to Bataan, abandoning the rest of Luzon to Homma.

Three years later, the situation was reversed. Although the Japanese, commanded by Gen. Tomoyuki Yamashita, were numerous and strong, they lacked air and naval support and were no match for the powerful ground, sea, and air forces that MacArthur had marshaled for his return to Luzon. Yamashita planned, therefore, to offer little resistance to the American invaders, and to fall back to inland delaying positions for a final stand. Other than Japanese suicide planes that punished the American convoys, there was no real opposition to the invasion. After a devastating preassault bombardment, the landing began at 9:30 A.M. on Jan. 9, 1945, on the south shore of Lingayen Gulf. Although practically unopposed, the Americans found their advance slowed by flooded rice fields, marshes, and streams, yet by evening they had secured a wide and deep beachhead, in preparation for the drive on Manila. The shores of Lingayen Gulf soon became a vast supply depot to support American operations inland.

[Louis Morton, *The Fall of the Philippines,* United States Army in World War II; Robert Ross Smith, *Triumph in the Philippines,* United States Army in World War II.]

STANLEY L. FALK

LINSEY-WOOLSEY, a stout homespun cloth having a wool weft and commonly a flax warp, although hemp or cotton was sometimes used, extensively manufactured in the American colonies and on the frontier. Its name, which is of British origin, first appears in colonial records soon after settlement. It was a homely fabric, conveniently made in country households from materials raised on the farm. Not only was it widely used for men's and women's garments by servants, laborers, and rural workers and therefore consumed for the most part in the households where it was made, it also appeared in local stores and was oc-

casionally receivable for taxes. No trustworthy statistics of the quantity produced in America exist, but linsey-woolsey probably formed a substantial fraction of the 18 or 20 million yards of mixed fabrics reported by the census of 1810.

[Rolla M. Tryon, *Household Manufactures in the United States;* William B. Weeden, *Economic and Social History of New England.*]

VICTOR S. CLARK

LIQUOR. *See* **Bootlegging; Rum Trade; Whiskey.**

LIQUOR LAWS. The history of liquor legislation in America mirrors a traditional and ongoing societal concern over the production, sale, transportation, and consumption of alcoholic beverages. Early laws were enacted primarily as efforts to encourage temperance and what was perceived as morality. Although liquor legislation for perceived moral reasons is still a common—and constitutional—goal, mid-20th-century statutes reflect a desire to protect those whose rights are threatened by liquor sellers and abusers.

As early as 1619 the colony of Virginia outlawed gaming, drunkenness, and other excesses. A little later, it enacted a number of liquor acts, including legislation against drunkenness among the clergy, and in 1676 it penalized judges who drank to excess on court days. Beginning in 1633 and during the rest of the 17th century, Massachusetts passed progressively stricter laws against drunkenness. New York first restricted the liquor business in 1638, and the remaining colonies soon did the same. The colonies one after another forbade the sale of liquor to Indians, with Connecticut first in 1645. Some colonies went so far as to make drunkenness grounds for disfranchisement. Paradoxically, at the same time—in the middle of the 17th century—the colonies started to reap considerable income from liquor taxes.

The 18th century saw little new liquor legislation, but by 1800 drinking had become enough of a problem to excite a temperance movement. In 1829 Maine was the first of many states to pass a local-option law, which permitted small subdivisions, such as counties, to prohibit liquor sales within their own boundaries. The period from 1830 to 1845 was an era of local option, but in 1846 Maine went still further and initiated a trend of statewide prohibition. In 1890 the Supreme Court held that the states' power to regulate commerce was preempted by that of the federal government under the Constitution and that they could not prohibit interstate liquor traffic without congressional sanction (*Leisy* v. *Hardin*, 135 U.S. 100). Congress then attempted to protect the "dry" states from liquor shipments with the Wilson Act (1890) and the more effective Webb-Kenyon Act (1913). The increasing momentum of the temperance movement stimulated twenty-eight states to go dry by 1918, the year the Eighteenth Amendment was ratified, prohibiting "the manufacture, sale, or transportation of intoxicating liquors" in the United States.

The violent Prohibition era lasted from Jan. 16, 1920, until the ratification of the Twenty-first Amendment on Dec. 5, 1933, which repealed the Eighteenth Amendment. The Twenty-first Amendment has been held to mandate the preeminence of states in liquor regulation, and a resultant diversity of legislation exists among the states. Although no state is completely dry any longer, several states permit local options by statute. Thus, many counties or other subdivisions are still dry, by their own choice. To control the liquor traffic better, some states have established a government monopoly on liquor sales, a practice that has been sustained by the courts.

All states outlaw sales of liquor to minors, the adult age varying from eighteen to twenty-one. Some states have "dram shop" acts that impose strict statutory duties on over-the-counter sellers, while others impose similar duties through the common law. All states forbid automobile operators from driving while intoxicated, with varying severity of punishment and a multitude of definitions of "intoxicated." There are 2 million arrests each year in the United States based on state public-drunkenness statutes.

Because of constitutional limitations, since passage of the Twenty-first Amendment the federal government has had no legal basis for involving itself in efforts at liquor control. But Congress, impressed by the magnitude and virulence of the problem, passed a law in 1970 under its power to spend for the general welfare to assist in the prevention of alcohol abuse and the treatment of alcoholism. It set up a National Institute on Alcohol Abuse and Alcoholism, made money available for state and local programs, and established prevention, treatment, and rehabilitation programs for federal civilian employees.

[Lloyd A. Wright, "Intoxicating Liquors," *American Jurisprudence*, vol. 45.]

HAROLD W. CHASE
ERIC L. CHASE

LISA, FORT, near the present site of Omaha, Nebr., was established by Manuel Lisa, probably in the spring of 1813, when he was forced to abandon Fort Manuel, in what is now Montana. The most important post on the Missouri River from 1813 to 1822, it controlled the trade of the Omaha, Pawnee, Oto, and neighboring Indians.

[Hiram Chittenden, *American Fur Trade of the Far West.*]

STELLA M. DRUMM

LISA AND COMPANY consisted of Manuel Lisa, Gregoire Sarpy, François M. Benoist, and Charles Sanguinet. After Auguste and Pierre Chouteau failed in their endeavor to renew their fur trade monopoly and moved their activities to the Arkansas River, Manuel Lisa and Company, in 1802, sought and obtained the exclusive trade with the Osage on the waters of the Missouri and Osage rivers. The territory involved was about 120 miles from the mouth of the Missouri. This monopoly ended with the establishment of U.S. territorial government in Upper Louisiana in 1804. In 1807 another firm called Manuel Lisa and Company was organized by Lisa, William Morrison, and Pierre Menard, with a capital of $16,000. An expedition consisting of about twenty-five men left Saint Louis for the upper Missouri River country on April 19, 1807. The party reached its wintering ground on Nov. 21, 1807, and immediately built a trading house. In the following spring Fort Raymond, later known as Fort Manuel, was built on the Yellowstone at the mouth of the Bighorn River, in what is now Montana.

[Richard E. Oglesby, *Manuel Lisa and the Opening of the Fur Trade.*]

STELLA M. DRUMM

LITCHFIELD LAW SCHOOL was established in 1784 in Litchfield, Conn., by Tapping Reeve, who was its only teacher until 1798. In that year he was succeeded by James Gould, who developed an institution that in the early years of the 19th century gave legal training to hundreds of young men from almost every state in the Union and numbered among its graduates some of the most prominent men in the public life of the next generation, including Henry Clay. Before it closed its doors in 1833, the Litchfield school had sent out more than a thousand graduates.

FRANCIS R. AUMANN

LITERACY TEST has been used by the federal government as an adjunct to its immigration and naturalization laws and by many states as a device to determine qualifications for voting. The federal government's use of the literacy test has not been a matter of major controversy, and the passage of immigration reform legislation in 1965, which abolished the national origins system, removed one of the primary objections raised when the literacy test act was passed in 1917.

As used by the states, the literacy test gained notoriety as a means for denying the franchise to blacks. Adopted by a number of southern states, the literacy test was generally combined with civic understanding tests (usually the interpretation of a portion of a state's constitution), and registration officials often applied it in a discriminatory manner against black potential voters. Effective federal action to counter this discrimination did not occur until the 1960's. In 1964, the Civil Rights Act provided that literacy tests used as a qualification for voting in federal elections be administered wholly in writing and only to persons who had not completed six years of formal education. The 1965 Voting Rights Act suspended the use of literacy tests in all states or political subdivisions in which fewer than 50 percent of the voting-age residents were registered as of Nov. 1, 1964, or had voted in the 1964 presidential election. In a series of cases, the Supreme Court upheld the legislation and restricted the use of literacy tests for non-English-speaking citizens. Under the 1970 extension of the Voting Rights Act, the use of the literacy test was suspended in all states and their political subdivisions until Aug. 6, 1975. The suspension of the literacy test has been accompanied by significant increases in black registration in the seven southern states covered by the 1965 law, and the registration problems faced by non-English-speaking citizens have been eased by subsequent judicial and legislative actions.

DENNIS IPPOLITO

LITERARY SOCIETIES were common in rural districts throughout the West during the last quarter of the 19th century and, in some remote communities, well into the 20th century. Their objectives were social, since they sought to create or stimulate interest in "things literary" and at the same time provide entertainment and an opportunity for social contacts. Possibly they represented a revolt against both the narrow, puritanical group, which seemed to find its chief pleasure in long sermons, prayer meetings, and hymn singing, and the wild, boisterous element found in every frontier or backwoods community. If so, they succeeded admirably, for the most ardent

churchgoers could find little to condemn while even the rowdiest of the rougher spirits gladly attended meetings because of the fun and good fellowship they afforded.

Meetings were generally held once or twice a month, usually at the schoolhouse, and the local schoolteacher often took a prominent part. Officers commonly consisted of a president, secretary, and program committee. This might be a standing committee or one specially appointed for each meeting. There was seldom a formal membership list; instead all interested persons were invited to attend and urged to take part in the programs. These consisted of readings, short plays, commonly called dialogues, and sometimes a vocal solo, duet, or quartet. Debates on various subjects, such as "Resolved that fire is more destructive than water" or "There is more pleasure in pursuit than possession," sometimes formed a part of the evening's entertainment. Often a newspaper was prepared and read aloud, providing some bits of news, but more often given over to gibes at various local leaders. Readings were humorous, dramatic, or pathetic, and new ones, as well as new dialogues, were eagerly sought in various books produced by publishers seeking to exploit this market. Such favorites as "Curfew Must Not Ring To-night," "The Face on the Barroom Floor," and "The Lips That Touch Liquor Can Never Touch Mine" were widely read. The program committee sought to provide well-balanced entertainment with enough comedy, pathos, drama, and ethical or religious teaching to cause everyone to be pleased with at least some part of the program.

[W. L. Wilkerson and B. A. Botkin, "The Oklahoma Literary Society," *Folk-Say, A Regional Miscellany*.]

EDWARD EVERETT DALE

LITERATURE. If the definition of American literature is confined to belles lettres, literary art in the United States can be said to begin with the random appearance of occasional poetry in the 17th century, broaden into a general acceptance of the patterns of British imaginative writing in the 18th century, and come to fruition only after the Republic was well established. But if American literature includes the literature of knowledge as well as that of power, it begins in the bosom of the Renaissance, speaks maturely from its beginnings, and continues to be full and rich until the present time.

On the first line of development a beginning was made by two minor figures—Anne Bradstreet (*The Tenth Muse Lately Sprung Up in America*, 1650) and

Edward Taylor (although his *Poetical Works* were not printed until 1937). The literary magazine was not effectively established until 1741, when Andrew Bradford printed the *American Magazine* and Benjamin Franklin established his *General Magazine and Historical Chronicle,* both emanating from Philadelphia. American fiction begins even later with *The Power of Sympathy,* by William Hill Brown, in 1789 and *Charlotte Temple,* by Susanna Haswell Rowson, in 1791. The great body of imaginative writing in the United States came after the Revolution.

The American mind has its truer beginnings in the great literature of discovery, exploration, and settlement from Richard Hakluyt's *Principal Navigations, Voyages, Traffiques and Discoveries* (1589) onward. A library of narratives by Capt. John Smith, Gov. William Bradford, Gov. John Winthrop, Edward Johnson, Thomas Morton, George Alsop, Mary Rowlandson, and others vigorously describes and thoughtfully interprets the first ventures of the English people into the New World. These books have the vitality of English prose of the 17th century. The writing shares the intellectual excitement of the eras of John Milton and Francis Bacon; it develops theories of history, of salvation, and of the relation of church and state that had a profound influence on American thought. The highest expression of the New England mind came in the next century in the work of Jonathan Edwards: *A Faithful Narrative of the Surprising Work of God* (1737) and *Enquiry Into the Modern Prevailing Notions of Freedom of the Will* (1754). Virginia, which has never lacked a literary culture, neatly counterpointed the metaphysics of Edwards with the secularity of William Byrd, whose *History of the Dividing Line* (1738, first printed 1841 in *The Westover Manuscripts*) remains a humorous minor masterpiece; whose secret journals, not published until 1941 and 1942, reveal an American Samuel Pepys; and whose career is a blend of the Renaissance and the Enlightenment. Byrd carried his considerable learning lightly, like a flower; Cotton Mather—whose *Magnalia Christi Americana* (1702) ends the New England 17th century and brings the New England mind face to face with the Enlightenment—boasts of erudition. More widely read than any of these, the first American to have worldwide influence was Benjamin Franklin, whose adroit *Autobiography* is a classic of Western literature and whose letters, satires, bagatelles, almanacs, and scientific writings are the work of a citizen of the world.

The intellectual brilliance of American thought between the end of the Seven Years' War (1763) and the creation of the federal government (1789) is among the wonders of the history of ideas. The constitutional issues of the 18th century could not have been more ably debated, as Edmund Burke, William Pitt, and other British statesmen testified. Franklin participated, but so did Samuel Adams, John Adams, Thomas Paine, Thomas Jefferson, and a company of others. Of this group Paine, the propagandist, whose *Common Sense* (1776) and *The Crisis* (1776–83) awakened American enthusiasm, and Jefferson, the principal author of the Declaration of Independence and the author of an unrivaled collection of letters and papers that reveal an encyclopedic mind, are best remembered today. The obsession of modern literary theory with problems of symbolism, depth psychology, and the like has turned attention away from this body of great argument, albeit many are willing to grant with the American historian Carl Becker that Jefferson's prose has a haunting felicity.

The Revolution, the Peace of Paris, and the adoption of the federal Constitution created a drive toward cultural independence. The satires of Philip Freneau, Francis Hopkinson, and John Trumbull are mainly of interest to scholars, but Freneau, in lyric poetry and in an exercise in Gothic romanticism, *The House of Night* (1779), marks the transition from the Enlightenment to romanticism. Trumbull was one of the Connecticut Wits, a group conscientiously endeavoring to create a national literature. The romances of Charles Brockden Brown have more vitality; *Wieland* (1798), *Arthur Mervyn* (1799), and *Edgar Huntley* (1799), compounded of Gothicism, romantic "science," propaganda, realism, and rodomontade, attracted Percy Bysshe Shelley by their power.

Maturer years began with the appearance in literature of three writers associated with New York. William Cullen Bryant—whose "Thanatopsis" (1817) was the product of a wunderkind, and whose philosophical poems, such as "The Prairies," have intellectual dignity—edited the *New York Evening Post* from 1829 to 1878, giving space in its columns to advocates of liberal and radical movements. More popular was Washington Irving, whose *History of New York by Diedrich Knickerbocker* (1809) gave that city a symbolic figure, whose *Sketch Book* (1819–20) created Rip Van Winkle and Ichabod Crane, and whose *Alhambra* (1832), an exercise in the sentimental exotic, scarcely prophesied his *Tour of the Prairies* (1835) and his substantial biographies. The third was James Fenimore Cooper, of worldwide fame, whose Leatherstocking series (*The Pioneers,* 1823; *The Last of the Mohicans,* 1826; *The Prairie,*

1827; *The Pathfinder*, 1840; *The Deerslayer*, 1841) has been called an American prose epic. Cooper's sea novels, of which *The Pilot* (1823) is most often read, were the best in the language before those of Joseph Conrad. Widely misjudged as a critic of American society, Cooper in later books endeavored to stem the tide of Jacksonian Democracy by plumping for a doctrine of *noblesse oblige* among a governing elite.

Of those who sought a cosmopolitan solution to the question of what literary culture should be, the Cambridge poets—James Russell Lowell, Oliver Wendell Holmes, and Henry Wadsworth Longfellow—are characteristic. The most influential was Longfellow, who appealed to religious, patriotic, and cultural desires, in translations (his version of Dante Alighieri, 1865–69, is notable), short lyrics, remarkable sonnets, and narrative poems of special interest to the American of the 19th century—*Evangeline* (1847), *The Song of Hiawatha* (1855), *The Courtship of Miles Standish* (1858), and *Tales of a Wayside Inn* (1863, 1872, 1873). Holmes, in verse and prose, sought to liberate Americans from the tyranny of theology, and Lowell, from cultural provincialism. Associated with this group is the Quaker abolitionist John Greenleaf Whittier, whose *Snow-Bound* (1866) is an unforgettable vignette of rural America.

Moderns find the Concord group—Ralph Waldo Emerson, Henry David Thoreau, Nathaniel Hawthorne, and, a little apart from them, Herman Melville—more exciting. Emerson was, par excellence, the mover and shaker in 19th-century American idealism, with *Nature* (1836), "The American Scholar" (1837), "The Divinity School Address" (1838), and the *Essays* (1841, 1844). His crisp Yankee accent penetrated where metaphysics could not reach. Industrial society pays more attention to Thoreau, whose *Walden* (1854) is more widely read and whose vigorous essays on what Americans of the late 20th century call civil rights are applicable to present problems. The modern appeal of Hawthorne in such books as *The Scarlet Letter* (1850), *The House of the Seven Gables* (1851), and *The Marble Faun* (1860), as well as in his short stories, was heightened in the 20th century with a spurt of interest in neo-Calvinist theories of human nature. A later, drastic revolution in literary values has placed Melville among the literary giants for much the same reason; and *Mardi* (1849), *Moby-Dick* (1851), *Pierre* (1852), and *Billy Budd* (not available until 1924) are studied for their symbolism of good and evil.

The South and the West had been developing writers of their own, but only one antebellum author rose to the importance of the writers just discussed—Edgar Allan Poe, if he can be called southern. Although the present tendency is to derogate his genius, his influence as critic, short-story writer (*Tales of the Grotesque and Arabesque*, 1840), and poet has been worldwide. The reputations of fictionists John Pendleton Kennedy and William Gilmore Simms are local in comparison, and the West did not speak with unmistakable authority until Mark Twain's *Roughing It* (1872).

The age of radio and television may not believe that oratory was ever a branch of literature, but in the second quarter of the 19th century the speeches of Daniel Webster and of his great rivals John C. Calhoun and Henry Clay approached Roman dignity in discussing the constitutional issues that led to the Civil War. Abolitionism lacked a similar great forum; yet Harriet Beecher Stowe's *Uncle Tom's Cabin* (1852), partisan, sentimental, and melodramatic, went around the world. After a great deal of unsuccessful hack writing, Walt Whitman produced the first version of *Leaves of Grass* (1855), a work he continued to rewrite and expand until 1892. Famous as metrical experimentation, this gospel was part of the 19th-century religion of humanity. In *Calamus* (1860), *Drum Taps* (1865), *Democratic Vistas* (1871), and *Specimen Days and Collect* (1882), Whitman caught the epic quality of the Civil War, as Abraham Lincoln caught its mystic quality in the Gettysburg Address (1863); or denounced political corruption as Mark Twain and Charles Dudley Warner did in the uneven novel they wrote together, *The Gilded Age* (1873), which gave its name to the postwar period.

The Civil War is a historical watershed dividing the culture of agrarian America from that of industrial America. But one of the results of that conflict was curiosity about the far-flung nation; and the increasing effectiveness of literary periodicals, notable in the creation of the *Atlantic Monthly* in 1857, gave rise to a varied literature of local color. The South found comfort in glamorous or sentimental pictures of its antebellum culture, as in George Washington Cable's *Old Creole Days* (1879); Joel Chandler Harris' *Uncle Remus: His Songs and Sayings* (1880), now dismissed as Uncle Tomism but a treasury of folklore; F. Hopkinson Smith's *Colonel Carter of Cartersville* (1891), a sentimental picture of the Confederate colonel; and Thomas Nelson Page's *Red Rock* (1898), an equally sentimental version of life in old Virginia, which the novels of Ellen Glasgow in the 20th century were to correct.

New England salved its hurts during its "decline"

in the charming and occasionally powerful genre stories of such writers as Sarah Orne Jewett, Mary Eleanor Wilkins Freeman, and Alice Brown. California produced Bret Harte's *The Luck of Roaring Camp* (1870), and partially through Harte the influence of Charles Dickens was filtered into the school of regional literature. Tennessee was pictured by Mary Nouailles Murfree ("Charles Egbert Craddock"), whose *In the Tennessee Mountains* (1884) preludes the exploitation of the mountaineer as subject, and New York State produced *David Harum* (1898), by Edward N. Westcott. Local color verse by John Hay, Joaquin Miller, Will Carleton, and James Whitcomb Riley, sometimes in dialect, accompanied the vogue.

After the Civil War the vigorous philosophic idealism of Concord deliquesced into the cultural propriety of the genteel tradition. The moderns find it difficult to be fair to the work of this tradition, exemplified by the poetic theories of Edmund Clarence Stedman (*The Nature and Elements of Poetry*, 1892), the aesthetic teachings of Charles Eliot Norton, and the criticism of W. C. Brownell. But the disciplinary quality of genteel criticism (for example, that of Brander Matthews) in curbing the excesses of romantic self-expression was an important contribution; and the postwar years also saw the rise of a mature literature of biography, history, and expository prose. Biography was of moment to the Puritans, but American biography really struck its stride with James Parton's *Life and Times of Benjamin Franklin* (1864) and has continued to produce masterly works ever since. American achievement in historical writing begins early and matures in such books as William Hickling Prescott's *History of the Conquest of Mexico* (1843) and Francis Parkman's distinguished series *France and England in North America* (1851–92)—these two, together with John Lothrop Motley, being classed as "romantic" historians. The influence of European scholarship is more directly evident after the Civil War in the work of Henry Harrisse, Justin Winsor, James Schouler, John Bach McMaster, and James Ford Rhodes. Stylistic craftsmanship is most evident in the work of Henry Adams, whose *History of the United States During the Administrations of Jefferson and Madison* (1889–91) challenges the literary supremacy of Parkman. All the world knows Adams' *Mont-Saint-Michel and Chartres* (1904) and *The Education of Henry Adams* (1904).

Historians had no monopoly on expository scholarship or propaganda. The *Personal Memoirs* of Ulysses S. Grant (1885) have the clarity and simplicity of Julius Caesar's *De bello Gallico;* Henry George's *Progress and Poverty* (1877–79) and Edward Bellamy's *Looking Backward* (1888) were as influential in their way as Paine's books had been in theirs; and a varied literature of science, philosophy, and theology developed as the country discovered Charles Darwin. Andrew Dickson White's powerful, if uneven, *History of the Warfare of Science With Theology in Christendom* (1896) is perhaps the single best monument of this debate, although writers as excellent as Asa Gray, John Fiske, and Josiah Royce participated. All this is the background for William James's classic *Principles of Psychology* (1890), the prelude to pragmatism; *The Will to Believe and Other Essays* appeared in 1897.

American fiction came of age in the late 19th century, however great the contributions of Hawthorne's generation. In *The Adventures of Huckleberry Finn* (1884), Mark Twain created a classic work; and if his collected writings are uneven, he moved steadily from the "oral" manner of *The Innocents Abroad* (1869) to the Voltairean irony of *The Mysterious Stranger* (1916) as hilarity gave way to pessimism. But the gathering forces of realism—evident, for example, in the work of John William De Forest and Albion W. Tourgée—found their spokesman in William Dean Howells. His *Criticism and Fiction* (1891) summed up realistic, but not naturalistic, theory; in *A Modern Instance* (1881), *The Rise of Silas Lapham* (1884), and *A Hazard of New Fortunes* (1890), he showed that the business of literature was with the here and now, not with trumpet-and-drum romances and sentimental tales. Beneath the serene surface of his prose there is a sardonic feeling, an ironic vision. Realists and naturalists (none of them consistent) were grouped around him—Hamlin Garland, Stephen Crane, Frank Norris, and others; and out of the excitement emerged the slow, awkward genius of Theodore Dreiser, whose *Sister Carrie* (1900) marks the transition in fiction between the realism of the 19th century and that of the 20th.

While realists and sentimentalists and naturalists and idealists argued, Henry James, self-exiled, opened the modern manner in fiction by concentrating on the subjective world. His progress from *The American* (1877) through *The Portrait of a Lady* (1881) to *The Wings of the Dove* (1902), *The Golden Bowl* (1904), and *The Sense of the Past* (1917) is for admirers a march toward subtlety of insight and of craftsmanship. For others he becomes so difficult that the game is not worth the candle. He was a theorist of literary art (for example, *Notes on Novelists*, 1914); and his example has profoundly influenced contemporaries and successors of the rank of Edith Wharton (*The House of Mirth*, 1905), Willa Cather (*A Lost Lady*, 1923), and Ellen Glasgow (*The Sheltered Life*, 1932). Indeed, the way leads from Henry James through William James to the stylistic experimentation of Gertrude Stein.

The end of the 19th century and the opening of the 20th saw a pause in the rhythm of American literature, as if the country awaited the coming of World War I and, so far as writing is concerned, the scarcely less powerful impact of Sigmund Freud and his successors on the literary imagination. Poetry seemed to recapture the great audiences it had lost since Longfellow, when Vachel Lindsay, Edgar Lee Masters, Edwin Arlington Robinson, Carl Sandburg, and Robert Frost achieved vast reading publics. But foreign influences from France and Italy and the impact of the war, summed up in T. S. Eliot's *The Waste Land* (1922) and in the energetic propaganda of Ezra Pound, diverted poetry into the more difficult styles of Conrad Aiken, Wallace Stevens, Hart Crane, and Marianne Moore.

Reacting against the canons of the 19th century, critical theory, whether it concerned literature or culture, took on new importance about 1910. Preluded by Joel Spingarn, Randolph Bourne, John Macy, and their elder fellow, George Santayana, critics turned to a reexamination of the American present and a reevaluation of the American past. Van Wyck Brooks, in *America's Coming of Age* (1915), campaigned for a "usable past," which he created in later volumes; H. L. Mencken demanded "sophistication" in various books of *Prejudices* (1919–27); and Walter Lippmann in *A Preface to Morals* (1929) and Joseph Wood Krutch in *The Modern Temper* (1929) declined to accept traditional canons of the dignity of man. In vain the neohumanists—Irving Babbitt, Paul Elmer More, Stuart P. Sherman, and others—asserted that long-run sagacity lay with tradition. The distinguished prose of Lewis Mumford, in such books as *Sticks and Stones* (1924) and *The Brown Decades* (1931), demonstrated that the modern spirit was not identical with iconoclasm.

In retrospect the 1920's resemble the 1850's—a great creative decade beginning with the smashing success of Sinclair Lewis' *Main Street* (1920) and closing with the troubled rhetoric of Thomas Wolfe's *Look Homeward, Angel* (1929), a singular specimen of the confessional literature associated with the European romantics. A brilliant ten years included F. Scott Fitzgerald's *The Great Gatsby* (1925) and the works of Ernest Hemingway; James Boyd's *Drums* (1925), which was a historical novel; and a spate of "sophisticated" writers, including James Branch Cabell, Joseph Hergesheimer, and Carl Van Vechten. Cabell's *Beyond Life* (1919) set forth a theory of sophistication that governed the whole movement of literary smartness. Possibly the soundest products of the self-conscious school were Thornton Wilder's philosophical contes, such as *The Bridge of San Luis Rey* (1927).

The cry was for "freedom," although no one quite knew what kind of freedom was meant; and the angry thirties, as they have been called, took revenge by nourishing proletarian fiction that included the *Studs Lonigan* trilogy (1932–35) of James T. Farrell, the three-volume national canvas of John Dos Passos' *U.S.A.* (1937), and the struggles of "the little man" in John Steinbeck's *In Dubious Battle* (1936) and *The Grapes of Wrath* (1939). The neonaturalistic novel also emphasized environment as the shaper of lives, especially in the social protest of Nelson Algren and the exposés of the black's plight in the work of Richard Wright, Erskine Caldwell, and Lillian Smith. The emerging genius of the 1930's was William Faulkner, an experimentalist in fictional forms who used his native Mississippi, as James Joyce had used Dublin, for a background to his criticism of the hollowness of modern society. A somber view of human failure and of race relations, *The Sound and the Fury* (1929), was followed, but not superseded in brilliance, by *Light in August* (1932), *Absalom, Absalom!* (1936), and twelve other novels. It more and more appeared that America was not promises; and foreign reporting of unexampled penetration by John Gunther, Edgar Snow, Vincent Sheean, and others not only pictured the death of Europe but also prepared Americans for a second world war. The spate of novels concerning World War I—John Dos Passos' *Three Soldiers* (1921), E. E. Cummings' *The Enormous Room* (1922), and Hemingway's *The Sun Also Rises* (1926) and *A Farewell to Arms* (1929) are examples—were at once the result of shock and of a return to European literary techniques. The novels of World War II lacked the shock techniques, but were frequently disturbing indictments and even previsions of future problems, notably James Gould Cozzens' *Guard of Honor* (1948), Norman Mailer's massive *The Naked and the Dead* (1948), and Joseph Heller's surreal *Catch-22* (1961).

The first three decades after World War II saw powerful pressures on the literary arts. The apocalyptic vision of total destruction in John Hersey's report *Hiroshima* (1946) not only heralded the postwar era's chief concern—survival—but also illustrated the difficulty creative writers experienced in matching the vitality and the violence in the world around them. As the American dream turned into a nightmare, the novelist and the poet have had to compete with an increasing public interest in theology and philosophy, history and sociology, and the phenomenon known as "the new journalism." David Riesman's study of human behavior, *The Lonely Crowd* (1950); Paul Tillich's argument for religious existentialism, *The Courage To Be* (1952); Erik H. Erikson's *Childhood and Society* (1950); the historical studies of C. Vann Woodward; the psychoanalytic critiques of Norman O. Brown; and revivals of Oriental mysticism have had wide currency. Even more popular are the essays of certain journalists who combine autobiography with polemic, historical facts with anecdote: such black writers as James Baldwin and Eldridge Cleaver; such novelists turned journalists as Mailer, Truman Capote, Wright Morris, and Gore Vidal; and such cultural observers as Tom Wolfe and John Cage—all of whom have reached an audience that might have chosen fiction over nonfiction in the decades before the war.

But to say that the traditional genres—fiction, poetry, and drama—have diminished beyond expectation since midcentury will not do. Philip Roth, author of the popular *Goodbye, Columbus* (1959), believes the postwar novelist "has his hands full in trying to understand, and then describe, and then make *credible* much of the American reality," but attempt it the novelist does in various guises. The hero is frequently an antihero, a rebel-victim, an outsider; yet he is not without vitality and diversity. Deriving from the works of Nathanael West and Henry Roth in the 1930's, the contemporary Jewish novel flourishes in the fiction of Saul Bellow, Bernard Malamud, and J. D. Salinger. The southern novel retains older traditions and more diverse talents, notably Eudora Welty, Carson McCullers, and Flannery O'Connor. Many novelists have recorded the black experience in America, but none more graphically than Ralph Ellison in his only novel, *Invisible Man* (1952). The fantasists express their subjectivism in satire, parody, and absurdist humor (John Barth, Donald Barthelme, John Hawkes, Thomas Pynchon) or in the prophetic visions of science fiction (Ray Bradbury, Robert A. Heinlein, Isaac Asimov). Virtuoso novelists who are difficult to classify—Vladimir Nabokov (*Lolita*,

1955) and John Updike (*Rabbit Redux*, 1971)—keep the genre alive by sheer linguistic agility.

The postwar poets have had a more difficult time. The Pound-Eliot tradition is waning as the reputations of Wallace Stevens and William Carlos Williams rise. The younger poets have had to begin afresh, seeking their own private faiths, and have focused on individualized and subjective experience. Chief among them is Robert Lowell, who admitted in 1961 that it was "hard to think of a young poet who has the validity of Salinger or Saul Bellow," but ten years later found himself with an international reputation, while Salinger was strangely silent. Lowell's early Catholic visions in clotted, elliptical verse forms gave way to intensely personal confessions (*Life Studies*, 1959) and public utterances on civil issues (*For the Union Dead*, 1964; *Notebook, 1967–1968*, 1969) that mark a major talent, a poet who has found his right métier. Had they lived past middle age, Theodore Roethke, a romantic lyricist and mystic; John Berryman, a learned, idiosyncratic original, the inventor of "dream songs"; and Randall Jarrell, the witty poet-critic-teacher, might have achieved Lowell's eminence. Had they not dissolved almost as quickly as they assembled, several groups of poets—namely, the Black Mountain poets (Charles Olson, Robert Creeley), the beat generation (Allen Ginsberg, Gregory Corso), the San Francisco group (Lawrence Ferlinghetti, Gary Snyder), the New York school (John Ashbery, Frank O'Hara, Kenneth Koch)—might have left a deeper impress upon American literary history.

The impress made by contemporary playwrights is probably even slighter, and Eugene O'Neill continues to be the leading dramatist of this century. Except for the meteoric careers of Arthur Miller and Tennessee Williams during the later 1940's and 1950's and the brief promise of Edward Albee in the 1960's, American writing for the theater declined, partly because of the high cost of producing plays, partly because of the competition of television.

Literary criticism seems also to have weakened. The death of Edmund Wilson in 1972 (*Axel's Castle*, 1931; *To the Finland Station*, 1940; *Memoirs of Hecate County*, 1946) removed from the scene America's one unquestioned man of letters, albeit Alfred Kazin (*On Native Grounds*, 1942; *The Inmost Leaf*, 1955) and Lionel Trilling (d. 1976) (*The Liberal Imagination*, 1950; *Beyond Culture*, 1965) maintain an intellectual tradition. Writers such as Leslie Fiedler and Richard Poirer breathe life into literary polemics, and E. B. White has kept the essay form alive. But belles lettres no longer hold the position of eminence they held in the 19th century.

[Jacob Blanck, *Bibliography of American Literature;* James D. Hart, *The Oxford Companion to American Literature;* Howard Mumford Jones and Richard M. Ludwig, *Guide to American Literature and Its Backgrounds;* Robert E. Spiller, Willard Thorp, Thomas H. Johnson, Henry Seidel Canby, Richard M. Ludwig, and William M. Gibson, eds., *Literary History of the United States;* William Peterfield Trent, John Erskine, Stuart P. Sherman, and Carl Van Doren, eds., *The Cambridge History of American Literature;* Moses Coit Tyler, *A History of American Literature, 1607–1765,* and *The Literary History of the American Revolution.*]

HOWARD MUMFORD JONES

LITERATURE, AFRO-AMERICAN, that literature written by black Americans of African heritage, has a long history. Definition in these terms is redundant but reflects the substance of diverse definitions that emerged during the 1960's. Historically, the literature includes the 18th-century classical poetry of Phyllis Wheatley, bought as a slave and educated in the Boston home of John Wheatley; slave narratives, collected and transcribed by northern abolitionists in the 19th century; the cultural "explosion" of the Harlem Renaissance of the 1920's; works of the World War II period; and experiments in fiction and drama spawned in the 1960's. The early poetry is in the traditional style of the 18th-century lyric and elegy and uses religious and patriotic themes. Racial emphases call for justice or look to the promise of a better life in the "hereafter."

By 1887 Charles W. Chesnutt had made his mark as a short-story writer with the publication of "The Goophered Grapevine." Born in Ohio, Chesnutt taught in the South and then returned to the North and studied law. His novels—*The House Behind the Cedars* (1900), *The Marrow of Tradition* (1901), and *The Colonel's Dream* (1905)—are considered to be overwritten, but the short stories present folk customs and beliefs effectively. During the same period Paul Laurence Dunbar became prominent as a poet, writing both in dialect and in formal English. Written in the latter style, his "We Wear the Mask" presents a theme that recurs frequently in Afro-American fiction.

From the cultural mix in Harlem in New York City and the sponsorship of artistic talent there the Harlem Renaissance erupted in 1921. Carl Van Vechten was probably the best known of the patrons. The range of production was broad, from poetry on West Indian themes by Claude McKay to Countee Cullen's lyrics in the style of John Keats and E. A. Robinson to Langston Hughes's scenes of the city and the novels of James Weldon Johnson, Wallace Thurman, and Zora Neale Hurston. Themes were as varied as approaches and style: recollection of home; miscegenation; "passing," urban poverty, love, and rebellion. And they included the traditional apostrophes to God and nature, and references to special events. The uniqueness of the period lay not so much in its cultural elitism as in the "interplay between white and black in American life, the illumination of the Afro-American experience within American culture," according to the historian Nathan I. Huggins. Hughes illustrates this point in an autobiographical work, *I Wonder As I Wander* (1964), in which he describes the plight of the black American as he travels through his native land and foreign countries. The interaction underscores the mutual dependence that Huggins describes. Interested in jazz, the music representative of the age, Hughes remarks on the mutual attention given it by both blacks and whites. He reveals the same respect for the jazz idiom as novelist Ralph Ellison and poet-dramatist LeRoi Jones, who in 1969 changed his name to Imamu Amiri Baraka. Baraka has pointed out the irony of dependence by showing that, even though Louis Armstrong and Bix Beiderbecke ushered in the Jazz Age, their styles were as dissimilar as can be imagined. Acculturation dictated style and attitude: Armstrong refined an Afro-American tradition, whereas Beiderbecke rebelled against midwestern conventionalism. Baraka wrote, in *Blues People* (1963), "the point is that [Americans believed] Afro-American music did not become a completely American expression until the white man could play it!"

For Alain Locke, writing in *The New Negro* in 1925, the Harlem Renaissance had depended on the verve and creativity of Harlem blacks. In an essay in the anthology, James Weldon Johnson predicted economic growth based on expansion in real estate and commerce in Harlem. He was optimistic for the future, assuming that Harlem would continue to be a "culture capital." Some disillusionment with patrons and the coming of the Great Depression cooled the ferment, as the intelligentsia moved to gain nationalistic aims through the National Association for the Advancement of Colored People and the masses, through Marcus Garvey's "Back to Africa" movement.

The next surge of literary activity occurred during the World War II period. From personal anger and agony sprang the social novels and stories of Richard Wright. The autobiographical *Black Boy* (1945) followed *Native Son* (1940), with its controversial hero, Bigger Thomas. In it Wright sought to show the destructive effect of prejudice, apathy, injustice, and poverty on Bigger and all his counterparts: he took an action that defied the society that had subjugated him; he forced it to notice him. This same theme, the repression of the black man, links the stories in Wright's collection *Eight Men* (1961). His protest pervades his short stories also, but it is turned to existentialist purposes in his novel *The Outsider* (1953), in which the hero places himself outside the code of moral responsibility.

The mélange of what some critics viewed as "exotic" themes of the Harlem Renaissance was replaced by a preoccupation with the search-for-identity theme of the 1940's and 1950's. Wright and, later, James Baldwin raised the question of the discovery of personal identity and its contribution to the achievement of "manhood" among blacks. It was left to Ralph Ellison in his monumental single novel, *Invisible Man* (1952), to combine the universality of this aim of all mankind with the specificity of the opposition blacks encounter in achieving it. The novel deals in different interrelated levels of understanding, utilizing a broad variety of style and form. It is mythic, allegorical, realistic, and symbolic. It tempers the protest of Wright by universalizing personal experience. Baldwin as essayist, novelist, and dramatist next inspected such personal experience. In his early novel *Go Tell It on the Mountain* (1953), he probes father-son relationships—that in his hero's own home and that emerging between him and God. It is in two striking collections of essays, *Notes of a Native Son* (1955) and *The Fire Next Time* (1963), that this prolific writer investigates motifs and motivations of prejudice in America. The novel *Giovanni's Room* (1956) treats the special problems of homosexual love, and his collected stories, *Tell Me How Long the Train's Been Gone* (1968), present several themes. Baldwin's dramatic works begin with the religious *Amen Corner* (1968) and then move on to attack racial prejudice in *Blues for Mr. Charlie* (1964).

The post–World War II period also included the "raceless" works of Frank Yerby and Lorraine Hansbery. Yerby's romantic fiction was of swashbuckling adventure; Hansbery's first play, *Raisin in the Sun* (1959), although concerned with a black family and its problems, did not adopt the militant stance engendered by some strains of the civil rights movement of the 1960's.

Afro-American literature returned to didacticism and emphasis on racial pride in the 1960's. Ed Bullins, Eldridge Cleaver, and Baraka stressed the responsibility of the black writer to sensitize the black audience to its racial history, to the need for personal growth, and to the imperative of attacking prejudice. Many of the writers had earlier employed traditional forms and subject matter, but in reply to the nonviolent philosophy of Martin Luther King, Jr., and in support of the militant approach, Cleaver and others adapted African themes and adopted the speech and subject matter of the black masses as vehicles of literary expression. Cleaver's collection of essays, *Soul on Ice* (1968), and Baraka's stunningly varied output of poetry, fiction, drama, and essays led the field. The evolution of Baraka's political philosophy can be traced in his work from the early poetry, *Preface to a Twenty-Volume Suicide Note* (1961) and *The System of Dante's Hell* (1965); essays, *Home* (1966); drama, *The Dutchman* (1964) and *The Toilet* (1966); and short stories, *Tales* (1967). It culminates in the revolutionary *Slave Ship* (1968) and *Four Revolutionary Plays* (1969).

The development of Afro-American literature has depended on available publishing opportunities, economic conditions, and the creative urge (and, often, the political commitment) of the writers.

[Nathan I. Huggins, *Harlem Renaissance*.]
CECELIA HODGES DREWRY

LITTLE BIGHORN, BATTLE OF (June 25, 1876). The Sioux in Dakota Territory bitterly resented the opening of the Black Hills to settlers in violation of the Treaty of Fort Laramie of 1868. Owing also to official graft and negligence they were facing starvation in the fall of 1875. They began to leave their reservations contrary to orders, to engage in their annual buffalo hunt. They were joined by tribesmen from other reservations until the movement took on the proportions of a serious revolt. The situation was one that called for the utmost tact and discretion, for the Sioux were ably led and the treatment they had received had stirred the bitterest resentment among them. But an order originating with the Bureau of Indian Affairs was sent to all reservation officials early in December, directing them to notify the Indians to return by Jan. 31 under penalty of being attacked by the U.S. Army. This belated order could not have been carried out in the dead of winter even if the Indians had been inclined to obey it.

Early in 1876 Gen. Philip H. Sheridan, from his

headquarters at Chicago, ordered a concentration of troops on the upper Yellowstone River, to capture or disperse the numerous bands of Dakota who were hunting there. In June Gen. Alfred H. Terry, department commander, and Col. George A. Custer, with his regiment from Fort Abraham Lincoln, marched overland to the Yellowstone, where they were met by the steamboat *Far West* with ammunition and supplies. At the mouth of Rosebud Creek, a tributary of the Yellowstone, Custer received his final orders from Terry—to locate and disperse the Indians. According to official records, there is no longer any doubt that Terry gave Custer absolutely free hand in dealing with the situation, relying on his well-known experience in such warfare.

With twelve companies of the Seventh Cavalry Custer set out on his march and soon discovered the Sioux camped on the south bank of the Little Bighorn River. He sent Maj. Marcus Reno with three companies of cavalry and all the Arikara scouts across the upper ford of the river to attack the southern end of the Sioux camp. Capt. Frederick Benteen, with three companies, was sent to the left of Reno's line of march. Custer himself led five companies of the Seventh Cavalry down the river to the lower ford for an attack on the upper part of the camp. One company was detailed to bring up the pack train.

This plan of battle, typical of Custer, was in the beginning completely successful. Suddenly faced by a vigorous double offensive, the Indians at first thought only of retreat. At this critical juncture Reno became utterly confused and ordered his men to fall back across the river. Thereupon the whole force of the Indian attack was concentrated upon Custer's command, compelling him to retreat from the river to a position at which his force was later annihilated. The soldiers under Reno rallied at the top of a high hill overlooking the river, and there they were joined by Benteen's troops and, two hours later, by the company guarding the pack train.

An official inquiry into Reno's conduct in the battle was made in 1879, and he was cleared of all responsibility for the disaster. Since that time the judgment of military experts has tended to reverse this conclusion and to hold both Reno and Benteen gravely at fault.

In Sheridan's *Memoirs* it is stated: "Reno's head failed him utterly at the critical moment." He abandoned in a panic the perfectly defensible and highly important position on the Little Bighorn River. Reno's unpopularity after the battle was one of the reasons he was brought up on charges of drunkenness and "peeping tomism" and court-martialed. Reno

was found guilty and dishonorably discharged. However, in December 1966 Reno's grandnephew, Charles Reno, asked the Army Board for the Correction of Military Records to review the court-martial verdict, citing disclosures in G. Walton's book *Faint the Trumpet Sounds*. In June 1967 the secretary of the army restored Reno to the rank of major and the dishonorable discharge was changed to an honorable one. The action was taken on the grounds that the discharge had been "excessive and therefore unjust." However, the guilty verdict still stands. In September 1967 Reno was reburied in Custer Battlefield National Cemetery in Montana.

As to Benteen, he admitted at the military inquiry following the battle that he had been twice ordered by Custer to break out the ammunition and come on with his men. Later, at 2:30 P.M., when he had joined Reno, there was no attacking force of Indians in the vicinity, and he had at his disposal two-thirds of Custer's entire regiment, as well as the easily accessible reserve ammunition. Gen. Nelson A. Miles, in his *Personal Recollections,* can find no reason for Benteen's failure to go to Custer's relief. He says, after an examination of the battlefield, that a gallop of fifteen minutes would have brought reinforcements to Custer. This opinion makes it hard to understand why, for more than an hour, while Custer's command was being overwhelmed, Reno and Benteen remained inactive.

[John Stands in Timber and Margot Liberty, *Cheyenne Memories;* Edgar I. Stewart, *Custer's Luck.*]

O. G. LIBBY

LITTLE CHURCH AROUND THE CORNER. In 1870 the rector of a New York church refused a burial service to George Holland because he had been an actor, but remarked, "I believe there is a little church around the corner where they do such things." He referred to the Church of the Transfiguration on Twenty-ninth Street, built 1849–56, which thereupon became a favorite sanctuary for actors, and still retains its whimsical nickname.

[George MacAdam, *The Little Church Around the Corner.*]

ALVIN F. HARLOW

LITTLE GIANT, the nickname given Stephen A. Douglas at a political rally in Jacksonville, Ill., 1834. So well did the youthful lawyer-politician uphold President Andrew Jackson and denounce "Emperor" Nicholas Biddle, president of the Bank of the United

States (*see* Panic of 1837), that the crowd hailed the diminutive Democrat by the sobriquet by which he was thereafter known.

[George Fort Milton, *The Eve of Conflict*.]
GEORGE FORT MILTON

"LITTLE GROUP OF WILLFUL MEN." By a five-day filibuster ending Sunday, Mar. 4, 1917, the passage of a bill to arm merchant ships against German submarines was prevented by a group of eleven senators: Robert M. La Follette, Frank Norris, Albert Baird Cummins, Asle J. Gronna, Moses E. Clapp, John D. Works (Republicans); William J. Stone, James A. O'Gorman, William F. Kirby, Harry Lane, James K. Vardaman (Democrats). Citing the passage of the bill by the House of Representatives, 403-13, President Woodrow Wilson, in a public statement, stigmatized the senators as "a little group of willful men, representing no opinion but their own, [who] have rendered the great government of the United States helpless and contemptible."

[F. L. Paxson, *Democracy and the World War: Pre-War Years, 1913–1917*; Mark Sullivan, *Our Times*, vol. V.]
HARVEY L. CARTER

LITTLE NIAGARA. *See* **Niagara, Carrying Place of.**

LITTLE NINE PARTNERS' PATENT, granted Apr. 10, 1706, to Samuel Broughton and seven associates, was in the northeastern part of Dutchess County, N.Y., and included the present towns of Milan and Pine Plains, the north half of North East, and small portions of Clinton and Stanford. The colonial assembly authorized its partition in 1734.

[Frank Hasbrouck, *History of Dutchess County*.]
A. C. FLICK

LITTLE RED SCHOOLHOUSE. From the 18th century well into the 20th, the country school stood as a symbol of American democracy and civilization founded upon the "three R's." The small, one-room school building, usually located on a small piece of wasteland that the farmers could readily spare, was painted, if at all, with red or yellow ochre, the cheapest possible paint. Such schoolhouses were found along country roads throughout New England and states farther west, serving several farm families in a central place. Pictures of such buildings became a sort

of patriotic fetish with the American Protective Association, successor of the Know-Nothing party, at the close of the 19th century.

[Clifton Johnson, *Old-Time Schools and School-Books*.]
ROBERT P. TRISTRAM COFFIN

LITTLE SARAH, an English ship captured by French privateers in 1793 and interned at Philadelphia. The French minister, Edmond Charles Genêt, by equipping the vessel and permitting its departure under the name *Little Democrat* in defiance of Secretary of State Thomas Jefferson's protest of July 12, forfeited the confidence of President George Washington and even of Jefferson, whose pro-French sympathies were outraged. Demand for Genêt's recall became insistent. The *Little Sarah* thereby imposed a strain upon Franco-American relations.

[J. B. McMaster, *History of the People of the United States*.]
LOUIS MARTIN SEARS

LIVESTOCK INDUSTRY. The livestock of the United States originated in the Old World, the bulk of the animals coming from Europe, although some came from Asia. Importations began in 1609 and the introduction of new breeds never fully ceased. The bulk of the livestock consisted of cattle, swine, sheep, and horses; but there were also some goats and mules. (Furbearing animals and fowl are not considered livestock.)

The several breeds of animals vary in size and special characteristics, such as disease resistance, docility, and yields of meat, fat, hides, and milk. Swine and sheep breeds also vary in gregariousness. The more readily herded animals flourished in open ranges; the less gregarious produced best when fenced in. Extensive animal husbandry long characterized frontier farming. Animals grazed with little attention paid to them. They were rounded up periodically, marked in some fashion to indicate ownership, and herded and trailed to market. Livestock trailed over long distances became tough and lean. As early as the 18th century some farmers near urban markets specialized in fattening livestock.

Intensive animal husbandry took place in areas of denser settlement and involved fencing the animals, growing feed for them, giving them shelter, and maintaining more animals on less land. It demanded more capital for barns, fences, feed, and machinery. From 1900 on, the livestock industry became progressively more intensive and more productive.

Technological advances, particularly the discovery in 1874 of silage and the development of the gasoline tractor (1892), helped change the industry. Stockmen could handle huge concentrations of animals on very little land and with very little labor. The tractor also caused a decline in the numbers of horses and mules, which by 1960 were so few that the Bureau of the Census did not count them. Disease and predators long caused considerable losses to stockmen. Advances in veterinary medicine, including the discovery of insect disease vectors (for example, tick fever, 1889), helped reduce losses, as did the discovery of antibiotics. Predator ravages declined as the industry intensified.

Most of the processing of animal products was done on the farm before 1800. Slaughtering, processing, and marketing rapidly became a specialized industry shortly thereafter. Coastal towns had developed meat-packing industries to supply the trade with the West Indies and Europe in the 18th century. Philadelphia led in the business before and after the Revolution. Processing shifted westward, and by the 1840's Cincinnati was a great processing center. Other centers arose, and Chicago had become "hog butcher of the world" by the 1870's.

Advances in refrigeration on both railroads and ships allowed packers to reach vast markets in America and abroad. The chief advantages of centering operations in Chicago and Omaha seemed to be that the industry could better exploit labor in those cities and that the railroads tended to direct the animals to central points. In the 1930's, changes in labor laws reduced the advantages of central location at the same time that the truck was gradually replacing the railroad. Slaughtering and processing drifted to the countryside. The Chicago Union Stock Yards, established in 1865, closed in 1971 for lack of business. The advent of chain stores accelerated the shift to small rural auction markets and to decentralized processing. Grocery chains and packers occasionally operated their own farms and feedlots, especially during the 1950's and 1960's, but did not gain control of that aspect of the industry. (*See also* Cattle; Hogs.)

[Lewis Corey, *Meat and Man;* Herrell DeGraff, *Beef Production and Distribution;* J. T. Schlebecker, *Cattle Raising on the Plains, 1900–1961;* Charles W. Towne and Edward N. Wentworth, *Pigs: From Cave to Corn Belt.*]
JOHN T. SCHLEBECKER

LLANO ESTACADO. *See* **Staked Plain.**

LOBBIES, groups of individuals acting for themselves or others who seek to influence the decisions of government officials primarily by informal off-the-record communications and exchanges. Their tactics range from such high-pressure techniques as bribery, threats of electoral retaliation, and mass mailings to such low-pressure methods as supplying research and information in support of their views. Intermediate forms of influence include campaign contributions and persuasion.

The objects and tactics of lobbying have shifted sharply in American history. In the 19th and early 20th centuries the typical lobbyist focused on the legislative arena and used high-pressure methods, including bribery, to influence legislators. By the 1950's many lobbyists had enlarged their focus to include the executive branch and shifted to soft-sell tactics. This shift in technique was a response to exposure of lobbying scandals at both state and national levels.

Congress began investigating lobbies in 1913 with a study of the National Association of Manufacturers (NAM). Since that time there has been at least one major investigation in every decade. The investigations were followed first by piecemeal legislation and then, in Title III of the Legislative Reorganization Act of 1946, by general legislation to regulate lobbies. These acts and subsequent legislation aim at control primarily through publicity, but many loopholes remain that permit lobbies such as the NAM and Washington, D.C., law firms to avoid registration and others to avoid full disclosure of their activities. While not eliminating lobbies, the investigations and legislation have encouraged lobbies to seek a lower profile by moving away from high-pressure methods.

With the rise of the executive branch as initiator of legislation and the growth of the administrative bureaucracy, the focus of lobbyists began to shift from legislative bodies to executive offices. As a corollary, the growing proportion of lobbying that occurs outside the legislative limelight reduces its overall visibility. Increasingly, chief executives and bureaucratic agencies lobby for legislative passage of bills they have initiated. They often appear to be the sole influence on legislation, even though it is not uncommon for regulatory agencies to be lobbying in the interests of the clientele they are supposed to be regulating. These changes have led critical observers to question the validity of distinguishing between private and public lobbies.

In the 1970's most lobbyists were still acting for associations with an economic interest—business, farm, labor, and the professions. Over half of all registered lobbyists in Washington, D.C., are specialized business associations such as the American

Petroleum Institute and Aerospace Industries Association. Although multiinterest peak associations such as the AFL-CIO, the Farm Bureau Federation, and the NAM continue to lobby on a variety of congressional issues, critics of lobbying have moved on to new targets—for example, the "military-industrial complex" and the impact of corporate campaign contributions on executive policymaking. In addition to primarily economic lobbies, the 20th century has seen major lobbying efforts by prohibition groups like the Anti-Saloon League, civil rights groups like the National Association for the Advancement of Colored People (NAACP), reform groups like Common Cause, and peace groups like the National Peace Action Committee.

[Grant McConnell, *Private Power and American Democracy;* Lester Milbrath, *The Washington Lobbyists;* Karl Schriftgiesser, *The Lobbyists.*]

EDWARD S. MALECKI

LOCAL GOVERNMENT is the designation given to all units of government in the United States below the state level. The number of such units is constantly changing, but the most reliable enumeration is that contained in the census of governments conducted every five years by the U.S. Bureau of the Census. The 1967 tabulation was as follows:

Unit	Number
Counties	3,049
Municipalities	18,048
Townships	17,105
School districts	21,782
Special districts	21,264
Total	81,248

In the original colonial settlements on the Atlantic coast, towns and counties played the most significant local governmental role. In New England the town was of central importance; but as one looked farther south, counties became increasingly important, and they formed the dominant pattern in the South. Local patterns were carried west by migrants, with few modifications. Increasing urbanization in the 19th century shifted the emphasis gradually from counties and towns to municipalities. By the mid-20th century, 70 percent of the population lived in incorporated urban places and received local government services through them to a much greater degree than through counties, towns, and townships.

The functions of local government have remained relatively constant throughout American history, even though the responsible local unit often has changed with increasing urbanization. These functions include law enforcement, fire protection, welfare, public health, public schools, construction and maintenance of roads, election administration, and assessment and collection of the property tax. Although local governments continue to perform these functions, increased federal and state activity in these areas has altered the political environment significantly.

The New England town that developed in the colonial period as a small unit devoted to direct democracy continues to be an important general purpose unit of government in rural New England. Increased population and governmental complexity have forced many towns to abandon direct democracy in favor of representative government, but the primary functions remain unaltered except in heavily urbanized areas in which municipalities have replaced towns as the prime general purpose unit.

In other regions the county has followed much the same pattern as the New England town—maintaining its significance as a general purpose government primarily in rural areas. But even in highly urbanized areas, the county frequently plays an important role in welfare, public health, tax assessment and collection, and election administration. Furthermore, as urban problems have outgrown the boundaries of municipal governments, more and more urban counties have begun to assume major general governmental responsibilities. The structures that counties utilize to perform these functions appear almost infinitely variable from state to state and frequently within states. The most common structural problem has been the absence of a single executive officer to administer the unit. A few counties have elected chief executives, and an increasing number have hired managers; the vast majority of counties have no executive leadership.

City governments in the United States initially followed the English model, with a mayor and a council. In the late 18th and early 19th centuries, fear of strong executives and a desire to copy the U.S. Constitution led to institutionally weak mayors and to bicameral councils. The bicameral council proved unworkable and was gradually abandoned. The weakness of the mayor and the corruption of political machines led to other reforms in city government, but these reforms were adopted unevenly across the country. Most major cities did provide for some strengthening of the office of mayor in the late 19th and early 20th centuries. The move to short ballots and nonpartisanship was more pronounced in middle-sized cities than in large, metropolitan centers. Other reforms of city government were attempted as well. In the first half of the 20th century several hundred cities experimented with a commission structure in which legislative and executive functions were combined in one body. This experiment proved to be unsatisfactory in all but a few communities, and only 111 cities still use this form of government.

Council-manager government has been much more popular, particularly in those medium-sized cities that are relatively homogeneous socially and economically. This type of structure began in Staunton, Va., in 1908 and spread rapidly, until by 1975 nearly one-half of all cities used it. Its major feature is a strong, centralized, professional executive branch under a city manager who is hired by the city council. Council-manager government has less of an impact in large, complex cities in which at-large, nonpartisan elections and an appointed chief executive are unpopular and in very small cities that are unable to afford the services of a professional manager and staff.

Widespread consolidations have reduced drastically the number of school districts in the United States. In the 1930's the U.S. Census Bureau reported over 128,000 such governmental units. By 1967, the number had been reduced by 100,000. Some school systems are administered by counties, towns, or municipalities, but most have separate governmental structures designed to insulate them from the normal political arena and to provide them with a separate tax base. Traditionally these districts are operated by elected boards of education that hire a professional superintendent as administrator.

Other special districts have proliferated, particularly in the mid-20th century. The majority of these local governments are established to provide a single service or to perform a single function. The functions include fire protection, water, sewerage, mosquito abatement, parks and recreation, airports, and a variety of other activities. In a few instances, special districts have been created for multiple purposes such as water and sewerage, but all are limited in scope. The governing boards of special districts are often appointed rather than elected, and this gives rise to some concern over the degree of popular control possible in these governments. Two major reasons exist for the rapid growth of special districts. First, many potential service areas do not coincide with the boundaries of existing local governments, and special districts can be created to fit these service areas. Second, many local governments have exhausted the taxing and bonding authority granted to them by the state legisla-

tures, and each special district can begin with a new grant of authority to tax and to borrow.

As the density of population in urban areas increased, particularly in the 20th century, local governments increased as well and began to overlap both functionally and geographically. This led reformers to suggest a rationalization of governmental structures, particularly in metropolitan areas. The most far-reaching of these suggestions would have merged counties and cities into a single unit of metropolitan government. This suggestion was followed with some modification in Nashville, Tenn.; Jacksonville, Fla.; and Indianapolis, Ind. Other reform efforts attempted to reallocate local governmental functions among counties and municipalities on an areawide rather than a local basis. The outstanding example of this latter approach is Miami-Dade County in Florida.

Local governments and their citizens have generally resisted sweeping reforms that would alter the basic structure of government in metropolitan areas. Instead, many local governments have sought other means to avoid duplication and inefficiency in the provision of services. One increasingly popular device is the intergovernmental agreement. By utilizing contractual agreements, existing governments can band together to provide services that single units are unable to afford. In other cases, as in California's Lakewood Plan, cities can contract for services with an urban county that can provide services across most of the local government spectrum. Such agreements are popular because they permit existing governments to continue operation and allow local citizens to maintain mechanisms for local control of policy.

Another way to address the problem of the proliferation of local governments is through the metropolitan council of governments or the regional planning agency. Although this coordinative mechanism was initially adopted in metropolitan areas, it has spread to more sparsely populated areas as well. Such agencies consist of representatives of local governments in the area. They have no formal governmental powers or status, but requirements in federal grant-in-aid legislation since 1960 have increased their importance. Most grant proposals from local governments to the federal government must now be endorsed by such a regional body before they can be considered by federal agencies. These councils and agencies do not address the fundamental problem of proliferation of local governments but they do provide a mechanism through which some of the more serious intergovernmental conflicts can be resolved if federal funds are to be forthcoming.

In the late 1960's another movement began that

was designed to make a fundamental change in the structure of local government. This movement focused its attention on large cities and proposed neighborhood governments within existing municipalities. Such efforts are diametrically opposed to the metropolitan consolidation movement. The values of local control of policymaking that have long sustained small-town and suburban governments have been recommended for units of comparable size within the big cities. The structure and functions of such local governments have not yet been clearly delineated. Experiments with limited neighborhood participatory mechanisms occurred under the Office of Economic Opportunity programs in the 1960's. After the passage of the Demonstration Cities and Metropolitan Development Act of 1966, broader participatory mechanisms were developed in the model neighborhoods of the designated model cities. These mechanisms have varied widely in form, and the pattern of social services to which they direct their attention also changes from city to city, with some general emphasis on health, welfare, and housing. Some large cities, particularly New York, have also experienced pressures for neighborhood control of the schools. Because of continuing requirements by the federal government, neighborhood participatory mechanisms will continue to develop. By the mid-1970's, none of these mechanisms had yet developed into a full-fledged local government, although because of the backing of the federal government, they sometimes possessed a veto over local governmental policy decisions.

[George S. Blair, *Local Government in America*.]

JOHN H. BAKER

LOCAL OPTION. *See* **Liquor Laws.**

LOCHABER, TREATY OF (Oct. 18, 1770), was negotiated by Col. John Donelson for Virginia with the Cherokee. Its purpose was to exclude from the Indian lands many whites who had settled west of the line fixed by the Treaty of Hard Labor of 1768. By the new treaty the dividing line was moved westward, to begin six miles east of Long Island of the Holston, running thence to the mouth of the Kanawha River, adding a vast area to Virginia. In the running of Donelson Line a wide departure from the treaty was made in fixing the northern terminus.

[S. C. Williams, *Dawn of Tennessee Valley and Tennessee History*.]

SAMUEL C. WILLIAMS

LOCHNER V. *NEW YORK,* 198 U.S. 45 (1905). At about the same time that Utah attempted to regulate hours of labor for men in dangerous industries, New York sought to extend such regulation to workers in baking and confectionery establishments. Although the Supreme Court upheld the Utah statute in *Holden* v. *Hardy,* 169 U.S. 366 (1898), it declared the New York statute invalid seven years later in *Lochner* v. *New York*. The law provided for a maximum sixty-hour week, with an average ten-hour day.

Lochner, proprietor of a Utica bakery, had been arrested, tried, and convicted for violation of the law. On appeal to the Supreme Court attorneys for the defendant argued that while such protections might be justified in dangerous industries, they were unnecessary in industries that, by their nature, required extreme care in matters of cleanliness and sanitation. The Court accepted this reasoning, holding the act void as a violation of freedom of contract. It held that this right is a part of the liberty of the individual, protected by the Fourteenth Amendment, along with the right to purchase or sell labor. The statute did not come under the legitimate police power of the state as a proper regulation of the health, safety, or morals of the people. (*See also West Coast Hotel* v. *Parrish.*)

[C. K. Burdick, *The Law of the American Constitution;* J. R. Commons and J. B. Andrews, *Principles of Labor Legislation;* W. Brooke Graves, *American State Administration.*]

W. BROOKE GRAVES

LOCHRY'S DEFEAT. When George Rogers Clark's proposed expedition of 1781 against Fort Detroit mobilized at Wheeling, Col. Archibald Lochry and about a hundred Pennsylvania volunteers had not arrived. On Aug. 8 Clark started down the Ohio with his Virginia and regular troops, leaving word for Lochry to follow. Separated thus from Clark, Lochry and his men were attacked on Aug. 24 about twenty miles below the site of Cincinnati by a band of Indians under Joseph Brant and Alexander McKee. A third of Lochry's men were killed, the rest captured; several of the captives, including Lochry, were later killed. This defeat contributed to Clark's abandonment of his projected expedition.

[J. A. James, *Life of George Rogers Clark;* C. H. Sipe, *Indian Wars of Pennsylvania*.]

SOLON J. BUCK

LOCKE'S POLITICAL PHILOSOPHY. John Locke (1632–1704), one of the leading English philosophers of the 17th century, carried political theory

173

to an advanced state of democratic development. His most characteristic contribution was in his doctrine of natural rights. He maintained that life, liberty, and property were the inalienable rights of every individual. He believed that the happiness and security of the individual were the ends for which government came into existence.

Locke believed in the social contract not only as a means of securing the grant of political authority but also as a means of securing political and social liberty. The contract not only originates and delegates the powers which a government is to possess but also it indicates the extent of liberty which the individual should retain. Locke justified the right of revolution not on the ground of hostile acts of the people but on usurpations of authority on the part of those to whom such authority has been delegated. In other words, the possession of authority by governmental officials is strictly on a fiduciary basis. However, the popular right of revolution should not be exercised for trivial reasons but only with the consent of the majority of the people. A controlling public opinion has the right to pass upon the acts of government.

At the time of the American Revolution, Locke was perhaps the most influential political authority and his theories were regarded with the greatest respect by the leaders in the American cause. "Almost every writer seems to have been influenced by him, many quoted his words, and the argument of others shows the unmistakable imprint of his philosophy . . . no better epitome of the Revolutionary theory could be found than in John Locke on civil government" (C. E. Merriam).

[W. S. Carpenter, *The Development of American Political Thought;* W. A. Dunning, *Political Theories From Luther to Montesquieu;* C. E. Merriam, *American Political Theories.*]

WILLIAM STARR MYERS

LOCKOUT, the temporary withholding of work by an employer or employer group, generally for one or more of the following purposes: (1) to defeat an organizational campaign, (2) to undermine an incumbent union, (3) to defend a multiemployer unit against "whipsaw strikes," (4) to avoid extraordinary losses from a partial strike or an anticipated strike, or (5) to secure a better bargain. There are many more strikes than lockouts, but the distinction between them is often essentially formal, because either type of stoppage may be a response to the prospect or actuality of the other. At common law, lockouts were largely unrestricted. The National Labor Relations Act (1935), as amended, produced unstable adjudications regarding the legality of lockouts. In the 1970's, only lockouts based on one of the first two foregoing purposes were clearly prohibited, but notice and waiting periods were required for some lockouts. Other federal legislation restricts lockouts, as well as strikes, that imperil national health, safety, or essential transportation.

[W. E. Oberer, "Lockouts and the Law: The Impact of American Shipbuilding and Brown Food," *Cornell Law Quarterly,* vol. 51 (1966); U.S. Bureau of Labor Statistics, *Strikes in the United States, 1880–1936,* bulletin no. 651.]

BERNARD D. MELTZER

LOCKS AND WATERWAYS. In the latter part of the 18th century dams and locks began to be employed to make rough rivers, such as the Mohawk, navigable for arks and flatboats. Usually short canals with locks in them were built around falls or rapids: for example, one around the rapids of the James at Richmond, built 1785–89; five along the Potomac, built 1785–1808; several on the Connecticut and Merrimack rivers in New England and one at the Conewago Falls in the Susquehanna, all constructed between 1790 and 1800. The height of the locks was then very modest. The Bellows Falls Canal on the Connecticut required nine locks in less than a mile to overcome a fall of fifty feet—or less than six feet of lift to each lock. Also in New England, the Blackstone Canal, built 1824–28, had forty-eight locks of cut granite in its forty-five-mile length. The Chemung Canal, completed in 1833, connecting Seneca Lake with the headwaters of the Susquehanna River, though only twenty-three miles long had forty-nine locks.

For the sake of economy, the lock walls of some early canals, such as the Chemung and Chenango in New York and the Middlesex between Boston and Lowell (built 1794–1803), were of wood, and in some instances they began to bulge and warp almost as soon as completed. Until cement rock was discovered in central New York in 1818, most stone lock walls had to be built with ordinary lime mortar, as cement imported from Europe was too costly. With the aid of cement, locks became higher, and in 1830 one with a lift of seventeen feet was built on the Delaware Division of the Pennsylvania Canal system.

Larger rivers were canalized—that is, improved with dams and locks—early in the 19th century. When the canal fervor swept Pennsylvania, beginning in 1826, not only was the Monongahela thus improved for a hundred miles, but also small streams, such as Bald Eagle Creek and Conestoga Creek from Lancaster to the Susquehanna. In Ohio nearly a hundred miles of the Muskingum were canalized between 1836 and 1840, and there for the first time in America the locks—36 feet wide and 180 feet long— were made large enough for steamboats. Before the end of the 19th century navigation dams and locks were placed on the upper Ohio, and later, on the Mississippi. With the development of steamboat traffic, the improvement of small rivers and creeks by locks became a favorite form of congressional patronage. (*See also* Canals.)

[Alvin F. Harlow, *Old Towpaths*.]
ALVIN F. HARLOW

LOCOFOCO PARTY, a radical faction of the Democratic party in New York allied with Jacksonian Democracy. At a meeting in Tammany Hall, Oct. 29, 1835, it wrested control of the city caucus from the conservatives by producing candles and lighting them with locofoco matches and thus continuing the meeting when opponents had darkened the hall by turning off the gas. Newspapers derisively called this faction the Locofoco party. Its program embraced suppression of paper money, curtailment of banking privileges, and protection of labor unions. From 1837 to 1860 the term was applied to the national Democratic party by its opponents.

[Lee Benson, *The Concept of Jacksonian Democracy: New York as a Test Case*.]
W. B. HATCHER

LOCOMOTIVES. Steam had been applied on railroads in England early in the 19th century, and locomotives were used on the first common-carrier railroad in England as well as on roads serving coal mines. These developments were known in the United States, and efforts were made to generate interest in the use of steam power and in the construction of railroads as superior to highways. In 1825 Col. John Stevens of Hoboken, N.J., built an experimental locomotive and demonstrated it on a circular track. The Baltimore and Ohio Railroad, chartered in 1827 as the first common-carrier railroad in the United States, early faced the question of what form of power to use. Peter Cooper of New York City, a director of the railroad, built the "Tom Thumb" for demonstration purposes. Success was sufficient to lead the railroad to sponsor a competition to secure a commercially useful locomotive. The competition was won by Phineas Davis of York, Pa., in 1831. His "York"

was the predecessor of a considerable group of vertical-boilered locomotives called "grasshoppers" that had walking-beam power transmission.

Meanwhile "Best Friend of Charleston," the first locomotive intended for commercial service, had been built by the West Point Foundry in New York for the South Carolina Canal and Railroad Company. Locomotives were imported from England during the early experimental period, notably for service on the Camden and Amboy Railroad and for test on the gravity railroad of the Delaware and Hudson Canal Company. These imports proved ill adapted to the light and uneven track of early American railroads and to the sharp curvature and heavy grades that were often employed. American locomotive design began to depart from British practice in order to adapt to these conditions. The leading truck was used to improve track-keeping qualities; headlights and cowcatchers were applied; and various devices, such as the Baldwin "flexible beam" truck, were developed to lend curve-keeping ability to freight locomotives of six- and eight-coupled design.

The early locomotive builders—Matthias W. Baldwin and William Norris of Philadelphia, as well as Davis—began in the jeweler's trade and shifted to machine shop practice. Baldwin and Norris proved to be highly inventive contributors to locomotive development. The Baldwin works, first in Philadelphia and later in Eddystone, Pa., became the nation's largest locomotive builder. Norris developed some early export business: one of his locomotives proved to have the ability to haul a train up the inclined plane of the Great Western of Great Britain; others supplied power for the first railroad built in Russia.

Numerous small locomotive works operated in the early period, ranging from the William Mason Company at Taunton, Mass., to the Richmond Locomotive Works at Richmond, Va. Some of these ultimately disappeared; a number were merged to form the American Locomotive Company, headquartered at Schenectady, N.Y., second of the country's great locomotive builders. Several railroads built locomotives in their own shops, but none so many as the Pennsylvania Railroad, principally at Altoona, Pa. The Pennsylvania also pioneered in the standardization of locomotives, beginning in the 1870's, and contributed much to the improvement of locomotive design.

The steam locomotive demonstrated its speed capabilities early, having attained 60 miles an hour by 1848. Hauling capability developed more slowly. The typical locomotive for freight and passenger work in the 1870's had four driving wheels (4–4–0, or American type) and a tractive effort of 8,000 to 12,000 pounds. Locomotives for heavy freight work were built with six or eight driving wheels. The Consolidation type (2–8–0), first built for the Lehigh Valley Railroad in 1866, became the most popular. Tractive efforts of leading specimens of this locomotive type increased from 24,000 pounds in the 1870's to 46,000 pounds by the end of the century. Apart from gradual perfection of design, improvement of materials, and increase of boiler pressures and weight on driving wheels, the greatest early post–Civil War challenge was the development of suitable grates and fireboxes for burning coal in place of wood.

Unlike stationary or marine plants, the locomotive power plant must be designed to fit into a small space and have a weight that tracks and bridges can carry. It must then function exposed to the weather and the vibration encountered in moving over the road. By the end of the century, at a time when railroad traffic was burgeoning, the locomotive had attained close to its maximum capacity under conventional design practice. Between 1895 and 1910, a series of innovations—trailing wheels to enable a wide firebox to be carried behind the rear drivers and the boiler to be lengthened, the brick arch, piston valves, and outside valve motion—enabled more than a doubling of tractive power.

Most important was the introduction of superheating, which allowed very hot, dry steam to be delivered to the cylinders, reducing condensation and increasing cylinder horsepower within existing dimensions. In 1904 the first Mallet type of articulated locomotive was placed in service on the Baltimore and Ohio Railroad, utilizing a system of compounding (use of steam first in high-pressure cylinders, then a second time in low-pressure cylinders) developed in Europe and of attachment of the front engine and driving wheel set by a pin to the main frame so that it could swing with curvature. Of particular use on lines of heavy gradient, the articulated locomotive increased rapidly in size, and by 1920 some examples exerted 120,000 pounds of tractive effort when working single expansion. The mechanical stoker, essential for firing such locomotives, had been perfected by then. Improved lateral-motion devices made the ten-coupled nonarticulated locomotive more practical, and typical examples of the 2–10–2 on eastern roads developed up to 84,000 pounds tractive effort prior to World War I.

The need for greater horsepower to permit sus-

tained high-speed operation with heavy loads led to a series of experiments from which emerged the first "superpower" locomotive, completed by the Lima Locomotive Works in 1925. This locomotive combined the elements already noted with a feedwater heater and four-wheel trailing truck to permit a much enlarged firebox. It became the prototype for hundreds of locomotives of the 2–8–4, 2–10–4, and, ultimately, 4–8–4 types that allowed for a major acceleration of freight service with greatly improved efficiency.

By this time the manufacture of locomotives for main-line railroad service was confined to three outside builders: Baldwin, American Locomotive, and Lima. Railroad shops, especially those of the Pennsylvania, Norfolk and Western, and Burlington railroads, continued to build new power. Railroads that built power also procured locomotives from outside builders. Railroad motive-power departments and the outside builders shared in the engineering, from which improved design emerged. But the manufacture of specialities—such items as superheaters, feedwater heaters, stokers, and boosters—moved more and more into the hands of the supply industries.

The depression of the 1930's brought a near-paralysis of locomotive building during the years 1932–35. Revival of railroad purchasing, although slow, was marked by the development of a new generation of locomotives—single-expansion articulateds especially made for service on the western transcontinental roads and several of the coal-hauling roads in the East. These locomotives combined the starting tractive effort of the Mallets with the speed capabilities of the later superpower locomotives. In these designs the steam locomotive reached its peak of development in the United States. Locomotives of this genus, differentiated somewhat in design to meet intended service conditions, could haul 18,000 tons or more in coal or ore service or move a 7,000-ton manifest freight at 70 miles per hour.

World War II interrupted steam locomotive development. So great had been the progress in diesel locomotives that many railroads bought no more steam power afterward. There were exceptions, especially the coal-hauling railroads of the Northeast, and several advanced designs were engineered for them. Locomotives built to those designs, however, had a short life as the superior efficiency of the diesel locomotive in all classes of service was recognized. The last steam locomotives built by Baldwin for service in the United States were delivered in 1949, and Lima's last locomotive for an American railroad, in the same year.

The steam locomotive was rugged, long-lived, and capable of being designed for any service. Hundreds of steam locomotives operated for forty years and more, often with few modifications. But the steam locomotive was never a very efficient machine, delivering, at the peak of its technical development, power at the drawbar equivalent only to 12 to 13 percent of the energy latent in the fuel. Since the greatest losses were in the cylinders of the reciprocating machine, late experiments were undertaken on three of the coal-hauling roads with steam turbine locomotives. This effort was made obsolete by the proven success of the diesel.

Straight electric locomotives were never extensively employed on American railroads. Although the Baltimore and Ohio used them after 1895 in its Baltimore tunnels, the Pennsylvania electrified the approaches to Pennsylvania Station in New York City in 1908, and the suburban lines out of Grand Central Station were electrified in the period 1906–13, use of the electric locomotive was always confined to special circumstances. The Milwaukee employed it over 641 route miles across the Rocky, Bitter Root, and Cascade ranges, the Great Northern between Skykomish and Wenatchee, Wash., and the Norfolk and Western and the Virginian on heavy-grade lines. The outstanding electrification was that of the Pennsylvania between New York and Washington, which was later extended over the main line to Harrisburg. The first segment, between New York and Philadelphia, was opened in 1932. Exceptionally heavy traffic density was considered to justify the investment in power transmission and distribution. Of the several types of locomotive employed on this 11,000-volt a.c. electrification, the GG-1 was outstanding, developing 8,500 horsepower on short-period rating and working both freight and passenger trains. Most of these locomotives were still in service forty years after the prototype was delivered.

Changes in technology have resulted in renewed consideration of the advantages of electric propulsion. The mercury arc and, later, the ignitron rectifier superseded the motor-generator set in a.c.-powered locomotives. The use of commercial frequencies became possible. Several western roads instituted studies of electrification of their more heavily trafficked main lines.

Except over the limited electrified mileage and on a few short lines, all service of American railroads was powered in the 1970's by diesel-electric locomotives. These use diesel engines to power generators that supply direct current to the traction motors. The first such locomotives were delivered for switching service in 1925. Baldwin and American Locomotive both went into their manufacture, but the Electric Motive Division of General Motors pioneered in the application of the diesel to both passenger and freight road service in the late 1930's. In the 1970's the business was dominated by General Motors and General Electric, the latter a past supplier of components to other manufacturers.

The diesel locomotive has the advantage of high efficiency and availability, compared with the steam locomotive. It can be operated in multiple units, any number of locomotives being controlled by a single engineman. Midtrain helper locomotives can now be controlled from the head end, making for a better distribution of power in long and heavy trains. The problem of water supply—a serious one for steam locomotives in many parts of the country—is eliminated. Unlike steam locomotives, diesels have been standardized by the manufacturers, and traction motors and other components can be removed and replaced by standby units to keep the locomotives in service. Although the first diesel road freight unit was tested in 1940, third-generation diesels were coming into service in the 1970's. Single units have been produced that generate more horsepower than four units of the original 5,400-horsepower freight diesel; yet locomotives in the 2,500-horsepower range remain popular because of their versatility in the systemwide locomotive pools that most railroads employed in the mid-1970's. The computer has been brought into use to manage such pools, to develop tonnage ratings, and to operate simulators that several railroads employ in training enginemen.

[Baldwin Locomotive Works, *History of the Baldwin Locomotive Works;* Alfred W. Bruce, *The Steam Locomotive in America;* Ralph P. Johnson, *The Steam Locomotive;* Angus Sinclair, *Development of the Locomotive Engine;* John White, *American Locomotives.*]

ERNEST W. WILLIAMS

LODE MINING. Gold, silver, and other metals are generally found in streaks that may range from a few inches to many feet in width and that are frequently traceable for a mile or more in length. These streaks are called lodes, veins, or ledges. A lode has been legally defined as mineral-bearing rock in place; extracting such mineral-bearing rock from the earth is lode mining. Distinguished from placer mining, geared to metals found in alluvial deposits near the surface, lode mining is conducted in hard rock and almost entirely underground. The ore is mined either by shafts sunk vertically downward or by tunnels driven horizontally into the mountainside.

The discoverer of a new lode, according to the laws of the early mining districts, could stake out two claims, but no more, along the lode. Others could stake one claim. Local laws and regulations determined the size of the claim—usually 100 or 200 feet—which was recognized by the first U.S. mineral patent law in 1866. On May 10, 1872, Congress fixed the size of lode claims at 600 feet wide and 1,500 feet along the lode. Consequently, there can be many rich mines on the same lode. Famous lodes are the Mother Lode in California and the Comstock Lode in Nevada.

[W. R. Crane, *Ore Mining Methods;* R. S. Morrison, *Mining Rights.*]

PERCY S. FRITZ

LODGE RESERVATIONS. The reservations attached to the Treaty of Versailles and the covenant of the League of Nations by a majority of the Senate in November 1919, and again in March 1920, bore the name of Sen. Henry Cabot Lodge as chairman of the Committee on Foreign Relations, not as their author. He probably drafted only the reservation asserting the Monroe Doctrine as long-established American policy and outside the league's jurisdiction.

The Foreign Relations Committee first reported to the Senate a series of strong reservations to the Treaty of Versailles, which might have been more appropriately called the "Lodge reservations," in early September. Republican senators who supported the League of Nations rejected them and a number of amendments proposed by senators wholly opposed to the treaty and the league.

During the next two months the pro-league Republicans negotiated a second set of milder reservations with Lodge and his supporters. They asserted the Senate's right to advise and consent to league agreements individually and to approve appointment of U.S. league representatives, reaffirmed congressional authority to appropriate funds for participating in league activities, and stated that the United States alone should determine what questions lay within its domestic jurisdiction or involved its "national honor and vital interest." Sen. Porter James McCumber

proposed the most vital reservation, declaring that Congress should decide what U.S. obligations were in each instance under Article X of the covenant, which called for collective action by league members against aggression.

Under orders from President Woodrow Wilson the Democrats boycotted these negotiations and voted against the proposed reservations. Combining with the league's "irreconcilable" opponents they defeated ratification in November.

In January 1920, public opinion forced a bipartisan committee headed by Lodge and Sen. Gilbert Monell Hitchcock, Wilson's minority leader, to negotiate a third group of reservations, including concessions requested by the British and French governments, which privately accepted the reservations in principle. Against the advice of his supporters, the president rejected even those compromises proposed by the Democrats. A majority of them then broke with the president to support the bipartisan compromises. When Wilson threatened to pocket veto any treaty with reservations attached, enough southerners remained loyal to him and voted again with the "irreconcilables" to defeat ratification the second time.

Wilson's position is difficult to understand because he publicly agreed to the substance of the Senate reservations, but from the very beginning he refused to accept them as legally binding reservations attached to the treaty.

[Thomas A. Bailey, *Woodrow Wilson and the Great Betrayal;* James E. Hewes, Jr., "Henry Cabot Lodge and the League of Nations," *Proceedings of the American Philosophical Society,* vol. 114 (August 1970); Henry Cabot Lodge, *The Senate and the League of Nations;* Ralph Stone, *The Irreconcilables: The Fight Against the League of Nations.*]

JAMES E. HEWES, JR.

LOEWE V. LAWLOR. *See* **Danbury Hatters' Case.**

LOFTUS HEIGHTS, the high eastern bank of the Mississippi, first called Roche à Davion for a French missionary (1699), is just north of the thirty-first parallel. It took its present name from an incident during the expedition led by British Maj. Arthur Loftus in 1764, from Mobile, to take possession of the Illinois country in accordance with the Treaty of Paris of 1763. At Roche à Davion the Loftus party, consisting of 300 men, was fired upon by the Tunica Indians. Several men were killed, and Loftus retreated precipitately down the Mississippi. Dominating the Spanish-

American boundary on the Mississippi, it became the site of Fort Adams, built 1798–99.

[J. F. H. Claiborne, *Mississippi;* Charles Gayarré, *History of Louisiana.*]

MACK SWEARINGEN

LOGAN'S FORT, also known as Saint Asaph Station, was located near Stanford, Ky. Its founder was Benjamin Logan, who arrived in Kentucky in 1775. On May 20, 1777, the fort was assaulted by Indians. Logan spurred his companions in the defense, and by sheer courage and surprising athletic prowess, he became the mainstay in his fort's defense. Stories of these exploits have given this station an important place in Kentucky's history.

[Richard Collins, *History of Kentucky.*]

T. D. CLARK

LOGAN'S SPEECH, popularly regarded as the most famous example of American Indian oratory, was made by the Mingo warrior John Logan, or Tahgahjute. The speech was made to John Gibson, who had been sent from Camp Charlotte (in present Pickaway County, Ohio) by the governor of Virginia, John Murray, Earl of Dunmore, to persuade Logan, then at his cabin a few miles distant, to attend the peace negotiations at the close of Dunmore's War (1774). Logan refused to come and recited his grievances in a speech so moving that Gibson translated and recorded it from memory after returning to Dunmore's camp. Thomas Jefferson later inserted it in his *Notes on the State of Virginia,* but the family and friends of Capt. Michael Cresap, whom Logan mistakenly charged with the murder of his relatives, took offense at the speech and denied its authenticity. A long controversy ensued. Most historians have reached the cautious conclusion that Gibson probably caught at least the spirit of Logan's impassioned remarks, if not the exact words.

[E. O. Randall and D. J. Ryan, *History of Ohio;* Theodore Roosevelt, *The Winning of the West.*]

EUGENE H. ROSEBOOM

LOG CABIN. It has been asserted that log construction was introduced into the New World by the Swedes who settled on the lower Delaware in 1638. But a log blockhouse, the McIntyre Garrison at York, Maine, far distant from the Delaware, built about 1640–45, is cited by others as evidence that the New England colonists, somewhere between 1620 and 1640, had learned log construction for themselves —though some one among them might have seen one of the log buildings that had long been in use in Scandinavia and northern Germany. Such construction increased rapidly in the 17th century, and the one-room or two-room log cabin became the typical American pioneer home, being supplemented by outbuildings also of log construction. For the dwelling, the sides of the logs facing each other were adzed flat, and the chinks between were luted with flat stones or chips of wood embedded in clay. In stables, the crevices were usually left unfilled. As the frontier was pushed westward across the continent, small log buildings became the first churches and schools, the first mills, stores, and hotels, and the first seats of town and county government and of the courts. In the South tall tobacco barns were built of long logs with wide, unfilled chinks between, so that the wind might blow through and dry the leaf tobacco racked inside. Many a solitary pioneer had to build his little log hut singlehanded or with the aid of his wife and children; but where there was a settlement, a houseraising became a pioneer social function, as neighbors gathered and completed the essential structure in one day. More prosperous farmers or villagers might erect two-story log houses of several rooms, which were shingled on the outside in New England or often weatherboarded farther west, though in Pennsylvania they were occasionally stuccoed.

[Carl W. Condit, *American Building: Materials and Techniques From the Beginning of the Colonial Settlements to the Present.*]

ALVIN F. HARLOW

LOG CABIN AND HARD CIDER CAMPAIGN. *See* **Campaigns, Presidential: Campaign of 1840.**

LOG COLLEGE, at Neshaminy, Pa., about twenty miles from Philadelphia, was a log schoolhouse, about 20 feet square, erected and conducted by William Tennent, an Irish Presbyterian minister. During its sixteen-year existence, 1726–42, it served to emphasize the need for an institution for the instruction of Presbyterian ministerial candidates. The Presbyterian Synod recognized this need, and in 1746 the charter for the organization of a college at Princeton, N.J. (later Princeton University), was issued.

[James Mulhern, *A History of Secondary Education in Pennsylvania.*]

H. H. SHENK

LOGISTICS

LOGISTICS is the application of time and space factors to war. If international politics is the "art of the possible" and war is its instrument, logistics is the art of defining and extending the possible. In short, it is the economics of warfare. Literally it provides the substance that physically permits a military force to "live and move and have its being." As the U.S. Army's *Field Service Regulations* puts it, "It envisages getting the right people and the appropriate supplies to the right place at the right time and in the proper condition."

The word itself is derived from the Greek *logistikos*, meaning "skilled in calculating." Although logistics has been a recognizable part of military science—together with strategy and tactics—since ancient times, Baron Henri Jomini, the French writer on military affairs, appears to have been the first to have made systematic use of the term in this sense, about 1838. One of the first to use the term in this way in a book in America was Henry B. Harrington in *Battles of the American Revolution, 1775–1781*, published in 1876.

In the triad of war, a more or less sharp distinction is maintained for each segment. Strategy is usually seen as the planning and management of campaigns toward achieving the object of the war, tactics as the planning and waging of battles or engagements toward achieving strategic objectives, and logistics as the planning and management of resources to support the other two. Yet in a broader sense these are all branches of the same thing. Frequently the objectives of strategic operations and tactical engagements are themselves aimed at weakening the enemy's logistics—whether through bombing an industrial center, mining a harbor, or seizing key terrain to threaten a line of supply.

It can be argued, for instance, that most of the major strategic decisions of World War II—Europe first, the cross-Channel invasion of 1944, the landings in southern France, the return to the Philippines, the bypassing of Formosa for Okinawa—were essentially logistic decisions. That is, the timing, the location, the scale, and the very purposes of those operations were based mainly upon logistic considerations—the evaluation of comparative resources and the determination that the seizure of Normandy or Marseilles or Luzon or Okinawa would facilitate further the support of forces by opening the way for additional bases and supply lines.

Logistics may be thought of in terms of scale as paralleling the scale of military operations. "Grand strategy" is used to refer to national policy and the object of the war; "strategy" to the planning and management of campaigns; and "tactics," to the planning and management of battles or engagements—and parallel terminology may be applied to logistics. Thus, "grand logistics" may be said to refer to the national economy and industrial mobilization; "strategic logistics," to the analysis of requirements and logistic feasibility of proposed campaigns and a determination of requirements to support a particular strategic decision and to the follow-up mobilization and assembly of forces and the moving of them, with their supplies and equipment, to the area, with provision for effective resupply; and "tactical logistics," to the logistics of the battlefield—the movement of troops to the battlefield and the supplying of these troops with the ammunition, food, fuel, other supplies, and services needed to sustain them in combat.

As a calculation of logistic efficiency, one may speak of "primary logistics" as that needed for the support of combat units and of "secondary logistics" as that required to support the means to meet the primary requirements, or what the satisfaction of requirements in one category may create for requirements in another. Thus, in delivering a given amount of gasoline to an armed force, for instance, the amount of fuel and other resources needed to deliver that gasoline must be taken into account. Gen. William Tecumseh Sherman during the Civil War reckoned that an army could not be supplied by horses and wagons at a distance greater than 100 miles from its base, for in that distance the horses would consume the entire contents of their wagons. Air transportation may create greater logistic problems than it solves. During the Korean War, for each 5 tons of cargo that a C-54 air transport carried across the Pacific, it consumed 18 tons of gasoline. To move a given 15,000 tons of cargo from San Francisco to Yokohama by sea required two Victory ships; to move it by air required 3,000 air flights plus eight ships to carry the gasoline for the airplanes. On the other hand, other secondary logistic requirements are built up in the maintenance of long supply lines and multiple storage facilities. At times a supply base, given to continuous proliferation, reaches the point at which it consumes more supplies than it ships out and thus becomes a net drain on the logistic system.

Another aspect of secondary logistics arises in the acceptance and manufacture of a new weapon or in the choice of one weapon over another for expanded production, in terms of the effect of the decision on the problem of ammunition supply.

180

[John W. Barriger, *Legislative History of the Subsistence Department of the U.S. Army From June 16, 1775 to August 15, 1876;* Benedict Crowell and Robert Forrest Wilson, *How America Went to War;* James A. Huston, *The Sinews of War: Army Logistics, 1775–1953;* Marvin A. Kreidberg and Merton G. Henry, *History of Military Mobilization in the United States Army, 1775–1945;* Richard M. Leighton and Robert W. Coakley, *Global Logistics and Strategy, 1940–1943,* and *1943–45;* Erna Risch, *Quartermaster Support of the Army: A History of the Corps, 1775–1939.*]

JAMES A. HUSTON

LOGROLLING, a practice among members of Congress of trading votes for each other's pet bills. The term is derived from the American frontiersmen's practice of helping one another in cutting down trees and rolling up the logs for building or burning. In Congress logrolling is usually practiced between friends who work together to secure appropriations, each seeking to benefit his own district. The pressure of local interests for these federal appropriations convinces the congressman of the necessity of seeking favors for his constituency in an effort to insure his reelection. While the practice normally obtains with reference to legislation applicable to local interests, it may be applied in national affairs when parties trade votes on certain bills on purely partisan grounds. The practice of logrolling often results in wastefulness and ill-advised legislation. Many such laws would not pass on their own merits.

[Charles A. Beard and Mary R. Beard, *The Rise of American Civilization.*]

GLENN H. BENTON

LOGSTOWN, an Indian village eighteen miles below the forks of the Ohio near the present Ambridge, Pa., was probably established by the Shawnee about 1728; it later became a mixed village of Shawnee, Delaware, and Iroquois. From 1747 to 1753 it was the most important Indian village on the upper Ohio, being the center of trade and the scene of Indian councils. It was visited by Pierre Joseph Céloron's expedition in 1749, by Christopher Gist in 1750, and by George Washington on his journey to Fort LeBoeuf in 1753. When the French and Indian War began in 1754, most of the Logstown Indians removed to Aughwick, just west of Philadelphia, and parties of them fought for the English in the Battle of Fort Necessity and joined Gen. Edward Braddock's expedition.

[S. J. Buck and E. H. Buck, *The Planting of Civilization in Western Pennsylvania.*]

SOLON J. BUCK

LOGSTOWN, TREATY OF (June 13, 1752), opening to settlement lands west of the Allegheny Mountains, was negotiated with the Iroquois, Delaware, Shawnee, Wyandot, and Miami Indians resident in what are now western Pennsylvania, Ohio, and Indiana. In 1751 negotiations with the same Indians had been conducted at Logstown by George Croghan of Pennsylvania, and presents had been distributed, but the Pennsylvania assembly had refused funds for erecting forts to hold the region against the French. In 1752 commissioners from Virginia distributed a royal present to the Indians and, with the help of Croghan and of Christopher Gist representing the Ohio Company, secured permission for Virginians to make settlements south of the Ohio and to build two fortified trading houses on the river. One of these was erected on the Monongahela at Redstone Old Fort, in southwestern Pennsylvania, and the other, in process of erection at the site of Pittsburgh in 1753, was surrendered to the French at the outbreak of hostilities (*see* Duquesne, Fort).

[S. J. Buck and E. H. Buck, *The Planting of Civilization in Western Pennsylvania.*]

SOLON J. BUCK

LOGWOOD TRADE. Logwood, also called blockwood and sometimes known as campeachy wood or, improperly, Brasiletto or Jamaica wood, comes from the leguminous tree *Haematoxylen campechianum,* found in Central America and the West Indies, and derives its name from the dark brownish red blocks in which it is shipped. Its chief use (prohibited in England from 1581 to 1662) was in dyeing, blacks and blues.

English activity in the trade, begun by the buccaneers and soon supplemented by colonial traders, centered in Spanish territory, first at Cape Catoche, then at Campeche Bay, Mexico, and finally around Belize (now British Honduras) and along the Mosquito Coast of Nicaragua. Spain made protests, occasional raids, and frequent seizures but in 1763 conceded limited wood-cutting rights to the British. Before 1670 England received almost all its logwood from Spain, but in 1773 England obtained 862 tons direct from Spanish America, 771 tons from Jamaica, 548 tons from other British colonies, and only 16 tons from Spain.

Most of the American colonists' logwood came from Yucatan and Honduras, but some came from surprisingly varied sources—to New York, for example, from Curaçao, Martinique, the Virgin Islands, Hispaniola, Havana, Veracruz, Saint Augustine, and eight British colonies. Logwood grown in an English colony was regulated by the Navigation Acts, but foreign logwood could be exported freely, and approximately one-fifth of the 3,480 tons exported in 1770 from the continental colonies went directly to Europe, which was also the ultimate destination of most of England's imports.

[G. L. Beer, *Old Colonial System;* M. Postlethwayt, *Dictionary.*]

LAWRENCE A. HARPER

LOMBOK STRAIT, BATTLE OF (Feb. 19–20, 1942). Allied naval forces opposing the Japanese invasion of the Netherlands East Indies consisted of a heterogeneous group of American, British, and Dutch cruisers and destroyers commanded by Dutch Rear Adm. Karel Doorman. On the evening of Feb. 19, 1942, Doorman set out to attack Japanese transports unloading troops on the island of Bali. With his warships scattered at different locations as a result of earlier actions and with no time to allow them to concentrate, Doorman was forced to carry out a disjointed and confused operation in the waters of Lombok Strait. In two separate, uncoordinated attacks, before and after midnight, a Japanese transport and destroyer were damaged, while Doorman lost a destroyer and sustained damage to another destroyer and a light cruiser. Other Japanese warships caught Doorman's second group of raiders as they were retiring, increasing the damage to the cruiser but suffering hits on one of their own destroyers. A raid on the Japanese anchorage by motor torpedo boats just before dawn on Feb. 20 revealed that the enemy ships, having finished unloading, had already departed. Doorman's attack was thus doubly unsuccessful: he had suffered more damage than the Japanese, and the enemy beachhead on Bali was established and secure.

[Samuel Eliot Morison, *History of United States Naval Operations in World War II*, vol. III.]

STANLEY L. FALK

LONDON, DECLARATION OF (Feb. 26, 1909), was a code of laws relating to maritime warfare drafted by the London Naval Conference. Ten naval powers, representing different viewpoints, thereby achieved a compromise agreement in the hope of enabling the international prize court, proposed at the second Hague Conference in 1907, to function.

Conspicuous in the declaration was the treatment of the issues of contraband and continuous voyage, entailing peculiar difficulties between belligerents and neutrals. Agreement was reached on definite lists of absolute and conditional contraband and on a third classification of goods that could not be declared contraband. Barring this third classification, a belligerent might add to the absolute and conditional lists. Noteworthy in the free list were raw cotton and metallic ores. Continuous voyage was restricted in application to absolute contraband, thus voiding in large part the precedents of the American Civil War. To illustrate: Arms (absolute contraband) were seizable anywhere on the high seas, if destined for the enemy; foodstuffs (conditional contraband) and cotton and copper (on the free list) were seizable only for violation of blockade. Since a blockading force could not bar access to a neutral port, neutral commerce was to be free from interruption except in cases of absolute contraband.

The declaration illustrates the strength and weakness of international legislation. It went unratified, but the United States, with the experience of the Napoleonic Wars in mind, tried to make it an important instrument of policy. To persuade Britain to follow the declaration during World War I, Secretary of State Robert Lansing secretly promoted a scheme to extend the doctrine of continuous voyage to conditional contraband: Britain might, by proclamation, attaint the ports of neutral countries adjoining Germany with enemy character with respect to trade in contraband and thus be permitted to seize foodstuffs and supplies en route to Germany but not to molest American goods on the free list. Britain rejected the plan, and the United States fell back on the traditional principles of international law.

[Bradford Perkins, *The Great Rapprochement: England and the United States, 1895–1914;* R. W. Van Alstyne, "The Declaration of London Policy of the United States at the Outbreak of the Great War," *Journal of Modern History,* vol. 7.]

RICHARD W. VAN ALSTYNE

LONDON, TREATY OF (1604), brought to an end the formal warfare that had been waged since 1585 between England and Spain, endangering all English colonizing projects in the New World. The treaty temporarily eradicated this danger and, among other things, reopened "free commerce" between the two kingdoms "where commerce existed before the war." Spain intended this clause to exclude English merchants from its colonies overseas, but the English gave it the opposite interpretation, causing continued warfare "beyond the Line" (*see* "No Peace Beyond the Line") and the rise of the buccaneers.

[Frances G. Davenport, *European Treaties Bearing on the History of the United States and Its Dependencies to 1648.*]

RAYMOND P. STEARNS

LONDON COMPANY. *See* **Virginia Company of London.**

LONDON NAVAL TREATY OF 1930. Through the efforts of Ramsay MacDonald, British prime minister, a naval conference met at London in 1930, attended by representatives of the United States, Great Britain, Japan, France, and Italy. The object was to reach an agreement to limit the size and number of warships, left unlimited by the Washington Treaty of 1922. The clash between the United States and Great Britain over parity and large cruisers, which had disrupted the Geneva Conference of 1927, was settled by a compromise arranged by MacDonald with President Herbert Hoover before the conference. The success of the conference was endangered, however, by the French demand for a tonnage beyond Italian needs and for a security pact with Great Britain, and by the Japanese claim for a 10:10:7 ratio in place of the 5:5:3 ratio agreed to in 1922 at the Washington Conference. The British were unwilling to give a guarantee to the French without American support, and the United States rejected the idea. The final treaty thus was confined to a three-power pact with provisions to include France and Italy if agreeable in the future. The 5:5:3 ratio was applied to large cruisers, but Japan won a 10:10:7 ratio in small cruisers and destroyers and equality in submarines, each nation being permitted to maintain a tonnage of 52,700 in the latter category. Not including capital ships and aircraft carriers, the total tonnage limitation under the treaty was 541,700 tons for Great Britain, 526,200 tons for the United States, and 367,050 for Japan. In order to meet the situation caused by the fact that neither France nor Italy signed the treaty, the so-called escalator clause provided that if the national security of any signatory power was endangered by new construction of ships by a nonsignatory power, the signatory power might increase its tonnage. Ratification of the treaty in Japan was obtained only after a struggle with the militarists. In 1931, after their invasion of Manchuria, the Japanese government took an expanded view of its naval requirements. Japanese demands for parity were rejected by the United States and Great Britain in parleys in London in 1934. Accordingly, under the provisions of the treaty, on Dec. 29, 1934, the Japanese government gave notice of its denunciation of the Washington Naval Treaty of 1922, to take effect on Dec. 31, 1936.

KENNETH COLEGROVE

LONDON NAVAL TREATY OF 1936. The Japanese government having, on Dec. 29, 1934, denounced the Washington Naval Treaty of 1922, a conference of the principal naval powers was held in London from Dec. 9, 1935, to Mar. 25, 1936. Great Britain and the United States refused to recognize the Japanese claim to parity or to accept a "common upper limit" for naval construction. Japan thereupon withdrew from the conference. By the treaty of Mar. 25, 1936, Great Britain, France, and the United States agreed not to exceed specified maximum limits for various types of warships (35,000 tons and 14-inch guns for battleships) and to exchange information concerning their building programs. But it was provided that the limits agreed upon might be set aside in the event of war or in the event they were exceeded by a power not a party to the treaty. Italy, indignant at the application of sanctions in the Ethiopian war, refused to sign the treaty, which was, however, left open for its adherence and for Japan's. The treaty, unlike those of 1922 and 1930 (*see* Naval Limitation Conferences), contained no provisions for quantitative limitation. In 1938 the contracting parties, unable to obtain information from the Japanese government about its building program, agreed to set aside the limit of 35,000 tons for capital ships.

BERNADOTTE E. SCHMITT

LONE JACK, ACTION AT (Aug. 16, 1862), was fought in southeastern Jackson County, Mo., between a body of Union state militia under Maj. Emory S. Foster and a Confederate force under Gen. Upton Hays, Col. John F. Coffee, and Col. Vard Cockrell. The Confederates attacked early in the morning and a six-hour fight ensued. The Union artillery was captured and held by the Confederates. About 800 men were in each force, and each side sustained losses of about 125 killed and wounded. The intense feeling between the two sides in this part of Missouri accounts for the vindictive nature of the struggle.

W. FRANCIS ENGLISH

LONG, HUEY, ASSASSINATION. On Sept. 8, 1935, Sen. Huey Pierce Long was shot at the state capitol at Baton Rouge, La., by Carl A. Weiss, the son-in-law of Judge B. H. Pavy, leader of an anti-Long faction. Weiss was shot dead on the capitol steps by Long's bodyguards; Long died two days later.

Nicknamed "Kingfish," Long exercised dictatorial control as governor (1928–31) through his political machine. He was also noted for organizing the Share-the-Wealth program, promising a homestead allowance of $6,000 and a minimum annual income of $2,500 for every American family.

[T. Harry Williams, *Huey Long.*]

LONG DRIVE. At the close of the Civil War cattle were plentiful and cheap in Texas. High prices in the North led cattlemen to seek a market. The building of the railroads to the Pacific opened the way. Beginning in 1866 cowboys drove herds of cattle, numbering on an average 2,500 head, overland to rail points on the northern Plains. Gradually homestead settlement pushed the trails westward, extinguishing them at the base of the Rocky Mountains about 1890. The average time consumed in driving a herd these hundreds of miles was from six weeks to two months (*see* Cattle Drives).

[Edward E. Dale, *The Range Cattle Industry.*]
EVERETT DICK

LONG EXPEDITION. To actively protest against the Adams-Onís Treaty with Spain, in 1819, by which the United States relinquished claims to Texas, a meeting of the citizens of Natchez, Miss., was held that year and an expedition into Texas was planned. Gen. John Adair of Kentucky was proffered the leadership but declined it. James Long of Virginia, a favorite of Andrew Jackson, was chosen as leader.

He left Natchez for Texas in June 1819 with about seventy-five men; the number had increased to more than 300 soon after his arrival at Nacogdoches. There he promptly declared Texas free and independent and set up a provisional government, a republic. Long was elected president of it. He made immediate military arrangements for conquering and holding the entire province. Failing to receive expected aid from the pirate Jean Laffite, and facing an overwhelming Spanish force, his entire scheme speedily collapsed.

In 1821 he returned to Texas from New Orleans with reinforcements and captured La Bahia, south of San Antonio. After holding it for a few days, he learned of Mexican independence from Spain and accepted an invitation from the new government to visit Mexico City, where he was killed, either by accident or design, in 1822.

[H. H. Bancroft, *History of North Mexican States and Texas;* H. S. Foote, *Texas and Texans.*]
J. G. SMITH

LONGHORNS, TEXAS. Although predominantly of the blood that Spaniards began bringing to Mexico in 1521, longhorn cattle achieved character and fame as a Texas product about 1845, which they maintained until almost the turn of the century. A strain out of cattle imported from southern states and the climate and ranges of Texas combined to develop an animal heavier and more "rangy" than Mexican cattle, but at the same time sharply different from the cattle of Colorado, Kansas, and elsewhere in the United States. In color the breed was earthlike—brindles, duns, smokies, blues, browns, dull reds, blacks, and paints of many variations, all mingling. Long of leg, body, and tail, a Texas steer carried a pair of horns that spread from 3 to 5 feet from tip to tip and occasionally over 8 feet.

The longhorn could, if necessary, go without water for days; many animals of this hardy breed are known to have thrived for months at a time while deriving all liquid nourishment from prickly pear and yucca stalks. Fortified by range grasses and browse, they could withstand the worst blizzards of the Northwest. They survived stampedes and milling roundups that would have killed other breeds. A longhorn cow was prepared to fight the fiercest panther or a pack of lobos off her calf; the bulls at times challenged grizzly bears. Hide and hoofs were tough against dagger thorns and the stones in trails over the Rocky Mountains. For driving thousands of miles and for stocking vast ranges vacated by buffalo and Indians, the breed was ideal (*see* Cattle Drives).

For the same reason that razorbacks have been supplanted by meatier hogs, the longhorn has been supplanted by bovine breeds that will better convert forage into beef—rather than into horns and bones. However, in addition to small herds along the Rio Grande, there were over 400 longhorns on the Wichita Mountains Wildlife Refuge near Cache, Okla., in 1975, and the total number in the United States was increasing.

[E. E. Dale, *The Range Cattle Industry;* J. Frank Dobie, *On the Open Range;* J. Evetts Haley, *Charles Goodnight, Cowman and Plainsman.*]
J. FRANK DOBIE

LONGHOUSES OF THE IROQUOIS. *See* **Architecture, American Indian.**

LONG HUNTERS, the term applied to residents of settled American frontier communities who, in the 1760's, spent months, sometimes eighteen, in hunting game together in the western wilds. Daniel Boone was one of the earliest and the most noted. Another and more typical was Elisha Walling, or Walden. Customarily each hunter took along two horses (one a packhorse), a trap, and a large supply of powder and lead, and each group carried a hand vise, bellows, files, and screw-plates to repair rifles. Long hunting required courage, initiative, and endurance, but the returns yielded a handsome profit and enabled those engaged to discover choice lands. Successive parties went farther and farther into the West, and their reports to their neighbors gave a decided impetus to migration to the regions described by the explorers. The Kentucky and Cumberland river valleys were favored hunting grounds.

[S. C. Williams, *Dawn of Tennessee Valley and Tennessee History*.]

SAMUEL C. WILLIAMS

LONG ISLAND, a part of New York State, 118 miles long and 1,682 square miles in area, lies parallel to the southern shore of Connecticut and is bounded on the north by Long Island Sound and on the south by the Atlantic Ocean. At its eastern end it divides into two forks, with Orient Point at the tip of the north fork and Montauk Point at the tip of the south fork. In 1620 it was included in the grant given by James I to the Virginia Company of Plymouth. In 1635 the territory held by the Plymouth Company's successor, the Council for New England, was divided into eight parts, and Long Island was assigned to William Alexander, Earl of Stirling.

In 1636, when Wouter Van Twiller was director general of New Netherland, Jacobus Van Curler (or Corlaer) was given the first Dutch patent for land on Long Island. During the Dutch period farms spread along the Long Island shore opposite Manhattan Island, and several settlements, both Dutch and English, sprang up in the interior: Hempstead, Flushing, Gravesend, Newtown, and Jamaica were English, and Breuckelen (Brooklyn), Midwout (Flatbush), Amersfoort (Flatlands), New Utrecht, and Boswyck (Bushwick) were Dutch.

While the western end of the island was thus being settled as a part of New Netherland, Puritan towns that reproduced the characteristic features and religious polity of New England were planted along the northern and southern forks of the island's eastern end. In 1640 English settlers from New Haven, Conn., laid out Southold, and others from Lynn in

Massachusetts Bay settled Southampton. Similar New England communities were established elsewhere, such as that at Oyster Bay in 1653 and those at Huntington and Setauket in 1660. An attempt was made to settle conflicting Dutch and English claims by means of a treaty signed at Hartford in 1650, which fixed a boundary by drawing a line southward across the island from Oyster Bay. The eastern towns in time fell under Connecticut jurisdiction, and thus eastern Long Island was politically a part of New England when the English conquered New Netherland in 1664. Charles II at that time granted all of Long Island to his brother, James, Duke of York, who cleared his title by promises of payments to Stirling and to Lord John Berkeley who had bought a half interest. Reconquest brought the Dutch back to the western district in 1673, but the Treaty of Westminster (1674) finally established Long Island's status as part of the English colony of New York.

The new English government attempted to change the original Dutch name of the island, Lange Eylandt, to Nassau. But residents of the island resisted the change, and the Dutch name continued to be used, although in its Anglicized form. In 1683 the island was divided into three counties: Queens, Kings, and Suffolk. A fourth county, Nassau, was created in 1898–99 by three townships formerly in the eastern part of Queens County, while the rest of Queens County became a borough of New York City. Kings County was gradually absorbed by the city of Brooklyn, so that by the end of the 19th century both city and county were coterminous. In 1898 Brooklyn (and Kings County) became a borough of New York City.

During the American Revolution the Battle of Long Island took place at Brooklyn on Aug. 27, 1776; the forces of British Gen. William Howe defeated those of Gen. George Washington. As a result of this victory the British were able to occupy New York City, which they held throughout the war.

During the 18th, 19th, and early 20th centuries Long Island was chiefly an agricultural region, with fishing, whaling, and shipbuilding as the important industries. In the 19th century Sag Harbor, at the eastern end of Long Island on Gardiners Bay, was the main whaling port, its most prosperous period occurring during 1840–60. In Great South Bay, off the south shore of the island, and Peconic Bay, just to the west of Sag Harbor, the oyster industry became very important during the 19th and early 20th centuries. The shipbuilding industry flourished in a number of north shore communities, such as Port Jefferson.

In the 20th century Long Island became one of the most prosperous and populous areas of its size in the

United States. Its two eastern counties, Nassau and Suffolk, witnessed extensive construction of single-family homes, especially after World War II, which helped increase their combined population from 604,103 in 1940 to 2,553,788 in 1970. Long Island's early concentration on agriculture, fishing, and ship-building gave way to increasing industrial development in the western section—especially in Queens and Kings counties. Aircraft manufacture became an important industry in Nassau County. Numerous summer resort areas developed in the eastern end, especially at East Hampton, Southampton, and Montauk.

[Ralph Henry Gabriel, *The Evolution of Long Island;* Jacqueline Overton, *Long Island's Story;* Benjamin F. Thompson, *A History of Long Island.*]

RALPH FOSTER WELD

LONG ISLAND, BATTLE OF

LONG ISLAND, BATTLE OF (Aug. 27, 1776). Between Aug. 22 and Aug. 25, 1776, British Gen. William Howe brought all but one of his brigades across from Staten Island in New York, landing them on Gravesend Bay beach, on the southwestern tip of Long Island. Gen. George Washington's outpost line was along Brooklyn Heights, a series of low hills crossed by four roads, through Jamaica, Bedford, and Flatbush passes, and along the shore from the Narrows. Washington strengthened his force by placing nearly a third of the entire American army on Long Island—under command of Gen. Israel Putnam.

On the night of Aug. 26–27 Howe attacked and captured Col. Samuel Miles's rifle regiment and most of Gen. William Alexander's command. Following this victorious outpost action, the British struck Washington's main position. Had this attack been pushed, all American forces on Long Island could have been captured. Instead, Howe switched to siege tactics. Realizing his danger, Washington determined to withdraw his forces to Manhattan, while giving the impression he was reinforcing. Withdrawal, begun the night of Aug. 29–30, was successfully completed, without interference from the British, by 7:00 A.M., Aug. 30.

[Ira D. Gruber, *The Howe Brothers and the American Revolution;* Christopher Ward, *The War of the Revolution.*]

ROBERT S. THOMAS

LONG ISLAND FLATS, BATTLE OF

LONG ISLAND FLATS, BATTLE OF (July 20, 1776). In June 1776 the Overhill Cherokee, under British incitement, determined to make war on the whites settled in what is now upper east Tennessee

and southwest Virginia. The invading force consisted of about 700 warriors, divided into three parties: the right wing, under Chief Old Abraham, was to strike Fort Watauga; the center, under Chief Dragging Canoe, was to attack Eaton's Station near Long Island of Holston, now Kingsport, Tenn.; a smaller detachment was to strike settlers in Carter's Valley. Near Long Island and Eaton's Station were level lands called the flats, where on July 20 a sharp battle was fought. After a severe conflict, the Indians were routed, with a loss of more than forty killed in addition to the wounded. Of the defending pioneers, five were wounded but not a man killed.

[J. M. G. Ramsey, *Annals of Tennessee.*]

SAMUEL C. WILLIAMS

LONG ISLAND OF HOLSTON, TREATY OF

LONG ISLAND OF HOLSTON, TREATY OF. The militia of southwest Virginia and North Carolina under Col. William Christian and Col. Joseph Williams made a successful punitive expedition in the fall of 1776 against the Cherokee, following raids by the Indians and the Battle of Long Island Flats in northeast Tennessee. A pledge was extorted from the Cherokee that they would come into a treaty the following year. In June and July 1777 the Cherokee met and negotiated with commissioners of the two states at Long Island, and ceded lands. North Carolina received a cession, the south line of which ran from Chimney Tops Mountain past the mouth of McNamee's Creek of the Nolichucky to the Allegheny range.

[John Haywood, *History of Tennessee.*]

SAMUEL C. WILLIAMS

LONG KNIVES. *See* **Big Knives.**

LONG'S EXPLORATIONS

LONG'S EXPLORATIONS. In the summer of 1819 Maj. Stephen H. Long, in the steamboat *Western Engineer,* left Saint Louis in command of the scientific part of the Yellowstone Expedition. Because of the delay and expense of the latter expedition, Congress refused further funds. As a compromise Long was authorized to make a scientific exploration to the Rocky Mountains.

On June 6, 1820, Long and twenty men set out to explore the Platte, the Arkansas, and the Red rivers. Marching up the Platte to the mountains, he discovered Long's Peak, Colo. Edwin James of his staff made the first recorded ascent of Pikes Peak, a hundred miles to the south. Capt. J. R. Bell marched down the Arkansas with part of the force; but Long, misled by Spanish information, explored the Canadian River and found it was not the Red only when he came to its confluence with the Arkansas. The expedition added little to the world's knowledge of geography; but the four scientists of the party, including Thomas Say, an entomologist, added much to knowledge of the botany, zoology, geology, and Indian lore of the Plains.

On Apr. 20, 1823, Long set out on another exploration, from Fort Snelling, Minn., and thence up the Saint Peter's (Minnesota) River. His mission was to explore the country, establish the location of forty-nine degrees north latitude, and take possession of all the territory below this newly authorized boundary line (*see* Convention of 1818 With England). The colony at Pembina, founded by Thomas Douglas, Earl of Selkirk, and North West Company posts in the Red River country were visited. The return trip was begun in August, the party going down the Red River to Lake Winnipeg and thence eastward to Lake Superior, through the Great Lakes to Niagara Falls, and on southward to Philadelphia, where they arrived Oct. 26, 1823.

[Harlan M. Fuller and LeRoy R. Hafen, eds., *The Journal of Captain R. Bell, Official Journalist for the Stephen H. Long Expedition;* William H. Goetzmann, *Exploration and Empire: The Explorer and Scientist in the Winning of the West.*]

BLISS ISELY

LOOKOUT MOUNTAIN, BATTLE ON (Nov. 24, 1863), an action in which Union Gen. Joseph Hooker, commanding the right wing of Gen. Ulysses S. Grant's army of about 56,000 men, cleared Lookout Mountain, Tenn., of the enfeebled and disheartened Confederate troops who had held it since the Battle of Chickamauga two months earlier. This initial stroke in Grant's effort to raise the siege of Chattanooga was dramatic, even if easily accomplished. It is popularly known in history as the "battle of the clouds" owing to the fact that low-hanging clouds hid the contending forces from observers below in the valley of the Tennessee.

The withdrawal of Confederate Gen. James Longstreet's corps from Lookout Mountain had left the Confederate left wing dangerously weak. Hooker's troops, scrambling up the mountain, drove off the remaining Confederates, swept on across Chattanooga Creek, and the next day participated in the fighting on Missionary Ridge, lying to the east. The battle, though not a hard fight, marked the beginning of final Union triumph in the Chattanooga campaign.

[R. U. Johnson and C. C. Buel, eds., *Battles and Leaders of the Civil War,* vol. III.]

ALFRED P. JAMES

LOOM. Primitive English looms, brought to America by the first settlers, were soon displaced by improved Dutch looms, to which the fly shuttle (invented by John Kay in 1733), which speeded their operation, was added. Power looms were invented in England, but original American types, adapted from the Scottish loom, were perfected by the Boston Manufacturing Company. Between 1825 and 1850 Samuel Batchelder, William Mason, and William Crompton of Massachusetts improved these looms to weave wool as well as cotton and to make pattern as well as plain fabrics, and Erastus B. Bigelow of the same state invented power looms to weave ingrain carpets and eventually Brussels and Wilton carpets. Another era of rapid improvement occurred after the Civil War, when James H. Northrop and George Draper perfected improvements that automatically changed shuttles and stopped a loom when a single warp thread broke. Early in the 20th century refinements were embodied in the Crompton loom and its successors. New, more completely automated looms were developed to offset the rising costs in labor and also to handle man-made yarns. One important development that has taken place in the 20th century is the shuttleless loom, including the water-jet loom, which uses a jet of water to force the weft between the warp. (*See also* Textiles.)

[Leander Bishop, *History of American Manufactures;* Victor S. Clark, *History of Manufactures in the United States.*]

VICTOR S. CLARK

LOOMIS GANG, consisting chiefly of the six Loomis brothers, terrorized Madison County, N.Y., during the 1850's and 1860's. Burglary, horse stealing, and even murder finally aroused the community. Vigilantes killed the oldest brother, burned the Loomis farmhouse, and frightened the remainder of the gang into quiescence.

[Carl Carmer, *Listen for a Lonesome Drum.*]

EDWARD P. ALEXANDER

LOOSE CONSTRUCTION. *See* **Constitution of the United States.**

LÓPEZ FILIBUSTERING EXPEDITIONS, armed attempts by Cuban revolutionists, in 1850–51, led by Narciso López, and American annexationists, chiefly southerners, to free Cuba from Spain. The expeditions were recruited and at least partly financed in the United States, and both set out from New Orleans. The first, consisting of 750 men, reached Cuba on May 18, 1850, and captured the Spanish garrison at Cárdenas, but was dispersed. The second expedition, consisting of 450 men, landed on Aug. 11, 1851; but it was captured and its members either executed or imprisoned. So extensive was popular approval of filibustering that the American government was powerless to enforce its own laws against it, including an inability to prevent the escape of the filibusters in the first instance and an inability to effect conviction for an illegal act upon their return.

López wanted independence for Cuba, but his American supporters desired annexation (*see* Ostend Manifesto). So grave a peril to the balance of power in the Caribbean did these expeditions appear to England and France that they threatened to intervene, and in 1852 they further urged a tripartite self-denying convention upon the United States.

[Samuel Flagg Bemis, *A Diplomatic History of the United States;* Earl W. Fornell, "Texans and Filibusters in the 1850's," *Southwestern Historical Quarterly,* vol. 59 (1956).]

RICHARD W. VAN ALSTYNE

LORAMIE'S STORE, a trading post on the Miami-Maumee portage in western Ohio, was founded by Pierre Louis Lorimier (Anglicized to Peter Loramie) about 1769. It remained an important center of British influence among the Ohio Indians until destroyed by George Rogers Clark in 1782, because of Lorimier's participation in Indian raids during the Revolution. Gen. Anthony Wayne later erected a fort on the site in 1794. "Loramie's" was used as a significant point of identification for the Indian boundary in the Treaty of Greenville in 1814.

[Henry Howe, *Historical Collections of Ohio,* vol. II; W. R. McFarland, "Forts Loramie and Pickawillany," *Ohio Archaeological and Historical Society Publications,* vol. VIII.]

EUGENE H. ROSEBOOM

LORDS AND GENTLEMEN, a designation applied by the people of Massachusetts to William Fiennes, Viscount Saye and Sele; Robert Greville, Baron Brooke; and others who, under the Old Patent of Connecticut, designed a settlement at Saybrook in 1635.

[C. M. Andrews, *The Colonial Period of American History,* vol. I.]

R. V. COLEMAN

LORDS OF TRADE AND PLANTATION. Constitutional practice provided that English provinces outside the realm were charges of the Privy Council. Beginning in 1624, British colonial administration was directed by special committees advising the Privy Council. As these committees were short-lived and often unskilled, confusion and inefficiency in imperial control resulted. To create an informed personnel with vigor and continuity in colonial policy, Charles II organized, by Order in Council, Mar. 12, 1675, the Lords of Trade and Plantation, twenty-one privy councillors, nine of whom held "the immediate Care and Intendency" of colonies, any five constituting a quorum. Although the lords represented nothing new in method and held powers only advisory to the Privy Council, because they were men of informed ability and great administrative capacity and had continuous existence for twenty years with relatively few changes in personnel, they achieved more systematic administration than any previous agencies for colonial affairs, serving as a transition to and a model for the Board of Trade and Plantations, which succeeded them, May 15, 1696. Holding 857 meetings (1675–96) and maintaining permanent offices in Scotland Yard, they established a permanent, salaried secretary (Sir Robert Southwell), assistant secretary (William Blathwayt), and clerical staff to handle colonial correspondence; became a bureau of colonial information by sending inquiries to colonial governors and agents (notably Edward Randolph) to colonies; recommended appointees as royal governors to crown colonies and prepared their commissions and instructions; developed the technique of judicial review of colonial cases appealed to the Privy Council; assaulted, in the interests of unity and efficiency, the charters of colonies—forcing surrender of two and instituting quo warranto proceedings against five others by 1686—and instituted the policy of consolidating colonies (the Dominion of New England). Although vigorous in its early years, the Popish Plot (1678) lessened activity, and as death took older members and political disorders (1685–89) interfered, the Lords of Trade became weak and ineffective. Their last meeting was on Apr. 18, 1696, a month before the Board of Trade was instituted.

[Ralph Paul Bieber, *The Lords of Trade and Plantations, 1675–1696.*]

RAYMOND P. STEARNS

LORDS PROPRIETORS. *See* **Proprietary Provinces.**

L'ORIENT, now Lorient, an important French port and naval base on the Bay of Biscay, from which, early in 1777, the ship *Amphitrite* cleared with a cargo of cannon, ammunition, tents, and other matériel for the American revolutionary army and succeeded in landing it safely at Portsmouth, N.H. In November 1777 two American frigates brought prizes into L'Orient and sold them. The port was thereafter a place of departure for American munitions and of entry for American products sold to the French during the Revolution.

[*Papers in the Case of Silas Deane.*]
ALVIN F. HARLOW

LORIMER CASE. On May 26, 1909, the Illinois legislature, after a deadlock of nearly five months, elected William Lorimer, a Republican, as U.S. senator. About a year later sensational charges of bribery and corruption were made in connection with this election. After an investigation the Senate by a close vote, on Mar. 1, 1911, declined to unseat him. After a committee of the Illinois senate had produced new evidence of corruption, the Senate ordered a second investigation, and on July 13, 1912, ousted him from his seat.

CLARENCE A. BERDAHL

LOS ADAES, a Spanish garrison in Louisiana established east of the Sabine River about 1718 to prevent French encroachment from Natchitoches, twenty miles eastward on the Red River. It remained a Spanish military and trading post on the route between Natchitoches and San Antonio until surrendered to the United States in the Louisiana-Texas boundary settlement of 1821 (*see* Adams-Onís Treaty).

[Isaac J. Cox, "The Louisiana-Texas Frontier," *Quarterly of the Texas State Historical Association* (continued as *Southwestern Historical Quarterly*), vols. 10 (1906) and 17 (1913).]
WALTER PRICHARD

LOST BATTALION, a misnomer applied to part of the U.S. 77th Division, which, during the Meuse-Argonne offensive in World War I, was surrounded in Charlevaux Ravine by German troops. The force was composed of companies A, B, C, E, G, and H, 308th Infantry; Company K, 307th Infantry; and two platoons from companies C and D, 306th Machine Gun Battalion, all under command of Maj. Charles W. Whittlesey. Adjoining French and American attacks launched Oct. 2 failed, whereas Whittlesey penetrated to his objective, where he was promptly encircled. For five days, from the morning of Oct. 3 until the evening of Oct. 7, he maintained a heroic defense against great odds until American relief troops broke through. Strictly speaking, Whittlesey's force was not a battalion, nor was it at any time lost.

[Thomas M. Johnson, *The Lost Battalion.*]
ROBERT S. THOMAS

"LOST CAUSE," a symbolic term descriptive of the ideals, aspirations, and memories of the southern Confederacy. It was probably first used by E. A. Pollard, a Richmond newspaperman, in a book *The Lost Cause,* published in 1866.

THOMAS ROBSON HAY

LOST COLONY. *See* **Raleigh's Lost Colony.**

LOST GENERATION, a term used to designate a group of American writers, notably Hart Crane, E. E. Cummings, John Dos Passos, William Faulkner, F. Scott Fitzgerald, Ernest Hemingway, Thornton Wilder, and Thomas Wolfe, most of whom were born in the last decade of the 19th century. These writers had in common the fact that their early adult years were framed not so much by their American cultural heritage as by World War I. Their psyches and their talents were shaped by the war and by self-imposed exile from the mainstream of American life, whether in Europe or in Greenwich Village in New York City—or, in Faulkner's case, in the small Mississippi town of his birth. Although the origin of the phrase is disputed, it probably derives from a remark made in the presence of Gertrude Stein by a hotel owner in Paris shortly after the end of World War I. Whether the characterization "You are all a lost generation" was originally addressed only to the French artisan class (specifically to a young mechanic) or to the whole international generation who had given the war their educable years—those in which they would probably have learned a culture or the skills of a trade—is moot. In 1926 Hemingway used it as the epigraph to *The Sun Also Rises* and thereby guaranteed its passage into literary history.

Malcolm Cowley, a chronicler of the era, has suggested that a distaste for the grandiose and sentimental language of the patriotic manifestos of the war gave them a common standpoint, though they are widely different in their techniques and responses to life. Salvation of the language was made doctrine by Dos Passos, who fulminated against the politicians and generals who, as he wrote, "have turned our language inside out . . . and have taken the clean words our fathers spoke and made them slimy and foul," and by Hemingway, who was the emblem of the movement. The influence of T. S. Eliot, James Joyce, and Stein and the encouragement of the editors and publishers of such little magazines as *Dial, Little Review, transition,* and *Broom* were significant in their development.

[Malcolm Cowley, *Exile's Return,* and *A Second Flowering;* Ernest Hemingway, *A Moveable Feast.*]

SARAH FERRELL

LOST ORDER, LEE'S. As the Confederate army advanced into Maryland in September 1862, Gen. Robert E. Lee, at Frederick, planned to capture Harpers Ferry and concentrate his army for an advance into Pennsylvania. Accordingly, on Sept. 9, he issued Special Order No. 191, outlining routes and objectives. Copies were sent to division commanders concerned. Gen. David H. Hill's division, formerly under Gen. Thomas J. ("Stonewall") Jackson's orders, had been transferred. Jackson, receiving the order before learning of Hill's transfer, sent him a copy in his own hand—which Hill preserved. Another copy from Lee's headquarters, also sent to Hill, was lost in some manner and later found by a Union soldier. It was sent to Union Gen. George B. McClellan, who sought to act on the information but moved too slowly, thus allowing Lee to concentrate his scattered troops. It is not certain when Lee learned that McClellan had been informed of his plans. The loss of the order nearly brought about Lee's complete defeat and created one of the most unusual situations in American military history.

[D. S. Freeman, *R. E. Lee,* vol. II.]

THOMAS ROBSON HAY

LOTTERIES have an ancient, even biblical, origin and exist in many forms in many nations. The word is of Italian derivation, although "lot" is Teutonic. A lottery may be defined as a scheme for the distribution of prizes by lot or chance; legally, it is a chance to win a prize for a price. A distinction historically exists between public and private lotteries. Governments have authorized lotteries for financial and eleemosynary purposes; private lotteries seek a private profit. The history of lotteries has followed a cyclical trend: they were utilized first by governments but then gave way to private schemes; these were then denounced legislatively and judicially, but today are occasionally permitted for churches and others; and, finally, they are again being run by some states and localities for the original reasons.

In Europe lotteries were used during the 16th century in Genoa (a numerical type) for political elections and in the Netherlands (a class type) to raise money. France and England (one of its earliest, in 1569, raised funds to repair harbors) also held lotteries for financial, as well as religious and charitable, causes but abolished them in the early 19th century, as did other nations, although England provided for exceptions for charities and local governments.

The earliest lawful form of lottery involving the United States, designed to overcome a dearth of company finances, is found in King James's third charter of Virginia (1612), which authorized "one or more . . . Lotteries" for one year "for the more effectual advancing of the said Plantation," to continue thereafter at his pleasure and to be held "within our City of London . . . or elsewhere within this our Realm." The American colonies speedily seized upon this method of raising money; by 1699, lotteries were numerous enough for a New England ecclesiastical assembly to denounce them as "a cheat" and their agents as "pillagers of the people."

One of the earliest printed references to lotteries in the United States occurs in Andrew Bradford's *American Weekly Mercury* for Feb. 23, 1720. To the end of that century lotteries were increasingly employed by most of the states to raise funds for schools, roads, bridges, canals, and other expenses. For example, in 1748 part of Philadelphia's fortifications were so financed, and lotteries for churches were especially popular. In 1759 Benjamin Franklin's *Pennsylvania Gazette* announced a lottery "solely for the promotion of honor and religion . . . in imitation of . . . neighbors in this and adjacent provinces." The public causes for which lotteries were held blinded to their evils many who would otherwise probably have opposed them. Franklin, George Washington, Thomas Jefferson, and other distinguished citizens favored them; Jefferson's later financial embarrassments were relieved by a lottery in 1826. The common use of lotteries for private gain came later.

Philadelphia was the center of lotteries during the

18th and early 19th centuries, but they were also held in many other places, sometimes sporadically and sometimes regularly. In 1761 Boston built the existing Faneuil Hall, after a fire destroyed the original, with the proceeds of a lottery; Harvard, Dartmouth, Yale, Williams, and other colleges so replenished their building funds; in 1777 the Continental Congress approved a national lottery; in 1793 the District of Columbia commissioners paid for improvements through a lottery, and in 1812 Congress approved the Maryland statute that authorized it; by 1790–91 lotteries had taken such a hold in New York City that its lists of drawings filled half a newspaper column.

Between 1820 and 1833 the traffic in lottery tickets rose to extraordinary proportions. Philadelphia's lottery offices increased from 3 to more than 200 between 1809 and 1833, and New York had fifty-two drawings in 1830, with the prizes aggregating $9.27 million. It is estimated that, nationally, 420 lotteries at that time offered annual prizes totaling about $53 million. Most of these were indigenous enterprises, although some were foreign-owned.

Philadelphia's experiences as the principal location of lotteries and the continued denunciation of this "pillager of the people" may have conduced to a somewhat restrictive Pennsylvania statute as early as 1729; but this act affected only those not operating under special legislative grants. No consistent attempt was made to suppress lotteries until Pennsylvania and Massachusetts passed repressive laws in 1833; New York followed the next year.

The earliest antilottery society appeared in Philadelphia in 1833, and its educational work did much to direct attention to what it considered the essential immorality of lotteries. During the next two decades one state after another ended them, until they survived only in Louisiana. That state's constitution of 1864 authorized its legislature to permit lotteries, and in 1868, for a $40,000 payment, that body chartered what was then the greatest lottery in American history; it quickly became a national scandal. In 1890 Congress, acting under its postal powers, made it a misdemeanor to use the mails to advertise or distribute lottery tickets; two years later Louisiana abolished its own internal lottery, and since then it has prohibited lotteries. In 1894 and 1897 Congress also forbade importing or advertising lottery tickets, and in 1895 it further exercised its commerce powers by excluding and making illegal any "lottery traffic through national and interstate commerce." Both statutes are still law.

Four years later the 1895 statute was challenged by one Charles Champion, who, having been indicted and arrested for its violation, brought habeas corpus proceedings against John C. Ames, a federal marshal. In 1903 the Supreme Court held that the national legislature could enact such laws in order to guard the people from the "pestilence of lotteries." This decision and similar ones in other fields have given rise to what is referred to as a "federal police power." Under this commerce-police power, the Supreme Court has continued to uphold federal laws regulating or excluding from interstate commerce impure food, drugs, stolen automobiles, gambling paraphernalia, and innumerable other items deemed injurious to the health, welfare, or morals of the people, as well as later applying these powers to economic, interpersonal, and civil rights questions.

Despite these federal laws, states may hold or permit lotteries within their own borders so long as no federal-state conflict arises. The constitutions and laws of the fifty states have to a degree reflected the changing times, allowing horse racing, bingo, and so on, so that in the mid-1970's the universal condemnation of lotteries had been modified in several states—for example, in New York, which had a state-owned lottery in aid of education; in New Jersey, where specified types were permitted to be engaged in by veteran, charitable, educational, religious, fraternal, and other organizations, but under prescribed restrictions and controls; and in Wisconsin, where a 1965 constitutional amendment permitted its legislature to authorize certain very limited types of activities. Whether or not the Irish hospitals sweepstakes, established after 1930 and resumed in 1947, influenced these actions is not material; the fact is that lotteries again obtained a foothold, albeit slight, in the United States.

[A. R. Spofford, "Lotteries in American History," *American Historical Association Annual Report* (1892).]

MORRIS D. FORKOSCH

LOUDON, FORT, in Pennsylvania, southeast of the present Loudon, was built by Col. John Armstrong of the Pennsylvania militia in 1756 as a protection against Indian forays into the Conococheague Valley. During the 1758 expedition of Gen. John Forbes it was used as a military storehouse and convalescents' camp. Lt. Charles Grant with a detachment of Highlanders occupied the post when, in November 1765, the Black Boys demanded the return of several guns that Grant had impounded following an assault upon a pack train of trading goods. Refused, they fired upon the fort, forcing its surrender and evacuation.

[G. O Seilhamer, "Old Fort Loudon and Its Associations," *Kittochtinny Historical Society Publications*.]

E. DOUGLAS BRANCH

LOUDOUN, FORT, in Tennessee, was built in 1756, to meet the French menace in the Old Southwest. Erected on the Little Tennessee River west of the Alleghenies by the English of South Carolina, it was named in honor of John Campbell, Earl of Loudoun, commander of the British forces in America. It was garrisoned by troops from South Carolina, and stood until 1760, when, under French incitement, it was besieged by the Cherokee, and surrendered on Aug. 7. The troops marched out only to be attacked by the Indians early in the morning of Aug. 10, when four officers, twenty-three privates, and some women and children were massacred. The fort was burned.

[S. C. Williams, *Dawn of Tennessee Valley and Tennessee History*.]

SAMUEL C. WILLIAMS

LOUISBURG EXPEDITION. After the loss of Acadia in 1713, France settled Louisburg on Cape Breton Island, constructing a mighty fortress and naval station to dominate the north Atlantic. A seat of Roman Catholicism and of privateers and pirates, Louisburg threatened Nova Scotia and preyed upon New England commerce, fishing, and peace of mind, though as the long peace progressed, France neglected it. When King George's War began in 1744, New Englanders, led by Gov. William Shirley of Massachusetts, determined to attack Louisburg. Well advised about French conditions, Shirley prevailed upon the general court (Jan. 25, 1745) to raise 3,000 men and necessary supplies and enlisted support from neighboring colonies. Without assurance of English assistance, Shirley hoped to capture Louisburg before the French fleet arrived in the spring. On Mar. 24 about 4,300 men, commanded by Sir William Pepperell, sailed from Boston. Landing at Canso, across the strait from Cape Breton Island, they were cheered by the arrival on Apr. 23 of Commodore Peter Warren with three English warships (eight others arrived later). On Apr. 30, while Warren blockaded Louisburg harbor, Pepperell landed his men at Gabarus Bay and laid siege to the town. Fortunate in capturing (May 3) the French battery of thirty heavy cannon, which they turned on the town, the colonials forced Louisburg to capitulate (June 15), and captured the

vessels of the French fleet as they arrived. Primarily achieved by colonial troops, this first important English victory in America was the result of careful planning, reckless fortitude, and good luck. The colonists held Louisburg despite ill-fated attempts at recapture, and were embittered when, by the Treaty of Aix-la-Chapelle of 1748, England sacrificed Louisburg for Madras, although England's reimbursements to the colonies for their expenses in the capture rescued Massachusetts, at least, from financial doldrums.

[Edward P. Hamilton, *The French and Indian Wars;* Jack M. Sosin, "Louisburg and the Peace of Aix-la-Chappelle, 1748," *William and Mary College Quarterly,* vol. 14 (1957).]

RAYMOND P. STEARNS

LOUISIANA, a southern state located at the mouth of the Mississippi River, is bounded on the north by Arkansas, the south by the Gulf of Mexico, the east and southeast by the Gulf of Mexico and the state of Mississippi, and the west by Texas.

French and Spanish Colonies. Spanish explorers touched the Louisiana coast before 1520, and Hernando de Soto died in the interior in 1542 while searching vainly for mines of precious metals. Spain then abandoned the region, which remained a sort of no-man's-land for nearly a century and a half, until Robert Cavelier, Sieur de La Salle, coming from Canada, followed the Mississippi to its mouth in 1682 and claimed the entire valley for Louis XIV of France, in whose honor it was named Louisiana. La Salle's expedition to plant a colony at the mouth of the Mississippi in 1684 missed its intended destination and landed on the Texas coast, and in 1687 he was assassinated while trying to make his way back to Canada by land. King William's War, beginning two years later, delayed the completion of La Salle's project, but after peace had been restored in 1697 Pierre Lemoyne, Sieur d'Iberville, planted the first permanent French colony on the Gulf coast in 1699 (*see* Biloxi), while Jean Baptiste Le Moyne, Sieur de Bienville, further explored the region. Queen Anne's War forced France to neglect the colony, but in 1712 Louis XIV, still anxious to develop Louisiana but faced with an empty treasury, granted to Antoine Crozat the exclusive privilege of exploiting Louisiana. Crozat exhausted his resources in futile searches for sources of quick wealth, and in 1717 surrendered his charter without having effected much development in the colony.

John Law, a Scotsman, recognized in France as a

successful banker and financier, organized the Western Company, which assumed control of Louisiana on Jan. 1, 1718. The scope of the company's operations was soon enlarged and its name changed to Company of the Indies. The anticipated immense and immediate profits were not realized, and in 1720 the company failed, and Law passed off the scene (*see* Mississippi Bubble). The company retained control of Louisiana until a series of bad harvests and the disastrous war with the Natchez Indians caused the surrender of the charter in 1731. Profiting by Crozat's mistakes, the company had brought some substantial development to the colony, although it had failed to make it a financial success.

Louisiana then passed under royal control, thus to remain for three decades. The colony developed slowly, handicapped by strife between France and England. France undertook to unite Louisiana with Canada by erecting fortified posts to exclude the English from the Mississippi Valley. The British quickly accepted the challenge, and King George's War (1744–48) and the French and Indian War (1754–63) seriously retarded the progress of Louisiana, culminating in the expulsion of the French from the mainland of North America. In 1762 Louisiana west of the Mississippi and the Isle of Orleans were ceded to Spain, and the remainder of Louisiana was surrendered to England in 1763 (*see* Fontainebleau, Treaty of; Paris, Treaty of).

Resentment of the French inhabitants at the transfer, Spain's tardiness in taking possession of the colony, general economic distress, and the unpopular measures of Antonio de Ulloa, the first Spanish governor, led to his expulsion in the so-called Revolution of 1768. But Alexander O'Reilly, an Irish soldier in Spanish service, crushed the rebellion and firmly established Spanish authority in 1769. Louisiana experienced a steady development under Spanish rule despite many difficulties. The international confusion accompanying the American and French revolutions kept alive the hope of French Louisianians for eventual reunion with France. Spanish Louisiana played an important part in the American Revolution. Needed supplies were forwarded from New Orleans to the patriot forces in the West (*see* Pollock's Aid to the American Revolution), and when Spain entered the war as an ally of France in 1779, Bernardo de Galvez, operating from Louisiana, captured the British posts in West Florida. Spanish discontent with the Definitive Treaty of Peace of 1783 led to intrigues with the Indians and with some of the western leaders for protecting Louisiana by holding back the influx of

American settlers or detaching the trans-Allegheny region from the United States (*see* Western Separatism). The Nootka Sound controversy between England and Spain in 1790 and the mission of Edmond Charles Genêt in 1793, involving threats of western attack upon Louisiana, alarmed Spanish authorities. Disputes between the United States and Spain over navigation of the Mississippi and the northern boundary of West Florida were adjusted by Pinckney's Treaty of 1795, but Spain still feared the outcome of American expansion in the Southwest.

When Napoleon Bonaparte became head of the French government in 1799, he planned a new colonial empire, and by the Treaty of San Ildefonso (Oct. 1, 1800) Spain retroceded Louisiana to France. But Napoleon's inability to subjugate the blacks in Haiti, the threat of renewal of the European war, the discontent of the United States over commercial restrictions at New Orleans (*see* Deposit, Right of), and Napoleon's pressing need for money induced him to sell Louisiana to the United States by the Louisiana Purchase Treaty of Apr. 30, 1803, before he had taken possession of the colony. In spite of Spanish resentment and threats, Louisiana was formally transferred by Spain to France on Nov. 30, 1803, and by France to the United States on Dec. 20, 1803 (*see* Louisiana Purchase).

WALTER PRICHARD

State of Louisiana. Louisiana was admitted to the Union in 1812. Near its close, the War of 1812 threatened Louisiana, but in a series of engagements ending on Jan. 8, 1815—two weeks after a treaty ending the war had been signed—British forces were decisively beaten by a motley American "army" of regulars, militia, frontiersmen, free blacks, and pirates led by Jean Laffite and Andrew Jackson. Aligned at first with Jeffersonian Republican national politics, Louisiana's interests later coincided with the principles of the John Quincy Adams–Henry Clay "American system" and with those of the Whigs, until the latter party's disappearance from the national scene after 1852. Despite its anti-Catholic bias, the American (Know-Nothing) party briefly acquired a sizable following in New Orleans, a major port of entry where immigrants were frequently viewed with disfavor.

Louisiana developed like all new states of the West and South. Agriculture and commerce expanded rapidly. Sugar culture, stimulated by a protective tariff and the introduction of hardier varieties of cane and improved processes of manufacture, became the favorite crop in lower Louisiana, extending to the Red

River by 1845. Cotton culture expanded greatly, particularly after the settlement of the region north of the Red River about 1840. The steamboat made New Orleans the commercial emporium of the entire Mississippi Valley. Agricultural and commercial expansion necessitated better transportation and banking facilities, and the state adopted the unsound policy of financing internal improvements by chartering several "improvement banks" backed by state credit, which brought financial distress in the panic of 1837. This disaster prompted the development of a sound state banking system and a saner program of internal improvements. Agriculture and commerce soon revived, followed by a new era of railroad and levee construction in the 1850's.

Cultural activities flourished in antebellum New Orleans if not throughout the state. Many talented authors wrote prose and verse in French and English, over a score of European operas received their American premieres in New Orleans, and the city's newspapers—some of them bilingual—were among the nation's best. On the other hand, state-supported public education had continually to compete with parochial schools and private academies and was additionally crippled by taxpayers' disinclination to provide adequate funds. Louisiana's penal laws were relatively humane, but the practice of leasing state convicts to private firms was begun as an economy measure in 1844. Subsequent leases were increasingly inhumane and avaricious, until in 1901 convict leasing came to an end and the penal system was returned to official hands.

As a colony initially of Bourbon France and then of Spain, Louisiana had been denied any exposure to democratic ideas or institutions from its establishment in 1699 to 1803. Ruled by appointed oligarchies prior to its admission to the Union, Louisiana was controlled for many years thereafter by powerful elected oligarchies of planters, lawyers, and businessmen. Louisiana, where dozens of lavish antebellum mansions can still be seen, shared with South Carolina on the eve of the Civil War the distinction of being the most aristocratic, conservative, and property-conscious state in the South.

The sectional crisis of 1860 found Louisiana aligned with the other disaffected slave states. The sixth state to secede, Louisiana early suffered from federal military and naval superiority. New Orleans was captured on May 1, 1862, and vital sections of the state remained in federal hands throughout the war. During the war President Abraham Lincoln used Louisiana as an experimental laboratory for testing his reconstruction theories. Louisiana emerged from the war with virtually no capital, an impoverished population, its traditional racial mores in limbo, and many of its former leaders dead, discredited, or exiled. Radical Reconstruction (1868–77)—which lasted longer and secured fewer positive accomplishments in Louisiana than anywhere else in the South—imposed upon the state a baleful legacy of corruption, violence, racial animosity, and political cynicism that endured into the 20th century.

Promising to "redeem" Louisiana from the evils of Reconstruction, a reactionary group of "home-rule Democrats" was voted into power (somewhat questionably) in 1877. For the next twenty years these men retained control of the state government by means of racist slogans, vote stealing, and various other forms of repression, frustrating in the process Republicans, independents, and Populists alike. Property and literacy qualifications for the franchise were written into the state constitution of 1898. By then Louisiana had become, as a result of Democratic indifference if not hostility to public education, the most illiterate state in the nation. The state's poor and ignorant farmers, black and white alike, were eliminated by the thousands from the voting rolls, leaving the Democrats of 1898 and their successors in secure possession of the government until the appearance of Huey P. Long more than twenty years later.

Louisiana's great industrial development began about 1900, with the exploitation of its petroleum and natural gas resources, as well as salt, sulfur, and timber, which had become important earlier. Limited social progress followed economic prosperity. Public education began to receive more support, yellow fever was eliminated and malaria brought under control, better levees were constructed, the tax base was broadened, a network of gravel roads was constructed, and the state university, moved to a superior location, was gradually upgraded.

A mild spirit of progressivism entered Louisiana politics about 1920 and became militant with the advent of Long as governor in 1928. Although bitterly assailed by the opposition, Long carried through in record time an elaborate program of public improvement and social amelioration. Paved roads and free bridges replaced gravel roads and toll ferries on main highways, a magnificent new state capitol was erected, more adequate financial support was accorded to all state educational and charitable institutions, free textbooks were supplied to all children, and the burden of taxation was more equitably distributed.

But Long was ruthless in suppressing those who opposed him, a trait that cost him his life when he was shot to death in 1935 by a relative of one of his political foes. Long remains historically controversial. To some he was an effective "mass leader," to others a dangerous demagogue. Still others view him as a popular dictator, who used his almost absolute power to remedy social ills rather than perpetuate a wealthy and corrupt few in office, as previous strongman governors of Louisiana had done.

From the time of Long's death until the 1960's, Louisiana politics operated within a "bifactional" state Democratic party, one faction appealing for voter support on the Longite platform of expanded public services, the other stressing the more conservative tenets of the anti-Longite opposition. Several factors, however, have combined to relegate the labels "Longite" and "anti-Longite" to history: (1) the continuing shift of population from countryside to cities and suburbs, (2) the migration into Louisiana of people from other states and nations, (3) the dramatic rise in Louisiana's standard of living as a result of the boom years of World War II and after, and (4) the resurgence of the Republican party in Louisiana.

Louisiana in the mid-1970's continued to enjoy the fruits of industrialization, mechanization of agriculture, and technological progress generally. In 1974 Louisiana voters ratified the state's eleventh constitution, replacing the document of 1921, which had been amended 536 times during its fifty-three years of existence. But several traditional afflictions were still in evidence. The state bureaucracy had become vast (over 250 agencies) and remained corrupt—hardly an administration since the Long era had been unblemished by nepotism, conflict of interest, outright theft, or underworld influence. While all of this went on, Louisiana remained low in literacy (forty-ninth of the fifty states) and in per capita income (forty-fifth). Most conservative politically, Louisiana is one of only three states (the others being Alabama and Mississippi) to have cast its electoral votes since 1948 for Strom Thurmond, Barry Goldwater, George Wallace, and Richard Nixon. Public schools in Louisiana (below the college level) were never integrated voluntarily but only as the inevitable result of irresistible federal pressure in the 1960's.

MARK T. CARLETON

[Henry E. Chambers, *History of Louisiana;* Alcée Fortier, *History of Louisiana;* Charles Gayarré, *History of Louisiana;* William I. Hair, *Bourbonism and Agrarian Protest in Louisiana;* Perry Howard, *Political Tendencies in Louisiana;* François Xavier Martin, *History of Louisiana;* Albert Phelps, *Louisiana;* Rogert W. Shugg, *Origins of Class Struggle in Louisiana;* Allan P. Sindler, *Huey Long's Louisiana;* T. Harry Williams, *Huey Long.*]

LOUISIANA, UPPER, was the Spanish designation for that part of Louisiana stretching from Hope Encampment (nearly opposite Chickasaw Bluffs) on the Mississippi northward to Canada and westward to the Rocky Mountains. Beginning in 1770 Saint Louis was the seat of government, presided over by a lieutenant governor, subordinate only to the governor of Louisiana at New Orleans. The first lieutenant governor was Pedro Piernas, and the last Carlos Dehault Delassus. The United States called Upper Louisiana the District of Louisiana, distinguishing Lower Louisiana with the name of Territory of Orleans. Upper Louisiana was further divided by the United States after the Louisiana Purchase in 1803 into five districts denominated respectively: Saint Louis, Saint Charles, Sainte Genevieve, Cape Girardeau, and New Madrid.

[Louis Houck, *History of Missouri;* Amos Stoddard, *Sketches, Historical and Descriptive, of Louisiana.*]

STELLA M. DRUMM

LOUISIANA LOTTERY was chartered by the Louisiana legislature in August 1868 for a period of twenty-five years. The capital stock was fixed at $1 million, but operations were to begin when $100,000 was paid in. In return for its monopoly of the lottery business in Louisiana, the company paid $40,000 annually to the state, but was exempt from other taxation. The business soon became immensely profitable. In March 1879 the legislature repealed the charter, but the U.S. District Court for Louisiana held that this was a violation of contract. In 1890, when the charter was about to expire, the company, through John A. Morris, one of its founders, offered the state $500,000 annually for an extension of twenty-five years. This offer was subsequently raised to $1 million and then to $1.25 million. Opposition immediately developed. Gov. Francis T. Nicholls sent to the legislature a message denouncing the proposal. Nevertheless, an act calling for a constitutional amendment embodying the lottery company's franchise was passed. This was vetoed by Nicholls. The house passed the bill over his veto, but the senate failed to do so. The latter body approved a resolution denying the governor's right to veto a bill proposing a constitutional amendment, whereupon the house sent the bill to the secretary of state to be promulgated. This the official refused to do. Morris took the matter into the courts, which decided against the secretary of state. On Sept. 19, 1890, the U.S. Post Office Department denied the lottery company the use of the mails. Morris thereupon withdrew his proposition. In the meantime a political organization unfavorable to the lottery had been formed and held a convention in Baton Rouge, Aug. 7, 1890. The agitation thus initiated resulted in the election of Murphy J. Foster to the governorship. After his election, Foster approved acts (June 28 and July 12, 1892) making the sale of lottery tickets unlawful in Louisiana. The lottery company continued in business in New Orleans until 1895 (see Lotteries), when it transferred its domicile to Honduras. From there it continued to sell tickets in the United States until April 1906, when the U.S. Department of Justice succeeded in breaking up the business.

[Alcée Fortier, *History of Louisiana;* Thomas C. Johnson, *Life and Letters of Benjamin M. Palmer.*]

JOHN S. KENDALL

LOUISIANA PURCHASE. In 1803 the French province of Louisiana embraced the Isle of Orleans on the east bank of the Mississippi and the vast area between that river, the Rocky Mountains, and the Spanish possessions in the Southwest. The purchase of the colony from France by the United States in that year ended forever France's dream of controlling the Mississippi Valley and began a program of expansion destined to carry the American flag to the Pacific.

For a generation Louisiana had been a pawn in European diplomacy. France ceded it to Spain in 1762 (see Fontainebleau, Treaty of). The first French minister to the United States, Edmond Charles Genêt, planned to attack it from the United States in 1793, but France turned to diplomacy as a means of recovering it between 1795 and 1799. By the Treaty of San Ildefonso, Oct. 1, 1800, and the Convention of Aranjuez, Mar. 21, 1801, Napoleon Bonaparte acquired Louisiana for France in return for placing the son-in-law of the Spanish king on the newly erected throne of Etruria.

The acquisition of Louisiana was part of an ambitious plan by which Napoleon and his minister of foreign affairs, Charles Maurice de Talleyrand-Périgord, hoped to build a colonial empire in the West Indies and the heart of North America. The mainland colony would be a source of supplies for the sugar islands, a market for France, and a vast territory for settlement. Two million francs were spent on an expedition for Louisiana assembled in Holland, at Hel-

voët Sluys, in the winter of 1802–03. Fortunately for the United States the ships were icebound in February, just as they were ready to sail.

By the Treaty of San Lorenzo, Spain, in 1795, had granted American citizens the privilege of depositing their goods at New Orleans for reshipment on ocean-going vessels. The United States was deeply aroused when Juan Ventura Morales, the acting intendant of Louisiana, revoked this right of deposit on Oct. 16, 1802, and failed to provide another site, as the treaty required. It was assumed at the time that France was responsible for the revocation, but all available documentary evidence indicates that the action was taken by Spain alone, and for commercial reasons.

President Thomas Jefferson handled the crisis in masterly fashion by appointing James Monroe as special envoy to assist Robert R. Livingston, the minister at Paris, in securing American rights. Monroe's instructions authorized an offer of $10 million for the Isle of Orleans, on which New Orleans stood, and the Floridas, erroneously thought to be French. If France refused this proposition, the ministers were to seek a commercial site on the Mississippi, or at least permanent establishment of the right of deposit at New Orleans.

In the meantime Livingston had pursued his country's interests with a zeal deserving even better results. He proposed the cession of New Orleans and the Floridas, belittled the economic value of Louisiana for France, and, after the closing of New Orleans, urged the cession to the United States of the Isle of Orleans and all the trans-Mississippi country above the Arkansas River. This was the first hint by anyone that France surrender any part of the right bank of the Mississippi.

By the spring of 1803 Napoleon's plans for his American empire had all gone astray. Spain refused to round out his possessions by ceding the Floridas. The resistance of resident blacks and yellow fever thwarted the attempt to subjugate Santo Domingo. War with Great Britain was imminent. In the United States there was growing hostility to France and talk of an Anglo-American alliance. Particularly disturbed at such a prospect, Napoleon decided to reap a nice profit and placate the Americans by selling them all of Louisiana.

When Monroe arrived in Paris on Apr. 12, the first consul had already appointed François de Barbé-Marbois, minister of the public treasury, to conduct the negotiations. On Apr. 11 Talleyrand had amazed Livingston by asking what the United States would give for the entire colony. Barbé-Marbois conferred with

196

Livingston on the evening of Apr. 13, thereby initiating the negotiations before the formal presentation of Monroe. Some jealousy arose between the American negotiators, but it did not handicap their work. Monroe was at first less inclined than Livingston to exceed their instructions and purchase all of Louisiana. By a treaty and two conventions, all dated Apr. 30, the United States paid $11.25 million for Louisiana, set aside $3.75 million to pay the claims of its own citizens against France, and placed France and Spain on an equal commercial basis with the United States in the colony for a period of twelve years.

Serious barriers to American ownership of Louisiana yet remained. Napoleon's action required the confirmation of the French legislature, and the sale was a violation of his solemn pledge to Spain never to alienate the colony to a third power. There was also grave doubt regarding the constitutionality of such a purchase by the United States. None of these dangers materialized. Napoleon ignored the legislature; Spain did nothing more than protest; and Jefferson put his constitutional scruples conveniently aside. On Nov. 30, 1803, Spain formally delivered the colony to Pierre-Clément Laussat, the French colonial prefect, who on Dec. 20 transferred the territory to William C. C. Claiborne and Gen. James Wilkinson, the American commissioners.

[E. Wilson Lyon, *Louisiana in French Diplomacy, 1759–1804;* Dumas Malone, *Jefferson the President: First Term, 1801–1805;* Francis S. Philbrick, *The Rise of the West, 1754–1830;* Marshall Smelser, *The Democratic Republic, 1801–1815.*]

E. WILSON LYON

LOUISIANA PURCHASE, BOUNDARIES OF.
The United States purchased Louisiana "with the same extent that it now has in the hands of Spain, and that it had when France possessed it; and Such as it Should be after the Treaties subsequently entered into between Spain and other States." The treaty of cession, incorporating these words, quoted verbatim from the treaty by which Spain retroceded Louisiana to France in 1800. When the U.S. commissioners requested a definition, Napoleon is reported to have said that "if an obscurity did not already exist, it would perhaps be good policy to put one there."

France, original settler of Louisiana, had not reoccupied it at the time of the U.S. purchase, but the extent of the region as then "in the hands of Spain" was ill defined. Before 1763 France claimed the entire Mississippi watershed eastward to the Alleghenies and westward to undetermined limits, as well as the

Gulf coast eastward to the Perdido River. French explorers had traversed Texas, and French traders controlled the Texas Indian trade, but the Arroyo Hondo, between Nacogdoches, Tex., and Natchitoches, La., was tacitly accepted as the frontier in the 18th century. Between French Louisiana and French Canada no clear line had been drawn.

France ceded western Louisiana to Spain in 1762 (*see* Fontainebleau, Treaty of), but there is no evidence that the two countries made a boundary delineation. Great Britain, by the Treaty of Paris, in 1763 completed its possession of all North America east of the Mississippi except New Orleans, making that river the eastern boundary of Louisiana. The province of West Florida was joined with the province of Louisiana, in administration only, from 1783, when Spain recovered both Floridas (*see* Definitive Treaty of Peace), until 1803 when Louisiana was surrendered to France and in turn to the United States (*see* Louisiana Purchase). But Spain governed West Florida separately after 1803 and asserted its independence of Louisiana. The United States claimed it and took over part of it in 1810 (*see* West Florida, Annexation of), further complicating the West Florida controversy.

Meanwhile Spain's acquisition of Louisiana in 1762 had postponed the need for a Texas-Louisiana delineation. Frontier disturbances began after 1803, and in 1806 rival commanders effected the Neutral Ground Agreement, mutually limiting their activities by a strip between the Arroyo Hondo and the Sabine River. The United States took French colonial exploration and the instructions to the intended French captain-general of Louisiana in 1802 as bases for its claim that the purchase extended to the Rio Grande.

The state of Louisiana as admitted to the Union in 1812 included part of West Florida and employed the Sabine River as its western limit, though without treaty sanction. In the Adams-Onís Treaty of 1819 Spain relinquished West Florida, though the negotiators consciously avoided saying whether or not it had belonged to Louisiana before 1819, and in exchange for other concessions the United States yielded Texas beyond the Sabine.

The natural limit between New Mexico and Louisiana was at the headwaters of the Rio Grande and the Arkansas River. But to keep the line far from Santa Fe, the Adams-Onís delineation left the Red River at one hundred degrees west longitude and proceeded west along the Arkansas to its source. Since colonial occupation gave no ground for boundary claims farther north, it was logical to assume that the purchase included the natural watershed of the Mississippi. President Thomas Jefferson's claim that Oregon was included had no foundation and no international recognition. The drawing of the line to the Pacific at forty-two degrees north latitude in the Adams-Onís Treaty was the result of bargaining on a larger scale.

An assertion that the northern boundary was defined in the Treaty of Utrecht of 1713 was ignored. In the Convention of 1818 a practical agreement between the United States and England placed the boundary at forty-nine degrees north latitude, from the Lake of the Woods to the Rocky Mountains. The United States had thus effected its ownership of almost the entire western Mississippi watershed through rights acquired in the Louisiana Purchase.

[Henry Adams, *History of the United States;* Samuel F. Bemis, *Diplomatic History of the United States;* Thomas M. Marshall, *History of the Western Boundary of the Louisiana Purchase.*]

PHILIP COOLIDGE BROOKS

LOUISIANA PURCHASE EXPOSITION, held in Saint Louis, Mo., from Apr. 30 to Dec. 1, 1904. Its 1,240 acres made it the largest of international expositions to date; its cost was more than $31.5 million and its attendance 19,694,855. The total deficit was considerable. Six years of preparation went to the celebration of the centennial of the purchase of the Louisiana territory. The technical marvel popularized by the exposition was the automobile, of which more than 100 were placed on display, including one that had made the trip all the way from New York ''under its own power.'' There were great chemical exhibits from Germany, thousands of articles from Japan, and an immense Philippine Reservation to show Americans the extent of the empire they had so recently acquired from Spain. Architecturally the fair followed the grandiloquent French style, and the ensemble formed an astonishing pattern of elaborate and universal chaos. The foreign governments contributed to this by building, for the most part, replicas of great European buildings and palaces—thus enhancing the architectural confusion.

FRANK MONAGHAN

LOUISIANA REVOLUTION OF 1768. The French inhabitants of Louisiana keenly resented being transferred to Spain by the Treaty of Fontainebleau of Nov. 3, 1762, and Spain's tardiness in taking possession of the colony induced the inhabitants to hope that the actual transfer would never take place. Economic distress, loyalty to France, and the unpopularity of Antonio de Ulloa, the first Spanish governor of Louisiana, culminated in Ulloa's expulsion from the colony in the so-called revolution of October 1768.

[Charles Gayarré, *History of Louisiana.*]

WALTER PRICHARD

LOUISIANA SPECIE RESERVE BANKING SYSTEM. The panic of 1837 destroyed the loose banking system of Louisiana. As a result of the distress there was a banking reform movement that culminated in the act of 1842, setting up a board of currency with large powers of supervision over all banks. The banks were required to separate their loans into two types: those made from capital and those made from deposits. Capital loans could be made on long-term paper, but those from deposits were limited to ninety-day paper, nonrenewable. In addition to this deposit protection was a requirement for a one-third specie reserve. Banks were prohibited from dealing in speculative ventures, and daily exchanges of notes and weekly specie settlements were required.

The strength of the Louisiana system was demonstrated during the panic of 1857, which had less effect in New Orleans than in any commercial city of the nation. This drew the attention of financiers and explains why the Louisiana system exerted such a marked influence on the national banking system. Its influence was second only to that of the New York act of 1838.

[Leonard C. Helderman, *National and State Banks—A Study of Their Origins.*]

LEONARD C. HELDERMAN

LOUISVILLE AND NASHVILLE RAILROAD. *See* **Railroads, Sketches.**

LOUISVILLE AND PORTLAND CANAL, around the Falls of the Ohio, at Louisville, was constructed by a Kentucky corporation chartered in 1825. The canal was begun in 1825 and opened in 1830. The original construction cost $742,869.94. The federal government, which had already subscribed heavily to the project, acquired complete possession of the canal in 1872, reducing the tolls to a nominal sum and none after 1880. The canal was twice enlarged, 1861–66 and 1870–82, and in 1927 it was rebuilt with federal aid to permit through navigation.

[*History of the Ohio Falls Cities and Their Counties.*]

W. C. MALLALIEU

LOVEJOY RIOTS. Elijah P. Lovejoy, an abolitionist clergyman, established a weekly newspaper, *The Observer*, at Saint Louis in 1833. Threatened with violence by proslavery men for editorials against slavery in 1834, he made a point of his rights to free speech and free press. Moving his press to free soil in Alton, Ill., in 1836, it was smashed on the Alton dock by local citizens. Sympathizers helped to purchase a new press, but when Lovejoy came out for immediate abolition and a state antislavery society (July 1837), a mob destroyed the press (August), smashed a third (Sept. 21), and, in an effort to destroy the fourth (Nov. 7), shot its defenders and killed Lovejoy who immediately came to be considered a martyr to the cause of abolition.

[Edward Beecher, *Narrative of Riots at Alton;* Joseph C. and Owen Lovejoy, *Memoir of the Reverend Elijah P. Lovejoy.*]

RAYMOND P. STEARNS

LOVELY'S PURCHASE. W. L. Lovely, Cherokee Indian agent in Arkansas, in an informal peace conference between Osage and Cherokee at the confluence of the Verdigris and Arkansas rivers in eastern Oklahoma, on July 9, 1816, obtained consent of the Osage to cede a large tract of land lying east of that stream if the government would pay claims for depredations held against them by white people. At Saint Louis, Sept. 25, 1818, representative members of the Osage ratified this cession in consideration of payment by the government of claims amounting to $4,000.

[Grant Foreman, *Indians and Pioneers.*]

GRANT FOREMAN

LOVEWELL'S FIGHT occurred at Pigwacket (Fryeburg), Maine, Sunday, May 9 (o.s.), 1725. Capt. John Lovewell, with thirty-three volunteers, was out for scalp bounty, and a chaplain with the party had just scalped an Indian when the troop was ambushed by about eighty Pequawkets (a branch of the Abnaki). Twelve white men, including Lovewell, fell at the onset; one deserted under fire; twenty-one were left. Ensign Seth Wyman, the only officer, placed his men for a finish fight, a pond at their backs and two large, fallen pines for breastworks. Toward nightfall, seeing the Indians preparing for a fresh attack, Wyman still-hunted and shot the medicine man. This ended the fight. Eighteen of the men eventually reached home. Rev. Thomas Symmes in his contemporary account changed the date from May 9 to May 8, supposedly to divert from the chaplain, who died, the odium of scalp hunting on Sunday.

[F. H. Eckstorm, "Pigwacket and Parson Symmes," *New England Quarterly,* vol. 9; Rev. Thomas Symmes, *The Original Account of Capt. John Lovewell's "Great Fight,"* Nathaniel Bouton, ed.]

FANNIE HARDY ECKSTORM

LOWER CALIFORNIA, also known as **Baja California,** was discovered in 1533 by Fortún Jiménez, a navigator in the service of Hernando Cortes. It was separated from Spanish Upper (Alta) California in 1772. The cession of the peninsula by Mexico was vainly sought by Nicholas P. Trist in making the peace treaty of Guadalupe Hidalgo in 1848. It was also the objective of William Walker's futile filibustering expedition of 1853–54; and James Gadsden failed to obtain it as part of the Gadsden Purchase completed in 1854. A number of efforts to purchase it for the United States in 1857, 1859, and later years were equally fruitless. The U.S. Navy for several years made use of Magdalena Bay on the west coast of the peninsula as a maneuvers base, by courtesy of the Mexican government; and an alleged Japanese effort to lease the bay in 1910–11 was the occasion leading to the Lodge Resolution of 1912, with its notable elaboration of the Monroe Doctrine, concerning the use by non-American governments of New World harbors and strategic points.

[H. H. Bancroft, *The North Mexican States and Texas;* J. M. Callahan, *American Foreign Policy in Mexican Relations.*]

RUFUS KAY WYLLYS

LOWER COUNTIES-ON-DELAWARE, comprising the counties of New Castle, Kent, and Sussex, or the present state of Delaware, evolved from Swedish and Dutch settlements. They were conveyed by the Duke of York (later James II) in 1682 to William Penn and shortly afterward annexed to the Province of Pennsylvania by the Act of Union. Because of disagreement in the provincial assembly the Lower Counties seceded from that body in 1704 and formed, at New Castle, their own assembly, by which they continued to be governed until the adoption of the constitution of the state of Delaware in 1776.

[J. Thomas Scharf, *History of Delaware;* Henry C. Conrad, *History of the State of Delaware*]

LEON DE VALINGER, JR.

LOWER LAKES. *See* **Upper and Lower Lakes.**

LOWER SOUTH, that part of the South lying wholly within the cotton belt, including South Carolina, Georgia, and the Gulf states of Florida, Alabama, Mississippi, Louisiana, and Texas. In the later antebellum period these states (Florida excepted) secured political leadership in the South, based on large-scale, slave-labor cotton culture and its concomitants.

[William G. Brown, *The Lower South in American History*.]

HAYWOOD J. PEARCE, JR.

LOYAL, FORT, CAPTURE OF (May 20, 1690). Toward the beginning of King William's War, under the command of the governor of New France, Louis de Buade, Comte de Frontenac, two French lieutenants, commanding a mixed force of French and Indians, besieged Fort Loyal on Casco Bay, Maine, and compelled its commander, Capt. Sylvanus Davis, to surrender. The pledge of kind treatment and quarter to the vanquished was grossly violated, and many of them were tortured and murdered.

[Francis Parkman, *Count Frontenac and New France*.]

ROBERT S. THOMAS

LOYALHANNA, BATTLE OF THE (Oct. 12, 1758), at Ligonier, Pa., was an unsuccessful attack of about 600 French and Indians upon 1,500 men, in an entrenched encampment, commanded by Col. James Burd. Its purpose was to delay the expedition of Gen. John Forbes by destroying horses and cattle and, if possible, to capture the post. Baffled by artillery behind fortifications, the French retired, after a four-hour conflict and slight losses. Burd's losses were considerable.

[Alfred P. James, "Fort Ligonier, 1758–1765," *West Pennsylvania Historical Review*, vol. 17 (1934).]

ALFRED P. JAMES

LOYALISTS, or **Tories,** those who were loyal to Great Britain during the American Revolution, comprised about one-third of the population of the thirteen revolting colonies. In Georgia and South Carolina they were a majority; in New England and Virginia, a minority; elsewhere they were more or less evenly matched by the patriots. Included in their ranks were all classes: great landowners such as the De Lanceys, Jessups, and Philipses of New York; rich merchants, such as the Whartons and Pembertons of Philadelphia and the Higginses and Chandlers of Boston; large

numbers of professional men—lawyers, physicians, and teachers; prosperous farmers; crown officials and Anglican clergy and laity; and dependents of Loyalist merchants and landlords. While a few of the more conservative stood for the rigid execution of imperial law, the majority opposed the objectionable acts of the British Parliament, served on the early extralegal committees, and were not hostile to the calling of the first Continental Congress in 1774, working hard to elect delegates of their own convictions to it. Although anxious to maintain their rights by means of petition and legal protest, and in some cases not even averse to a show of force, they were strongly opposed to separation from the British empire. The Declaration of Independence gave finality to their position.

Before April 1775 few efforts were made to arrest or suppress the Loyalists, but after the Battle of Lexington the war fervor rapidly grew more intense. Great numbers of Loyalists flocked to the royal colors or, in a few instances, organized militia companies of their own under commissions from the crown. Although they probably contributed 60,000 soldiers, their military service was not commensurate with their numerical strength: their only outstanding exploits were an expedition against the coast towns of Connecticut; frontier raids; and a savage guerrilla warfare against patriots in the South.

As the struggle progressed, the patriots resorted to more and more drastic measures against the Loyalists. All who refused to take an oath of allegiance to the new governments were denied the rights of citizenship and could not vote, hold office, or enjoy court protection. In many cases they were forbidden to pursue professions or to acquire or dispose of property. Free speech was denied them, and they were not allowed to communicate with the British. When these laws failed to accomplish their purpose, the more ardent Loyalists were jailed, put on parole, sent to detention camps, or tarred and feathered. Nearly all the new state governments eventually enacted legislation banishing those who refused to swear allegiance. It is probable that before the war was over 200,000 Loyalists died, were exiled, or became voluntary refugees to other parts of the British empire—a large number of citizens for struggling frontier communities to lose.

To banishment was added confiscation of property. In the early days of the Revolution Thomas Paine advised confiscation of Loyalist property to defray the expenses of the war, and several states followed his suggestion. The definition of treason by Congress supplied a legal basis for action, and late in 1777 Congress advised the states to confiscate and sell the real and personal property of those who had forfeited "the right of protection" and to invest the proceeds in Continental certificates. Although some of the more conservative patriots protested that confiscation was "contrary to the principles of civil liberty," statutes of condemnation and forfeiture were enacted in all the states before the end of the war.

Many persons were the victims of private grudges and persecution. Evidence abounds that the execution of the sequestration laws was frequently attended by scandal and corruption. The amount of property seized is uncertain. Claims totaling £10 million were filed with the commission established by the British Parliament in 1783, and the claims for less than £1 million were disallowed (*see* British Debts).

On the whole, throughout the conflict, the Loyalists lacked organization and good leadership. They were conservatives who were suspicious of the innovations demanded by a crisis. The triumph of the patriots accentuated their hesitancy. They had placed implicit trust in the invincibility of the British army, and the unexpected development of the conflict dazed them.

All things taken into consideration, the treatment of the Loyalists was moderate. The period was one in which the most bitter and most harsh human emotions were aroused—a civil war within a state. Although the laws of banishment and sequestration were severe, there was no such slaughter and terrorism as prevailed later during the French Revolution, and surprising care was taken to make sure that punishment of Loyalists was carried out only in accordance with law.

[Wallace Brown, *The Good Americans: The Loyalist in the American Revolution;* North Callahan, *Flight From the Republic: The Tories of the American Revolution.*]

A. C. FLICK

LOYAL LAND COMPANY. The spirit of speculation in western lands was rife in Virginia in the later years of the first half of the 1700's. The first grant to a company organized to deal in such lands was to the Loyal Land Company. A grant of 800,000 acres was made to it by the Council of State of Virginia, on July 12, 1748, John Lewis, founder of Staunton, Va., being the leading spirit for four years. In launching the company's activities Thomas Walker was chosen on Dec. 12, 1749, as field agent, and soon became the directive force of the enterprise. In 1750 he led a group on a tour of exploration into the Tennessee and Kentucky country in the interest of the company and kept a journal that is one of the most valuable sources

on the early history of that region. On that tour Walker named the Cumberland mountains, gap, and river in honor of King George II's son William Augustus, Duke of Cumberland.

The lands actually taken up by the company were located east of the Cumberland Mountains, and by the autumn of 1754 lands had been sold to about 200 settlers. The French and Indian War of 1754–63 brought a cessation of activities, and the Proclamation of 1763 gave Walker and his associates concern and trouble. In order to render lands west of the proclamation line available, Walker took an active part in removing the claims of the Indian tribes to the region. He participated in negotiating the treaties of Fort Stanwix and Lochaber in 1768 and 1770. Until his death in 1794 Walker was persistent in salvaging all he could for the company, and southwest Virginia owes much to his enterprise and assiduity in bringing in settlers.

[Archibald Henderson, "Dr. Thomas Walker and the Loyal Land Company," *Proceedings of the American Antiquarian Society* (1931).]

SAMUEL C. WILLIAMS

LOYAL LEAGUES, generically the Union League of America, were formed to restore northern morale that had been shaken by military and political reverses in 1862. The movement had its origin at Pekin, Ill., on June 25, 1862. Eventually leagues were set up in every northern state, and clubs were organized in many cities and towns. A convention, which assembled at Cleveland, May 20–21, 1863, created the national Grand Council with headquarters at Washington, D.C. Public meetings were sponsored, and broadsides, pamphlets, and posters were circulated by the millions. Union leagues insisted upon unconditional loyalty, promoted the formation of the Union party, contributed to the renomination and election of President Abraham Lincoln, and aided in state and local political contests. In the Reconstruction period pamphlets on southern "outrages" and the plight of the blacks were issued, but many leagues continued mainly as local social clubs. Agents sent to the South were welcomed by upland loyalists who joined the Union League to wrest political control from the lowland aristocracy. Most native southern whites deserted upon the admission of blacks, who were organized into local lodges by secret and mysterious ritualistic ceremonies. As a political machine designed to inculcate the tenets of the Radical Republicans, the league was partly responsible for the formation of the

Ku Klux Klan. By 1870 the league ceased to exert influence in the South.

[H. W. Bellows, *Historical Sketch of the Union League Club of New York;* G. P. Lathrop, *History of the Union League of Philadelphia.*]

WENDELL H. STEPHENSON

LOYAL LEGION, MILITARY ORDER OF THE. *See* **Military Order of the Loyal Legion of the U.S.A.**

LOYAL PUBLICATION SOCIETIES were formed during the Civil War to distribute "journals and documents of unquestionable loyalty." Strongly opposing Copperheads and Democrats, they were active in state politics and the national campaign of 1864. Under the leadership of Francis Lieber, prominent author and publisher and professor at Columbia College, the New York society from 1862 to 1865 raised $30,000, with which it published 900,000 copies of ninety pamphlets. The New England Loyal Publication Society, at Boston, spent $4,000 to print more than 200 broadsides. The two organizations cooperated with each other. In addition to their own publications, they distributed newspapers, pamphlets, and broadsides favorable to the Union cause.

[Loyal Publication Society of New York, *Annual Reports;* E. E. Ware, *Political Opinion in Massachusetts During the Civil War and Reconstruction.*]

FRANK FREIDEL

LOYALTY OATHS are statements of allegiance to a cause, a concept, an institution, a community, a party, a group, a political or religious association, a leader, or even a symbol, as in the pledge of allegiance to the flag. Historically the loyalty oath has been intended to increase the security of authority from real or fancied refusals to accord it legitimacy; to mark nonjurors for ostracism, expulsion, or punishment; and to bind the compliant to obligation. It is also a ceremony of faith and submission. In 1086, for example, William the Conqueror at Salisbury imposed an oath on the most prominent lords of the land that they would be faithful to him. After his break with Rome, Henry VIII—and later Elizabeth I—enforced oaths to secure the new religious establishment. They were employed by James I after the Gunpowder Plot as a measure to secure the realm against religious subversion. In the earliest colonial charters all those immigrating to the New World were required

to take oaths of loyalty to the crown. The Massachusetts Bay Colony and other colonies enforced oaths of loyalty to the colonial regime.

During the American Revolution, loyalty oaths were used by radicals to enforce boycotts against the Tories, and both rebel and royal loyalty oaths were freely employed to maintain the security of the conflicting forces. Perhaps because colonial-state loyalties were so strong, no provision for oaths of loyalty to the new central government was made in the Articles of Confederation in 1781. But in the federal Constitution of 1787, a specified oath is required of the president in Article II, Section 1, Clause 8, that he will faithfully execute his office and, to the best of his ability, "preserve, protect, and defend the Constitution of the United States." And Article VI does require an oath of all federal and state officers to "support this Constitution."

Tensions over loyalty led to the adoption of the Alien and Sedition Acts of 1798, but it was through prosecutions rather than oaths that the Federalists sought to silence critics. Tensions over nullification in South Carolina in 1833 led to the widespread enforcement of oaths of loyalty to the state in its conflict with the federal authority. During the Civil War, test oaths were enforced in both the North and the South. The center of Abraham Lincoln's program for reconstruction in 1863 was a pledge of future loyalty to the Union, unlike the test oath enacted by Congress in 1862, which required pledges of past loyalty. The Supreme Court in *Cummings* v. *Missouri* (1866) held unconstitutional a state oath requiring voters, teachers, candidates for public office, and others to swear that they had not participated in rebellion against the United States. On the same day, in *Ex Parte Garland,* the Court held unconstitutional a congressional statute requiring a similar oath of attorneys practicing in the courts of the United States.

Although loyalty testing was carried to excessive lengths in World War I, it (like the actions of 1798) was carried on primarily in the courts, under the Espionage and Sedition Acts of 1917 and 1918, and through private groups operating under the doubtful auspices of the Department of Justice and the Department of War. Oaths did not play a primary role in either of the two world wars, although both these conflicts contributed to a new kind of concern about loyalty as an aftermath. Issues of property and social structure were not absent from questions of loyalty during the Revolution, the nullification controversy, and the Civil War, but the primary conflict in all three was political difference over the relations between the central and local governments in two kinds of confederation, imperial and national. Out of the two world wars, concern grew for what was perceived to be a threat by social radicals to the security of all political authority and the prevailing distribution of property. The Hatch Act of 1938 required as a condition of federal employment that the applicant swear that he did not belong to an organization advocating the violent overthrow of the government.

Loyalty testing programs were conducted by federal officials during World War II as a minor routine. But in the agitation over Communists in the postwar period, loyalty testing became a prominent activity in the executive establishment. It was also a principal feature of the work of congressional committees in both the House of Representatives and the Senate and punishments for contempt or perjury were meted out to many who refused to make exculpatory statements or who swore falsely. Many state legislatures and municipal bodies required loyalty oaths of teachers, public and private, and governmental employees, most of which were upheld by the Supreme Court, especially in the 1950's. Although the Court later showed some tendency to decide such cases in favor of defendants, as late as 1972 the Supreme Court upheld a Massachusetts statute that required a public employee to swear "to support and defend" the Constitution and to oppose the overthrow of government by violent means.

Although loyalty oaths have an Anglo-American history of a thousand years, it is doubtful that they contribute much to the security of authority; more likely, they reflect its anxiety rather than its strength.

[Eleanor Bontecou, *The Federal Loyalty-Security Program;* Morton Grodzins, *The Loyal and the Disloyal;* Harold M. Hyman, *To Try Men's Souls;* John H. Schaar, *Loyalty in America.*]

EARL LATHAM

LUDLOW RESOLUTION, a proposed constitutional amendment introduced by Rep. Louis Ludlow of Indiana in 1935. It was a by-product of the Senate munitions investigation of 1934 and the keep-America-out-of-war movement, which culminated in the Neutrality Acts of 1935, 1936, and 1937. Proceeding on the theory that the people who have to do the fighting should make the decision, this proposal limited the power of Congress by requiring a popular referendum to ratify a declaration of war except in case of actual attack on the United States or its outlying territories. The resolution gained considerable popularity, and only strenuous efforts by President Franklin D. Roosevelt's administration prevented its coming to a final vote in the House of Representatives in January 1938.

[Stephen and Joan Raushenbush, *The Final Choice, America Between Europe and Asia.*]

HAROLD H. SPROUT

LUDLOW'S CODE. A common complaint of the early American colonists was that, in the absence of an established body of laws, the decisions of the magistrates tended to be capricious. To meet this situation the general court of Connecticut in 1646 requested Roger Ludlow, a member of the court and trained in the English law, to compile a body of laws for the commonwealth. The result was Ludlow's Code of 1650, which, under seventy-eight headings, established the law of the colony—prefaced by the assurance that no man's life, reputation, or goods should be endangered "unless it be by the virtue or equity of some express law of the country warranting the same, established by a General Court, and sufficiently published. . . ." Although revised many times, this code remains as the foundation of the laws of the state of Connecticut.

R. V. COLEMAN

LUMBEE, or Croatan, Indians, numbering more than 30,000, constitute a group of obscure origin, with a mixed ancestry of white, Indian, and black strains. They seem to constitute a hybridized remnant of once-powerful Atlantic coast tribes and claim to be descendants of Sir Walter Raleigh's lost colony of 1587–91, intermarried with the Hatteras Indians. They speak no Indian language and have few distinctively Indian traits. The group is centered in Robeson County, N.C., although some 2,000 urban Lumbee live in Baltimore, Md. The Lumbee attracted national attention in 1958 when they drove hooded Ku Klux Klansmen from their North Carolina lands with shotguns.

[Brewton Berry, *Almost White.*]

KENNETH M. STEWART

LUMBER INDUSTRY. The great American forest, with coniferous arms that encircled a central hardwoods belt, stretched from the Atlantic Ocean, with occasional open meadows, to the edge of the Great Plains. Early logging gave winter employment to farmers and their work animals, who worked to remove this forest to create arable land, and in addition provided a variety of forest products. If the logs were piled up and burned, the ashes could be scattered as fertilizer, used to surface primitive roads, or sold to soapmakers and glassmakers. Timbers and boards could be used in fences, buildings, or ships. It was a wooden world, and scarcely any part of colonial life was not based on wood.

The farmer cut down all of the trees that shaded his fields, but the commercial lumberman tended to specialize in a single species of tree, both in logging and in milling. Beginning in New England, for example, the lumberman logged the white pine in ever-widening swathes north from Maine into New Brunswick and west into Pennsylvania. By the 1830's the white pine in the Great Pineries of Michigan, Wisconsin, and Minnesota was falling to the lumberman's ax, and by the 1890's the pursuit of this noble tree led the lumberman to the Inland Empire centered around Spokane, Wash. In the same decade other lumbermen crossed the Great Lakes into Canada or changed species and began to cut the Norway pine and other previously neglected species. Still others moved south to stands of Southern pine or cypress or jumped to the West Coast, where the redwoods, Douglas fir, Port Orford cedar, and other giant trees awaited ax and saw. Southern forests also provided oak for the stout warships of the Old Ironsides era and pitch, tar, and turpentine from the pine barrens of the Carolinas.

The principal production problem of the lumberman has always been transportation. He has to move heavy, bulky, cheap materials to a sawmill and then to a distant market. For many years the solution was to cut the trees in the winter, when frozen ground provided a hard roadway for each tree. The logs could then be moved over the frozen ground to streams and lakes, piled until the spring thaw, and then floated to the sawmills. Driving logs down a frigid torrent was hard, dangerous work for the lumberjack, and an occasional logjam caused special perplexities. Since about 1920 logging has tended to be done in the summertime or has become an all-year occupation. The road-building bulldozer and the heavy-duty truck have ended the old log drives; now temporary roads can be built to within an economical distance of each tree.

The chain saw has almost completely displaced the ax and handsaw in the felling occupation, but even greater technological advances have been made in sawmills. Pit sawing, in which a log was inched over a pit or trestle and sawed into boards or planks, was replaced in colonial times by the muley saw, operated by waterpower. Early in the 19th century the buzz, or circular, saw partially replaced the muley saw. The buzz saw was fast and reliable but turned much of the log into sawdust. The increasing value of hardwoods, used in furniture and vehicles, led to the introduction of the band saw, which reduced the amount of wood wasted in sawdust. A toy in the 18th century, the band saw became a practical tool with the development of special steels, hard rubber, and resistant glues. Today sawmills, planing mills, drying kilns, and other associated plants are largely automated. Important developments since the middle of the 19th century include the making of paper from wood pulp, the burgeoning of the plywood industry, and the use of wood fibers for insulating material or wallboard. But the forest industry as a whole, which played such an important role in early America, has become only a very minor part of the industrial system.

The lumber industry has been the principal target of the conservationists over the years, but forest conservation was impossible as long as wood was literally less than dirt cheap, a situation that lasted until the 1890's. Cheap raw material, unfavorable land laws, a cutting cycle that might vary from 15 to 150 years, and unfair local taxes led to a cut-out-and-get-out attitude among lumbermen, to desolate, eroded hillsides, or to thickets of weed trees and brush. Many large companies maintain tree farms, practice conservation measures, and plan for a century ahead. Some small self-serving loggers still pursue ruthless ways. However, many of America's timber reserves are in the national forests and are subject to the rules established by the U.S. Forest Service. Large-scale forest management is still a subject for development and debate, and the use of controlled fire may be a tool of the future.

[Agnes M. Larson, *History of the White Pine Industry in Minnesota;* Richard G. Lillard, *The Great Forest;* William G. Rector, *Log Transportation in the Lake States Lumber Industry, 1840–1918.*]

RODNEY C. LOEHR

"LUNATIC FRINGE," a phrase used by Theodore Roosevelt in his *Autobiography* to characterize the "foolish fanatics," such as extreme pacifists, "who form the lunatic fringe in all reform movements." The term has since been used by journalists to describe crackpots and rabble-rousers who proclaim impractical schemes.

STANLEY R. PILLSBURY

LUNDY'S LANE, BATTLE AT (July 25, 1814), the most sharply contended engagement in the War of

1812, occurred about three weeks after Gen. Jacob Brown's army, invading Canada, had won the important victory at Chippewa, eighteen miles north of Fort Erie. Brown's invading army encountered the British under Gen. Phineas Riall at Lundy's Lane, in Canada near Bridgewater and Niagara Falls. Col. Winfield Scott's First Brigade failed to carry the position in a frontal attack and was reinforced by Gen. Eleazar Ripley and Col. Peter B. Porter's brigades. Maj. Thomas Jesup, with the Twenty-fifth Infantry, executed a turning movement, driving in the British left and capturing Riall. Gen. Gordon Drummond, arriving with reinforcements, took command. Protracted and savage fighting ensued. Col. James Miller's Twenty-first Infantry stormed the hill and took the British artillery, the Americans repulsing determined counterattacks until midnight. Brown and Scott, both severely wounded, withdrew. Ripley, left in command, brought off the army when ammunition failed, but lacking horses, abandoned the captured cannon. Both sides claimed victory, but Drummond remained in possession of the field. Losses were heavy: British, 30 percent; American, slightly less.

[E. A. Cruikshank, *The Battle of Lundy's Lane*.]
CHARLES WINSLOW ELLIOTT

LUSITANIA, SINKING OF THE. The Cunard liner *Lusitania* was sunk without warning by the German submarine U-20 off Old Head of Kinsale, Ireland, on May 7, 1915. Of the 1,959 passengers and crew, 1,198 perished, including 128 (out of 197) Americans. Since on May 1, the day of sailing, the German embassy in Washington, D.C., had published an advertisement in American papers warning Atlantic travelers that they sailed in British or Allied ships at their own risk, it was widely believed that the sinking was premeditated. The log of the U-20, published years later, shows, however, that the submarine had sunk other ships, met the *Lusitania* by chance, and sank it from fear of being rammed. The ship carried 4,200 cases of small-arms ammunition and 1,250 shrapnel cases, allowed by American law; this cargo, stored well forward, about 150 feet from the spot where the torpedo struck, may have exploded and contributed to the rapid (eighteen minutes) sinking of the ship. A thorough examination prior to sailing revealed no evidence that the liner was armed. Why the captain of the ship had reduced speed, failed to follow a zig-zag course, and kept close to shore, in violation of orders from the British admiralty, was not satisfactorily explained.

The catastrophe created intense indignation in the United States, especially since, on Feb. 10, 1915, the American government had denied the legality of submarine warfare (as practiced by Germany) and had warned that it would hold the German government to "a strict accountability" for the observance of American rights on the high seas. In May, President Woodrow Wilson resisted considerable popular clamor for war (chiefly in the East), and in three successive notes (May 13, June 9, and July 21, 1915) demanded that Germany make reparation for and disavow the sinking; the last note concluded with the statement that a repetition of the act "must be regarded by the Government of the United States, when they affect American citizens, as deliberately unfriendly." Secretary of State William Jennings Bryan thought the American demands too severe and likely to lead to war, and resigned on June 8. The German government agreed to make reparation and eventually gave a promise (after the sinking of the *Arabic*) that liners would not be sunk without warning and without safety of the lives of noncombatants; but it steadfastly refused to disavow the sinking of the *Lusitania*. No settlement of this question was reached before the United States entered World War I.

[T. A. Bailey, "The Sinking of the Lusitania," *American Historical Review*, vol. 61; Adolph A. Hoehling and Mary Hoehling, *The Last Voyage of the Lusitania*; Charles Seymour, *American Diplomacy and the World War*.]
BERNADOTTE E. SCHMITT

LUSK COMMITTEE was authorized in 1919 by the New York legislature and headed by state senator Clayton R. Lusk. It published a monumental report of 4,450 pages on radical and seditious activities.
W. BROOKE GRAVES

LUTHERAN CHURCHES in America trace their heritage to the Reformation of the 16th century in Germany and northern Europe. Historically, Lutheranism has placed heavy emphasis on its confessional statements. The Augsburg Confession, drawn up by Melanchthon in 1530, is the primary doctrinal symbol, but many Lutherans also adhere to the 1580 Book of Concord, which was drafted to end theological disputes within the second generation of reformers. Lutheran theology is centered around the doctrine of justification by faith and stresses the role of the Word of God and the sacraments of baptism and the Lord's Supper in the communication of grace.

Although there were Lutherans in both New Sweden and New Netherland, the primary growth of colonial Lutheranism was the result of German immigration. Salzburg Lutherans began settling in Georgia in 1734, but even larger numbers, drawn by William Penn's skillful advertisements, immigrated to Pennsylvania. The outstanding leader of the young church was Henry Melchior Mühlenberg, who—by means of extensive traveling and strong personal leadership—managed to unite the various pastors in the colony in the Ministerium of Philadelphia (1748). Despite the formation of the Ministerium, the church did not have a national organization until the General Synod was formed in 1820.

As the 18th century progressed, Lutheranism tended to become more Americanized, and both its liturgical practices and theology assumed features characteristic of the Reformed churches around it. The conflict between those who supported the emerging "American Lutheranism" and those who wished to emphasize tradition came in the first half of the 19th century. The leader of the "American" Lutherans was the theologian Samuel S. Schmucker, who founded the seminary at Gettysburg. An active churchman, Schmucker believed that the Protestant churches should cooperate to promote the spiritual welfare of the new nation. In his *Fraternal Appeal to the American Churches* (1838), he called for an organization similar to the present National Council of Churches, and he was both a founder and an active member of the Evangelical Alliance. His principal opponent in the dispute was Charles Philip Krauth, who conducted a running debate with Schmucker in the Lutheran press. The controversy reached its climax in 1853 when the Definite Synodical Program was presented to the General Synod. It called for a revision of the Augsburg Confession in the direction of commonly held American religious beliefs and provoked a decade of conflict that effectively removed the partisans of American-oriented Lutheranism from power.

In many ways, the pattern of immigration made the dispute academic. The vast majority of new German immigrants had been influenced by the confessional revival in Europe, and they moved the whole church in that direction. Immigration also tended to fragment Lutheranism, for the new settlers hoped to reproduce the pattern of church life that they had known in their home churches. Different synods, representing different European communities and nationalities, struggled to provide an adequate ministry and to find marks of distinction.

One of the most successful of these immigrant churches was the Missouri Synod, which was founded by Saxon immigrants who left Germany to escape the laxity and rationalism of their national church. The leader who most shaped this branch of Lutheranism was Carl F. W. Walther. His own theology, which became the foundation of the synod, was both pietist and confessional, and the organization of the church reflected this dichotomy. Against the "high church" party in Lutheranism, the synod affirmed a congregational polity and a "low" transfer theory of the ministry; against the Americanizers, it affirmed pure doctrine and the need for a strict theological consensus. In the 20th century, the confessional stance of the synod has led to intense controversy over the higher criticism of the Bible.

The fragmentation of the 19th century seemed to be coming to an end in the 20th century. In the mid-1970's, as the result of almost a half-century of mergers, 95 percent of all Lutherans were members of three synods: the Lutheran Church in America, with 3,138,057 members; the Lutheran Church–Missouri Synod, with 3,055,254 members; and the American Lutheran Church, with 2,464,744 members. In 1967 these synods took a step toward further unification when they joined together in the Lutheran Council in the United States. Other Lutheran denominations are the Apostolic Lutheran Church, 7,000 members; the Church of the Lutheran Brethren of America, 9,010 members; the Evangelical Lutheran Church in America, 2,500 members; the Evangelical Lutheran Synod, 17,321 members; the Protestant Conference, 2,660 members; the Synod of Evangelical Lutheran Churches, 21,000 members; the Wisconsin Evangelical Lutheran Synod, 388,411 members; and Church of the Lutheran Confession, 9,490 members.

[Gothard E. Arden, *Meet the Lutherans: Introducing the Lutheran Church in North America;* Herman O. A. Keinath, *Documents Illustrating the History of the Lutheran Church in America, With Special Emphasis on the Missouri Synod;* Fred W. Meuser, *The Formation of the American Lutheran Church: A Case Study in Lutheran Unity;* Abdell Wentz, *A Basic History of Lutheranism in America;* Richard Charles Wolf, ed., *Documents of Lutheran Unity in America.*]

GLENN T. MILLER

LUTHER V. BORDEN, 7 Howard 1 (1848), was an attempt to make the Supreme Court decide between the charter government of Rhode Island and the new government arising from the rebellion led by Thomas W. Dorr in 1842. Chief Justice Roger B. Taney's opinion evaded that issue, recognized state law and state courts as completely competent, and declared existing state authority legally empowered to use martial methods to maintain itself against violence.

[Charles Warren, *Supreme Court in United States History.*]

ELBRIDGE COLBY

LYCEUM MOVEMENT, an important phase of the early adult education and public school movements, utilizing, principally, lectures and debates. It was begun by an article in the *American Journal of Education* (October 1826) by Josiah Holbrook, containing a plan for "Associations of Adults for Mutual Education." The first society was organized by Holbrook in November 1826 at Millbury, Mass. Within a year more than a dozen lyceums had sprung up in Worcester County, Mass., and in Windham County, Conn. The movement was endorsed by a meeting of eminent Bostonians, presided over by Daniel Webster, in 1828. By 1831 lyceums existed in all the New England states and in northern New York. State lyceums were organized in 1831 in Massachusetts, Maine, and New York, and in the same year the New York State Lyceum called a meeting in New York City to organize a national lyceum. Holbrook journeyed as far west as Missouri and found active interest in the western states, including Kentucky and Tennessee. National lyceums were held each year until 1839, although often poorly attended. The town lyceums, estimated by Holbrook at 3,000 in 1835, were the heart of the movement. Their number probably increased greatly thereafter. After 1840 the main emphasis was upon self-improvement by means of lectures, readings, and discussions on science, literature, and morality. Politics and religion were generally avoided because of their controversial nature, but the lyceums often developed interest in topics that later became political issues, such as slavery and prohibition.

The lyceums continued to grow until the early 20th century. In 1915 their number was estimated at 12,000. In 1924–25 it was found that they existed mostly in small towns and were concentrated mostly on semipopular music and "sanitated vaudeville." Besides improving the public schools and giving a supplementary education to those unable to attend high school or college, the early lyceums led to certain permanent institutions, such as Lowell Institute in Massachusetts and Brooklyn Institute in New York. The Lyceum Village was founded at Berea, Ohio, in 1837. Holbrook conducted the Central Lyceum Bureau from 1842 to 1849, and in 1867–68 a number of commercial lecture bureaus were founded, among them the Boston Lyceum Bureau of James Redpath, whose successor, J. B. Pond, was a successful lecture promoter. Some lyceums developed into historical or literary societies, public libraries, or museums. Later the same idea was developed by the Chautauqua movement and women's clubs.

[C. B. Hayes, *The American Lyceum.*]

W. C. MALLALIEU

LYGONIA, a grant, commonly called the Plough Patent, made by the Council for New England, June 26, 1630, of an area forty miles square, west of the Kennebec River in Maine. Settlement by the original grantees failed, and the grant was purchased, Apr. 7, 1643, by Sir Alexander Rigby, an influential member of Parliament, whose interest had been aroused by George Cleeve, whom he appointed deputy president of the province. Cleeve was involved in a bitter quarrel over land with John Winter, agent of the Trelawney plantation, and the revival of the dormant Lygonia patent not only gave him a legal basis for his own defense but also placed the Trelawney grant within his jurisdiction. The Rigby title was confirmed Mar. 27, 1647, by the Warwick Commission, and thus Sir Ferdinando Gorges was deprived of more than half of his province, including Saco, Black Point, Spurwink, Richmond's Island, and Casco. Litigation between Gorges' deputy governor and Cleeve was a chief cause of the difficulties of Gorges' government in its formative years, while Cleeve's constant appeals to Massachusetts Bay for aid paved the way for that colony's expansion northward to include jurisdiction over Lygonia in 1658. The records of the province have disappeared, and only a few official documents dealing with its brief history have survived. The king's commissioners of 1664 did not recognize the legality of the Rigby claim, and in 1686 Edward Rigby, Alexander's grandson and heir, filed a claim with Massachusetts that was not accepted. In 1691 the new Massachusetts charter put an end to the Province of Lygonia.

[James Phinney Baxter, *George Cleeve of Casco Bay.*]

ROBERT E. MOODY

LYMAN'S COLONY. *See* **Georgiana.**

LYNCHING, whereby a mob without any authority at law inflicts injury or death upon a victim, has its roots deeply embedded in American life. The term derives from a Virginian, Col. Charles Lynch, who presided over the flogging of local criminals and Tory sympathizers during the revolutionary war. Since then, mob justice has taken many other forms: lynchings of alleged desperadoes along America's expanding southern and western frontiers throughout the 19th century; of blacks from the Reconstruction era to mid-20th century; and occasionally of unpopular immigrants and of outspoken labor, radical, or antiwar figures. Since 1882 (the earliest year for which there is reliable data) lynch mobs have killed over 4,730 persons; at least 3,341 of these were blacks. The sustained lynching of blacks in southern and border states coincided with the disfranchisement and Jim Crow prohibitions inflicted upon the Afro-American community at the turn of the century. From 1886 through 1916 alone, lynch mobs murdered 2,605 black men and women. Despite assertions about ''protecting'' white womanhood, less than 30 percent of black victims were accused—let alone tried and convicted—of rape or attempted rape.

Given the diversities of time, place, and victims, generalizations about American lynchings are difficult to establish. Certainly the search for quick solutions, an enthusiasm for force as an instrument of public conduct, a strong sense of conformity to local or regional mores, a determination to impose majority rule upon a vulnerable minority, and support for a mechanism of control in a biracial environment have all applied.

Lynching did not go unchallenged. Founded in 1909, the National Association for the Advancement of Colored People (NAACP) conducted a national drive against mob violence for over four decades. The Atlanta-based Association of Southern Women for the Prevention of Lynching campaigned diligently throughout the 1930's. The numbers of reported lynchings declined after 1935. The long years of antilynching work, the growing political power of Afro-American voters in northern and western urban centers, concerns about America's international cold-war image, and the widely publicized recommendations of President Harry S. Truman's Committee on Civil Rights (1947) all contributed to that decline. For the first time ever, no reported lynchings occurred in a three-year period (1952–54). Lynchers did kill three black persons in 1955 and at least one in 1959, and the murders and beatings of civil rights workers during the 1960's reaffirmed that certain segments of the United States had not fully disavowed a lynching mentality.

Lynching Legislation. Legislation to deal with anticipated lynchings, lynchers, or delinquent officials—or to indemnify survivors—was enacted in several states during the 1890's (Georgia, North Carolina, South Carolina, Kentucky, Texas, Tennessee, Ohio, and Indiana among them). Public attitudes and fears of political reprisals impeded corrective action; when black victims were involved, 99 percent of mob members escaped prosecution and punishment. From 1918 to 1950, the NAACP tried, unsuccessfully, to secure a federal antilynching statute. Its first effort in Congress resulted from a bill introduced by Rep. L. C. Dyer of Missouri. The measure passed the House of Representatives in 1922, as did other bills in 1937 and 1940, but none made it through the Senate. Notwithstanding the 1947 recommendations of Truman's Committee on Civil Rights, Congress still refused to enact an antilynching law. Belatedly, the 1968 Civil Rights Act authorized federal action if two or more persons should conspire to intimidate a citizen in the free exercise of constitutional rights, whether or not death ensued. Formerly, civil rights advocates relied on Title 18, Sections 241 and 242, of the U.S. Code. Derived from Reconstruction statutes and difficult to implement, these sections were central in two U.S. Supreme Court rulings in 1966 (one involved three slain civil rights workers). On three earlier occasions (1923, 1936, 1940), the Court had invoked the due process clause of the Fourteenth Amendment to undercut ''legal lynchings'' by reversing convictions based on ''evidence'' and ''confessions'' obtained through torture.

[Richard Bardolph, ed., *The Civil Rights Record: Black Americans and the Law, 1849–1970;* James H. Chadbourn, *Lynching and the Law,* and *To Secure These Rights: The Report of the President's Committee on Civil Rights;* Richard Hofstadter and Michael Wallace, eds., *American Violence: A Documentary History;* Arthur F. Raper, *The Tragedy of Lynching;* Walter White, *Rope and Faggot: A Biography of Judge Lynch.*]

ROBERT L. ZANGRANDO

LYON, FORT, was built in Colorado Territory near Bent's new fort on the Arkansas River, thirty-eight miles below Bent's old fort, destroyed in 1852. It was named successively Fort Fauntleroy, Fort Wise, and Fort Lyon, the last after the hero of Wilson's Creek. In 1866 the river cut the banks, so that Fort Lyon was moved twenty miles upstream, two miles below the mouth of the Purgatoire.

[George Bird Grinnell, ''Bent's Old Fort and Its Builders,'' *Kansas State Historical Society Collections,* vol. 15.]

PAUL I. WELLMAN

McALLISTER, FORT, CAPTURE OF (Dec. 13, 1864). Fort McAllister, six miles from Ossabaw Sound and eighteen miles southwest of Savannah, Ga., commanded the mouth of the Ogeechee River and held up Union Gen. William Tecumseh Sherman's "march to the sea" for several days. At 5:00 P.M. on Dec. 13 Union Gen. W. B. Hazen effected its capture. This made possible Sherman's junction with the gunboat fleet, and opened the gates to Savannah.

[R. U. Johnson and C. C. Buel, eds., *Battles and Leaders of the Civil War,* vol. IV.]

ROBERT S. THOMAS

McCARDLE, EX PARTE, 7 Wallace 506 (1869), marked the summit of Radical Republican power (*see* Reconstruction) by confirming the supremacy of a legislative majority over the executive and judicial branches of the government. President Andrew Johnson's impeachment trial was under way and the Fourteenth Amendment was about to become effective.

In two cases in 1867—*Mississippi* v. *Johnson* and *Georgia* v. *Stanton*—an effort had been made to restrain Congress from effecting military reconstruction in the South, but in each case the Supreme Court had refused jurisdiction. Another case soon reached the Court. McCardle, a Mississippi editor, had criticized Gen. E. O. C. Ord, the military commander in the "conquered province" of Mississippi. Worse, he had criticized the policy of Congress. He was promptly arrested and jailed and denied the benefit of habeas corpus. To secure freedom, McCardle endeavored to take advantage of a Radical Republican law providing for an appeal to the Supreme Court of "all cases where any person may be restrained of his or her liberty in violation of the Constitution or of any treaty or law of the United States," a statute passed to protect federal officials and other "loyal persons" against the state courts of the South.

As a decision in the McCardle case was imminent, the alarmed Radicals hastened to restrain the Supreme Court from fear that the precedent of *Ex Parte Milligan* might be used to declare the Reconstruction acts unconstitutional. After failure of a proposal to require a two-thirds vote of the Court to invalidate a law, the Court was stripped of its power of judicial review so far as it concerned the Reconstruction acts. Johnson vetoed the act, but the Radicals promptly repassed it. The Supreme Court unanimously decided it had no jurisdiction because of the new restriction and dismissed the case.

[Stanley T. Kutler, *Judicial Power and Reconstruction Politics,* and "Ex Parte McCardle: Judicial Impotency? The Supreme Court and Reconstruction Reconsidered," *American Historical Review,* vol. 72 (1967).]

THOMAS ROBSON HAY

McCARRAN-WALTER ACT of June 27, 1952, was the basic United States immigration law from 1952 until passage of the Immigration and Nationality Act, which went into effect Dec. 1, 1965. The McCarran-Walter Act revised all previous laws and regulations regarding immigration, naturalization, and nationality, and brought them together into one comprehensive statute. The law retained the national-origin system of the Immigration Act of 1924, under which the United Kingdom, Germany, and Ireland were allotted more than two-thirds of the annual maximum quota of 154,657 persons (380 more than the previous maximum). The most significant changes effected by the McCarran-Walter Act were: (1) It removed race as a bar to immigration and naturalization; thus, countries whose citizens were previously ineligible for naturalization were assigned annual quotas of not fewer than 100 persons. (Far Eastern countries, particularly, had bitterly resented the exclusion policy.) (2) It removed discrimination between sexes. (3) It gave preference to aliens with special skills needed in the United States. (4) It provided for more rigorous screening of aliens in order to eliminate security risks and subversives, and for broader grounds for the deportation of criminal aliens.

The law aroused much opposition, mainly on the grounds that it discriminated in favor of northern and western European nations, and that its provisions for eliminating undesirable aliens were unduly harsh. It was passed over President Harry S. Truman's veto.

CHARLES S. CAMPBELL, JR.

McCARTHY-ARMY HEARINGS. In 1954 the Permanent Investigations Subcommittee of the Senate Committee on Government Operations, commonly known as the "McCarthy Committee," conducted hearings on the charges and countercharges arising out of its investigation (beginning October 1953) of alleged spying at the army base at Fort Monmouth, N.J. These hearings proved to be a crucial turning point in the career of Sen. Joseph R. McCarthy of Wisconsin. Although "McCarthyism" (a term that came to mean unsubstantiated charges of communism) continued to flourish, the hearings dealt his reputation a blow from which it never recovered.

The hearings were the outgrowth of McCarthy's

charges that the army was lax in ferreting out Communist spies. He claimed it was protecting those responsible for granting a left-wing dentist at Fort Monmouth a promotion and honorable discharge following the discovery of his political sympathies.

After some unsuccessful attempts to mollify McCarthy and have him call off his investigation, Robert T. Stevens, the secretary of the army, charged that McCarthy and his subcommittee's chief counsel, Roy M. Cohn, had intervened to obtain special treatment for Private G. David Schine, the recently drafted son of a millionaire hotel chain owner who, as a good friend of Cohn, had acted as a sometime subcommittee "expert" on communism. The army charged that, having failed to obtain an officer's commission for Schine, McCarthy and his staff were using the Fort Monmouth hearings to harass the army into granting Schine an assignment to the subcommittee in New York rather than the overseas tour he could normally expect. McCarthy and Cohn then charged that the army was, in effect, holding Schine "hostage" in an effort to force them to abandon their investigation of subversion.

McCarthy temporarily gave up his seat on his own subcommittee to allow it to investigate the charges, insisting, however, on the right to cross-examine witnesses at any length. In return, the army was granted the same privilege. This privilege proved disastrous to McCarthy, for the hearings soon turned into a seemingly interminable shambles. The tone was set on the very first day (Apr. 22) when, during the reading of the army's charges against him, McCarthy repeatedly interrupted with "points of order" that merely presaged rambling, seemingly irrelevant speeches. Characteristically, he also challenged the testimony of the army's first witness, a high-ranking officer, with the apparently irrelevant (and false) charge that the officer's brother had been forced to resign from the State Department as a "security risk."

The hearings were shown daily on national television. As they dragged on, McCarthy's "points of order" and rambling, bulldogged, monotonic interjections became the object of widespread exasperation and (worse for his reputation as a serious enemy of dangerous Communists) standard fare of television and nightclub comedians. His vicious attacks on Maj. Gen. Ralph Zwicker, the highly decorated war hero who was the commanding officer at Fort Monmouth, shocked many Americans, raising questions about the nature of McCarthy's own vaunted "patriotism." Meanwhile, Cohn looked like McCarthy's *éminence grise,* whispering in McCarthy's ear and scowling at adversaries. Only too late, halfway through the hearings, did McCarthy and Cohn realize what was happening and begin an effort to project a new image.

Just as they seemed to be making headway in establishing a new, less sinister look, McCarthy made his major blunder. Angered by the cross-examination of Cohn by the army's wily old Boston counsel, Joseph N. Welch, McCarthy blurted out that he had information that one of the junior members of Welch's law firm had belonged to a left-wing lawyers' organization. Welch was prepared for the attack. Tears welling in his eyes, he said that until this moment, when McCarthy had tried to wreck the promising career of a brilliant young lawyer, he had not realized how cruel and reckless he could be. In a short statement redolent of sadness and bitterness, he lashed out at McCarthy and his methods, making him appear like a vicious bully. McCarthy himself was taken aback by Welch's emotional attack. Moreover, for the first time many Americans gained an insight into the kind of human tragedy McCarthy's "investigations" had caused. From then on, despite the efforts of McCarthy and Cohn to be on their best behavior, they were discredited in the eyes of a majority of the television viewers, if not in the eyes of a majority of the subcommittee.

After the subcommittee ended its thirty-six days of hearings, it issued four separate reports. The Republican-dominated majority report cleared both McCarthy and the army of most of the charges against them but agreed that Cohn had intervened inordinately to obtain special treatment for Schine. The army was at fault for not reporting his intervention, they said, and McCarthy was negligent in not controlling the actions of the subcommittee staff. Cohn was thereupon forced to resign (July 20) his position as chief counsel.

With McCarthy's prestige and public support greatly damaged by the hearings, his opponents in the Senate initiated hearings to censure McCarthy for contempt of the Senate Privileges and Elections Committee and for unwarranted abuse of Zwicker. The Zwicker charge was eventually dropped, but, by a vote of sixty-seven to twenty-two on Dec. 2, the Senate "condemned," but did not "censure," McCarthy.

[Richard H. Rovere, *Senator Joe McCarthy.*]

HARVEY LEVENSTEIN

McCONNELSVILLE ORDINANCE. Citizens of McConnelsville, Ohio, passed an ordinance in April 1869 for the purpose of restraining the liquor traffic.

This first ordinance proved unsatisfactory and a new one was unanimously adopted in September 1869. This was repealed in 1871 but was reenacted on Mar. 14, 1874. The later ordinance, which was taken to the Supreme Court and declared constitutional, was adopted in many cities and villages.

[T. W. Lewis, *History of Southeastern Ohio and the Muskingum Valley;* Charles Robertson, *History of Morgan County, Ohio.*]

HARLOW LINDLEY

McCORMICK REAPER. The machine with which the name of Cyrus Hall McCormick has always been associated had many inventors, notably Obed Hussey, who patented his machine in 1833, a year before the first McCormick patent, and whose machine was the only practicable one on the market before 1840. It was the McCormick reaper, however, that invaded the Middle West, where the prairie farmer was ready for an efficient harvester that would make extensive wheat growing possible. In 1847 McCormick moved from the Shenandoah Valley in Virginia, where the first machine was built, to Chicago.

Perhaps, as his biographer contends, McCormick, or his father, Robert McCormick, did most effectively combine the parts essential to a mechanical grain cutter. Other improvements came in the 1850's and 1860's—the self-raker, which dispensed with the job of raking the cut grain off the platform, and then the binder, first using wire to bind the sheaves and later twine. The first self-raker was sold in 1854, seven years before McCormick produced such a machine. The first wire binder was put on the market in 1873, two years before the McCormick binder. Through effective organization the McCormick reaper came to dominate the field.

[H. N. Casson, *The Romance of the Reaper;* Victor S. Clark, *History of Manufactures in the United States;* W. T. Hutchinson, *Cyrus Hall McCormick.*]

ERNEST S. OSGOOD

McCRAY V. UNITED STATES, 195 U.S. 27 (1904). An act of Congress imposing a prohibitory tax of ten cents per pound on artificially colored oleomargarine was upheld by the Supreme Court in *McCray* v. *United States* as a valid exercise of the constitutional power to lay taxes.

[Charles K. Burdick, *The Law of the American Constitution.*]

EARL E. WARNER

McCREA, JANE, MURDER OF. Jane McCrea of Fort Edward, N.Y., was seized by some Indians in 1777 and accidentally shot when her captors were pursued by the colonials. She was scalped by an Indian in revenge for losing the reward given for white prisoners. This act contributed to British Gen. John Burgoyne's defeat, for the frontiersmen were greatly aroused and rallied to support Horatio Gates, general in the Continental army and in command of Fort Ticonderoga. Many Indians deserted Burgoyne, angered by his orders to end murder and pillage, leaving the English without sufficient scouts or guides.

[W. L. Stone, *The Campaign of Lt. Gen. John Burgoyne.*]

NELSON VANCE RUSSELL

McCULLOCH V. MARYLAND (4 Wheaton 316) was decided by the Supreme Court of the United States on Mar. 6, 1819. Congress had incorporated the second Bank of the United States, a branch of which was established in Baltimore. The state of Maryland required all banks not chartered by the state to pay a tax on each issuance of bank notes. When James W. McCulloch, the cashier of the Baltimore branch of the bank, issued notes without paying the tax, Maryland brought suit. Two questions were involved in the case: first, whether Congress had power under the Constitution to establish a bank and, second, whether Maryland could impose a tax on this bank.

Chief Justice John Marshall wrote the opinion for a unanimous court upholding the power of Congress to charter a bank as a government agency and denying the power of a state to tax the agency. Marshall's discussion broadly interpreting the powers of Congress is still a classic statement of the implied powers of the federal government. Congress has been granted the power "to make all laws which shall be necessary and proper for carrying into execution" the expressed powers in the Constitution. Since the Constitution empowers the government to tax, borrow, and engage in war, Congress by incorporating a bank was creating the means to attain the goals of these powers. The chief justice phrased the basic point as follows: "Let the end be legitimate, let it be within the scope of the Constitution, and all means which are appropriate, which are plainly adapted to that end, which are not prohibited, but consist with the letter and spirit of the Constitution, are constitutional." Along with this principle Marshall expounded the notion of federal supremacy, noting that the national government "though limited in its powers, is supreme within its sphere of action."

This led to the second question in the case, the power of the state of Maryland to tax a branch of the U.S. bank located in that state. The answer of the

Court was the sum total of several propositions. The power of the federal government to incorporate a bank had been established; the supremacy of the federal government in legal conflicts with state authority had likewise been set forth; and there was agreement that "the power to tax involves the power to destroy." It followed from all of this that an admittedly legal function of the federal government could not be subjected to possible destruction by an inferior government through taxation. The state tax was void.

[A. J. Beveridge, *The Life of John Marshall;* Charles Warren, *The Supreme Court in United States History.*]

PAUL C. BARTHOLOMEW

McDONALD'S EXPEDITION (1774). Angus McDonald, a Scotsman living at Winchester, Va., responded to the call by John Murray, Lord Dunmore, for an expedition against the hostile Indians. Enrolling 400 militia, he left Wheeling on July 26 and marched ninety miles across country to the Shawnee villages on the Muskingum River. The Indians had previously deserted these villages, but had returned and were in ambush. After a skirmish they retreated; the whites then cut up the standing corn and retired. The expedition only led to fresh hostilities by the Shawnee.

[R. G. Thwaites and L. P. Kellogg, *Dunmore's War.*]

LOUISE PHELPS KELLOGG

MACDONOUGH'S LAKE CHAMPLAIN FLEET. When Lt. Thomas Macdonough took command of the American naval force on Lake Champlain on Sept. 12, 1812, it consisted of two gunboats. By acquisition and construction he gradually built it up to approximately a dozen active vessels, two or three of which compared favorably with some of the famous seagoing warcraft of the period. Macdonough was commissioned master commandant in July 1813, and after a few minor brushes with the British, in which no serious damage was done to either side, he went into winter quarters at Vergennes, Vt., on Otter Creek to prepare for the 1814 campaign. A heavy English attack by land and water from Canada was pending. Ships were built and stores accumulated to meet it. To maintain control of the lake was imperative. On Apr. 14, 1814, the British fleet appeared off the mouth of Otter Creek, but was driven away by a land battery. The British advance came in September. Macdonough met the English fleet on Sept. 11, 1814, off Cumberland Head, near Plattsburgh, N.Y., where between 15,000 and 20,000 British and American

troops had joined battle. The American fleet consisted of fourteen battlecraft, mounting eighty-six guns and carrying 882 men. The British had sixteen fighting vessels, ninety-two guns, and approximately 937 men. The fight, one of the most bitter naval engagements of the war, was won by Macdonough through superior seamanship and strategy.

[Theodore Roosevelt, *Naval War of 1812.*]

LEON W. DEAN

McDOWELL, BATTLE AT (May 8, 1862). The combined Confederate forces of Gen. Thomas J. ("Stonewall") Jackson and Gen. Edward Johnson gained a decisive victory in the engagement at McDowell, Va. Union forces were compelled to retreat toward Franklin, suffering the loss of great quantities of stores and ammunition.

[R. U. Johnson and C. C. Buel, eds., *Battles and Leaders of the Civil War,* vol. II.]

ROBERT S. THOMAS

MACEDONIAN. In 1821 Chilean forces in southern Peru under Lord Thomas Cochrane seized $70,400 in silver from the captain of the American merchant ship *Macedonian,* asserting that it was Spanish property. Twenty years later the United States submitted a claim for repayment. After a long diplomatic controversy, the matter was arbitrated by the king of Belgium, who, on May 15, 1863, awarded the American owners three-fifths of the amount claimed.

[J. B. Moore, *International Arbitrations,* vol. II.]

DANA G. MUNRO

McFADDEN BANKING ACT of Feb. 25, 1927, permitted national banks to operate home-city branch offices in cities in which the state banks were allowed similar privileges. It also tended to delimit the growth of out-of-town branches by providing that no state bank that was a member of the Federal Reserve System might establish such a branch after date of passage of the act, and that no nonmember bank might join the Federal Reserve System, after the same date, without relinquishing any out-of-town branches established after that date. The act also changed the restrictions on real estate loans of national banks and provided indeterminate charters for national and Federal Reserve banks.

[F. A. Bradford, *Money and Banking.*]

FREDERICK A. BRADFORD

McGILLIVRAY INCIDENT. On Aug. 7, 1790, Alexander McGillivray and other Creek chiefs signed two treaties in New York with Henry Knox, sole American commissioner. The treaties, one public and one secret, had to do with peace, boundary, and trade and abrogated, in effect, the Creek-Spanish Treaty of Pensacola (June 1784). McGillivray was commissioned an American brigadier general, with a salary of $1,200 a year, twice his Spanish salary as Indian *comisario*.

Creek and Spanish opposition prevented ratification of these treaties. Spanish intrigues, including gradually raising his *comisario* salary almost sixfold, finally induced McGillivray to sign a convention with Barón Francisco Luis Héctor de Carondelet on July 6, 1792, abrogating the New York treaties. McGillivray's death on Feb. 17, 1793, left both Spanish and American treaties unratified.

[J. W. Caughey, *McGillivray of the Creeks;* A. P. Whitaker, "Alexander McGillivray," *North Carolina Historical Review,* vol. 5.]

ELIZABETH HOWARD WEST

McGUFFEY'S READERS formed a series of textbooks that molded American literary taste and morality, particularly in the Middle West, from 1840 until the early 20th century. The total sales reached 122 million copies by 1920. Only the Bible and *Webster's Spelling Book* have enjoyed equal acceptance in the United States. William Holmes McGuffey undertook the preparation of the Eclectic Series of school readers at the request of Winthrop B. Smith, a Cincinnati publisher interested in books adapted to the western schools. The *First Reader* (1836) followed the conventional pattern of readers, as indeed did its successors. Its fifty-five lessons with accompanying pictures taught principles of religion, morality, and patriotism. The *Second Reader* (1836) contained eighty-five lessons and sixteen pictures. It included considerable lore about nature, games and sports, manners, and attitudes toward God, relatives, teachers, companions, unfortunates, and animals. Here the pioneer youth found a code of social behavior to carry him safely through any experience. This book plagiarized *Worcester's Readers;* in 1838 damages were paid and the offending pages changed. In 1837 the *Third Reader* and *Fourth Reader,* for older pupils, completed the series. The *Third,* with only three pictures, contained many rules for oral reading. The *Fourth,* an introduction to standard British and American literature, elaborated the objectives of the whole series, the ability to read aloud with sense, clearness, and appreciation. Several revisions were made. In 1844 a *Fifth Reader* was added; in 1857 the material was regraded and a *Sixth Reader* (by Alexander H. McGuffey, a brother) and a *High School Reader* were added; in 1879 the books were completely remade; and in 1901 and 1920 the series was recopyrighted with slight changes.

The popularity of the McGuffey Readers arose partly from the happy adaptation of the substance to frontier interests. The lessons enforced proverbial wisdom, advising accuracy, honesty, truthfulness, obedience, kindness, industry, thrift, freedom, and patriotism. The problems of the world were simplified, so that in the end right always conquered and sin or wrong was always punished. In defense of the many religious selections McGuffey wrote: "In a Christian country that man is to be pitied who at this day can honestly object to imbuing the minds of youth with the language and spirit of the word of God."

[H. C. Minnich, *William Holmes McGuffey and His Readers.*]

HARRY R. WARFEL

MACHAULT, FORT, was built by the French under Chabert Joncaire on the site of Franklin, Pa. (*see* Venango), in 1754. It served as a link in their chain of communications from Lake Erie to the Ohio River. The fort was abandoned along with other small posts in western Pennsylvania when the loss of Fort Niagara in 1759 cut off communications with Canada.

[F. H. Severance, *An Old Frontier of France.*]

SOLON J. BUCK

McHENRY, FORT, built in 1799 on a small island in Baltimore harbor at the time of the Quasi-War with France, was named for Secretary of War James McHenry. During the War of 1812 a British fleet in Chesapeake Bay bombarded the fort (Sept. 13, 1814). A spectator, Francis Scott Key, who watched through the night, was moved to write "The Star-Spangled Banner," which later became the national anthem of the United States. Subsequently the fort was used as a storage depot and an army headquarters post.

[B. C. Steiner, *The Life and Correspondence of James McHenry.*]

THOMAS ROBSON HAY

MACHINE, PARTY. For many Americans party machines and party bosses connote a bad, sinister, or undesirable image. The machine often conveys the image of an all-powerful and ruthless professional politician—the boss—who commands a small army of dedicated precinct and ward leaders. Moreover, the machine connotes a very small group that is in actual control of the organization and aims at perpetuating its own power within the organization. The machine was built around the precinct and ward leaders, who maintained systematic communication with the voters in their neighborhoods.

Party machines varied in style from city to city. There were differences between the machines of Tammany Hall in New York, of William Hale ("Big Bill") Thompson in Chicago, of Thomas J. Pendergast in Kansas City, of Ed Crump in Memphis, of Abe Ruef in San Francisco, and of Richard J. Daley in Chicago. At the apex of the party machine are the city or state bosses. Not all machine bosses ran their organization for selfish motives. Many bosses entered the political arena solely with the idea of public service. On the other hand, there were those whose political machine was built on the spoils system, corruption, fraud, waste, and graft.

Certain broad preconditions in American society and political culture have aided the rise and continued existence of party machines controlled by professional politicians. These preconditions included the long ballot, the tradition of freewheeling individualism, the spoils system, the presence of unassimilated subgroups in the larger society, the lack of civic pride, opportunism, urban expansion, and the convention method of nomination.

The machine performed many services for its clientele in return for votes on election day. It focused on the personal needs of the diverse subgroups or minority groups in the community. The precinct and ward leaders provided rent money, fuel, food, and jobs for the needy families. They aided the diverse subgroups or ethnic minorities when they got in trouble with the state and its agents. Moreover, the party functionaries provided sympathy, hospitality, friendship, and social intercourse for the unassimilated minorities. Frank J. Sorauf, in *Political Parties in the American System,* has aptly described the functions of the machine:

> In its fabled heyday the urban machine in America offered the new arrivals to the cities a range of services that made it, in contemporary terms, a combination of employment agency, legal aid society, social worker, domestic relations counselor, and community social center. And in the new style, urban "club" parties in the American cities and suburbs, the parties cater to the social and intellectual needs of a mobile, educated, ideological, often isolated upper middle class.

As Robert K. Merton put it, the political machine performed an important social function of personalizing and humanizing all kinds of assistance to those who needed it.

The machine was interested in political patronage, which was contrary to the principle of selecting personnel on the basis of merit. Political bosses practiced "dishonest" and "honest" graft, both of which benefited the interests of particular individuals rather than the interests of the larger community.

The party machine began to decline in the middle of the 20th century, in part because of the efforts of reformers. Perhaps the advent of the civil service, with its recruitment procedures emphasizing the merit principle, reduced the sources of patronage. Also, modern methods of accounting and auditing have restricted the opportunities for "honest" graft. The voters have become more independent and sophisticated and increasingly disinterested in the rewards distributed by party politicians. Direct primaries, the nonpartisan system of elections, voting machines, and strict registration requirements have dealt severe blows to the political boss and his machine. In addition, the Social Security program, minimum-wage laws, and the various relief programs have alleviated some of the conditions on which the machine thrived. Finally, it should be noted that the nature of mature urban and technological society demands that close attention be paid to the experts and urban planners. All these determining factors have taken away from the political machine the opportunity to serve as a center for charity and employment in return for political support.

Although the party machine and the political boss have declined, the urban machine and its functionaries continue to exist in some American cities. The events at the Democratic National Convention in Chicago in the summer of 1968 called to the attention of many millions of Americans the political machine of Cook County, Ill., and its political boss, Mayor Richard J. Daley.

[Hugh A. Bone, *American Politics and the Party System;* Lyle W. Dorsett, *The Pendergast Machine;* Charles Garrett, *The LaGuardia Years;* Mike Royko, *Boss: Richard J. Daley of Chicago.*]

GEORGE S. MASANNAT

MACHINE GUNS. The first machine gun, the *mitrailleuse,* was designed in 1851 in Belgium, but the weapon is largely a product of American inventors. In 1862 Dr. Richard J. Gatling patented a gun with six barrels that rotated around a central axis by a hand crank. During the Civil War, conservative officers of the Union Ordnance Corps rejected Gatling's invention; however, the army purchased 100 improved Gatling guns in 1866. Although it was the best machine gun available, the Gatling was given a minor role as an auxiliary artillery weapon. Hiram S. Maxim, an American engineer, patented the first automatic machine gun in 1884. Powered by recoil energy, Maxim's gun was smaller, lighter, and easier to operate than the Gatling and later proved to be an excellent infantry weapon. In 1890 John M. Browning patented a machine gun powered by the expansion of powder gases. Although it failed commercially, Browning's gun introduced the principle of gas operation that is used by the U.S. M-60 machine gun and that constituted the last basic development in machine-gun design.

The interest of the army in machine guns was rekindled by the Spanish-American War, but it was not until 1916 that a regimental machine-gun company with 6 weapons was authorized. By November 1918, each infantry regiment had a 12-gun company and each division included 3 machine-gun battalions—a total of 168 weapons. Entering World War I with only 1,453 obsolescent machine guns of four different types, the army finished the war partially equipped with the superb new Browning machine guns. Browning's guns remained standard equipment for U.S. forces during World War II and the Korean War. Light machine guns were assigned to the rifle company, while .30-caliber water-cooled and .50-caliber machine guns were placed in the heavy weapons company in each infantry battalion. In 1945 the infantry division had 448 machine guns. During World War II Browning guns also served as the principal armament for fighter aircraft and as antiaircraft weapons for tanks and other vehicles. During the mid-1950's American ordnance officers procured a replacement for the Browning .30-caliber guns; designated the M-60, this weapon is distributed at the infantry platoon level. Through continued physical and doctrinal development, the machine gun has gradually shifted from classification as an artillery weapon to the backbone of infantry firepower.

[George M. Chinn, *The Machine Gun*, vol. 1.]
DAVID ARMSTRONG

MACHINE TOOLS, part of a larger classification of power-driven, nonportable metalworking machines. There are many processes by which metals may be shaped: hammering, stamping, punching, forging, bending, shearing, rolling, and extruding. The distinctive characteristic of machine tools—whether they be lathes, borers, drilling machines, milling machines, planing machines, or grinding machines—is that they employ a cutting tool and are used to impart shape to metal objects by the progressive cutting away of chips.

This characterization, while technically adequate, in no way conveys the historical importance of this class of machinery. Machine tools played a strategic role in the industrialization process because they constituted the primary method employed in the precision shaping of large quantities of metal products. The Industrial Revolution of the 19th century centered upon the exploitation of unprecedented quantities of metal—primarily iron—products. But a society that relied increasingly on the use of metals and machinery needed methods for shaping metal to precise specifications and tolerances. Traditional craftsmen, using tools controlled and guided by the human hand and eye, were obviously inadequate. Industrialization required reliable techniques for shaping metals not only with increasing precision but also at progressively lower and lower cost. Machine tools, historically, were central in fulfilling that need. America did not originate the machine tool, but it did lead the world in the application of these tools to novel production methods that played a major role in the development of modern industrial technology.

In the first few decades of the 19th century a group of British engineers and machinists, responding to the growing need for techniques for shaping metal products, developed the main categories of modern machine tools. The machinist, working with such equipment as hammer, chisel, and file, gave way by midcentury to the machine-tool operator, employing engine lathes equipped with slide rests, boring machines, planers, and shapers. The basic British inventions were transferred to America, where mechanics and engineers soon began to make their own unique contributions to the growing pool of machine-tool techniques.

As late as the 1820's no separate category of American firms specializing in the production of machine tools existed. The machines were typically made in the workshops of factories that were engaged in producing a final product, such as textiles or firearms. These workshops at first produced machinery to serve the requirements of their own firms. The more successful workshops sometimes produced machinery on order from other firms. By the 1840's the demand for machinery in many sectors of the economy was great enough for the manufacture of machine tools to begin to be a specialized activity of firms engaged solely in their production. The pattern in subsequent decades was for the number of firms to grow and for individual firms to specialize in a narrow range of products. In some cases this meant that a firm produced only one type of machine tool with perhaps minor modifications with respect to size, auxiliary attachments, or implements. By 1900 the U.S. Bureau of the Census made the following observations:

> In late years . . . manufacturers starting in this branch of industry [metalworking machinery] have very generally limited their operations to the production of a single type of machine, or at the most to one class embracing tools of similar types. For example, there are large establishments in which nothing is manufactured but engine lathes, other works are devoted exclusively to planers, while in others milling machines are the specialty. This tendency has prevailed in Cincinnati perhaps more than in any other city, and has been one of the characteristic features of the rapid expansion of the machine-tool industry in that city during the past ten years. During the census year there were in Cincinnati 30 establishments devoted to the manufacture of metal-working machinery, almost exclusively of the classes generally designated as machine tools, and their aggregate product amounted to $3,375,436. In 7 shops engine lathes only were made, 2 were devoted exclusively to planers, 2 made milling machines only, drilling machines formed the sole product of 5 establishments, and only shapers were made in 3 shops.

By 1914 there were over 400 machine-tool manufacturers in the United States.

The unique American contributions to machine tools arose out of techniques developed to meet special requirements. Although textile manufacturers and firearms makers were the earliest substantial users of machine tools, each of a series of subsequent technological innovations—for example, the railroads in the 1830's and later, the sewing machine in the 1850's, the bicycle toward the end of the 19th century, and the automobile in the opening decades of the 20th century—generated its own production problems and therefore its own machine-tool requirements.

America's most important contributions to machine-tool design and operation—Thomas Blanchard's profile lathe, turret lathes, milling machines, drilling and filing jigs, taps and gauges—were associated with specialized, high-speed machinery devoted to the production of standardized components of complex products. This system of interchangeability of parts is feasible only if individual components can be produced in very large quantities.

It requires a high degree of standardization of the final product, as well as the ability to produce individual components with a high degree of precision. When these conditions have been achieved, the tedious, time-consuming, and expensive processes of fitting can be replaced by the rapid, progressive assembly of parts that readily fit together without any need for adjustment. These principles will be recognized as underlying much of the mass-production technology of the 20th century. They were sufficiently well developed in the American firearms industry in the first half of the 19th century for the method to be referred to by British observers, at the London Crystal Palace Exhibition in 1851, as the "American system of manufactures." American innovations in machine-tool design and operation were an essential element in the emergence and perfection of this new system of industrial production.

[Joseph Wickham Roe, *English and American Tool Builders;* L. T. C. Rolt, *A Short History of Machine Tools;* Nathan Rosenberg, "Technological Change in the Machine Tool Industry, 1840–1910," *Journal of Economic History,* vol. 23 (1963).]

NATHAN ROSENBERG

McINTOSH, FORT, on the north bank of the Ohio River within the limits of the present Beaver, Pa., was built in 1778 by Gen. Lachlan McIntosh as a base for a projected expedition against Detroit. From October of that year to the following spring it was the headquarters of the Western Department of the Continental army. In 1783 the fort was transferred by the War Department to the state of Pennsylvania, and in 1788 it was demolished.

[J. H. Bausman, *History of Beaver County, Pa.*]

SOLON J. BUCK

McINTOSH, FORT, TREATIES OF. After the second Treaty of Fort Stanwix in 1784 it was thought desirable to extinguish the claims of western Indian tribes to some of the lands covered by the Iroquois cession. United States and Pennsylvania commissioners therefore met at Fort McIntosh with representatives of the Wyandot, Delaware, Chippewa, and Ottawa. By the treaty signed on Jan. 21, 1785, these tribes ceded much of what is now the state of Ohio and agreed to give hostages for the return of prisoners taken during the Revolution. By the Pennsylvania treaty, signed on Jan. 25, the Wyandot and Delaware, for a consideration of goods worth $2,000, deeded to Pennsylvania the lands previously claimed by them within the limits of that state. Many of the western Indians later repudiated these treaties, and stable peace in the region involved was not secured until the Treaty of Greenville of 1795.

[J. H. Bausman, *History of Beaver County, Pa.*]

SOLON J. BUCK

MACKENZIE'S TREATY. Kenneth Mackenzie, director of the Upper Missouri Outfit of John Jacob Astor's American Fur Company, anxious to keep the rich domain under his governorship open to his traders, arranged a peace between warring Indian tribes. This treaty between the Blackfoot and Assiniboine was signed at Fort Union, N.Mex., in 1831. It pledged the two tribes and certain related groups to perpetual peace, thus opening a large section of the upper Missouri country to exploitation by the American Fur Company.

[H. M. Chittenden, *History of the Fur Trade in the Far West.*]

THEODORE G. GRONERT

MACKEREL FISHERIES occupy a place in the development of New England only less prominent than that of the cod fisheries. The first public free school, opened in 1671, received aid directly from the profits of the mackerel fishery of Cape Cod, Mass. Mackerel supplemented codfish as an important commodity in the profitable trade with the West Indies during the 18th century. However, the taking of the mackerel lagged far behind that of cod until after the conclusion of the Convention of 1818 with England. The failure of this instrument to provide facilities for the mackerel fisheries became an important factor in the fisheries question when Americans began sending large mackerel fleets to the Gulf of Saint Lawrence. In 1840 Gloucester passed Boston as the leading mackerel port. To Gloucester went the credit for the introduction of such improvements as the clipper fishing schooner. The adoption about the middle of the century of the purse seine enabled the mackerel vessels to fish profitably off the New England coast. Fishing vessels also went as far south as Cape Hatteras, N.C., to take mackerel. The fisheries reached their height in the decade from 1880 to 1890, after which they suffered an abrupt decline. The varying abundance of the Atlantic mackerel from year to year has often determined the extent of the industry on the Atlantic coast. With the settlement of the Pacific coast and Alaska, the Pacific mackerel became a commercially important product, and the annual catch gradually surpassed that of the Atlantic mackerel.

In 1970, 57 million pounds of mackerel, valued at $2 million, were caught by U.S. fishermen; 622,000 pounds of the total catch came from Alaska. (In 1950 the total catch exceeded 165 million pounds.) Catches by Japanese and Norwegian fishermen meet more of the world's mackerel requirements; in 1970 the United States exported only 98,000 pounds (valued at $20,000).

[G. B. Goode and others, *Materials for a History of the Mackerel Fishery;* Raymond McFarland, *A History of the New England Fisheries.*]

F. HARDEE ALLEN

MACKINAC, STRAITS OF, AND MACKINAC ISLAND, formerly the **Straits of Michilimackinac** and **Michilimackinac Island.** The waters of lakes Michigan and Superior unite with Lake Huron by the Straits of Mackinac and the Saint Marys River. Lying at the crossroads of the upper Great Lakes, in the middle of the straits and within striking distance of the outlet of the Saint Marys, is Mackinac Island, widely famed for its scenic beauty and as a summer resort. When waterways were the chief highways of travel it was renowned as a strategic center of military and commercial operations.

Historically, the Indian name Michilimackinac, and its shortened form, Mackinac, applies not only to the straits and to the adjacent mainland, but also specifically to three distinct place sites—the island, Saint Ignace on the northern mainland, and Mackinaw City on the southern mainland. Although today the final syllables of both island and mainland names—*nac* and *naw*—are pronounced alike (rhyming with "paw"), originally the French pronounced *nac* as they spelled it (rhyming with "pack").

French rule was established at Mackinac in the 1660's. The French missionary Claude Dablon wintered in 1670 with the Huron, and in 1673 Louis Jolliet launched his successful search for the Mississippi River from Mackinac. The first marine disaster on the Great Lakes occurred at Mackinac in 1679, when the *Griffon,* the ship of Robert Cavelier, Sieur de La Salle, vanished. British rule was established in 1761, and during the Revolution the British moved their fort from Mackinaw City to Mackinac Island. The United States gained possession of Mackinac by the Treaty of Paris of 1783, but during the War of 1812 the British forced the surrender of the garrison and Fort Mackinac was in British hands until 1815.

After the war and until the 1830's Mackinac Island

was the center of John Jacob Astor's fur trading business. The advent of the railroad and the decline of the fur trade wrought the doom of Mackinac as a military and commercial center. Since then it has been promoted as a summer resort. In 1895 most of Mackinac Island was made a state park, and it has retained its turn-of-the-century setting by banning automobiles from the island.

Construction of the Mackinac Bridge, from Mackinaw City over the straits to a point near Saint Ignace, began in July 1954 and the bridge was opened in November 1957. It connects the upper and lower peninsulas of Michigan. The population of Mackinac Island in 1970 was 517.

[M. M. Quaife, "The Romance of the Mackinac Country," *Michigan History Magazine,* vol. 13; E. O. Wood, *Historic Mackinac.*]

M. M. QUAIFE

MACKINAW BOAT, a light, strongly built, flat-bottomed boat, pointed at both ends. It was used for travel and more especially for the transportation of goods on the rivers of the interior of the North American continent. Mackinaw boats varied greatly in size; they were commonly propelled by oars and, when conditions permitted, by a sail. Apparently the Mackinaw boat was adapted from the Indian Northwest canoe, long the favorite vehicle of the fur trader and explorer.

M. M. QUAIFE

McLANE-OCAMPO TREATY, between the United States and Mexico, was signed on Dec. 14, 1859. Its terms granted the United States right of way over the Isthmus of Tehuantepec, including the right to transport troops across the isthmus and other parts of Mexico. It also provided for reciprocal trade relations and for a loan of $4 million by the United States to Mexico. The treaty was ratified by Mexico, but not by the United States.

[William R. Manning, *Diplomatic Correspondence of the United States, Inter-American Affairs, 1831–1860,* vol. IX.]

N. ANDREW N. CLEVEN

McLEOD CASE arose out of the arrest at Lockport, N.Y., of Alexander McLeod, deputy sheriff of Niagara, Upper Canada, on Nov. 12, 1840, on charges of arson and of murdering Amos Durfee when the *Caroline,* an American steamship being used by Canadian rebels to bring supplies from New York to Canada, was destroyed on Dec. 29, 1837, by order of the Canadian authorities. Despite British demands for McLeod's release on the ground that the destruction of the *Caroline* was a public act, the New York Supreme Court held that he had been rightfully indicted for murder and remanded him for trial in a lower court, where he was acquitted on Oct. 12, 1841, by proving an alibi.

Meanwhile much excitement was generated in England over a bellicose report on foreign affairs in Congress, and the New York court's decision. Minor naval preparations for war were undertaken in case of McLeod's execution. Both federal and New York State governments took every precaution to safeguard McLeod's person. In both the United States and Canada additional appropriations were made to strengthen border defenses. To prevent jurisdictional conflicts in similar cases in the future, a congressional act of 1842 provided for the removal of an accused alien from a state court to a federal court on a writ of habeas corpus.

[J. M. Callahan, *American Foreign Policy in Canadian Relations;* Alastair Watt, "The Case of Alexander McLeod," *Canadian Historical Review,* vol. 12 (1931).]

ALBERT B. COREY

McLOUGHLIN LAND CLAIM. Dr. John McLoughlin, a chief factor of the Hudson's Bay Company, laid claim in 1829 to the land at the falls of the Willamette River, where he later platted Oregon City. Because of disputed national possession until 1846 (*see* Oregon Question) all land claims rested on squatters' rights. As a nonresident, McLoughlin found his claim contested by a group of early settlers; the contest was settled by a compromise. Even after he became a resident of Oregon City in 1846 his claim was disputed, and by the terms of the federal law known as the Donation Land Law of 1850 a portion of McLoughlin's claim was given to a rival claimant. The remainder, with its valuable waterpower rights, was given to the territory of Oregon for the benefit of a university. This injustice was not corrected within McLoughlin's lifetime, but the land claim was restored to his heirs by an act of the state legislature in 1862.

[Charles H. Carey, *A General History of Oregon.*]

ROBERT MOULTON GATKE

McNAMARA CASE. Efforts of union labor to organize Los Angeles culminated on Oct. 1, 1910, in the bombing of the plant of the *Times,* which had campaigned for an open shop. Twenty persons were killed, and the building demolished. Labor leaders claimed the explosion was due to escaping gas, but James B. McNamara, his brother John J. McNamara, and Ortie McManigal, an accomplice, were arrested and charged with the crime. McManigal confessed, but the brothers pleaded "not guilty."

After their arrest, the prisoners became symbols of labor's struggle against capital, and their trial was a national issue. Employers' organizations supported the prosecution, while the American Federation of Labor issued an official appeal to the working class to stand by the McNamaras. Samuel Gompers visited the brothers and declared the trial a "frame-up." McNamara defense leagues raised a large fund, which enabled the brothers to hire Clarence Darrow as defense attorney.

The trial began on Oct. 11, 1911, coinciding with a heated political campaign in Los Angeles. It proceeded slowly, and was marked by the arrest of two of Darrow's agents on charges of jury bribing. After asserted negotiations with the prosecution, the defense on Dec. 1 withdrew its pleas of "not guilty." James B. McNamara pleaded guilty to bombing the *Times,* and John J. McNamara to bombing the Llewellyn Iron Works, a Los Angeles concern. They were sentenced to life imprisonment and fifteen years, respectively. Their confessions were a decided blow to the organized labor movement throughout the country.

[Louis Adamic, *Dynamite, The Story of Class Violence in America.*]

FRANK FREIDEL

McNARY-HAUGEN BILL had for its purpose the rehabilitation of American agriculture by raising the domestic prices of farm products. At the end of 1920, overexpansion of agricultural lands, the decline of foreign markets, the effects of the protective tariff, and the burdens of debt and of taxation had created a serious agricultural depression. It grew steadily worse in the middle 1920's. The basic idea of the McNary-Haugen, or equalization-fee, plan was to segregate the amounts required for domestic consumption from the exportable surplus. The former were to be sold at the higher domestic price (world price plus the tariff), using the full advantage of the tariff rates on exportable farm products, and the latter at the world price. The difference between the higher domestic price and the world price received for the surplus was to be met by the farmers of each commodity in the form of a tax

or equalization fee. The legislation was before Congress from 1924 to 1928. It received powerful and united support from agricultural interests in 1927 and in 1928, respectively, when it passed both houses, only to meet two vigorous vetoes by President Calvin Coolidge.

[Paul Murphy, "The New Deal Agricultural Problem and the Constitution," *Agricultural History,* vol. 29 (1955); Theodore Saloutos and John D. Hicks, *Twentieth Century Populism: Agricultural Discontent in the Middle West, 1900–1939.*]

THOMAS S. BARCLAY

MACOMB PURCHASE. In accordance with an act of the legislature for the sale and disposition of lands of the state of New York, Alexander Macomb contracted with the commissioners in 1791 for the purchase of 3,635,200 acres of land in the present counties of Saint Lawrence, Franklin, Jefferson, Lewis, and Oswego, at eight pence per acre. The application was accepted and a patent issued to Macomb who, soon becoming financially embarrassed, deeded the tract to William Constable and others.

[E. B. O'Callaghan, *Documentary History of New York,* vol. III.]

ROBERT W. BINGHAM

MACON. *See* **Dirigibles.**

MACON'S BILL NO. 2 was enacted by Congress on May 1, 1810, to compel Great Britain and France, the major belligerents, to stop their illegal seizures of American commercial vessels. Designed as a substitute for the unsuccessful Nonintercourse Act, it forbade British and French armed vessels to use American waters, unless forced in by distress, except to carry dispatches. The measure opened American trade to the entire world. If France removed its restrictions on neutral commerce by Mar. 3, 1811, and Great Britain failed to do so within three months, the president would continue to trade with the former and prohibit trade with the latter and vice versa.

[U.S. Congress, *American State Papers,* vol. III.]

GEORGE D. HARMON

MADISON, FORT, sometimes called Fort Bellevue, was built during the winter and spring of 1808–09, on the west side of the Mississippi River, where the city of Fort Madison, Iowa, now stands. Housing a garrison for the protection of a government post for

Indian trade (*see* Factory System, Indian), Fort Madison had from the beginning a precarious existence among tribes that were under the influence of English traders, and suffered repeated attacks both before and during the War of 1812. On Sept. 3, 1813, its garrison, out of firewood, food, and ammunition, and closely besieged by hostile Indians, set fire to the buildings and escaped through a trench to boats on the Mississippi River.

[Jacob Van der Zee, *Iowa and War.*]

KATE L. GREGG

MADISON COUNTY ANTISLAVERY WAR. The existing controversy over slavery in the border states frequently brought proslavery and antislavery forces face to face. This was the case in the so-called Madison County Antislavery War in 1859. Earlier in the decade an antislavery colony had been established in Berea in southern Kentucky under the leadership of Cassius M. Clay. With the aid of Rev. John G. Fee a union church was organized in 1853 and Berea School was founded in 1855. These moves were opposed by the community's slaveowners who were alarmed over the abolition doctrine preached by Fee, James S. Davis, John G. Hanson, and others and by the educating of blacks in the same school with whites. Opposition was intensified by John Brown's raid in October 1859. Mass meetings were held in Richmond, the county seat, and resolutions were passed that the abolitionists be driven out. On Dec. 23 an armed mob called at the homes of Fee and other antislavery families and ordered them to leave Kentucky under penalty of death. An appeal to Gov. Beriah Magoffin on Dec. 24 brought no protection. The antislavery families moved to Cincinnati, but Fee returned the next year to resume his abolitionist work. Again there was considerable excitement, and warfare similar to that in Kansas seemed imminent. Conditions eased only after Fee was forcibly removed to Ohio by slaveowners. The work of Berea School (later Berea College) was resumed in 1865 at the end of the Civil War.

[John G. Fee, *Autobiography;* John A. R. Rogers, *The Birth of Berea.*]

HENRY N. DREWRY

MADISON'S ISLAND, the name given, in honor of President James Madison, by Capt. David Porter to the island of Nuku Hiva in the Marquesas Islands in the south Pacific. Porter, commanding the U.S. frigate *Essex,* spent several weeks at Nuku Hiva in

1813, where he erected a fort and on Nov. 19 formally proclaimed U.S. sovereignty. The United States never ratified Porter's act of annexation, and the Marquesas Islands became a French colony in 1842.

[David Porter, *Journal of a Cruise Made to the Pacific Ocean by Captain David Porter in the U.S. Frigate Essex, in the Years 1812, 1813, and 1814.*]

JULIUS W. PRATT

MADISON SQUARE GARDEN. In 1879 William K. Vanderbilt took control of Gilmore's Garden in New York City and renamed it Madison Square Garden for its location on Madison Square (Madison Avenue and Twenty-sixth Street). Vanderbilt turned the exhibition hall into a center for athletic events. The limitations of the original structure soon necessitated construction of a new one, and Stanford White was commissioned to design a second Madison Square Garden, which rose on the site in 1890. (It was in the roof garden restaurant of this building that White was murdered by Harry K. Thaw in 1906.) The new Garden was capped by Augustus Saint-Gaudens' famous statue of Diana (now in the Philadelphia Museum of Art) and housed musical and theatrical performances, horse and dog shows, balls, circuses, public meetings, and athletic events, notably boxing.

In 1924 the holders of the mortgage on the land decided to tear down the Garden, whereupon George ("Tex") Rickard, a boxing promoter, organized a group to construct a third Madison Square Garden at Eighth Avenue and Fiftieth Street, to be designed by Thomas Lamb. Completed in 1925, the third Garden became the world's most famous sports arena, but it had outgrown its usefulness by the late 1950's. Consequently, on Nov. 3, 1960, plans were announced for the construction of a fourth Madison Square Garden, to be built atop Pennsylvania Station. Madison Square Garden Center, which includes a new Garden, a bowling center, the Felt Forum (a 5,000-seat amphitheater), and a twenty-nine-story office building, was completed in 1968. The fourth Garden is the home of New York's basketball, hockey, and tennis teams and continues to present major athletic events and musical performances.

LELAND S. LOWTHER

MADRID, TREATY OF, between Spain and Great Britain in 1670, provided for peace between the colonial possessions of the respective powers, excluding the subjects of each party from trade and navigation to the other's colonies. Thus by implication, Spain recognized for the first time the legal existence of British colonies in the New World over which it had hitherto (with Portugal, now annexed to Spain, 1581–1640) asserted a monopoly of sovereignty based on the papal decrees of 1493 and afterward, and the Treaty of Tordesillas of 1494.

[Francis Gardiner Davenport, *European Treaties Bearing on the History of the United States and Its Dependencies*, vol. II.]

SAMUEL FLAGG BEMIS

MADRID CONFERENCE of 1880 was the first international conference arising from imperialistic rivalry in Morocco, an antecedent of the Algeciras Conference. Great Britain and Spain tried to strengthen the sultan's government and to limit extraterritorial rights, especially that of protection to Moroccans in foreign employ. France, backed by Germany, insisted on earlier treaty rights. The conference accomplished little beyond a convention defining current practices. The United States, not closely involved, participated for the first time in a European political conference, partly because of humanitarian interest in the welfare of Moroccan Jews. Secretary of State William M. Evarts' instructions show a firm but moderate assertion of extraterritorial rights important to the United States in the Far East.

[S. F. Bemis, *A Diplomatic History of the United States*; J. B. Moore, *A Digest of International Law*.]

CHARLES C. GRIFFIN

MAFIA. *See* **Crime, Organized.**

MAFIA INCIDENT. On Oct. 15, 1890, David C. Hennessey, New Orleans chief of police, was assassinated at the gate of his house by a lurking group of men with sawed-off shotguns. Hennessey had been relentless and courageous in efforts to curb local groups that, using the name made infamous by a Sicilian secret society, Mafia, had a record of a dozen murders. His murder was certainly the work of such a group. Nineteen men were indicted, and nine of these were the first put on trial. The case made by the state was overwhelming. Yet the jury brought in a verdict of acquittal for four; a mistrial was declared for three; and two were cleared by direction of the judge, and by public feeling. There was strong conviction in New Orleans that improper influences had defeated elementary justice. A mass meeting of 6,000 to 8,000

people, led by prominent citizens, was held the next morning (Saturday, Mar. 14) at which the results of the trial were denounced. The mob marched from Canal and Saint Charles streets to the old Parish Prison, on what was then Congo (now Beauregard) Square. Eleven of the accused were lynched by the mob. Only three of the eleven were Italian subjects; the others were either naturalized citizens or had expressed the intention of becoming American citizens. The Italian government protested the lynchings, denounced the inaction of the New Orleans authorities, and demanded protection for the Italian colony in New Orleans and some form of indemnity for the families of those killed. When the United States did not meet these demands, and an investigation into the incident did not prosecute any of the mob, Italy recalled its minister; the United States then recalled its minister to Rome. Finally, in April 1892, President Benjamin Harrison instructed Secretary of State James G. Blaine to offer $25,000 to the families of the victims and expressed regrets to Italy for the incident. The Italian government accepted and full diplomatic relations were restored.

[John E. Coxe, "The New Orleans Mafia Incident," *Louisiana Historical Society*, vol. 20 (1937); John Higham, *Strangers in the Land: Patterns of American Nativism, 1860–1925*.]

PIERCE BUTLER

MAGAZIN ROYAL. *See* **Niagara, Carrying Place of.**

MAGAZINES. Magazine publishing in America began with the almost simultaneous appearance in 1741 of Andrew Bradford's *American Magazine, or Monthly View* and Benjamin Franklin's *General Magazine and Historical Chronicle*. Franklin indignantly alleged he had already begun to plan his publication when Bradford stole his idea; but it was not really a very serious matter, since neither magazine lasted a year. Bradford was able to bring out three issues, Franklin six, before both ceased publication. Since then, magazine publishing has remained a perilous venture, and it is no wonder Noah Webster remarked in 1788 that "the expectation of failure [was] connected with the very nature of a Magazine."

Conditions for magazine publishing at first made success nearly impossible. Such reading public as existed habitually read newspapers and books, very largely theology and the English classics, with some Greek and Latin. Mails were few and slow, and circulation by mail was thus difficult; newsstand circulation was so limited as to be nearly useless. Promotion was nearly impossible. National advertising, with its large profits, for all practical purposes did not exist. There were practically no writers or editors able to capture and hold the attention of a fairly wide public. Woodcuts or expensive metal engravings were the only possible illustrations.

In spite of difficulties, stubborn printers continued to undertake what proved to be short-lived ventures; and it was natural, since writers were few, that the reprint magazines, based mainly on clippings from British reviews, became fairly abundant. There seems to have been no difficulty about copyright, although a copyright statute had been on the books since the reign of Queen Anne. Reprint magazines, although fewer in number, continued far into modern times. *Littell's Living Age,* founded in 1844, was published for nearly a century. The *Literary Digest* lasted until its unfortunate prediction of President Franklin D. Roosevelt's defeat at the polls in 1936. *Reader's Digest,* originally a reprint magazine, still contains some reprinted material.

A change came as education became more widespread, enlarging the reading public; as printing processes, photography, and photoengraving improved; as the development of industry made national advertising, and thus financial profit, possible; and as improved postal organization and generous second-class mailing privileges for periodicals made distribution cheap and easy. Advertising, at first unimportant, became the main source of revenue for both magazines and newspapers as a huge advertising industry sprang up and became a major influence in American life. *Reader's Digest,* nevertheless, proved highly profitable for many years, even without advertising, which it began including in April 1955. Advertising was for a time regarded as faintly discreditable to a publication. As late as 1864, *Harper's Magazine* refused to carry any advertising except its own announcements of Harper books. The publishers felt seriously insulted when offered an $18,000 contract for sewing-machine advertising.

Among early magazine successes were *Godey's Lady's Book,* Robert Bonner's *New York Ledger,* and later "quality" magazines, such as *Century, Harper's, Scribner's, Atlantic,* and *Forum.* During the latter part of the 19th century, these were important influences in American literature and life, but they began to disappear fairly early in the 20th century as a mass culture arose, rigorous educational standards slackened, and many new distractions began to inter-

est and amuse the mass public. *Atlantic* and *Harper's* still remain, although much changed.

As the reading public became vastly larger and much less thoroughly educated, a group of elaborately illustrated popular magazines, with very large circulations justifying much profitable advertising, developed. The *Saturday Evening Post,* which traced a somewhat tenuous ancestry to one of Benjamin Franklin's 18th-century periodicals, developed into a successful and highly profitable "mass" magazine. *Liberty, Look, Life,* and *Collier's* developed enormous circulations.

The rise of radio and television has drawn off great numbers of possible readers and has provided an enormous market for advertising. The huge mass magazines have succumbed one by one to this competition, especially when a formidable rise in mailing and other costs developed in the early 1970's.

Successful news magazines, such as *Time* and *Newsweek,* continued; various university reviews more or less replaced the "serious" quality magazines; the *New Yorker* took the place of the older humorous magazines, making an especial point of avoiding their somewhat monotonous "he-she" jokes; and *Playboy* ventured into daring illustrations and text that would have been quite impossible even one generation earlier. Innumerable smaller magazines still represented the special interests of special groups.

[John Bakeless, *Magazine Making;* Frank Luther Mott, *History of American Magazines;* Lyon N. Richardson, *History of Early American Magazines;* Roland E. Wolseley, *The Magazine World;* James Playsted Wood, *Magazines in the United States.*]

JOHN BAKELESS

MAGAZINES, CHILDREN'S. The first American juvenile periodical was the *Children's Magazine* (Hartford, 1789), a work designed to supplement the schoolwork of students between the ages of seven and twelve and to lead children "from the easy language of the spelling books up to the more difficult style of the best writers." The rising Sunday-school movement produced the *Youth's Friend and Scholar's Magazine* (Philadelphia, 1823–64), the first of many such papers, some interdenominational and some denominational, devoted to inculcating religious truth through fiction, verse, and essay. Samuel G. Goodrich ("Peter Parley") founded *Parley's Magazine* in 1833 (New York) and eleven years later merged it with *Merry's Museum for Boys and Girls* (Boston, 1841–72), also established by him and edited between 1867 and 1870 by Louisa May Alcott. Lydia Maria Child's *Juvenile Miscellany* (1826–34) had an early success under her and for two more years under Sarah Josepha Hale.

Of special significance for authors and artists as well as for young readers were five famous magazines initiated in the 19th century. Longest lived was the *Youth's Companion* (Boston, 1827–1929), founded by Nathaniel P. Willis, a conservative Congregationalist anxious to exert a positive religious influence. *Our Young Folks* (Boston, 1865–73), edited by John T. Trowbridge, Mary Abigail Dodge ("Gail Hamilton"), and Lucy Larcom, published Louisa May Alcott, Thomas Bailey Aldrich, and Lucretia P. Hale. It merged with *St. Nicholas, An Illustrated Magazine for Young Folks,* in 1874. *The Little Corporal* (Chicago, 1865–74), under the editorship of Edward Eggleston and Emily C. H. Miller, also merged with *St. Nicholas,* in 1875. Extolled above all other juvenile periodicals, the monthly *St. Nicholas* (1873–1943) was founded and edited for over thirty years by Mary Mapes Dodge. Writers for adults as well as for children were encouraged to contribute to it: Rudyard Kipling; Mark Twain; Alfred, Lord Tennyson; Henry Wadsworth Longfellow; Bret Harte; Robert Louis Stevenson; Joel Chandler Harris; Ring Lardner; and William Cullen Bryant. Many later recognized novelists and poets sent youthful contributions to the famous "St. Nicholas League." Another popular 19th-century magazine was *Harper's Young People* (1879–95), which cared much for good writing and illustration, like the distinguished *Riverside Magazine* (1867–70), edited by the great Horace E. Scudder, who secured original, hitherto unpublished tales by Hans Christian Andersen.

Among the most successful periodicals of the 20th century was the *American Boy* (1899–1941), devoted chiefly to fiction (the *Youth's Companion* merged with it in 1929). Its emphasis upon achievement and the contemporary also characterizes the official scouting papers, *Boys' Life* (1911–) and the *American Girl* (1917–).

Later established were *Scholastic* (1920–), which was to serve classroom interests on four age levels. It bought *St. Nicholas* in 1940. *Story Parade* (1936–54) faced the problem of nearly every independent children's magazine, the difficulty of maintaining a large enough subscription list when readers are continually lost because they grow up. Periodicals initiated in 1973 include *Kids,* written by children; *Ebony Junior,* designed to meet black interests; and a literary magazine, *Cricket,* with the high

aims of securing the best in writing and art from both American and foreign contributors.

VIRGINIA HAVILAND

MAGDALENA BAY RESOLUTION, also known as the Lodge Corollary to the Monroe Doctrine. In 1911 a Japanese syndicate offered to buy a large tract of land on Magdalena Bay in Lower (Baja) California. Fearing that a foreign colony on the bay would endanger California and the Panama Canal, Sen. Henry Cabot Lodge, chairman of the Committee on Foreign Relations, introduced a "statement of policy, allied to the Monroe Doctrine," which was adopted by the Senate on Aug. 2, 1912, by a vote of fifty-one to four. This resolution declared that when "any harbor or other place in the American continents" is so located that its occupation "for naval or military purposes might threaten the communications or the safety of the United States," the United States could not without grave concern see that land pass into the possession of any corporation or association that would ensure its control by a non-American power. This was the first time the Monroe Doctrine was applied to an Asiatic power.

[Eugene K. Chamberlin, "The Japanese Scare at Magdalena Bay," *Pacific Historical Review,* vol. 24 (1955).]

WILLIAM SPENCE ROBERTSON

MAGEE-GUTIÉRREZ EXPEDITION. See **Gutiérrez-Magee Expedition.**

MAGEE-KEARNY EXPEDITION (July 1820). War Department plans for the simultaneous movement of troops up the Missouri River toward the Yellowstone River, and up the Mississippi to the mouth of the Saint Peters (Minnesota) River in 1819, contemplated contacts and close cooperation between the two forces in case of Indian hostilities (*see* Yellowstone River Expeditions). Col. Henry Atkinson's force, wintering at old Council Bluffs, Nebr., on Apr. 10, 1820, received orders to open roads from this camp to Chariton and to Col. Henry Leavenworth's post on the Saint Peters.

On July 2, 1820, Capt. Matthew J. Magee of the Rifles, commanding a detachment comprising a lieutenant, an engineer officer, and fifteen soldiers, and accompanied by Lt. Col. Willoughby Morgan and Capt. Stephen Watts Kearny, left Council Bluffs to lay out the road to Saint Peters. After traveling twenty-three days through unsettled, sparsely timbered country, the party reached Saint Peters and reported this route impracticable. The force returned to Saint Louis by boat (see Long's Explorations).

[Valentine M. Porter, ed., "Journal of Stephen Watts Kearny," *Missouri Historical Collections*, vol. III; Edgar B. Wesley, *Guarding the Frontier*.]

WILLOUGHBY M. BABCOCK

MAGNA CHARTA, or **Magna Carta.** By the early spring of 1215 England was in the throes of a civil war. King John's blundering foreign policy had disrupted the Angevin Empire and had alienated a considerable number of his former followers. His clash with Rome over the vacant See of Canterbury had outraged the nation's religious sentiments. More significant were his repeated violations of feudal and common law. The accumulative effect of these factors, plus unrivaled despotism, led to armed revolt by most of John's barons. Military success crowned the efforts of the latter and John capitulated at Runnymede on June 15, 1215. Here he gave his consent to the Magna Charta.

No document in all English history equals the Magna Charta, although none has been more misunderstood or misinterpreted. Stripped of its wording, the great charter was a treaty won by a victorious barony from a defeated king. In its essence, the charter simply meant that John, like all other Englishmen, was to be subject to the spirit and letter of the law. His past conduct was condemned; in the future he was to rule in accordance with law and custom. The charter was not a document of human liberties. It contained no reference to habeas corpus, jury trial in criminal cases, or Parliament's control over taxation. Several centuries were to pass before these basic rights became an integral part of England's organic law. Between the 13th and 17th centuries it was not thought that the Magna Charta had been drafted in the interests of the masses. Indeed, though it was frequently reissued during these years, it was gradually shoved into the background and ultimately forgotten. The civil conflicts attending the War of the Roses and the strong arm of the Tudors blotted out the memory of the Magna Charta. Contemporary literature of the Tudor period (1485–1603) is strangely silent about the charter, and William Shakespeare in *King John* made no reference to what probably was the most important event in the life of that monarch. Had the great dramatist known of the charter, he would hardly have passed over so significant an episode.

It remained for the Puritans, lawyers, and members of Parliament of the 17th century, in their contest with the Stuarts, to resurrect the Magna Charta and interpret it as an impregnable bulwark of democracy. Although they were wrong in their conclusions and laid the foundation of the myth of the Magna Charta, they fashioned it into an obstacle to arbitrary government and paved the way for the present constitutional monarchy. When the Puritans migrated to the New World they imbedded their ideas in American political philosophy. The Magna Charta was viewed in the United States as a priceless heritage, never to be lost sight of, and bravely to be defended. Historical research has removed the myth and fancy that have surrounded the charter, but its essential truths have become more significant than when John reigned. Human rights, individually or collectively, are not to be destroyed by arbitrary and despotic government; the law of the land is supreme and inviolable and must be respected; and no individual or government may transcend law.

[Anne Pallister, *Magna Carta*.]

W. E. GALPIN

MAGUAGA, BATTLE AT (Aug. 9, 1812). Commanding a force consisting of Michigan and Ohio volunteers and the Fourth Regular Infantry, Col. James Miller defeated a British and Indian force at Maguaga, Mich. Fighting with the British was the Shawnee chief Tecumseh, who had been commissioned a brigadier general in the British army for his part in this fight.

[Benson J. Lossing, *Pictorial Field Book of the War of 1812*.]

ROBERT S. THOMAS

MAHICAN. *See* **Mohegan and Mahican.**

MAIDEN'S ROCK, in Pepin County, Wis., is a picturesque rocky bluff overhanging the eastern shore of Lake Pepin. From this rock, according to an Indian legend long believed and possibly true, Winona (meaning "first-born girl child"), a comely Sioux maiden, hurled herself to death rather than marry an Indian brave of another tribe, probably a Winnebago, selected by her parents. The legend was first brought to the attention of the reading public in William H. Keating's narrative of Stephen H. Long's expedition to the Saint Peters River, published in 1823.

[F. Curtiss-Wedge, *Wabasha County, Minnesota*.]

RICHARD J. PURCELL

MAIL-ORDER HOUSES. In the mid-1970's several thousand establishments in the United States were engaged primarily in mail-order retailing, with sales accounting for approximately 1 percent of total U.S. retail volume. Total U.S. mail-order volume is substantially larger than the catalog sales of the mail-order houses as reported in the U.S. Census of Business, since numerous department and specialty stores supplement in-store volume through direct mail solicitation to selected groups of prospective customers. A rough measure of the breadth of interest in buying by mail is *The Catalogue of Catalogues* (1972).

Most mail-order houses sell limited lines of merchandise, although the recognized industry leaders (primarily headquartered in Chicago) are among the largest American companies and offer much broader lines than even the largest department store. Sears, Roebuck and Company (founded 1886) reported total corporate sales in excess of $10 billion in 1972; Montgomery Ward (founded 1872) is also a multibillion dollar business. Less than one-third of their total volume, however, is accounted for by catalog sales.

Agricultural expansion and the completion of a continental rail network after the Civil War supported the early growth of the great mail-order companies. These developments and the characteristic large-farm pattern of American agriculture provided a hospitable environment to fledgling companies that offered a variety of merchandise through periodical advertisements and catalogs to relatively isolated farm dwellers at comparatively low prices. Mail-order prosperity was further accelerated by the advent of rural free delivery at the turn of the century and the extension of the parcel post system beginning in 1913.

Mail-order buying offers easy access to a vast variety of merchandise and shopping convenience both for consumers located in rural communities with limited retail facilities and increasingly for urban consumers in traffic-congested areas. On the supply side, the major catalog houses are characterized by the economies of large-scale buying and selling, including the mechanization of order processing, handling, and shipping.

Traditionally, mail-order houses received customer orders by mail, processed them, and dispatched merchandise by parcel post, freight, or express. The general catalog was a "display case" from which customers selected merchandise. Present operating methods are characterized by a very large volume of telephone-order buying and selling—and, indeed, catalog-order desks and stores. Just as urbanization prompted the major mail-order companies to program further expansion through a system of retail stores to parallel the catalog, technological developments—notably the computer—stimulated the development of various special seasonal, promotional, and limited-line catalogs for distribution to special customer classes.

JOHN E. JEUCK

MAINE, the most northeasterly of the fifty states of the United States, was an official part of Massachusetts from the late 1600's to 1820, when it became the twenty-third state. It has an extremely long and irregular coastline, with numerous bays and inlets. Portland and Searsport have two of the finest deep-water ports on the Atlantic coast. Its approximately 31,500 square miles of territory make it about the size of the rest of New England combined.

Maine is believed to have been visited by French, British, and Portuguese explorers in the 1500's, but no attempts at permanent settlement were undertaken before the early 1600's, when almost simultaneously the British and French began colonization in the area southward from the Bay of Fundy. The French under Pierre du Guast, Sieur de Monts, and Samuel de Champlain established a small settlement on an island in the Saint Croix River in 1604. It failed after one miserable winter. The English under the auspices of Sir John Popham and Sir Ferdinando Gorges in August 1607 planted a colony on the lower reaches of the Kennebec River, but it too expired after only one winter. Gorges remained the chief English promoter of Maine settlement and in 1622 he and John Mason received a grant for all lands between the Merrimac and Kennebec rivers. The name Maine was first used in this grant. Maine is a perpetuation of the usage by sailors of the mainland to distinguish it from the numerous islands that dot the coast. In 1629 Mason and Gorges divided their lands and Gorges took the area between the Piscataqua and Kennebec rivers for his share. In the early days most settlements were populated directly from England and were largely confined to the area from Kittery to Casco Bay. Pemaquid, Georgetown, and Monhegan Island were notable exceptions.

The English civil war of the 1640's had an adverse effect on settlement from the mother country and afforded Massachusetts an opportunity to assert its influence and control as early as 1652. Temporarily displaced in 1664 by action of Charles II, Massachusetts reasserted its authority in 1668 and fortified it in 1677 by purchasing all claims of the Gorges family for £1,250. If James II had prevailed as king of England, events probably would have had a different outcome. However, James was driven from the throne and his successors, William and Mary, in 1691 granted a new charter to Massachusetts that confirmed its title to Maine.

The struggle between England and France for control of North America had a decisive influence on the course of Maine history. The first blood in the conflict was shed on Mount Desert Island in 1613, when Captain Samuel Argall destroyed a developing French post and Jesuit mission. The Indians, whose villages dotted the valleys of the principal rivers and whose numbers in 1600 were estimated to be somewhere between 25,000 and 60,000, were pawns in the struggle. Six wars were fought between the Indians and the English between 1675 and 1763. The French were active allies of the Indians in four of these wars. Although these allies in the early wars largely destroyed all English towns except Kittery, Indian power was so reduced by the end of the fourth war (mid-1720's) that the Indians were never again a serious menace. During King George's War in the 1740's and the French and Indian War (1754–63), Maine communities supplied considerable soldiery for the campaigns against Louisburg, the "Gibraltar of the West," and in New York Colony and Quebec. A Kittery native, William Pepperell, was the commander of the first expedition against Louisburg (1745) and was made a baronet for his successes.

The transfer of Canada from the French to the British in 1763 afforded Maine the long-awaited opportunity for expansion of settled territory and population. As a part of Massachusetts, Maine was active in defiance of the various measures imposed by the British as they tightened imperial control. The Sugar Act, Stamp Act, and Townshend Acts were greeted with evasion and violent opposition. Falmouth, as Portland was known until 1786, was in the forefront of defiance and was destroyed by British ships in October 1775 in partial retribution. During the revolutionary war, Benedict Arnold marched heroically through the Maine wilderness on his ill-fated expedition against Quebec. The first naval contest of the war, the battle of the *Margaretta,* was fought off Machias in June of 1775. In the summer of 1779 a monumental disaster occurred at Castine when Massachusetts tried, through amphibious assault, to recapture that town

from the British. The Treaty of Paris that ended the war created a boundary dispute between Maine and Canada that was not settled until the conclusion of the Webster-Ashburton Treaty in 1842.

Between the end of the revolutionary war and 1820, Maine's population increased severalfold and expanded into the backcountry of western and central Maine and along the coast and up the rivers of eastern Maine. This growth was accompanied by a growth of sentiment for statehood. Differences of opinion between the hardy Maine frontiersmen and the Boston capitalists and Federalists over land policies, taxes, representation in the legislature, internal improvements, banking, and commercial rights and privileges finally led to a successful campaign for separation in 1819. It was led by a self-made Bath entrepreneur, William King, who presided over Maine's constitutional convention and became the first governor in 1820.

Between 1820 and 1860, Maine's population doubled again, from about 300,000 to about 600,000. Most of the population were farmers and lumbermen. The Jeffersonian-Jacksonian party dominated politics until the mid-1850's, when Democrats were rent asunder by the questions of slavery in the United States and prohibition in Maine. An organized temperance movement began developing in Maine right after the War of 1812 and was in full swing between 1825 and 1837. Under the dynamic leadership of Neal Dow of Portland, Maine was the first state to adopt prohibition on a statewide basis (1851) and retained it until the early 1930's. Amply blessed with many navigable rivers, the state had its needs effectively served by water transportation until after the Civil War. For years Maine was the leading producer of wooden ships in America. Its clippers and downeasters and schooners were constructed in dozens of yards up the rivers and along the coast. Bath, Thomaston, Searsport, Bucksport, and Calais were among the leading towns that had yards. The *Red Jacket,* a clipper out of the Thomas yards at Rockland, in 1853 set the record for west-to-east passage from New York to Liverpool—thirteen days, one hour, and twenty-five minutes.

Maine railroading began in 1836 with the completion of the Bangor and Old Town Railroad, but as late as 1860 the state had less than 500 miles of railroad. The era of greatest construction was between 1865 and 1900, when the state was crisscrossed with railroads. Trackage reached its peak of 2,200 miles in 1919. In the first decade of the 19th century cotton and woolen textile mills made a modest appearance at several river towns in western Maine. The numbers and locations dramatically increased after the Civil War and textile making became the most important manufacturing activity. Cities like Biddeford, Lewiston, and Waterville were conspicuous as cotton communities, while Skowhegan, Brunswick, Wilton, Corinna, Dover-Foxcroft, and many others had impressive woolen mills. After 1900 a decline set in as mills began moving southward.

Although paper mills using rags were first established in the 1700's, it was not until the use of wood pulp was developed that Maine's pulp and paper industry mushroomed. In the years from 1880 to 1910, mills were constructed at many locations and new towns like Rumford and Millinocket sprang up. Soon pulp and paper surpassed textiles as the most important industry, and it remained so in the mid-1970's. The industry rests on the solid foundation of the Maine hardwood and softwood forests. The state is more than 86 percent forested, with more and more abandoned farmland being added to the forest each year.

Agriculture, which once featured the small subsistence farms, is now characterized by the large farm, with its dairy cattle, poultry, or potatoes. Fishing is relatively unimportant, with lobsters, clams, and herring as the principal products. There are few mineral resources in the state.

In 1856 the Republican party began a domination of politics that, except for the late 1870's, the early 1910's, and the depression years of the 1930's, lasted for a century. Beginning with the appearance of Edmund Muskie as governor in 1954, the Democratic party began a resurgence. Resting on the increasing role of the city, the maturing of the large Franco-American segment of society, reapportionment, the welfare state, and the increased activity of organized labor, an effective two-party system now exists in the state.

[Henry S. Burrage, *Beginnings in Colonial Maine;* Louis Hatch, *Maine: A History;* Maine League of Historical Societies and Museums, *Maine: A Guide "Downeast'';* W. H. Rowe, *Maritime History of Maine;* William Williamson, *History of Maine.*]

ROBERT M. YORK

MAINE, DESTRUCTION OF THE (Feb. 15, 1898). In January 1898, the second-class battleship *Maine,* under the command of Capt. Charles D. Sigsbee, was ordered from Key West, Fla., to Havana, Cuba, during that island's revolt against Spanish rule, as an "act of friendly courtesy." Spanish authorities in Havana objected to the arrival of the *Maine.* For three weeks the ship lay moored to a buoy 500 yards off the Havana arsenal. There was considerable ill feeling against the United States among the Spaniards, but no untoward incident took place until 9:40 P.M. on Feb. 15, when two explosions threw parts of the *Maine* 200 feet in the air and illuminated the whole harbor. A first dull explosion had been followed by one much more powerful, probably that of the forward magazines. The forward half of the ship was reduced to a mass of twisted steel; the after section slowly sank. Two officers and 258 of the crew were killed or died soon afterward. Most of these were buried in Colón Cemetery, Havana.

Separate investigations were soon made by the American and Spanish authorities. Their conclusions differed: the Spaniards reported that an internal explosion, perhaps spontaneous combustion in the coal bunkers, had been the cause; the Americans, that the original cause had been an external explosion that in turn had set off the forward magazines.

News of the disaster produced great excitement in the United States, and accusations against the Spaniards were freely expressed by certain newspapers, including the *New York Journal.* Without doubt the catastrophe stirred up national feeling over the difficulties in Cuba, crystallized in the slogan "Remember the *Maine,''* and was a major factor in bringing the United States to a declaration of war against Spain on Apr. 25 (retroactive to Apr. 21).

The wreck remained in Havana harbor until 1911, when U.S. Army engineers built a cofferdam about the wreck, sealed the aft hull of the ship, the only part still intact, and floated it out to sea. There, on Mar. 16, 1912, appropriate minute guns boomed as the *Maine* sank with its flag flying. The remains of sixty-six of the crew found during the raising were buried in Arlington National Cemetery, Va. During the removal of the wreck, a board of officers of the navy made a further investigation. Their report, published in 1912, stated that a low form of explosive exterior to the ship caused the first explosion. "This resulted in igniting and exploding the contents of the 6-inch reserve magazine, A–14–M, said contents including a large quantity of black powder. The more or less complete explosion of the contents of the remaining forward magazine followed." The chief evidence for this was that the bottom of the ship had been bent upward and folded over toward the stern. European experts, perhaps influenced by several internal explosions in warships in the intervening years, still maintained the theory of an internal explosion. No further evidence has ever been found to solve the mystery.

[F. E. Chadwick, *The Relations of the United States and Spain: Diplomacy;* Charles D. Sigsbee, *The Maine.*]

WALTER B. NORRIS

MAINE BOUNDARY DISPUTE. *See* **Aroostook War; Northeast Boundary; Webster-Ashburton Treaty.**

MAIZE. *See* **Agriculture; Agriculture, American Indian; Corn.**

MAJORITY RULE. A fundamental American concept, evolved from the principle of the sovereignty of the people, is that when two candidates are running for an office, the one who receives more than half of the total votes cast shall be elected and his policies shall be entitled to a fair trial. If three or more candidates are seeking the same office, the concept holds that an absolute majority is not required but that the one who receives a mere plurality, or more votes than any other candidate, shall be elected.

The operation of majority rule was well illustrated when the election of Thomas Jefferson to the presidency was accepted as sufficient warrant for refusing to approve Federalist changes in the judiciary (*see* Judiciary Act of 1801). President Andrew Jackson interpreted his reelection in 1832 as approval of his hostility to the second Bank of the United States. During the Reconstruction period, the Radical Republicans believed their 1866 election victories justified them in imposing a harsh program of military reconstruction on the South. In 1933 President Franklin D. Roosevelt and the public generally interpreted his overwhelming victory at the polls as authority for inaugurating his far-reaching New Deal.

Majority rule is limited somewhat by the Constitution. Civil liberties are specifically protected by the fundamental law and cannot be suppressed by a temporary majority. The Constitution itself cannot be amended without the consent of three-fourths (thirty-eight) of the states. Because of constitutional guarantees of freedom of speech and of the press and other liberties, minority groups in the United States are able to oppose the majority. Minority criticism and the ever-present possibility that the minority will

become the majority have operated to make majority rule work well.

[James Bryce, *The American Commonwealth,* vol. II; Alexis de Tocqueville, *Democracy in America.*]

ERIK MCKINLEY ERIKSSON

MAKAH, a native American tribe that numbered about 2,000 in 1780, still has lands at the extreme northwestern end of the Olympic Peninsula of the state of Washington. Their closest relatives appear to have been the Nootka of Vancouver Island, who spoke the language usually classified as Wakashan. Their native culture, like that of other tribes centering around the Strait of Juan de Fuca and Puget Sound, was a southern variation of the rich Northwest Coast development. The basic salmon dependence, the use of wood for both tools and housing, and the emphasis on wealth seen in potlatches constitute elements shared with the neighboring peoples. But the Makah, along with other groups of the southern parts of the area, did not achieve the sophistication in art and society characteristic of the more northern Haida and Tlingit or the central Kwakiutl-Nootka. Elements of these cultures are still in existence; generally, however, following contact with Europeans, the gradual erosion of the native cultures took place.

[June M. Collins, *The Valley of the Spirits: The Upper Skagit Indians of Western Washington,* American Ethnological Society monograph 56; Elizabeth Colson, *The Makah Indians.*]

ROBERT F. SPENCER

MAKASSAR STRAIT, BATTLE OF (Jan. 24, 1942). Shortly after the Japanese began their invasion of the Netherlands East Indies, an American force of two light cruisers and four destroyers commanded by Rear Adm. William A. Glassford II sortied from Timor to make a night attack on a large Japanese convoy heading south through Makassar Strait for Balikpapan, Borneo. An accident to one cruiser and engine trouble on the other left only the destroyers to carry out the attack. These ships reached the waters off Balikpapan at about 3 A.M. on Jan. 24, 1942, and found the Japanese transports, their principal targets, silhouetted against the light of burning oilfields on shore. Attacking with torpedoes and gunfire, for forty-five minutes the destroyers raced back and forth unhindered through the startled and confused Japanese. Then, having exhausted their torpedoes, the American vessels retired south through Makassar Strait and made good their escape. They had sunk or left sinking four heavily loaded transports and a patrol boat at the cost of only slight damage to themselves. Their one-sided victory was an unusual event at a time of widespread Allied defeats, but it did not prevent the Japanese from swiftly seizing Balikpapan and using it as a base for further advances.

[Samuel Eliot Morison, *History of United States Naval Operations in World War II,* vol. III.]

STANLEY L. FALK

MAKIN RAID (Aug. 17–18, 1942). To divert Japanese attention from embattled Guadalcanal, early on Aug. 17, 1942, some 200 U.S. Marines under Lt. Col. Evans F. Carlson landed unopposed from two submarines on Makin Atoll in the Gilbert Islands. They wiped out the eighty-five-man Japanese garrison, gathered intelligence data, and destroyed installations and supplies before withdrawing the following evening. Carlson lost thirty men, including nine marines left ashore and later captured and beheaded by the Japanese. The raid attracted considerable attention in the American press and served as a morale builder at home but was of little military significance.

[Philip A. Crowl and Edmund G. Love, *Seizure of the Gilberts and Marshalls,* United States Army in World War II.]

STANLEY L. FALK

MALARIA is a disease characterized by chills and fever that recur at regular intervals, anemia, and an enlarged spleen; it is caused in man by four species of *Plasmodium,* a protozoan. Long prevalent in Europe and Africa, malaria was probably brought to the Americas by European colonists and black slaves. By 1700 it had become established from South Carolina to New England. The ague, chills and fever, and intermittents of 18th- and early 19th-century medical literature were commonly malaria, as were many of the autumnal bilious remittent fevers. Malaria spread into the Mississippi Valley with the American settlers, where it became a commonly accepted part of life. Generally chronic and debilitating to all ages and often fatal, it placed a heavy burden of ill health on settlers, especially along the waterways that formed the chief routes of commerce. Its effects are portrayed in the sallow countenances and listless, emaciated forms described by travelers.

Malaria was at its height in New England in the 18th century and after 1800 appeared only sporadically. In the Midwest it reached its peak about 1875,

declining thereafter quite rapidly in the North. Associated since antiquity with marshes, malaria in the United States tended to rise with the initial clearing of land and to fall with cultivation and drainage, as Benjamin Rush noted in 1785. Better housing, an increase in dairy cattle (which the mosquito may prefer to man), and the development of railroads, moving settlement out of the river bottoms, were other factors in the decline of malaria.

Cinchona bark, a specific for malaria, was brought to Europe in the 1630's from Peru, and by the 18th century it was widely used, although often incorrectly. Well into the 19th century, many American doctors also relied on bloodletting and cathartics. The isolation of quinine by French chemists in 1820 made rational therapeutics more practicable, and from the 1850's there was a great upsurge in the use of quinine not only to cure or suppress malaria but also to prevent its appearance. While prophylactic use of quinine cannot eradicate malaria, its enormous use in the 1880's and 1890's no doubt helped directly by abating sickness and indirectly by enabling people to make the improvements that led to the virtual disappearance of malaria in the North by about 1900 without specific antimosquito measures.

In 1880 a French army surgeon, Alphonse Laveran, demonstrated the parasitic cause of the disease in the blood of man. Dr. A. F. A. King of Washington, D.C., speculated on mosquito transmission in 1882, and William George MacCollum added significantly to knowledge of the complex life history of the plasmodium in 1897 by elucidating the significance of the extramammalian flagellated form. A British physician, Ronald Ross, made the crucial demonstration of mosquito transmission in avian malaria in 1898; others soon confirmed this for man. Using antimosquito measures and prophylactic quinine, William C. Gorgas in 1901 initiated a campaign that reduced the malaria rate in Havana from 909 per 1,000 in 1899 to 19 per 1,000 in 1908. Later he obtained comparable results in the Canal Zone and made possible the building of the Panama Canal.

Extended campaigns began in the United States in 1912, when the U.S. Public Health Service instituted malaria surveys in cooperation with several southern states and the Rockefeller Foundation. A decline in antimalaria programs in the 1920's, followed by the depression, led in the early 1930's to a resurgence of the disease, which was attacked by drainage and other measures under New Deal relief programs. During World War II both the Public Health Service and the army increased antimalaria programs in the United

"MALEFACTORS OF GREAT WEALTH"

States, while overseas actions brought home the global importance of the disease. With quinine supplies cut off, new and more effective drugs were developed. After the war the Public Health Service, using the newly developed insecticide DDT, inaugurated a program to eradicate malaria in the United States. In 1935 there were about 4,000 malaria deaths in the country, in 1945 about 400, and by 1952 only 25. In the 1970's the United States was free of significant indigenous malaria, although the possibility of importation in troops from Korea in the 1950's and Vietnam in the 1960's had been a continuing threat. Since World War II the United States has also participated in antimalaria campaigns in other countries, through various bilateral and international agencies. Although these efforts have greatly reduced the incidence of malaria, it remains a major health problem in many of the less developed countries.

[Erwin H. Ackerknecht, "Malaria in the Upper Mississippi Valley 1760–1900," *Bulletin of the History of Medicine,* Supplements, no. 4 (1945); Paul F. Russell, *Man's Mastery of Malaria.*]

JOHN B. BLAKE

"MALEFACTORS OF GREAT WEALTH." On Aug. 20, 1907, President Theodore Roosevelt defended his antitrust policy in an address at Provincetown, Mass., blaming the depression of that year (*see* Panic of 1907) partly on "certain malefactors of great wealth," who he believed had brought about some of the financial stress in order to force the government to relax its control over corporations.

[Mark Sullivan, *Our Times,* vol. III.]

STANLEY R. PILLSBURY

MALLET BROTHERS EXPLORATIONS (1739–42). The first known Santa Fe traders to cross the Plains from the Missouri River were eight Canadians led by Pierre and Paul Mallet, who, in 1739, driving packhorses, explored a route from the Platte River's mouth to Santa Fe. Returning, they explored the Arkansas River from the Rockies to the Mississippi in 1740. They guided Fabry de Bruyère on a second Santa Fe expedition from New Orleans by boat up the Mississippi, Arkansas, and Canadian rivers to the present central part of Oklahoma. Inability to float boats in the shallow Canadian River and Fabry's reluctance to use Indian horses caused abandonment of the expedition in 1742.

[Pierre Margry, *Découvertes et Établissements des Français dans l'Amérique,* vol. VI.]

BLISS ISELY

MALMÉDY MASSACRE (Dec. 17, 1944). During the Battle of the Bulge, troops of the First SS Panzer Division under Lt. Col. Joachim Peiper overran a convoy of Battery B, 285th Field Artillery Observation Battalion, in the Belgian Ardennes near the town of Malmédy. Capturing approximately 100 Americans, the Germans marched the prisoners unarmed into a field on Dec. 17, 1944, and systematically shot them. A few feigned death and escaped; eighty-six died. Elsewhere in the Ardennes, Peiper's command killed at least 100 Belgian civilians and more than 250 American prisoners, but the massacre near Malmédy was the worst single atrocity committed against American troops in Europe during World War II. Peiper, three of his superior officers, and sixty-nine SS troops were subsequently tried by an American tribunal for their part in the massacre. Forty-three, including Peiper, were sentenced to death by hanging; the others, to imprisonment ranging from ten years to life. After sensational, although generally unsubstantiated, allegations that harsh methods had been used in the trial were made in the German and American press and the U.S. Senate, the death sentences were commuted, and none of the convicted served a full prison sentence. Peiper was paroled after ten years.

[Hugh M. Cole, *The Ardennes: Battle of the Bulge,* United States Army in World War II; Richard Gallagher, *Malmédy Massacre.*]

CHARLES B. MACDONALD

MALVERN HILL, BATTLE OF (July 1, 1862), last of the Seven Days' battles, ended Union Gen. George B. McClellan's Peninsular campaign. After the Battle of Frayser's Farm, McClellan fell back to a prepared position on Malvern Hill, a plateau protected by streams on its flanks, with an open field of fire at the immediate front, located fourteen miles south of Richmond, Va. When Gen. Robert E. Lee's artillery attack failed, through poor organization and staff inefficiency, several divisional attacks were launched against Malvern Hill. These assaults were not successful in driving the Union army from its position that day, but on July 2 McClellan felt forced to withdraw to his base at Harrison's Landing.

[Matthew Forney Steele, *American Campaigns.*]

GEORGE FREDERICK ASHWORTH

MAMMALS. The study of American mammals may be divided into two periods: an exploratory-descriptive period, lasting until the 1880's, and an analysis-management period, extending from the 1880's to the

MAMMALS

present. The transition from one to the other was gradual, and so it may be more useful to think in terms of trends rather than periods.

Mammals are among the dominant forms of life, but since many species are nocturnal or secretive, they are not as easily observed as plants or birds. The early explorers in America, therefore, did not provide much reliable information about the mammals. Since Europeans were eager to learn about the products and curiosities of the New World, various explorers and settlers attempted to satisfy the demands for knowledge. William Wood, after living four or five years in Massachusetts, related useful information about the moose and beaver in his *New Englands Prospect* (1634). John Josselyn visited New England in 1638–39 and returned to live there from 1663 to 1671. Yet, in his *New England Rarities* (1672), which was devoted to the region's flora and fauna, he provided only brief accounts of eleven species. William Byrd provided the speciman for the first outstanding contribution to American mammalogy when he sent a female opossum to the Royal Society of London. The science of anatomy was further advanced than was field natural history, and Edward Tyson published in 1698 an outstanding study on this first known species of marsupial. In 1704 William Cowper, a leading English anatomist and surgeon, obtained a male specimen and published a supplementary paper of comparable quality.

Progress in describing American mammals was slow during the 18th century, and the center of this activity shifted to the South. John Lawson, after being appointed surveyor general of North Carolina, traveled in the eastern parts of North and South Carolina from 1700 to 1708. In 1709 he published *A New Voyage to Carolina,* which contained accounts of over thirty mammals. Substantial portions of his accounts were later incorporated by John Brickell into his *Natural History of North Carolina* (1737), along with his own observations made when he practiced medicine at Edenton in 1731. The British naturalist Mark Catesby lived in Virginia from 1712 to 1719 and then returned to America to travel into the Carolinas from 1722 to 1725. His second trip was supported by patrons for whom he collected interesting plants and other natural curiosities. Catesby made important contributions to the knowledge of American birds and plants, but he contributed much less to American mammalogy. However, his illustrations of seven species were the first good illustrations of American mammals. The Swedish naturalist Pehr Kalm, who was primarily interested in American

plants, traveled through Pennsylvania and New York and published accounts of over twenty mammalian species in his *Resa til Norra America* (three volumes, 1753–61).

In the second half of the 18th century the French naturalist Comte Georges Louis Leclerc de Buffon published accounts of all known mammals in his *Histoire naturelle* (fifteen volumes, 1749–67; seven-volume supplement, 1774–89). This was one of the most widely read natural histories ever published. As director of the Jardin du Roi (now Jardin des Plantes) in Paris, Buffon had unparalleled resources available to him in the zoo, museum, and biological library. Louis Jean Marie Daubenton contributed many fine anatomical studies of mammals to the *Histoire naturelle*. Buffon was interested in the geographical distribution of species and attempted to explain their anatomical similarities as being based on climatic modifications of a few basic types. Because America was still largely a wilderness, he assumed in 1766 that America's climate was less favorable than Europe's and that American mammals had degenerated from European species after migrating from Eurasia.

Thomas Jefferson responded with a long, effective argument in his *Notes on the State of Virginia* (1785), including tables that compared the weights of European and American species and indicated that many American mammals were as large or larger than their European counterparts. To further his claims, while American ambassador in Paris, he presented Buffon with the skeleton, antlers, and skin of a moose. Jefferson also developed a keen interest in the fossil remains of large American mammals. He obtained the bones of *Megalonyx*, the giant sloth, which he named and described in a scientific paper in 1799. He also encouraged the successful recovery of mammoth bones by Meriwether Lewis and William Clark and by Charles Willson Peale.

A minor effect of the American Revolution was to change the plans of the British naturalist Thomas Pennant. He had intended to write an account of the zoology of North America, but after the loss of the colonies he wrote instead *Arctic Zoology,* the first volume of which (1784) contains accounts of only those mammals of the independent states that were also found in Canada. But Pennant's attitude was not typical, and however little was lost to mammalogy by political offense was more than recompensed by the nationalistic fervor among the Americans to discover their own natural resources and to make their own contributions to scientific knowledge. Following Jefferson's example of writing an account of his state,

231

Jeremy Belknap wrote *The History of New Hampshire* (1784–92), the third volume of which included a discussion of thirty-one of the state's native mammals. Peale established a museum in Philadelphia where he displayed his fossils and many other natural history specimens. His collections came to include birds and mammals brought back by the Lewis and Clark expedition.

In the 19th century a number of natural history surveys that made useful contributions to mammalogy were written. Some of these were state surveys, of which James E. De Kay's *Zoology of New York* (four volumes, 1842–44) was an outstanding example. The federal government sponsored a series of exploratory expeditions—beginning with Lewis and Clark in 1804–06—that collected mammalian specimens, but it was only after the establishment of the Smithsonian Institution at midcentury that federal sponsorship of biological research became regular. The early comprehensive surveys of American mammals were private endeavors. Philadelphia was still the center of scientific activity during the first half of the 19th century. Dr. Richard Harlan of that city published in 1825 a natural history of North American mammals that included 136 living and 11 fossil species. Since he compiled it mainly from the scientific literature and it was not illustrated, it was quickly eclipsed by Dr. John D. Godman's treatise on the same subject (three volumes, 1826–28), written while he was also living in Philadelphia. George Ord of Philadelphia, who may have been the best naturalist of the three, had planned to publish his own work on the subject but succeeded in publishing only a number of descriptive papers. Sir John Richardson, a Scottish naturalist, explorer, and surgeon who had accompanied Sir John Franklin on his land explorations in Canada, published in 1829 the first volume of his *Fauna Boreali-Americana,* which capably described eighty-two mammalian species.

In spite of the growing thoroughness of the surveys of American mammals, they provided little information on the mammals of the West. In 1839 John James Audubon and a Lutheran minister from Charleston, S.C., John Bachman, began their treatise on American mammals, excluding bats, seals, and whales. It was a much greater task than they imagined. Audubon's strength began to wane in 1846, and his son John Woodhouse Audubon had to paint about half of the 155 color illustrations. Bachman was in charge of the text and contributed most of it, although he used notes from the expeditions of both Audubons and from other naturalists. Audubon's other son, Victor, was indispensable in handling the business aspects of publishing *The Viviparous Quadrupeds of North America* (three volumes, 1845–54). This great work, describing 197 species, was the culmination of privately initiated surveys on mammals.

With the appointment in 1850 of Spencer F. Baird as assistant secretary of the newly established Smithsonian Institution, description zoology entered a new phase. There was now a permanent museum for specimens—the Peale Museum had not long survived its creator—and more regular government support of both field studies and scientific publications. As assistant secretary, and after 1878 as secretary, Baird made excellent use of his position to further American mammalogy. He efficiently organized the zoological representatives for the government's Pacific Railroad surveys, and the specimens and notes from the returning naturalists provided the basis for his careful and lengthy report (1857) on western mammals. It was truly a museum report, being limited to physical descriptions. It also opened the final phase of the explorative-descriptive period, a phase dominated by museum monographs. These were usually written for specialists, but sometimes the author of a monograph managed to write for the general public and still provide the technical information that made the work scientifically useful. Successful examples of this synthesis are Charles M. Scammon's *The Marine Mammals of the North-western Coast of North America, Described and Illustrated: Together With an Account of the American Whale-Fishery* (1874), Dr. Elliott Coues' *Fur-Bearing Animals: A Monograph of North American Mustelidae* (1877), and John Dean Caton's *The Antelope and Deer of America* (1877).

Another aspect of descriptive mammalogy that flourished in 19th-century America was paleontology. The first leader in this field was Dr. Joseph Leidy of Philadelphia, who wrote over 200 papers on fossils of the West. His greatest contribution to paleontology was his monograph *On the Extinct Mammalia of Dakota and Nebraska* (1869). During the last three decades of the 19th century, American paleontology was led by Leidy's student Edward Drinker Cope and by the Yale professor of paleontology Othniel Charles Marsh. A fierce rivalry developed between them. Both became famous for their discoveries and reconstructions of mammals and dinosaurs from the western states. Their work was continued in the early 20th century under the leadership of Henry Fairfield Osborn, whose many publications include *The Age of Mammals* (1910).

The fame of the early paleontologists derived considerably from the display of their discoveries in America's museums. Most of Cope's collections were sold to the American Museum of Natural History, which was founded in 1869. Louis Agassiz, who had established the Museum of Comparative Zoology at Harvard University in 1859, trained the outstanding museum mammalogist Joel A. Allen. Allen was associated with the Museum of Comparative Zoology from 1862 to 1885, when he became curator of ornithology and mammalogy at the American Museum of Natural History. He published a monograph on the living and extinct American bisons in 1876 and his most comprehensive monograph, on the walruses and seals of North America, in 1880.

The analysis-management period began, on the one hand, with phylogenetic studies, which arose from interest in evolution and paleontology, and, on the other hand, with a concern for wildlife management. C. Hart Merriam led both scientific and applied mammalogy in America from the 1890's to the 1920's. In 1877, when Merriam was only seventeen, his father, Congressman C. L. Merriam, obtained an appointment for him as a collector of birds with the Hayden Survey of the Yellowstone region. His *Mammals of the Adirondacks* (1884) set new standards for regional studies and prepared the way for his appointment as director of the Department of Agriculture's Division of Economic Ornithology and Mammalogy when it was created in 1888. His first priority was to establish the geographical ranges of American birds and mammals. In the West he correlated these ranges with elevations and temperatures to establish ecological life zones. Under his direction, the division (renamed the Bureau of Biological Survey in 1905) studied the economic importance of many species, publicizing the value of hawks and owls, which eat rodents, but was also responsible for the eradication of wolves, coyotes, and other animals considered detrimental to agriculture. Merriam became the first president of the American Society of Mammalogists when it was founded in 1919. Problems of wildlife management have increased in importance during the 20th century and have continued to provide a major, although not the sole, stimulus for scientific studies of American mammals.

[Theodore Gill and Elliott Coues, "Bibliography of North American Mammals," *Report of the United States Geological Survey of the Territories*, vol. 11; W. J. Hamilton, Jr., "Mammalogy in North America," in Edward L. Kessel, ed., *A Century of Progress in the Natural Sciences, 1853–1953*; Donald F. Hoffmeister, "The First Fifty Years of the American Society of Mammalogists," *Journal of Mammalogy*, vol. 50 (1959); John C. Phillips, *American Game Mammals and Birds: A Catalogue of Books, 1582 to 1925. Sport, Natural History, and Conservation*; Tracy I. Storer, "Mammalogy and the American Society of Mammalogists, 1919–1969," *Journal of Mammalogy*, vol. 50 (1959).]

FRANK N. EGERTON

MAMMOTH CAVE, in Edmonson County, Ky., is mentioned in county records as early as 1797. Evidences of Indian occupation were found for miles inside its entrance by early explorers. Saltpeter was taken from it to make gunpowder during the War of 1812. Within a quarter century after the war it began to attract tourists. The first official guide, Stephen Bishop, did much of the dangerous work of exploring the cave as it is known today. The cave and surrounding area were established as a national park under National Park Service administration on May 22, 1936. Total acreage of the park is 51,354.

[Helen F. Randolph, *Mammoth Cave and the Cave Region of Kentucky*.]

ALVIN F. HARLOW

MANAGED MONEY projects and value-measuring devices to implement them date back to the colonial period. The colony of Massachusetts, in the throes of a price inflation in 1748, adopted a tabular standard made up of an assortment of goods, in specified quantities, to be used as a test of the value of money. All money payments had to be made according to the changes in the value of money as reflected by this goods assortment. Astronomer Simon Newcomb suggested the need for managing money to achieve a stable price level in an article in the *North American Review* (September 1879). Economist Irving Fisher in 1911 outlined a plan for stabilizing the dollar in his *Purchasing Power of Money* and again in 1920 in his *Stabilizing the Dollar*. Fisher's system presupposed no gold coins in circulation. To correct the trend of the price level, he would increase or decrease the amount of gold representing a dollar, such dollars being disbursed in ingots and chiefly in international payments. In 1922 he wrote *The Making of Index Numbers*, explaining how to measure the price level scientifically. Americans were particularly conscious of price level changes at this time. In the previous sixty years wholesale prices more than doubled during the Civil War, fell by two-thirds between 1865 and 1896, rose moderately until 1913, then more than doubled between 1914 and 1920, and plummeted 40 percent in one year, mid-1920 to mid-1921. All these changes had political repercussions, some of which were quite severe.

Many prominent economists who felt there must be some way to improve the situation helped Fisher organize the Stable Money League in 1921. Rep. T. Alan Goldsborough of Maryland introduced a bill in 1922 based on Fisher's ideas, but it got nowhere. Because some league members differed with Fisher as to the appropriate solution, the organization changed its name that autumn to the National Monetary Association. Dissension among its members killed the association in early 1924. The next year Fisher promoted a new group called the Stable Money Association, whose avowed goal was educational instead of legislative. It nevertheless gave thinly veiled support to other bills by Goldsborough and by Rep. James G. Strong of Kansas. The organization died in 1932.

Meanwhile a Cornell University agricultural economist, George F. Warren, also concluded that decreasing the gold content of the dollar was the way to raise the general price level. In early 1933 farm prices were only 59 percent of what they had been in "normal" 1926 and he felt the way to restore prosperity, especially agricultural prosperity, was to raise the price level to that 1926 level. Warren influenced then Under Secretary of the Treasury Henry Morgenthau, Jr., his former student, who had the ear of President Franklin D. Roosevelt. The United States temporarily abandoned the gold standard in March 1933 and called in all gold coins. In an Oct. 22 radio address Roosevelt, discussing his gold purchase plan (to drive up the price of gold), said, "We are thus continuing to move toward a managed currency." On Jan. 30, 1934, Congress passed the Gold Reserve Act and the next day, acting on its authority, the president created a new gold dollar (never coined) of 13.71 grains, 59 percent the size of the old gold dollar. Warren estimated that this would quickly raise the price level by 69 percent (100/59 is 169), but the rise did not take place as expected. There were other managed money bills introduced in the 1930's, especially by Rep. Wright Patman of Texas, who thought himself a modern "populist," but nothing came of them.

In the early 1960's a school of economists, soon known as monetarists, headed by Milton Friedman of the University of Chicago, achieved prominence. They believed that the quantity of money in circulation, measured in a sophisticated manner, greatly affected both the severity of business cycles and the general price level. Their solution was to increase the money supply by a steady 4 percent a year, the coun-

try's annual average rate of economic growth. The Treasury and the Federal Reserve have never fully accepted the monetarists' formula, but it has influenced them at times.

Under any money system, whether gold, silver, or irredeemable paper, central bankers or others in power may to some degree manage the money supply with an economic goal in mind. Since they may do it most easily under irredeemable paper money, that form of money is most often employed.

[I. Fisher, *Stable Money;* M. Friedman, *A Program for Monetary Stability.*]

DONALD L. KEMMERER

MANASSAS, BATTLE OF. *See* **Bull Run, First Battle of; Bull Run, Second Battle of.**

MANCHAC, a British trading post established shortly after 1763 at the junction of Bayou Manchac (Iberville River) and the Mississippi River, from which an extensive trade was conducted with French planters along the Mississippi as far south as New Orleans. Manchac was captured by Spanish forces under Bernardo de Galvez in September 1779.

[Charles Gayarré, *History of Louisiana.*]

WALTER PRICHARD

MANCHURIA AND MANCHUKUO. Manchuria, where the Manchu people originated, was administered separately from "China proper" by the Manchu dynasty (1644–1911) after the Manchu conquered China in 1644. In the 1890's, Russia penetrated the region by obtaining railroad concessions and a leasehold that included Dairen and Port Arthur. As Western and Japanese imperialists vied for concessions in China and Manchuria after China's defeat by Japan in 1895, American policy was expressed in John M. Hay's Open Door notes of 1899 and 1900. The notes reflected an American assumption that the interests of the United States were served best by preserving both equal opportunity to trade throughout China and China's independence and territorial integrity. Manchuria was of particular concern because American exporters fared better there than in China proper and because Russian domination threatened to exclude American goods. From 1901 to 1903, the administration of Theodore Roosevelt quarreled with the Russians in an effort to preserve American opportunities in Manchuria. In 1904, the Japanese, considering their interests in Manchuria to be vital, attacked Russian forces there. Japanese successes led to control over southern Manchuria, conceded by the Russians in the Treaty of Portsmouth (1905). Roosevelt aided negotiation of the settlement and acquiesced in the parceling of spheres of interest in Manchuria. He rejected subsequent Chinese overtures for help in regaining control of the region. Later, the administration of William Howard Taft challenged both Japan and Russia in Manchuria. As part of their program of "dollar diplomacy," Taft and Secretary of State Philander C. Knox attempted to internationalize the railroads that were the foundation of the Japanese and Russian spheres. The American plan failed, driving Japan and Russia together.

A note by Secretary of State William Jennings Bryan in 1915 and the Lansing-Ishii agreement in 1917 appeared to constitute American recognition of the Japanese sphere of interest in southern Manchuria. In neither instance was American intent clear. The four-power consortium agreement of 1920 and the Nine-Power Treaty of 1922 were also ambiguous about Japan's special interests in Manchuria. Without legitimizing Japanese political pretensions in the region, the United States conceded Japanese economic hegemony. The governments of the Republic of China (1911–49) never exercised more than nominal control over the area.

By the 1920's, control of Manchuria was considered by Japanese leaders to be vital to Japan's economic development and security. Threatened by the growth of Chinese nationalism there, the Japanese army staged an incident on Sept. 18, 1931, occupied all of Manchuria, and, on Feb. 18, 1932, created the puppet state of Manchukuo. Concerned less with who controlled Manchuria than with Japanese violations of the Nine-Power Treaty and the Pact of Paris (1927), the United States, independently and in concert with the League of Nations, exerted pressure on Japan. Foreign protests were ignored by the Japanese military, and the civilian government was unable to restrain the army. With none of the powers willing to impose sanctions, the United States resorted in January 1932 to the Hoover-Stimson Doctrine—a refusal to recognize conditions brought about by Japanese treaty violations.

The United States never recognized Manchukuo and refused to concede Japanese dominance over the region during the efforts of Cordell Hull and Nomura Kichisaburo to avoid war in 1941. At Yalta (February 1945), Franklin D. Roosevelt secretly agreed to give the Soviet Union Japan's sphere of interest in Manchuria in return for Soviet intervention in the war in Asia. The Red Army entered Manchuria in August 1945 and remained there until April 1946. After Soviet forces withdrew, Mao Tse-tung's People's Liberation Army defeated Chiang Kai-shek's Kuomintang armies in Manchuria as in the rest of China. An agreement between Mao and Joseph Stalin in 1950 led to complete Chinese sovereignty in 1955. A separate American policy toward these northeastern provinces of China ceased to exist after 1947, when the administration of Harry S. Truman rejected Gen. Albert C. Wedemeyer's proposal for a five-power or United Nations trusteeship for Manchuria.

[Warren I. Cohen, *America's Response to China;* Michael H. Hunt, *Frontier Defense and the Open Door;* Charles E. Neu, *The Troubled Encounter;* Christopher Thorne, *The Limits of Foreign Policy.*]

WARREN I. COHEN

MANDAN, FORT, was built by the expedition of Meriwether Lewis and William Clark at Five Villages, now Stanton, N.Dak. The party remained there from Oct. 26, 1804, to Apr. 7, 1805. This was an advantageous wintering place because of neighboring Mandan and Hidatsa villages.

O. G. LIBBY

MANDAN, HIDATSA, AND ARIKARA. The northern Plains of America, in which most Indian tribes depended on bison hunting, were the home of three peoples that practiced river-bottom agriculture along the Missouri River in the general area of North Dakota. This is the northernmost point of the aboriginal spread of maize cultivation. The three tribes, the Mandan, Hidatsa, and Arikara, although sharing this common economic mode, were from different geographic areas and spoke mutually unintelligible languages. The Arikara appear to have branched off from the Skidi Pawnee, a Caddoan-speaking tribe, before the arrival of Europeans. Both the Mandan and the Hidatsa spoke Siouan languages, but those of subbranches long separated from each other. The Hidatsa language is closest to the Crow of Montana, while the Mandan language, in its structure, seems most closely allied to the East, to Winnebago. The Arikara are believed to have brought knowledge of farming up the Missouri, and the Hidatsa and Mandan are said to have been introduced to agriculture by contact with the Arikara.

Although farming appeared in the eastern Plains, among such sedentary peoples as the Omaha, Osage, and Oto, it is somewhat out of place so far north and east, but the Mandan, Hidatsa, and Arikara tended toward residential stability. Although they used the tipi and shared other distinctive elements of the culture of the nomadic bison hunters of the Plains, their use of a complex earth lodge, possibly Pawnee and thus southeastern in origin, suggests a trend toward permanent villages. Even so, bundles, the vision quest, ranked clubs or fraternities, the Sun Dance, and the war complex were as much a part of the life of these groups as they were of the life of such other nonagricultural peoples of the area as the Crow, Cheyenne, Assiniboine, and the various Dakota.

The three Missouri River tribes were first known from the account of Pierre Gaultier de Varennes, Sieur de La Vérendrye, who visited the area in 1738. He and his contemporaries created some confusion in the designation of local tribes, identifying the Hidatsa as ''Gros Ventres''; this is a misnomer, the designation ''Gros Ventre'' probably being more properly applied to the Algonkin-speaking Atsina, a group related to the Arapaho and culturally identified with the hunters of the Plains. Meriwether Lewis and William Clark mention in some detail their encounters with the Mandan, Hidatsa, and Arikara in 1805, and there are accounts and depictions of them from the 1830's by the German naturalist Prince Maximilian zu Wied and the American painter George Catlin.

Never large groups, the three tribes suffered greatly from smallpox, which reduced their population in the mid-19th century. At times hostile to European incursion, their effectiveness was curtailed by both geographic location and epidemics.

[Robert F. Spencer, ''Introduction'' to Washington Matthews, *Ethnography and Philology of the Hidatsa Indians*.]

ROBERT F. SPENCER

MANDATES. Under the treaties of Versailles and Lausanne and the Covenant of the League of Nations, conquered German and Turkish colonies were assigned for administration to individual powers, subject to general supervision by the league, after World War I. The United States, although not a party to the treaties nor a member of the league, took a keen interest in these mandates and insisted on equal rights with the other powers in them. Its claims were based on the provision in the Treaty of Versailles turning the German colonies over to the principal allied and associated powers, of which the United States was one, even though it did not ratify the treaty. The United States also put forth the ingenious argument that al-

though it had not been at war with Turkey, it had by its participation in the war against Germany helped win the war against Turkey and was entitled to share in the results.

Both claims were finally granted by the other powers, and the United States thereupon insisted on being consulted concerning the terms of the individual agreements. Again it won its point. Treaties were negotiated incorporating the text of the mandate agreements entered into between the mandatory power and the league council and making its terms applicable to the United States. Ten such treaties, securing for the United States all the rights it would have had automatically had it joined the League of Nations, were ratified by the Senate. They included treaties with Japan, respecting the mandate over Yap and other Pacific islands (Feb. 11, 1922); with France, respecting the French Cameroons, now the Republic of Cameroon, and French Togoland (Feb. 13, 1923), since 1958 the Republic of Togo; with Belgium, respecting Ruanda-Urundi (Apr. 18, 1923, and Jan. 21, 1924), since 1962 Burundi and Rwanda. Treaties with Great Britain concerned the mandates of Palestine (Dec. 3, 1924), which is now divided between Israel and Jordan, with the Gaza Strip administered by Egypt (although under Israeli control since 1967); and concerning the British Cameroons (Feb. 10, 1925), now Nigeria; British Togoland, since 1957 part of Ghana; and Tanganyika, since 1964 united with Zanzibar as the United Republic of Tanzania; and Iraq (Jan. 9, 1930).

[Whitney T. Perkins, *Denial of Empire: The United States and Its Dependencies*.]

CLARENCE A. BERDAHL

MANGAS COLORADAS WARS, a series of Apache hostilities led by Mangas Coloradas (''Red Sleeves''), a chief of the Mimbreño Apache of southwest New Mexico. Mangas Coloradas became chief in 1837 upon the death of his predecessor, Juan José, who was killed when American trappers led by James Johnson fired a howitzer into a group of Mimbreño, seeking bounties for their scalps. Mangas Coloradas then became an enemy of the Anglo-Americans and with his Apache warriors was a scourge to the white settlements of a large part of the Southwest for decades. In 1861, at the age of seventy, he joined forces with Cochise after the incident at Apache Pass, in which Lt. George N. Bascom had ordered the hanging of Apache hostages. Mangas Coloradas and Cochise together resisted the troops of the California volunteers who had reoccupied the Southwest when it was abandoned by federal troops at the beginning of the Civil War. Mangas Coloradas was wounded in a battle with those troops at Apache Pass on July 15, 1862. He recovered but was taken prisoner by the soldiers in January 1863; he was killed while allegedly trying to escape.

[Jack D. Forbes, *Apache, Navajo, and Spaniard;* Dan L. Thrapp, *The Conquest of Apachería.*]

KENNETH M. STEWART

MANGEURS DE LARD, or "pork eaters," was a term applied to the new crop of recruits for the fur trade imported annually and bound for a period of five years' service. While en route from Canada they were fed on pea soup, bread, and pork, but chiefly on the latter. They were scorned by the aristocracy of the trapping fraternity and assigned only the most menial tasks, and their wages were so low that they customarily ended the five years' apprenticeship in debt to the company and were forced to remain as employees. The term was frequently applied to any newcomer in the sense of greenhorn or tenderfoot.

[H. M. Chittenden, *History of American Fur Trade in the Far West.*]

CARL L. CANNON

MANHATTAN, an island and borough of New York City bounded on the south by New York Bay, on the west by the Hudson River, on the east by the East River, and on the north by the Harlem River and Spuyten Duyvil Creek. The island is 13.5 miles long and 2.25 miles wide (22.6 square miles) and includes Roosevelt (Welfare), Randall's, and Ward's islands in the East River, and a small portion of the mainland, the Marble Hill section, just south of Riverdale in the Bronx. The island was discovered by Giovanni da Verrazano in 1524 and visited by Henry Hudson in 1609. Its name and insularity were first shown on a Dutch printed map of 1617. The name is derived from that of a small tribe of Indians called the Manhattan, who then lived on the island. There were white settlers on the island in 1613–14. In 1626 Peter Minuit, an agent of the Dutch West India Company, bought the island—then covered with forest and abounding in game and wild fruits—from the Canarsie Indians, who had no claim to it, for about $24 worth of trinkets. Later, other payments had to be made to the Manhattan, the true claimants. New York City spread rapidly over the island in the 19th century, and by 1860 streets were being planned to the northernmost tip of Manhattan. The city was confined to this island alone until Greater New York was created on Jan. 1, 1898.

The borough of Manhattan became the financial, commercial, and cultural center of the United States. It contains Wall Street, with the New York and American stock exchanges; miles of docks, making it one of the nation's great ports; the headquarters of many U.S. and foreign corporations; and numerous colleges and universities. There is also Lincoln Center for the Performing Arts, home of the Metropolitan Opera, the New York City Opera, and the New York City Ballet; the Broadway theater district; the Metropolitan Museum of Art, the largest in the United States; and the Museum of Modern Art. Manhattan is also the seat of the United Nations. The population in 1970 was 1,524,541. (*See also* New York City.)

[I. N. Phelps Stokes, *The Iconography of Manhattan Island.*]

ALVIN F. HARLOW

MANHATTAN PROJECT. After the discovery of nuclear fission in Germany in late 1938, physicists the world over recognized the possibility of utilizing the enormous energy released in this reaction. From 1939 on, experiments were performed to determine whether neutrons were released during fission and, if so, how to utilize them to achieve a sustained process, called a chain reaction, in which at least one neutron produced in fission of a uranium nucleus strikes another uranium atom, causing it to break apart. If the chain reaction could be controlled at a suitable rate, a power source, or reactor, was envisaged. Alternatively, if the reaction proceeded unchecked, an instant release of energy—of a magnitude greater than that obtainable from any chemical explosive—was likely.

Frustrated by the leisurely pace of progress in America and fearful that Germany might produce a bomb first, Leo Szilard and some other refugees from Nazi persecution convinced Albert Einstein to use his influence to urge government support from President Franklin D. Roosevelt. This tactic was successful, and after the fall of 1939 funding was at a significantly higher level, allowing theoretical and experimental research to move faster. With the entry of the United States into World War II, British and French scientists joined the efforts in the Western Hemisphere.

By mid-1942, it was obvious that pilot plants—and eventually full-sized factories—would have to be built, and that the scientists were ill prepared for this sort of activity. Because the work was now being done in secrecy and considerable construction was foreseen, Gen. Leslie R. Groves of the U.S. Army Corps of Engineers was given controlling authority. Scientific direction was retained by the National Defense Committee and subsequently by the Office of Scientific Research and Development, both under Vannevar Bush. Because much early research was performed at Columbia University in New York, the Engineers' Manhattan District headquarters was initially assigned management of such work, from which came the name "Manhattan Project" for the nationwide efforts.

Groves, possessed of great energy and willing to use his authority, soon had most research consolidated at the University of Chicago, under Arthur H. Compton. Groves purchased the Oak Ridge, Tenn., site for separation of the fissionable uranium-235 isotope, found to the extent of only 0.7 percent in uranium ores, and began bringing industrial giants, such as the contracting company of Stone and Webster and the Dupont Chemical Company, into the project. Funds, totaling an enormous and unforeseen $2 billion by the war's end, came from a special account that Congress voted the president for secret purposes. With such backing and under pressure to produce a weapon for use in the current war, Groves proceeded simultaneously on as many fronts as possible. No approach could be disregarded until proven unsatisfactory. Hence, liquid thermal diffusion, centrifuge, gaseous diffusion, and electromagnetic separation processes were all tried to extract U-235 from U-238. The last two techniques, developed in huge plants at Oak Ridge, ultimately proved to be the most successful.

In December 1942, Enrico Fermi succeeded in producing and controlling a chain reaction in the pile, or reactor, he built at the University of Chicago. This reactor not only provided necessary information for construction of a weapon but also furnished the means for a second path to the bomb. Uranium-238, while it does not fission in a reactor, can capture neutrons and ultimately be transformed into a new element, plutonium, not found in nature but highly fissionable. Plutonium, moreover, was seen to have the advantage of possessing different chemical properties, which would permit its extraction from uranium in processes simpler than the physical means required to separate the uranium isotopes. Five gigantic reactors were constructed on the banks of the Columbia River, near Hanford, Wash., to produce plutonium.

Appreciable quantities of U-235 from Oak Ridge and plutonium from Hanford were not produced until 1945, although means to employ these materials in a bomb were studied earlier. In late 1942, Groves placed J. Robert Oppenheimer in charge of a newly created weapons laboratory on an isolated mesa at Los Alamos, N.Mex. Oppenheimer's stature as a leading theoretical physicist encouraged many scientists to "drop out of sight" and work on the project for the duration of the war. Relatively little difficulty was encountered in designing a uranium weapon. Ballistics was a well-developed subject; one piece of U-235 could, with confidence, be fired at another in a gun barrel, with the knowledge that together they would form a critical (explosive) mass. The atomic bomb dropped on Hiroshima, Japan, on Aug. 6, 1945, was of this construction. The technique was unsuitable for plutonium, because an isotope that fissioned spontaneously was discovered and it was feared that the neutrons released might cause predetonation. Therefore, a new approach called implosion was conceived. A small sphere of plutonium is surrounded by a chemical high explosive; and when this outer covering is ignited the pressure wave compresses the plutonium core into a mass dense enough to reach criticality (enough neutrons strike plutonium nuclei to maintain the chain reaction). Since this process was entirely novel, a test was held at Alamogordo, N.Mex., on July 16, 1945, before the weapon was used against Nagasaki, Japan, on Aug. 9, 1945.

The Manhattan Project was unique in the size and cost of the effort, the employment of large numbers of scientists for military purposes, the standards of purity and performance required of materials, the one-step scaling-up of several microscopic laboratory processes to full-size industrial production facilities, and the skill and speed with which basic science was brought to application. Numerous confounding technical problems ultimately were overcome—for example, production of a suitable porous membrane for the gaseous diffusion process and discovery of a means of canning uranium cylinders in aluminum jackets.

The nontechnical problems were less tractable: scientists chafed under military supervision, particularly the security regulations that permitted them knowledge only of their own specific topic. More significantly, some scientists, Szilard and James Franck prominent among them, feared a postwar arms race and questioned the planned use of nuclear weapons against a nearly defeated Japan. Because the public knew nothing of the project and could not debate the issue, they felt their own insights should be accorded more weight by those in government. The wisdom and necessity of the Hiroshima and Nagasaki bomb-ings are, of course, still being debated. After the war scientists, and nuclear physicists in particular, were regarded with considerable public awe and veneration and were able to capitalize on this in several ways; but the effect of science on society and the question of morality in science were to become increasingly important issues. Finally, the Manhattan Project may be seen as the starting point for a qualitative change in weaponry that figured large in the postwar arms race.

[Richard G. Hewlett and Oscar O. Anderson, *The New World, 1939/1946*.]

LAWRENCE BADASH

"MANIFEST DESTINY," a phrase in common use in the 1840's and 1850's, suggesting the supposed inevitability of the continued territorial expansion of the United States (*see* Westward Movement). The phrase first appeared in the *Democratic Review* for July-August 1845, in an article in which the editor, John L. O'Sullivan, spoke of "our manifest destiny to overspread the continent allotted by Providence for the free development of our yearly multiplying millions." Although this article referred specifically to the annexation of Texas, the phrase was quickly caught up by the expansionists of the period and utilized in the controversy with Great Britain over Oregon and in the demand for annexations of territory as a result of the war with Mexico in 1846–48. It was also used, in the next decade, in connection with the desire to annex Cuba.

Believers in "manifest destiny" derived their faith in part from the phenomenal rate of population growth in the United States, in part from a conviction of the superiority of American talents and political institutions over those of neighboring countries. Although at first a tenet chiefly of the Democratic party, "manifest destiny" also had its devotees among Whigs and, later, Republicans—notably William H. Seward, who as secretary of state purchased Alaska and sought vainly to annex sundry Caribbean and Pacific islands. "Manifest destiny" was revived as a Republican doctrine in the 1890's and was in evidence in connection with the annexation of Hawaii and the islands taken from Spain in 1898 in the Spanish-American War.

[Julius W. Pratt, "The Origin of 'Manifest Destiny,'" *American Historical Review*, vol. 32; A. K. Weinberg, *Manifest Destiny*.]

JULIUS W. PRATT

MANILA BAY, BATTLE OF (May 1, 1898). Selected for the command of the U.S. Asiatic Squadron through the influence of Assistant Secretary of the Navy Theodore Roosevelt, Commodore George Dewey thoroughly fitted out at Hong Kong his four cruisers, *Olympia* (flagship), *Baltimore, Boston,* and *Raleigh,* and the gunboats *Concord* and *Petrel*. Upon the declaration of war with Spain in April 1898, Dewey received orders to attack the Spanish squadron under Adm. Patricio Montojo y Pasarón at Manila: "You must capture vessels or destroy." On Apr. 30 Dewey reached Manila Bay and entered safely at midnight, disregarding serious risks from shore batteries and mines. Off Manila at dawn, he sighted Montojo's force ten miles westward under the guns of Cavite dockyard. It consisted of some ten small wretchedly equipped cruisers and gunboats, mounting not one-third the American broadside. At 5:41 A.M. Dewey opened fire, swinging his column in long ovals past the enemy ships at 5,000 to 2,000 yards' range. On a mistaken report of ammunition shortage he withdrew at 7:35, but renewed action at 11:16 and ended it an hour later, when the shore batteries were silenced and every Spanish ship, to quote Dewey's report, "was sunk, burned, or deserted." The Spanish suffered 381 casualties, the Americans but nine wounded. Manila was blockaded and surrendered on Aug. 13 after merely formal bombardment. For his easily won victory Dewey's promotion to full admiral in 1899 was high reward, yet justified by his prompt, resolute movements and correct discounting of the dangers in entering enemy waters defended by mines and heavy guns on shore.

[H. W. Wilson, *The Downfall of Spain*.]

ALLAN WESTCOTT

MANILA CONFERENCE (Oct. 24–25, 1966) was held in the Philippines between the United States, represented by President Lyndon B. Johnson, and its allies in the Vietnam War. It resulted in a reaffirmation of American policy rather than in concessions acceptable to the government of North Vietnam, and so the war in Vietnam continued as before.

JACOB E. COOKE

MANITOULIN ISLANDS stretch across northern Lake Huron and include Cockburn, Drummond, Grand Manitoulin, and Little Manitoulin islands. They became known to the Jesuit missionaries of Huronia about 1640, and were subsequently seen, or skirted, by most voyagers between lower Canada and the upper Lakes. The French explorer Simon François

Daumont, Sieur de Saint Lusson, wintered on or near Great Manitoulin in 1670–71, when the island teemed with big game. After the War of 1812 the Joint International Boundary Survey Commission awarded Drummond Island (now part of Michigan) to the United States and the remainder of the group to Canada. The islands have become popular resorts and fishing grounds.

M. M. QUAIFE

MANN, FORT, in Kansas, is supposed to have been built about 1845; part of William Gilpin's battalion was quartered there in 1847–48 (*see* Doniphan's Expedition). The exact location is in doubt. Randolph B. Marcy in his *Prairie Traveler* (1859) located Fort Mann near the Arkansas River on the route to Santa Fe from Fort Leavenworth, about 359 miles from Fort Leavenworth and 423 miles from Santa Fe. A later writer, R. M. Wright, says: "At this side of Point of Rocks, 8 miles west of Dodge City, used to be the remains of an old adobe fort. Some called it Ft. Mann; others, Ft. Atkinson."

[F. W. Blackmar, *Kansas*.]

CARL L. CANNON

MANN ACT. In 1910 Congress enacted the so-called Mann Act, the title of which was "An Act Further to Regulate Interstate and Foreign Commerce by Prohibiting the Transportation therein for Immoral Purposes of Women and Girls, and for Other Purposes." The object of the legislation was the suppression of the white-slave traffic. The law is an example of federal police legislation for the protection of public morals, based constitutionally upon the commerce power. Although attacked as denying to American citizens the privilege of free access in interstate commerce, as invading the legislative domain of the states, and as exceeding the proper scope of the commerce power, the law was declared constitutional. The Supreme Court held that no person has any constitutional right to use the channels of interstate commerce to promote objectionable or immoral transactions, that the act is a proper exercise of the power to regulate commerce, and, as such, that its effect on the normal scope of state police power is irrelevant. The act was further upheld in the sections forbidding the interstate transportation of women for immoral purposes without any pecuniary element; "the mere fact of transportation" was sufficient. The act is significant in the extension of congressional control over a social and economic problem for the general welfare of the country. The Mann Act was reinforced by antiracketeering laws passed by Congress in 1961 that made interstate travel or transportation for illegal purposes—such as prostitution—illegal.

[R. E. Cushman, "National Police Power," *Minnesota Law Review,* vol. 3 (1918–19).]

THOMAS S. BARCLAY

MANNERS have always been a problem in America. Both immigrants from Europe and frontiersmen moving west were cut off from the usages of the best society. The wilderness had to be settled before there was time for cultivating manners. And of course there was no hereditary aristocracy, as in Europe, to set the standards for the rest of society. In the colonial period, both a hierarchical social structure and a corresponding code of deferential manners were modeled on the society of Puritan and Restoration England. Morals were equated with religion, and manners with morals. The colonial authorities, backed by church leaders, were harsh with offenders, punishing them in public (pillory, stocks, branding irons, and whips) for disobeying a wide variety of laws regarding dress, scandalmongering, cursing, lying, name-calling, flirting, and making ugly faces. The importance of manners in this new society of Englishmen in the wilderness is suggested by the fact that Cotton Mather, Benjamin Franklin, and George Washington thought it necessary to concern themselves with drawing up elaborate codes of good behavior, an activity that would be deemed superficial for men of such stature in the 20th century.

The real problem of manners came after the nation's founding and especially after the election of Andrew Jackson to the presidency in 1828. Until then, the gentry, Virginia planters in the style of Washington, Thomas Jefferson, James Madison, and James Monroe, and northern Federalists had set a more or less hierarchical tone. The problem, after Jackson, was to create a democratic code of manners. Some measure of the size of the task is the fact that some twenty-eight etiquette manuals were published during the 1830's, thirty-six in the 1840's, and thirty-eight more during the 1850's, an average of three a year. Their prices were kept down and they sold widely. The *Dime Book of Practical Etiquette* (1859) was extremely popular. Americans of all classes in this rapidly changing and egalitarian period were interested in "learning how to behave" correctly. The writers of these manuals were backed by educational leaders who thought it their duty to inculcate good manners in the classroom; textbook writers obliged with sections on "Politeness" and "Manners at the Table."

There were two schools of thought on the subject of manners: manners (1) as "character in action" and (2) as a set of rules to be learned (in the style of Lord Chesterfield). In the pre–Civil War period, the former school, which stressed truthfulness, sobriety, modesty, temperance, piety, chastity, and fidelity, was more typically in the American tradition of democratic manners. Almost all the manuals avoided references to Old World deferential manners; the use of the word "help" when referring to servants and the antipathy to tipping were indicative.

Although the educated classes before the Civil War were interested in comfort and the manners of character, after the war, and especially during the Gilded Age, the quest for luxury and the manners of fashion came to the fore. New York became the financial and manners manufacturing capital of the nation. There was a mushrooming of "high tone" manners, aping the British aristocracy for the most part, but also importing the lighter *ton* of the French. *Au fait, recherché,* and *de rigueur* entered the language of fashionable drawing rooms, and British nannies were imported to impart proper accents to the children of the newly rich. Between 1870 and 1917, the publication of etiquette books averaged from five to seven a year; the drawings of Charles Dana Gibson brilliantly satirized the manners of "high society"; and the striving middle classes avidly read the newly popular society columns in the newspapers.

World War I was a watershed in American manners. After the war, as a contemporary writer put it, "Formality was pushed aside with a barbaric shout." The career of Emily Post was indicative of this trend. Born to wealth and position, launched as a debutante in 1892, and widely traveled abroad, she was schooled in the rigid code of the Gilded Age. A failed marriage and the need to support herself and her children prompted her to publish her *Etiquette, The Blue Book of Social Usage,* in 1922, with the firm desire to preserve the punctilious standards of her own heritage. The revision of 1927 partly succumbed to the *négligé* manners of flaming youth. The original chapter on "Chaperons and Other Conventions" became "The Vanishing Chaperon and Other New Conventions." She even countenanced smoking for women.

The revolution in manners after World War I was mild compared with the changes that took place in the course of the two decades following World War II. Informality and an infinite variety of styles took hold in an affluent society of mass communications and mass manners. The celebrity replaced the socialite and the gossip column the society column. The natural replaced the conventional and rules of behavior of any kind became suspect. Perhaps the advice of the editor of the social page of the *New York Times* is most revealing: "Up with women, down with ladies, and take off the little white gloves."

[Arthur M. Schlesinger, *Learning How to Behave.*]
E. DIGBY BALTZELL

MANORS were self-sufficient agricultural communities, embracing one or more villages or towns over which seignorial rights and privileges generally obtained and within which both independent farmers and servile tenants lived. At the time of colonial settlement the manor was the prevailing mode of agricultural life in England, but the manorial lord was becoming more a country proprietor and less an administrative figure. Because the country gentlemen wanted to secure landholdings in the New World the manorial system was established in the proprietary colonies, principally in New York, Maryland, and Carolina.

Under the Dutch regime in New Netherland numerous patroonships, virtually manors, were authorized, but only one, that of Rensselaerswyck, was successfully established. The early English governors of New York created numerous manors in Westchester, on Long Island, and elsewhere. Their legal and political characteristics were feudal, and confirmed the manorial jurisdiction of Rensselaerswyck. The manorial jurisdiction, however, could not withstand the encroachments of town and county authority, although the manorial landlords, through their control of the sheriffs and the manorial or local courts, and through their influence in the provincial legislature, long dominated the local government of the province. The chief grievances tenants had against the manor system were insecurity of tenure and perpetual rents. The tenants on the Rensselaerswyck manor agitated against their leasehold estates and perpetual rents, and the controversy was a burning one into the 19th century.

In Maryland proprietors set up the manorial system extensively, erecting some sixty manors in the 17th century, not including those that the proprietary and his relations laid out in 6,000-acre tracts, each for his own use. The manors were divided more or less unevenly into demesne land reserved for the lord and freehold lands—both called plantations—where tobacco was cultivated.

Under the Fundamental Constitutions of Carolina of 1669 an aristocratic system of landholding was set up, two-fifths of the land being granted to the hereditary nobility and three-fifths to the manorial lords and the common freeholders. Seignories, baronies, and manors were provided for, although no seignory or barony ever contained more than 12,000 acres, and there is no evidence available of any manor in the strict sense actually having been set up. In these large estates manorial jurisdiction such as that found in Maryland and New York in the 17th century (*see* Court Leet) does not appear to have existed. Over a hundred proprietary manors were set up by William Penn for his colony in Pennsylvania but in no case does it appear that manorial jurisdiction was ever exercised.

[C. M. Andrews, *Colonial Period of American History;* S. G. Nissenson, *Patroon's Domain;* John Kilty, *Land-Holder's Assistant.*]

RICHARD B. MORRIS

MANSFIELD, BATTLE OF. *See* **Sabine Crossroads, Battle at.**

MANUEL'S FORT was the first American outpost in present-day Montana. It was built by Manuel Lisa, a Saint Louis fur trader, at the junction of the Yellowstone and Bighorn rivers in 1807 to serve as a trading post for Crow Indians and as headquarters of trapping brigades. Various trapping expeditions started from this post and explored the region. Most noted were two ventures of John Colter, who, traveling alone, explored what is now Yellowstone Park and first reported the geysers. He later explored a route to the three forks of the Missouri.

Hostility of the Blackfoot caused the abandonment of the fort, first in 1810, and finally in 1811. Trappers returning to the site after the War of 1812 found no remains of the fort. Later trading posts built at this location were headquarters for trappers who explored most of the present state of Wyoming. (*See also* Saint Louis Missouri Fur Company.)

[Hiram Martin Chittenden, *History of the American Fur Trade in the Far West.*]

BLISS ISELY

MANUFACTURES, COLONIAL. *See* **Industries, Colonial.**

MANUFACTURES, RESTRICTION OF COLONIAL. During the 17th century the colonies were regarded by Englishmen as sources of supplies, chiefly raw materials, that England did not produce itself. By the 18th century the plantations came to be prized as markets for English manufactured goods in addition to being reservoirs of raw materials. English manufacturers now felt that it was imperative to keep the colonies from manufacturing goods that they themselves could produce, and various attempts were made to restrict the development of colonial manufactures. Also, to free Great Britain from dependence on Baltic countries for naval stores and other supplies, a policy of granting bounties on such commodities was inaugurated in 1705.

Restrictions of colonial manufactures were attempted not only through the passage of laws but also by administrative action. For instance, the Board of Trade in its instructions to royal governors frequently emphasized that the restriction of colonial manufacturing was one of the duties of governors. In few cases, however, were such instructions taken seriously. Another example can be seen in the action of the Privy Council, when in 1724 it ordered the colonists to refrain from imposing tariffs on English goods, thus discouraging colonial legislation that favored manufacturing.

The first important step in the direction of parliamentary restriction of colonial manufactures was made in connection with the production of woolens. In 1699, at the demand of English woolen manufacturers, a law was passed that forbade the export of wool, raw or manufactured, from one colony to another "or to any other place whatsoever." The law was not prohibitory, for any colony could still manufacture woolen goods for consumption within its own borders.

Another colonial enterprise that became the subject of restrictive legislation was the beaver hat industry. An inquiry in 1731 disclosed that thousands of hats were being manufactured annually in the colonies, especially in New England and New York. The Hat Act of 1732 provided that no American-made hats could be exported from any colony, that no one could engage in hatmaking who had not served an apprenticeship of seven years, that no hatmaker could have more than two apprentices, and that no blacks should be employed in the industry. The Iron Act of 1750 prohibited the further erection of slitting mills, steel furnaces, and plating mills in the colonies. However, it also encouraged the production of colonial pig iron and bar iron by relaxing the duties when such iron was to be imported into England.

The colonists, whenever they wished, disregarded all administrative measures and laws that restricted manufactures. But manufacturing did not develop more rapidly in the colonies for other reasons, such as the difficulty of securing skilled labor, poor transportation, the lack of capital, and competition from agriculture.

[G. L. Beer, *British Colonial Policy, 1754–1763;* Arthur C. Bining, *British Regulation of the Colonial Iron Industry;* Curtis Nettels, "The Menace of Colonial Manufacturing," *New England Quarterly,* vol. 4.]

ARTHUR C. BINING

MANUFACTURING. Colonial Period to the Civil War. Most manufacturing in the United States was still in the handicraft stage when George Washington became president. The only power-using plants were mills for making flour, lumber, paper, and gunpowder and for grinding plaster. Establishments in the fuel-using industries were limited to charcoal furnaces and forges for working iron; kilns for making lime, tar, and potash; distilleries; brickyards; and a few small glassworks and potteries.

During the next quarter of a century, ending with the War of 1812, such enterprises increased in size and number. More significant were the introduction of machine spinning and weaving, the erection of nearly 200 cotton mills in New England and the middle states, and the use of steam to move machinery. Meanwhile, a manufacturing interest, which had been vocal in a small way when the first federal revenue laws were drafted in 1789, had acquired sufficient influence by 1816 to give a protectionist color to subsequent customs legislation.

Between the War of 1812 and the Civil War American manufacturing acquired its characteristic pattern. Faced by a scarcity of accumulated funds and entrepreneurial experience, its leaders adopted corporate organization as a device for assembling capital and economizing management. This was particularly true in New England. Funds came at first from the accumulations of merchants engaged in trade with Europe and the Far East. Later the investment reserves of insurance companies and other financial institutions were a source of capital. The mercantile origin of many factories accounted for the early appearance of the agency or factor system and through it of larger corporation groups.

During this period the growth of manufacturing was encouraged by a rapidly expanding market protected to some degree by tariffs and held together by canals and steam transportation on land and water.

Factories specialized in the quantity production of standardized goods to supply the multiplying demands of middle-class consumers. Native ingenuity and scarcity of labor stimulated the use of power devices. Yankee inventors designed textile machinery that enabled relatively inexperienced operatives to make plain fabrics for common use cheaply and efficiently. Americans developed interchangeable mechanisms and their correlative, automatic machinery, for working wood and metals, in order to produce tools, agricultural implements, household utensils, firearms, shelf clocks, and vehicles on a large scale and at low cost. These goods were demanded in ever larger quantities by the expanding population of the older settlements and the rapidly growing West. At the same time, imperative tariff demands led to the establishment of shops and foundries to build steamboat machinery and locomotives, and improved transportation hastened the urbanization of industry.

During these fifty years the advent of factory goods in place of household and homespun manufactures revolutionized consumption. Although in 1860 plain fabrics, hats, footwear, axes and nails, plowshares, and hoes still dominated manufacturing output, refinements and modifications of these staples as well as new inventions and novelties already held a conspicuous position in the market. The production of machine-knit goods, collars and cuffs, garment accessories, and silks had become important industries. Manufactures of rubber were familiar. Pressed glass and porcelain, plated metalwares, lamps, and numerous minor conveniences turned out in quantities by machinery had ceased to be luxuries. Changing fashions increasingly determined consumer demand and the industries that served it.

Quantitative evidence of progress was even more imposing. Between 1810 and 1860, or within the memory of people still alive at the latter date, the number of factory cotton spindles in the country increased from a few hundred thousand to over 5 million, each doing far more work than its predecessors. Output of pig iron rose from less than 60,000 tons to nearly 1 million tons. The factory system extended from textiles to the production of clocks and watches, firearms, sewing machines, and other metal manufactures. In 1853 American methods of making interchangeable mechanisms with automatic machinery had aroused European attention and were studied by special commissioners from Great Britain.

Meanwhile a division of labor developed along sectional lines, so that by 1860 the northeastern states were engaged chiefly in mechanical production, the South in growing staple crops such as cotton, and the

MANUFACTURING

West in producing and processing other raw materials and provisions.

Reconstruction to World War I. The outcome of the Civil War gave the industrial states control over federal policies and inaugurated a period of high protection during which new branches of manufacture were brought to America from Europe. The discovery of petroleum, the introduction of Bessemer steel, the opening of new mines on Lake Superior and in the South, the growth of inland cities, and a great influx of immigrants from Europe combined to turn the nation's energy increasingly toward manufacturing and to move industries from older sites to centers near new sources of raw material and recently created markets. This phase of American manufacturing development was passing at the close of the century and ended by World War I.

Inventions and scientific discoveries multiplied at an accelerated rate as the industrial organism grew more complex. Some of these, suggested at first by an immediate need, later created new industries. In the 1840's, ten years after the advent of railways, the electric telegraph arrived to facilitate their operation. But a major electric industry did not arise until forty years later, when the incandescent lamp and alternating current changed illumination and power distribution and substituted electric power for shaft and belt transmission in large plants. In 1851 William Kelly, a Kentucky ironmaster, invented a rudimentary Bessemer-type process for steel that enabled him to make better boiler plates for steamboats. The perfected process did not come to America until nearly twenty years later, after heavier traffic made steel rails and bridges a necessity. Petroleum appeared at the opportune moment to provide lubricants for millions of machine-age bearings and subsequently suggested the development of internal combustion engines, which made oil an indispensable source of power.

Public enthusiasm for industrial development was increased by a series of international expositions. Two years after the Crystal Palace Exhibition at London in 1851, where American manufacturers first exhibited their skill to Europe, a similar though smaller exhibition in New York testified to a national awakening on the subject. America was officially represented at the Paris Exposition of 1867 and at subsequent international fairs in Europe and learned much from this participation. At home the Centennial Exhibition at Philadelphia in 1876 for the first time enabled the public to compare foreign and domestic manufacturing attainments in a systematic way.

The economy continued the rapid rate of expansion of the pre–Civil War decades. By 1890 the United States had surpassed its nearest rivals, England and Germany, in the production of iron and steel and was by almost any method of reckoning the leading industrial nation. Between 1869 and 1914 the number of wage earners engaged in manufacturing more than trebled. Meanwhile, the horsepower employed in factories increased nearly tenfold and the gross value of manufactured products rose from $3.4 billion to $24.2 billion.

Before the turn of the century important manufacturing enterprises had begun to assemble all operations, from extracting raw materials to marketing finished products, under unified control. Along with this vertical integration a horizontal grouping of plants engaged in similar processes of production but situated in different parts of the country occurred under the ownership and direction of giant companies such as the United States Steel Corporation, formed in 1901. This movement necessitated large-scale financing from a center such as New York City and caused control over many large companies to pass from the major stockholders to investment bankers. Simultaneously, management was increasingly entrusted to professional salaried administrators rather than to the chief owners. Although proprietary establishments and moderate-size corporations continued to grow in number, large companies dominated the highly capitalized industries and made big business a characteristic of American manufacturing.

During the 19th century most manufacturing consisted of processing or shaping materials with hand tools or power machinery. The development of new substances was a relatively minor part of industrial activity. The factory overshadowed the laboratory. Only in the 20th century was organized research, made possible in part by the concentration of industrial capital in great corporations, directed consciously and continuously to the discovery of processes and products hitherto unknown. As early as the Civil War, when Abram S. Hewitt watched his furnace assays and introduced gunmetal from Great Britain, research into the structure and qualities of metals and alloys began slowly to emancipate American metallurgy from rule-of-thumb limitations. A line of advance indicated by the requirements of the Bessemer process in the 1870's and of high-test armor plate in the 1880's as well as the development of electrolytic processes and the commercial production of aluminum in the same decade eventually gave industry the metals that made airplanes and automobiles possible. Plastics such as celluloid film led to motion pictures, and the development of synthetic fibers such as rayon greatly changed the textile industry. While the domestic dye industry was largely the result of interrupted trade with Germany in World War I, chemical processes in general were gaining in importance.

Post–World War II. Up to 1940 continuously pursued research was largely confined to the electrical, chemical, rubber, and power machinery industries; in other lines innovation came from outside or by chance more than by design. World War II added aircraft and scientific instruments, over 60 percent supported by government orders or grants, to the research-oriented industries.

Research directed toward the perfection of existing processes inevitably spawned ideas for new ones, and firms engaged in research tended to diversify their products. Large corporations also saw added security in product diversification, while high corporate taxes added an incentive to absorb companies with "carry-over" tax losses regardless of the type of product. Thus rubber companies came to produce moving pictures, and chemical companies made scores of unrelated items. By the second quarter of the 20th century the control of production was so well understood that companies did not fear the problems of managing plants making strange products; the difficulties arose in marketing. Here there were several failures by very large concerns that found that their dealer organizations, educated for a particular purpose, could not efficiently take on radically different tasks.

The unusual needs and taxes of World War II increased the pace of diversification. In World War I, the United States had been chiefly a supplier of raw materials and semifinished goods; in World War II it became the chief source of finished military supplies. And these supplies took on a complexity never dreamed of before. The automobile industry, converted to military products, was the great mass supplier of motors and various assemblies. Wartime needs expanded small electronics operations into the manufacture of radar, computers, and other devices that had continuing postwar importance. Meanwhile, government-financed research penetrated some of the secrets of atomic fission and fusion and laid the base for atomic power in future decades. The development of rockets, confined in the United States to hand and traditional artillery weapons, also led quickly to navigation in outer space. The war also raised real wages and thereby created a permanently larger consumer demand.

Outwardly, the most striking change in United States industry between 1940 and 1960 was its reloca-

tion. The breakup of large urban industrial complexes with their high land values and congestion of population had always been inherent in the use of electricity and motor transportation, but it accelerated only after 1940, when massive government and private investments led to the construction of new plants and the underwriting of new housing. Electric power that could make the small plant as efficient as the large one, and automobiles and trucks that could carry small shipments more cheaply than the railroads, opened the whole countryside to factory location. Typically, the movement of factories was from central cities to urban fringe areas, and plants that used highly skilled or middle-income employees moved before those requiring large numbers of unskilled workers.

The most spectacular industrial developments of the mid-20th century were in electronics and the many new products made by airplane companies. In the electronics field the total value added by manufacture was not great, but the digital computer promised wide future effects on all types of technology. By the late 1960's jets, missiles, and aerospace equipment made the "airplane" census subdivision of the manufacturing list second only to motor vehicles in value added.

By the early 1970's the largest aggregate industrial groups, based on value added, were transportation equipment, machinery other than electrical, food, electrical supplies, and chemical products. Machinery other than electrical, electrical supplies, transportation equipment, and food were also the major employers, each utilizing about 2 million workers.

[Victor S. Clark, *History of Manufactures in the United States;* Thomas C. Cochran, *American Business in the Twentieth Century.*]

THOMAS C. COCHRAN

MANUFACTURING, HOUSEHOLD, employed a substantial part of the annual working time of American colonists and settlers for 200 years and continued in rural and frontier communities until after the Civil War. During much of this period clothing, household goods, tools, implements, and other articles of home consumption were made largely by members of the family. Wool cards, flax hatchels, spinning wheels, hand looms, and dye tubs were even more universal than the sewing machine is today.

Throughout their history the American colonies experienced cycles of prosperity and depression comparable for their day with those under the Republic. In hard times household manufactures expanded; in good times, when the people had money to pay for imported goods, they declined. Since periods of distress and their accompanying indebtedness to British merchants were commonly ascribed to the colonists' buying too many imported goods, public and private agencies exerted themselves at such times to encourage household manufacturing by establishing spinning schools, levying taxes payable in homespun yarn, and similar measures.

No comprehensive statistics exist concerning these manufactures. Contemporary observers before the Revolution testified to their prevalence except in towns and on plantations producing export crops. British colonial governors described them in reports to their London superiors, for they curtailed the market for British goods. Alexander Hamilton's report on manufactures in 1791 was the first systematic attempt to gather information about them. A more ambitious effort was made to enumerate them in the census of 1810, but its figures are fragmentary. Thereafter factory goods rapidly replaced the products of family industry, though values of household manufactures were reported by the census until 1860.

The most important household manufactures were textiles and garments. According to the incomplete returns of 1810 over 72 million yards of cotton, flax, woolen, and mixed fabrics valued at nearly $38 million were made in households. Maple sugar, cheese, cider, soap, candles, shoes, harness, furniture, woodenware, plows, harrows, tools, nails, and other unrecorded or imperfectly recorded articles of household production probably added several million dollars to this total. But the output of local factories and workshops was already displacing household products. According to later censuses the total value of family-made goods produced in the United States declined from $29 million in 1840 to less than $25 million in 1860, and by the latter date their per capita value, which had exceeded $5 in 1810, had fallen to less than $1.

[Carl Bridenbaugh, *The Colonial Craftsman;* Alex Croner, *American Heritage History of American Business.*]
VICTOR S. CLARK

MANUMISSION during the years 1790–1860 was the formal liberation of a slave by means of an instrument of writing, such as a will or a deed of manumission, as prescribed by state law. Often the slaves purchased their freedom, especially in the border states, over a period of years. Personal considerations, religion, the doctrine of natural right, and the schemes for African colonization (*see* American Colonization Society) influenced the slaveowners to free their slaves. Changes in the attitude toward slavery within each state were reflected in the changing laws on manumission. Manumission was advocated by the moderate antislavery groups in opposition to the extreme abolitionist program for immediate, unconditional emancipation. By 1831 the northern states had adopted measures for the gradual emancipation of their black population, but fear for the loss of white supremacy and increasing sectional strife caused the southern and border states to restrict or prohibit manumissions. In 1860 Maryland had the largest number of free blacks, 49 percent of its black population, with Virginia holding second place. In the United States the number of slaves increased from 697,897 to 3,950,531 between 1790 and 1860. During the same period the number of free blacks increased from 59,527 to 488,070, due largely to manumissions and the natural growth of population.

[A. D. Adams, *The Neglected Period of Antislavery in America;* James Wright, *The Free Negro in Maryland.*]
ELIZABETH W. MEADE

MAPLE SUGAR. The Indians were familiar with maple sap, either drinking it fresh or boiling it down to syrup and sugar, usually in bark troughs into which hot stones were dropped. The French in Canada soon learned of the merits of maple sap, but not until the late 17th century did English settlers take it up. Then the sugar rapidly became an article of food and commerce, especially in the northern states, with Vermont leading all the rest. It was said in 1809 that probably two-thirds of Vermont's population worked in spring at making sugar and syrup. In one town alone in 1794, eighty-three families produced 14,080 pounds of maple sugar; the state's total output was estimated at 1,000 tons. (More than 30 gallons of maple sap are needed to yield 1 gallon of syrup; 1 gallon of syrup yields about 8 pounds of maple sugar.) The sap was first boiled in iron kettles; the introduction of shallow pans in the middle 19th century was revolutionary. On the frontier, where cane sugar and molasses were scarce or unprocurable, the maple tree sweetened the pioneer's food and drink; its sugar was his confection. Small quantities of maple sugar were made even in the Gulf states in early days, but this soon ceased. The use of maple sugar declined in the 19th century, but the syrup gained in popularity. By 1900 Ohio was competing sharply with Vermont in its production, but cane sugar gradually replaced maple sugar in popularity because it is less expensive to produce. Maple sugar production is now confined to the Northeast, particularly in Vermont and New York, and takes place from February to April.

[W. F. Fox and W. F. Hubbard, *The Maple Sugar Industry.*]

ALVIN F. HARLOW

MAPPING OF AMERICAN COASTS. Every phase of exploration and discovery in America is represented by one or more contemporary maps. Christopher Columbus plotted his course to the westward in 1492 either from Paolo dal Pozzo Toscanelli's world map (1474) or from Martin Behaim's globe (1492). On his return to Spain with news of islands in the "Great Western Sea" between Europe and the Orient, Columbus drew a map of his discoveries. Only a copy, after the original, survives in the "Admiral's Map" (ca. 1507), first published in the 1513 edition of Ptolemy's *Geography.* By the end of the 15th century several voyages had been completed, a series of explorations that probed the coastlines of both North and South America in an attempt to find a passage through the land barrier to the Orient. The mapping of America was a slow process, made slower by the unwillingness of navigators to exchange information and maps. In 1500 Juan de la Cosa, experienced navigator and pilot, compiled a large map of the world based on his own voyages across the Atlantic with Columbus and with Alonso de Ojeda. On it he incorporated all he knew of the Spanish, Portuguese, and English discoveries in America, including those of Amerigo Vespucci and John and Sebastian Cabot. Two years later (1502) the discoveries of Gaspar Corte-Real were outlined on a map drawn by Alberto Cantino. But only four maps are known that were actually printed between 1492 and 1510, so closely were new discoveries guarded in Spain and Portugal. And those four were printed in other countries. The earliest, by Giovanni Contarini (1506), was closely followed in 1507 by a globe and large wall map by Martin Waldseemüller. The globe gores of Waldseemüller were published with a text (*Cosmographiae Introductio*) that suggested for the first time that the New World be called America. The fourth printed map, by Johann Ruysch, appeared in 1508.

Two general theories became current regarding the size and shape of America. The first, propagated in a series of maps by Oronce Fine, whose heart-shaped world was published in 1531, assumed that America was joined to Asia—that by sailing far enough north or south along the Atlantic coast a passage would be discovered that would lead to Asia, lying not far

beyond. Others believed that America was a continent beyond which, at some distance, lay the Orient. But just how far beyond, nobody knew. This second theory was championed by Waldseemüller, whose ideas were developed and extended in a long series of maps by Johannes de Stobnicza. After Ferdinand Magellan had circumnavigated South America in 1520 and Hernando Cortes had launched several expeditions in the Pacific Ocean, the western coast of America began to take shape. It was first drawn on a map in 1529, but there was no other good map of the coast until 1544, when one attributed to Sebastian Cabot was published, probably based on the *Padron Real* in Seville. This master chart, maintained under the supervision of the Casa de Contraction, was supposed to have added to it all new discoveries as soon as they were made. Many inaccuracies crept into this chart, and many discoverers failed to report their findings. The first authentic map of the coast of California, undated, but based on the discoveries of Cortes in 1535, was followed by a map of the same region by Alonso de Santa Cruz (1542–45).

The latter half of the 16th century saw many map publishing firms spring up in Europe. They issued hundreds of maps of America and parts thereof; these were strange combinations of factual and legendary information. Two cartographic productions by Gerhardus Mercator led to a revolution in the mapping of America. On his world map of 1538 and his globe of 1541, Mercator, though unfamiliar with the discoveries of Cortes, separated America from Asia and rejected the Asiatic names commonly found in the heart of the New World. Meanwhile, three manuscript maps were produced in the Dieppe school of cartography (1541–53). These maps gave the world its cartographic knowledge of the three voyages of Jacques Cartier along the northeast coast. They incorporated much that was new, including the discoveries of Giovanni da Verrazano (1524–28). With the publication of Mercator's large-scale chart of the world (1569), revised and improved by Edward Wright in 1655, the science of cartography came into its own, and mariners were able to navigate with a degree of certainty. Mercator's projection, in a modified form, is still in use today.

In the 17th century, three maps made by Capt. John Smith added to the knowledge of the Atlantic coast; these were a map of Virginia (1608), a map of New England (1614), and a general map of the Atlantic coast (1624). Samuel de Champlain's map of the northeast coast, published in his *Voyages* (1613), represents the first attempt to lay down the latitudes and longitudes of the region, at the same time adding a great deal of information on the interior of the country. On the West Coast, beginning with a map in the 1622 edition of the work of Antonio de Herrera, and later on the map by Henry Briggs of 1625, California was shown as an island. This erroneous idea persisted for many years, although not all cartographers subscribed to it. Chief among the notable maps of the West Coast printed in the 17th century were those of Robert Dudley, an expatriated Englishman who explored the entire West Coast. His large-scale map of the region was included in his atlas, the *Arcano Del Mare,* published in Florence, Italy, in 1646–47. On this map he supplied the world with a precise and elaborate nomenclature for the West Coast.

In the 18th century an elaborate survey of the Atlantic coast was projected by the British government. The work was begun in 1765 under the direction of Capt. Samuel Holland, who worked with a detail of men until 1772. At that time it was estimated that it would take five more years to complete the job. In 1774 Capt. J. F. W. Des Barres replaced Holland, and from that date until 1781 his charts were printed and published as they were completed. Later they were bound in various atlas formats and issued under the title *The Atlantic Neptune* (1774–81). On the West Coast Capt. George Vancouver completed two years of surveying in 1792 and published his findings in three volumes (1798), including a valuable atlas, giving the world the first accurate maps of the region. Surveys of the Pacific coast were climaxed by Alexander von Humboldt and Aimé Bonpland, whose monumental works, including many maps, published over a period of nearly fifty years, added greatly to the knowledge of the Northwest. The mapping of the United States by the Coast Survey, a branch of the federal government, began in 1807; the field work of this agency has been practically uninterrupted since its inception. After the Civil War geodetic operations were added to the function of the Coast Survey, and in 1878 the name of the agency was changed to Coast and Geodetic Survey. (*See also* Cartography.)

[Ralph H. Brown, *Mirror for Americans: Likeness of the Eastern Seaboard;* James Clement Wheat and Christian F. Brun, *Maps and Charts Published in America Before 1800: A Bibliography.*]

LLOYD A. BROWN

MARAIS DES CYGNES MASSACRE (May 19, 1858), an incident of the Kansas Border War. Charles A. Hamilton, a proslavery settler from Georgia, with a party of about thirty men, arrested a number of Free-State men, eleven of whom were taken to a ravine near the Marais des Cygnes River in Kansas and shot. All were left for dead, though five were only wounded, and one, falling with the rest, escaped unhurt. The shooting, without political significance, was probably an act of revenge. John Greenleaf Whittier commemorated the event with a poem.

[L. W. Spring, *Kansas, The Prelude to the War for the Union.*]

SAMUEL A. JOHNSON

MARBURY V. MADISON, 1 Cranch 137 (1803), was decided by the U.S. Supreme Court on Feb. 24, 1803. The importance of the decision in American constitutional history lies chiefly in the position taken that the Court would declare unconstitutional and void acts of Congress in conflict with the Constitution. By this decision the doctrine of judicial review was firmly entrenched in the governmental system, and the position of the judiciary was strengthened in the balance of powers among the legislative, executive, and judicial branches of the government.

The case grew out of the attempt of William Marbury to compel James Madison, secretary of state, to turn over to Marbury a commission as justice of the peace that had been made out to Marbury by Madison's predecessor in office. The Supreme Court had to decide whether it could and should issue a mandamus to compel the secretary of state to act. Intimately involved were issues of contemporary politics. The appointments of Marbury and other Federalists to newly created offices had been made as the Federalist administration under John Adams was retired, to be succeeded by Republicans under the leadership of Thomas Jefferson (*see* Midnight Judges). At the head of the Supreme Court was Chief Justice John Marshall, a staunch Federalist. Granting the writ of mandamus would therefore be regarded as an exertion not merely of judicial power on the executive, but of Federalist power on Democratic-Republican party leadership as well. The customs of the Constitution were not yet well established, and it was not known whether the writ would be obeyed even if issued.

The opinion of the Supreme Court, written by the chief justice, began not with the constitutional question, the existence of which was not generally recognized, but with the question of Marbury's right to the commission. He found that Marbury had such a right. Reasoning from accepted principles of government, he concluded that the laws of the country must provide a remedy for the violation of a vested legal right, and that the writ of mandamus was the proper form of remedy. The remaining question was whether the Supreme Court could issue the writ. The power was not included among the grants of original jurisdiction made to the Supreme Court in the Constitution, but it was given by a section in the Judiciary Act of 1789, which had the effect of expanding the original jurisdiction of the Court beyond the group of powers enumerated in the Constitution. The chief justice argued that Congress could not expand the original jurisdiction of the Court. The act was therefore in conflict with the Constitution, and it became necessary to decide whether an act repugnant to the Constitution could become the law of the land. The Court answered in the negative. It held the statutory provision unconstitutional, and decided that the writ of mandamus could not be issued by the Supreme Court.

Contemporary interest lay less in the doctrine of judicial review than in the political aspects of the case. The chief justice succeeded in condemning the acts of the Jefferson administration, and then, by a step that appeared superficially to be an act of judicial self-restraint, avoided a resulting decision that might have terminated in mutiny when it came to enforcement. Only gradually did emphasis in appraisal of the case shift to the topic of the power of the courts to invalidate federal legislation deemed by them to be in conflict with the Constitution.

[A. J. Beveridge, *The Life of John Marshall;* Charles Warren, *The Supreme Court in United States History.*]

CARL BRENT SWISHER

MARCH TO THE SEA, SHERMAN'S. *See* **Sherman's March to the Sea.**

MARCY'S EXPLORING EXPEDITION (1852) was ordered by the War Department for the purpose of exploring the Red River to its source. Capt. R. B. Marcy, by reason of his previous exploration of the territory between Fort Smith, Ark., and Santa Fe, N.Mex., to determine the best route to California from the Mississippi, and his experience in exploring the Canadian River and locating sites for forts in that region, was selected to command the expedition. His report, printed by Congress in 1853, disclosed that there were two main branches of the Red River, whereas earlier treaties, including the one between Mexico and Texas, admitted but one. Between the two stretched valuable lands, which were made the object of litigation between the United States and Texas in 1896 (*see* Greer County Dispute). No survey of the Red to its source had been made before

Marcy's expedition. In addition to mapping the country, Marcy brought back much valuable scientific information and wrote one of the most interesting reports of the Southwest.

[G. Foreman, ed., *Adventure on Red River.*]

CARL L. CANNON

MARCY'S MARCH (1857). Because of menacing conditions in the Mormon country a military department was constituted in Utah. In the summer of 1857 troops commanded by Col. A. S. Johnston were sent there (*see* Mormon Expedition). The command wintered at Fort Bridger, Wyo. A detachment under Capt. R. B. Marcy was sent to New Mexico for supplies. It marched on Nov. 24, 1857, into a mountainous wilderness, without pathway or habitation, through deep snow and in bitter cold, to Fort Massachusetts, Colo. Preparing to return, Marcy was instructed to delay for reinforcements, because of information that hostile Mormons planned to intercept him and destroy the supplies. On June 9, 1858, Marcy reached Fort Bridger.

[O. L. Spaulding, *The United States Army in Peace and War.*]

THOMAS ROBSON HAY

MARDI GRAS, the name applied to the elaborate series of outdoor pageants and indoor balls held annually during the winter social season in the United States, especially in New Orleans, and culminating on Shrove Tuesday, the day before Ash Wednesday, the first day of Lent. Introduced on a small scale from Paris in 1827, this interesting spectacle still survives, in a greatly enlarged and refined form, after many lapses and revivals. The unique and colorful pageants, each sponsored by one of the numerous carnival organizations, are based upon themes drawn from history, fiction, or mythology; and the balls given by the several groups are elaborate and exclusive. Mardi Gras, or carnival, is also celebrated in other parts of the world, notably Brazil.

[John S. Kendall, *History of New Orleans;* Lyle Saxon, *Fabulous New Orleans.*]

WALTER PRICHARD

MARE CLAUSUM is a term in international law indicating the principle of the "closed sea" as against *mare liberum,* or a "free sea." The United States has been in favor of the free sea (*see* Freedom of the Seas), though it asserted the principle of *mare clau-*

sum when it sought to break up pelagic sealing in Alaskan waters. In the summer of 1886, the United States seized three English sealers operating well upon the high seas. America contended that with Alaska it had acquired the privilege of closing the sea. A Russian ukase of 1821 was cited. In arbitration, America had to surrender the principle. It had invoked the principle of *mare liberum* too often, including a protest against the ukase in question, which had resulted in Russian treaties with the United States (1824) and Great Britain (1825) keeping the Bering Sea open.

[John Bassett Moore, *International Arbitrations.*]
JIM DAN HILL

MARIA MONK CONTROVERSY originated in 1836 with the publication of the *Awful Disclosures of the Hotel Dieu Nunnery of Montreal,* which, although purporting to be Maria Monk's autobiography, was actually written by a group of New York clergymen. Its stress on priestly immorality aroused a storm of controversy that persisted even after several committees had investigated the Hotel Dieu Convent and pronounced Maria Monk a fraud. She retained some prestige until after her death in 1849 in a Five Points brothel. The *Awful Disclosures,* an immediate bestseller, was one of the most influential pieces of nativistic propaganda ever printed in the United States.

[R. A. Billington, ''Maria Monk and Her Influence,'' *Catholic Historical Review,* vol. 12, and *The Protestant Crusade.*]
RAY ALLEN BILLINGTON

MARIANA, the territory in present-day Massachusetts between the ''Naumkeck'' River (Salem) and the Merrimack River from the sea to their heads and including Cape Ann, was granted to Capt. John Mason by the New England Council on Mar. 9, 1622. The evidence of Mason's actual occupation is slight. In 1679 his heirs claimed that his agent, Ambrose Gibbons, took possession in 1622 or 1623 and that he was ousted in 1630 by the Massachusetts Bay Company. Neither Mason nor his heirs were ever able to make good their title to the territory, which by the charter of 1629 was incorporated into that of the Massachusetts Bay Colony.

[J. W. Dean, ed., *Captain John Mason.*]
ROBERT E. MOODY

''MARIANAS TURKEY SHOOT.'' *See* **Philippine Sea, Battle of the.**

MARIETTA, the first settlement made under the provisions of the Ordinance of 1787, was settled on Apr. 7, 1788, when forty-eight men under the leadership of Gen. Rufus Putnam of the Ohio Company of Associates concluded their journey from Massachusetts to the mouth of the Muskingum River in the present state of Ohio. It was at first named Adelphia, but on July 2, 1788, in honor of Queen Marie Antoinette of France, the name was changed to Marietta. The machinery of government in the Northwest Territory first functioned here, when Gen. Arthur St. Clair, governor of the territory, arrived on July 9, 1788.

T. N. HOOVER

MARIN, EXPEDITION OF, planned by Marquis Abraham Duquesne de Meneval and executed by Capt. Paul Marin, established French authority in western Pennsylvania. Routes and sites were reconnoitered in 1752. Moving by water from Montreal in 1753, Marin occupied Presque Isle (now Erie, Pa.). Later Fort LeBoeuf and Venango were garrisoned. The expedition alarmed the Indians and precipitated British-American resistance.

[William Kingsford, *The History of Canada,* vol. III; Frank Hayward Severance, *An Old Frontier of France.*]
ALFRED P. JAMES

MARINE BIOLOGICAL LABORATORY AT WOODS HOLE. Established in 1888, when the summer school for teachers sponsored by the Woman's Education Association of Boston (founded 1871) moved from Annisquam, Mass., to Woods Hole, Mass., MBL (as it is universally known) became almost at once the summertime center of American biological research. Many of the leaders of American biology have spent their summers as students, teachers, and researchers in MBL's seaside laboratories in Massachusetts. Research at MBL has broken new paths in three areas especially. Before World War I, important advances were made in cytology and genetics. Developmental biology occupied center stage for the following two decades. Then, in 1936, the British biologist J. Z. Young discovered that the Woods Hole squid contains a single giant axon, or nerve fiber, into which electrodes can be inserted, inaugurating a line of research into nerve conduction that continues to occupy the largest single group of investigators at MBL.

The research of independent investigators is complemented at MBL by a teaching program centered since the 1890's in four courses: invertebrate zoology, marine botany, general physiology, and embryology. Other courses, such as protozoology (1919–29), have been taught from time to time; since 1957 there have been postdoctoral training programs in neurobiology, fertilization and gamete physiology, and excitable membrane biophysics.

The laboratory's ability to exert leadership in the rapidly growing domain of biology has been greatly aided by a governmental structure unique among American scholarly institutions. The laboratory began by modeling itself on the Stazione Zoologica, founded by Anton Dohrn in Naples in 1872, where income came largely from two sources: the collecting of specimens for other laboratories and the renting of laboratory "tables" to educational and scientific institutions. To this European tradition of research, MBL joined the American tradition of instruction, begun by Louis Agassiz at Penikese Island (off Woods Hole) in 1873 and continued by his student Alpheus Hyatt at Annisquam. In 1897, the scientists, led by the director, C. O. Whitman, professor successively at Tokyo, Clark, and Chicago universities, eliminated from the control of MBL both the women who had founded the laboratory and the Boston financiers who had supported its rapid growth. In spite of a financial crisis that nearly led in 1902 to the laboratory becoming a department of the Carnegie Institution of Washington, MBL remains, as Whitman had envisaged, under the control of the scientists who came to work there from all over the United States and from many foreign countries. Lay trustees are in a small minority, and the director is chosen more for scientific reputation than for managerial skills.

The laboratory expanded steadily until 1971, financed before 1945 by the Carnegie Corporation, the Rockefeller Foundation, and private donors (chiefly Charles R. Crane of Chicago, father-in-law of MBL's second director, Frank R. Lillie, a professor at the University of Chicago). Since 1950, the federal government has been the laboratory's largest single supporter through the National Science Foundation and the National Institutes of Health.

Woods Hole was chosen as the site for MBL because Spencer F. Baird had established the U.S. Fish Commission's laboratories there. More recently, MBL has itself been the nucleus of an expanding scientific community. In 1930, the Woods Hole Oceanographic Institution was founded under the aegis of Lillie, then president of MBL and the National Academy of Sciences. Biologist-presidents of the academy following Lillie have also spent summers in Woods Hole and vicinity, leading the acad-

emy to set up a summer studies center there in 1956. In the 1960's MBL replaced its old wooden buildings with modern ones, permitting it to add year-round research programs to the summertime instruction and research that have made the laboratory a world center in biology.

[F. R. Lillie, *The Woods Hole Marine Biological Laboratory*.]

HAROLD L. BURSTYN

MARINE CORPS, UNITED STATES. The U.S. Marine Corps traditionally dates its history from Nov. 10, 1775, when the Continental Congress authorized that "two Battalions of Marines be raised." These first marines executed a successful amphibious raid into the Bahamas in March 1776; joined George Washington at Princeton, N.J., in January 1777; wintered at Morristown, N.J.; and participated in the defense of the Delaware River and Philadelphia in the autumn of 1777. A small number of Continental marines were included in the Penobscot expedition in July–August 1779. This expedition, aimed at uprooting the British from the area near present-day Castine, Maine, ended in disaster and was the last effort in the American Revolution at a large-scale amphibious operation. At sea, marines—Continental, state, or privateer—served on board virtually all armed ships of the embattled colonies. Both the Continental navy and marines were disbanded at the end of hostilities.

In 1794 Congress, spurred by the depredations of Algerian pirates, authorized the building of six frigates. Marine quotas were included in their complements, although actual recruiting did not begin until 1797. On July 11, 1798, concomitant with the separation of the navy from the War Department, Congress authorized "a Marine Corps." In the Quasi-War with France (1798–1800) the new U.S. Marines fought in virtually all sea actions—notably the victories of the *Constellation* over the *Insurgente* (1799) and *Vengeance* (1800). Some minor landings were made, including those in Curaçao and in Puerto Plata, Santo Domingo, in 1800. Next came operations against the Barbary pirates (1801–15), including the celebrated march "to the shores of Tripoli" by eight marines as part of the polyglot "army" that moved 600 miles across the Libyan desert from Alexandria to Derna (1805).

In the War of 1812 the U.S. Marines' chief service continued to be at sea, notably in the great frigate duels and in the cruise of the *Essex* to the Pacific (1812–14). A provisional battalion fought well at Bladensburg, Md. (1814), as did another battalion at

New Orleans (1815), but there were neither resources nor opportunities for significant amphibious employment.

The next three decades saw operations against the pirates in the Caribbean (1822 to the 1830's), landings in such diverse places as the Falkland Islands (1832) and Sumatra (1831–32), and patrolling off West Africa to suppress the slave trade (1820–61). A marine regiment was improvised for the Seminole War of 1836–42.

In the Mexican War (1846–48) marines were used in many amphibious operations on both the Gulf and Pacific coasts. A marine battalion drawn from the Gulf Squadron executed raids against Frontera, Tampico, and Alvarado (1846–47) and landed with Gen. Winfield Scott at Veracruz (Mar. 9, 1847). A second marine battalion joined Scott at Puebla and marched with him to Mexico City, coming into prominence in the storming of Chapultepec and the taking of San Cosmé Gate (Sept. 13, 1847). Meanwhile, the Gulf Squadron was conducting successful landings at Alvarado, Tuxpan, Frontera, and up the Tabasco River to San Juan Bautista. In the West, marine landing parties from the Pacific Squadron were repeatedly used in the conquest of California (1846) and against Mexico's west coast ports (1847).

The U.S. Marines were in China with the East India Squadron as early as 1844 and were with Commodore Matthew C. Perry when he forced open the doors of Japan to foreign commerce in 1853. A marine detachment from Washington, D.C., captured John Brown at Harpers Ferry, W.Va. (1859).

In the Civil War (1861–65), a battalion fought at the first Battle of Bull Run (1861), but most service was with the navy. Overshadowed by the larger scope and drama of the land campaigns, the series of amphibious operations in which marines participated—beginning with the capture of Fort Clark on Hatteras Inlet, N.C., on Aug. 28, 1861, and ending with the assault of Fort Fisher, a guardian of Wilmington, N.C., on Jan. 15, 1865—has been largely overlooked.

In the last third of the 19th century, marine involvement in the Orient and in the Caribbean increased. From 1865 until 1898 there were some thirty-two landings, including Formosa (1867), Japan (1867 and 1868), Mexico (1870), Korea (1871, 1888, and 1894), Colombia (1873), Hawaii (1874 and 1889), Egypt (1882), Panama (1885 and 1895), Samoa (1888), Haiti (1888), China (1894 and 1895), and Nicaragua (1894 and 1896).

In the Spanish-American War (1898) a marine bat-

talion seized an advanced base at Guantánamo Bay in support of the American blockade of the Spanish squadron at Santiago de Cuba. Elsewhere, marine landing parties accepted the Spanish surrender of Guam and several Puerto Rican ports. A regiment was formed for service in the Philippine Insurrection (1899–1904). This regiment also joined the allied relief column sent to Peking in the Boxer Rebellion (1900) to succor the besieged legation quarter, whose defenders, in turn, included marine ship's detachments detailed as legation guards.

Between the turn of the century and World War I, the Marine Corps was expanded gradually and structured more permanently into companies, regiments, and brigades for expeditionary service. Landings and expeditions of this period include Samoa (1899), Nicaragua (1899, 1909–10, 1912–13), Panama (1901, 1902, and 1903–04), Honduras (1903), the Dominican Republic (1903, 1916–24), Syria (1903), Ethiopia (1903), China (1905), Cuba (1906–09, 1912), Mexico (1914), and Haiti (1915–34).

In World War I the Fifth Marine Regiment was in the first convoy to sail for France (June 14, 1917). The Fifth Regiment was joined by the Sixth Marine Regiment and together, as the Fourth Brigade, Second U.S. Division, they fought at Belleau Wood (June 1918), Soissons (July 1918), Saint-Mihiel (September 1918), Blanc Mont (October 1918), and in the final Meuse-Argonne offensive (November 1918). Four marine squadrons, forming the day wing of the navy's northern bombing group, operated primarily over Belgium in support of the British.

Marine involvement in the occupation of Haiti and Santo Domingo continued through these war years. The marines served along the Mexican border, the Sixth Brigade was used in the sugar intervention in Cuba (1917–19), and there were minor expeditions to Siberia (1918–20). After the war large-scale involvement in Nicaragua (1926–33) and China (1926–41) was renewed. At home, marine planners at Quantico, Va., envisioned the probability of a war with Japan in which amphibious operations of unprecedented size and complexity would be required. These studies led to the development and testing of amphibious doctrine and equipment that served the United States and its allies well in World War II. Concurrently, marine aviation was experimenting with close air support. The organization of the Fleet Marine Force in 1933 provided a framework that was expanded by 1945 to two corps headquarters, six divisions, and five large aircraft wings.

A marine brigade was sent to occupy Iceland in the

summer of 1941. In the Pacific, when the Japanese struck on Dec. 7, 1941, U.S. Marines were involved not only in the defense of Pearl Harbor but also in the Philippines and at Guam, Wake, and Midway islands. Beginning with Guadalcanal (August 1942), marine divisions or corps later conducted amphibious assaults at Bougainville (November 1942), Tarawa (November 1942), New Britain (December 1943), Kwajalein (January 1944), Eniwetok (February 1944), Saipan (June 1944), Guam (July 1944), Tinian (July 1944), Peleliu (September 1944), Iwo Jima (February 1945), and Okinawa (April 1945). Separate marine raider operations included Makin (August 1942) and New Georgia (June 1943). Marine aviation, in addition to providing air defense and close air support incident to these and other, including army, operations, contributed to the neutralization of bypassed Japanese-held islands. During World War II the Marine Corps reached a peak strength of 485,113.

Marine units, originally of corps size, took part briefly in the occupation of Japan (1945–46) and for a longer term in the occupation of northern China (1945–49). Renewed studies at Quantico concentrated on the use of the helicopter to achieve a "vertical envelopment" capability.

Immediately after the outbreak of the Korean War (June 1950), a marine brigade was sent to reinforce the Pusan perimeter. Joined by the remainder of the First Marine Division and supported by the First Marine Aircraft Wing, these marines executed the assault at Inchon and the subsequent recapture of Seoul (September 1950). At the time of the Chinese intervention, the marines were near the Chosin Reservoir in northeastern Korea. With the collapse of the UN front on both flanks, the marines fought their way back to Hungnam (December 1950). The division next joined the United Nations forces in the counteroffensives of spring and summer 1951 until the truce line was reached. Two years of trench warfare followed.

A brigade-size force was landed in Lebanon (July 1958); a large amphibious force was marshaled, but not landed, in the Cuban missile crisis (October 1962); and a brigade of marines was used in the Dominican intervention (April 1965).

Involvement in Vietnam began with the assignment of U.S. Marine advisers to the Vietnamese Marine Corps in 1954. Marine transport helicopter units arrived in 1962, and in 1965 the landing of the Ninth Marine Expeditionary Brigade at Da Nang marked the first significant introduction of U.S. ground forces. Marine ground operations were concentrated in First Corps Tactical Zone, the northern five provinces of South Vietnam. By summer of 1968, the Third Marine Amphibious Force in Vietnam included over 85,000 marines, more than the number who fought at Iwo Jima or Okinawa. This force had completely left Vietnam by June 1971. In reaction to the North Vietnamese Easter offensive of 1972, two marine aircraft groups were reintroduced into Vietnam, but no marine ground forces were used.

Legislation passed during the Korean War (June 1952) requires that the active Fleet Marine Force be maintained at a minimum of three divisions and three wings, with requisite supporting units. A fourth marine division and wing are contained in the Organized Reserve. Strength of the regular Marine Corps in 1975 was 196,000.

[R. D. Heinl, Jr., *Soldiers of the Sea*; J. A. Isely and P. A. Crowl, *The U.S. Marines and Amphibious War*; E. N. McClellan, *History of the U.S. Marine Corps*; C. H. Metcalf, *History of the U.S. Marine Corps*; R. Sherrod, *History of Marine Corps Aviation in World War II*; U.S. Marine Corps, *History of Marine Corps Operations in World War II*, and *U.S. Marine Operations in Korea*.]

EDWIN H. SIMMONS

MARION, BATTLE AT (Dec. 18, 1864). Union Gen. George Stoneman, raiding southwestern Virginia from eastern Tennessee, struck the Confederates under John C. Breckinridge at Marion, Va. During the battle Stoneman detached a force that moved back to Saltville, Va., and destroyed the salt works there. This was his original purpose, even though he could gain no decision against Breckinridge.

[R. U. Johnson and C. C. Buel, eds., *Battles and Leaders of the Civil War*, vol. IV.]

ROBERT S. THOMAS

MARION, FORT, at Saint Augustine, Fla., called by the Spaniards, at various times, San Juan de Pinos, San Augustine, and San Marco, and by the British (1763–83) Saint Marks, was finally brought to completion, at enormous cost, in 1756. In the meantime it had withstood South Carolina Gov. James Moore's attack in 1702 and James E. Oglethorpe's siege in 1740. The fort is a regular, coquina structure of four equal, huge outer walls and four equal bastions, each with a tower. It has about thirty rooms (one was the chapel), which enclose an open court 103 by 109 feet. A moat, drawbridge, and portcullis suggest a medieval castle. When the United States acquired Florida in 1819 the place was renamed for Gen. Francis

Marion. The fort and the great coquina pillars of the ancient gate to Saint Augustine still stand as monuments of the Spanish regime in America.

[J. T. Connor, ''The Nine Wooden Forts at St. Augustine,'' *Florida Historical Quarterly,* vol. 4; Charles B. Reynolds, *Old Saint Augustine.*]

JONATHAN T. DORRIS

MARIPOSA LAND GRANT is the best known of the 800 grants or claims to land given by the Spanish and Mexican governments in California. Like most of the grants, except for small plots near the missions, it was intended as a grazing ranch, but because it was a floating grant, its owner was privileged to locate it within a broad area roughly equivalent to present-day Mariposa County. The grant given to the former Mexican governor Juan Bautista Alvarado was for ten leagues, or 44,368 acres. The claim was purchased by John C. Frémont in 1847, even though there were grave questions as to its validity because it had not been occupied or surveyed, juridical possession had not been given by the local magistrate, and Alvarado had been interdicted from selling, alienating, or hypothecating it in any way. Not long after, gold was discovered and the Mariposa area was quickly flooded with miners washing the sands and pecking into the quartz veins. Frémont, finding that his claim, despite its questionable title, was most promising, swung it around to include the richest of the gold-bearing quartz deposits on which miners were working high in the foothills of the Sierra, land unsuited for grazing. With the aid of his brother-in-law, William Carey Jones—a strong-minded, arrogant, and self-assured attorney—he pushed the claim with the utmost dispatch through the courts to win early confirmation by the Land Commission, whose members were not well versed in claim litigation. Later, before Judge Ogden Hoffman of the District Court of Northern California, the claim was rejected because of the failure of Alvarado to conform to the requirements of Mexican land law. On appeal to the Supreme Court by a battery of top-ranking lawyers, the chief of whom made an impassioned harangue calling for confirmation because of the brilliant service of Frémont to the country, the claim was confirmed, although only after numerous precedents for rejecting it had been arbitrarily swept aside. The decision opened the way to the confirmation of other equally questionable grants, until Chief Justice Roger B. Taney was finally persuaded to hold more rigidly to previous decisions and to Mexican law.

The action of the Supreme Court in upholding Frémont's right to the minerals of Mariposa brought him a flood of gold and enabled him to live the life of an oriental nabob for a decade. But his difficulties were not over, for he had to evict the miners on his claim. His ejectment proceedings and his refusal to pay taxes on the claim until the title of Mariposa was confirmed incurred deep hostility toward him. In the presidential election of 1856 he was badly cut in the mining counties. Lacking in business experience, he was taken advantage of by wily financiers and lost ownership of Mariposa. In his later days Frémont lived in poverty, which was only relieved by a patronage job as territorial governor of Arizona. Mariposa itself was in trouble in the courts and in international finance for much of its existence as a mining enterprise, because of divided authority, exaggerated estimates of its potential, and wasteful management. It was said that $20 million in gold was taken from Mariposa by 1872, but operating costs, investments in machinery, road costs, and litigation costs left little profit.

[Allan Nevins, *Frémont, Pathmarker of the West;* Raymond F. Wood, *California's Agua Fria.*]

PAUL W. GATES

MARITIME COMMISSION, FEDERAL, an independent regulatory agency, was established under the provisions of Reorganization Plan No. 7 on Aug. 12, 1961, to administer the functions and discharge the regulatory authorities of the shipping statutes (for example, the Shipping Act of 1916, Merchant Marine Act of 1920, Intercoastal Shipping Act of 1933, and Merchant Marine Act of 1936).

The Federal Maritime Commission protects the interests of the public by regulating waterborne shipping in the foreign and domestic offshore commerce of the United States. The statutory authorities and functions of the commission embrace eight principal areas: (1) regulation of services, practices, and agreements of common carriers by water and certain other persons (as defined in the Shipping Act of 1916) engaged in the foreign commerce of the United States; (2) acceptance, rejection, or disapproval of tariff filings of common carriers engaged in foreign commerce; (3) regulation of rates, fares, charges, classifications, tariffs, regulations, and practices of common carriers by water in the domestic offshore trade of the United States; (4) licensing of independent ocean freight forwarders; (5) investigation of discriminatory rates, charges, classifications, and practices in the waterborne foreign and domestic offshore commerce; (6) issuance of certificates of financial responsibility to passenger shipowners and charterers to ensure payment of judgments for personal injury or death, and repayment of fares in the event that voyages do not take place; (7) issuance of certificates of financial responsibility for any vessel over 300 gross tons using any port or place in the United States or the navigable waters of the United States, to meet the liability to the United States to which the vessel could be subjected to meet the costs of cleanup for spilled oil or hazardous substances; and (8) rendering of decisions and issuance of orders and rules and regulations governing and affecting common carriers by water, terminal operators, freight forwarders, and other persons subject to the shipping statutes. The commission, in conjunction with the Department of State, conducts activities to effect the elimination of discriminatory practices on the part of foreign governments against U.S. flag shipping.

HELEN DELICH BENTLEY

MARKETING. *See* **Distribution of Goods and Services.**

MARKETING RESEARCH is the systematic collection and analysis of data to help managers solve the problems they encounter in moving goods and services to market. More research is done for sellers than for buyers; more for consumer goods than for industrial goods; and more for profit-seeking organizations than for nonprofit organizations. Much of it tries to measure factors in the environment to which marketing plans must be adjusted; but the underlying objective generally is to develop aggressive programs for the promotion of sales. It is no accident that research men borrow from the military and speak of devising the best strategy for achieving their objectives in the market. The range of topics covered is wide. They include measuring and forecasting markets, testing the effectiveness of advertising (past or projected), developing new products, forecasting reactions to price changes, selecting and controlling channels of distribution, and organizing marketing staffs.

Formal marketing research is said to have begun in 1911, when the Curtis Publishing Company appointed Charles Coolidge Parlin as its first director of commercial research. Some early practitioners were inspired by the efforts of Frederick W. Taylor and others to establish what had come to be called ''scientific management.'' More influential was the pressure of events, notably the growth in scope and complexity of managerial problems in marketing. Reliance upon intuitive judgments guided by maxims derived from personal experience could no longer provide acceptable controls.

Once started, marketing research grew rapidly. By the early 1970's, rough estimates indicate, expenditures for marketing research in the United States amounted to $300 million or more per annum. The research is done partly by employees of the firms that use the results and partly by consultants of many types, who are employed under contracts, usually for individual projects.

The growth of expenditures for research has been accompanied by a corresponding increase in the power and sophistication of the techniques used. Marketing research has been a major beneficiary of sweeping improvements since the 1920's in statistical methodology, quantitative analysis, and behavioral science, as well as in the use of computers. Individual agencies differ widely in the extent to which they use advanced technology. Efforts have been made by various organizations to professionalize marketing research in order to set standards of competence and to control various abuses; they have been only moderately successful.

[Harper W. Boyd, Jr., and Ralph Westfall, *Marketing Research: Text and Cases;* Kenneth P. Uhl and Bertram Schoner, *Marketing Research: Information Systems and Decision Making.*]

REAVIS COX

MARKETS, PUBLIC. When the New World was being settled every European town of any importance had its public market, and so in laying out their towns it was not unusual that the early settlers provided for them. There was a marketplace in Jamestown as early as 1617 and one in New Amsterdam as early as 1647. As in Europe, forestalling, regrating, and engrossing were generally prohibited. The sale of meats and vegetables was permitted only in the public market. A sale of these articles at any other place was illegal. The system was quite general in America in the colonial and early national periods. By the time of the Civil War, the public market system was well on its way to disintegration. It was inconvenient for the city householder to travel some distance to make daily purchases. As a result meat shops, although at first illegal, were established outside the public market, nearer the householder. The public market buildings were then either abandoned or converted into predominantly wholesale markets.

[Thomas F. DeVoe, *The Market Book.*]

FRED M. JONES

255

"MARK TWAIN." On the old Mississippi River steamboats, the leadmen created a series of characteristic terms for the various markings on the leadline that were chanted as they called the soundings, thus: "quarter twain," indicating 2¼ fathoms; "mark twain," 2 fathoms or 12 feet. "Mark Twain" was first used as a pen name for newspaper articles by the Mississippi River pilot Isaiah Sellers. It was later adopted and made famous by Samuel L. Clemens.

[Mark Twain, *Life on the Mississippi*.]
ROBERT W. BINGHAM

MARQUE AND REPRISAL, LETTERS OF, are papers from a belligerent government authorizing privately owned vessels, commonly known as privateers, to engage in warfare against enemy commerce. The Constitution gives Congress power to "grant Letters of Marque and Reprisal, and make Rules concerning Captures on Land and Water" (Article I, Section 8). According to former practice, the legality of captures was decided in prize courts, and the profits went chiefly to the privateer owners, officers, and crews. During earlier wars, privateering was widely practiced and highly profitable. During the Revolution, letters of marque were issued by both Congress and state governments to 1,150 vessels, and in the War of 1812 privateers numbering 515 captured about 1,450 prizes. Among European nations privateering was abolished by the Declaration of Paris (1856). It was practiced only briefly by the South in the Civil War, and in subsequent wars the destruction of enemy commerce has been limited to government-owned vessels.

[E. S. Maclay, *History of American Privateers*.]
ALLAN WESTCOTT

MARRIAGE. One of the major differences between the colonial settlers of British North America and those of Spanish Central and South America is that the former came to America as family units rather than as male adventurers, traders, or priests. From the beginning, marriage and the family has been a central North American institution. Not only were the thirteen original colonies largely settled by English men and women and their children, but the first settlers were predominantly Protestant and, in the 17th century, mainly Puritan. For them marriage was both a civil contract and a religious sacrament. The Puritan ethic has made for strict monogamy, even among the upper classes. The mistress among the wealthy or extramarital affairs among the middle classes have existed to a far lesser extent than in Europe.

From their first crossing of the Atlantic, the American people have been highly mobile, both geographically and up (and down) the class ladder. This mobility has made the conjugal family unit far more important than the extended consanguine family that was more characteristic of the settled village and agricultural societies of Europe. The only consanguine units of any durability are to be found among the upper classes, especially along the eastern seaboard. Such consanguine families as the Adamses, Cabots, and Lowells of Boston; the Schuylers, Van Rensselaers, and Roosevelts of New York; the Cadwaladers and Biddles of Philadelphia; and the Byrds, Lees, and Randolphs of Virginia stand out as exceptions to the generality of conjugal families. Until the Industrial Revolution and the urbanization of America, the conjugal family extended to three generations. Gradually, and especially in the 1970's, the aged tended to live apart and were less likely to be supported by the conjugal unit. The welfare state is an important factor here.

Social mobility has not only encouraged small conjugal families, it has also affected courtship and marriage patterns. Except among the upper classes, marriage in America, more than in any other country in the world, has been based on romantic love rather than on economics or class. A majority of young people did marry within their own religious group and socioeconomic class; but there were free choice and many exceptions, especially among the college generation since World War II. Since the war courting has taken place on campuses made up of students of mixed ethnic and religious origins.

Although the colonial family was patriarchal, industrialization and urbanization have weakened male authority and made for far more equality between husband and wife. These factors have also weakened parental control over children, reinforcing romantic love as a reason for marriage. Parental control is also weakened in the highly mobile urban U.S. society, in which children are not only geographically removed from their parents but are often at a higher educational and occupational level.

With the decline of parental control and of the need for long apprenticeships and, in the second half of the 20th century, with the trend toward accepting marriages between college students, Americans have been marrying at younger ages throughout the century. Women have had fewer children, at younger ages (and used birth control devices more), so that more and more married women are entering the labor force.

Increased mobility, weakening of traditions of endogamy, women's acceptance in the labor force, and the fact that childbearing and child-rearing functions end at younger ages all make for a looser family structure and a rising divorce rate. Much of the increase in the divorce rate has come in the later years of marriage, when the family functions have been fulfilled, and women and men are living longer. It must be remembered that up to the late 19th century, many men had been married two or more times without ever having been divorced. The increase in divorces after the age of forty is also due to the new equality between the sexes (the decline of alimony) and the increase of hedonistic values at the expense of duty, loyalty, and lifelong commitments.

Taking into account the steady weakening of the American family in the 20th century, it is no wonder that the restless and more affluent young in America were experimenting with new marriage forms in the 1960's, or avoiding marriage altogether in the 1970's. As a result, there have been increasing numbers of middle-class unmarried mothers living alone with their children. But at the same time a higher proportion of the population was married than at any other time in U.S. history, hardly a sign of the disintegration of marriage in America.

[William M. Kephart, *The Family, Society and the Individual.*]

E. DIGBY BALTZELL

MARSHALL CONVENTION, a gathering of the governors of Texas, Louisiana, Mississippi, and Arkansas at Marshall, Tex., in May 1865. It was called by Confederate Gen. Edmund Kirby-Smith for the purpose of obtaining more favorable terms of surrender than had been granted by Gen. Ulysses S. Grant and Gen. William Tecumseh Sherman. The Confederate army in the Southwest was rapidly disintegrating after the news of Robert E. Lee's surrender and a strong effort was made to check this disintegration and try for time and better terms. The convention drew up terms and attempted to present them directly to the federal government but failed.

[C. W. Ramsdell, *Reconstruction in Texas.*]

J. G. SMITH

MARSHALL ISLANDS, a group of coral atolls and reefs located 2,000 nautical miles southwest of Hawaii. Seized by Japan in 1914, the Marshall Islands

were granted as a mandate to Japan after World War I by the League of Nations. The Marshalls lay astride the route through the central Pacific chosen to carry U.S. forces to Japan during World War II. After taking Makin and Tarawa in the neighboring Gilbert Islands in November 1943 to provide bases for bombing the Marshalls, Adm. Chester W. Nimitz, Central Pacific Area commander, focused on Kwajalein atoll, in the center of the Marshalls and headquarters for Japanese defense of the islands. Heavy naval and air bombardment began on Jan. 29, 1944. Two days later landing craft carried the Fourth Marine Division under Maj. Gen. Harry Schmidt toward causeway-connected Roi and Namur islands in the north of the atoll and the Seventh Infantry Division under Maj. Gen. Charles H. Corlett toward Kwajalein in the south.

First landings on Jan. 31 were on smaller islands near the main objectives, to establish artillery positions; the main landings took place the next day. The marines cleared Roi in one day and Namur in two. U.S. Army troops encountered more resistance on Kwajalein but cleared it on Feb. 4. A battalion of the army's 106th Infantry occupied nearby Majuro Island unopposed.

Since a reserve U.S. Marine regiment and two battalions of the 106th had not been needed, Nimitz directed capture of Eniwetok atoll on the western fringe of the Marshalls. The marines took Engebi and Parry islands in one day each, Feb. 18 and 22, respectively. Resistance again was stouter for army infantry on Eniwetok, requiring four days, until Feb. 21, to reduce.

Total American losses in the Marshalls were 671 killed, 2,157 wounded; the Japanese dead totaled 10,000. The airfields and fleet anchorages that subsequently were established facilitated further advance to the Caroline and Mariana islands and neutralization of a strong Japanese base on Truk Island.

In 1947 the Marshall Islands became part of the U.S. Trust Territory of the Pacific.

[Philip A. Crowl and Edmund G. Love, *Seizure of the Gilberts and Marshalls,* United States Army in World War II.]

CHARLES B. MACDONALD

MARSHALL PLAN, the popular name of the European Recovery Program (1948–52), which grew out of a proposal by Secretary of State George C. Marshall in a speech at Harvard University on June 5, 1947. Designed to revive the European economy in order to provide political and social conditions under which free institutions could survive, the plan proposed that European countries take the initiative in assessing their resources and requirements to show what they could do to give effect to American economic aid.

Sixteen countries, led by Great Britain and France, established the Committee of European Economic Cooperation to outline a four-year recovery program. This was later replaced by the permanent Organization of European Economic Cooperation (OEEC), to which West Germany was also ultimately admitted. The U.S. Congress in April 1948 enacted legislation for a recovery program that was placed under the control of the Economic Cooperation Administration (ECA), headed by Paul J. Hoffman. In an effort to restore agricultural and industrial production to prewar levels, create financial stability, promote economic cooperation, and expand exports, the United States in a four-year period appropriated some $12 billion (plus $1.5 million for assistance on credit terms). This period saw great efforts made toward European reconstruction; the gross national product of Western Europe rose 25 percent, or 15 percent over prewar levels. The Soviet Union and its satellites refused to participate in the program.

[Harry Bayard Price, *The Marshall Plan and Its Meaning*.]

FORREST C. POGUE

MARTHA'S VINEYARD, an island off the southwestern coast of Cape Cod, Mass., was discovered in 1602 by Bartholomew Gosnold. It was granted by derivation from the crown of England to Thomas Mayhew, an English merchant, and his son as a proprietary grant with rights of government. The first settlement was made at Edgartown in 1642. The community was an outpost of feudalism in a new world of democratic tendencies. The Mayhew family held manors and offices for life until the Revolution put an end to hereditary pretensions. Formerly an important whaling center, in the 20th century Martha's Vineyard became a well-known summer resort.

[L. C. M. Hare, *Thomas Mayhew, Patriarch to the Indians.*]

LLOYD C. M. HARE

MARTIAL LAW is the use of military forces to control part or all of an area in which the civil authorities are losing or have lost control or in which their continued functioning would be dangerous. In practice in the United States, martial law may exist side by side

with civil courts, and military commanders may find themselves subject to judicial review for actions that, judged against the pressures, apparent facts, and necessities of the moment, appear unreasonable. Martial law must be declared by the president in federal cases; this is a power he cannot delegate. Governors may declare martial law within their states.

Martial law in the United States is directly descended from English practice of the 17th and 18th centuries. President George Washington set the precedent when he dispatched troops to quell the Whiskey Rebellion of 1794 by ordering all rebels to be delivered to civil courts for trial. Thereafter, martial law was rarely invoked until World War II, even though troops have been called to assist civil authorities. Andrew Jackson declared martial law in New Orleans in the face of imminent British attack in 1814. It was also declared in Indiana in 1864 in the face of Copperhead threats and led to the important Supreme Court decision in *Ex parte Milligan* (1866) protecting civilians from being arbitrarily tried by the military authorities when civil courts are still functioning. Troops were called out during the railroad strikes of 1877, in Idaho in 1899, and again during the coal strikes in Colorado in 1893–94, 1896–97, 1902–03, and 1927–28.

Martial law was not actually declared in all cases. In a few instances the declaration did not come from the president or *eo nomine* ("in his name") as the law requires. The state governments involved have often hesitated to invoke martial law, and the reasons have sometimes been more political than legal, as can well be seen in the exchanges between President Lyndon Baines Johnson and his potential Republican opponent in the 1968 elections, Gov. George Romney of Michigan, at the time of the July 1967 Detroit riots. Martial law has also been used on occasion after natural disasters, as in Wilkes-Barre, Pa., when the Susquehanna River flooded following Hurricane Agnes in June 1972.

Martial law has been declared within the United States thirty times during the period 1789–1975. The pattern apparent by 1972 was the use of martial law to bolster civil authority rather than to replace it, with lawmen making arrests and taking the prisoners before civil rather than military courts. This suits the military, who are rarely happy in the legal morass of a civilian situation, especially since 1932, when the Supreme Court modified the 1909 *Moyer* v. *Peabody* decision by a ruling in *Sterling* v. *Constantin* that placed martial law under judicial review. Later court decisions upholding the rights of individuals rather than those of society in criminal cases have made even such matters as preventing looting more difficult.

For a short period right after World War I, martial law was declared and the War Department made illegal use of troops because the National Guard had not yet been reorganized. Regulations that were in other respects quite clear were not violated, except that the president's approval was not obtained (Woodrow Wilson was unavailable). Much more patent abuses of martial law were its invocation by the governors of Oklahoma (1935), South Carolina (1935), Arizona (1935), Tennessee (1939), and Georgia (1940) for political purposes. In Arizona the state attempted to interfere with a federal project on federal land. Rhode Island also employed martial law against horse racing (1937).

Martial law was used in June 1943 to stop a race riot in Detroit. It was also used in Hawaii in the aftermath of the attack on Pearl Harbor. There for the first time the federal government was involved in the consequences. Faced with the apparent threat of invasion and concerned over the possibility that the Japanese population in the islands would prove to be fifth columnists, the governor called upon the military authorities to take over. He acted in violation of the Hawaiian Organic (Territorial) Act and invoked the concept of military government, which was only proper in an invaded enemy territory. What was required was a declaration of martial law. The proper procedure would have been for the military to have supported, rather than supplanted, the local police forces. A much more serious mistake was the closing of the civil courts and the trial of civilians in military courts. The cases of White, an embezzling stockbroker, and of Duncan, a civilian who scuffled with a marine guard, reached the Supreme Court (*Duncan* v. *Kahanamoku*, 327 U.S. 304 [1946]). In *Duncan* the Supreme Court went beyond judicial review in declaring military trials of nonmilitary personnel unlawful. Further cases may arise, since army manuals in 1969 still envisaged military trials of civilians.

After the milestone Supreme Court decision in *Brown* v. *Board of Education of Topeka* (1954), the use of martial law accelerated. Incidents at Little Rock, Ark., in 1957; Oxford, Miss., in 1962; and Selma, Ala., in 1965 recalled the old doctrine that the entire force of the nation could be used to uphold the Constitution and the Court, revived the use of the anti–Ku Klux Klan legislation of 1871, and saw the federalization of the state National Guard after U.S. troops appeared and the employment of

U.S. marshals supported by troops. In April 1968, after the death of Martin Luther King, Jr., the Riot Act of 1792 was read to the crowds in Washington, D.C., and troops were then employed. Of the ten declarations of martial law from 1945 to 1969, five were to support the federal government, four were to aid the states, and one was to disperse "Resurrection City" in Washington, D.C., in June 1968.

[Robin Higham, ed., *Bayonets in the Streets;* Frederick Bernays Wiener, "Martial Law Today," *American Bar Association Journal,* vol. 55 (1969).]

ROBIN HIGHAM

MARTIN-TOLLIVER FEUD. In an election brawl in Morehead, the county seat of Rowan County, Ky., in 1884, John Martin was wounded by Floyd Tolliver. Later, Martin killed Tolliver. While he was under arrest for the shooting, Martin in turn was slain by Tolliver kinsmen. A vendetta ensued, lasting three years, causing such a state of anarchy that many peaceable citizens left the county and the population of Morehead shrank from 700 to 300. The Logan family was drawn in on the Martin side, and after twenty-three men had been killed in the war, Daniel Boone Logan armed a large force, closed in on Morehead on June 22, 1887, and in a pitched battle killed the Tolliver leaders, ending the feud.

[Charles G. Mutzenberg, *Kentucky's Famous Feuds and Tragedies.*]

ALVIN F. HARLOW

MARTIN V. HUNTER'S LESSEE, 1 Wheaton 304 (1816), upheld the right of the U.S. Supreme Court to review the decisions of state courts, which right had been challenged by the Virginia court of appeals. The opinion of Justice Joseph Story (Chief Justice John Marshall not participating because of personal connection with the litigation) held that the Supreme Court's jurisdiction depended on the nature of the case rather than on the court from which it was appealed, and that Congress could confer appellate jurisdiction on the Supreme Court in all cases involving the laws, treaties, and Constitution of the United States.

[A. J. Beveridge, *Life of John Marshall;* Charles Warren, *Supreme Court in United States History.*]

LAWRENCE A. HARPER

MARTIN V. MOTT, 12 Wheaton 19 (1827). Considering an incident of the War of 1812, the Supreme

Court decided that when Congress under the Constitution authorizes the president to call militia against actual or imminent invasion, his decision as to "whether the exigency has arisen" is "conclusive upon all persons." Prompt obedience, said Justice Joseph Story, obviates maintaining huge standing forces.

[J. Story, *On the Constitution*.]

ELBRIDGE COLBY

MARTLING MEN, a faction of the Democratic-Republican party of New York City, composed of followers of Aaron Burr, who opposed De Witt Clinton, governor of New York. They received their name from the fact that they met in the Long Room of Martling's Tavern, at the southeast corner of Nassau and Spruce streets, which was also the first "wigwam" of the Tammany Society, to which most of the Martling men belonged.

[D. R. Fox, *The Decline of Aristocracy in the Politics of New York*.]

STANLEY R. PILLSBURY

MARY AND JOHN, the ship that sailed from Plymouth, England, on Mar. 20, 1630, and landed the pioneers of the Great Migration, on May 30, at Massachusetts Bay, where they founded a town to which they gave the reminiscent name of Dorchester.

R. V. COLEMAN

MARYLAND. The Proprietary Province of Maryland was granted in 1632 by Charles I to George Calvert, first Baron of Baltimore in Ireland. Calvert had risen to membership in the Privy Council and to principal secretary of state when he resigned and announced his adherence to the Church of Rome. He had, prior to the 1632 grant, received a grant to the Peninsula of Avalon in Newfoundland, where he invested and lost a great deal of money and where he himself spent a bitter winter. The climate persuaded him that he would have to seek farther south for a profitable as well as a habitable plantation. He returned to England via Virginia and pressed the king for a grant of land south of the James River. This project was opposed by the Virginians, and he finally compromised for a plantation north of the Potomac. His death prevented his receiving this grant after he had written a charter for it modeled after that of the bishopric of Durham on the Scottish border. George's son Cecil received this grant on June 20, 1632. Shortly thereafter he

began gathering colonists and materials for the settlement that he expected to make in his province, which he named Maryland, after Queen Henrietta Maria. The expedition under the command of Leonard Calvert, Cecil's younger brother, sailed Nov. 22, 1633, from Cowes, Isle of Wight, on the *Ark* and the *Dove*. These two small vessels were soon separated by a fierce storm. Reunited two months later at Barbados, they set sail again Jan. 24, 1634, arriving off the capes of the Chesapeake Bay on Feb. 27. Proceeding up the bay, the two parties next landed at Saint Clement's Island, where on Mar. 25, Annunciation Day, they celebrated mass.

The first settlement was established at Saint Marys City, 20 miles from Saint Clement's Island. The settlement is particularly noteworthy as the first in which freedom of religion was permitted by all those who believed in the Trinity. Lord Baltimore's instructions to his brother Leonard regarding religious problems were reinforced by the Maryland general assembly in the 1649 Act Concerning Religion, commonly called the Act of Religious Toleration. The situation was altered by the Protestant Revolution of 1689, when the dominant Catholics of Saint Marys City were replaced by the Puritans and Episcopalians of Annapolis. The Anglican church became the established church of Maryland and continued as such until 1776; until the Revolution, Catholics could not practice their religion openly.

Maryland, like its sister colony Virginia, established its economy on a money crop, tobacco. A plantation system developed, based on slavery, which proved profitable through the 18th century and well into the 19th.

The citizens of Maryland were divided about loyalty to England at the start of the Revolution. The justices of Frederick County repudiated the Stamp Act, while the commissioner in charge of the stamps removed himself to New York fearing for his life in Annapolis. Anthony Stewart was compelled to burn his vessel, the *Peggy Stewart,* laden with taxed tea, in the harbor of Annapolis. Maryland declared its independence by the adoption of the first state constitution in November 1776. Maryland's troops marched to New York and there made a reputation as reliable and enduring soldiers, which they maintained throughout the war. After the Revolution Maryland ceded the land to the central government for what was to become the District of Columbia. Virginia also gave part of this area just south of the Potomac but this grant was later returned. Maryland also provided the funds for the first buildings of the central government.

The reputation of Maryland's troops was fortified during the War of 1812 by its defense of Baltimore during the siege of Fort McHenry (1814) and at the Battle of North Point. These engagements distinguished them in an otherwise militarily disappointing war. During the siege of Fort McHenry, Francis Scott Key was a prisoner on a British man-of-war, where he wrote the lyrics to the "Star-Spangled Banner."

During the Civil War, southern Maryland and the eastern shore favored the Confederacy. About half of Baltimore City and the western counties were inclined toward the Union. The quick takeover of the state by federal troops preserved Maryland for the Union. Marylanders fought on both sides, about 20,000 for the South and about 60,000 for the Union. The major battles of Antietam (or Sharpsburg) and South Mountain (or Boonesboro) were fought on Maryland soil in 1862. The assassination of Abraham Lincoln was plotted in Maryland, and the chief culprit, John Wilkes Booth, was a Marylander who, after the murder of the president, fled through southern Maryland to Virginia and his death. The words of Maryland's official song, "Maryland! My Maryland!" were written at this time by John Ryder Randall, who, although a Marylander, was temporarily in New Orleans.

Maryland abolished slavery in 1864, anticipating the Thirteenth Amendment to the Constitution. However, Maryland did not ratify the Fourteenth Amendment until 1959, ninety years after the required number of three-fourths of the states had adopted it.

After the war, Maryland converted to a commercial and industrial economy. This had begun earlier with the building of the Chesapeake and Ohio Canal and the construction of the Baltimore and Ohio, the country's first railroad, effectively connecting Chesapeake Bay with the Middle West. After 1865 Baltimore became the banker of the South. The development of its port encouraged Baltimore to become a manufacturer and distributor of fertilizer, both natural and chemical. Later it became a center of the steel and copper industries. Its port continued to grow until by 1970 it was the fourth largest port in the United States for foreign trade.

During the 20th century, politics in Maryland achieved national importance. Albert C. Ritchie, governor from 1920 to 1935, became prominent nationwide because of his resistance to the Volstead Act. He declined to be the running mate of Franklin D. Roosevelt, with whose policies he disagreed. Harry Whinna Nice was nominated at the Republican convention of 1936 for vice-president but nothing

came of that nomination. In 1968 Spiro T. Agnew was chosen for the second place on the Republican ticket led by Richard Nixon; he served only part of his term as vice-president, resigning in 1973 after pleading no contest to a charge of tax evasion.

Maryland enjoyed a flowering of cultural and scientific institutions during the late 19th century and early 20th century, some of the most noteworthy being the Johns Hopkins University and hospital; the Peabody Institute of Music and its great library; the Walters Art Gallery; the Shepheard and Pratt Mental Hospital; and the Enoch Pratt Free Library. Military installations were created at Annapolis by the U.S. Naval Academy, founded in 1845.

[Mathew Page Andrews, *History of Maryland: Province and State;* Morris L. Radoff, ed., *The Old Line State, A History of Maryland.*]

MORRIS L. RADOFF

MARYLAND, INVASION OF (September 1862). The defeat of Union Gen. John Pope in the second Battle of Bull Run, and his retreat to the Washington, D.C., lines, imposed upon Gen. Robert E. Lee the necessity of adopting a new plan of operations. He wrote Confederate President Jefferson Davis, "The present seems to be the most propitious time . . . to enter Maryland." Regardless of objections, Lee added, "We cannot afford to be idle." Aggressive movements, he thought, would insure the safety of Richmond, Va.

On Sept. 2, 1862, marching orders were issued. Within a week troops were concentrating at Frederick, Md. Union Gen. George B. McClellan, who had been restored to command, began organizing a force to defend Maryland. The "uncertainty" as to Lee's intentions was dispelled by the finding of the "lost order." McClellan accelerated his movements.

Meantime, Lee detached Gen. Thomas J. ("Stonewall") Jackson to capture Harpers Ferry (in present-day W. Va.), while he led his army westward to an expected junction with Jackson in the vicinity of Hagerstown, Md. Once across South Mountain, Lee's line of supply would be through the Shenandoah Valley.

On Sept. 13, McClellan reached Frederick. He hurried troops after Lee. Sharp fights took place at gaps in South Mountain; Lee sent reinforcements, but by nightfall, finding the positions no longer tenable, he directed a retirement toward Sharpsburg, Md. McClellan advanced slowly, diverted by Jackson's movement against Harpers Ferry. As soon as that place surrendered, Jackson hurried to Sharpsburg,

"MARYLAND! MY MARYLAND!"

leaving A. P. Hill to dispose of captured property and prisoners and then follow promptly.

McClellan reached Sharpsburg on Sept. 16 and spent the day testing Lee's line. His attacks the following day brought on the Battle of Antietam, characterized by more hard fighting than any other battle of the war. Lee, outnumbered, remained in possession of the field, but severe losses and heavy odds made it inadvisable to stay. McClellan did not attack again. On the night of Sept. 18, Lee recrossed the Potomac "without loss or molestation," ending the campaign.

[R. U. Johnson and C. C. Buel, eds., *Battles and Leaders of the Civil War*, vol. II.]

THOMAS ROBSON HAY

"MARYLAND! MY MARYLAND!" is a poem written by James Ryder Randall in April 1861. Randall, a college professor in Louisiana but a native of Maryland and a strong southern adherent, was inspired to write this famous poem when he heard that Massachusetts troops had been attacked as they passed through Baltimore (*see* Baltimore Riot). In the hope that this episode would swing Maryland to the southern cause, Randall made his appeal to the people of his state in verses that, set to the music of the old German song "O Tannenbaum," soon became one of the marching songs of the Confederate army.

[M. P. Andrews, *The Poems of James Ryder Randall*.]

E. H. O'NEILL

MASERS AND LASERS are devices employed for the generation and amplification of electromagnetic radiation. Essentially they convert atomic or molecular energy into radiation by a process called stimulated emission.

During the last decades of the 19th century, physicists specializing in the science of spectroscopy explored the natural resonances of many elements at optical wavelengths. The introduction of quantum theory at the beginning of the 20th century and the Bohr theory of the atom in 1913 created a fresh approach to the understanding of atomic structure.

Under normal circumstances an atom in an upper energy state falls to a lower level and emits light "spontaneously," as in a discharge lamp. If energy hits a neutral atom, that atom may also absorb the energy and become "excited." In 1917 Albert Einstein postulated a third circumstance: If electromagnetic radiation of proper resonant frequency is incident upon an atom in an upper energy state, it may "stimulate" the atom to radiate a packet of energy

identical to that of the incoming signal, the net result being amplification of the original radiation.

Under usual conditions, the amount of stimulated emission present in any lighting system is negligible, and few physicists gave the matter serious consideration prior to World War II. The field of spectroscopy entered a new phase when techniques developed during and after the war permitted the exploration of atomic resonances far below the optical range.

In 1934 C. E. Cleeton and N. H. Williams of the University of Michigan, using magnetron oscillators, demonstrated the absorption of energy in a sample of ammonia gas near the 24,000-megahertz line. On the basis of important advances in microwave engineering made during World War II, spectroscopists were quick to apply several types of oscillators to the exploration of various resonance lines. At the same time, some thoughts were given to the possibility of creating an atomic amplifier by purposely designing an "excited" system in which more atoms existed in the higher energy state. In 1952, J. Weber of the University of Maryland suggested a method for amplifying an electromagnetic wave by stimulated emission. A molecular generator was also proposed by Soviet scientists N. G. Basov and A. M. Prokhorov. The first successful generator and amplifier was operated at Columbia University in 1954 by Charles H. Townes and research students J. P. Gordon and H. J. Zeiger. A beam of ammonia molecules was split into two energy levels by a system of electrostatic focusing. Operational frequency was the ammonia absorption line near 24,000 megahertz. The Columbia group coined the term "maser," an acronym for "microwave amplification by stimulated emission of radiation."

The ammonia maser had limited practical application. In 1956, N. Bloembergen of Harvard University suggested a solid-state maser that employed three energy levels. The first device of this type was operated at Bell Telephone Laboratories. In 1957 a four-level ruby maser was designed by Chihiro Kikuchi of the University of Michigan and applied to radioastronomy use for the amplification of weak galactic signals.

Thoughts of extending the maser principle to optical frequencies quickly developed, although some uncertainties existed about the most suitable material for achieving laser ("light amplification by the stimulated emission of radiation") action. In 1958, Townes and Arthur Schawlow described a system suggesting the use of excited potassium vapor and a built-in resonator called a Fabry-Perot interferometer. The first

262

operational device employed a cylindrical ruby crystal with silvered ends to form the Fabry-Perot resonator. This laser was demonstrated by T. H. Maiman of Hughes Research Laboratories in July 1960. Developments occurred rapidly thereafter; significant contributions were made by several research groups, including Bell Telephone Laboratories, International Business Machines, the General Electric Company, and the Lincoln Laboratory of the Massachusetts Institute of Technology.

[David Fishlock, ed., *A Guide to the Laser*.]
ELLIOT N. SIVOWITCH

MASON, FORT, was established by the federal government in Mason County, Tex., in 1851, as frontier protection against the Comanche and Kiowa. It was situated on the divide between the Llano and San Saba rivers. When Texas seceded in 1861, it was abandoned. There was also a fort of that name in Missouri, and one called Mason's Fort in Pennsylvania.

[F. W. Johnson and E. C. Barker, *History of Texas*.]
CARL L. CANNON

MASON AND SLIDELL INCIDENT. *See* **Trent Affair.**

MASON BAND consisted of highwaymen and river pirates led by Samuel Mason who operated in pioneer days at Cave-in-Rock, in Hardin County, Ill.; on the Ohio and Mississippi rivers; and over the Natchez Trace, between Natchez, Miss., and Nashville, Tenn. Mason was killed by two of his men in 1804.

[Otto A. Rothert, *The Outlaws of Cave-in-Rock*.]
OTTO A. ROTHERT

MASON-DIXON LINE is the southern boundary line of Pennsylvania, and thereby the northern boundary line of Delaware, Maryland, and West Virginia, formerly part of Virginia. It is best known historically as the dividing line between slavery and free soil in the period of history before the Civil War, but to some extent it has remained the symbolic border line between North and South, both politically and socially.

The present Mason and Dixon line was the final result of several highly involved colonial and state boundary disputes, at the bottom of which was the Maryland Charter of 1632, granting to the Calvert family lands lying "under the fortieth degree of Northerly Latitude." Acute trouble arose with the grant and charter to William Penn in 1681 that contained indefinite and even impossible clauses with regard to boundaries. The terms of the two charters were inconsistent and contradictory. A full century of dispute with regard to the southern boundary of Pennsylvania was the result. At first the trouble was between Pennsylvania and Maryland. Had all Pennsylvania claims been substantiated, Baltimore would have been included in Pennsylvania, and Maryland reduced to a narrow strip. Had all Maryland claims been established, Philadelphia would have been within Maryland. There were conferences, appeals to the Privy Council, much correspondence, attempted occupation, temporary agreements, all without permanent solution. The Maryland and Pennsylvania proprietors continued the quarrel until 1760, when an agreement was finally made. Under its terms, two English surveyors, Charles Mason and Jeremiah Dixon, began the survey of the boundary line in 1763. Completed after four years' work, the boundary line between Maryland and Pennsylvania was set at 39°43'17.6" north latitude. The results were ratified by the crown in 1769. In the meantime, Virginia contested the boundary west of Maryland in a dispute that lasted for many years and ended with the extension of the Mason and Dixon line westward, a settlement not completed until 1784. Historically the line embodies a Pennsylvania boundary triumph. (*See also* Pennsylvania-Maryland Boundary Dispute; Pennsylvania-Virginia Boundary Dispute.)

[John E. Potter, "Pennsylvania and Virginia Boundary Controversy," *Pennsylvania Magazine of History and Biography*, vol. 38; James Veech, *Mason and Dixon's Line: A History*.]
ALFRED P. JAMES

MASON TITLE. English Capt. John Mason commanded an expedition against the Hebrides Islands in 1610 for which he advanced money that he never recovered. This debt was indirectly repaid by land grants later. From 1615 to 1621 he was governor of Newfoundland, and while there explored the New England coast. On returning to England he became associated with Sir Ferdinando Gorges and others on the Council for New England. On Mar. 9, 1622, he received from the council the grant of Mariana in Massachusetts, and on Aug. 10, jointly with Gorges, the province of Maine between the Merrimack and Kennebec rivers. European wars hindered settlement. With peace, the proprietors divided their land. On Nov. 7, 1629, the council granted Mason the province of New Hampshire, extending from the Merrimack to the Piscataqua and running inland sixty miles up each river. On Nov. 17 Mason and Gorges were granted Laconia. Mason sent settlers to the Piscataqua and spent about £22,000, with no return. In 1635 the council, breaking up, confirmed Mason, by then its vice-president, in his title to Mariana, New Hampshire, Masonia on the Kennebec, and the south half of the Isles of Shoals. He died soon after and his widow allowed the colony to shift for itself.

In 1675 his heirs recovered title, but collected little money from the settlers. Samuel Allen bought the title in 1691 for £2,750, but received no return on his investment. The sale was voided by the Privy Council in 1739 and John Tufton Mason, the heir, sold his lands in New Hampshire in 1746 to a group of twelve leading citizens, called the Masonian Proprietors. Their offer to sell to the province of New Hampshire was not met, and they granted out about 2 million acres. The last meeting of the Proprietors was in 1846; their records have been printed by the state. The long quarrels between the people and government of New Hampshire, the heirs of Mason, and those of Allen were very important in determining the political and economic history of the state, its settlement, its boundaries, and indeed its separate existence.

[W. H. Fry, *New Hampshire as a Royal Province;* Otis G. Hammond, "The Mason Title and Its Relation to New Hampshire and Massachusetts," *Proceedings of the American Antiquarian Society* (1916); C. W. Tuttle, *Captain John Mason.*]

HERBERT W. HILL

MASSAC, FORT, was erected in 1757 by Charles Philippe Aubry by order of the commandant of the Illinois. Originally named Fort Ascension, it was renamed Fort Massiac in 1758 in honor of the Marquis de Massiac, French minister of marine. In 1763 Aubry described it as "a Picqueted Fort with four Bastions and eight pieces of Cannon" garrisoned by 100 men, but in the following year it was abandoned and soon afterward destroyed by the Indians.

The site remained unfortified until 1794, when Maj. Thomas Doyle, under orders from Gen. Anthony Wayne, erected a new fort. Mistakenly attributing the former name to a legendary massacre, Doyle called the post Fort Massac. The fort was built of pickets with a small bastion at each angle. Its garrison, which was maintained until 1814, varied from a handful to nearly 100 men.

Fort Massac was of minor military significance, and is known principally because George Rogers Clark landed on its site at the outset of his Illinois campaign.

[C. W. Alvord, *The Illinois Country, 1673–1818;* M. T. Scott, "Old Fort Massac," *Transactions of Illinois State Historical Society* (1903).]

PAUL M. ANGLE

MASSACHUSETTS. The first European landfalls along Massachusetts shores were probably made by Norsemen from Greenland in the 11th century. Next came the voyages of John Cabot in 1497 and 1498 and reports of abundant codfish from Newfoundland to Cape Cod. Hundreds of Portuguese, French, and English fishermen and fur traders soon followed. Spanish charts showed Cape Cod in 1527, but before 1600 little exploration occurred south of Maine.

Englishmen made the first documented Massachusetts landings: Bartholomew Gosnold around Cape Cod in 1602 and Martin Pring at Plymouth in 1603. French explorer Samuel de Champlain mapped Massachusetts harbors during 1605–06. In 1614 the Dutchman Adriaen Block and the Englishman John Smith charted Cape Cod and Massachusetts Bay; Smith's expedition carried the Patuxent Indian Squanto from Plymouth to Europe, and Thomas Dermer returned him to Massachusetts in 1619.

The Colonial Period. The first settlement in Massachusetts was made in 1620 by English Pilgrims—Separatists from the Puritan church who had fled persecution to Holland in 1608. Determining to make an English settlement in the New World, they obtained merchant financing for their voyage, contracting repayment by seven years' business enterprise. On Sept. 16, 1620, thirty-five of these Pilgrims and sixty-seven others—including fourteen servants and artisans and a hired military leader, Myles Standish—set sail in the *Mayflower* from Plymouth, England, for Massachusetts, using Smith's map. Having reached Provincetown in November, they decided to proceed south, and en route, by their Mayflower Compact, they established a "civill body politick," controlled by the Separatists. Sighting Plymouth on Dec. 11, they chose it for their settlement, and using the *Mayflower* as their winter barracks, they built Plymouth Plantation. During the winter, half of the colonists and crew died, but in the spring the survivors negotiated the Peace of Massasoit with the Wampanoag, and with the help of Squanto, they planted corn, fished, and hunted. In October of 1621 they celebrated their harvest, the first Thanksgiving. A Jamestown ship brought trade goods, with which Gov. William Bradford extended trade with the Indians to Cape Cod and Maine, as Standish fended off unfriendly Indians. New settlers arrived, and by 1622, when Squanto died, the untrained Pilgrim families had secured their beachhead.

Competitive English merchants exploited Pilgrim successes: unrestricted by the Mayflower Compact, they built trading bases at Weymouth, Wollaston, and Gloucester, some of which were sponsored by Sir Ferdinando Gorges' Council for New England. The Pilgrims provided protection, but they envied better-located plantations at Medford, Charlestown, Boston, and Salem. Gloucester went bankrupt; Roger Conant reorganized the settlement at Salem, and there John Endecott brought new colonists and supplies in 1628.

England's deep economic depression and Charles I's dissolution of Parliament in 1626 led wealthy Puritan merchants to resolve to emigrate to Massachusetts to escape religious and economic persecution, and in 1629 a group secured a royal charter for the Massachusetts Bay Company, partly displacing the Council for New England. Its usual trading-company provisions for governor, assistants, and a general court of stockholders lacked requirements for meetings in England, enabling them to establish a self-governing commonwealth. And in 1629 and 1630 the first ships reached Boston, carrying Gov. John Winthrop, assistants, general court, and the Massachusetts Bay Company—the home office complete—together with 800 colonists and horses, cattle, and building supplies. The owners believed themselves divinely chosen to govern their Bible commonwealth solely by interpreting Holy Scripture.

By 1633 several thousand colonists inhabited twelve Bay Company towns, from Hingham to Saugus. Shipyards, gristmills, fisheries, and fine estates abounded. By 1640, when the Puritan Long Parliament reduced emigration incentives, 18,000 Bay Company planters populated thirty towns, whereas Plymouth Plantation's nine towns held only 3,000 people. Theocratic intolerance exiled from the Bay Company to neighboring colonies the harshly persecuted Quakers and other dissenters, and Oliver Cromwell's government rarely interfered with the Massachusetts Puritans' theocracy. Reforms did occur within, however. The founding of Harvard College (1636), endowed grammar schools, and free elementary schools initiated nonreligious education; the body of liberties (1641) and *The Book of the General Lawes and Libertyes* (1648) liberalized the legal system, and the election of administrative selectmen was instituted.

The permissiveness of Cromwell's government to-ward the Massachusetts Puritans came to an end with the restoration of the monarchy in 1660, and a royal commission was dispatched to New England in 1664 to investigate the state of affairs in those colonies. It reported that Massachusetts was resisting England's mercantile law, disobeying the Navigation Acts, minting its own currency, restricting suffrage to church members, denying free worship to dissenters, and generally vitiating the authority of Parliament. The refusal of the Massachusetts Bay Company leaders to send representatives to England to answer charges, and the even harsher reports of Edward Randolph, who became collector of customs of New England in 1678, led to the annulment of the Massachusetts Bay Company's charter in 1684.

As part of the Dominion of New England, Massachusetts chafed under the governorship of Edmund Andros after 1685, and in 1689, coincident with the Glorious Revolution, Boston rebelled. King William abolished the Dominion of New England and granted the moderate Massachusetts Province Charter, joining Plymouth, Maine, and the Massachusetts Bay Colony under Gov. William Phips. During much of his governorship Phips was away from Massachusetts, fighting King William's War (1689–97) against French Canada, and the theocrats regained some influence—it was the time of the Salem witchcraft trials (1693). Resumption of war with French Canada (Queen Anne's War, 1702–13) and a few more years of Indian raids delayed western expansion of the province until 1715.

In the peaceful years that followed, nineteen new western Massachusetts towns were founded. Shipbuilding, overseas commerce, and waterpower industries developed a wealthy, moderate, merchant leadership that replaced the theocrats. Economic opportunity for freeholders reduced class distinction; representative assemblies balanced between freeholders and theocrats attained control over royal governors' salaries. Boston's harbor, triangular trade, and banks made Boston America's principal seaport.

As maritime competition grew, so did smuggling and evasion of customs duties. Commercial quarrels were exacerbated by day-to-day conflicts with the English bureaucracy, resentment of militia mobilization for the Canadian campaigns of King George's War (1745) and the Seven Years' War (1756–63), and outrage at the conspicuous presence of British regulars. The Molasses Act (1733) and the Stamp Act (1765), the first strictly enforced imperial taxes for revenue, brought merchants, small landholders, and debtors into boycotts, riots, and attacks on tax collectors. Although the Committees of Correspondence (initiated in Massachusetts by Samuel Adams) and the Sons of Liberty organized nonimportation agreements so effective that the Stamp Act was repealed and the Molasses Act was modified, the English ministry initiated the Townshend Acts (1768), whereupon the Massachusetts Assembly petitioned other colonies to oppose what they called an English usurpation of power. After Gov. Francis Bernard dissolved the assembly and asked Gen. Thomas Gage for British troops to protect his government, riots ensued in Boston, notably the Boston Massacre of 1770. Although the Townshend Acts were substantially repealed, the tax on tea remained, and the Boston Tea Party (1773) precipitated a crisis that resulted in the closing of the port and establishment of military government under Gage. Committees of Correspondence of all the colonies sent supply caravans to Massachusetts, and militia were mustered and armed.

The Revolution and the Federal Period. Massachusetts minutemen numbering 15,000 drilled weekly and stored powder in the churches. In April 1775 Gage, now governor of Massachusetts, using 1,500 of his 4,000 Boston regulars, determined to seize the colonists' military stores at Concord, but the Boston Committee of Safety learned of the plan and on Apr. 18 sent Paul Revere to alert the militia at Lexington. There, on Apr. 19, 70 minutemen confronted 700 grenadiers and infantrymen, giving the Concord militia time to hide its powder; later the same day 400 minutemen from surrounding towns routed three British companies at Concord Bridge. Following the Battle of Bunker Hill (June 17), George Washington arrived to take command of the Massachusetts forces. The British evacuated Boston on Mar. 17, 1776.

Massachusetts was the sixth state to ratify the Constitution (Feb. 6, 1788). Postwar economic depression gripped Massachusetts, and currency inflation and wartime shipping losses hindered recovery. England closed its ports to Yankee ships and poured European goods into American harbors, where profiteering speculators intensified inflation. Massachusetts shipmasters found exports embargoed even to the West Indies. Inflation bankrupted farmers and storekeepers and landed them in debtors' prisons. This produced the abortive Shays's Rebellion in 1786. Many pioneer families abandoned Massachusetts and moved westward.

Federalist merchants first responded to West Indian export embargoes by smuggling, but with the opening of the China trade in 1784 the Massachusetts econ-

omy began to revive. Bostonian vessels joined other American ships in enormously profitable voyages to China and India, via Africa or across the Pacific, and brought Asian goods directly to Massachusetts warehouses. Profits built richly furnished mansions in Bay State seaports and shipyards in every river mouth. Marine societies, libraries, navigation schools, banks, and countinghouses flourished. A quarterdeck Federalist aristocracy replaced the Puritans.

Elected second president of the United States in 1796, Massachusetts Federalist John Adams averted a confrontation with Napoleon that would have dealt a blow to Massachusetts' maritime prosperity, but Republican President Thomas Jefferson's embargo of 1807–09 bankrupted Massachusetts merchants. When the War of 1812 was declared during the next Republican administration, the remnants of the Massachusetts Federalists repudiated "Mr. Madison's War" and occasionally collaborated with the blockading enemy. Despite the disruption of commerce caused by the war, the China trade continued and Massachusetts prospered.

The Industrial Revolution. After the War of 1812 England repeated its post-Revolution maneuver, dumping manufactures on American seaports, aiming to stifle infant U.S. industries born of the embargo and the war. Outraged American manufacturers gained from Congress the high protective tariff of 1816. And although Massachusetts' East India cotton trade declined by half, textile manufacturing burgeoned in Fall River, New Bedford, and eventually Lowell. China traders invested in industry; shipfitters and ironworkers turned their skills to making clocks, cotton gins, cutting tools, shoe-sewing machines, spinning mills, and power looms. By 1840 Taunton, Brockton, Chelsea, Cambridge, Waltham, Worcester, and Gardner were industrial cities manufacturing cotton and woolen textiles, shoes, ironwares, and furniture, using water-powered mill wheels. At the same time, Boston's domestic mercantile trade swelled, and smaller harbors sent Yankee products to southern ports, bringing back cotton and hides. Briefly in the 1850's enormously profitable domestic trade in supplies for the California gold rush, aboard fast clipper ships, rivaled the earlier China trade. But the advent of steam vessels soon made uncompetitive these great racing clippers, which required huge crews. Scheduled steam packet ships replaced them.

Volume production in huge textile and shoe mills similarly replaced the handicraft industries. Steam replaced waterpower; steam railroads replaced ox carts and domestic shipping; petroleum replaced whale oil; and huge factories replaced the millpond economy. The Irish potato famine of 1846 brought 50,000 unskilled immigrant laborers to perform standardized machine tasks. Soft coal, and later electricity, supplied the muscle.

Moving from its quarterdeck economy, Massachusetts was becoming a prosperous industrial society, and the wealth and leisure abounded to bring about a literary renaissance. The quarterdeck prosperity had already produced educational and benevolent institutions, such as the Phillips Academy at Andover, the Massachusetts General Hospital at Boston, the American Academy of Arts and Sciences, the Massachusetts Medical Society, the Handel and Haydn Society, the Massachusetts Historical Society, libraries, and charitable and missionary societies.

When George Ticknor returned from Europe in 1819 after four years of conferences with Johann Wolfgang von Goethe; George Gordon, Lord Byron; Robert Southey; Sir Walter Scott; and other European romantics to teach belles lettres at Harvard, the stage was set for change. William Ellery Channing, Daniel Webster, Edward Everett, Richard Henry Dana, William Cullen Bryant, George Bancroft, Jared Sparks, William Hickley Prescott, and John Gorham Palfrey often came to his newly assembled library. To these founders of the renaissance were added the dour novelist Nathaniel Hawthorne, the Concord transcendentalist philosopher-poet Ralph Waldo Emerson, and the poet-abolitionist John Greenleaf Whittier. Henry David Thoreau joined Concord neighbor Emerson in philosophic commentaries on man's relationship to nature. Dana and Herman Melville wrote novels on life aboard sailing ships. James Russell Lowell's whimsical Yankee verse, Oliver Wendell Holmes's patriotic poetry and trenchant autocrat prose, and Henry Wadsworth Longfellow's poetic versions of New England legends rounded out Boston's literary golden age at midcentury.

Stimulated in some measure by the philosophical challenge of the literati, successive state constitutional amendments began to liberalize the tight governmental control previously held by the Congregational church. Compulsory church attendance and taxes to support the church were abolished. Religious and property qualifications for officeholders disappeared. Election of state senators and governors' councillors, long controlled by "the rich, the wise and the good," was determined by popular vote.

Horace Mann pioneered in the establishment of tax-supported public high schools and teacher-training normal schools, supported by such leaders as Josiah Quincy, Rufus Choate, and Charles Sumner.

Liberal aristocrats Sumner and Wendell Phillips and poets Whittier, Longfellow, and Lowell joined the abolitionists who had been mobilized in Massachusetts by William Lloyd Garrison, and former President John Quincy Adams offered antislavery petitions in Congress. When six southern states seceded from the Union, Massachusetts' foresighted Gov. John Albion Andrew instantly put three regiments at President Abraham Lincoln's disposal, and during the Civil War, Massachusetts sent 146,000 men to fight for the Union, of whom 13,942 died.

After the Civil War, Massachusetts' production quadrupled as Massachusetts manufactured half the nation's shoes and a third of its woolens. Boston's land-filled Back Bay accommodated mansions for affluent investors in new railroading, banking, and mining enterprises. Postbellum affluence built colleges—Tufts, Boston College, Holy Cross, Massachusetts Institute of Technology, Boston University, Wellesley, Smith, Radcliffe, Clark, Simmons, Northeastern, and scores of vocational schools. Boston's affluence produced its Arnold Arboretum, Boston Museum of Fine Arts, and Boston Symphony Orchestra and also pioneering social institutions—employers' liability laws, sanitary systems, health departments, kindergartens, research laboratories, civil-service reforms, and public welfare. Civic conscience was digesting immigration pressures by 1900.

The 20th Century. During the transition from the horse age to that of the automobile, Massachusetts not only built state roads but also, by 1910, had standardized local budgets, accounting, civil service, assessing, taxation, and sanitation, fire, police, school, welfare, and health departments through state subsidies. Intense industrial competition continued to centralize manufacturing in urban centers and their immediate suburbs. Distant towns languished, their water-powered industries no longer competitive. Although taken as a whole the Massachusetts economy flourished through World War I and the 1920's, the state's isolation from raw materials and markets in the depression of the 1930's destroyed its preeminence in textile and shoe manufacture, which moved to the South and West. Deprived of bulk freight and already reduced by bus, truck, and airplane competition, the rail services fell apart. By 1940 only diversified industries, using skilled labor to make products that sold for ten times the cost of raw materials, could survive in Massachusetts. Enormous factory complexes disappeared or were occupied by hundreds of small specialty companies in all the shoe and textile cities. The balance of industry moved into electronics, machinery, metal fabrication, paper specialties, chemicals, tools, and airplane engines. Service industries—notably finance and insurance—thrived. The continued development of Cambridge's "Research Row" and ample vocational schools fostered skills to support new clusters of technological factories around Boston's periphery—such as Polaroid and General Electric—as the researchers at the Massachusetts Institute of Technology and Arthur D. Little, Inc., developed the nuclear physics, chromatography, lasers, solar energy, computers, and analytical chemistry to shape the future of the U.S. economy.

As the early intellectual leadership of Massachusetts revived in the 20th century, so also did the national prominence of the state's political leaders. Having produced the second and sixth presidents of the nation—John Adams (1797–1801) and John Quincy Adams (1825–29), Massachusetts produced two presidents in the 20th century—Calvin Coolidge (1923–29) and John F. Kennedy (1961–63). It also produced such national leaders as Henry Cabot Lodge, Louis Brandeis, Leverett Saltonstall, Felix Frankfurter, Christian Herter, Edward Brooke, John Volpe, Elliot Richardson, and Robert and Edward Kennedy.

In 1970 three-quarters of Massachusetts' population of 5.6 million inhabited less than half the state's area, largely concentrated in Greater Boston's crescent of 150 communities from Newburyport to Fall River. This congested urban-suburban crescent has all the modern metropolitan problems of inadequate commuter rail services, crowded arterial highways, pollution, and overburdened public utilities. Historically formidable local community pride has sometimes retarded areawide planning and restricted change, although preserving jealously the major historic sites and many green areas and recreational parks in the outlying suburbs. Boston, now mostly a distributional center, is recovering from its central-city blight by redevelopment of many of its degenerated core areas; other formerly industrial cities often lack the resources to do so.

Meanwhile, supplemented by the nation's bicentennial celebrations, the recreational and tourist industry in Massachusetts grows unceasingly. Sturbridge Village, the Cape Cod National Seashore, the Berkshire Music Festival, and Plymouth Plantation draw thousands of summer visitors. Fall foliage tours; skiing, hunting, and fishing; and Concord and Bunker Hill battle reenactments carry tourism through the other seasons. The convention trade is brisk, and clambakes and lobster dinners popular. Sailing yachts and power cruisers fill the harbors.

Although Massachusetts' population increased 10.5 percent from 1960 to 1970, the city populations of Boston, Worcester, Springfield, and New Bedford all decreased in the same years. But the Standard Metropolitan Statistical Areas of these cities continue to increase in population, demonstrating that the flight from cities to the suburbs is a factor in the state's overall population growth.

[James Truslow Adams, *Revolutionary New England, 1691–1776,* and *New England in the Republic;* V. W. Brooks, *The Flowering of New England, 1815–65,* and *New England Indian Summer, 1865–1915;* Oscar Handlin, *Boston's Immigrants, 1790–1865: A Study in Acculturation;* A. B. Hart, ed., *Commonwealth History of Massachusetts;* Henry F. Howe, *Prologue to New England, Salt Rivers of the Massachusetts Shore,* and *Massachusetts—There She Is—Behold Her;* Samuel Eliot Morison, *Builders of the Bay Colony,* and *Maritime History of Massachusetts, 1783–1860;* A. H. Rubenstein, *Problems of Financing and Managing: New Research-based Enterprises in New England.*]

HENRY F. HOWE

MASSACHUSETTS, FORT, in Colorado, was established in 1852, at the foot of Blanca Peak on Ute Creek in the San Luis Valley, by Maj. George A. H. Blake to protect the settlers on the upper Rio Grande against the Ute Indians. The buildings and stockade of pine logs accommodated 150 men, infantry and cavalry. In 1858 the post was moved six miles south and the name changed to Fort Garland.

[M. L. Crimmins, "Fort Massachusetts," *Colorado Magazine* (July 1937).]

COLIN B. GOODYKOONTZ

MASSACHUSETTS, FORT, in Williamstown, Mass., was one of the three "Province Forts" erected for the protection of the Deerfield Valley. It was built in 1744 by order of the Massachusetts court. In August 1746, it was attacked by a party of French and Indians, led by Pierre François, Marquis de Vaudreuil, and its garrison, which had been depleted to render assistance in the war to the east, was destroyed. It was rebuilt in 1747, put in command of Capt. Ephraim Williams, and came to serve as headquarters for the surrounding forts and blockhouses. On Aug. 2, 1748, it was again subjected to attack.

[Justin Winsor, *Narrative and Critical History of America,* vol. V.]

LEON W. DEAN

MASSACHUSETTS BALLOT. Before July 20, 1629, all voting in New England was by acclamation or by the uplifted hand, but on that date the Salem church used the ballot in choosing a pastor. By 1634 the ballot was used in electing the governor of Massachusetts. In 1645 Dorchester ordered that all "elections be by papers," that is, by ballots. Paper being scarce, kernels of wheat and Indian corn were sometimes used, the wheat for the affirmative and the corn for the negative; in Dedham, in 1643, assistants were chosen by the use of Indian beans, white for the affirmative and black for the negative, from which the term "black ball" came to signify a negative vote. The Australian, or secret, ballot was introduced into the United States by Massachusetts in 1878.

[A. B. Hart, *Commonwealth History of Massachusetts;* J. F. Sly, *Town Government in Massachusetts.*]

R. W. G. VAIL

MASSACHUSETTS BAY, FRANCHISE IN, was limited to church membership under the first charter and to property holders under the second. The charter of 1629 contained no such specific provisions, but because it gave to stockholders, or freemen, the right to vote in the trading company's general court, and to the general court the authority to admit new freemen, the Puritan leaders, after the Great Migration, were able to limit suffrage to those in sympathy with their religious beliefs. Only about one-fifth of the adult males had any share in the colony's government. Charles II's protest against the suffrage limitations brought occasional gestures of compliance, but the Massachusetts leaders could not submit to such demands without endangering the theocracy itself. This close union of church and state was broken by the annulling of the charter in 1684. Under the Dominion of New England (1686–89), in the absence of a representative assembly, there was no colony franchise. In 1689, when the leaders of revolution, without authority from England, reestablished the old charter government, they made a wide extension of suffrage in order to win support for restoring the charter. To their disappointment, the new charter of 1691 did not confirm the old freemanship, but gave the suffrage to 40-shilling freeholders and to others who had property worth £40 sterling. The state constitution of 1780 contained a similar property qualification, but when a general national movement for a freer suffrage set in, Massachusetts fell into line, first abandoning the property qualification in favor of a small taxpaying restriction and later adopting the generally accepted white manhood suffrage (*see* Franchise).

[F. N. Thorpe, *The Federal and State Constitutions.*]

VIOLA F. BARNES

MASSACHUSETTS BAY COMPANY. The history of the Massachusetts Bay Company is in reality not the history of a trading company, but of a theocracy, one of the most interesting of the early American experiments in utopias. The royal charter of 1629 confirmed to a group of merchants and others land already granted to them, presumably, by the Council for New England in 1628, with power to trade and colonize in New England between the Merrimack and the Charles rivers. Under the council's patent the Massachusetts group had local powers of self-government, subject to the general government to be established by the council over all New England. The royal charter removed Massachusetts from its position of dependence on the council's general government and allowed the company to establish whatever government it chose for its colony, subject to no superior authority except that of the king. The company in its beginnings closely resembled other trading companies operating in the New World, but almost immediately after receiving its charter, it changed the emphasis of its interest from trade to religion. Puritan stockholders who considered prospects for religious and political reforms in England increasingly hopeless under Charles I decided to migrate to New England with their families, possessions, and the company charter (*see* Cambridge Agreement). Some compromises concerning the business administration were made with the merchants remaining behind, but control of the enterprise for the future lay with those who left England in the Great Migration of 1630, and the government designed for the trading company in England became that of the colony of New England.

The charter of 1629 provided for the usual organs of government—governor, assistants, and general court of the stockholders—but omitted the clause requiring the company to hold its business sessions in England. This omission made it possible for Puritan leaders among the stockholders to transfer the company with its charter to the colony in New England and to superimpose upon the colony the government designed for the company. By so doing they could use the power of the general court to admit new members as a means of limiting the suffrage (*see* Massachusetts Bay, Franchise in) in the colony to those of their own religious faith and in a few years to transform the enterprise from a trading company existing for profit into a theocracy practically free from outside control. As a further safeguard, the assistants tried to govern the colony without the share of the general court except in annual elections, but when this breach of charter terms was objected to, the general court received back its legitimate authority. With the expansion of settlement, representative government evolved and the general court came to be composed of deputies from the towns who sat with the governor and assistants, until a bicameral court was established in 1644. Dissent within the theocracy resulted in the voluntary exile of the group that founded Connecticut, and the forced exile of Roger Williams and Anne Hutchinson, founders of Rhode Island towns.

The Council for New England under the leadership of its president, Sir Ferdinando Gorges, almost immediately charged that the charter had been surreptitiously obtained, and, aided by leading officials of government, including Archbishop William Laud, began a campaign to have it annulled. In 1635 the council surrendered its own charter and asked the king to regrant the land in eight charters to eight members of the council, a process that would give the new patentees an opportunity to inspect all previous grants for purposes of confirmation. It was expected that the Massachusetts charter would be caught in this net. The plan failed because only one of the eight patents, that for Maine, passed the seals before the outbreak of the Puritan Revolution.

Massachusetts Bay Company remained neutral during the Puritan Revolution in England, but joined with Plymouth, Connecticut, and New Haven in a defensive confederation in 1643, perhaps partly as a protection against being drawn into the struggle (*see* United Colonies of New England). The Massachusetts government considered itself an independent commonwealth after 1649. Nevertheless, when the monarchy was restored in 1660, the company recognized the relationship to the mother country that the charter defined. After the Navigation Acts were passed, the leaders in the theocracy found it extremely difficult to be reconciled to the dependent position of the colony. Because they refused to accept many features of England's new colonial policy, they

gradually incurred the displeasure of the crown. The commission sent over in 1664 to conquer New Netherland was instructed also to visit the New England colonies and investigate conditions. The commission and others reported Massachusetts at error in many respects: coining money without authority, extending government over the region of Maine and New Hampshire at the north, restricting the suffrage to church members, denying freedom of worship to dissenters, and, most important of all, refusing to obey the Navigation Acts or to recognize Parliament's authority over them (*see* Nicoll's Commission). The company avoided trouble for a while by a policy of procrastination and evasion, but in 1676 Edward Randolph was dispatched on another mission of investigation. His report was even more damning than that of the 1664 commission. At the king's demand the company sent over agents to negotiate some sort of compromise, but thereafter failed to fulfill the promises made by the agents. The Lords of Trade, exasperated by the long delays and the failure to get results, recommended annulling the charter on the ground that the company had not lived up to its terms. Formal charges were made against the company and the charter withdrawn by *scire facias* proceedings in 1684, after which the company as a corporation ceased to exist. Its government, however, continued to function without legal status until the establishment of the Dominion of New England in 1686.

Although the company very early lost its character as a trading company and became a theocracy, the charter itself was necessary to the maintenance of that theocracy because of the almost complete governmental control it gave to the company's general court. Under that outer shell the colony developed a very close union of church and state, a theocracy more or less on the Calvinist pattern. To maintain the purity of the religious ideals of the leaders, the very limited suffrage was necessary, as was the weeding out of dissenters, the control of the school system, and the refusal to recognize the power of Parliament over it. Yet the colony was too weak to resist the authority of the mother country by force; it had to resort to strategy. The faith of the leaders in God's protection of them led them to believe that in a crisis He would come to their aid. This faith allowed them to dare to procrastinate and at times even to defy the mother country. If they had been more conciliatory they might have preserved the charter. As it was, their actions and attitude made England believe that no policy of colonial administration could ever be successful as long as the Massachusetts Bay theocracy existed. The only way to destroy it was to destroy the company through its charter.

[C. M. Andrews, *The Colonial Period in American History*, vol. I; H. L. Osgood, *The American Colonies in the Seventeenth Century*, vol. I.]

VIOLA F. BARNES

MASSACHUSETTS BODY OF LIBERTIES. To curb the power of the magistrates, deputies in the Massachusetts general court agitated for a code of laws (1635). Committees appointed (May 6, 1635; May 25, 1636; and Mar. 12, 1638) accomplished little, although a member of one committee, John Cotton, presented (October 1636) a code that was not accepted. In June 1639 the court referred the task to Cotton and Nathaniel Ward, formerly an English lawyer. Each was to frame a model code. In November 1639 both models were referred to a committee, which adopted Ward's code. Sent to the towns for suggestions and reduced to 100 items by the court, the code was adopted as law on Dec. 10, 1641. This body of liberties was to be in force for three years and, if found satisfactory, made perpetual. Similar to bills of rights and based largely on English common law, the code left too much authority to the magistrates. Deputies, at the end of the probation period, renewed the agitation and, after a long survey, replaced the body of liberties with *The Book of the General Lawes and Libertyes* (1648).

[Charles M. Andrews, *The Colonial Period of American History*, vol. I; J. W. Dean, *A Memoir of the Reverend Nathaniel Ward*.]

RAYMOND P. STEARNS

MASSACHUSETTS "CIRCULAR LETTER." On Feb. 11, 1768, the Massachusetts House of Representatives, fearing the commercial, political, and constitutional effects of the Townshend Acts of 1767, petitioned George III and his ministers and drafted a letter to all colonial legislatures "to inform them of the measures this House has taken" with regard to the acts. This step toward colonial unity was punished by dissolution of the general court on July 1, 1768.

[Edward Channing, *A History of the United States*, vol. III; John C. Miller, *Sam Adams: Pioneer in Propaganda*.]

RAYMOND P. STEARNS

MASSACHUSETTS GOVERNMENT ACT, or Regulating Act, second in order of the Coercion Acts, was passed by the English Parliament in May 1774, with the intention of quelling the recent disturbances created by New England merchants and radicals protesting against the tea tax. Its purpose, Lord North announced, was "to take the executive power from the hands of the democratic part of the government." To this end, the act provided that the charter of Massachusetts be abrogated; that members of the council be appointed by the governor instead of by a convention of the preceding council and assembly, as formerly; that salaries of councillors be paid by the crown rather than by appropriation of the assembly; and that all councillors be subject to dismissal at the king's pleasure. The judges were also to be chosen by the governor and receive their stipend from the crown. Sheriffs were to be appointed in like manner, and they alone had the right of selecting juries. Last and most drastic, the town meeting was abolished, except for the function of electing municipal officers. The immediate reaction to the act was one of intense indignation throughout English North America, and in Massachusetts it crystallized public opinion in favor of an armed revolt, if need be, to safeguard the liberties of the colony.

[John R. Alden, *General Gage in America*; John Shy, *Toward Lexington: The Role of the British Army in the Coming of the American Revolution*.]

FRANK J. KLINGBERG

MASS MEDIA. In the latter half of the 20th century "mass media" was the term employed to designate, comprehensively, all forms of public communication. Until after World War I, local newspapers and weekly journals and magazines, supplemented by public meetings and personal interchange, constituted the means by which people were informed on current issues. After 1920 the means both broadened and intensified. Radio, starting with crystal sets, came into popular favor. After World War II, television evoked an even greater mass appeal. In many communities newspaper managements reached out to include ownership of electronic facilities—a development later opposed by the Federal Communications Commission. As newspapers merged under economic pressures, print competition lessened, and more and more people relied on broadcasts for reports and interpretations of the news. Tabloids, paperback books, and mass magazines, many sold in supermarkets, were elements of the wide-spreading communications media. Professional lobbying associations, public relations firms, advertising and consulting groups proliferated, all with the media as targets.

By the decade of the 1960's the social and political influence and power of the mass media had become a matter of national concern and controversy. The newspaper trade weekly, *Editor & Publisher* (May 4, 1974), noting unfavorably the trend among elected officials, the public, and the press itself to refer to "the media," protested: "It is a short-cut word used to avoid specifics. . . . The First Amendment guarantee is to 'the press.' There is no mention of 'the media.' . . . Let's talk and write about 'the press,' and if we mean broadcasting or magazines let's say so!" Although these were not fully accounted by the public, important differences in legal status did distinguish the various media. Print journalism, thanks to its constitutional enshrinement, knew almost no regulation, while radio and television airwave channels, limited in number, were licensed and controlled almost as public utilities using a public resource.

[Harry M. Clor, ed., *The Mass Media and Modern Democracy;* Peter M. Sandman, David M. Rubin, and David B. Sachsman, *Media: An Introductory Analysis of American Mass Communications;* John Tebbel, *The Mass Media in America.*]

IRVING DILLIARD

MASS PRODUCTION, perhaps the most outstanding contribution of the United States to technology, represents a synthesis of several distinct traditions. The various strands of mass production were brought together by Henry Ford in the manufacture of the Model T automobile in 1903, but all extended deep into the American past.

The core of mass production is a system of production based on interchangeable parts. Although anticipated by several Europeans, it was first developed by Eli Whitney after 1798 when he undertook to manufacture muskets for the federal government. In essence, Whitney sought "to substitute correct and effective operations of machinery for that skill of the artist which is acquired only by long experience." This required special-purpose machines that were precisely guided by devices called "jigs." By use of jigs Whitney could utilize relatively unskilled labor. He made important progress, but his success was not complete. His muskets still required hand fitting and the parts could only be interchanged for groups of ten muskets.

Whitney was not the only pioneer: Simeon North and John H. Hall made fundamental contributions, notably in developing the milling machine. It took a generation to bring interchangeable-parts manufacturing to perfection, involving the collective labors of dozens of engineers both in the federal arsenals and in private firms. This required many new machines

(such as Thomas Blanchard's copying lathe) and new precision instruments (such as the micrometer gauge). Two events signaled the maturity of interchangeable-parts manufacturing: the award of a gold medal for the mass-produced Robbins and Lawrence rifle at the London Crystal Palace Exhibition of 1851 and the installation of what was termed the "American system" of manufacturing at Britain's Enfield Arsenal by the same firm. The American system was subsequently adopted by the national arsenals of all the leading European states. Although developed for the arms industry, the idea was applied to a wide range of industries, including the manufacture of clocks, sewing machines, typewriters, locomotives, farm machinery, and bicycles.

The symbol of modern mass production is not, however, the machine tool or the gauge; it is the moving-belt assembly line. This too has historical roots. In 1785, Oliver Evans invented an automatic flour mill that used moving belts and other devices to transport grain. By the 1830's the Cincinnati meatpacking plants were moving carcasses on overhead conveyors in what might be described as a disassembly line. Ford combined interchangeability and the assembly line. When Ford applied the moving belt principle to the assembly of automobiles, the increase in productivity was immediate and spectacular. The increase resulted only partially from the more minute division of labor and automatic materials handling; in addition, the moving belt was a tool of management, for by means of it the manager could set the pace of work. A good part of the increase in productivity came simply from forcing workers to work faster.

Mass production has been accompanied almost invariably by plant integration, the idea being to combine several stages of manufacturing to eliminate the profits of middlemen and to achieve the economies inherent in large-scale production. Whereas the American textile mills founded by Samuel Slater in Rhode Island in 1793 confined themselves to a single stage of production, the Boston Manufacturing Company, established at Waltham, Mass., in 1813, adopted plant integration; it combined all the processes needed to convert raw cotton into finished cloth in the same factory. Plant integration and economies of scale were also exploited by Andrew Carnegie for the steel industry, leading to "vertical combination"—that is, a company that controlled every stage of the productive process from the mining of the raw materials to the marketing of the finished product. The Ford Motor Company's River Rouge plant, built during World War I, was an extreme example of plant integration. Although it eliminated the profits of countless middlemen and its size permitted many economies, it was not totally successful, for it was too large and too complex to be managed efficiently by traditional methods.

The Ford Motor Company's managerial difficulties point up another aspect of mass production—rational management. Railroads were America's first truly big businesses, and they were the first to find traditional management inadequate and to pioneer in the development of new methods. Daniel C. McCallum, as superintendent of the Erie Railroad in the 1850's, attempted a precise, written definition of the duties and responsibilities of each employee. Albert Fink, when head of the Louisville and Nashville Railroad in the 1870's, instituted methods of modern cost accounting. The Pennsylvania Railroad employed a chemist, Charles B. Dudley (1882–1901), who devised methods of quality control and specifications in purchasing. But modern management was revolutionized at the turn of the century by Frederick W. Taylor's scientific management. Although his use of the stopwatch to analyze and measure work is the best known of Taylor's methods, his most important contribution was his view of every facet of management as an object of scientific inquiry and conscious design. He developed many tools of modern management, including routing, cost accounting, and the organization of management along functional lines. Founded in 1908 as a competitor of the Ford Motor Company, the General Motors Corporation, under Alfred P. Sloan, developed a more flexible, decentralized management during the 1920's and 1930's. Since World War II the use of systems analysis and the computer has opened a new era; the application of these newer techniques to the Ford Motor Company by Robert S. McNamara was an important element in revitalizing that almost moribund company after the war.

Mass production affects not only management but also consumers and workers. Oversimplification of the complex interaction of mass production and society has led to assertions that it manifests the American democratic spirit and, conversely, that it leads to tyranny and the negation of democratic principles. In terms of consumption it requires a market that is both large and capable of absorbing relatively standardized products. The absence of rigid class gradations in America contributes to the uniform mass market required, the luxury trade being small and few being very poor. Mass production in turn tends further to blur class distinctions, at least in consumption. High productivity makes possible high wages, and thus

American workers, as consumers, can support the mass-production industries that employ them. Americans are more nearly equal in the consumption of mass-produced products, such as automobiles and home appliances, than in the consumption of craft-produced commodities, such as houses.

In mass-production industries, such as the Ford Motor Company, management was long able to manipulate and exploit employees almost at will. The workers lacked skills and were easily replaced, and management's position was further strengthened by the fact that many of the workers were recent immigrants without either social or economic security. Management could exploit workers by setting an excessive pace (the "speed-up") or by reducing the number of workers on the line (the "stretch-out"). These practices resulted in mounting discontent, leading to strikes and unionization of workers in mass-production industries by the Congress for Industrial Organization (later the Congress of Industrial Organizations) in the 1930's and 1940's.

The unions were able to achieve marked rises in wages, especially after World War II. They gave mass-production workers the power to bargain with management, and they provided the basis for political organization as well. But complaints of dehumanizing working conditions persist. Individual tasks are often monotonous and highly repetitive. The pace of work still puts great pressure on the individual and denies him freedom to determine the rate at which he works. These deeper questions of worker alienation have been receiving much attention, and both in America and Europe experiments are underway that look toward replacing the "line" by a "work team" that would set its own pace. The ideal solution would be one combining the phenomenal productivity of mass production with the pride of workmanship and individual autonomy that characterize the craftsman's work.

[Horace L. Arnold and Fay L. Faurote, *Ford Methods and the Ford Shops;* Greville Bathe and Dorothy Bathe, *Oliver Evans, A Chronicle of Early American Engineering;* Roger Burlingame, *Backgrounds of Power: The Human Story of Mass Production;* Charles H. Fitch, "Report on the Manufactures of Interchangeable Mechanism," in U.S. Bureau of the Census (10th Census), *Census of Manufactures,* vol. II; Nathan Rosenberg, compiler, *The American System of Manufactures;* Merritt Roe Smith, "John H. Hall, Simeon North, and the Milling Machine," *Technology and Culture,* vol. 14 (1973); Charles R. Walker and Robert Guest, *Man on the Assembly Line;* Robert S. Woodbury, "The Legend of Eli Whitney and Interchangeable Parts," *Technology and Culture,* vol. 1 (1960).]

EDWIN T. LAYTON

MATAMOROS EXPEDITION, an incident in the Texas Revolution. After the capture of San Antonio in December 1835, many Texans wished to carry the war to Mexico by launching an expedition to seize Matamoros. The provisional government of Texas was divided over the plan; a violent quarrel between Gov. Henry Smith and the council disorganized the military forces of Texas and wrecked the proposed expedition. Meanwhile, the rival commanders, James W. Fannin, Jr., and Frank W. Johnson, who had been commissioned by the council to lead the expedition, were left at the frontier, where their forces were annihilated by the Mexicans early in 1836 (*see* Goliad, Massacre at).

[H. H. Bancroft, *History of the North Mexican States and Texas;* George P. Garrison, *Texas: A Contest of Civilizations.*]

C. T. NEU

MATANZAS, FORT, was constructed by the Spaniards in 1743 on an islet at the south entrance to the Matanzas River as a part of the defenses of Saint Augustine, Fla. The immediate occasion for the fortification was fear of the British after James E. Oglethorpe's victory on Saint Simon's Island in 1742 and his second attack on Saint Augustine in March 1743. This coquina structure is maintained by the federal government.

[Herbert E. Bolton and Mary Ross, *The Debatable Land;* Amos A. Ettinger, *James Edward Oglethorpe, Imperial Idealist.*]

JONATHAN T. DORRIS

MATCHES. Although phosphorus was discovered in 1669 by Hennig Brand of Hamburg, the ease of manufacture and economic conditions were not favorable for the production of matches until about 1825. The friction match, a match that can be lighted by striking on any surface (an outgrowth of the "lucifer," made of chlorate of potassium and sulfide of antimony), arrived in New England in the early 1830's. The first American patent was issued to Alonzo D. Phillips of Springfield, Mass., on Oct. 24, 1836, for a match using only phosphorus, chalk, and glue. This patent was sold to Ezekiel Byam, also of Massachusetts, who manufactured the "locofoco," celebrated in the presidential campaign of 1840.

The major contribution of the United States in match production was in the development of match-making machinery. Machinery was developed by Jonathan Morgan (1839), Thaddeus Hyatt (1840), Harvey Law (1844), and, most notably, by William Gates, Jr., and H. J. Harwood, who, in 1854, patented the first continuous match machine. This was improved in detail until it became the standard machine.

In 1892 a patent was issued to Joshua Pussey for his book matches. The patent was purchased in 1894 by the Diamond Match Company, but book matches did not become a successful commercial product until a brewing company purchased 10 million books to advertise its product.

The alarming development of phossy jaw in workers in American match factories, caused by the inhalation of white phosphorous fumes, prompted President William H. Taft to urge preventive legislation. In December 1910 William A. Fairburn of the Diamond Match Company announced the development of nonpoisonous sesquisulfide matches and deeded the patent to the public, eliminating the payment of royalties. Congress followed Fairburn's action by placing a two-cent tax on each box of white phosphorous matches, making their production unprofitable. Since 1913 all matches produced in the United States have been of the nonpoisonous variety.

[W. H. Dixon, *The Match Industry: Its Origin and Development;* Herbert Manchester, *The Diamond Match Company.*]

ROGER BURLINGAME

MATERNAL AND CHILD HEALTH CARE. Medical theory and practice relating to maternity and children date from ancient times and form an integral part of the history of medicine. Concepts of organized maternal and child health care and significant differential treatment of children are, however, of relatively recent origin, having evolved in the last decades of the 19th century. Only with the development of the public health movement in the post–Civil War era, the advance of scientific medicine, the growing responsibilities of state medicine, and the social reforms of the Progressive period did maternal and child health care become clearly defined.

From colonial times to about the beginning of the 20th century the mortality rate for infants and children was extremely high. Most dangerous was the first year of life, and a child's chances for reaching maturity remained precarious for the first five years. In 1789 about 40 percent of all deaths were among children under five years of age. By 1850 there had been no significant decline in this mortality rate, and although children under one year of age constituted less than 3 percent of the total population of 23,191,876, they accounted for 16.8 percent of the deaths. Children from one to four years, inclusive, made up 12.3 percent of the population and accounted for 21.2 percent of the total mortality.

Aside from poor diet, austere treatment, and unhygienic care in the home, disease took a high toll of lives. Gastrointestinal infections—especially cholera infantum, dysentery, and diarrhea—produced a high morbidity and mortality rate among infants. Epidemic diseases that particularly affected children were smallpox, scarlet fever, and diphtheria. The diphtheria epidemic, or "throat distemper," that ravaged fifteen New Hampshire communities between July 1735 and July 1736 took 984 lives; 802 of those who died were children under ten years of age, and 139 were youths from ten to twenty years old. The inferior state of obstetrical care not only contributed to the rate of infant death but was also a cause of high maternal mortality. Puerperal fever was widespread and in the majority of cases proved fatal.

The single most important medical contribution to benefit children prior to the modern era was inoculation for smallpox, first practiced in the United States by Zabdiel Boylston in 1721. An improved form of immunization against the disease, vaccination with cowpox virus, was introduced by Benjamin Waterhouse in 1800. Although the general state of medicine changed little until after the Civil War, some achievements did contribute to better maternal and child care. In 1825, William P. Dewees, of the University of Pennsylvania, published a treatise on the physical and medical treatment of children that may be considered the first comprehensive work on the subject. The American Medical Association (AMA) was established in 1847, and during the 1850's the first two American hospitals for children were founded in Philadelphia and New York. In 1872 the American Public Health Association was organized, and the following year the AMA formed a section on obstetrics and diseases of women and children. During the decades of the 1870's and 1880's numerous states established health departments, and scientific research broadened the level of medical knowledge, both in the laboratory and in the clinic. There was also a tremendous growth of medical literature at the time, accelerating the interchange of ideas and knowledge. In 1888 the American Pediatric Society was organized.

To Abraham Jacobi, an immigrant from Germany in 1853, belongs the credit for putting pediatrics on a firm and lasting basis. By 1857 Jacobi was lecturing on pediatrics at the College of Physicians and Surgeons of New York, and in 1860 he was appointed to the first special chair of diseases of children, in the New York Medical College. He became clinical professor of pediatrics in the Medical Department of Columbia College in 1870 and taught there until 1902. During his sixty years of active practice, Jacobi produced a vast number of publications, and his influence as a physician and teacher in the cause of child health care is unequaled in American pediatrics.

Of the numerous health problems relating to child care in the late 19th and early 20th centuries, none evoked more concern among physicians and public health officials than dirty and unsafe milk. The issue of milk as a vital element in infant feeding and a factor in the spread of disease was the first significant problem confronted by the pediatric profession. Among the pioneers in the clean milk movement were Henry L. Coit, founder of the certified milk program; Rowland G. Freeman; Charles E. North; and the philanthropist Nathan Straus, a staunch advocate of the pasteurization of milk who, in 1893, established the first of his systems of milk depots. Only with the acceptance and refinement of the pasteurization process in the first decades of the 20th century was the milk problem solved.

The expansion of modern public health methods brought the public school into the field of preventive medicine. In 1894 Samuel H. Durgin, a physician and member of the Boston Board of Health, inaugurated regular medical inspection of schoolchildren to detect and prevent the spread of disease. In 1902, on the initiative of Lillian Wald, the first school nurse in America was appointed in New York City, and by 1911 systems of medical inspection had been adopted by 411 cities. In 1903 Vermont passed a statewide law that required annual eye examination of all schoolchildren. School lunches were first provided in New York City in 1908.

In the quest for better child health services the year 1908 is significant because in that year New York established its Division of Child Hygiene, with Dr. S. Josephine Baker in charge. This government agency, devoted exclusively to the health of children, was to set a pattern for city and state health department administrations throughout the country. In 1909 the first White House Conference on Children, called by President Theodore Roosevelt, recommended the creation of a federal children's bureau. President William Howard Taft endorsed the proposal in 1910 and on Apr. 9, 1912, signed the bill establishing the bureau. Julia C. Lathrop, a social worker, was appointed chief, and for nine years she guided the bureau in its mission to "investigate and report upon all matters pertaining to the welfare of children and child life among all classes of our people."

The early work of the bureau, in cooperation with

state health departments, and the efforts of medical and welfare organizations resulted in important contributions for the betterment of maternal and child health care. Subjects studied included the reduction of maternal and infant mortality; the improvement of birth registration; the promotion of maternal, prenatal, and infant health care; the prevention of illness at home and in school through proper diet, clothing, exercise, and good health habits; and the general health and welfare of children in rural areas. Crippled children also received an attention that had been unknown previously, and work continued to better conditions for the care and education of blind, deaf, and mentally ill children. In 1921 Congress passed the Sheppard-Towner Act, which allocated funds to the states for health services for mothers and children, particularly in rural communities. Although Congress failed to renew this Maternity and Infancy Act in 1929, the projects of the period were a precedent and incentive for many of the programs that came with the Social Security Act, signed into law by President Franklin D. Roosevelt on Aug. 14, 1935.

In 1931 the American Academy of Pediatrics held its first meeting, and by that time maternal and child health care had made tremendous gains. Whereas in 1907 no state had had an agency dealing with child health problems, by 1926 all but one state had established a child hygiene division or its equivalent. Whereas in 1906 the infant mortality per 1,000 live births had been 148, by 1926 it had been reduced to 71. By 1945 it was reduced to 38.3; the maternal mortality rate for 1965, 31.6 deaths per 100,000 live births, was the lowest recorded in the United States to that time. This progress was a result of efforts by individuals, private organizations, and federal and state governments, emphasizing scientific research, public health education, and community health services.

In the period after World War II the advancement of maternal and child health care was focused on the needs of special groups of children and mothers, the conquest of particular diseases, and the social and psychological welfare of children, as well as their medical welfare.

[Dorothy E. Bradbury, *Five Decades of Action for Children;* Robert H. Bremner, ed., *Children and Youth in America;* Harold K. Faber and Rustin McIntosh, *History of the American Pediatric Society, 1887–1965.*]

MANFRED WASERMAN

MATILDA LAWRENCE CASE.
In 1837 Matilda Lawrence, a slave, left a steamboat at Cincinnati, and later, through her attorney, Salmon P. Chase, claimed her freedom on the ground that she had been brought by her master to free soil. The local court remanded her to slavery, but the conviction of James G. Birney for harboring her was reversed by the Ohio Supreme Court as a result of Chase's defense. The issue raised was ultimately resolved by the Supreme Court in *Dred Scott* v. *Sanford* in 1857.

[A. B. Hart, *Salmon P. Chase;* J. W. Schuckers, *Life and Public Services of Salmon Portland Chase.*]

EUGENE H. ROSEBOOM

MAUMEE INDIAN CONVENTION.
At this fateful conference, held in August 1793, the confederated Indian tribes of the Northwest Territory, encouraged by the British through their agent, Alexander McKee, and puffed up by two recent defeats of the American army (*see* Harmar's Expedition; Saint Clair's Defeat), decided to insist that the United States give up to the Indians all the lands of the Northwest Territory. As a result, U.S. commissioners, who were on their way to Sandusky with compromise proposals concerning the Indian-American boundary, declined to meet with the tribes, and the American army under Gen. Anthony Wayne proceeded to carry out its final campaign against the Indians. The tribes represented at the convention included the Delaware, Wyandot, Miami, and Shawnee.

[R. C. Downes, *Frontier Ohio, 1788–1803.*]

RANDOLPH C. DOWNES

MAUREPAS, FORT,
was erected by Pierre Lemoyne, Sieur d'Iberville, in 1699 on the Bay of Biloxi, near the present town of Ocean Springs, Miss. Iberville chose Fort Maurepas as the seat of the first French colony in Louisiana after he had explored the lower reaches of the Mississippi River without finding a suitable site for a colony on its banks. The seat of colonial government was moved from Fort Maurepas (Biloxi) to Dauphin Island, near Mobile, in 1702, but the fort appears to have been occupied continuously until it was destroyed by fire in 1719. When Louisiana was divided into districts for local administration, Biloxi became the chief post in the new district of that name.

[Alcée Fortier, ed., *Louisiana;* Dunbar Rowland, *History of Mississippi, The Heart of the South.*]

WALTER PRICHARD

MAURY'S CHARTS.
In the autumn of 1847 Matthew Fontaine Maury, then in charge of the Depot

of Charts and Instruments of the Navy Department, published his first *Wind and Current Chart of the North Atlantic,* founded on information collected from old, discarded naval log books. Through the co-operation of navigators all over the world, Maury secured data that enabled him not only to revise this chart but also to prepare similar charts for the South Atlantic, North Pacific, South Pacific, and Indian oceans. To explain and illustrate these charts he issued a pamphlet of ten pages, which grew to 1,257 pages in two quarto volumes, called *Sailing Directions.* By demonstrating to navigators how to take advantage of winds and currents and thus shorten the time of their voyages, Maury saved shipowners enormous sums of money. It has been estimated that the annual saving to British commerce in the Indian Ocean amounted to at least $1 million, while the United States saved at least $2.25 million a year in the outward voyage alone from Atlantic and California ports to South America, Australia, and the Far East. For this achievement Maury has been called the "pathfinder of the seas."

[Charles Lee Lewis, *Matthew Fontaine Maury: Pathfinder of the Seas.*]

CHARLES LEE LEWIS

MAUVILLA, BATTLE OF (October 1540). The only surviving sources, partly historical, partly romantic Portuguese accounts, record the southwesterly march of Hernando de Soto to meet the cacique Tuscaluza near the present site of Montgomery, Ala. De Soto, contemptuous of the Indians' kindness, held Tuscaluza practically a prisoner, forcing him to lead the way to Mauvilla, a populous and splendidly fortified town. Tuscaluza, outwardly friendly but inwardly resentful, forwarded a secret message, warning of the Spaniards' vicious characteristics. Unsuspecting, de Soto entered Mauvilla. A few hours later a Spaniard killed an Indian in a street brawl. In the ensuing fight, Mauvilla was burned, hundreds of its citizens perishing; Tuscaluza committed suicide; and de Soto was seriously wounded. The Spaniards suffered eighty casualties and lost many horses and practically all their baggage.

[Lambert A. Wilmer, *The Life, Travels and Adventures of Ferdinand de Soto.*]

ROBERT S. THOMAS

MAVERICK. In 1845 Samuel A. Maverick, a lawyer in San Antonio, Tex., reluctantly took over 400 head of stock cattle on a $1,200 debt. He kept them for eleven years under charge of an irresponsible hand and had fewer cattle than he started with. Neighbors had done most of the branding of the increase. They came to refer to any unbranded animal older than a calf and running at large as "one of Maverick's." The usage spread, the noun becoming common. After the Civil War there were hundreds of thousands of maverick cattle in Texas. Mavericking became an occupation that sometimes bordered on and often led to thieving, though any range man had—and still has—a right to brand any maverick found on his range.

[J. Frank Dobie, *A Vaquero of the Brush Country;* Mary A. Maverick, *Memoirs.*]

J. FRANK DOBIE

MAXENT, LACLEDE AND COMPANY, a firm established in 1762 by Pierre Laclede Liguestе, Antoine Maxent, and others for stimulating and maintaining a large-scale commerce with Indians. An exclusive license to carry on this trade with the Indians of the Missouri, which included the Illinois and the Peoria, and all nations residing west of the Mississippi was granted to them, and confirmed in 1763 by M. D'Abbadie, director general of Louisiana. The company imported large supplies of goods from Europe for trading. Laclede, a man of great experience, skill, and prudence, was placed in charge of a considerable armament that left New Orleans on Aug. 3, 1763. Proceeding into the Illinois country he stored his goods at Fort de Chartres in present-day Randolph County, Ill. Locating the present site of Saint Louis for his post, from which he planned to control the territory included in the grant, he ordered his lieutenant to clear the spot and form a settlement. Meanwhile, he traded with various tribes of Indians. In May 1769, Laclede bought the three-fourths interest of Maxent for 80,000 livres in silver, and the partnership was dissolved. The trade established by Laclede extended as far north as Saint Peters River (present-day Minnesota River) and came in competition with the British traders. Laclede carried on the trade until his death in 1778.

[John Francis McDermott, "The Exclusive Trade Privilege of Maxent, Laclede and Company," *Missouri Historical Review,* vol. 29.]

STELLA M. DRUMM

MAXIM GUN. Hiram S. Maxim, a native of Maine, invented the first automatic, quick-firing gun. He conceived the idea and made the first drawings while on a visit to Paris, and going from there to London, perfected the gun in 1884. It used a belt of cartridges, the first model firing more than ten times per second. Maxim manufactured automatic guns of various calibers (up to 12-pounders) for many governments, modifying them to suit the ideas of each. His guns' aid to Great Britain in winning the Egyptian campaigns of 1897–99 led to his being knighted in 1901. He had become a British subject several years before.

[Hiram S. Maxim, *My Life*.]

ALVIN F. HARLOW

MAXWELL LAND GRANT was made by the Mexican government on Jan. 11, 1841, to Guadalupe Miranda and Carlos Beaubien. It included roughly a rectangle of land whose eastern boundary was the line connecting Trinidad, Colo., and Springer, N.Mex., and reaching west to the Sangre de Cristo Range. Congress confirmed the title on June 21, 1860, and Beaubien's son-in-law, Lucien Maxwell, eventually acquired 1,714,765 acres by inheritance and purchase. His successor, the Maxwell Land Grant Company, successfully maintained its title to this vast estate in four suits before the Supreme Court and against armed resistance of the settlers.

[R. E. Twitchell, *Leading Facts of New Mexican History*.]

PERCY S. FRITZ

MAY DAY. The festivity at Merry Mount in Quincy, Mass., in 1627 seems to have marked the introduction of the Maypole to America. Naturally, such frivolity could not continue in Puritan Massachusetts; nor was the medieval May Day, with its dance around the Maypole, much celebrated anywhere else in early America. During the 19th century it became the traditional family moving day in cities. In 1889 an International Socialist Congress selected it as a world labor holiday; and on May Day (the first day in May), 1890, for the first time there were demonstrations in Europe and America in favor of the eight-hour working day. Thus May Day is celebrated both as a festival of spring and, in some countries, as Labor Day.

[Mary Caroline Crawford, *In the Days of the Pilgrim Fathers*.]

ALVIN F. HARLOW

MAYFLOWER, a three-masted, double-decked, bark-rigged merchant ship of 180 tons, with a normal speed of 2.5 miles per hour. Christopher Jones became its master in 1608 and its quarter owner in 1620.

The *Mayflower* was chartered in London to take the Pilgrims to America. They left Leiden, Holland, on July 31, 1620 (all dates are new style), for Delsthaven, and the next day they sailed for Southampton, England, aboard the *Speedwell,* a smaller but older craft that they had outfitted for the voyage to America. There they met the *Mayflower* and took on supplies for the voyage. The two ships sailed on Aug. 15, but put back into Dartmouth harbor about Aug. 23 because of the leaky condition of the *Speedwell.* They sailed again about Sept. 2, but the *Speedwell* continued unseaworthy and they were again forced to return, this time to Plymouth harbor, where the smaller ship was abandoned. Some of the passengers returned to shore and 102 passengers and crew finally sailed on the *Mayflower* on Sept. 16, sighted Cape Cod on Nov. 19, and arrived in what is now the harbor of Provincetown, Cape Cod, Mass., on Nov. 21. Some time was spent in taking on wood and water, in mending their shallop, and in exploring the bay and land, so that they did not reach the site of Plymouth, Mass., until Dec. 21, 1620. The *Mayflower* followed the land-exploring party and sailed into Plymouth harbor on Dec. 26, where it remained until houses could be built for the new settlement. It sailed for England on Apr. 5, 1621, reaching London safely. It was in the port of London again in 1624, after which its history is uncertain because of confusion with several other contemporary ships of the same name.

[William Bradford, *History of the Plymouth Plantation;* W. S. Nickerson, *Land Ho!—1620.*]

R. W. G. VAIL

MAYFLOWER COMPACT, the agreement signed on Nov. 11, 1620, by the male passengers on the *Mayflower,* before coming ashore, that they would form a body politic and submit to the will of the majority in whatever regulations of government were agreed upon. Its purpose, according to William Bradford, was to hold in check the restless spirits on board who had threatened to strike out for themselves when the Pilgrim leaders decided to land in New England instead of Virginia. The Pilgrims held a patent from the Virginia Company granting rights to the soil and to local self-government, but this patent was of no use after they settled in New England. The compact appears therefore to have been a voluntary agreement to establish a local government that, although having no legal status until a patent could be obtained from the Council for New England, would at least have the strength of common consent. Its significance lies rather in its similarity to later ideas of democratic government than in any new philosophy of popular government in the minds of its authors. Plymouth Colony, though never so completely theocratic as Massachusetts, nevertheless leaned more toward theocracy than toward democracy.

[H. L. Osgood, *The American Colonies in the Seventeenth Century*.]

VIOLA F. BARNES

MAYNARD TAPE PRIMER consisted of a waterproofed paper roll of fifty fulminate caps and a mechanism to operate it, designed to speed operation of the percussion lock rifle. Offered by Edward Maynard to an ordnance board on Jan. 29, 1845, it was used, with some improvements, on many Civil War firearms, notably the rifle and rifle-musket models of 1855.

[Claude Fuller, *U.S. Shoulder Arms, 1795–1865*.]

DON RUSSELL

MAYO FOUNDATION, located in Rochester, Minn., is a charitable, nonprofit corporation devoted to the conduct and advancement of medical education and research as integral parts of medical and health care. Originally known as Mayo Properties Association, the foundation was incorporated on Oct. 8, 1919, when Dr. William J. Mayo and his brother Dr. Charles H. Mayo signed a deed of gift conveying all the assets of Mayo Clinic to the association. The name Mayo Properties Association was changed to Mayo Association in 1947 and to Mayo Foundation in 1964. Also in 1964 the name of the teaching arm of the Mayo institutions was changed from Mayo Foundation for Medical Education and Research to Mayo Graduate School of Medicine.

Mayo Foundation owns all the physical assets utilized by Mayo Clinic, a private group practice of medicine. Net earnings from patient care are used to support the foundation's research and teaching programs. The foundation conducts the Mayo Graduate School of Medicine, established in 1915 in affiliation with the University of Minnesota; the Mayo Medical School, opened in 1972; training in health-related sciences; and a broad program of medical research.

NORMAN K. NELSON

MAYSVILLE VETO, an episode in the long struggle over internal improvements. In 1830 Congress passed a bill authorizing a subscription of stock in the Maysville, Washington, Paris and Lexington Turnpike

Road Company. In vetoing the bill President Andrew Jackson pointed out that the project lay entirely within one state (Kentucky), that it had no connection with any established system of improvement, and that it therefore violated the principle that such works, to receive federal aid, had to be national and not local in character. The attitude of Jackson was in accord with prevailing Democratic principles but he was perhaps not unmindful of its political effect. "The veto," wrote Martin Van Buren, "was the wedge which split the party of internal improvements, a party which was wielded by a triumvirate of active and able young statesmen as a means through which to achieve for themselves the glittering prize of the Presidency."

[Archer Butler Hulbert, *Historic Highways of America*.]

J. HARLEY NICHOLS

MAZZEI LETTER. A letter by Thomas Jefferson to Philip Mazzei, an Italian physician and merchant and former colonial agent in Europe, on Apr. 24, 1796, was published in translation at Florence, Italy, on Jan. 1, 1797. Retranslated for the French *Moniteur*, it was republished in English for the *Minerva* on May 14, 1797. In the letter Jefferson severely criticized Federalist leaders, and certain phrases were interpreted in the Federalist press as direct attacks on George Washington. Jefferson was nearly ostracized by polite society, and the incident precipitated a permanent rupture between Washington and Jefferson.

[Dumas Malone, *Jefferson and the Ordeal of Liberty*.]

LOUIS MARTIN SEARS

MEAT INSPECTION LAWS in the United States originated with the campaign for pure food legislation. After 1887 the publications of the Department of Agriculture, under the supervision of H. W. Wiley, did much to stimulate national and state interest. Spurred to action by the "embalmed beef" scandal at the time of the Spanish-American War, Congress passed in 1906 the Meat Inspection Act, a comprehensive meat inspection statute. This act gave the secretary of agriculture, under the interstate commerce clause, power to inspect all meat and condemn such products as are "unsound, unhealthful, unwholesome, or otherwise unfit for human food." Although modified and amended, this enactment has remained the basis of activity by the federal government.

[C. W. Dunn, ed., *Food and Drug Laws, Federal and State*; Gustavus Weber, *The Food, Drug and Insecticide Administration*.]

BENJAMIN F. SHAMBAUGH

MEAT-PACKING. As long as the early colonists produced their own livestock and other food, meat-packing was strictly a local business, but in 1692, John Pynchon of Springfield, Mass., began buying hogs and shipping the meat to Boston, for the growing city population and the provisioning of ships. Colonial farmers at first found a market for their surplus meat in coastal towns and in the West Indies, and later the growing cities and the plantations of the South provided additional outlets. Early meat-packers were given that name because they literally packed cuts of pork and beef into barrels with brine. Meat-packing in those days was essentially a seasonal industry; there was no mechanical refrigeration to aid in keeping the meat from spoiling. Even when salt treatment was used, operations were confined almost entirely to the winter months. The custom was to pack meat through the winter, pile the barrels on the ground outside, and then sell in the spring.

Packinghouses were originally concentrated in New England and on the western frontiers of the Atlantic states. The shift westward began in the 19th century with the development of the livestock industry in the Middle West. Settlers found that the new land grew corn abundantly but that there was no way to sell the grain to the growing industrial centers of the East; shipment overland cost more than the grain was worth. Ohio settlers found the answer in feeding their corn to cattle that were driven over the Alleghenies to the seaboard or by stuffing some 15 bushels of corn into a pig and subsequently packing the pork into a barrel. But prior to 1825 most beef, pork, and mutton from the Middle West moved eastward on the hoof, since the era of canals and railroads and a major meat-packing industry was yet to come. At midcentury animals were trailed from farms and ranches to the cities, often hundreds of miles away. Slaughter took place close to the ultimate consumers because of the impossibility of storing fresh meat or shipping it any considerable distance, except occasionally during the winter in the northern areas. Local butchers predominated in the meat business. With the introduction of ice for cooling, curing activities were extended to the summer months.

Commercial meat-packing came into existence around 1818 in Cincinnati, soon called "Porkopolis" because by 1850 it was packing 27 percent of the meat products in the West. Chicago, Louisville, and Saint Louis soon became rivals. During the Civil War Chicago reached first rank, largely because of favorable rail and water transportation facilities. Beef had come to equal pork in importance, and competition developed in Kansas City, Omaha, Sioux City, and Saint Paul, in particular. As the livestock population grew in the West and the human population increased in the East, refrigerated packing plants were built to bridge the meat gap from the farm to the table. In the 1870's several large packing firms with headquarters at Chicago came to dominate the U.S. meat-packing industry, namely Armour and Company, Swift and Company, and Libby, McNeill and Libby. After the Civil War the vast western rangelands became a new major center for beef cattle because of the advancing railroads. Each fall cattle traveled north to Kansas, Nebraska, and Wyoming and terminated at Abilene, Kans., on the newly built Kansas Pacific Railroad, at Dodge City, Kans., on the Atchison, Topeka and Santa Fe, and at other centers, such as Ogallala, Nebr., and Miles City, Mont.

Meat-packing subsequently moved farther west with the introduction of efficient motor trucks and the extension of hard-surfaced roads that facilitated the trucking of livestock. Other cost changes largely eliminated the locational advantage of large rail terminals. Slaughter became feasible at almost any location. The big California market surpassed that of the state of New York, and even Chicago closed down its famed stockyards in 1971.

Until 1865 meat-canning establishments, which had originated in Massachusetts and Maine in 1815, were small and located in the East. Meat-canning got a considerable boost through the Civil War in providing for the army, and after 1868 P. D. Armour and others developed a canned corned beef and roast beef trade. Other companies packed ox and pork tongues and potted meats, chicken, rabbits, ham, and soups.

Corned beef was packed by the Libby company in quadrangular cans that were awkward in shipping, but in 1875 a method was developed for pressing corned beef into tapered tin cans that were easily shipped. A European market was created and the demand for canned corned beef became so great in the United States that it affected the sale of fresh cuts.

Methods of drying meat were long established, as shown by the pemmican devised by the American Indians and the charqui of the South American Indians. They were the forerunners of jerked beef. Meat powder was introduced in the United States about 1870; lean meat was dried on steam-heated plates and ground into powder to be used in soups or to be mixed with flour and made into biscuits.

Considerable quantities of meat were still smoked (chiefly with hickory wood) in the United States in 1900, when one Chicago firm had in operation forty-three smokehouses, each of which held 60,000 pounds of ham or shoulder or 120,000 pounds of side meat.

The introduction of efficient railroad refrigerator cars soon after 1880 made possible the transportation of fresh meat from as far west as Omaha to New York City without spoilage, and improvements in refrigeration created the possibility of marketing less salty ham and bacon, less heavily smoked meat, and glandular meats throughout the United States and the year round by the start of the century. Freezing later became a method for bulk storage of raw material for subsequent production of canned and dried items, as well as sausages, meat dishes, and soups. The industry has further profited by the utilization of an ever-increasing number of by-products, such as fertilizers, leather, wool, glue, and many pharmaceuticals, including hormones and sterols. In 1906 Upton Sinclair's novel *The Jungle* focused attention on unsavory conditions in the packing plants and led to the federal Meat Inspection Act of 1906. One consequence of the book, despite the new law, was substantial loss in foreign business, and the United States subsequently resorted to importation from Mexico, Argentina, Australia, Central America, and Brazil.

[O. E. Anderson, Jr., *Refrigeration in America;* R. A. Clemen, *The American Livestock and Meat Industry;* E. E. Dale, *The Range Cattle Industry, 1865–1925.*]

GEORG BORGSTROM

MECHANICS' INSTITUTES. Along with lyceums, apprentices' libraries, and other organizations that emphasized self-improvement through education in science and its applications, mechanics' institutes grew out of the reform spirit of the early 19th century. As the founders of Baltimore's Maryland Institute proclaimed in 1825, their goal was "to establish that equality so particularly recognized in our Bill of Rights."

Although the founders of these societies in America often looked abroad for the comfort of Old World precedent, the movement began simultaneously in Great Britain and the United States. The New York Scientific and Mechanic Institution was established in 1822; the Glasgow Mechanics' Institute, Britain's first, was formed in the following year. In both countries large numbers of institutes were started during the ensuing quarter-century. British organizations tended to follow a single institutional pattern and were often joined into regional unions. In America, however, the prevailing characteristic was diversity. Many institutes—in New York, Balti-

more, Philadelphia, and Cincinnati, for example—employed academics in their evening lecture programs. Other societies, the Boston Mechanics' Lyceum in particular, argued for a system in which artisans educated themselves.

The library was an important feature of mechanics' institutes in Chicago and San Francisco, while in Louisville the emphasis was on exhibitions of industry. The most successful organizations, notably Philadelphia's Franklin Institute, carried on all these activities as well as major programs in technical research and publication.

By midcentury, mechanics' institutes had lost much of their original mission—to provide low-cost technical education to the poor—and had largely departed from their early institutional patterns. Evening lectures tended increasingly to be patronized by the middle classes, who wanted general talks on a miscellany of topics. The widening establishment of private schools better supplied the educational needs of artisans. Furthermore, technical instruction was more effectively carried out in formal classroom situations than by evening lectures. In time, some institutes merged with temperance societies; others were absorbed into the lyceum movement, became a basis for town libraries, were incorporated into new agencies for vocational training, or disappeared for lack of purpose.

Although often short-lived, mechanics' institutes played a significant role in making Americans aware of technical skill and its relation to industrial advancement: their educational efforts reflected the need for a better system of technical training, and they dramatized, especially in exhibitions of domestic manufactures, America's emergence as an industrial power.

[C. A. Bennett, *History of Manual and Industrial Education up to 1870;* C. Bode, *The American Lyceum;* B. Sinclair, *Philadelphia's Philosopher Mechanics: A History of the Franklin Institute, 1824–1865.*]

BRUCE SINCLAIR

MECHANICSVILLE, BATTLE OF (June 26, 1862), sometimes called the Battle of Beaver Dam Creek. Aware that Union Gen. George B. McClellan, endeavoring to contact Gen. Irvin McDowell's advance from Fredericksburg, Va. (*see* Jackson's Valley Campaign), had dangerously extended his right, consisting of Gen. Fitz-John Porter's Fifth Corps, north of the Chickahominy, Gen. Robert E. Lee determined to crush the exposed wing. Leaving 21,000 troops east of Richmond to contain the 75,000 troops of McClellan's center and left, he threw 36,000 troops across the Chickahominy toward Porter's front, east of Mechanicsville. Confederate Gen. Thomas J. ("Stonewall") Jackson, marching from the Shenandoah Valley via Ashland with 18,500 troops, was to envelop the Union flank. Five brigades of A. P. Hill and James Longstreet's divisions of Lee's army assaulted Gen. George A. McCall's division, entrenched behind Beaver Dam Creek, and were severely repulsed. Jackson arrived too late to participate. During the night McCall withdrew and Porter concentrated behind Boatswain's Creek. (*See also* Peninsular Campaign.)

[R. U. Johnson and C. C. Buel, eds., *Battles and Leaders of the Civil War*, vol. II; Douglas S. Freeman, *R. E. Lee.*, vol. II.]

JOSEPH MILLS HANSON

MECKLENBURG DECLARATION OF INDE-PENDENCE. On Apr. 30, 1819, the *Raleigh Register* printed what was purported to have been a document adopted by the citizens of Mecklenburg County, meeting at Charlotte, N.C., on May 20, 1775, in which they declared themselves "a free and independent people, are and of right ought to be a sovereign and self-governing association under the control of no other power than that of our God and the General Government of Congress." This account was based on the recollections of old men, who insisted that there had been such a meeting and that the original records had been destroyed by fire in 1800. Thomas Jefferson denounced the document as "spurious," but its authenticity was not seriously questioned until 1847, when a copy of a Charleston newspaper of June 16, 1775, was found containing a full set of the Mecklenburg Resolves adopted at Charlotte on May 31, 1775. The available evidence leads one to believe that there was only one meeting. Confusion as to dates probably arose because of the old style and new style calendars. The resolves of May 31 did not declare independence, and they were drafted by the same men who claimed the authorship of the May 20 document, and who, after 1819, insisted that there was one meeting and one set of resolutions. Although the date May 20, 1775, is in the state seal and the state flag of North Carolina, most historians agree that the Mecklenburg Declaration of Independence is a "spurious document."

[William Henry Hoyt, *The Mecklenburg Declaration of Independence*.]

HUGH T. LEFLER

MECKLENBURG RESOLVES. On May 31, 1775, the Mecklenburg County Committee of Safety, meeting at Charlotte, N.C., drew up a set of twenty resolves, declaring "that all laws and commissions confirmed or derived from the authority of the King and Parliament are annulled and vacated and the former civil constitution of these colonies for the present wholly suspended." One resolve stated that the provincial congress of each colony under the direction of the Continental Congress was "invested with all legislative and executive powers within their respective Provinces and that no other legislative or executive power does or can exist at this time in any of these colonies." The committee proceeded to reorganize local government, elected county officials, provided for nine militia companies, and ordered these companies to provide themselves with proper arms and hold themselves in readiness to execute the commands of the provincial congress. Any person refusing to obey the resolves was to be deemed "an enemy to his country." The resolves were to be "in full force and virtue until instructions from the Provincial Congress shall provide otherwise or the legislative body of Great Britain resign its unjust and arbitrary pretensions with respect to America." This revolutionary document must not be confused with the so-called Mecklenburg Declaration of Independence of May 20, 1775, the authenticity of which has never been established.

[Hugh T. Lefler, *North Carolina History Told by Contemporaries*.]

HUGH T. LEFLER

MEDAL OF HONOR. *See* **Decorations, Military.**

MEDIATION. *See* **Arbitration; Labor.**

MEDIATION AND CONCILIATION SERVICE, FEDERAL. *See* **Federal Agencies.**

MEDIATION BOARD, NATIONAL. *See* **Federal Agencies.**

MEDICAL EDUCATION. The planting of British and continental cultures in the New World in the 17th century highlighted the need to perpetuate various arts and skills vital to the growth and permanence of the colonies. At an early date it was apparent that there were not enough medical immigrants, and sending young men abroad to study medicine was not economically feasible. Of necessity the apprenticeship system came into use, with a preceptorial period usually lasting no more than three years.

After the founding of Jamestown, 158 years elapsed before the establishment (1765) of the first collegiate curriculum in medicine in the colonies at the College of Philadelphia. During the latter part of that period a few brief lecture courses in anatomy and midwifery had been offered, and the apprenticeship system had produced a community of practitioners who were generally of the apothecary-barber type and who worked as family physicians. Some members of the clergy and other callings incorporated the healing art in their services to the colonists. There were also practitioners of folk and Indian medicine. It has been estimated that of the 3,500 physicians in the colonies in 1776, no more than 400 had medical degrees, principally from schools in Edinburgh, London, and Leiden, which a few young Americans began attending in the middle of the 18th century.

Fourteen years before John Morgan and William Shippen opened the College of Philadelphia medical school, Benjamin Franklin and other citizens had secured a charter (1751) for the Pennsylvania Hospital, the first such institution in the English colonies designed to be a community general hospital. King's College (now Columbia University) in New York City established (1767) the second medical school. Before the revolutionary war interrupted these two collegiate programs, the College of Philadelphia had conferred twenty-nine M.B. degrees and five M.D.'s; King's College had conferred twelve M.B.'s and two M.D.'s, besides four *ad eundem* M.D.'s.

By the end of 1800, thirty-two American colleges possessed charters sufficiently broad in wording to justify conferring medical degrees, but only ten instituted any kind of medical instruction before Jan. 1, 1801. Frederick C. Waite of Western Reserve University, writing in the 1830's and 1840's, calculated that 335 medical degrees of all types had been conferred on 312 candidates by that date—199 in Philadelphia, 85 in New England, and 49 in New York. Only Pennsylvania, Harvard, and Dartmouth medical schools entered the 19th century with fair prospects for the future, the College of Philadelphia having come under the aegis of the University of Pennsylvania in 1779.

The quality of medical education reached a low level during the 19th century for reasons peculiar to the history of the century. The founders of the College of Philadelphia (chiefly Morgan) had conceived of their two-term curriculum as a supplement to, and not a substitute for, the preceptorial system. The admission requirement was a college degree or its equivalent, including a satisfactory knowledge of Latin, mathematics, and natural and experimental philosophy. Required were courses in anatomy, materia medica, chemistry, and theory and practice of physic; practical clinical lectures; and one year attending the practice of Pennsylvania Hospital. A certificate of apprenticeship and examinations were required before the M.B. was conferred. Then, after three or more years of experience and preparing and defending a thesis in Latin, a candidate was eligible for the M.D. degree.

After 1792 the M.B. degree was abolished. A successful candidate for the M.D. degree served three years of apprenticeship and two terms of lectures, which could run concurrently with the apprenticeship. A required course in natural and experimental philosophy in the medical curriculum took the place of the admission requirement, and the thesis was acceptable in English or Latin.

Early in the history of the University of Pennsylvania and other medical schools shortages in textbooks and other teaching materials led to the custom of giving the same lectures each year instead of a graded curriculum, thus making the second year a repetition of the first. It was argued that repetition was an effective method of instruction. King's College probably set the pattern when in its early experience it required candidates for the advanced M.D. degree to return to school and repeat the regular lectures as a partial requirement. At first justified as necessary, this pedagogic foible became by 1820 the universal practice in American medical schools.

Two schools established under the corporate authority and control of medical societies, the College of Physicians and Surgeons under the Medical Society of the City and County of New York and the College of Medicine of Maryland in Baltimore under the Medical and Chirurgical Faculty of Maryland, had short-lived security under politically minded societies. The faculty of the latter institution envisioned itself as the nucleus of a university and reorganized in 1812 under a charter authorizing it to "annex to itself" faculties in law, divinity, and the arts and sciences. The act constituted the professors and provost a self-perpetuating board of trustees, and when the other schools failed to materialize, the medical professors found themselves to be both faculty and trustees. This arrangement, a departure from sound practice, created the first proprietary medical school in the United States. In the decades from 1820 to 1850 other state legislatures chartered independent groups of self-appointed professors over whom little or no restraint was exercised.

Not all proprietary schools had uniformly low standards, but the pressure of competition and the absence of detached governing boards forced standards down. Many such schools closed from lack of patronage in the period 1840–60 because they failed to provide cadavers for dissection and to establish hospitals for clinical instruction.

By 1830 nearly every state had laws designed to control licensing and malpractice, but the ground swell of the Jacksonian emphasis on the rights of the common man swept away these laws and left the medical profession and the public without reasonable protection. Thus, the portals to medical practice were opened to many hundreds of Americans with scant education, not to mention hordes of irregulars who rode the crest of succeeding waves of immigration from Europe. The times were also propitious for American practitioners who embraced Thomsonianism, homeopathy, eclecticism, hydropathy, and other cults that thrived on the declining popularity of the regulars.

A sense of default and unfulfilled mission felt by some medical educators and leaders in the profession led to the establishment of the American Medical Association (AMA) in 1847, its major goal being to elevate the standards of medical education. Because the association was extralegal, persuasion was its only weapon; nothing substantial was accomplished by it before the Civil War.

With one or two exceptions the Civil War closed southern medical schools. Hundreds of southern students in northern schools departed in a flurry of secessionism. Some northern schools introduced courses in military medicine. It was common for schools to give credit for a second term of attendance to students who spent their second year of medical study in military service as medical cadets. Because bacteriology was not yet an established science and heavy medication dominated therapeutics, internal medicine made little advance during the war. The introduction of ether (1846) and chloroform (1847) as anesthetic agents inspired surgeons to develop speed and skill in performing amputations, Joseph Lister's antisepsis (1867) coming too late to influence wartime surgery. The knowledge of personal and public hygiene and the construction of hospitals benefited empirically from the war experience.

Medical veterans and other physicians, sensing their need, began going to Europe, especially to German universities and to Vienna, for postgraduate study after 1870. Returning scholars, some of whom became teachers, started a renaissance in medical education. Progress was slow; the tyranny of utilitarianism and competition in the establishment of low-grade medical schools threatened education and care. The U.S. Commissioner of Education in his *Report* (1899–1900) listed 151 of the active medical schools, of which eight were eclectic and physiomedical and twenty-two homeopathic. Little more than 15 percent of 25,000 matriculates held a baccalaureate degree, and many students entered medical school with less than a high school diploma.

In 1877 a group of courageous medical educators formed the American Medical College Association. They foundered in 1883 over the proposal to require three, instead of two, terms of graded education; but in 1890, representatives of sixty-six medical schools revived the organization as the Association of American Medical Colleges (AAMC). Jointly with the AMA's Council on Medical Education and Hospitals (1904), this association became a potent force in shaping the course of medical education. In its formative years the AAMC was encouraged by pressure from the American Academy of Medicine and the Confederation of State Medical Examining and Licensing Boards. New state medical practice laws were slowly enacted, and medical schools—notably Pennsylvania and Harvard—began making improvements. The most encouraging advance in medical education during the late 19th century was the opening of the Johns Hopkins Hospital (1889) and the Johns Hopkins Medical School (1893). Although under separate boards they operated essentially as a unit, patterned principally after the German system.

In 1910 a dramatic exposé, the Flexner Report, called attention to the condition of medical education throughout the United States and Canada. Under the auspices of the Carnegie Foundation, but arranged by the AMA's Council on Medical Education, this survey (1907–10) by Abraham Flexner and N. P. Colwell, secretary of the council, brought to public attention the existence of numerous diploma-mill schools and the large number of mediocre institutions, both proprietary and university-related. There were only a few schools with graded curricula of university caliber.

Several mergers of weak schools to form stronger programs took place during the course of the survey. Numerous substandard institutions disappeared entirely. The AAMC and the council began to classify schools as A, B, or C in quality. States began to reject graduates of class C schools as candidates for certification to practice. Of the 165 medical schools that had existed in 1900, fewer than 70 remained within a few years of the publication of the report. By 1929 the A–B–C classification had been dropped, and all schools thereafter in existence were classified as approved, on probation, or not approved—the last classification constituting a death sentence.

Certain standards came to be common during the post-Flexner years: basic medical training was constituted as two years of preprofessional college education, a four-year graded curriculum, and an approved internship; medical schools were called upon to maintain a substantial full-time clinical faculty. The age of specialization gave rise to the demand for residency teaching programs and to the AMA's formation of specialty examining boards beginning in 1917.

After World War I, American and foreign physicians needing postdoctoral education turned to large American teaching hospitals. Facilities were expanded after World War II to accommodate returning American veterans and foreign physicians seeking refresher or residency opportunities. Curricula were frequently upgraded in the light of the information explosion in medical science, initiated in the 1930's. The dramatic acceleration of research in the postwar years was aided by government grants and subsidies through the National Institutes of Health and other federal agencies. In the 1970's there was an active trend away from specialization, with emphasis on family medicine as an area needing particular attention.

In addition to their search for scientific truth, medical educators are continually reviewing medicine's obligations to society. In response to an intensified public demand for more and better-distributed medical care, twenty-four new medical schools were opened in the period between 1967 and 1974. Many older schools enlarged their facilities. In 1973–74 there were 50,886 students enrolled in 108 medical schools, and 11,613 students were graduated.

[Abraham Flexner, *Medical Education: A Comparative Study*, and *Medical Education in the United States and Canada;* William Frederick Norwood, *Medical Education in the United States Before the Civil War;* C. D. O'Malley, ed., *The History of Medical Education;* Francis R. Packard, *History of Medicine in the United States;* Richard H. Shryock, *Medicine in America: Historical Essays.*]

WILLIAM FREDERICK NORWOOD

MEDICAL RESEARCH. The evolution of medical research in the United States has in some measure followed European experience, but there have also been significant differences. Until the end of the 19th century the United States was essentially a developing country, with a largely colonial culture. A scientific tradition was evolving, but research had small prestige, and certainly few institutions in which to develop. From the last decades of the 19th century until the mid-1970's, however, American medicine, as aptly described by H. E. Sigerist, has "rushed in a short time through all the successive stages of European development."

Early American medical research was sporadic, conducted by individuals, and most often clinically oriented. The most important influence was that of the Paris school of clinical pathologists, introduced by Americans who had studied in France. The work of William W. Gerhard in demonstrating the clinical-pathological distinction between typhoid and typhus fevers (1837) and that of Oliver Wendell Holmes on the contagiousness of puerperal fever (1843) are illustrative. Other important contributions were the experimental studies of gastric function by William Beaumont (1833), the introduction of ether anesthesia (1846) through the work of William T. G. Morton and Horace Wells, and the clinical experiments by J. Marion Sims leading to his discovery of a technique for the repair of vesicovaginal fistula (1852). The role of government in fostering medical research throughout most of the 19th century was more potential than actual. A National Board of Health was established in 1879 and for several years made grants to university scientists for specific studies concerned chiefly with quarantine, epidemic diseases, sanitation, and vital statistics. These grants covered expenses in the execution of research. The board was abolished after five years, and support for research ceased.

By the latter part of the 19th century a number of institutional forms for organizing and furthering medical research had been developed in Europe, particularly in Germany and France, and had demonstrated their effectiveness. Leading American physicians and medical scientists were fully cognizant of these developments. Many had been trained or had spent some time working abroad, particularly in Germany, and on their return they applied the ideals and the knowledge they had acquired to their work in the United States. In large measure German research provided the models Americans used and adapted to their own needs. Thus, the first laboratory for experimental physiology in the United States—and one might better say for experimental medicine—was founded in 1871 by Henry P. Bowditch, who had worked for two years with the German physiologist Carl Ludwig in Leipzig. The influence of the German experience may also be seen in the establishment of clinical laboratories in teaching hospitals. Illustrative are the opening of the William Pepper Laboratory of Clinical Medicine in 1894 at Philadelphia and the establishment of laboratories in the medical department at Johns Hopkins, beginning in 1905. Similar influences may also be seen in the organization of laboratories for medical research by governmental agencies, such as the Hygienic Laboratory of the U.S. Public Health Service (1887) and the research laboratories of the New York City Health Department (1892–93).

Such developments brought widespread public attention to the idea of medical research by showing the great practical benefits in the prevention and treatment of disease that resulted from discoveries in microbiology, nutrition, and experimental medicine. Increasingly the press, especially magazines, carried articles on medicine, science, and technology and brought to public notice problems of health and welfare that required investigation. Thus, it was not merely coincidence that a growing public recognition of the need to advance health research became evident just before and during the first decade of the 20th century. A nationwide discussion of health problems was aroused by the publication in 1909 of the *Report on National Vitality, Its Wastes and Conservation* by Irving Fisher, a Yale economist. He urged the federal and state governments, as well as municipalities, to undertake vigorous action to protect people from disease and thus conserve a national resource—and Fisher considered research a major weapon for this endeavor.

Concurrently a reform of medical education was in the making. Progressive medical schools and hospitals had established pathological, bacteriological, and clinical laboratories. The number of trained researchers was increasing. Relative progress had been made, but the process and scope of change were still slow and limited. Because of insufficient financial support, facilities in many places were still not adequate for many kinds of research, while many persons who were capable of fruitful contributions in medical research lacked the necessary professional stimulation and support. What was needed was action to establish medical research firmly as a significant social activity worthy of support in its own right and to create the means by which it could be stimulated, fostered, and developed.

Action of this kind might possibly have been taken by the federal government; actually, the response of private wealth provided the necessary stimulus and example. From 1900 to 1940 the influence of private agencies and funds was stronger than that of the federal government in medical research, owing largely to the impact of those extraordinary organizations established by John D. Rockefeller during the first two decades of the century—the Rockefeller Institute for Medical Research, the Rockefeller Foundation, and the General Education Board.

The Rockefeller Institute, founded in 1901, was officially opened in 1906. Its importance resides not so much in the scientific contributions of its staff, although they have been outstanding, or in the example it set for the establishment of independent organizations for medical research. More fundamental is the fact that those who created and guided it, especially William H. Welch, thought through the problems of medical research in the United States. They envisioned the need for large-scale support of medical education in relation to research and indicated the major instruments for the achievement of the desired goals. In addition to the establishment of research laboratories, these means included endowment support of research-centered schools of medicine and public health, grants-in-aid for specific research projects, and training for research through fellowships and other means of support. The various Rockefeller boards entered actively and effectively into such activities.

During the first decades of the 20th century other wealthy men and women followed the Rockefeller example. Foundations and endowments stimulated research in medicine and public health and created facilities in which it could be carried on. Universities were provided with greater means for research, and the growing scientific tradition was reinforced. This development was in large measure possible because vast surpluses of wealth had been accumulated and were available. Among the foundations that provided support for research in medicine and public health are Rockefeller, Carnegie, Duke, Milbank, Commonwealth, and Josiah Macy, Jr. Indeed, by 1930 some forty organizations were active in endowing research, education, and training.

By the end of the 1920's an era in philanthropic, private support of medical research was coming to an end. These private funds had played an indispensable role in creating and supporting the scientific environment for medicine and public health—for example, the General Education Board had given over $90 million for endowment of American medical schools. It became increasingly clear after 1929 that the decline in interest rates and difficulties in inducing other donors to match foundation funds made this a dubious and uncertain way to finance medical research. These factors were also reflected in the situation of other foundations, and the problem was noted in 1935 by

President Franklin D. Roosevelt's Science Advisory Board.

At a time when the conditions for productive medical research had been created and research was increasing in volume and effectiveness, the major agencies that had been instrumental in developing such a climate were unable, because of limited financial capacity, to meet the growing demands of research. Moreover, these demands were not just financial in nature. At the beginning of the century Simon Flexner had recognized that developments in organic and physical chemistry and in physics would increasingly affect biology and, therefore, medicine. By the 1930's it was becoming clear that significant advances in medical research would come from the exploration of the phenomena of living systems and that such work would require powerful and precise instrumentation. During and after World War II, the federal government emerged as the major source of support of medical research, especially through the research arm of the U.S. Public Health Service, the National Institutes of Health (NIH).

Although late in assuming a major role, medical research under federal auspices began in 1887 with the founding of the Hygienic Laboratory of the U.S. Marine Hospital Service, later the U.S. Public Health Service. The laboratory dealt with problems encountered by the service in carrying out its mission—foreign and interstate quarantine and medical inspection of immigrants, in particular. Accurate knowledge of the causes, sources, modes of spread, and means for diagnosis and prevention of major communicable diseases was thus required. As the work of the service grew and field investigations were undertaken that were not under the administrative control of the Hygienic Laboratory, the need for a central agency to coordinate the research work of the service was recognized, and the Division of Scientific Research was created in 1901, with the Hygienic Laboratory as a unit in the division.

Although the initial work of the Hygienic Laboratory was concerned with microbiology and communicable diseases, signs of a shift in emphasis appeared in 1910 when the Public Health Service turned its attention to cancer. During the 1920's there was an increasing emphasis on the study of chronic, noncommunicable diseases. By 1930 attention was being directed to the investigation of heart disease as one of the major causes of premature death and to studies of mental hygiene from the standpoint of biochemistry and endocrinology.

Another indication of the change in research policy that was slowly taking place was the act of May 26, 1930, which changed the name of the Hygienic Laboratory to the National Institute of Health and provided for its expansion. Although a program of basic research was being formulated, the means to carry it out barely existed. Funds were needed; an organizational pattern had to be developed within which the money could be applied; and legislative authority had to be secured. These aims were achieved during the 1930's and 1940's, largely through the efforts of Lewis Ryers Thompson, who in 1930 became assistant surgeon general in charge of the Division of Scientific Research; Thomas Parran, who became surgeon general of the Public Health Service in 1936; and Rolla E. Dyer, who became director of the National Institutes of Health in 1942. One of the first fruits of their efforts was Title VI of the Social Security Act of 1935, which authorized the expenditure of up to $2 million annually for research on disease. Thereafter the medical research funds available to NIH began to increase, although they did not reach the amount allocated by law until after World War II.

The interest in chronic diseases materialized first in the National Cancer Institute, created in 1937, which became a prototype of the other national institutes that followed. It had funds for intramural research; it was authorized to award grants-in-aid and fellowships to outside researchers and to establish a trainee program to help physicians learn to diagnose cancer. With it was established a National Advisory Cancer Council to aid in the selection of grantees and trainees.

With the beginning of World War II the federal government set up another agency, the Office of Scientific Research and Development (OSRD), with the Committee on Medical Research which arranged for research to be done on a contract basis. In 1945, after the OSRD went out of existence, forty-four of the contracts that still ran were turned over to the NIH. The following year the Research Grants Office was set up. A pattern originally established in the National Cancer Institute was then used to create a series of advisory groups, councils, and study sections. These advisory units continued their work into the 1970's and formed an important mechanism by which the federal government and the medical research community were tied together.

In the mid-1960's the agencies of the U.S. Department of Health, Education, and Welfare provided about 70 percent of the federal funds for the support of medical and health research. In 1963 the research programs of that department amounted to about $70 million; the National Institutes of Health, the principal health research agency of the federal government, provided more than three-fifths of the total federal support. In the 1970's a group of solidly established national institutes for medical research existed with impressive intramural programs as well as broad extramural programs for the furtherance and support of research. Medical scientists in universities were conducting medical research on a scale undreamed of in the early decades of the 20th century, owing in no small measure to the commitment of large public funds for the support of such investigations. Despite a slowdown in appropriations for medical research, there was in the mid-1970's no indication that the federal government would not continue as the major source of support of medical research in the United States.

Medical research has produced results. Elucidation of the mysteries of pellagra and other nutritional disorders; development of means for the control of poliomyelitis, measles, and other communicable diseases; elimination of retrolental fibroplasia—these illustrate what medical research in the United States has meant to its people and to people in other parts of the world.

[A. Hunter Dupree, *Science in the Federal Government. A History of Policies and Activities to 1900*; George Rosen, "Patterns of Health Research in the United States, 1900–1960," *Bulletin of the History of Medicine*, vol. 39 (1965); Richard H. Shryock, *American Medical Research, Past and Present*.]

GEORGE ROSEN

MEDICAL SECTS. As the American population expanded throughout the 19th century, the demand for health care increased. The number of traditionally educated physicians was inadequate, and there was widespread doubt about the efficacy of orthodox practices. Undergirding these concerns was a pervasive Jacksonian distrust of professional monopoly. Sectarian practitioners flourished in these conditions. The major groups were the botanical practitioners, the homeopaths, the hydropaths, and the osteopaths.

Samuel Thomson used sweat-producing, emetic, and purgative herbs as well as steam baths and enemas in treating all diseases. He wrote *A New Guide to Health; or, the Botanic Family Physician*, acquired a patent on his therapeutic package, and established Friendly Botanic Societies as a way to spread his medical gospel. Between 1827 and 1845 Thomson's followers established the reformed botanic, the physiomedical, and the eclectic groups. With more than 10,000 physiomedical and eclectic practitioners active in 1901, these sects remained significant in the early decades of the 20th century.

A German physician, Samuel Hahnemann, created a system of treatment based on the belief that drugs would cure if they caused the symptoms of the disease being treated and that the effectiveness of a drug would be significantly increased by dilution. By 1850 American homeopathic disciples had developed societies and schools as well as a large clientele. There were twenty-two homeopathic schools by 1900. The homeopathic sect declined extensively in the 20th century, and only a few practitioners were still active in the 1970's.

Water was employed in cure treatments evangelically prescribed by an Austrian layman, Vincent Priessnitz, between 1826 and 1851. Proclaimed as a panacea, water was used by a growing number of American practitioners beginning in the 1840's. Hydropathic colleges, societies, and journals were established. Water-cure establishments appeared throughout the country, and thousands of patients "took the cure." By the latter part of the 19th century hydropathy had expanded from a simple treatment to a complex regimen of personal hygiene.

Dr. Andrew Taylor Still, the founder of osteopathy, became disillusioned with orthodox remedies after watching three of his children die from meningitis in 1864. Still developed a system of medical practice based on the belief that diseases resulted from malalignment of bones, especially those in the spine. By 1910 there were twelve schools of osteopathy, and doctors of osteopathy were eventually licensed to practice in all states. The requirements for education and practice are similar to those of orthodox practice, and the sectarian characteristics of osteopathy have become less and less distinctive as the 20th century has progressed. Symbolic of this process was the conversion in 1962 of the California College of Osteopathy into the California College of Medicine.

These sectarian groups caused orthodox professionals to reexamine their practices, to raise their educational standards, and to develop professional organizations that could withstand the social and political exigencies of the day. With the growing uniformity of practices based on an experimentally validated science of pharmacological therapeutics, sectarian groups have become less acceptable to the public and to health professionals.

[Martin Kaufman, *Homeopathy in America*.]

CHESTER R. BURNS

MEDICAL SOCIETIES. Colonial practitioners made several attempts to organize medical societies in Boston, New York, New Haven, Philadelphia, and Charleston. In 1766, New Jersey was the first of the North American colonies to form a medical society that has endured.

In the first half of the 19th century numerous societies were established that did not survive. For example, the state legislature of Illinois incorporated short-lived medical societies on three different occasions between 1817 and 1825. In 1840 a state society was established in Illinois, but it stopped functioning in 1847. In 1850 an Illinois State Medical Society was founded that did survive, and enduring societies were established in thirty-four states prior to the Civil War.

Using the American Medical Association (AMA, 1847) as a model, voluntary medical societies became predominant during the middle third of the 19th century. These voluntary societies attempted to advance medical knowledge, elevate professional character, and protect the interests of their members. Scientific specialization led to a host of additional societies.

Although the Association of Medical Superintendents of American Institutions for the Insane was established in 1844, societies of clinical specialists became quantitatively significant only in the 1880's. A few examples are American Pediatric Society (1888), American Urological Association (1902), American College of Surgeons (1913), American College of Physicians (1915), Aerospace Medical Association (1929), and American Academy of General Practice (1947).

As the 20th century unfolded, physicians had opportunities to participate in city, county, state, regional, national, and international societies. An individual physician usually belonged to several societies. Membership in the AMA required membership in both a state and a county medical society. Beyond that, physicians specializing in allergic diseases, for example, could belong to two national societies, the American College of Allergists and the American Academy of Allergy, and also to the ultraspecialized Association of Allergists for Mycological Investigations; a voluntary health agency, the Allergy Foundation of America; and the International Allergy Association. A similar pattern of organizations existed for other diseases (for example, diabetes), for clinical specialties (for example, pediatrics), for medical sciences (for example, histochemistry), and for various conditions of life (for example, aging). New societies continued to be established, such as the American Association of Planned Parenthood Physicians (1963) and the Society of Eye Surgeons (1969).

By 1972 there were more than 2,500 medical societies in the United States.

[Ralph Bates, *Scientific Societies in the United States;* W. B. McDaniel, ''A Brief Sketch of the Rise of American Medical Societies,'' in Felix Marti-Ibañez, ed., *History of American Medicine*.]

CHESTER R. BURNS

MEDICARE. The national program of health insurance for the aged, commonly called Medicare, was enacted in 1965. It finances most of the cost of hospital and nursing-home care for persons over sixty-five years of age through the Social Security system. It also provides voluntary reduced-cost insurance covering doctors' bills. Enactment of the measure followed one of the longest and bitterest legislative struggles of the postwar period.

The controversy began in 1945 when President Harry S. Truman advanced a proposal for a system of health insurance for the entire population, to be financed through Social Security. The American Medical Association (AMA), spending the largest sums ever reported in a lobbying campaign, succeeded in branding that proposal ''socialized medicine,'' bottling it up in Congress and defeating a number of its backers in the congressional elections of 1950. Proponents then came forward with a scheme limited to older people, who have the heaviest per capita medical costs and are least well covered by private insurance.

The drive for passage of this measure began in earnest in 1957, when the American Federation of Labor–Congress of Industrial Organizations (AFL-CIO) made the bill its foremost legislative objective. The AMA renewed its campaign of opposition, but the American Nurses Association, joined later by the American Hospital Association, supported the plan, and a ground swell of popular support rapidly developed—one of the most powerful grass roots political movements of the time. Republican President Dwight D. Eisenhower joined Democratic party spokesmen in acknowledging that some kind of measure was needed, and the question became not whether a program should be instituted, but rather what kind of program. Differences over the form the program should take were sufficient to deadlock the measure in Congress until after the Democratic landslide of 1964. Then a bill could be passed embodying the basic AFL-CIO approach, endorsed by presidents John F. Kennedy and Lyndon B. Johnson, but the final measure incorporated major features sponsored by Republicans as well. President Johnson went to Independence, Mo., to sign the bill in the presence of Truman.

The Medicare program is in two parts. The first part of the program, which covers all Social Security beneficiaries and is financed as are other Social Security benefits through a payroll tax, provides payment for the costs of 90 days of hospital care, 100 days of nursing-home care, and 100 home health care visits, after an initial payment by the beneficiary, originally set at $40 but increased to $92 by mid-1975. The payroll tax was set at 0.7 percent initially (equally divided between employer and employee), scheduled to rise to 1.6 percent by 1987. A rapid rise in hospital costs, coupled with a rate of use of the program 20 percent higher than forecast, soon threatened the fund with bankruptcy, and in 1972 an act was passed raising the tax to 2.0 percent effective in 1973, with further increases scheduled to bring it to 2.9 percent in 1985. In the same act benefits were extended to the 1.7 million disabled persons under sixty-five years of age who were receiving Social Security payments.

The second part of the program offers insurance covering 80 percent of a patient's bills over $60 (originally $50) a year for doctors' fees, laboratory tests, and related expenses—such as ambulance service and durable medical equipment—originally at only $3 a month, although the premium had been raised to $6.70 a month by July 1974.

Benefits under the hospitalization program rose from $2.5 billion in the 1967 fiscal year to $6.5 billion in 1973, with 7 million beneficiaries. Payments under the second program rose from $664 million to $2.5 billion in the same period, there being 11 million beneficiaries in 1973.

JAMES L. SUNDQUIST

MEDICINE, MILITARY. Military medicine, as a specialty, has focused on the surgical management of mass casualties; on the prevention and treatment of infectious diseases, especially tropical diseases; and, in the 20th century, on the interactions of man and military machines. As part of a military hierachy, the organization of structured medical command and administrative systems has been important for interaction with the line and for function in combat.

Army Medicine. Medical support for an American army began on July 27, 1775, when the Continental Congress established a medical service for Gen. George Washington's army when it was besieging Boston. The organization followed the model of the British army. Several texts on surgery, on preventive medicine, and on pharmacy were written by military physicians during the revolutionary war and were the first American publications of their kind.

On Apr. 14, 1818, Congress reorganized the staff departments of the army and established the present medical department. Medical officers were granted military rank in 1847. A hospital corps, providing formal instruction for enlisted men as physicians' assistants, was established in 1887; the present civilian programs for paramedical physician extenders have their philosophical base in this system. The army's Nurse Corps was established in 1901, the Dental Corps in 1911, the Veterinary Corps in 1916, and the Sanitary Corps in 1917; the latter became the Medical Service Corps in 1947 when the Women's (since 1966, Army) Medical Specialist Corps enrolled dietitians and physical and occupational therapists. Corps functions had existed previously in the Medical Department, but organization into a corps not only formalized the position of the specialty in the military bureaucracy but also regularized the status of the individuals and provided for commissions, tenure, and pensions. Thus, because she was chief of her corps, it was possible for Col. Anna Mae Violet McCabe Hays, Army Nurse Corps, to become the first female general officer in American history in 1970. One consequence of formal organization, with command overview of health-care delivery, including the supporting infrastructure, was the development of a centrally managed health-care program outside the civilian fee-for-service system, which was later adapted to the Veterans Administration Hospital program.

The major military contributions of the surgical disciplines have been in mass casualty management, the evacuation of wounded, and in the treatment of battle wounds. Although the removal of the sick and wounded from the battlefield has always been a part of military operations, the development of an organized system did not come until 1862. Jonathan Letterman, the medical director of the Army of the Potomac, established a system of staged and echeloned medical care and of forward treatment followed by evacuation of patients by medical elements in the rear that is now the practice of all armies. The next major advance was the use of airplanes for evacuation of hospitalized patients in World War II and of helicopters as forward tactical air ambulances in the Korean War: having proved its worth in Vietnam, the helicopter was adopted by the civilian community for the evacuation of the injured from highway accidents. Army studies of wound ballistics, beginning in 1892, established the scientific rationale for wide debridement of wounds and led to reduction in gas gangrene and wound infection, as well as to the development of individual body armor. Systems for mass blood collection, distribution, and transfusion were developed by Charles Drew, Douglas B. Kendrick, and others in World War II and introduced the civilian medical community to the concepts of massive blood transfusions for shock and trauma. An army burn research and treatment center, founded in 1947, was the first in the United States, and the use of sulfamylon to prevent skin infection was a major contribution of the burn research program.

Communicable and infectious diseases have always been the major causes of morbidity among troops, and military medicine has made its greatest contributions in this area. In World War I mortality from disease was for the first time less than that from battle wounds, and the application of infectious disease research to military sanitation produced this milestone in the history of war.

From 1818 to 1860 the army's Medical Department was mostly concerned with patient care at the small army posts scattered over the southern and western frontiers. Morbidity and mortality data were reported in a uniform format, and the collected reports, which included some civilian data, were published beginning in 1840; they were the first national public-health statistics and the beginning of a national approach to public-health epidemiology. Because disease etiology and occurrence were thought to be related to climate, post surgeons also included meteorological data with their reports. The weather observations were separately published as the only nationwide data, and the National Weather Service remained a Medical Department function until 1870.

When bacteriology became a science in the 1860's, military physicians were among the first to explore this new field. Joseph J. Woodward and Edward Curtis in 1864 introduced aniline dyes in the United States for staining in microscopy and were the pioneers of photomicroscopy of tissues and bacteria. George M. Sternberg of the U.S. Army published the first American bacteriology textbook in 1892; later, as surgeon general, he was responsible for the establishment and direction of the two "Walter Reed boards" for the study of typhoid and yellow fever, in 1898 and 1900, respectively.

The history of Walter Reed's work on the transmission of yellow fever in 1900 is well known: he and his colleagues, using volunteer test subjects, took only a few months to disprove fomite infection, document mosquito transmission, and define the organism as

nonbacterial. Less well known is the story of the "Typhoid Board" of 1898, which studied recruit camp epidemics, documented that contact was more important than water in transmission, and suggested that a carrier state existed.

The founding by Sternberg, in 1893, of the Army Medical School—the first school of public health and preventive medicine in the United States—was the beginning of formal postgraduate education in the basic sciences for army medical officers. Renamed the Walter Reed Army Institute of Research, the organization became the largest tropical medicine research organization in the United States.

Tropical parasitic diseases occupied the attention of military physicians. Bailey K. Ashford, working in Puerto Rico after the Spanish-American War, isolated the American hookworm, *Necator americanus,* as the cause of anemia in Puerto Rican farm laborers. His program for detection, therapy, and prevention was the model used later by the Rockefeller Foundation to attack hookworm in the American South. Charles F. Craig wrote an early text on medical parasitology in 1911, developed serological tests for amebiasis, and described new intestinal parasites. Work at the Army Medical Research Board in the Philippines from 1900 to 1934 proved that dengue was a virus and that mosquitoes were the vector; documented the usefulness of emetine in treating amebiasis; showed that *Aedes* mosquitoes were major vectors for equine encephalitis; and made critical contributions in new rabies and rinderpest vaccines, in the treatment of beriberi, and in zoonotic diseases.

Frederick F. Russell developed an American typhoid vaccine in 1909 at the Army Medical School. In 1911 the army was immunized—the first time for an entire army—and typhoid disappeared as a major cause of morbidity and mortality. Carl Rogers Darnall's introduction of the use of anhydrous chlorine to purify drinking water in 1910 is the basis for present systems of municipal water purification. William C. Gorgas used the new findings on mosquito transmission to control yellow fever and malaria and permit the building of the Panama Canal. In 1933 the Army Medical Research Board in Panama did the first American studies on the efficacy of atabrine as a prophylactic drug against malaria; this standard drug of World War II was replaced by the chloroquine-primaquine combination tablet following definitive studies in Korea in 1960. In 1963 the army's Medical Department began the support of the only large international research program for the development of new antimalarial drugs.

During World War II the United States of America Typhus Commission, a joint military-civilian organization, did broad-scale work on the typhus fevers and was responsible for the application of DDT to delousing of populations and for field trials of vaccines. Similarly, military-civilian investigators of the Army Epidemiological Board investigated viral hepatitis, separated infectious and serum hepatitis as entities, and demonstrated the usefulness of gamma globulin for passive protection. After World War II the concept of joint military-civilian teams persisted and led to such contributions as the use of chloramphenicol to treat typhoid fever and scrub typhus and the use of broad-spectrum antibiotics in the treatment of plague.

During and after the Korean War, studies of communicable and infectious diseases by Medical Department members led to the description of the ecology of the transmission cycle of Japanese B. encephalitis in 1955; the isolation of the Asian influenza virus in 1957; the isolation of the German measles virus in 1962, for later development by the National Institutes of Health of the vaccine; and the development of effective vaccines against adenovirus infection in recruit camps in 1967. Vaccines against meningococcal meningitis were developed while a vaccine against Venezuelan equine encephalitis was used by Central American countries during epizootics in 1969 and 1970.

Other discoveries and contributions made by Medical Department members have been important to general medicine. In 1833, William Beaumont published his classic work on the physiology of digestion from his ten-year study of the gastric fistula of Alexis Saint Martin. In that decade the surgeon general established a collection of medical books, which grew over time—and especially after the Civil War—to become the Army Medical Library; in 1956 it was transferred to the Department of Health, Education, and Welfare to become the National Library of Medicine.

Involvement in the main stream of American medicine is typified by the career of John Shaw Billings. In 1870 his investigation and recommendations changed the Marine Hospital System to its present U.S. Public Health Service structure. He designed Johns Hopkins Hospital and was responsible for the selection of William H. Welch and William Osler as faculty for its medical school. As librarian of the Army Medical Library, he developed the *Index-Catalogue* and, with Dr. Robert Fletcher, developed and published the *Index-Medicus*. He recommended the use of electrically sorted punch cards for medical record keeping and saw to the testing of such a system by Herman Hollerith at the surgeon general's office. (Hollerith's company later became part of International Business Machines.) In retirement, Billings organized and built the New York Public Library and became its first director.

The Civil War period saw the founding of the Army Medical Museum, renamed the Armed Forces Institute of Pathology in 1949, from which, in the next thirty years, came the *Medical and Surgical History of the War of the Rebellion,* the first detailed account of the medical and surgical findings of the impact of war on an army and the beginning of formal research in pathology in the United States.

Navy Medicine. Congressional appropriations on Nov. 2, 1775, provided for surgeons on naval ships, but it was not until 1842 that the Bureau of Medicine and Surgery was established. The surgeon general was authorized flag rank in 1898. The navy's Nurse Corps was established in 1903, and its Dental Corps in 1912.

A naval laboratory for the production of pure drugs was founded in 1853 by Edward R. Squibb, who later founded the pharmaceutical firm. The Naval Medical School was established in 1902. Annual physical examinations for officers were introduced in 1903, laying the foundation for programs of multiphasic health screening.

Edward R. Stitt, later surgeon general, wrote the first modern American text on tropical medicine in 1914. In 1958, navy physicians developed methods for fluid replacement in the treatment of cholera, which became standard procedures, especially during epidemics. Toxicological research on trace-element effects in the closed environment of submarines produced some of the earliest data now useful for civilian pollution studies.

Aviation Medicine. Aviation medicine began in Europe as an army medical problem. In 1917, with the entry of the United States into World War I, an army research laboratory and the School for Flight Surgeons were established. Louis H. Bauer, the first commandant of the school, wrote the first American textbook of aviation medicine in 1926 and became the first director of civil aviation medicine for the Department of Commerce. In 1936, Harry E. Armstrong, later surgeon general of the U.S. Air Force, built the first centrifuge to study the effects of acceleration on man.

A separate Air Force Medical Department was established in 1949. In 1950 the School of Aerospace Medicine began biological research on the effects of space flight, and the great majority of the medical work in the National Aeronautics and Space Administration was done by air force officers. John Paul Stapp's studies in 1954 on abrupt deceleration founded the present field in crash injury. Air force studies of anthropometry, human factors, designs of instruments, displays, and basic work in vibration effects and noise-level tolerance have had widespread application to design.

[P. M. Ashburn, *A History of the Medical Department of the United States Army;* S. Bayne-Jones, *The Evolution of Preventive Medicine in the United States Army, 1607–1939;* R. C. Engelman and R. J. T. Joy, *Two Hundred Years of Military Medicine;* F. H. Garrison, *Notes on the History of Military Medicine;* E. E. Hume, *Victories of Army Medicine;* G. Peyton, *Fifty Years of Aerospace Medicine;* L. H. Roddis, *A Short History of Nautical Medicine.*]

ROBERT J. T. JOY

MEDICINE, OCCUPATIONAL. Daily occupations can actually be inimical to human health. Adverse working conditions can cause acute and chronic illnesses and disabling accidents. Low wages, long hours of work, emotional stress, and inferior status or social role may also adversely affect the general health of the worker. Occupational medicine attempts first to maintain the worker's health and to prevent disease. Emphasis is then placed on prompt treatment and rehabilitation through focus on recovery of function if disease or accident occurs. Health counseling and health maintenance have evolved as important facets of contemporary occupational medicine, along with psychological testing and industrial psychiatry. As safety engineering has emerged as a key aspect of accident prevention, so environmental engineering has emerged as a concern of occupational medicine.

In ancient societies, as well as in the New World, slaves had the worst working conditions and therefore suffered most. Mining has been dangerous to health throughout history and is still so. It was only in the 18th century in America, however, that occupational diseases began to be recognized as such. Benjamin Franklin noted that typesetters suffered from abdominal cramps and wrist or foot paralysis from the lead used in their work.

Access to health services was the first principal theme in occupational medicine. After the first American mutual benefit society, or lodge, was formed by workers in 1793, such lodges strove to make a lodge doctor available to their members. In 1798 the Marine Hospital Service was created by the U.S. Congress to provide care for American seamen, since their disabilities and illnesses had exceeded the abilities of

local communities to handle them under poor-law arrangements. In the early 19th century, labor unions began to concern themselves with safe working conditions, among the earliest being the Pennsylvania Society of Journeymen Cabinetmakers, founded in 1806. Led by Massachusetts in 1836, the states began to enact laws limiting child labor and women's hours of work.

Not until 1837 was a systematic examination of occupations and related health problems published in the United States. In that year, a New York physician, Benjamin W. McCready, modeling his study after the work of the Englishman C. Turner Thackrah, wrote a prize essay for the Medical Society of the State of New York, entitled "On the Influence of Trades, Professions and Occupations in the United States in the Production of Disease." McCready dealt with the health problems of agricultural workers, laborers, seamen, factory operatives, artisans, professionals, and literary men, and he also discussed housing and "the general conditions of life" stemming from poverty and unhealthy cities. Long hours of work, slum living, and the effects of insufficient fresh food and sunshine were commented on. McCready, far ahead of his time, also commented on anxiety as a health factor, remarking that in America "all classes are either striving after wealth or endeavoring to keep up its appearances."

As the 19th century unfolded, some diseases were diagnosed as occupational. The expression "mad as a hatter" was traced to mercury poisoning in hattery workers by J. Addison Freeman of Orange, N.J., in 1860. The lung problems among anthracite coal miners, particularly the illness now known as black lung, were vividly described in 1869 in the *Transactions of the Medical Society of Pennsylvania.* Lead colic among lead miners was described in 1884 in the *Saint Louis Medical Journal.* Safety conditions were considered a national scandal. Railroads, factories, mines, the construction industry, and lumbering all vied for "worst place" in work-connected accidents. Safety inspection and compensation for the results of accidents became leading subjects of public discussion.

The first major industrial medical-care prepayment plan to endure was organized by the Southern Pacific Railroad in 1868. The first company-financed medical department with a full-time staff providing complete medical care for employees and families was established by the Homestake Mining Company of Lead, S.Dak., in 1887. Although some U.S. coal miners had been prepaying their medical and accident care at $1 per month at least since 1869, the check-off for hospitalization, doctor care, and drugs became general throughout U.S. coalfields by the end of the century. It was a compulsory deduction required by the coal companies until the 1920's, after which it became voluntary in most places. The coal companies' doctors practiced both industrial medicine and family medical care. This system was a cause of much protest and dissatisfaction.

In the cities, mutual benefit societies multiplied, 38,000 societies having been formed by 1867, although many were financially unstable and failed. A high proportion had a lodge doctor, and some built and administered hospitals.

In the 20th century much of the impetus in occupational medicine came from Dr. Alice Hamilton, who wrote on lead poisoning in 1911; she followed it with work on coal-tar dye toxicities and many other hazards. Later in the century, Dr. Harriet Hardy, a protégée of Hamilton, detected the toxicity of beryllium as the cause of "Salem sarcoid" in workers in fluorescent bulb factories and in beryllium-smelter workers. Hamilton's contemporary John Andrews tackled the use of phosphorus in making matches in the United States, recognized as the cause of "phossy jaw." Andrews founded the American Association for Labor Legislation in 1906, and in 1910 the first U.S. Conference on Industrial Diseases was held under its auspices. In 1911, an excessive prevalence of tuberculosis among garment workers in New York City was clearly demonstrated by a Public Health Service physician, J. W. Schereschewsky.

The first American academic program in industrial medicine was established at Harvard University in 1917. In the following year, the *Journal of Industrial Hygiene* made its appearance; the *Journal of Industrial Medicine* appeared in 1932.

In 1914 the U.S. Public Health Service created a Division of Industrial Hygiene and Sanitation. This grew into the National Institute of Occupational Safety and Health. The formation of state industrial hygiene units was stimulated by the 1935 Social Security Act. In 1937 the American Medical Association created the Council on Industrial Health and joined in work with the National Safety Council.

The first state to enact a workmen's compensation law was New York, in 1910, but not until 1955 had all the states enacted such legislation. By 1960 dissatisfaction with state workmen's compensation and safety rules led to passage of the federal Coal Mine Safety Act. In 1970 Congress authorized the use of the Social Security system to compensate for industrial diseases by providing work-connected disability payments and required the inclusion of occupational health and safety inspection and occupational health services in the Industrial Health and Safety Act of 1970.

Collective bargaining contracts as sources for medical-care payment grew rapidly during World War II and afterward. In 1947 the United Mine Workers of America began services to miners paralyzed from rock falls and to silicotics. It then developed a comprehensive medical care program. Although most industrial workers had insurance coverage for hospitalization costs through their places of work in the 1970's, the coverage was inadequate, and agitation for a national health security or insurance program was widespread.

Excessive heat, cold, noise, and vibration are among the basic hazards. Farm labor is often exposed to pesticide chemicals, including organic phosphates, and to farm machinery accidents. Each technical advance has tended to produce its own occupational and environmental problems. For example, radioactivity burst upon the scene as a killer of fluorescent wristwatch workers who painted luminous dials. After World War II uranium mining and fallout from atomic bomb testing constituted a new health hazard. Radiation hazards remain a problem. Carbon tetrachloride, which is used in cleaning establishments, came rapidly to the fore as a toxic agent, causing liver poisoning. Coal tar derivatives emerged as major contributors to cancer of the bladder, of the skin, and of the blood-forming organs. Hot metal fumes, such as arise in the smelting of mercury cadmium, lead, nickel, and beryllium, have come to be recognized as major causes of occupational disease.

Dusty trades, such as pottery-making, glassworking, quarrying, sandblasting, tunneling, and mining cause the lung diseases silicosis and black lung. Textile industries tend to cause brown lung, or byssinosis. Exposure to asbestos fiber has become a major problem, in some cases causing lung cancer; 3.5 million U.S. workers were exposed as of 1970. Fiberglass is suspect. Organic solvents are common producers of skin disorders, called dermatoses. Polyvinyl chloride used in plastics is a cause of liver cancer.

Environmental hazards in the community and home must be considered as additive to those in occupations. Many are similar to those listed above.

[Leslie A. Falk, "Coal Miners' Prepaid Medical Care in the United States," *Medical Care,* vol. 4 (1966); Alice Hamilton, *Exploring the Dangerous Trades;* Alice Hamilton and Harriet Hardy, *Industrial Toxicology;* George Rosen, *A History of Public Health,* and *The History of Miners' Disease;* Ludwig Teleky, *History of Factory and Mine Hygiene.*]

LESLIE A. FALK

MEDICINE AND SURGERY. The early settlers of the American colonies faced the hardships of the frontier and most of the same infectious illnesses they had encountered in their European homelands. Malnutrition and a "starving time" were also common. Few physicians were among the early migrants, and so medical care fell to the traditional sources of comfort and wisdom—grandmothers, clergymen, and other sympathetic souls. When the United States came into being, there were only about 400 physicians with an earned M.D. degree in the nation. The many others who called themselves doctors were trained locally by apprenticeship, but in most cases they were no less successful in coping with the prevalent malaria or the outbreaks of smallpox, diphtheria, and yellow fever than were their European-trained medical colleagues.

Also lacking in the English colonies was the professional focus for medicine. Books were in short supply, and medical schools nonexistent. An occasional ordinance regulating practitioners was passed, but no regular licensing boards, medical societies, or hospitals existed until the late 18th century.

Life expectancy around 1750 was about thirty to thirty-five years, although precise figures are difficult to obtain. Sickness rates were high and malnutrition still rife. Fevers (including malaria), tuberculosis, diphtheria, and measles all continued to abound. Smallpox was a particular scourge. Unlike their European counterparts who were exposed to the disease in infancy, North American children often escaped exposure and thus failed to build up immunity; in times of epidemics of smallpox, American adults often succumbed because they had not met the disease earlier in life.

Medical developments in the colonies during the 18th century were sparse. In 1721, Cotton Mather, a clergyman, and Zabdiel Boylston, a physician, both of Boston, were among the first to try the new procedure of variolation to immunize against smallpox, and they also added significantly to the store of proven medical knowledge. Using simple statistics, they clearly demonstrated that of those who had been immunized, only about 2 percent were likely to succumb to the epidemic form of the disease, whereas in the rest of the population mortality was about 15 percent.

From its opening in 1752, the Pennsylvania Hospital in Philadelphia played an important role in medical teaching and in care of patients, and in 1765 the first American medical school opened its doors in the same city. By the end of the century three additional schools had been founded. These developments were strikingly meager in comparison to those in the more settled countries of Europe. Even as late as 1800 only a bare beginning had been made in developing a profession of medicine in the United States with requisite educational institutions, such as schools and hospitals, and collegial bodies, such as medical societies and licensing authorities.

As Americans moved westward, disease continued to burden the early settlers, even after they established themselves permanently. Malaria, scurvy, dysentery, and the respiratory diseases of winter were prevalent in New England as well as in the South and the West. Many Americans of the 18th and 19th centuries, especially those living on the frontier, had little understanding of medical education and cared less about their doctors' training. As the regular doctors began to dose more and more vigorously and yet became no more effective in curing, their patients began to look toward others professing medical knowledge, especially the homeopaths and the botanical practitioners. The high disease rate in all parts of the country continued to create a great demand for the doctor's craft. Tuberculosis was, throughout most of the 19th century, the leading cause of death. All physicians were powerless in its wake, although sanatoriums built in many healthful mountain retreats were of some help. Against the repeated outbreaks of cholera and yellow fever, physicians were no more effective, but these epidemics did spur local and national public health legislation that led to sanitary improvements.

In view of the great number of widespread settlements and the dearth of physicians, especially in the rural areas, it is not surprising that home medical advisers sold well. Such books as *Every Man His Own Doctor; or The Poor Planter's Physician,* in the 18th century, and John C. Gunn's *Domestic Medicine,* in the 19th century, were found in many homes. Some of these were written by laymen, such as John Wesley's *Primitive Physic,* very popular after its initial appearance in England in 1747. Others were written by physicians—notably Gunn—and like similar volumes written in the 20th century, contained enough information about regulating the family diet, tending to fevers, and treating the injured to enable most families to manage quite well.

By 1837 there were about 2,500 medical students enrolled in thirty-seven schools. Many more schools were founded as the century progressed, reaching a total of 457 by 1910. Although more and more schools existed, teaching did not improve much. Medical instruction could, after all, be only as good as the state of medical knowledge would allow. Not until the advent of the research-oriented, laboratory-based medical schools of the late 19th century did they add appreciably to the store of medical knowledge and to the understanding of disease processes.

Most American medical schools prior to 1900 were of the proprietary type, meaning that fees paid by students went into the pockets of their professors. Failing a student resulted in an economic loss for the faculty, as did stringent entrance requirements. By the 1880's there were some three-year schools teaching a graded course, but most still awarded the M.D. degree after two years. In most cases the "year" included only four months of didactic lectures, the second year being a repeat of the first. Limitation of books, equipment, and—in some schools—professors led to the need for repeating everything to assure each student's exposure to the necessary fundamentals of medicine. Many students attended lectures in two schools so as to avoid complete duplication. This nongraded curriculum was less expensive for both teachers and students.

As late as 1892 philanthropic aid to medical schools amounted to only about $600,000, whereas schools of theology received over $17 million. Medical students were generally ill prepared and often rowdy and boisterous. Better students usually went into schools of theology or law; the course work relied mainly on lectures, there being only a few demonstrations. Anatomical dissection was often slighted; rarely did students help with surgical operations, and rarely did they see, much less assist in, the delivery of a baby until they were faced with the realities of practice. Yet for all this the results often seemed better than the system.

Even though Jacksonian notions of democracy had led to the suspension of license requirements in many states in the 1830's, a man was expected to fulfill several requirements before he could call himself a doctor. He was to have attended two courses of lectures at a medical school; he was to have studied medicine for at least three years (as an apprentice); he must have reached the age of twenty-one; and, finally, he was expected to possess "proper morals." Often the apprenticeship was the most important part of these requirements, since the medical school term lasted only sixteen weeks and since the second course might be a mere repetition of the first. With the advent of the American Medical Association (AMA) in 1847, there was increasing talk of reform in medical education, but the apprenticeship was still an important means by which a young man learned about disease and how to treat it. Apprenticeship continued to be a major means of medical education until the latter years of the 19th century. It was an efficient method of practical instruction. Not until medical science developed sufficiently to require the student to learn the contents of a theoretical body of knowledge did the medical school almost completely replace the preceptorship. The preceptor usually took the apprentice into his practice as a junior assistant. The student, in return for the privilege of observing his teacher and reading what books the older man might possess, was expected to help mix potions and pills, bleed patients, clean the office, and do other general chores; in addition he paid a fee to the preceptor. Often the apprentice was taken into the family home of his teacher. The chief virtue of the preceptorial system was that it gave the student a practical clinical experience and prevented him from becoming a mere theorist. The most apparent weakness of the system was that everything depended on the training and conscientiousness of the preceptor. If he had few books or little interest in passing on what meager knowledge he himself had acquired, the preceptor did not aid much in the development of the fledgling physician.

Several factors were basic to the problems and concerns facing medical men and the public in the mid-19th century. The gravest issue was the limited effectiveness of the physician to cure patients. There were purges and sedatives, sudorifics and anodynes, but physicians had to rely most heavily upon nature for cures. In the 1840's more physicians began to appreciate this fact, and their understanding culminated in a call for a "rational medicine" in the 1850's. Because Americans were activists, they demanded some form of "dosing," even though effective therapy did not always exist. This was still a problem in the late 20th century. The American physician Worthington Hooker typified the thought of the 1850's when he wrote, "Perhaps the disposition to demand of the physician an active medication in all cases exists to a greater degree in this than other countries. We are preeminently an energetic and enterprising people, and therefore the bold 'heroic' practitioner is apt to meet with favor from the public." (From "Nature of Evidence in Practical Medicine," *New Englander*, vol. II.)

A major problem that the regular medical profession had to face was the increasing popularity of the irregulars, and so the AMA, immediately after its founding, concerned itself with sectarianism. The medical journals repeatedly strove to disprove the claims and charges made by homeopaths, botanics, and others. But this was no easy task. The public was not readily convinced that the practice of calomel-prescribing physicians was better than that of homeopaths who prescribed in minute doses; and, of course, the regulars often achieved no better results. Much of the public realized this full well. It was not merely the uneducated who consulted the sectarians, as was so often the case in the 20th century. George T. Strong, a well-educated New York lawyer and diarist, wrote that he would renounce allopathy and become a zealous convert to homeopathy if the latter were to give relief to his headaches: "Certainly if there be any substitute for the old system, that dispenses with emetics and cathartics and blistering and bleeding and all the horrors anticipation of which makes 'the doctor's' entry give me such a sinking of spirit, it's worth trying."

The regular physicians frequently argued the question of nature versus art. Following the 1835 essay on "Self-Limited Diseases" by Jacob Bigelow, a degree of skepticism regarding therapeutics was engendered. Nature's healing powers had been recognized since antiquity, but in the heyday of heroic medicine as favored by Benjamin Rush during the 1810's and 1820's, nature had been forced to take a back seat to vigorous dosing with drugs and bleeding with the lancet and by leeches. To have been a patient with a febrile disease before the late 19th century must have been an exceedingly unpleasant experience. To the patient already weakened by fever, further insult was brought by blood loss, followed by calomel or castor oil to induce copious diarrhea. The theory was that the disease was caused by a maldistribution of the basic humors of the body—blood, phlegm, yellow bile, and black bile. Purging and bleeding, or perhaps counterirritation by means of blisters, would serve to redistribute the humors to their proper place and normal balance.

Moreover, the practice of medicine in the 19th century was generally not the lucrative business it has become. Where local medical societies existed, they usually published a fee bill stating the standard charges for house calls, bleeding, and other medical services, but payment often went uncollected. The situation was aggravated by the fact that there was an excess of physicians in many urban locales. Many doctors turned to nonmedical activities—such as farming, running drug stores, and other business ventures—simply because of economic necessity.

It would be misleading to assume that the work of the profession was entirely futile. In the first place, as has continued to be the case, many of the physician's therapeutic abilities rested not merely on the use of drugs but also on his skill and art. Second, there were some effective drugs—such agents as cinchona, opium, and digitalis. But American medical advances appeared slowly in the 19th century. Medicine, as was true of American culture in general, still looked to Europe for its lead. By the 1830's the profession had established enough permanent institutions to be able to withstand the continuing encroachment by the sectarians. A number of important discoveries stemming from the work of Americans also began to appear. The physiological studies of digestion carried out by William Beaumont, using the gastric fistula of Alexis Saint Martin, a French-Canadian trapper who had been wounded by a musket shot, captured European interest as well as praise. Beaumont published his findings as a monograph in 1833. Four years later William W. Gerhard of Philadelphia clearly differentiated typhus from typhoid; these two distinct diseases, with different epidemiological characteristics, had been lumped together as one. In 1846, after several false starts and some unreported success, ether anesthesia was announced to the world with immediate acclaim. "Anesthetics constitute our chief claim in the eyes of the civilized world," wrote Oliver Wendell Holmes, Sr., who had witnessed its successful use on Oct. 16, 1846, during a surgical operation at the Massachusetts General Hospital. The surgical work of J. Marion Sims, who devised an effective repair for vesicovaginal fistula in 1849, using several very patient slave women with this troublesome disorder; the abdominal operations for gall bladder disease and for appendicitis; and the work in cardiac surgery in the 20th century, are but a few examples of American surgical innovations.

American medical education was of decidedly uneven quality, and often poor, throughout the 19th century, but many young American physicians spent from a few months to several years studying medicine and doing research in the leading medical centers of Europe, returning with substantial competence. Late in the colonial period they went to Leiden and to Edinburgh. In the Jacksonian period Paris was the favorite, and in the decades after the Civil War the German clinics and laboratories were especially popular.

From the Paris hospitals, these Americans returned

with a zeal for clinical observation and correlation of premortem with postmortem findings. An example of the fruitfulness of this approach may be seen in Gerhard's work on typhus. Others returned with knowledge and enthusiasm for using new diagnostic instruments, such as the stethoscope and the ophthalmoscope as well as the microscope.

Toward the end of the 19th century the laboratories of Germany, as well as that country's elaborate postgraduate clinical training systems, became the basis for the "new medicine," which combined the laboratory and the clinic. Among the first medical schools to adopt the German pattern were those of Harvard and Michigan universities, and especially the Johns Hopkins Medical School after its opening in 1893; they exposed their students to four years of rigorous study. William S. Halsted and William Osler, professors of surgery and of medicine respectively at Johns Hopkins, introduced the residency system into postdoctoral training, taken from the German model. They also took the medical student out of the lecture room and put him in the laboratory, in the clinic, and on the hospital wards. Abraham Flexner's well-known report about American medical schools in 1910 pointed to Johns Hopkins and a few other schools as exemplary. Already during the previous decade proprietary schools had begun closing, and stimulated by Flexner's work, this trend continued. With the advent of an increasingly scientific basis for medicine, the proprietary schools simply could not keep up because medical education became an increasingly expensive proposition.

American scientific medicine came into its own in the 1890's with such work as that of William H. Welch and his co-workers at Johns Hopkins, where numerous young men received excellent training in basic research methods. Although Welch himself discovered the gas-gangrene bacillus, it was of minor significance: the climate for research he created was of much greater importance. One group of his students, headed by Walter Reed and Jesse W. Lazear, clearly demonstrated the mosquito spread of yellow fever. This was a monumental piece of work carried out in Cuba and reported in 1900. Its impact on public health was immediate and widespread. Of equal scientific importance was the earlier work of Theobald Smith, who about 1890 determined the causative parasite of Texas cattle fever and clearly showed that it was spread by ticks, thus establishing the model for a vector-borne disease.

The growing importance of U.S. medicine and surgery in the 20th century may be demonstrated by a variety of yardsticks. Increasingly, discoveries were made in the leading centers of research. Some of those centers were in the medical schools; others were in privately endowed institutes, such as Rockefeller, Sloan-Kettering, and McCormick. The numbers of Nobel prizes awarded to Americans also began to increase as more and more of the influential medical literature in the form of monographs, texts, and journals stemmed from the western side of the Atlantic. Accompanying this rise in American medical literature in the mid-20th century was the reversal of the flow of students. Europeans, as well as students from other continents, began to make the medical pilgrimage to the United States.

As one attempts to account for the American rise to the top of the scientific ladder of medicine, neither men alone nor the creation of educational and research institutions will furnish a satisfactory explanation. Again and again one must return to economic reasons. A high standard of living available to a nation with a highly industrialized economy allows money to be spent on basic and applied research, and the result is greater scientific and technological advance.

Closely related to the striking scientific developments in medicine and surgery during the 20th century have been the increasing specialization of practitioners and the pronounced increase in hospitals and their use. An 1873 survey showed that there were only 149 hospitals for the care of the sick in the entire country, of which only six had been established prior to 1800; by 1973 there were more than 7,000 hospitals with 1.65 million beds. In the 19th century, only the poorer classes generally used hospitals. The upper classes not only delivered their babies at home, as was generally custom but also nursed their sick in the home and submitted to surgery on the kitchen table. Postoperative infection rates were actually lower under these circumstances than in the large, urban hospitals. Not until the acceptance of Lister's principles of antisepsis in the 1870's, which Americans were quite slow to adopt, and the advent of heat sterilization of operating-room equipment in the 1890's did surgery of the cavities of the body become feasible and safe. It is primarily the rapid strides in surgery that account for the changing locus of medical practice from the home to the hospital in the 20th century.

Along with changing patterns of medical care have gone changing patterns of disease and a slowly rising life expectancy. In 1900 the commonest causes of death were infections, such as tuberculosis, influenza, and dysenteries. By midcentury heart disease, cancer, stroke, and accidents accounted for the majority of mortality. The age distribution of the population had changed as well, as the elderly and the very young came to constitute larger percentages. This demographic pattern had implications for medical care because it is precisely these two age groups that require the most physician visits and hospital beds.

The overall drop in mortality rates from 17.2 per 1,000 in 1900 to about 9.4 per 1,000 in 1972 is a reflection of both medical and nonmedical factors. Specific preventive measures for some infectious diseases (notably smallpox, tetanus, and diphtheria), antibiotic therapy for many infectious illnesses, hormone therapy, and surgical advances account for some of the change. Improved housing and nutrition and a higher level of education have also been significant. Improved prenatal and postnatal care has been extremely important in helping to lower infant mortality, probably the most significant factor in increasing life expectancy from about fifty years in 1900 to seventy years in the 1970's. Diarrheas, malnutrition, and respiratory disorders no longer threaten young children as they once did. By the mid-20th century most families could expect all their children to grow to maturity—which was not the case during the 19th century when between 25 and 50 percent of children died before reaching the age of five.

In the latter part of the 20th century, as advances in scientific medicine continued apace, a paradox continued to puzzle the medical profession, the public, and health planners. The more effective medical services have become, the greater has been the demand for them; at the same time, they have become more expensive and so more difficult of access for many. Two conflicting concepts of medical care have always existed in American medicine—as a public service and as private enterprise.

[G. H. Brieger, *Medical America in the Nineteenth Century;* Joseph Kett, *The Formation of the American Medical Profession;* W. F. Norwood, *Medical Education in the United States Before the Civil War;* W. Rothstein, *American Physicians in the Nineteenth Century;* R. H. Shryock, *American Medical Research: Past and Present,* and *Medicine and Society in America, 1660–1860.*]

GERT H. BRIEGER

MEDICINE CREEK COUNCIL was conducted in October 1867 by the commissioner of Indian affairs of the Department of the Interior with the Kiowa, Comanche, and Apache tribes and some parts of the Arapaho and Cheyenne tribes, on Medicine Creek, in present-day South Dakota, eight miles south of the Arkansas River. The Comanche and Kiowa agreed to relinquish their claims to the lands embraced in the Texas Panhandle, and they, with all the other Indians participating, accepted removal to new reservations set aside for them. Although the negotiations did not bring final peace on the southwestern frontier, they went far toward doing so, and after 1875 Indian disturbances there practically ceased.

JOSEPH MILLS HANSON

"MEDICINE MAN." *See* **Indian Medicine.**

MEDICINE SHOW. About 1830 Gideon Lincecum, a practicing physician and Indian trader of Mississippi who was later to earn a name as a botanist and entomologist, went to live alone in the wilderness with a Choctaw medicine man in order to absorb his herbal knowledge—some of it secret. Lincecum represented a public that believed in some herbs as strongly as a preceding age had believed in the fabled Fountain of Youth. The widespread dissemination of patent medicines was at hand. The stage was prepared for the prevalence of the medicine show, although it had existed in a small way in the 18th century.

The showman had a cure-all medicine to sell. In order to sell this bottled magic, he gave his show free, on town squares, on street corners, wherever he could find a drawing place for crowds. Often he claimed to be Indian or part Indian, or he might be accompanied by a human being of complexion and garb professedly Indian. He employed blackface comedians. Songs and repartee jokes were his stock in trade, and he was an artist at "kidding" the crowd while he mixed in praise of the supernal drug.

[R. Wright, *Hawkers and Walkers in Early America.*]

J. FRANK DOBIE

MEDITERRANEAN FUND was projected in 1786 by Thomas Jefferson while minister to France. It provided for international cooperation against the Barbary pirates. Jefferson proposed that, "As miscarriages often proceed from the want of harmony among officers of different nations the parties shall now consider & decide whether it will not be better to contribute their quotas in money to be employed in fitting out, and keeping on duty, a single fleet of the force agreed on." The project was too visionary to be realized.

LOUIS MARTIN SEARS

MEEKER MASSACRE. Because of his arbitrary ways, agent N. S. Meeker of the Ute agency on White River, Colo., created so much ill will among the Indians that on Sept. 10, 1879, one of them assaulted him. He requested military aid, and Maj. T. T. Thornburgh marched with 200 men on Sept. 24 from Fort Fred Steele, Wyo., bearing orders also to arrest Indians suspected of setting forest fires in the district. The Ute ambushed this detachment near Milk River on Sept. 29, killing Thornburgh and nine men and wounding forty-three others. The survivors were besieged for six days in hastily prepared barricades. Meanwhile, on Sept. 29, other Ute attacked the agency, thirty miles south of Milk River, killing Meeker and seven employees, and carrying away three women. Gen. Wesley Merritt relieved Thornburgh's men on Oct. 5, the Ute disappearing. Through the efforts of Ouray, Ute chief, who was absent deer hunting during the fights, further hostilities were averted and the three captured women released.

[J. P. Dunn, *Massacres of the Mountains;* Philip H. Sheridan, *Record of Engagements With Hostile Indians.*]

PAUL I. WELLMAN

MEETINGHOUSE became best known in connection with the New England Puritan (Congregationalist) churches. Reserving "church" to designate a covenanted ecclesiastical society, the Puritans used "meetinghouse" for the church's assembly place, the more appropriately because the same place often served for town meetings and other public gatherings. Church membership was restricted but attendance at church services was a community requirement. Services included baptism and the Lord's Supper, lengthy sermons, prayers, and psalm singing. Marriages and funerals were excluded from the meetinghouse, although commemorative funeral sermons were preached there for notable persons. Most typically a white frame structure, the early square meetinghouse, with central tower, gave way to an oblong style with end tower topped by a spire. The pulpit dominated the simple but dignified interior. In much of New England taxes as well as offerings and pew receipts long were available to support the meetinghouses' religious activities. Population expansion necessitated new meetinghouses for new churches, closely related to the increase in the number of new townships. In late colonial times the meetinghouse became a center of revolutionary activities. It also fostered local responsibility and community spirit.

[W. Walker, *A History of the Congregational Churches in the United States.*]

LOUISE B. DUNBAR

MEIGS, FORT, was built in 1813, on order of Gen. William Henry Harrison, on the south bank of the Maumee River opposite the present town of Maumee, Ohio, primarily as a general depot for supplies and a base of operations against Detroit and Canada. It was in the form of an irregular ellipse, with blockhouses equipped with cannon. From Apr. 28 to May 9, 1813, it was besieged, unsuccessfully, by Gen. Henry A. Proctor with a force of British, Canadians, and Indians, aided by Tecumseh.

[E. O. Randall and D. J. Ryan, *History of Ohio,* vol. III.]

HARLOW LINDLEY

MELLON INSTITUTE OF INDUSTRIAL RESEARCH was founded in 1913 to bring to American industry the fruits of scientific research, especially in chemistry. Concerted research by teams of scientists had begun in the German dye industry in the last quarter of the 19th century, and major American firms—notably General Electric and Eastman Kodak—established their own laboratories after 1900. Between 1875 and 1900, American agriculture had improved dramatically as the research of the land grant colleges was applied on the farm. At one such college, the University of Kansas, Robert Kennedy Duncan brought the problems of industry into the campus chemical laboratory after 1907. His program of fellowships sponsored by industry influenced Andrew W. Mellon to support Duncan's move to the University of Pittsburgh in 1911. Two years later Andrew Mellon and his brother Richard founded the institute as a part of the University of Pittsburgh.

After Duncan's death in 1914 the institute prospered under his protégé Edward R. Weidlein by providing, in a university setting, research facilities for companies that did not have their own. After 1922, when the institute could support itself from industrial fellowships alone, the Mellons' funds were freed to subsidize pure research in chemistry. Growth of the research enterprise made the Mellon Institute a separate entity by 1927, and in 1937 the institute's monumental building was erected. Novel processes and products that emerged from the institute's laboratories formed the basis for new companies or new divisions of old companies (for example, Dow-Corning, Union Carbide, and Gulf Oil). Success turned many of the fellowships into separate research facilities at the parent company, and the institute replaced them with new ones.

To the increasing prestige of fundamental research, the Mellon Institute responded when it obtained in 1957, under Weidlein's successor, Gen. Matthew B.

Ridgway, who was assisted by Paul J. Flory as scientific director, a substantial endowment from the Mellon family for fundamental research. It was raised to parity with industrial research, and the institute became an important center for the training of postdoctoral fellows in science. However, following a study of Pittsburgh institutions in response to a financial crisis at the University of Pittsburgh in 1965, the Mellon Institute was merged into the Carnegie Institute of Technology (founded in 1900) to form Carnegie-Mellon University (1967), whose college of natural sciences has been known since 1970 as the Mellon Institute of Science. From headquarters in the Mellon Institute building, this college continues the programs of both institutions of research and teaching in biology, chemistry, computer science, mathematics, and physics. The system of industrially supported research programs begun at Mellon Institute continues under the Division of Sponsored Research.

[Robert Kennedy Duncan, *The Chemistry of Commerce: Some Chemical Problems of Today;* "Industrial Fellowships: Five Years of an Educational Industrial Experiment," *Journal of the Franklin Institute,* vol. 175 (1913); and "Industrial Fellowships of the Mellon Institute," *Science,* vol. 39 (1914); Edward R. Weidlein, "Historical Sketch of Mellon Institute," *Fiftieth Annual Report of the Mellon Institute.*]

HAROLD L. BURSTYN

MELUNGEONS, from French *mélange,* are a people of mixed blood who have long lived in a remote mountain section of Hancock County, Tenn. The Bureau of American Ethnology classes them as an offshoot of the Croatan Indians, but W. A. Dromgoole claimed that the original stock was Cherokee that had settled on Newman's Ridge in 1797 and intermarried with the English and the Portuguese traders and settlers. There have been many disputes over alleged Afro-American blood; most of the families alleged to have such blood have lived separately.

[Will Allen Dromgoole, "The Malungeon Tree and Its Four Branches," *Arena* (May 1891); Paul D. Converse, "The Melungeons," *Southern Collegian* (December 1912).]

P. D. CONVERSE

MEMORIAL DAY (May 30), or **Decoration Day,** began in 1868 when members of the Grand Army of the Republic heeded the request of their commander, Gen. John A. Logan, to decorate the graves of their fallen compatriots on the thirtieth day of May. It has since become the day on which the United States honors the dead of all its wars and is observed as a

legal holiday in all but several southern states. Ceremonies have traditionally included decoration of graves, parades, and commemorative speeches. National services are held at the Tomb of the Unknowns in Arlington, Va.

SEDDIE COGSWELL

MEMORIAL OF THE PLANTERS AND MERCHANTS OF LOUISIANA. Immediately after the Louisiana Revolution of 1768, in which the Spanish governor Antonio de Ulloa was expelled from the colony, the leading citizens of Louisiana drew up and sent to Louis XV of France a lengthy memorial, in which they sought to justify the recent revolutionary proceedings against Spanish authority. The memorial set forth a sort of bill of indictment against Ulloa, whom they charged with having ruined the colony by oppressive restrictions on commerce, navigation, and industry, prohibition of importation of slaves, and the granting of monopolies to favorites. They also complained of his introduction of the Spanish legal system and of his contempt for the ecclesiastical laws of the colony. They stressed the great value of Louisiana to France and its uselessness to Spain, professed their love for Louis XV, and begged him to take back the colony. The memorial may be regarded as a sort of antidote or rebuttal to the reports on the revolution that they knew the last French commandant and Ulloa, the expelled Spanish governor, would send to their respective governments. Their pleadings were ineffective. Louis XV refused to consider taking back the colony, and Spain sent Alexander ("Bloody") O'Reilly, who crushed the revolution and firmly established Spanish authority in Louisiana in 1769.

[Alcée Fortier, *History of Louisiana;* Charles Gayarré, *History of Louisiana.*]

WALTER PRICHARD

MEMPHIS, a city in the southwest corner of Tennessee on the east bank of the Mississippi River. Comparatively speaking, Memphis is a modern city, but its site (on the lowest of the Chickasaw Bluffs) figured in the dawn of the history of the Mississippi Valley. The legend of the Chickasaw fixed it as the place where they crossed the Mississippi in their migration from the West. A number of historians say Hernando de Soto crossed the river there in 1541. Father Jacques Marquette in 1673 stopped at the site on his journey down the river. Fort Assumption was built by Jean Baptiste Le Moyne, Sieur de Bienville, on the bluff in 1739 as a base for his campaign against the Chickasaw. In 1795 the Spanish government erected

Fort San Fernando, which stood until 1797, when it was dismantled (*see* Guion's Expedition). Settlement was encouraged by a group of proprietors that included Andrew Jackson, and the town was laid out in 1819 and given the name of the ancient city on the Nile. Memphis was incorporated as a town in 1826, as a city in 1840, and made a customs port in 1850. Serving as the state's temporary capital in 1862, it was captured by Union troops and remained in Union hands until after the Civil War.

Rail and river transportation aided in the city's rapid development as a cotton center. But three yellow fever epidemics struck the city in the 1870's, and many of the survivors fled. By 1879 the city was bankrupt and surrendered its charter to the state. Sanitation reforms aided in the city's being rechartered in 1893, and by 1900 Memphis was once again a thriving cotton center and the state's largest city. It soon became a hardwood lumber market and eventually added the manufacture of chemicals, agriculture machinery, and pharmaceuticals to its industry. Memphis is also known as the home of the "blues," particularly as popularized by W. C. Handy. The population in 1970 was 623,530.

[Gerald M. Capers, *Biography of a Rivertown;* Shields McIlwaine, *Memphis Down in Dixie;* S. C. Williams, *Beginnings of West Tennessee.*]

SAMUEL C. WILLIAMS

MEMPHIS, NAVAL BATTLE AT (June 6, 1862). The Union western flotilla, five ironclad gunboats mounting sixty-eight guns, under Flag Officer Charles H. Davis, was anchored across the Mississippi River two miles above Memphis at about sunrise on June 6, 1862. It was attacked by the Confederate river defense fleet, eight improvised steam rams carrying twenty-eight guns, commanded by Capt. J. E. Montgomery. Col. Charles Ellet with three unarmed Union rams ran down past Davis' flotilla and broke the double Confederate line. The gunboats followed, firing rapidly, and Montgomery's fleet was destroyed in an hour and ten minutes. Three Confederate vessels were sunk, four captured, and one escaped. Memphis immediately surrendered to Davis. The Union suffered four men wounded, including Col. Ellet, who later died of his wounds. (*See* Mississippi Squadron.)

[R. U. Johnson and C. C. Buel, eds., *Battles and Leaders of the Civil War,* vol. I; A. T. Mahan, *Gulf and Inland Waters.*]

JOSEPH MILLS HANSON

MEMPHIS AND CHARLESTON RAILROAD. Between 1830 and 1850, by means of railroads, the prin-

cipal Atlantic ports sought to break the monopoly of New Orleans on the lucrative export trade of the Mississippi Valley. Charleston, S.C., no less than New York, sought to obtain this commerce for itself by constructing an east-west railroad terminating at some point on the Mississippi. Such a rail route was begun in 1829. By 1845 the road had reached Atlanta, and in the same year Memphis was selected by the Charleston promoters as the western terminus. In 1857, after twelve years of further construction, both from Atlanta westward and Memphis eastward, the Memphis and Charleston Railroad was completed.

[R. S. Cotterill, "Southern Railroads and Western Trade," *Mississippi Valley Historical Review,* vol. 3.]

GERALD M. CAPERS, JR.

MENDOZA EXPEDITION. In 1683 the Jumano Indians who lived in central Texas appealed to the governor of New Mexico for missionaries. In response to this request Juan Dominguez de Mendoza and Father Nicholás López, starting from El Paso in December 1683, traveled to the country of the Jumano, where they hoped to meet a delegation of Indians. They established a temporary mission on the Colorado River that, on their return to El Paso in July 1684, they recommended be made permanent. Their recommendation was not followed because the intrusion of Robert Cavelier, Sieur de La Salle, had drawn the attention of Spanish officials to eastern Texas.

[Herbert E. Bolton, *Spanish Exploration in the Southwest, 1542–1706;* Carlos E. Castañeda, *The Winning of Texas.*]

C. T. NEU

MENÉNDEZ IN FLORIDA AND GEORGIA. On Aug. 28, 1565, Pedro Menéndez de Avilés arrived at Saint Augustine, Fla., with 2,646 persons, for the purposes of colonization and driving out the French. In a short time most of the French were exterminated, and the first Jesuit missionaries began their work in Florida. To Menéndez, Florida meant the whole of eastern North America and he intended to make it self-supporting and rich. Within two years he had established a line of posts between Tampa Bay and Santa Elena, S.C., and had made an attempt to colonize Virginia. He erected forts at Guale in northern Georgia, at Tampa and Charlotte bays on the west coast of the peninsula, and at Biscayne Bay and the Saint Lucie Inlet on the east coast. The projected settlement at Chesapeake Bay failed and the missionaries left. In 1570 more missionaries were sent to Virginia but the next year they were killed by the Indians. In 1572 Menéndez was recalled to Spain to take charge of the armada, but he died in 1574. His work gave Spain another important colony in America, and by 1615 more than twenty missions were established in Florida, Georgia, and South Carolina.

[H. E. Bolton, *Spanish Borderlands;* J. T. Lanning, *The Spanish Missions of Georgia.*]

LILLIAN ESTELLE FISHER

MENNONITES are descendants of an Anabaptist group that received its distinctive form from the teachings of Menno Simons, first propounded in the 1530's and 1540's. Mennonites are generally pacifists who maintain a high degree of community discipline through moderate use of the ban—a disciplinary power of the congregation over the believer, for public and private sins—and who practice adult baptism. The Amish, a conservative body of Mennonites founded by Jacob Amman in the 1690's, are particularly notable because they maintain strict customs of dress and advocate separation from the world.

The first Mennonite settlers to come to the New World settled in Pennsylvania in 1683, coming to be known as the Pennsylvania Dutch. Renewed persecutions of Mennonites in Russia in the 1870's led to a second wave of immigrants, who settled primarily in the American and Canadian Midwest.

The principal Mennonite denominations and their 1974 membership figures are Beachy Amish Mennonite Churches, 4,069 members; Church of God in Christ (Mennonite), 6,204 members; Evangelical Mennonite Brethren, 3,784 members; General Conference of Mennonite Brethren Churches, 13,000 members; Hutterian Brethren, 3,405 members; General Conference of the Mennonite Church, 36,129 members; Old Order Amish Church, 14,720 members; Old Order (Wisler) Mennonite Church, 8,000 members; Reformed Mennonite Church, 500 members.

[Harold S. Bender, *Two Centuries of American Mennonite Literature . . . 1727–1928;* Cornelius Dyck, *An Introduction to Mennonite History: A Popular History of the Anabaptists and the Mennonites;* John A. Hostetler, *Amish Society,* and *Annotated Bibliography on the Amish;* Charles Henry Smith, *The Story of the Mennonites;* John C. Wenger, *The Mennonite Church in America, Sometimes Called Old Mennonites.*]

GLENN T. MILLER

"MEN OF THE WESTERN WATERS," a term used by people living along the frontiers of the eastern states between 1642 and 1785. There was no specific group of men to whom this applied, but it referred generally to persons hunting or exploring in the neighborhood of the Ohio and Mississippi rivers and their tributaries. The Long Hunters, Daniel Boone, and, later, George Rogers Clark's men, were referred to as "men of the western waters." Sometimes settlers of Kentucky were referred to as living on the western waters.

[C. W. Alvord and Lee Bidgood, *The First Explorations of the Trans-Allegheny Region by the Virginians.*]

T. D. CLARK

MENOMINEE IRON RANGE. About two-thirds of the iron ore produced in the United States comes from six iron ranges adjacent to Lake Superior. Three of these are in Michigan and three in Minnesota. Of these six ranges, the Menominee is the second to have been developed—the Marquette Range is the oldest. The Menominee Range is situated mainly in the valley of the Menominee River, which lies on the boundary between the upper peninsula of Michigan and northern Wisconsin. That iron was located here seems to have been known before the Civil War, but mining dates from the 1870's. The Breen Mine was opened in 1872 and other locations opened soon afterward, but active shipments had to await the construction of a branch of the Chicago and North Western Railroad from Powers, Mich., on the main line of the Peninsular Division, which reached the district in 1877. The best outlet for the range was at Escanaba on Little Bay De Noc of Lake Michigan, to which the North Western constructed a direct line. The Chicago, Milwaukee and Saint Paul Railroad also penetrated the region and shipped ore over the Escanaba and Lake Superior line until it reached a pooling agreement for shipment over the North Western. Mines were opened at Vulcan, Norway, Iron Mountain, and Iron River, Mich., and at Florence, Wis. The most remarkable producer was the Chapin Mine at Iron Mountain, which produced nearly 26 million tons of iron ore from its opening in 1879 to its closing in 1934. Most of this ore reached Lake Michigan at Escanaba, where ore docks were erected. From there bulk freighters carried the ore to lower lake ports. Between 1854 and 1972 the Michigan part of the Menominee Iron Range produced 297,883,000 long tons. Wisconsin produced considerably less—887,000 tons in 1972 as compared with 2,533,000 tons from the Michigan area of the range in the same year.

[Peter Temin, *Iron and Steel in Nineteenth Century America: An Economic Inquiry;* Fremont P. Wirth, *Discovery and Exploration of the Minnesota Iron Lands.*]

L. A. CHASE

MENTAL HYGIENE MOVEMENT. Measures to improve mental health as well as physical health were part of the popular health movements that began before the Civil War. In the late 19th century the perceived "increase in insanity" that seemed to accompany urbanization and immigration intensified concern for the nation's mental health, and the medical professionals concerned with the mentally ill in the 1880's tried briefly to launch a formal campaign to improve mental health.

Although the organizational expression soon faded away, this concern continued among psychiatrists and was galvanized into action in the Progressive era by a voluntary health organization, the National Committee for Mental Hygiene, patterned in part after the National Anti-Tuberculosis Association. In 1908 a young Yale graduate, Clifford W. Beers, published a bestselling account of his bout with serious mental illness, *A Mind That Found Itself*. With the cooperation of leading psychiatrists, Beers founded, first, in 1908, the Connecticut Society for Mental Hygiene and, in 1909, the National Committee for Mental Hygiene.

The committee came under the leadership of an able and enthusiastic psychiatrist, Thomas W. Salmon, and conducted educational campaigns and recommended reforms in the hospitalization of the mentally ill. The great accomplishment of Salmon and his associates was obtaining full recognition for specialists in nervous and mental disease in the World War I military medical services. The work of the committee, along with the "shell shock" scare, did much to popularize psychiatry in the 1920's. In 1930 an International Congress on Mental Hygiene was held at Washington, D.C. In later years, especially near the middle of the century, the mental hygiene movement was largely directed toward defending and advocating psychiatry as it was then practiced.

During the first half of the twentieth century, the major contribution of the mental hygiene movement was to foster a broad approach to mental health that involved educators, social workers, and other lay persons as well as psychologists and medical specialists. During those decades, therapy to restore psychological well-being was relatively ineffective. The leaders of the mental hygiene movement therefore concentrated their efforts upon programs of prevention, particularly programs that affected children. By the 1960's mental hygiene was associated increasingly with the community psychiatry movement and, as in the 1920's, the use of paramedical personnel as well as physicians.

[George K. Pratt, "Twenty Years of the National Committee for Mental Hygiene," *Mental Hygiene,* vol. 14 (1930); Barbara Sicherman, "The Quest for Mental Health in America, 1880–1917" (dissertation, Columbia University); Francine Sobey, *The Nonprofessional Revolution in Mental Health*.]

JOHN C. BURNHAM

MENTAL ILLNESS, TREATMENT OF. The line between so-called mental illness and mental health has always been tenuous, and so definitions of mental illness have always been varied and ambiguous. Many persons who would not be considered mentally ill by currently accepted definitions were institutionalized in mental hospitals, as for example, epileptics, severe retardates, and homeless senile men and women. This article deals primarily with the treatment afforded persons previously called insane and today termed psychotic.

With some exceptions, American approaches to the care of the mentally ill have been derived from European models, and even periodic reform movements that have had uniquely American characteristics can be related to similar developments abroad. Thus, as in Europe, prevailing ideas and practices have tended to run a cyclical course: times of pessimism and custodial care have alternated with periods of optimism and active treatment, and commitment to physical and pharmacological therapies has alternated with belief in psychological, environmental treatment.

By the early 18th century the ancient idea of mental disorder as divine retribution or satanic possession had given way among physicians and sophisticated laymen to the view that it was a physical disease of the brain, amenable to treatment by physicians in institutions established for the purpose.

In British North America, as elsewhere, the vast majority of mentally disordered persons did not receive such treatment. Instead, friends, relatives, or town authorities supplied care for "madmen" or "lunatics," often secreted and physically restrained in attics, outhouses, cellars, or shacks. If the town assumed responsibility and the "lunatic" was not considered dangerous, he might be auctioned off to anyone who would care for him at the least public cost. Sometimes he might be surreptitiously abandoned far away so that another community would be burdened with his support, or he would be left free to wander about begging for food and lodging. At the close of the colonial period, the newly constructed workhouses and jails frequently also housed the insane, where on rare occasions a physician might visit them.

The opening in 1752 of the first general hospital in the British colonies, the Pennsylvania Hospital at Philadelphia, marked what was more a portent of better care than an achievement of it, but conducted on somewhat more humane principles was the first hospital in the colonies devoted exclusively to mental patients, now the Eastern State Hospital at Williamsburg, Va., opened in 1773 by a family of physicians and keepers, the Galts. Lay keepers administered the small asylum with the advice of a physician, who came weekly to see patients and prescribed the conventional contemporary medical therapy—cathartics, emetics, bloodletting, cold and warm showers, and special diets and tonics. More famous were the reforms introduced at the Pennsylvania Hospital by Dr. Benjamin Rush, often called the father of American psychiatry, after he took charge of the mental patients in 1783. Although Rush adhered dogmatically to the traditional belief in bloodletting, as well as dosing with mercury, as a cure for all ills, he took an innovative stance, endeavoring to deal with the emotional condition of the mental patients under his care. He tried to establish a kindly, albeit authoritarian, relationship with them and initiated improvements in their living conditions, including opportunity for some sort of occupation.

More thoroughgoing reforms were proposed in France, England, and Italy, where physicians and lay activists originated a new system called moral treatment; transplanted to the United States, it flourished during the first half of the 19th century. A precursor of what were considered innovative theories of treatment in the mid-20th century, moral treatment emphasized the emotional needs of patients through the creation of a total therapeutic, benevolent environment. Although initially conventional medical therapy was not rejected in moral treatment asylums, it did not predominate, and by 1850 bloodletting was virtually abandoned, depletive drugs and low diets infrequently prescribed, and most mechanical restraints eliminated. The stress was on kindness and activity: occupational therapy (especially farming and gardening) was encouraged, and there were recreational programs, such as lectures, lantern-slide showings, scientific demonstrations, and musical concerts. Open hospital practices were variously adopted in the form of open wards, freedom of the grounds, the right of patients to visit the neighboring town, and group activities.

From 1817 to 1824 four new hospitals on the moral treatment model opened, all of them nonprofit corporate institutions under private management; they tended to cater mainly to middle-class and upper-class patients. Later, in the 1830's and 1840's, several state hospitals established during the wave of antebellum social reform also practiced moral treatment, the best

known being the asylum at Worcester, Mass., under Dr. Samuel Woodward. The most original American practitioner of moral treatment was Woodward's mentor, Dr. Eli Todd, first superintendent of the Hartford Retreat (later the Institute of Living), which opened in 1824. The founding of a professional organization, the Association of Medical Superintendents of American Institutions for the Insane (later the American Psychiatric Association) in 1844 and of the *American Journal of Insanity* (predecessor of the *American Journal of Psychiatry*) during that same year by Dr. Amariah Brigham, the chief of the new state hospital at Utica, N.Y., helped to spread the idea of moral treatment and fostered the acceptance of institutionalized medical care for the insane. The latter trend was accelerated by the philanthropist and reformer Dorothea Lynde Dix's success in persuading state legislatures to establish some twenty mental hospitals. In all, there were approximately 26 mental hospitals in the United States by 1849, over 60 by 1866, and 200 by 1900. In 1844 approximately 3.1 percent of the persons estimated to be insane (probably no more than half are so recognized at any time) were in mental hospitals, and by 1900, 24 percent; not until 1940 did the figure rise to 60 percent, most of the patients living in giant state hospitals.

Institutional care changed after the Civil War, often for the worse, and especially at the state hospitals, which had to cope with inadequate funding and too many patients. Moral treatment declined, as did reported therapeutic successes—from 20 to 30 percent of yearly admissions as compared with from 40 to 60 percent during the 1830's and 1840's. Social resentment against the large immigrant population of the latter 19th century brought with it a revival of theories of the hereditary and incurable nature of insanity. Concomitantly new scientific discoveries, most notably the germ theory of disease, encouraged a reversion to a physiological approach to mental illness. Such drugs as opium compounds, bromides, belladonna, and cannabis were used to subdue agitated patients, but most hospitals became primarily custodial.

There were some bright spots at the turn of the 20th century as a result of research into disorders that cause mental abnormalities. In 1891 G. R. Murray's work led to the prevention of goitrous cretinism, and in 1914 J. Goldberger described his method of preventing and treating pellagra by diet. Interest in the psychological and administrative aspects of the care of the mentally ill also revived at this time, partly under the influence of physicians' work with noninstitutionalized patients. Significant in this respect was the new medical specialty neurology, which expanded to include "nervous diseases" that had no visible physical basis as well as those that did and whose practitioners came to dominate psychiatry; leading mental hospitals had as their chiefs men trained in neurology. A large proportion of the neurologists' patients seemed to be suffering from a supposedly newly discovered disorder; named neurasthenia in 1868 by the neurologist Charles A. Beard, it actually resembled the hysteria and hypochondria of old and the conditions called neuroses in the 20th century. The preferred treatment for neurasthenia, which was characterized by weakness, lassitude, tension, and anxiety, was that prescribed by the famous neurologist and novelist Silas Weir Mitchell—bed rest, nourishing food, and isolation, with a dose of moralizing about self-control. Although some neurasthenics were hospitalized, most were treated by neurologists in their private offices, and thereby was initiated a dual system of dealing with emotional disorders: psychotics within hospitals and neurasthenics (neurotics) in private practice.

Psychoanalysis, another influential therapeutic system, was first applied to nonpsychotic patients and then tried with psychotics in some hospitals. Sigmund Freud introduced his theories to Americans at Clark University in 1909, and his work was brought to the attention of the psychiatric profession by prominent psychiatrists like Abraham A. Brill (his American translator) and William Alanson White.

An institutional trend that began at about the same time was the establishment of the psychopathic hospital as a teaching and research center associated with a general hospital, where the latest therapeutic methods were employed. The prototype was the Phipps Psychiatric Clinic at Johns Hopkins, which opened in 1913 with Adolf Meyer as chief. Another new idea was the training of social workers to serve in mental hospitals.

A new reform movement was launched in 1909 with the founding of an organization designed to improve hospital conditions, the National Committee for Mental Hygiene. It was founded by Clifford W. Beers, a former mental patient whose description of his unhappy experiences in mental hospitals in *A Mind That Found Itself* created a sensation when published in 1908. The committee's call for nonrestraint and emphasis on prevention encouraged improvements in the leading mental institutions and the establishment of child guidance clinics; but for the vast majority of institutionalized patients there was little change.

During World War I the high incidence of "shell shock" made the mental health of servicemen a national concern. Dr. Thomas W. Salmon, medical director of the National Committee for Mental Hygiene, developed an effective program of prompt psychiatric treatment of soldiers in the field that consisted mainly of reassurance and return to active duty. Hospitalization of "shell-shocked" men had proven counterproductive, leading to chronic invalidism or disability, a lesson quickly forgotten and relearned only during World War II.

The first effective treatment for what had always been an intractable mental illness was the fever therapy first tried in Vienna in 1917 by J. Wagner-Jauregg for general paresis, the final stage of syphilis (by then known to be caused by the spirochete). It was not until 1943, however, when J. F. Mahoney and co-workers suggested the use of penicillin and the National Research Council furnished the expensive new drug to a few psychiatrists, that physicians thought it possible to all but eradicate paresis.

During the 1930's somatic treatments developed in Europe became popular in American mental hospitals, most notably the shock therapies, which seemed to be helpful in cases of depression—insulin shock, metrazol, and then electroshock. Because electroshock had fewer side effects, it became in the 1940's the method of choice among nonpsychoanalytically oriented psychiatrists. Another "new" treatment, psychosurgery, came into widespread use, commonly in the form of lobotomy, the removal of white tissue from the frontal lobe of the brain, advocated by W. Freeman to modify the behavior of chronic psychotics. Condemned later as mutilation of helpless patients, lobotomy declined by the 1960's as more effective drugs came into use. At the same time that shock therapy and psychosurgery became fashionable, a number of psychiatrists in the United States—including Harry Stack Sullivan, Frieda Fromm-Reichman, Fritz Redlich, and Silvano Arieti—practiced psychoanalysis on schizophrenic patients in private hospitals. During World War II some American psychiatrists also turned to hypnotherapy; the Society for Clinical and Experimental Hypnosis was formed in 1949.

One of the most significant developments in the history of psychopharmacology occurred in 1950 when the Swiss chemist Paul Charpentier synthesized the tranquilizer chlorpromazine. Thereafter the number of psychopharmacological compounds used in the treatment of mental illness proliferated; tranquilizing drugs dramatically decreased patients' excitement and thereby the "need" for violent wards, and antidepressant drugs seemed to relieve the anxiety of depressed patients. Both kinds made it possible for many patients to live outside the hospital. The success of these drugs also stimulated scientific searches for biochemical and genetic features of mental illness.

Concomitant with the appearance of the new drugs and to some extent made possible by the relative calm they produced in patients, new psychologically and sociologically oriented approaches to patient care gained popularity, especially milieu therapy, which, unknown to its originators, resembled the moral treatment of a century before. Also gaining ground during the 1950's and 1960's was the application of behaviorist theories, especially B. F. Skinner's work in operant conditioning, whose popularity among psychotherapists can be related to disillusionment with psychoanalysis.

Some reformers wanted to deinstitutionalize patients altogether. In recognition of the observation that long-term hospitalization not only failed to help but frequently harmed patients, the first American hospital where patients not needing constant supervision could come only at night to sleep was established, on the model of similar institutions inaugurated in Moscow and Montreal. This approach received recognition and funds in 1963 from the federal government, through the National Institute for Mental Health, by then the major research and funding agency for mental health programs in the United States. The goal set by community mental health advocates was the return of the majority of mental patients to their original communities, to live at home or in specially supervised residences (halfway houses), with therapeutic support from local mental health centers.

In the 1960's, under the influence of radical and humanist critics within the professions of psychiatry and psychology and coinciding with the growth of sociopolitical movements in behalf of oppressed minorities, a new wave of questioning and change seemed to be upon psychiatry. Former mental patients began to form organizations to change hospital conditions; psychosurgery was being challenged in the courts; and legal steps were being taken to prevent involuntary commitment of persons in mental hospitals and to require adequate treatment of patients in state hospitals. The question whether mental illness was illness or an understandable response to a disturbed familial and social environment was raised, as well as the propriety and usefulness of conventional institutions for persons deemed mentally ill.

Whatever power the various reform movements gained began to erode in the late 1960's with the federal government's retrenchment of social and health programs. By the mid-1970's this decline, intensified by economic recession, had reached a level that threatened the collapse of reforms in the mental hospitals as well as of the community health programs designed as alternatives to hospital care and as agencies of prevention of serious mental illness.

[Clifford W. Beers, *A Mind That Found Itself: An Autobiography;* Norman Dain, *Concepts of Insanity in the United States, 1789–1865,* and *Disordered Minds: The First Century of Eastern State Hospital in Williamsburg, Virginia, 1766–1866;* Albert Deutsch, *The Mentally Ill in America: A History of Their Care and Treatment From Colonial Times;* Gerald N. Grob, *The State and the Mentally Ill: A History of the Worcester State Hospital in Massachusetts, 1830–1920;* Nathan G. Hale, *Freud and the Americans: The Beginnings of Psychoanalysis in the United States, 1876–1917;* David J. Rothman, *The Discovery of the Asylum: Social Order and Disorder in the New Republic.*]

NORMAN DAIN

MERCANTILE AGENCIES grew up after the panic of 1837, when there was an urgent need for credit information. The first agency was started in 1841 in New York by Lewis Tappan, who had accumulated a great deal of credit information for the wholesale firm of A. Tappan and Company. He offered this information for sale following the failure of the Tappan company, and the demand was such that the business grew from the first. In 1859 it became R. G. Dun and Company. In 1849 the Bradstreet Company was started by John M. Bradstreet, a Cincinnati lawyer who had accumulated a great deal of credit information while settling an estate. Many other agencies were started, but these were the only two general agencies to survive and they were merged into Dun and Bradstreet, Inc., in March 1933. Several special agencies cover only particular trades or limited areas. Dun and Bradstreet, Inc., supplies financial and credit ratings and information on concerns in all trades in all parts of the United States and in many foreign countries.

P. D. CONVERSE

MERCANTILISM, as applied to the British colonies, did not follow the general theories of that doctrine very closely. It was always tempered by the fact that the colonies were self-governing subdivisions of the British Empire, inhabited by Englishmen. The mercantilist trading company was used to initiate the first colonies, but was soon abandoned for direct imperial control (*see* Colonial Policy, British). This control took the form of many measures intended to regulate the trade, production, and manufacture of both England and the colonies with the object of promoting the prosperity of all. These included the Navigation Acts, by which the trade within the empire was confined to English seamen and English ships. The word English in these and subsequent acts referred to nationality and not to residence. Thus, a merchant from Boston was just as English as a resident of London.

Other phases of the Navigation Acts required that certain colonial products be shipped from their place of production to England, or to another British or colonial port, and not directly to a foreign country. Asian goods and European manufactured goods were in turn required to reach the colonies only by way of England. This program permitted the profits from colonial trade and commerce to center in England, promoted English shipping, and enabled the British government to support itself by taxing this trade as it flowed through England.

The colonies were chiefly producers of raw materials, homes for surplus British population, and markets for goods produced in the home country. Colonial manufacture for an export trade that competed with that of the home country was discouraged by prohibitive legislation: wool in 1699, hats in 1732, and wrought iron and steel in 1750. On the other hand, colonial production of articles needed within the empire was encouraged. The sugar islands were given a practical monopoly of the colonial market for molasses (1733). Virginia and its neighbors were given a monopoly of the tobacco market in England by acts forbidding the growing of tobacco in England and by prohibitive tariffs on competing Spanish tobacco. Direct bounties, paid from the British treasury, were used to promote the colonial production of hemp, tar, pitch, and other naval stores, and very large sums were paid out for this purpose between 1705 and 1774. Other colonial products that benefited from bounties were raw silk, masts, lumber, and indigo. Payments from the British treasury on this account averaged more than £15,000 a year in the decade preceding the Revolution. Preferential tariffs gave colonial products favored treatment in the British markets. Colonial products like sugar and tobacco that were not needed for the British market were, on exportation, assisted by drawbacks of the import duties so that they reached their European markets burdened by a minimum of British taxes. Drawbacks

also were used to promote American colonial use of such goods from the British colonies in Asia as tea after 1767. The total export drawbacks paid out by Great Britain in an average year—for example, 1772—amounted to £2,214,508 in a total export trade valued at £16,159,412, nearly one-third of its exports to America. Exports from Scotland show a similar relationship. Thus colonial and foreign goods flowed through Great Britain to the colonies without too much burden.

The colonial markets were developed by favors instead of compulsion. The usual inducement was export bounties, especially in the case of British manufactures that had foreign competition. The chief articles so aided were cordage, gunpowder, linen, sailcloth, silk manufactures, and refined sugar. The total payments by England alone averaged about £40,000 a year at the close of the colonial period, but had amounted to more than £61,000 in 1771, according to treasury reports. In this way the British market was made attractive to colonial purchasers. Both England and the colonies profited from this 18th-century policy of enlightened mercantilism.

The opposition to mercantilism in its later stages came from free traders like Adam Smith, who admitted that the system worked, but insisted it was wrong in theory. It is difficult to find opposition to the system among revolutionary Americans, so long as measures were purely regulatory and did not levy a tax on the colonists. The system was specifically approved by the First Continental Congress in the Declaration of Rights of Oct. 14, 1774.

[Lawrence A. Harper, *English Navigation Laws*.]

O. M. DICKERSON

MERCER, FORT, ENGAGEMENTS AT (Oct. 22 and Nov. 20, 1777). British Gen. William Howe dispatched 1,200 Hessian troops to attack Col. Christopher Greene's force of 400 at Fort Mercer, a dirt fort, mounting but fourteen guns, at Red Bank, N.J., on Oct. 22, 1777. When the Hessian troops attacked, Greene's men raked them with grapeshot and musketry fire, forcing their retreat with heavy losses. A month later, on Nov. 20, Gen. Charles Cornwallis, with greater numbers, compelled Greene to evacuate the fort, which was then dismantled.

[B. J. Lossing, *Pictorial Field-Book of the Revolution*.]

ROBERT S. THOMAS

MERCHANT ADVENTURERS. *See* **Adventurers.**

MERCHANT FLEET CORPORATION. *See* **Emergency Fleet Corporation.**

MERCHANT MARINE. The history of American shipping in the foreign trade has been spectacular but not invariably profitable. There was marked activity, especially in New England, in the colonial period. The Revolution brought short-lived dislocations of trade; then, in the neutral trading during the long Anglo-French conflict, the merchant fleet quickly expanded and prospered until enmeshed in the War of 1812. Shortly after that, the New York sailing packets began to give American seamanship high prestige. The old merchant marine reached its peak between 1845 and 1855. This peak was followed by a long depressed period in which the American flag was virtually withdrawn from the distant sea lanes. After World War I, the United States returned to foreign trade with the largest merchant marine in the world.

Less familiar has been the less spectacular, but steadier, story of the long major role in the nation's transportation of the domestic "enrolled" shipping, as distinct from vessels "registered" for foreign trade. The lack of adequate statistics comparable to the wealth of "commerce and navigation" figures for foreign trade doubtless accounts for part of the failure to appreciate the full significance of the domestic merchant marine, which, since 1817, has been protected by law from foreign competition. Many American coastal runs have been longer than many foreign ones in Europe. A voyage equivalent to the Boston–New Orleans passage, for instance, would carry a vessel from London on a foreign run to numerous nations in western Europe. Until the early 20th century a large share of the cargo movements in the Atlantic, Gulf, and Pacific coastal regions were seaborne; so, too, was a considerable part of the passenger traffic. The protection against competition from foreign shipping was extended to the lengthy intercoastal routes between Atlantic and Pacific ports, whether by clippers around Cape Horn or, later, by steamships through the Panama Canal. Likewise protected in later days was commerce with the noncontiguous possessions: Alaska, Hawaii, and Puerto Rico. In the meantime steamboats on the Mississippi and other western waters and barges on the Erie and other canals handled a large amount of internal transportation from about 1820 to 1860, when the railroads began to take over. In the second quarter of the 20th century, barge traffic on the inland waterways revived in vigorous fashion. The most consistently flourishing

segment of domestic shipping has been the Great Lakes movement of ore, grain, and other heavy cargo in great ships specially designed for the purpose.

The New England colonists took to the sea almost at once. Their rocky acres were poor for farming, but they had a rich supply of oak and pine to build vessels that they could load with lumber and fish that could be swapped and reswapped until they got what they wanted. Much of that cargo went to the West Indies to be exchanged for sugar, molasses, or rum; some went along the coast to be exchanged for grain or flour; and some crossed the Atlantic. England's Navigation Laws, aimed at developing a self-sufficient empire, benefited them, for a vessel built and manned on Massachusetts Bay or Casco Bay counted as an English ship with an English crew; many of the cheaply built New England vessels, moreover, were sold to English owners. By 1700, Boston ranked third, after London and Bristol, among all English ports in the tonnage of its shipping. By 1730, Philadelphia passed it in commerce, but the New England coast remained the center of shipping activity.

After the Revolution, American vessels no longer enjoyed British registry, could not be sold in England, and were barred from the profitable and mutually advantageous triangular trade with the British Caribbean sugar islands. On the other hand, American ships no longer had to buy all their return cargoes in Britain and were free to trade with the Mediterranean, the Baltic, India, and China. Salem, in particular, was quick to take advantage of this. The long Anglo-French wars, starting in 1793, put a premium on the neutral status of American-flag shipping, which could visit ports where the British or French belligerent flags would be vulnerable. At the risk of occasional capture and confiscation in this "heroic age" as they ran afoul of belligerent regulations, the Americans reaped a rich profit. Their registered tonnage rose from 346,000 tons in 1790 to 981,000 in 1810, while the combined exports and imports in those same years jumped from $43 million to $152 million, about 90 percent of which was carried in American bottoms. Eventually the American embargo and Nonintercourse Acts hurt the trade, while the British blockade during the War of 1812 eventually almost cut off the United States from the sea. The difficulty in bringing southern cotton and other products overland to New York and New England during the blockade illustrated the importance of the normal coastwise trade.

In the fairly quiet period between 1815 and 1845, the two principal developments were the rapid expansion of steam navigation and the performance of the transatlantic sailing packets. Although there were numerous early American, British, and French experiments in steam, successful steam navigation is normally dated from the voyage of Robert Fulton's *Clermont* up the Hudson River from New York to Albany and back in 1807. New York quickly utilized the sheltered waters of Long Island Sound as a steam approach to New England, while other local uses of steam for ferries and tugs developed. The ability of steamboats to ascend the Mississippi and its tributaries quickly revolutionized and promoted traffic on western waters. On the longer ocean runs, however, the early engines required so much coal, in contrast to wind, which was free, that steam did not pay. The pioneer ocean crossing of the auxiliary steamer *Savannah* (1819) was not a success. Permanent transatlantic steam navigation dates from 1838, when two British steamships, the *Sirius* and the *Great Western,* arrived at New York on the same day. In the meantime the American sailing packets from New York to Liverpool, London, and Le Havre had dominated the North Atlantic run since 1818. These "square-riggers on schedule," sailing on specified dates with passengers, mail, and fine freight, had demonstrated the value of regular line service, previously unknown.

By the 1840's the Irish potato famine, Britain's repeal of its Corn Laws and Navigation Laws, and the discovery of gold in California were combining to bring the American merchant marine to its golden age in the early 1850's, almost equaling Britain's shipping in tonnage and surpassing it in quality. The starving Irish swarmed across the Atlantic in huge numbers, followed shortly by a large migration of Germans. The Yankee ships that brought them over could, with the repeal of the Corn Laws, carry back American grain. The California gold rush led to the construction of large numbers of beautiful, fast clippers, in which cargo capacity was sacrificed for speed, and to the establishment of subsidized steamship lines converging from New York and San Francisco upon the Isthmus of Panama. The British example of subsidizing the mail steamers of Samuel Cunard led Congress to support steamship lines to Bremen and Le Havre. Finally, it gave even more generous support to Edward K. Collins for a line to Liverpool to "beat the Cunarders." For a while he achieved that; his *Baltic*'s speed won the "blue riband." But after that, speed led to the loss of two ships; Congress withdrew its support, and the line failed.

By the late 1850's a decline, which would lead to the long Dark Ages of the merchant marine, had al-ready set in, accentuated by the panic of 1857. The clipper craze had been overdone; it no longer paid to sacrifice one-third of a vessel's cargo capacity for a few extra knots of speed. The building of square-rigged ships, which reached its peak in 1855, fell off sharply, but the total tonnage registered for foreign trade was a trifle higher in 1860 than it had been in 1855—at 2,379,000 tons, a level that was not to be equaled again until World War I. With the tonnage enrolled or licensed for domestic trade, however, it was a different matter. In 1860, at 2,974,000 tons, it was well ahead of the registered tonnage and would gradually increase. But the oceangoing shipping was to suffer during the Civil War from the depredations of the *Alabama* and other British-built Confederate naval raiders. Actually, they caught barely one Union ship in a hundred, but the panic they generated so raised war-risk insurance rates that shippers sought foreign flags that called for no such extra expense. Scores of the finest American square-riggers were consequently transferred to foreign registry and were not permitted to return afterward. After the war the shift of the nation's interest and its capital investment from the sea to the opening of the West contributed to this decline.

Probably the basic cause of the decline in American oceangoing shipping stemmed from the upward surge in the use of steam. The development of the compound, reciprocating marine engine at last made it practicable to transport bulk cargoes, such as coal, wheat, and sugar, by steamship rather than by sailing vessel; the opening of the Suez Canal in 1869 further accentuated the trend, for sailing ships had great difficulty in traversing it and the adjacent Red Sea. Steam gradually pushed sail off all except a few of the longest runs to Europe, such as those carrying grain from California, nitrates from Chile, jute from India, and wool and grain from Australia. The big American Down Easter square-riggers found employment on some of these runs for a while but were gradually crowded out. The most important cause of the new difficulties, however, probably lay in the effect of the cost of steam and iron or steel on shipbuilding. In the past, wooden vessels had been built more cheaply on the American side of the Atlantic because of the ample supplies of ship timber close to the seaboard, but Europe had gained the advantage of lower costs because of its iron deposits and technological advantages for manufacture.

Congress tried to stimulate American shipping with subsidies for lines to Brazil and the Far East and with the 1891 program for mail subsidies in general, but they accomplished little. The tonnage registered for foreign trade fell off from 2,379,000 in 1860 to 782,000 in 1910. Although the value of foreign commerce in that half century grew from $762 million to nearly $3 billion, the share carried in American bottoms shrank from 66 percent to 8 percent.

With the protected domestic trade, it was a different story. From the 2,974,000 tons of enrolled and licensed shipping in 1860, it fell off slightly during the 1860's and 1870's, but by 1890 it had climbed to 3,496,000 tons, continuing on to 6,726,000 by 1910, almost nine times the foreign-trade total. Certain river, Great Lakes, and Long Island Sound steamers were of too specialized construction for oceangoing use, but between the major coastal ports some quite substantial and effective vessels performed regular cargo and passenger service, which long held its own against railroads parallel to the coast. Much of the coastal bulk cargo was still carried by sail, especially in the Northeast, in little two-masted schooners for lumber, granite, anthracite coal, and lime. Gradually, larger schooners came into use, with three- and four-masters carrying ice and southern lumber. Eventually, big five- and six-masters competed with barges and later with steam colliers in carrying bituminous coal northward from Hampton Roads. Tankers began to carry Gulf petroleum up around Florida to ports "north of Hatteras." On the West Coast, small "steam schooners" carried lumber southward to California, while big secondhand square-riggers brought the salmon catch down from Alaska. The sizable fishing fleet, operating chiefly out of Gloucester and other Northeast ports, consisted chiefly of two-masted schooners for fishing from rowed dories on the Grand Banks.

The experiences of World War I produced a drastic transformation in the American merchant marine, leading it once more back to the distant sea routes. On the eve of the war some 92 percent of the nation's foreign commerce was carried by British, German, and other ships that offered generally satisfactory service. When that was suddenly disrupted by the war in 1914, the United States suddenly realized how serious it was to lack shipping flying its own flag. This was especially brought home to the nation when South America, Africa, Asia, and Australia suddenly offered rich opportunities for American exporters. American-owned vessels, which had been under foreign flags for reasons of economy, were glad to be admitted to neutral registry under the American flag, while sailing vessels were to have their last chance for large-scale useful service in supplying those distant markets. In 1916, Congress established the U.S. Shipping Board, the first body specifically charged with supervision of the merchant marine.

An amazing expansion of American shipping resulted from the emergency building program undertaken in 1917 to offset the heavy Allied losses from Germany's unrestricted submarine warfare. The Shipping Board's ambitious program set up numerous new yards, the largest being at Hog Island just below Philadelphia. Much of this activity was continued after the war suddenly ended late in 1918. By 1921 the United States had overtaken Great Britain for first place among the world's merchant fleets; it had some 700 new large steel freighters and 575 smaller ones.

About a third of those new large ships found employment in a new intercoastal trade between the East and West coasts through the Panama Canal, opened in 1914, which cut the New York–San Francisco run from 13,122 to 5,263 miles. It was thus possible to carry steel, machinery, and similar heavy cargo westward and to bring back lumber and canned goods at rates about one-third cheaper than by rail.

More nearly permanent in national merchant-marine policy, however, was the use of many of the other new freighters on government-supported "essential trade routes" to all parts of the world. The wartime experience had shown how important it was to have regular service on certain runs to provide outlets for American exports and dependable sources of essential imports. At first the new lines were operated directly for the Shipping Board, which absorbed the initial deficits, but as soon as they were on a paying basis, the ships were auctioned off at bargain rates to private operators who would agree to maintain regular service on their lines for a period of years. In 1929 the Jones-White Act provided generous grants, in the name of mail payments, to those approved lines that agreed to build new ships. The falling-off of trade during the depression that started that year left the shipping industry in difficulties, particularly because of competition against cheaper foreign costs of operation and construction.

To meet that situation, Congress in 1936 passed the Merchant Marine Act, which remained the basis of American shipping policy a quarter century later. The former supervisory functions of the Shipping Board passed to the Maritime Commission, which in 1950 gave way to the Federal Maritime Board for policy and the Maritime Administration for operation. To enable American-flag vessels to compete with the foreigners, Congress established "operating-differential" and "construction-differential" subsidies that would meet the difference between American and foreign costs both in the operation and in the building of vessels.

The operating subsidies went only to lines approved for specific "essential trade routes"; there were usually from a dozen to fifteen such lines on thirty-odd routes from Atlantic, Gulf, or Pacific ports. To avoid excessive profits in boom periods, the government would "recapture" half of all profits in excess of 10 percent. About three-quarters of the operating subsidies went to meet the difference in pay between American and foreign officers and crews. Aggressive action on the part of new maritime unions in about 1936 began to push American wages far ahead of foreign wages; the daily wage cost on a medium-sized American-flag freighter rose from $141 in 1938 to $552 in 1948 and to $1,234 in 1960, that figure being about four times as much as in the principal foreign merchant marines. Consequently, unsubsidized vessels found it increasingly difficult to operate under the American flag, and large numbers of them shifted to the "flags of convenience" of Panama or Liberia. In 1960, the subsidized fleets, in order of size, were United States Lines, Lykes Brothers, Moore-McCormack, Grace Line, American President Lines, American Export Lines, Pacific Far East Lines, Farrell Lines, Mississippi Shipping Company (Delta Lines), Oceanic Steamship Company, American Mail Lines, Gulf and South America Line, Prudential Steamship Company, and Bloomfield Steamship Company.

The construction-differential subsidies, designed to keep American shipyards going, absorbed up to half the cost of construction in foreign yards. Lines receiving operating-differential subsidies had to build in American yards, and certain other shipowners were also eligible. For replacement, as vessels approached the conventional twenty-year age limit, the Maritime Commission developed several standard types of freighters designated "C" for "cargo"—especially the C-2 and C-3.

During World War II the subsidized merchant marine fully demonstrated its high value, through its adequate ships, trained mariners, overseas contacts, and operational skill, which did much to provide logistical support for the far-flung military operations across the Atlantic and Pacific. Once again the government undertook a tremendous emergency building program, which produced 5,777 vessels, about half of them slow, capacious "Liberty ships."

The foreign services on the essential trade routes continued on a fairly successful basis after the war, and some of the other shipping also benefited by the congressional "50-50" stipulation that at least half of the cargo sent abroad in the various foreign-aid programs must be carried in American-flag vessels. Domestic shipping, however, fell off sharply in the coastal and intercoastal trades. Part of this decline was blamed by the shipping industry on the "railroad-minded" Interstate Commerce Commission, which in 1940 was given control of all transportation rates. Part of the trouble also arose from the still mounting wages of mariners and longshoremen and from the competition of trucks. Efforts were made to combat the stevedoring costs by containerization, with truck bodies, railroad freight cars, or other preloaded containers carried aboard ship. Barge traffic on inland waterways, on the other hand, gained heavily during the middle years of the century, while the Great Lakes traffic, stimulated by the Saint Lawrence Seaway, likewise flourished. In 1959, the shipping in domestic trade, at 13,284,000 gross tons, was almost equal to the 15,000,000 tons in foreign trade.

The shipping picture suddenly brightened when Congress passed the Merchant Marine Act of 1970, which generously extended and liberalized the terms of the 1936 act. No longer were the fifteen or so lines of the specific "essential trade routes" to have a virtual monopoly of the subsidy benefits. The construction-differential subsidies were expanded to produce thirty new ships a year for the next ten years. Partly because of the growing need for oil and gas from overseas, bulk-cargo ships became potential beneficiaries. The act declared that "the bulk cargo carrying services should, for the promotion, development, expansion, and maintenance of the foreign commerce of the United States and for the national defense or other national requirements be provided by United States-flag vessels whether or not operating on particular services, routes, or lines." The construction subsidy was cut below the old 55 percent maximum; the operating-differential subsidy was extended in a more tentative and restrictive manner but was made to apply to areas rather than rigid lines, and the basis of computation was modified.

The act had an immediate quickening effect on merchant shipping; numerous applications for both kinds of subsidies were made, and plans were laid to build vessels far larger than any previously built in the United States, together with facilities to accommodate their construction. But the initial exuberance was suddenly dampened when President Richard M. Nixon's 1973 budget slashed the funding of the program. As the figures first stood, before the congressional reaction could set in, the overall sum was slashed from $455 million to $275 million.

It was remarked that shipping underwent more drastic changes around 1970 than in any period since the mid-19th century. The increased speed resulting from jet airplanes virtually drove out regular ocean passenger service (the transatlantic passage had dropped from five weeks with the sailing packets and five days with the crack liners to five hours); the passenger liners were laid up, sold, or participated in the fast-growing development of pleasure cruises. The old economic self-sufficiency gave way to increasing need for seaborne cargoes. Oil tankers increased more than tenfold in size, special ships were developed for natural gas, and bulk carriers were developed to bring iron and other ore from overseas.

[R. G. Albion, *Seaports South of Sahara: The Achievements of an American Steamship Service,* and *Square-Riggers on Schedule;* N. R. P. Bonsor, *North Atlantic Seaway;* C. C. Cutler, *Greyhounds of the Sea;* Walter Havighurst, *The Long Ships Passing;* John G. B. Hutchins, *The American Maritime Industries and Public Policy;* Lane C. Kendall, *The Business of Shipping;* Samuel H. Lawrence, *United States Merchant Shipping, Policies and Politics;* E. A. Stackpole, *The Sea Hunters.*]

ROBERT G. ALBION

MERCHANTMEN, ARMED. Absence of international law at sea in the colonial and postrevolutionary periods motivated American shipping interests to arm their vessels against piracy and privateering. This self-defense for their merchantmen was linked to freedom of the seas, a condition essential to national economic survival. As an example, the *Ranger,* out of Salem, Mass., and engaged in West Indian trade in 1782, carried seven guns, plus muskets, cutlasses, and pikes.

To control operations of U.S. armed merchantmen, Congress on Mar. 3, 1805, provided that such ships post bond that their ordnance would be used for defense only. Again, on Apr. 20, 1818, Congress passed similar legislation, upheld by the Supreme Court in January 1832.

During the War of 1812, U.S. merchant ships, typically armed with 6-pounders, sailed clandestinely in and out of British ports, including the West Indies. U.S. ships engaged in trade in China, the West Indies, and South America carried armament for self-defense.

The Declaration of Paris (Apr. 16, 1856) abolished privateering. This action, coupled with the gradual disappearance of piracy, rendered the practice of arming merchantmen virtually obsolete. Nevertheless, in

1877 and again in 1894, the U.S. Department of State, taking note of world trouble spots endangering U.S. merchant ships, held that such ships could be armed for self-defense.

During World War I, Germany, in disregard of freedom of the seas, announced on Jan. 31, 1917, a policy of unrestricted submarine warfare. Consequently, President Woodrow Wilson authorized the arming of U.S. merchant ships with naval gun crews manning 3-inch, 4-inch, or 5-inch guns. During 1917–18 hundreds of naval armed guards sailed on U.S. oceangoing merchant ships.

During World War II, Congress at first passed the Neutrality Act of 1939 forbidding the arming of U.S. merchant ships. After German submarines had attacked U.S. ships in the Atlantic, Congress on Nov. 13, 1941, authorized the use aboard merchant ships of naval armed guards similar to those of World War I.

The convoy routes to Murmansk and to the Mediterranean were among the most dangerous in the history of armed merchantmen. German U-boats and bombing aircraft continually harried the Allied cargo ships supplying Russia in the Baltic and Allied armies in North Africa and in South Asia (the last via the Mediterranean and Suez Canal). The Allied combat campaigns would never have succeeded without the merchant ship convoys.

[H. I. Chapelle, *History of American Sailing Ships;* Lewis P. Clephane, *History of Overseas Transportation Service in World War I;* Alexander Laing, *American Sail;* Samuel Eliot Morison, *History of United States Naval Operations in World War II,* vols. I, II, IX, X, XI; Carlton Savage, *Policy of the United States Toward Maritime Commerce.*]

PAUL B. RYAN

MERIDIAN CAMPAIGN (February 1864). In preparation for the spring campaign, Gen. Ulysses S. Grant sent a force of 20,000 men under Gen. William Tecumseh Sherman to Vicksburg for advance eastward to Meridian, Miss., to destroy Confederate supply depots and railroads. If advisable, Sherman was authorized to move on to Selma, Ala., or southward toward Mobile. He left Vicksburg on Feb. 3, 1864, opposed only by weak Confederate forces under Leonidas Polk. Sherman expected cooperation from cavalry under Sooy Smith coming from Memphis. On Feb. 20 Confederate cavalry under Gen. Nathan B. Forrest stopped Smith's advance and at Okalona, Miss., decisively defeated him. Lacking Smith's cooperation and fearing for his communications, Sherman returned to Vicksburg, having accomplished nothing of importance. Several weeks later his troops were ordered to Chattanooga to prepare for the campaign against Atlanta.

[R. U. Johnson and C. C. Buel, eds., *Battles and Leaders of the Civil War*.]

THOMAS ROBSON HAY

MERRILL'S MARAUDERS. In 1943 global priorities sorely limited the assignment of American infantry to Gen. Joseph W. Stilwell's forthcoming operation to retake north Burma and reopen the land route to China (*see* Burma Road and Ledo Road). Stilwell's command was scaled down from a 30,000-man corps to a three-battalion, or 3,000-man, all-volunteer force. Coded GALAHAD, numbered the 5307th Provisional Unit, and nicknamed Merrill's Marauders by the press after the field commander, Gen. Frank D. Merrill, the three battalions were each broken down into two 472-man combat teams (the remainder of the men had noncombat duties), plus pack animals.

Based on the experience of British army officer Brigadier O. C. Wingate, GALAHAD's strength lay in its tactical mobility, in its potential to hit Japanese flanks and rear areas, and in its unique air supply. The Marauders were to spearhead short envelopments while Stilwell's main Chinese columns pushed back the enemy's front.

Entering combat Feb. 24, 1944, GALAHAD made sharp attacks down the Hukawng Valley and by Mar. 29 entered the Mogaung Valley, gateway to the Irrawaddy River and its rail system. Stilwell's goal was the river town of Myitkyina from which a fair road led to the Burma Road junction at Wanting, China. Reduced to 1,400 men, the Marauders struck directly at Myitkyina through a 6,100-foot pass in the Kumon Range, surprising the 700-man Japanese garrison at Myitkyina's strategic airfield on May 17. Quickly the Japanese brought 4,000 men to Myitkyina, and a seige began that ended Aug. 3. By June 4 GALAHAD was spent: 123 were dead, 293 wounded, 8 missing, 1,970 ill. Grievances that had mounted during a five-month, 500-mile campaign broke out dramatically at Myitkyina. A Distinguished Unit Citation and Stilwell's praise for taking Myitkyina were only appreciated when he explained how they had given heart to the Chinese soldiers to fight on to their homeland.

[Charles N. Hunter, *GALAHAD;* U.S. Army, *Merrill's Marauders*.]

CHARLES F. ROMANUS

MERRIMAC, SINKING OF (June 3, 1898). When the Cuban squadron of Pascual Cervera y Topete was blockaded by Adm. William T. Sampson at Santiago in the Spanish-American War, Assistant Naval Constructor Richmond Pearson Hobson with seven men volunteered to sink the collier *Merrimac* across the narrow entrance, blocking Cervera's escape. Under heavy enemy fire the *Merrimac* was anchored in position about 2 A.M., but its steering gear was injured, only two of its sinking charges exploded, and as finally sunk it did not lie athwart the channel or close it effectively. Surviving almost miraculously after their hazardous exploit, Hobson and his crew were taken prisoners and courteously treated until their exchange on July 7.

[R. P. Hobson, *The Sinking of the Merrimac*.]

ALLAN WESTCOTT

MERRIMACK. *See Monitor* and *Merrimack*, **Battle of.**

MERRYMAN, EX PARTE, Federal Cases No. 9487 (1861), involved President Abraham Lincoln's exercise of extraordinary war powers, specifically his right to suspend habeas corpus. John Merryman, a Baltimore County secessionist, was imprisoned in Fort McHenry in Baltimore harbor by military order on May 25, 1861. The commanding officer refused to comply with a writ of habeas corpus issued by Chief Justice Roger B. Taney, on the grounds that he had been authorized by the president to suspend the writ. Taney wrote an opinion, widely denounced in the North, that the writ could be suspended constitutionally only by Congress, not by the president. Lincoln did not alter his policy (*see Milligan, Ex Parte*).

[C. B. Swisher, *Roger B. Taney;* Charles Warren, *The Supreme Court in United States History*.]

RANSOM E. NOBLE, JR.

MERRY MOUNT, or Mount Wollaston, in Quincy, Mass., was the site of an early conflict between the public interest and commercial greed. About 1625 Thomas Morton established an Indian trading post there, and later added a Maypole, around which he and his men sported with the "lasses in beaver coats." Of the dozen settlements then scattered along the New England coast only that at Plymouth would have objected to the customary May Day promiscuity that Morton, according to his own story, gleefully introduced, and Plymouth was too busy trying to get out of debt; but the combination of neglected Indian husbands, liquor, and gunpowder was recognized as a public menace. Every settlement from Maine to Nantasket Beach, Mass. (none of them Puritan), complained. Plymouth, being nearby, was asked by the others to suppress Morton. Twice the Pilgrims protested to him that he was endangering the common safety, but each time he insisted that he would "trade peeces [guns] with the Indeans in despite of all." As a result, Myles Standish was sent in June 1628 to arrest him in the king's name. Fortunately Morton's crew was so drunk that the only bloodshed came from one of his men who ran his nose onto a sword. Morton was sent off to England, from which he returned shortly to set up the Maypole again and resume his practices. The Massachusetts Bay Colony having been founded in the interval, it was Gov. John Endecott who cut down the pole this time. The Puritans offered to take Morton into the fur-trading monopoly, but he refused because its methods were less profitable than his practice of getting the Indians drunk before trading. So he was again shipped off to England, where he got revenge by writing his amusing *New English Canaan,* the first of the attacks on the New Englanders.

[S. E. Morison, *Builders of the Bay Colony.*]
CLIFFORD K. SHIPTON

MESA, a flat-topped area of land with bluffy walls, sometimes hundreds of feet high, standing above eroded terrain. A mesa may comprise an acre or a thousand acres. This geological formation is characteristic of the Southwest. Acoma, N.Mex., the "city in the sky," is a noted example.

[C. F. Lummis, *Mesa, Cañon and Pueblo.*]
J. FRANK DOBIE

MESABI IRON RANGE contained the richest deposit of iron ore in the United States, but the peculiar quality of the soft hematite ore (nonmagnetic and powdery rather than rock) delayed discovery and exploitation until the 1890's. The ore existed in some eighteen townships in northeastern Minnesota. When its great value became known, there was an unparalleled scramble to enter the land through abuse of the Preemption Act (1841) and the Homestead Act (1862) and for the choicer deposits with the rarer forms of land scrip. Some of the greatest finds were made by Leonidas Merritt and his seven brothers, who, lacking capital to build a railroad to Lake Superior, were unable to market their ore and lost their rich deposits to

John D. Rockefeller. He in turn sold them to Andrew Carnegie, who transferred them to the United States Steel Corporation. More than 2.5 billion tons of ore have been mined from the Mesabi range, but by the middle 1960's the richest of the hematite ore was gone. Only then were the deposits of taconite appreciably valued.

[Theodore C. Blegen, *Minnesota, A History of the State;* Fremont P. Wirth, *Discovery and Exploitation of the Minnesota Iron Lands.*]
PAUL W. GATES

MESA VERDE, PREHISTORIC RUINS OF. In the southwest corner of Colorado stands Mesa Verde National Park (52,073 acres), established in 1906 to preserve the pre-Columbian cliff dwellings. Not all the remains of cliff dwellings are found in Colorado; many have been located in the adjacent parts of New Mexico, Arizona, and Utah. But the most extensive and best preserved, particularly the communal houses, lie in the canyon walls of this sloping plateau. There are hundreds of ruins scattered through these canyons; among the most important are Spruce Tree House, Cliff Palace, Balcony House, and Sun Temple. The builders were a race of Indians, supposedly the predecessors of the present Pueblo. For purposes of defense, they constructed their communal houses in recesses high up on the sides of precipices. The dwellings and temples were composed of stone, clay, and supporting poles. The cliff dwellers flourished in the 11th and 12th centuries, and it is supposed that they were forced to abandon the mesa canyons by a severe drought that came upon the land in the year 1276.

[U.S. Department of the Interior, *Mesa Verde National Park.*]
ROBERT PHILLIPS

MESILLA, an unincorporated town in Dona Ana County, N.Mex., was originally situated on the west side of the Rio Grande, but since 1865, because of a change in the river's channel, is on the east. It was founded after the conclusion of the Mexican War by persons who wished to retain Mexican citizenship. A conflict over jurisdiction ensued, which threatened a renewal of hostilities, until the Gadsden Purchase (1853) definitely placed the region within the United States. During the Confederate invasion of New Mexico in 1861–62, Mesilla was made the capital of a Confederate territory of Arizona.

P. M. BALDWIN

MESQUITE, a spiny shrub or small tree characteristic of the Southwest. Its astounding root system (sometimes to depths of 70 feet) enables it to withstand the severest droughts and produce beans, which horses thrive on, cattle can exist on, and of which Indians and Mexicans make brew and bread. During the days of the open range its leaves were used for browse, its trunks as fence posts, its limbs and roots as an aromatic fuel. The more arid the land, the slimmer are its leaves—to avoid evaporation. It is always spinous. It is now considered a pest in warmer climates of the United States and is eradicated.

J. FRANK DOBIE

MESSIAH WAR (1890–91), an outgrowth of the Ghost Dance excitement, which so affected the Sioux Indians that R. F. Royer, the Indian agent at Pine Ridge, S.Dak., wired for troops. When the soldiers arrived on Oct. 19, 1890, thousands of Indians fled to the Badlands, and many settlers left their homes in fear of a major Indian war. Gen. Nelson A. Miles, commanding the troops in the area, ordered the apprehension of the chief, Sitting Bull, then living on Grand River, but on Dec. 15 the chief was killed, together with six Indian police and eight of his own followers, while resisting arrest.

Skirmishing in the Badlands followed, but on Dec. 28 Maj. S. M. Whitside, Seventh Cavalry, discovered the principal band of hostile Indians, under Big Foot, camped on Wounded Knee Creek. Big Foot surrendered, but the following morning, while his warriors were being disarmed by the troops, fighting broke out, and the so-called Battle of Wounded Knee, really a massacre of the Indians, followed. An estimated 200 to 300 Indians were killed and 29 whites lost their lives. This battle was the only important action. After a few more skirmishes, the overwhelming force under Miles overawed the Sioux and compelled their surrender at Pine Ridge Agency early in January 1891.

[James Mooney, *The Ghost Dance Religion and the Sioux Outbreak of 1890;* Stanley Vestal, *Sitting Bull.*]
PAUL I. WELLMAN

METEOROLOGY. The first contributions to scientific meteorology in America were the famous experiments of Benjamin Franklin in the fields of lightning, atmospheric electricity, cyclone theory, and ocean circulation, during the years from 1748 to 1775. Franklin suggested the experiment that was to prove that electric sparks created artificially in the laboratory were no different from deadly and destructive lightning bolts, except in magnitude. He also proved that there were electric charges in the atmosphere both in cloudy (or thunder) weather and in fine weather. Franklin showed that storms may move progressively "into the wind," by observing that a cyclonic storm with a northeast wind hit Philadelphia a day or so before it hit Boston, which lies to the northeast of Philadelphia. Finally, while crossing the Atlantic between 1746 and 1775, Franklin made observations determining that there is a warm current off the New England coast setting to the northeast—the Gulf Stream—and was able to chart its boundaries fairly accurately.

Thomas Jefferson was one of the first observers to apply statistical methods (in advance of his era) to comparative climatology. Simultaneous observations made by Jefferson at Monticello and Williamsburg with the help of James Madison (not the president) were analyzed and published in terms of frequencies of winds from different directions and not merely in terms of averages or mean values. Thus, Jefferson could compare climates with a much greater sophistication and more meaningfully, as when he noted how much more often a northeast or northwest wind, or a freezing or adversely high temperature, occurred in the tidewater part of Virginia than in the Piedmont area.

In the 19th century three important forerunners of modern scientific meteorology were William Redfield, James Pollard Espy, and Elias Loomis. Redfield, an engineer and one of the leaders in American science in the middle of the century, in 1821 observed the pattern of fallen trees after a hurricane had struck Connecticut and correctly deduced the rotary, progressive nature of the storm. Ten years later he published the first of a series of papers leading to the first nearly correct mathematical theory and proof of the "law of storms." He also correctly predicted that such storms would rotate in the opposite direction (clockwise) in the Southern Hemisphere because of the rotation of the earth. Espy was the first to attempt (in 1828) an explanation of the initial cause and maintenance of the energy of a cyclonic storm on thermodynamic principles—that is, by means of the heat liberated by condensation of the water vapor as heated air ascends in the center of a storm. He became world famous because of his "convective" theory of clouds and thunderstorms as well as cyclones. Espy also prepared the first long series of daily analyzed weather charts and was the first official government meteorologist in the United States. Loomis, a professor of mathematics at Yale, introduced the modern weather chart. He collected observations from all over the eastern and central states and lower Canada and drew colored charts showing the boundaries of clear, cloudy, rainy, and snowy weather. Some of the features of Loomis' charts are similar to those of modern classical synoptic charts made with the latest theoretical and observational techniques.

M. F. Maury, a naval officer and founder and director of the U.S. Hydrographic Office in Washington, D.C., pioneered in the compilation of marine charts and sailing directions for all the world's oceans (1847), in international cooperation in oceanography and meteorology (1853), and in publication of the first comprehensive popular-scientific textbook on marine meteorology and oceanography—*The Physical Geography of the Sea and Its Meteorology,* which went through eight editions from 1855 to 1861. Maury developed the first global graphic model of the earth's atmospheric and oceanic circulation, based mainly on his analyses of merchant and naval vessel observations on the seven seas. Where he had factual data, his conclusions were correct, but where little or no data existed, he resorted to speculation. In the case of the circulation, pressure, and temperature conditions in the Arctic and Antarctic his conjectures were wrong, as were his hypotheses on the causes of the trade winds and the circulation of the air and sea. However, Maury's pioneer work received so much publicity that it served as a challenge to mathematical physicists in the United States and abroad to improve on his models and explanations of the entire range of geophysical phenomena.

Joseph Henry's work on the various aspects of magnetism and induction helped to usher in the age of electrical technology with the telegraph, which he was the first to employ (1849) for transmitting weather observations to Washington from a network of observers scattered throughout the United States. His pioneer work in telegraphic exchange of weather reports led to the later continental telegraphic networks (1870–71) and subsequent worldwide exchange of reports and warnings from, and to, land, sea, and air—in other words, to modern, scientific meteorology. As the first secretary of the Smithsonian Institution, Henry was not content merely to collect, analyze, and post daily synoptic weather reports. He had the data carefully observed, recorded, submitted, compiled, analyzed, and published for climatological purposes, and he had manuals and guides issued for standardizing observations and ensuring their quality

and accuracy. He also had instruments carefully calibrated and compared with standard instruments of all varieties for physical atmospheric and solar observations. One of the most fundamental contributions of Henry and of subsequent scientific pioneers in the Smithsonian Institution was in the study of the light and heat radiated by the sun and received at various places on earth, at sea level and at high altitudes. These scientists not only developed instruments capable of measuring solar heat in various areas of the spectrum to a sufficient degree of sensitivity to detect day-to-day changes but also calculated normal and abnormal solar heat emission, especially from or during sunspots and other solar events. The Smithsonian standard instruments have become the basis for worldwide comparisons of instruments and observations.

An obscure professor of physics in Tennessee, William Ferrel, published his first classical paper on motions in the atmosphere in 1856. Although this paper constituted an extremely lucid exposition of the mechanical forces acting on air parcels moving on a rotating earth in the presence of such modifying forces as heating from below in the tropics, cooling in the Arctic, and evaporation and condensation of water vapor, little attention was paid to Ferrel's work until 1886. His models include those of the earth's planetary circulation and, by extension, of the effects of this circulation on pressure, temperature, and weather and climate, as well as on the monsoons, trade winds, cyclones, tornadoes, waterspouts, and thunderstorms and on the composition of the atmosphere. Ferrel is recognized in Europe, even more than in the United States, as the father of modern dynamic meteorology and oceanography.

Cleveland Abbe, another mathematician turned astronomer and meteorologist and the first government weather forecaster, encouraged a generation of scientists, including Ferrel, through his research laboratory in Washington, D.C.

The 20th century saw the development in Europe of the Norwegian School of Hydrodynamic Meteorology and Oceanography and in the United States of numerical prediction (computer forecasting), which began with the work of L. F. Richardson during the first two decades of the century and evolved into the computer models and forecasting method of the 1950's and 1960's. The contributions of Carl-Gustav A. Rossby and other contemporary associates of V. and J. Bjerknes (father and son), Sverre Petterssen, Tor Bergeron, and others, first in Bergen, Norway, and from 1925 to the 1960's in the United States

(Massachusetts Institute of Technology, University of Chicago, and the University of California, Los Angeles), Norway, and Sweden, vastly improved the models of atmospheric motions, thermodynamics, precipitation and cloud-physics processes, air masses, fronts, hurricanes, severe storms, and the water-vapor cycle (ocean-atmosphere-continent) and ultimately resulted in more successful prediction of disastrous, as well as normal, weather phenomena.

[James Espy, *Philosophy of Storms;* William Ferrel, *A Popular Treatise on the Winds;* Joseph Henry, *Smithsonian Institution Annual Reports* (1849, 1853, 1854); Patrick Hughes, *A Century of Weather Service;* M. F. Maury, *The Physical Geography of the Sea and Its Meteorology.*]

MALCOLM RIGBY

METES AND BOUNDS, the ancient system of indicating boundaries of landholdings by reference to natural objects such as trees and stones, as opposed to the modern system based on astronomical lines as first exemplified in the National Survey System. The metes and bounds system, which prevails generally in that portion of the country settled before 1785, has caused much uncertainty concerning legal titles and boundaries of holdings.

M. M. QUAIFE

METHODISTS. The Methodist church was founded as a separate entity by John Wesley in 1744 in England. He had initially hoped to reawaken the Church of England to the demands of vital piety. Wesley's theology was a warm-hearted evangelicalism that stressed the experience of Christ within the heart, man's capacity to accept Christ's offer of redemption, and the need for a disciplined life. In his later years Wesley came to believe in the possibility of entire sanctification or holiness (a state of perfection) and taught that it should be the goal of every Christian. This latter doctrine has contributed to many of the divisions within Methodism.

Methodist ideas entered the American colonies informally at first, notably through the efforts of Robert Strawbridge and Philip Embury, and their success prompted Wesley to send Richard Broadman and Joseph Pilmoor to America in 1769. Two years later he sent Francis Asbury, who was to become the great apostle of early Methodism in America. At first, Methodism was an extremely small movement that existed on the fringes of the Anglican church, but after the revolutionary war, the Methodists completely separated from that body. The Christmas Con-

ference, held in Baltimore in 1784, marks the beginning of the Methodist church in America. At that meeting sixty preachers joined with Richard Vassey, Richard Whitcoat, and Thomas Coke, delegates from Wesley, in ordaining Francis Asbury and establishing an order for the church. The conference decided on a form of government by deacons, elders, and superintendents (later bishops); adopted the Book of Discipline, which regulated the life of the church and its members; and elected Coke and Asbury as its first superintendents.

Almost immediately after the Christmas Conference, Methodism entered a period of rapid expansion. The system of circuit riders, which Wesley had experimented with in England, met the need for clergymen in outlying regions and allowed relatively uneducated men to enter the ministry. Wherever the circuit rider could gather a crowd, he would stop, preach a sermon, and organize a Methodist class to continue the work until he was able to return. Methodist theology was also easy for the average man to understand, and the Methodist emphasis on discipline was invaluable to communities that were far from the ordinary restraints of civilization. The Methodist combination of simplicity, organization, and lay participation not only made it the largest Protestant denomination but also decisively influenced the other frontier churches. Other denominations, even those of Calvinist background, were forced to accept elements of Methodist theory and practice in order to survive.

The 19th century was a period in which the Methodists, like many other American denominations, experienced internal division. The question of slavery, an important issue for churches located in both the North and the South, led to the formation of three separate ecclesiastical bodies: the Methodist Episcopal church (1844); the Methodist Episcopal church, South (1844); and the Wesleyan Methodist Connection, a small antislavery church founded in 1843. After the Civil War most black Methodists formed their own denominations. In the same period, the increasingly middle-class nature of the church contributed to disputes over the issue of entire sanctification, and the lower-class membership largely withdrew into the "Holiness" or "Pentecostal" movement.

In the 20th century, Methodism has been involved in both the ecumenical movement and the Social Gospel. The Methodist Social Creed was adopted by the Federal Council of Churches in 1908 as its own statement of social principles. Methodism has also begun to heal the divisions within its own ranks. In 1939 the Methodist Episcopal church; the Methodist Episcopal church, South; and the Methodist Protestant church merged. In 1968 this church merged with the Evangelical United Brethren to form the United Methodist church.

The principal Methodist groups and their 1974 membership figures are United Methodist church, 10,192,265 members; African Methodist Episcopal church, 1,500,000 members; African Methodist Episcopal Zion church, 1,024,974 members; African Union First Colored Methodist Protestant church, 8,000 members; Christian Methodist Episcopal church, 466,718 members; Evangelical Methodist church, 10,519 members; Free Methodist church of North America, 65,066 members; Fundamental Methodist church, 722 members; Primitive Methodist church, U.S.A., 11,945 members; Reformed Methodist Union Episcopal church, 5,000 members; Reformed Zion Union Apostolic church, 16,000 members; Southern Methodist church, 9,917 members; Union American Methodist Episcopal church, 28,000 members.

[Emory Stevens Bucke and others, eds., *History of American Methodism;* Hunter Dickinson Farish, *The Circuit Rider Dismounts: A Social History of Southern Methodism;* Gerald K. Kennedy, *The Methodist Way of Life;* Ralph Ernst Morrow, *Northern Methodism and Reconstruction;* Warren William Sweet, *Methodism in American History.*]
GLENN T. MILLER

METROPOLITAN STATISTICAL AREAS, STANDARD. *See* **Population.**

MEUSE-ARGONNE OFFENSIVE (Sept. 26–Nov. 11, 1918). In April 1917, when the United States declared war against the Central Powers, the contending European powers had long been stalemated in trench warfare. The erstwhile subtleties of strategy and tactics had vanished into grim attrition. The entry of the United States was a true light at the end of the tunnel, but hostilities persisted for another bloody year and a half before the American Expeditionary Forces (AEF) were ready for a major part in the decisive Allied offensive.

When the war began in 1914, U.S. regulars consisted of 5,033 officers and 93,511 men—not quite enough to have filled four divisions of the 1917 organization. The National Guard had about 67,000 men; the U.S. Marines, a mere 10,386. The sinking of the *Lusitania* in May 1915 angered Congress into the creation of reserves and some expansion of the standing forces, but realistic expansion awaited the declaration of war.

French and British leaders wanted the existing American regiments to be replacements for veteran Allied divisions, and the new units to consist of infantrymen and machine gunners. Controversy smoldered over the U.S. decision—resolutely embodied by Gen. John J. Pershing—to build the AEF into a power able to assume responsibility for a part of the front. Pershing's original goal of 1 million troops was in fact tripled.

During the seemingly interminable buildup, American units reaching France were first trained by Allied instructors and then given front experience in quiet sectors, starting near Saint-Mihiel on Feb. 5, 1918. In emergencies created by German offensives, some Americans fought under Allied commanders. Units performed well at Lunéville in October-November 1917 and at Seicheprey in April 1918. Meeting the Champagne-Marne crisis of May-July 1918, Americans at Château-Thierry and Belleau Wood sealed a German break through the French lines. In these operations, the way the French command squandered American lives, particularly the marine half of the U.S. regular Second Division, by ordering open attack rather than a dug-in defense was taken as vindication of Pershing's obdurate insistence on making an organic, self-contained American force. Compromising by the gradual allocation of about one division in every three to serve under the French, the British, or the Belgians, Pershing by early August had gathered nineteen divisions to form the First American Army, responsible for nearly 100 miles of the Lorraine front. Personally directing the successful September operation that erased the Saint-Mihiel salient, Pershing made ready for what proved to be the grand Allied offensive that ended the war.

On Sept. 26, 1918, the First Army jumped off on a twenty-five-mile front, advancing northward with the ultimate goal of reaching Sedan, thirty-five miles distant and the strategic hub of German lateral railroad communications maintaining their defense. Precipitating heavy combat, the American left deployed via the Argonne forest, the center for the towering Montfaucon bastion, and the right deployed along the marshes of the Meuse River. The long-standing German defenses were in four lines ten miles deep. Continual rain compounded difficulties of terrain and severely hampered action and supply. The third German line checked the advance on Oct. 3. The results to that date—such as destroying sixteen German divisions—were far better than the French had ever managed to win over the same ground but less than Pershing had hoped for. He did not know that Field

Marshal Paul von Hindenburg was impressed into advising Kaiser Wilhelm II to seek peace, while Gen. Erich F. W. Ludendorff was warning the Reichstag that defeat was inexorably nearing.

During a relatively slack period while he awaited fresh troops and supplies, Pershing formed the Second Army under Robert L. Bullard and gave the First Army to Hunter Liggett. Pershing in the meantime had been granted equality with the commander in chief of the French armies, Henri Philippe Pétain, and the British commander in chief of expeditionary forces in France and Flanders, Douglas Haig. On the American front, by Oct. 31 the third German line had been fragmented by the Americans. In the clearing of the deadly Argonne was the saga of the "Lost Battalion" and the unparalleled exploit of Sgt. Alvin C. York.

All along the western front, the Germans were near exhaustion. A fourth of their divisions, forty-seven, had been committed in a hopeless attempt to halt the American advance. On Nov. 1, a renewed attack carried the Americans six miles through the last German line and onto the heights of Barricourt. Capture of that high ground compelled the Germans to withdraw west of the Meuse. In retreat and disarray, German troops still fought sharply, but their cause everywhere to the English Channel was being rendered militarily chaotic.

In the climactic Meuse-Argonne offensive, Pershing deployed twenty-one divisions, comprising some 1.2 million men, of whom one-tenth were casualties in capturing 48,800 prisoners and 1,424 guns. Overshadowed by the giant American drive, ten U.S. divisions simultaneously fought under Allied control in other sectors. Of two who, under the British, took the maze of Saint-Quentin, the 107th Infantry Regiment on Sept. 29 suffered the heaviest one-day losses of all U.S. units. Of two divisions in the French Fourth Army, the redoubtable Second Division of regulars particularly distinguished itself in capturing Mont Blanc ridge. On Armistice Day, as supreme U.S. commander, Pershing had 1,981,701 men.

[J. M. Hanson, *The Stars and Stripes,* and *Order of Battle of the United States Land Forces in the World War;* Frederick Palmer, *Our Greatest Battle;* J. J. Pershing, *My Experiences in the World War;* Laurence Stallings, *The Doughboys;* T. S. Stamps and V. J. Esposito, *A Short Military History of World War I.*]

R. W. DALY

MEXICAN ASSOCIATION, one of several similar organizations formed to secure the liberation of Mexico from Spanish rule. Organized in 1805, it consisted of some 300 men who were interested in reviving the commerce of New Orleans, securing the spread of American ideas, and building a sentiment favorable to the United States. Any undertaking that gave promise of furthering these objectives was readily supported. Aaron Burr hoped to utilize the Mexican Association in his land conquest conspiracy of 1806. Despite government opposition, the association continued to function actively and was one of the backers of the filibustering expeditions of Francisco Javier Mina and of James Long.

[W. F. McCaleb, *The Burr Conspiracy.*]
THOMAS ROBSON HAY

MEXICAN BOUNDARY. The history of the boundary between the United States and Mexico may be said to begin in 1803 with the Louisiana Purchase. The frontier of the United States marched with the possessions of Spain along the western limits of the Louisiana Territory; but the western boundary of the Louisiana Territory was not, either then or thereafter, internationally or juridically delimited.

After prolonged negotiations, a conventional line was established between American and Spanish sovereignties by the Adams-Onís Treaty of Feb. 22, 1819. The boundary fixed by that treaty, with a reference to John Melish's map of 1818, began in the Gulf of Mexico at the mouth of the Sabine River, ran up that river to the 32nd parallel, from there north to and up the Red River to 100° longitude, and then north to and up the Arkansas River. From the source of the Arkansas the line extended north to the 42nd parallel and followed that parallel from near 109° longitude (in Wyoming) west to the Pacific. John Quincy Adams had given up the American claim to Texas and in return had acquired for the United States the Spanish rights to the Oregon country, north of California, as well as a definitive cession of all Spanish territory east of the Mississippi, that is, the Floridas.

The treaty of 1819 did not go into effect until Feb. 22, 1821, the same year Mexico gained its independence; so the line of the treaty of 1819 became the first boundary between the United States and Mexico. The treaty of Jan. 12, 1828, which did not enter into force until Apr. 5, 1832, confirmed this boundary. Before survey of the line, events intervened; the independence of Texas (Mar. 2, 1836) was recognized by the United States on Mar. 7, 1837. Accordingly, the boundary of the treaty of 1819 was not demarcated either with Spain or with Mexico.

The boundary between the United States and Mexico during the period of Texas independence (1836–45) is not internationally definable; not only was there great divergence of view as to the western and northern limits of Texas, but Mexico never recognized the independence of Texas, and only a brief interval separated the admission of Texas into the Union (Dec. 29, 1845) and the outbreak of the Mexican War (May 13, 1846).

The boundary of the treaty of peace, signed at Guadalupe Hidalgo on Feb. 2, 1848, ran from the Gulf of Mexico up the Rio Grande to the southern boundary of New Mexico, "which runs north of the town called Paso" (Ciudad Juárez), and from there along the southern and western boundaries of New Mexico (as those boundaries were laid down in John Disturnell's map of 1847) to the intersection of the western boundary of New Mexico with the Gila River. The boundary then proceeded down the Gila to its junction with the Colorado, and from there by a straight line to a point on the Pacific one marine league due south of the southernmost point of the port of San Diego (as shown on a plan of that port drawn in 1782).

Owing to inaccuracies in Disturnell's map, controversy arose during the demarcation of the boundary between the Rio Grande and the Colorado. The Mexican boundary commissioner proposed a line beginning on the Rio Grande at 32°22' north latitude (this was the latitude of the southern boundary of New Mexico at the Rio Grande according to Disturnell's map), running from there about one degree west to the Mimbres, up that stream to its source, and from there by direct line to the Gila. The line agreed upon by the two boundary commissioners (Apr. 24, 1851) ran from the Rio Grande at 32°22' three degrees west, and from there due north to the Gila; but the surveyor of the United States, whose assent was necessary under the treaty, did not accept the line of the commissioners and contended (correctly) that the beginning point at the Rio Grande should be at 31°52' north latitude, according to the position of the Chihuahua–New Mexico boundary on Disturnell's map relative to the true latitude of Paso. This starting point is some thirty miles south and a few miles east of the point on the Rio Grande at latitude 32°22'; the line of the surveyor ran from the Rio Grande at 31°52' three degrees west, then due north to the Gila. The territorial difference between the line of the surveyor and the line of the commissioners was about 6,000 square miles. Congress approved the line of the surveyor; the work of demarcation ceased; the boundary of the United States with Mexico between the Rio Grande and the Colorado under the Treaty of Guadalupe Hidalgo was never internationally agreed on.

Dispute as to the boundary from the Rio Grande to the Colorado under the Treaty of Guadalupe Hidalgo was ended by the Gadsden Purchase. By the Gadsden Treaty of Dec. 30, 1853, as it went into force on June 30, 1854, after extensive Senate amendments, the line westward from the Rio Grande ran, as it does now, from 31°47' north latitude due west one hundred miles, then south to 31°20' north latitude, and from there along that parallel to 111° west longitude, then going in a straight line to a point on the Colorado River twenty English miles below the junction of the Gila and Colorado, and, finally, up the middle of the Colorado some twenty miles to a point nearly seven miles to the west of the junction of the Gila and Colorado and about ten miles by water below that junction, meeting at that point the boundary from the Colorado to the Pacific. That line of the Gadsden Treaty is now the boundary between Mexico and the states of New Mexico and Arizona, and throughout its entire course from the Rio Grande to the Colorado is well to the south of any possible line under the Treaty of Guadalupe Hidalgo. No change from the treaty of 1848 was made by the Gadsden Treaty in the line from the Pacific to the Colorado River (the southern boundary of California) or in the boundary of the Rio Grande between Texas and Mexico, from 31°47' to the Gulf of Mexico.

The boundary resulting from the treaties of 1848 and 1853 remains the boundary between the two countries, except for the reciprocal elimination, pursuant to various agreements, of *bancos,* which have been defined as "small tracts of land in the valleys of the Rio Grande and the Colorado which are isolated by the river when it cuts through a sharp bend and forms a new channel." Because of the shifting course of the Rio Grande a strip of land known as the Chamizal tract of about 600 acres around El Paso, Tex., and Ciudad Juárez, in Mexico, was the subject of dispute until 1963, when, by the Chamizal Treaty, Mexico received 437 acres and the United States, 133 acres. An artificial riverbed was dug to prevent the Rio Grande from shifting again.

[Robert V. Hine, *Bartlett's West: Drawing the Mexican Boundary.*]

HUNTER MILLER

MEXICAN CESSION. *See* **Guadalupe Hidalgo, Treaty of.**

MEXICAN DECREE of Apr. 6, 1830, sought to save Texas for Mexico by stopping immigration from the United States and substituting for it an inflow of native Mexicans, and perhaps Europeans. Garrisons were sent to Texas to enforce the law. This abrupt change in policy so adversely affected the Americans already in Texas that to a large extent they ignored its provisions and resorted to violence. The American colonists declared the independence of Texas from Mexico on Mar. 2, 1836.

[Alleine Howren, "Causes and Origin of the Decree of April 6, 1830," *Southwestern Historical Quarterly,* vol. 16.]

JIM DAN HILL

MEXICAN GULF PORTS, BLOCKADE OF (1846–48). War with Mexico was declared on May 13, 1846. Not long afterward Commodore David Conner, in command of the Home Squadron, was ordered to blockade or seize the Mexican Gulf ports. The first success was the capture of Frontera at the mouth of the Tabasco River, on Oct. 23, by Capt. Matthew Calbraith Perry, commanding the *Mississippi* and six gunboats. He also forced the state of Tabasco, eighty miles up the river, to surrender on Oct. 26, but the same day returned to Frontera. On Nov. 14 Conner captured Tampico. On Dec. 8 the brig *Somers,* commanded by Lt. Raphael Semmes, while chasing a blockade runner off Veracruz, capsized with the loss of about forty men. Conner was replaced, on Mar. 20 during combined naval and military operations against Veracruz, by Perry, who was considered a more aggressive officer. Only a week later the city surrendered to Perry and Gen. Winfield Scott. Meanwhile the gunboat *Hunter* was lost in a gale on Mar. 21, though all were saved. Lt. C. G. Hunter, commanding the *Scourge,* captured Alvarado on Mar. 30, prematurely against orders, and for this was dismissed from the service. Perry proceeded with his squadron of sixteen vessels to Tuspan. On Apr. 18 the town, located five miles above the mouth of the Tuspan River, was captured by ships' barges towed by six small gunboats. Leaving two vessels here, Perry sailed with the rest to Frontera. Ascending the river again to Tabasco on June 15 and 16, Perry, despite serious resistance from the fortifications, took and held the place. With all Mexican Gulf ports taken, Perry's squadrons cruised up and down the coast until the signing of the Guadalupe Hidalgo Treaty on Feb. 2, 1848; yellow fever had proved a more dangerous foe than the Mexicans.

[Edward M. Barrows, *The Great Commodore: Exploits of Matthew Calbraith Perry;* Charles Lee Lewis, *Admiral Franklin Buchanan.*]

CHARLES LEE LEWIS

MEXICAN OIL CONTROVERSY. Article 27 of a new constitution adopted in Mexico in 1917 asserted Mexican public ownership over subsoil resources, beginning a series of disputes over exploitation of petroleum deposits. Involved were the Mexican government, British and U.S. oil companies, and the companies' governments, which provided the firms with diplomatic support and legal protection as "nationals."

Until 1938 the companies maintained their essential positions despite Mexican efforts to dispossess them. In 1936, however, a serious labor dispute developed and the U.S. companies, more intransigent than the British, rejected a settlement approved by the highest Mexican labor board. President Lázaro Cárdenas ordered the expropriation of the companies' concessions on Mar. 18, 1938, a day still celebrated in Mexico as marking "economic independence." It complements the political independence from Spain, which is marked by the *grito de Dolores* celebrated in Mexico on Sept. 16 of each year.

Cárdenas' action was bold and novel. The companies claimed their investments and land holdings were worth nearly $500 million. Washington's reaction was uncertain, but the companies themselves brought economic pressure to bear. Secretary of State Cordell Hull, in a note of Mar. 26, 1938, requested "a prompt reply" to his request for "just compensation" to the companies. Cárdenas agreed to provide compensation, but as the result of an unorthodox diplomatic action by American Ambassador Josephus Daniels, Cárdenas did not reply to the note. Further, Cárdenas refused arbitration as a means of deciding the amount of compensation, and the companies, other than Sinclair, refused to accept any other method.

After the outbreak of World War II, Hull, with the strong support of the U.S. defense agencies and in spite of the disapproval of the remaining oil companies, agreed to solve the compensation issue by a board of commissioners consisting of one Mexican and one U.S. citizen. This agreement was reached on Nov. 19, 1941, three weeks before the attack on Pearl Harbor, and it made possible the use of Mexican airfields for refueling U.S. airplanes on their way to the Panama Canal. The commission members, Manuel J.

Zavala and Morris L. Cooke, agreed in April 1942 that Mexico should pay $24 million to the United States companies, and a later settlement was also reached with British companies.

[E. David Cronon, *Josephus Daniels in Mexico;* Josephus Daniels, *Shirt-Sleeve Diplomat.*]

BRYCE WOOD

MEXICAN WAR (1846–48) had remote or indirect causes in the increasing distrust arising from diplomatic indiscretions, quibblings, and misunderstandings of the first decade of American-Mexican diplomatic relations. Its more immediate cause was the annexation of Texas, which the Mexican government regarded as equivalent to a declaration of war and which was followed by withdrawal of the Mexican minister from Washington, D.C., in March 1845 and the severance of diplomatic relations. Another cause was the American claims against Mexico arising from injuries to and property losses of American citizens in the Mexican revolutions.

The American government strove to preserve peace. It adopted a conciliatory policy and made the first advances toward renewal of diplomatic relations. Recognizing that the chief aim of American foreign policy was the annexation of California, President James K. Polk planned to connect with that policy the adjustment of all difficulties with Mexico, including the dispute over jurisdiction in the territory between the Nueces River and the Rio Grande.

In September 1845, assured through a confidential agent that the new Mexican government of José Joaquín Herrera would welcome an American minister, and acting on the suggestion of James Buchanan, secretary of state, Polk appointed John Slidell as envoy-minister on a secret peaceful mission to secure California and New Mexico for $15 million to $20 million if possible, or for $40 million if necessary—terms later changed by secret instructions to $5 million for New Mexico and $25 million for California. In October, before Slidell's departure, Buchanan sent to American consul Thomas O. Larkin at Monterey, Calif., a confidential statement of the American "goodwill" policy to acquire California without war and with the spontaneous cooperation of the Californians.

Mexico refused to reopen diplomatic relations. In January 1846, after the first news that the Mexican government under various pretexts had refused to receive Slidell, partly on the ground that questions of boundary and claims should be separated, Polk ordered Gen. Zachary Taylor to advance from Corpus Christi, Tex., to the Rio Grande, resulting shortly in conflicts with Mexican troops (*see* Palo Alto, Battle of; Resaca de la Palma, Battle of).

On May 11, after arrival of news of the Mexican advance across the Rio Grande and the skirmish with Taylor's troops, Polk submitted to Congress a skillful war message, stating that war existed and that it was begun by Mexico on American soil. He obtained prompt action authorizing a declaration of war, apparently on the ground that such action was justified by the delinquencies, obstinacy, and hostilities of the Mexican government; and he proceeded to formulate plans for military and naval operations to advance his purpose to obtain Mexican acceptance of his overtures for peace negotiations.

The military plans included an expedition under Col. Stephen W. Kearny to New Mexico and from there to California, supplemented by an expedition to Chihuahua; an advance across the Rio Grande into Mexico by troops under Taylor to occupy the neighboring provinces; and a possible later campaign of invasion of the Mexican interior from Veracruz.

In these plans Polk was largely influenced by assurances received in February from Col. A. J. Atocha, a friend of Antonio López de Santa Anna, then in exile from Mexico, to the effect that the latter, if aided in plans to return from Havana, Cuba, to Mexico, would recover his Mexican leadership and cooperate in a peaceful arrangement to cede Mexican territory to the United States. In June, Polk entered into negotiations with Santa Anna through a brother of Slidell, receiving verification of Atocha's assurances. Polk had already sent a confidential order to Commodore David Conner, who on Aug. 16 permitted Santa Anna to pass through the coast blockade to Veracruz (*see* Mexican War, Navy in). Having arrived in Mexico, Santa Anna promptly began his program, which resulted in his own quick restoration to power, but he gave no evidences whatever of his professed pacific intentions.

On July 3, 1846, the small expedition under Kearny received orders to go via the Santa Fe Trail from Fort Leavenworth, Kans., to occupy New Mexico (*see* Doniphan's Expedition; Kearny's March to California). It reached Santa Fe on Aug. 18, and a part of the force (300 men) led by Kearny marched to the Pacific at San Diego. From there it arrived (Jan. 10, 1847) at Los Angeles to complete the work begun at Sonoma by insurgents under John Charles

Frémont, and at Monterey and San Francisco Bay by Commodore John Drake Sloat, shortly succeeded by Robert Field Stockton.

The expedition of Taylor into northern Mexico, which was organized to carry out the plan for an advance southward into the interior of Mexico, began to cross the Rio Grande to Matamoros on May 18, 1846, and advanced to the strongly fortified city of Monterrey, which after an attack was evacuated by Mexican forces on Sept. 28. Later, in February 1847, at Buena Vista, Taylor stubbornly resisted and defeated the attack of Santa Anna's Mexican relief expedition.

Soon thereafter the theater of war shifted to Veracruz, from which the direct route to the Mexican capital seemed to present less difficulty than the northern route. In deciding on the campaign from Veracruz to Mexico City, Polk probably was influenced by the news of Sloat's occupation of California, which reached him on Sept. 1, 1846. In November 1846, Polk offered the command of the Mexico City expedition to Gen. Winfield Scott, who promptly accepted. After the capture of the fortress of Veracruz on Mar. 29, 1847, Scott led the army of invasion westward via Jalapa to Pueblo, which he entered on May 15, and from which he began (Aug. 7) his advance to the mountain pass of Cerro Gordo.

Coincident with Scott's operations against Veracruz, Polk began new peace negotiations with Mexico through a "profoundly secret mission." On Apr. 15 Buchanan had sent Nicholas P. Trist as a confidential peace agent to accompany Scott's army. In August, after the battles of Contreras and Churubusco, Trist arranged an armistice through Scott as a preliminary step for a diplomatic conference to discuss peace terms—a conference that began on Aug. 27 and closed on Sept. 7 by Mexican rejection of the terms offered. Scott promptly resumed his advance. After hard fighting (Sept. 7–11) at the battles of Molino del Rey and Chapultepec, he captured Mexico City on Sept. 14 and with his staff entered the palace, over which he hoisted the American flag.

Practically, the war was ended. Santa Anna, after resigning his presidential office, made an unsuccessful attempt to strike at the American garrison Scott had left at Pueblo, but he was driven off and obliged to flee from Mexico.

The chief remaining American problem was to find a government with enough power to negotiate a treaty of peace to prevent the danger of American annexation of all Mexico. Fortunately, Trist was still with the army and in close touch with the situation at the captured capital. Although recalled, he determined

(Dec. 3–4) to assume the responsibility of remaining to renew efforts to conclude a treaty of peace even at the risk of disavowal by his government. After some delay, he was able to conclude with the Mexican commissioners a treaty in accord with the instructions that had been annulled by his recall. The chief negotiations were conducted at Mexico City, but the treaty was completed and signed on Feb. 2, 1848, at the neighboring town of Guadalupe Hidalgo. By its terms, which provided for cessation of hostilities, the United States agreed to pay $15 million for New Mexico and California. Polk received the treaty on Feb. 19 and promptly decided to submit it to the Senate, which approved it on Mar. 10 by a vote of thirty-eight to fourteen. Ratifications were exchanged on May 30, 1848.

Among the chief results of the war were expansion of American territory; increased American interest in the problems of the Caribbean and the Pacific and in the opening and control of isthmian interoceanic transit routes at Panama, Nicaragua, and Tehuantepec; and ebullitions of "manifest destiny" in the period of "young America" from 1848 to 1860. In domestic affairs the large acquisition of territory was reflected in political controversies relating to the slavery problem (see Compromise of 1850).

[Seymour V. Connor and Odre B. Faulk, *North America Divided: The Mexican War, 1846–1848;* Otis A. Singleton, *The Mexican War;* George Winston Smith and Charles Judah, eds., *Chronicles of the Gringos: The United States Army in the Mexican War, 1846–1848.*]

J. M. CALLAHAN

MEXICAN WAR, NAVY IN. The dry cactus barrens of southern Texas together with the wider mountainous wastes of northern Mexico constituted a greater barrier to military invasion of Mexico from the United States than did the Mexican armies. Gen. Zachary Taylor, from his navy-supported base at Brownsville, Tex., easily vanquished, or drove off, all military opposition on his front but experienced supply troubles as soon as his lines of communication became extended. In Washington, D.C., it was decided the main effort should be made from a naval-supported base at Veracruz, in eastern Mexico, hundreds of miles closer to Mexico City than Brownsville.

Meanwhile the Pacific Squadron was circumventing distance and wilderness in another direction by seizing Monterey, San Diego, San Francisco, and other key points on the Pacific. These seizures guaranteed American possession of California.

Thereafter the squadron not only rendered mobility, reinforcements, and indispensable aid to the military commands of Stephen Watts Kearny and John C. Frémont, but also blockaded, threatened, and harassed the principal Mexican seaports on the Pacific.

While Taylor was invading from the north, and long before Gen. Winfield Scott's Veracruz disembarkation on Mar. 9, 1847, men-of-war under Commodore David Conner were engaged in blockading Tampico, Veracruz, and lesser Gulf ports. Raids by landing parties were frequent. The most pretentious expedition was the capture by Capt. Matthew C. Perry of Frontera and Tabasco. During the nineteen-day siege of Veracruz, the navy rendered invaluable assistance by covering landing parties, bombarding forts, and providing a siege battery.

[K. Jack Bauer, *Surf-boats and Horse Marines: U.S. Naval Operations in the Mexican War, 1846–1848.*]

JIM DAN HILL

MEXICAN WAR CLAIMS were settled by a commission created under a convention of 1867 with the Mexican government. American citizens presented 1,017 claims against Mexico amounting to $470,126,613, and Mexicans countered with 998 claims totaling $86,661,891.15. To the former, 186 awards, totaling $4,125,622.20, were allowed; to the latter, 167 awards amounting to $150,498.41. Claims against the United States arose largely from Indian depredations and excesses committed by American soldiers. Those presented against Mexico were largely for the seizure and destruction of property, forced loans, illegal arrests and imprisonments, and murder. The work of the commission was not completed until November 1876.

[J. F. Rippy, *The United States and Mexico.*]

FRANK FREIDEL

MEXICO, CONFEDERATE MIGRATION TO. After the Civil War many Confederate military and civil leaders, despondent and dreading Reconstruction, sought homes in Mexico. The exact number who went to Mexico will probably never be known, but an estimate of 2,500 seems reasonable. Southerners settled in all parts of the empire—on farms, in seaport towns, and in villages of the interior. Colonies were planted in the provinces of Chihuahua, San Luis Potosí, Jalisco, and Sonora. The best known was the Cordova Valley Colony (*see* Carlotta, Confederate Colony of).

Ferdinand Maximilian (*see* Mexico, French in) encouraged migration to Mexico by offering low-priced public lands, free transportation for the needy, and toleration for the Protestant churches and schools, but the movement failed because of unforeseen circumstances. There was a hostile northern and southern press; the U.S. government opposed the movement; and the settlers had little cash. The disturbed political conditions under Maximilian's regime aided in the downfall of the project. By 1867 most of the adventurers had returned to the United States.

[George D. Harmon, "Confederate Migration to Mexico," *Hispanic American Historical Review*, vol. 17.]

GEORGE D. HARMON

MEXICO, FRENCH IN. In October 1861, England, France, and Spain signed a treaty by which they undertook coercive action to secure reparation for their subjects and the execution of certain obligations contracted by Mexico. They agreed to refrain from intervention in Mexico's internal affairs and neither to make any territorial aggrandizements nor to influence its form of government. Spanish armed forces promptly seized Veracruz. After French and English soldiers arrived on the Mexican coast, a conference of commanders of the allied forces held at Orizaba could not agree. The English and the Spaniards decided to withdraw from Mexico. The French army, which was strongly reinforced, captured Mexico City in June 1862. The invaders convoked an assembly of notables, which decided in favor of the establishment in Mexico of a monarchy headed by Ferdinand Maximilian, archduke of Austria, who had been selected by Napoleon III.

Attracted by the glittering dream of a throne in a fair land over which his ancestors had ruled, Maximilian accepted the invitation. On Apr. 10, 1864, he signed the Convention of Miramar, which specified that Napoleon III would support the exotic empire until 1867. After Maximilian's arrival in Mexico, he sought to secure recognition by the United States, but that government continued to support the republican leader, President Benito Juárez, who took refuge on the northern frontiers of his country.

The fortunes of the empire of Maximilian largely depended on the outcome of the Civil War. During that struggle the United States made mild protests against French intervention in Mexico, but after the defeat of the South, the French secretary of foreign affairs was informed by Secretary of State William H. Seward that the "presence and operations of a French army in Mexico and the maintenance of an authority there resting upon force and not the free will of the people in Mexico is a cause of serious concern to the United States." In vain did France attempt to secure the recognition of Maximilian's government by the United States or to postpone the withdrawal of its troops. Finally, on Mar. 12, 1867, the last detachment of French soldiers left Mexican soil. The soldiers of Juárez soon captured Maximilian, who was deserted by his Mexican followers. The unfortunate prince was court-martialed, and, despite the pleas of the United States for mercy, was shot on June 19, 1867. Thus a clear violation of the Monroe Doctrine was repelled, and republican government was restored in Mexico.

[E. C. Corti, *Maximilian and Charlotte of Mexico;* D. Perkins, *The Monroe Doctrine, 1826–1867.*]

WILLIAM SPENCE ROBERTSON

MEXICO, GULF OF, which by its form and position has had a profound influence on the climate of the southeastern part of the United States and all the eastern coast, has also had a large influence in American national history, especially on American foreign policy. Its early importance was determined by the Spanish search for a possible water passage through the continental barrier, the Spanish settlement at Havana, Cuba, in 1519, the expedition of Hernando Cortes into the interior from Veracruz, Mexico, and the subsequent discovery of gold in Mexico. Later it was also influenced by several settlements along the northern coast, a Spanish permanent settlement at Pensacola in 1696, and French settlements at Mobile in 1702 and New Orleans in 1718.

Its subsequent increased importance was especially due to its relations as the receiver of the Mississippi drainage and as the natural commercial outlet of the trans-Allegheny West. Its strategic geographic importance was recognized by the British seizure of Havana in 1762 and by the British colonial opposition to the surrender of Havana in 1763, by the American hope to secure the Floridas from England in the Revolution, by Napoleon's dreams of a circum-Gulf colonial empire before 1803, by the American acquisition of Louisiana by purchase in 1803 in order to secure for the increasing American trans-Allegheny settlements free access to the Gulf via the mouth of the Mississippi, and by the consequent American claim to the entire Gulf coast from the Perdido on the east to the Rio Grande on the west.

In 1819, influenced in part by the British use of Spanish harbors on the Gulf in the War of 1812, the American government obtained a cession of all the Floridas (*see* Adams-Onís Treaty) in order to secure the safety of a logical American abutment on the Gulf and the complete control of the American rivers that reached the Gulf through this territory. The United States also wanted to prevent the danger of a transfer of the strategic territory by Spain to some other European power. In the decade of 1825–35, the United States unsuccessfully negotiated to extend the Gulf frontage west of the Sabine River; in 1845 it was able to extend it to the Rio Grande by annexation of the independent state of Texas.

As a result of increasing interest in the Gulf after it obtained control of the mouth of the Mississippi, the American government had a vital interest in the political condition and destiny of Cuba, which guarded the commercial portal water between the Gulf and the Atlantic and which was regarded as the strategic key to the Gulf, and therefore to the Mississippi.

After the Mexican War and the subsequent opening of practical transit routes across Panama and Central America, American interest in the Gulf was extended by the increasing use of the Yucatán Channel, the natural line of communication between the mouth of the Mississippi and the new interoceanic transits. In the 1850's such prominent southern quixotic leaders as Robert Toombs and Judah P. Benjamin urged the acquisition of Cuba (*see* Ostend Manifesto) as a means of making the Gulf a *mare clausum*, on the ground that the Gulf was the reservoir of the Mississippi and must be practically an American lake for purposes of American security.

The commercial and political interests and relations that were influenced or determined by geographic conditions of the Gulf region reached a logical consequence in the expulsion of Spain (1898) from its last foothold in the Western Hemisphere (*see* Spanish-American War), in the later significant advance of American influence and control and ascendancy in the Caribbean and in Panama and Central America, and in the subsequent growing commercial importance of the American southern seaboard. The Gulf of Mexico continues to be of great economic significance. In addition to its geographical importance there are vast oil and gas reserves and great supplies of fish and sulfur. During the 1970's approximately 1 million barrels of oil were being taken from the Gulf daily, and several million tons of sulfur were taken annually. By the mid-1970's, however, the Gulf was becoming increasingly polluted with wastes, especially pesticides and other pollutants from the Mississippi River.

[J. M. Callahan, *Cuba and International Relations;* Ellen C. Semple, *American History and Its Geographic Conditions.*]

J. M. CALLAHAN

MEXICO, INDIANS OF. Middle America, in pre-Columbian times, developed a major civilization, comparable to any in such Old World centers as the ancient Near East, India, or China. This civilization depended for its growth on factors of geographic location and of control of food supply for large populations. Location permitted a continuing interchange of ideas between peoples of differing cultures. Similarly, the intensive development of maize farming made for population increase and for the elaborate controls that leisured classes of priests and nobles exerted on production and imposed on the growth of politicolegal systems and religion. The cultural developments of North America north of Mexico pale in comparison with the rich Mexican heritage. Agriculture, invented in Middle America at about the same time it was emerging in the fertile crescent of the Near East, spread slowly northward, reaching the Arizona-New Mexico Southwest, the Gulf area, and the riverine systems associated with the Mississippi Valley. Here and there may be found suggestions of Mexican influences among North American tribes—temple mounds in the lower Mississippi region, for example, and ideas of calendars, the new fire rite, and world renewal. North American hunters show no Mexican influence; the farmers, however, appear to owe their mode of subsistence to southern influences.

The civilization of Mexico did not spring from one people. Over considerable periods of time, considering that the formative phases go back 3,500 years, local and differing cultural systems arose. The Maya, Olmec, Zapotec, Mixtec, and Toltec reflect differing developments in time and space. The Aztec, who spoke a language of the same Uto-Aztecan family as the languages of the North American Great Basin, were viewed as barbarian upstarts. It is known that this group came from the north, conquered, but was assimilated into the existing cultural systems of the Valley of Mexico. Preconquest Mexico represents a complex history of the rise and fall of states and their interrelations.

Mexican achievements were considerable. The tendency in the growth of the various states was to build ceremonial centers rather than cities as such. Maize-raising peasant villages clustered about these centers, a situation in some measure still existing. In such centers, the priests of the Maya, for example, invented a system of writing, developing in this the sole example of New World writing, a script not yet wholly deciphered. Concerned with an agricultural calendar, they, like their counterparts in Egypt and Babylonia, evolved systems of higher mathematics, even inventing, quite independently of the Old World, the algebraic concept of zero. Art and architecture were highly developed, each center among the linguistically and culturally different peoples having its own styles of building, artistic depiction, carving, sculpture, and ceramics.

These special inventions, together with the striking architectural remains such as are seen at Chichén Itzá, Teotihuacán, Monte Albán, and Mitla in Mexico—or, to move into a parallel New World area, in the Peruvian Cuzco and Pachácamac—have suggested to some that Middle American civilization owes its origins to influences from the Old World. But this seems emphatically not to be the case; the prehistory of Middle America is one of a gradually evolving continuum.

[Robert Wauchope, ed., *Handbook of the Indians of Middle America.*]

ROBERT F. SPENCER

MEXICO, PUNITIVE EXPEDITION INTO (1916–17). On Mar. 9, 1916, Francisco (Pancho) Villa, with 485 men, crossed the border from Mexico and raided Columbus, N.Mex., killing 18 people; the raid was the culmination of a series of border troubles involving murder and robbery of Americans by Mexican bandits. In hopes of stopping it, Brig. Gen. John J. Pershing was ordered into the state of Chihuahua in northern Mexico with a force that eventually numbered over 11,000. At the start the United States concluded an agreement with Mexico, giving each country the right to cross the boundary in pursuit of bandits. Mexico understood the agreement to take effect in the event of future raids, whereas the United States interpreted it retroactively, to authorize the Pershing expedition after Villa, which it actually did not. A long series of diplomatic correspondences ensued. Venustiano Carranza's government rightly considered the uninvited Pershing force an infringement of its sovereignty, and the United States rightly considered that something must be done to protect American life and property in the face of chaotic conditions in northern Mexico, since Carranza's government seemed helpless to do so. Mexicans generally were hostile to the expedition, and on two occasions, at Parral on Apr. 12 and at Carrizal on June 21, armed clashes occurred between American and Mexican troops. For a time war seemed imminent. President Woodrow Wilson called out the National Guard of three border states on May 9 and that of the whole United States on June 18. Negotiations between the governments took place from September 1916 to January 1917 but ended without a settlement. The United States ordered Pershing's force withdrawn in February 1917. Although Villa had not been caught, a number of his chieftains had been killed or wounded and his band was generally broken up. The expedition provided valuable training for the national guardsmen on the border and the regular army in Mexico, served as a testing ground for equipment, and demonstrated the command capacity of Pershing, as a result of which he was appointed to head the American Expeditionary Forces in World War I.

[Haldeen Braddy, *Pershing's Mission in Mexico;* Clarence C. Clendenen, *Blood on the Border;* Herbert M. Mason, Jr., *The Great Pursuit.*]

DONALD SMYTHE

MEXICO, RELATIONS WITH. Relations between the United States and Mexico have been marked variously by suspicion, hostility, and friendly cooperation. Contentions have centered on territorial boundaries, claims, trade regulations, and the status of American investments in Mexico. Less frequent periods of harmony have reflected mutual desires for economic advantage and solidarity in resisting extrahemispheric threats.

Boundary problems predominated for thirty years after the United States recognized Mexican independence in 1822. By 1830 some 20,000 Americans had settled in Texas. When Mexico tried to restrict immigration and impose tighter control the Texans rebelled; they won independence in 1836. U.S. annexation of Texas in 1845 led to war the next year. By the Treaty of Guadalupe Hidalgo (1848), Mexico acknowledged the loss of Texas and ceded over a half million square miles to the United States for a consideration of $18,250,000. In 1853 the United States bought 54,000 square miles of the Mesilla Valley (Gadsden Purchase) for use as a railroad route to California.

The seizure of power by Mexican liberals in 1855 triggered internal strife and foreign intervention. The defeated conservatives appealed to France for aid, and in 1862 Napoleon III dispatched an army to place Archduke Maximilian of Austria on the Mexican throne. The United States, engulfed in the Civil War, was unable to counter France's violation of the

Monroe Doctrine until after Appomattox. Then the United States sent troops to the border, and Napoleon, already disillusioned with his imperial adventure, withdrew from Mexico.

During the long rule of Porfirio Díaz (1876–1911) official relations became increasingly cordial. Díaz welcomed foreign capital, and U.S. investments in mining, land, and manufacturing rose to over a billion dollars, earning huge profits but also arousing resentment among Mexican opponents of the dictatorship.

The revolution that began in Mexico in 1910 produced a generation of conflict between the two nations. The U.S. government recognized the moderate Francisco I. Madero, but Woodrow Wilson's antipathy toward Victoriano Huerta, who overthrew Madero in 1913, culminated in the American occupation of Veracruz in 1914. U.S. forces invaded again in 1916 in response to Francisco (Pancho) Villa's raid on Columbus, N.Mex. Although Washington accredited an ambassador to Venustiano Carranza's government in 1917, the promulgation that year of a revolutionary constitution containing severe restrictions on foreign economic activities aroused new animosities in the United States. In 1923 President Álvaro Obregón agreed to moderate the application of the objectionable regulations and to arbitrate U.S. claims through mixed commissions, but the intractable policies of his successor, Plutarco Elías Calles, nullified the attempt at conciliation. Ambassador Dwight W. Morrow's success in persuading Calles to soften his anti–United States stand and to end a serious church-state conflict reduced American hostility to the revolutionary regime and paved the way for better relations. A 1934 accord provided for partial payment of U.S. claims for damage suffered during the revolution. Lázaro Cárdenas' expropriation of major U.S. petroleum holdings in 1938 created a crisis (*see* Mexican Oil Controversy), but Franklin D. Roosevelt, committed to his Good Neighbor policy and anxious to secure Mexican benevolence at a time when war threatened in Europe, arranged a peaceful solution. A Mexican-American general agreement signed in 1941 settled most outstanding issues. Mexico joined the war against the Axis powers and became a charter member of the United Nations.

After World War II, relations were harmonious despite periodic Mexican dissatisfaction over American trade policy. The presidents of both countries regularly exchanged visits. Government personnel cooperated to eliminate the aphthous fever epidemic and to combat the illicit narcotics trade. Diplomacy assuaged Mexico's ire over treatment of its migrant laborers in the United States and settled the century-old dispute over ownership of the Chamizal district in El Paso. Mexico asserted its autonomy in foreign affairs by maintaining relations with Fidel Castro but aligned itself with the United States in other cold war conflicts.

[J. M. Callahan, *American Foreign Policy in Mexican Relations;* H. F. Cline, *The United States and Mexico.*]

DAVID C. BAILEY

MEXICO CITY, CAPTURE OF (Sept. 13–14, 1847). The fall of Chapultepec made possible a combined advance by Gen. William J. Worth's and Gen. John A. Quitman's divisions against the western gates of Mexico City. By dusk on Sept. 13, Worth, despite desperate resistance, arrived at the San Cosmé gate. Quitman, on the Belén Causeway, was held up before the citadel. During the night Antonio López de Santa Anna evacuated the city, the citadel surrendering to Quitman at dawn. Marching immediately to the plaza, Quitman raised the flag on the palace. Worth's troops, followed by Gen. Winfield Scott, then entered, and Scott announced the capture of the capital.

[C. W. Elliott, *Winfield Scott;* J. H. Smith, *The War With Mexico.*]

CHARLES WINSLOW ELLIOTT

MIAMI, FORT, or Fort Miamis, at present-day Fort Wayne, Ind., where the Saint Marys and Saint Joseph rivers unite to form the Maumee, was built by the French about 1749. It replaced an older fort of the same name. It was garrisoned by the British under Lt. Robert Butler of Rogers' Rangers. In May 1763, the fort was evacuated, and shortly thereafter it was seized by the Indians in Pontiac's uprising.

[C. Moore, *The Northwest Under Three Flags;* E. O. Randall and D. J. Ryan, *History of Ohio.*]

RANDOLPH G. ADAMS

MIAMI, FORT, in the present state of Ohio, at the foot of the Maumee rapids, on the left bank of the Maumee River, was built by the British in April 1794, under orders of Lt. Gov. J. G. Simcoe of Upper Canada. The command was given to Maj. William Campbell. The position of the fort, "an encroachment of nearly forty miles upon the American soil," was protested by George Washington, Thomas Jefferson, and John Jay. On July 26, 1796, according to Article II of Jay's Treaty, signed in 1795, the fort was yielded to the Americans. During the War of 1812 it

was retaken by the British and used as Gen. Henry Proctor's headquarters.

[E. O. Randall and D. J. Ryan, *History of Ohio;* J. Winsor, *Narrative and Critical History.*]

RANDOLPH G. ADAMS

MIAMI AND ERIE CANAL. *See* **Ohio State Canals.**

MIAMI PURCHASE, the next important colonization project in the Old Northwest after the grant to the Ohio Company of Associates, was first settled about eight months after Marietta (April 1788). The Miami purchase represented an important step in the American advance on the north bank of the Ohio. Extending northward from the Ohio, between the Miami and the Little Miami rivers, it commanded not only the increasingly important Ohio River route but also the Miami-Maumee roadway to Lake Erie, while southward the Licking River gave ready access to the Kentucky bluegrass region. Benjamin Stites, an Indian trader, represented the possibilities of the Miami country to Judge John Cleves Symmes, of Morristown, N.J., an influential member of the Continental Congress. After a personal inspection Symmes enlisted the support of Jonathan Dayton, Elias Boudinot, and other important men to found a colony between the two Miamis. A contract with the Treasury Board on Oct. 15, 1788, granted Symmes and his associates 1 million acres, for which, under the Land Ordinance of 1785, they agreed to pay $1 per acre, with certain deductions, in Continental certificates, and one-seventh in military warrants. As in the Ohio Company purchase, section sixteen in each township was reserved for the support of education and section twenty-nine for that of religion. Also, one entire township was set aside for a college. Eventually, Symmes could not meet the payments in full, and in 1794 he received a patent for the Miami purchase that covered only 311,682 acres.

Symmes started for his new colony in July 1788 and made a temporary stop at Limestone, Ky. The first permanent settlement in the Miami purchase was made on Nov. 18, 1788, by Benjamin Stites, at Columbia, at the mouth of the Little Miami. The next settlement, on Dec. 28, 1788, opposite the mouth of the Licking, was led by Israel Ludlow and Robert Patterson, and was given the fanciful name Losantiville, which the first governor of the Northwest Territory, Arthur St. Clair, changed to Cincinnati, in honor of the Society of the Cincinnati. The third settlement Symmes himself founded, on Feb. 2, 1789, at North Bend. At first the constant danger of Indian attacks confined the settlers, the majority of whom were from New Jersey, to the vicinity of Fort Washington, but gradually they went up the watercourses into the interior. Fort Hamilton, founded in 1791, became the nucleus of an advanced settlement, and after the Treaty of Greenville (1795), population spread quickly through the lands of the Miami purchase.

[Beverley W. Bond, Jr., ed., *The Correspondence of John Cleves Symmes;* Charles T. Greve, *Centennial History of Cincinnati,* vol. I.]

BEVERLEY W. BOND, JR.

MIAMISBURG MOUND. *See* **Adena; Archaeology and Prehistory, North American.**

MIAMI TRAIL, an early Indian trail running from the towns of the Miami in the valleys of the Miami and Little Miami rivers of southwestern Ohio to the Cherokee country of the South. It had several branches north of the Ohio but these converged to cross that river near the mouth of the Licking River. From that point it followed the Licking and Kentucky valleys to the watershed between the Cumberland and Green rivers, where it divided, one branch joining the Scioto Trail leading to Cumberland Gap, the other passing southward into the Cherokee country of Tennessee. It was much used in Indian invasions of Kentucky.

[A. B. Hulbert, *Indian Thoroughfares.*]

EUGENE H. ROSEBOOM

MICHABOUS, GOD OF MICHILIMACKINAC.
The island of Mackinac, at the junction of lakes Superior, Michigan, and Huron, was regarded by the surrounding Indians as the home of their greatest supernatural sponsor, known as Michabous, Manabozhu, Manitou, and other names. The term Michilimackinac, with various spellings, was originally applied to the whole region embracing the union of the lakes but eventually was restricted to Mackinac Island. Jesuit missionaries first visited the region about 1641 but the name does not occur in the Jesuit *Relations* until 1670. Forms of the term Michabous appear among all Algonkin-speaking tribes with such synonyms as Gloskap and Wisakedjak (corrupted into whiskey jack). Ethnologists prefer to speak of the basic concept implied in these terms as the Manitou, for although in Algonkin mythology the various names

given above apply to animal as well as human gods, these in turn are but personifications of the "life-force" in the world as formulated in the Algonkin philosophy.

[Ellen R. Emerson, *Indian Myths or Legends;* Reuben G. Thwaites, "Story of Mackinac," in *Wisconsin Historical Collections,* vol. XIV.]

CLARK WISSLER

MICHIGAN. The story of France in Michigan began when Étienne Brulé, a protégé of Samuel de Champlain, reached the Sault Sainte Marie area about 1622. The first formal community in Michigan began in 1668 when Father Jacques Marquette established a mission at Sault Sainte Marie. Three years later he founded the mission of Saint Ignace on the Straits of Mackinac. By 1671, the French had become aware of the potential riches from the fur trade of the upper country and claimed the area for the king of France. In 1701, Detroit, which became the most important French fur-trading center in Michigan, was founded by Antoine de la Mothe Cadillac. Michigan remained a great center for the lucrative fur trade throughout the French regime, which officially ended in 1763, at the close of the French and Indian War.

In the first year of British jurisdiction, Pontiac utilized the power of his great Indian confederacy to wage unsuccessful war against the British. British policy was stabilized by the Proclamation of 1763, which restricted the settlement in the area to licensed fur traders and Indians. In 1774, by the terms of the Quebec Act, Michigan was attached to Quebec in an effort to maintain the region as the western fringe of the recently acquired French-Canadian empire. At the close of the American Revolution, Michigan was ceded to the United States, but the British retained jurisdiction until 1796. During the thirteen-year interval of irregular government many aspects of British civil authority were introduced, and beginning in 1792, Michigan was administered as part of Upper Canada. In accordance with the terms of Jay's Treaty, the British withdrew from Michigan posts in 1796.

During the period of English occupation, the American government outlined its new favorable western policy. In 1787, Congress passed the Northwest Ordinance and made Michigan a part of the newly created Northwest Territory. In 1794 an American force under the command of Anthony Wayne defeated a British-inspired Indian confederacy. Indian opposition to the American government was ended by the Treaty of Greenville (1795). Consequently, in 1796, the political institutions recognized by the

Northwest Territory were gradually implemented. By 1803, Michigan had become a part of Indiana Territory. However, in response to the petitions of Detroit residents, Congress authorized the creation of Michigan Territory, which began to function as a governmental unit on July 1, 1805, with Detroit as the capital.

William Hull was the first governor of the territory, but Augustus B. Woodward, one of the three judges, was the dominant personality. The early years of the territorial government were given over to the settlement of land claims growing out of the rebuilding of Detroit, the cession of Indian lands in southeastern Michigan, the further organization of local government, and routine matters of administration. In 1812, Michigan was subject to a second disastrous interval of British occupation as the result of the War of 1812. American rule was not restored until 1813, following the naval victory of Capt. Oliver Hazard Perry.

The growth of the territory began after the close of the struggle. Many factors contributed to this expansion. Lewis Cass, who became the territorial governor in 1813, used his tireless energies to encourage and promote settlement, by demonstrating that the interior of Michigan was well adapted to profitable agriculture. Changes in transportation were significant. In 1818 the *Walk in the Water,* the first steamboat to operate successfully on the Great Lakes, made its maiden journey from Buffalo to Detroit. The completion of the Erie Canal in 1825 assured relatively inexpensive water transportation between the East and Detroit. A network of highways outlined by Cass, some constructed by the federal government as military roads, radiated out from Detroit into the most fertile counties in the territory. The most important of these crudely constructed arteries was the Chicago Road, which linked Detroit with Chicago. The Gratiot Road connected Detroit with Port Huron, and the Saginaw Road ran northward from Detroit to Saginaw.

In 1835 a constitution was carefully drafted for the projected state of Michigan. It was approved by the electorate, but admission to the Union was delayed until Jan. 26, 1837, because of a boundary dispute with Ohio and the resultant Toledo War. In spite of a disastrous experiment with internal banking, largely the result of inexperience, the state grew rapidly. Both native-born and foreign-born agricultural settlers established new homes in Michigan. In the 1840's, the vast mineral resources of the upper peninsula were publicized, Dr. Douglass Houghton made known the presence of large copper reserves, and

William A. Burt gave an inkling of the huge deposits of iron ore. By 1850 the population was 397,000.

Although Michigan residents supported many reforms, none matched the intensity of the antislavery crusade. The electorate was divided over the issue of the expansion of slavery. On the weekend of July 4, 1854, enthusiastic antislavery devotees formed the present-day Republican party at Jackson, Mich. This new party won control of the state government in 1854 and soon dominated the Michigan political scene.

The growth of the state was unusually rapid after the Civil War. By the beginning of the 20th century, when the population was 2,242,000, all counties had been settled. Agriculture was the leading source of wealth, and the rural population outnumbered the urban population. Lumbering served as a basis for the first economic activities in the northern portions of the lower peninsula and many counties of the upper peninsula. Here, pine was king and ruthless exploitation gave rise to great wealth and lumbering cities. The growth of manufacturing in Detroit, Grand Rapids (a major furniture center), and other Michigan cities contributed to the great economic wealth, which included an ever-expanding commerce.

Modern industrial Michigan really began in the 20th century, when the economy was rapidly modified by the great expansion of the automotive industry. Detroit became the automotive capital of the nation. The economy of Flint and several other cities also came to be largely dependent on the new industry. As the automotive industry was centralized, Michigan became the home of the Big Three—General Motors Corporation, Ford Motor Company, and Chrysler Corporation.

Progressivism was the theme of state politics prior to the outbreak of World War I. In 1912, Michigan was one of the few states that gave its electoral vote to Theodore Roosevelt. Michigan played an important role throughout World War I; its increased industrial production included the manufacture of civilian and military supplies.

During the 1920's, the increase in manufacturing surpassed the gains of earlier eras. The growth of cities was highly significant. The lumbering industry became virtually extinct, and the percentage of wealth contributed by agriculture declined. A modernized state government recognized the growing influence of the automobile, and an extensive program of state highway construction, including the building of superhighways, was authorized. Tourism also made great strides.

The Great Depression was unusually severe in Michigan. The mining counties of the upper peninsula and the large industrial cities of the lower peninsula had unusually high rates of unemployment. Many workers were forced to accept a shorter workweek. Welfare programs placed almost unbearable strains upon local governments. On Feb. 14, 1933, Gov. William A. Comstock was forced to declare the famous eight-day Michigan bank holiday.

In 1932, Michigan entered the Democratic column and thereafter remained a doubtful political state. James Couzens, a Republican U.S. senator, and Frank Murphy, a Democrat who served in many high capacities, were among the outstanding political personalities of the early years of the depression.

In World War II some 673,000 men and women from Michigan served in the military. Detroit and other cities became great production centers. Michigan plants met staggering industrial goals. All civilian automobile production was terminated. Factories were converted to the manufacture of many military items.

In 1970 Michigan's population was 8,875,083, which represented an increase of 13.4 percent over the 1960 total. Some 88.3 percent were white and 11.7 percent were other races, primarily black. The gains in the black population were most noticeable in Detroit, but high percentages of increase were observable also in many smaller cities. The nine large metropolitan areas in Michigan indicate the growing dependency of the state on urban industry and commerce.

In 1974 and 1975, primarily because of the depressed condition of the automotive industry, Michigan faced the worst unemployment market since the 1930's. In February 1975 the unemployment rate of the Michigan work force was 15.8 percent, and Detroit's was 16.2 percent. All levels of local government took steps to alleviate the plight of the unemployed.

[F. Clever Bald, *Michigan in Four Centuries;* Willis Dunbar, *Michigan: A History of the Wolverine State;* George N. Fuller, ed., *Michigan, A Centennial History;* M. M. Quaife and Sidney Glazer, *Michigan From Primitive Wilderness to Industrial Commonwealth.*]

SIDNEY GLAZER

MICHIGAN, LAKE, one of the Great Lakes and the largest lake lying wholly within the United States. It extends 321 miles from north to south. The first known European discoverer was Jean Nicolet in 1634, but not until four decades later did the French (Father Jacques Marquette; Louis Jolliet; Robert Cavelier, Sieur de La Salle) become familiar with the lake's entire shoreline. From this time forward Lake Michigan became a highway for explorers, traders, and others. After 1760 the British developed a naval establishment on the upper Great Lakes, and occasional voyages for commercial or military reasons were made to Lake Michigan, at whose northern outlet lay the important fur trade center of Michilimackinac. The chief historical importance of Lake Michigan dates from the early 19th century, when the tide of American settlement began pouring into the adjacent country and such thriving cities as Milwaukee, Kenosha, Chicago, and Michigan City were founded. The vast importance of Lake Michigan as a route of travel and commerce during the 19th century can only be suggested. Because the Ordinance of 1787 fixed an east and west line through the southern extreme of Lake Michigan as the boundary between the three southern and the two northern states of the Old Northwest and because in every instance this provision was later violated, Lake Michigan figured importantly in the determination of the boundaries of the states of Ohio, Indiana, Illinois, Michigan, and Wisconsin. Lake Michigan is now part of the Great Lakes–Saint Lawrence Seaway and handles a vast amount of international commerce, particularly in coal, iron ore, limestone, and grain. Despite some pollution the lake has been restocked with trout and salmon, enabling part of the lake's shores to remain popular fishing and resort areas.

[Louise P. Kellogg, *The French Régime in Wisconsin and the Northwest.*]

M. M. QUAIFE

MICHIGAN TERRITORIAL ROAD was authorized by the territorial legislature in 1829 and laid out in 1830. It ran from Detroit to the mouth of the Saint Joseph River and followed approximately the route of the present highway U.S. 12. It paralleled the national turnpike (*see* Chicago Road) from Detroit to Fort Dearborn (now highway U.S. 112) that was authorized in 1824. These two roads are sometimes called "extensions of the Erie Canal" and were the chief routes followed by immigrants who settled the southern part of the lower peninsula of Michigan. A stage line over the territorial road connecting at Saint Joseph with steamers for Chicago was established in 1834.

[M. M. Quaife, *Chicago's Highways Old and New.*]

WILLIS DUNBAR

MICHILIMACKINAC. *See* **Mackinac, Straits of, and Mackinac Island.**

MICMAC. *See* **Abnaki.**

MICROWAVE TECHNOLOGY. Microwave detection and communications systems have come to play a major, but little appreciated, role in American life since 1940. Perhaps the application best known to the general public is the microwave oven, but microwaves have also made possible live television from space and between continents. Microwave technology is also essential for safe all-weather operation of commercial and military aircraft as well as for intercity telephone traffic. The high cost of microwave systems has tended to limit their use for mass-produced consumer products. This situation seems likely to change as a result of the introduction of comparatively inexpensive solid-state microwave sources suitable for such applications as collision-avoidance devices for automobiles, burglar alarms, mobile telephones, and health-data telemetry.

Microwave technology has gone through several stages. Some theoretical and experimental work was done by European physicists in the late 19th century, but interest languished because of the dominance of long waves in early radio communication. Fundamental advances in the transmission of microwaves through hollow metal pipes or waveguides were made by George C. Southworth, John R. Carson, and others at the Bell Telephone Laboratories during the 1930's. An important new microwave generator known as the klystron was developed by Russell H. and Sigurd Varian at Stanford in 1939. The waveguide, klystron, and cavity magnetron, brought to the United States in a famous "black box" by a British team in 1940, became key elements in a wide variety of radar systems developed by several groups, including the Radiation Laboratories formed at the Massachusetts Institute of Technology in 1941.

The prototype for a major microwave communications system by means of repeating stations separated by distances of about thirty miles was installed between New York and Boston by the Bell System in 1947. By 1960 microwave chains carried about 40 percent of Bell's intercity traffic. Similar apparatus was adapted for use in satellite repeating stations, beginning with the launch of Pioneer 3 in 1958. Further innovations and the increasing congestion of the electromagnetic spectrum aroused renewed inter-est in the use of Southworth's hollow pipes for communications by 1970. A single circular pipe is believed capable of carrying 250,000 simultaneous conversations over long distances. The discovery in the 1960's by J. B. Gunn of IBM and others that semiconductor devices such as the Gunn oscillator and IMPATT diode can generate and amplify microwave signals is expected to stimulate a variety of consumer and industrial applications of microwave technology.

[Raymond Bowers and Jeffrey Frey, "Technology Assessment and Microwave Diodes," *Scientific American* (February 1972); George C. Southworth, "Survey and History of the Progress of the Microwave Arts," *Proceedings of the Institute of Radio Engineers* (May 1962).]

JAMES E. BRITTAIN

MIDCONTINENT OIL REGION, a vast mineral fuel–producing region situated in the nation's heartland, extending from Nebraska to south Texas and flanked by the Mississippi River and the Rocky Mountains. From earliest times an oil sign in the form of a green slick on springs and creeks was observed at widely scattered locations. In the age before kerosine lamps and internal-combustion engines oil slick was used as a lubricant and as medicine. Teamsters crossing the Plains from the Missouri settlements to the Rio Grande towns greased their wagon axles with oil slick. Before the Civil War, oil springs in the Chickasaw Nation (in south-central Oklahoma) and north Texas served as spas. Oil was believed to have therapeutic properties, particularly in the treatment of rheumatism, dropsy, and other chronic diseases. Natural gas is a ubiquitous associate of oil in the midcontinent region. Indians in the region lighted their council grounds with surface leakage of natural gas, using gun barrels thrust into the gas seepage crevices as tubes to control the gas flow and to serve as burners.

Early discoveries of subsurface oil in the midcontinent region were inadvertent, largely the result of digging wells for water and saline solution used in salt manufacture. One of the earliest discoveries occurred in 1859 when Lewis Ross, an Indian operating a saltworks in the Cherokee Nation on Grand River in Mayes County (in northeastern Oklahoma), dug a well to increase the flow from his salt springs. He struck oil, which flowed at the rate of ten barrels a day until the gas pressure producing the free flow dissipated. A year later at Paola, Kans., oil was found in a well at a depth of about 300 feet. Thereafter, from Kansas to Texas, oil discoveries through digging water wells became a regular occurrence.

Prospecting for oil in the midcontinent region began in the 1880's. In 1882, H. W. Faucett from the Pennsylvania oil fields received a concession from the Choctaw tribal government for drilling rights in the Choctaw Nation (in southeastern Oklahoma). On Boggy Creek near Atoka he produced a shower of oil and gas 1,400 feet high. Successive discoveries in Kansas, Indian Territory, and Texas opened oil and gas fields. The production was used as a lubricant, an illuminant (kerosine, coal oil, and rock oil), and medicine. The natural gas fields of southern Kansas became an important source for fuel for smelters refining lead and zinc ores from the nearby Tri-State District, for ceramic manufacture (particularly bricks), and for other industrial purposes. Also, natural gas was widely used as a home fuel and as an illuminant for lighting city streets and homes.

The premier oil well of the midcontinent region was Spindletop, a dramatic gusher brought in by Anthony F. Lucas near Beaumont, Tex., on Jan. 10, 1901, which produced 75,000–100,000 barrels a day. The advent of the internal-combustion engine with the concomitant increase in demand for petroleum products led to a sustained flurry of wildcatting (exploration by drilling) throughout the midcontinent region, opening new fields in every state of the region from Nebraska to Louisiana. Around 1945 midcontinent petroleum production peaked and began to level off. Discovery of extensive new fields in eastern New Mexico, the Permian Basin in Texas, and the Wilburton Field in Oklahoma dramatically increased the oil and gas resources of the region. Also, deeper drilling in the Hennessey and Garber fields of Oklahoma, and other points where marginal production from shallow wells had forced abandonment, yielded rich petroleum-bearing sands at deeper levels. Water flooding of wells abandoned at Paola, the Osage Nation field in Oklahoma, and other points because of low production recharged the oil-bearing sands and caused the wells to resume production. Advances in petroleum technology have increased pool discovery and well production. The South Alex Field in Oklahoma has several wells extending to a depth of nearly 20,000 feet.

The oil industry of the midcontinent region has provided a legacy of bonanza wealth and boomtowns reminiscent of the California gold rush in 1848–49. The region's petroleum industry has been a major influence in state and regional economic development, urban evolution, and politics. The midcontinent region petroleum production is controlled by allow-

ables set by the various states for individual wells and by the regional Interstate Oil Compact Commission.

[Max W. Ball, *This Fascinating Oil Business;* W. L. Connelly, *The Oil Business As I Saw It;* Carl Coke Rister, *Oil! Titan of the Southwest.*]

ARRELL M. GIBSON

MIDDLE CLASS originally referred to the urban craftsmen and the mercantile class in medieval towns. The middle class was easily distinguished from the hereditary nobility, on one hand, and from the largely nonowning peasantry, on the other. During this period, "middle" referred to the position of the class between nobility and peasantry in social esteem or honor. In most European nations, the numbers and power of the class grew with the Industrial Revolution. By the 19th century, the middle class was clearly dominant and had evolved political and economic doctrines, political parties, and life-styles peculiar to itself.

Such clear demarcation of class was generally lacking in the United States, where society was established after the advent of the middle class in Europe. Aristocrats were few, and most farmers were landowners and thus shared many attitudes with the urban middle class. There is no generally accepted definition of the middle class in the United States, or even of the number and composition of classes other than the middle class.

Under Communist theory, the middle class consists of those who own the means of production, such as land, tools, materials, and factories. This definition applied quite well at the time of the founding of the Republic, when the class was composed chiefly of self-employed craftsmen, small businessmen, independent professionals such as doctors and lawyers, and landowning farmers. In 1800, four-fifths of Americans owned their means of livelihood.

The United States has been described as the most middle class of nations. The class is the embodiment of the "American way," with its dedication to business, emphasis on ambition, faith in progress, and devotion to the pervasive influence of the Protestant ethic.

Since the Civil War, class lines have remained unclear because of the movement into the middle class of salaried officials and government clerks, paid professionals such as teachers, growing numbers of white-collar workers, and well-paid managers, none of whom owned the means of production but all of whom shared the income levels and life-style of the middle class. A further dilution of the class occurred in the 20th century as skilled workers reached and surpassed the income levels of the lower middle class; also, since World War II, semiskilled workers have been able through credit to adopt middle-class life-styles.

Although less than one-fifth of Americans own their means of livelihood, most social researchers agree that belonging to the middle class has become primarily a matter of sharing middle-class attitudes and of self-perception as a member of the class. By these criteria, up to nine-tenths of the American people regard themselves as middle class. More than three-quarters of the working class, by occupation, consider themselves middle class.

Although the middle class has on occasion been influential in public life, such as during the reform movement of the 1890's and 1900's, it is now so large and diverse that it lacks the cohesion to produce major social or political change.

[A. N. Holcombe, *The Middle Classes in American Politics;* C. Wright Mills, *White Collar*.]

PAUL J. HOFFMANN

MIDDLE-OF-THE-ROAD POPULISTS, the name given during the presidential campaign of 1896 to those members of the People's (Populist) party who objected to fusion with either of the older parties, and who insisted that the proper policy was to "keep in the middle of the road." At their national convention in Saint Louis, on July 22, they were unable to prevent the party from accepting the Democratic candidate, William Jennings Bryan, as its candidate for president, but they forced the convention to nominate a Populist, Thomas E. Watson of Georgia, for vice-president. After 1896 the Middle-of-the-Road Populists formed a separate organization, which endured feebly for a dozen years.

[J. D. Hicks, *The Populist Revolt*.]

JOHN D. HICKS

MIDDLE PASSAGE, the term applied to the trip from Africa to the West Indies, the second leg of the triangular voyage of a slave ship (*see* Triangular Trade). During the passage the slaves, packed in holds 18 inches to 5 feet deep, and allowed above only for air, food, and exercise, died in large numbers.

[U. B. Phillips, *American Negro Slavery;* J. R. Spears, *The American Slave Trade*.]

FLETCHER M. GREEN

MIDDLESEX CANAL was constructed (1793–1803) between Boston and the Merrimack River near the site of Lowell, Mass., to bring that river's commerce to Boston without a sea voyage. The Merrimack River flows between southern New Hampshire and northeastern Massachusetts, and the canal was of great economic value in developing New Hampshire, but the building of railroad lines made it less valuable, and the last boat passed through in 1852.

[Alvin F. Harlow, *Old Towpaths*.]

ALVIN F. HARLOW

MIDEWIWIN, or **Grand Medicine Lodge,** was a secret society of medicine men, widespread among the Chippewa, which attracted the attention of early missionaries by its use of the cross in ceremonies of initiation. The order centered around the cult of Minabozho, traditional source of men's knowledge of medicine. Candidates for membership (either men or women) served an apprenticeship with older mide, and prepared for admission to each of the degrees of the lodge with sweat baths, fasting, ceremonial smoking, and gifts to the mide. The initiation ceremonies centered around shooting the sacred *migis* (shell) into the body of the candidate. The mide possessed an extensive native pharmacopoeia, practiced bloodletting and simple surgery, and used songs and formulas of exorcism. The *djesakid* class interpreted dreams and foretold the future. The sorcerers were known as *wabeno*. The Midewiwin was the principal means for transmitting legends, songs, and traditional religious lore preserved in pictographs on birch bark. Because the order represented a tendency to evolve into a mystic, priestly religion, and because it was so widespread, its members resisted Christianization stubbornly. (*See also* Indian Medicine.)

[Frances Densmore, *Chippewa Customs;* W. J. Hoffman, *The Mide-wiwin or Grand Medicine Society of the Ojibwa*.]

HAROLD E. DAVIS

MIDNIGHT JUDGES refers to the judicial appointments made by John Adams just before he was succeeded in the presidency by Thomas Jefferson. The action of Adams was assailed as an attempt "to make permanent provision for such of the Federalists and Tories as cannot hope to continue in office under the new administration." Congress, dominated in the next session by the partisans of Jefferson, reconstructed the inferior courts and legislated most of the midnight judges out of their commissions (*see* Judiciary Act of 1801). In the case of a justice of the peace for the District of Columbia the delivery of his commission was refused. This act led to the famous Supreme Court case of *Marbury* v. *Madison*.

[W. S. Carpenter, *Judicial Tenure in the United States*.]
WILLIAM S. CARPENTER

MIDNIGHT ORDER was issued on Dec. 5, 1872, by U.S. District Judge E. H. Durell. It cited in contempt the members of a board appointed by the governor of Louisiana, H. C. Warmoth, to canvass the returns in the gubernatorial election of that year. Durell had previously enjoined this board from functioning save under very great restrictions. It had ignored the injunction and declared the Democratic ticket elected. The order also directed the U.S. marshal to prevent the state legislature from meeting on Dec. 9, pursuant to Warmoth's call. The "midnight order" had the effect of making the Republican candidate, W. P. Kellogg, governor of Louisiana.

[Albert Phelps, *Louisiana*.]
JOHN S. KENDALL

MIDWAY, BATTLE OF (June 4–6, 1942), a major engagement of aircraft carriers that reversed Japan's initial tactical successes in the Pacific during World War II. After ravaging the U.S. Battle Fleet at Pearl Harbor, the Japanese steamed unimpeded across the western Pacific. Their progress was delayed only briefly by the indecisive Battle of the Coral Sea (May 3–8, 1942), the first carrier duel in naval history. At this point, Adm. Isoroku Yamamoto, commander of Japan's Combined Fleet, resolved to take Midway Island and force Adm. Chester W. Nimitz, commander of the U.S. Pacific Fleet, to commit his weakened forces to a final clash at sea.

At Nimitz' disposal were the carriers *Enterprise* and *Hornet* and their support ships, constituting Task Force 16 under Rear Adm. Raymond A. Spruance. Also available to him was Task Force 17, built around the carrier *Yorktown*, which had been badly mauled in the Coral Sea engagement but patched up at Pearl Harbor miraculously in two days. In overall sea command was Rear Adm. Frank J. Fletcher, who flew his flag from the *Yorktown*. Yamamoto drew together one of the most prodigious armadas of modern times—185 warships in all—battleships, carriers, cruisers, destroyers, and submarines, along with numerous auxiliary vessels.

Late in May, Yamamoto's great fleet steamed eastward from various Japanese bases, while the Northern Area Force, a diversionary assault fleet under Vice Adm. Moshiro Hosogaya, steamed toward the Aleutians in an ill-fated bid to draw the Americans away from the Midway area. The First Mobile Force, under Vice Adm. Chuichi Nagumo, included the carriers *Akagi, Kaga, Hiryu,* and *Soryu*. Nagumo's task was to shatter Midway's defenses with his aircraft and clear the way for Vice Adm. Nobutake Kondo's Transport Group, an invasion force of some 5,000 troops. Yamamoto, flying his flag from the gigantic battleship *Yamato,* steamed toward Midway, far behind Nagumo and Kondo, convinced through intelligence reports that there were no American carriers in the area of Midway.

Nimitz' naval intelligence was not as faulty as that of his Japanese adversary, and he was able to visualize the enemy's battle plans precisely. He sent a few warships northward to cover the Aleutians, but he stationed his three carriers 350 miles northeast of Midway and waited for Yamamoto to make his first tactical move. On June 3 the Japanese mounted their deceptive strike at Dutch Harbor in the Aleutians, and on June 4 the first wave of enemy aircraft hit Midway. Fletcher, with search planes aloft, promptly ordered Spruance to "proceed southwesterly and attack enemy carriers when definitely located."

Shortly after 7 A.M., Spruance launched his air strike on Nagumo, while island-based army and navy aircraft were making fruitless attacks on the zigzagging Japanese fleet. At the same time, the flight leader of the returning Japanese air strike radioed Nagumo that one more bombing attack on Midway was needed. Accordingly, the Japanese admiral ordered his torpedo-laden reserve aircraft to rearm with bombs for another strike at the island. This was the first fatal decision of the battle. Yet, despite the fact that within the next few hours Nagumo was attacked by island-based planes and the U.S. submarine *Nautilus,* no hits were scored. He seemed invulnerable until, during this critical period, one of his scout planes finally sighted units of the U.S. naval force. At once Nagumo halted the rearming operation and ordered part of his second wave to attack the American ships with torpedoes, the rest to hit Midway again with bombs; but before launching these attacks, he decided to recover the planes of his returning first Midway strike. This was his second fatal decision. Shortly after recovery was made, Nagumo had to dodge the torpedo planes of the *Enterprise, Hornet,* and *Yorktown*. The U.S. torpedo aircraft were massacred, but behind them came U.S. dive-bombers that struck the Japanese carriers while their flight decks were loaded with fueled and armed aircraft. The *Akagi, Kaga,* and *Soryu* burst into flame. The *Hiryu,* farther to the north, temporarily escaped the holocaust and was able to mount two heavy attacks on the *Yorktown,* forcing its captain to abandon his badly damaged ship. Spruance soon retaliated, and by late afternoon the *Hiryu* was burning out of control. All four Japanese carriers finally went down with their planes.

On June 5, Yamamoto accepted the immensity of his losses and canceled the invasion of Midway, but Spruance pressed further his attack on the retreating Japanese fleet and sank the cruiser *Mikuma.* The American naval triumph was flawed when a lurking Japanese submarine fatally torpedoed the listing and vulnerable *Yorktown,* along with a lone ministering destroyer. Early in the morning of June 7, the *Yorktown* succumbed to its many wounds and the Battle of Midway was over. The U.S. Navy, having inflicted enormous and irreparable damage on a vastly superior fleet, effectively turned the tide of the naval war in the Pacific. It was appropriate that Nimitz, whose strategic insight had made victory possible, should later pun that "we are about midway to our objective."

[Samuel Eliot Morison, *History of United States Naval Operations in World War II,* vol. IV; T. V. Tuleja, *Climax at Midway.*]

THADDEUS V. TULEJA

MIDWAY ISLANDS, located 1,200 miles northwest of Honolulu, are part of a coral atoll containing two islands (Sand and Eastern), with a total area of about two square miles. Discovered in 1859 by Capt. N. C. Brooks, they were annexed by the United States in 1867. The U.S. Navy was given administrative responsibility over the islands in 1903, and they became a station link in the transpacific cable in 1905. Attacked by the Japanese in World War II, Midway was the scene of a naval aircraft battle (June 1942) that resulted in a severe defeat for Japan. By checking the Japanese advance toward Hawaii, the battle proved to be one of the decisive American victories of the war. Since World War II the islands have served as a naval and air base and as a stopover point for commercial transpacific flights.

SEDDIE COGSWELL

MIDWAY PLAISANCE, the amusement center of the World's Columbian Exposition in Chicago in 1893. Extending from the exposition grounds to Washington Park, it was lined with restaurants, music halls, and concessions contrived by the people of all

nations to draw profit from the exposition's visitors. Most memorable were a huge ferris wheel and the Streets of Cairo, featuring "Little Egypt," the hootchy-kootchy dancer. The Midway has been preserved as a parkway, which is bordered by the University of Chicago, and the term is regularly used as a Chicago place name.

[Edgar Lee Masters, *The Tale of Chicago.*]

PAUL M. ANGLE

MIDWINTER INTERNATIONAL EXPOSITION, the first international exposition held on the Pacific coast, formally opened Jan. 27 and closed July 4, 1894. The exposition covered 100 acres in San Francisco's Golden Gate Park and cost $1,193,260; there were 1,315,022 paid admissions. The purpose was to "enhance the commercial and industrial interests of the Pacific Coast." It was directly inspired by the World's Columbian Exposition held in Chicago in 1893, of which it was a smaller edition in many respects. Many of the exhibits were transported directly from Chicago to San Francisco. Four American states, besides California, and nine foreign nations participated officially.

FRANK MONAGHAN

MIER EXPEDITION. Mexico refused to recognize the independence of Texas in 1836 and as late as 1842 made an invasion and took possession of San Antonio for a short time. A counterexpedition into Mexico was ordered by Texas President Sam Houston. This expedition left San Antonio for the border in November 1842 under Gen. Alexander Somerville, with 750 troops. Because of lack of enthusiasm by the leaders and dissension among the troops, only 250 crossed into Mexico and these surrendered to an overwhelming Mexican force at Mier on the lower Rio Grande. After an attempt to escape, one-tenth were shot and the others marched to a prison near Mexico City. Here some died, some escaped, and the others were released two years later.

[H. H. Bancroft, *History of North Mexican States and Texas;* Thomas J. Green, *Journal of the Texan Expedition Against Mier.*]

J. G. SMITH

MIFFLIN, FORT, was originally built as Mud Fort in 1762 on Mud Island, Delaware River, below the mouth of the Schuylkill. The most important of Philadelphia's revolutionary war defenses, it was besieged by the British from Sept. 27 to Nov. 16, 1777, when, razed by gunfire, it was abandoned. After the British evacuation of Philadelphia, it was rebuilt and named for Thomas Mifflin, then governor of Pennsylvania. It was frequently modernized but ceased active use shortly after World War II.

[J. T. Scharf and Thompson Westcott, *History of Philadelphia*.]

MARION V. BREWINGTON

MIGRATION, GROUP. The single family was the typical unit in the westward movement that resulted in the settlement of America. Nevertheless, a large number of communities in the West were settled by groups of people previously associated with each other who migrated in one body to a new home. Usually, although not always, the destination of these groups was predetermined by agents sent out in advance to select favorable locations, and often even to purchase land before the movement was undertaken.

These group migrations fall into two classes. The first class was made up of groups of people who were governed by the same motives that in general impelled settlers westward, but who decided to move and settle in a body for mutual aid and protection, or in order to make sure of having friendly neighbors in the new home, or for other reasons. The second class was composed of religious groups or experimental colonies seeking more favorable environments in which to carry out their particular purposes. In both classes were to be found not only groups migrating westward from eastern communities, but also groups that came directly from Europe.

From earliest colonial times the westward advance presented examples of groups of the first class moving into the interior. The first settlements in the Connecticut Valley were made by the groups that followed Roger Ludlow from the Massachusetts Bay Colony (*see* River Towns of Connecticut). In fact, community migration into new lands previously surveyed was quite typical of the method of early frontier expansion in the New England colonies. The original settlement of Germans and their subsequent migrations in New York were of this type, as were many of the German and Scotch-Irish movements to Pennsylvania. In the early 1770's there was mention of a group of adventurers from Connecticut who settled on a tract of land on the Mississippi in West Florida (*see* Georgiana).

Frequent examples of the same phenomena were found throughout the years when the country west of

the Alleghenies was being occupied by settlers. One authority states that Rev. Lewis Craig's congregation moved in a body from Virginia to Kentucky in 1781. In 1788 the Ohio Associates from New England founded Marietta in Ohio. Two decades later *Niles' Weekly Register* commented on the tendency of the people of Connecticut to move in groups, after previous investigation, to new homes in the Western Reserve in northern Ohio. About the same time a New York editor described "a cavalcade of upwards of twenty waggons containing one company of 116 persons, on their way to Indiana, and all from one town in the district of Maine." In 1819 a party of 120 persons was seen on its way to Illinois. In Michigan in 1822 there were said to be numerous individuals spying out lands for groups of settlers who were to follow. A colony of Quakers on the River Rouge was mentioned the following year.

In 1839 an Iowa editor reported that "whole neighborhoods in Illinois, Indiana and Ohio are 'organizing' for emigration." To one locality in Wisconsin a few years later came a group of more than 100 persons from Rochester, N.Y., of whom 62 were members of one family. During the 1850's the rush to the newly opened Kansas-Nebraska country contained many groups, such as the one made up of friends and acquaintances from Outagamie County, Wis., which founded Fremont, Nebr., in 1856. Illustrations of this nature might be multiplied indefinitely to show the part played by groups in the westward movement.

In the second class of group migrations, various experimental colonies and religious groups migrated westward. The Harmony Society, led by George Rapp and made up of a sect from southern Germany, established a settlement in western Pennsylvania in 1805 and moved to Indiana ten years later. The Zoarites came to Ohio in 1817 from Württemberg, Germany. In the 1830's a group of ministers in New York's Mohawk Valley drew up a plan for a religious and educational community in the West. An exploring committee sent out in 1835 selected land in Illinois and the result was the founding of Galesburg and Knox College. The establishment of Oberlin, Ohio, and Oberlin College was accomplished in a similar manner a few years earlier. The Mennonites nearly always moved in groups, after previous investigations of localities, when they established their various communities throughout the country, whether they came directly from Europe or moved from their earlier centers of settlement in America. Another instance of group migration may be found in the history of the

Iowa community known as Amana—a religious colony that for almost a century was communistic in organization.

The final illustration of this type of group migration may be in many respects the most notable of all. The Mormon church had its origin about 1830 in western New York. In that year a temporary domicile was selected at Kirtland, Ohio, but at the same time Independence, Mo., was chosen as a permanent location, and by 1831 more than 1,000 members of the sect had moved there. Two years later the Mormons were forced to move to the Far West, north of the Missouri River. In 1839 the hostility of the neighboring settlers caused another move, this time to Nauvoo, on the eastern bank of the Mississippi River in Illinois. After seven years at Nauvoo, the leaders decided to seek an asylum in the Rocky Mountains, and the result was the historic hegira of the Mormons to Utah, which began in 1846.

[Earnest E. Calkins, *They Broke the Prairie;* William A. Linn, *The Story of the Mormons.*]

DAN E. CLARK

MILAN DECREE. *See* **Napoleon's Decrees.**

MILEAGE is an allowance toward the expense of legislators in traveling to and from sessions of their respective bodies. Members of Congress are entitled to one round trip to their district per month while Congress is in session, plus one additional trip to and from Washington, D.C., at the beginning and end of each session. The allowance for one of these trips is determined at the rate of twenty cents per mile via the most direct highway route. No compensation is allowed for transportation of family or household goods, and only travel fares, meals, and incidental expenses of the legislator are covered by the allowance. In the case of state legislators, mileage allowances vary from five cents a mile in Arkansas and South Dakota to fifteen cents a mile in Kentucky for one round trip during regular sessions; from ten cents a mile in twelve states to fifteen cents a mile in Illinois for round trips once a week during sessions; and from eight cents a mile in Rhode Island to twenty cents a mile in Hawaii for unlimited round trips during sessions. Mileage is also commonly provided by law for national and state officials who are required to travel in the performance of their duties, and for witnesses summoned to testify in state and federal courts or before legislative committees.

[Council of State Governments, *The Book of the States 1974–1975,* vol. 20; Donald G. Tacheron and Morris K. Udall, *The Job of the Congressman.*]

DONALD HERZBERG

MILITARY, AFRO-AMERICANS IN THE. Afro-Americans have served in the U.S. Army and Navy during all American wars. Fear of the black man under arms limited their numbers and duties during colonial wars and the revolutionary war. It is estimated that some 5,000 black soldiers and sailors served in the patriot forces during the revolutionary war, but many more sought and found their freedom behind British lines. At the end of the war the British evacuated 14,000 blacks from Savannah, Charleston, and New York harbors as a reward for their loyalty and service to the British fighting forces.

Afro-Americans fought conspicuously well during the War of 1812. Praise for their valor came from Andrew Jackson, who had sought and received black enlistments at the Battle of New Orleans. Enlistment of free blacks was specifically provided for by the navy under an act of Mar. 3, 1813. Blacks formed approximately one-sixth of all naval personnel during the War of 1812, serving faithfully and bravely through all the battles of the Great Lakes.

The army, under general order of the Adjutant and Inspector General's Office, issued Feb. 18, 1820, prohibited black recruits. The order stated, "No Negro or Mulatto will be received as a recruit of the army." In 1839 the secretary of the navy restricted blacks to 5 percent of all naval personnel. Few blacks served in the conflict with Mexico. And at the outset of the Civil War the Union War Department had "no intention to call into the service of the Government any colored soldiers." It was not until white northern manpower had been drained that blacks appeared in the ranks. In January 1863, as part of the Emancipation Proclamation, President Abraham Lincoln provided for the enlistment of blacks. By 1865 some 186,000 blacks had worn Union blue, participating in battles at Milliken's Bend, Olustee, Fort Wagner, the Crater, and Fort Pillow. The navy suffered from a severe shortage of manpower throughout the Civil War and encouraged the enlistment of black sailors. It is estimated that 30,000 blacks, some 25 percent of the Union navy, saw service.

As a reward for loyal and valiant Civil War service Congress, on July 28, 1866, established two regular regiments of cavalry and two of infantry to be manned by black regular troops. These regiments were to serve at remote posts in Texas, Montana, and the

Dakotas. Black soldiers participated in the subjugation of the Apache, Kiowa, Cheyenne, and other Indian tribes. These black regiments, the Ninth and Tenth Cavalry and the Twenty-fourth and Twenty-fifth Infantry, were viewed as being excellent in all areas of military operation, be it combat or spit and polish.

During the Spanish-American War the four regular black regiments were sent to Cuba. Of the 24,123 members of the 1898 navy some 2,000 were Afro-Americans. Twenty-two black sailors went down with the *Maine* in Havana harbor. The involvement of black troops in the war with Spain was more extensive than in any other conflict up to that time except for the Civil War. The Tenth Cavalry was especially honored for valor. Three hundred black regulars were awarded commissions in the sixteen Afro-American volunteer regiments. The volunteer regiments were raised by congressional action and state sponsorship, did not see combat, and were used for labor and nursing duty in Cuba and Puerto Rico. After the war the black regular regiments were sent to the Philippines, where they fought against the insurgent forces led by Emilio Aguinaldo. The volunteer units were disbanded, and the black officers who led them were returned to the ranks in their former regular regiments.

Between 1863 and 1898 forty-four black men—thirty-six soldiers and eight sailors—were awarded the Medal of Honor. In August 1906, the Twenty-fifth Infantry, newly arrived at Brownsville, Tex., station, was charged with riot and murder during an alleged fray in the town of Brownsville. President Theodore Roosevelt dismissed nearly all the men of the First Battalion without honor. The charges were false, but it was not until 1972 that the army exonerated all those accused. On Aug. 23, 1917, the Twenty-fourth Infantry Regiment was involved in a race riot in Houston. Seizing rifles and ammunition, one hundred black soldiers marched to Houston and killed seventeen whites and wounded twelve. Thirteen black soldiers were hanged for murder and mutiny, and forty-one were sentenced to life in prison.

The hostility generated by the events in Brownsville and Houston destroyed the high regard for the regular black regiments and black service of any sort. In 1912 the navy began to refuse enlistment to blacks into any but the messman branch. Three hundred and fifty thousand black soldiers served in the army during World War I, but only 40,000 saw combat; the rest were employed as laborers. Of the army's 213 labor battalions, 106 were all-black. Two black divi-

sions were established, the Ninety-second and the Ninety-third, but both were poorly trained and regarded as ineffective.

In World War II black soldiers and sailors, operating in a segregated military force, served largely in quartermaster, engineer, and transport units. This segregated, largely noncombat, status engendered much bitterness among blacks. Not until President Harry S. Truman ordered the racial integration of the armed forces in 1948 did blacks begin to appear in nonsegregated military units. The wisdom of this order was demonstrated by the creditable performance of black servicemen in the Korean War and in Vietnam. In the 1970's, blacks were serving in significant numbers in all branches of the armed forces, occupying all ranks, and holding many positions of command responsibility.

[R. M. Dalfiume, *Desegregation of the United States Armed Forces;* Ulysses Lee, *The Employment of Negro Troops;* Benjamin Quarles, *Negro in the American Revolution;* T. G. Steward, *The Colored Regulars in the United States Army;* G. W. Williams, *A History of Negro Troops in the War of the Rebellion.*]

DONALD W. CORRIGAN

MILITARY ACADEMY, UNITED STATES. During his presidency George Washington constantly urged on Congress the creation of a military academy for professional military training of promising youths. In 1794, Congress did establish a School for Artillerists and Engineers at West Point, N.Y., but it was a training school, not a professional one. The establishment of a true military academy awaited the passage under President Thomas Jefferson of the Act of Mar. 16, 1802, providing for the creation of a corps of engineers consisting of five officers and ten cadets, with a chief of engineers, designated superintendent of a military academy at West Point. Jonathan Williams was the first superintendent (1801–03, 1805–12), followed by Joseph G. Swift (1812–14) and Alden Partridge (1815–17).

The academy languished for lack of congressional support and, when the War of 1812 began, existed only on paper. By an act of Apr. 29, 1812, Congress provided for a reorganization, authorized a maximum of 250 cadets, and set age and mental requirements for admission that had not previously existed. Not until Maj. Sylvanus Thayer took over as superintendent on July 28, 1817, did the academy begin truly to fulfill the purposes envisioned by its founders. Thayer, known as the father of the military academy, was superintendent for sixteen years (1817–33). He expanded the curriculum; introduced a new system of order, organization, and discipline; and left a lasting mark on the academy. He founded his system on the bedstone of character development, insisting on absolute honesty and integrity and on each cadet's exercising his faculties to the utmost. The traditional West Point honor system had its origins in Thayer's work.

The U.S. Military Academy was for many years the only engineering school in the country, and its graduates, working both as civil and military engineers, were largely responsible for planning and directing the building of major canals, roads, and railroads in the period before the Civil War. The Mexican War meanwhile proved the value of West Point education in the training of army officers; academy graduates in the middle and lower officer ranks were largely responsible for the new professionalism demonstrated by the U.S. Army in Mexico. In the Civil War, West Point graduates dominated the higher positions on both sides, furnishing about 150 Confederate and 300 Union generals.

After the Civil War, with the rise of civilian engineering schools, the Military Academy lost its preeminent position in this field and, with appropriate curriculum changes, became an institution for training officers of all branches of the army. An act of Congress of July 13, 1866, transferred supervision from the Corps of Engineers to the War Department. During the period of 1865–1914 most academy graduates pursued military careers, and in World War I they nearly monopolized the higher ranks, furnishing all commanders of armies and above and about 90 percent of those of corps and divisions. Although this dominance was less in World War II, as graduates of the Reserve Officer Training Corps claimed an increasing place in the sun, still 70 percent of full generals and 65 percent of all lieutenant generals were graduates of the academy.

During each of the two world wars the course at West Point was accelerated to provide for graduation in three years rather than four. And after each of these wars there were extensive changes in organization and curriculum to keep abreast of new developments in military art and technology and, at least to some extent, to adjust to changes in methods and courses in civilian institutions. After World War II there was a progressive increase in the use of modern technology in the cadet's education. The Thayer system of providing a uniform curriculum for all cadets underwent considerable modification with the introduction of electives and fields of concentration. Authorized cadet strength has grown progressively from the 10 of 1802 and the 250 of 1812 to 1,960 in 1935, 2,496 in 1942, and 4,417 in 1975.

[Stephen E. Ambrose, *Duty, Honor, Country: A History of West Point*.]

ROBERT W. COAKLEY

MILITARY AID TO THE CIVIL POWERS is an area that has become more and more confused. By 1940 there had been some 100 instances of troops called out to aid the civil authorities. Since then, the number has increased considerably because of the number of riots and other disturbances as well as natural disasters. Although the president is the sole judge of the necessity to use federal troops, state governors can on their own responsibility call out the National Guard. During the 1960's the prevalence of disorder in civil-rights confrontations and on campuses made some governors reluctant to see the National Guard called out of state, and in many cases they successfully avoided its involvement in the Vietnam War except as a reserve at home to release other units for overseas service.

The president is empowered to employ troops under Article IV, Section 4, of the Constitution and under the "insurrection" statutes, which allow him to make use of troops with or without the request of the state legislature or executive to maintain the Constitution, to support federal law enforcement, or to protect interstate commerce and federal property. At least since the New Deal, each president, as commander in chief, has taken a wider view and has also employed troops in humane tasks, such as aiding flood and tornado victims and feeding weather-isolated cattle. Coast Guard, naval reserve, air force, and army aircraft and helicopters have been most active in the latter cases. In these circumstances, troops have worked with civil authorities, with or without the benefits of martial law.

Because the states of Indiana (1919) and West Virginia (1920–21) were stripped of troops by demobilization after World War I, regular troops were employed in these two states to quell disturbances. Regulars were sent into the aircraft industry in California in 1940 to break a strike that threatened the national defense, and into Little Rock, Ark., in 1957 when there was doubt that the National Guard would respond to orders to help desegregate the schools. However, the federalized National Guard gave no cause for concern. Troops were called into Detroit in 1967, to the Democratic convention in Chicago in 1968—where the police bore the odium of action—and to many other cities when tensions flared. They were even employed on occasion on college campuses, culminating in the unfortunate incident that led to the death and wounding of several students at Kent State University, Ohio, in May 1970. The National Guard, having been trained as a reserve for a European campaign, was singularly unfitted for the role of campus policeman, although recommendations for its retraining had been made after the Detroit riots of July 1967.

The use of troops to aid civil authorities has always been fraught with danger in a country with strong feelings about the employment of troops at home. Training, lack of understanding, and restrictions on freedom of action, together with increasing legal constraints, make the job of troops in police roles, rather than constructive (Corps of Engineers) or rescue roles, difficult. They may face not only court review but also congressional scrutiny of their internal-security role.

In the period 1945–65, regulars were used fifty-six times and National Guardsmen forty times in riots and civil disturbances. In 1967 alone, troops were called out fifty-nine times. The number of troops employed varied from 5 guardsmen to a combined 20,600 in Oxford, Miss., during 1962–63.

[Department of the Army, Office of the Chief of Military History, *Use of Troops in Civil Disturbances Since World War II, 1945–65;* Robin Higham, ed., *Bayonets in the Streets, 1969;* Arthur D. Larson, compiler, *Civil-Military Relations and Militarism: A Classified Bibliography;* Willis E. Schug, ed., *United States Law and the Armed Forces: Cases and Materials on Constitutional Law, Courts-Martial, and the Rights of Servicemen.*]

ROBIN HIGHAM

MILITARY COMPANIES, VOLUNTARY, were a feature of the social and recreational activities of the youth of the 1850's. The companies appeared in considerable numbers as a result of the interest in military affairs aroused by the Mexican War. Young men joined the companies because they combined athletic activity with social recreation. In 1856–59 every important newspaper carried records of their activities, which included dress parades, competitive drills, and interstate encampments. These companies sometimes received aid from the state, but generally maintained an independent existence, depending on some rich patron and the proceeds from military balls and other entertainments for funds.

The movement developed simultaneously in every section of the country, and spread from the larger cities to the towns and villages. The Chicago Zouaves attained a national reputation for their discipline and their military proficiency. Most of the voluntary companies had disbanded before the Civil War began and they did not contribute much to the officer personnel of the war.

[T. G. Gronert, "The First National Pastime in the Middle West," *Indiana Magazine of History,* vol. 29.]

THEODORE G. GRONERT

MILITARY COMPANY OF ADVENTURERS. *See* **Georgiana.**

MILITARY INTELLIGENCE. *See* **Intelligence, Military and Strategic.**

MILITARY LAW regulates the military establishment. For the United States the primary source of military law is legislative enactments of Congress, which receives its authority to enact legislation regarding military law from various provisions of the U.S. Constitution. Its powers include the power to raise and support armies; provide and maintain a navy; make rules for government of the land and naval forces; provide for calling forth the militia to execute the laws of the Republic, suppress insurrections, and repel invasions; provide for organizing, arming, and disciplining the militia and for governing such part of it as may be employed in the service of the United States; and make all laws necessary and proper for carrying into execution the foregoing powers.

Evolving from a few laws implemented by a small number of government workers and service personnel, the amount of legislation and regulation associated with military law has reached huge proportions. It encompasses implementing regulations from the executive branch of the government, including the president, the secretary of defense, and the secretaries of the military services, and decisions of reviewing courts in the military justice system and federal courts. Military law includes diverse subjects, such as the military justice system, veterans' benefits, retirement, government contract law, the laws of war, civil claims for and against the government, draft law, martial law, international law, military commissions, and courts of inquiry and other fact-finding bodies.

[Edward M. Byrne, *Military Law.*]

EDWARD M. BYRNE

MILITARY ORDER OF THE LOYAL LEGION OF THE U.S.A., an organization resembling the Society of the Cincinnati, was established at Philadelphia in 1865 by a group of officers who had served in the Union army during the Civil War. Membership was originally limited to such officers and their eldest male descendants, according to the laws of primogeniture; membership is now open to all male descendants of Union officers. The order, whose headquarters are still in Philadelphia, publishes the *Loyal Legion Historical Journal*. Membership in 1975 was 1,100.

ALVIN F. HARLOW

MILITARY POLICY. The development of the military policy of the United States may be divided into two periods—the period from the founding of the Republic to World War II and the period after World War II. During the first period the United States, relatively safe behind its ocean barriers, followed a foreign policy of isolation and maintained a minimum of military forces in peacetime, rapidly expanding them in time of war and just as rapidly demobilizing them at the end of each conflict. World War II brought an end to isolation as the nation assumed a leading role in world affairs. Ocean barriers lost much of their former importance with the development of terrible new weapons and means for their delivery over vast distances. These changed conditions required new military policies stressing the maintenance of adequate forces in being to protect against attack and discharge new international responsibilities.

The essential elements of the military policy shaped by President George Washington and his immediate successors were (1) a professional regular army of strictly limited size to police the frontiers, to guard the borders and coasts, and to keep alive knowledge of the military arts; (2) a militia based on universal military service, theoretically well trained and organized, to reinforce the regulars in local emergencies when necessary, to maintain internal order, and to supply a reserve from which national armies might be raised in case of major war; and (3) a navy of sufficient size to protect American commerce and, in conjunction with coastal fortifications, to provide a first line of defense against invasion. This policy was much influenced by a traditional distrust of standing armies in peacetime and a belief in the efficacy of a militia as the primary bulwark of defense in a democratic state.

The militia was, in fact, neither well organized nor well trained, and thus, it did not fulfill its role as a national reserve. It proved a weak reed in the War of 1812. In the Mexican War, the Civil War, and the Spanish-American War the nation relied primarily on volunteers (recruited in state units) to fill the ranks of its armies. These volunteer citizen armies were quickly demobilized after each conflict.

America's emergence as a world power after the Spanish-American War brought some modifications in the old military policy. The navy, by then charged with defense of possessions overseas as well as of American coasts, began to build toward the supremacy at sea advocated by Adm. Alfred T. Mahan and his disciples. Both the army and the navy modernized their systems of administration and command. The Dick Act of 1903 ended the old universal militia system for all practical purposes and substituted an organized volunteer militia, known as the National Guard, as the main U.S. Army reserve, under state control. The National Defense Act of 1916 added a volunteer organized reserve under national control, and the three components were recognized by the National Defense Act of 1920 as making up the army of the United States. Meanwhile, in World War I, a great national army was raised by conscription, and the whole national economy was for the first time tightly organized to support a military effort.

In the wave of disillusionment after World War I the United States reverted to isolationism and to military policies to match it. The World War I army was rapidly demobilized, and Congress rejected all schemes for universal military service in peacetime to maintain a trained reserve. Neither the regular army structure nor the volunteer reserve structure contemplated in the National Defense Act amendments of 1920 was funded by Congress or supported by the public. The goal of a "navy second to none" was abandoned in the naval limitation treaties negotiated at the Washington Conference in 1921–22. The place of the new element in the military picture—airpower—remained ill-defined and controversial.

With the approach of World War II these policies of neglect were reversed, and in the war itself the nation simply sought to provide the largest military forces its resources would permit. Despite new responsibilities in the postwar world, the massive World War II military structure was dismantled as hastily and almost as completely as after earlier wars. But in the midst of demobilization, growing tensions with the Soviet Union forced attention to the necessity for military strength sufficient to guard against Communist encroachments around the globe. In the development of military policies for this purpose, the new element, for which historic policies provided no guidance, was the development by both major powers of nuclear weapons of ever-increasing destructive power and of sophisticated means for delivery on their targets.

The central feature of American military policy in the postwar world was the maintenance of an atomic striking power that would serve to deter any attack on the United States or its principal allies. But with treaty obligations and military interests in every corner of the globe, the United States had to give consideration to preparation for contingencies other than atomic war, particularly as the Soviet Union moved closer to atomic parity with the United States. Every administration in the postwar era attempted to maintain forces in being or in reserve to deal with a whole spectrum of possible conflicts from full-scale atomic war to guerrilla warfare in outlying areas of the world. The central question of military policy was that of a proper mix of the elements in the military structure— within army, navy, and air force, joined together in a single Department of Defense, and within the forces of all services required for different contingencies. Different administrations adopted different approaches to the problem. The administration of President Harry S. Truman, after initial retrenchment and tacit reliance on air atomic power, undertook a massive rearmament program after the outbreak of the Korean War, stressing balanced forces to meet a Soviet threat in Europe. President Dwight D. Eisenhower modified this policy to place more explicit reliance on air atomic power under the doctrine of massive retaliation. Under presidents John F. Kennedy and Lyndon B. Johnson a policy of flexible response was adopted, emphasizing balanced forces, both conventional and nuclear, to meet the spectrum of threats without sacrificing atomic supremacy.

These policies of maintaining large forces in being required a level of military expenditure undreamed of before World War II and reliance on conscription to maintain military strength. Reserve policy came gradually to emphasize readiness of small, select elements rather than masses of semitrained reserve manpower. Although President Richard M. Nixon, after 1969, continued the general policies of his predecessors, he started a retrenchment of conventional forces as the United States withdrew from Vietnam, accepted a doctrine of nuclear sufficiency rather than absolute superiority in the face of a great growth in Soviet

atomic strength, and ended conscription as a means of recruiting military manpower.

[Samuel Huntington, *The Common Defense: Strategic Programs in National Politics;* Library of Congress Legislative Reference Service, *United States Defense Policies Since World War II;* Walter Millis, *Arms and Men: A Study in American Military History;* Raymond G. O'Connor, ed., *American Defense Policy in Perspective;* Emory Upton, *The Military Policy of the United States.*]

ROBERT W. COAKLEY

MILITARY ROADS. *See* **Roads, Military.**

MILITARY TRACTS. Military land bounties were offered in the early national period by the states and the federal government to attract people into the armies or to reward soldiers and officers for their services. In the revolutionary war such bounties varied in size according to military rank, the upper limit being 5,000 to 10,000 acres in some cases. To satisfy the warrants issued for these bounties military tracts were set aside in which the warrantee had to locate his land. New York set up two such reserves, one in the Finger Lakes district and the other in the extreme northern part of the state. North Carolina created a military tract in the Cumberland basin of Tennessee, and Virginia established a similar tract in western Kentucky. When it was seen that the Kentucky tract would not satisfy outstanding warrants of Virginia, a second military tract, consisting of 3.85 million acres, was created in south central Ohio, which Virginia reserved to itself from the cession it made of its western lands to the federal government. In this latter tract the United States had no control over the lands; it is the only part of Ohio that was not surveyed in rectangles in advance of lawful settlement (*see* Virginia Military Reserve in Ohio).

The United States created four military tracts to satisfy the warrants it gave in the revolutionary war and the War of 1812. The first of these was located in central Ohio, adjacent to the Virginia military tract, and consisted of 2,539,000 acres. Warrantees of the revolutionary war located their lands here. The other three tracts of 2 million acres each were originally located in Michigan, Illinois, and Arkansas; but when it was reported that the Michigan tract was poorly drained and unsuited to farming, it was abandoned and the Illinois tract was increased to 3.5 million acres and a tract of 500,000 acres was established in Missouri. In these three tracts soldiers of the War of 1812, who received 160 acres each, were required to locate their warrants by lottery.

Most of the soldiers or their heirs refused to move to these tracts to take up their claims, as the law contemplated, because they were too far from zones of settlement. Instead, they sold their warrants or locations to speculators for prices as low as ten cents an acre. The result was a high percentage of absentee or speculative ownership in each of the military tracts. For example, twenty-four persons, including Nathaniel Massie, Duncan McArthur, and Thomas Worthington, owned 1,035,000 acres in the Virginia military tract of Ohio. In the military tract of Illinois, located in the triangle between the Illinois and Mississippi rivers, the New York and Boston Illinois Land Company acquired 900,000 acres, Romulus Riggs of Philadelphia owned 40,000 acres, and other easterners had large possessions.

Such large-scale land monopolization in the military tracts aroused all the latent frontier hostility against absentee speculators. Squatters settled upon the absentee-owned lands, plundered them of their timber, defied ouster proceedings, and flouted all efforts to make them pay rent for their use of the land. Local governments frequently levied discriminatory taxes on absentee-owned lands, raised their valuations, and built public improvements in their vicinity to force higher taxes. Many speculators with little capital lost their lands at tax sales; others, better financed, sooner or later would sell or lease to tenants. Residents of the military tracts long cherished their dislike of nonresident proprietors.

[B. H. Hibbard, *History of the Public Land Policies;* P. J. Treat, *The National Land System, 1785–1820.*]

PAUL W. GATES

MILITARY WARRANTS. *See* **Land Bounties.**

MILITIA. The militia system is based on the idea that every able-bodied man owes military service to his country. Traditionally militiamen have been enrolled and drilled in military organizations other than regular forces and subject to call to duty in times of national or other emergency.

Early American colonists faced Indian attack and famine, and survival dictated that every male colonist be both settler and soldier. With manpower at a premium and regular troops unavailable, the colonies reverted to the old English fyrd, general levy, or militia, as it was coming to be known. Under this system every able-bodied man was enrolled for local defense. Virginia and other southern colonies followed the British organization, dividing the colony into counties, each supervised by a lieutenant. In New England, New Jersey, and New York the town was the militia's basic unit, although the county was retained as an element of higher control.

As the population increased and the frontier moved west a gradual change occurred. Dangers became less frequent along the seaboard, and so universal service was maintained only along the frontier. Colonial troops for service in King William's War (1689–97), Queen Anne's War (1702–13), King George's War (1740–48), and the French and Indian War (1754–63) were raised largely by selection or ordinary recruiting, although the legal militia obligation remained in force and local musters were still held. This change occurred because the entire male population was no longer needed for military campaigns. With the approach of the American Revolution the patriot faction gained control of the militia, which reinforced the Continental army, provided local security, and harassed British detachments. About 164,087, or 41 percent, of the 395,864 troops employed in the formal campaigns were militia.

After the Revolution, Congress cut the army to eighty men, believing it to be "dangerous to the liberties of a free people" to have a large standing army. From 1784 to 1786 Congress asked the states to furnish militiamen for a required force. Although it had the constitutional power to provide for organizing, arming, and disciplining the militia, Congress chose not to exercise that option. In 1789, Congress raised a regular regiment of infantry and a battalion of artillery but also reaffirmed its faith in the militia concept. In 1792, Congress enacted a law to the effect that all free, able-bodied, white male citizens between eighteen and forty-five years of age were to be enrolled in the militia by local authorities and that the units were to be organized by the state governors, thus committing the United States to the militia concept for defense. Although the militia could quell domestic disturbances, such as Shays's Rebellion (1786–87) and the Whisky Insurrection (1794), it proved almost useless on the frontier and had to be replaced by regular troops. The law of 1792 was virtually unenforceable, and annual musters degenerated into drinking brawls in many cases. Except when led by such outstanding commanders as Andrew Jackson and Jacob Brown, militiamen performed poorly in the

War of 1812. Many units refused to leave the state or cross the border into Canada. Thereafter the militia idea as a workable plan was slowly abandoned. Local groups organized into military units with little or no help from any governmental source. Many units were composed of socially elite and wealthy men who had considerable political influence; others were formed from immigrant groups, especially Irish and German. In 1840, Massachusetts abolished all the militia except for these volunteer units, and other states soon followed suit. The militia played no part in the Mexican War, but the volunteers formed an important part of the army. In the years just before the Civil War the volunteer units increased in number, and they provided cadres for units, North and South, during the war and many partially trained officers. Aside from President Abraham Lincoln's initial call for 75,000 militiamen for three months' service, all Civil War levies were for individuals, either volunteers or draftees.

The general demobilization following the Civil War left the volunteer militia units as the nation's only reserve force. During this time these units generally adopted the name National Guard. Most of them volunteered for the Spanish-American War, although some refused. This reticence, a general lack of efficiency in the volunteering units, and the recognition that the militia concept was unworkable led to the Dick Act of 1903, which declared that the armed forces of the United States, in addition to the regular army, consisted of the organized and unorganized militias, with the understanding that the latter was nonexistent. The volunteer National Guard became the organized militia, organized, equipped, and trained as the regular army. In 1916 it became subject to federal standards of efficiency and federal control for any type of emergency, the federal government assuming responsibility for the guard's drill pay. In 1917, National Guard units lost their historic state designations, and in 1933 the guard was given the status of a reserve component of the army. In 1956 the regular army took over the basic training of all guardsmen, although when not on active federal service they are under state control.

The militia, as called for in the Militia Act of 1792, is still in existence—both the organized militia, consisting of the National Guard and the Naval Militia, and the unorganized militia, consisting of all ablebodied males between 18 and forty-five years of age who are not members of the organized militia. Female citizens of the United States who are commissioned officers in the National Guard are also members of the militia. The former function of the fyrd or general levy is fulfilled by the draft, even when in suspension.

[J. D. Hill, *The Minute Man in Peace and War;* W. H. Riker, *Soldiers of the States.*]

WARNER STARK

MILLE LACS, BATTLE OF (ca. 1745). As part of their general tribal advance, Lake Superior Chippewa, equipped with firearms, surprised three Sioux villages on the southwest shore of Mille Lacs, Minn. In a fierce three-day battle, the Sioux were decisively defeated and, retreating down Rum River, abandoned these villages. This encounter is sometimes called the Battle of Kathio.

[W. W. Warren, *History of the Ojibway Nation.*]

WILLOUGHBY M. BABCOCK

MILLERITES. *See* **Adventist Churches.**

MILLIGAN, EX PARTE, 4 Wallace 2 (1866), a Supreme Court case in which the trial and conviction of Lambdin P. Milligan by a military commission in 1864 were invalidated. Milligan had been arrested at his Indiana home by order of the general in command of the military district of Indiana and was charged with conspiring against the United States, with giving aid and comfort to the enemy, and with inciting insurrection and disloyal practices (*see* Copperheads). The charges grew out of Milligan's activities as an officer of a secret order whose general purpose was to cooperate with the Confederate government. Milligan was tried before a court-martial established under the authority of the president, found guilty, and sentenced to be hanged. Before execution of the sentence, proceedings were instituted in the federal circuit court denying the legality of the military trial, and asserting that Milligan had been deprived of his constitutional right to trial by jury.

The Supreme Court held that neither the president nor Congress has the power to set up military tribunals except in the actual theater of war, where the civil courts are no longer functioning; and that elsewhere courts-martial have jurisdiction only over persons in the military or naval service of the United States. Milligan was not in the military or naval service; war did not exist in Indiana; nor was the state invaded or threatened with invasion; and the civil courts were open and in the proper and unobstructed exercise of their jurisdiction. The substitution of trial before a court-martial for the regular civil procedure was therefore unwarranted, and Milligan had been deprived of his constitutional right. He was released, after having been held in confinement for eighteen months. Later, because the decision seemed to cast grave doubt upon the legality of the military government established by Congress in former rebellious states, the Court was widely denounced, especially by Radical Republicans.

[W. D. Foulke, *Life of Oliver P. Morton;* S. Klaus, ed., *The Milligan Case;* B. Pitman, *Trials for Treason at Indianapolis.*]

P. ORMAN RAY

"MILLIONS FOR DEFENSE, BUT NOT ONE CENT FOR TRIBUTE," a toast offered by Robert Goodloe Harper, South Carolina member of the House of Representatives, at a dinner given by Congress in Philadelphia on June 18, 1798, in honor of John Marshall. Marshall, Charles Cotesworth Pinckney, and Elbridge Gerry were the commissioners sent to France in October 1797 by President John Adams to negotiate with France concerning that country's hostile actions against United States shipping. Charles Maurice de Talleyrand-Périgord, minister of foreign affairs, solicited a bribe of $250,000 and a "loan" to France (actually a gift) of several million dollars before he would receive the commissioners. Pinckney's reply to Talleyrand's agent was "Not a sixpence!" The Quasi-War with France followed soon afterward. (*See also* Franco-American Misunderstanding; XYZ Affair.)

[A. J. Beveridge, *Life of John Marshall.*]

CHARLES LEE LEWIS

MILL SPRINGS, ENCOUNTER AT, took place on Jan. 19, 1862, in Pulaski County, Ky., between about 4,000 Confederates led by George B. Crittenden and an equal number of Union troops under George H. Thomas. Before the end of the day, with the arrival of about 8,000 reinforcements, the Union troops had disastrously defeated the Confederates and killed Felix K. Zollicoffer, second in command. This was one of a number of disasters that overtook the Confederates and resulted in their expulsion from Kentucky.

[L. Collins and R. H. Collins, *History of Kentucky;* E. M. Coulter, *Civil War and Readjustment in Kentucky.*]

E. MERTON COULTER

MILL STREAMS. That the pioneers could think of no more appropriate name than Mill Creek or Mill River for dozens of streams in the eastern United States attests to the widespread use of waterpower. There are two Mill Rivers flowing into the Connecticut in Massachusetts alone. When dams and short canals with locks began to be constructed in the late 18th and early 19th centuries for the improvement of navigation by arks, flatboats, and rafts of such rough rivers as the Merrimack, the Connecticut, the Blackstone, the Mohawk, the Potomac, the James, the Schuylkill, and others, the fall of the water at the locks was often employed to operate mills and factories. The village of Manchester, N.H., was developed into an important industrial city after 1800 through the utilized waterpower of the little canal around the Amoskeag Falls in the Merrimack River. Those early mills had to be actuated directly by a water wheel or turbine, and therefore had to be close to the fall or rapid. Woonsocket and Pawtucket, R.I., were built up on the Blackstone by the power from that stream and from the canal locks later (1824–28) built alongside it. Paterson, N.J., and Rochester, N.Y., became large cities because of the cataracts of the Passaic and the Genesee, around which they were built. The Falls of Saint Anthony in the Mississippi aided in the establishment of Minneapolis. The name of the city of Fall River, Mass., tells its own story. Lowell on the Merrimack, Turner's Falls, Holyoke, and Chicopee on the Connecticut, and Richmond on the James are other cities made large and prosperous by the adjacent waterpower that in their earlier history was almost their only reason for being. Even larger canals often sold waterpower at their locks; one frequently finds the prospectus of a new canal project estimating that the waterpower would operate, say, "thirty run of millstones."

ALVIN F. HARLOW

MIMS, FORT, MASSACRE AT, occurred on Aug. 30, 1813, when the fort was attacked by a force of about 1,000 Creek. The fort was a mere stockade built the preceding July around the house of Samuel Mims on the eastern bank of Lake Tensaw, near Mobile, Ala. The families of the vicinity had taken refuge in the stockade, fearing a Creek uprising in revenge for the Burnt Corn attack in July. Not expecting an attack, the commanding officer, Maj. Daniel Beasley, neglected to keep out patrols, to maintain a watch, or even to keep the gates closed. The Creek surprised the fort and after desperate fighting burned the fort and massacred all but 36 of the fort's 553 inhabitants.

[T. M. Owen, *History of Alabama and Dictionary of Alabama Biography.*]

R. S. COTTERILL

MINA EXPEDITION. In an attempt to liberate Mexico, Francisco Xavier Mina, a Spanish exile in the United States, reached Galveston, Tex., in November 1816 with some 200 volunteers. He landed at Soto la Marina, Tamaulipas, in April 1817. Receiving additional recruits from New Orleans, he marched into the interior of Mexico. After some preliminary successes most of his followers deserted him. On Oct. 17 he was surprised and captured by a superior Spanish force and sent to Mexico City, where he was executed on Nov. 11, 1817.

[H. H. Bancroft, *History of Mexico;* H. I. Priestley, *The Mexican Nation.*]

WALTER PRICHARD

MINERALOGY. Observations on minerals in the New England and Virginia colonies appear in the writings of John Josselyn and other early 17th-century travelers. In the mid-17th century John Winthrop, son of the first governor of the Massachusetts Bay Colony, actively engaged in the search for and development of mineral deposits. His grandson, John Winthrop, Jr., who had similar interests, formed a notable mineral collection that was presented to the Royal Society of London in 1734 and later incorporated into the British Museum. Throughout the colonial period, questions about the nature and use of minerals and rocks and about the development of known mineral deposits were usually answered by sending specimens or trial shipments of ore abroad or by importing skilled workmen or experts from Europe. The first American study of mineralogy in a professional sense began after the Revolution—led by Adam Seybert, Gerard Troost, and the mineral chemist James Woodhouse, all of Philadelphia. The first mineral collections of scientific importance began to be acquired at about the same time. Most of the specimens were brought from Europe, chiefly by Americans traveling abroad for educational purposes and by immigrants of scientific or technological bent. It was the acquisition of these European collections, with their store of correctly identified and labeled material illustrating European textbooks, that provided the basis for American study instruction.

The formal teaching of mineralogy—the term then usually included earth history and other aspects of geology—began in American colleges shortly before 1800. Benjamin Waterhouse, a Rhode Island Quaker who had been trained in medicine and the natural sciences in Leyden and London, lectured on mineralogy and botany at Brown University in 1786 and at the medical school at Harvard between 1788 and 1812.

The first textbook on mineralogy written in the United States, Parker Cleaveland's *Elementary Treatise on Mineralogy and Geology,* was published in Boston in 1816. Cleaveland, a Harvard graduate of 1799, was self-taught in mineralogy. He was professor of natural philosophy and mathematics at Bowdoin College. The work received good reviews in Europe and remained a standard text for many years. In 1837 James Dwight Dana of Yale brought out the *System of Mineralogy,* which became an international work of reference, reaching a sixth edition in 1892. Both of these books drew heavily on European works, especially those of the German Friedrich Mohs and of French crystallographer R. J. Haüy.

The main development of mineralogy and geology in the United States took place in the first three decades of the 19th century, centering in the New England colleges. The leading figure was Benjamin Silliman, appointed professor of chemistry and natural science at Yale in 1802, in response to a move on the part of the college, then, like other New England colleges chiefly theological and classical in its leanings, to develop the sciences. Silliman was active as a teacher, editor, and public lecturer, rather than as an investigator. Among his students, Amos Eaton, Charles Upham Shepard, and Dana became important in the further development of the geological sciences.

The marked growth of the geological sciences in American colleges in the early 19th century was accompanied by the formation of numerous state and local academies, lyceums, and societies concerned with natural history. These organizations afforded public platforms from which such men as Silliman and Eaton and, later, Louis Agassiz, spread scientific ideas. The Academy of Natural Sciences of Philadelphia, organized in 1812, was a leading factor; it began the publication of its journal in 1817 and of its proceedings in 1826. The Boston Society of Natural History, formed in 1830—the year the first state geological survey was begun, in Massachusetts—and the Lyceum of Natural History of New York, organized in 1817, also were important.

The *American Journal of Science and Arts,* started by Silliman in 1818, published the bulk of American mineralogical contributions for the next five decades. (A forerunner, the *American Mineralogical Journal,* edited by Archibald Bruce of New York City, had published only four issues, 1810–14.)

Toward the middle of the 19th century courses in analytical chemistry, emphasizing ores, minerals, and agricultural materials, were introduced into many colleges and medical schools. Mineral chemistry and geochemistry developed strongly during the late 1800's, fostered especially by the U.S. Geological Survey, organized in 1879, and American work on minerals and rocks was outstanding in those fields. The publications of the U.S. Geological Survey and of the state geological surveys carried much descriptive mineralogical and petrographic material. Toward the end of the 19th century, as the organization and interests of science enlarged and specialized, the various academies and their attendant periodicals were joined and ultimately virtually supplanted by national and regional professional societies. The Mineralogical Society of America was founded in 1919, and the *American Mineralogist,* an independent journal first published in 1916, became its official journal.

The great private mineral collections, to which public museums and universities are deeply indebted, were developed during the last decades of the 19th century and the first decades of the 20th century, a period coinciding with the major development of America's mineral resources and the accumulation of large personal fortunes. Commercial dealing in mineral specimens, as by A. E. Foote of Philadelphia, developed on a large scale. Exhibits at national and international fairs, notably at the Saint Louis World's Fair of 1904, also spread interest.

Crystallography, particularly in its theoretical aspects, did not attract much attention in the United States during the 19th century, when American interest in minerals was primarily concerned with chemical composition, occurrence, and use. It was not until the early 20th century that advanced instruction and research in the formal aspects of crystallography became widespread. Charles Palache of Harvard was one of the leaders.

[I. B. Cohen, *Some Early Tools of American Science;* G. P. Fisher, *Life of Benjamin Silliman;* John C. Greene, "The Development of Mineralogy in Philadelphia, 1780–1820," *Proceedings of the American Philosophical Society,* vol. 113 (1969).]

CLIFFORD FRONDEL

MINERAL PATENT LAW. The discovery of gold in California in 1848 occurred in a legal vacuum. The regulation of the race for wealth on the public domain was accomplished by rules growing out of the necessities of the miners through the organization of districts and the adoption of bylaws for those districts. It gradually became apparent that a national policy for the administration and disposal of the mineral resources of the public lands was essential. The resulting Mining Law of 1866 adopted the idea of open mineral exploitation of the public lands. A claimant who discovered a mineral lode, made a minimum investment in labor and improvements, and complied with filing and posting prerequisites could secure a patent from the United States on the lands covered by his claim. In 1870 similar legislation was enacted specifically covering placers—that is, surface deposits of gravels of mineral value, as opposed to lodes or veins of ore.

The legislation of 1866 and that of 1870 were combined in the Mineral Location Law of 1872. Locations based on discovery of a lode were limited to 1,500 feet by 600 feet, while placer claims were limited to 20 acres. Patents were issued upon payment of $5 per acre for lode claims and $2.50 per acre for placers. Although there are some differences in ownership rights between locators who have proceeded to a patent and those who have not, a valid location is sufficient without patent to allow the removal of the minerals from the claimed location.

Although there were a number of supplementing and limiting statutes, such as the Wilderness Act of 1964, the 1872 act still governed most of the public domain of the United States in the late 1970's, except in states derived from the original thirteen colonies, Texas, and several other specific exemptions. Oil and gas were included under the placer mining provisions of the federal legislation and could be acquired without the payment of any royalty to the United States; but under the Mineral Leasing Act of 1920 rights of exploration and production of those substances came to be leased, not patented, with royalty paid to the United States as landowner.

[Rocky Mountain Mineral Law Foundation, *American Law of Mining,* vol. 1, and *Law of Federal Oil and Gas Leases.*]

RICHARD C. MAXWELL

MINERAL SPRINGS, estimated at 10,000 in the United States, influenced the location of settlements. Salt deposits, or licks, attracted deer and buffalo, and the abundance of game made desirable sites. With crude diet, intemperance, and primitive medicine, convenient medicinal waters were a blessing. The most famous springs were at Saratoga, N.Y., and White Sulphur Springs, W.Va. After settlement, springs were important as resorts; visiting "spas" became fashionable. In 1809 Natchez ladies "took the waters" at nearby springs. Saratoga was nationally popular by 1820; White Sulphur by 1830. Most abundant east of the Mississippi, springs were especially important in the South. After 1870 improved transportation boomed resorts. Many were small, drawing patronage only from surrounding areas, but they became an important part of social routine. They were the scene of famous entertainments, honeymoons, family vacations, protracted "cures," political horsetrading, and gambling. (*See also* Resorts and Spas.)

MACK SWEARINGEN

MINE RUN CAMPAIGN (1863). The Army of the Potomac under Union Gen. George G. Meade forced its way across the Rappahannock River in Virginia on Nov. 7–8, 1863. Then, after some delay, the army crossed the Rapidan unopposed on Nov. 26. Gen. Robert E. Lee took a strong position in the forest back of a brook called Mine Run. There Meade, confronting him on Nov. 29, ordered flanking movements by G. K. Warren on the left and John Sedgwick on the right. Warren's advance was detected by Lee and blocked in such force that Warren refused a major attack. Meade thereupon halted Sedgwick, and the following day the Union army retired across the Rapidan.

[R. U. Johnson and C. C. Buel, eds., *Battles and Leaders of the Civil War*, vol. IV.]

ALVIN F. HARLOW

MINES, U.S. BUREAU OF. The U.S. Bureau of Mines was established in the Department of the Interior by an act of Congress approved May 16, 1910. The work of the new bureau had been initiated in 1904 under the U.S. Geological Survey in response to public demand for a federal program to alleviate coal mine hazards, which caused 2,000 deaths per year. Legislation in 1913 and 1915 expanded the bureau's responsibilities and provided for the establishment of ten experimental stations and seven mine-safety stations. The bureau was transferred to the Department of Commerce by President Calvin Coolidge in 1925, assuming additional functions previously assigned to the Geological Survey and the Commerce Department's Bureau of Foreign and Domestic Commerce.

President Franklin D. Roosevelt transferred the bureau back to the Department of the Interior in 1934.

The bureau's primary and continuing activities may be summarized as scientific, technologic, and economic research aimed at improving health, safety, efficiency, and conservation in mining, mineral processing, and mineral use. Health and safety responsibilities of the bureau were extended in May 1941 when Congress authorized the bureau to inspect coal mines. Legislation in 1952, 1966, and 1969 further increased the bureau's responsibility for health and safety in coal mines. The Federal Metal and Non-metallic Safety Act in 1966 extended the bureau's health and safety regulatory authority to other types of domestic mining. In May 1973 the Department of the Interior transferred responsibility for enforcing federal mining health and safety laws from the Bureau of Mines to the newly created Mining Enforcement and Safety Administration.

The bureau was the sole U.S. producer of helium from 1918 to 1961, initially for use in lighter-than-air craft. The bureau became involved because the federal government wanted the helium for defense purposes and apparently there were no commercial sources or commercial interest. After World War II, with five extraction plants (helium is extracted from natural gas) in operation, the bureau produced helium for the space program. Starting in 1963 much of the helium recovered was recharged underground for future use.

By 1930 the bureau had established its role as the principal governmental source of mineral intelligence, and this capability was expanded during World War II. The bureau's *Minerals Yearbook* (published annually) and the quintennial *Mineral Facts and Problems,* started in 1955, have become worldwide mineral references.

The bureau has been called upon for many special defense and civilian studies, including such diverse assignments as the control of civilian use of explosives; exploration for strategic minerals; research on military gases and gas masks; development of metallurgical technology and initial production of zirconium as a structural reactor material for the Nautilus nuclear submarine; recovery of radium when its first medical use was recognized; and investigation of explosions outside of mines.

Legislation in 1944 authorized the bureau to construct and operate demonstration plants to produce synthetic liquid fuels from coal, oil shales, agricultural products, and other substances. The program continued until 1955 and laid the groundwork for a renewed emphasis on energy research in the early 1970's. In early 1975, under the Energy Reorganization Act of 1974, the energy research activities were transferred to a newly created Energy Research and Development Administration.

By 1975 there were twelve Bureau of Mines metallurgy or mining research centers and four field operation centers. By that year the bureau had gained worldwide recognition as a result of its investigations, published in more than 18,000 principal reports.

[*Annual Reports of the Director of the Bureau of Mines* (1911–63).]

PAUL F. YOPES

MINES AND MINING. *See* **Ferrous Metals; Nonferrous Metals;** *and separate articles on the mining of individual metals, such as* **Lead, Copper,** *and* **Zinc.**

MINESWEEPING, the systematic clearance of mines from an area where they have been planted by submarines, surface ships, or aircraft, is simple if they are of the type set off by contact but difficult if they are of the influence type—that is, acoustic, magnetic, or pressure mines. Contact mines can be swept by a ship towing a serrated wire that cuts the mooring line and thus causes the mine to surface, where it can be destroyed by gunfire. One minesweeper can tow two sweep wires in a V-shaped arrangement called "both sides out," or two minesweepers can tow opposite ends of a sweep wire in a "single catenary sweep." Acoustic mines, which are set off by a built-in hydrophone that amplifies the sound of a ship's engines, are swept by towing a mechanical noise-maker near them. Magnetic mines, which are set off when a magnetic field causes a delicate needle to complete an electrical circuit, are swept by creating such a magnetic field over them with a towed cable in which a pulsating current is maintained. Pressure, or oyster, mines are set off only when a passing ship creates a change in water pressure. Pressure mines, sitting on the bottom, cannot be swept in the conventional sense. However, they are set to sterilize themselves after a certain period, when they become harmless.

Minesweeping is a tedious and dangerous operation. During the Civil War, Union forces cleared a few Confederate mines by dragging for them with chains strung between boats, but it was impossible to make a mined area completely safe. After World War

I, during which the United States and Great Britain laid the immense North Sea barrage of some 56,000 mines, 230 miles long and from 15 to 35 miles wide, minesweepers spent months clearing mines, with no assurance that all of them had been disposed of. Sometimes mooring cables broke and the mines floated away; sometimes cases leaked and they sank. Mines have been found on beaches, twenty or thirty years after they were laid.

An estimated 500,000 mines were laid in all the oceans of the world during World War II. In European waters alone, after the war ended, more than 1,900 minesweepers spent a couple of years clearing mines. American minesweepers cleared some 17,000 square miles of water in the Japanese area. Influence mines were particularly difficult to clear: at Nagoya, 1,900 sweeper-days were spent locating only six mines.

No extensive mining operations have been conducted since World War II, although the North Koreans laid influence mines off Korean coasts during the Korean War, and U.S. Air Force planes dropped mines in Haiphong harbor during the Vietnam War. Minesweepers cleared the mines in Korea, and minesweepers and helicopters went into Haiphong later and cleared mines there. Helicopters have virtually taken over minesweeping; they are faster, safer, and more efficient. When the Suez Canal was reopened in 1974, U.S. helicopters did all the minesweeping. There was no room for a minesweeper to tow conventional gear in the narrow canal, but helicopters towing acoustic and electronic sweeps were highly effective.

[Arnold S. Lott, *Most Dangerous Sea.*]

ARNOLD S. LOTT

MINGO BOTTOM, a region in Ohio about three miles south of Steubenville, so named for Mingo Indians who frequented it in the 18th century. During the revolutionary war it became a rendezvous for white expeditions against Indians farther west. From Mingo Bottom frontiersmen under Col. David Williamson marched to Gnadenhutten on Mar. 4, 1782, and massacred nearly 100 Christian Indians.

[Theodore Roosevelt, *Winning of the West.*]

ALFRED P. JAMES

MINIATURE in America, like its European prototype, was a small, portable, generally oval, portrait painted on ivory that was highly popular during the

18th and early 19th centuries. Whereas both portraits in oil and in miniature were considered primarily as family documents, the oil portrait, with its frame, served as an article of interior furnishing, while the miniature, with its gold case, was used for personal adornment as a locket or as part of a bracelet.

John Singleton Copley, better known as a portrait painter in oils, his half brother, Henry Pelham, John Ramage, James Peale, and Charles Willson Peale were some of the prominent 18th-century miniature painters. The most important miniature painters during the 19th century were Edward Greene Malbone, who worked in Boston, New York, and Charleston; Charles Fraser, who worked in Charleston; Benjamin Trott, who worked in Philadelphia and Baltimore; and Robert Field, an Englishman who worked in Boston, Washington, D.C., and Halifax, Nova Scotia.

In spite of their artistic quality, the value of miniatures is largely historic, as records of likenesses. There is a small but excellent collection of miniatures at the Metropolitan Museum of Art in New York City.

[T. Bolton, *Early American Portrait Painters in Miniature;* H. B. Wehle, *American Miniatures;* A. H. Wharton, *Heirlooms in Miniatures.*]

THEODORE BOLTON

MINIATURIZATION. Prior to the advent of the transistor in 1948, miniaturization had been a major design objective in only a few applications, such as hearing aids, proximity fuses, and portable radio transceivers. Although the earliest transistorized equipment was compact in comparison with older apparatus using vacuum-tube amplifiers, the discrete transistor marked only the beginning of a series of innovations in microelectronic technology. These innovations enabled the size of electronic devices to be reduced by a factor of approximately 100,000 between 1948 and the early 1970's. Major external stimuli for the astonishing achievements in miniaturization were provided by the aerospace programs, in missile guidance systems, for example, and by the adoption of entirely electronic switching by the telephone industry. By the mid-1970's the impact of microelectronics on consumer products had already been substantial, as in such popular and inexpensive applications as the pocket-sized electronic calculator, which may contain more than 10,000 microtransistors.

The most significant single technical innovation other than the discovery of the transistor itself in making possible the microelectronics revolution was the silicon oxide masking technique worked out by Carl Frosch and associates of the Bell Telephone Laboratories during the 1950's. This made the large-scale integrated circuit feasible with component densities of the order of 100,000 per square inch. In the mid-1970's studies were progressing toward a still further increase in component density by means of an electron beam fabrication method.

[A. N. Broers and M. Hatzakis, "Microcircuits by Electron Beam," *Scientific American* (November 1972); Horace D. Gilbert, *Miniaturization;* F. G. Heath, "Large-Scale Integration in Electronics," *Scientific American* (February 1970).]

JAMES E. BRITTAIN

MINIÉ BALL, a bullet invented in 1849 by Capt. Claude Étienne Minié of the French army. This bullet had a deep tapered cavity in the base with a hemispherical iron cup fitted into it. The bullet was easily fitted into a muzzle-loading rifle, and the force of the explosion expanded the base of the bullet against the rifling of the barrel with resultant greater accuracy and range. The Minié ball was used extensively in the Civil War in the Model 1842 U.S. Rifle, caliber .69. In the American service a wooden plug was substituted for Minié's iron ring, the force of the explosion driving the plug into the cavity and expanding the bullet.

[A. O. P. Nicholson, *Reports of Experiments With Small Arms for the Military Service.*]

H. A. DeWEERD

MINIMUM-WAGE LEGISLATION. The concept of a minimum wage may be said to go back to pre-Christian times, in the sense that a slaveowner was required to provide minimum subsistence for his bondsmen lest they perish. In many other societies wages were set at a "just" level (the medieval period) or, as with England's 16th-century legislation, at fixed maximums. Legal recognition of the idea of a minimum wage as a humanistic, as well as economic, desideratum is found first in a New Zealand law of 1894. In the United States the first such law was passed in 1906 in California; it provided for a minimum wage of $2 a day for almost all public employees. In 1912 Massachusetts enacted the first minimum-wage law that applied to private enterprise, but it affected only women and children. Fourteen other states and the District of Columbia and Puerto Rico had similar laws on their books within the next ten years. But the apogee of the minimum-wage movement had already been passed. In 1919 and 1921 Nebraska and Texas repealed their enactments. In

1923, in the case of *Adkins* v. *Children's Hospital,* the Supreme Court declared a District of Columbia minimum-wage statute to be unconstitutional on the ground that it violated the due process clause of the Fifth Amendment. The majority reasoned that in arbitrarily fixing a wage on the basis of the employee's minimum cost of living, the law might be requiring the employer to pay more than the services were worth and thus taking the employer's property. Within the next few years the Supreme Court invalidated several other state laws on the basis of similar reasoning but based its ruling on the Fourteenth Amendment. Kansan and Puerto Rican courts declared their own laws unconstitutional, and the Minnesota attorney general's opinion excepted only girls under eighteen from such a judicial ban.

Not until the effects of the Great Depression were felt in the early 1930's did the states revive their efforts in the area of minimum-wage legislation. In 1933, Connecticut, Illinois, New Hampshire, New Jersey, New York, Ohio, and Utah enacted such laws, followed by Massachusetts in 1934 and Rhode Island in 1936, but they sought to avoid the judicially rejected cost-of-living base by adopting a new approach. The states did not now attempt to regulate or fix wages directly but, through an investigation of any occupation in which women and minors received less than a living wage, set wages on the supposed judicially approved standard of what is "fairly and reasonably commensurate with the value of services rendered" and yet sufficient for the minimum necessary for health and well-being. This new attempt also failed at first, but only because of a procedural technicality. In a 1936 decision (*Morehead* v. *Tipaldo*) it was only a bare majority that ruled against the New York State minimum-wage law, and it rested its determination on the fact that "no application [had] been made for reconsideration of the constitutional question" decided in the *Adkins* case. Within ten months such an application was made in a Washington State case, *West Coast Hotel Company* v. *Parrish* (1937), and a new five-to-four majority upheld the law because of "the economic conditions which [had] supervened [since the *Adkins* decision] and in the light of the reasonableness of the exercise of the protective [police] power of the state." Thus, as long as a reasonable procedure is utilized that takes into account all economic views and factors, such as the relation of the type, hours, and conditions of the work to the employer's required payment, so that no judicially unreasonable wage determination eventuates, then such minimum-wage laws are constitutional.

After 1937 numerous state and federal laws involving or affecting minimum wages were quickly enacted. By 1974 forty-one states had such laws on the books, the exceptions being Alabama, Georgia, Iowa, Mississippi, Nebraska, South Carolina, Tennessee, Texas, and Virginia. Most of these laws cover only women over eighteen, but others also cover minors, with a few including men. In most states a general minimum wage is set by the legislature and in the others machinery is provided for administrative determinations. There are also state and federal laws relating to particular minimum-wage considerations—for example, setting minimums for apprentices and minors, affecting farm laborers, and establishing minimum overtime payments.

The principal federal law affecting wages is the Fair Labor Standards Act of 1938, commonly called the Wages and Hours Law, the enforcement of which is supervised by an administrator and ultimately enforced by the courts. (Where a state fixes a higher minimum, it, rather than the federal one, applies; furthermore, since the Fair Labor Standards Act is limited to industries in or affecting interstate commerce and therefore does not cover all employees and since it also contains several exemptions, state laws are a necessary adjunct to it.) The Fair Labor Standards Act was amended in 1947 by the Portal-to-Portal Act, which overturned a Supreme Court decision permitting extra pay for preparation and cleaning up work, so that only such work as is an integral and indispensable part of the employee's principal activities is today compensable. In 1963 another amendment, the Federal Equal Pay Act, provided equal pay for equal work in industries engaged in commerce. In addition, legislation has been passed specifically relating to the federal government as an employer and as a purchaser of goods and services, requiring it to pay set (minimum) wages to its employees and requiring the payment of minimum wages by parties that hold government contracts—the Davis-Bacon Act of 1931 and the Walsh-Healey Public Contracts Act of 1936.

Originally the Fair Labor Standards Act was aimed at establishing a 40 cents per hour minimum wage—raised to 75 cents per hour in 1949 and $1.00 per hour in 1956. By 1975 the federally established minimum wage had reached $2.10 per hour for nonfarm workers and $1.80 for farm workers, first covered in 1966.

[Barbara N. Armstrong, *Insuring the Essentials;* Bureau of National Affairs, *Wage and Hour Manual;* J. R. Commons and J. B. Andrews, *Principles of Labor Legislation;* Morris D. Forkosch, *A Treatise on Labor Law.*]

MORRIS D. FORKOSCH

MINING CAMP, LAW OF THE. The early mining camps of California and Colorado had a law of their own because the United States had not yet established civil government in the regions suddenly made populous by the goldseekers. When a group of miners found a promising spot they quickly formed a mining district, defined its boundaries, passed laws regulating the filing and working of claims, and elected officers. A president and recorder kept track of each miner's claims. A sheriff preserved order. Disputes were settled by the miners' court, an open meeting of miners at which both sides were heard and decisions rendered by those present. Usual punishments were hanging, shaving the head, banishment, whipping, and fines. To promote discovery the finder of a new vein or placer was given the right to file two claims. To insure equality of opportunity others could then preempt one claim each on that vein. The size of claims varied in each district, but 100 feet long by 50 feet wide was most common for lode claims. Claims had to be recorded and worked a specified number of days each year. This born-of-necessity and extralegal law of the mining camps established titles to the mines that were recognized by the United States in its mineral patent law of 1866.

[P. S. Fritz, *Constitutions and Laws of Early Mining Districts;* C. H. Shinn, *Mining Camps.*]

PERCY S. FRITZ

MINING TOWNS. The location of mining towns is determined by the location of the deposits, whether mineral, coal, or oil. All are monuments to the drama of mining, but none more so than the mining towns born in a gold rush. The towns originate in the desire of the miners to be near their place of work. Others come flocking to serve the miners' needs.

Most of America's mining towns began as boom-towns. Flimsy temporary structures were dominant, and most early mining towns were destroyed by fire. San Francisco, gateway to the California mining towns, had five fires in the million dollar class between 1849 and 1851. The fire of May 4, 1851, almost completely destroyed the city. Denver, born in the Colorado gold rush (*see* Pikes Peak Gold Rush), was swept by fire on Apr. 19, 1863. Central City, Colo., completely destroyed by fire in 1874, was rebuilt mostly of stone. More recent mining towns have not escaped the same fate—for example, Cripple Creek, Colo., in 1896 and Nome, Alaska, in 1934. More substantial structures were usually built after such fires.

Another characteristic of mining towns is their rapid growth. Leadville, Colo., started in 1877, grew to a city of 10,000 inhabitants within two years. Nevada City, Calif., was a town that showed phenomenal growth in a few months. Mining towns show a much greater fluctuation in population than other towns, except seasonal resorts. Some early mining towns have developed other dominant interests, such as Oroville, Calif., with its fruit raising, and Gold Hill, Colo., which is a mountain resort. Other mining towns are now "ghost cities," their buildings still standing, but deserted. Kokomo, Colo., a ghost town, claims historic interest because it is the highest incorporated town (altitude 10,618 feet). Nevadaville, Colo., and Rhyolite, Nev., are other ghost cities. But as some die, new ones are born. Climax, Colo., is the site of the greatest molybdenum mine in the world. Uravan, Colo., has both name and prosperity based on two rare metals—uranium and vanadium.

[H. H. Bancroft, *Works,* vol. XXIII; G. C. Quiett, *Pay Dirt;* C. H. Shinn, *Mining Camps.*]

PERCY S. FRITZ

MINISINK INDIAN RAID. To divert attention from the expedition by Gen. John Sullivan and Gen. James Clinton against Iroquois strongholds, the Mohawk Indian Chief Joseph Brant and his men raided Minisink, N.Y., on July 20, 1779. They were pursued by 149 men and attacked on July 22 near Lackawaxen ford. Although considerably outnumbering the troops that attacked him, Brant won only after a hard struggle, losing many men. The principal object was not achieved; Sullivan and Clinton proceeded as planned.

[Howard Swiggett, *War out of Niagara;* H. E. Twichell, *History of the Minisink Country.*]

ARTHUR POUND

MINISINK PATENT, granted in 1704 by Edward Hyde, Lord Cornbury, to Stephen De Lancey, Matthew Ling, and twenty-two associates, was a vast tract, lying in the southern parts of Orange and Sullivan counties, N.Y., bounded on the south by Pennsylvania and on the north by the Hardenbergh patent.

[Russel Headley, *The History of Orange County;* C. E. Stickney, *A History of the Minisink Region.*]

A. C. FLICK

MINNEAPOLIS. *See* Twin Cities.

MINNESOTA. The central geographic position of Minnesota was fundamental in determining the course of its history. The state occupies the Lake Superior highlands, a portion of the prairie plains, and the upper limits of the Mississippi Valley. It looks eastward through the Great Lakes, northward down the Red River to Canada, and southward along the Mississippi, serving as the northern gateway to the western United States and to central Canada. Minnesota is not only the Star of the North, as its official seal proclaims; it is also the crest of the Middle West and the approximate geographic center of the continent.

More than 11,000 lakes are Minnesota's most distinctive feature. Minnesota's waters flow into three great systems: the Mississippi River, which rises in Lake Itasca, drains about 57 percent of the area; the Red River of the North and others channel the waters of about 34 percent of the region northward into Hudson Bay; and the Great Lakes–Saint Lawrence River system is the outlet for the remaining 9 percent.

The two great Indian families of major importance in Minnesota history were the Dakota Sioux and the Chippewa (Ojibwa). The Sioux occupied most of Minnesota when the first white men to record a journey to Minnesota arrived. Two Frenchmen, Pierre Esprit Radisson and Médart Chouart, Sieur de Groseilliers, may have traveled into the interior of Minnesota in 1654 and again in 1659. In 1679 another Frenchman, Daniel Greysolon, Sieur Duluth, went to Minnesota to make peace between the warring Sioux and Chippewa. After holding a council not far from the site of the city that now bears his name, he and his men pushed on to the Sioux villages at Mille Lacs. There Duluth asked for the Indians' friendship and claimed possession of the area for Louis XIV. In 1686, Nicholas Perrot, in command of the French in the West, established a trading post, Fort Saint Antoine, on the east side of Lake Pepin. There in 1689 he proclaimed the sovereignty of Louis XIV over the lands of the Sioux. In 1695, Pierre Charles Le Sueur established a post on Prairie Island, and in 1700 he led an expedition up the Minnesota River to the great bend where the city of Mankato now stands. There, at the mouth of the Blue Earth River, he built Fort L'Huillier and spent the winter. In 1731, Pierre Gaultier de Varennes, Sieur de La Vérendrye, started on a journey that took him deeper into the West than any of his fellow Frenchmen. He reached Grand Portage and the following year built Fort Saint Charles on Lake of the Woods. During the next fifteen years La Vérendrye's men traveled far into the Dakota plains

and built a chain of forts into the Saskatchewan Valley.

French control of the Northwest was broken by 1760. Piece by piece the French empire crumbled during the French and Indian War before the attacks of the English and the American colonists. When peace was made in 1763, the French surrendered to the British their extensive dominions in America. But the French had earlier ceded to Spain their claim to lands west of the Mississippi River, which thus did not fall into British hands.

At the close of the American Revolution, when England acknowledged the sovereignty of the United States over the region east of the Mississippi River, the new nation was too feeble to govern the area effectually. Whatever law and order existed was administered by the British fur-trading companies, then at the zenith of their power. From 1783 until after the War of 1812 the North West Company was in practical control of the Minnesota country, with at least twenty-four posts. The most important were those at Grand Portage (western headquarters for the whole British trade), Fond du Lac, and Sandy, Leech, Cass, and Red lakes.

After President Thomas Jefferson had completed the negotiations for the Louisiana Territory in 1803 he sent Meriwether Lewis and William Clark to explore the western wilderness. Lt. Zebulon M. Pike was dispatched to explore the upper Mississippi Valley. Pike arrived in the Minnesota country in September 1805 and went into camp on an island at the mouth of the Minnesota River, still known as Pike Island. There for the first time the U.S. flag was raised on Minnesota soil, and, at a council, Pike persuaded the Sioux to cede land at the mouth of the Saint Croix River and at the junction of the Minnesota and Mississippi rivers for army posts.

The fall of American garrisons in the Northwest during the War of 1812 caused the U.S. government to hasten its occupation of the northern lands. In 1815 a treaty was negotiated with the Sioux whereby they accepted the sovereignty of the United States. The following year Congress passed a law prohibiting all but Americans from trading with the Indians on American soil and established the first three of a contemplated chain of forts on the frontier—Fort Armstrong at Rock Island, Ill.; Fort Howard at Green Bay, Indiana Territory; and Fort Crawford at Prairie du Chien, Indiana Territory. In 1819 the post first known as Fort Saint Anthony and later as Fort Snelling was established at the junction of the Minnesota and Mississippi rivers. For a generation it remained the northwesternmost military post in the United States, and around it developed the fur-trading center of the region.

In 1823 the steamboat *Virginia* overcame the obstacles to navigation in the Mississippi River and triumphantly steamed upriver to Fort Snelling, making the first step toward closer contact for Minnesota with the outside world. This demonstration of the practicability of navigation on the upper Mississippi encouraged the development of commerce and led to increased activity in the fur trade.

In 1834, Henry Hastings Sibley and Hercules L. Dousman were appointed to manage the American Fur Company, which had gradually gained control of the fur trade in the Minnesota country, and began handling the trade with the Sioux in the Northwest. Sibley's success was immediate but short-lived. His agents were to be found in all parts of the area, and trading posts permanently occupied by white men appeared at favorable locations throughout the region. After 1837 the fur trade declined in importance, in part because of the depletion of fur-bearing animals but more because of the encroachment of settlement. In 1842, under the impact of the disastrous panic of 1837, the American Fur Company went into bankruptcy and the reign of that enterprise in the Northwest ended.

As early as the 1820's men had looked with covetous eyes at the rich stands of white pine in the valley of the Saint Croix and wondered about the farming possibilities of the area. Except for the Fort Snelling military reservation, the Indians held title to the entire Minnesota region. In 1837 the federal government negotiated treaties with the Sioux and Chippewa whereby they gave up their lands in a triangle bounded by the Saint Croix and Mississippi rivers and by a line drawn eastward from the mouth of the Crow Wing River.

On Mar. 3, 1849, Minnesota Territory was created by the U.S. Congress, and Alexander Ramsey, a Pennsylvania Whig, was appointed governor. According to the federal census of 1850 the territory had 6,077 inhabitants. Treaties with the Sioux in 1851 and with the Chippewa in 1854 and 1855 opened up vast areas west of the Mississippi, and an unparalleled rush to the new lands took place. An 1857 census indicated a population of 150,037. The towns of Stillwater and Saint Anthony (the latter merged with Minneapolis in 1872) prospered, and Saint Paul, at the head of navigation on the Mississippi, became the commercial center of the territory. In July 1857 a con-

vention met and drew up a state constitution, and on May 11, 1858, Minnesota became the thirty-second state in the Union.

Minnesota provided 22,000 men for the Union armies during the Civil War. Ramsey, who, as the infant state's governor, was in Washington, D.C., in April 1861 when Fort Sumter fell to the Confederacy, at once offered 1,000 troops to President Abraham Lincoln, who readily accepted them. Minnesota, less than three years old, was the first state to volunteer soldiers to defend the Union. Sixteen months later—in August 1862—Minnesota faced a war within the larger war, one within its own borders. When the Santee Sioux bands gathered in the spring of 1862 to elect a speaker, Little Crow was defeated by Traveling Hail, the former having fallen into disfavor with many of his people, who felt he was too friendly with white fur traders and public officials in treaty negotiations. As Indian grievances against the whites piled up—loss of ancestral lands, dissatisfaction with reservation life, crop failures, starvation, and delay on the part of the government in paying overdue annuities—Little Crow joined other Sioux leaders in appealing to Indian agents at the Lower and Upper Sioux agencies for food. Their appeals were met with indifference. The murder of five white settlers by four young Sioux on Aug. 17, 1862, provided the fuse that ignited a bloody and tragic uprising throughout the Minnesota River valley. The lives of some 500 white settlers and an unknown number of Indians were lost in the short space of thirty-eight days. The war rolled back the frontier at least a hundred miles and for a time resulted in white emigration from the state. Its tragic aftereffects kept the northwestern frontier in a turmoil throughout the Civil War. By 1869, however, westward immigration resumed.

Waves of migration richly diversified Minnesota's population. The state census of 1865 showed a population of 250,000; the federal census of 1900, 1,751,394. In 1881 the state had a population of 780,773 residents; of these, 267,676, about 30 percent, were foreign-born. By 1880, 71 percent of the population was first- or second-generation immigrants from Europe. The largest single immigrant group in 1880 was German born, 66,592 of the total; the Scandinavians numbered 107,768—62,521 Norwegians, 39,176 Swedes, and 6,071 Danes. The third largest immigrant group was composed of English-speaking peoples (Irish, English, Scottish, and Welsh), who totaled 38,504. In addition, 29,631 Minnesotans traced their ancestry to British America.

By 1858, Minnesota farmers were devoting 66 percent or more of their acreage to wheat, and in that year wheat was for the first time shipped commercially from the state. A year later wheat exports exceeded fur exports in value, and the wheat crop increased from 2 million bushels in 1860 to 19 million in 1870, to 34 million in 1880, and to 95 million in 1890—far more than the yield from any other crop. Wheat was king, and it was shipped by rail and boat to markets all over the East and to Europe. Because repeated planting of this grain exhausted the soil, a kind of wheat frontier moved across the state. By 1890 it had reached the Red River valley. As the wheat frontier moved on, farmers turned their attention to other crops. Milk, butter, and cheese had been produced from the beginning, but it was not until the 1880's that dairy products took a leading position in the state's agricultural economy. In the north the forests began to be felled under the organized attack of lumber companies. Agricultural conditions revived; railroads were again being built; and the basis was laid for steady growth in the following decades.

In 1861 one railroad company—the Saint Paul and Pacific—managed to build about 1,500 feet of track, an amount sufficient to run its lone locomotive from the steamboat wharf, where it had been landed, to the roundhouse the company had erected. In the spring of 1862 the firm pushed its work with such vigor that in early July it opened service over the first ten miles of its line, from Saint Paul to Saint Anthony, which became Minneapolis. By 1865 there were 210 miles of railroad in operation in the state, and two years later Minnesota had achieved a major goal, an all-rail link with Chicago. By the end of 1872 fifteen companies had built almost 2,000 miles of track, covering the settled portions of the state and, in the case of the Northern Pacific and the Saint Paul and Pacific, reaching into the wilderness itself. The main outlines of Minnesota's 20th-century railroad system were already discernible, and in the next thirty years almost 5,000 additional miles of track were laid.

In 1884 the mining of iron ore was begun in the Vermilion Range, and in 1890 and 1891 the much larger deposits of the Mesabi Range were discovered. With the opening of the Cuyuna Range in 1911, Minnesota became the primary U.S. source of iron ore. The granite quarries of Saint Cloud were also being exploited.

Flour milling developed as an adjunct to Minnesota's wheat production, and as that declined and the raising of livestock increased, South Saint Paul and Austin became meat-packing centers. As an adjunct to the lumber industry the manufacture of paper became a major industry, particularly in International Falls.

Minnesota has had an unconventional political history. While the Republican party was dominant during much of the state's history, a vigorous liberal tradition nurtured a number of third parties. The source of the state's liberal tradition can be traced to the cooperative social and economic ideas imported by Scandinavian immigrants; to a strong labor movement forged in the lumber and mining camps, as well as in the cities; to recurring economic depressions in the midwestern farm belt; and to a remarkable series of farm-protest leaders who articulated the keenly felt grievances of the Minnesota farmer.

During the first half-century after the establishment of the territory in 1849, the frontier had been settled, and Minnesota emerged as a rich, rural, agricultural state. After 1900, Minnesota became an urban, industrial commonwealth—with its nonidentical twin cities of Minneapolis and Saint Paul as the metropolitan center for the upper Midwest. Its industrial power, once closely tied to its varied natural resources—soil, water, timber, and iron—continued to develop, but electronics, adhesives, and abrasives were introduced, adding much diversification. In 1860 less than 10 percent of the population lived in the three communities with more than 2,500 people, Saint Paul, Saint Anthony, and Minneapolis; Saint Paul, the largest, had only 10,401 citizens. By 1970 one-half of the 3.8 million people in Minnesota lived in the seven-county area surrounding Minneapolis and Saint Paul.

The 1930's was a pivotal period for forging public policies that would strongly influence political leaders of the future toward progressive social and economic programs. Under the leadership of Gov. Floyd B. Olson and the Farmer-Labor party, a state income tax was enacted in 1935, and it laid the foundation for one of the most progressive state tax structures in the nation.

By the middle of the 20th century, Minnesotans long accustomed to thinking of their state as agricultural found that fundamental shifts had occurred in the state's economy. The 1950 census figures showed that for the first time the value of goods manufactured in Minnesota exceeded that of its agricultural products. By the 1970's the great extractive industries like lumber, mining, and, to some extent, agriculture had been supplanted by manufacturing and service industries, and close to two-thirds of Minnesota's people lived in urban areas. The variety of industrial production was enormous, ranging from food processing and taconite pellets to such industries as printing, electronics, and computer manufacture. In 1962, although Minnesota ranked twenty-sixth in the country in per capita income and thirtieth in disposable income after taxes, it ranked fifth in public school revenue from state and local sources and second highest in the percent of its students who graduate from high school. The state has also been among the leaders of progressive taxation as well as in the first rank among states providing high quality public services—a combination of public policies that has helped to make possible the much-heralded "quality of life" for which Minnesota is known.

[Theodore C. Blegen, *Minnesota: A History of the State;* Russell W. Fridley, *Minnesota: A State That Works,* and *Minnesota: A Student's Guide to Localized History.*]

RUSSELL W. FRIDLEY

MINNESOTA MORATORIUM CASE, or *Home Building and Loan Association* v. *Blaisdell et al.,* 290 U.S. 398 (1934). At the height of the depression that began in 1929, many property owners whose properties were covered by a mortgage were unable to meet the regular interest payments. Under long-established rules of law, the holders of these mortgages had a right to foreclose. Property owners importuned their legislators for relief. In 1933, in Minnesota and some other states, so-called mortgage moratorium acts were adopted. These acts were immediately attacked on constitutional grounds. On the one hand, it was contended that they constituted a violation of the contract clause in the federal Constitution (*see Fletcher* v. *Peck*) and of the due process and equal protection clauses of the Fourteenth Amendment, while on the other the existence of an emergency situation was stressed. The Minnesota act was sustained by the state supreme court and, on appeal, by the U.S. Supreme Court. While the latter contended that an emergency does not create power, it admitted that an emergency may furnish occasion for the exercise of power. The conditions upon which the period of redemption was extended did not appear to the majority of the Court to be unreasonable; furthermore, the act was definitely temporary in character, its life being limited to the exigency that called it forth.

[Robert E. Cushman, "Constitutional Law in 1933–34," *American Political Science Review* (February 1935).]

W. BROOKE GRAVES

MINORITY RIGHTS. Doctrines of natural rights, under whose aegis the Declaration of Independence was issued, enunciate the view that while governments must indeed make certain binding decisions for society, there are rights of human beings that must not be impaired by those decisions. Thus, while governments may have to restrict liberty in controlling crime, they should do so only under fixed procedures ("due process of law"); and certain rights such as freedom of speech, association, and the press are particularly sacrosanct. Basic rights of minorities are to be respected, according to many thinkers, for a number of reasons. First, human beings should be valued as ends in themselves and not merely as means to other ends. Second, the idea of majority rule itself requires that respect be given the rights of minorities: thus if freedom of speech is suppressed by today's majority, present minorities will not be able to become tomorrow's majority through peaceful discussion and persuasion. Federal and state checks and balances and constitutional bills of rights were thus designed to protect minorities against established governments. James Madison argued (*Federalist Papers,* No. 10) that protection against the pressures of a potentially monolithic public opinion may be undergirded by diversity of interests, parties, factions, and sects, or what has since been termed social, economic, and cultural pluralism.

American history has been characterized by an almost constant struggle to protect minority rights against various kinds of encroachments. In 1798, for instance, the Alien and Sedition Acts imposed restrictions on freedom of speech and the press; and the acts were vigorously opposed. Before the Civil War, proponents of slavery attempted to limit antislavery agitation through gag rules involving petitions to Congress and other measures, but they were overcome by the war itself.

After the Civil War increasing social and economic complexity, expanded use of government regulatory power, and several wars posed new problems and dramatized old ones. Workers, particularly industrial workers, seeking to form unions, were restricted in their attempts to organize labor unions throughout the 19th century, and only in the 1930's were these restrictions somewhat abated. Alleged abrogations of the rights of religious minorities have been the occasion for Supreme Court decisions, as when the Court upheld the right of the children of Jehovah's Witnesses not to salute the U.S. flag in *West Virginia State Board of Education* v. *Barnette,* 319 U.S. 624 (1943). Political minorities have often found it difficult to express themselves freely: they were jailed during World War I for circulating anticonscription pamphlets; investigated by constitutionally and morally questionable methods, particularly in the 1920's and 1950's; often confronted by state statutes making it difficult for minority parties to be listed on the ballot; and punished, not for overt acts, but for allegedly conspiring to organize the Communist party and to teach and advocate the forcible overthrow of the government, as in *Dennis et al.* v. *United States,* 341 U.S. 494 (1951). During World War II, without trial and solely on the grounds of race, the U.S. government forced thousands of Japanese-Americans to leave their homes and to reside in camps. Afro-Americans were long relegated to racially segregated and inferior schools until in *Brown* v. *Board of Education of Topeka,* 347 U.S. 483 (1954), the Supreme Court held that racially segregated schools were inherently unequal; and the civil rights movement of the 1960's sought to secure the rights of racial minorities in public accommodations and other areas. Also in the 1960's and 1970's efforts were made to buttress the rights of the poor and the aged, of prisoners, and of Indians.

The American experience suggests that minority rights are always in peril and that their protection depends not only on law and the courts but also on the development of economic and organizational power by the minorities themselves. Minorities, many have argued, must struggle for their own rights through such activities as public agitation, strikes, and, on occasion, civil disobedience.

[Robert E. Cushman, *Civil Liberties in the United States;* Robert B. Downs, ed., *The First Freedom;* Paul L. Murphy, *The Meaning of Freedom of Speech.*]

MULFORD Q. SIBLEY

MINOR V. *HAPPERSETT,* 21 Wallace 162 (1875). The first section of the Fourteenth Amendment provides that ''No State shall make or enforce any law which shall abridge the privileges or immunities of citizens of the United States.'' Virginia L. Minor, a citizen of Missouri and the wife of a Saint Louis lawyer, when rejected in her attempt to register in 1866 as a voter in that state, maintained that the right of suffrage was a privilege of U.S. citizenship. In rejecting this contention, the Supreme Court held that the right of suffrage is not coextensive with citizenship, that the Fourteenth Amendment does not add to the privileges or immunities of citizens of the United States, but merely furnishes an additional guarantee for those in existence, and that, if the purpose of the amendment had been to make all citizens voters, it would have been unnecessary to adopt the Fifteenth

Amendment. In the opinion, the Court, for the first time, also gave a definition of citizenship, declaring that a citizen is one who owes allegiance to the state of which he is a member, and to whom the state owes protection.

[K. H. Porter, *A History of Suffrage in the United States;* B. R. Trimble, *Chief Justice Waite.*]

THOMAS S. BARCLAY

MINSTREL SHOWS. The first appearance of a comic black character on the American stage is said to have taken place in Boston in 1799. There were few such appearances until 1830, when Thomas D. Rice introduced his enormously popular song, ''Jim Crow,'' in blackface makeup. The first known minstrel troupe was a quartette—including Dan Emmett, who later wrote the song ''Dixie''—that appeared on the Bowery in New York City in 1843. Thereafter, many new troupes sprang up and grew in size. By 1857, when the famous Christy Minstrels appeared, the performance had settled into the standard pattern that has endured. The ''first part'' had the company seated in a semicircle, with a white interlocutor and two ''end men'' who bandied jokes with him between vocal solos by others in the circle. Following this came the ''olio,'' a variety entertainment, with dances, comic sketches, and acrobatic turns. In the late 19th century, when such entertainment was highly popular and there were scores of companies on the road, Haverly's was perhaps most famous, although Lew Dockstader, Primrose and West, Al G. Fields, and others shared popularity with him toward the end and carried on after him. Beginning in 1853, Philadelphia had a permanent minstrel organization for three-quarters of a century. Minstrelsy gradually died out in the 20th century and was practically extinct by 1930, though the ''first part'' was heard in its original form on the radio as late as 1935.

[Edwin LeRoy Rice, *Monarchs of Minstrelsy.*]

ALVIN F. HARLOW

MINT, FEDERAL. Robert Morris, secretary of finance, urged the Continental Congress in 1782 to establish a mint. In 1786 Congress ordered the Board of the Treasury to study the subject, but not until Apr. 2, 1792, three years after the birth of the new government, was the creation of a mint authorized. It was set up in Philadelphia, then the national capital, in 1793, and remained there permanently after other government agencies had been moved to Washington, D.C. Silver coinage began in 1794 and gold coinage in

1795. The staff at first consisted of eleven officers and clerks, nineteen workmen in the coining department, and seven men at the furnaces. The total coinage produced in 1794–95 was less than $500,000. By 1807 the output exceeded $1 million; in 1851 nearly $63.5 million was struck, all of it gold save about $800,000. In the earlier years the mint often lacked gold and silver with which to work. In 1820 it operated only part of the time because of this scarcity and the small demand for copper coins. In 1835 Congress established three branch mints—one at New Orleans and two in the new goldfields, at Charlotte, N.C., and Dahlonega, Ga. The one at New Orleans was taken over by the Confederates at the beginning of the Civil War and operated by them from Jan. 26 to May 31, 1861, when operations were suspended. It did not resume work until 1879; in 1909 it ceased to coin and became an assay office. The mint at Dahlonega closed in 1861; that at Charlotte was used as barracks by Confederate soldiers and never operated after that. A branch mint was installed at San Francisco in 1854 and operated until 1955. Another was legally established at Denver in 1862, but no coins had yet been made there when in 1870 it was turned into an assay office. In 1895 it was again authorized to coin, but no money was made there until 1906. A sixth branch mint began work at Carson City, Nev., in 1870, but its production was not great, and it closed in 1893. Another, authorized in 1864 at the Dalles, Oreg., was in process of construction in 1871 when it was destroyed by fire and the project was abandoned. A mint authorized in 1902 at Manila, in the Philippines, had a comparatively small output. By acts of 1846 and later, the various mints were made public depositories. The Bureau of the Mint was created by Congress on Feb. 12, 1873, as a division of the Treasury Department, and supervises the two remaining coinage mints—Denver and Philadelphia; the two assay offices—San Francisco and New York City; and the two bullion depositories—Fort Knox, Ky. (gold), and West Point, N.Y. (silver). The minting of gold coins ceased in 1934.

[Jesse P. Watson, *The Bureau of the Mint*.]
ALVIN F. HARLOW

MINTS, PRIVATE, frequently appeared in new gold-producing areas, up to about 1860—first in Georgia and North Carolina, later in the West—when there was a scarcity of U.S. minted coins. Their coins, of original design, circulated freely. In California, in 1849–51, government money was so scarce that sev-

eral private mints were set up; their coins, though not legal tender, were often accepted as such. They circulated widely and were accepted on deposit by banks. A little later, private mints functioned in Oregon, Utah, and Colorado. With the establishment of the U.S. mint at San Francisco in 1854 the scarcity diminished, and the need for privately minted coins disappeared. No private mint has ever been requested by the federal government to mint U.S. coins.

[John S. Dye, *Dye's Coin Encyclopedia*.]
ALVIN F. HARLOW

MINUTEMEN. While the term "minuteman" goes back at least to 1756, the famous body developed under that name first appeared in the reorganization of the Massachusetts militia by the Worcester convention and the Provincial Congress in 1774. To rid the older militia of Tories, resignations of officers were called for in September in the three Worcester regiments, which were broken into seven. New officers were elected. These officers were to enlist a third of the men in new regiments, which were specifically called (Sept. 21) regiments of minutemen, who were to elect their officers. The Provincial Congress, meeting in October, found the same process voluntarily going on in the militia of other counties, and directed its completion (Oct. 26). Thus a double system of regiments was established in the province, the minutemen to be ready for any emergency "at a minute's warning."

The formation of the minuteman regiments proceeded slowly. On Feb. 14, 1775, as returns that had been called for were not forthcoming, the Provincial Congress set May 10 for a complete return. None was ever made, and only scattered records show that while Marblehead organized its company on Nov. 7, 1774, Woburn, though close to Boston, did not vote to establish its minutemen until Apr. 17, 1775, two days before the outbreak of war. No complete list of minuteman companies and regiments was possible, and only from town records, a few lists, and the "Lexington alarm lists" of minutemen and militia can a fragmentary roster be patched together of an organization that never was completed.

On Apr. 19 militia and minutemen turned out together to resist the British expedition to Concord, Mass. The men whom the British killed on Lexington green were minutemen, and minutemen led the march down to Concord bridge. But militia were also in the column, and men of both kinds harried the British back to Boston. The minuteman organization was then abandoned by the Provincial Congress in organizing the Eight Months Army (*see* Washington's Eight Months Army). As this was formed, it drew men from both minutemen and militia; those who could not join went back into the militia, and the minutemen thenceforth disappeared in Massachusetts.

Other colonies organized their minutemen on the recommendation of the Continental Congress (July 18, 1775) to use them for rounds of service on special brief enlistments. Maryland (August), New Hampshire (September), and Connecticut (December) are on record as accepting this plan, and Connecticut minutemen are credited with resisting William Tryon's expedition against Danbury. There are statues commemorating the minutemen in Concord and Lexington, Mass., and Westport, Conn.

[Allen French, *First Year of the American Revolution.*]
ALLEN FRENCH

MIRAMAR, CONVENTION OF, signed at Miramar Castle near Trieste on Apr. 10, 1864, by Archduke Ferdinand Maximilian of Austria. Infringing upon the Monroe Doctrine, it was an attempt by Napoleon III to establish a French monarchy in Mexico. He induced an assembly of notables made up of Mexican conservatives to offer the Mexican throne to Archduke Ferdinand Maximilian of Austria. Under the conditions of the convention, the French army was to withdraw from Mexico, but 25,000 French troops would remain to become a part of Maximilian's Mexican army and to support his regime against rebel forces. Mexico was to pay 1,000 francs a year per man, plus other sustaining costs, and an additional 270 million francs for previous costs of French intervention in Mexico.

The United States, in the midst of the Civil War, objected to the French intervention in Mexico and continued to recognize the government of Benito Juárez. But, fearing that France would side with the Confederacy should the United States intervene, Secretary of State William H. Seward moved cautiously. Strengthened by its victory in the Civil War, the U.S. government was prepared to enforce the Monroe Doctrine. On Feb. 12, 1866, Seward requested a specific date as to when French military operations would cease in Mexico. Napoleon, realizing that the intervention in Mexico was a costly failure, wished to withdraw, without, however, appearing to violate the Convention of Miramar. He therefore began withdrawing French troops from Mexico in separate de-

tachments, and the last French soldiers left Mexico on Mar. 12, 1867. The withdrawal of the French from Mexico strengthened the European opinion of the Monroe Doctrine.

[Clyde E. Duniway, "Reasons for the Withdrawal of the French From Mexico," *American Historical Association Annual Report* (1902); Percy F. Martin, *Maximilian in Mexico.*]

MIRANDA'S INTRIGUES. Threatened with incarceration in Cuba in 1783, Francisco Miranda, a native of Caracas, Venezuela, fled from the Spanish military service to the United States. During a tour of the country that ended in December 1784, Miranda made the acquaintance of Gen. George Washington, Gen. Henry Knox, and Alexander Hamilton. To several Americans he disclosed in more or less detail his plan to emancipate the Spanish Indies by the aid of foreign powers. From London, on the occasion of the Nootka Sound controversy in 1790, Miranda attempted in vain to interest Knox and Hamilton in the liberation of the Spanish colonies. After war broke out between England and Spain in 1796, he tried to get the American government to enter into an alliance with England and with alleged Spanish-American emissaries for revolutionizing the Indies, but largely because of the reluctance of President John Adams this scheme was frustrated. Still, he continued to correspond with parties in America. Upon landing in New York from London toward the end of 1805, Miranda renewed his acquaintance with Col. W. S. Smith, Richard Rush, and Rufus King; he met Aaron Burr, Secretary of State James Madison, and President Thomas Jefferson. Miranda managed to recruit a few American troops and made two attempts (1805 and 1806) to liberate Venezuela, but was repulsed by the Spanish. He continued his intrigues throughout the rest of the decade, but was captured and imprisoned by the Spanish in 1812.

[W. S. Robertson, *The Life of Miranda.*]
WILLIAM SPENCE ROBERTSON

MIRANDA V. ARIZONA, 384 U.S. 436 (1966). Up to the 1960's the admissibility of confessions in state cases was governed by the "voluntariness" test. By the 1950's the voluntariness test had come to mean not only that a confession must be free of influences that made it untrustworthy or "probably untrue" but also that it must not be the product of police methods offensive to a "sense of fair play and decency"—

such as "relay" interrogation or "incommunicado" detention. Even as expanded, the voluntariness test had serious shortcomings. Because it developed on a case-by-case basis and depended upon the totality of circumstances of each particular case (for example, the particular defendant's intelligence, age, education, and powers of resistance), it seemed unlikely to furnish much guidance to the police. The courts also found it extremely difficult to reconstruct the tenor, atmosphere, and conditions of police questioning behind closed doors.

In *Miranda* v. *Arizona*, a five-to-four majority of the Supreme Court scrapped the voluntariness–totality-of-circumstances test in favor of what the dissenters called a "constitutional code of rules for confessions." The so-called *Miranda* rules provide that the prosecution may not use statements obtained by "custodial interrogation" (questioning initiated by law enforcement officers after a person has been taken into custody) unless the person is warned prior to any questioning that "he has a right to remain silent, that any statement he does make may be used as evidence against him, and that he has a right to the presence of an attorney, either retained or appointed." Moreover, if the defendant "indicates . . . at any stage of the process that he wishes to consult with an attorney before speaking [or continuing to speak] there can be no questioning."

The *Miranda* case was bitterly criticized by many law enforcement officials and politicians for unduly restricting police interrogation during a national crime crisis, and in 1968 Congress passed the Crime Control Act, which purports to "repeal" the decision. The validity of the statute had not been tested by the Supreme Court by the mid-1970's.

[Fred Graham, *The Self-Inflicted Wound;* Yale Kamisar, "A Dissent From the Miranda Dissents," *Michigan Law Review,* vol. 65 (1966); Yale Kamisar, Fred Inbau, and Thurman Arnold, *Criminal Justice in Our Times.*]

YALE KAMISAR

MIRO, FORT, was the Spanish post established on the Ouachita River in 1785 by Don Juan Filhiol, on the site of present-day Monroe, La. First called Ouachita Post and later Fort Miro, after Esteban Miro, Spanish governor of Louisiana from 1785 to 1791, it was renamed Monroe in 1819.

[J. Fair Hardin, "Don Juan Filhiol and the Founding of Fort Miro, the Modern Monroe, Louisiana," *Louisiana Historical Quarterly,* vol. 20.]

WALTER PRICHARD

MISCEGENATION. The idea of a prohibition against interracial marriage originated in America, for at the time the colonies were settled, England had no ban on miscegenation. Among the colonists marriage between black slaves and whites (especially white women who were indentured servants) caused great moral concern and concern about potential economic loss, for the children of a marriage between a slave and a free person were free.

The first antimiscegenation statutes were enacted in Maryland (1661) and Virginia (1691); Massachusetts, North Carolina, and Pennsylvania soon followed suit. When the nation moved west, similar laws were passed in many of the frontier states. It was argued that such laws were designed to preserve racial integrity, but they generally prohibited only interracial marriages involving a white person and a person of another color, not, for example, those between an Indian and a black. As late as 1950 some thirty states still had such laws on their books.

Between 1950 and 1967 the widespread attention given a 1948 decision of the California Supreme Court holding its state antimiscegenation law unconstitutional and the momentum of the general movement for legal and political racial equality led fourteen states to repeal their statutory bans on miscegenation. In 1967, in the case of *Loving* v. *Virginia* (388 U.S. 1), a unanimous U.S. Supreme Court declared such laws unconstitutional. Restricting the individual's "fundamental freedom" to marry solely on the basis of race, ruled the Court, violated both the equal protection clause and the due process clause of the Fourteenth Amendment. If racial classifications are ever to be upheld, observed the Court, "they must be shown to be necessary to the accomplishment of some permissible state objectives independent of the racial discrimination which it was the object of the Fourteenth Amendment to eliminate." The Court could find no such legitimate independent purpose.

The *Loving* ruling was expected, for, on a related question, in *McLaughlin* v. *Florida* (1964), the U.S. Supreme Court had held it a denial of equal protection of the laws for a state to prohibit cohabitation by a white and black not married to each other while not restricting cohabitation by unmarried couples generally.

[Harvey Applebaum, "Miscegenation Statutes: A Constitutional and Social Problem," *Georgetown Law Journal,* vol. 53 (1964); Alfred Avins, "Anti-Miscegenation Laws and the Fourteenth Amendment: The Original Intent," *Virginia Law Review,* vol. 52 (1966).]

YALE KAMISAR

MISCHIANZA was the name given to the most elaborate, extravagant, and romantically feudal *fête champêtre* given in 18th-century America. It was held at the Wharton estate, Walnut Grove, on May 18, 1778, in honor of Sir William Howe, commander of the British forces occupying Philadelphia. The directing geniuses were Maj. John André and Capt. Oliver Delancey. The entertainment lasted from four o'clock on the afternoon of May 18 until four o'clock in the morning of the following day. Seven hundred and fifty invitations were issued; 330 covers were laid. The staff officers paid 3,312 guineas, and a London firm sold, it is said, £12,000 worth of silks, laces, and other fine materials.

JULIAN P. BOYD

MISIONES AWARD, the decision ending an Argentine-Brazilian dispute over part of the Misiones Territory between the Iguaçu and Uruguay rivers. After direct negotiations failed, the two governments asked President Grover Cleveland to arbitrate. On Feb. 5, 1895, he rendered an award upholding Brazil's contentions.

[M. W. Williams, "The Treaty of Tordesillas and the Argentine-Brazilian Boundary Settlement," *Hispanic American Historical Review* (1922).]

MARY WILHELMINE WILLIAMS

MISSILES, MILITARY, include the spectrum of rockets and jet vehicles, ballistic or winged in flight, capable of carrying destructive payloads ranging from tactical weapons to "nation buster" thermonuclear warheads at intercontinental ranges (intercontinental ballistic missiles, or ICBM's). World War II saw the development of missilery by the major participants: the U.S. hand-held bazooka antitank weapon; the artillerylike Soviet Katyusha and U.S. naval barrage rocket; a variety of antiaircraft missiles for air and ground forces; the innovative German V-1 pulse-jet buzz bomb; and the German supersonic, liquid-fuel V-2 ballistic missile with a range of 200 miles, launched by the hundreds against London and Antwerp. Military missilery after 1945, its evolution, and its influence on American security policies and international crises—for example, the Cuban missile crisis in 1962—were compounded by dynamic technological advances and interactions of the cold war.

American military needs for the North Atlantic Treaty Organization (NATO) and the Korean War in the 1950's and for the Vietnam War in the 1960's forced accelerated development of improved tactical rockets. Missiles designed to destroy aircraft included the Falcon (radar-guided), the Sidewinder (heat-seeker homing, effective against jet aircraft), and the Genie (nuclear warhead). Missiles fired from aircraft to attack surface targets included the Bullpup, Hound Dog, Maverick, Walleye (television-guided glide bomb), and later the "smart bomb" (laser-guided). Operational decoys, such as the Quail subsonic missile, were also developed. Antiaircraft and antimissile missiles included the U.S. Army Nike-Hercules and the U.S. Air Force Bomarc as well as the shorter-range Redeye, Sea Sparrow, Hawk, and Terrier. Missiles for continental defense against ICBM's were under development in the early 1970's; one such missile was the Safeguard. An antisubmarine missile, the Asroc, and a missile to be fired from submarines, the Subroc, were developed. Missiles developed for battlefield support of ground forces included the Lance, Dragon, Honest John, Sergeant, SS-11B1, and TOW (antitank or antihelicopter). Missiles saw service during the Vietnam War when applicable; prominent among them were the Soviet SAM antiaircraft missiles massively deployed in North Vietnam and the numerous small rockets of guerrilla forces fired into South Vietnamese cities.

The German V-2 and the American atomic bomb proved the major innovations of World War II, leading directly to the development of strategic missile weapons systems by the 1960's. Lacking a long-range bomber and the atomic bomb in 1947, the Soviet Union immediately gave highest priority to the development of an intercontinental-range missile, nuclear weapons, and long-range jet aircraft. Premier Josef Stalin is reported to have said that such a policy "could be an effective strait jacket for that noisy shopkeeper Harry Truman." By 1954 the United States was faced with a much altered situation, both because of Soviet missile progress and because of the invention of the thermonuclear warheads, far more powerful although of reduced size. Thereupon President Dwight D. Eisenhower initiated priority development of 5,000-mile ICBM's and 1,500-mile intermediate-range ballistic missiles (IRBM's). When the USSR launched Sputnik 1 on Oct. 4, 1957, it was clear that it had already developed an ICBM rocket as announced in August, quite apart from launching the first man-made space satellite to orbit the earth. Thus, the first generation of ICBM's (Atlas and Titan 1) and IRBM's (Jupiter, Thor, and nuclear-powered submarine-carried Polaris A1) were quickly followed by subsequent generations. In 1959 Thors were deployed to England and Jupiters to Turkey for NATO. Second-generation ICBM's by the mid-1960's included a solid-propellant and silo-sited Minuteman 1 and 2. In the third generation the Minuteman 3 with MIRV (multiple, independently targeted reentry vehicle) warheads and the submarine-based Polaris A3 (2,500-mile range) were developed. They were to be followed by the Poseidon (2,500-mile-range MIRV warhead, for an advanced Trident submarine) for the late 1970's.

Strategic missile weapons systems—deployed in hardened sites or on ocean-legged nuclear-powered submarines, each carrying sixteen missiles and held in readiness to retaliate instantly against nuclear attack—came to serve during the 1960's as the fulcrum of the strategic balance of military power between the United States and the Soviet Union. In the 1970's lateral negotiations between Washington and Moscow were undertaken to consider the control and limited development and deployment of strategic weapons. These were known as the SALT (strategic arms limitation treaty) talks. A limited agreement on "basic principles" was reached in May 1972 between the United States and the Soviet Union. At that time relative strategic forces, including missilery, were estimated as follows:

	United States	Soviet Union
ICBM's	1,054	1,618
Submarine missile launch tubes	656	580
Heavy bombers	531	140
Antimissile launchers	0	64
Total strategic warheads	5,700	2,500

The United States had installed MIRV's in most of its then-current 16 missiles on each of 41 Polaris submarines and 550 of its 1,000 Minuteman land-based ICBM's, while the Soviet Union was constructing additional missile-firing submarines. In June 1975, the Soviets demonstrated new large strategic missiles, each with five or six MIRV accurate warheads, according to the U.S. secretary of defense. The Space Treaty of 1968 had previously outlawed nuclear weapons in space. SALT talks continued after 1972, while the Soviet Union greatly increased, as expected, the number of its warheads.

The development of nuclear warhead missiles by the People's Republic of China increasingly erected a tripolar strategic world for the 1970's, but the existence of nuclear weapons continued to enforce an uneasy peace among the major nations. The United States endeavored to avoid possible strategic surprise, partly by means of passive military satellites and by the establishment of direct communications ("hot lines") with Moscow and Peking. Since 1945 no nuclear weapons involving missile technology have been exploded in anger.

[E. M. Emme, *The History of Rocket Technology*, and "The Contemporary Spectrum of War," in M. Kranzberg and C. W. Pursell, Jr., eds., *Technology in Western Civilization*, vol. II; U.S. Department of Defense, *U.S. Guided Missiles*.]

EUGENE M. EMME

MISSIONARY ACTIVITY IN THE PACIFIC. American missions in the Pacific were preceded by those of the French Jesuits and other Catholic orders as well as by the London Missionary Society, which began its labors in Tahiti in 1797. The American missionary activity in this area had its origin with the American Board of Commissioners for Foreign Missions, founded in 1810 in Massachusetts. Interest in Hawaii was stimulated when a Hawaiian boy, Obookiah (a refugee from tribal wars who had been brought to America), was found weeping at the door of a classroom in Yale College because of his desire for an education. In 1820 the American Board sent a party of seventeen led by Hiram Bingham and Asa Thurston to Honolulu to build churches and schools and to heal the sick. Members of the royal family of Hawaii were among the early adherents. American missions were established in Samoa and Micronesia. Before 1898 American missionary effort was not directed toward the Philippine Islands. There is abundant testimony regarding the beneficent work of American missions in the South Seas. Especially in Hawaii, they gave the natives an alphabet, grammar, and dictionary and preserved their language from extinction, translated the Bible and scientific books, and established schools, teaching the people to read and write.

[Rufus Anderson, *History of the Sandwich Islands Mission*; J. J. Jarves, *History of Hawaii*.]

KENNETH COLEGROVE

MISSIONARY RIDGE, BATTLE OF (Nov. 25, 1863). To prevent reinforcement of Confederate Gen. James Longstreet and his troops, besieging Knoxville, Tenn., on Nov. 24, 1863, Gen. Ulysses S. Grant ordered Gen. Joseph Hooker to attack Gen. Braxton Bragg's left on Lookout Mountain. The movement was successful. The next morning Union Gen. George H. Sherman was ordered to turn Bragg's right and sever his communications southward; Hooker was to advance from Lookout Mountain and get across Bragg's line of retreat. Sherman made repeated unsuccessful attacks against the Confederate right, commanded by William J. Hardee and Patrick R. Cleburne; Hooker's attack was held up. To prevent Bragg from reinforcing either wing of his army, Thomas, about noon, was ordered forward.

Bragg's defense was faulty. He had put one-half his center at the foot of Missionary Ridge, with orders to retire and join the other half, stationed on the crest of the ridge, if Thomas' advance should get within 200 yards. Bragg's artillery was nearly useless as it could not be sufficiently depressed to sweep the slope of the ridge effectively. The Union troops had orders to halt at the foot of the ridge, but as the Confederates promptly retreated, the Union soldiers took matters into their own hands. They either had to go forward or retreat. Stopping only momentarily, the men rushed on, driving the disorganized Confederates from their positions on the top. Bragg's routed center and left moved eastward to the protection of Cleburne's command, which had successfully resisted Sherman. Before dark the battle was practically over. It only remained for Bragg to withdraw his defeated troops as best he could southward to Chickamauga Station and Dalton. Cleburne covered the retreat, halting Hooker's vigorous pursuit at Ringgold Gap. A week later Bragg relinquished his command of the Army of Tennessee. Hardee, temporarily in command, was soon succeeded by Gen. J. E. Johnston.

[R. U. Johnson and C. C. Buel, eds., *Battles and Leaders of the Civil War,* vol. III.]

THOMAS ROBSON HAY

MISSIONARY SOCIETIES, HOME, are voluntary associations, usually under denominational control, for the advancement of religion in the needy parts of the United States. In the 18th century missions to the new settlements were sponsored on a small scale by such ecclesiastical units as Presbyterian synods and Baptist and Congregational associations. A revival of interest in evangelical religion, the growing spirit of humanitarianism, and the realization of the vastness of the expanding frontier resulted in the establishment of many local missionary societies, especially in New England and New York, in the latter part of the 18th and early part of the 19th centuries. Among these were the Missionary Society of Connecticut (1798), Massachusetts Missionary Society (1799), Maine Baptist Missionary Association (1804), and the United Domestic Missionary Society of New York (1822). Competition among the local societies led the

members of Congregational, Presbyterian, Associate Reformed, and Dutch Reformed churches to form the American Home Missionary Society in 1826. The society was intended to be national in scope and, within limits, interdenominational. Successive withdrawals of three of the constituent groups left this society entirely Congregational after 1861 (name changed to Congregational Home Missionary Society in 1893). The chief agency for those Presbyterians who did not cooperate with the American Home Missionary Society was the General Assembly's Board of Missions (1816). In order to advance their own interests, as well as to spread the gospel, the principal Protestant denominations created similar organizations; in addition to those mentioned above, they included the Missionary and Bible Society of the Methodist Episcopal Church (1819), the Domestic and Foreign Missionary Society of the Protestant Episcopal Church (1821), and the Baptist Home Mission Society (1832). The slavery controversy and church schisms on the eve of the Civil War resulted in the formation of both the antislavery American Missionary Association (1846) and, on the other hand, of missionary societies affiliated with the southern churches.

Throughout most of the 19th century the chief aim of home missionary societies was to send preachers to, and maintain churches on, the western frontier; later more attention was paid to the foreign-born in the cities, to Afro-Americans, and to decadent rural communities in the eastern states. The formation in the latter part of the 19th century of national denominational societies composed chiefly of women showed the influence of the feminist movement. Although concerned primarily with preaching, the home missionary movement has helped in the establishment of many colleges and academies in the West.

During the 1930's, following a study by the Institute of Social and Religious Research, home missionary societies were transformed into social agencies, deemphasizing church programs and intensifying efforts to increase the immigrant's social and economic well-being.

[H. L. Burleson, *The Conquest of the Continent;* H. P. Douglass, *The New Home Missions;* O. W. Elsbree, *Historical Sketch of Board of Home Missions of the Presbyterian Church;* J. M. Reid and J. T. Gracey, *Missions and Missionary Society of the Methodist Episcopal Church.*]

COLIN B. GOODYKOONTZ

MISSION INDIANS OF CALIFORNIA. Between 1769 and 1823 a chain of twenty-one Franciscan missions was established in California by Father Junípero

MISSIONS

Serra. The Indians were rounded up by the Spaniards and were concentrated around the missions, to be Christianized and taught agriculture and trades. Soon the tribal names were forgotten, and the Indians came to be known by the names of the missions at which they lived. Their numbers were much reduced both by the ravages of epidemics and by their inability to make the transition from a free, migratory mode of life to the more confined mode of living around the missions. In 1833, little more than a decade after Mexican independence from Spain, the missions were closed for lack of funds, and the Indians were turned out to shift for themselves. They proved, however, to have lost much of their capacity for self-support, and for years they drifted around in misery on the margins of the expanding settlements of the whites. Between 1870 and 1907, small parcels of land were purchased for these Indians by the government. In southern California the descendants of the mission Indians now live on twenty-eight tiny reservations under the jurisdiction of the Mission Agency at Riverside. The principal surviving groups in southern California are the Diegueño, Luiseño, and Cahuilla. Some groups, such as the Gabrielino of what is now Los Angeles County, are extinct.

[Sherburne F. Cook, *The Conflict Between the California Indians and White Civilization;* Jack D. Forbes, *Native Americans of California and Nevada;* Robert F. Heizer and Mary A. Whipple, *The California Indians.*]

KENNETH M. STEWART

MISSIONS. *See* **Dominicans; Franciscans; Indian Missions; Jesuit Missions.**

MISSIONS, FOREIGN, constitute a phase of the expansion of Christianity. More specifically, they represent a modern movement since the early 18th century analogous to the rise in earlier times of the orders of preaching friars. Protestant missions followed, at first, Dutch, English, and Danish conquests and colonization, whether in India, the East Indies, or North America. The German Moravians were the first Protestants to undertake (in 1732) foreign missions apart from colonial expansion. The American movement received its initial impulse from England, where William Carey, the first great missionary herald, founded (1792) the Baptist Missionary Society, and himself undertook service in 1793 in India. In England Protestant churches began the formation of missionary societies, which were organized to spread the gospel to the "uttermost parts" of the world, and to convert all non-Christian peoples. There was at the time little critical reckoning with certain substantial elements in the non-Christian cultures and religions.

American participation began in 1810 with the organization of the American Board of Commissioners for Foreign Missions, a society that served the interests of Congregational, Presbyterian, and Reformed churches. Thereafter, separate societies were formed by Baptists (1813), Methodist Episcopalians (1819), Protestant Episcopalians (1820), Presbyterians (1836–37), Lutherans (1839), and others, in turn. Bible societies, such as the American Bible Society, undertook the translation of Holy Scripture into the tongues of mission lands. The development of the foreign-missions enterprise was most notable between 1850 and 1930. In 1920, 236 American Protestant societies were operating through about 9,000 missionaries, on an income of about $30 million. Reduction in income, unrest in mission lands, opposition from foreign cultures and religions, and a reappraisal by the churches themselves of the gospel in relation to non-Christian faiths have caused a cutback in foreign missions, although many continue to be active.

[Wade C. Barclay, *History of Methodist Missions;* Robert F. Berkhofer, Jr., *Salvation and the Savage: An Analysis of Protestant Missions and the American Indian Response, 1787–1862;* Joseph L. Grabill, *Protestant Diplomacy and the Near East: Missionary Influence on American Policy, 1810–1927.*]

JOHN CLARK ARCHER

MISSIONS, FRONTIER, grew out of the feeling among Christians in the older parts of the United States that it was their duty to send the gospel to the new settlements in the West. The frontier was usually regarded in the East as a region of crudeness, lawlessness, and low moral standards. In religion it was thought to be characterized paradoxically both by irreligion and by excessive emotionalism (*see* Camp Meetings); unorthodox creeds, such as Mormonism, were thought to flourish there. But as the new territories increased in population and were admitted to the Union it became evident that the West would sometime hold the balance of power in the nation; hence it was important that "sound principles" be established in the frontier communities. Another powerful motive was the rivalry between the various denominations to win adherents and to hold their own constituents in the new settlements; the spread of Roman Catholicism especially was an incentive for Protestant missionary activity. Disinterested Christian benevolence, however, is the chief explanation of home missions.

366

Missions to the frontiers began early in the 18th century. By the opening of the 19th century the rapidly expanding field led to the organization of many local home missionary societies in New England and New York. These in turn generally grew into or merged with national denominational societies between 1820 and 1835. Preachers and churches were the chief agencies employed, but academies and colleges were useful adjuncts. Among the more important Protestant denominations it appears that a majority of their congregations west of the Alleghenies have at some time received missionary assistance. Indian missions, since they normally operated beyond the frontier of settlement, were regarded as foreign missions.

[O. W. Elsbree, *The Rise of the Missionary Spirit in America;* Colin B. Goodykoontz, *Home Missions on the American Frontier;* P. G. Mode, *The Frontier Spirit in American Christianity;* W. W. Sweet, *The Rise of Methodism in the West.*]

COLIN B. GOODYKOONTZ

MISSIONS OF THE SOUTHWEST. As a Spanish frontier institution the mission was meant to be a temporary, not a permanent, device. It envisaged the training of the aborigines for citizenship and economic self-dependence, a process that the first lawmakers expected would last some ten years only, after which period the mission regime was to give way to civil and parochial organization. Along with the mission went the presidio or military guard. The two mutually supporting institutions formed in combination the essential spearhead of the Spanish advance into the wilderness.

In 1539 Fray Marcos de Niza made his famous journey along the road to Cíbola and the year following Francisco Vásquez de Coronado led his expedition in the same direction. With the latter were four Franciscans, whose missionary activities in present-day New Mexico and beyond are the earliest recorded for the Southwest. One of their number, Fray Juan de Padilla, settled among the Indians of Quivira but, while on his way to evangelize a tribe farther afield, was slain by the natives, about 1544, being the first missionary so to die on American soil.

The Jesuit order of missionaries began work in Mexico in the 1570's and was particularly influential in the northwest part of New Spain. The Jesuits were active among the Indians of the Sierra Madre, including the Tarahumare, and among the Yaqui and Mayo of lowland Sonora. Meanwhile, Franciscan missionaries were establishing missions among the Pueblo of Arizona and New Mexico.

Numerous missions were established within the limits of present-day New Mexico, Arizona, and Texas. In New Mexico, Fray Francesco de López and the lay brother Augustin Rodriguez were at work as early as 1581 among the Tugua Indians at Puaray, now Sandia, where they were martyred. Mission centers multiplied with the years. In 1630 they were twenty-five in number, staffed by fifty friars and serving ninety pueblos with a Christian population of some 60,000. In 1680 the New Mexico missions, then numbering thirty-three, were destroyed in the great Pueblo revolt of that year, which cost the lives of thirty-three missionaries. With the reconquest of New Mexico under Gov. Diego de Vargas in the last decade of the 17th century the missions were restored. In Arizona the three missions set up among the Hopi or Moqui Indians, the first of which dated from 1628 or 1629, were swept away in the Pueblo revolt. Near the site of Tucson the Jesuit Eusebio Kino, "superb missionary, church-builder, explorer and ranchman," founded in 1700 Mission San Xavier del Bac. Within the two years following he founded also San Gabriel de Guevavi and San Cayetán del Tumacácori, all three missions being within the limits of Arizona. Upon the expulsion of the Jesuits in 1767, the three missions were taken over by the Franciscans, one of whom, Fray Francisco Garcés, labored at San Xavier del Bac with distinguished zeal. The first of the Texas missions was planted among the Jumano of La Junta near present-day Presidio, in 1683; the last foundation, Refugio, on Mission River, was in 1791. Outstanding among the Texas missionaries was Fray Antonio Margil de Jesús.

The missions of the Southwest declined during the 18th century and, by the time of the Mexican War, were practically nonexistent. Chief among the causes of decay was the process of secularization, which withdrew the Indians from the tutelage of the friars and transferred administration of the mission temporalities from the latter to civil functionaries.

[Herbert E. Bolton, *The Rim of Christendom: A Biography of Eusebio Francisco Kino,* and *Spanish Explorations in the Southwest, 1542–1706;* Peter M. Dunne, *Early Jesuit Missions in Tarahumare;* Edward H. Spicer, *Cycles of Conquest.*]

GILBERT J. GARRAGHAN
KENNETH M. STEWART

MISSISSINEWA, BATTLE OF (Dec. 17, 1812), the result of an expedition led by Col. John B. Campbell against the Miami Indian villages on the Mississinewa River within the limits of the present Grant County, Ind. Nearly all the Miami were in the service of the

British, and Gen. William Henry Harrison decided to destroy them. Campbell left on Nov. 25, 1812, but was delayed at Dayton until Dec. 14. In the early morning of Dec. 17 the troops attacked an Indian town, which was captured and burned; three other villages were destroyed shortly thereafter.

[Logan Esarey, *History of Indiana.*]

HARLOW LINDLEY

MISSISSIPPI was inhabited prior to European exploration by several Indian tribes, the most important of which were the Chickasaw, Choctaw, Natchez, Biloxi, Tunica, and Pascagoula. The name of the state is probably derived from either the Choctaw "mish sha sippukin," meaning "beyond age," or the Choctaw phrase "meact chassipi," meaning "the ancient father of waters."

Hernando De Soto discovered the Mississippi River in May 1541. Little interest was shown in the lower Mississippi Valley region until Robert Cavelier, Sieur de La Salle, became convinced of its trading potential and its strategic location in halting English expansion inland from the Atlantic. La Salle claimed the entire Mississippi Valley for France in 1682. French control of the lower valley was established by the founding of Biloxi by Pierre Lemoyne, Sieur d'Iberville, in 1699; the expansion of settlement to Mobile and Natchez; and the founding of New Orleans by Jean Baptiste Le Moyne, Sieur de Bienville, in 1718. Colonial rivalry led to the French and Indian War (1754–63), which resulted in England's acquisition of all French territory east of the Mississippi River except New Orleans, and of Spanish Florida. The new English colony of West Florida included the southern portion of the present states of Alabama and Mississippi and the Florida parishes of Louisiana. During the American Revolution, Spain reacquired Florida, the northern border of which remained in dispute until Pinckney's Treaty of 1795.

The Mississippi Territory, created on Apr. 7, 1798, included the land area within 32°28′ north latitude on the north, 31° north latitude on the south, the Mississippi River on the west, and the Chattahoochee River on the east. Territorial organization was patterned after the Northwest Ordinance, with the important exception that slavery was permitted in the Mississippi Territory. To facilitate an ordered western expansion after the Louisiana Purchase (1803), the area between 32°28′ north latitude and the state of Tennessee was added to the Mississippi Territory in 1804. After a revolt in Spanish Florida in 1810 resulted in the es-

tablishment of the Republic of West Florida, President James Madison, claiming that area had been a part of the original Louisiana Purchase, declared the Florida republic American territory, and it was incorporated into the Mississippi Territory by Congress in 1812 and later divided between Louisiana and Mississippi.

On Dec. 10, 1817, Mississippi was admitted to the Union—a north-south line dividing the territory into the states of Mississippi and Alabama. The first constitution of the state of Mississippi, a very conservative document reflecting the dominance of the commercial-planter aristocracy in the river counties, alienated residents in the backcountry and stimulated sectional animosities that became a prominent, and permanent, aspect of Mississippi politics. Land ownership was required of both voters and public officials.

After a series of Indian cessions (1820, 1830, and 1832) the northern half of the state was opened to white settlement, and Mississippi experienced a massive population increase and economic development, known as the Flush Times, during the decade 1830–40. Speculation drove land and slave prices to unrealistic levels. The panic of 1837 caused severe depression and repudiation of state bonds and drove many residents to seek refuge and fortune in Texas. Early in the Flush Times the influence of Jacksonian Democracy led to a new and much more democratic constitution in 1832.

During the 1840's and 1850's Mississippi developed an agrarian system based almost exclusively on a one-crop (cotton) economy. By 1860 the state's slave population of 436,631 was substantially larger than its white population of 353,899. Mississippi was naturally committed to the expansion of slavery and participated actively in the sectional controversies that characterized the American political scene prior to the Civil War. Mississippi was the second state to secede, on Jan. 9, 1861, and provided the Confederacy's only president, Jefferson Davis. During the Civil War more than 100 battles and skirmishes were fought in Mississippi, the most important being the Battle of Vicksburg, which fell to a Union siege July 4, 1863. Mississippi contributed to the Confederacy 78,000 troops, of which 28,000 never returned—a heavy toll on the state's manpower for leadership and labor. (Indicating that the war was perhaps not so popular as has been assumed, 11,000 Mississippi soldiers were listed as deserters or otherwise "dropped" from the ranks.)

Following the devastation of the Civil War, Mississippi experienced a decade of strife during Reconstruction. Initially, under President Andrew Johnson's plan, Reconstruction in Mississippi was to be conducted on a lenient and magnanimous basis that would allow many ex-Confederates an active and important role in shaping postwar policy. However, Mississippi's refusal to ratify the Thirteenth Amendment, its enactment of restrictive Black Codes, and its rejection of the Fourteenth Amendment undermined the president's policy and, along with similar developments elsewhere, led to the adoption of the congressional plan of reconstruction in 1867. Military rule was instituted until a civil government could be established consistent with the Radical Republican Reconstruction program. After five years of confusion and delay Mississippi complied and was readmitted to the Union on Feb. 23, 1870. Although many Mississippians were willing to acquiesce in the democratic and even radical innovations of Reconstruction, the prewar power elite, capitalizing on racial prejudice and anxiety, managed to restore itself to power in 1875, claiming that it would "redeem" the state government from Republican control.

The Redeemers, later called Bourbons, established the iron rule of a one-party system by maintaining the color line in Mississippi politics, as was done elsewhere in the South. Throughout the 1880's, Bourbon favoritism toward railroads and industry was challenged by spokesmen of the small farmers in the white hill counties. In 1890 a new constitution, disfranchising blacks and marking the rise of the "rednecks," reduced political rivalry to the planter-industrial power elite and the small farmers and laborers. James Kimball Vardaman became the undisputed leader of the rednecks and, immediately after the enactment of the primary law, was elected governor in 1903. Mississippi politicians succeeding Vardaman after 1911 achieved many progressive reforms in Mississippi.

Theodore Gilmore Bilbo (governor, 1916–20, 1928–32; senator, 1935–47) became the dominant political figure in Mississippi. Both Vardaman and Bilbo exploited white supremacy in their rise to power, and both were often abusive of wealthy industrialists while stimulating and exploiting class antagonism. Many progressive reforms were instituted in Mississippi in the first decades of the 20th century, in medical and geriatric care, the penal system, education, and transportation.

The rule of the rednecks ended in the midst of the depression of the 1930's when a businessman governor, Martin Sennett Conner, inaugurated a state-sponsored industrial-development program that reversed the antibusiness policies of the rednecks. The Balance Agriculture With Industry program of 1937 and postwar economic expansion combined to increase industrial jobs significantly, although Mississippi remained largely rural and agrarian.

From 1932 until the mid-1950's, Mississippi political campaigns were largely free of racial overtones; no governor from 1932 to 1955 owed his election to exploitation of the race issue. The civil rights movement, however, reactivated race as a major political issue, especially after the Supreme Court's school desegregation decision in 1954.

The election of Gov. Ross R. Barnett in 1959 and the application of James Meredith to the University of Mississippi in 1961 set the stage for the most dramatic confrontation between federal and state authorities since the Civil War. Following an almost two-year legal delay and one night of rioting, in the fall of 1962, Meredith became the first black admitted to the university and graduated in August 1963. Subsequently, the state's segregated dual-school program was replaced by a unitary system. These changes, along with industrial development and an incipient breakdown in the monolithic party system, inaugurated major readjustments in the state's long-standing economic, social, and political traditions.

The impact of large-scale black voter registration in the 1960's is typified by the fact that for the first time in the state's history a black, Charles Evers, waged a vigorous, although unsuccessful, campaign for governor in 1971. Both a contributing factor to, and a result of, racial and political readjustment in Mississippi after the mid-1950's was the shift from a one-crop cotton economy to a diversified agricultural and industrial system. The percentage of the labor force employed in agriculture dropped from 43 percent in 1950 to 7.3 percent in 1970. Although the population increased only slightly from 2,178,141 in 1960 to 2,216,912 in 1970, the number of industrial wage earners rose 42.1 percent in the same period.

[J. F. H. Claiborne, *Mississippi as a Province, Territory and State;* J. W. Garner, *Reconstruction in Mississippi;* A. D. Kirwin, *Revolt of the Rednecks;* R. A. McLemore, ed., *A History of Mississippi;* P. L. Rainwater, *Mississippi: Storm Center of Secession.*]

DAVID G. SANSING

MISSISSIPPI, CONFEDERATE ARMY OF. On Mar. 27, 1862, the Confederate troops under Gen. A. S. Johnston, known as the Army of Kentucky, retiring from Kentucky to Corinth, Miss., were united with other troops gathered from various southern points. The combined forces were called the Army of Mississippi (not to be confused with Union forces of the same name). Gen. P. G. T. de Beauregard was made second in command. At the death of Johnston at Shiloh in Tennessee, Beauregard became commander of the army, but was soon succeeded by Gen. Braxton Bragg. In the summer of 1862, the army unsuccessfully invaded Kentucky. Following its return to Tennessee, it was reorganized, and on Nov. 20, 1862, it was designated the Army of Tennessee.

THOMAS ROBSON HAY

MISSISSIPPI, UNION ARMY OF THE, was first constituted late in March 1862, and consisted of troops, under Gen. John Pope, gathered to operate against Island No. 10. Later the army joined the forces collected by Gen. Henry W. Halleck after the Battle of Shiloh to besiege Corinth, Miss. When Pope was ordered to Virginia, Gen. William S. Rosecrans assumed command. The Army of the Mississippi with that ''of the Tennessee,'' combined under Gen. Ulysses S. Grant, fought Confederate forces at Iuka and Corinth. On Oct. 24, 1862, the Army of the Mississippi became the Thirteenth Army Corps. In January 1863, under Gen. John A. McClernand, it enjoyed a brief existence as an independent army during the operations against Arkansas Post. (*See also* Mississippi, Confederate Army of.)

THOMAS ROBSON HAY

MISSISSIPPIAN CULTURES. The prehistoric Mississippian cultures dominated the lower and middle Mississippi Valley from about A.D. 700 to the historic period. Some of the most famous archaeological sites in eastern North America are Mississippian settlements. Cahokia, Ill.; Moundville, Ala.; Aztalan, Wis.; Etowah, Ga.; and Spiro, Okla., are among the many sites of this culture that are visited yearly by tourists. Settlements ranged in size from small villages to the city of Cahokia, with an estimated population of 30,000 inhabitants. Characteristic traits of the cultures are centralized political organization; social stratification; the platform mound-and-plaza complex; intensive cultivation of corn, beans, and squash; and pottery with crushed-shell temper. A highly religious cult referred to as the Southern Cult or the Southeastern Ceremonial Complex was an important social institution within most Mississippian cultures. The cult is characterized by monolithic stone axes,

macelike batons, ceremonial flint knives, and a wide variety of iconographic symbols and other objects. Monks Mound at Cahokia is the third largest temple mound in the New World, measuring 200 by 300 meters (650 by 967 feet) at the base and 30 meters (97 feet) in height. A chiefdom has been suggested as the level of political organization reached by many of these cultures, and a state-level society may have existed at Cahokia. Many features of these Mississippian cultures—including the mound-and-plaza complex, religious symbolism, and elements in shapes and decorations of pottery vessels—indicate a Middle American stimulus, or at least extensive borrowing from that center. But the main impetus leading to the emergence of these prehistoric Mississippian cultures apparently came from indigenous developments, such as population growth and the adoption of an economic system sustained by domesticated plant foods.

[Jesse D. Jennings, *Prehistory of North America;* Gordon R. Willey, *Introduction to American Archaeology,* vol. I.]

GUY GIBBON

MISSISSIPPI BUBBLE, the term commonly applied to the disastrous failure of John Law's scheme for exploiting the resources of French Louisiana. After Antoine Crozat surrendered his charter in 1717, John Law, a Scot who had previously gained an enviable reputation in France as a successful banker and financier, organized the Compagnie de l'Occident (Western Company), also known as the Mississippi Company, to assume control of Louisiana on Jan. 1, 1718. Law's reputation caused the stock to sell readily, and the organization soon enlarged the scope of its activities by absorbing several other commercial companies, and changed its name to the Company of the Indies. Enormous profits were anticipated from the operations of the company, and the increasing demand for its stock led to wild speculation that drove the price of shares to high figures, without any sound basis in tangible assets. Many Frenchmen invested their all in the company's stock. A few, who sold at the right moment, reaped fortunes from their speculation; but the majority held their stock in expectation of greater profits. The anticipated immense and immediate profits were not realized, and soon the scheme revealed itself as a purely speculative venture. In 1720 the company failed, the ''bubble'' burst, and the stockholders lost their entire investments; many were completely ruined. Law's connection with the venture ceased, but the company retained control of Louisiana until 1731.

[Alcée Fortier, *History of Louisiana;* Charles Gayarré, *History of Louisiana.*]

WALTER PRICHARD

MISSISSIPPI COMPANY OF VIRGINIA

MISSISSIPPI COMPANY OF VIRGINIA was organized in 1763 by a group of men, most of whom were members of the original Ohio Company of Virginia, including Thomas and Arthur Lee, George Washington, and others. Its purpose was to procure a huge tract of land at the junction of the Ohio and Mississippi rivers. The hopes of the members were soon dampened by the Proclamation of 1763, which prohibited land grants and settlements west of the Appalachian Mountains. The company continued its existence, however, and Arthur Lee was its representative in London in 1768 when the Treaty of Fort Stanwix again opened opportunities for western settlements. He pressed the claims of the Mississippi Company, which was now asking for 2.5 million acres to lie between the Alleghenies and the Ohio and the thirty-eighth and forty-second parallels. From that time to 1775 the British secretary of colonial affairs was besieged by the Ohio Company, the Indiana Company, and the Vandalia Company for grants of land that overlapped the grant sought by the Mississippi Company. The approach of the American Revolution terminated the hopes of the Mississippi Company, as well as the hopes of the other companies.

[Jack M. Sosin, *Whitehall and the Wilderness.*]

R. J. FERGUSON

MISSISSIPPI DELTAS, BLOCKADE OFF THE.

MISSISSIPPI DELTAS, BLOCKADE OFF THE. Before the capture of New Orleans in April 1862, the chief task of Union naval ships in the Gulf of Mexico was to blockade the mouths of the Mississippi River. Late in May 1861 the two main ship channels, Pass à L'Outre and South West Pass, were blockaded by Comdr. C. H. Poor in the screw sloop *Brooklyn* and Lt. D. D. Porter in the side-wheeler *Powhatan.* Deep draft and poor maneuverability in narrow waters prevented these vessels from entering the river in chase of suspicious craft, and unsupported by light auxiliaries they could do little to police the four secondary passes between the two main channels. When Poor ill-advisedly left his station on June 30 to block a secondary pass, Comdr. Raphael Semmes in the Confederate raider *Sumter* made his famous escape through Pass à L'Outre. The difficulty of stopping all the mouths of the Mississippi from the outside led to an

effort to establish a base within the river at Head of the Passes; but this was thwarted by the Confederate ironclad ram *Manassas.* Since New Orleans had, in addition to the Delta passes, lateral outlets via Lake Pontchartrain and Barataria Bay, it proved impossible for the Union forces with their shortage of ships to establish an effective blockade, a fact that materially influenced the decision to attempt the capture of New Orleans itself.

[R. S. West, Jr., *The Second Admiral.*]

RICHARD S. WEST, JR.

MISSISSIPPI PLAN

MISSISSIPPI PLAN, the name given to two attempts in the South to disfranchise the Afro-American.

The first Mississippi Plan was a practice occurring in the 1870's, and even as late as the 1890's, under various names, such as the Edgefield, or Shotgun, policy to discourage blacks from voting. In contrast to the violence of the earlier Ku Klux Klan, this device was a more subtle means of intimidation, and it did not become customary until federal troops were withdrawn from the southern states. It refers to the practice by whites of carrying firearms on election day, ostensibly for hunting, but actually as a veiled threat to blacks. Occasionally a gun would "accidentally" go off in the direction of a black near the polls.

The second Mississippi Plan was adopted by the Mississippi constitutional convention of 1890. It required every citizen from twenty-one to sixty to be able to display his poll tax receipt. It also required the would-be voter to be able to read the U.S. Constitution, or understand it when read to him, or give a reasonable interpretation thereof. This requirement permitted registration officials to discriminate between white and black illiterates. Six other southern states made similar constitutional changes between 1895 and 1910. In *Williams* v. *Mississippi* (1896) the Supreme Court upheld these suffrage provisions. However, the Supreme Court reversed itself in *Harper* v. *Virginia Board of Elections* (1966) when it invalidated the poll tax as a requirement for voting in state elections. Two years earlier the Twenty-fourth Amendment eliminated the poll tax in federal elections. These actions, along with federal legislation passed in 1957, 1960, 1964, and 1965, have removed the effectiveness of the Mississippi Plan as an instrument for disfranchisement.

[Mary Frances Berry, *Black Resistance and White Law: A History of Constitutional Racism in America;* A. D. Kirwin, *Revolt of the Rednecks: Mississippi Politics (1896–1925);* Milton R. Konvitz and Theodore Leskes, *A Century of Civil Rights;* J. G. Randall, *The Civil War and*

Reconstruction; C. Van Woodward, *The Strange Career of Jim Crow.*]

GERALD M. CAPERS, JR.
OSCAR S. DOOLEY

MISSISSIPPI RIVER, the greatest of the North American rivers, has the fifth largest drainage area in the world (1.2 million square miles) and is one of the world's busiest commercial waterways. The river has two main lateral branches—the Ohio River to the east and the Missouri to the west. The length of the Mississippi proper is 2,348 miles, and the waters of its system pass through two Canadian provinces and thirty-one states into the Gulf of Mexico. Its source is Lake Itasca in northwestern Minnesota.

Although other Spaniards had doubtless seen the mouth of this great river, its discovery is rightly accredited to Hernando de Soto, who reached it near the site of Memphis, Tenn., early in May 1541. There is no indisputable evidence that another European saw the Mississippi River until 1673, and then the new discoverers were Frenchmen. On June 17 of that year Louis Jolliet and Father Jacques Marquette paddled their canoes out of the Wisconsin River into the larger stream. They proceeded down the river to a point near the mouth of the Arkansas River, where they turned back. In 1682 Robert Cavelier, Sieur de La Salle, explored the river from the Illinois to its mouth, where on Apr. 9 he took possession of the country for France and named it Louisiana.

La Salle realized the full significance of the Mississippi River and planned to establish a colony at its mouth. Unfortunately, when in 1684 he sailed from France to carry out his purpose, he missed the mouth of the Mississippi and landed on the coast of Texas. Three years later he was murdered by one of his followers and his plan for a French colony seemed to have perished with him.

Scarcely more than a decade elapsed before two Frenchmen, Pierre Lemoyne, Sieur d'Iberville, and Jean Baptiste Le Moyne, Sieur de Bienville, sailed from Brest in two vessels carrying 200 soldiers and colonists. In March 1699, they entered the Mississippi, explored it for some distance, and warned away an English vessel that had arrived on a mission similar to their own (*see* Carolana). The French established themselves first at Biloxi, then on Mobile Bay, and in 1718 they founded New Orleans. Thereafter for nearly a half-century the Mississippi was used and controlled by the French.

At the close of the French and Indian War in 1763 France lost its possessions in the New World, and the Mississippi River became an international boundary. From 1763 to 1783 Spain and Great Britain confronted each other across the "Great River." During the American Revolution the river witnessed hostilities between the British and the Spanish and was the avenue for the supplies by which George Rogers Clark was able to maintain his hold on the Illinois country. According to the Definitive Treaty of Peace of 1783, the United States was to extend to the Mississippi between Spanish Florida and the Canadian boundary, and Americans were to have the free navigation of the river (*see* Mississippi River, Free Navigation of).

The Spanish were not party to this treaty and they had their own ideas about the navigation of the Mississippi—ideas they were able to enforce because they controlled the mouth of the river. They imposed duties that were regarded as exorbitant and prohibitive by the settlers in the Ohio Valley, for whom the river was the only feasible outlet to market. The West seethed with unrest, intrigues, and threats of disunion (*see* Western Separatism), and the "Mississippi question" became one of the most troublesome problems facing federal officials and diplomats. In 1795, in accordance with Pinckney's Treaty with Spain, the river was opened to Americans (*see* Deposit, Right of). In 1800, however, Spain ceded Louisiana back to France (*see* San Ildefonso, Treaty of). Shortly afterward the river was closed once more, and again there was consternation and turmoil in the West until the Louisiana Purchase settled the question and made the Mississippi an American river.

Thereafter the Mississippi River served without restriction as the great artery of trade and commerce for the whole upper valley (*see* Mississippi Valley). The first successors of the canoes or pirogues of the Indians and traders were the flatboats on which the farmers floated their produce to market. Then came the keelboats, which could be propelled upstream by prodigious effort. But river transportation received its greatest impetus in 1811 when the steamboat *New Orleans* made its historic trip from Pittsburgh to New Orleans. The number of steamboats on the Mississippi and Ohio increased slowly at first, but by 1825 there were 125, and by 1860 more than 1,000 were in service. It was not without reason, therefore, that the southerners counted on the Mississippi to bind the Middle West to them in economic interest. That it failed to do so at the critical time was due to the counteracting influence of the railroads and other factors.

During the Civil War the vital importance of the Mississippi to the Confederacy was recognized by both sides, and the struggle for its control was one of the principal aspects of the war. When, after the fall of Vicksburg, the Union forces came into full possession of the river, the Confederacy was cut in two and seriously weakened (*see* Mississippi River, Opening of the).

Steamboating revived somewhat after the war but the railroads, with their greater speed, convenience, and certainty, have frustrated all hope of a return of the glamorous river life about which Mark Twain wrote so vividly. Commercial traffic dwindled and towboats replaced steamboats on the river. The Mississippi River Commission was established by act of Congress in 1879 to supervise the maintenance and improvement of the river as a commercial waterway. By deepening and widening some of the Mississippi's channels, the commission has helped to increase the river's traffic. During World War I, as traffic on other waterways became congested, new barge lines were created on the Mississippi. By 1970 traffic had increased on the river to 230 million tons annually, just slightly less than that on the Great Lakes. The main products being moved along the river are petroleum and petroleum products, coal, coke, and iron and steel.

Disastrous floods have made flood control one of the principal concerns of the state and federal governments. Following the flood of 1927 the federal government established a flood control program that, through the construction of 1,870 miles of main stem levees and other measures, has greatly reduced the threat of inundation.

[Julius Chambers, *The Mississippi River;* Timothy Severin, *Explorers of the Mississippi;* Mark Twain, *Life on the Mississippi;* Arthur P. Whitaker, *The Mississippi Question, 1795–1863.*]

DAN E. CLARK

MISSISSIPPI RIVER, FREE NAVIGATION OF, from its headwaters to its mouth was important to inhabitants of the interior Mississippi Valley during the 17th and 18th centuries, when the river was their main highway of commerce and its mouth was owned by a foreign power. The establishment of the right was an important step in the worldwide liberation of commerce. It was first granted by France, which then owned Louisiana, in favor of Great Britain and was a by-product of the territorial settlement at the end of the French and Indian War in 1763. At the same time France ceded Louisiana to Spain (*see* Fontainebleau, Treaty of). During the American Revolution both British subjects and American citizens claimed the right of free navigation and Spain permitted both of them to navigate it for a time—the British until 1779, when Spain went to war with Britain, and the Americans until 1784, when Spain closed the river to all foreigners, mainly in the hope of checking the growth of American settlements in the West. During and just after the revolutionary war, the United States sought repeatedly, but in vain, to obtain from Spain treaty recognition of its claim, which was based upon natural law, its inheritance of the British right of 1763, and its treaty of peace with Great Britain (*see* Definitive Treaty of Peace), by which the two powers guaranteed the right to each other. Spain persisted in its refusal when the subject was discussed in the Jay-Gardoqui negotiation of 1785–87. In 1786 John Jay, convinced that Spain would not yield, advised Congress to agree to suspend the claim for a term of years in return for commercial privileges that would have been mainly beneficial to the middle and northern states. By a sectional vote Congress instructed Jay to negotiate on this basis; but its action aroused such vehement protest in the South and West that he decided not to proceed, especially since the creation of a new federal government was already in prospect. The negotiation hung fire until 1795. In 1788 Spain undertook a separatist intrigue (*see* Spanish Conspiracy) with the westerners and, in order to promote it, granted them limited privileges of navigation; but they were not satisfied, French revolutionary influence soon increased their unrest, and by 1794 their threats of violent action had become so menacing that the governments of both the United States and Spain were prodded into renewed activity. Further alarmed by the Jay Treaty of 1794 (by which Britain and the United States renewed their mutual guarantee of free navigation) and by the ill success of its war with France, Spain at last yielded in the Pinckney-Godoy Treaty of San Lorenzo (Oct. 27, 1795). Article IV established the free navigation of the Mississippi by the United States, which also gained the ancillary right of deposit at New Orleans (*see* Deposit, Right of). These rights gave a great impetus to American commerce on the Mississippi, which was shared by the eastern seaboard as well as the West, and paved the way for the Louisiana Purchase of 1803. The right of free navigation, as distinguished from the right of deposit, was never thereafter disturbed and this phase of the question was ended by the Louisiana Purchase. The

MISSISSIPPI RIVER, NAVIGATION ON

British right was lost by the War of 1812 and never recovered.

[S. F. Bemis, *Pinckney's Treaty;* E. W. Lyon, *Louisiana in French Diplomacy;* A. P. Whitaker, *The Mississippi Question.*]

A. P. WHITAKER

MISSISSIPPI RIVER, NAVIGATION ON. The primitive craft used on the Mississippi were the bull boat, or coracle, made of buffalo hide stretched on a frame, and the pirogue, or dugout canoe. The French introduced the bateau, which was essentially a large flat-bottomed skiff propelled by oars, and the barge, which was built with keel and ribs and propelled by sails, oars, or cordelle. The Spanish maintained on the river a fleet of galleys that were probably large barges or small ships.

The Americans seem to have introduced the flatboat, or ark, which handled much of the downstream transportation until the Civil War. The keelboat also seems to have been an American adaptation. It was a long, narrow craft built on ribs and keel and propelled by setting poles or cordelle. The barge and the keelboat were the most important upstream carriers until the period of steamboat dominance began, shortly after 1820.

The first Mississippi steamboat was the *Orleans* or *New Orleans,* built at Pittsburgh by Nicholas Roosevelt, which entered the Natchez–New Orleans trade in 1811. The steamboat was not successful on the western rivers until 1816, when Capt. Henry Shreve built the *Washington,* which carried the boilers on deck and skimmed the surface of the water instead of plowing the depths as Robert Fulton's steamboats did. Steamboats multiplied rapidly after 1820 and this multiplication necessitated river improvements. Some dredging of sandbars was done by the government after 1824 and Henry Shreve invented a snag-pulling apparatus with which he cleared river channels and picked apart the famous Red River raft.

By 1840 steamboat traffic had reached its zenith, though much heavy freight was brought downstream in flatboats. East-west railroads soon began sapping trade from the steamboats. The western phase of the Civil War was largely based on the Union campaign to open the Mississippi. Fleets of armored river gunboats aided in this effort (*see* Mississippi Squadron), and other fleets of boats were essential in supplying the armies. After the war steamboat commerce revived for almost twenty years, but the railroads finally conquered. The navigation of the river remains important to carry bulky freight (petroleum, coal,

steel), much of it on steel barges, and to check railway rates.

In the early years ocean vessels came as far as New Orleans along the Mississippi, and that city is still the most important transfer point. There has been much difficulty in keeping bars from forming in the mouth of the river and the problem requires constant vigilance.

The modern system of improvements since the establishment of the Mississippi River Commission in 1879, largely under the direction of army engineers, has provided vast lines of levees, dams, dikes, cutoffs, reservoirs, spillways, and dredged channels over more than 2,000 miles of river. The low-water channel above Saint Louis is 6 feet deep, and below Saint Louis 9 or more feet deep. These operations have also aided in flood control.

[Harry Sinclair Drago, *The Steamboaters, From the Early Side-Wheelers to the Big Packets;* Walter Havighurst, *Voices on the River: The Story of the Mississippi Water Ways;* L. S. Hunter, *Steamboats on the Western Rivers.*]

LELAND D. BALDWIN

MISSISSIPPI RIVER, OPENING OF THE. The strategic importance of controlling the Mississippi River was recognized by both Union and Confederate leaders early in the Civil War. In the hands of the former it would afford an easy avenue for penetrating into enemy territory and separating the important states of Arkansas, Louisiana, and Texas from the rest of the Confederacy; to the latter it served as a valuable artery for transporting troops and supplies and a connecting link between two important sections of their territory.

Thwarted in 1861 in their plan to hold the line of the Ohio River, the Confederates fortified Columbus, Ky., on the Mississippi; but the Union capture of forts Henry (Feb. 6, 1862) and Donelson (Feb. 16, 1862) led to the evacuation of Columbus. Island No. 10, in the Mississippi River near the Kentucky-Tennessee boundary, was then fortified by the Confederates, but Union gunboats captured the island on Apr. 7, 1862, leaving Fort Pillow, about midway between Island No. 10 and Memphis, as the northernmost river defense. However, Union occupation of Corinth, Miss., soon rendered Fort Pillow useless to the Confederates and it was abandoned; and on June 6, 1862, Memphis fell into Union hands, opening the Mississippi as far south as Vicksburg.

Meanwhile, a Union squadron under David G. Farragut, operating from the Gulf of Mexico, had forced its way past the Confederate defenses at forts Jackson and Saint Philip, some sixty miles below New Orleans; it appeared before that city on Apr. 25, 1862. New Orleans surrendered on May 1, 1862, and other river points as far up as Baton Rouge, La., soon fell into Union hands. The Confederates now strongly fortified the high bluffs at Port Hudson, twenty-five miles above Baton Rouge, and at Vicksburg, Miss., 200 miles to the north, in an effort to preserve the valuable communication between the fertile Red River valley and Confederate territory east of the Mississippi.

After several months of preliminary operations, Ulysses S. Grant closed in on Vicksburg in the early summer of 1863, and Gen. Nathaniel P. Banks soon attacked Port Hudson from the rear, after Farragut had made an unsuccessful attempt to pass the fortifications with his gunboats on Mar. 14, 1863, to go to the aid of Grant before Vicksburg. After a siege of nearly two months Vicksburg surrendered on July 4, 1863. When the news reached Port Hudson that post also surrendered, on July 9, 1863, since it was no longer of value to the Confederates. This completed the opening of the Mississippi, and Abraham Lincoln could write: "The Father of Waters again goes unvexed to the sea."

[J. K. Hosmer, *The Appeal to Arms, 1861–1863;* James Ford Rhodes, *History of the Civil War, 1861–1865.*]

WALTER PRICHARD

MISSISSIPPI SQUADRON. At the beginning of the Civil War the importance of controlling the great river system of the Mississippi Valley stimulated both Union and Confederate governments to construct war vessels to cooperate with their land forces. By the end of July 1861, the Union Flotilla in the Western Waters consisted of three wooden gunboats converted from river packets by Commodore John Rodgers II under orders from the War Department. In December 1861 and January 1862 the completion of nine ironclad vessels made the fleet formidable.

The first major operation of the flotilla was the capture of Fort Henry, Tenn., and the ascent of the Tennessee River into Alabama. The fleet also contributed to the capture of Fort Donelson and the occupation of Nashville. The reduction of the Confederate strongholds at Columbus, Island No. 10, and Fort Pillow, and the naval victory at Memphis, June 6, 1862, opened the river to Vicksburg, Miss., and led to the attack on its fortifications during June and July. To guard the rivers against incursions by guerrilla bands, large numbers of light-draft steamers were purchased, armed, and kept on patrol duty. Additional ironclads

and monitors were added as rapidly as they could be completed. This expansion of the fleet necessitated its transfer to the Navy Department, and on Oct. 1, 1862, it was rechristened the Mississippi Squadron.

A second unsuccessful attack on Vicksburg in December was followed by the capture of Arkansas Post, Jan. 11, 1863. Henceforth, much of the squadron worked in close cooperation with Gen. Ulysses S. Grant in his campaign against Vicksburg. Also, the vessels in the upper rivers were frequently called on to help defeat the plans of the Confederate cavalry raiders. After the fall of Port Hudson, La., July 9, 1863, the only important variation from the monotony of patrol and convoy duty was the Red River campaign, Apr. 8 to May 22, 1864, when a sudden fall in the river threatened the destruction of many of the best vessels of the squadron. During the summer of 1865 most of the squadron was taken out of commission and the vessels either returned to peacetime traffic or dismantled and sold for scrap.

[A. T. Mahan, *Gulf and Inland Waters.*]

T. R. PARKER

MISSISSIPPI VALLEY. Until it came into the possession of the United States the Mississippi Valley was the prize sought by the leading nations of Europe. Spaniards—Hernando de Soto and Francisco Vásquez de Coronado (1541)—discovered the lower valley, but Spain did not follow up the discoveries and more than two centuries elapsed before that country became really interested in the region. It was far different with the French. Their explorers and *coureurs de bois*—Jean Nicolet (1634); Pierre Esprit Raddison and Médard Chouart, Sieur de Grosseilliers (1654–60); Louis Jolliet and Father Jacques Marquette (1673); Robert Cavelier, Sieur de La Salle (1669–84); and many others—penetrated far and wide into the valley. When in 1699 Pierre Lemoyne, Sieur d'Iberville, and Jean Baptiste Le Moyne, Sieur de Bienville, established a colony near the mouth of the Mississippi River, the French were in almost undisputed control of the great valley—a control they maintained for half a century. Although claiming the region on the basis of their sea-to-sea charters, the English colonists were slow in finding their way to the "western waters." But when English traders and land companies became actively interested in the Ohio Valley, about the middle of the 18th century, the great struggle between the French and English, known as the French and Indian War, was precipitated.

At the close of the war in 1763 France lost its possessions in America, relinquishing its claims west of the Mississippi to Spain and the region east of that river to the English. In the Definitive Treaty of Peace, 1783, the new United States received jurisdiction westward to the Mississippi and north of Spanish Florida. Twenty years later the Louisiana Purchase gave the United States the entire valley, after Spain had ceded Louisiana back to France in 1800 (*see* San Ildefonso, Treaty of). Even before the revolutionary war there were American settlements in Kentucky and Tennessee. After 1783 the floodgates were opened and Americans poured across the mountains in ever-increasing numbers to take possession of their new domain.

The influences and problems arising out of the settlement of the Mississippi Valley made the United States a strong nation. In meeting the demands of the westerners for protection against the Indians, for autonomous local governments, for roads and river improvements, for mail service, and for liberal land legislation, the powers of the federal government were vastly extended and strengthened. It was in the Mississippi Valley that the frontier had its most characteristic influence on American life and institutions. At the same time, in the Mississippi Valley the sectionalism that culminated in the Civil War developed its greatest bitterness.

[Dan E. Clark, *The West in American History;* James K. Hosmer, *A Short History of the Mississippi Valley.*]

DAN E. CLARK

MISSISSIPPI V. JOHNSON, 4 Wallace 475 (1867), a suit filed on Apr. 5, 1867, by Gov. William L. Sharkey of Mississippi, Alexander H. Garland, and Robert J. Walker, asking the U.S. Supreme Court for permission to file a plea to perpetually enjoin President Andrew Johnson from "executing or in any manner carrying out" the Reconstruction acts passed a few weeks before by the Radical Republican Congress. Although he had vetoed the acts as unconstitutional, the president ordered Attorney General Henry Stanbery to oppose the Mississippi plea before the Court. Speaking for a unanimous Court, Chief Justice Salmon P. Chase denied the petition for lack of jurisdiction. The Court pointed out that no question of person or property was involved. Furthermore, "the Congress is the legislative department of the government," Chase said. "The President is the executive department. Neither can be restrained in its action by the judicial department." Mississippi's counsel

sought desperately to introduce person or property. But after reargument, by a four-to-four vote the plea was disallowed.

[G. F. Milton, *The Age of Hate: Andrew Johnson and the Radicals.*]

GEORGE FORT MILTON

MISSOURI history began with the exploration by French traders and missionaries of the Mississippi Valley in the late 17th century. The explorations of Father Jacques Marquette and Louis Jolliet; Robert Cavelier, Sieur de La Salle; Charles Claude Du Tisne; and Étienne Venyard, Sieur de Bourgmont, resulted in the occupation of the area by the French, with the migration of a few French settlers. The first permanent settlements after 1700 were on the east side of the Mississippi River opposite present-day Saint Louis and Sainte Genevieve. Temporary settlements—soon abandoned—were made in 1703 on the River Des Peres within present-day Saint Louis and in 1722 on the Missouri River at Fort Orleans near the mouth of the Grand River.

A permanent settlement was not made west of the Mississippi until about 1735, when a small group built a few cabins across from the mouth of the Kaskaskia. Their village was Sainte Genevieve, and it was followed by Pierre Laclede's fur-trading village of Saint Louis in 1764. Laclede, a well-educated Frenchman, came with a monopoly grant to trade with the Osage. The dissatisfaction of the Illinois French with English, and later American, rule caused many to cross the river and join Laclede.

The French villages and fur traders were pawns of European politics. France handed over all of Louisiana to Spain by the Treaty of Fontainebleau in 1762, but Spain did not send a lieutenant governor until 1770. From 1770 to 1803 the Spanish lieutenant governors, with all civil and military powers, mildly ruled the quiet French settlements. Settlements were made at Saint Charles (1769), Carondelet (1767), New Bourbon (1793), Cape Girardeau (1793), and several other places. But the population grew slowly; furs, lead, and salt were exported, and the people established Roman Catholic communities that reflected the life-style of Old France. In 1780 the British and Indians mounted an attack on Saint Louis, but Lt. Gov. Fernando De Leyba and the inhabitants of the town succeeded in defending it with hastily built fortifications.

New threats faced the Spanish after the close of the American Revolution. A new breed of men had crossed the Alleghenies and were swarming into Kentucky and the Old Northwest. In 1795 Spanish Lt. Gov. Zenon Trudeau was told to relax the requirement that emigrants had to be Roman Catholic and to admit American settlers and give each as much as 500 acres of land. As a result, by 1804 more than half the 10,000 settlers in Missouri were American. Spanish rule came to an end in 1803 when Napoleon Bonaparte suddenly changed his ambitious plans to reestablish New France and sold Louisiana to the United States.

The establishment of U.S. hegemony was a rude shock to the Louisiana French. The presence of American lawyers, land speculators, and public officials contrasted sharply with the Spanish system. The last Spanish lieutenant governor, Don Carlos De Lassus, had granted huge tracts of land, based on incomplete and illegal claims, to his friends and family; for over twenty years American officials were engaged in an effort to settle the bitter struggle that resulted from these disputed claims. It attracted land speculators and lawyers in large numbers. After a short period of military government under Capt. Amos Stoddard and a temporary attachment to the Indiana Territory, Louisiana became a first-class territory in 1804; in 1812 it was made a second-class territory, and the name "Missouri" was adopted. In 1816 it was made a third-class territory.

After the end of the War of 1812 a mass of immigrants, mainly from Virginia, Kentucky, Tennessee, and North Carolina, had crowded the road to Missouri, many of them bringing slaves. This group as well as the earlier immigrants stood fast against the attempt in 1820 to make Missouri a free state.

Missouri's population had grown rapidly, from about 10,000 in 1804 and about 20,000 in 1810 to about 66,000 in 1820, just previous to statehood; by 1830 the state's population had reached 140,000, and by midcentury, 682,000. Missouri had become Jacksonian in politics by 1830; and one of its senators, Thomas Hart Benton, was Andrew Jackson's leader in the Senate. All governors from 1830 to the Civil War were Democrats; only one Whig was elected by the state to the U.S. Senate.

Economically the state grew rapidly. The staple crops were corn and wheat; hemp and tobacco became money crops of importance in a few counties. The trade and transportation of military equipment across the Plains enriched some Missourians. After 1820 the Santa Fe trade was an important business for a limited number of Missourians, significant largely because of the silver, furs, and mules that were

brought back; large fur companies under the leadership of William H. Ashley, the Chouteaus, and John Jacob Astor were prosperous. Also, because of its location, Missouri was considered the gateway to the West by those going to Oregon's rich farmland or California's gold fields.

In 1832, Joseph Smith, the prophet and founder of the Mormon church, selected Jackson County as the Promised Land. The large Mormon settlement and the Mormons' insistence that they were God's chosen people caused bitter conflict with Missourians and open warfare. The Mormons were brutally harried out of Jackson County in 1833 and out of the state in 1838. Gov. Lilburn Boggs ordered that they be expelled or exterminated.

The struggle over slavery from 1850 through the Civil War was acute in Missouri. In 1849 Benton was being hewn down in Missouri because he would not accept John C. Calhoun's demands that slavery be protected in the territories. During the 1850's Missouri became a divided state, both political parties splitting over the slave issue. In 1860 and early 1861 Missouri had three elections with four factions contending, but each time the moderates, who were for peace and compromise, won overwhelmingly.

From 1845 to 1857 slaveholding Missourians played a disgraceful role by invading Kansas Territory and voting illegally in order to make Kansas slave territory. These inroads were organized and led by prominent proslavery leaders, notably Missouri's Sen. David Rice Atchison. The effort failed as the free-soil group in Kansas was augmented by immigrants from free states, but conflict continued until 1865.

At the beginning of the Civil War, western Missouri was the scene of guerrilla warfare. Doc Jennison and James Henry Lane led antislavery gangs from Kansas that wrought havoc on Missouri's western border, while William Clarke Quantrill, Confederate guerrilla commander, led the Missouri bushwhackers into Kansas, sacking and leveling Lawrence in 1863.

The Union armies threw the pro-Confederate state government out early in 1861, for although initial battles at Wilson's Creek and Lexington were favorable to the Confederates, Union strength prevailed. The state suffered from guerrilla warfare for four years; and more than 400 skirmishes were fought on Missouri soil before the end of the war. A provisional state government struggled successfully to keep Missouri in the Union.

After the Civil War, Missouri still had close ties with the South, but it looked principally to the West.

The railroads, partially built before 1860, were pushed to the state's western boundaries and across the Plains. Farming was productive, and manufacturing in Saint Louis grew rapidly, supported by the immigrant labor that had begun to flow into the state in the 1830's, largely from Germany and Ireland. Kansas City, a struggling village on the riverfront in 1850 and a battered victim of the border wars in 1865, grew into a rough railroad center in a decade. Its growth continued as the cattle and wheat from the Plains flowed in to be converted into beef and flour; before 1900 it was clearly the second metropolis in the state.

Missouri has established a balanced economy of agriculture, manufacturing, and commerce. Neither conspicuously Democratic nor Republican since 1900, Missouri is usually classed as a conservative state, slow to adopt new ideas but vigorous in using them once they are accepted. The population of the state in 1970 was 4,677,399.

[William F. Foley, *A History of Missouri, 1671–1820*, vol. I; Perry McCandless, *A History of Missouri, 1820–1860*, vol. II; David D. March, *The History of Missouri*; Duane Meyer, *The Heritage of Missouri: A History*.]

W. FRANCIS ENGLISH

MISSOURI, THREE FORKS OF THE, a picturesque and strategically important spot in Montana, so named because three principal source streams of the Missouri unite there—the Jefferson, the Madison, and the Gallatin. The place was named by Meriwether Lewis and William Clark, who camped at the junction on their exploratory trip to the Pacific Ocean in 1805. A fort was established there by the Missouri Fur Company in 1810 but persistent attacks by the Blackfoot caused its abandonment the same year.

[Q. D. Wheeler, *The Trail of Lewis and Clark*.]

CARL L. CANNON

MISSOURI BOTANICAL GARDEN was established in 1895 by Henry Shaw, a merchant who came to Saint Louis from England in 1819. Shaw's business efforts in Saint Louis were so successful that in 1840, at the age of forty, he was able to retire as a wealthy man. Influenced by a close friend, the physician and botanist George Engelmann, Shaw decided to establish a botanical garden on the grounds of his estate. For the remaining forty years of his life, he devoted himself to the development and direction of this garden, eventually called the Missouri Botanical Garden.

When Henry Shaw died in 1889, he left the garden to the people of Saint Louis, under the control of a board of trustees. His legacy, in addition to a sizable endowment for the support of the garden, includes the garden's basic design, several major buildings, a herbarium (a collection of dried plant specimens), and a botanical research library. His Victorian country home, located on the grounds of the garden, was later restored.

The Missouri Botanical Garden continued to expand and develop, both as a research facility and as a major public attraction. In 1960 the Climatron, the world's first geodesic-domed greenhouse, was constructed to simulate tropical environments. The Japanese garden, designed by Koichi Kawana, is the largest public garden of this type in the Midwest.

The garden's scientific program, instituted under the guidance of Engelmann, has made significant contributions to the study of botany and is one of the nation's major centers of biosystematic research. Research done by garden staff members has included studies of insect pollination of yucca, and in the 1920's a study of tobacco virus done by B. M. Duggar resulted in a breakthrough in modern understanding of viruses. Other contributions have included the development of the process of preserving wood with creosote and the hybridization of many popular varieties of water lilies and orchids. The garden has also become the national center for the study of African plants and has also continued major research programs on Latin-American floristics, particularly in Panama.

Expansion and development have not been limited to the original 70 acres in the city of Saint Louis. During the 1920's the board of trustees purchased land near Gray Summit, with the intention of removing the garden's plant collections from the badly polluted atmosphere of industrial Saint Louis. Greenhouses were built and the orchid collection was moved, but during the 1930's the pollution decreased and the collection was returned to its original location. At that time a collection representing native and exotic conifers was planted on a portion of the Gray Summit facility. By 1972, when the Arboretum and Nature Reserve at Gray Summit had expanded to include 2,200 acres, it was dedicated as a National Environment Education landmark by the Department of the Interior.

JAMES REED

MISSOURI COMPROMISE. The Missouri Territory comprised that part of the Louisiana Purchase not organized as the state of Louisiana in 1812. Ever since it had been a French province, slavery had existed in the territory. From 1817 to 1819 the Missouri Territorial Assembly petitioned Congress for statehood, with boundaries limited to approximately those of the present state. In 1819 there was an equal number of slave and free states. When the House of Representatives reported a bill authorizing Missouri to frame a constitution, James Tallmadge of New York proposed an amendment prohibiting the further introduction of slaves into Missouri and providing that all children born of slaves should be free at the age of twenty-five. The amendment was passed by the House on Feb. 16–17, 1819, but rejected by the Senate. Congress adjourned without further action but the South was stricken with fear.

When Congress reconvened in December 1819, Maine had formed a constitution and was requesting admission as a free state. The House passed an act admitting Maine. The Senate joined this measure to the one admitting Missouri without mention of slavery. Sen. J. B. Thomas of Illinois offered an amendment to the Senate bill for the admission of Missouri as a slave state, but with the provision that, in the remainder of the Louisiana Purchase, slavery should be prohibited north of 36°30′ north latitude. A debate followed that startled the nation. It came, said Thomas Jefferson, "like a fire bell in the night." A sectional alignment threatened the Union.

The House passed a bill, Mar. 1, 1820, admitting Missouri as a free state. The Senate took up the measure, struck out the antislavery provision, and added the Thomas amendment. A compromise was effected by admitting Maine as a free state, Mar. 3, 1820 (effective Mar. 15), and by authorizing Missouri to form a constitution with no restriction on slavery, Mar. 6, 1820. The region of the Louisiana Purchase north of 36°30′, except for the state of Missouri, was thus dedicated to freedom.

Missouri called a constitutional convention to meet at Saint Louis on June 12, 1820. The constitution empowered the legislature to exclude free blacks and mulattoes from the state. This restriction caused another bitter debate in Congress. A second compromise was, therefore, effected on Mar. 2, 1821. This stipulated that Missouri would not be admitted until it agreed that nothing in its constitution should be interpreted to abridge the privileges and immunities of citizens of the United States. The pledge was secured. On Aug. 10, 1821, Missouri became a state.

The compromise was respected and regarded as almost sacred until the Mexican War, when the power of Congress to exclude slavery from the territories was again questioned, by the Wilmot Proviso. In 1848 Congress passed the Oregon Territory bill prohibiting slavery. President James K. Polk signed it on the ground that the territory was north of the Missouri Compromise line. Soon afterward proposals were made to extend the compromise line of 1820 through the Mexican cession to the Pacific. These efforts failed to secure the extension of the 36°30′ line across the continent. Instead, the principle of popular sovereignty prevailed in the Compromise of 1850. The admission of California in 1850 gave the free states a majority of one. In 1854 the Missouri Compromise was repealed (see Kansas-Nebraska Act).

[George Dangerfield, *The Awakening of American Nationalism, 1815–1828;* Glover Moore, *The Missouri Controversy.*]

GEORGE D. HARMON

MISSOURI FUR COMPANY. *See* **Saint Louis Missouri Fur Company.**

MISSOURI-KANSAS-TEXAS RAILROAD. *See* **Railroads, Sketches.**

MISSOURI PACIFIC RAILROAD. *See* **Railroads, Sketches.**

MISSOURI RIVER, in the central and northwest central United States, is a major tributary of the Mississippi River and the longest river in the United States (2,466 miles). It drains a watershed of approximately 580,000 square miles. Father Jacques Marquette and Louis Jolliet reached the mouth of the Missouri in 1673. It was known to them as Peki-tan-oui, so named on some of the early maps, and later as Oumessourit. From its source in southwestern Montana, where the Jefferson, Gallatin, and Madison rivers join together, it winds around hills and bluffs, through one of the most fertile valleys in the world, to its junction with the Mississippi (ten miles north of Saint Louis).

The lower part of the Missouri was known to the French trappers, traders, and voyageurs, who ascended it as far as the Kansas River in 1705. In 1720 a Spanish caravan was sent from Santa Fe to the Missouri to drive back the French (see Villasur Expedition). The early French called the river Saint Philip. They probably did not go higher than the Platte, which was considered the dividing line between the upper and lower river. In 1719 Claude Charles du Tisne and party went up the Missouri in canoes as far as the Grand River. Credited with being the first white man to visit the upper Missouri country, Pierre Gaultier de Varennes, Sieur de La Vérendrye, led a party from one of the posts of the Hudson's Bay Company in 1738 to the Mandan villages. Other explorations followed, searching for the "Western Sea" by way of the Missouri River. The Missouri was first explored from its mouth to its source by Meriwether Lewis and William Clark (1804–05).

Although it was thought for years that no keelboat could ascend the Missouri, it later became the great highway into the West. Gregoire Sarpy is said to have first introduced the keelboat, but the real father of navigation on the Missouri was Manuel Lisa. The first steamboat ever to ascend the river was the *Independence,* which pushed off from Saint Louis in 1819, reached Old Franklin in thirteen days, and turned back at Old Chariton, in Missouri. In 1831 Pierre Chouteau succeeded in ascending the Missouri in his steamboat *Yellowstone.* As a result of steamboating many cities grew up along the edge of the river and several states built their capitals on its bank. Steamboating on the river reached its peak in the late 1850's and declined following the completion in 1859 of the Hannibal and Saint Joseph Railroad.

The Missouri River has always carried in suspension an immense amount of solid matter, mostly very fine light sand, discoloring the water and justifying the name of "Big Muddy." It is said that the yearly average of solid matter carried into the Mississippi by this river is over 500 million tons, brought along for an average distance of 500 miles. While the Missouri has a greater annual flow of water than the Mississippi above its mouth, it is subject to greater fluctuations. These have affected its navigability in certain seasons and caused the shoreline to shift, some farms and villages to disappear, and others to be left far back through deposits of the soil in front of them.

In 1944 Congress authorized a Missouri River basin project to control flooding of the Missouri, improve navigation, develop hydroelectric power, irrigate over 4.3 million acres in the basin, halt stream pollution, and provide recreation areas. By the 1970's there were seven dams on the Missouri and eighty on its tributaries. The Missouri Basin Interagency Committee, with representatives from seven federal agencies and the governors of the ten Missouri basin states (North Dakota, South Dakota, Wyoming, Nebraska, Kansas, Minnesota, Missouri, Colorado, Iowa, and Montana), oversees the project.

[J. V. Brower, *The Missouri River and Its Utmost Source;* Bernard de Voto, *Across the Wide Missouri.*]

STELLA M. DRUMM

MISSOURI RIVER FUR TRADE. The Missouri River and its tributaries constituted one of the three great systems of importance to the fur trader and trapper. The several companies engaged in the fur trade operated, generally speaking, in distinctive fields, usually identified with some one or another of the great drainage systems that mark off the natural divisions of the country. The Spanish Commercial Company, Saint Louis Missouri Fur Company, and thereafter in succession the Missouri Fur Company, the Columbia Fur Company, and the American Fur Company, all confined their operations to the Missouri and Mississippi watersheds. Although the Rocky Mountain Fur Company competed with these to some extent at the headwaters of the Missouri, its operations were largely confined to some of the tributaries and to regions farther inland.

Many establishments, variously designated as forts, posts, and houses, were scattered along the Missouri in the wilderness long before the tide of western immigration set in. After the expedition of Pierre Gaultier de Varennes, Sieur de La Vérendrye, in 1738, whose main purpose was one of exploration, came Pierre Menard, fourteen years earlier than Jacques D'Église (1791–95), and then Jean B. Truteau of the Spanish Company. This last-named company erected Truteau's Post in 1794. In 1800 Regis Loisel's post, known also as Cedar Post, was established in the Sioux country, thirty-five miles below the present site of Pierre, S.Dak. The most important early post was that of the Saint Louis Missouri Fur Company. Known as Fort Lisa, it was located near Council Bluffs, in present-day Iowa. Outstanding forts of the American Fur Company were received from the Columbia Fur Company. The largest and most important of the American Fur Company's forts was Fort Union, in present-day North Dakota. The Missouri River made Saint Louis the greatest center of the fur trade. All the early expeditions were outfitted and started from this point. In 1843 in the country tributary to Saint Louis there were 150 fur trading posts, a great majority of which lay along the Missouri River. Although the upper reaches of the Missouri were at first walled off by the British and the Blackfoot and Arikara, these obstacles were eventually overcome.

The fur trade was the principal commerce of the early days in the West and it was able to develop to such a great extent because of the Missouri River. As facilities for navigation improved the fur trade increased. The pirogue, bateau, and barge of the French voyageur gave way to the keelboat and mackinaw boat, and these in turn yielded to the steamboat in 1831. The Missouri River was said to be the most difficult in the world to navigate. Nevertheless, it was the most dependable medium of transportation in the days of the fur trade.

[Phil E. Chappell, *A History of the Missouri River;* Hiram M. Chittenden, *The American Fur Trade of the Far West.*]

STELLA M. DRUMM

MISSOURI V. HOLLAND, 252 U.S. 416 (1920), a Supreme Court case in which it was determined whether the treatymaking power extends the exercise of federal power to a field not specifically delegated to the national government. Two federal district courts had held an earlier Migratory Birds Act, passed under the commerce power, unconstitutional. An identical statute of 1918, passed after the ratification of the Migratory Bird Treaty of 1916 with Great Britain, was upheld in *Missouri* v. *Holland* on the grounds that it contravened no express limitations of the Constitution and that the treatymaking power is not limited by any "invisible radiation from the general terms of the Tenth Amendment."

PHILLIPS BRADLEY

MITCHELL'S MAP, or *Map of the British and French Dominions in North America With the Roads, Distances, Limits, and Extent of the Settlement,* on a scale of 1:2 million, was published in London on Feb. 13, 1755, under the auspices of the Board of Trade by John Mitchell. A successful physician and botanist, Mitchell practiced medicine in Urbana, Va., between 1735 and 1746. He wrote well on many subjects, but is best remembered for his large-scale map. On the fourth English edition (London, 1775) the words *British Colonies* were substituted for *British and French Dominions.* The map, engraved on copper and printed on eight sheets, measures when joined 52.75 by 76.25 inches. More than twenty editions were published before 1792, after which parts of the map were published with new titles by numerous authors, many times without acknowledgment to Mitchell.

Since its publication, Mitchell's map has figured in nearly every boundary dispute involving the United States or parts thereof. On it were laid down the first boundaries of the United States following the Treaty of Paris (1783).

LLOYD A. BROWN

MIWOK, native Californian peoples spread through the central river valley and to the north of San Francisco Bay in the coast ranges. Lacking political organization outside their tightly knit and separatistic villages, the Miwok were distinguishable by their language, a branch of the Penutian phylum, and by their brand of central Californian culture. With other Californians, such as the Pomo, Maidu, and Wintun, the Miwok depended on acorns for subsistence, made fine basketry, and focused their lives within the confines of several hundred small hamlets. Like other California peoples the Miwok were numerous, an estimated 11,000 in 1770. Contact with Europeans after 1850 proved highly destructive both to their numbers and to their native culture.

[A. L. Kroeber, *Handbook of the Indians of California,* Bureau of American Ethnology, bulletin 78.]

ROBERT F. SPENCER

MIXED COMMISSIONS are instruments of international law established by bilateral or multilateral agreements and composed of members of different nationalities for the purpose of achieving the peaceful settlement of disputes. According to their functions they may be mixed claims commissions, commissions of conciliation, or commissions of inquiry.

Mixed claims commissions have the task of arbitrating disputes arising from claims of one state or its nationals against another state regarding damages, debts, boundary questions, and other matters involving claims. The procedure of establishing such commissions was initiated by the United States and Britain with the Jay Treaty of 1794, which set up a joint international commission consisting of an equal number of lawyers appointed by each party, who appointed an umpire with a casting vote. In subsequent mixed claims commissions it was not necessary that the members be lawyers; frequently they were nationals of third neutral countries. Following the success of the Jay Treaty, other claims commissions were established by the United States and other countries. Among those in which the United States participated were the United States–Mexican Commission established in 1868, which disposed of over 2,000 claims, and the United States–German Mixed Claims Commission created after World War I to settle war damage claims.

Mixed commissions of conciliation elucidate the facts underlying an international dispute and make proposals for settlement. The parties to the dispute are under no obligation to accept the proposals, which, in contrast to arbitrated settlements, are not binding. Claims commissions occasionally have also been called commissions of conciliation, as was the commission established by the United States and its allies with Italy after World War II to settle claims of American and Allied nationals.

Conciliation commissions were developed first by the "Bryan treaties," concluded by the United States and some American and European states between 1913 and 1915 on the initiative of Secretary of State William Jennings Bryan. Conciliation commissions were also established by the Locarno treaties of 1925. The concept was later embodied in the Revised General Act for the Pacific Settlement of International Disputes adopted in 1949 under United Nations General Assembly Resolution 268A(III). The commissions are composed of one member chosen by each party to a dispute from among its nationals and three members appointed by agreement from among nationals of third countries. Since World War II nearly 200 commissions of conciliation have been established by different states through bilateral and multilateral agreements, but these commissions have not been used often, because usually each of the parties was free to reject the commission recommendations. Therefore other procedures for the settlement of disputes were preferred.

Mixed commissions of inquiry are similar in nature and composition to conciliation commissions, but their functions are limited to determining the facts in a controversy.

[Werner Feld, *The Court of the European Communities: New Dimension in International Adjudication,* and *Nongovernmental Forces and World Politics: A Study of Business, Labor, and Political Groups.*]

WERNER J. FELD

MOBILE, a city and seaport in southwest Alabama, located on Mobile Bay, thirty-one miles from the Gulf of Mexico. In 1702 Jean Baptiste Le Moyne, Sieur de Bienville, established a fort twenty-seven miles from the mouth of the Mobile River. Flooding forced the movement of the fort to the present site of Mobile in 1711. The French colony served as the capital of Louisiana from 1711 to 1719. At the close of the French and Indian War (1763), it passed into the hands of the British; during the American Revolution Bernardo de Gálvez seized Mobile for Spain. It re-

mained a Spanish city until the War of 1812, when Gen. James Wilkinson took possession of the city in 1813, alleging that it was being used as a base by British vessels (*see* Mobile Seized). Mobile was incorporated as a town in 1814 and as a city in 1819.

During the Civil War, Mobile was one of the most important Confederate ports. It was strongly fortified and was much used by blockade runners. Adm. David G. Farragut closed the port in the Battle of Mobile Bay (Aug. 5, 1864), but the city did not fall into Union hands until Apr. 12, 1865. Bankruptcy forced the city to relinquish its charter in 1879; it was, however, rechartered in 1887.

After the Civil War, Mobile burgeoned as one of the nation's major ports. Banana importing began in 1893, and the city continues to export vast amounts of lumber, cotton, and naval stores. Mobile is also a major shipbuilding center and was especially active in this area during the world wars. The population of the city in 1970 was 190,026.

[Peter Joseph Hamilton, *Mobile Under Five Flags;* A. B. Moore, *History of Alabama;* C. G. Summersell, *Mobile, History of a Seaport Town.*]

HALLIE FARMER

MOBILE ACT. During a dispute with Spain over the boundaries of West Florida, Congress, at President Thomas Jefferson's insistence, passed an act on Feb. 24, 1804, directing that the territories ceded by France in the Louisiana Treaty of 1803, "and also all the navigable waters, rivers, creeks, bays, and inlets, lying within the United States, shall be annexed to the Mississippi District." The words "lying within the United States" avoided a precise boundary, and thus left it to executive action to determine just what territory should be annexed. Spain had contended, with much force, that there was no territory on the Gulf of Mexico lying within the United States east of the Mississippi River. In proclaiming the annexation Jefferson repeated the latitudinarian but ambiguous language of the act and thus evaded the issue. The region (eastward from the Mississippi to the Perdido River, and bordering on the Gulf, but not including Mobile) was not actually occupied by the United States until 1810 (*see* West Florida, Annexation of).

[Samuel Flagg Bemis, *A Diplomatic History of the United States.*]

SAMUEL FLAGG BEMIS

MOBILE BAY, BATTLE OF (Aug. 5, 1864). A Union fleet of four monitors and fourteen wooden vessels of war, commanded by Adm. David G. Farragut, forced an entrance into Mobile Bay in Alabama through a narrow passage protected by mines, by Fort Morgan, and by the ironclad *Tennessee* and three small wooden gunboats, commanded by Adm. Franklin Buchanan. The Union monitor *Tecumseh* was sunk by a mine; "Damn the torpedoes!" cried Farragut, as his *Hartford* took the lead. All his vessels eventually reached the bay, though some were injured by gunfire from Fort Morgan and from the *Tennessee*. The *Tennessee* then fought the whole Union fleet. Three of the larger wooden vessels were injured, but the powerful guns of the three monitors finally forced the ironclad to surrender. Farragut lost 52 killed, 93 drowned, and 170 wounded. Buchanan lost 12 killed and 20 wounded. Fort Morgan surrendered on Aug. 23, and the city of Mobile was completely blockaded.

[C. L. Lewis, *Admiral Franklin Buchanan;* A. T. Mahan, *Admiral Farragut.*]

CHARLES LEE LEWIS

MOBILE SEIZED (1813). At the beginning of the War of 1812, Mobile, Ala., was in the possession of Spain. The United States had long coveted the port (*see* Mobile Act) and when the English navy began using it as a base for attacking the United States, President James Madison ordered Gen. James Wilkinson, commanding the United States forces at New Orleans, to capture Mobile. The Spanish commander had few soldiers at his command and surrendered to avoid bloodshed, although he protested against the invasion of Spanish territory by the United States in time of peace. The town passed into the possession of the United States on Apr. 13, 1813 (*see* West Florida, Annexation of).

[Peter Joseph Hamilton, *Mobile Under Five Flags.*]

HALLIE FARMER

MOBILIZATION is the process of assembling and organizing troops and matériel for the defense of a nation in time of war or national emergency. It has become a central factor in warfare since the French Revolution and the rise of nationalism. Whereas 18th-century powers most often hired mercenaries to fight limited wars, 19th-century nations increasingly demanded that every able-bodied citizen respond to mobilization calls. American attitudes toward war further reinforced the concept of total war because threats to public tranquility were interpreted as being illegal and immoral and thus as calling for nothing short of total war to reestablish the peace. In 20th-century wars it has been necessary to mobilize not only men and matériel but also psychological support, as illustrated by President Woodrow Wilson's vow to "make the world safe for democracy" and President Franklin D. Roosevelt's call for Germany's "unconditional surrender."

While embracing the notion of total war, the United States, until the 20th century, was notoriously inept at mobilizing troops and retaining them for the duration of the wars it fought. Congress was ever suspicious of standing armies and of all efficient means that would enable the executive to mobilize the state militia forces, feeling that these instruments might serve partisan causes.

The mobilization problems experienced in the War of 1812 and the Mexican War (1846–48) continued to plague U.S. military efforts throughout the 19th century. For instance, the militia system was never workable. This fact, together with the unreliability of the volunteers and the vices of the bounty system, demonstrated the necessity for conscription in any extended war in which the United States was involved. Furthermore, the tendency to mobilize manpower before mobilizing matériel was to create confusion down to World War I.

In the Mexican War, mobilization was based largely upon an expansible standing army and the calling of volunteers, because the militia's poor performance in the War of 1812 had demonstrated that the militia system was irredeemable. There were traces of preplanning in this first foreign war, as arms and supplies were provided by the federal government based on the needs of the whole mobilized army.

The Civil War was a total war and thus a modern conflict, even though many of the mobilization mistakes of previous wars were repeated. At the outset, few were able to perceive the conflict's full dimensions, and thus mobilization proceeded sporadically. Initially President Abraham Lincoln called 75,000 state militia troops. But since this element had not been called since 1836 at the outset of the second Seminole War, the 2,471,377 troops on its rolls represented only a paper force in 1861. Next, a call was issued for volunteers; with no effective mobilization plan, the War Department was unable to process the overwhelming number of recruits. Later, when the ardor of volunteering cooled, other methods of raising troops were resorted to, such as the draft, implemented by the Conscription Act of 1863. Although the act netted few draftees, it forced many to volunteer who otherwise would not have. Other extraordinary measures employed to mobilize manpower included accepting blacks for army service and organizing special service units to receive invalid volunteers for noncombatant duty.

All the old nightmares of poor mobilization were present in the Spanish-American War (1898), plus some new ones. With no plan of mobilization there was no integration of manpower with matériel and no training in combined naval and military operations. Only the fact that the war was short and successful helped to ameliorate some of the potentially disastrous problems. A series of postwar reforms was instituted to remedy the worst mobilization shortcomings, among which was the founding of the Army War College in 1901 to study the mobilization process.

U.S. participation in World War I (1917–18) and World War II (1941–45) introduced speed into the warmaking equation. Although the urgency of mobilization was slightly cushioned by the prior entry of America's allies into both wars, the gigantic scale of mobilization, the increased importance of technology, the total absorption of a sophisticated industrial economy into the war effort, and the huge number of troops all raised mobilization planning to the highest councils of war.

By the National Defense Act of 1916 the United States avoided some of the desperate measures used to raise manpower in previous wars: uncertain calls for militiamen and volunteers were no longer to be relied on, and draftees were not to make substitutions, purchase exemptions, or receive bounties. Whereas in earlier American wars estimates of manpower requirements had been based largely on guesses of what public sentiment would allow, in World War I the calls for manpower were limited only by the manpower requirements for industry. Therefore, the great mobilization problems of World War I were not those of recruiting, but of equipping, training, organizing, and transporting the army to the front.

The Japanese attack on Pearl Harbor in 1941 catapulted the United States into the most massive mobilization effort in history. As in World War I the armed forces and the war industries were in competition for manpower. In addition, there were the requirements of not one but five theaters of war, the need of maintaining lines of communication to each theater, and the need to dovetail efforts with coalition partners. The squeeze upon American manpower extended the search for able hands to the enlisting of women, indigenous personnel, prisoners of war, and the physically handicapped.

The leading role of the United States in the cold war significantly altered its traditional mobilization techniques. Although never implemented, universal military training, authorized in principle by the Universal Military Training and Service Act of 1951, was supposed to provide a peacetime pool of manpower that could be drafted in time of national emergency. Until the Korean War (1950–53) the emphasis on air power and nuclear arms allowed the army's strength to slip.

Selective-service legislation passed in 1955 assured that reserve units would be manned by trained men; but instead of the reserves being called for the Vietnam War, as had been done in the Korean War, forces were raised through increased draft calls. The decision to do so was prompted by problems experienced in the reserve call-up during the Berlin crisis in 1961 and by political exigencies. But not calling the reserves was generally considered to have been a mistake, for it gravely weakened the army's strategic reserve.

[M. G. Henry and M. A. Kreidberg, *History of Military Mobilization in the United States Army 1775–1945;* M. Matloff, *American Military History.*]

DON E. MCLEOD

MOCCASIN, from an Algonkin word for shoe, is specifically a foot covering of soft skin, with soft or hard soles. All the American Indian tribes wore moccasins except some barefoot Indians of the Pacific coast and southeast Texas and the sandal-wearing Indians along the Mexican border. The eastern Indian moccasin had a soft sole and was often made by folding a piece of soft tanned skin up over the foot, the seams at the top. The uppers and the toes offered fields for decoration with quills and beads. The Plains Indians preferred a moccasin with a hard sole, but decorated the uppers with attractive designs in porcupine quills and beads. Tribal styles in shape and other nonessentials made possible the identification of tracks in soft earth. Women made the moccasins and both sexes of all ages wore them. Moccasins were adopted by the whites and universally worn by early traders and trappers. They are still in use in parts of Canada and the United States, and to some extent Indian models have influenced certain modern styles of shoes.

[G. Hatt, *Moccasins and Their Relation to Arctic Footwear.*]

CLARK WISSLER

MODOC WAR (1872–73), last of the Indian wars to affect northern California and southern Oregon, had complex causes. The war was a final desperate resistance to the impact of the white man's culture on an Indian way of life, as well as a reaction to mistreatment of the Indians by the settlers. The removal of the Modoc to the Klamath reservation in Oregon in 1864 antagonized them for several reasons: no cognizance was taken of a rivalry between a Modoc chief named Sconchin and a younger chief, Captain Jack (Kintpuash), which had resulted in a physical division of the tribe; the Modoc were dissatisfied with reservation life; and they were not welcome among their hereditary enemies, the Klamath.

In 1872 Captain Jack led the more aggressive elements among the Modoc back to their former habitat in the vicinity of the Lost River in northern California and refused to return to the reservation, although Sconchin's faction remained quietly on the reservation. An attempt by a detachment of cavalry to return Captain Jack's Modoc to the reservation failed after a skirmish in which there were casualties. The situation was aggravated when fourteen settlers were killed by the Modoc. Captain Jack and his band then retreated south of Tule Lake to the lava beds, which constituted an impregnable natural stronghold. The Modoc band consisted of only 75 warriors and about 150 women and children, but they held out in the lava beds for six months against all attempts by troops to dislodge them. The first attack on the lava beds, on Jan. 17, 1873, in a dense fog, was an utter failure; sixteen U.S. soldiers were killed and fifty-three were wounded, while not a single Modoc died in the battle. On Apr. 11, Gen. Edward R. S. Canby and another member of a peace commission that had entered the lava beds to negotiate were killed by the Modoc. The Modoc were finally dislodged only after military operations involving more than 1,000 U.S. soldiers and after dissension had developed among the Modoc themselves. In June 1873 the Modoc left the lava beds and scattered. They were pursued by soldiers and captured, thus ending the war. Captain Jack and three others were tried by a court-martial for murder, found guilty, and hanged, while the rest of the band was exiled to Indian Territory.

[Keith A. Murray, *The Modocs and Their War;* Erwin N. Thompson, *Modoc War: Its Military History and Topography.*]

KENNETH M. STEWART

MODUS VIVENDI, a temporary agreement or protocol made by an executive to cover questions that will later be covered in a formal treaty. In the United States these arrangements are made by the president to meet emergencies in foreign relations where Congress has failed to act. The method was first used by President Grover Cleveland for a temporary settlement of the North Atlantic fisheries dispute. A notable instance of this use of executive power was Theodore Roosevelt's agreement establishing a financial protectorate over the Dominican Republic.

[J. M. Mathews, *American Foreign Relations.*]
THEODORE G. GRONERT

MOGOLLON. The prehistoric Mogollon, or Western Pueblo, culture developed on the forested slopes and in the grassy valleys of the mountains of southern New Mexico and southeastern Arizona. Even though primitive corn dating back to 2000 B.C. has been discovered in a Desert culture context in Bat Cave and Tulorosa Cave, N.Mex., a distinctive Mogollon tradition did not appear until about 1000 B.C., when squash and beans became available. The transition to the Mogollon culture from a Desert culture base was completed by 300 B.C., with the introduction of pottery from Middle America. The Mogollon were in an important sense ancestral to other Southwest groups, for they adopted and transmitted many features of Middle American culture at an early date, but their mountain habitat lacked the potential for high agricultural yields that later supported the elaborate ceremonialism characteristic of the Hohokam. After A.D. 900 the Mogollon even became the recipients of innovations developed by the more northern Anasazi. The earliest Mogollon villages and hamlets consisted of from two to about twenty semisubterranean, or pit, houses irregularly scattered throughout the settlement. Large buildings in these settlements may have served as community or ceremonial centers. Mogollon artifacts include wickerwork sandals; ornaments of shell, wood, stone, and bone; string aprons; fur and feather robes; textiles; figurines; pottery; and many tools for collecting and processing food. Corn, beans, and squash were the staples. Various animal and human forms were portrayed on the attractive Mogollon painted pottery. Settlements containing multiroomed pueblo or apartment-type surface dwellings appeared by about A.D. 1000. Some of these settlements grew to large apartments containing well over a hundred rooms. Each community probably remained autonomous and maintained an essentially democratic social organization. Traits derived from the Anasazi include stone masonry and black-on-white decoration on pottery. Complex social factors and perhaps climatic change resulted in a contraction of the area inhabited by the Mogollon after A.D. 1400. The historic Zuni tribe is the probable descendant of this early Southwest culture.

[Jesse D. Jennings, *Prehistory of North America;* John C. McGregor, *Southwestern Archaeology.*]

GUY GIBBON

MOHAVE. The so-called River Yumans, including such native American tribes as the Halchidhoma, Yuma, and Cocopa, as well as the Mohave, were unique in their adaptation to their native terrain and in their cultural development. All four, the Mohave being the northernmost, settled along the lower reaches of the Colorado River at the present-day Arizona-California border. The Maricopa, historic residents of the middle Gila drainage, were earlier associated with the Colorado River groups. The largest tribe, however, was the Mohave, having a population of about 3,000 in 1680. All spoke Yuman languages, Yuman being a subgrouping of a conceptual Hokan or Hokan-Siouan macrophylum.

The ethnographic problem posed by the River Yumans is one of cultural affinities. They appear to be a California Basin archetype, over which have been laid Southwestern elements. An original gathering mode of life was enriched by the addition of knowledge of maize cultivation. In the rich alluvial soils of the Colorado the Mohave raised corn but at the same time gathered mesquite beans. The absence of regulated land ownership suggests a late, yet still prehistoric, integration of agriculture. Unlike other Californian tribes, the Mohave abandoned basketry in favor of pottery making, a Southwestern trait.

The distinctiveness of aboriginal Mohave culture lies in several features not seen among other Indian tribes. With the other Yumans they shared a strong nationalist sense even though formal political officials were lacking. The exception was the war chief, who organized formalized battles, virtual games that the tribes of the area carried on among themselves. It is in religion, however, that the Mohave and their related neighbors were most distinctive. Among them, ceremonials of a group nature were subordinated to dream cycles that formed an integral part of Mohave life: individual dream experiences, either of tribal history and lore or of individual fantasy life were recounted in association with a ritual that suggests a view of reality different from that general among native North Americans.

Contacts of the Mohave with Europeans may have taken place as early as 1540, and it is certain that Juan de Oñate visited them in 1604. But the Mohave and their neighbors remained essentially free of contact with outsiders, and although relegated to the Colorado River Reservation by 1876 by executive order, they entered into no treaty with the United States.

[A. L. Kroeber, *Handbook of the Indians of California,* Bureau of American Ethnology, Bulletin 78 (1925); William J. Wallace, "The Mohave Indians of the Lower Colorado River," in R. F. Spencer, J. D. Jennings, and others, eds., *The Native Americans.*]

ROBERT F. SPENCER

MOHAWK AND HUDSON RAILROAD was chartered by the state of New York in 1826. Construction began in 1830 and it was opened on Aug. 9, 1831, when the first steam locomotive in New York State, the *De Witt Clinton,* was put into service. The line connected Albany with Schenectady. In 1853 the Mohawk and Hudson was joined with other short lines between Albany and Buffalo to become the New York Central Railroad.

[H. U. Faulkner, *American Economic History.*]

JAMES D. MAGEE

MOHAWK VALLEY, the northern gateway to the West, was the only natural east-west passage through the Appalachian barrier and hence was prized by both Indians and whites from earliest times. From the earliest days of the Dutch period the fur trade moved along this route to Albany. This trade increasingly depended on the Iroquoian conquests in the West. Inevitably there was a clash with the interests of the French in Canada. To protect the New York frontier and to maintain the Iroquois alliance—of necessity cardinal objectives of English policy—control of the Mohawk Valley was essential. Both the French and English claimed the Iroquois as subjects. In 1701 the Iroquois signed a treaty (*see* Iroquois Beaver Land Deed) deeding their hunting grounds to the king of England, in effect placing themselves under the protection of the British, and in 1713, by the Treaty of Utrecht, the suzerainty of England over the Iroquois was acknowledged by the French. This protection was to be used, first by the English and later by the state of New York, as a basis for claiming the western lands conquered by the Iroquois. During the colonial wars the valley settlements suffered cruelly from French and Indian raids (*see* Schenectady). The Iroquois wavered in their alliance, and only the influence of Sir William Johnson held them to the English. Again in the American Revolution the strategic importance of the valley was recognized. In 1777 Col.

Barry St. Leger planned to take the valley on his way to Albany but was checked at Oriskany and Fort Stanwix, both on the upper Mohawk River in New York, and forced to retreat.

A part of the only continuous water route from the Atlantic to the Great Lakes, the valley became the natural route along which turnpikes and other highways, railroads, canals, and airports were built. A stream of immigration moved through the valley westward with the opening of the Erie Canal in 1825. The products of midwestern states were carried to eastern markets and eastern goods were sold in the West.

[Nelson Greene, *History of the Mohawk Valley*.]

A. C. FLICK

MOHEGAN AND MAHICAN, two native American tribes speaking differing Algonkin languages, are easily confused with each other. The Mohegan were spread through the upper Thames Valley in Connecticut and were often identified with the Pequot, another Algonkin people of the same area. The destruction of the latter in 1637, as well as of other Algonkin tribes following the onset of King Philip's War in 1675, left the Mohegan the dominant Algonkin group in southern New England. Their fame through this period rests largely on their paramount chief, Uncas, who sided with European settlers.

The Mahican, on the other hand, a somewhat larger tribe with an estimated population of 3,000 in 1600, inhabited the upper Hudson Valley and the territory toward Lake Champlain. Under pressures from the Mohawk and from Europeans they gradually shifted westward. One band of the Mahican settled on the Housatonic in Massachusetts and in 1737 was located at the mission at Stockbridge, a name that followed this group even on to Wisconsin.

Culturally much alike, falling into the general pattern of the Woodland Algonkin, the two tribes were influenced in their political organization by the Iroquois. The Mahican are best known through James Fenimore Cooper's novel *The Last of the Mohicans* (1826).

[John R. Swanton, *The Indian Tribes of North America*, Bureau of American Ethnology, bulletin 145.]

ROBERT F. SPENCER

MOHEGAN CASE, involving a century of protracted litigation, arose from a deed in 1640 given by Uncas, Mohegan chief, to the colony of Connecticut. The deed conveyed virtually the whole Indian country, including the north parish of New London and the townships of Windham, Colchester, Lynne, and Hebron, for a paltry consideration. The Indians later looked upon the deed as merely constituting a right of preemption. In 1659 the famous Norwich tract was deeded by Uncas to Capt. John Mason and others. The Indians and Mason's descendants claimed this deed merely set up a trusteeship in the Indians' behalf. But as Mason was agent for the colony, Connecticut maintained that he had obtained the deed to eliminate whatever remaining title to the lands the Mohegan might have possessed. Further sales of the area known as the Mohegan hunting grounds were made by Uncas' son. A royal commission set up in 1703 by Queen Anne decided that Connecticut should restore all the lands they had at the time of Uncas' death to the Mohegan. But in 1715 a commission appointed by the general assembly decided nearly all claims in favor of the colony. Similar findings were returned by a royal commission of review in 1738, which virtually repealed the 1703 decision. These findings were set aside on appeal, but a new commission in 1743 sustained the ruling substantially upholding the Uncas deed. An appeal to the king in council finally settled the issue in favor of the colony as late as 1773.

[G. A. Washburne, *Imperial Control of the Administration of Justice in the Thirteen American Colonies, 1684–1776*.]

RICHARD B. MORRIS

MOHONK, LAKE, CONFERENCE. The Lake Mohonk Conference was held annually between 1883 and 1912 at Lake Mohonk, N.Y., for the purpose of discussing reforms in Indian affairs and was attended by clergymen, educators, government officials, senators, representatives, ethnologists, and other interested persons. It was inaugurated by Albert K. Smiley, a Quaker educator and then a member of the Board of Indian Commissioners. The policies recommended by the conference aimed at the assimilation of Indians into the mainstream of American life and were influential in the passage of the Dawes Severalty Act of 1887, which provided for the allotment of tribal land to individual Indians.

[Hazel W. Hertzberg, *The Search for an American Indian Identity*.]

KENNETH M. STEWART

MOLASSES ACT, passed in 1733, laid a prohibitive duty of ninepence on every gallon of rum, sixpence a gallon on molasses, and five shillings a hundred-weight on sugar imported from foreign colonies into Great Britain's American colonies, to be paid before landing.

The act originated in the conflicting economic interests of continental and island colonies. Barbados, which was suffering from the effects of a recent hurricane, the exhaustion of its soil, the restraints of the Navigation Acts, and a burdensome export tax, led the other British sugar colonies in petitioning Parliament to prohibit the "Bread Colonies" from selling provisions to, or buying sugar products from, the more fertile foreign West Indies. The continental colonies had a sound economic answer, that the British West Indies could not consume all their provisions nor satisfy their demand for molasses; but the sugar colonies had the better political connections in Parliament.

Colonial smuggling minimized the act's effects. Although one cannot measure the exact extent of the illicit trade, it is clear that New England distilled considerably more rum than could have been produced from legally imported molasses. Yet it was expensive to evade officials or to procure their connivance, and the act probably served as a mildly protective tariff in favor of the British West Indies until its repeal in 1764 by the Sugar Act.

[G. L. Beer, *British Colonial Policy;* C. W. Taussig, *Rum, Romance and Rebellion.*]

LAWRENCE A. HARPER

MOLASSES TRADE was the keystone of colonial commerce, supplying as it did a product that enabled the colonists to offset their unfavorable balance of trade with England. Except for experimental attempts to produce molasses locally from corn, the source of supply was the West Indies. It centered at first in the English sugar colonies, but by the early 18th century it had shifted to the other West Indies.

Molasses had obvious advantages for sweetening purposes, and it provided a "money cargo" almost as current as cash; but once exported from the islands, there was surprisingly little trade in molasses as such. Its real potency came when distilled into rum. Most important, it served as the basis for the triangular trade in which rum sent to Africa brought slaves to the West Indies, where they were exchanged for cash or bills of exchange and more molasses.

At first the trade was unrestrained except for local taxes, but in 1704 Parliament confined the exportation of molasses to England or its colonies. In 1733 the Molasses Act unsuccessfully attempted to eliminate trade with the foreign West Indies by prohibitive taxes, and after 1764 the Sugar Acts tried to raise revenue from that trade. Independence freed the thirteen colonies from such restraints, but hampered their trade with the British West Indies. Modifications of the law permitted the direct importation of molasses, but the Navigation Acts continued to limit American shipping until 1830.

[C. W. Taussig, *Rum, Romance and Rebellion.*]

LAWRENCE A. HARPER

MOLECULAR BIOLOGY is the term commonly used to denote the study of living organisms with special reference to the role of certain large molecules—particularly the nucleic acids and proteins—that are the chief bearers of biological specificity. Research in this field has demonstrated the role of the nucleic acids as carriers of genetic information, in which they serve to specify the precise structure of the proteins. Since all enzymes, which catalyze the immense variety of metabolic processes, are proteins, molecular biology is central to almost all aspects of the study of living organisms. No sharp line can be drawn between molecular biology and biochemistry. The whole subject is built on a biochemical foundation, and many of the chief contributors to it would call themselves biochemists. Likewise, molecular biology is deeply involved with genetics, and much of molecular biology represents the extension of classical Mendelian genetics to the structure and action of genes as defined in biochemical terms. The development of molecular biology began about 1930 and increased rapidly after 1950.

Major contributions to molecular biology, as to all sciences, have come from many countries. American contributors have been of central importance, but their work cannot be considered in isolation. Moreover, several of the major American contributors have been immigrants from Europe and Asia.

Chemical knowledge of the proteins and nucleic acids grew slowly, with much arduous research, throughout the 19th and early 20th centuries. By about 1930 it had been established that proteins from all kinds of organisms are composed of about twenty amino acids, which link together in long chains by what are known as peptide bonds. The virtually infinite number of possible arrangements of the different amino acids in these chains appeared adequate to account for the immense variety and specificity of the proteins. Protein molecules are very large, as shown especially by the colloid chemist T. Svedberg in

Sweden, who developed the ultracentrifuge, with which he found for various proteins molecular weights ranging from about 10,000 up to many millions. (On the same scale the weight of a single carbon atom is 12.) The ultracentrifuge became a tool of crucial importance in the development of molecular biology. In 1926, J. B. Sumner at Cornell University and, from 1930 on, J. H. Northrop at the Rockefeller Institute produced decisive evidence that enzymes were indeed proteins. About a decade later, G. W. Beadle and E. L. Tatum, then at Stanford University, showed from genetic studies on bread molds (*Neurospora*) and bacteria that the action of genes directs the production of enzymes; they summarized their conclusions by the slogan "One gene, one enzyme." By about 1940 it was clear that all enzymes are proteins and that their production is directed by the genes, but the chemical nature of the genes was still obscure.

In 1935, W. M. Stanley, at the Rockefeller Institute, obtained the virus of tobacco mosaic disease as a very large protein molecule. Thenceforth viruses were no longer regarded as mysterious entities, but as defined substances that could be obtained in a pure form. F. C. Bawden and N. W. Pirie in England soon showed that Stanley's virus also contained nucleic acid, a fact of the utmost importance for the development of molecular biology.

In the period 1930–40, nucleic acids were less well understood than proteins. They were known to contain phosphate groups, certain organic bases, and a particular kind of sugar that was linked at one end to one of the bases and at the other end to the phosphate. This combination of base, sugar, and phosphate was called a nucleotide. The phosphate group also served to link one nucleotide to another. Thus, nucleic acids, like proteins, were composed of long chains, with a repeating pattern of similar units. Whereas proteins contain about twenty different kinds of amino acids, nucleic acids contain only four different kinds of nucleotides. Nucleic acids are of two kinds: deoxyribonucleic acid (DNA) and ribonucleic acid (RNA). In DNA the sugar is deoxyribose and the four bases are adenine (A), guanine (G), cytosine (C), and thymine (T). In RNA the sugar is ribose, and the bases are the same except that thymine is replaced by the closely related base uracil (U). The size of nucleic acid molecules was still obscure, but later work showed it to be very large.

One of the pioneers of molecular biology was W. T. Astbury of England, a pupil of W. H. and W. L. Bragg, the discoverers of crystal-structure determination by diffraction of X rays. Astbury extended the X-ray method to the study of fibrous proteins, such as keratin and collagen, and obtained preliminary indications of the arrangements of the amino acid groupings of the proteins in space. In 1934, J. D. Bernal and Dorothy Crowfoot Hodgkin, in Cambridge, England, opened a new era in the study of crystalline globular proteins, including enzymes, by obtaining highly detailed X-ray diffraction patterns from these protein crystals—patterns that showed that the protein molecules must possess very definite and compact internal structures. Although these diffraction patterns provided a wealth of information, it could not at that time be fully interpreted. Another quarter-century passed before interpretation became possible, primarily through the work of Max F. Perutz and of John C. Kendrew, also in Cambridge, England.

A very different kind of advance in molecular biology came a few years later at the California Institute of Technology. Max Delbrück, a physicist turned biologist, who had come from Germany, and Salvador Luria, from Italy, joined in the study of the genetics of bacteria. It was then widely believed that the principles of Mendelian genetics did not apply to bacteria and that the variations that constantly turned up in carefully cultivated strains of bacteria were somehow induced by the media in which they grew and had no genetic basis. Delbrück and Luria showed, in a series of searching experiments, that the variations were indeed genetic; the variations were caused by mutations and by subsequent selection of the mutant forms, which would then breed true in later generations. This discovery opened the whole field of bacterial genetics, which was soon to revolutionize all of genetics. Delbrück and his colleagues also made fundamental advances in the study of bacteriophages, the viruses that enter bacteria, multiply within them, and are liberated with the destruction of the host bacterium.

Oswald T. Avery at the Rockefeller Institute, with C. M. MacLeod and M. McCarty, produced the first decisive evidence for the chemical nature of the gene. It was already known, from the work of F. Griffith in England, that a culture of "rough" nonvirulent pneumococci could be transformed into the "smooth" virulent variety by exposure to an extract from killed virulent pneumococci. The active factor in the extract was clearly producing a genetic change. After some ten years of work, Avery and his associates announced in 1943 that the active transforming factor was pure DNA. This conclusion was revolutionary, for nearly everyone believed at that time that proteins were the essential genetic material. It took several years for the full import of Avery's work to be appreciated.

About 1950, E. Chargaff at Columbia University found a remarkably simple relation for the relative amounts of the various bases in DNA from many different organisms. The amounts of adenine and of thymine were always equal within experimental error, and the amounts of guanine and cytosine were also equal, although the ratio A/G, which was of course equal to the ratio T/C, varied greatly from one organism to another.

The next and greatest advance in understanding the structure and function of DNA followed a similar advance in the understanding of protein structure. In 1951, Linus Pauling and R. B. Corey at the California Institute of Technology proposed that the peptide chains of protein molecules could coil into the form of a helix, known as the alpha helix, which was stabilized by hydrogen bonds between the amino acid groups at different levels along the axis of the helix. They also proposed other, more extended, arrangements of amino acids in peptide chains, known as pleated sheets. These structures proved to explain many aspects of the three-dimensional structure of proteins; they also made other workers aware of the possible importance of helical arrangements in other molecules.

In London, at King's College, M. H. F. Wilkins and Rosalind Franklin were obtaining X-ray diffraction pictures of fibers of DNA. The patterns suggested that the DNA was helical, but the nature of the helix was not clear. It was elucidated in 1953 by J. D. Watson and F. H. C. Crick at Cambridge University. (Watson was a young American who had been a pupil of Luria at Indiana University; Crick, who was English, had been trained as a physicist.) After a period of puzzled confusion, characteristic of scientific research in general, they concluded from the data of Wilkins and Franklin that DNA was built as a double helix, somewhat like a double spiral staircase, of two polynucleotide chains wound around each other. The bases of each chain, A, T, G, and C, lie on the inside of the double helix, and the two chains are complementary to one another; the base A in one chain always lies opposite T in the other; there is a neat geometric fit between A and T and a similar complementary fit between G and C, the complementary bases being held together by hydrogen bonds. This discovery gave a simple structural explanation of Chargaff's rule that A = T and G = C; and the existence of this rule was one of the factors that led Watson and Crick

to the correct solution. A small segment of the helix might, for example, contain the following sequence:

The vertical lines in this formula represent hydrogen bonds between the two chains. Each of the two chains may contain thousands of such units, but the corresponding pairs are of only four kinds: A – T, T – A, G – C, and C – G.

The two chains could, on occasion, unwind and peel apart, and then, in the presence of the necessary enzymes and with nucleotides as building materials, each chain could direct the synthesis of another complementary to itself. Since each chain produces its complement, both chains are in fact faithfully reproduced. Since it was clear from Avery's work and that of others that DNA was the genetic material, the structure proposed by Watson and Crick provided a plausible mechanism for explaining how genes replicate themselves. Their predictions led to an enormous amount of new experimental work in many laboratories, which fully sustained the fundamental concepts. Moreover, it was shown that DNA, located in the nucleus of the cell, could do more than replicate itself; it could also, in the presence of suitable enzymes and the essential chemical building materials, direct the synthesis of RNA. The RNA then migrates out from the nucleus to the cytoplasm in the outer part of the cell. Only one of the two strands of DNA (which might be called the master strand) directs this synthesis, but the same complementary relations hold; G in the DNA strand determines the formation of C in RNA, and vice versa; A in DNA gives rise, in complementary RNA, not to T but to the closely related base uridine (U). This process, by which DNA directs the synthesis of RNA, is known as transcription.

The RNA in turn was found to direct the synthesis of protein. This process is called translation and is much more complicated than transcription. It was apparent that the sequence of the bases in the RNA must somehow specify the sequence of amino acids in the peptide chain of the protein: the RNA contains only four bases, and yet these must somehow specify twenty different amino acids. This was the problem of the genetic code, first clearly formulated about 1954. Crick and others soon pointed out that a sequence of at least three bases in RNA was necessary to provide more than twenty possible arrangements to specify all the amino acids. In fact, from four bases one can make 4^3, or sixty-four, triplets. The first fruitful experiments directed to this problem were those of M. Nirenberg and J. H. Matthaei at the National Institutes of Health in Bethesda, Md., in 1961. They showed, in a protein-synthesizing system, that adding a synthetic nucleotide polymer of the repeating structure – U – U – U – U – U – U – (polyuridylic acid) gave rise to an amino acid polymer composed entirely of the amino acid phenylalanine (Phe). Thus, if the code was a triplet code, as Crick had (correctly) proposed, the triplet UUU was translated as Phe. By making other combinations of the bases A, U, G, and C, the entire code was worked out by 1966. Nirenberg played a major role in this work, as did S. Ochoa and his collaborators at New York University. H. G. Khorana, a native of India who came to the University of Wisconsin, carried out particularly remarkable chemical syntheses that were essential in unraveling the code. The fact that there are sixty-four possible triplets and only twenty amino acids indicated that several triplets (or codons) can all specify the same amino acid. Thus, UCU, UCC, UCA, and UCG all specify the amino acid serine. Three of the sixty-four codons are "stop" signals, to indicate the point at which the synthesis of the peptide chain of the protein is complete. Experiments on a wide variety of organisms showed clearly that the code was indeed universal—the same for bacteria and for all plants and animals.

These discoveries provided an explanation for the simplest kind of genetic mutation—one that results in a change in a single amino acid in a large protein molecule that is otherwise unaltered. Thus, a serious disease—sickle-cell anemia—is caused by an alteration at one single point in the molecule of human hemoglobin, which corresponds to a single base change at one point in human DNA.

Under special circumstances, by means of a suitable enzyme system, RNA can direct the synthesis of a complementary DNA, thus reversing the usual order of events described above, in which DNA furnishes the specific sequence patterns that are transcribed into a complementary RNA. This "reverse transcription" from RNA to DNA is found in certain RNA-containing tumor viruses, and was first reported independently, in 1970, by Howard M. Temin at the University of Wisconsin and by David Baltimore at the Massachusetts Institute of Technology. However, the process of translation, from nucleotide sequences in nucleic acids to amino acid sequences in proteins, always goes from nucleic acid to protein; no reversal is possible here.

The genetic code specifies how the sequence of bases in DNA and RNA determines the amino acid sequence in the resulting proteins; these chains of amino acids then fold into well-defined three-dimensional structures, to give functional proteins. The folding, in a normal physiological medium, is spontaneous; the sequence determines the three-dimensional structure, as shown experimentally by C. B. Anfinsen at the National Institutes of Health, and by others. The details of the three-dimensional structure, for many proteins, have been worked out by X-ray diffraction, the first definitive achievements (1958–61) being the work of Kendrew on myoglobin, the oxygen-binding protein from muscle, and of Perutz on hemoglobin, the oxygen-transporting protein of blood. Work on other proteins followed rapidly, both in England and the United States. And this work led to a detailed picture of how enzymes and other proteins work—revolutionizing the study of metabolism—while comparative studies of proteins of a given class, from a wide variety of species, are throwing fresh light on the rate and mechanisms of evolutionary change.

[R. E. Dickerson and I. Geis, *The Structure and Action of Proteins;* J. S. Fruton, *Molecules and Life;* R. Olby, *The Path to the Double Helix;* G. Stent, *Molecular Genetics;* J. D. Watson, *Molecular Biology of the Gene.*]

JOHN T. EDSALL

MOLINO DEL REY, BATTLE OF (Sept. 8, 1847). During the Mexican War, Gen. Winfield Scott, believing "King's Mill," a stone building at the base of Chapultepec hill, near Mexico City, contained an operating gun foundry, ordered Gen. William J. Worth to storm the building. Worth's tactics proved uninspired and the Mexican defense unexpectedly resolute. It was only after a bloody initial repulse that the "mill" was captured. The victory proved disappointingly barren, the foundry nonexistent. The heavy casualties, including valuable senior officers, temporarily depressed the army's spirits. Later the "mill" provided cover from which Gen. Gideon J. Pillow assaulted Chapultepec.

[R. S. Ripley, *The War With Mexico;* Justin H. Smith, *The War With Mexico.*]

CHARLES WINSLOW ELLIOTT

MOLLY MAGUIRES, a secret and eventually criminal society, also known as the Buckshots, White Boys, and Sleepers, that terrorized the anthracite region of Pennsylvania from about 1865 until it was broken up in a series of sensational murder trials between 1875 and 1877. The name of the society was taken from a group of anti-landlord agitators in the 1840's led by a widow named Molly Maguire. Most members of both groups were of Irish origin.

The Molly Maguires used their power in labor disputes for the benefit of their members and intimidated or murdered recalcitrant mine bosses and colliery superintendents. In 1874, at the height of their power, Franklin B. Gowen, president of the Philadelphia Coal and Iron Company and the Philadelphia and Reading Railroad Company, determined to suppress them. A Pinkerton detective, James McParlan, posing as a counterfeiter and killer, established himself in the coal regions, joined the organization, and rose to be secretary of his division.

After a particularly outrageous murder in 1875, one assassin was condemned to death, the first capital conviction of a Molly. In view of evidence brought out at the trial, suspicion arose that a detective was at work and quickly centered on McParlan. Evading one plot to murder him, he continued his pose for some time and then quietly withdrew. The murder prosecutions that followed were based largely on his evidence and shattered the organization forever.

[Anthony Bimba, *Molly Maguires;* F. P. Dewees, *The Molly Maguires;* Allan Pinkerton, *The Molly Maguires and the Detectives.*]

JOHN BAKELESS

MONEY. Money is any generally accepted medium of exchange, standard of value, or store of value. Although this definition is universally accepted, there has always been some disagreement about what the term "money" includes.

In the 19th and early 20th centuries some authorities insisted that only specie (gold and silver) should be considered money, but most defined money to include currency—that is, coin and paper money—as well as specie. The definition of money was gradually broadened, so that by the mid-1920's, money was considered to include demand deposits in commercial banks. Later, authorities came to include commercial bank time deposits and other assets that could be quickly turned into cash (U.S. Treasury bills and deposits in savings banks and savings and loan associations) as "near money." The money supply, or stock of money, differs from money in that it does not include currency and deposits owned by commercial banks and by the federal government; it includes only currency and demand deposits owned by the public.

The Monetary Standard. The monetary standard of the United States is the commodity that the U.S. Congress designates as the basis of the monetary system. It is the commodity for which all other kinds of money can be exchanged at a fixed ratio. Money that is not redeemable in a specific commodity at a specific rate is fiat money—that is, money backed only by the credit of the issuer.

During the colonial period there was no specific monetary standard: colonists used many commodities as money—wampum in New England, beaver skins in the Middle Colonies, and tobacco and many kinds of foodstuffs in the South. During the 18th century individual colonies issued paper currency.

Soon after the United States became an independent republic, Congress in 1791 established a bimetallic standard at a ratio of 15 ounces of silver to 1 ounce of gold. The mint was authorized to accept silver and gold and to issue in exchange silver dollars of 371.25 grains and gold pieces containing 24.75 grains of gold per dollar. In 1834 the administration of President Andrew Jackson devalued the gold dollar, but it retained the bimetallic standard. The ratio of silver to gold was changed to approximately 16 to 1, by reducing the gold content of the dollar to 23.2 grains (23.22 in 1837). Soon thereafter, silver ceased to circulate, because it was undervalued at the mint; consequently, the country, although legally on a bimetallic standard, was actually on a monometallic gold standard. During the Civil War the monetary standard ceased to have any real significance, because the right to redeem paper money in specie was suspended. Gold became a commodity that could be bought and sold in a free market, and its value in paper money was no longer fixed but fluctuated from day to day. To be sure, this suspension of specie payments had occurred in every previous depression, but each previous suspension had been short-lived. The suspension that began in the Civil War lasted for eighteen years, until Jan. 1, 1879.

Although the United States continued on a bimetallic standard *de jure* until the turn of the century, Congress in 1873 stopped the minting of silver dollars, but in 1878 it adopted a limping standard by authorizing the coinage of a debased silver dollar. Bimetallism officially came to an end when the Coinage Act of 1900 established a monometallic gold standard. A series of presidential executive orders and acts of Congress in 1933 severely compromised the gold standard by abrogating the right to redeem paper money in gold. The last vestiges of a metallic standard disappeared in the acts of Mar. 3, 1965, and

Mar. 18, 1968, which eliminated the gold reserve against Federal Reserve deposits, and the act of July 23, 1965, which ended the coining of silver dollars. Thereupon, all money in the United States came to be fiat money, although U.S. dollars were still accepted internationally on a severely modified gold bullion standard.

Purchasing Power of Money. The value of money, or its purchasing power, is the reciprocal of the price level. Its relative rise and fall can, therefore, be measured by a price index. Such an index of wholesale prices dates from 1720 (it is discussed here with the 1957–59 value of $1.00 as the basis).

In most of the colonies, prices rose sharply and the purchasing power of money dropped under the pressure of large infusions of paper money. A similar experience occurred in the revolutionary war. The dollar's value fell from $3.79 at the start of the war to 28 cents in 1780. From there it sprang back to $3.15 in 1789 and then receded to about $2.00 in 1801, where it remained for the next decade. With the War of 1812, prices again rose, and the dollar's purchasing power fell to about $1.60 in 1814.

After the War of 1812, prices declined significantly until 1821. From $2.80 in 1821, the dollar's value declined to $2.40 in 1836 but resurged to $3.90 in 1843. The late 1840's and 1850's produced little change, but the Civil War brought money's purchasing power down to $1.30. There followed a long period of declining prices, so that the dollar's purchasing power had risen to $3.90 by 1896. In the first years of the 20th century, prices rose more than in any previous time of peace. By 1915 the dollar's purchasing power had declined to $2.70.

Prices soared during World War I, and the dollar's value dropped to $1.30 by 1920. It quickly recovered to $1.90 in 1921—around which level it fluctuated narrowly for the rest of the decade. The depression of the 1930's brought the price level almost back to where it had been in the 1840's and 1890's. At its highest point in 1932, the dollar's value was again close to $3.00.

From 1934 on, the price level rose—slowly at first, but at a greatly accelerated pace during World War II. By 1948 the dollar was worth $1.14 in 1958 prices. By 1970 it was worth 85 cents and still going down at a rate of between 4 and 7 percent a year.

Currency. During much of American history gold and silver coins issued first by the crown and then by the federal government have not circulated. Instead Americans have used many different kinds of currency.

In the colonial period most transactions were handled through barter or open-book accounts. Although the money of account was the same as in England, only a small amount of pounds, shillings, and pence circulated. Most of the money that the colonists used consisted of commodities, non-English coins, and paper money. The coins were of two types: foreign coins, especially Spanish dollars, and occasional colonial coin issues, such as the Pine Tree shilling of 1652. The paper money was of four types: bills of credit or government notes; paper certificates representing deposited coin, bullion, or other commodities; bank notes issued by land banks; and fractional currency (that is, notes in denominations of a shilling or less). Each colony set its own legal value for current coin, and gradually nominal and arbitrary valuations for the current Spanish coins were established, giving rise to an extraordinary confusion of values. A New Yorker accustomed to a shilling value for the Spanish real had to adjust himself to a nine-pence value in Boston and an eleven-pence value in Philadelphia. The confusion was rendered worse by a multitude of paper-money issues. When the first issue (or "first tenor") depreciated, it was replaced by a "second tenor" and then a "third tenor." The first issue by Massachusetts in 1690 was the first authentic government paper money in history, although the 1685 "playing-card money" issued to French troops in Canada somewhat resembled government paper.

The issuance of colonial money ended in New England in 1751 and in other colonies in 1764 when it was proscribed by the crown. During the Revolution the colonists embarked on a new money splurge. To assist in financing the war, the Continental Congress authorized $241,552,780 of bills of credit between June 22, 1775, and Nov. 29, 1779. In addition, the individual states issued $209,524,776, and there were doubtless other batches of unauthorized issues. Much of this paper money was fractional currency. In an effort to make it conform to the differing valuations of Spanish coins, which circulated widely, the individual states issued denominations ranging from 1 penny to 10 pence and from $1/16$ to ¾ of $1. The paper money depreciated, slowly at first and then more rapidly. Only a negligible quantity of the fractional currency was ever redeemed, although the Funding Act of 1790 provided for the redemption of the higher values of paper money at a rate of $1 of specie for $100 of Continental currency. In 1779 the depreciation, in relation to specie, rose from 8 to 1 on Jan. 14, to 38½ to 1 on Nov. 17. In spite of partial redemption and retirement after 1779, the old Continental currency depreciated more rapidly than ever. By January 1781 it was valued at 100 to 1 and by May had practically lost its value. The phrase ''not worth a Continental'' comes from this period.

The currency history of the United States under the Constitution began with the Mint Act of Apr. 2, 1792. Based on the suggestions and proposals of Alexander Hamilton, Thomas Jefferson, and Robert Morris, the act authorized the establishment of a mint to coin gold eagles ($10 gold pieces), containing 247.50 grains of pure gold, half eagles, and quarter eagles; dollars, containing 371.25 grains of pure silver, half dollars, quarter dollars, dismes, and half dismes; and cents, containing 11 pennyweight of copper, and half cents. The weight of the cent was changed to 208 grains of copper in 1793. Although the Mint Act demonstrated an impressive familiarity with monetary principles, the system it created did not work. Gold was vastly undervalued at the mint, and consequently by the early 1800's, gold coins ceased to circulate. The silver coins disappeared because they were accepted at face value in Spanish America even though they contained less silver than the Spanish dollar. The circulation of cents also ran into sporadic difficulties, for the market value of the copper in a cent was often higher than 1 cent. Immediately, bills were introduced in Congress to abolish the mint, but none was adopted; in 1806, President Jefferson, by executive order, stopped the minting of silver dollars.

Even if mint ratios had been the same as market ratios, gold pieces and silver dollars would not have circulated in everyday transactions. They were too cumbersome. What Americans actually used for currency, in addition to foreign coins, consisted of a hodgepodge of paper money issued by state-chartered commercial banks, by the two United States banks (1791–1811 and 1816–36), and, occasionally, by nonbank corporations. Although the absence of large-denomination coins was not a hardship, the absence of fractional coins (halves, quarters, dimes) was. To some extent, paper fractional currency, so-called ''shinplasters,'' filled the need for currency in denominations of less than $1, but it was never completely satisfactory.

The devaluation of the gold dollar in 1834 increased the circulation of gold coins. Congress further encouraged gold circulation by authorizing the minting of $1 and $20 gold pieces. But whatever was done for gold made the circulation of silver even more remote, because the metal in the subsidiary silver coins was worth more as bullion in the open market

than its face value as money. In 1851, Congress tackled the problem of providing a fractional currency by creating a 3-cent piece composed of silver and copper. But no halves, quarters, or dimes circulated. Then, in 1853, Congress brought subsidiary coinage back by reducing the silver content of the half dollar from 206.25 grains to 192 grains, $9/_{10}$ fine. The other fractional silver coins were reduced proportionately. Because of the 1853 reform it was no longer necessary to use foreign coins, and Congress removed their status as legal tender in 1857. At the same time, the half cent was eliminated and the composition of the cent was changed to 72 grains, 88 percent copper and 12 percent nickel. From then until the Civil War the money and currency used by the public consisted of state bank notes in various denominations upward from a few cents, gold coins, and subsidiary silver coins and copper cents.

The Civil War revolutionized the American money system. To help pay for the war, Congress authorized $450 million in paper money, officially known as United States notes but more popularly called greenbacks or legal tender notes. This was the first paper money printed by the federal government, and eventually the U.S. Treasury issued $431 million in paper money. (After the war some greenbacks were retired, but in 1878 Congress fixed their circulation at the amount then outstanding, $346,681,016.)

Early in the war the banks stopped redeeming paper money in specie. The government also stopped paying its obligations in specie. Gold became a commodity, and its value climbed in terms of paper money, $100 in gold eventually commanding $250 in paper. In March 1863, Congress authorized the issue of gold certificates, which were really warehouse receipts, because they were issued in denominations of $20 or more in exchange for gold coin and bullion deposited with the U.S. Treasury. These certificates were temporarily discontinued between January 1879 and July 1882 and permanently ended by executive order in April 1933; the Gold Reserve Act of January 1934 created a new gold certificate that could be held only by Federal Reserve banks.

The Civil War also drove subsidiary silver coins out of circulation, because the wartime increase in the demand for silver pushed its price above the face value of the coins. After an unhappy experience with the use of postage stamps, Secretary of the Treasury Salmon P. Chase authorized the issue of fractional notes, commonly called postage currency. Congress legalized Chase's action in July 1862. In March 1863, Congress authorized $50 million in fractional paper currency. To further alleviate the currency shortage, Congress, in April 1864, changed the weight of the cent to 48 grains, 95 percent copper and 5 percent tin and zinc. It also provided for a 2-cent piece. Then, in 1865, it authorized the coinage of a 3-cent piece of 30 grains, 75 percent copper and 25 percent nickel.

The federal government also effected a major change in bank currency. The National Bank (or Currency) Act of February 1863, amended in June 1864, established a federally chartered banking system; each national bank was authorized to issue bank notes against federal bonds. Subsequently, in July 1866, Congress imposed a 10 percent tax on nonnational bank notes, driving them out of circulation.

Controversies over money characterized the last quarter of the 19th century. Farmers, silver-mine owners, and some businessmen called for the reinstatement of bimetallism, which had been effectively ended with the so-called Crime of 1873. Bankers and other sound-money adherents resisted, and much legislation was passed attempting to reconcile the two opposing views. Whereas the Crime of 1873 had eliminated the silver dollar and also provided for a trade dollar of 420 grains of silver, 9/10 fine, the Bland-Allison Act of February 1878 authorized the purchase of between $2 million and $4 million of silver per month to be coined into silver dollars containing 412.50 grains of silver, 9/10 fine. The latter act also provided for silver certificates in denominations of $10 or more to be issued against deposits of silver coin. In 1886 the denominations were changed to include $1, $2, and $5. The Sherman Silver Purchase Act of 1890 replaced the Bland-Allison Act by providing for the purchase of 4.5 million ounces of silver a month. The Treasury was to pay for these purchases with Treasury notes, redeemable in coin. After considerable struggle, sound-money adherents succeeded in repealing the Sherman Silver Purchase Act in November 1893. The Gold Standard Act of Mar. 14, 1900, ended the silver controversy by adopting a monometallic gold standard.

Minor coinage laws in the late 19th century included the authorization in May 1866 of a 5-cent piece of 77.16 grains, 75 percent copper and 25 percent nickel; the authorization in March 1875 of a 20-cent piece, which was discontinued in May 1878; and the discontinuance of the $1 and $3 gold pieces and the 3-cent nickel. The Federal Reserve Act of December 1913 made additional basic changes in the currency by providing for a Federal Reserve note secured by gold and commercial paper and a Federal Reserve bank note secured by government bonds.

Although few currency changes occurred in the two decades after 1913, the depression of the 1930's created a new flurry in currency and banking. In April 1933, President Franklin D. Roosevelt issued a proclamation recalling gold coin, gold bullion, and gold certificates, in effect taking the country off the gold standard. In January 1934 the dollar was devalued from 23.22 grains pure to 13.714 grains. The price of gold was raised from $20.67 to $35 per ounce. Further changes in the currency were made in July and August 1935 by retiring the last of the bonds with the circulation privilege, thus ending the issuance of national bank notes.

The depression made silver a controversial issue again. The Thomas amendment to the Agricultural Adjustment Act of May 1933 authorized the president to accept $200 million in silver in payment of international debts. Further congressional acts during the New Deal ordered the Treasury to buy all newly mined domestic silver and to issue silver dollars or silver certificates against the purchases.

Since the 1930's the gold cover has been removed from Federal Reserve notes and deposits. In July 1965 the minting of standard silver dollars came to an end, and the silver certificate was also discontinued. In the mid-1970's the currency system consisted of fractional, subsidiary silver and copper currency ($7 billion), a few silver dollars, and $60 billion of paper money issued by Federal Reserve banks. By far the largest part of the money supply was the $200 billion in demand deposits in commercial banks.

The evolution of the American money system has been from bimetallism through a monometallic gold standard to what has been called "managed money." The payments mechanism has evolved from a hodge-podge of currencies in the 19th century to a standard fiat money. Checks drawn against demand deposits constitute 75 percent of the money supply and cover well over 90 percent of the dollar volume of transactions. Indications are that in the mid-19th century they covered about 60 percent. By 1837 checks were more important than cash in the cities; by 1850, for the country as a whole; and in 1890, in the rural areas.

[Milton Friedman and Anna Jacobson Schwartz, *A Monetary History of the United States;* Herman E. Krooss, *A Documentary History of Banking and Currency;* Paul Studenski and Herman E. Krooss, *Financial History of the United States.*]

HERMAN E. KROOSS

MONHEGAN ISLAND, a small, rocky island, the westernmost of the outlying islands off Penobscot

Bay, is the most prominent landmark on that section of the Maine coast, and as such was the sailing objective of most of the early voyagers to New England. Perhaps frequented by the Basque and Portuguese fishermen of the 16th century, the island itself was described by David Ingram in 1569 and was visited by George Weymouth in 1605 and by Capt. John Smith, who spent some time fishing there in 1614. Its present name first appeared in Smith's account. Later he tells us that eighty ships came there to fish between 1614 and 1622. It was from these fishermen that Samoset, who greeted the Pilgrims at Plymouth in March 1621, learned to speak English. The owner of one of these fishing ships, Abraham Jennings of Plymouth, England, became a member of the New England Council on Nov. 27, 1622, and in the following year, his agent, Abraham Shurt, took possession. Under Shurt's auspices, Jennings' establishment became the largest fishing and trading post in New England and the frequent resort of ships from Virginia, Plymouth, and other settlements. Fishing had so declined by 1626, owing to the dispute in Parliament over fishing rights in New England, that Jennings decided to sell out. His stock of goods was purchased by David Thomson of Piscataqua and William Bradford of Plymouth for over £800. The place itself was sold to merchants in Bristol, England, for £50. These merchants established their post at Pemaquid, for which they received a grant from the New England Council in 1632, and Monhegan became merely a resort for fishermen, though during some periods down to the abandonment of the area by the English in 1689, there were some settlers. Until 1665 there was no settled government; from 1665 to 1668, and from 1677 to 1686, New York governed under the patent of James Stuart, Duke of York, of 1664.

The modern settlement of the island dates from 1790. Since Sept. 4, 1839, the island has had the form of government known in Maine as the "plantation." Fishing is still the only year-round economic activity for the approximately 100 (1970) permanent residents.

[Charles Francis Jenney, *The Fortunate Island of Monhegan.*]

ROBERT E. MOODY

MONITOR AND *MERRIMACK,* BATTLE OF

(Mar. 9, 1862). The principle of the ironclad was introduced by the French during the Crimean War, and about 100 ironclads were built or projected—none in the United States—before the American Civil War.

When Stephen Mallory, who had been chairman of the Senate Committee on Naval Affairs since 1851 and was thus exceptionally well informed on naval matters, became Confederate secretary of the navy, he saw the Confederacy's only chance of beating the North at sea in ironclad production. Unfortunately for Mallory, his program was subordinated to the greater needs of equipping the Confederate army from meager industry. He managed to commission thirty-two ironclads, of which fewer than a dozen were ever fully ready.

The Confederates salvaged the U.S.S. *Merrimack,* which had been scuttled in the Union evacuation of Norfolk. Upon its sound hull the Confederates built a sloping casemate of 20-inch-square heart pine, sheathed by 4-inch-square live oak, and a double layer of 2-inch-thick iron, the outermost vertical. The conversion dragged on for months, time that allowed the Union to recognize the danger and begin its own program. The *Merrimack* was rechristened the C.S.S. *Virginia,* a name that did not gain contemporary usage. It was unique in not having a captain, inasmuch as Flag Officer Franklin Buchanan preferred to have it commanded by its able young executive officer, Lt. Catesby Jones.

On Mar. 8, 1862, the *Merrimack* sortied from Norfolk to demonstrate Buchanan's conviction that it could vitally assist Maj. Gen. John Magruder if he wished to expel Union forces from the lower Yorktown peninsula. Control of Hampton Roads and the James River was the issue. The wooden warships *Cumberland* and *Congress* were protecting the water flanks of the Union position at Newport News, and Buchanan sank them easily, although he was wounded by imprudent exposure during the fight with the *Congress.* The Union squadron on duty at the blockading station outside the Roads hastened in and was driven back by the ironclad. The *Minnesota* was stranded beyond the *Merrimack's* reach, and Jones brought it to anchor for the night off Sewell's Point.

During the night, the U.S.S. *Monitor* arrived after a dramatic dash from New York on Mar. 6, into blue water that nearly foundered it. When Jones got up steam on Mar. 9 to destroy the *Minnesota,* it was no longer helplessly alone. The *Monitor,* under Lt. John Worden, successfully engaged the *Merrimack* until tide and cumulative damage required Jones to head for Norfolk. Worden was blinded by a shell explosion.

Union claims of victory were founded on the misconception that the *Merrimack* was trying to break the blockade. For multiple reasons the lumbering *Mer-*

rimack was incapable of making headway three miles into the open Atlantic. Buchanan had aimed at clearing Hampton Roads and did so. By naval semantics, both antagonists won: the *Monitor* tactically because Worden kept the *Merrimack* from destroying the *Minnesota,* and the *Merrimack* strategically because the Union navy thenceforward stayed out of the Roads until the *Merrimack* was destroyed by its own crew when the Confederates evacuated Norfolk on May 11, 1862. By then, Gen. George B. McClellan, who had initially planned using the Roads and the James River for a swift stab at Richmond, was fully committed to the limited wharfage of Fort Monroe, safely outside the Roads, to mount tediously and slowly his famous Peninsular campaign, which ended in defeat.

The strategic victory of the *Merrimack* in buying time for the Confederacy to shift forces from the Potomac to defend Richmond is a classic American illustration of the influence of sea power on history. The career of the *Merrimack* is an example of a successful strategic deterrent. It is noteworthy that a hugely exaggerated notion of its power was responsible for McClellan's self-defeating decision to use the Union-controlled York River for his supplies.

[J. P. Baxter, *The Introduction of the Ironclad Warship;* R. U. Johnson and C. C. Buel, eds., *Battles and Leaders of the Civil War.*]

R. W. DALY

MONITORS, or ironclad warships with hulls nearly awash and equipped with revolving gun turrets, were first built by the Swedish engineer John Ericsson for the U.S. government in 1862. Ericsson had submitted plans for a similar vessel to Napoleon III in 1854, but they had been rejected. In Great Britain an English naval inventor, Capt. C. P. Coles, had patented a similar vessel with a revolving turret in 1859. Ericsson's contract for the original *Monitor* was made Oct. 4, 1861. It was to be completed within 100 days, but it was not ready for sea until Mar. 3, 1862. It was towed to Hampton Roads, Va., where it took part in the historic engagement with the *Merrimack* on Mar. 9, 1862. It foundered at sea in a storm off Cape Hatteras, N.C., Dec. 31, 1862. After its success at Hampton Roads the U.S. government built a number of monitors all patterned on Ericsson's plans. They were used on Apr. 7, 1863, in Adm. Samuel F. DuPont's attack on Charleston, S.C., but their performance was disappointing. However, the success of the original *Monitor* gave a worldwide impetus to the adoption of the revolving armored turret. As a type of warship it was abandoned speedily by naval powers because of its limited radius of action, its slowness of fire, its low speed, and its almost total lack of ability to maneuver and to keep the sea.

[J. P. Baxter, *The Introduction of the Ironclad Warship;* C. H. Davis, *Life of Charles Henry Davis.*]

LOUIS H. BOLANDER

MONKS MOUND. *See* **Cahokia Mounds; Mounds and Mound Builders.**

MONMOUTH, BATTLE OF (June 28, 1778). The British army, under Sir Henry Clinton, evacuated Philadelphia, June 18, and arrived at Monmouth Courthouse (Freehold, N.J.) on June 26, on its march to New York. George Washington planned a telling blow against the enemy and assigned Maj. Gen. Charles Lee to command the advanced corps, then near Englishtown, with orders to attack the British rear. About 5 P.M., June 28, word arrived that Clinton's huge baggage train was moving—the signal for Lee's advance. When Lee, after long delays, reached Monmouth Courthouse, he attempted to cut off 1,500 to 2,000 troops of the rear guard, but failed. His entire division of over 4,000 men then retreated until halted by Washington, two and one-half miles to the rear. After rebuking Lee, Washington skillfully reformed his lines to meet the enemy, now heavily reinforced. One of the fiercest contests of the war followed. Repeated assaults of crack troops of the British army under Gen. Charles Cornwallis failed to break the American lines. Fought in intense heat and engaging some 10,000 men on each side, the battle ended only with darkness. During the night Clinton's army quietly withdrew. Washington reported his loss at 69 killed, 161 wounded; the Americans buried 249 British on the field. A court-martial sustained charges against Lee of disobeying orders and making an unnecessary retreat.

[Leonard H. Ludin, *Cockpit of the Revolution;* Samuel F. Smith, *The Battle of Monmouth.*]

C. A. TITUS

MONMOUTH PURCHASE included the region in present-day New Jersey extending "west from Sandy Point [Sandy Hook] along the coast and up the Raritan River and south for twelve miles from any part of this northern line." The original settlers were Quakers and Baptists from Long Island, N.Y., and Newport, R.I., who established Middletown and Shrewsbury on the model of New England towns.

Relying on their patent from Gov. Richard Nicolls (Apr. 8, 1665) they opposed proprietary government and quitrents, and passed laws, administered justice, and held their own general assemblies. James Stuart, the Duke of York (later James II), annulled their patent on Nov. 25, 1672, as being in conflict with his prior grant of the territory to John Berkeley and George Carteret.

[C. M. Andrews, *The Colonial Period of American History*.]

C. A. TITUS

MONOCACY, BATTLE OF THE (July 9, 1864). Gen. J. A. Early's Confederate army of approximately 11,000 men, advancing on Washington, D.C., had marched some fourteen miles on July 9 when about 6,000 Union troops under Gen. Lew Wallace were found strongly posted on the east bank of the Monocacy River, southeast of Frederick, Md. The Confederate right wing crossed the river and broke the Union left, which enabled the Confederate center and left to cross. The Union force was routed and reported 98 killed, 594 wounded, and 1,188 missing. The Confederates captured nearly 700 prisoners and lost between 600 and 700 killed and wounded. At dawn, July 10, Early resumed the march on Washington.

[R. U. Johnson and C. C. Buel, eds., *Battles and Leaders of the Civil War*.]

GEORGE FREDERICK ASHWORTH

MONONGAHELA, BATTLE OF THE (July 9, 1755). When the vanguard of British Gen. Edward Braddock's expedition at the site of Braddock, Pa., encountered French and Indians marching from Fort Duquesne, about eight miles away, in a desperate effort to check the English, both sides were taken by surprise. The British guns opened fire immediately, scattering the enemy. After some wavering, the Indians occupied a commanding hill and worked through a gully on the other British flank. Caught between two fires, the vanguard retreated, abandoning its guns. The main body, instead of standing to receive the retreating men, rushed forward hastily and in disorder. The advance of the main body forced the flankers in to avoid being cut off, and the whole army became an unmanageable huddle.

The legend of the cowardice of the troops seems to have less foundation than the charge of incompetence among the officers. Certainly the soldiers displayed extraordinary fortitude, withstanding a withering fire

for over three hours from a foe concealed behind trees. Attempts to form the ranks and one gallant effort to storm the hill were in vain. Most of the officers were killed or wounded, but Lt. Col. George Washington, who was one of Braddock's aides, was almost miraculously unscathed. Finally Braddock, mortally wounded, ordered a retreat. The general was carried from the field by two provincial officers; the soldiers fled in disorder.

[Stanley Pargellis, "Braddock's Defeat," *American Historical Review* (1936); Francis Parkman, *Montcalm and Wolfe*.]

SOLON J. BUCK

MONONGAHELA RIVER, an important tributary of the upper Ohio, drains the western slopes of the Allegheny Mountains in northern West Virginia, Maryland, and southern Pennsylvania. Its existence was known through Indians and fur traders long before it became historically significant. Possibly utilized by earlier expeditions, notably in 1694, 1739, and about 1745, its great importance dates from the Ohio Company of 1748 and the expedition of Pierre Joseph de Céloron de Blainville in 1749. Christopher Gist explored the region for the Ohio Company in 1750 and 1752, and Thomas Cresap and the Indian Nemacolin blazed a path from the Potomac to the Monongahela. George Washington, 1753 and 1754, and Edward Braddock, 1755, used this path. After 1759 Virginia and Maryland frontiersmen pushed west to the Monongahela, which even Pennsylvania pioneers reached by connecting roads. The Monongahela Valley was the first trans-Appalachian English-speaking frontier. Much of later westward migration traveled through it and down the river.

[Alfred P. James, "The First English-Speaking Trans-Appalachian Frontier," *Mississippi Valley Historical Review*, vol. 17; James M. Veech, *The Monongahela of Old*.]

ALFRED P. JAMES

MONOPOLY in its most elementary form is the exclusive control of the output of a good or a service by a single seller. The significance of monopolistic control lies in the power to restrict output in order to increase the price of the commodity or service above the competitive level and, therefore, above the necessary economic costs of production.

Monopolistic power may exist in markets of more than one seller, and in fact few markets are so monopolized as to contain but a single supplier. In the medieval guild system local craftsmen were able to monopolize their markets by exercising control over entry into their trades; while a town might have several artisans in each craft, this control over entry and guild discipline served to keep the prices of goods or services above the competitive level. As the guild system declined in the face of technological change and the expanding geographical dimensions of economic markets, other forms of monopolization developed. The most important of these was the English patent system, utilized by the crown to grant to its favored subjects the exclusive right to manufacture or to distribute a commodity in domestic or foreign markets. Popular pressures against this system culminated in Parliament's enactment of the Statute of Monopolies in 1623, limiting patents to important inventions.

American public policy against monopoly derives in part from early English laws against engrossing, forestalling, and regrating—practices that were also illegal under ancient Roman law: they involve the purchase of essential commodities in order to influence their prices and to reap considerable profits from resale. The Anglo-American tradition has also frowned on formal or informal agreements to limit output or to raise prices, although the common law that prevailed until the late 19th century did not make the practice illegal: public disapproval was manifested in the fact that the parties to the agreement could not enlist the court's assistance in enforcing its terms. The pervasive price-fixing and market-sharing agreements of numerous American enterprises in the 19th century—notably trunk-line railroads, cast-iron pipe manufacturers, pig-iron producers, and whiskey distillers—eventually brought about statutory restraint of such practices through the Sherman Antitrust Act of 1890. These overt price-fixing and market-sharing agreements have been ruled to be per se violations of the Sherman Act, and more direct attempts to monopolize through acquisitions and mergers have been found unlawful under the Clayton Antitrust Act of 1914 (as amended in 1950).

A more direct route to monopoly lies in the acquisition of competing firms. J. P. Morgan built the United States Steel Corporation in this manner, acquiring companies that produced more than one-half of all finished steel in the United States in 1901. Similarly, John D. Rockefeller acquired a large number of competing refiners to gain control of nearly 90 percent of the U.S. market for refined petroleum products by the end of the 19th century. Rockefeller also utilized the trust form of organization through which the control of ostensibly independent refiners was vested in a single board of trustees, but this form of control was adjudged a violation of the Sherman Act in 1906. The acquisition of monopoly power through merger has since been sharply curtailed by the Clayton Act and the subsequent amendment in 1950.

The growth of markets in the United States and throughout the world has greatly reduced the incidence of pure monopoly in the production and distribution of goods and services. The Aluminum Company of America held one of the closest approximations to a pure monopoly in the United States, but its monopolistic position ended in 1945. Nevertheless, sellers of such products as computers, flat glass, office equipment, automobiles, and office copiers continue to enjoy some monopolistic power because either patents, large capital requirements, or both limit competitive enterprise in these areas.

[F. Machlup, *The Political Economy of Monopoly;* H. Thorelli, *The Federal Antitrust Policy.*]

ROBERT W. CRANDALL

MONROE, FORTRESS, one of the principal fortifications on the Atlantic coast, was foreshadowed in the early settlement of Virginia by Fort Algernourne (1609) and forts Henry and Charles (1610). In the 18th century Fort George was built near the site of the present fort but was destroyed by a hurricane in 1749. The strategic position of Point Comfort, commanding the entrance to Chesapeake Bay, engaged the attention of the federal government, which began the construction of Fortress Monroe in 1819; it was not completed until 1834. The Confederates made no attempt to capture it, and it remained in Union hands. The first engagement in Virginia, Big Bethel, was fought nearby (June 10, 1861). The action of the *Monitor* and *Merrimack,* Mar. 9, 1862, took place just off the fort. Gen. George B. McClellan began the Peninsular campaign from it in 1862. Jefferson Davis was confined in Fortress Monroe from 1865 to 1867.

[Robert Arthur, *History of Fort Monroe;* R. U. Johnson and C. C. Buel, eds., *Battles and Leaders of the Civil War.*]

H. J. ECKENRODE

MONROE DOCTRINE. Since the adoption of the U.S. Constitution there has been a strong tendency to differentiate America from Europe and to assume that as little political connection should exist between the two as possible. Expressions of this viewpoint can be found in President George Washington's farewell address and in President Thomas Jefferson's first inaugural. President James Monroe's message to

Congress of Dec. 2, 1823, supplemented this previous formula by seeking to exclude European intervention from the Western Hemisphere. The message was the result of two different sets of circumstances. The pretensions of the Russian government to exclude all but Russian vessels from the Northwest coast of the United States north of fifty-one degrees precipitated a diplomatic controversy in the course of which Monroe's secretary of state, John Quincy Adams, laid down the principle that European governments could establish no new colonies in the Western Hemisphere, every portion thereof having been already occupied. In his message of 1823 Monroe repeated Adams' formula virtually in Adams' own words, declaring that "the American continents, by the free and independent condition which they have assumed and maintained, are henceforth not to be considered as subjects for future colonization by any European powers." A second reason for the message lay in the fear that the continental European powers were planning the reconquest of the Spanish American republics that had declared their independence of Spain (see Latin-American Republics, Recognition of). Suggestions of such a purpose came to Monroe and his cabinet from Richard Rush, U.S. minister in London, who got them from George Canning, the British foreign secretary, and more directly from the language of Czar Alexander I in a memorandum addressed to the U.S. government in October 1823. After long cabinet discussions, the president fixed upon a pronouncement that warned against intervention, and, with regard to the Spanish colonies, declared that "we could not view any interposition with the view of oppressing them or controlling in any other manner their destiny by any European power, in any other light than as the manifestation of an unfriendly disposition toward the United States."

While the message was enthusiastically received in the United States, it had little practical influence at the time. The European powers never intended intervention on any considerable scale and viewed the message with irritation and contempt.

The United States itself, on four separate occasions in the years immediately following 1823, refused to make any commitments looking to the carrying out of the policy outlined by Monroe, and the debates on the Panama Congress in 1826 showed that, beyond the shadow of a doubt, U.S. opinion was hostile to any alliance with the new states in the hemisphere. They themselves, as a matter of fact, became economically and financially, if not politically, more dependent on Great Britain than on the republic to the north.

For some time after 1826 Monroe's message remained virtually unnoticed, and minor violations of it occurred in the British encroachments in Central America and in the acquisition by Great Britain of the Falkland Islands.

The first great revival of interest in the doctrine came in 1845. This was produced by the intrigues of Great Britain and France to prevent the annexation of Texas to the United States, by the difference of opinion over Oregon between Britain and the United States, and by fear of British purposes in California (see Oregon Question). On Dec. 2, 1845, President James K. Polk reiterated the principles of Monroe, condemning not only intervention but also the application of the principle of the balance of power to the Western Hemisphere (see Polk Doctrine). He emphasized particularly the significance of this principle with regard to North America. Again, as in 1823, the immediate results were not important, but the principle had begun to sink into the American mind, and Polk gave it new expression. On Apr. 29, 1848, in a message in which he declared that an English or Spanish protectorate over Yucatán would be a violation of the principles of 1823, Polk declared that the threat of such action might compel the United States itself to assume control over the region in question. In this message, for the first time, the Monroe principle was made the basis for measures of expansion (see "Manifest Destiny"). No action was taken, however.

In the 1850's, the message figured again and again in connection with the dispute over the Central-American question and attained increasing popularity (see Clayton-Bulwer Treaty). From a partisan or democratic dogma, it began to rise to the rank of a national principle. It was cited in international correspondence and its significance was recognized (although its validity was denied) by more than one European statesman.

The Civil War offered to the powers of Europe an excellent opportunity to challenge Monroe's principles. Taking advantage of the situation, Spain intervened in Santo Domingo, and France sought to establish in Mexico an empire under the rule of the Austrian Archduke Maximilian (see Mexico, French in). When, at the outbreak of the war, Secretary of State William H. Seward attempted to invoke the Monroe Doctrine against the first of these powers, he received a sharp rebuff, but learning from experience, he waited before challenging the French in Mexico until the success of American arms made it possible for him to assert the doctrine with increasing vigor. While other circumstances contributed to the collapse of Maximilian's empire, there can be no question that the diplomatic pressure exerted by the U.S. government in 1865 was keenly felt in Paris, and that fear of the United States was a factor in the French decision to withdraw its troops from Mexico. The doctrine, in the meantime, had attained immense popularity at home.

The events of the 1870's and the 1880's are less dramatic, but a steady tendency developed to expand the scope of the doctrine. The principle that no territory might be transferred in the New World from one European power to another, not altogether unknown in the previous epoch, became more and more closely linked with Monroe's principles, especially through the efforts of President Ulysses S. Grant and his secretary of state, Hamilton Fish. The doctrine was cited even less in consonance with its original terms, or with Polk's interpretation of it, as forbidding the construction by Europeans of a transisthmian canal (see Panama Canal), and still more as implying that such a canal must be under the exclusive guarantee of the United States. This point of view, the cause of acute diplomatic controversy in the 1880's, was accepted by Great Britain in the first Hay-Pauncefote Treaty (Feb. 5, 1900).

One of the most dramatic extensions of the doctrine was President Grover Cleveland's assertion that its principles compelled Great Britain to arbitrate a boundary dispute with Venezuela over the limitations of British Guiana. Cleveland's position produced a serious diplomatic crisis, but the moderation displayed by the British government permitted a peaceful solution of the difficulty (see Olney Corollary of Monroe Doctrine).

The growing nationalism of the United States toward the end of the 19th and the beginning of the 20th century was not without its effect upon the doctrine. The joint intervention of Great Britain, Germany, and Italy against Venezuela, looking to the satisfaction of pecuniary claims, concealed no ulterior purpose, but it produced widespread irritation in the United States. The story of German designs of conquest is pure legend, but it is certainly true that the administration of Theodore Roosevelt, which began with an attitude of great moderation, was gradually rendered more and more nervous by the intervention and was considering diplomatic measures to bring it to an end (see Venezuela, Blockade of). On Roosevelt himself the effect of the intervention was important. He moved toward the position that the United States must assume a measure of control of the more unruly of the Latin-American states in order to prevent European action against them, and in 1905 a treaty for American control of customs in Santo Domingo was negotiated (see Dominican Republic). While it met with

opposition in the Senate, it was ratified in 1907. In the meantime the president, in his annual message to Congress in 1904, had definitely laid down the doctrine (later called the Roosevelt Corollary to the Monroe Doctrine) that chronic wrongdoing by a Latin-American state might compel American action. The precedent that he established was applied or attempted more than once, especially in the Caribbean area. And, in general, the doctrine has figured as justification in the not infrequent interventions in the affairs of Caribbean states (see Caribbean Policy).

During the two decades following World War I, a change took place. Increasing resentment against American interference in the affairs of the republics of Latin America has been reflected in actual policy (see Latin America, U.S. Relations With). The interventions of the United States in Haiti and Santo Domingo in 1915 and 1916, during the administration of President Woodrow Wilson, were liquidated, respectively, in 1934 and 1924. The intervention in Nicaragua during the administration of Calvin Coolidge was short-lived. Under President Franklin D. Roosevelt pledges against armed intervention were given, and at the seventh Pan-American Conference (Montevideo, Dec. 3–26, 1933) a definite treaty was signed, pledging the signatories not to intervene in the internal and external affairs of one another. At Buenos Aires in 1936 the practice of collecting pecuniary obligations by armed force was declared illegal (see Peace Conference at Buenos Aires).

The Monroe Doctrine has never obtained a true international status. At the World War I peace conference in 1919, in order to placate domestic opposition to the covenant of the League of Nations, Wilson was obliged to incorporate in that document an article declaring that nothing therein contained should affect the legal validity of a regional understanding such as the Monroe Doctrine. The exact interpretation of such a phrase must remain doubtful, and it is difficult to maintain that it implies complete European recognition of the American dogma. It was certainly far from acceptable to the more nationalistic supporters of Monroe's principles in the United States.

In the United States, as the evolution of the American attitude toward intervention shows, there has been somewhat of a reaction against extreme interpretations of the principles of 1823. Secretary of State Charles E. Hughes attempted to dissociate various U.S. interventions in the Caribbean area from the Monroe Doctrine. In 1929 the Committee on Foreign Relations of the Senate of the United States, in transmitting the Kellogg-Briand Pact, added a separate report in which the Monroe Doctrine was conservatively interpreted and based on the principle of self-defense. The Roosevelt Corollary of 1904 was definitely excluded.

But Argentina's policy of neutrality during World War II was a major obstacle to hemispheric unity against the Axis powers. The Inter-American Conference on Problems of War and Peace, called to strengthen arrangements for collective security in the Western Hemisphere during the war and to discuss problems in Argentina, was assembled in February 1945, and on Mar. 6 adopted the Act of Chapultepec, which broadened the Monroe Doctrine by incorporating the principle that an attack on one country of the hemisphere was to be considered an act of aggression against all the countries of the hemisphere. The act also contained a provision for the negotiation of a defense treaty among the American states after the war. Meeting at Petrópolis, outside Rio de Janeiro, Aug. 15–Sept. 2, 1947, the United States and nineteen Latin-American republics drew up the Rio Pact (Inter-American Treaty of Reciprocal Assistance), a permanent defensive military alliance that legally sanctioned the principle that an attack on one is an attack on all. The following year the Organization of American States was established, its charter going into effect in December 1951, through which the principles of the Monroe Doctrine could be effected by a system of Pan-Americanism. Despite this emphasis on hemispheric unity, the U.S. fear of Communist infiltration in Latin America led it to take action unilaterally in Guatemala (1954), Cuba (1960–61), and the Dominican Republic (1965) without prior approval or with only very tardy approval by inter-American consultative bodies. But, in general, the United States has maintained an active interest in the Organization of American States and continued to support Pan-Americanism.

[A. Alvarez, *The Monroe Doctrine;* Samuel Flagg Bemis, *The Latin American Policy of the United States;* Phillips Bradley, *A Bibliography of the Monroe Doctrine, 1919–1929;* Worthington C. Ford, "Genesis of the Monroe Doctrine," *Proceedings of the Massachusetts Historical Society,* vol. 15, series 2; C. H. Haring, *South America Looks at the United States;* Charles Evans Hughes, *The Pathway of Peace;* C. C. Hyde, *International Law Chiefly as Interpreted and Applied by the United States;* J. B. Moore, *A Digest of International Law;* Dexter Perkins, *A History of the Monroe Doctrine;* David Y. Thomas, *One Hundred Years of the Monroe Doctrine, 1823–1923.*]

DEXTER PERKINS

MONROE MISSION TO FRANCE (1794–96). The rapid development of the French Revolution made Gouverneur Morris unpopular as the American minister to France. His sympathies were strongly monarchal. The French government suggested his recall when Edmond C. E. Genêt was recalled from the United States. James Monroe was selected to replace Morris because of his known friendship for the French republic. He arrived in Paris in August 1794 and found the French Revolution rapidly changing. He took a fraternal tone toward the revolutionary government and immediately became popular. Monroe, however, faced a double difficulty that eventually deprived him of the confidence both of the French government and of President George Washington. Jay's Treaty was negotiated with England in 1794. Monroe, having been kept in ignorance of the real character of John Jay's mission, was instructed to allay French suspicions. He informed the French government that Jay, in his negotiations with England, had been positively forbidden to weaken the ties between the United States and France. Monroe was in no position to defend the Jay Treaty when its text was revealed, containing provisions harmful to France, particularly the placing of England on a most-favored-nation basis. Monroe tried to palliate what seemed to him to be the ill faith of Washington's cabinet. The Federalist leaders were able to convince Washington that Monroe's conduct was disloyal to the administration and the president recalled him. Washington's decision was approved by many Americans whose sympathies had been alienated by the bloody excesses of the French Revolution.

[Edward Channing, *A History of the United States.*]

CHARLES MARION THOMAS

MONROE-PINKNEY TREATY. On Dec. 31, 1806, James Monroe and William Pinkney, as joint U.S. special envoys, signed an agreement with Great Britain replacing Jay's Treaty, which was just expiring. Notwithstanding some concessions from Great Britain, impressments and indemnities for previous ship and cargo seizures remained an issue. President Thomas Jefferson refused to submit the treaty to the Senate, but sought to utilize it as a base for further negotiation. In this he was rebuffed by the British foreign secretary, George Canning. Monroe was displeased at this treatment of his labors, and a temporary rift occurred within the ranks of the Democratic party.

[Charles E. Hill, "James Madison," in Samuel Flagg Bemis, ed., *The American Secretaries of State and Their Diplomacy,* vol. III.]

LOUIS MARTIN SEARS

MONTANA. The area of Montana first came into national focus with the Louisiana Purchase (1803) and the reports of the Lewis and Clark expedition, 1804–06. A detailed report by Gen. Isaac I. Stevens of his expedition in 1853 for a western railroad publicized its advantages. Early explorers met the major Indian tribes of the region: the Sioux to the east, the Blackfoot and Gros Ventres on the upper Missouri River, the Flathead in the Bitterroot Valley, and the Crow in the Yellowstone Valley. In the mid-1970's some 27,000 Indians still lived in Montana, concentrated in seven areas.

Montana's growth is linked with several important economic periods. The first was that of the rich fur trade. Manuel Lisa and the Missouri Fur Company opened the trade on the Yellowstone River in 1807. Kenneth McKenzie built Fort Union for the American Fur Company in 1830, and Alexander Culbertson, with Andrew Dawson, opened Fort Benton in 1846. The influence of Jesuit missionaries was extended out from the Bitterroot Valley after 1842, especially by Father Pierre Jean DeSmet and Father Antonio Ravalli.

A spectacular mining period opened with the fabulous strikes that took place at Bannack in 1862, at Virginia City in 1863, and at Helena and nearby Confederate Gulch in 1864. Emphasis shifted from placer mining to quartz veins and to silver mining in the 1870's and then to Butte's copper and zinc deposits in the 1880's. The migration to the mines carved out important trails, such as the Mullan Road from Fort Benton to Fort Walla Walla, the Virginia City–Corinne Road, and the Bozeman Trail. Missouri River steamboating also flourished; boats reached Fort Benton in 1860. Miners who did not find conditions favorable in the camps branched out into farming, especially in the Bitterroot and the Gallatin valleys. Disorderly conditions in the mining camps led to the rise of local government, and the famous vigilantes of Montana helped to enforce law and order even after the Montana area became part of Idaho Territory on Mar. 3, 1863. Continued increase in population led to the organization of Montana Territory on May 26, 1864.

Another distinct economic period in Montana's history was that of the cattleman; enormous ranches for both cattle and sheep were built up on the eastern plains. The several homestead acts brought an influx of farmers that eventually led to a balance between stock raising and crop farming. Permanent settlement encouraged railroad building to the region. The Utah and Northern Railroad reached Butte in 1881; the Northern Pacific was completed in 1883; the Great Northern reached Great Falls in 1887; the Chicago, Burlington and Quincy built to Billings in 1894; and the Chicago, Milwaukee, Saint Paul and Pacific completed its line in 1908. Industry grew up around mining, forestry products, and agricultural manufacturing. Petroleum manufacturing and natural gas were developed after 1915.

Montana became a state on Nov. 8, 1889. It has been repeatedly subject to political-economic controversy. The most colorful episode was the War of the Copper Kings, at the turn of the century, during which Marcus Daly, William A. Clark, and Frederick A. Heinze used every means, including their great wealth, to promote their mining interests and their political leadership. Continuing problems include the severe problems of aridity, the polarization between the eastern plains and the diversified western section, and the "space cost" of maintaining public services over an extremely large land area with a thin population. Amid strong conservative influences, the state has been kept abreast of progressive trends in the nation, led by such men as Joseph M. Dixon, Thomas J. Walsh, Burton K. Wheeler, and Mike Mansfield, all U.S. senators of considerable influence in national legislation and national political party decisions.

Montana's economic growth has been assisted by improvements in agriculture, its major source of income, developed during the extreme drought of the 1930's. The metals mining of the 19th century has been replaced by equally large petroleum production and manufacturing and especially by enormous coal deposits made available by strip mining. Forests approaching depletion in the 1950's are being placed on a perpetual yield management basis. Environmental studies have led to major laws restricting the exploitation of resources and regulating the use of water. The crucial factor of transportation is being solved by international pipelines for oil and gas, fast shipments of train-load lots of coal and wheat, and international air shipments of valuable livestock. Tourism is in third place as a source of income, just behind mineral production and manufacture. Montana's population growth was exceptionally rapid to 1920. Between 1920 and 1930 it was the only state in the Union to lose population. The 2.9 percent increase between 1960 and 1970 to a total of 694,409 is slightly below the average growth maintained since 1930.

[M. G. Burlingame and K. R. Toole, *A History of Montana;* J. M. Hamilton, *History of Montana;* K. R. Toole, *Montana, An Uncommon Land,* and *Twentieth Century Montana.*]

MERRILL G. BURLINGAME

MONTDIDIER-NOYON OPERATION (June 9–13, 1918). Stopped in the Marne area of France by June 4, the German army launched a new attack, on a twenty-mile front, June 9, west of Soissons, between Montdidier and Noyon. The resistance of the French Third Army, weak at first, stiffened as the Germans penetrated. On June 10, the attack having slowed, French Gen. Marie Émile Fayolle entrusted a counterattack to Gen. Charles M. E. Mangin. Working feverishly, Mangin collected his forces, established his supply, and, on June 11, launched a counterattack that drove the victorious Germans back for three miles. The American First Division at Cantigny came under artillery preparation fire and sustained raids directed against it during this operation.

[John J. Pershing, *My Experiences in the World War.*]
ROBERT S. THOMAS

MONTE CASSINO. A mountain, 1,674 feet high, about fifty miles north of Naples, and crowned by the famous Benedictine abbey, Monte Cassino was the place of protracted conflict during the first five months of 1944. Overlooking the Rapido River valley on the south and the Liri River valley on the west, Monte Cassino provided German troops with superb observation over the Allied forces approaching from the south and trying to enter the Liri Valley, which was deemed the best route to Rome. The Germans incorporated the hill into their strong Gustav Line defenses, although they exempted the monastery itself from their fortified positions. Yet the presence of the massive buildings so close to the German defensive posts made it virtually impossible to attack legitimate military targets without striking the abbey.

Failure of American troops to cross the Rapido and gain access into the Liri Valley on Jan. 21–22, 1944, was ascribed to the dominating eminence of Monte Cassino. Under the mistaken belief that Germans occupied the abbey, the Allies on Feb. 15 destroyed the buildings and their artistic and cultural treasures with an air bombardment by 250 planes. German troops then moved into the abbey and in a fierce battle denied the height, as well as entrance into the Liri Valley, to the Allied forces.

On Mar. 15 the Allies heavily bombed the town of Cassino at the foot of Monte Cassino but again failed to advance into the Liri Valley. Not until a powerful spring offensive broke the Gustav Line did the Allies gain entrance into the Liri Valley and, on May 18, capture the mountain.

The abbey and the town were rebuilt after the war, but controversy continued about whether the destruction had been justified.

[Martin Blumenson, *Salerno to Cassino;* Dominick Graham, *Monte Cassino;* Fred Majdalany, *The Battle of Cassino;* Jacques Mordal, *Cassino.*]
MARTIN BLUMENSON

MONTEREY, a city on the central coast of California, was discovered in 1542 by Juan Cabrilla. A settlement was made by Gaspar de Portolá in 1770 and served as the capital of Spanish and Mexican California from 1777 to 1845. Although in the latter year Los Angeles became the seat of civil government, Monterey remained the fiscal and military headquarters, as well as the center of social life. The town was under the U.S. flag for one day, Oct. 19, 1842, when Commodore Thomas ap Catesby Jones seized it in the belief that war existed between Mexico and the United States. Permanent American control came during the Mexican War, with Monterey's surrender, without resistance, to Commodore John D. Sloat on July 7, 1846. Monterey was incorporated in 1850, but the city was replaced by San Francisco in importance. Monterey has grown in popularity as a resort area. The population in 1970 was 26,302.

[C. E. Chapman, *A History of California: The Spanish Period;* L. B. Powers, *Old Monterey: California's Adobe Capital.*]
CHARLES EDWARD CHAPMAN
ROBERT HALE SHIELDS

MONTERREY, BATTLES OF (Sept. 21–23, 1846). In the Mexican War, Gen. Zachary Taylor's invading army of 6,000 attacked Monterrey (in northeastern Mexico—not to be confused with Monterey in California), which was defended by Gen. Pedro de Ampudia with 9,000 men. The first day's fight outside the city paved the way for the assault on three fortified hills that guarded the approach and that was carried before daybreak on Sept. 22. On that day and the next the Americans completed the conquest of the city. An eight-weeks' armistice was agreed on, but repudiated by Congress, and the fighting was renewed within six weeks.

[W. E. Connelley, *History of the Mexican War, 1846–48.*]
ALVIN F. HARLOW

MONTGOMERY CONVENTION assembled at Montgomery, Ala., Feb. 4, 1861, to organize the Confederate States of America. Representatives were present from six states of the lower South (South Carolina, Georgia, Alabama, Mississippi, Florida, and Louisiana). The convention drafted a provisional constitution for the Confederate states. It then declared itself a provisional legislature and set up a government without waiting for the ratification of the constitution. The next important step in setting up this government was the selection of the president and vice-president. For president, the convention selected Jefferson Davis of Mississippi, a conservative who had not actively supported secession. For vice-president, Alexander H. Stephens of Georgia, who had actively opposed secession, was chosen.

The convention continued to sit in Montgomery until May 20, 1861, when it adjourned to meet in Richmond on July 20. It added new members as other states seceded and acted interchangeably as a constitutional convention and a provisional legislature. It completed a permanent constitution (adopted Mar. 11, 1861), and supervised its ratification. It directed the election in November 1861 at which a congress and a president and vice-president were elected; it also passed all laws necessary to adapt the existing laws and machinery of the government of the United States to the needs of the new government. With the inauguration of the permanent government (Feb. 22, 1862) it adjourned.

[J. G. Randall, *The Civil War and Reconstruction*.]

HALLIE FARMER

MONTICELLO was the home of Thomas Jefferson, on a "little mountain," near Charlottesville, Va. The spot came into Jefferson's possession by inheritance from his father. Excavation and the preparation of lumber were started in 1767–68. The following summer the summit was leveled and brickmaking begun. A small brick house, still standing, was constructed, into which Jefferson moved in 1770. For a decade the big house was under construction. Jefferson, as his own architect, built in Italian style, on the model of Andrea Palladio. But after five years in Europe and examination of many buildings, Jefferson greatly altered Monticello. The result was an Italian villa with a Greek portico, a Roman dome, and many colonial features. The home of Jefferson for fifty-six years, Monticello was the mecca of tourists and visitors, the entertainment of whom impoverished Jefferson. On his death the estate passed from his heirs to Uriah Levy, who willed it to the people of the United States, but the will was overthrown. Eventually the estate came under the control of the Thomas Jefferson Me-

morial Foundation. Jefferson is buried on the grounds.

[Paul Wilstack, "Jefferson's Little Mountain," *National Geographic Magazine* (April 1929).]

ALFRED P. JAMES

MONTREAL, CAPTURE OF (1760). British Gen. James Wolfe's victory over the French at Quebec in 1759 was followed on Sept. 8, 1760, by the surrender of Montreal. The spirits of the French had been raised by the success of François Gaston de Lévis at Sainte Foy on Apr. 28, but not for long. Everything depended on whether the French or the English fleet would first come to the rescue. On May 15 the vanguard of the English ships appeared below Quebec. Lévis, abandoning hope of help from France, raised the siege and retreated up the river. The English, knowing that Montreal was doomed, prepared at their leisure for the final stroke. The plan of campaign had been carefully prepared. While Gen. Geoffrey Amherst moved north from New York to Lake Ontario and descended the Saint Lawrence River, Gen. James Murray with another army and the fleet moved up the river, and Col. William Haviland approached by way of Lake Champlain. On Sept. 8, 1760, the governor, Pierre François de Rigaud, Marquis de Vaudreuil-Cavagnal, at Amherst's demand, surrendered Montreal, and with it Canada.

[William Wood, *The Fight for Canada*; George M. Wrong, *The Fall of Canada, 1759–1760*.]

LAWRENCE J. BURPEE

MONTREAL, CAPTURE OF (1775). After the fall of Saint John's, Newfoundland, Nov. 2, 1775, the main body of the American force under Gen. Richard Montgomery pushed on toward Montreal, which Ethan Allen had failed to take by a *coup de main* in September. Gov. Guy Carleton was in the city, but, as the fortifications were weak and ruinous, he made no attempt to defend it, and on Nov. 11 slipped away with the garrison down the river toward Quebec. American batteries at Sorel barred the way, and the flotilla and the troops were captured; but Carleton himself reached Quebec in safety. On Nov. 13 the American troops marched into Montreal without encountering resistance. The city remained in American hands until June 15, 1776.

[A. L. Burt, *The Old Province of Quebec*; Justin H. Smith, *Our Struggle for the Fourteenth Colony*.]

C. P. STACEY

MONTREAL, WILKINSON'S EXPEDITION AGAINST. In 1813 Gen. James Wilkinson assumed command of the northern troops distributed from Champlain to Niagara, N.Y., with headquarters at Sackets Harbor. Wilkinson arrived at Sackets Harbor in late August, and spent two months assembling forces. According to War Department plans his objective should have been the British base, Kingston, directly opposite. Wilkinson chose to advance on Montreal. It was Nov. 1 before the expedition—about 7,000 men in 300 boats—started down the Saint Lawrence, constantly harried by British gunboats and batteries on shore. On Nov. 10 the flotilla reached the Long Sault Rapids, still 100 miles from Montreal. Troops were landed to protect their subsequent progress, but reembarked after hard fighting at Chrysler's Field on the Saint Lawrence River. Further disheartened by wintry weather, sickness, and nonarrival of troops from Lake Champlain, Wilkinson retreated up the Salmon River to winter quarters at French Mills. In February 1814 his army was further withdrawn to Plattsburgh (*see* Lacolle Mill, Battle of) and Sackets Harbor, ending this badly mismanaged campaign.

[J. R. Jacobs, *Tarnished Warrior*.]
ALLAN F. WESTCOTT

MONUMENTS, NATIONAL. *See* **Parks, National, and National Monuments.**

MOONEY CASE. During a strike in 1913 Thomas J. Mooney, a minor labor leader, and his wife, together with Warren K. Billings and two others, all connected with labor organizations, were arrested and tried on the charge of unlawful possession of explosives. Mooney was acquitted; Billings served two years in prison.

On July 22, 1916, a Preparedness Day parade was in progress in San Francisco when a bomb exploded on the sidewalk, killing outright or mortally injuring ten persons and wounding forty others. Mooney and Billings were among those charged with the outrage; Mooney was sentenced to death and Billings received a life sentence. The case against Mooney was weak and some of the evidence so questionable that the judge who presided at his trial finally became convinced that the trial had been unfair and joined in the long fight to save Mooney. In 1918 President Woodrow Wilson asked Gov. William Stephens of California to delay the execution, with the result that Stephens eventually commuted Mooney's sentence to life imprisonment. Labor and other organizations fought steadily in his behalf. Governor after governor was petitioned for pardon or a rehearing. On Jan. 7, 1939, Gov. Culbert L. Olson, only a few days after his inauguration, pardoned Mooney, and, on Oct. 16, 1939, he released Billings through a commutation of his sentence.

[E. J. Hopkins, *What Happened in the Mooney Case.*]
ALVIN F. HARLOW

MOON HOAX. On Aug. 25, 1835, the *New York Sun* first announced wonderful discoveries on the moon by Sir John Herschel through an improved telescope at the Cape of Good Hope in South Africa. Batlike beings, temples of polished sapphire, and a beautiful inland sea were described and illustrated. The hoax, really written by Richard A. Locke, an Englishman reporting for the *Sun,* fooled most New Yorkers, and even some Yale professors. It was finally explained as a satire, but it put the *Sun* on the road to prosperity and led to later hoaxes, such as Edgar Allan Poe's *Balloon Hoax,* also published in the *Sun.*

[F. M. O'Brien, *The Story of the Sun;* E. A. Poe, *The Literati.*]
WALTER B. NORRIS

MOON LANDING. On Wednesday, July 16, 1969, half a million people gathered near Cape Canaveral (then Cape Kennedy), Fla. Their attention was focused on three astronauts—Neil A. Armstrong, Edwin E. Aldrin, Jr., and Michael Collins—who lay in the couches of an Apollo spacecraft bolted atop a Saturn V launch vehicle, awaiting ignition of five clustered rocket engines to boost them toward the first lunar landing. This event took place eight years after President John F. Kennedy, in the wake of Soviet Sputnik and Vostok successes, issued a challenge to land men on the moon before 1970 and thus give the United States preeminence in space exploration. After twenty manned missions—two to the vicinity of the moon itself—the United States was ready to achieve that goal.

At 9:32 A.M., eastern daylight time, the historic voyage, watched by millions via television, began without incident. After less than two revolutions of the earth to check out their spacecraft, the Apollo 11 crew fired the 200,000-pound-thrust Saturn S-IVB stage to escape earth's gravitational field. The flight path was so nearly perfect that only one of four planned trajectory corrections had to be made. On their way to the moon, the astronauts monitored systems, ate, and slept. Several times via television they showed scenes of the receding earth and their own cabin activities.

Early Saturday afternoon (July 19), seventy-six hours after launch, the crew slowed their ship while on the back side of the moon to enter lunar orbit. Following this maneuver, Aldrin slid through a passageway into the lunar module, called Eagle, to test its systems and then returned to the command module Columbia so that he and the other crew members could sleep before the descent to the lunar surface.

On Sunday (July 20) Armstrong and Aldrin in the lunar module told Collins, "The Eagle has wings," as they cut loose from the command module and headed toward the surface of the moon. Dodging a boulder-strewn area the size of a football field, Armstrong set the craft down at 4:17 P.M. (EDT), reporting: "Houston, Tranquility Base here. The Eagle has landed." Six and one-half hours later, after donning a protective suit and life-sustaining backpack, Armstrong climbed down and set foot on lunar soil, saying: "That's one small step for [a] man, one giant leap for mankind." Aldrin soon followed. From the first step through the ensuing walk, half a billion people watched on television as the two astronauts moved about on the lunar surface with its gravity one-sixth that of earth's.

While on the Sea of Tranquility, Armstrong and Aldrin deployed a television camera, raised the American flag, collected about 47 pounds of samples, talked with President Richard M. Nixon, set up scientific equipment that would remain on the moon, and gave millions of listeners a description of their experiences. After two hours of exploring, they returned to the lunar module, rested for eight hours, and then started the engine of the ascent stage to rejoin Collins, who was orbiting the moon in Columbia, late Monday afternoon (July 21). Discarding the Eagle, the astronauts fired the service module engine shortly after noon the next day to escape the lunar gravitational field for the return to earth. During the return flight, they tended their ship, conducted television transmissions to earth, and told their fellow men what going to the moon had meant to each of them.

Apollo 11 splashed down in the Pacific Ocean on Thursday (July 24), a week and a day (195 hours) after departing the Florida launch site. The astronauts, greeted by Nixon aboard the U.S.S. *Hornet*, were kept in quarantine for sixteen days, because scientists feared the introduction of pathogens from outer space. None was found. Thus ended man's first visit to a celestial body.

[James Byrne, ed., *10:56:20 PM EDT, 7/20/69: The Historic Conquest of the Moon as Reported to the American People by CBS News Over the CBS Television Network;* Michael Collins, *Carrying the Fire;* Richard S. Lewis, *Appointment on the Moon.*]

JAMES M. GRIMWOOD

MOONSHINE, an old cant term in southern England for smuggled liquor, indicating that it was customarily transported by night. The name "moonshiner" for an illicit distiller in the southern Appalachian area came into popular use in the 19th century, some of that functionary's work and many of his deliveries being accomplished at night. His still was apt to be in a wild place among thickets or rocks, in a gorge or a cave. His product was known locally as "brush whiskey" or "blockade"; the term "moonshine" was not used to describe the liquor itself. The blockader, as he most often called himself, made illicit whiskey because he believed that a man had as much right to do so as to make his own molasses, and because this was the only way in which a fair monetary return could be obtained for the mountain corn crop (*see* Whiskey Rebellion). After 1877, when the government intensified its campaign against moonshining, armed revenue officers were constantly active in the southern mountains, killings were frequent, and sometimes pitched battles were fought, but the business was never quite eliminated. During the Prohibition era, the word "moonshine" came to be popularly applied to liquor illicitly made anywhere, even in the home. (*See also* Bootlegging.)

[Horace Kephart, *Our Southern Highlanders.*]

ALVIN F. HARLOW

MOORE'S CREEK BRIDGE, BATTLE AT (Feb. 27, 1776), a decisive victory of North Carolina Whigs over North Carolina Loyalists. Aptly called "the Lexington and Concord" of the South, this battle, fought eighteen miles above Wilmington, crushed the Loyalists, aroused the Whigs, stimulated the independence movement, and prevented British invasion of the state in 1776. In the battle, which lasted only three minutes, 1,600 Loyalists were overwhelmed by 1,100 Whigs. The latter had one killed and one wounded; the former, fifty killed or wounded and 850 prisoners. The Whigs also captured 350 guns, 150 swords, 1,500 rifles, 13 wagons, medical supplies, and £15,000 sterling.

[Hugh T. Lefler, *North Carolina History Told by Contemporaries.*]

HUGH T. LEFLER

MORALS. From the arrival of colonists until World War I the American moral code was absolutist, puritanical, and individualistic and applied a single standard for all men. It was absolutist in that all persons were bound, in all situations, to uniform standards of right and wrong. They were not excused by extenuating circumstances, especially environmental influences. The source of authority was the one God, as revealed in the Bible, and not one's peer group. It was a principled rather than a situational morality; pervasive conduct contrary to the code was, in theory at least, no excuse for breaking it. The code was puritanical in that it was dominated by ascetic and anti-aesthetic values. The sabbath was strictly kept and the enforcement of "blue laws" was widespread. Actors and the theater, pleasure for pleasure's sake, all forms of display or conspicuous consumption, and gambling were morally suspect and often forbidden by law. The code was individualistic in that the main emphasis was placed on personal morality (mainly sexual). Men faced their God (the ultimate judge of right and wrong) as individuals, without the mediation of a church with priests, sacraments, and confessionals. Conscience was the only guide, and a sense of guilt was a major factor in social control. Both puritanical Protestantism and a secular democratic creed of equality made for a single standard of morality; that is, rich and poor, men and women, and ministers and laymen were held to one uniform standard of conduct. The poor were not to be excused because of a debilitating environment; the rich were not to be allowed moral license on the basis of privileged status; and men were to be held to substantially the same standards of chastity as were women, particularly with regard to marital fidelity.

Despite avowals of religious tolerance, a *de facto* Protestant establishment ruled—in requiring prayer and chapel attendance in schools and colleges. Ascetic Protestant moral standards were applied to all, whether Catholic, Protestant, or Jewish—as well as to the unchurched and the atheists. Moreover, the Protestant ethic was related to the gospel of success: since it was believed that the moral and ascetic individual would become economically successful, economic failure implied immorality. In a society in which most people were self-employed—and which was predominately rural through the first decade of the 20th century—this individualistic and ascetic morality of success was more or less in accord with, and reinforced by, circumstances. And until about the same time there were new opportunities in the West for the unsuccessful.

With the development of the Industrial Revolution new factors developed in society—urbanization, industrialization, large-scale immigration, and especially the growth of an extremely affluent minority at the top and a large laboring class, as well as slum-dwellers, at the bottom. New ideas also developed, including secular and Christian socialism, the social gospel, and deterministic social science. Within this matrix a new, more collectivist, more political, and more situational and relativist morality emerged. Although no exact dates can be given for the transition, the signs of change extended all the way from the moral indignation over slavery to indignation over the evils of the sweatshop, the assembly line, and capitalism in general—all examples of institutional or situational, rather than purely personal, immorality.

In many ways the career of Woodrow Wilson marked the change from an individualistic to an institutional sense of morality in America. In a 1909 speech he said:

> For my part, I do not see any promise of vitality either in the church or in society except upon the true basis of individualism. . . . He, the minister, must preach Christianity to men, not to society. He must preach salvation to the individual, for it is only one by one that we can love, and love is the law of life.

In a 1919 speech in Pittsburgh he said:

> For one, I am not fond of thinking of Christianity as a means of saving individual souls. . . . Christ came into this world to save others, not to save himself, and no man is a true Christian who does not think constantly of how he can lift his brother, how he can enlighten mankind, how he can make virtue the rule of conduct in the circle in which he lives.

World War I was the great watershed. Puritanical, confident, and success-worshipping Americans who went to war came home to view themselves, in a social context, as the "lost generation." Freudianism, Marxism, and the cultural relativism of social science, combined with the antipuritanical diatribes of H. L. Mencken and the debunking historians, all contributed to the decline of an absolutist and individualistic morality in postwar America. In the mid-1970's moral relativism, situational rather than principled, and all forms of environmental determinism had come to hold the field, especially among creative and educated groups. Some even went so far as to replace the religious categories of good and evil, as well as the morality of right and wrong, with the scientific categories of the sick and the well. While moral relativism and scientific determinism seemed in the ascendency in the area of personal morality, there were signs among the younger generation in the 1960's and 1970's of a rigid moral absolutism regarding institutions; in other words, if institutions as a whole are not evil in themselves, according to this new collectivist morality, there were at least good and bad institutions in a world where men and women were, at the same time, merely more or less psychologically or emotionally adjusted.

[Joseph Wood Krutch, *The Measure of Man,* and *The Modern Temper;* Walter Lippmann, *A Preface to Morals.*]

E. DIGBY BALTZELL

MORAL SOCIETIES. The religious upsurge beginning late in the 18th century brought innumerable associations into being whose general intent was expressed by the names of the Society for the Reformation of Morals, organized in 1813, and the New York Moral Reform Society, chartered in 1834. Many of them had temperance as one of their cardinal principles. There were dozens of groups printing and distributing moral and religious pamphlets; about fifty of these were absorbed by the American Tract Society, organized in 1825. Antislavery, antitobacco, and peace societies sprang up. The National Lord's Day Society had former President John Quincy Adams presiding at its annual meeting in 1844. The American Female Guardian Society aimed to "throw good influences around poor young women," while the Young Men's Association for Mutual Improvement had a similar intent toward the other sex. The Young Men's Christian Association, the Young Women's Christian Association, the Societies for Ethical Culture (first one organized in 1876), and others are later manifestations of the same tendencies.

[E. Douglas Branch, *The Sentimental Years;* Gilbert Seldes, *The Stammering Century.*]

ALVIN F. HARLOW

MORATORIUM, HOOVER. The ominous financial situation throughout the world in the spring of 1931 and its disastrous effects on American conditions led President Herbert Hoover, on June 20, to propose a one-year international postponement "of all payments on intergovernmental debts, reparations, and relief debts, both principal and interest, of course not including obligations of governments held by private parties." He hoped that such action would promote a worldwide restoration of confidence and economic stability. By July 6 the fifteen nations involved had accepted the proposal.

[John D. Hicks, *The Republican Ascendancy, 1921–1933;* Herbert Hoover, *Memoirs.*]

W. A. ROBINSON

MORAVIAN BRETHREN trace their ancestry back to the Hussite movement in 15th-century Bohemia. They were almost destroyed by persecution in the 16th and 17th centuries, but a small community of survivors in Moravia was able to reconstitute itself on the Saxony estate of Count Nicholaus Ludwig von Zinzendorf in 1722. At Herrnhut, as they called their sanctuary, they came under the influence of German pietism, and the estate became the center of a widespread missionary enterprise that included America, Africa, and Greenland. The first Moravian settlement in America, in Georgia in 1735, was unsuccessful, but enduring settlements were made in Nazareth, Pa., in 1740 and in Salem, N.C., in 1753. Although closed communities for about a century, these and other Pennsylvania communities exercised considerable influence, largely through their music. The principal Moravian churches are the Moravian Church in America (Northern Province), with 33,687 members in 1974; the Moravian Church in America (Southern Province), 22,411 members; and the Unity of the Brethren, 6,142 members.

[John Taylor Hamilton and Kenneth G. Hamilton, *History of the Moravian Church: The Renewed Unitas Fratum, 1722–1957;* Gillian Lindt, *Moravians in Two Worlds: A Study of Changing Communities.*]

GLENN T. MILLER

MORAVIAN MASSACRE. *See* **Gnadenhutten.**

MORAVIAN TOWN, BATTLE AT. *See* **Thames, Battle of.**

MOREY LETTER, a campaign document in the presidential election of 1880 in which James A. Garfield was purported to have declared himself in favor of "Chinese cheap labor." While it was immediately denounced as a forgery, agitation over the issue of Chinese exclusion was so intense on the West Coast that the suggestion that Garfield might support free immigration has been held responsible for his loss of the electoral votes of California. The forged letter was first published in the *New York Truth* on Oct. 20, 1880.

[T. C. Smith, *The Life and Letters of James A. Garfield.*]
FOSTER RHEA DULLES

MORFIT'S REPORT. President Andrew Jackson sent Henry M. Morfit to Texas in 1836 to obtain information upon which to base a recommendation for or against recognition of Texan independence. Morfit's written report consisted of ten letters, dated in Texas between Aug. 13 and Sept. 14, 1836. On the basis of these letters and a conversation with Morfit on his return to Washington, D.C., Jackson recommended delay.

E. C. BARKER

MORFONTAINE, TREATY OF. *See* **Convention of 1800.**

MORGAN, FORT, SEIZURE OF. *See* **Mobile Bay, Battle of.**

MORGAN-BELMONT AGREEMENT was a contract (Feb. 8, 1895) between the U.S. Treasury Department and the banking houses of J. P. Morgan and August Belmont, American representative of the Rothschilds of Paris. Under the contract these financiers agreed to buy $62 million worth of thirty-year government bonds and pay for them in gold, thus replenishing the government's rapidly diminishing gold reserve.

[D. R. Dewey, *National Problems;* A. Nevins, *Grover Cleveland.*]
P. ORMAN RAY

MORGAN'S RAIDS (1862–64). After taking part in some minor engagements as a Confederate cavalry leader, Col. John Hunt Morgan began a career as a raider by a spectacular dash into Kentucky from Knoxville, Tenn., in July 1862, going as far as Georgetown and Cynthiana and causing alarm in Cincinnati and Lexington. He retired with 1,200 men across the Cumberland after having destroyed quantities of Union arms and supplies with little actual fighting. He assisted Edmund Kirby-Smith's northward advance in September 1862 (*see* Kentucky, Invasion of), captured a Union force at Hartsville, Tenn., in December, and continued his activities

the next spring. His most spectacular achievement came in July 1863, when he led 2,460 men across Kentucky, reaching the Ohio River in five days. Without authority from his superiors and pursued by Union cavalry, he crossed the Ohio River at Brandenburg, Ky., drove off some Indiana militia, dashed northeastward into Ohio at Harrison, and, passing through the suburbs of Cincinnati at night, bewildered Union and state forces by the speed of his march and the boldness of his plan. His dash across southern Ohio ended disastrously in a battle at the ford at Buffington Island but Morgan and 1,200 men escaped, only to be captured at Salineville, Ohio, on July 26. After several months' confinement in the Ohio penitentiary Morgan escaped, with six others, to resume his military career as commander of the Department of Southwestern Virginia. His raiding activities ended suddenly when he was surprised and killed in eastern Tennessee in September 1864. His raid of 1863 had given Indiana and Ohio a bad fright, had inflicted property damages of over $500,000 in Ohio, and had helped relieve the pressure on the Confederate forces in Tennessee.

[B. W. Duke, *History of Morgan's Cavalry;* Whitelaw Reid, *Ohio in the War.*]
EUGENE H. ROSEBOOM

MORGAN TRIALS (1827–31). The disappearance of William Morgan of Batavia, N.Y., in September 1826, as he was about to publish a book revealing the secrets of Freemasonry, led to a prolonged investigation and numerous court trials. It was believed that Masons had abducted and perhaps murdered him. A special prosecutor was appointed by the governor, but it proved impossible to determine Morgan's fate or satisfactorily to place responsibility. Several Masons pleaded guilty of conspiracy in abducting Morgan and were given jail sentences and fined; others refused to testify and were imprisoned for contempt. The inconclusive trials and the suspicion aroused contributed to the anti-Masonic movement.

[Samuel D. Greene, *The Broken Seal;* Rob Morris, *William Morgan.*]
MILTON W. HAMILTON

MORMON, BOOK OF, is said by Mormons to be a translation by Joseph Smith of the sacred history of the ancestors of the American Indians who were, at the time the history was written, a white people with inspired prophets similar to those among the Hebrews, from whom it is said they descended. Joseph

Smith claimed that this record was delivered to him by an angel in the year 1827, who gave him instructions by which he was able to translate the engravings as the Book of Mormon. This work is held by the Mormons as sacred and equal in authority with the Bible as the word of God.

[William Muelder, *The Mormons in American History.*]

J. F. SMITH

MORMON BATTALION, a company of U.S. soldiers who served in the war with Mexico (1846–48). They were enlisted from the Mormon camps in Iowa Territory, and were furnished by Brigham Young. In all, there were 549 persons, including several families, who marched to Fort Leavenworth, Kans., where the battalion was properly equipped with clothing and firearms. Under the command of Col. Philip St. George Cooke, the Mormon volunteers marched to California by way of Santa Fe and the Gila River. Due to short rations, lack of water, and excessive toil in roadmaking and well digging, many fell sick and some died. They reached San Diego, Calif., in January 1847, where the battalion was disbanded, and most of the members joined the Mormon company under Brigham Young that had arrived in the valley of the Great Salt Lake in Utah in July 1847.

[Orson F. Whitney, *History of Utah.*]

L. E. YOUNG

MORMON EXPEDITION (1857–58) was caused by the refusal of the Mormons, led by Brigham Young, to obey federal laws. President James Buchanan ordered the Fifth and Tenth Infantry and two batteries of artillery from Fort Leavenworth, Kans., to subdue them; the force totaled about 1,500 officers and men. The Second Dragoons were to follow with Col. Albert Sidney Johnston, designated as commander of the expedition. The lateness of the season (it was September before the troops crossed Green River) and the guerrilla tactics of the Mormons compelled the troops to go into winter camp near Fort Bridger, Wyo. Johnston arrived at the fort on Nov. 11; despite continuous Mormon depredations on federal supplies, he found that by strict rationing his force could remain there until the following summer. However, the shortage of animals caused by hardships of the journey and Mormon raids was serious and on Nov. 27, 1857, Capt. R. B. Marcy and thirty-five volunteers started an almost incredible journey to Fort Massachusetts, N.Mex. They returned on June 8, 1858, with 1,500 horses and mules and an escort of five companies of

infantry and mounted riflemen. Meanwhile, promises of amnesty by Buchanan, coupled with the threat of federal military intervention, induced Young and his followers to submit, and on June 26, 1858, Johnston's expedition marched into Salt Lake City, Utah, without bloodshed.

[W. A. Ganoe, *The History of the United States Army;* W. A. Linn, *The Story of the Mormons.*]

C. A. WILLOUGHBY

MORMON HANDCART COMPANIES. In the immigration of the *Latter-Day Saints* to Utah, those with insufficient means to procure horses resorted to the use of handcarts after reaching Iowa City, Iowa. From that point the companies continued on their way a distance of 1,300 miles. One or two persons were assigned to each handcart, which they pushed and pulled across the dreary wastes to the Salt Lake Valley; the average daily journey was about twenty miles. Most of these companies successfully made the journey, but two companies that started late in the summer of 1856 were caught in the early winter storms and some of the members perished before rescue parties, sent out from Salt Lake City, arrived with food and clothing. Travel with handcarts began in 1856 and continued until 1860.

[J. F. Smith, *Essentials in Church History;* O. F. Whitney, *History of Utah.*]

J. F. SMITH

MORMONS. *See* **Latter-Day Saints, Church of Jesus Christ of.**

MORMON TRAIL. The Mormons, after their expulsion from Nauvoo, Ill., in February 1846, took a westerly route along a well-beaten trail, through what is now Iowa, to the Missouri River. By permission of the Omaha Indians, they crossed the Missouri River into Nebraska Territory, and established winter quarters, where they remained during the winter of 1846–47. In April 1847 the first company, consisting of 143 men, 3 women, and 2 children, started west, under the leadership of Brigham Young. They followed the north bank of the Platte River to Fort Laramie, Wyo. At this point they continued their journey over the old Oregon Trail, until they reached Fort Bridger in Wyoming. Traveling to the southwest through Echo Canyon to the Weber River, they ascended East Canyon, crossed the Big and Little mountains of the Wasatch Range, and entered the valley of the Great Salt Lake in Utah through Emigration Canyon on July 24, 1847.

[Orson F. Whitney, *History of Utah.*]

L. E. YOUNG

MORMON WAR (1844–46), a series of disorders between the Mormon residents of Nauvoo in Hancock County, Ill., and the non-Mormon population of the neighboring territory. Upon their settlement at Nauvoo in 1839 the Mormons had been warmly welcomed, but resentment at the excessively liberal terms of their city charter, fear of their political power, which they demonstrated by mass voting, and envy of their apparent prosperity soon generated suspicion and then hate on the part of the non-Mormon population.

By June 1844 mutual antagonism had reached such a pitch that the Mormon militia was under arms in Nauvoo, while at least 1,500 armed men, bent on the expulsion of the Mormons, had assembled in the county. The situation was so critical that Gov. Thomas Ford took personal charge. When Joseph Smith, leader of the sect, surrendered on a charge of riot, a peaceful solution appeared possible, but on June 27 Smith and his brother Hyrum were murdered by a mob in the county jail at Carthage. The state militia kept peace throughout the winter of 1844–45 and the summer of 1845 was relatively quiet, but violence flared in the fall, and the militia was called out again. On Oct. 1 the Mormons promised to leave Illinois the following spring. Their migration began in February and continued steadily, but the anti-Mormons, professing to believe that many intended to remain, moved in force against the city in the fall of 1846. A general engagement, with several casualties, resulted. Peace was patched up and the Mormons hastened their exodus. By mid-December, when nearly all had gone, the trouble came to an end.

[W. A. Linn, *The Story of the Mormons;* T. C. Pease, *The Frontier State, 1818–1848.*]

PAUL M. ANGLE

MORRILL ACT. Long agitation by agricultural societies, farm journals, and other advocates—especially Jonathan Baldwin Turner of Illinois—of vocational training for farmers and mechanics influenced Sen. Justin S. Morrill of Vermont to introduce into Congress a bill to aid in the establishment of agricultural and mechanical arts colleges in every state in the Union. The measure passed Congress in 1858, but constitutional objections induced President James Buchanan to veto it. A similar measure, since called the Morrill Act, was signed by President Abraham Lincoln in 1862. States were offered 30,000 acres of land for each representative and senator they were entitled to in the national legislature as an endowment for the proposed schools. In some states the lands were given to existing institutions, as in Wisconsin, where the state university was the beneficiary; elsewhere they were conveyed to newly established agricultural and technical colleges, such as Purdue University and the Illinois Industrial University, now the University of Illinois. Morrill was henceforth called the "father of the agricultural colleges." (*See also* Land Grants for Education.)

[Paul W. Gates, *Agriculture and the Civil War;* Fred A. Shannon, *The Farmer's Last Frontier, 1860–1897;* John Y. Simon, "The Politics of the Morrill Act," *Agricultural History,* vol. 37 (1963).]

PAUL W. GATES

MORRIS CANAL AND BANKING COMPANY was organized in 1824 to build a canal across New Jersey from the mouth of the Lehigh River to New York harbor, thus giving a direct water route to the seaboard for Lehigh coal. The canal, completed in 1832, was one of the engineering wonders of America. In its ninety-mile course, it passed over an elevation of 914 feet above tidewater, largely through the agency of twenty-three inclined planes designed by James Renwick, a professor at Columbia College, which carried the boats up and down steep grades on tram cars. The banking privilege in the company's charter brought it into disgrace and ruin. During the speculative mania of 1835–36, it bought large quantities of the bonds issued by Indiana and Michigan for internal improvement purposes, sold them, and, instead of paying the states, used the money for the extension and improvement of its canal. Two Indiana officials, one of them a stockholder in the Morris Company, aided in the jobbery and participated in the profits. The panic of 1837 compelled the company to mortgage the canal for $750,000, and in 1841 it collapsed in one of the most noisome bankruptcies of the period, owing the state of Indiana alone $2,536,611—a very serious matter for so young a commonwealth in those days. In 1844 a new canal and banking company was organized. After 1866 the business of the canal declined because of railroad competition. It was leased to the Lehigh Valley

Railroad in 1871, was taken over by the state in 1904, and went out of use in 1924.

[Alvin F. Harlow, *Old Towpaths*.]
ALVIN F. HARLOW

MORRISSEY NOMINATION. In September 1965, Francis J. X. Morrissey, a municipal judge of high church and political connections but disputed legal credentials, was nominated for a Boston federal judgeship by President Lyndon Johnson. The request for the nomination had come from Sen. Edward Kennedy, and it was believed that Morrissey's devoted service to the family of Joseph Kennedy completely explained the nomination. The American Bar Association staunchly opposed Morrissey, and its judiciary committee, seeking influence in the selection process, led a campaign against confirmation. Witnesses disparaged Morrissey's ability and charged that he had obtained a law degree from a "diploma mill" in Georgia. Kennedy claimed a bare majority for confirmation but deemed it unwise to cash his pledges by forcing a Senate vote. In an emotional floor speech on Oct. 21 he asked to recommit the nomination to committee. A relieved Senate consented. Although defeated, Kennedy won political credit for loyalty. By exposing the vulnerability of judicial nominations, the case served as a dress rehearsal for later defeats of three Supreme Court nominees (1968, 1969, and 1970).

[Harold W. Chase, *Federal Judges: The Selection Process*.]
JOHN P. MACKENZIE

MORRISTOWN, ENCAMPMENT AT. The natural fortress of the Watchung Mountains to the south, roads leading to the Hudson and Delaware rivers, the proximity of important iron works and a powder mill, and the residents' patriotism determined the selection of Morristown, N.J., as a camp site for the Continental army during the winters of 1776–77 and 1779–80. The first troops, three regiments from Ticonderoga, N.Y., arrived Dec. 17, 1776. These were joined on Jan. 6, 1777, by the main army of about 4,000 men, fresh from Trenton and Princeton, N.J. With headquarters at Jacob Arnold's tavern, George Washington located the general camp at Lowantica Valley (now Spring Valley), one and one-half miles southeast of the town. Suffering from smallpox and depleted by desertions the army remained here until late May. Two years later (1779–80) the army was

encamped from November until early June at Jockey Hollow, four miles southwest of the general's headquarters at the Jacob Ford Mansion.

[A. M. Sherman, *Historic Morristown*.]
C. A. TITUS

MORSE GEOGRAPHIES. In 1784 the first edition of *Geography Made Easy,* the work of Jedediah Morse, New England politician and divine, also known as the "father of American geography," appeared. The little book was the first geography to be published in the United States. As the title implies, *Geography Made Easy* attempted to simplify existing notions about America, which was poorly treated in English geographies. More than twenty-five editions were published during the author's lifetime. Other publications followed the first. An enlarged work, *The American Geography,* later called *The American Universal Geography,* appeared in 1789. A child's book, *Elements of Geography,* appeared in 1795, and *The American Gazetteer* was published in 1797. All these works were reedited and reprinted many times.

[W. B. Sprague, *The Life of Jedediah Morse*.]
RANDOLPH G. ADAMS

MORTARS, CIVIL WAR NAVAL, heavy guns designed to throw shells with a high angle of fire, were built at Pittsburgh in 1862 for use in the New Orleans campaign (*see* Mississippi, Opening of the). They were mounted on twenty schooners, one mortar to a schooner, and, escorted by six steamers, were brought to the Mississippi Passes in April 1862 by Comdr. David Dixon Porter. From Apr. 16 to Apr. 24 they bombarded forts Jackson and Saint Philip, the principal defenses below New Orleans, with 13-inch shells, throwing in all 16,800 shells. The forts' buildings were burned, the casemates flooded, the cannon dismounted, and fourteen Confederates were killed and thirty-nine wounded. The mortar bombardment materially aided Adm. David G. Farragut in passing the forts with the Union fleet. After New Orleans' surrender, the flotilla ascended the Mississippi to Vicksburg, Miss., which, from June 27 to July 9, 1862, it bombarded, enabling Farragut's fleet to run past the city. During the siege of Vicksburg the following year, a mortar fleet bombarded the city for forty-two days prior to its surrender, throwing 7,000 shells into the beleaguered town. Porter claimed that the mortar firing was one of the main factors in forcing the surrender. At the close of the war the navy possessed twenty-six such mortars.

[D. D. Porter, *Naval History of the Civil War;* R. S. West, *The Second Admiral: A Life of David Dixon Porter.*]

LOUIS H. BOLANDER

MORTGAGE RELIEF LEGISLATION. Since the early 19th century the relationship between mortgagor and mortgagee in the United States has undergone substantial modification—not continuously, but as the result of emergency measures taken at times of widespread financial distress arising from economic or natural causes. The alterations were generally to the apparent advantage of the borrower, and thus are referred to as relief for mortgage debtors, or, when statutory, simply as mortgage relief legislation.

Because the law of real property (including mortgage law) is a function of the states, mortgage relief legislation has also come primarily from the states. The major episodes of mortgage debtor relief followed periods of farm mortgage distress in the late 19th century and in the period between World War I and World War II, especially in the 1930's.

One feature of the settlement of the 1870's and 1880's in the Plains states was a large-scale overextension of farmer indebtedness, primarily in land mortgages. When farm incomes deteriorated and land values declined in subsequent years, mortgage debt became very burdensome to the borrower. As a result, delinquency, default, and finally foreclosure or some other form of distress transfer often occurred. The inevitable agitation for debtor relief included demands for inflation of the money supply (such as the Free Silver movement) and for public regulation of business monopolies. Two kinds of mortgage relief legislation in the narrow sense emerged from this period of farm mortgage distress: (1) the establishment of statutory periods of redemption that continued after foreclosure sale and (2) the requirement of appraisal of mortgaged property prior to sale and the prohibition of sale at less than a specified proportion of the appraised value. Such legislation resulted from criticism of sales at unreasonably low prices and deficiency judgments based on those sales.

A similar period of farm mortgage distress occurred in the 1920's, primarily in the High Plains region. There rapid expansion of agriculture during the World War I years was followed by deteriorating farm income and declining land values, which led to numerous foreclosures and other distress transfers of mortgaged farms. After 1929, general economic de-pression—in conjunction with severe drought in some areas—made mortgage distress a national concern. As a result of the extent and severity of the problem in both rural and urban areas, mortgage relief legislation reached a peak in the 1930's.

Although voluntary adjustments between debtors and creditors involving extensions of unpaid obligations, deferral of payments, and refinancing of loans occurred, these remedies proved insufficient in the face of the economic catastrophe of the 1930's. Government action seemed to be required and came first from the states. By early 1936, twenty-eight states had passed mortgage relief legislation in one or more of the following forms: (1) moratoria on foreclosures, (2) extensions of redemption periods, and (3) restrictions on the use of deficiency judgments. A moratorium halted foreclosure proceedings for a temporary period identified as an economic emergency. Legislation extending the period of redemption specified a definite period during which the debtor continued to have the right to redeem the mortgaged property. Restrictions on the use of deficiency judgments took several forms, for example, the establishment of a minimum sales price, the use of an appraised "fair value" rather than sales value as a base for figuring the amount of deficiency, and a limitation on the time within which a deficiency judgment could be executed. State mortgage relief legislation was generally upheld in the courts when the following provisions were included: the relief afforded was conditional and temporary, related to the existence of the economic emergency; the integrity of the mortgage indebtedness contract was not impaired; and creditors were assured appropriate compensation in the form of rental payments during the period of relief. The key decision on constitutionality was made by the U.S. Supreme Court in *Home Building and Loan Association* v. *Blaisdell,* 290 U.S. 398 (1934), when it upheld the Minnesota Moratorium Act of 1933.

State mortgage relief legislation met with only limited success as a solution to the mortgage distress problems of the 1930's, partly because the measures were not enacted until after much of the damage had been done. More important, the problem of mortgage distress was only part of the much larger problem of general economic depression. In the mortgage relief area, as in so many others, the search for solutions was transferred from the states to the federal government. An attempt at a federal moratorium, the Frazier-Lemke Act of 1934, was declared unconstitutional in 1935, but two years later an amended version was judged constitutional. More effective were the actions of the federal farm-credit agencies in refinancing mortgage loans—actions that benefited lenders by providing welcome liquidity while enabling debtors to escape foreclosure. Similar steps were taken in the field of urban mortgage finance.

When the general economic depression succumbed to the prosperity induced by World War II, the farm sector returned to relative well-being. Widespread mortgage distress calling for mortgage relief legislation did not occur in the postwar period. Farm ownership transfers by foreclosures, assignments, bankruptcies, and related defaults averaged 22 per 1,000 farms annually from 1929 through 1938, and peaked at 39 per 1,000 in 1933. Such distress transfers averaged about 1.5 per 1,000 farms annually during the twenty-five years from 1950 through 1974.

[Miles L. Colean, *The Impact of Government on Real Estate Finance in the United States;* William G. Murray and Aaron G. Nelson, *Agricultural Finance;* Purdue University Agricultural Experiment Station, *Improving Land Credit Arrangements in the Midwest;* Robert H. Skilton, *Government and the Mortgage Debtor.*]

GLENN H. MILLER, JR.

MORTIMER, FORT, was built on the upper Missouri at the present site of the old military post of Fort Buford, in what is now North Dakota. The site was first occupied by Fort William, a trading post belonging to the Saint Louis firm of Sublette and Campbell. Fort William was built in 1833 and abandoned in 1834 when the firm sold out to the American Fur Company.

A New York firm, Fox, Livingston and Company, organized the Union Fur Company. It was induced to take this step by the favorable representations made to it by a fur trader who had succeeded during 1841 in carrying on a very successful trade in opposition to the American Fur Company. In the spring of 1842 the new company sent the steamboat *New Haven* up the Missouri River with a complete outfit for establishing opposition posts. It established Fort George just below the mouth of the Cheyenne River and Fort Mortimer on the site of old Fort William. The Union Fur Company was also known as Ebbetts and Cutting, after the agents who represented the firm on the upper Missouri. After three years of unsuccessful competition the firm sold out to the American Fur Company, and in 1845 Fort Mortimer was abandoned.

[H. M. Chittenden, *The American Fur Trade of the Far West;* Charles Larpenteur, *Forty Years a Fur Trader on the Upper Missouri River.*]

O. G. LIBBY

MOSBY'S RANGERS, an irregular body of Confederate troops commanded by Col. John S. Mosby, operated, 1863–65, south of the Potomac behind the Union lines. This organization began with a scouting assignment from Confederate Gen. J. E. B. Stuart in January 1863. From a few troopers the rangers gradually grew to eight companies by 1865. Apart from participation with Stuart in the Gettysburg, Pa., campaign, their main activities consisted of sudden attacks on Union outposts, followed, when pursued, by quick dispersion. To Gen. Philip H. Sheridan, Gen. George A. Custer, and others, Mosby's men were a thorn in the flesh. Efforts to destroy the rangers were provokingly unavailing.

[James J. Williamson, *Mosby's Rangers, A Record of the Forty-Third Battalion Virginia Cavalry.*]

ALFRED P. JAMES

MOSCOW CONFERENCE OF FOREIGN MINISTERS (Oct. 19–30, 1943) was held by U.S. Secretary of State Cordell Hull, British Foreign Secretary Anthony Eden, and Soviet Foreign Minister V. M. Molotov. Hull and Eden had some success in allaying Soviet suspicions over the failure to open a second front in Europe, and in promoting closer cooperation with the Soviet Union. In addition, a European Advisory Commission was established to make studies of European questions, with a view to a peace settlement; and a four-power declaration (signed also by China) was made pledging the four countries to set up at the earliest practicable date an international organization for peace. To implement the declaration, steps were taken after the conference that led eventually to the Dumbarton Oaks Conference and the United Nations Conference, San Francisco.

CHARLES S. CAMPBELL

MOSES HIS JUDICIALS, the earliest compilation of New England legislation, was prepared by John Cotton and presented to the general court of Massachusetts Bay in October 1636. Although bulwarked by many scriptural citations, it was not of biblical origin, but embodied the trading-company government, the early laws, and the practices of Massachusetts. Only the chapters dealing with inheritance and the punishment of crime were drawn from the Bible. Although eventually rejected by Massachusetts in favor of the Body of Liberties adopted in 1641, for the years the compilation was under consideration copies of it were carried to New Haven, Southampton, and possibly Portsmouth, R.I., where it received at least partial acceptance, and it did influence the Body of Liberties.

[I. M. Calder, "John Cotton's Moses His Judicials," *Colonial Society of Massachusetts Publications,* vol. 28.]

ISABEL M. CALDER

MOSQUITO FLEET, a small naval squadron selected by Commodore David Porter in 1823 to wipe out the West Indian pirates. The fleet consisted of eight small schooners, a steamer, a transport ship, and five barges. The fleet scoured the coasts of Santo Domingo, Cuba, and part of Yucatán thoroughly, but encountered few pirates. Yellow fever broke out in August 1823, and Porter was obliged to sail north. He returned in 1824 and made several captures, then was succeeded by Commodore Lewis Warrington, who captured a pirate vessel and destroyed a pirate stronghold. By 1829 the fleet had captured about sixty-five pirate craft, virtually destroying their power.

[F. B. C. Bradlee, *Piracy in the West Indies and Its Suppression;* E. S. Maclay, *A History of the United States Navy From 1775 to 1894.*]

LOUIS H. BOLANDER

MOSQUITO QUESTION, one of the several delicate issues between Britain and the United States involving rivalry for the dominance of the Caribbean. Mosquito comprised the present east coast of Nicaragua, strategically located for a canal. An Indian tribe inhabited only a small portion, the remainder having been taken up by English traders. To supervise the relations between the natives and the whites the British government in 1844 converted a long-standing tradition of protection over the tribe into a formal protectorate.

American jealousy was aroused in 1849, when Nicaragua was seen to be a vital link in American intercoastal communications (*see* Hise Treaty; Squier Treaty). The issue thus joined was the occasion for the Clayton-Bulwer Treaty (April 1850), a clever formula instituting an alliance between the two countries under cover of which the Mosquito and other Central American issues were to be settled and the entire region neutralized. The Mosquito question thenceforth became inseparable from the general Central American question, the United States presently putting a Monroe Doctrine interpretation on the treaty and Britain maintaining its right to continue supervision in behalf of the Mosquito Indians. Honors were even in 1860 when Mosquito was incorporated into

Nicaragua but a reserve was created for the Indians with guarantees. The guarantees were terminated in 1895 by arrangement between Britain and Nicaragua.

[J. B. Moore, *Digest of International Law,* vol. III; R. W. Van Alstyne, "The Central American Policy of Lord Palmerston," *Hispanic American Historical Review,* vol. 16.]

RICHARD W. VAN ALSTYNE

MOST-FAVORED-NATION PRINCIPLE. One of the fundamental objects of American foreign policy from the beginning has been to break through the dikes of colonial trade monopoly and the barriers of discriminatory national tariffs. The first expression of this was the so-called conditional most-favored-nation article, which was inserted into the Treaty of Amity and Commerce with France of 1778 (*see* Franco-American Alliance), by which "The most Christian King, and the United States engage mutually not to grant any particular Favour to other Nations in respect of Commerce and Navigation, which shall not immediately become common to the other Party, who shall enjoy the same Favour freely, if the Concession was freely made, or on allowing the same Compensation if the Concession was Conditional." The conditional feature was inserted at the initiative of the French negotiators. The conditional most-favored-nation formula became a standard article of treaties of commerce of the United States whenever it could be secured, until 1923, when the Department of State changed over to the unconditional formula.

Before World War I it had become the tendency of European powers to accept the unconditional formula in their treaties, and American theorists argued in favor of this practice as more liberal, and, if universally pursued, more efficacious in lowering tariff walls everywhere. But by the time the reform of American policy had taken place, the European nations, following World War I, in a wave of neomercantilism, had gone back to the old conditional most-favored-nation formula. As a result a network of such treaties was erected, known as compensation trade treaties.

[Samuel Flagg Bemis, *A Diplomatic History of the United States.*]

SAMUEL FLAGG BEMIS

MOTION PICTURES. Scientists of many lands acquired over a period of centuries the knowledge needed for motion pictures. Motion pictures involve three elements: (1) a working knowledge of light and vision; (2) camera and projector apparatus; and (3) photography, including a flexible base for the emulsion. Only the third is of modern origin. The key to motion pictures was the discovery of a suitable plastic, a flexible film base. Motion pictures were the first great modern industry founded on plastics.

As a commercial activity motion pictures are a modern development paced by Americans. Thomas A. Edison deserves more than anyone the title "Father of Motion Pictures." He made the first thoroughly workable camera and viewer for motion pictures. The first practical projectors in the United States and elsewhere were based on his apparatus. In 1887 Edison began his quest for an apparatus to do for sight what his phonograph had done for sound, ultimately wishing to reproduce both pictures and sounds. The same year, Hannibal Williston Goodwin obtained a U.S. patent on a photographic pellicle described as "transparent, sensitive and like celluloid." In 1889 Edison and an assistant, William Kennedy Laurie Dickson, obtained from George Eastman film stock that proved workable. On Dec. 10, 1889, Eastman applied for a patent on "the manufacture of flexible photographic films." This patent was issued in 1898, after a legal battle with the Goodwin estate had been compromised.

In 1891 Edison's Kinetograph camera and Kinetoscope viewing apparatus were completed, and application was made for a patent, which was issued in 1893. The peep-show Kinetoscopes went on public display on Apr. 14, 1894, at 1155 Broadway, New York City. Later that year they were shown in Paris and London. These demonstrations influenced many in the United States and abroad who finally solved the problems of projecting continuous motion pictures on a screen.

Screen projection was achieved in 1895 in France by Louis and Auguste Lumière with the Cinématographe; in London by Robert W. Paul with films made by Birt Acres shown in the Bioscope; and in the United States by Thomas Armat, C. Francis Jenkins, Woodville Latham and his sons, Grey and Otway, and others. In 1896 motion pictures were commercial successes on screens in many parts of the world. In New York the significant premiere was held at Koster and Bial's Music Hall, Herald Square, on the evening of Apr. 23, 1896.

The first "movies" were only brief sequences, inserted in a vaudeville show. Before long, personalities of the stage agreed to appear in films. Productions became more elaborate as pictures began to tell a story. Public interest grew rapidly, especially among immigrants in the large industrial cities of the United States. In the movies these people found a universal language as well as inexpensive recreation. In April 1902 the first modest theater was established to show movies exclusively. It was the Electric Theater, Los Angeles, owned by Thomas L. Tally. Early in 1903 Harry M. Warner and his brothers opened the Cascade Theater in New Castle, Pa. These and other early theaters soon became known as nickelodeons because the admission price was five cents.

Initial production centers in the United States were in, and adjacent to, New York City and in Chicago and Philadelphia. In larger cities throughout the country, "exchanges" were established that serviced the nickelodeons with complete programs at a fixed weekly rental. Such a system did not encourage quality or experimentation.

The Motion Picture Patents Company, which controlled the industry through patented devices in the early years of the 20th century, did not believe that the public would accept "features." The Patents Company came under attack by independent producers led by Carl Laemmle, William Fox, and others. In 1912 Adolph Zukor imported a four-reel film made in France, *Queen Elizabeth* with Sarah Bernhardt. The success of this long film was a spur to American producers to attempt more ambitious subjects. In 1913 Jesse L. Lasky formed an association with Cecil B. De Mille and Samuel Goldwyn. The resulting picture was *The Squaw Man* with Dustin Farnum. It was the first feature made in Hollywood. The lure of good weather and remoteness called producers west, and Hollywood became the American production headquarters while corporate management, financial, and sales departments centered in New York.

American films first achieved real stature during World War I. In 1915 the film classic, D. W. Griffith's *The Birth of a Nation,* was released. That film was popular with the public and also made intellectuals realize the dramatic power of the screen. At that time Mary Pickford and Charles Chaplin were so popular that stars became more important than stories. From then on American films were usually made with players selected for "star value."

Hollywood during the golden age of the silent film, from the days of World War I to the mid-1920's, sought story material and creative workers throughout the world. This gave the American film an international flavor and appeal. Hollywood films had a substantial export market from the early 1920's; by the

1950's almost half the gross revenue of American pictures was being earned abroad.

At a time when many observers felt the silent films were becoming routine, sound became a reality. At first the industry leaders did not view "talkies" with favor, but the public wanted them and in 1927 and 1928 the entire industry shifted to talking pictures. On Aug. 6, 1926, the first sound film (synchronized with music on discs but with no dialogue), *Don Juan,* made by Warner Brothers, was presented at the Warner Theater, New York. Although Edison and others experimented with sound, the first acclaimed talking picture was *The Jazz Singer,* made by Warner Brothers with Al Jolson, and shown in 1927. Also in 1927 the first pictures with sound on film, Movietone films, were shown. In 1928 came the first all-talking picture, *The Lights of New York* (also Warner Brothers).

As pictures and sound were improved there was increasing interest in color. Experiments of Herbert T. Kalmus of Technicolor and others resulted in successful three-color features, the first being *Becky Sharp* in 1935. Although there had been experiments with color from the beginning of motion pictures, Technicolor was the first commercially successful process and long remained the standard of comparison of other screen color systems. From the time of the release of the record-breaking *Gone With the Wind* in 1939, an increasing proportion of important motion pictures were in color.

Following record attendance enjoyed during World War II, the American motion picture industry entered upon a long-deterred period of technical improvement. This took two forms—one, the large screen and the other, improved sound. The traditional screen proportions of four (width) to three (height) had been set by Edison. In order to compete with television's small screen and to give movies a new look, motion picture theaters, first in the United States and then throughout the world, installed large screens permitting pictures to be two to three times as wide as they were high. Cinerama, a three-film-strip process developed from an aerial gunnery trainer of World War II and which opened in New York on Sept. 30, 1952, stimulated interest in wide screens. Cinerama, Inc., also introduced a highly developed multitrack stereophonic sound system. CinemaScope, introduced in 1953 by Twentieth Century-Fox with *The Robe,* became an important wide-screen and stereophonic sound system.

In the booming 1950's and 1960's the American motion picture was confronted with intense competition for the public's leisure time. Television was the principal competitor, but there was a host of others, including vacation travel and various sports. The economic strength of the film industry to respond had been weakened by a government antitrust suit filed in 1938 and settled in 1950 by the divorcement of the five largest theater chains from the film-producing companies. Thereafter production activity at Hollywood studios declined.

After nearly two decades of unsatisfactory profits, interrupted by only a few good years, in 1970 the American film industry reached its nadir; five major companies reported a total loss of $500 million. This was a sum larger than all the film companies had lost during the Great Depression. The trend toward merging firms into multicompany conglomerates accelerated, and by the early 1970's the major American film companies had either lost their independence through mergers or come under the control of new managements interested in diversification into nonfilm fields.

The American film industry has had a stormy record of conflict about censorship. At the dawn of the feature film era the Supreme Court had ruled that motion pictures were not entitled to freedom of expression, and it took a half century for the Court to reverse itself. By the 1920's a number of states and cities had established boards of film censors. In 1929, shortly after sound films supplanted silent pictures, the American film industry adopted a plan formed by Martin Quigley, an editor and publisher of film trade journals, and instituted a system of self-regulation based on a production code. For twenty-five years the Production Code, mostly under the direction of Joseph I. Breen and Geoffrey Shurlock as administrators, guided Hollywood production in a way that stopped the spread of boards of censors. The objective of the Production Code was not to avoid the portrayal of crime, wrongdoing, or sin—essentials in most dramas—but to have films produced that would not lower the moral level of the spectators—that is, to see that the people leaving a theater were as good human beings as they had been when they entered.

A series of decisions by the Supreme Court in the 1950's struck down most local and state censorship. These decisions, together with changes in public taste, resulted in the replacement of an enforced code by one that was merely advisory. Later emphasis shifted to a rating system intended to guide patrons concerning the nature of each feature.

By the 1970's, restrictions on the creative filmmaker were more commercial than legal: a film intended for a general audience, for example, had to be restrained in matters of sex and violence to avoid the "adults only" label or one that would restrict the audience. Films planned only for adults avoided "hard-core" pornography and obscenity out of practical concern for the fact that these concepts were not clearly defined in court decisions.

All through the history of motion pictures producers of films have had to guess what types of subjects would have audience appeal, but by the early 1970's the odds against guessing correctly had become substantial. Most films of that era were disappointing from both critical and financial standpoints. However, when a picture did capture public attention, attendance reached high levels and gross receipts were often record-breaking.

By about 1970 a new generation of filmmakers and executives had replaced the individuals who had dominated the American film industry for more than forty years. The American film had grown up, matured, and grown old under the leadership of about a score of men who became involved in the decade prior to World War I. How soon—or whether—the American film would rise from the plateau on which it had been during the 1950's and 1960's depended on the successors to the pioneers. In the early years of the 1970's many were hoping for some potent new factor to increase the appeal of films, as had the advent of sound, of color, and of the wide screen with stereophonic sound.

[Bosley Crowther, *The Great Fifty;* Arthur Knight, *The Lively Art;* Arthur L. Mayer and Richard Griffith, *The Movies;* Martin Quigley, Jr., *Magic Shadows: The Story of the Origin of Motion Pictures;* Martin Quigley, Jr., and Richard Gertner, *Films in America: 1929–1969;* Terry Ramsaye, *A Million and One Nights.*]

MARTIN QUIGLEY

MOTOR TRUCK TRANSPORTATION had its inception in France about 1769 with Nicolas J. Cugnot's experimental artillery tractor. It was introduced in America in the 19th century, but neither the times, nor the technology, nor the roads were prepared for such an innovation, and the occasional builders of experimental vehicles received little encouragement for their efforts.

In the 1890's numerous experimental motor vehicles began to appear throughout the country, and among them were a few motor wagons. During the last three years of the century a few commercial motor vehicles were marketed. Like the passenger vehicles, the motor wagons resembled their horse-drawn predecessors; motors and other machinery were suspended under the bodies. This design prevailed through the first decade of the 20th century. At first, electric wagons were more common than those powered by gasoline or steam engines; the latter never were serious contenders in America. Early trucks were rarely efficient or reliable, and most carried only small loads. Consequently, people found them most valuable as advertisements, because of their novelty. During these years use of the motor truck was retarded by inexperienced drivers who abused and neglected the vehicles, by the conservatism of the business world, and by inadequate design; some manufacturers attempted simply to fit a truck body to a modified automobile chassis.

By 1910, improvements in truck design had begun to break down the conservatism, and the increased profits for the manufacturers enabled more rapid development. Vertical four-cylinder engines, located under a hood in front of the driver, began to replace the single-cylinder and double-opposed engines. Planetary transmissions and the less efficient friction transmissions were superseded by sliding gear transmissions. During the period 1913–15, there was a noticeable trend away from chain drive in favor of several forms of gear drive.

Important developments of 1912 were the tractor and semitrailer, the former having been introduced for use with the many serviceable wagons designed to be drawn by horses, the tractor and its rear wheels replacing the horses and front wheels of the wagons. Truck use increased rapidly during that decade. The production of 25,000 trucks in 1914 was tripled in 1915, and total registrations of 99,015 in 1914 rose to 1,107,639 by 1920. Poor rural roads and the 15 mile per hour speed of the solid-tired trucks restricted most of these vehicles to city streets.

World War I and its aftermath had an immense effect on truck use and development. The immediate need for trucks by the military and the army's truck-standardization program focused the attention of truck engineers on component design and furthered the cause of the assembled truck as against the manufactured truck. As the railroads became woefully congested and inefficient because of the tremendous increase in traffic when the United States entered the war in 1917, the first long-distance truck shipments were made, the trucks hauling military supplies to ports of embarkation. At that time, too, pneumatic tires capable of withstanding heavy truck loads were being developed; previously pneumatic tires had rarely been used on anything heavier than a three-quarter-ton truck. The improved tires enabled trucks to double their former speed, an enormous advantage and a practical necessity for intercity trucking. Immediately after the war the good-roads movement began to achieve results, and many previously unpaved highways were surfaced.

Interstate trucking increased steadily during the 1920's. As the decade closed such developments as power-assisted brakes, six-cylinder engines, and three-axle trucks began to contribute to the safety and efficiency of highway operation. The lean years of the early 1930's had some adverse effects on trucking, but there was also some progress, as the use of the semitrailer, adapted to heavier loads, increased 500 percent from 1929 to 1936. Likewise, in the early 1930's cooperative trailer-switching arrangements between carriers permitted through service by eliminating the extra freight handling previously necessary and, at the same time, led to standardization in size, fifth wheels, brakes, and other new components. The diesel truck was introduced in the early 1930's, although it was not found in significant numbers until the 1950's.

Growth of motor freighting was curtailed during the war years of the 1940's, but trucks served as a mobile assembly line on the home front and were often the decisive factor in the theaters of war, causing Gen. George S. Patton to remark, "The truck is our most valuable weapon." After the war the trucking industry resumed a steady and rapid growth. An important development of the late 1950's and 1960's was "piggybacking," or the long-distance movement of loaded semitrailers on railway flatcars; 1,264,501 semitrailers were loaded on flatcars in 1970. By 1968 there were 75,000 U.S. truck fleets with ten or more units each, and the 1970 truck total of 18,747,781 more than tripled the 1941 figure. In 1970 trucks moved 596 million tons of intercity freight, while giving employment, through manufacture, operation, and service, to over 10 million persons.

[Automobile Manufacturers Association, *Motor Truck Facts;* A. F. Denham, *Twenty Years' Progress in Commercial Motor Vehicles;* R. F. Karolevitz, *This Was Trucking.*]

DON H. BERKEBILE

MOULTRIE, FORT, BATTLE OF (June 28, 1776).

Throughout a ten-hour bombardment, Fort Moultrie, a palmetto fort on Sullivan's Island in Charleston harbor, in South Carolina, commanded by Col. William Moultrie, successfully beat off a British attack under Sir Henry Clinton and Peter Parker. American loss was slight, while that of the British, both in lives and

damage to ships, was large. The victory kept the British out of the South for the next two years.

[Benson J. Lossing, *The Pictorial Field Book of the Revolution.*]

ROBERT S. THOMAS

MOUNDS AND MOUND BUILDERS, terms used to designate, respectively, the numerous ancient artificial structures of earth and stone widely scattered over the eastern United States and the primitive peoples responsible for their construction.

What may be termed the General Mound Area corresponds approximately to the basins of the Mississippi and its tributaries, particularly those to the east, and the Gulf and southeastern seaboard regions. There are few major remains east of the Appalachians, from the Carolinas northward through New England.

In its broader interpretation the word "mounds" comprises all major remains of prehistoric man within the area: conical mounds, truncated temple mounds, effigy and linear mounds, defensive earthworks, geometric enclosures, and shell heaps. Conical mounds are artificial hillocks of earth, earth and stone, and, occasionally, stone only, and more or less conical in form; in height they range from almost imperceptible elevation to 70 feet. They occur generally throughout the mound area and were intended mainly as places of interment and as monuments to the dead. Two striking examples of conical mounds are the Grave Creek Mound in Marshall County, W. Va., and the Miamisburg Mound in Montgomery County, Ohio, each of which is a trifle short of 70 feet in height.

Truncated mounds occur mostly in the lower Mississippi Valley. Most are quadrangular flat-topped pyramids, which served as bases or platforms for sacred and domiciliary structures. Surprisingly, the greatest of the truncated mounds lies near the northern limit of their occurrence—the great Monks Mound, the third largest mound in the New World, near East Saint Louis, Ill. This tumulus, one of more than eighty comprising the Cahokia group, is 100 feet high and covers 16 acres of ground.

The effigy mounds (so called because they are built in the images of animals, birds, and men) and the associated linear mounds center in southern Wisconsin and adjacent parts of Iowa, Minnesota, and Illinois. Within this area are numerous examples, occurring both singly and in groups, particularly in and adjacent to the city of Madison, Wis. The greatest of the effigy mounds, however, is the Serpent Mound, in Adams

County, Ohio. This effigy, following the sinuous coils of the serpent, measures 1,330 feet in length. It is supposed that the effigy mounds were adjuncts of the religious observances of their builders.

The defensive earthworks, or fortifications, usually occupy the more or less level tops of isolated hills and consist of walls of earth and stone following the outer circumferences of such areas, supplementing the natural barriers against intrusion. The walls were usually fortified by means of pointed upright stakes or pickets. They are of general occurrence, having their greatest development in southern Ohio, where Fort Ancient, in Warren County, is the most striking example.

Geometric enclosures, as contrasted to the defensive works, invariably occur in level valley situations, without consideration of defensive factors, and are strictly adjuncts of the Hopewell culture of southern Ohio and adjacent regions. They are usually low walls of earth, in the form of circles, squares, octagons, and parallel walls, occurring singly or in combination. Their function apparently was social and ceremonial, rather than defensive. Examples are the Hopewell, Mound City, and Seip groups, in Ross County, Ohio; and the Newark Works, at Newark, Ohio.

Shell mounds are accumulations of shells of both marine and fresh-water mollusks, and are incidental to the use of these as food. They occur to some extent adjacent to inland streams, but mainly along the Atlantic tidewater, particularly in Florida, and often are of great extent. Other major fixed remains of aboriginal occupancy are village sites, cemeteries, and flint quarries, occurring generally throughout the area.

Builders of the ancient mounds were once thought to have been a separate and distinct race of people, but archaeological investigations have demonstrated that they were members of the single great race to which the Aztec, Maya, and Inca and others of the native stocks pertained. While some of the cultures of mound-building peoples cannot be directly identified with historic tribes and nations, it is probable that for the most part they were the ancestors of Indian nations living in the same general area at the time of the discovery of America. It is further probable that the Creek, Choctaw, and Natchez to the south, the Cherokee and Shawnee in the Ohio Valley, and the Winnebago and some others of the Siouan family, at some time and to some extent, were builders of mounds. Hernando De Soto and other explorers of the 16th

century found certain tribes in the South using, if not actually building, mounds. The occasional occurrence of objects of European manufacture as original inclusions in mounds toward the southeast and to the west of the Great Lakes indicates a limited survival of the trait in early Columbian times, but mound building had for the most part disappeared by that time.

Since mounds and their builders antedate the historic period of America, their age must be established by the radiocarbon dating technique and other techniques independent of the historical record. The shell mounds in general date to the Archaic period—in particular the middle and late Archaic period, between 5000 B.C. and 1000 B.C. Earthworks and burial mounds were both constructed from shortly before 1000 B.C. to the historic period. Temple mounds were built beginning about A.D. 700. While the mound-building peoples were still in the Stone Age era, certain of them had achieved a considerable degree of advancement. Copper was hammered into implements and ornaments; very creditable potteryware was made; and woven fabric of several types was produced. In the lower Mississippi Valley and to an even greater extent in the Ohio Valley, a surprising artistic development, in the form of conventional design and small sculptures in the round, probably was not surpassed by any people in a similar stage of development.

[Henry Clyde Shetrone, *The Mound Builders.*]
HENRY C. SHETRONE

MOUNTAIN MEADOWS MASSACRE occurred in southern Utah in September 1857. In the summer of that year, two companies of emigrants, one from Arkansas and the other from Missouri, passed through Salt Lake City, Utah, on their way to California. In southern Utah, as they reached the country beyond the fringe of settlement, the Missouri company was attacked by the Indians and was saved by the help of the Mormon militia. This company reached the Pacific coast in safety. The Arkansas company met with a terrible fate. It numbered thirty families, a total of 137 persons, including a lawless band known as the Missouri Wildcats. At a point forty miles from Cedar City, a party of Indians and a few white men, led by John D. Lee, a farmer, attacked the company, and all were massacred except seventeen children, who were spared. It was primarily an Indian outbreak, and was due to the insolent and lawless conduct of certain members of the emigrant party. Gov. Brigham Young had admonished his people to allow all emigrants to pass through the territory unmolested, to furnish them food when necessary, and to protect them from the Indians. John D. Lee was later executed for the crime on the spot where it was committed.

[H. H. Bancroft, *History of Utah*.]

L. E. YOUNG

MOUNTAIN MEN, the pioneers of the Rocky Mountain West, came first as fur trappers, lured to the West by beaver as these animals were lured to traps by castor bait. With virgin streams producing the prize catches, trail blazing was rewarded, and the trappers thus became the explorers of the Far West. Frenchmen, the most experienced fur gatherers, mingled with Americans and Spaniards at Saint Louis in the first decades of the 19th century and made this the great western emporium of the fur trade. Trapping parties and trading company caravans laden with supplies and Indian goods for the mountain trade left from Saint Louis. A season or two of trapping and the adventurer boasted the sobriquet of "mountain man."

Trapper life held an irresistible appeal to a variety of men—to the restless and daring it offered adventure; to the homeless, a home; to the lawless, an asylum. Wedded to the wilds and usually to the Indian, the mountain man became a recognizable type. The mixed racial strains produced a polyglot jargon, spiced with metaphor and figure, and known as mountain talk. Mingling with the Indian, he adopted the aborigine's manner of life, his food, shelter, morals, and frequently his superstitions. He took on the Indian love of adornment, bedecking himself in moccasins and fringed buckskin suit, adorned with dyed porcupine quills or colored glass beads. An Indian buffalo skin lodge provided winter shelter. His rifle, steel traps, skinning knife, and horse made him independent and free. Jim Bridger, Christopher ("Kit") Carson, Thomas Fitzpatrick, and Bill Williams were examples of the fraternity. There were three classes: the hired trapper, paid annual wages by a fur company; the skin trapper who dealt with one company only; and the free trapper, who trapped and disposed of his furs when and where he pleased.

The summer rendezvous at Green River, Wyo., or other appointed mountain valley, became the most interesting and typical institution of fur trade days. White trappers and Indians gathered there. Fur companies from Missouri brought out their supplies and trade goods, and barter flourished. With drinking, gambling, racing, and contests of skill the mountain man had a holiday. His regular meat diet was now varied by limited supplies of flour, coffee, and similar luxuries from the "states." In a few days of prodigal living he frequently spent his year's earnings (*see* Trappers' Rendezvous).

With the introduction of the silk hat and the consequent decline in beaver skin prices, from six or eight dollars apiece to two dollars or less, the mountain man forsook his traps and began to trade with the Indian. Buffalo robes replaced beaver pelts, and the trading post supplanted the rendezvous. With the coming of emigrant homeseekers and government exploring and military expeditions, the trapper-trader became scout and guide to lead newcomers over the paths he broke. Advancing civilization "rubbed out" the mountain man.

[LeRoy R. Hafen, *The Mountain Men and the Fur Trade of the Far West;* Carl P. Russell, *Firearms, Traps, and Tools of the Mountain Men*.]

LEROY R. HAFEN

MOUNT DESERT, an island off northeastern Maine with an area of about 100 square miles, was called Pemetic by the Indians. It was named by Samuel de Champlain in 1604 while he was exploring the Maine coast. Jesuit missionaries arrived about 1611 and established a small settlement, which was wiped out in 1613 by a raid of Virginia colonists. The French relinquished claim to the island in 1713, and during the next few decades the island changed hands frequently. In 1762 it was given outright to Sir Francis Bernard in return for services rendered the crown as governor of Massachusetts.

The island's beauty began to attract summer vacationers in 1855; steamboat service from Boston was established in 1868. Lafayette National Park was established on the island in 1919, and in 1929 the name of the park was changed to Acadia National Park (41,642 acres). Mount Cadillac on the island is the highest elevation (1,530 feet) on the East Coast of the United States. The population of the town of Mount Desert in 1970 was 1,659.

[Samuel Eliot Morison, *The Story of Mount Desert Island*.]

ELIZABETH RING

MOUNT HOPE, a hill in the present town of Bristol, R.I., was, in 1676, in the colony of Plymouth. It was the home of the Wampanoag sachem Metacom (King

Philip), the leading spirit in King Philip's War. Metacom was slain in a swamp at the west foot of the hill on Aug. 12, 1676. His spring and "stone seat" are on the east side of the hill.

[W. H. Munro, *The History of Bristol, R.I.*]
HOWARD M. CHAPIN

MOUNT VERNON, the home of George Washington, is situated on the south bank of the Potomac River, near Alexandria, Va. The Washington family acquired title to Mount Vernon by division of a 5,000-acre grant in 1690. The central part of the existing house was built about 1743 for Lawrence Washington, half-brother of George Washington. Lawrence died in 1752 and the property passed to George Washington a short time later.

In 1759 Washington and his wife Martha established their household at Mount Vernon. Here Washington lived the peaceful life of a southern planter until the outbreak of the Revolution. At the close of the war he returned to his home and completed improvements that had been started under his own supervision in 1773 and carried forward by his manager during his absence. Buildings, gardens, and grounds were developed substantially to their present form and extent during this period. The wood mansion and thirteen subsidiary structures have survived. Several others have been reconstructed. Together they constitute one of the best remaining examples of the plantations around which centered the highly developed social and economic life of the South in the 18th century.

Washington retired from public life at the close of his presidency in 1797 and again returned to Mount Vernon. Here he died on Dec. 14, 1799; here he was buried. Martha Washington died in 1802 and was interred with him in the family vault.

Mount Vernon has been restored and is maintained by the Mount Vernon Ladies' Association, an organization founded by Ann Pamela Cunningham of South Carolina in 1856. The property was acquired from the last private owner, Col. John Augustine Washington, in 1858.

[Paul Wilstach, *Mount Vernon, Washington's Home and the Nation's Shrine.*]
CHARLES C. WALL

MOUNT WASHINGTON, EARLY EXPLORATION OF. The first white man to explore Mount Washington, the chief eminence of the White Mountains in northern New Hampshire, was Darby Field.

In June 1642, accompanied by two Indians, he reached its summit; later that summer with a small party of white men he made the ascent again. The White Mountains were first mentioned in print in John Josselyn's *New England's Rarities Discovered* (1672). In the later colonial period Mount Washington was occasionally ascended by ranging parties, as in April 1725 and in March 1746. Careful exploration did not take place until after the Revolution. In July 1784 a party that included the clergymen Manasseh Cutler and Jeremy Belknap climbed the mountain and gave it the name it now bears. Cutler ascended the peak again in 1804; and in Belknap's third volume of his monumental *History of New Hampshire* (1812) the name "Mount Washington" was formally recognized.

[Thomas Starr King, *The White Hills.*]
JAMES DUANE SQUIRES

MOUNT WILSON AND PALOMAR OBSERVATORIES. *See* **Hale Observatories.**

MOURNERS' BENCH stood at the emotional center of the backwoods religious revival: in the open space between pulpit and audience. It varied from the rude seat of unplaned boards used in remote schoolhouses to a varnished bench in the town churches. Before it kneeled the repentant seeking salvation; around it grouped exhorters and evangelist to counsel and pray with the contrite.

GENE GEER

MOURT'S RELATION, printed in London in 1622, a valuable source of information on the Pilgrims' first months in America, was naively propagandist as it described the "safe arival" of these "English Planters" and their "joyfull building of . . . the now well defended Towne of New Plimoth." G. Mourt, signer of the recommendatory preface, is identified as George Morton, who settled in Plymouth in 1623. William Bradford and Edward Winslow generally have been considered the chief authors of the book.

[H. M. Dexter, ed., *Mourt's Relation.*]
LOUISE B. DUNBAR

MOVERS. After the Civil War (about 1870) a great migration into the trans-Missouri region began and continued, with intermittent lulls and temporary retrogressions, into the beginning of the 20th century. A canvas-covered farm wagon carried the belongings of the "mover," consisting of a few articles of furniture, cooking utensils, and a scanty supply of farming equipment. Perhaps a plow, spades, a coop of chickens, or a beehive adorned the outside of the overloaded vehicle. Not infrequently the mother drove the team and rode in the wagon while the father and the children drove the loose livestock. The family dog trotted contentedly under the wagon or helped drive the stock. The large amount of food prepared before leaving the old home was supplemented by that prepared around the campfire. The cows were milked and butter was sometimes churned by hanging a can of cream on the jolting wagon. Winter movers built a wooden frame on the wagon and kept a stove inside to make the occupants cozy. Sometimes the wife drove a buggy, and one or more wagons were driven by the men. Often movers would make two or three such pilgrimages to successive frontiers in a career.

[Everett Dick, *The Sod-House Frontier*.]

EVERETT DICK

MOVIES. *See* **Motion Pictures.**

MOWING MACHINE. As late as 1840 practically all the hay crop in the United States was still being harvested with the scythe. The reapers offered to the American farmer in the 1830's by Obed Hussey and Cyrus Hall McCormick could be used as mowers by removing the platform at the rear of the cutter bar on which the wheat fell. The hay fell behind, to be raked up after the machine had passed. The use of the reaper as a mower was unsatisfactory, for such machines could operate only on comparatively level fields and not on the uneven pastures and uplands where hay was often grown. In 1856 Cyrenus Wheeler put on the market a two-wheeled mower with a hinged cutter bar that could operate on rough and uneven ground. By 1860 several machines were manufactured that did not differ essentially from the mowers in use today. The hand rake disappeared along with the scythe. As early as 1812 wooden horse-drawn rakes were in use in the East. The invention of the mowing machine hastened this development. In the Middle West the enclosure of the prairie pastures and the sowing of part of them to cultivated grasses increased the forage crops of that region enormously.

[P. W. Bidwell and J. I. Falconer, *History of American Agriculture in the Northern United States, 1620-1860*.]

ERNEST S. OSGOOD

MOYNIHAN REPORT. *The Negro Family: The Case for National Action,* written by Assistant Secretary of Labor Daniel P. Moynihan, attempted to define the plight of black Americans in 1965. Intended as a prelude to formulating national policy, it provoked a bitter controversy instead, especially concerning the alleged deterioration of the black family.

[Lee Rainwater and William L. Yancey, *The Moynihan Report and the Politics of Controversy*.]

JOSEPH E. ILLICK

MRS. O'LEARY'S COW. According to popular legend the great Chicago fire of Oct. 8-9, 1871, started at Jefferson and DeKoven streets when Mrs. O'Leary went to the stable to visit the family cow and the cow inconsiderately upset the lamp she was carrying. No one really knows how the fire started (Mrs. O'Leary herself flatly denied the cow story) but the verdict of *vox populi* is firmly rooted in the public mind.

M. M. QUAIFE

MUCKRAKERS, a group of young reformers who, through novels and popular magazine articles, laid bare the abuses that had crept into American political, social, and economic life. The era of the muckrakers began in 1903 with the publication of Lincoln Steffens' "The Shame of the Cities" and Ida M. Tarbell's "History of the Standard Oil Company" in *McClure's Magazine*. These were followed by numerous other articles, delving into every phase of American life—the most important of which were Ray Stannard Baker's "The Railroads on Trial" (*McClure's*, 1905–06), Thomas W. Lawson's "Frenzied Finance" (*Everybody's*, 1905–06), and David Graham Phillips' "The Treason of the Senate" (*Cosmopolitan*, 1906–07). *Collier's* exposed food adulteration, traffic in women and children, and fraudulent advertising of patent medicines. Of the novelists, the most important was Upton Sinclair who, in *The Jungle* (1906), revealed the unsavory conditions in the packing plants of Chicago. Although the authors were specific in their charges, no major suit was ever entered.

An irresponsible host of sensation mongers was soon attracted and a reaction threatened that would have hindered reform. President Theodore Roosevelt, thoroughly annoyed, in two addresses (Mar. 17 and Apr. 14, 1906), likened the authors of the exposure literature to the man with the rake in John Bunyan's *Pilgrim's Progress,* who was more interested in the filth on the floor than in a celestial crown, and referred to them as "muckrakers." He declared that the time had come to cease exposure for its own sake and to turn to constructive reform. In 1909 muckraking attached itself to the Progressive movement. The muckrakers, primarily responsible for most of the progressive legislation of the period, passed into oblivion after 1912.

[Roy Stannard Baker, *An American Chronicle;* David Mark Chalmers, *The Social and Political Ideas of the Muckrakers.*]

RAYMOND C. WERNER

"MUD MARCH" (January 1863). After his bloody repulse at Fredericksburg, Va., Union Gen. A. E. Burnside planned to move his army across the Rappahannock River and seize positions behind Gen. Robert E. Lee's left flank. Union Gen. William B. Franklin's two corps, followed by two under Gen. Joseph Hooker, marched on Jan. 20 and bivouacked near Banks' Ford. That night a torrential rain began and continued for days. Pontoon wagons, artillery, trains, in fact the whole army, were mired down in the soft clay soil. Lee scarcely needed to move a soldier; the Union offensive was defeated by the mud. On Jan. 21 Burnside's army returned to Falmouth.

[R. U. Johnson and C. C. Buel, eds., *Battles and Leaders of the Civil War.*]

JOSEPH MILLS HANSON

MUGLER V. KANSAS, 123 U.S. 623 (1887). Kansas had passed an act in 1881, under its police power, that forbade the manufacture and sale, except for medicinal purposes, of all intoxicating liquors. Mugler was convicted under this act of selling beer. In his defense, it was argued that since he had invested his money in a brewing business, and had done so with the sanction and under the authority of the state government, he could not be denied the right to continue the operation of his business. To require such discontinuance, it was contended, would be to deprive him of his property without due process of law. The Supreme Court refused to accept this position. The decision established the principle that those who choose to engage in a business that is, or that may come to be, regarded as objectionable have no redress if at some future time the public decides that its discontinuance is desirable. Thus the right of the public to protection takes precedence over the property-owning right of the individual.

[C. K. Burdick, *The Law of the American Constitution;* Ernst Freund, *The Police Power;* Rodney L. Mott, *Due Process of Law.*]

W. BROOKE GRAVES

MUGWUMPS, one of many derisive terms applied to those liberal, or independent, Republicans who bolted the party ticket in the presidential campaign of 1884 to support actively the candidacy of Grover Cleveland. They held one national and many regional meetings and were credited with being a strong factor in the defeat of James G. Blaine.

[E. E. Sparks, *National Development.*]

ASA E. MARTIN

MULCT LAW was a form of local option adopted in Iowa in 1894. Statewide prohibition, existing since 1884, had met strong opposition in some counties. A compromise resulted by which the prohibitory law was retained, but provision was made for an annual mulct tax of $600 to be paid by all persons selling intoxicating liquor. The payment of this tax was a bar to prosecution for the sale of liquor in municipalities in which a statement of consent had been signed by a majority of the voters. For a municipality of fewer than 5,000 inhabitants, the signatures of a majority of the voters in the township and of 65 percent of the voters in the county outside cities of 5,000 or over had to be secured. Municipal authorities might add license fees and make additional regulations. The mulct law was repealed in 1915, and on Jan. 1, 1916, prohibition again went into effect throughout Iowa.

[Dan E. Clark, "The History of Liquor Legislation in Iowa," *The Iowa Journal of History and Politics,* vols. 6 and 15.]

RUTH A. GALLAHER

MULE. Introduced into the colonies from Spain, the mule—hybrid offspring of a jackass and a mare—became important in America in 1785, when George Washington received first an Andalusian jack and jennets from the king of Spain, and, shortly after, a similar Maltese group from Marie Joseph du Motier, the Marquis de Lafayette. By crossing the two breeds Washington secured a mule stock that found ready favor with fellow planters. Another center of origin was in Kentucky, where Henry Clay and other leading stockmen imported asses—including the famous jack "Warrior"—from the two main sources. The mule proved particularly adapted to plantation needs and by 1860 nine-tenths were in the plantation region, with the source of supply in the Ohio Valley. Mules were extensively used in the Civil War in the supply trains, and from that time the ''army mule'' has become proverbial. Mules have been classified according to the main uses to which they have been put; the most common are draft, farm, sugar, cotton, and mining mules. Extensive breeding developed only since the 1880's and centered in the Southwest. As mechanization grew, the demand for mules decreased, and there were less than a quarter as many mules in the United States in 1970 as in 1930.

[C. S. Plumb, *Types and Breeds of Farm Animals;* Harvey Riley, *The Mule.*]

EARLE D. ROSS

MULE SKINNER (or mule driver) and his complement the bullwhacker (freighter with oxen) flourished during the 1850's and through the 1870's, when millions of tons of freight were being pulled by mules and oxen across the Great Plains. In the early 1860's the great firm of Russell, Majors and Waddell operated 6,250 wagons and 75,000 oxen pulling freight west of the Missouri River. Mules and mule skinners were probably as numerous as oxen and bullwhackers at that time. The mule skinner used a long whip with which he could, aided by ''language,'' take the skin off a mule.

[W. F. Hooker, *The Bullwhacker.*]

J. FRANK DOBIE

MULLAN TRAIL, one of the most important wagon trails of the Pacific Northwest. It was 624 miles long, from the head of navigation of the Missouri River (Fort Benton, Mont.) to Walla Walla, Wash. It was built largely for military purposes, but played an important part in opening the Montana mines. Lt. John Mullan directed the building of the trail. Work started at Walla Walla, July 1, 1859, and the trail reached Fort Benton in 1860. Work during the summers of 1861 and 1862 made it a passable pioneer road.

[George W. Fuller, *A History of the Pacific Northwest.*]
ROBERT MOULTON GATKE

MULLIGAN LETTERS, letters written by James G. Blaine during the years 1864–76 to Warren Fisher, Jr., a businessman of Boston that indicated Blaine had used his official power as speaker of the House of Representatives to promote the fortunes of the Little Rock and Fort Smith Railroad. On May 31, 1876,

James Mulligan, an employee of Fisher, testified before a committee of Congress that he had such letters in his possession. On motion of a member of the committee, who pleaded illness, the committee immediately adjourned. That afternoon Blaine obtained possession of the letters, promising to return them. On June 5 he read the letters on the floor of the House and defended himself. Friends of Blaine claimed a complete vindication. Eight years later, when he was the Republican candidate for the presidency, the letters were published and were probably an important factor in his defeat.

[D. S. Muzzey, *James G. Blaine.*]
J. HARLEY NICHOLS

MUNFORDVILLE, CAPTURE OF. Early in the Civil War a Union earthwork was built on a hill near Munfordville, Ky., to guard the important railroad bridge of the Louisville and Nashville Railroad across Green River. When the Confederate army under Gen. Braxton Bragg invaded Kentucky in September 1862, this fort's garrison of about 3,600 men held out for three days (Sept. 14–17) against the attacks of a considerable portion of Bragg's force, finally surrendering on the afternoon of Sept. 17 (*see* Kentucky, Invasion of).

[R. U. Johnson and C. C. Buel, eds., *Battles and Leaders of the Civil War.*]
ALVIN F. HARLOW

MUNICIPAL GOVERNMENT refers to the governmental structure, powers, and processes of incorporated local governments—primarily cities—in the United States. The governmental structure of municipalities was adopted from English models introduced in the colonial period. Councillors and aldermen were chosen by the electorate and performed legislative functions, and a mayor was appointed by the colonial governor to serve in an executive capacity.

The American Revolution and the U.S. Constitution each modified the system somewhat. In some cities mayors were directly elected and gradually received significant appointment and veto powers, while in others the chief executive was selected by the city council and had few formal powers. Councils in the large cities followed state and federal practice and were bicameral throughout much of the 19th century. Jacksonian Democracy in the 1830's and 1840's encouraged a proliferation of directly elected administrators in municipalities and a resultant weakening of the mayor's position. There was also widespread use of appointed boards of citizens to oversee major administrative responsibilities in the 19th century. Structural reforms at the end of the century led to unicameral city councils and the strengthening of the office of mayor through greater powers of appointment. Many of these reforms were limited to large cities, and a number of smaller communities continued to have a relatively weak mayor but a unicameral council.

In the 20th century, structural reforms have centered on medium- and small-sized cities. The major movement has been toward council-manager government, with movement in a few cities toward commission government. The major characteristics of council-manager government are a nonpartisan council elected at large, a mayor selected from the council with relatively few formal powers, and a professional manager hired by the council to perform executive and administrative functions. In commission government, executive and legislative functions are merged in the commission, whose members act individually as administrators and collectively as legislators. Further reform of the mayor-council form in larger cities has strengthened the hand of the mayor by permitting him to hire professional administrative help.

The powers of municipal governments have traditionally been a matter of great debate. In both England and the United States, the very existence of the municipal corporation has presupposed some inherent local governmental powers. The powers of the municipality have, in fact, always depended heavily on a grant from the chartering authority. Colonial American cities drew their powers from the colony, which in turn received its grant from the crown. When states replaced colonies in postrevolutionary America, they became the source of municipal charters and, therefore, the source of much of the power exercised by municipal governments. In the late 18th and early 19th centuries, most cities received individually tailored special charters from the state. By the end of the 19th century, states had rejected this practice in favor of general charter laws that applied, with some exceptions, to all municipalities. The 20th century has seen a move toward home rule charters that in theory emphasize the autonomy of the cities but in fact grant flexibility primarily with respect to governmental structure.

The debate over the significance of municipal governments has continued unabated into the last half of the 20th century. Those who have watched the rapid growth of the national government and its concern for urban problems and who have stressed the absolute discretion of the states in granting and withholding power from municipalities have insisted that municipal government is of decreasing importance. However, municipal governments have proven to be surprisingly durable. As staunch defenders of local self-government, they have modified unfavorable state policies and encouraged the introduction of requirements for municipal participation in federal urban programs.

Although municipal reform and home rule have introduced greater variety in the structures of municipal governments and the powers of these governments remain ill-defined, municipal governments have maintained their historic position at the heart of the American political process.

[John H. Baker, *Urban Politics in America;* Jewell Cass Phillips, *Municipal Government and Administration in America.*]

JOHN H. BAKER

MUNICIPAL OWNERSHIP. In the years of greatest public concern, 1898–1913, the term ''municipal ownership'' was primarily associated with the provision of water, gas, electricity, and transit. Also, even in earlier years, cities occasionally operated markets, harbor facilities, and ferries.

During the 19th century all cities coveted the services of utilities. Because financial risks were involved in private development, an eager city was usually ready to grant promoters liberal franchises. When profits mounted, competing companies were extended similar favors.

Yet a utility is inherently a monopoly, and by 1900 it was clear that the ethics of competition were not the answer to the problems inherent in monopolies. The needs of the public were ignored as streets were torn up indiscriminately. The profits of trolley companies, for example, often came as much from land speculation and the issuance of watered securities as from actual operations, even as operational profits were enhanced by rapidly improving technology. As a by-product, corrupt deals between utility companies and political bosses and political machines had become the order of the day.

Thus, the stage was set for the issues of the Progressive era. Lincoln Steffens and others relentlessly exposed utility machinations in city after city. Local leaders, following the example set by Hazen Pingree of Detroit in the early 1890's, took up the reform battle. To many crusaders municipal ownership seemed the only answer—bypassing the corruption, the inordinate profits, the high rates, and the poor service. European examples of success were cited. Despite the agitation, increases in municipal ownership of public utilities were unimpressive. Its existing trend toward municipally owned waterworks was given some momentum. The initial tendency of the small towns west of the Alleghenies to opt for municipal ownership of electric light and power, as well as of water, was strengthened, but only a few cities took over municipal street lighting, and still fewer, private power plants. In 1912 San Francisco adopted the goal of municipalization of its trolleys, and in 1919 the first fully municipalized trolley system was completed in Seattle. Lest the work of the progressive reformers of the day be regarded as largely futile, it should be noted that corruption by the private utilities was lessened, rates were reduced, service was improved, and yardsticks were provided. Regulation by the states emerged as the eventual answer.

The trend toward municipal ownership of waterworks continued gradually in the 20th century, as it had before—based as it was on the visible practical failures of private ownership: insufficient water for firefighting, for example, and impure water for domestic use. The need to seek supplies outside the municipality proper was an additional factor, manifested in the Boston area, for example, by a multiplicity of independent jurisdictions. In 1895 the state of Massachusetts established a metropolitan water district, which gave a central supply source, each community providing its own pipe system. By 1897, 41 of the 50 largest cities had publicly owned systems, as did 100 of the 142 cities with populations between 30,000 and 100,000. By 1968, 40 of the 43 largest cities had publicly operated waterworks.

The course of public ownership of gas and electric plants was quite different. Municipally owned electric plants were numerous, but mostly in smaller cities or for street lighting only. Yet, in spite of a continuous barrage of statistics on comparative rates, by 1968 only six of the forty-three largest cities operated electric utilities and only three used municipal gas. Priorities granted to publicly owned power plants by federal installations, such as those of the Tennessee Valley Authority and the great dams of the West, gave them some stimulus.

Problems in commuter transport across city boundaries were foreshadowed as early as the turn of the century in New York and Boston, both of which adopted a policy of public financing and private leasing for their subways. And it has since been demonstrated that in the largest communities only the metropolitan

area has been adequate to deal with the problems of mass transit, whether under public or private ownership. For example, the Washington area public transportation system requires the cooperation of the District of Columbia, the states of Maryland and Virginia, and the units of local government; and a major federal subsidy was a prerequisite.

There was a mid-20th-century increase in publicly owned transportation systems as a by-product of the financial difficulties that the private systems encountered because of the advent and growth of automobile use. By 1970 the publicly or privately operated bus had all but superseded the trolley. While the private systems, however precarious their finances, were still more numerous, the trend was toward city, county, or regional transit authorities. Public and private transit authorities alike increasingly faced the necessity of taxpayer subsidy. In New York City, by 1974 this subsidy (federal, state, and municipal) grew to 50 percent of the costs. These costs had almost doubled since 1970, while the receipts from fares had stabilized at slightly over $500 million. In 1975 fares were increased, and certain revenue-producing activities had been transferred from the Port Authority of New York and New Jersey, but a deficit was still anticipated. The spectacular new rapid-transit system of the San Francisco area was made possible only by a major federal grant. In 1975 fares were increased on this system, too; the system was incomplete; and its future was uncertain.

Both public and private rapid-transit systems were facing operating deficits in the 1970's. In 1963 these amounted to only $880,000. By 1973, according to the American Transit Association, their total revenues, which amounted to $1.8 billion, still left a deficit of $681 million. In fiscal year 1974 the federal government was bearing 80 percent of the cost of the public construction it approved.

Private commercial and public municipal efforts both figure in the early stages of airports, but national planning and subsidies soon gave preference to the governmental units. Predominantly urban counties and special districts as well as cities shared the responsibilities.

The most controversial development has been municipally constructed and owned housing. The three major stimuli were the depression of the 1930's, World War II, and the Great Society programs of President Lyndon B. Johnson's administration. In the depression some subsidized low-rent public housing took place under "local housing authorities." During and after World War II housing shortages were such that the federal government had to subsidize and build houses as a defense measure, utilizing numerous public, private, and nonprofit agencies, including municipalities.

Eventually, at the instigation of both the states and the federal government, low-rent housing was explicitly linked with slum clearance and urban renewal. By 1964 this concept evolved into inclusive programs that might also include community facilities, transit, and streets. Federal subsidies direct to the local authorities were generous. By 1964 there were 1,454 such projects; of these 60 percent were either under construction or completed. The completed projects were, for the most part, modest ones, as to the size of the city and the funds committed. By 1975 the remaining ones were often in deep fiscal trouble.

Great Society policies accelerated a trend to join these ventures into municipal ownership with a number of costly further objectives that were admirable in themselves but created political and financial obstacles. "Equal opportunity" was one of these, and its racial overtones aroused much local opposition—especially acute in situations in which the central city, where the problems were, was hemmed in by a suburban ring often adamant against low-income housing projects within its borders. The use of union labor, a political requirement, drove up the costs of construction. Neighborhood participation in decisions introduced procedural delays. At the same time, many earlier housing projects were approaching bankruptcy: Saint Louis, for example, was forced to tear down much of its municipal housing. Rent collections or payments toward ownership fell into arrears.

High standards in facilities or amenities either brought costs out of the reach of the poor or required large subsidies from the taxpayers. The need to provide alternative housing for those displaced was obvious, but it created further delays. On the other hand, where local leadership was imaginative and adequate, as in New Haven, Conn., initial achievements in clearance and new low-cost homes (subsidized) were considerable. But the future course of municipal housing is uncertain, as one after another of the municipal projects has become insolvent, required increased subsidies, or (as in Saint Louis) been torn down.

[Charles R. Adrian and Ernest S. Griffith, *History of American City Government, 1775–1870;* Charles R. Adrian and Charles Press, *Governing Urban America;* Ernest S. Griffith, *History of American City Government, 1870–1900,* and *History of American City Government, 1900–1920;* U.S. Department of Housing and Urban Development, *Annual Reports;* U.S. Office of Economic Opportunity, *Catalog of Federal Assistance Programs.*]

ERNEST S. GRIFFITH

MUNICIPAL REFORM is a movement in American local government that has traditionally focused on achieving the goals of honesty in public officials and efficiency and economy in government. The movement has attempted to realize these goals by working for changes in local electoral systems and in the structure of municipal governments. No clear date can be established for the beginning of the campaign for municipal reform; the first efforts in this area probably occurred with the creation of formal municipal governments in the colonial period. Such governmental reform efforts have been tied closely to an ever-present dissatisfaction with policy decisions on the part of a dissident group in the community.

The municipal reform movement became clearly identifiable on a large scale at the close of the 19th century, when the corruption of machine-dominated big cities received publicity in the popular press. Reforms of the electoral system that involved nonpartisan elections and the at-large election of councilmen were designed to destroy the power of party machines. Most of the structural reform emphasized the introduction of professional management personnel in the executive branch of municipal government. The main thrust of this reform has been embodied in the campaign for council-manager government that was first suggested by Haven Mason in 1899 and was fully articulated by Richard Childs in the form adopted by Sumter, S.C., in 1912.

The council-manager plan continues to be the main focus of the municipal reform movement in the United States. This reform effort has been most successful in middle-sized cities, which are homogeneous enough to support nonpartisan and at-large electoral reforms but large enough to afford professional executives. Reform had touched large cities as well.

The council-manager type of government has led to the concentration of greater power in the executive. Large cities have also tended to reduce the number of executive offices and to concentrate power in the office of the mayor. In addition, the complexities of big city government have increased the need for professional managers in the executive branch, and these professionals have been hired as deputies or assistants to the elected mayor.

[Charles R. Adrian, *State and Local Governments;* John H. Baker, *Urban Politics in America;* Hugh L. LeBlanc and D. Trudeau Allensworth, *The Politics of States and Urban Communities.*]

JOHN H. BAKER

MUNITIONS. Derived from a Latin word meaning "fortification," "munitions" through long usage has come to mean, in a strict sense, weapons and ammunition, although broadly it embraces all war materials. "Ammunition" has the same derivation, but it has come to apply strictly to propellants, projectiles, and explosives. The broader term "munitions" takes on legal significance in neutrality legislation and embargoes and in definitions of contraband of war. But in the way of legal language it almost never stands alone. In treaties, legislative acts, and proclamations it usually forms part of a redundancy as "arms and munitions of war" or gives way to the synonymous triplet "arms, ammunition, or implements of war."

In March 1912 the attorney general issued a "practical working definition" of "arms or munitions of war" for the use of border officials in enforcing an embargo on such items to Mexico. His list included

> weapons of every species used for the destruction of life, and projectiles, cartridges, ammunition of all sorts, and other supplies used or useful in connection therewith, including parts used for the repair or manufacture of such arms, and raw material employed in the manufacture of such ammunition; also dynamite, nitroglycerin, or other explosive substances; also gun mountings, limber boxes, limbers, and military wagons; field forges and their component parts, comprising equipment of a distinctively military character; articles of camp equipment and their distinctive component parts; and implements manufactured exclusively for the manufacture of implements of war, or for the manufacture or repair of arms or war material.

President Franklin D. Roosevelt's list of items to be considered as arms, ammunition, and implements of war prohibited for export to belligerents under the Neutrality Act of 1935 included firearms, machine guns, artillery, bombs, torpedoes, mines, tanks, war vessels of all types, aircraft, aircraft engines and certain parts, and poison gas.

Development. During the American Revolution the colonial militia and Continental forces depended largely on British and European models of muskets and artillery, although some American innovations were already apparent. Perhaps the most important of these were rifles, usually referred to as Pennsylvania or Kentucky rifles. Made practical by the use of a greased patch that would permit muzzle loading with a tightly fitting ball down the grooved bore, these rifles, in the hands of frontiersmen, were far superior in range and accuracy to smooth-bore muskets. The principal artillery pieces of the period were cast-iron, bronze, and brass cannon, taking shot of 4, 9, 12, or 32 pounds—and thus known as 4-pounders, 9-pounders, and so on—and siege mortars.

The first major improvements in small arms after the Revolution and the War of 1812 were in breechloaders and repeaters. Although the first breech-loading rifle, the Hall, was adopted in 1819 and adjusted to percussion ammunition in 1833, the muzzle-loading musket remained the standard infantry arm in the U.S. Army until after the Mexican War, and muzzle loaders were still the chief arm during the opening phase of the Civil War.

One of the greatest advantages the Union infantry and cavalry had in the Civil War was in the quality and quantity of their repeating rifles and carbines, although these were slow in winning acceptance. At first, numbers of Springfield rifles were converted to breechloaders, which were still single-shot. But the spectacular success of Colt revolvers (pistols) in the Mexican War made nothing seem more reasonable than the development of a repeating rifle that operated on the same principle—that of using a rotating cylinder. The first repeating rifle, the Colt revolving rifle, was introduced in 1858. The missing link was the metallic cartridge, just being developed, for the paper cartridges might accidentally ignite in the cylinder, causing severe burns on the hands or face. The Sharps repeating rifle showed well in tests in 1860, but it still used paper cartridges. The best of the newer models were the fifteen-shot Henry and the seven-shot Spencer—"the seven-forked lightning"—which had a great impact on the last year of the war.

Even after the demonstrated success of repeating rifles in the Civil War, U.S. soldiers were still carrying single-shot Springfields twenty-five years later. The Winchester model of 1873 became famous throughout the West and was used by everyone except the army. Other models by Remington and by the Springfield Armory were tested but not accepted. The Winchester Company was so discouraged by government policies that it did not even enter the competition in 1890, when a repeating rifle was accepted at last. This was the Danish-designed Krag-Jörgensen magazine rifle, which became the standard shoulder weapon of U.S. forces in the Spanish-American War.

The all-time favorite U.S. rifle among marksmen was the .30-caliber Springfield Model 1903, but it found only slight use in World War I, when the U.S. Army mainly used an adaptation of the British Enfield in the interest of making maximum use of industrial capacity. During World War II and the Korean War, the eight-shot Garand, or M-1, a semiautomatic rifle that was not as accurate as the 1903 but fired more rapidly and with less "kick," was the standard rifle. In Vietnam the M-16, a lighter rifle that used .22-

caliber ammunition, was favored. Ironically, the United States had adopted the M-14 rifle, which took the standardized NATO 7.62 mm (.30-caliber) cartridge, and then proceeded to go into mass production of the M-16.

Probably the most significant change in artillery during the period immediately preceding the Civil War was the adoption of the "Napoleon" gun in 1857. Introduced by Napoleon III in an effort to simplify his field artillery system with a single general-purpose weapon that could perform the functions of howitzers as well as guns and that, as a 12-pounder, would be efficient enough and maneuverable enough to reduce the need for other calibers, this smooth-bore bronze cannon had proved itself in the Crimean War. Its ammunition included solid shot, cannister, grape, explosive shell, spherical case, and carcass (incendiary).

Artillery improvements during the Civil War were mostly in the direction of greater size and strength and in the introduction of rifled cannon on a large scale. A process devised by Maj. Thomas J. Rodman for casting guns on a hollow core and cooling from the inside added considerable strength to the Dahlgren gun. Robert P. Parrott found that it was possible to add great strength to the breech of a gun—and so to its power and range—by encasing it with coiled wrought-iron hoops mounted red hot and then shrunk to a tight fit by cooling. Some of these guns were of tremendous size and strength. The "Swamp Angel" was a Parrott that hurled 200-pound shells more than four miles into Charleston, S.C. With one 4.2-inch (30-pounder), Parrott fired 4,605 rounds before the tube burst. At that time the greatest limitation on artillery was the lack of a good recoil mechanism.

That deficiency was overcome before World War I, the war of artillery par excellence. By far the best recoil system and "recuperators" were those on the French 75-millimeter gun the Allied forces used as their main field artillery weapon. This gun fired a 16-pound shell over a range of three miles at a rate of thirty rounds a minute. Many heavy guns were mounted on railroad cars for long-range bombardment. The American Expeditionary Force, while relying on the French for most of its artillery, did bring in a number of U.S. 14-inch naval guns for use in land warfare.

The other weapon that dominated the battlefield in World War I and remained prominent until after World War II was the machine gun, which had its beginning in the multibarreled Gatling gun of the Civil War. Hiram S. Maxim, an American inventor,

developed the first practical automatic machine gun. John M. Browning developed his recoil-operated machine gun in 1900, and in 1917 the U.S. Army adopted this "best of all machine guns"—a .30-caliber, recoil-operated, belt-fed, water-cooled, heavy weapon fired from a tripod mount. A version of this gun with an air-cooling jacket served as a light machine gun, but the favorite of this kind was the Browning automatic rifle, introduced near the end of World War I and widely used in World War II. The Browning rifle was a gas-operated, air-cooled, magazine-fed, shoulder weapon, with a cyclic rate of 550 rounds a minute, usually fired from a bipod. Turned down by the U.S. Army just before the outbreak of World War I, the Lewis light machine gun, fed from a revolving drum, came into widespread use in the British Army early in that war. It was widely used on airplanes and was adopted by the Marine Corps, but the U.S. Army never adopted it for general ground use.

Other important developments in munitions in World War I were the tank, the airplane, and poison gas. Both the tank and the plane were the results of American inventions, but both were slow to be adopted by the United States.

World War II was fought largely with the improved weapons of World War I. The numbers and effectiveness of tanks and airplanes—including especially the long-range heavy bombers—characterized the military operations of that war. Jet fighter planes had come into use by the time of the Korean War, and helicopters were being used for supply and medical evacuation. In Vietnam the jet bomber, the B-52, having a range of over 12,000 miles and carrying a weapons load of 75,000 pounds, was the chief instrument of heavy aerial bombing.

Naval vessels have gone through periods of swift change. Steam power came into use during the Mexican and Civil wars, and the ironclad was introduced during the Civil War. The "Great White Fleet" of U.S. armored cruisers and battleships impressed the world in the round-the-world cruise of the battle fleet in 1907–09. The 1906 British battleship *Dreadnought*, carrying ten 12-inch guns in center-line turrets and having a speed of 21 knots, established a new standard for battleships. This same period saw the conversion from coal to oil and the introduction of the steam turbine for the propulsion of vessels.

The greatest innovation of World War I in naval warfare was the widespread use of the submarine, which in World War II was a major weapon. Development has been continual and spectacular since the advent of nuclear propulsion gave submarines practically unlimited range. In the 1970's about 60 percent of the U.S. attack submarine fleet of over ninety vessels was nuclear-powered.

After World War I the aircraft carrier began to come into prominence. During World War II, battleships were used more for the support of landing operations than for direct ship-to-ship combat. By the end of the war the battleship had given way almost completely to the aircraft carrier. In the post–World War II period nuclear power came into use in the 76,000-ton supercarrier *Enterprise,* and in 1973 it was authorized for use in another supercarrier that would be the world's first billion-dollar weapon system.

The most spectacular development of all in munitions was the intercontinental ballistic missile with its nuclear warhead. The atomic bomb introduced near the close of World War II had a rating of 20 kilotons; that is, its explosive force was about the equivalent of 20,000 tons of TNT. In 1961 the Soviet Union deployed the SS-7 "Saddler" missile, said to have a warhead with a yield of 5 megatons, the equivalent of 5 million tons of TNT. The U.S. Titan, deployed a year later, was of equal or greater magnitude, but in 1965 the Soviets claimed their SS-9 "Scarp" had a warhead of 20 to 25 megatons. The race was on.

Manufacture. A major problem of public policy has always been the determination of what kind of industry should provide munitions of war and what measures should be instituted for encouragement, on the one hand, and control, on the other. Generally the assumption in the United States has been that the munitions industry should combine public and private ownership—that government armories and arsenals and shipyards should set standards of quality, provide experience for accurate pricing, and fill essential armaments needs for the peacetime military forces and that private contractors should provide most of the capacity and flexibility needed for war mobilization.

Most of the weapons used by American colonists in the colonial wars came from England; perhaps one-third were of domestic manufacture. Gunpowder mills were operating and cannons were being cast at several colonial foundries. These activities increased during the Revolution, but most munitions came from French and other European sources and from the raids of privateers against British ships.

After the Revolution, American leaders were anxious to free the country of dependence on Europe for the means of defense. Two men of genius, Alexander Hamilton and Eli Whitney, probably more than any other men, set the course for the national arms policy of the United States. In his report of 1783 on a military peace establishment, Hamilton urged the founding of "public manufactories of arms, powder, etc." In his celebrated report on manufactures eight years later the development of domestic industries for national security was once again a central theme. In 1794 Congress authorized the construction of some national armories, and four years later it authorized contracting for the private manufacture of arms. The site chosen for the first national armory was Springfield, Mass., and the site for the second, chosen by George Washington himself, was Harpers Ferry, Va., where the manufacture of muskets began in 1797.

Whitney's great contribution—a contribution indeed to the whole of American industry—was the manufacture of muskets with interchangeable parts. At his arms plant in New Haven, Conn., he was able to substitute machinery for much of the skill of individual gunsmiths, laying the basis for the system of mass production when he set to work on his first government contract in 1798.

One of the most important steps in the development of a domestic arms industry in the United States was the enactment in 1808 of a bill that provided for the appropriation of an annual sum of $200,000 "for the purpose of providing arms and military equipment for the whole body of the militia of the United States," either by purchase or by manufacture. Nineteen firms signed contracts to produce 85,200 muskets over a period of five years. None delivered satisfactorily on schedule, but the effort set a pattern for encouraging private arms manufacture over the next forty years. Six private armories enjoyed contract renewals until the late 1840's: Whitney, Lemuel Pomeroy of Pittsfield, Mass., and Asa Waters of Sutton, Mass., all of whom specialized in muskets; Henry Deringer of Philadelphia, who made small arms; Simeon North of Middletown, Conn., who specialized in pistols; and Nathan Starr, also of Middletown, who made swords.

The production of artillery was also on a more secure basis after the War of 1812. The West Point Foundry began to make cannon in 1816 under the direction of Gouverneur Kemble and quickly became the leading supplier of heavy ordnance. This and several other foundries were established and maintained on the basis of assurances of continued support from the government. While depending on them for guns, the government itself went into the business of constructing carriages, limbers, and caissons at arsenals in Washington, D.C.; Pittsburgh, Pa.; and Watervliet, N.Y.

The biggest single munitions contractor of the Civil War was Parrott (West Point Arms and Cannon Foundry), who was awarded 2,332 contracts with a total value of $4,733,059. Close behind was Samuel Colt's Patent Fire Arms Company at Hartford, Conn., which held 267 contracts for a total value of $4,687,031. No fewer than fifteen companies—including such names as J. T. Ames, Herman Baker and Company, Alfred Jenks and Son, Naylor and Company, E. Remington and Sons, Sharpe's Rifle Manufacturing Company, Starr Arms Company, and Spencer Arms Company—had contracts amounting to at least $1 million each. The old firm of Eli Whitney of Whitneyville was still in the picture, but only to the extent of $353,647. Private industry was the source of all the artillery (although carriages and caissons were made at the arsenals), all the gunpowder, and a large part of the small arms. The Springfield Armory turned out 802,000 rifled muskets, some of which used parts manufactured by private industry. Private arms makers produced 670,600 of these Springfield weapons. Other purchases, from domestic industry and from abroad, included nearly 1,225,000 muskets and rifles; over 400,000 carbines; and 372,800 revolvers.

With the advent of World War I, American leaders looked for every possible facility, government or private, that could be put to use. Not only were the government's arsenals and factories expanded, but vast new government-owned or government-financed plants were constructed. Probably the most ambitious, disappointing, dramatic, and controversial production story of the war was that of aircraft. And the brightest spot in that story was the development and production of the Liberty engine. Packard, Ford, General Motors (Buick and Cadillac), Nordyke and Marman, Willys-Overland, Olds, and Trego Motors shared in this mass-production effort. All of the difficulties of trying to start an aircraft industry practically from scratch appeared. In addition to the problems of finding aeronautical engineers, building factories, developing designs, and organizing production, serious shortages of materials had to be overcome. These steps included developing long-staple cotton cloth, used for covering the airplanes, to replace linen; developing a new dope for applying to the cloth for weatherproofing; cultivation of castor beans to supply the necessary lubricants until a satisfactory mineral oil could be developed; and increasing the supplies of spruce, the principal wood used in airframes. The Liberty engine was designed to incorporate all the best features of known engines in a way suited to mass production. Within less than six weeks after engineers began drawing plans in May 1917, the first working model of an eight-cylinder Liberty engine was delivered, and within another six weeks a twelve-cylinder model had completed its fifty-hour test. By August 1917 the Aircraft Production Board had placed contracts with Ford for 10,000 of the eight-cylinder engines, and with Packard for 22,500 of the twelve-cylinder. Total orders went above 64,000. Actual production to the date of the armistice amounted to 13,500, of which 4,400 were shipped overseas to the American Expeditionary Forces and 1,000 to the Allies.

Industrial mobilization and production of munitions during World War II generally followed the pattern of World War I, but on a vastly larger scale. The biggest and most complex single project of the war undoubtedly was the making of the atomic bomb. This was a $2.2 billion undertaking under the direction of the Manhattan Project of the Corps of Engineers. It involved the coordinated efforts of scientists, engineers, and laborers; of universities; and of industrial corporations. Secretary of War Henry L. Stimson called it "the greatest achievement of the combined efforts of science, industry, and the military in all history."

But production of war materials on a great scale has always brought questions about profiteering, corrupt bargains, the selling of influence, and the influence of special interests on national policy in a way that might be contrary to the national interest. Such serious charges have arisen in every war, and the seriousness tends to be proportional to the magnitude and duration of the war, although peacetime arms production may be no more free of such practices or suspicions.

One of the most dramatic appeals against the munitions makers as "merchants of death" came in 1935–36 with the hearings of the Senate's Special Committee Investigating the Munitions Industry, under the chairmanship of Sen. Gerald P. Nye of North Dakota. Although the committee failed to establish that munitions makers were a major cause of war, it probably fanned the flames of isolationist sentiment then rising in the country. This sentiment produced the arms embargo provisions in the neutrality acts of 1935, 1936, and 1937. Secretary of State Cordell Hull later wrote in his *Memoirs:* "It is doubtful that any Congressional committee has ever had a more unfortunate effect on our foreign relations, unless it be the Senate Foreign Relations Committee considering the Treaty of Versailles submitted by President Wilson.'' Others would minimize its influence on legislation.

In the ever-growing complexities of munitions manufacture since World War II, nagging questions remain about the extent to which companies dependent on government contracts for their very existence influence national security policy so as to retain, adopt, or emphasize certain weapon systems—whether aircraft, naval vessels, or missiles—in which they have a direct financial interest. President Dwight D. Eisenhower himself brought this question into focus when, in his farewell speech, he warned:

> In the councils of Government, we must guard against the acquisition of unwarranted influence, whether sought or unsought, by the military-industrial complex. The potential for the destructive use of misplaced power exists and will persist. . . . Only an alert and knowledgeable citizenry can compel the proper meshing of the huge industrial and military machinery of defense with our peaceful methods and goals, so that security and liberty may prosper together.

[Vannevar Bush, *Modern Arms and Free Men;* George M. Chinn, *The Machine Gun: History, Evolution, and Development of Manual, Automatic, and Airborne Repeating Weapons;* Wesley F. Craven and James L. Cate, eds., *The Army Air Forces in World War II,* vol. VI; J. G. W. Dillin, *The Kentucky Rifle;* Claud E. Fuller, *The Whitney Firearms;* James E. Hicks, *Notes on United States Ordnance;* Melvin M. Johnson, Jr., and Charles T. Haven, *Ammunition: Its History, Development and Use, 1600 to 1943;* Jeannette Mirsky and Allan Nevins, *The World of Eli Whitney;* Donald M. Nelson, *Arsenal of Democracy;* Charles W. Sawyer, *Firearms in American History;* Harold T. Williamson, *Winchester, The Gun That Won the West;* John E. Wiltz, *In Search of Peace: The Senate Munitions Inquiry, 1934–36.*]

JAMES A. HUSTON

MUNN V. ILLINOIS, 94 U.S. 113 (1877), one of the Granger cases, involved the validity of an Illinois law of 1871 that fixed maximum rates for the storage of grain. A Chicago warehouse firm, Munn and Scott, found guilty in 1872 of violating the law, appealed first to the state supreme court, where the decision of the lower court was affirmed, and then to the U.S. Supreme Court, which upheld the Illinois statute. To the argument that the fixing of maximum rates constituted a taking of property without due process of law, the Court replied that the warehouse business was sufficiently clothed with a public interest to justify public control; and to the argument that Congress alone had the right to regulate interstate commerce, of which the storage of grain was a part, the Court replied that until Congress made use of its power a state might act, ''even though in so doing it may indirectly operate upon commerce outside its jurisdiction.'' (*See Wabash, Saint Louis and Pacific Railroad* v. *Illinois.*)

[S. J. Buck, *The Granger Movement.*]
JOHN D. HICKS

MURCHISON LETTER. *See* **Sackville-West Incident.**

MURDERING TOWN, probably an Indian encampment, was located on Connoquenessing Creek, in Butler County, Pa. Both George Washington and Christopher Gist mention, in their diaries, passing the place Dec. 27, 1753, on their return from Fort Le-Boeuf. Some miles farther on an Indian from the encampment fired on Gist, who named it Murthering town.

[W. M. Darlington, ed., *Christopher Gist Journals;* J. C. Fitzpatrick, *The Diaries of George Washington.*]
ALFRED P. JAMES

MURFREESBORO, BATTLE OF (Dec. 31, 1862–Jan. 2, 1863). After the Battle of Perryville, Gen. Braxton Bragg withdrew his Confederates through eastern Tennessee. The Union Army of the Cumberland under Gen. William S. Rosecrans concentrated at Nashville. Both forces were reorganized and refitted during November and December, Bragg facing and annoying Rosecrans from Murfreesboro thirty miles away. After a five-day deployed advance Rosecrans confronted Bragg drawn up astride Stone River protecting Murfreesboro. Each general aimed against his enemy's right on Dec. 31. Bragg, striking first against the flank and rear of Gen. Alexander McDowell McCook's unready corps, would have won save for inspired resistance by Gen. Philip H. Sheridan's division and stern pertinacity by Gen. G. H. Thomas' (central) corps. Rosecrans' attack lagged. He recalled T. L. Crittenden's advancing (left) corps and hurried reinforcements to the Union right, which was bent back, repeatedly charged, dented, but not broken. By nightfall the two nearly equal armies had fought themselves into fatigue, with ground, spoils, and many prisoners in Confederate hands, and Rosecrans' Unionists clinging desperately to the Nashville pike and pinned against the river. For a full day the forces took breath as sporadic Confederate advances were checked. Instead of withdrawing his shaken army, Rosecrans was waiting for ammunition and moving one of Crittenden's divisions back across the river. On Jan. 2, Bragg sent nearly 10,000 men against Crittenden's division and broke it, but an insane counterattack made without orders by 1,500 Union troops from Indiana across the stream cracked the assault; sudden artillery concentration shattered it; and the battle stopped. Next day Bragg retreated toward Chattanooga.

[H. M. Cist, *Army of the Cumberland;* D. C. Seitz, *Braxton Bragg;* W. J. Vance, *Stone's River.*]

ELBRIDGE COLBY

MURMANSK. An ice-free Russian port on the Barents Sea, Murmansk became important in World War I with the completion by prisoner-of-war labor of a railway from there to Petrograd (later Leningrad). Uncertainties created by the 1917 Russian revolution induced the Allies to land a guard there to protect their stockpiles of military goods. In 1918 some 720 U.S. military engineers helped to improve and maintain the new railroad.

In World War II the "Murmansk run" was the bloodiest of routes for convoys delivering lend-lease supplies to the Soviet Union, whose naval and air forces did not provide adequate protection even in the harbor itself. The Soviets have tried to exculpate themselves of any responsibility for the fact that in July 1942 only thirteen of the thirty-six merchantmen in Convoy PQ 17 reached Murmansk.

R. W. DALY

MUSCLE SHOALS PROJECT. *See* **Tennessee Valley Authority.**

MUSCLE SHOALS SPECULATION is significant mainly as a spectacular, but characteristic, phenomenon of American frontier life in 1783–89, during the period of the Confederation. The Muscle Shoals region on the Tennessee River was then thought to have great potential value for the commerce of the westerners, since it might afford them an outlet via Mobile, Ala., at a time when Spain denied them the use of the Mississippi River (*see* Mississippi River, Free Navigation of). The project for establishing a colony at Muscle Shoals passed through three phases, in all of which it was resisted by many of the neigh-

boring Indians, who were supported by Spain. The Confederation, too, opposed it, but less effectively. In the first phase, 1783–85, it was a private enterprise organized by six North Carolinians (John Sevier and two other frontiersmen, and William Blount and two other easterners) who, under a purchase from some Indians and a grant from Georgia, planned to colonize the Muscle Shoals region as a colony of that state. In the second phase, 1785–86, the project was made a part of the expansionist program of the new State of Franklin, of which Sevier was governor, and it contemplated cooperation with Georgia in a war of conquest against the neighboring Indians. When these plans went awry, the project entered its third phase, 1786–89, which was marked by an intrigue with Spain (*see* Spanish Conspiracy), the Franklinites offering to secede from the Union in return for Spanish support of their project. Spain rejected the proposal, Sevier became a loyal supporter of the new federal government, and the project again became a private enterprise. In the 1790's it was actively prosecuted by Blount, Zachariah Cox, and others; but the opposition of the U.S. government, the Indians, and Spain prevented its execution.

[A. P. Whitaker, *The Spanish American Frontier.*]

A. P. WHITAKER

MUSEUMS exist principally to care for significant objects that, having outlasted their original function, would otherwise be in danger of loss or destruction. Since they do for objects what libraries do for books, it is not surprising that the earliest learned and historical societies in the United States maintained "cabinets," as museums were often called in the 18th century. The 1769 by-laws of the American Philosophical Society provided for curators "to take charge of, and preserve, all *Specimens of natural Productions,* whether of the *Animal, Vegetable* or *Fossil* Kingdom; all Models of Machines and Instruments, and all other matters and things belonging to the Society, which shall be committed to them; to class and arrange them in their proper order." An 18th-century cabinet might also include coins, medals, paintings, prints, and sculpture; almost anything that was rare, curious, or from distant parts, whether natural or man-made, was grist for such a mill.

The Massachusetts Historical Society, the first of its kind (having been founded in 1791), included among its purposes "the collection and preservation of materials for a political and natural history of the United States," but almost from the start, the physical difficulties of preserving birds, fishes, and animals were recognized. Books, manuscripts, and maps predominated in the earliest accessions. Some indication of the relative values of the society's interests is indicated by its vote of Oct. 25, 1796, which authorized the cabinet keeper "to exchange some of the shells belonging to the Society for Governor Hutchinson's picture." As specialized scientific organizations were created during the 19th century, the older societies devoted less attention to their undifferentiated collections of objects. The founding of the Boston Society of Natural History in 1830, for example, permitted the Massachusetts Historical Society to relinquish any obligations that it had originally assumed in that field. By 1897 the American Philosophical Society had deposited practically all its museum holdings that had any scientific or educational value with other institutions.

The Peabody Museum of Salem, Mass., is the oldest museum in continuous operation in the United States, by virtue of perpetuating the collections of the East India Marine Society, founded in 1799. This group of shipmasters, whose requirements for admission were as exacting as those for a club restricted to astronauts would be today, had, in addition to sociable and benevolent purposes, the following objectives: "to collect such facts and observations as may tend to the improvement and security of navigation" and "to form a Museum of natural and artificial curiosities, particularly such as are to be found beyond the Cape of Good Hope and Cape Horn." While some of the objects brought back to the museum by members were mere curiosities, some—particularly those from the Pacific islands—provide continuingly important evidence of indigenous methods of hunting, fishing, and agriculture. Although Nathaniel Hawthorne's 1842 story entitled "A Virtuoso's Collection" satirized the contents of East India Marine Hall, this shipmasters' cabinet of "natural and artificial curiosities" has evolved into an important modern museum, specializing in maritime history, the ethnology of the Pacific islands and Japan, and the natural history of Essex County, Mass.

Private individuals also created early museums. The painter Charles Willson Peale in 1794 rented part of the American Philosophical Society's hall in Philadelphia for his natural-history museum, begun in his home in 1786, but the association lasted only until 1811. By the time its founder died in 1827, Peale's museum had become a commercial venture. The explorer William Clark created a museum devoted to the American Indian in Saint Louis in 1816; its collec-

tions were dispersed shortly before his death in 1838. The Western Museum of Cincinnati, founded in 1820 with high scientific purpose, lapsed into commercialism within three years; until its disappearance in 1867 it offered chiefly entertainment in the manner of an amusement park.

In the second third of the 19th century the word "museum" often connoted entertainment for the commercial advantage of the proprietor. A British visitor of the period, Edward P. Hingston, observed:

A "Museum" in the American sense of the word means a place of amusement, wherein there shall be a theatre, some wax figures, a giant and a dwarf or two, a jumble of pictures, and a few live snakes. In order that there may be some excuse for the word, there is in most instances a collection of stuffed birds, a few preserved animals, and a stock of oddly assorted and very dubitable curiosities; but the mainstay of the "Museum" is the "live art," that is, the theatrical performance, the precocious mannikins, or the intellectual dogs and monkeys.

A Boston showman, Moses Kimball, a friend and collaborator of P. T. Barnum, built a theater in 1845 that he called the Boston Museum. To justify the use of the name he exhibited the gigantic painting by Thomas Sully of George Washington crossing the Delaware, as well as Chinese curiosities, two stuffed elephants and a giraffe, live Indians, and similar attractions. But the theater was the heart of the place; Kimball's motive, like Barnum's, was personal profit, based on attracting and amusing a crowd.

The federal government's involvement with museums dates from the 1846 act creating the Smithsonian Institution and providing for the formation of a museum of natural history and a gallery of art under its auspices. With the establishment of the American Museum of Natural History (1869) and the Metropolitan Museum of Art (1870) in New York City and of the Museum of Fine Arts (1870) in Boston, the word "museum" ceased to suggest a sideshow. Like the U.S. National Museum, these were institutions concerned with the preservation of objects for the highest of motives. During the 20th century establishment of museums of art, history, and science in all parts of the United States accelerated rapidly; in some cases buildings were constructed before objects worthy of preservation were collected. The 1975 edition of the *Official Museum Directory* of the American Association of Museums listed 5,225 museums in the United States and Canada and stated that since 1965 six new museums had been founded every seven days; the 1974 edition of the *Encyclopedia Britannica* gives a lower, but still disquieting, estimate of the rate of creation of new museums—one every 3.3 days.

Late 19th-century museums tended to exhibit objects of the same kind together, whether they were stuffed bears or silver teapots. In the 20th century an attempt was made to place objects in an approximation of their natural setting. While "habitat groups" in natural history museums required work by artists and model-makers, art museums cannibalized ancient buildings to procure structural elements for their "period rooms." The American Wing of the Metropolitan Museum in 1924 brought together architectural elements from widely scattered sources to provide a background for examples of American decorative arts, as did the Henry Francis du Pont Winterthur Museum in 1951 in Winterthur, Del. The restoration of Williamsburg, Va., substantially completed between 1926 and 1941, turned an entire 18th-century town into a museum. Its popularity inspired the foundation of several historical museums in rural areas where, with space available, the re-creation of an image of the American past was attempted, following the precedent of the open-air museums of Scandinavia, where buildings were moved to new locations for preservation. Typical examples are a New England village synthetically re-created in Sturbridge, Mass., and a seaport at Mystic, Conn. In contrast to such general evocations of the past are such institutions as the Hagley Museum in Greenville, Del., and the Merrimack Valley Textile Museum in North Andover, Mass., which specialize in local economic and industrial history.

Although a museum is actually a mausoleum, in the sense that it preserves objects that have passed out of current use, the didactic urge has long led museum directors and curators to evoke the educational usefulness of their institutions. George Brown Goode, assistant director in charge of the Smithsonian Institution from 1887 until his death in 1896, defined "an efficient educational museum as a collection of instructive labels each illustrated by a well-selected specimen." His notion called for a museum that was essentially a vast "dictionary," illustrated by original, three-dimensional objects. But such an institution, although like the dictionary, admirable for specific reference and for desultory browsing, could not be counted on to provide systematic knowledge of any subject; moreover, it would be vast and necessarily incomplete, for not even the U.S. National Museum could illustrate everything in three-dimensional form. In the 20th century the dictionary-type collection of the American Museum of Natural History was transformed, through the efforts of Henry Fairfield Osborn and Roy Chapman Andrews, into a "textbook," wherein exhibits were designed to aid self-instruction in a great variety of subjects. Theoretically the visitor could educate himself by a careful study of the exhibits. The idea, although elevated and appealing, had the disadvantage of requiring an immense amount of space; moreover, as scientific discoveries proliferated, exhibits constantly became obsolete. The Museum of Science in Boston, under the leadership of Henry Bradford Washburn, Jr., who became its director in 1939, abandoned the notion that a museum could be an all-inclusive organization, providing the possibility of self-instruction in science and technology through its exhibits and lectures. Washburn's policies were directed at exciting the visitor's imagination and inspiring him to pursue the study of a subject in school or college, or by independent study.

[Whitfield J. Bell, Jr., Clifford K. Shipton, John C. Ewers, Louis L. Tucker, and Wilcomb E. Washburn, *A Cabinet of Curiosities: 5 Episodes in the Evolution of American Museums;* Walter Muir Whitehill, *Independent Historical Societies, Museum of Fine Arts, Boston: A Centennial History,* and *The Salem East India Marine Society and the Peabody Museum of Salem.*]

WALTER MUIR WHITEHILL

MUSIC. During the colonial period, American music was a provincial replica of European patterns, with the chief influences coming from Great Britain, France, Italy, and Germany. Professional musicians who emigrated from these countries assumed control of public concerts, as well as of church music and opera. They were often assisted by "gentlemen amateurs" who practiced music as an avocation. This situation prevailed through the early decades of independence, but after 1800 the number of professional musicians, both European and American-born, increased considerably. The Handel and Haydn Society of Boston (1815) and the Musical Fund Society of Philadelphia (1820) were formed to sponsor public concerts. The first permanent symphony orchestra was that of the New York Philharmonic Society, founded in 1842.

The earliest "grass roots" movement in American musical composition originated in New England as a result of the Puritan predilection for singing psalms— not only as a religious duty but also as a social pastime. From about 1720, informal singing schools were organized to promote group singing among the people in both urban and rural communities. These created a demand for books containing the music to be sung, usually written in four parts for men's and women's voices. After 1770 several hundred "tune-books" were published in New England, and during the early 19th century they could also be found in the South and the Midwest. They included not only paraphrases of the psalms of David but also evangelical hymns, anthems, spiritual songs, and some secular numbers, usually odes for public occasions or patriotic songs. The composers were mostly native-born Americans. They often had limited musical training but a gift for melody, and they were always responsive to the needs and tastes of the people. Prominent among them were William Billings, Supply Belcher, Daniel Read, Jeremiah Ingalls, Oliver Holden, and Andrew Law.

Although much secular music was published during the 18th century, it was mostly of European origin. An exception was *Seven Songs for the Harpsichord* (and voice), published by Francis Hopkinson of Philadelphia in 1788 and dedicated to George Washington. After 1800, more secular music by Americans, both vocal and instrumental, began to be published. It was mostly in the form of sheet music, with a prevalence of marches, dances, and sentimental, humorous, patriotic, and topical songs. From about 1820 many pseudo-"Negro" songs began to appear, engendered by the vogue for blackface (or "burnt-cork") minstrelsy—a type of popular entertainment that flourished through most of the 19th century. The earliest blackface entertainers appeared individually, but in the 1840's they began to form groups, at first with four members but gradually increasing in numbers to the "mammoth" minstrel troupes of the last decades of the century. The best-known composers of minstrel-show songs were Daniel Decatur Emmett and Stephen Foster. The former is famous as the composer of *Dixie;* the latter wrote many of America's best-loved songs, among them *Old Folks at Home, Old Black Joe,* and *Oh Susanna.* The instrumental music of blackface minstrelsy was derived largely from the syncopated banjo tunes of the blacks on the southern plantations.

This Afro-American music influenced the style of America's first internationally famous composer, Louis Moreau Gottschalk, a native of Louisiana who studied in France and won European celebrity with such piano pieces as *La Bamboula, La Savane,* and *Le Bananier,* based on black Creole melodies of Louisiana. *The Banjo* was more directly related to the spirit of minstrelsy. Gottschalk was also the first American to achieve international fame as a pianist.

The first American to compose a grand opera—in the Italian style but with a libretto in English—was William Henry Fry of Philadelphia, where his opera *Leonora* was produced (at his own expense) in 1845. Ten years later, George F. Bristow's *Rip Van Winkle* was successfully produced in New York. Both Fry and Bristow composed symphonies and other works in the larger forms, such as cantatas and oratorios. By the end of the century, many other Americans were busily cultivating the traditional forms of European art music, mainly under German influence. Eminent among them was Edward MacDowell, also an excellent pianist, best known for his two piano concertos, his numerous piano pieces, and his *Indian Suite* (1896) for orchestra. From about 1880 to 1920 there was widespread interest in the use of American Indian themes by American composers. Charles W. Cadman wrote three "Indian" operas, including *Shanewis;* Arthur Farwell wrote his Indian pieces for piano, for voice, and for orchestra.

What may be called the "Indianist" movement in American composition was only one phase of a general trend toward seeking American themes from various sources, such as Anglo-American and Afro-American folk music. John Powell of Virginia drew on both of these sources, as did Farwell and Daniel G. Mason. Henry F. B. Gilbert was attracted mainly to Afro-American sources in such works as *Comedy Overture on Negro Themes* (1905) and *The Dance in Place Congo* (1906). Black composers also drew on their own cultural heritage, most notably William Grant Still in his *Afro-American Symphony* (1931).

John A. Carpenter was among the first to draw on American popular music, notably in his ballets *Skyscrapers* and *Krazy Kat.* George Gershwin, with a background in popular music, moved into the sphere of concert music with *Rhapsody in Blue* (1923), *Concerto in F* (1925), and *An American in Paris* (1928), creating a unique blend of the popular and the artistic. With *Porgy and Bess* (1935), his opera based on DuBose Heyward's novel about blacks in South Carolina, he achieved a dramatic masterpiece while preserving the tunefulness and vivacity of his earlier musical shows for Broadway. Marc Blitzstein, in his satirical opera *The Cradle Will Rock* (1937), turned to the American musical and verbal vernacular in depicting the ruthless efforts of big business to suppress the incipient labor-union movement. Leonard Bernstein used pop-music elements in his one-act opera on American domestic life in suburbia, *Trouble in Tahiti* (1952), and gave a new social-dramatic dimension to the Broadway musical with *West Side Story* (1957).

Douglas Moore, working in the more traditional vein of grand opera, but on a totally American subject, was very successful with *The Ballad of Baby Doe* (1956), based on the life of Horace Tabor, who made his fortune in the mining boom in Colorado. Virgil Thomson shunned realism in *The Mother of Us All* (1947), with a libretto by Gertrude Stein, but packed a great variety of musical Americana into this historical allegory of Susan B. Anthony's struggle for woman's rights.

Thomson, along with Aaron Copland, Roy Harris, and Walter Piston, belonged to the generation of composers who turned toward France rather than Germany for training and creative stimulation. Of the same generation are Henry Cowell, an extraordinary innovator, and Roger Sessions, a highly respected composer of deeply serious works. Undoubtedly the most famous composer of this generation is Copland, who was remarkably successful in writing music that is both personal and unmistakably American. He drew on jazz elements in *Music for the Theater* (1925) and a piano concerto and on American folk music in his ballets *Billy the Kid* (1938), *Rodeo* (1942), and *Appalachian Spring* (1944) and in *Lincoln Portrait* (1942) for narrator and orchestra. He has also written much "abstract" or formal music, such as the Piano Variations, Short Symphony, and Piano Quartet, as well as an opera, *The Tender Land* (1954). Roy Harris has striven to express the American spirit in many of his works, including twelve symphonies of which the Third (1937) proved to be the most popular.

Charles Ives is generally recognized as America's greatest and most original composer. He wrote nearly all of his music between 1894 and 1921, but it was so far ahead of its time that recognition of its unique qualities was long delayed. The process of recognition began in the 1920's; however, his extraordinary Fourth Symphony, completed in 1916, did not have its first complete performance until 1965. In many of his works, such as *Three Places in New England* (1903–14) for orchestra and the Piano Sonata no. 2 (*Concord, Mass., 1840–60;* 1909–15), Ives drew on his personal memories and on his spiritual affinities with the life and culture of 19th-century New England. His music is full of quotations of American tunes of many kinds—patriotic, sentimental, humorous, religious, popular. Thus, he looked to the past for much of his inspiration, but in the daring originality of his musical language he was one of the greatest innovators of the 20th century.

Of the composers born after 1900, Elliott Carter, John Cage, and Milton Babbitt are among the most influential. Carter represents the height of cultivated elitism, with compositions of great complexity and intellectual depth. Babbitt is in a somewhat similar position, except that, with a mathematical background, he has concentrated on developing the twelve-tone method of Arnold Schoenberg and Anton von Webern into a system of "total serialization" (or "total structuralization"), whereby "the twelve-tone set must . . . determine *every* aspect of the piece." He has also done important work with electronic music, which from the 1950's attracted a rapidly increasing number of composers.

Except for his interest in electronic music, Cage embodies the antithesis of all that Babbitt and Carter represent. Instead of "ideas of order," he proposes "no ideas of order." Instead of predetermined structures, he proposes "composition as process." The prevailing principle is that of "indeterminacy," leading to what became known as "chance music." The aim, says Cage, is "to make a musical composition the continuity of which is free of individual taste and memory (psychology) and also of the literature and 'traditions' of the art." Cage is the Marcel Duchamp of American music: a dedicated iconoclast. Like other American composers of the mid-20th century, he was much influenced by the music and philosophy of the Far East.

The most original and creative currents in American popular music—ragtime, jazz, blues, rock— came from Afro-American traditions, even though both whites and blacks participated in their development. Ragtime has its antecedents in the syncopated banjo tunes played for dancing by black musicians. In the 1890's it emerged as a type of music primarily for piano, with a syncopated melody in the treble (right hand) and a strong regular beat in the bass (left hand). It also acquired a definite form, consisting of three to five "themes" disposed in sixteen-bar "strains," which were usually repeated. This is "classical ragtime," as represented superlatively in such piano "rags" of Scott Joplin as *Maple Leaf Rag* and *The Entertainer*. Joplin was black, but one of the outstanding composers of classical piano rags, Joseph Lamb, was white. In the early 1900's ragtime— much of it adapted for dance orchestras, brass bands, and popular songs—became a national craze. This passed, but in the 1970's classical ragtime enjoyed an extraordinary revival.

More deeply rooted in folk tradition were the blues—the quintessence of Afro-American folksong. The blues are a personal expression of feeling, concerned with deprivation, bad treatment, regret, loneliness, misfortune, and infidelity. They do not preclude humor, satire, or mockery—often sexual. The usual form is a three-line stanza, with the first verse repeated. Musically the twelve-bar pattern prevails, with a fixed harmonic sequence. In country blues the singer usually accompanies himself on the guitar. As the blues reached the cities they were often accompanied by the piano or by various instrumental combinations. W. C. Handy's *St. Louis Blues* (1914) became a favorite of jazz musicians. The early great women blues singers, such as Gertrude ("Ma") Rainey and Bessie Smith, were accompanied by jazz "combos" during the 1920's. The modern urban blues, featuring big, hard-driving bands, were developed chiefly in Kansas City, Memphis, and Chicago, by such black bluesmen as Bobby Bland and B. B. King. The blues also engendered a percussive piano style called "boogie-woogie." What came to be known as "soul music" developed from a synthesis of blues, jazz, and gospel. Its leading exponents were Ray Charles and Aretha Franklin.

The music called "jazz"—a term of uncertain origin—absorbed both ragtime and blues, as well as gospel hymns, marches, dances, popular songs, and even some "classical" numbers. It was essentially an instrumental style that could assimilate and transform any kind of music. Its origins are chiefly associated with New Orleans around the turn of the century, when Charles ("Buddy") Bolden formed a band that included cornet, clarinet, trombone, guitar, string bass, and drums. The most influential early jazz pioneer, also from Louisiana, was Joseph ("King") Oliver, who in 1918 went to Chicago, where in 1923 he made a series of historic recordings with his Creole Jazz Band. These were the first jazz recordings by black musicians; but a white group from New Orleans calling itself the Original Dixieland Jazz Band made some recordings in New York in 1917, following a sensational success at Reisenweber's Restaurant—a foretaste of the Jazz Age to come. Thereafter whites and blacks were to vie in developing both the commercial and the creative potential of jazz. Among black jazzmen, Louis Armstrong, beginning in the 1920's, set new standards for solo improvisation with his creative playing on cornet and trumpet.

Many of the early jazz musicians could not read music: they played by ear and relied largely on improvisation, facilitated by the small size of the groups—usually five to seven players. By the 1930's big bands were the vogue—in the so-called Swing Era—and

their music was arranged and written down by musicians with some professional training, such as Fletcher Henderson, Benny Carter, and Edward Kennedy ("Duke") Ellington, who became an important composer in the jazz idiom. Benny Goodman, a white clarinetist and bandleader, is credited with starting the vogue of "swing" with his nationwide tour in 1934.

By this time the saxophone had acquired a prominent role in jazz, and such performers on that instrument as Lester Young, Coleman Hawkins, and Charlie ("Bird") Parker were widely influential. Parker, together with the trumpet player John Birks ("Dizzy") Gillespie and other "progressive" jazz musicians, developed the style called "bebop," which (in the words of Ross Russell) was a revolt against commercialized music and a reassertion of "the individuality of the jazz musician as a creative artist."

Certain eccentricities and excesses of the bebop scene led to a countermovement that was characterized as "cool," in which the black trumpet player Miles Davis was a leader, along with the white jazzmen Gil Evans and Gerry Mulligan, who brought into jazz such concert instruments as the flute and the French horn. The cool style reached its utmost refinement in the Modern Jazz Quartet, organized by composer-pianist John Lewis in the 1950's. Vibraphone, string bass, and drums completed the quartet, which performed many of Lewis's neoclassical compositions.

Jazz has developed dynamically in ever-changing directions. The cool phase was followed by the style known as "hard bop" or "funky," marked by a return to the more primitive roots of jazz, combined with a hard-driving rhythm, as exemplified by the Jazz Messengers, led by Art Blakey, described as "the most emotionally unbridled drummer in jazz." The saxophonists John Coltrane and Sonny Rollins were also identified with this trend.

Modern jazz has its avant-garde innovators, among whom Charles Mingus and Ornette Coleman emerged as powerfully creative figures in the 1950's. Both tried to maintain the basic principle of improvisation within the framework of extended compositions. There has also been a fusion of jazz and rock, notably in the later work of Miles Davis.

The music called "rock and roll" developed from "rhythm and blues," a type of urban blues with a strong beat that originally was aimed at black audiences and record-buyers (the recording industry, together with radio, has had a decisive role in American popular music). During the 1950's, elements of "pop" music and the style known as "country and western" were fused with rhythm and blues to produce the fast, rocking beat of rock and roll, geared primarily toward the white youth market, although the performers were both blacks and whites. Prominent among the latter were Bill Haley and the Comets, with their big hit *Rock Around the Clock,* and Elvis Presley, whose background was in country and western but whose 1956 recording of *Heartbreak Hotel* started him on the way to superstardom as a rock and roll singer. Among black performers, none was more influential than Chuck Berry, whose songs appealed strongly to teenagers. His electric guitar style also influenced the whole field of rock-and-roll music, including that of the Beatles, an English quartet. When the latter came to the United States in 1964, they had a tremendous impact. The unprecedented success of their personal appearances and recordings stimulated the growth of American bands and launched the era of modern rock.

In the mid-1960's, San Francisco became the chief locus for American rock groups, such as the Jefferson Airplane, Grateful Dead, Country Joe and the Fish, and Big Brother and the Holding Company. These were white groups; among the important innovative black groups of the 1960's were the Jimi Hendrix Experience, and Sly and the Family Stone. High-powered electronic amplification characterized the performances of rock groups.

Bob Dylan started out as an urban folksinger, in the tradition of Woody Guthrie and Pete Seeger, writing his own songs and accompanying himself on the guitar and harmonica. In 1965 he made the transition from folk to rock, adopting the electrified guitar and the basic rock beat. Rather than creating a dichotomy, he helped to create a synthesis known as "folk rock." As a songwriter involved with social-political-moral issues of the time, he became a symbol of protest and alienation.

Politicized folk music came to the fore in the 1930's, largely under the influence of leftist ideology and the struggle for unionized labor. This was not traditional folk song, orally transmitted from generation to generation in rural communities, like the old narrative ballads or love ditties, but rather an adaptation of folk styles to the political issues of an industrialized and urbanized society. New songs of protest and propaganda were often set to traditional melodies, or even to popular tunes. Such urbanized folksingers as Woody Guthrie and Pete Seeger also wrote words and music for their songs, while adhering to basic folk styles. The aim was to make folk music a weapon of the "class struggle." Seeger was associated with a group called the Almanac Singers and later with the Weavers (1944–52). The former became a target of the House Un-American Activities Committee; the latter, toning down its radicalism, enjoyed a commercial success. Seeger himself became a favorite on college campuses and in the 1970's concentrated his musical message on the need for environmental protection.

Country-and-western (or, more simply, country) music had its origins in so-called "hillbilly music"— folk music of the southern uplands developed from the heritage of Anglo-Celtic ballads and folksongs. The commercialization of hillbilly music began in the 1920's, largely through the media of radio and recordings. The first big successes were achieved by the Carter family and by Jimmie Rodgers, famous for his "blue yodel." Rodgers was much influenced by the music of the blacks in his native Mississippi, whose blues he adapted to his own style.

The term "hillbilly" persisted until the late 1940's, when it was replaced by "country" or "country and western." By that time it was a flourishing phase of American popular music, with dozens of highly paid stars appearing on radio and making records that sold in the millions. Its headquarters were in Nashville, Tenn., from which two very popular radio shows, "The National Barn Dance" and "The Grand Ole Opry," carried country music across the nation. From 1926 until his death in 1956, Uncle Dave Macon, a versatile banjo-picker, was the star of "Grand Ole Opry." The fiddle, five-string banjo, and guitar were the typical instruments in country music, although many others were also used, including the mandolin. This last was particularly identified with the style called "bluegrass," named after the Blue Grass Band, led by Bill Monroe. Another name associated with bluegrass is that of Earl Scruggs, famous for perfecting the three-finger style of banjo playing. Together with guitarist Lester Flatt, he was highly influential in popularizing the bluegrass style.

Amid the variety and mutability of American music, a constant factor has been the expression of national themes and aspirations. No composer more effectively expressed this national spirit, in its historic moment of confident affirmation, than did John Philip Sousa in his famous marches, such as *Semper Fidelis* (1888), *The Washington Post March* (1889), and *The Stars and Stripes Forever* (1897). Music of this kind transmits both an emotional experience and a historical testimony.

Beginning with the vogue of European-style operetta by such composers as Sousa (*El Capitan,* 1895), Reginald De Koven (*Robin Hood,* 1890), and Victor Herbert (the most successful and durable, with such hits as *The Red Mill,* 1906, and *Naughty Marietta,* 1910), the popular musical theater developed a more characteristically American expression in the musical comedy. Following the pioneer entertainer George M. Cohan came Irving Berlin, Jerome Kern, George Gershwin, Cole Porter, and Vincent Youmans, who established the basic type, with a perfunctory plot carried by memorable tunes and an attractive chorus line. Gershwin and Berlin occasionally ventured into political satire, the former with *Strike Up the Band* (1930) and the latter with *As Thousands Cheer* (1933).

With *Show Boat* (1927), based on the novel by Edna Ferber, Kern broadened the dramatic scope of the popular musical show, particularly in characterization, and pointed the way toward what came to be known as the "musical." Although always aiming at entertainment, this was not limited to comedy and often drew on literary sources for its plot, as well as giving more prominence to integrated ballet sequences. An early example is *Pal Joey* (1940), with music by Richard Rodgers and libretto by Lorenz Hart. After the latter's death, Rodgers teamed with Oscar Hammerstein II to write such famous musicals as *Oklahoma!* (1943), *Carousel* (1945), and *South Pacific* (1949). This vein was continued by Frank Loesser, with *Guys and Dolls* (1950), and by Leonard Bernstein, with *West Side Story* (1957), a Manhattan ethnic transposition of the Romeo and Juliet story. A high point of this trend was *My Fair Lady* (1956), by Frederick Loewe and Alan Jay Lerner, based on George Bernard Shaw's play *Pygmalion.*

The world of the musical show is closely interrelated with that of the popular song, as many of the hit tunes have originated in the theater. American popular singers such as Bing Crosby, Frank Sinatra, Nat "King" Cole, Ella Fitzgerald, Billie Holiday, Ethel Merman, Peggy Lee, and Barbra Streisand have impressed their personal styles on songs of every kind, from blues to ballads, from show tunes to pop hits. Others, like Hank Williams and Johnny Cash, have done the same with country music, while Mahalia Jackson became the great interpreter of gospel hymns. Gospel, blues, and rock have fused in the music of blacks associated with such recording centers as Detroit (Motown), Memphis (Albert King, the Staple Singers), and New York (Otis Rush, Otis Spann). Nina Simone and James Brown brought "soul" to frenzied heights.

In the area of musical composition, the most significant trend that developed in the 1970's, besides the widespread use of electronics (which cuts through all categories), was that of increasing influences from non-European cultures, particularly Asia and Africa. Concomitantly, this involved a decreasing reliance on the traditional forms of composition and the standard instrumental media, such as the symphony orchestra and the string quartet. The trend was toward emphasizing percussive instruments of every kind, both European and exotic, and relying on complex metrical patterns rather than on preestablished forms, with latitude for improvisation. These trends are represented in the work of such influential composers, performers, and group leaders as Steve Reich, Terry Riley, and La Monte Young. American music had entered an era of irreversible pluralism.

[C. Belz, *The Story of Rock;* G. Chase, *America's Music;* G. Chase, ed., *The American Composer Speaks;* R. S. Denisoff, *Great Day Coming: Folk Music and the American Left;* C. Gilliat, *The Sound of the City: The Rise of Rock and Roll;* H. W. Hitchcock, *Music in the United States;* Bill Malone, *Country Music U.S.A.;* W. J. Schafer and J. Riedel, *The Art of Ragtime;* E. Southern, *The Music of Black Americans.*]

GILBERT CHASE

MUSIC, AFRO-AMERICAN, reflects many different types of experience in the history of black Americans. African rhythms transferred to the southern plantations by slaves from various African tribes, the mingling of these rhythms with the work and new experiences of slavery, the input of spirituals and hymns and, later, the infusion of personal loss and desire into blues, and the evolution of syncopated, traditional melodies into jazz—all of these combined to create Afro-American music. They have been the usual divisions presented in studies of Afro-American music. In 1971 Eileen Southern treated the subject in full detail, including discussions of hymnody in the New England colonies, the camp meeting, the "shout" music in the Confederate and Union armies, and 20th-century concert music.

Music and dance, even to the present day, are the core of all West African ceremony and are inextricable from the chanted or sung message of the ritual. African work, hunting, and boat songs contributed to the spirit of cotton field and railroad work songs in America, just as African drum rhythms (although, as

Southern points out, the talking drum is not a musical instrument) are reflected in Afro-American band and vocal music. Another characteristic of African vocal and instrumental performance, its aural nature, is the result of complex and varied use of melody: the falsetto, nasality, growls, glides, the pentatonic scale, and (in Ghana), according to J. H. Kwabena Nketia, the "ornamental devices such as glissando, rising attack, or falling release . . . though the extent of use varies from area to area." The oral tradition was "an invaluable medium for recording traditions and for creating social commentary and criticism." Further, Nketia reemphasizes the heterogeneous aspects of African music and its all-important correlation with daily life: "In its setting, [traditional music] is part of a complex of activities; singing, drumming, dancing and non-musical activities may take place simultaneously, for traditional music is essentially music organized and performed as part of a living drama and as an essential component of everyday life."

For the slave in America, this "essential component" offered escape from his degrading new life. He sang in coffles marching to slave trading posts; he sang in the fields and on the auction block. On certain holidays in the South and in the New England colonies he joined in parades and celebrations using the dance steps and verses, mingled with English words, of Africa. Because of the less harsh attitude toward slaves in New England and the prevalent urge there to convert them to Christianity, the singing of psalms and hymns was undertaken early by the slaves, and the imprint of their perception that might have been expected was made as early as 1641. The slaves' own religious comment was made in the spiritual, with its promises of future reward. The use of spirituals to bear messages in plans for escape or uprising is well recognized, although it seems to have been indecipherable to the slaveowners. The hymns chosen for a hymnbook for the first black independent church (Mother Bethel African Methodist Episcopal Church in Philadelphia, 1794) were selected from the white Methodist hymnbook, with some changes and additions by the founder, Richard Allen. But the introduction of choral singing and "spiritual" song in the mid-1800's caused conflict. The spiritual then moved to a concertized version as has happened in the formalizing of the blues and jazz.

Roots of the early blues can be identified in early forms: the African call-and-response, the "shout," and the spiritual. Writing in 1963, LeRoi Jones (who changed his name to Imamu Amiri Baraka about 1969) stressed the personal nature of the blues and the

very important shift in emphasis from future reward to present expectation:

> The metaphysical Jordan of life after death was beginning to be replaced by the more pragmatic Jordan of the American master: the Jordan of what the ex-slave could see vaguely as self-determination. . . . Not that that idea or emotion hadn't been with the very first Africans who had been brought here. . . . The Negro began to feel a desire to be more in this country, America, than chattel. "The sun's gonna shine in my back door someday!"

The very personal touch was, perhaps, most often on the theme of love, or, more accurately, the loss of it. Both "primitive" blues and "classic" blues reiterate this experience. The later form was carried to its peak by Bessie Smith and her teacher, Gertrude "Ma" Rainey, and W. C. Handy, the latter in composition rather than singing. It turned away from the communal context of African, work, and religious music to themes with a universal attraction; it moved beyond the primitive to "classic" professionalism and stylizing. It moved, also, to an urban emphasis that made itself evident in the Jazz Age.

During the black literary renaissance of the 1920's, the upsurge in creativity and volume of artistic endeavor occurred in the music world as well. Jazz, a direct descendant of the blues, captured the senses and imagination of performer and listener alike. Improvisatory and "native" American, it was recorded first, ironically enough, by a white group, the Original Dixieland Jazz Band, in 1917. It too is a vocal music, with the instruments recreating the ancient whines and glides of the talking drums. Its new characteristic was syncopation—new only in the arrangement of the rhythm, not in the attention to rhythm itself. The form continued, immortalized by Louis Armstrong and imbued, sometimes, with country emphases.

Afro-American music has evolved in identifiable steps from African music. At the same time, it has embroidered upon the old forms new departures and patterns.

[LeRoi Jones, *Blues People: Negro Music in White America*; J. H. Kwabena Nketia, *Ghana—Music, Dance and Drama: A Review of the Performing Arts of Ghana*; Eileen Southern, *The Music of Black Americans: A History*.]

CECELIA HODGES DREWRY

MUSKINGUM RIVER CANAL ROUTE. The canal in Ohio connecting Cleveland on Lake Erie with Portsmouth on the Ohio River was completed in 1832 (*see* Ohio State Canals). As a supplement to this canal a project was authorized in 1836 to canalize the Muskingum River and join it with the canal at Dresden Junction. It was finished in 1841. The chief benefit was steam navigation from Marietta on the Ohio up the river to Zanesville.

[C. P. McClelland and C. C. Huntington, *History of Ohio Canals*.]

JAMES D. MAGEE

MUSSEL SLOUGH INCIDENT (May 11, 1880). Known locally as the Mussel Slough tragedy, an outbreak of gunfire seven miles northwest of Hanford, Calif., brought to a head a long controversy between settlers on railroad lands and the Southern Pacific Company and left seven men dead and one wounded. The company had invited settlers to occupy lands of a federal grant, assuring them that they could buy the lands in due time at reasonable prices from $2.50 to $5.00 an acre. Occupation in the area took place mainly in the late 1860's and early 1870's. Conveyance of patent to the company was effected on four dates, from December 1874 to December 1880. After conveyance, the company specified prices, ranging mostly from $25 to $35 an acre.

The settlers organized and raised money by assessment and solicitation to finance legal resistance. The impact of their activities was far-reaching. Their plight was linked with national conditions widely viewed as a struggle between farmers and capitalists. In court they tried to prove that the Southern Pacific, having failed to meet the government's terms, lacked title to the land. They stressed discrepancies between company promises and prices, claiming that asking prices were based on their improvements on the land. Since both lower and higher court decisions were unfavorable to them, they appealed to President Rutherford B. Hayes for time to have a hearing before the Supreme Court.

Accompanied by a representative of the Southern Pacific Company, U.S. Marshal A. W. Poole drove out from Hanford on May 11, 1880, with a court order to dispossess certain occupants. A crowd of men, some carrying arms, gathered; among them were Walter J. Crow and Mills D. Hartt, who had submitted bids on parcels of the land. The marshal, unarmed, counseled restraint, but an unidentified man fired, and a quick blast of shots followed. Hartt and five other men died from that shooting, some having no connection with the controversy. Crow, having walked away after the shooting, was killed by an unknown person more than a mile from the scene.

Tensions relaxed perceptibly after the tragedy. Some settlers purchased lands they had occupied; many did not. The Southern Pacific reduced prices by small amounts in some cases.

[J. L. Brown, *The Mussel Slough Tragedy;* Jerome Madden, *Lands of the Southern Pacific*.]

J. L. BROWN

MUSTANGS. The expeditions of Hernando Cortes, beginning in 1518, explored the New World on horseback and raised horses on unfenced ranges. For twenty-four years after the landing of Cortes a royal edict prohibited an Indian's riding a horse. But horse stock strayed from the haciendas; on explorations that took their riders thousands of miles into the unknown, horses were lost. The wild increase of these lost and strayed animals were called *mesteños*—mustangs.

On the plains of Alberta, down the corridor between the Mississippi and the Rocky Mountains, and along the length of the Mesa Central of Mexico, wild horses, the mustangs, ran with the deer, the antelope, and the buffalo. No estimate of the numbers is possible. In 1846 Lt. U. S. Grant saw in Texas between the Neuces River and the Rio Grande so many mustangs that he doubted "if the State of Rhode Island" could hold them. On old maps this region is marked "Mustang Desert." On the Staked Plains the wild horses were hardly less numerous.

The mustangs ran in bands, called *manadas,* each under the leadership of a stallion, who fought other stallions off and managed his mares like a general. Like the longhorns, the mustangs were of many colors. Some stallions gained wide fame—the Pacing White Mustang became one of the legends of America. Early in the 19th century mustanging began to develop into one of the occupations of the Southwest. Mustangers used various methods to capture the wild horses, sometimes "walking them down," keeping after a single band until it was utterly exhausted from lack of sleep, food, and water; trapping them in pens; snaring them singly along trails; "creasing" them—shooting so that the bullet grazed a cord along the top of the neck, thus stunning but not permanently injuring the animal; often catching colts and raising them by hand.

The ranches and missions of early California raised tens of thousands of Spanish horses that were mustangs, many of which were stolen by Indians and herds of which were "lifted" by mountain men and driven east. Synchronous with the great cattle drives from Texas, at least a million horses of the mustang breed were driven north.

444

With the development of ranching, mustangs were recognized as a nuisance and were killed off. The wild horses ranging today in certain parts of Arizona, Wyoming, and other western states are not of the unmixed Spanish mustang breed. The wild horses along the Carolina seaboard were another breed. The mustang—even though Mark Twain satirized "A Genuine Mexican Plug"—influenced the history of the West tremendously. (*See also* Horse.)

[J. Frank Dobie, *Tales of the Mustang;* R. B. Cunninghame Graham, *The Horse of the Conquest;* Clark Wissler, "The Influence of the Horse in the Development of Plains Culture," *American Anthropologist,* vol. 16.]

J. FRANK DOBIE

MUSTER DAY. Under the militia act of 1792, in effect for more than a century, every able-bodied citizen between the ages of eighteen and forty-five was a member of the militia. Actual enrollment was accomplished through the annual muster day, which soon degenerated into an annual spree. After the Civil War muster day was generally neglected.

[Reuben Davis, *Recollections of Mississippi and Mississippians;* A. B. Longstreet, *Georgia Scenes.*]

DON RUSSELL

MUTINY. An examination of various military authorities leads to a welter of contradiction in defining mutiny. From actual conditions a working definition may be evolved and stated as "concerted insubordination, or concerted opposition or resistance to or defiance of lawful military authority, by two or more persons subject to such authority, with the intent to usurp, subvert, or override such authority, or to neutralize it for the time being." When examples of mutiny are sought, difficulty is encountered in that the larger number of cases that might possibly be so designated are tried for lesser charges, such as insubordination or refusal to obey orders. This gives rise to many borderline cases. U.S. history does afford some definite examples. The most striking is that of the entire Pennsylvania Line, six regiments, which mutinied at Morristown, N.J., on Jan. 2, 1781, and started for Philadelphia to lay their grievances directly before Congress (*see* Pennsylvania Troops, Mutinies of).

A year before, on May 25, 1780, two regiments of the Connecticut Line paraded without their officers in a spirit of mutiny. They were brought back under authority by a Pennsylvania brigade. On Jan. 20, 1781, three New Jersey regiments sought to imitate the Pennsylvania Line. George Washington ordered Gen. Robert Howe to handle the situation. He surrounded the mutineers with infantry and artillery at Ringwood and gave them five minutes to come to time. They yielded; the ringleaders were immediately tried and two of them hung, whereupon the regiments returned to duty. In June 1783, recruits of the Pennsylvania regiments marched on Congress at Philadelphia. When Congress fled to Princeton, N.J., Gen. Howe again stepped in and settled matters.

In the War of 1812, the Twenty-third Infantry mutinied at Manlius, N.Y.; the Fifth Infantry at Utica; a company of volunteers at Buffalo; and, in 1814, a regiment of Tennessee militia, part of Gen. Andrew Jackson's forces, had a sergeant and five privates condemned to death for inciting mutiny.

A conspicuous maritime case was that on the U.S. brig *Somers* in 1842 when Midshipman Phillip Spencer (son of the then Secretary of War Ambrose Spencer) was one of three prisoners hanged on shipboard as a mutineer. As of the mid-1970's no later case of mutiny on a U.S. Navy vessel had occurred.

[William Hough, *Precedents in Military Law;* Oliver L. Spaulding, *The United States Army in War and Peace;* James Thacher, *Military Journal During the American Revolution;* William Winthrop, *Military Law and Precedents.*]

ROBERT S. THOMAS

MUTINY ACT OF 1765 was a routine parliamentary enactment. The feature affecting the American colonies was the quartering provision that, like the Stamp Act, was designed to shift the burden of supporting British troops in America from British taxpayers to the colonists. It required provincial legislatures to provide barracks, fuel, and certain other necessities for the soldiers stationed within their borders. Colonial Whigs feared that the Mutiny Act was designed to pave the way for the introduction of a standing army to enforce the Stamp Act; but after the repeal of the Stamp Act, the cry was raised in the colonies that the Mutiny Act violated the principle of no taxation without representation. Most of the colonies attempted to evade the act, and New York refused point-blank in 1767 to obey it. To punish the colony, Parliament passed an act suspending the New York legislature on Oct. 1, 1767, but the New York assembly had already grudgingly provided for the troops. Thus the Mutiny Act served to keep alive the controversy over taxation without representation during the interval between the repeal of the Stamp Act and the passage of the Townshend duties. (*See also* Billeting.)

[C. H. Van Tyne, *The Causes of the War of Independence.*]

JOHN C. MILLER

MUTUAL FUNDS. *See* **Investment Companies.**

"MY COUNTRY, 'TIS OF THEE." In 1832 Lowell Mason, musical educator and hymn writer of Boston, handed Samuel F. Smith—then a theological student at Andover and becoming known as an amateur poet—a book of German songs, asking him to look it over. If he found any good tunes, he was to make an English translation of the words thereto, or write original songs to the meter, for use in schools. One air, simple yet strong and pleasing, gave Smith a patriotic inspiration, and within half an hour he had written five stanzas of the now familiar hymn to his native land, "My Country, 'Tis of Thee." The third stanza he later discarded, and the remaining four stand almost as originally written. Not until some time afterward did Smith learn that the tune he had used was that of the British national anthem, "God Save the King," which had been taken over into the musical literature of several other lands. Even the melody is of gradual growth, though in its present form it is generally attributed to the early 18th-century English composer, Henry Carey. Smith's hymn was first sung in the Park Street Church in Boston, July 4, 1832. Anti-British feeling was still strong in the United States then, but strangely enough, the knowledge that the air was that of the British national anthem did not deter the growth of the song's popularity. It was first published in Mason's collection *The Choir* in 1832. With the tune rechristened "America," and without any official action, the song—simple, melodious, easily sung and remembered—became within two or three decades as close to a national anthem as anything in the United States—perhaps even closer than the "Star-Spangled Banner," which is essentially a paean to the national flag, and is frequently under attack because of its alleged unsuitability.

[Samuel F. Smith, *Poems of Home and Country*.]
ALVIN F. HARLOW

MYERS V. UNITED STATES, 272 U.S. 52 (1926). The power to appoint federal officers resides primarily in the president. In most cases such appointment requires confirmation by the Senate. The power to remove is considered concomitant with the power to appoint, but from time to time Congress has stipulated that removal is restricted and subject to the consent of the Senate. Presidents have opposed this view, and in 1920 President Woodrow Wilson removed Frank S. Myers, the Portland, Oreg., postmaster, without first obtaining the consent of the Senate. Myers sued in the Court of Claims, challenging the president's right to remove him. He lost, and on appeal the Supreme Court held in *Myers* v. *United States* that officers named by the president were subject to removal at his pleasure. In so holding, the Supreme Court declared unconstitutional the law that had been passed in 1876 limiting removal of postmasters.

Although presidential authority to appoint carries with it the right to remove, exceptions have been made by the Court after *Myers* with respect to members of several independent regulatory and administrative agencies, such as the Federal Trade Commission and the War Claims Commission. These exceptions apply if the Congress has decreed in the statute creating the office that removal is subject only to specific cause made explicit by the statute and if the official involved exercises adjudicatory function. The cases of *Humphrey's Executor* v. *United States* (1935) and *Wiener* v. *United States* (1958) distinguished between officials like Myers, who exercised only ministerial and administrative authority, and those like W. E. Humphrey, a member of the Federal Trade Commission, and Wiener, a member of the War Claims Commission, who functioned in a quasi-judicial capacity.

In *Myers* the Court justified unlimited removal power by the president on the basis of the executive power granted in the Constitution: control over administration rests in the president; therefore, he must have complete control over those officers through whom he discharges his administrative responsibilities.

[E. C. Hargrove, *The Power of the Modern Presidency;* C. H. Pritchett, *The American Constitution;* D. Vinyard, *The Presidency.*]
PAUL DOLAN

MYITKYINA, BATTLE OF (May 17–Aug. 3, 1944). Climaxing a ten-month Sino-American campaign in 1943–44 across north Burma, the bitter World War II siege of the railhead and river town of Myitkyina on the Irrawaddy River ended Japan's blockade of China. The siege had the immediate effect of driving away Japanese air power so that American transports could fly a lower-altitude route carrying increased tonnage to China. Thus, an American air effort from east China bases could be intensified in support of Pacific operations.

On the ground, Gen. Joseph W. Stilwell's Allies believed that Myitkyina could not be taken and held without heavy reinforcements and that even if it could be held, was not worth taking. Before the monsoon Stilwell decided to make a bold strike against Myitkyina's 700-man garrison. Stilwell's main Chinese columns kept Lt. Gen. Shinichi Tanaka's attention fixed on the Kamaing-Mogaung corridor leading south and into the rail system of the Irrawaddy Valley. On Apr. 21, 1944, Stilwell set up an Allied task force that included depleted GALAHAD teams (GALAHAD was the designation given a 3,000-man volunteer force that had been sent to Asia in September 1943). On Apr. 28 the march across the Kumon Range through a 6,100-foot pass for a back-door attack on the Myitkyina airfield began. A prearranged code message, "Merchant of Venice," received May 17, meant GALAHAD had taken the airstrip. It was safe to launch air reinforcements. Stilwell was exultant as Chinese units landed, hopeful of occupying the town. The Japanese were stunned and frantically called for troops all over Burma as the green Chinese columns reached the center of Myitkyina on May 18. Then mishaps occurred, as the Chinese became confused, fought among themselves, and drove themselves right back out of Myitkyina. GALAHAD was fatigued and riddled with tropical disease; their commander, Brig. Gen. Frank D. Merrill, suffered a heart attack. The Japanese won the race to reinforce and hold Myitkyina's well-stocked base during the monsoon. By June 4 Myitkyina was surrounded, but the 4,600-man garrison was well dug in, willing to die for the emperor. Stilwell had no reinforcements except some combat engineers to throw into the struggle, but it finally ended in a victory for the Allies on Aug. 3. The costs were high: the Americans lost 272 killed, 955 wounded, 980 ill; the Chinese, 972 killed, 3,184 wounded, 188 ill. Captured Japanese totaled 187, most of them wounded, while about 600 Japanese made good their escape.

Meanwhile, Mogaung fell to the Allies, and with Myitkyina secured, Stilwell had a great supply base squarely on the road and rail net of Burma and within easy distance of China itself.

[Charles F. Romanus and Riley Sunderland, *Stilwell's Command Problems*.]

CHARLES F. ROMANUS

"MY OLD KENTUCKY HOME" is perhaps the finest work of Stephen Foster, the great composer of folk songs. Although its origin is shrouded in legend, it seems probable that the original inspiration came from a visit that Foster made to Federal Hill at Bardstown, Ky., some time in the 1840's. This old southern mansion was the home of Judge John Rowan, a relative of Foster's. The song has become a part of American history because, in words and music of singular beauty, it perpetuates the romantic tradition associated with Kentucky and the antebellum South.

[John T. Howard, *Stephen Foster, America's Troubadour*.]

E. H. O'NEILL

MYSTICISM has many meanings in the study of the history of religions. In general it refers to a type of faith that emphasizes the direct experience of a unity with the divine. Theologically, mystical faiths tend to stress the divine immanence, and they often identify God with the structure of being. In the United States, mystical forms of faith can be seen as a protest against the dominant religious tradition, which highlights the divine transcendence and the necessity of obedience to the divine will.

The most famous mystic in early American history was Anne Hutchinson, whose mysticism was evolved from the Puritan emphasis on the Holy Spirit as the means of grace. Her teachings were controversial, and for stating that she believed in immediate revelation, she was exiled from Massachusetts Bay Colony in 1637.

The early Quakers attempted to combine a mystical emphasis on the Inner Light with the organization of English Puritan sects, and these two elements in early Pennsylvania Quakerism frequently pulled in opposite directions. Quaker history illustrates the difficulty in transmitting a mystical faith to second and third generations. As time passed, many Quakers identified the mystical experience of the Inner Light with the universal human experience of conscience, and their descendants were often only "birthright" members.

Although Jonathan Edwards was primarily interested in traditional forms of religious experience, many elements in his writings suggest mystical leanings. His description of his wife's religious experience in *Some Thoughts Concerning the Present Revival* (1742) is one of the classic accounts of mystical experience in American literature. Edwards' own theology presented a view of the world as filled with shadows and images of things divine and had elements in it similar to those found in mystical faiths.

Ralph Waldo Emerson was perhaps the most prominent proponent of 19th-century romantic mysticism in America. Building on ideas ultimately derived from German philosophy and—in his later years—from the religions of the East, Emerson evolved a unique American mysticism that stressed the unity of man with all nature. Through man's communication with the world, Emerson argued, he could come to transcend it and recognize himself as part of it at the same time. Unlike many Old World mystics, Emerson argued that the world showed a moral, as well as a natural, balance. Again unlike other mystics, he understood the will to be essential in the mystical experience, not something to be overcome preparatory to it.

Mysticism became better known to Americans through the World Parliament of Religions, held in Chicago in 1893. Representatives of Eastern religions and Western mysticism presented their views of the religious life to a large audience, and a number of groups were formed to explore aspects of mystical faith.

The popularity of the psychology of religion following the publication of William James's *Varieties of Religious Experience* (1902) also contributed to interest in mysticism. Although James had played down the place of the mystic in the history of religion, many later psychologists believed that mysticism was the fullest form of the religious life, and the topic received a great deal of attention and study.

The Roman Catholic church has always found more of a place for mysticism than the Protestant churches, although in the United States, the problems of establishing the church and absorbing millions of immigrants from diverse ethnic backgrounds have absorbed much of its energy. Still, the mystical experience has continued to be important in the lives of many Roman Catholic religious orders. Thomas Merton, a convert to Catholicism, was one of the influential voices for Catholic mysticism in America in the 20th century. His exposition of the mystical way was marked by clarity and philosophic insight. His works reveal a deep concern for social justice and a keen analysis of political issues.

The drug culture of the 1960's brought with it a widespread interest in mysticism among the young. Many who tried the new mind-expanding drugs believe the states they induce to be similar to, or even identical with, the experiences of the great mystics of the past.

[Thomas Merton, *Gift From the Sea;* Perry Miller, *Jonathan Edwards;* Ruth Underhill, *Mysticism: A Study in the Nature and Development of Man's Spiritual Consciousness.*]

GLENN T. MILLER

NACOGDOCHES, the oldest town in eastern Texas, was a strategic frontier outpost until the disturbances of the Mexican war for independence from Spain in 1821 almost destroyed it. Under Mexican rule it became a gateway for Anglo-American immigrants to Texas; a center of some revolutionary disturbances, notably the Fredonian Revolt of 1826; and the capital of a political subdivision of Texas. Its inhabitants took a leading part in the Texas revolution in 1836 and in the affairs of the Republic of Texas.

[George L. Crockett, *Two Centuries in East Texas;* George P. Garrison, *Texas: A Contest of Civilizations.*]

C. T. NEU

NADER'S RAIDERS. In the summer of 1968, Ralph Nader, a noted consumer advocate, selected seven students from the Harvard and Yale law schools to investigate the operations of the Federal Trade Commission (FTC). After testifying before an FTC hearing in November 1968, they were dubbed "Nader's Raiders" by a headline in the *Washington Post.*

During subsequent summers Nader recruited hundreds of college students and young lawyers from the nation's campuses, which, at the time, were teeming with distrust of the "Establishment." Operating from Nader's Center for Study of Responsive Law, established in Washington, D.C., in May 1969, the group compiled critical reports on such bureaucratic strongholds as the Interstate Commerce Commission and the Food and Drug Administration and on such national problems as care of the elderly, occupational safety, and the misuse of natural resources. Some reports from the center stimulated important reforms (as in the FTC), and their activities encouraged the consumer movement throughout the country.

[Robert F. Buckhorn, *Nader, The People's Lawyer;* Charles McCarry, *Citizen Nader.*]

RICHARD R. BENERT

NAILS, TAX ON. In its first session in 1789 the U.S. Congress levied an import duty of one cent per pound on "nails and spikes," but not on tacks and brads. Several southern members opposed this duty, but ultimately agreed to a small tax to protect this industry, which engaged farmers' families through the long winter evenings.

[Richard Hildreth, *History of the United States.*]

CHARLES MARION THOMAS

NANTUCKET, an island south of Cape Cod, Mass., was discovered in 1602 by Bartholomew Gosnold and settled by the English in 1659. Sterile soil directed the attention of settlers to the capture of whales offshore. Eventually deep-sea vessels of 30 tons burden were fitted out for cruises of six months' duration. After the American Revolution new boats were built, and Nantucket vessels rounded Cape Horn in 1791 and thereafter ventured to Asia. The spread of whaling into the uncharted Pacific opened an era of discovery and trade and the expansion of American diplomacy into South American, Polynesian, and Asian lands, which may be attributed in measure to Nantucket enterprise and hardihood. A fleet of six sloops in 1715 had grown to a marine of eighty-six large and four smaller vessels by 1842. Voyages of from four to six years were common. A waterfront fire in 1846, the California gold rush, and the discovery of petroleum contributed to the downfall of Nantucket whaling, always handicapped by an inadequate harbor. In 1869 the last whaling ship cleared port and brought to a close a brilliant chapter in American economic history.

After the Civil War the fine beaches, good fishing, and picturesque bluffs of Nantucket Island brought it a new reputation as a summer resort, and tourism had become its principal industry before the turn of the century. The town of Nantucket on the island, incorporated in 1687, has many historic features, including a whaling museum and the fine 19th-century homes built during the whaling days. The 1970 population of the town was 3,774.

[Alexander Starbuck, *The History of Nantucket.*]
LLOYD C. M. HARE

NAPLES, AMERICAN CLAIMS ON, arose from seizures of American vessels and cargoes, beginning in 1809, ordered by Joachim Murat, Napoleon I's brother-in-law, as king of Naples. William Pinkney, U.S. minister to Russia, attempted negotiations in 1816, but the Bourbon government denied responsibility for acts of the usurper. A fresh effort by special agent John J. Appleton in 1825–26 yielded like results, although it established the amount of actual losses. The French spoliation treaty of 1831, which ended the legitimist pretentions of irresponsibility, the visit of an American squadron after the French refused to pay the first installment, and the lure of a commercial treaty helped John Nelson, U.S. chargé d'affaires, to reach an agreement in 1836. By 1842 the last payment was made, the total being $2,049,033.12.

[Hunter Miller, ed., *Treaties and Other International Acts of the United States of America;* P. C. Perrotta, *The Claims of the United States Against the Kingdom of Naples.*]
HENRY M. WRISTON

NAPOLEON'S DECREES. Throughout his long struggle with Great Britain, Napoleon Bonaparte was torn between the desirability of excluding British commerce and the undesirability of economic suffocation for continental Europe. His arbitrary policies, alternating between such impositions as the Berlin, Milan, and supplementary decrees and a system of licenses, not only had the effect of cutting off burgeoning American trade with the Continent but also of subjecting American shipping to the British licensing system and, indirectly, to British impressment of seamen.

The Berlin Decree of Nov. 21, 1806, in belated response to the Orders in Council of May 16, 1806, imposed a paper blockade of the British Isles, outstripping in its defiance of neutral rights Britain's own blockade. The Milan Decree, of Dec. 17, 1807, eclipsed even this, by declaring lawful prey ships submitting to the British Orders in Council. The Bayonne Decree of Apr. 17, 1808, further mocked neutrals by representing the seizure of American shipping as cooperation with President Thomas Jefferson in enforcing the embargo begun in December 1807. Similarly, the Rambouillet Decree, drafted Mar. 23, published May 14, 1810, legalized seizure of American shipping as retaliation for a proviso in the U.S. nonimportation law. Climaxing Napoleonic hypocrisy was the letter of the French foreign minister, Jean Baptiste Nompère Champagny, Duc de Cadore, of Aug. 5, 1810, deceptively revoking the continental decrees contingent upon British abandonment of the Orders in Council.

[L. M. Sears, *Jefferson and the Embargo.*]
LOUIS MARTIN SEARS

NARCOTICS TRADE AND LEGISLATION. Many characteristics of American narcotics trade and legislation have developed from three conditions: almost no opium poppies (the source of morphine, heroin, codeine) and coca bushes (the source of cocaine) have been grown commercially in the United States; until the early 20th century importation of crude narcotics, their domestic manufacture into purified drugs, and public distribution were almost unrestricted; and when restrictions began to be imposed, long-standing constitutional barriers between federal and state powers complicated the task of creating nationally uniform and flexible restraints on domestic traffic and consumption.

Except for a sharply increased tariff on smoking (or "prepared") opium in the 1880's, import duties on crude and manufactured narcotics were modest or even absent in the 19th century. Importation records for opium dating from 1840 provide an approximate indication of American opium demand until restrictive legislation was enacted shortly before World War I. One can infer that consumption rose steadily from 1840 to about 1890, when imports leveled off at about half a million pounds of crude opium annually. The battlefield use of opium during the Civil War, so often cited as a cause of American appetites for the drug, does not appear to have affected this rate of consumption, which had already been rising before the conflict. Extensive use of narcotics can probably be attributed to a reliance on them by the rapidly growing, but poorly trained, medical profession; the lack of laws limiting uses to even broadly defined medical purposes; the increasingly effective marketing of proprietary nostrums without any restraints on claims or contents; and the difficulty of legally controlling unorganized and unlicensed health professions. Between 1905 and 1919, after state controls had been judged ineffective, federal statutes and Supreme Court rulings curbed each of these features of American narcotics distribution.

American reliance on foreign supplies of narcotics was dramatically emphasized during the Civil War, when the Confederacy attempted unsuccessfully to grow its own poppies to supply opium for the battlefield. Largely because of the position of the United States as a victim of foreign production, as early as 1909 Americans sought an international agreement to limit production and manufacture of narcotics to strictly medical uses, a category U.S. diplomats insisted did not include maintenance of simple addiction. Worldwide reporting and regulation of opium and coca products gradually evolved after the American-inspired International (or Hague) Opium Convention of 1912, although control sufficient to end the American addiction problem had not yet been attained by the mid-1970's.

The United States has occasionally sought to enact legislation that would influence the control practices of other nations, but without great success. Instances include the three Harrison acts of 1914, which implemented the Opium Convention, and the Porter Heroin Act of 1924, which prohibited importation of crude opium for the manufacture of heroin, a policy the United States desired all other countries to adopt so as to curtail the smuggling of foreign-manufactured heroin.

Controlling the domestic narcotics trade has always been difficult. Reducing the number of narcotics addicts after the easy availability of drugs in the 19th century was complicated by constitutional separation of federal and state powers. Federal assumption of traditional states' rights was much more sharply limited by the Supreme Court than in the mid-20th century after almost a half-century of rapidly increasing centralization of health, police, and welfare powers. Federal legislation with a moral object, therefore, often had to be enacted as a tax measure (as in stopping the manufacture of phosphorous matches by a prohibitive tax) or as a regulation of interstate commerce (the Mann Act), two unquestioned prerogatives of the federal government. A classic example of such legislation is the third of the Harrison acts (approved Dec. 14, 1914), the one usually identified by the eponym, which sought to control the distribution of narcotics to the general public.

Tax powers were again used to control the use of narcotics in 1937 when the transfer of marijuana from one person to another was prohibitively taxed unless the transferrer was registered with the Treasury Department and paid an annual fee—an ingenious legal device suggested by the National Firearms Act of 1934, which had forbidden nonofficial transfer of certain firearms, primarily machine guns, without the payment of a $200 tax on each gun.

Since the development of relatively effective federal and state regulation of the distribution of narcotics by legitimate dealers and health professionals, smuggling has become a focus of attention. The amount of drugs smuggled into the country, like the number of drug users or addicts, has been difficult, if not impossible, to determine objectively. Estimates have been profoundly affected by political and popular attitudes, found in retrospect to be influenced often by fears of minority groups, a desire to exculpate authorities for social disorder, or simple misconceptions of the dangers of some drugs.

The international stance of the United States in relation to narcotics has shifted with changes in the nation's attitudes toward its position within the world community. Thus, before World War I, when the United States initiated the international control of narcotics traffic, it was at the same time pursuing the larger question of peace between nations through such instruments as the "cooling-off" treaties. After the war a deep distrust of other nations, most dramatically exemplified in refusal to join either the League of Nations or the World Court, led the United States also to abandon not only leadership, but even cooperation, in the international struggle against narcotics until the 1930's.

Federal penalties for domestic narcotics violations gradually increased until 1955, when Congress passed both mandatory minimum sentences for many narcotics-related offenses and the death penalty, at the jury's discretion, for some heroin violations. A reaction to severe penalties, particularly to mandatory minimum sentences, set in during the 1960's, led by the American Bar Association. In that decade, as faith in medicopsychological treatment of deviance gained strength among legislative and executive bodies, there was a corresponding decline in the long-standing primacy of law enforcement in the drug-control effort. Further, a rapid rise in drug use—particularly psychedelic substances and cannabis—by young people, in spite of the harshest penalties, supported arguments against such statutory controls as effective deterrents.

Drug abuse, and particularly heroin addiction, became a major public issue in the mid-1960's, as addiction came to be popularly construed as the cause of a large percentage of both property and violent street crime. Like estimates of the number of addicts, the link between drugs and crime seems to have been heavily influenced, as in the past, by many factors, especially by the desire of both government institutions and the public for simple explanations of fearful and complex social problems. Reliance on therapy or other alternatives to prison for drug abuse did not dramatically reduce the crime rate by the early 1970's. As had a similar frustration after attempts to treat addiction medically before and during World War I, public frustration at this "failure" led to enactment of severe prison penalties in several states, most notably New York, the state having perennially the largest addict population. A trend toward relaxation of penalties for possession of small amounts of marijuana continued in the face of this public demand for stricter drug control, both because extensive research had not shown dangers convincing to most scientists and because the large numbers of marijuana users made jailing impracticable.

Changes in response to narcotics use illustrate the difficulties facing legislators when they seek appropriate legal formulas. Extreme punishments, such as the death penalty for drug possession, have in the past diminished the willingness of juries to convict or even indict those accused, while moderate and flexible penalties may not satisfy an insistent popular demand for dramatic action to end drug abuse, as the federal government urged in 1972, "once and for all." Unfortunately, bribery and corruption of public officials have muddied enforcement from the beginning and, along with delays and crowded criminal justice systems, are the realities that, until reformed, sabotage carefully framed legislation.

[Richard J. Bonnie and Charles H. Whitebread II, *The Marihuana Conviction: A History of Marihuana Prohibition in the United States;* Peter D. Lowes, *The Genesis of International Narcotics Control;* David F. Musto, *The American Disease: Origins of Narcotic Control;* Arnold H. Taylor, *American Diplomacy and the Narcotics Traffic, 1900–1939: A Study in International Humanitarian Reform.*]

DAVID F. MUSTO

NARRAGANSETT BAY, an inlet of the Atlantic Ocean in southeastern Rhode Island, was visited in 1524 by Giovanni da Verrazano and described in his letter to King Francis I of France, printed in 1556 and reprinted in English in 1582. The bay was called "G [Gulf] del Refugio" on the 1529 map of Hieronymus da Verrazano. It was called "Bahia de San Johan Baptista" by the Spanish chronicler Gonzalo Fernández Oviedo y Valdéz in 1535. This name in various forms continued to be used until the end of the 16th century.

Dutch explorers and traders recognized the three branches of the bay and called the west passage Sloep Bay (Sloup Bay, Chaloup Bay), the east or middle passage Anker Bay, and the Sakonnet River the Nieuwe River or the Bay van Nassau. English settlers called it Narragansett Bay, though with much variation in spelling, naming it after the native Narraganset, who lived on its west shore. Aquidneck Island is the largest island in the bay.

[H. M. Chapin, *Cartography of Rhode Island.*]

HOWARD M. CHAPIN

NARRAGANSETT PLANTERS, a group of 17th-century stock and dairy farmers living in the southern portion of the colony of Rhode Island. By careful breeding they developed the renowned Narragansett pacer, the best horse of the time for speed. From the last quarter of the 17th century their prosperity, derived from intercolonial and West Indian trade and slaveholding, increased until curbed by the strict enforcement of trade regulations prior to the Revolution. Wealth, and the opportunities afforded by the cultural influences of Newport, developed a mode of life unique in the northern colonial countryside, resembling more that of the South.

[Edward Channing, *The Narragansett Planters, A Study in Causes,* Johns Hopkins University Studies in Historical and Political Science; William Davis Miller, "The Narragansett Planters," *Proceedings of the American Antiquarian Society,* new series, vol. 43.]
WILLIAM DAVIS MILLER

NARROWS, a strait connecting the upper and lower New York bays, was entered by the explorer Giovanni da Verrazano in 1524, and first shown on a map made by the Italian scholar Giambattista Ramusio in 1556. It was fortified about 1710, and more strongly for the War of 1812, providing for an effective defense of New York harbor. A semaphore telegraph, to announce the sighting of vessels, was erected there in 1812. In 1964 the Narrows were spanned by the world's longest suspension bridge (4,260 feet), the Verrazano-Narrows Bridge.

[I. N. Phelps Stokes, *The Iconography of Manhattan Island.*]
ALVIN F. HARLOW

NARVÁEZ EXPEDITION. Pánfilo de Narváez received from Charles V of Spain on Nov. 17, 1526, a patent to explore and reduce to Spanish rule all the lands from Soto la Marina, which empties into the Gulf of Mexico just south of Laguna Madre, northeastward around the Gulf to the "Isle of Florida." With 600 men and eighty horses, he landed from his five ships at Tampa Bay, Apr. 14, 1528. Marching north along the coast in search of the Indian country of Apalachee, he lost contact with his ships, and, after battles with the Indians, he and his men were reduced by famine to the desperate plan of building crude flatboats in which to follow the coast from Apalachee Bay westward to the Spanish settlements on the Rio Pánuco, just south of Tampico. Despite bad weather and starvation the surviving 247 men managed to follow the Gulf coast as far as Texas, where the flotilla broke up among the coastal islands near Galveston Bay, and Narváez perished there in a storm in November 1528. The treasurer of the expedition, Álvar Núñez Cabeza de Vaca, with a few survivors, lived among the coastal Texan Indians for about six years. Then, utilizing their reputations as healers and traders, Cabeza de Vaca and three companions, including a Moorish slave, Estebanico, sought to reach the Pánuco on foot. Turned back in

northeastern Mexico, they performed the justly famous feat of traversing the continent by ascending the valley of the Rio Grande, crossing the Sierra Madre ranges, and wandering down through Sonora, to be rescued by Spaniards near Culiacán, only forty miles from the Gulf of California in modern Sinaloa, in March 1536. The account of their journey and of the Indian lands they had visited or heard about seems to have been a stimulus to the viceroy of New Spain, Antonio de Mendoza, in dispatching the expedition of Francisco Vásquez de Coronado in 1540. Narváez's patent was taken over by Hernando de Soto in 1537.

[F. Bandelier, trans., *The Journey of Álvar Nuñez Cabeza de Vaca;* M. Bishop, *The Odyssey of Cabeza de Vaca;* J. B. Brebner, *The Explorers of North America, 1492–1806;* W. Lowery, *The Spanish Settlements Within the Present Limits of the United States, 1513–1561.*]
RUFUS KAY WYLLYS

NASHOBA, a cooperative or communistic settlement of slaves near Memphis, established in 1825 by Frances Wright, a social reformer from Scotland. Through the organization of such communities of from fifty to a hundred members each, she planned to prepare slaves for their freedom, after which they were to be colonized outside the United States. But Wright soon became too ill to continue its management, and those left in charge proved incompetent. Within five years the experiment was completely abandoned.

[William Randall Waterman, *Frances Wright.*]
L. W. NEWTON

NASHVILLE, a port city and the capital of Tennessee, was founded in the winter of 1779–80 as Fort Nashborough by migrations under James Robertson and John Donelson from the Holston Valley settlements to French Lick near the Cumberland River in north central Tennessee. Although the fort was a frontier outpost constantly threatened by Indians until 1800, it had by then the first government west of the Alleghenies based on a written constitution. In 1784 the community within the fort was incorporated as the town of Nashville by the North Carolina legislature. In 1806 it was chartered as a city. The fertility of the Cumberland Basin attracted wealthy investors and speculators, and soon after the arrival of the first steamboat in 1818 Nashville developed into a commercial and manufacturing center. Politically and economically it had already outdistanced Knoxville and the older eastern section of Tennessee, and as a result of the suitability of its hinterland to cotton, its population increased from 7,000 in 1830 to 17,000 in 1860. Three of its citizens, Andrew Johnson, Andrew Jackson, and James K. Polk, became president of the United States, and in national politics it wielded an influence out of all proportion to its size.

One of the more cultured and aristocratic cities of the antebellum South—largely because it did not experience the mushroom growth of some of its rivals, such as Memphis—Nashville, the "Athens of the South," was so strongly Whig that its citizens were able to defeat the secession movement at the Nashville Convention in 1850. Occupied by Union troops in February 1862 without a fight, Nashville suffered less from the war than most important southern cities and made a speedy recovery afterward. A crossroads of turnpike, rail, and steamship facilities, it had soon recovered its position as a commercial and investment center. By the turn of the 20th century it was becoming a manufacturing center as well, and it burgeoned as such after cheap electric power became readily available with the creation of the Tennessee Valley Authority in 1933. As a religious center Nashville became the home of three major religious publishing houses—the Methodist Publishing House, the National Baptist Publishing Board, and the National Baptist Sunday School Publishing Board—and publishing became one of its principal industries. Beginning about 1925 Nashville became an entertainment center; it is now the home of the country music hall of fame and Opryland, U.S.A., and the mecca of the country music industry. The population of Nashville in 1970 was 447,877.

[T. P. Abernethy, *From Frontier to Plantation in Tennessee.*]

GERALD M. CAPERS, JR.

NASHVILLE, BATTLE OF (Dec. 15–16, 1864), a dramatic winter conflict in which Gen. George H. Thomas, with a hastily organized army of heterogeneous troops, moved out of Nashville and fell upon the Confederate forces of Gen. John B. Hood. On the first day the Confederates were pushed back. On the following day, while feinting and holding on his left wing, Thomas pressed forward on his right and drove the Confederates in disorderly retreat from the battlefield. Sometimes described as exemplifying perfect tactics, Thomas' victory freed Tennessee of organized Confederate forces and marked the end of Hood's Tennessee campaign.

[Thomas Robson Hay, *Hood's Tennessee Campaign.*]

ALFRED P. JAMES

NASHVILLE AND CHATTANOOGA RAILROAD, chartered in 1845 and completed in 1854, was the first Tennessee railroad to be completed. Designed as an extension of a railroad line from Charleston by way of Atlanta to Chattanooga, it assisted in providing the Middle West with an outlet to the southern Atlantic seaboard, contributed to the development of Atlanta and Chattanooga as important antebellum railway centers, and attained considerable military significance during the Civil War. Following the acquisition of several connecting lines it became the Nashville, Chattanooga, and Saint Louis Railroad in 1873.

[T. D. Clark, "Development of the Nashville and Chattanooga Railroad," *Tennessee Historical Magazine,* series 2, vol. 3.]

S. J. FOLMSBEE

NASHVILLE CONVENTION. As sectional strife reached a peak following the opening of the first session of the new Congress of December 1849, many southern statesmen believed that a united southern party was necessary if slavery and southern rights were to be maintained within the Union. The leaders of a caucus of southern delegates in Congress adopted and published an "Address . . . to their Constituents" in 1850, but the leaders felt that a southern convention would be more effective. Sen. John C. Calhoun of South Carolina wrote a letter to Collin S. Tarpley of Mississippi suggesting that his state issue the call for the convention. The Mississippi state convention, which opened in Jackson, Oct. 1, 1849, resolved "that a convention of the slave-holding States should be held in Nashville, Tenn., . . . to devise and adopt some mode of resistance" to northern aggressions. In response to this call delegates from nine states—chosen by popular vote, by conventions, or by state legislatures or appointed by governors—assembled at Nashville on June 3, 1850. Both Whig and Democratic delegates were chosen, but the latter predominated. Many of the outstanding political leaders of the South were among those elected. The convention unanimously adopted twenty-eight resolutions, which maintained that slavery existed independent of, but was recognized by, the Constitution. They asserted that the territories belonged to the people of the states, that the citizens of the several states had equal rights to migrate to the territories, and that Congress had no power to exclude them but was obligated to protect them. The resolutions then expressed a willingness to settle the matter by extending the Missouri Compromise line to the Pacific. The convention also adopted an address to the people of the southern states that condemned the compromise resolutions of Sen. Henry Clay of Kentucky, then before Congress. Reassembling six weeks after Congress had adopted the Compromise of 1850, the convention, with a changed and more radical membership, rejected the compromise and called upon the southern states to secede from the Union. The second session of the convention was a fiasco because southern sentiment rapidly crystallized in support of the compromise.

[Cleo Hearon, *Mississippi and the Compromise of 1850;* D. T. Herndon, "The Nashville Convention of 1850," *Alabama Historical Society Publications,* vol. 5; St. G. L. Sioussat, "Tennessee, the Compromise of 1850 and the Nashville Convention," *Mississippi Valley Historical Review,* vol. 2.]

FLETCHER M. GREEN

NASSAU, FORT, on the Delaware River, was built by Cornelius Jacobsen May in 1623, at the mouth of Big Timber Creek in Gloucester County, N.J. Garrisoned intermittently until 1636, the fort gave the Dutch fur traders a dominant position in the valley. When Gov. Peter Stuyvesant erected Fort Casimir on the lower Delaware in 1651 to compel the evacuation of the Swedish Fort Elfsborg, to the southeast, he abandoned and destroyed Fort Nassau.

[Christopher Ward, *The Dutch and Swedes on the Delaware.*]

C. A. TITUS

NASSAU PACT (Dec. 18–21, 1962) was made by President John F. Kennedy and Great Britain's Prime Minister Harold Macmillan at Nassau, Bahama Islands. It provided that the two countries, in consultation with other North Atlantic Treaty Organization (NATO) allies, would cooperate in establishing a NATO multilateral nuclear force. The agreement was undermined by President Charles de Gaulle, who announced that France would build its own nuclear weapons.

JACOB E. COOKE

NAST CARTOONS. Thomas Nast's cartoons, appearing in *Harper's Weekly* between 1862 and 1886, not only marked the beginning of the modern political cartoon but were a great force in contemporary politics. Nast, a German-born artist, began as a news illustrator for *Frank Leslie's Illustrated Newspaper* in 1855 but later joined *Harper's* and stirred emotions with his Civil War pictures. In 1864 he satirized the compromise "Chicago platform" and the Copperheads, and thenceforth his pictures were largely political.

During Reconstruction Nast was relentless in his attacks on President Andrew Johnson and Secretary of State William H. Seward and began to employ his talent for caricature. His greatest work was in the exposure of political boss William M. Tweed and his cohorts in New York City in 1870. One cartoon asked, "Who stole the people's money?" as each member of the ring pointed to his neighbor, " 'Twas him." In another cartoon Tweed and his minions were vultures on the body of New York City, "Waiting for the storm to blow over." And finally they bowed before the gallows, "The only thing they respect." It was a Nast cartoon that identified Tweed in Europe and thus effected his capture.

In national politics *Harper's* was usually Republican, and in 1872 Nast mercilessly caricatured liberals Horace Greeley and Carl Schurz. After the publication of the "cipher dispatches" in 1878 Samuel J. Tilden was shown repeatedly as an Egyptian mummy on whose wrinkled brow was the word "Fraud." In 1884 *Harper's* bolted with the Mugwumps, and Nast's pen depicted James G. Blaine with three dilapidated plumes and a carpetbag labeled, "Are 20 Years of Blaine Enough?"

Beginning with elaborate pictorial cartoons and long, descriptive captions, often utilizing Shakespearean themes, Nast later evolved a direct and simple design. He invented the symbolic Republican elephant and the Democratic donkey and popularized the Tammany tiger, borrowed from a political club emblem. His skill in caricature and composition and the variety of his conceptions made him extremely popular, and his cartoons are still regarded as incisive commentaries on the politics of the period.

[Morton Keller, *The Art and Politics of Thomas Nast;* J. C. Vinson, *Thomas Nast: Political Cartoonist.*]

MILTON W. HAMILTON

NATAQUA, PROPOSED TERRITORY OF, originated in a movement of the citizens of Honey Lake Valley, Calif., in 1856, to organize an independent territory. Believing they were too far east to be in California and not liking the government of adjacent Carson County in Utah Territory, they met and adopted laws and regulations for the new territory and elected a recorder and surveyor. Nothing came of the movement.

[Asa M. Fairfield, *History of Lassen County, California.*]

JEANNE ELIZABETH WIER

NATCHEZ, a city in southwestern Mississippi and the oldest city on the Mississippi River. In 1716 Jean Baptiste Le Moyne, Sieur de Bienville, in accordance with his policy of extending the French colonial domain up the Mississippi Valley from the Gulf of Mexico, established Fort Rosalie on the site of the present city of Natchez, on the lowest of the several bluffs on the Mississippi. By 1729 it had become a settlement of 700, but in that year the Natchez, resenting the treatment they had received from the French, destroyed the fort.

Not until 1763, when the site came into English possession, was any attempt made at the reestablishment of Natchez (*see* Panmure, Fort). During the Revolution its population, fewer than a hundred at the time and mostly English, was divided into two bitter factions of patriots and Loyalists. After several years of fighting both groups were overpowered by the Spanish, who in turn surrendered the post to the United States in 1798, in compliance with the terms of Pinckney's Treaty of 1795 (*see* Guion's Expedition).

Under the lenient Spanish rule after 1780 Natchez prospered. Tobacco, indigo, and cotton were introduced, and in the first decade of the 19th century the town became a commercial center as the southern terminus of the new road from Nashville, the Natchez Trace. It grew so rapidly that by the end of the second decade of American settlement it contained over 2,000 inhabitants. With the increasing production of cotton and the advent of the steamboat on the Mississippi, it was converted from an isolated frontier outpost into a center of planter aristocracy, second only to New Orleans in the entire Southwest. By the middle of the century, however, because of the rush of population to richer sections of Mississippi and the proximity of New Orleans, it had become apparent that the early commercial promise of Natchez would not be fulfilled.

Following a decline after the Civil War, Natchez regained its economic health in some measure as a shipping point and soon began to capitalize on its natural resources, particularly timber and oil. In the 20th century Natchez gained a reputation as an embodiment of the antebellum South and developed a large tourist industry. The population of Natchez in 1970 was 19,704.

[Dunbar Rowland, *History of Mississippi;* C. Sydnor, *A Gentleman of the Old Natchez Region.*]

GERALD M. CAPERS, JR.

NATCHEZ. The Muskogean-speaking Natchez constituted the largest and most fully unified of the native tribes of the lower Mississippi in the 17th century. Their number is estimated to have been 4,500 in 1650. Hernando De Soto is believed to have fought them in 1541; their presence in the Gulf area in 1682 is noted in the narratives of the expedition of Robert Cavelier, Sieur de La Salle, in that year; and Pierre Lemoyne, Sieur d'Iberville, entered into negotiations with them in 1699. The 18th century saw them driven from their original towns along Saint Catherine's Creek in Mississippi as a result of their continuing hostilities with the French and Choctaw. Segments of the Natchez were assimilated by the Creek and Cherokee, and they were settled with their hosts in Oklahoma in the 19th century. Both the culture and the language of the Natchez were destroyed, with the result that the tribe can be said to be extinct.

Despite the disappearance of the Natchez, enough remains in the accounts of the 18th century to form a picture of their society. The sensitive accounts of Iberville; Du Pratz; Le Petit; Charles Gravier, Comte de Vergennes; and others in various sources of the period provide a fairly clear description of one of the most unusual American Indian tribes. The uniqueness of Natchez culture lay in its patterns of social and political development, especially in the sociopolitical hierarchy the Natchez created. Although their mode of life, village organization, intensive maize cultivation, warfare, and religion relate them closely to other Gulf tribes, such as the Creek, Choctaw, and Cherokee, their concept of hereditary chieftainship has no parallel among American Indians. It is so unusual, in fact, that students of comparative society have devoted considerable effort to tests of the inherent logic of the system.

Like other tribes of the Southeast and Gulf areas, the Natchez structured their societal organization on maternal principles. To matrilineal inheritance they added the concept of social ranking, an element seen in incipient form among the Creek, for example, but considerably extended and strengthened by the Natchez. They evolved a noble class, made up of three ranks: "Honored Men" made up the bottom rank of the nobility; the rank above was made up of "Suns"; and from this rank was drawn the "Great Sun," the chief. Although most American Indians lacked autocratic chiefs, this seems not to have been the case with the Natchez, for the Great Sun was given considerable political power, as indeed were his brothers who were sons of the same mother, the "White Woman," a member of the Sun group. The matrilineal principle was operative in that a woman's offspring took her class. There is some suggestion of class exogamy, a noblewoman's rank being conferred on her husband—with the result that the father of the Great Sun could be drawn from any one of the other ranks. A slight concern with patrilineal ordering was present in that if a man of the noble class married a commoner, the children were Honored Men. That the Natchez were acutely concerned with rank is suggested by the fact that they referred to commoners as "Stinkards"—not only members of their own tribe but also members of other tribes, such as the Tunica, drawn into the Natchez orbit. Although the system created by the Natchez made use of a number of the patterns known to adjacent peoples, it was uniquely put together and emerges as a sociological puzzle.

[C. W. M. Hart, "A Reconsideration of the Natchez Social Structure," *American Anthropologist*, vol. 45 (1943); Theodore Stern, "The Natchez," in R. F. Spencer, J. D. Jennings, and others, eds., *The Native Americans*.]
ROBERT F. SPENCER

NATCHEZ, TREATY OF (May 14, 1790), between Gov. Manuel Gayoso de Lemos of Mississippi Territory and the Choctaw and Chickasaw nations, confirmed boundaries of the Natchez District as set originally by the British and the Indians: on the west, the Mississippi; on the east, a line from the Yazoo River, a few miles above Walnut Hills, running south into Florida.

MACK SWEARINGEN

NATCHEZ CAMPAIGN OF 1813 was waged by U.S. forces against the Creek of the Tombigbee and Alabama rivers region, then the eastern frontier of Mississippi Territory. The Indians threatened hostilities early in 1813, and a brigade of volunteers from Natchez country, commanded by Gen. F. L. Claiborne, was ordered to Fort Stoddert, on the Tombigbee. Following the Creek attack on Fort Mims on the east bank of the Alabama River about thirty-five miles above Mobile, Aug. 30, 1813, Claiborne was reinforced and was able to destroy the Creek stronghold at the Holy Ground in present Lowndes County, Ala., Dec. 23, 1813 (*see* Creek War).

[Dunbar Rowland, *History of Mississippi*.]
EDGAR B. NIXON

NATCHEZ TRACE, a road running more than 500 miles from Nashville, Tenn., to Natchez, Miss., on the Mississippi River, roughly following an old Indian trail. After the United States acquired a clear title from Spain (*see* Pinckney's Treaty) to the Old South-

west in 1795 and eight years later purchased Louisiana, the economic and military necessity of adequate roads through the southwestern wilderness to the Gulf of Mexico spurred the government into action. By far the most famous and important of the roads that resulted was the Natchez Trace. In 1801 Gen. James Wilkinson obtained the right of way by treaties with the Chickasaw and Choctaw (*see* Adams, Fort), and in 1806 Congress authorized construction to begin. In a few years wagons were using the road, but for several decades most of its traffic was northward, since settlers would float their produce down the Mississippi to market on flatboats and return over the robber-infested Natchez Trace by foot or on horseback. Construction of a 450-mile parkway following the trace began in 1934. In 1938 it was designated the Natchez Trace National Parkway.

[E. B. Stanton, *Natchez Trace;* Robert Coates, *Outlaw Years*.]

GERALD M. CAPERS, JR.

NATCHITOCHES, a city in Louisiana, began as a French trading post, established by Louis Juchereau de Saint Denis in the winter of 1713–14 among the Natchitoch, near the site of the present city on the Red River. Soon thereafter it was garrisoned and fortified, becoming an outpost against neighboring Spanish establishments in Texas. For a century the settlement was a military-commercial center with a cosmopolitan population composed eventually of French, Spanish, Anglo-American, and other elements. Besides the Indian trade it carried on an extensive traffic, mostly contraband, with the Spaniards to the west, French manufactured articles and foodstuffs being exchanged for cattle, horses, mules, hides, and silver, which went in turn to other points on the Mississippi. In the late 18th century local produce exported from Natchitoches included indigo, tobacco of superior quality, bear oil, tallow, dressed skins, and meats.

During the Franco-Spanish war of 1719 the commandant of Natchitoches drove the Spaniards temporarily from their posts in northeastern Texas. In 1731 Saint Denis, with Spanish assistance, repulsed an attack of the Natchez on the fort. In 1735–36 and again in 1751–53 Natchitoches figured in inconclusive Franco-Spanish boundary controversies. In 1806, as a U.S. border post, it became the center of military and diplomatic maneuvers culminating in the Neutral Ground Agreement.

Natchitoches served as a gateway for explorers, notably Saint Denis (1713, 1716), Bernard de la Harpe

(1719), Athanase De Mézières y Clugny (1770–79), and Zebulon M. Pike (1807); for adventurers and filibusters entering Texas, notably Philip Nolan (1799–1801), Bernardo Gutiérrez de Lara and Augustus Magee (1811–13), and James Long (1819); and for Anglo-American colonists brought to Texas after 1821 by Stephen F. Austin and others, as well as for settlers going to Arkansas. The town was a military post of some importance at the time of the Texas Revolution (1836) and the Mexican War (1846–48). During the Red River campaign of the Civil War it was captured (Mar. 31, 1864) by Union forces, being evacuated by them following the failure of Gen. Nathaniel P. Banks's campaign against Shreveport, ten days later.

Natchitoches yielded its primacy as head of navigation for the Red River steamboat traffic to Grand Ecore after 1850, when the main channel of the Red River shifted. Local industries, notably fish breeding and lumber manufacture, developed during the early 20th century and continue to provide the basis for the state's economy, along with the production of dairy products and cottonseed oil and the raising of poultry. The population of Natchitoches in 1970 was 15,674.

[H. E. Bolton, *Athanase de Mézières and the Louisiana-Texas Frontier, 1768–1780;* Alcée Fortier, *A History of Louisiana;* G. Portré-Bobinski and C. M. Smith, *Natchitoches.*]

CHARMION SHELBY

NATIONAL ACADEMY OF SCIENCES was established by Congress on Mar. 3, 1863, as a private organization to investigate and report on any subject of science or art (technology) whenever called upon by any department of the government. For example, in 1871 the academy drew up instructions for the government-sponsored Arctic expedition of the *Polaris* commanded by Charles F. Hall.

The National Research Council was established by the academy in 1916 at the request of President Woodrow Wilson to organize research needed for national preparedness in time of war. Two years later an executive order made the National Research Council a permanent and broadly based agency of the National Academy of Sciences to aid the military and civil branches of the government during World War I and after, to stimulate research—particularly cooperative research—in both pure and applied science, and to conduct scientific studies as the need for them arose. Since that time the research council, supported by both public and private funds, has acted as the principal operating arm of the academy. In 1950 the National Academy of Sciences and its research council became a single administrative and operating unit, the National Academy of Sciences–National Research Council.

The National Academy of Engineering was created by Congress in 1964 under the original 1863 charter of the National Academy of Sciences as a private, permanent agency through which engineers could advise the government on the needs and uses of technology and engineering as it affected public policy. The National Academy of Engineering was organized with twenty-five founding members and with no limitation on membership. The parent organization, the National Academy of Sciences, had originally been limited by its charter to fifty members. In 1870 that restriction in the enabling act was removed, and membership was limited only by the maximum number that could be elected annually. The National Research Council drew its membership from scientists, engineers, and other professionals in universities, industry, and government to serve on its several hundred study committees.

Both the National Academy of Sciences and the National Academy of Engineering annually elect foreign associates who meet the qualifications for membership; they are privileged to attend meetings and to communicate papers to the academies. In 1970 the parent academy established an Institute of Medicine to provide advisory services in the areas of medicine and public health on a national scale. The home of the National Academy of Sciences is in Washington, D.C.

REXMOND C. COCHRANE

NATIONAL ADVISORY COMMISSION ON CIVIL DISORDERS. The wave of urban ghetto riots that began in New York City and Rochester, N.Y., in 1964 and in the Watts section of Los Angeles in 1965 reached its peak in the summer of 1967 when a total of sixty-six people were killed in Newark, N.J., and Detroit, Mich. Only days after these two riots, President Lyndon B. Johnson created the National Advisory Commission on Civil Disorders, headed by Judge Otto Kerner of Illinois. On the basis of formal hearings and a series of studies by a large number of distinguished social scientists, the commission issued a widely circulated report in March 1968. This report concluded that America's tradition of white racism was responsible for the riots. The commission deplored the polarization of the nation into two societies, one black and one white, and recommended a massive program of federal spending to correct the inequities produced by centuries of racial discrimination. Shortly after the report was issued, the assassination of Martin Luther King, Jr., produced a new wave of riots. Thereafter civil disorders quickly subsided, and at least partly for that reason, only a few of the commission's recommendations were carried out. But its widely read report, which gave official sanction to the view that the blame and the remedy for racial inequalities lay with white America, had appreciable impact upon public opinion and governmental actions.

ELLIOTT RUDWICK

NATIONAL ADVISORY COMMITTEE FOR AERONAUTICS was created in 1915 in response to war-stimulated advances in Europe. NACA, as it became known, was charged by Congress "to conduct the scientific study of the problems of flight, with a view to their practical solution." It consisted of twelve unpaid members (increased to seventeen in 1948) appointed by the president from the federal establishment plus recognized leaders from the scientific community. It was headed by a chairman, most of whom were members of the National Academy of Sciences. It began with one employee (John F. Victory) and acquired a director of aeronautical research (George W. Lewis) in 1924. By 1947, when Hugh L. Dryden became its second director, NACA had become an independent research agency with some 7,000 employees.

NACA recommendations exercised influence during World War I on such urgent national policy questions as research needs, technical coordination, cross-licensing of patents, and airmail, but the committee's policy role had ended by 1926. It was served by technical committees and increasingly by dedicated in-house research, beginning at the Langley Aeronautical Memorial Laboratory (Hampton, Va.) after 1917. With unique wind tunnels and other research tools NACA-sponsored research was focused on areas neglected by industry and the military or prompted by such foreign innovations as jet propulsion. Aviation leaders attended annual inspections, and the excellence of NACA technical reports earned an international reputation and congressional support. By the mid-1930's all modern aircraft were said to bear the mark of NACA research.

World War II prompted NACA's greatest expansion. The Ames Aeronautical Laboratory at Moffett Field, Calif., was founded in 1940, and the Lewis Flight Propulsion Laboratory at Cleveland in 1941. By 1945 NACA had a station for rocket research at Wallops Island, Va., and one for support of the NACA role in the flight test program conducted jointly with the air force and navy at Edwards Air Force Base, Calif. When the Bell X-1 made the first supersonic flight on Oct. 14, 1947, it symbolized the future of flight in space. The Soviet Sputnik of Oct. 4, 1957, precipitated the creation of a more far-reaching agency, and the National Advisory Committee for Aeronautics emerged as the organizational nucleus of the National Aeronautics and Space Administration (NASA) on Oct. 1, 1958.

[E. M. Emme, *Aeronautics and Astronautics, 1915–1960;* G. W. Gray, *Frontiers of Flight;* J. C. Hunsaker, "Forty Years of Aeronautical Research," *NACA Annual Report* (1958).]

EUGENE M. EMME

NATIONAL AERONAUTICS AND SPACE ADMINISTRATION. During the decade of the 1960's the United States became a space-faring nation, primarily as a result of intense international rivalry with the Soviet Union. The establishment of the National Aeronautics and Space Administration (NASA) was the foremost legislative manifestation of a mood of national anxiety—often approaching hysteria—that followed the orbiting of the earth by the first two artificial satellites, belonging to the Soviet Union, in the fall of 1957. The Soviet Sputniks were immediately associated in the thinking of government officials, military strategists, and the general public with the Soviet news agency's announcement late the previous summer that the Soviet Union had successfully tested an intercontinental ballistic missile (ICBM) capable of carrying a nuclear warhead to targets in the United States. In the winter of 1957–58 the conviction that the "space lag" and the alleged "missile gap" constituted a severe national security crisis became even more pronounced as the Vanguard rocket (which was to orbit a small scientific payload as part of the U.S. contribution to the International Geophysical Year) exploded on its launch stand and as a Senate subcommittee investigation revealed delays, duplication, and rampant interservice rivalry in the nation's missile programs.

In early 1958, two U.S. satellites—Explorer and Vanguard—were sent into orbit, and within a few years, the United States had deployed several times as many intercontinental nuclear-tipped missiles as had the Soviet Union. Eventually it became apparent that

the party. Membership includes one man and one woman from each state and most of the territories. First used by the Democrats in 1848 and by the Republicans in 1856, a committee is formally designated by each party every four years by the national convention. Actually, its members are selected according either to state law or to party rule. The committee is usually of little significance in its collective capacity; the chairman, named by the presidential candidate, and a small executive committee usually dominate the situation. The members are active and influential, however, in state politics.

[E. B. Logan, ed., *American Political Scene;* E. M. Sait, *American Parties and Elections.*]

THOMAS S. BARCLAY

NATIONAL CONGRESS OF AMERICAN INDIANS, an intertribal organization founded in 1944, includes both individual and tribal members. The purpose of the organization is political action, and it has used the political technique of lobbying for the advancement of Indian interests. Its political philosophy has been relatively moderate, although it has pressed for changes in the Bureau of Indian Affairs. It has sought primarily to improve the position of Indians within the federal governmental structure. It has opposed the termination of federal responsibilities to Indians and the transfer of federal functions pertaining to Indians to the states.

[Hazel W. Hertzberg, *The Search for an American Indian Identity.*]

KENNETH M. STEWART

NATIONAL DEBT. *See* **Debt, Public.**

NATIONAL DEFENSE. *See* **Defense, National.**

NATIONAL EDUCATION ASSOCIATION. The NEA, the largest professional educational organization in the United States, grew out of the National Teachers Association (NTA), which was established in 1857. Through the activity of the NTA a department of education was established in the federal government in 1867. The NTA was reorganized as the National Education Association in 1871, and in 1906 it was chartered by Congress.

The purpose of the NEA is to promote educational efforts and excellence and to secure teachers' rights. On the federal level it actively lobbies for education

legislation, much of which it drafts. On the local level it acts as a bargaining unit. The NEA publishes an important educational journal, *Today's Education* (formerly the *NEA Journal,* begun in 1913); the quarterly *NEA Research Bulletin,* yearbooks, and research and other studies. In 1975 it had 50 state and 9,000 local affiliates and a membership of 1.7 million.

[Edgar B. Wesley, *NEA, The First Hundred Years.*]

NATIONAL GAZETTE was started in Philadelphia, Oct. 31, 1791, under the patronage of Thomas Jefferson, then secretary of state, who subsidized its editor, Philip Freneau, with the position of translator in the Department of State. It was intended to oppose the Federalist *United States Gazette;* but its attacks on Secretary of the Treasury Alexander Hamilton's policies angered President George Washington, who held Jefferson responsible. It was discontinued shortly after Jefferson's resignation in 1894.

[W. G. Bleyer, *Main Currents in the History of American Journalism.*]

MILTON W. HAMILTON

NATIONAL GUARD, the modern counterpart of the militia, with the longest continuous history of any American military component, the oldest units being the 182nd Infantry (Fifth Massachusetts-Middlesex) Regiment and the 101st Engineer Battalion (Eighth Massachusetts-Marblehead Regiment), both organized in 1636. The name "National Guard" was first used in 1824 by New York units to honor the Marquis de Lafayette, commander of France's Garde Nationale.

From the Federal Militia Act of 1792 to the Dick Act of 1903, the United States lacked a uniform, enforced militia policy. The modern National Guard began with the Dick Act, which divided the militia into the organized militia, or National Guard, and the unorganized militia. Units were to conform with the standards of the regular army and receive increased state and federal aid, but they were separate from the army. A 1908 amendment authorized the president to send guard units outside the country. The National Defense Act of 1916 made the guard an army component while in federal service and provided for regular training.

The National Defense Act of 1920 established a three-component army: National Guard, organized reserves, and regular army. Although the guard was considered the first-line reserve, it still was not an army component. An amendment of June 15, 1933, created the National Guard of the United States (NGUS) as a reserve component of the army. Although the composition of this force was identical to that of the state National Guard, it was subject to a call to active duty by the president without his having to go through the governor. For a short time after World War II there was no guard, but in 1945 the War Department established the guard as a twenty-seven–division force, available for immediate service in event of war. Upon the creation of a separate air force in 1947, the Air National Guard was formed. Under terms of the Reserve Forces Act of 1955 the army became responsible for at least six months' training of guard recruits.

A reorganization in 1962 cut four divisions from authorized guard strength. In 1965 Secretary of Defense Robert S. McNamara tried to amalgamate the guard with the reserves, but he encountered powerful opposition from Congress. Two years later fifteen divisions were cut from the force structure, leaving six infantry and two armored divisions. National Guard units must undergo at least forty-eight drills and fifteen days of field training annually. Aside from being used in wartime, guard units have given aid in times of natural disasters and maintained order during civil disturbances. (*See also* Military Aid to the Civilian Power.)

[J. D. Hill, *The Minute Man in Peace and War;* W. H. Riker, *Soldiers of the States.*]

WARNER STARK

NATIONAL INDIAN YOUTH COUNCIL, an all-Indian organization, started in 1961 by Indian college students and recent college graduates. The council is more militant than the National Congress of American Indians, which it has criticized as being too conservative. It manifests the influence of the civil rights movements of the period of its founding and has used tactics of demonstration and confrontation. It favors the abolition of the Bureau of Indian Affairs.

[Hazel W. Hertzberg, *The Search for an American Indian Identity;* Alvin Josephy, *Red Power.*]

KENNETH M. STEWART

NATIONAL INDUSTRIAL RECOVERY ACT. *See* **National Recovery Administration.**

NATIONAL INSTITUTE FOR THE PROMOTION OF SCIENCE, founded on May 15, 1840, in Washington, D.C., as the National Institution for the Promotion of Science, was referred to as the National Institution; but the word "Institution" was changed to "Institute" by common assent on July 27, 1842, when Congress granted it a twenty-year charter. The National Institute reflected the ambitions of its Washington predecessor, the Columbian Institute, and followed the tradition of other philosophical societies in America. Its areas of inquiry ranged over the natural and physical sciences and applied science and agriculture, as well as American history, literature, and the fine arts. Membership was broadly defined, and invitations went to resident politicians, diplomatic representatives, and interested Americans throughout the nation.

Its founding coincided with congressional acceptance of Englishman James Smithson's bequest for an "institution for the promotion of science." The leaders of the new institute, Joel R. Poinsett and Frances Markoe, were especially interested in establishing a permanent national museum with the Smithson fund. They hoped to base the museum on specimens from the United States Exploring Expedition under Charles Wilkes (1838–42). The Washington group began publishing its *Bulletin* in 1841, and circulars solicited membership and contributions. By 1842, despite the new federal charter, the institute had inadequate funds to care for its growing collections and had not gained support from scientists. In addition, Congress seemed sympathetic to several rival claims for the Smithson bequest.

Hoping to gain a reputation as the national spokesman for science in the eyes of Congress and the public, the local membership sponsored a gala meeting in April 1844. Political speeches, enthusiastic amateurs, and varied entertainment could not camouflage the distrust or lack of interest of many leading scientists. Without the support of these leaders, many of whom attended a rival meeting of the Association of American Geologists and Naturalists the following month, the institute produced few substantive results. Lack of federal funding, establishment of the independent Smithsonian Institution in 1846, and disaffection among the leaders led to the disintegration of the institute. Despite attempted revivals in 1847–48 and 1854, the institute became merely a local group, meeting irregularly. Gradually its collections were deposited at the new Smithsonian Institution. In 1862 the charter expired, and no attempt was made to renew it.

The National Institute during the early 1840's reflected a transition in American science. Unprofessional and eclectic, it could not meet the needs of an increasingly sophisticated, specialized scientific community. By its activity, however, the institute demonstrated the need for an alternative kind of organization. More positively, the institute sustained the idea of a national museum for science by its preservation of the Wilkes collection and served as a partial model for the later development of the Smithsonian Institution.

[Sally Kohlstedt, "A Step Toward Scientific Self Identity in the United States: The Failure of the National Institute, 1844," *Isis,* vol. 62 (1971); Madge Pichard, "Government and Science in the United States: Historical Backgrounds," *Journal of the History of Medicine and Allied Sciences,* vol. 1 (1946).]

SALLY GREGORY KOHLSTEDT

NATIONAL INSTITUTES OF HEALTH originated as the Laboratory of Hygiene and was established at the Marine Hospital, Staten Island, N.Y., in 1887 for research on cholera and other infectious diseases. In 1891 it was renamed the Hygienic Laboratory and moved to Washington, D.C., and in 1930, as a result of the Ransdell Act, it became the National Institute of Health. In 1937 the National Cancer Institute was added, and the following year Congress authorized the construction of new, larger laboratory facilities and the transfer of the National Institute of Health (NIH) to Bethesda, Md. Legislation in 1948 established a National Heart Institute and changed the name of the National Institute of Health to National Institutes of Health.

An agency of the Department of Health, Education and Welfare since that department's establishment in 1953, NIH has the mission of improving the health of all Americans. To achieve this goal it conducts biomedical research; provides grants to individuals, organizations, and institutions for research, training, and medical education; assists in the improvement and construction of library facilities and resources; and supports programs in biomedical communications. From its beginnings in a one-room laboratory, NIH has developed into a great research center consisting of ten institutes (Cancer; Heart and Lung; Allergy and Infectious Diseases; Dental Research; Arthritis, Metabolism, and Digestive Diseases; Neurological Diseases and Stroke; Child Health and Human Development; General Medical Sciences; Eye; and Environmental Health Sciences); four divisions (Computer Research and Technology; Research Grants; Research Resources; and Research Services); the National Library of Medicine; and two centers,

the research hospital Clinical Center and the John E. Fogarty International Center.

The NIH campus consists of over 300 acres and includes laboratories, libraries, and clinical facilities for highly sophisticated research into the biomedical sciences. NIH also has annual lectures, honors, exhibits, and symposia. Among its scientists are three Nobel laureates, and since 1938 NIH has supported the work of another fifty-six Nobel Prize winners, thirty-nine of whom received grant support for research conducted prior to their awards and were thus directly assisted by NIH in making their discoveries.

[U.S. Department of Health, Education and Welfare, Public Health Service, National Institutes of Health, *NIH Almanac* (1975); Ralph Chester Williams, *The United States Public Health Service, 1798–1950.*]

MANFRED WASERMAN

NATIONAL INTELLIGENCER, a conservative triweekly newspaper, issuing a weekly edition, styled *National Intelligencer and Washington Advertiser,* was established by Samuel Harrison Smith in Washington, D.C., Oct. 31, 1800, as the official organ of Thomas Jefferson's Democratic-Republican party. *Washington Advertiser* was dropped from the title in 1810, and in 1813 the *Intelligencer* became a daily. Smith sold it in 1810 to Joseph Gales, Jr., who in 1812 took William W. Seaton into a partnership that lasted until Gales's death in 1860. The *Intelligencer* was the organ of administrations until the presidency of John Quincy Adams. It became a Whig paper during Andrew Jackson's regime but was supplanted by the *Republic* as the Whig official organ during Zachary Taylor's presidency. It was returned to favor during Millard Fillmore's administration. The daily edition was merged with the weekly in 1870, moved to New York, and was soon discontinued.

[W. G. Bleyer, *Main Currents in the History of American Journalism;* F. Hudson, *Journalism in the United States From 1690 to 1872.*]

W. B. HATCHER

NATIONALIZATION OF U.S. PROPERTY ABROAD. Prior to World War I, few countries ever expropriated the property of aliens, and when they did, it generally was upon the payment of just compensation to the former owners. Starting with the Russian Revolution in 1917, expropriations became more commonplace, often taking the form of vast nationalization programs under which countries took the private property of citizens and aliens alike. Between

World War I and World War II, many U.S. nationals, both individuals and corporations, lost their property in this fashion. Whereas some countries compensated the former owners for their losses—Mexico is a prime example—often such was not the case. Half a century after its revolution, the Soviet Union still had not settled claims. Moreover, even when compensation was paid it was often inadequate.

Since the end of World War II, nationalizations have become increasingly common. The Communist countries of Bulgaria, Czechoslovakia, Hungary, Poland, Rumania, and Yugoslavia all engaged in such programs, nationalizing not only the means of production but in most instances all real and personal property as well. All but Czechoslovakia eventually entered into lump-sum settlement agreements, under which the United States received over $100 million to distribute among U.S. claimants in return for its waiver of their claims. The amount of compensation received under these agreements averaged well under 50 percent of the value of the claims. Additionally, as was the case with China in 1949–50 and Cuba in 1959–60, negotiations looking toward a lump-sum settlement frequently proved impossible.

In the 1960's and 1970's, numerous nationalizations took place in Latin America, the most noteworthy being the taking of the International Petroleum Company by Peru in 1968 and of the Kennecott and Anaconda corporations by Chile in 1971. Both countries, while offering what otherwise might be considered adequate compensation, demanded the right to deduct therefrom amounts for "unjust enrichment" and "excess profits," amounts that actually exceeded the tendered compensation. The United States, while acknowledging the right of all countries to nationalize the property of foreigners in the course of making structural changes in their economies, has insisted in all such cases that U.S. claimants be paid, in the words of the United Nations Resolution on Permanent Sovereignty Over Natural Resources (1962), "appropriate compensation . . . in accordance with international law."

With the advent of the United Nations and the passing of "gunboat" diplomacy, the United States no longer can legally intervene in foreign countries that nationalize the property of U.S. citizens, even when the nationalization amounts to actual confiscation. Hence, alternative strategies have had to be developed. One is a pattern of bilateral treaties now in force between the United States and several dozen countries, all of which provide that the taking of property shall be conditional upon "prompt payment of just

compensation." Another is the so-called Hickenlooper Amendment to the Foreign Assistance Act of 1961, under which the United States suspends foreign aid to countries that have not taken appropriate steps to provide suitable compensation within six months after the nationalization of U.S. property. Still another is the Investment Guarantee Program, administered by the Overseas Private Investment Corporation, which allows U.S. investors to insure against losses caused by nationalizations in developing countries.

None of the above techniques, however, can mandate the payment of compensation by a foreign country bent upon confiscating the property of U.S. nationals. Only the realization by such countries that their access to foreign capital and, perhaps even more important, to foreign technology will be cut off if they engage in confiscatory nationalizations can prevent such action, and even the possibility of economic sanctions will not deter governments motivated by ideological reasons or domestic political considerations.

[R. B. Lillich, *The Protection of Foreign Investment;* R. B. Lillich, ed., *The Valuation of Nationalized Property in International Law;* R. B. Lillich and B. H. Weston, *International Claims: Their Settlement by Lump Sum Agreements;* G. M. White, *Nationalisation of Foreign Property.*]

RICHARD B. LILLICH

NATIONAL LABOR RELATIONS ACT. Enacted in 1935, the National Labor Relations Act (NLRA) is the cornerstone of national labor policy. Known initially as the Wagner Act, it guarantees the rights of workers to organize and to bargain collectively with their employers. It encourages collective bargaining and provides governmental processes for the selection of employee bargaining representatives. It provided for the establishment of the National Labor Relations Board (NLRB) to administer its provisions.

As originally enacted, the NLRA prohibited unfair labor practices by employers but not by labor organizations. Employers were prohibited from interfering with, restraining, or coercing employees in the exercise of their rights to form unions, to bargain collectively, and to engage in other concerted activities. The right to strike thus was protected for employees subject to the law. The act outlawed company unions or employer-assisted unions. It prohibited discrimination in employment to encourage or discourage membership in a labor organization but permitted "closed shops" established by collective-bargaining agreements between employers and unions with exclusive bargaining rights. It prohibited employers from discharging or otherwise discriminating against employees who file charges or give testimony under the act. It also made it unlawful for an employer to refuse to bargain collectively with the representative chosen by a majority of employees in a group appropriate for collective bargaining.

The NLRA was amended in 1947 by the Labor Management Relations Act, commonly known as the Taft-Hartley Act. The most important 1947 amendments were those that made it unlawful for unions to engage in certain unfair labor practices. Among other things, unions were prohibited from restraining or coercing employees in exercising their rights under the law, refusing to bargain in good faith with an employer when the union is the representative of employees, and engaging in secondary boycotts and certain types of strikes and picketing. Closed shops were outlawed by the Taft-Hartley amendments, but a proviso permitted an employer and a union to agree to a "union shop," requiring employee membership thirty days after date of hire to the extent of tendering the uniformly required dues and initiation fees. Another proviso stated that union-shop agreements could not be authorized in states where they were forbidden by state law; in all other respects the NLRA preempted state laws. The 1947 amendments also reorganized the NLRB, providing for the president to appoint the general counsel, who was assigned statutory responsibility for the investigation of charges of unfair labor practice, the issuance of complaints, and the prosecution of complaints before the board.

The NLRA was amended again in 1959 by the Labor-Management Reporting and Disclosure Act, commonly known as the Landrum-Griffin Act. By the more important 1959 amendments, unions were precluded from picketing or threatening to picket to force recognition by the employer or to force the employees to accept the union as their representative if the union was not certified to represent the employees. Unions and employers were barred from entering into "hot cargo" contracts; that is, with certain exceptions the law declared void and unenforceable any contract by which a company agreed to cease handling, using, selling, transporting, or otherwise dealing in the products of any other company.

The NLRA generally applies to all employers engaged in interstate commerce. It does not apply to railroads and airlines, which are covered by the Railway Labor Act, or to governmental agencies. As a matter of policy the board has not exercised its legal jurisdiction to the fullest extent so as to take cases in all businesses or industries that affect interstate commerce. Some groups of employees—such as agricultural laborers, domestic employees, and supervisors—are excluded from coverage.

The board is composed of five members appointed by the president subject to approval by the Senate, with each member having a term of five years. The general counsel, whose appointment also must be approved by the Senate, has a term of four years. Headquartered in Washington, D.C., the agency has thirty-one regional offices and eleven smaller field offices throughout the country. Total Washington and field staffs numbered approximately 2,400 in 1972. Between 1935 and 1972 the agency processed more than 300,000 cases in which unfair labor practices were alleged and it conducted more than 190,000 secret-ballot employee self-determination elections. Millions of employees have cast ballots in these elections; 25 million voters entered the polling place by 1967.

The board members act primarily as a quasi-judicial body in deciding cases on formal records, generally upon review of findings of fact and decisions by its administrative law judges (formerly called trial examiners) in cases of unfair labor practice or upon review of regional director decisions in representation cases. The NLRB has no independent statutory power of enforcement of its orders, but it may seek enforcement in the U.S. courts of appeals; parties aggrieved by board orders also may seek judicial review.

[H. A. Millis and E. C. Brown, *From the Wagner Act to Taft-Hartley;* National Labor Relations Board, *Summary of the National Labor Relations Act,* and *Annual Reports;* Louis G. Silverberg, *How to Take a Case Before the NLRB.*]

FRANK M. KLEILER

NATIONAL LABOR RELATIONS BOARD V. *JONES AND LAUGHLIN STEEL CORPORATION,* 301 U.S. 1 (1937), a Supreme Court decision that, by a five-to-four decision, upheld the validity of the National Labor Relations Act of 1935. The Court accepted the findings of the National Labor Relations Board, designed to show that the Jones and Laughlin Corporation was engaged in interstate commerce. By bringing in raw materials from other states and then shipping its finished products to points outside the state in which they were made, the Court ruled, the company was engaged in activities that were in the "stream" of commerce. The "stoppage" of these activities "by industrial strife would have a most serious effect upon interstate commerce," an effect that "would be immediate and might be catastrophic," the Court majority declared. This majority had "no doubt that Congress had constitutional authority to safeguard the right of respondent's employees to self-organization and freedom in the choice of representatives for collective bargaining." The Court thus reversed the lower court, which had ruled that the federal government had no constitutional right to regulate labor relations in a manufacturing establishment. This was the first of fifteen formal decisions won by the National Labor Relations Board.

ERIK MCKINLEY ERIKSSON

NATIONAL MEDIATION BOARD. *See* **Federal Agencies.**

NATIONAL MONETARY COMMISSION was appointed in accordance with the provisions of the Aldrich-Vreeland Act of May 30, 1908, which provided for the appointment of a commission of eighteen members, to be composed of nine members of the Senate and nine members of the House of Representatives. The act further stated that it was to be the duty of this commission "to inquire into and report to Congress . . . what changes are necessary or desirable in the monetary system of the United States or in the laws relating to banking and currency."

The commission, with Sen. Nelson Aldrich as chairman, was duly appointed and proceeded to carry out its designated task. Experts were appointed to make studies of banking history and existing conditions in the United States and other countries, and in the summer of 1908 members of the commission visited England, France, and Germany to ascertain their banking arrangements, methods, and practices by personal observation and interviews.

On Jan. 8, 1912, the commission submitted its report to Congress. The report contained a summary of the work done by the commission, and by experts and others employed by it, as well as a description and text of a proposed law to remedy a number of existing defects as enumerated in the report. The proposed law contained provisions for the establishment of a National Reserve Association with branches to act as a central bank for the United States (*see* Federal Reserve System). The monographs and articles, prepared for the commission by experts and published in conjunction with the report, numbered more than forty, and constituted, at the time, one of the most comprehensive banking libraries available.

[J. L. Laughlin, *The Federal Reserve Act, Its Origin and Problems;* P. M. Warburg, *The Federal Reserve System.*]
FREDERICK A. BRADFORD

NATIONAL MUSEUM. The concept of a national museum is as old as the American nation. In 1788 both James Madison and Benjamin Rush embodied it in a plan for a federal university, but its actual development was tentative and haphazard, and a century had passed before it was built. Among its several sources was the Patent Office, containing an "American Museum of Arts," which included patent models as well as specimens accumulated on various scientific expeditions. Between 1840 and 1862 there was the privately initiated, but publicly incorporated, National Institute for the Promotion of Science in Washington, D.C. Most important was the Smithsonian Institution, established in 1846, which inherited James Smithson's cabinet of minerals. Other collections were acquired, including those of the Patent Office and the extinct National Institute, and these were unified in a single museum under the skillful guidance of Spencer F. Baird, first assistant to Joseph Henry, the founding secretary.

The National Museum was created as an outgrowth of the Centennial Exposition of 1876 at Philadelphia. Plans were made to participate, and Congress was asked for funds to construct a building at Philadelphia, subsequently to be moved and "used as a National Museum at the capital of the nation." Instead, a large rambling structure adjoining the Smithsonian Institution was begun in 1879 to house the exhibits; it opened in 1881 as the National Museum. G. Brown Goode became its first curator, and he served it well for some twenty years. He also became the leading authority on museums in the nation, formulating and disseminating a broad theory of museum functions. A museum, according to Goode, is not merely a "cemetery of bric-a-brac," but should become "a nursery of living thoughts." The National Museum collected and preserved specimens in all fields of natural and human history, and fostered research and education by scholarly study and publication.

Under the direction of successive directors the National Museum prospered and expanded in both scope and purpose. It became the depository of collections in many fields, ranging from geology and zoology to anthropology, ethnology, and arts and industries. Indeed, its very multiplication of collections rendered the original unifying entity of the National Museum obsolete and inadequate, and it passed "into disuse" both as a name and as a concept under the museum reorganization of 1968. The director of the National Museum became the director-general of museums, of which there were three main groupings, in natural history, history and technology, and air and space, each housed in its own building in Washington, D.C. Together they virtually eclipse their parent, the Smithsonian Institution, which continues to supervise and integrate them administratively.

[George Brown Goode, "The Genesis of the National Museum," *Report of the United States National Museum for 1891;* Paul H. Oehser, *The Smithsonian Institution;* Frederick W. True, "An Account of the United States National Museum," *Report of the United States National Museum for 1896.*]

SAMUEL REZNECK

NATIONAL PARKS AND MONUMENTS. *See* Parks, National, and National Monuments; Park Service, National, and National Park System.

NATIONAL RECOVERY ADMINISTRATION.

The National Industrial Recovery Act (NIRA), a New Deal emergency measure, became law on June 16, 1933. It included provisions to give the nation temporary economic stimulation and provisions intended to lay the ground for permanent business-government partnership and planning. The act provided for codes of fair competition, for exemption from antitrust laws, and for the government licensing of business; in section 7a it guaranteed the right of collective bargaining and stipulated that the codes should set minimum wages and maximum hours.

The National Recovery Administration (NRA) was created under Administrator Hugh S. Johnson after the NIRA went into effect. From its inception through March 1934 the NRA was chiefly engaged in code-making. Industrial councils were authorized to draw up codes of fair competition. Administered by a code authority in each industry, the codes were supposed to stop wasteful competition, effect more orderly pricing and selling policies, and establish better working conditions. Every code had to guarantee freedom of workers to join their own unions and provide for maximum hours and minimum wages; a group offering a code had to be truly representative of the trade or industry involved; and no code could be designed to promote monopoly or oppress or eliminate small enterprises. Within a year nearly all American industry was codified.

In the fall of 1934 Johnson was replaced by Donald R. Richberg as administrator. On Feb. 20, 1935, the president recommended to Congress the extension of the NIRA for two years beyond its expiration date of June 1935. On June 14, Congress voted to extend the recovery legislation until Apr. 1, 1936, but repealed the provisions authorizing the president to approve or prescribe codes of fair competiton. (On May 27, 1935, in *Schechter Poultry Corporation* v. *United States,* the Supreme Court had invalidated the code-making provisions of the act.) The NRA was terminated on Jan. 1, 1936.

The chief purpose of the NRA was recovery—to increase purchasing power by the net reduction of unemployment, the spreading of work through shorter hours, and the increase of wages. In 1933 it helped to generate employment. Beyond that, it established the principle of maximum hours and minimum wages on a national basis, abolished child labor, and made collective bargaining a national policy, transforming the position of organized labor.

[Broadus Mitchell, *Depression Decade;* Basil Rauch, *The History of the New Deal;* Arthur M. Schlesinger, Jr., *The Coming of the New Deal.*]

MORTON J. FRISCH

NATIONAL REPUBLICAN PARTY. All the presidential electors chosen in 1824 were Jeffersonian Republicans, but the party failed to unite on a candidate and the electors divided their votes among four Republican leaders who sought the presidency. Election by the House of Representatives followed in 1825 and resulted in the choice of John Quincy Adams on the first ballot. Because Adams won partly through the support of Henry Clay (*see* Corrupt Bargain) and his friends and then placed the Kentuckian in the Cabinet as secretary of state, opposing elements drew together in support of Andrew Jackson. Thus the Jeffersonian Republicans became divided into two parties. Leaders and members of both wings continued to call themselves Republicans, but often those who adhered to the administration were called Clay-Adams men, while those who rallied to the standard of Jackson were called Jackson men. As the years passed, members of the Clay-Adams party were referred to as National Republicans and those of the Jackson faction as Democratic-Republicans. Most of the Federalists remaining on the scene in 1825 gravitated to the National Republicans, though many of them joined the Jackson party. Accurately speaking, there were no Whigs and no Democrats until 1834. Then the National Republican party was absorbed by the new and larger Whig party, and Demo-

cratic-Republicans took on the name Democrats during the next few years.

[William O. Lynch, *Fifty Years of Party Warfare.*]
WILLIAM O. LYNCH

NATIONAL RIFLE ASSOCIATION (NRA) was founded in 1871 by National Guard officers in an effort to encourage marksmanship. The organization maintained close ties to the Defense Department, which until 1967 provided substantial financial support for NRA-sponsored rifle contests. Partly as a result of these subsidies, which provided ammunition to NRA members at low prices, the organization had grown to approximately 1 million members by the early 1970's.

The main importance of the NRA lies in its efforts to prevent strict gun control legislation. Some of the organization's efforts have taken conventional lobbying form. In 1968 Franklin L. Orth, the executive vice-president of the group, finally registered as a lobbyist, and he frequently appeared before congressional committees to oppose gun control bills. More impressive have been the NRA campaigns to get their members to write members of Congress, urging them to oppose such legislation. Similar campaigns have been directed toward state and local governments, generally with great success in preventing laws restricting the ownership of guns.

The association has gained its greatest political support in small towns and rural areas, especially of the West and South, where hunting is particularly popular. NRA members insist that strict gun controls would not really prevent crime, since criminals would readily evade the restrictions. They also insist that the Second Amendment to the U.S. Constitution, providing "the right of the people to keep and bear arms," should be interpreted as prohibiting strict gun control legislation. The Supreme Court has not so interpreted the amendment, but the association continues to urge the correctness of this view and generally to attempt to persuade the public that gun control laws will not solve the problems of crime and violence in American society.

[Jonathan Cottin, "The National Rifle Association," *National Journal,* vol. 2, no. 18.]
ROBERT H. SALISBURY

NATIONAL ROAD, the name often given to the section of the Cumberland Road extending from Wheeling (in present-day West Virginia) to its western terminus in Ohio. This western portion was probably not so significant as was the section built from Cumberland, Md., to Wheeling (1815–18), for much of the traffic in the West was diverted to steamboats on the Ohio River. As the interior of Ohio was developed, the National Road through that state became a crowded highway; as many as a hundred teams might be encountered in a journey of twenty miles.

For some years construction west of Wheeling was uncertain because of constitutional questions, raised especially by old-school Republicans. The work was begun from Wheeling toward Zanesville, Ohio, in 1825, following (Ebenezer) Zane's Trace. By 1833 the road was opened to Columbus. The last appropriation for the road—in Ohio, Indiana, and Illinois—was made by Congress in 1838. Parts of the road had been surrendered to the states following President James Monroe's veto of a bill for the collection of tolls by the federal government in 1822. The states undertook repairs and erected tollgates to ensure the financing of such operations. The road through Indiana was completed only in 1850 by a state corporation. When Illinois received the custody of its portion, it was unfinished, although graded and bridged as far west as Vandalia, then the state capital.

The road meant less to Indiana and Illinois than to Ohio, and after 1850 the canal, the railroad, and the telegraph contributed generally to the decline of its importance. With the advent of the automobile the National Road became U.S. Route 40, a primary route for motor travel in the United States.

[Philip D. Jordan, *The National Road.*]
FRANCIS PHELPS WEISENBURGER

NATIONAL SCIENCE FOUNDATION. The NSF was created as a result of the report *Science—The Endless Frontier,* made by Vannevar Bush to President Harry Truman in July 1945, and congressional hearings chaired by Sen. Harley M. Kilgore. Drawing on the wartime experience of the Office of Scientific Research and Development (OSRD), both Bush and Kilgore urged the government to establish a science agency that would continue federal subsidies to basic research in the areas of defense, public health, the natural sciences, and science education. Such suggestions had been rejected during the New Deal, but the success of the OSRD led to eventual acceptance of the plan.

The original NSF legislation was debated for two years, during which time there was a division of opinion over such issues as how properly to dispose of patents arising from federally funded research;

what degree of independence from political control the agency should enjoy; whether funds should be distributed on a geographical basis or awarded to individually excellent projects; and whether the social sciences should be supported along with the natural sciences. Legislation passed in 1947 was vetoed by Truman because it failed to provide for presidential appointment of the governing National Science Board. Compromise legislation establishing the NSF was passed in 1950.

Between 1945 and 1950, such important areas of science as medical research, atomic energy, and military research were provided for by separate agencies set up or expanded by Congress. By 1950 the potential areas of NSF responsibility had shrunk to support of basic research, science education, and the establishment of science policy for the government as a whole (a mission never vigorously pursued). The NSF began modestly, with a budget of only $3.5 million and a staff (including Director Alan T. Waterman) drawn in part from the very successful Office of Naval Research.

Under the governance of a twenty-five–man National Science Board, made up of prominent scientists and educators appointed for six-year terms by the president, the NSF has expanded steadily, and its budget had grown to $511 million in fiscal 1971. Even so, in that year it spent less than one twenty-fifth of the total federal research and development dollars, including about 8 percent of the federal funds for basic research. Although it has had a disproportionate influence in supporting basic research on college campuses, its research budget has always been dwarfed by those of the Department of Defense, the Atomic Energy Commission, the National Aeronautics and Space Administration, and the National Institutes of Health.

The administration of President Richard M. Nixon placed a new emphasis on research and development geared more toward practical application than toward basic knowledge. Accordingly, in 1970 a major new direction opened up for the NSF with the implementation of a program called Interdisciplinary Research Relevant to the Problems of Our Society (IRRPOS). In 1971 the NSF established a Research Applications Directorate to "help scientists increase societal benefits from research." For the fiscal year 1972, the directorate, which oversees IRRPOS, obligated 10 percent of the NSF's funds.

[Committee on Science and Astronautics, House of Representatives, *The National Science Foundation—A General Review of Its First 15 Years,* 89th Congress (1966); National Science Foundation, *Annual Report* (1971); D. Schaffter, *The National Science Foundation.*]

CARROLL PURSELL

NATIONAL SECURITY COUNCIL. See Federal Agencies.

NATIONAL TRADES' AND WORKERS' ASSOCIATION was started in 1910 at Battle Creek, Mich., by C. W. Post to fight trade unions. It replaced the Citizens' Industrial Association founded in 1902, also by Post. *The Square Deal,* the new association's organ, was filled with accounts of the evils of organized labor. It advocated arbitration for labor disputes and was against the closed shop, strikes, lockouts, boycotts, and blacklisting. Only a few locals were established, and the association came to an end soon after Post's death in 1914.

[C. E. Bonnett, *Employers' Associations in the United States.*]

JAMES D. MAGEE

NATIONAL TRIBUNE was founded as a soldiers' newspaper in 1877, in Washington, D.C., by George E. Lemon, the leading claim agent in securing pensions for soldiers of the Union army (*see* Grand Army of the Republic). Within seven years after it was established, the newspaper boasted of a circulation of 112,000 paid subscribers. Filled with articles of general appeal to the former soldiers, its particular purpose was to keep them apprised of all pension legislation and urge them to work constantly for more liberal pensions. In 1884 it became a political campaign sheet, and week after week called upon the soldiers to demand a "Soldier President." As the years passed and the ranks of the veterans thinned out, it became a family newspaper, but in 1926 it resumed its original character in some measure by absorbing the Washington, D.C., continuation of the World War I *Stars and Stripes.*

JOHN W. OLIVER

NATIONAL TRUST FOR HISTORIC PRESERVATION, a private, nonprofit organization chartered by Congress in 1949 to encourage public participation in the preservation of sites, buildings, and objects significant in historical and cultural aspects of America's environment. More than 71,000 individuals and 2,100 organizations support the National Trust through membership. Its services—to the public and the membership—include counsel and education on preservation and interpretation and administration of historic properties. Such assistance is carried out from its Washington, D.C., headquarters, in the Decatur House, a National Trust property, on Lafayette Square, and at Chicago and San Francisco field offices. The trust also operates a New England field office, which is cosponsored by the Society for the Preservation of New England Antiquities.

The trust owns a number of historic properties, ten of which are maintained as house museums open to the public: Belle Grove (Middletown, Va.), Chesterwood (Stockbridge, Mass.), Cliveden (Philadelphia, Pa.), Decatur House (Washington, D.C.), Lyndhurst (Tarrytown, N.Y.), Oatlands (Leesburg, Va.), Pope-Leighey House (Mount Vernon, Va.), Shadows-on-the-Teche (New Iberia, La.), Woodlawn Plantation (Mount Vernon, Va.), and Woodrow Wilson House (Washington, D.C.). Casa Amesti (Monterey, Calif.) has been put to adaptive use as a men's club and is open to the public on a limited schedule; the Cooper-Molera Adobe (also in Monterey) is leased to the California Department of Parks and Recreation, which will maintain it as part of the Monterey State Historic Park.

Four offices carry out the National Trust programs: preservation services, properties, public affairs, and the Preservation Press. Two programs of financial assistance are administered by the Office of Preservation Services: the Consultant Service Grant Program and the National Historic Preservation Fund. The Preservation Press produces two major items for members: *Preservation News,* a monthly newspaper, and *Historic Preservation,* a quarterly color magazine. The Preservation Bookshop, located at National Trust headquarters, offers a catalog on request.

TERRY B. MORTON

NATIONAL UNION ("ARM-IN-ARM") CONVENTION, held in Philadelphia, Aug. 14–16, 1866, was an effort by President Andrew Johnson's supporters to unite opposition to the Radical Republicans. The convention platform stressed conciliation, equality among the states, and acceptance of the results of the Civil War and called for election of conservatives to Congress. Copperhead delegates withdrew to preserve harmony. Although the convention was widely acclaimed at first, Radical Republican successes in the congressional elections of 1866 demonstrated its failure.

[Howard K. Beale, *The Critical Year.*]
CHARLES H. COLEMAN

NATIONAL UNION FOR SOCIAL JUSTICE, organized by Charles E. Coughlin, a Roman Catholic priest and popular radio speaker, Apr. 25, 1935, had as its stated object the protection of the masses against "domination of and exploitation by powerful vested interests." Units were quickly organized in many states. The union denounced President Franklin D. Roosevelt's New Deal policies and advocated the nationalization of banks and utilities. The union was officially disbanded by Coughlin in the autumn of 1936, but it continued to operate independently in many places. In October 1937 Coughlin sold its weekly magazine, *Social Justice,* to one of its members, but in December he returned to the editorial staff. On Feb. 17, 1938, he suspended all units of the union, but many continued to function for a few more years. *Social Justice* ceased publication in 1942 after it was barred from the U.S. mails, because of its anti-Semitic and pro-Nazi statements, under the Espionage Act.

ALVIN F. HARLOW

DICTIONARY OF AMERICAN HISTORY